UNGER'S
BIBLE
HANDBOOK

UNGER'S BIBLE HANDBOOK

*An Essential Guide
to Understanding the Bible*

BY MERRILL F. UNGER, TH.D., PH.D.

MOODY PRESS · CHICAGO

1967

ISBN: 0-8024-0419-7

L. C. catalog card number: 66—16224

FIRST EDITION

Moody Paperback Edition, 1983

1 2 3 4 5 Printing/LC/Year 87 86 85 84 83

Over 350,000 in print

As this view through the open door of the Church of All Nations, looking across the Kidron Valley, focuses on the Golden Gate and the wall of old Jerusalem, so this volume is designed to lead you to the very heart of biblical truth. (*Courtesy* Decision *magazine and Russell Busby*)

FOREWORD

As a lover of the sacred Scriptures from childhood, I have always realized what a tremendous treasure the Word of God is and what an indescribable blessing to all who study and receive its great soul-transforming truths into heart and life. Thus, a keen desire has been aroused to stimulate others to read God's Word and to share in the vast benefits of Bible study.

To accomplish this purpose, for years I have had in mind a simple and concise Bible handbook that could appeal to all classes of people—the layman as well as the clergyman, the young convert as well as the seasoned saint, the non-Christian as well as the Christian believer.

The plan called for full array of the latest scientific information *about* the Bible, such as geography, chronology, history, archaeology and biblical criticism. Although this information is an important aspect of this book, and extremely essential in a day of vast strides in technical studies, yet this is not the principal feature. The chief emphasis is the message of *the Bible itself.* To achieve this feature a complete commentary on the entire sixty-six books is presented. Each verse is related to its chapter, each chapter to the book, each book to the entire Bible. Careful interpretation is striven for from the original Hebrew and Greek and related to the overall message and purpose of divine revelation.

An attempt is made to face difficulties. The aim is to place in the hands of the Bible student a ready reference tool in which he may at a glance relate chapter and verse to the immediate as well as the overall context in which they occur, and thus obtain light on the accurate interpretation of any passage that may be desired.

Acknowledgment is made to innumerable sources from which I have drawn—commentaries, learned journals, histories, Bible geographies, dictionaries, handbooks, travel in Bible lands, and personal study. But above all I have striven to be guided by the Holy Spirit in expounding the written Word and in exalting Christ the living Word.

It is my prayer that *Unger's Bible Handbook* will kindle love in the hearts of many for the precious oracles of God, revealing that "more to be desired are they than gold, yea, than much fine gold: sweeter also than honey and the honeycomb" (Ps. 19:10).

MERRILL F. UNGER

ACKNOWLEDGMENTS

Special acknowledgment is given to those who have supplied photographs for this book: Israel Information Services; The Oriental Institute of the University of Chicago; The University of Michigan Library; Dr. Howard F. Vos; The Wellcome Archaeological Research Expedition; and The Matson Photo Service, 1428 South Marengo, Alhambra, California, 91803.

CONTENTS

Old Testament

Between the Testaments

New Testament

How the Bible Came to Us

Appendix

ILLUSTRATIONS

MAPS

CHARTS

ABBREVIATIONS
Books of the Bible

OT	Old Testament	Prov	Proverbs
Gen	Genesis	Eccl	Ecclesiastes
Ex	Exodus	Song	Song of Solomon
Lev	Leviticus	Isa	Isaiah
Num	Numbers	Jer	Jeremiah
Deut	Deuteronomy	Lam	Lamentations
Josh	Joshua	Ezk	Ezekiel
Jud	Judges	Dan	Daniel
Ruth	Ruth	Hos	Hosea
1 Sam	1 Samuel	Joel	Joel
2 Sam	2 Samuel	Amos	Amos
1 Kgs	1 Kings	Ob	Obadiah
2 Kgs	2 Kings	Jon	Jonah
1 Chr	1 Chronicles	Mic	Micah
2 Chr	2 Chronicles	Nah	Nahum
Ezr	Ezra	Hab	Habakkuk
Neh	Nehemiah	Zeph	Zephaniah
Est	Esther	Hag	Haggai
Job	Job	Zech	Zechariah
Ps	Psalms	Mal	Malachi
NT	New Testament	2 Thess	2 Thessalonians
Mt	Matthew	1 Tim	1 Timothy
Mk	Mark	2 Tim	2 Timothy
Lk	Luke	Tit	Titus
Jn	John	Phm	Philemon
Acts	Acts	Heb	Hebrews
Rom	Romans	Jas	James
1 Cor	1 Corinthians	1 Pet	1 Peter
2 Cor	2 Corinthians	2 Pet	2 Peter
Gal	Galatians	1 Jn	1 John
Eph	Ephesians	2 Jn	2 John
Phil	Philippians	3 Jn	3 John
Col	Colossians	Jude	Jude
1 Thess	1 Thessalonians	Rev	Revelation

Apocrypha

1 Esd	1 Esdras	Bar	Baruch
2 Esd	2 Esdras	Bel	Bel and the
Tob	Tobit		Dragon
Wisd	Wisdom of Solomon	1 Macc	1 Maccabees
Sir	Wisdom of Jesus the son of Sirach, or Ecclesiasticus	2 Macc	2 Maccabees

Others

A.D.	*anno domini* (in the year of our Lord)
ASV	American Standard Version
AV	Authorized Version (King James Version)
B.C.	before Christ
c.	*circa* (about)
cen.	century
cf.	*confer* (compare)
ch.	chapter
E	east
e.g.	*exempli gratia* (for example)
et al.	and others
f., ff.	following
Gr.	Greek
Heb.	Hebrew
i.e.	*id est* (that is)
IIS	Israel Information Services
Jos	Josephus' *Antiquities*
KJV	King James Version
LXX	Septuagint (Greek translation of Old Testament)
marg.	margin, marginal reading
MPS	Matson Photo Service
MS., MSS.	manuscript, manuscripts
N	north
ORINST	Oriental Institute of the University of Chicago
p., pp.	page, pages
q. v.	*quod vide* (which see)
RSV	Revised Standard Version
S	south
UML	University of Michigan Library
v., vv.	verse, verses
W	west

INTRODUCTION

WHAT THE BIBLE IS

The word "Bible" designates the Scriptures of the Old and the New Testaments recognized and used by the Christian churches. Judaism recognizes only the Scriptures of the OT. Other religions such as Buddhism, Hinduism, Zoroastrianism and Islam, have their sacred writings.

But there is only *one* Bible—incomparable, unique as far as all other "sacred" literature is concerned, because: (1) It is *the* revelation of God. (2) It is "God-breathed" (2 Tim 3:16) and inspired in a different sense from all other literature. (3) It discloses God's plans and purposes for the ages of time and eternity. (4) It *centers in God incarnate in Jesus Christ,* the Saviour of mankind (Heb 1:1-2).

MEANING OF THE NAME "BIBLE"

The word "Bible" comes from the Greek word *biblia* ("books"), a diminutive from *biblos* ("book"), denoting the inner bark of the papyrus reed (ancient paper) from which ancient books (scrolls) were made. Daniel 9:2 refers to the OT prophetic writings as "the books" (*ta biblia* in the Gr.).

The prologue to Ecclesiasticus (an apocryphal book dating *c.* 130 B.C.) calls the OT writings outside the Law and the Prophets "the rest of the books." The writer of 1 Maccabees (another apocryphal book) styles them "the holy books" (12:9). The usage passed over into Christian terminology (2 Clement 14:2) and by the 5th cen. A.D. came to be applied to the whole Scriptures. Jerome (*c.* A.D. 400) called the Bible *Bibliotheca Divina* ("the Divine Library").

By the 13th cen. "the Books" (*biblia* neuter plural) by a happy solecism became styled "the Book" (regarded as a feminine singular *biblia*), and thus passed into usage in modern European languages. The evolution of the term "the Bible" from the plural to the singular concept is to be viewed as providential, stressing the *unity* of the 39 books of the OT and the 27 of the NT.

SCRIPTURAL DESIGNATIONS OF THE BIBLE

Our Lord customarily referred to the OT books as "the scriptures" (Mt 21:42; Mk 14:49; Jn 5:39). His followers did likewise (Lk

1

24:32; Acts 18:24; Rom 15:4). Paul styled them "the sacred writings" (2 Tim 3:15, RSV), "the holy scriptures" (Rom 1:2), "the oracles of God" (Rom 3:2).

Jesus once referred to them as "the law of Moses, and the prophets, and the psalms" (Lk 24:44), echoing the formal arrangement in the Hebrew. The OT is more briefly termed "the law and the prophets" (Mt 5:17; 11:13; Acts 13:15). Even more briefly the term "law" comprehends the other divisions (Jn 10:34; 12:34; 15:25; 1 Cor 14:21).

There is no name in the Bible for the complete body of Scripture. The only Scriptures then known were those of the OT and the earliest NT books. In the latter category Peter refers to Paul's epistles as "scriptures" (2 Pet 3:16).

THE TERMS "OLD TESTAMENT" AND "NEW TESTAMENT"

Since the close of the 2nd cen. the terms "Old Testament" and "New Testament" have been used to differentiate the Hebrew from the Christian Scriptures. The formal collection of Christian writings made after the middle of the 2nd cen. was called the New Testament. This collection was placed alongside the Hebrew canonical books as of equal inspiration and authority. The Hebrew Scriptures were then styled the Old Testament. Tertullian, an early Latin father (c. 200), first employed the term *Novum Testamentum*. Thereafter it came into general use, and the concept of a Christian Bible was crystallized.

Applied to the Scriptures the terms Old Testament and New Testament mean strictly Old and New Covenant. The Covenant (Heb. *berith;* Gr. *diathēkē*) is a continuation of the OT designation for the Mosaic law, the book of the covenant (2 Kgs 23:2). Paul in this sense uses it of "reading of the old testament," i.e., the old covenant (2 Cor 3:14).

The NT use of *diathēkē* is not testament or will (except in Heb 9:16,17), as in classical Greek, but covenant. The older usage, however, is too firmly fixed to be changed. Even the designation "the new covenant" for the NT writings is not completely accurate. Most of the events catalogued in the four Gospels occurred under the old covenant. Not until Christ's death, attended by the tearing of the curtain which separated the holy place from the most holy place (Mt 27:51), did the legal age end, and the new testament (covenant) actually begin.

THE LANGUAGES OF THE BIBLE

The OT was written almost entirely in Hebrew, a Semitic dialect akin to Phoenician and Ugaritic. The only portions written in Aramaic, another Semitic language akin to Hebrew, were Ezr 4:8—6:18; 7:12-26; Dan 2:4—7:28, and Jer 10:11. The NT was written entirely in Greek. Archaeology has shown this to be the common everyday language (*Koine*) of the contemporary Graeco-Roman world.

ORDER OF BOOKS IN THE HEBREW OLD TESTAMENT

The canonical books in a present-day Hebrew Bible number 24 and are arranged in a threefold division—the Law (*Torah*), the Prophets (*Nebhiim*) and the Writings (*Kethubhim*). This division is old, being clearly implied in the prologue to the apocryphal book of Ecclesiasticus (*c.* 180 B.C.), known by Philo and referred to by our Lord (Lk 24:44). The threefold division, however, experienced some evident shifting of books from the second to the third section in the early Christian centuries.

The form as it has come down to us from the Masoretic period (600-900) is as follows:

1. *The Law* (*Torah*), 5 books: Genesis, Exodus, Leviticus, Numbers, Deuteronomy
2. *The Prophets* (*Nebhiim*), 8 books
   Former Prophets, 4 books: Joshua, Judges, Samuel, Kings
   Latter Prophets, 4 books: Isaiah, Jeremiah, Ezekiel, the Twelve
3. *The Writings*, 11 books
   Poetical Books, 3 books: Psalms, Proverbs, Job
   The Scrolls (*Megilloth*), 5 books: Song of Solomon, Ruth, Lamentations, Ecclesiastes, Esther
   Prophetic-Historical Books, 3 books: Daniel, Ezra-Nehemiah, Chronicles

Josephus, expressing current Jewish opinion of the 1st cen. A.D., reckons 22 books (5 of the Law, 13 of the Prophets, 4 of the Writings), instead of the later 24. In the books of the Law he, of course, included Genesis, Exodus, Leviticus, Numbers and Deuteronomy. Josephus' 13 books of the Prophets included all the historical and prophetic Scriptures, counting as *one* book each Judges-Ruth, 1 and 2 Samuel, 1 and 2 Kings, 1 and 2 Chronicles, Ezra-Nehemiah, Jeremiah-Lamentations, and the Twelve Minor Prophets (total 7 books). Josephus also included in the Prophets Joshua, Isaiah,

Jeremiah, Ezekiel, Job and Esther. In the Writings he placed Psalms, Proverbs, Canticles and Ecclesiastes.

Josephus' 22 books were, therefore, those of the Hebrew canon only (no apocryphal books were included). His arrangement in 22 books apparently represented an earlier order than the rabbinic arrangement in 24 books which has come down to us in modern Hebrew Bibles.

Melito of Sardis (c. A.D. 170), Origen (c. 250) and Jerome (c. 400), following Jewish authorities, confirm Josephus' 22-book division with some variation of enumeration. Jerome was also acquainted with the rabbinic 24-book division, which was obtained by separating Ruth from Judges and Lamentations from Jeremiah.

THE 39 BOOKS OF THE OLD TESTAMENT
(English Order)

Historical (17 books)	Poetical (5 books)	Prophetic (17 books)
Genesis ⎫	Job	Isaiah
Exodus ⎪ Law of	Psalms	Jeremiah
Leviticus ⎬ Moses	Proverbs	Lamentations
Numbers ⎪	Ecclesiastes	Ezekiel
Deuteronomy ⎭	Canticles	Daniel
Joshua		Hosea
Judges		Joel
Ruth		Amos
1 Samuel		Obadiah
2 Samuel		Jonah
1 Kings		Micah
2 Kings		Nahum
1 Chronicles		Habakkuk
2 Chronicles		Zephaniah
Ezra		Haggai
Nehemiah		Zechariah
Esther		Malachi

Note on the 39 Books of the Old Testament. The content of the English OT is identical with that of the Hebrew. The only difference is in arrangement of the material. The English translators followed the order of the books in the Septuagint (Greek) translation made about 280-150 B.C. Roman Catholics followed the Septuagint tradition further in including 11 apocryphal books.

THE 27 BOOKS OF THE NEW TESTAMENT

Biographical (4 books)	Historical	Pedagogical (21 books)	Prophetic
Matthew	Acts	Romans	Revelation
Mark		1 Corinthians	
Luke		2 Corinthians	
John		Galatians	
		Ephesians	
		Philippians	
		Colossians	
		1 Thessalonians	
		2 Thessalonians	
		1 Timothy	
		2 Timothy	
		Titus	
		Philemon	
		Hebrews	
		James	
		1 Peter	
		2 Peter	
		1 John	
		2 John	
		3 John	
		Jude	

Note on the 27 Books of the New Testament. The Gospels, although composed later than many of the epistles, in completed collections were placed before Acts and the epistles for chronological reasons. Cataloging the earthly life and ministry of our Lord, they naturally precede the book of Acts, which describes the formation and history of the early church.

The 21 epistles consist of 13 by Paul, one (Hebrews) anonymous and addressed to Hebrew Christians, another (James) also addressed to "the twelve tribes of the diaspora," with two by Peter, three by John and one by Jude. James, 1 and 2 Peter, 1, 2 and 3 John, and Jude are called the Catholic epistles.

Revelation, the capstone of biblical prophecy, completes the NT books.

THE INSPIRATION OF THE BIBLE

Inspiration has reference to the influence God exerted over the human authors of Scripture so that the words and thoughts they recorded in the original autographs were without error (cf. 2 Tim 3:16; Jn 10:35; 2 Pet 1:19-21). This inspiration comprehends the original writings only, although a high degree of accuracy in the transmitted text is not only what is to be expected if God directed the process, but a fact demonstrated by textual criticism. Ferreting out any scribal errors which may have crept into the transmitted text is an activity belonging to the domain of lower criticism and the legitimate labors of consecrated scholars.

Divine inspiration makes the Bible uniquely the Word of God and not merely a book containing the Word of God, and as such is different from any other book sacred or secular. It is an inspired revelation of God's redemptive plan and purposes in Christ on behalf of man, and not a revelation of natural science or a book of secular history. Alleged scientific discrepancies are due either to faulty scientific theories or inadequate interpretations of Bible thought forms. Alleged historical blunders may be due to such factors as a faulty textual tradition, or wrong interpretation of historical or archaeological evidence or of the biblical text itself.

THE AUTHORITY OF THE BIBLE

Authority resides in God's inspired Word (the Bible) interpreted by God's Spirit operating through Spirit-taught human agents. Orthodox Protestantism differs from Catholicism in claiming no other authority than canonical Scripture as the voice of the Holy Spirit.

During the Middle Ages the Church of Rome concentrated in itself through its episcopacy all the authority of tradition, bishops, councils and anything else that held sway over the mind of the church. This movement culminated in the decree of Papal Infallibility of 1870, which holds that "the Roman Pontiff, when he speaks *ex cathedra*, has that infallibility with which the Divine Redeemer endowed his church, in defining a doctrine of faith or morals."

Neo-orthodox and liberal wings of Protestantism deny final authority to Scripture as inerrant and infallible, substituting some internal authority such as feeling, conscience, experience, "Christ speaking through the Holy Spirit," etc.

CHRIST THE UNIFYING THEME OF THE BIBLE

Although the Bible consists of 66 books (39 in the OT and 27 in the NT), it is nevertheless *one* book. The unifying theme of Scripture is Christ. The OT prepares for Him and predicts Him in both type and prophecy. The Gospels present Him redemptively in divine-human manifestation. The Acts portrays Him preached and His gospel propagated in the world. The epistles expound His redemptive work. The Revelation reveals Him as the consummation of all the plans and purposes of God. From "the Seed of the woman" (Gen 3:15) promised in paradise lost, to the "Alpha and Omega" (Rev 22:13) realized in paradise regained, He is "the beginning and the end," "the first and the last" in God's revealed ways with man.

THE PURPOSE OF THE BIBLE

The Bible was given to bear witness to *one* God, Creator and Sustainer of the universe, through Christ, Redeemer of sinful man. It presents one continuous story—that of human redemption. This story is a progressive unfolding of the central truth of the Bible that God in His eternal counsels was to become incarnate in Jesus Christ for the redemption of fallen man.

The unfolding of this central truth of redemption is set forth through history, prophecy, type and symbol. This revelation of human redemption through Christ orients man in the larger framework of God's plans for him in the ages of time, as well as the divine purpose for him in eternity.

TYPOLOGY OF THE BIBLE

Definition. A type (from the Gr. *typos*, "a blow or mark left by a blow; a pattern or impress") is a double representation in action, the literal being intended and planned to represent the spiritual. A type is thus the divine impress of spiritual truth upon a literal event, person or thing. Rightly understood and appreciated, typology offers a strong proof of divine inspiration. It is in reality the divine redemptive program of the ages deftly woven into the warp and woof of Scripture by God Himself.

Extent. All Scripture is not equally typical. The book of Hebrews is a NT witness to the concentrated typical quality of the Pentateuch and Joshua. Likewise, the book of Ruth, because of its illustration of the Kinsman-Redeemer and the truth of redemption, has a deeper typical meaning than a mere love story. First Corinthians 10:11 offers a NT basis for the rich typology of the Pentateuch. "Now all these things happened to them [that is Israel in the wilderness] for ensamples [Gr. *tupikōs*, typically or as types]; and they are written for our admonition, upon whom the ends of the world [ages] are come."

Purpose. Typology as the divine inworking of God's purposes in

INTRODUCTION

Scripture is a means of making the Word of God relevant for every age and situation. Since Jesus Christ is the constant subject of all Scripture, His person and work are divinely impressed upon it in type, symbol and prophecy.

Varieties of Types. (1) Typical *persons*, such as Cain, a type of the natural man, destitute of any adequate sense of sin or atonement (Gen 4:3; 2 Pet 2:1-22; Jude 11). Abel, by contrast, is a type of the spiritual man whose sacrifice of blood (Gen 4:4; Heb 9:22) evidenced his guilt of sin and his reliance upon a substitute. Similarly numerous other OT saints are typical of some aspect of the Messiah or some phase of redemption. (2) Typical *events* include the Flood, the Exodus, the desert sojourn, the giving of manna, the brazen serpent, the conquest of Canaan. (3) Typical *institutions* include the Levitical ritual where there is a concentration of typology. For example, the whole Levitical ritual in which lambs or other animals were slain to atone for sin (Lev 17:11) prefigured the Lamb of God (Jn 1:29; Heb 9:28; 1 Pet 1:19). The Passover (Lev 23) portrayed Christ our Redeemer (1 Cor 5:6-8). (4) Typical *offices* include prophets, priests and kings. For example, Moses as a prophet was typical of Christ (Deut 18:15-18; Jn 6:14; 7:40). (5) Typical *actions* include Jonah's experience with the great fish, a prophetic type of our Lord's burial and resurrection (Mt 12:39).

Type As a Prophecy. Typology has been called a species of prophecy. This is true, but the typical import may not be made known in the age in which the type appears. Much of the typology of the OT deals with events and truths concerning a period which was unrevealed to the OT seers (Mt 13:11-17), so that it may be stated that this period, known to us as the Church Age, although undisclosed to OT prophets, was nevertheless impressed upon OT institutions, persons and things through the omniscient authorship of the Holy Spirit. For this reason OT ritual, institutions and experiences have an interest and instructive value to NT saints. This fact, when properly understood and appreciated, is a wonderful evidence of the divine authorship of Scripture, making it practical and omnitemporal in its instruction and everyday relations.

HISTORICAL BACKGROUND OF THE OLD TESTAMENT

Date	Biblical Event[1]	Contemporary Scene[2]
Undated past	Universe created.	Various geologic eras. Prehistoric Stone Ages.

Date	Biblical Event	Contemporary Scene
Probably 10,000-8000 B.C. or earlier	Man created.	First farming and cattle raising. Beginnings of urban life. Crude arts.
Probably before 5000	Noahic Flood.	
c. 5000	Noahic descendants (Shem, Ham, Japheth) develop into the first nations.	Earliest culture in Mesopotamia. Beginning of Chalcolithic (stone-copper) Age, first pottery. Badarian and Amratian cultures (Egypt).
c. 4800	Tower of Babel. Earliest languages.	First large buildings in Babylonia. Earliest occupational levels at Tepe Gawra, Nineveh, Tell ed-Judeideh, etc.
4500-3000	City-states in Babylonia. Urban civilization develops.	Halafian culture (c. 4500), Obeidan culture (c. 3600) at Tell Obeid near Ur. Warka (Erech, Uruk, c. 3200) flourishes, earliest writing, first cylinder seals; Jemdet Nasr culture (c. 3000).
3000-2200	Noahic descendants develop in civilizing arts but lapse into polytheism. Knowledge of the one true God lost (Gen 11).	Rise of perverted tradition of creation and Flood, preserved in Sumerian and Babylonian literature. Union of Lower and Upper Egypt (c. 2900). Dynasties I and II (2900-2700). Old Kingdom (c. 2700-2200). Pyramids. Early dynastic (Sumerian period) in Babylonia. First Semitic dynasty in Babylonia founded by Sargon I (c. 2360-2180).

[1] The chronology underlying the Hebrew Bible is followed.
[2] W. F. Albright and Jack Finegan are generally followed.

Date	Biblical Event	Contemporary Scene
c. 2225	Terah born.	First Intermediate Period (Dark Ages) in Egypt (c. 2200-1989).
c. 2161	Abram (Abraham) born (chronology of Hebrew Bible).	Gutian rule in Babylonia (c. 2180-2070). Third Dynasty of Ur arises to power in Abraham's birthplace (c. 2070-1960).
c. 2110	Abram migrates to Haran ("caravan city," prominent in Cappadocian Tablets of 19th cen. B.C. and Mari Texts of 18th cen.).	Ur-Nammu, Dungi, Bur-Sin, Gimil-Sin and Ibi-Sin rule at Ur. Flourishing donkey caravan trade between Ur, the greatest commercial capital of the world to that time, and Haran, Damascus, Egypt.
c. 2086	Abram enters Canaan.	Central highland ridge of Palestine, wooded and sparsely settled.
c. 2074	Invasion of Transjordan by a coalition of Mesopotamian kings (Gen 14).	The 'Apiru (donkey caravaneers) carry on a flourishing trade on the Fertile Crescent between Ur in Mesopotamia and Egypt, via Syria-Canaan. Abraham, "the Hebrew" (Gen 14:13), one of this class.
c. 2050	Sodom and Gomorrah destroyed.	
c. 1950	Isaac.	Ur destroyed by the Elamites. Elamite princes in Isin and
c. 1900	Jacob.	Larsa in Lower Babylonia and Elamite city-states in other parts of Babylonia.
c. 1871	Israel enters Egypt. Joseph viceroy in Egypt.	Strong Middle Kingdom (Dynasty XII) in Egypt. Amenemes I-IV, Senwosret I-III (c. 1989-1776).
c. 1780	Israel in Egypt.	First Dynasty of Babylon (c. 1850-1550); Hammurabi (c.

Date	Biblical Event	Contemporary Scene
		1728-1686). Mari a powerful city-state on Middle Euphrates. Hyksos (Asiatic foreigners) invade and dominate Egypt (c. 1720-1570). Dynasties XV-XVII.
c. 1520	Moses born.	Dynasty XVIII (c. 1570-1310); Kamose, Thutmose I, II, Queen Hatshepsut (c. 1570-1490).
c. 1490	Enslavement of Israel.	Thutmose III (c. 1490-1445).
c. 1441	Exodus from Egypt. Israel in the desert.	Amenhotep II (c. 1445-1425). Thutmose IV (c. 1425-1412).
c. 1401	Fall of Jericho.	Amenhotep III (c. 1412-1375) and Amenophis IV or Akhnaton (c. 1375-1359). Period of the Amarna Letters. Wane of Egyptian control over Palestine.
c. 1400-1361	Conquest of Canaan. Joshua and elders rule.	Invasion of Habiru (Hebrews?). Advance of Hittites. Greek world. Downfall of Crete (c. 1400).
c. 1360	Invasion of Cushan-Rishathaim.	Tutankhamn in Egypt (1359-1350).
c. 1354	Othniel rescues Israel —40-year period of peace.	Harmhab (c. 1350-1319).
c. 1314	Eglon of Moab oppresses the Israelite tribes.	Dynasty XIX in Egypt. Seti I (c. 1319-1299).
c. 1296	Ehud's deliverance.	Raamses II (c. 1299-1232), wars with Hittites at Kadesh
c. 1295	80-year peace.	(c. 1286), and concludes a Hittite treaty. Merneptah stele alludes to Israel in Palestine (c. 1224).

Date	Biblical Event	Contemporary Scene
c. 1215	Jabin of Hazor over-runs Israel.	Egyptian Pharaohs (Amenmose, Siptah, etc.) weak.
c. 1200	Deborah's judgeship.	Raamses III (c. 1198-1167) repulses invasion of Philistines and other "sea peoples."
c. 1195-1155	40-year peace.	
c. 1155	Midianites invade Canaan.	
c. 1150	Gideon's judgeship.	Weak successors of Raamses III (Raamses IV and V).
c. 1150	40-year peace after Gideon.	
c. 1110	Abimelech is king at Shechem.	Increase of power of Peleste (Philistines) in SW Palestine.
c. 1105	Jephthah's judgeship.	
c. 1099	Philistines begin to harass Israel.	
c. 1085	Samson's exploits.	Decline of Hittite, Assyrian and Egyptian imperial power making possible David's conquests (c. 1010-970) and Solomon's empire (c. 970-931).
c. 1065	Eli priest, Hophni and Phinehas at Shiloh.	
c. 1050	Philistines defeat Israel at Ebenezer. Ark captured.	
c. 1035	Samuel judge and prophet.	
c. 1025	Saul and beginning of monarchy.	
c. 1010	David king of Judah.	
c. 1003	David reigns over Israel at Jerusalem.	
c. 970	Solomon succeeds David.	
c. 931	Division of the kingdom.	

Date[3]	Judah Kings	Judah Prophets	Israel Kings	Israel Prophets	Contemporary Scene
c. 931-913	Rehoboam		Jeroboam I (c. 931-910)		Rezon seizes power in Damascus. Ascendancy of Damascene state as foe of Israel. Pharaoh Shishak's invasion (c. 925).
c. 913-911	Abijam				
c. 911-870	Asa		Nadab (c. 910-909)		
			Baasha (c. 909-886)		
			Elah (c. 886-885)		
			Zimri (c. 885)		
			Tibni (c. 885-880)		Rise of Assyria. Ashurnasir-pal II (883-859).
			Omri (c. 880-874)		

13

Date[3]	Biblical Event				Contemporary Scene
	Judah		Israel		
	Kings	Prophets	Kings	Prophets	
c. 873-848	Jehoshaphat		Ahab (c. 874-853)	Elijah	Conquest of Shalmaneser (859-824).
			Ahaziah (c. 853-852)		Battle of Karkar (853). Palestine-Syrian coalition vs. Assyrian advance.
			Jehoram (c. 852-841)	Elisha	
c. 848-841	Jehoram				
c. 841	Ahaziah		Jehu (c. 841-814)		
c. 841-835	Athaliah				
c. 835-796	Joash		Jehoahaz (c. 814-798)		
			Joash (c. 798-782)		
c. 796-767	Amaziah				

14

Date[3]	Judah		Israel		Contemporary Scene
	Kings	Prophets	Kings	Prophets	
c. 791-740	Uzziah		Jeroboam II (c. 782-753)	} Amos	
			Zachariah (c. 753/752)		
			Shallum (c. 752)		
			Menahem (c. 752-742)		
			Pekahiah (c. 742-740)		
				Isaiah	
c. 750-736	Jotham	Isaiah	Pekah (c. 740-732)		Syro-Ephraimite war (c. 734).
c. 736-716	Ahaz				Tiglath-pileser III invades Israel (733-732).
			Hoshea (c. 732-722)		Assyrians lay siege to Samaria (724-722).
			Fall of Samaria (c. 722)		Sargon takes Samaria (722).
c. 716-687	Hezekiah	} Micah		Micah	Sennacherib invades Judah (701).
c. 696-642	Manasseh				

[3] Discrepancies between the years assigned to a reign and the actual years computed in the Bible are due to a number of factors, such as overlapping coregencies reckoned in the actual reign, antedating or non-accession year system, or post-dating or accession year system of computing the reign, corruption of numbers in transmission, etc. No absolute chronology as yet exists. Many of the dates used here are those of Edwin R. Thiele, *The Mysterious Numbers of the Hebrew Kings* (Chicago: University of Chicago Press, 1951), p. 283.

15

Date	Biblical Event	Contemporary Scene
	Judah Kings Prophets	
c. 642-640	Amon	
c. 640-608	Josiah ⎫	Josiah slain by Pharaoh-Necho (608).
608	Jehoahaz ⎬	
c. 608-597	Jehoiakim ⎰ Jeremiah	Nabopolassar's death (605). First siege of Jerusalem (605).
c. 597	Jehoiachin	
c. 597-586	Zedekiah	Nebuchadnezzar's second invasion (598-597). His third invasion (588-586).
586	Fall of Jerusalem ⎬ Ezekiel	
	Daniel's career in exile.	Lachish Letters (c. 589). Nebuchadnezzar's conquest of Egypt. Evil-Merodach (562-560).
		Liberation of Jehoiachin (c. 561).
		Neriglissar (560-556).
		Nabunaid (Nabonidus) (556-
c. 539	Fall of Babylon.	539).
c. 538	Edict of Cyrus.	Belshazzar (coregent with Nabunaid).
c. 537/6	Remnant of about 50,000 return. Foundation of temple laid.	Cyrus ruled the Persian Empire till his death (530).
c. 537/6-520	Temple construction delayed.	Cambyses (530-522).
c. 520	Ministry of Haggai and Zechariah. Temple resumed.	Darius I (522-486).

Date	Biblical Event	Contemporary Scene
	Judah *Kings Prophets*	
c. 515	Temple completed by Zerubbabel. Joshua as high priest.	Behistun Stone, key to Assyrian-Babylonian cuneiform script.
c. 481	Esther is queen.	Greeks defeat Persians at Marathon (490). Xerxes I (Ahasuerus) (486-465). Greeks defeat Persians at Salamis (480).
c. 458	Ezra's return. Law revived.	Artaxerxes I (465-424).
c. 445	Nehemiah rebuilds walls.	Age of Pericles (Golden Age) in Greece (460-429); Herodotus, "Father of History" (*c.* 485-425); Socrates (*c.* 470-399); Plato (*c.* 428-348); Aristotle (384-322).
c. 432	Malachi's prophecy.	

Note: Background of the intertestamental period is found in the section titled "Between the Testaments."

American School of Oriental Research, Jerusalem, Jordan, an important agency for archaeological work in Palestine. (*Courtesy* The Biblical Archaeologist)

17

THE BIBLE AND ARCHAEOLOGY

Biblical Reference	Archaeological Illustration
Creation Gen 1:1—2:25	The Creation Tablets record a perverted polytheistic version of creation in cuneiform writing on seven clay tablets. They were found at ancient Nineveh A.D. 1848-1876 in the library of the Assyrian king Ashurbanipal (669-626 B.C.), but composed earlier in the reign of Hammurabi (1728-1686 B.C.). See Gen 1.
The Garden of Eden Gen 2:8-14	Archaeology has established the lower Tigris-Euphrates Valley (the location of Eden) as the cradle of civilization. The Hiddekel (Babylonian *Idigla, Diglat*) is the Tigris River. F. Delitzsch located Eden just N of Babylon; Sayce, near Eridu, anciently on the Persian Gulf.
The Fall Gen 3:1-24	The Myth of Adapa was discovered on four cuneiform fragments, three from Ashurbanipal's famed library in Nineveh (7th cen. B.C.) and the fourth from the archives of Amenhotep III and IV at Amarna, Egypt, c. 1375 B.C. The myth is not a parallel to the biblical story of the Fall, but offers suggestive illustration to the fruit of the tree of life (Gen 3:3, 22) and other details.
Earliest Civilization Gen 4:1-26	Farming and cattle raising (Cain's and Abel's occupations) are shown by archaeology to be the beginning of man's civilization. Arts, crafts, music (Gen. 4:16-24) and the rise of urban life are illustrated at Tell Hassuna, Nineveh, Tepe Gawra, Tell Obeid, Tell Chagar Bazar and other Mesopotamian mounds (lowest levels).
Metallurgy Gen 4:22	Copper has been attested as early as 4500 B.C. By 3000 B.C. it had displaced stone for tools and weapons. Henri Frankfort attests an iron dagger handle

Biblical Reference	Archaeological Illustration
	at Tell Asmar *c.* 2700 ʙ.c. From Ur has come an iron ax.
Pre-Flood Longevity Gen 5:1-32	The Weld-Blundell Prism preserves a very ancient Sumerian King List. It contains eight pre-Flood rulers said to have reigned a total of 241,200 years over the Lower Mesopotamian cities of Eridu, Badtibira, Larak, Sippar and Shuruppak. The shortest reign was 18,600 years, the longest 43,200. This discovery at least puts the comparatively modest biblical figures in a different light.
The Flood Gen 6:1—9:29 (Its historicity)	C. L. Woolley's 8-foot flood stratum at Ur and S. Langdon's at Kish were the result of local Tigris-Euphrates inundations, not evidence of the universal Noahic deluge. Evidence of the latter must be sought in geology before 4000 ʙ.c.
The Flood (Its reality)	The Flood Tablets (both Sumerian and Babylonian) give evidence that this event *did* occur. The oldest account is the Sumerian from Nippur, dating before 2000 ʙ.c. The Babylonian is recorded in the 11th book of the Epic of Gilgamesh. The Flood Tablets were unearthed at Nineveh by H. Rassam (1853) from Ashurbanipal's library (669-626 ʙ.c.) and furnish the most striking extrabiblical parallel to any biblical event, even including sending out of the birds from the ship by the Babylonian Noah.
The Table of the Nations Gen 10:1-32	The names and places of this marvelous ethnographical table have been largely illuminated and clarified by modern scientific archaeology. See notes on Gen 10.
The Tower of Babel Gen 11:1-9	The location of more than two dozen ancient temple-towers of Mesopotamia, called ziggurats and possibly illustrative of the Tower of Babel, are now known.

Biblical Reference	Archaeological Illustration
	These towers were gigantic artificial mountains of sun-dried bricks. The oldest one recovered is that at Uruk (biblical Erech, Gen. 10:10), from the fourth millennium B.C. Other famous ziggurat ruins remain at Ur, Borsippa and Babylon.
Abraham's Birthplace Gen 11:27-31	C. L. Woolley's excavations in 1922-34 have made Ur one of the best-known ancient sites of southern Babylonia. Under the famous Third Dynasty (*c.* 2070-1960 B.C.), when Abraham left the city, it was at the height of its splendor as a commercial and cult center dedicated to the moon-god Nanna. The famous ziggurat, temple and sacred precincts of the moon-god have been uncovered.
Terah's Religion Gen 11:31-32	Terah was apparently a worshiper of Ur's god Nanna. Terah's stay at Haran is singular, since Nanna was also worshiped there (cf. Josh 24:2).
Abraham at Haran Gen 11:31; 12:5	Cuneiform sources confirm the existence of Haran in the 19th and 18th cen. B.C. The city appears in Assyrian documents as *Harranu* ("road"), because it was on the great E-W trade route between Nineveh, Damascus and Carchemish.
Patriarchal Sojourn in Mesopotamia (Padan-aram) Gen 25:20; 26:6	Nahor, Rebekah's home (Gen 24:10), often occurs in the Mari Tablets, discovered in 1935 and dating from the 18th cen. B.C. Also attested as cities in this region are Terah, Peleg (Paligu) and Reu (cf. Gen 11:10-30).
Patriarchal Sojourn in Canaan Gen 12:1—50:26	Archaeology has corroborated the semi-nomadic life of the patriarchs as pictured in Genesis in the Middle Bronze Age (2000-1500 B.C.). Shechem, Bethel, Dothan, Gerar and Jerusalem (Salem) are all known from excavations to have existed in Abraham's day. Canaan, the older native name of Palestine, seems

Biblical Reference	Archaeological Illustration
	derived from Hurrian, meaning "belonging to the land of red purple," and applied to traders in red purple dye obtained from the murex shells on the Phoenician seacoast.
Abraham in Egypt Gen 12:10-20	This visit occurred during the Middle Kingdom under Dynasty XII (*c.* 1989-1776 B.C.). Archaeology has resurrected ancient Egypt for the Bible student.
Abraham and the *Mesopotamian Kings* Gen 14:1-24	The antiquity and historicity of this chapter are supplied by archaeology, including such ancient sites as Ashtaroth and Karnaim in Bashan, as well as Ham (Gen 14:5). The line of march over the later designated King's Highway is perfectly in accord with archaeological knowledge of this region of eastern Gilead and Moab, where the Early Middle Bronze city at Ader was discovered in 1924.
Sodom and Gomorrah Gen 19:1-32	*Vale of Siddim* (Gen 14:3) is known to be the area now covered by the southern end of the Dead Sea. This region was populous *c.* 2065 B.C. The city of Bab ed-Dra, which belongs to this era, came to an abrupt end at this time, as Kyle and Albright have shown. An earthquake and explosion of the salt and free sulphur made the area a burnt-out region of oil and asphalt.
Patriarchal Customs Gen 15:1—50:26	The tablets from Nuzu (1925-41) near Kirkuk illustrate such patriarchal customs as adoption, marriage, rights of the firstborn, the teraphim and many other details of local color. The Mari Letters from Tell el Hariri on the Middle Euphrates, discovered in 1933, also illustrate this period, as well as the Code of Hammurabi from 1700 B.C., discovered in 1901.

Biblical Reference	Archaeological Illustration
Israel's Entrance into Egypt Ex 1:1-6	A fine archaeological parallel is the sculpture on a tomb from about 1900 B.C. at Beni Hasan showing the entrance of a group of Semites into Egypt under "Sheik of the highlands, Ibshe."
Evidence of Israel's Sojourn in Egypt Ex 1:7—12:41	(1) Egyptian personal names of Levites (Moses, Assir, Pashhur, Merari, Hophni, Phinehas and Putiel). (Cf. 1 Sam 2:27.) (2) Authentic Egyptian local color in accord with data from Egyptian monuments, such as titles "chief of the butlers" and "chief of the bakers" (Gen 40:2).
Moses' Birth Ex 2:10	The story of how the Egyptian princess, perhaps the famous Hatshepsut (1504-1482), found Moses in the ark of papyrus is paralleled by Sargon I of Akkad (c. 2350). Moses' name is apparently Egyptian Mase ("child"), pronounced *Mose* after the 12th cen. B.C.
The Exodus Ex 12:1—14:31	Under early view Thutmose III (1490-1445) was the oppressor; Amenhotep II (1445-1425 B.C.), the pharaoh of the Exodus. Late views place the events under Raamses II after 1280 or under Merneptah, whose famous stele contains the first extrabiblical mention of Israel (c. 1224 B.C.). The Amarna Letters, discovered 1886, deal with the period c. 1380-1360, and mention the Habiru, whom some archaeologists identify in part with the invading Hebrews.
Fall of Jericho Josh 6:1-27	Illustrated by Ernst Sellin's excavations 1907-09, John Garstang's in 1930-36 and Kathleen Kenyon's in 1950's.
Laws of Moses Ex, Lev, Deut	Illustrated by the Code of Hammurabi (c. 1700 B.C.) discovered at Susa in 1901; the laws of Lipit-Ishtar of Isin (c.

Biblical Reference	Archaeological Illustration
	1875 B.C.), and the even earlier laws of Eshnunna.
The Conquest Josh 1:1—11:23	Illuminated by: (1) excavation at Jericho, Ai, Lachish, Debir and Hazor. (2) The Amarna Letters discovered in 1886 in Egypt which, apparently, describe the invasion of Palestine by the Habiru (Hebrews?). (3) The religious literature from Ras Shamra (Ugarit), 1929-37, which illuminates the culture, religion and morals of the Canaanites.
Period of the Judges Jud 1:1—21:25	Archaeological resurrection of Egyptian, Hittite, Aramaean, Assyrian, Phoenician and Hurrian history now furnishes background to this period. Also excavations at Megiddo and Bethshan.
Period of Samuel 1 Sam 1:1—8:22	Shiloh, as a religious center, is illustrated by great pagan central sanctuaries at Nippur in Babylonia, Nineveh in Assyria, at Haran (temple of Sin), at Qatna (temple of Belit-ekalli) and at Byblus (temple of Baaltis). Excavations at Shiloh show that the city fell to the Philistines c. 1050 and was destroyed (cf. Jer 7:10-15).
Saul's Reign 1 Sam 9:1—31:13	Saul's rustic palace-fortress of Gibeah (Tell el-Ful) about four miles N of Jerusalem was identified by Edward Robinson, the pioneer Palestinian explorer (19th cen.) and excavated by W. F. Albright in 1922 and 1933, shedding much light on the king's reign. Saul's resort to occultism (1 Sam 28:7-25) is abundantly illustrated by Hittite, Assyrian, Hurrian texts and the Mari Letters.
David's Conquests 2 Sam 1:1—24:25	Archaeology has shown that the Jebusite city David took (2 Sam 5:6-8) was the SE part of Jerusalem above the Gihon spring. Old Jebusite walls and the an-

Biblical Reference	Archaeological Illustration
	cient water tunnel and shaft have been explored, dating from 2000 B.C., like similar water works found at Gezer and Megiddo.
Solomon's Empire 1 Kgs 3:1—11:43	Archaeology has brilliantly illuminated Solomon's reign. (1) Excavations at Hazor, Megiddo, Gezer have confirmed his army and chariotry (1 Kgs 9:15-19; 10:26). (2) Excavations of Nelson Glueck at Ezion-geber (cf. 1 Kgs 7:46) have uncovered Solomon's copper furnaces. (3) Solomon's matrimonial alliances (1 Kgs 11:1-5, 33) are illustrated by royal records of Egypt, Mitanni, etc. (4) His "fleet of Tarshish" (smeltery or refinery fleet) is illustrated by Phoenician inscriptions. (5) His horse and chariot trade and commerce with Hiram I of Tyre (c. 969-936 B.C.) are illustrated by archaeology, (6) as well as the temple he built in Jerusalem, especially by the sanctuary at Tell Tainat in northern Syria excavated in 1936.
Jeroboam's Calves 1 Kgs 12:25-33	This was a dangerous religious innovation which apparently represented the invisible Deity (Yahweh) enthroned or as standing on the bulls, rather than Yahweh as bull-god. Pagan deities, as Baal, are pictured on seals, etc., in the form of a bolt of lightning on a bull's back.
Shishak's Invasion 1 Kgs 14:25-28	The gold-masked body of Shishak (Sheshonk I, Dynasty XXII, c. 945-924 B.C.) was discovered at Tanis in 1938-39. His Karnak Inscription lists his conquests in Judah in the coastal plain at Megiddo, where a part of his stele was discovered, and his advance into Gilead.

Biblical Reference	Archaeological Illustration
Benhadad of Damascus 1 Kgs 15:18	His stele discovered in northern Syria (1940) confirms the dynastic order of "Benhadad, son of Tabrimmon, son of Hezion, king of Syria, who dwelt in Damascus."
Omri and Mesha 1 Kgs 16:21-27; 2 Kgs 3:4-27	Famous stele of Mesha of Moab set up at Dibon c. 840 B.C., discovered in 1868, mentions Omri, Ahab, Mesha, Chemosh (Moab's god) and many place names.
Omri and Samaria	Excavations of G. A. Reisner, C. S. Fisher, D. G. Lyon (1908-10) and J. W. Crowfoot, K. Kenyon and E. L. Sukenik (*The Buildings at Samaria,* 1942) have traced the city of Omri, Ahab, Jeroboam II and later periods.
Omri and Assyria 1 Kgs16:23-27	From Omri's time on, Israel is mentioned in Assyrian records as *Bit-Humri* ("house of Omri"), and Israelite kings as *mar-Humri* ("son," i.e., royal successor of Omri).
Ahab and Assyria 1 Kgs 17:1—22:39	"Ahab, the Israelite" is mentioned by name on the monolith Inscription of Shalmaneser III (859-824).
Jehu and Assyria 2 Kgs 9:1—10:36	Hazael of Damascus (2 Kgs 8:7-15) is mentioned in a text from Ashur, and Jehu is actually pictured on the Black Obelisk of Shalmaneser III (found 1846) kneeling in tribute before the Assyrian emperor—"tribute of *Iaua* (Jehu), son of Omri."
Benhadad II of Aram 2 Kgs 13:25	Mentioned in the stele of Zakir, king of Hamath, found in 1903 in northern Syria, published 1907 by H. Pognon.
Jeroboam II 2 Kgs 14:23-29	Jasper seal of "Shema, servant of Jeroboam," was found at Megiddo by Schumacher. Jeroboam II's capital at Samaria is illuminated by excavations there (see "Omri" above).

Biblical Reference	Archaeological Illustration
Menahem 2 Kgs 15:19	This event is mentioned in the annals of Pul (Tiglath-pileser III, 745-727 B.C.).
Fall of Damascus 2 Kgs 16:9	Described in Tiglath-pileser's Annals but lost. Mentioned in Assyrian records also are Azariah of Judah (2 Kgs 15:1-7), Rezin (Rasunna) of Aram, Ahaz of Judah (2 Kgs 16:7-8), Pekah and Hoshea (2 Kgs 15:30).
Fall of Samaria 2 Kgs 17:3-23	Siege begun by Shalmaneser V (726-722 B.C.) completed by Sargon II (722-705 B.C.); cf. Isa 20:1. In his Khorsabad Annals Sargon relates how he deported 27,290 Samerinai (people of Samaria). He does the same in the "Display Inscription" at Khorsabad, his capital.
Hezekiah and *Sennacherib* 2 Kgs 18:13—19:37; Isa 36:1—37:38	In the Annals of Sennacherib (705-681) preserved on the Taylor Prism in the British Museum, the Assyrian monarch tells of his siege of Jerusalem (701 B.C.) in which he says he shut up Hezekiah "like a caged bird." Sennacherib's great capital Nineveh, excavated by Austen Layard, yielded the royal palace (1849-51), besides many other archaeological treasures.
Hezekiah's Tunnel 2 Kgs 20:20	The Siloam Inscription, discovered in 1880, was carved on the conduit about 19 feet from the Siloam end of Hezekiah's aqueduct to mark the completion of the 1777-foot-long rock tunnel (*c.* 700 B.C.).
Manasseh's Idolatry 2 Kgs 21:1-15	The Ras Shamra Epic literature from Ugarit has shed a great deal of light on Baal, Asherah, and Canaanite fertility cults. Manasseh's compulsory visit to Nineveh (cf. 2 Chr 33:10-13) is mentioned in Assyrian monuments.

Biblical Reference	Archaeological Illustration
Isaiah's Prophecy Isa 1:1—66:24	The Isaiah Scroll, discovered with other Dead Sea Scrolls at Qumran (1947), is the entire prophecy, antedating other known texts by 1,000 years.
Jeremiah's Age Jer 1:1—52:34	The Lachish Letters discovered in 1935 and 1938 at Lachish (Tell ed-Duweir) illustrate Jeremiah's age and Nebuchadnezzar's invasion of Judah 588-586 B.C.
Jehoiachin's Exile 2 Kgs 25:27-30	This is confirmed by Babylonian records which list Yaukin of the land of Yahud ("Jehoiachin of Judah") as one of the recipients of royal rations in Babylon. This text was published in 1940.
Ezekiel's Prophecy Ezk 1:1—48:35	The genuineness of this prophecy is supported by archaeology in such details as dating by King Jehoiachin's captivity. Jar handles from Tell Beit Mirsim and Bethshemesh are stamped "Eliakim steward of Yaukin."

Lachish, 25 miles southwest of Jerusalem, was located on a 22-acre mound excavated by J. L. Starkey 1932-38. Sennacherib of Assyria took the city in 701 B.C. (II Chron. 11:9). Lachish was one of Judah's last remaining strongholds when Nebuchadnezzar laid final siege to Jerusalem (Jer. 34:7). (© MPS)

Biblical Reference	Archaeological Illustration
Nebuchadnezzar II Cf. Jer, Ezk and Dan 2:1—4:37	The splendors of his capital city Babylon are now well known from R. Koldewey's excavations 1899 onward (cf. Dan 4:30). The Ishtar Gate, the palace, the ziggurat, Marduk's temple and the Hanging Gardens have been discovered. Bricks stamped with Nebuchadnezzar's name attest his building activities.
Jewish Exile 2 Kgs 25:1-30; Ezk, Dan, Ezr	Three hundred cuneiform tablets found near the Ishtar Gate in Babylon, dating between 595-570 B.C., include the name of Jehoiachin of Judah among other captive princes, besides many Jewish names similar to those in the OT.
Belshazzar Dan 5:1-31	Belshazzar is corroborated as the eldest son and coregent of Nabonidus by contemporary Babylonian records. Belshazzar reigned in Babylon (Dan 5:1-31; 7:1; 8:1) from 553 B.C. to the fall of Babylon 539 B.C., as the Nabunaid Chronicle indicates.
Fall of Babylon	The Nabunaid Chronicle relates how Cyrus and his general Gobryas took Babylon (539 B.C.).
Cyrus' Edict Ezr 1:2-3; 2 Chr 36:22-23	Cyrus' Cylinder, discovered by H. Rassam in the 19th cen., tells of Cyrus' restoration of peoples and their gods, and is in line with the spirit of the decree recorded in the Bible.
The Return Ezr 1:1—10:44	Prominent leaders, such as Sheshbazzar (Ezr 1:11) and Zerubbabel (Ezr 2:2) bear good Babylonian names illustrated by discoveries in this area. The "daric" (Ezr 2:69, RSV) is the Greek drachma, and shown to be authentic for this date.
Ezra-Nehemiah	The Elephantine Papyri (discovered 1903) dating 500-400 B.C., written in Aramaic by Jews on the island of Elephantine at the First Cataract of the

Biblical Reference	Archaeological Illustration
	Nile, are the chief archaeological source for illustrating detail and the genuineness of the books of Ezra and Nehemiah.
Haggai, Zechariah	Illustrated by the trilingual (Babylonian, Elamite and Persian) Behistun Inscription set up by Darius I, the Great (522-486 B.C.). (Zech 1:1, 7.)
Xerxes and Esther	The book of Esther is illustrated by inscriptions from Persepolis, the Persian capital. Xerxes (486-465 B.C.) suffered defeat by the Greeks at Salamis and Plataea. "Shushan" (Est 1:2) is Susa where Xerxes' palace was discovered by the French (1880-90). The casting of the lot (Pur, 3:7) is illustrated by archaeology as well as details of local color.
Between the Testaments	Illustrated by the Dead Sea Scrolls: two scrolls of Isaiah, Habakkuk Commentary, Manual of Discipline of the pre-Christian sect of the Essenes, War Between the Children of Light and Darkness, and fragments of almost all OT books, aiding textual criticism. Excavations of the Essene Community at Qumran (1953-56) have filled in historical gaps of the period 150 B.C.-A.D. 70.
Luke's Census Lk 2:1-5	Papyri suggest that Quirinius was twice governor of Syria, probably briefly before 4 B.C. as well as in A.D. 6-7. Papyri also show that a Roman census was conducted every 14 years and that people were required to go to their ancestral homes for it. Archaeology supports Luke as far as available evidence goes, showing how invalid was the old liberal charge that Lk 2:1-5 was a medley of errors.
Pontius Pilate Mt 27:11-25	Coins attest the procurator Pontius Pilate A.D. 26-36, as well as other procurators from Coponius to Antonius Felix.

Biblical Reference	Archaeological Illustration
Last Supper Mt 26:17-29	Illustrated by the Chalice of Antioch, discovered 1910, which is not the original communion cup but a product of early Christian art.
Synagogues Mk 1:21; Lk 7:1, 5	The most famous and best preserved of these is the synagogue at Capernaum (late 3rd cen.), probably built on the site of the one Jesus ministered in. Other synagogues have been uncovered at Chorazin, Bethsaida Julias, and Beth Alpha.
Crucifixion Mt 27:32-60	Two views of the site prevail: (1) one within the Church of the Holy Sepulchre, thought then to be outside the walls (Heb 13:12-13); (2) the other at Gordon's Calvary near the Damascus Gate, outside the present walls on the north side.
Burial of Jesus Jn 19:41-42	One view favors the site of the Church of the Holy Sepulchre; the other the Garden Tomb unearthed by Gen. Christian Gordon (1881) near Gordon's Calvary.
Resurrection	The Nazareth Inscription is an imperial ordinance brought to Paris from Nazareth (1878) and now in the Bibliotheque Nationale. It concerns the crime of the violation of tombs with the death penalty. By those who assign it to Tiberius or Claudius it has been interpreted as evidence of Christ's resurrection. However, some connect it with later emperors, so the proof is not decisive.
NT Jericho Lk 10:30-37	NT Jericho, excavated in 1950, was Herod the Great's and Archelaus' elegant winter capital. Ruins include a theater, palace, fortress and a hippodrome, like those at Jerash.

Biblical Reference	Archaeological Illustration
Herod's Temple Mt 24:2; Mk 13:2	Two signs from Herod's temple forbidding non-Jews to enter the court of the Jews have been found at Jerusalem, one in 1871 and another in 1935, near St. Stephen's Gate (see Acts 21:28-31). The stones read: "No alien may enter within the balustrade and enclosure around the sanctuary. Whoever is caught will render himself liable to the death penalty, which will inevitably follow."
Bethlehem Mt 2:1; Lk 2:4	A short distance SE of Bethlehem are the ruins of the Herodium, Herod the Great's fortress palace, and farther SE was his "Mountain Stronghold" at Masada.
Nazareth Mt 2:23; Lk 1:26	Site of Mary's Well. The important city of Sepphoris, just three miles N of Nazareth, was walled and embellished by Herod Antipas. Japha lay only one and a half miles SW.
Other Cities	Tiberias (Jn 6:23), Magdala, Capernaum, Chorazin and Bethsaida were all on or not far from the Sea of Galilee and have been illuminated by archaeology. Caesarea Philippi near Hermon (Mk 8:27) and the Decapolis (Mt 4:25; Mk 5:20), the latter a ten-city confederation, are now much better known.
Samaria (Sebaste) Cf. Acts 8:5	Excavations have resurrected the Hellenistic-Roman city, especially the fortifications of Herod the Great and his grandiose Temple to Augustus and stadium.
Caesarea (Palestine) Acts 10:1, 24	This brilliant Hellenistic city built by Herod the Great was the scene in 1960 of undersea exploration of Herod's sea mole by the Link Expedition. Excavation of the city has uncovered a forum, theater, stadium, amphitheater, etc.

INTRODUCTION

Biblical Reference	Archaeological Illustration
Antioch on the Orontes Acts 13:1; 14:26-28	Extensive excavations since 1932 have shown the beauty and size of this third city of the empire and birthplace of Christian missions. Beautiful mosaics, the Chalice of Antioch (see Last Supper above), numerous Christian churches, etc., together with important diggings at Antioch's seaport Seleucia Pieria (Acts 13:4), are the result of these researches.
Proconsul vs. Propraetor Acts 13:7 (ASV)	Luke has been proved correct in calling Sergius Paulus "proconsul," not "propraetor." An inscription was found reading: "under Paulus, the proconsul," dated A.D. 52-53.
Antioch of Pisidia Acts 13:14-52	The site of this city was discovered in 1833. William Ramsay excavated the sanctuary of the god Men 1910-1913. Numbers of inscriptions were found. Later excavations by the University of Michigan have uncovered the Roman city.
Other Asiatic Cities	Iconium, Lystra and Derbe have also been identified and important inscriptions and other data gained.
Philippi Acts 16:12-40	Excavated between 1914 and 1938, the site has revealed forum, porticoes, public temples, etc., of the Roman colony.
Thessalonica Acts 17:6, 8	Accuracy of Luke's use of "politarchs" (in original, for "rulers") has been vindicated by some 17 inscriptions. The most famous from the Vardar Gate is now in the British Museum.
Athens Acts 17:15-34	Since 1930 excavations of the American School of Classical Studies have uncovered the ancient agora.
Corinth Acts 18:1-17	Extensive excavations since 1896 have resurrected the ruins of the ancient city. Gallio's proconsulship is attested.

Biblical Reference	Archaeological Illustration
Ephesus Acts 19:1-41	Discovery of the Artemision, Dec. 31, 1869, was followed by the excavation of this most famous temple of antiquity, next to Solomon's. Later excavations uncovered the theater, stadium, Odeon, Arkadiane, forum (agora), etc.
Cities of the Lycus Valley	Colossae was identified and explored in 1835 and challenges further excavation. Laodicea, now Eski-Hissar (cf. Col 2:1; Rev 3:14), shows extensive remains for further excavation. Hierapolis (Col 4:13) also shows extensive Graeco-Roman ruins.
Pergamum Rev 1:11; 2:12 (RSV)	Since 1878 this brilliant Hellenistic Roman city has yielded its exquisite works of art. Recent digging was done 1955-58.
Sardis Rev 3:1-2	Excavations reveal how Christianity eventually supplanted the worship of Artemis. Latest campaigns began in 1958.
Rome Acts 28:16-31	"The Eternal City" is an archaeological paradise. Excavations and researches have greatly illuminated and clarified temples, forums, theaters, circuses, palaces, inscriptions, arches, etc.
NT as Literature	The papyri, ostraca and inscriptions discovered from the Graeco-Roman period show that NT Greek was the common language of the period (Koine) with some literary element, not a special "holy" tongue.
Text of the NT	The NT text has been attested by 240 uncial mss., 2,533 minuscles, 1,678 lectionaries, 63 papyri and 25 ostraca. Particularly significant are the Chester Beatty papyri from the 3rd cen. A.D., edited by F. Kenyon 1933-37.

ANCIENT WRITING

Writing in the Time of Abraham. By Abraham's day (*c.* 2050 B.C.) writing had already become hoary with age. Cylinder seals were invented about 3400 B.C. in the Warkan culture at Uruk, biblical Erech (Gen 10:10), modern Warka on the Lower Euphrates in Babylonia. Writing soon followed. In the Red Temple of Uruk a number of clay tablets were found inscribed in the earliest known crude pictographic script (*c.* 3300 B.C.), the direct ancestor of cuneiform (wedge-shaped writing) of early Sumer (lower alluvial plain of the Tigris-Euphrates Valley). By Abraham's time Sumerian and later Babylonian cuneiform writing had become well-known and widespread. This fact is attested by finds at Kish, Larsa, Fara, Ur (Abraham's own town), Nippur, Eridu, Accad, Lagash.

Writing in the Time of Moses. By the time of Moses, 1520-1400 B.C. (early chronology), alphabetic writing had become common, as attested by the religious literature found at Ras Shamra (ancient Ugarit, 1929-37). The Ugaritic dialect (*c.* 1400 B.C.) is very close to Hebrew, so Moses could have written the Pentateuch in old Hebrew.

Since Moses was educated in Egypt, he could also have written in Egyptian hieroglyphics. The Rosetta Stone, discovered in 1799 at Rashid (Rosetta) at the westernmost mouth of the Nile, proved the key to deciphering ancient holy writing of Egypt called hieroglyphics.

Since Moses was elevated to prominence in Egypt, he could also have written the Pentateuch in Akkadian cuneiform. This fact is established by the discovery of the Tell-el-Amarna Tablets in 1886, at Amarna in Egypt halfway between Cairo and Luxor. Written in Akkadian cuneiform, the international diplomatic language of the era, the Amarna Tablets belong to about 1380-1360 B.C., just after Moses' death, when Israel was entering Palestine.

The discovery of a great cuneiform library at Boghaz-Keui (1906) in the Hittite center there shows that Babylonian writing and literature were widely spread throughout the world around 1400 B.C. The Code of Hammurabi dates three centuries earlier around 1700 B.C.

AUTHORSHIP OF THE PENTATEUCH

Archaeology fully demonstrates that Moses could have written the Pentateuch either in early Hebrew, Akkadian cuneiform or Egyptian hieroglyphics, had he desired. The traditional view is that Moses did write it substantially as we have it today. It is, accordingly, authentic, historical and reliable, worthy of the name Holy Inspired Scripture.

The higher critical view is that Moses did *not* write it. It is a patchwork of discordant and conflicting oral traditions, written centuries after Moses. The J tradition (using the name YHWH) was written *c*. 850; the E tradition, *c*. 750; D tradition (Deuteronomy), *c*. 621 B.C.; and P, a priestly invention, *c*. 500 B.C. It is, on this supposition, unauthentic, unhistorical and unreliable, a fabrication of men, not the work of God.

Reasons Why Moses Did Write the Pentateuch

1. He was well-qualified scholastically to do so (Acts 7:22), and there is no rational reason archaeologically, historically or in the nature of the case why he should not have done so. Would he have been so foolhardy as not to? Would he have been so unwise as to entrust his whole life's work and teaching to oral tradition, especially when he was the founder and father of the Hebrew nation?

2. The Pentateuch claims that Moses wrote it, at least in part (cf. Ex 17:14; 24:4; 34:27; Num 33:2; Deut 31:19, 24-26).

3. The rest of the Bible claims that Moses did so (Josh 1:7; 1 Kgs 2:3; Lk 24:44; 1 Cor 9:9).

4. Our Lord Himself claimed that Moses wrote of Him (Jn 5:46-47; cf. Gen 3:15; 49:10; Num 24:17; Deut 18:15-18, etc.).

5. The foundation of all revealed truth and of God's redemptive plan is based on the Pentateuch. If this foundation is unreliable, the whole Bible is unreliable.

6. The partition of the Pentateuch on the ground of the divine names is based on the unsound presupposition that the original redactors followed one name, mechanically piecing together contradictions and discordant accounts on this artificial and utterly unnatural basis. But on this supposition how can the redactors qualify for more than being either simple-minded blunderers, and no redactors at all, or plain dishonest deceivers?

GENESIS

THE BOOK OF CREATION

Nature of the Book. Genesis, "the Book of Beginnings," is the indispensable introduction to the entire Bible, the foundation of all revealed truth. The book takes its name from the title given to it by the Septuagint (Greek) Version, derived from the heading of its ten parts *he biblos geneseos* (2:4; 5:1; 6:9; 10:1; 11:10; 11:27; 25:12; 25:19; 36:1; 37:2).

Genesis records nine beginnings:

1. The beginning of the earth as man's habitation. 1:1—2:3.
2. The beginning of the human race, 2:4-25.
3. The beginning of human sin, 3:1-7.
4. The beginning of redemptive revelation, 3:8-24.
5. The beginning of the human family, 4:1-15.
6. The beginning of godless civilization, 4:16—9:29.
7. The beginning of nations, 10:1-32.
8. The beginning of human languages, 11:1-9.
9. The beginning of the Hebrew race (covenant people), 11:10—50:26.

Genesis records ten family histories:

1. The generations of the heavenly posterity and the earthly seed, 1:1—4:26.
2. The generations of Adam, 5:1—6:8.
3. The generations of Noah, 6:9—9:29.
4. The generations of Noah's sons, 10:1—11:9.
5. The generations of Shem, 11:10-26.
6. The generations of Terah, 11:27—25:11.
7. The generations of Ishmael, 25:12-18.
8. The generations of Isaac, 25:19—35:29.
9. The generations of Esau, 36:1—37:1.
10. The generations of Jacob, 37:2—50:26.

Outline

Primeval History of Humanity, Ch. 1—11
   Creation, Ch. 1—2
   The Fall, Ch. 3
   From the Fall to the Flood, Ch. 4—5
   The Flood, Ch. 6—9
   From the Flood to Abraham, Ch. 10—11

CHAPTER 1. THE BEGINNING OF THE EARTH AS MAN'S HABITATION

God. In the first phrase of revelation occurs the declaration of the existence of God, whose eternal being is assumed and asserted, and in no sense argued and defined. He is presented here as the infinite First Cause, the Originator and Fashioner of all things.

"In the Beginning." These opening words of Genesis have been commonly assumed to refer to the original creation of the earth and the universe, and well they might. But the question is asked, May they not envision a *relative* beginning as to God's creative activity of the earth in a much later period in preparation for earth's late-comer man? For example, the phrase "in the beginning" of John 1:1 antedates the time "in the beginning" of Gen 1:1, even if the latter is interpreted as the original creation of the earth and the universe.

"God Created." If "in the beginning" is a relative beginning with regard to the late-comer man, then "created" docs not refer to God's activity in bringing the universe into being *ex nihilo* (out of nothing), but His *refashioning* the earth and its sidereal heavens at a much later period in geological history. The original earth created *ex nihilo* was brought into being by the hand of God *before* sin entered God's moral universe, (Ezk 28:13-14; Isa 14:12) and was designed to be the habitation of God's first sinless angelic creatures (Job 38:4,7; cf. Isa 45:18). The pristine sinless earth was evidently the *place* where sin began in God's hitherto sinless universe in connection with the revolt of Satan and his angels (Isa 14:12-14; Ezk 28:13, 15-17).

Genesis 1:2 and the Gap Theory. This verse has been sometimes held to portray a chaotic visitation of divine judgment upon the original earth and made a slot to pigeonhole scientific difficulties. To place this gap in 1:2 is untenable as is proved by the Hebrew text, which shows that all three clauses of 1:2 are circumstantial either to the main clause in 1:1 or that in 1:3. Presumably 1:2 is circumstantial to 1:1, putting the gap not in 1:2 but *before* 1:1. This is a possible interpretation that must be reckoned with in an era of alleged conflict between the Genesis account of creation and modern science.

Genesis 1:1 and 1:2 a Unit. These two pivotal verses must not be separated. They form an introduction to the activity of the seven days (1:3—2:3), because they tell us the condition of the earth *when* God began to remake or refashion it. It *"was"* (not "became") wasteness and emptiness, with darkness upon the surface of the chaotic mass. However, the Spirit of God was brooding over the waters, showing that God had not utterly forsaken and forgotten the earth, ruined by the sin of former angelic inhabitants (cf. Gen 6:1-6; Isa 14:13-14; Ezk 28:12-15). When sin entered the universe, God gave the first intimation that He would deal with it in mercy as well as in judgment.

Creation and the Six Days of Genesis 1. If Gen 1:1 does not describe the original creation of the earth *ex nihilo* before the entrance of sin into the pristine sinless earth (Job 38:7), then the six days represent either (1) literal 24-hour days of re-creation, (2) literal 24-hour days of the divine *revelation* of re-creation to man, (3) or extended geologic ages or epochs preparatory for the eventual occupancy of man. Since the Genesis account itself is indecisive, view (2) or (3) is possible, view (1) being sometimes assumed as untenable in an age of science. If Gen 1:1 describes the original creation of the earth out of nothing, and not the refashioning of an earth that suffered chaos in connection with the entrance of sin into the universe, then the six days represent the same possibilities, 1-3, as indicated above.

First Day—Light, 3-5. This is not the original creation of light, but the penetration of the sun's rays through the absolute darkness of the chaotic earth and atmosphere by divine fiat. The Bible does not tell us when God created our solar system or the vast solar systems of the universe. Certainly it was in the illimitable and unfathomable past as the science of geology shows. Certainly it was before Gen 1:1, since the light of Gen 1:3 is obviously from the sun, which does not become visible and function normally *with respect to the regenerated earth* till the fourth day (Gen 1:14-18). This interesting feature is further evidence that Gen 1 is re-creation, not original creation.

Second Day—Firmament, 6-8. The second day involved the separation of the chaotic mixture of atmospheric waters from terrestrial waters. This can only mean that an immense foggy, watery blanket had shut out all sunlight and shrouded the judgment-ridden earth in impenetrable gloom, obliterating any idea of heaven or sky in the primeval chaos. This chaotic celestial water mass condensed to unite with the land watery chaos, producing the firmament or atmospheric heavens. The condensation was only partial, since this re-creative process resulted in the separation of the waters "under the firmament" from the atmospheric vapor or waters "above the firmament" (1:6-8). That this particular climatic condition prevailed until the Flood is suggested by the 40-day diluvial downpour and the postdiluvian rainbow (Gen 7:11-12; 9:11-15).

Third Day—Land, Sea, Plants, 9-13. After the separation from the atmospheric waters on the second day, the terrestrial waters were separated from the land to constitute the earth and to form the seas, making possible luxuriant plant and tree growth.

Fourth Day—Sun, Moon and Stars, 14-19. These heavenly bodies (together with the vast solar system of space) had been brought into existence in the original creation *ex nihilo* prior to the re-creative work of Gen 1:1. On the first day of re-creation their light began to pierce the chaotic vapors enshrouding the judgment-ridden earth. Now due to the separation of the vast quantities of atmospheric waters ("waters above the heavens") from their chaotic mixture with terrestrial waters ("waters below the heavens") on the third day, their light became visible on the earth. With the earth becoming dependent on the sun as its only source of heat, while its surface gradually cooled, seasons ensued and geological developments slowed down.

Fifth Day—Sea Life and Birds Created, 20-23. As conditions in the reconstituted earth became suitable, God created marine and bird life. Earth's restoration proceeded progressively to prepare for God's highest earthly creature.

Sixth Day—Land Life and Man Created, 24-31. Man was created (not evolved) and appeared as the crown and goal of all God's re-creative activity with regard to the earth as man's special home. The expression "let us" (1:26) intimates the Triune God's counsel and activity in man's creation (cf. Jn 1:3; Col 1:16), as well as God's foreordained redemptive plan and purpose for man upon the earth (Eph 1:4-6). Man was given dominion over the earth.

ARCHAEOLOGICAL LIGHT

Creation Tablets Discovered. Between 1848 and 1876 the first tablets and fragments of tablets of the Babylonian creation epic called *Enuma elish* were found. Written in cuneiform characters the seven cantos of the epic were inscribed on seven tablets and were recovered from the library of the Assyrian emperor Ashurbanipal (669-626 B.C.) at his capital Nineveh. This version, though late, goes back in its political mold to the days of Hammurabi the Great

(1728-1686 B.C.), and beyond that to the Sumerians, the earlier pre-Semitic inhabitants of Lower Babylonia.

Tablet 1. Tablet 1 presents the primitive scene when only living uncreated world matter existed, personified by two mythical beings. These two, Apsu (male) representing the primeval fresh water ocean and Tiamat (female) the primeval salt water ocean, gave birth to a brood of gods who were so ill-behaved that their father Apsu determined to slay them. But Ea, the father of Marduk, the city-god of Babylon, instead slays Apsu, thereby transforming Tiamat into a raging avenger of her slain husband.

Tablets 2-7. Tablets 2 and 3 recount how Marduk is selected to fight with the raging Tiamat. Tablet 4 tells how Marduk is chosen on the basis of ability to remake a destroyed garment. Marduk defeats Tiamat (chaos) and brings about an ordered universe out of Tiamat's carcass. Tablet 5 describes Marduk's setting up the heavenly bodies for light. Tablet 6 sets forth the creation of man out of the blood of Kingu, Tiamat's commander-in-chief, who is slain. Tablet 7 describes Marduk's elevation as the chief of Babylon and head of the Babylonian pantheon because of his role in creation.

Similarities and Differences with Genesis. The Babylonian account and that of the Bible are similar in that (1) both accounts know of a chaos, although *tehom* is a common noun with no mythological connotations like Tiamat. (2) Both accounts have a similar order of events—light, firmament, dry land, luminaries, man, and God or the gods of Babylon at rest. (3) Both accounts have a predilection for the number seven, seven days, seven cantos. But this similarity is superficial, and the differences between the gross polytheistic Babylonian version and the Genesis account are vast. The Babylonian account is a corrupted version of an original tradition, the truth of which was granted to Moses by inspiration and thus freed from its polytheistic incrustations.

CHAPTER 2. MAN IN EDEN

God's Rest, 1-3. God rested from His re-creative work of Gen 1 on the seventh day. This sabbath rest of God became the basis of the Mosaic sabbath (Ex 20:11) and a type of the believer's rest in God's redemption to be realized in Christ. Elohim, the generic name of God, appears (1:1—2:3).

Edenic Climate, 4-6. The re-creative work of God is summarized and the prediluvian climate is described: "a mist used to ascend" (no rain apparently fell till the Flood). The earth was evidently watered by an ascending vapor from subterranean waters (cf. Gen 7:11-12).

Man's Creation, 7. The creative act of 1:27 is here described in detail. Jehovah, the redemptive name of Deity, is introduced, 4, 7, when man filled the scene and assumed control of the earth re-created for him. In His Jehovah character, God is introduced in special revelatory and redemptive relationship to man.

The Garden of Eden, 8-14. It was provided for unfallen man, 8-9. Its location, 10-14, was somewhere in the Tigris-Euphrates region, evidently in the easternmost end of the Fertile Crescent (the moon-shaped rim of ancient civilization, with one point at Palestine-Syria and the other point in the lower Tigris-Euphrates Valley). The Hiddekel is the ancient name of the Tigris River (Babylonian *Idigla, Diglat*). The Pishon and the Gihon were probably smaller channels which connected the Tigris and the Euphrates as ancient river beds. The accumulation of vast deposits of silt has changed the coastline of the Persian Gulf, pushing it farther out to sea.

A. H. Sayce and others located Eden near Eridu, anciently on the Persian Gulf (*Higher Criticism and the Verdict of the Monuments*). Friedrich Delitzsch (*Wo Lag das Paradies?*) placed it just N of Babylon where the Tigris and the Euphrates come close together. But changing topography renders any precise location now only a guess. It is significant, however, that both archaeology and the Bible concur that the Eastern Mediterranean Basin and the region imme-diately to the E of it (Breasted's Fertile Crescent) is indeed the cradle of civilization and the scene of the earliest activity of man.

Man's Testing in Eden, 15-17. Created innocent, placed in a per-fect environment, man was put under a simple test of obedience, to abstain from eating the fruit of "the tree of the knowledge of good and evil." The penalty for disobedience was death—*immediate* spiritual death (Mt 8:22; Eph 2:1-5), *eventual* physical death (Rom 5:12; 1 Cor 15:21-22). "And all the days that Adam lived were nine hundred and thirty years: and he died" (Gen 5:5), and ever afterward death has "reigned" in the fallen human family (Rom 5:14).

Man Provided a Companion, 18-22. The Lord God declared that a sexless or unisexual race would not be good and enunciated His purpose to create "a help suitable to man to be in his presence" (lit.), "a help meet for him" (AV). Adam named the animals and birds; but these, although companions in a sense, were not help meets on the same physical, mental, moral and spiritual plane as he.

41

Woman Created, 21-23 (cf. 1:27). The Lord God made woman from the man, and presented her to him. Only in this manner could man have "a help suitable for him to be in his presence." Man is man by that spirit by which he *differs* from the beast. Gen 2:21-23 with 2:7 presents the details of man's creation in distinction to 1:26-27 which presents the general truth that man was created, not evolved, and that woman was created in man (*ishah*, because she was taken out of *ish*, man).

Marriage Instituted, 24-25. The union of husband and wife prefigured the union of Christ and His Church, the woman becoming a picture of the Church as Christ's Bride (Eph 5:28-32; cf. Mt 19:5; 1 Cor 6:16; Eph 5:31).

CHAPTER 3. THE FALL OF MAN

The Tempter, 1. This verse introduces Satan, identified by subsequent Scripture (2 Cor 11:3,14; Rev 12:9; 20:2), with his tool the Edenic serpent. Although formally presented here, this mysterious personage's majestic and sinless creation, his fall, and his strange interest in and enmity toward newly created man given *dominion* over the earth, are described elsewhere (Ezk 28:12-19; Isa 14:12-14). The Edenic serpent (Satan's agent) was not a writhing serpent, which was the result of God's curse (Gen 3:14), but doubtless the most cunning and beautiful of God's animal creatures.

The Woman Tempted, 2-5. Satan began by questioning the inspiration God's word: "Yea, hath God said?"1. Then he denied its teaching: "Ye shall not surely die," 4. Finally he substituted his own gospel, the immanence of God: "You shall be as Elohim," 5. The woman made the mistake of parleying with the tempter, adding to the word of God: "Neither shall ye touch it," 3; misquoting it: "We may eat," 2, instead of "We may freely eat"; and "Lest we die," 3, instead of "Ye shall surely die"; and succumbing to the appeal of pride, 5, as Satan himself had done in the original entrance of sin into the universe (Isa 14:12-14).

The Fall, 6-7. The woman was deceived, but Adam sinned knowingly (1 Tim 2:14-15). Both lost their innocence, became sin-and-shame conscious, and tried to cover this guilt and nakedness by some form of human effort (works).

The Lord God Seeks Fallen Man, 8-13. God's sabbath rest of creation was broken by sin, 8, and He took the first steps in His new work of redemption to rescue fearful, ashamed, alienated and confused fallen man. Adam hid from God, because of a change in him, not in God. His self-provided clothing seemed all right till God appeared and then it was found to be worthless. Similarly, sinners attempt to clothe themselves with their own righteousness.

The Curse of Sin in the Serpent, 14-15. Satan's tool, the serpent, was cursed and transformed from what probably was an upright, beautiful, intelligent animal to a revolting, crawling snake, 14. But in connection with the serpent not only was the deepest mystery of redemption-atonement hinted (typified by Moses' brazen serpent in Num 21:5-9; Jn 3:14-15; 2 Cor 5:21), but the first promise of a Redeemer was made, 15. This predicted that He would be of the human race, and would come through Abel, Seth, Noah (Gen 6:8-10), Shem (9:26-27), Abraham (12:1-3), Isaac (17:19-21), Jacob (28:10-14), Judah (49:10), David (2 Sam 7:5-17), culminating in Christ (Mt 1:1).

The Curse and the Woman, 16. The status of woman in the fallen state is outlined and characterized by increased conception and childbearing attended with pain and sorrow, and the headship of the man, made necessary by the disorder brought in by sin (1 Cor 11:7-9; Eph 5:22-25; 1 Tim 2:11-14).

The Curse and the Man, 17-19. The ground was cursed for fallen man's sake, for he could not wisely use too much leisure in his fallen condition, 17. Life was conditioned by inescapable sorrow, 17. Evidently a vegetable diet was prescribed, 18. Light occupation of Eden (2:15) changed to heavy labor, 18-19. Physical death, 19, was pronounced (Rom 5:12-21), although man had already demonstrated spiritual death in his shame and fear in God's presence, 8-13 (cf. Eph 2:1-5; 4:18-19).

Unity of the Race and Typified Redemption, 20-21. Adam named his wife Eve ("living") "because she was the mother of every living person," i.e., of every human being. On unity of the human race in Adam, here declared, is based the atonement of Christ, illustrated in 21. The coats of skin which God made typify "Christ made unto us righteousness," which alone fits the sinner for God's presence.

Expulsion from Eden, 22-24. As a result of disobedience man lost his innocence and experienced knowledge of evil. Through this knowledge conscience was awakened, and he entered a new time period in which God dealt with him not in innocence as in the garden but under conscience. He was responsible to do all known good and to avoid all known evil, and as a sinner to come before God through sacrifice.

Man was accordingly expelled from Eden lest by eating of the tree of life he should perpetuate his misery. The cherubim at the gate of Eden vindicated God's holiness against the presumption of sinful man who, in spite of his sin, would "put forth his hand and take also of the tree of life." Later, in the Israelite tabernacle, cherubim hovered over the sprinkled blood in the holiest and portrayed the maintenance of the divine righteousness through sprinkled blood typifying the sacrifice of Christ (Ex 25:17-20; Rom 3:24-26).

ARCHAEOLOGICAL LIGHT

The Myth of Adapa. This account of creation was discovered on four cuneiform fragments, three from Ashurbanipal's library in Nineveh (7th cen. B.C.) and the fourth from the archives of the Egyptian kings Amenhotep III and IV at Amarna (14th cen. B.C.). This legendary tale, although not really parallel to the fall of Gen 3 as sometimes claimed, does contain striking similarities, such as "the food of life" corresponding to the fruit of the tree of life (Gen 3:3, 22). The two accounts agree that eternal life could be obtained by eating a certain kind of food or fruit. Adam, however, forfeited immortality for himself because of a wrong desire to be like God. Adapa was already endowed with wisdom by the gods and failed to become immortal, not on account of disobedience or presumption, like Adam, but because of his obedience to his creator, Ea, who deceived him. Both accounts deal with the problem of why man must suffer and die, but are poles apart in the matter of an actual fall from a state of innocence, of which the Adapa myth knows nothing.

The Temptation Seal portrays two persons sitting beside a fruit-bearing tree, and behind one the upright figure of a serpent. But this is scarcely a picturization of the temptation scene, since both figures are fully clothed, contrary to the fact that both are explicitly said to be unclothed in Gen 2:25.

The Cherubim placed eastward of Eden (Gen 3:24) are now abundantly shown by ancient Near Eastern iconography to have been a sphinx, i.e., a winged lion with human head.

Adam and Eve Seal is from the fourth millennium B.C. level at Tepe Gawra near Nineveh, and now in the University Museum at Philadelphia. This small stone engraving found in 1932 shows a dejected naked man and woman followed by a serpent, and suggests to some the expulsion from Eden.

Worldwide Traditions of the Fall are found among Chinese, Hindu, Greek, Persian and other peoples and, like similar creation and flood stories, go back to an actual event in history, being corrupted in transmission.

CHAPTER 4. THE FIRST MURDER AND CIVILIZATION

Cain and Abel and Their Worship, 1-5. Cain ("acquisition") was a type of a natural man of the earth. His religion was of works, destitute of saving faith, a sense of sin and need of atonement (cf. "the way of Cain," Jude 11). How mistaken Eve was concerning her first child, when she said, "I have gotten a man—the Lord!" 1, by which she meant, "I have gotten the man promised by the Lord," that is, the posterity of the woman who should bruise the serpent's head (Gen 3:15). Instead of getting the Saviour she got a murderer, illustrating the ignorance in which she was plunged because she trusted Satan for knowledge. When she gave birth to Abel she again misgauged the situation crying, "Vanity!" In contrast to Cain the farmer, typifying the natural man, Abel the shepherd is a type of the spiritual man. His sacrifice in which blood was shed expressed his consciousness of sin and his faith in an expiatory substitute. "The firstlings of his flock" were typical of the coming divine Substitute (Jn 1:29; Isa 53:7; Lk 23:9) and contrast saliently with Cain's bloodless offering of the fruit of his own works. It is for this reason the Lord had respect to Abel and not to Cain, for the divine attitude here enunciated from the very beginning of the human race that "without the shedding of blood is no remission" (Heb 9:22; 11:4).

The Lord's Plea with Cain, 6-7. Abel's worship was based on prior revelation (Gen 3:21), for it was by faith (Heb 11:4). Cain's unacceptable offering rejected God's word. But the Lord made a final appeal to Cain to bring the stipulated sacrifice. "If thou doest well, shall it [thy fallen countenance] not be lifted up, and if thou doest not well, sin coucheth [like a wild beast] at the door, and its desire shall be realized in you, but you get the better of it [by dealing with it in the divinely prescribed way]."

Cain's Refusal and Result, 8-15. Cain's religion was too fastidious to kill a lamb, but not too cultured to murder his brother. The divine way of salvation fills man's heart with love. Man's way of religion inflames it with hatred. Religion was at the bottom of the first murder and has always been a prolific cause of bloodshed. In Adam who sinned against God and Cain who sinned against man, sin appeared in its full gamut, and on the first pages of divine revelation.

The First Civilization, 16-24. Cain left the place of God's manifested Shekinah presence above the cherubim eastward of Eden (3:24) and "went out from the presence of the Lord," 16, taking up residence in the land of Nod ("wandering"). Departure from God's presence always involves the absence of divine guidance.

Cain "knew" (euphemism for having sexual relations with) his wife, one of his innumerable sisters since by this time Adam's progeny was numerous. Cain's son Enoch built a city (the first civilization). With Lamech polygamy was introduced, 19, in violation of God's original monogamous standard (2:24). In succeeding generations of Cain appear the arts (metal craftsmanship) and music, 21-22, and poetry, 23. Pride, lust and lawlessness increased in this line.

Seth and the Spiritual Progeny, 25-26. The Lord raised up Seth ("set") and Enosh ("mortal") to be depositories of the Messianic promise. Their birth closes the first section of Genesis (1:1—4:26), giving "the generations of the heavens [the family history of the heavenly posterity, the children of Seth] and [the generations] of the earth [the earthly seed—the descendants of Cain]."

ARCHAEOLOGICAL LIGHT

Beginnings of Urban Life. Excavations at Tell Hassuna, Nineveh and Tepe Gawra in northern Mesopotamia reach down to Neolithic times, 5000 B.C. or earlier, showing stone tools, beautiful pottery and architectural remains of skill. Around 4500 B.C. copper was introduced alongside stone. To the Copper-Stone Age, 4500-3000 B.C., belong such sites as Tell Halaf, Chagar Bazar and Tell Arpachiya in northern Mesopotamia. In southern Mesopotamia, the Tell Obeid culture about 3600 B.C. underlies Ur, Erech, Lagash and Eridu. Excavations here elucidate the succession of cultures in this prehistoric epoch, and bear out the biblical representations. Iron ore (cf. Gen 4:22) was occasionally smelted in Mesopotamia at an early date (or some suggest meteoric iron was used). At Tell Asmar (Eshnunna) Henri Frankfort found evidence of an iron blade dating about 2700 B.C. A small steel ax has been recovered from Ur. But iron smelting was not followed up on an industrial scale till after the Bronze Age, 3000-1200 B.C. The Iron Age extended from 1200 to 300 B.C.

CHAPTER 5. FROM ADAM TO NOAH

The Messianic Line from Adam to Enoch, 1-24. The second division of the book of Genesis is introduced by the words: "This is the book of the generations of Adam," not "these are the generations of Adam," as in the other nine divisions (see listing at beginning of Genesis). The reason is that this gives the line of Christ, the last Adam (cf. Mt 1:1). The godly race is marked by physical death, although long-lived. The dirge "and he died" tolls like a funeral bell throughout this chapter. Enoch alone escaped death by translation, 24 (Heb 11:5), before the cataclysm of the Flood. Enoch was evidently 65 years old when regenerated, and "walked with God" for 300 years. Before the Fall God walked with man; after it, man walked with God.

The great age of the pre-Flood patriarchs was due probably to greater physical vitality and a more healthful pre-Flood climate. Listed in tabular form the ages were:

Adam	930 years	Jared	962 years
Seth	912 years	Enoch	365 years
Enosh	905 years	Methuselah	969 years
Cainan	910 years	Lamech	777 years
Mahalaleel	895 years	Noah	950 years

ARCHAEOLOGICAL PARALLEL

It has been customary for critics to treat the longevity of the pre-Flood patriarchs as obviously legendary or mythical. According to the Weld-Blundell Prism, eight antediluvian kings reigned over the lower Mesopotamian cities of Eridu, Badtibira, Larak, Sippar and Shuruppak; and the period of their combined rule totaled 241,200 years (the shortest reign being 18,600 years, the longest 43,200). Berossus, a Babylonian priest (3rd cen. B.C.), lists ten names in all (instead of eight) and further exaggerates the length of their reigns. Other nations too have traditions of primeval longevity.

Attempts to correlate Berossus' ten kings with the ten patriarchs from Adam to Noah have failed. However, the names as preserved by the Sumerian King List and Berossus evidently represent a corrupted tradition of the historical facts as preserved in Gen 5, besides giving extrabiblical indication of the greater length of human life before the Flood.

The Messianic Line from Methuselah to Noah, 25-32. Methuselah, the longest-lived patriarch (969 years), begat the shortest-lived patriarch Lamech (777 years), who in faith begat Noah ("rest"). Enoch, having been translated without dying, is an exception to the long-lived patriarchs, of course.

CHRONOLOGICAL LIGHT

It is highly improbable that the genealogical framework of Gen 5 was intended to be used, or can be used, for calculating the number of years (1656) between the creation of man and the Flood, thus dating man's creation 4004 B.C. (Ussher). There are several reasons: (1) The Hebrew terms "begat," "son," "daughter" are used with great latitude and may involve a distant as well as an immediate descendant. (2) The ten generations from Adam to Noah and the ten from Noah to Abraham evidently aim at brevity and symmetry, rather than unbroken father-to-son relation. (3) Abbreviations due to symmetry are common features of Scripture genealogies (as in Mt 1). (4) In the recurring formula A lived____ ____years and begat B, and A lived after he begat B____years and begat sons and daughters, B *may* not be the literal son of A. If so, the age of A is his age when his descendant was born from whom B was descended. An indefinite time interval may therefore be intended between A and B. (5) Man is now scientifically known to have existed long before 4000 B.C., as both paleontology and archaeology show.

CHAPTERS 6—8. THE FLOOD

The Moral Cause of the Flood, 6:1-7. Two common views are held as to the cause of the Flood: (1) the intermarriage of godly Sethites with the ungodly Cainites; (2) the intermarriage of "the daughters of men," i.e., "women in the flesh," with the *bene Elohim,* "sons of God," i.e., angels. The main argument against the first view is that it fails to meet the scope of the passage or account for the nephilim (Septuagint *gigantes;* not "giants" but of mixed human and angelic birth, like the Titans of Greek and Roman mythology, who were partly human and partly divine—angelic). The argument that angels are sexless because marriage is unknown among them (Mt 22:30) ignores the fact of evil fallen angels as well as the pure unfallen spirits (cf. Gen 19:1, 5). Moreover, *bene Elohim* is an expression used consistently of angels in the OT (Job 1:6; 2:1, etc.); and the breaking down of God-ordained orders of beings (cf. 2 Pet 2:4-5; Jude 6) is the only exegesis of this passage that will satisfy its scope.

The Lord's Grace Toward Noah, 6:8-12. Noah found grace in the sight of God because of his faith in the promised Redeemer and the need of vicarious atonement (Heb 11:7). Therefore he is said to have been "righteous" and "perfect" (possessed of spiritual integrity, *not* sinless). Like Enoch, he was an antediluvian of whom it was said, "He walked with God" (Gen 5:24; 6:9). The ark Noah was told to construct was a type of Christ as the preserver of His people from judgment (Heb 11:7), specifically of the remnant of Israel who will turn to the Lord during the Great Tribulation (Isa 2:10-11; 26:20-21).

Instructions for Building the Ark, 6:13-22. "Pitch," 14, is the same word translated "atonement" (Lev 17:11, etc.) and illustrates the atoning work of Christ, which keeps out the waters of judgment. The ark was 300 cubits (450 feet) long, 50 cubits (75 feet) broad, and 30 cubits (45 feet) high with a displacement of 43,300 tons.

ARCHAEOLOGICAL LIGHT

The Babylonian flood story is preserved in the eleventh book of the famous Assyrian-Babylonian Epic of Gilgamesh, unearthed at Kuyunjik (Nineveh) in 1853. It describes a boat about five times larger than Noah's ark with a displacement of some 228,500 tons and cubical in structure. In both the Babylonian and the biblical accounts, bitumen or pitch to close up the seams of the vessel appears prominently. Both accounts hold that the catastrophe was divinely planned. But in striking contrast to the monotheistic Hebrew account, the Babylonian is polytheistic and has no adequate moral concept of the cause of the Flood. Both accounts assert that the hero of the deluge (Noah, Utnapishtim) was divinely instructed to build a huge boat to preserve life. Of all extrabiblical parallels that have come down to us from the vast cuneiform literature of the Tigris-Euphrates Valley of antiquity, the most striking remains the Babylonian account of the Flood.

Instructions Concerning the Flood, 7:1-9. "Clean animals" (i.e., acceptable for sacrifice, cf. Gen 4:3-5) are specified to be taken, in addition to male and female of each species for future increase (Gen 6:19). Such distinctions antedate the Mosaic law, which stipulates ten such animals fit for sacrifice.

The Physical Causes of the Flood, 7:10-24. The causes of the Noahic flood suggest a world-engirdling catastrophe, not a local flood (cf. 2 Pet 3:4-6). The displacement of vast quantities of subterranean water (Gen 7:11), certainly by earthquake, involved sinking of land levels and raising of sea bottoms. This is mentioned first. The violent 40-day precipitation was only a secondary source of water and occasioned radical climatic changes. Up to that time the earth had evidently been watered by these subterranean fountains and an ascending mist (Gen 2:5-6), so that atmospheric conditions did not yet exist to form a rainbow (Gen 9:13) as in the changed postdiluvian world.

ARCHAEOLOGICAL LIGHT

Both the Babylonian and the biblical accounts specify the duration of the Flood. The pre-Babylonian (Sumerian) account specifies seven days and nights, the Babylonian six days and nights. The Bible account indicates a little more than a year (371 days). The Bible also espouses supernatural catastrophism against the modern naturalistic theory of uniformity (2 Pet 3:5-6).

The Waters Recede, 8:1-6. A wind dried up the water, 1; land and sea levels shifted back to normal positions, 2. Condensation of watery vapor which had surrounded the pre-Flood earth stopped, 2 (cf. Gen 1:6-8). The ark touched dry ground on one of the mountains of Ararat, 4, the name being identical with Assyrian *Urartu*, signifying the general mountainous territory of Armenia (cf. 2 Kgs 19:37; Jer 51:27; Isa 37:38), W of the Caspian Sea and SE of the Black Sea. Mt. Nisir (Pir Omar Gudron), E of the Tigris and S of the lower Zab River, is mentioned as the landing place of Utnapishtim's vessel in the Gilgamesh Epic.

The Sending Out of the Birds, 8:7-14. A raven was sent out first, 6-7; then a dove was released on three occasions. The return of the second dove with a fresh-plucked olive twig showed that the valleys where the olive groves grew were almost dry.

Noah Leaves the Ark and Worships, 8:15-22. Noah offered burnt offerings on the altar which he built, 20, gratefully worshiping the Beloved One who had saved him and his family. Accepting Noah's act of worshipful gratitude, the Lord "smelled the soothing fragrance," 21.

ARCHAEOLOGICAL LIGHT

In the Babylonian flood story, Utnapishtim offered sacrifice, poured out a libation, and burned "sweet cane, cedar, and myrtle" after he left the boat, partly to appease the wrath of the angry deities who had decreed the complete extermination of mankind and partly to express his gratitude to the god Ea for sparing him. In both accounts the expression "smell" occurs. Before he left the boat, like Noah, Utnapishtim sent out birds—a dove seven days after the boat landed on Mt. Nisir, followed by a swallow and finally a raven.

CHAPTER 9. GOD'S COVENANT WITH NOAH

Elements of the Covenant, 1-19. (1) Promise that every living thing should never again be destroyed, 8:21. (2) Order of nature confirmed, 8:22. (3) Noah and his sons commanded to increase and subdue the earth, 9:1, 7. (4) Meat diet permitted but not with the blood, 3-4. (5) Human government (capital punishment) instituted, 5-6. (6) Rainbow appeared as the sign of the covenant, indicating changed climate after the Flood, 8-19.

Noah's Prophecy of the Moral and Spiritual History of the Nations, 20-29. Noah in an unguarded moment dishonored himself, 20-21. His son Ham, exhibiting the lascivious bent of his character, shamefully dishonored his father, 22-23. Noah by the spirit of prophecy foretold the inevitable outworking of this lascivious tendency in the curse that lighted upon Ham's "son" (descendant) Canaan, who represented the progenitor of that branch of the Hamitic peoples that later occupied Palestine before Israel's conquest (Gen 10:15-20).

The purpose of this prophecy was to indicate the origin of the Canaanites and to show the source of their moral pollution (cf. Gen 10:15-19; 19:5; Lev 18, 20; Deut 12:31). That Canaan's curse was fundamentally religious is shown by the fact that Shem's contrasting blessing was religious, 9:26, with a knowledge of God and God's salvation coming through the Semitic line. Likewise Japheth's blessing was also religious, 27. He would dwell in the tents of Shem. The Japhethites have been grafted into the good olive tree (Rom 11:17) and Shem's spiritual heritage through Abraham has become ours.

ARCHAEOLOGICAL LIGHT

The Canaanites were enslaved by one of the most terrible and degrading forms of idolatry, which encouraged their immorality. Discovered in 1929-37, Canaanite religious literature from Ras Shamra (ancient Ugarit in North Syria) reveals the worship of the immoral gods El and Baal and the sacred courtesans Anath, Asherah and Astarte. This literature fully corroborates the OT notices of the religious debauchery and moral degradation of the Canaanites. Cult objects, figurines and literature combine to show how sex-centered was Canaanite religion, with human sacrifice, cult of serpents, sacred courtesans and eunuch priests excessively common. The sordid depths of social degradation to which the erotic aspects of Canaanite cults led can scarcely be imagined.

CHAPTER 10. THE SONS OF NOAH
JAPHETHITES

Noah's panoramic prophecy of moral and spiritual history (cf. 9:24-27) forms an indispensable introduction to the principle that underlies the ethnographical table of Gen 10, viz., that in God's ways with men the moral character of a nation cannot be understood unless its source is known. The nation Israel, divinely elected to be the medium of redemptive blessing to the world, needed to know the source from which the various nations surrounding her sprang, that she might know how to act toward them. The table stands unique in ancient literature, without a remote parallel even among the Greeks, for their framework is mythological and the peoples are only Greek or Aegean tribes. W. F. Albright calls the Table of Nations "an astonishingly accurate document" (in Young's *Analytical Concordance to the Bible*, p. 25). Although numerous names have been known from ancient Greek and Roman sources, modern archaeology of the past century and a half has elucidated many of them by its discoveries.

The Descendants of Japheth, 2-5. These formed the northern nations. *Gomer* (Assyrian *Gimirraya*), Cimmerians of antiquity (Ezk 38:6), is mentioned in the annals of Assyrian emperors Esarhaddon and Ashurbanipal (7th cen. B.C.). *Magog* (Ezk 38:2; 39:6) were Scythians (according to Josephus), but probably this is a comprehensive term for northern barbarians.

Madai are the well-known Medes (2 Kgs 17:6; 18:11; Isa 21:2) mentioned in the Assyrian inscriptions. *Javan,* Ionian Greeks of Homer and particularly the Asiatic Ionians, was first mentioned by Sargon II (722-705 B.C.) and subsequently known in Jewish history (Ezk 27:13; Isa 66:19; Joel 3:6; Zech 9:13; Dan 8:21; 10:20). *Tubal and Meshech* (Ezk 27:13; 32:26; 38:2; 39:1; Isa 66:19) were the Tabali and Mushki of the Assyrian cuneiform records from the time of Tiglath-pileser I (c. 1100 B.C.) onward. *Tiras* was probably the ancestor of the Tirsenoi, a pirate Aegean people.

Ashkenaz are the Scythians (Assyrian *Ashkuz*). *Riphath* were probably preserved in the Riphaean Mountains far to the N (Josephus calls them Paphlagonians).

Elishah is Kittim or Cyprus (Ezk 27:7), the Alashiya of the Amarna Tablets. *Tarshish* was the Phoenician copper smelting center at Tartessus, Spain, or one in Sardinia (Ezk 27:12). *Kittim* is Cyprus, connected with the ancient south coast city Kition (present-day Larnaka). *Dodanim* was perhaps the Dardana (Dardanians) of Asia Minor; also read *Rodanim* in 1 Chr 1:7 (RSV) and in the Greek and Samaritan texts of Gen 10:4, in which case the Aegean island of Rhodes is indicated.

HAMITES

Descendants of Ham, 6-20. These were southern nations. The earliest empire builders were in southern Babylonia and later in Egypt. *Cush* is connected with *Kish,* the ancient city-state in lower Babylonia. From Kish, where Babylonian emperors of the third millennium B.C. took their titles as kings of the world (cf. Nimrod, 8-12), the Cushites migrated to Africa (Kosh or Nubia). *Mizraim* is Egypt whose civilization dates from about 5000 B.C. and includes the Predynastic period to 2900 B.C. and 30 dynasties of splendid kings from 2900 B.C. to 332 B.C. *Phut (Put)* is Cyrenaica in North Africa W of Egypt, as is now known from the inscriptions of Darius I of Persia (522-486 B.C.). *Canaan* represents the original Hamitic peoples settling in Palestine who yielded to racial amalgamation and became predominantly Semitic.

Seba is connected with South Arabia and is mentioned in the Assyrian inscriptions of the 8th cen. B.C. *Havilah* was ancestor to a people in central and southern Arabia partly Cushite and partly Semitic Joktanite (10:7-29). *Sabtah* is Shabwat, ancient capital of Hazarmaveth (10:26), modern Hadramaut. *Raamah, Sabteca, Sheba* and *Dedan* are representative of Cushite tribes of Arabia.

Hamitic Imperial Power, 8-10. This appeared in human history in Nimrod, founder of the kingdom of Babylon, plausibly explained as Sumerian (early non-Semitic Babylonian) Nin-Maradda ("Lord of Marad"), a town SW of Kish. The Sumerian King List names the dynasty of Kish with 23 kings first in the enumeration of Mesopotamian dynasties which reigned after the Flood. However, the name Nimrod suggested "rebel" against God to the Hebrews, who took note of his character as a hunter, the opposite of the divine ideal of a king, that of a shepherd (2 Sam 5:2; 7:7).

Nimrod's Kingdom is mentioned in its inception in the land of Shinar (the entire alluvial plain of the Tigris-Euphrates River, the last 200 miles of their course to the Persian Gulf) with *Babel, Erech, Akkad* and *Calneh,* 10, all of which have been resurrected by archaeology. *Akkad (Agade)* and *Babel (Babylon)* were in the northern part of Shinar, called Akkad, and in the southern portion, called Sumer, was Erech (ancient Uruk), modern Warka, where the first ziggurat (temple tower) and cylinder seals were discovered. The name *Akkad* was given to the district of northern Babylonia from its chief city Agade, which Sargon made the capital of a Semitic empire 2360-2180 B.C. *Calneh* is still obscure, but is thought to be a shorter form of Hursagkalama (Kalama), a twin city of Kish.

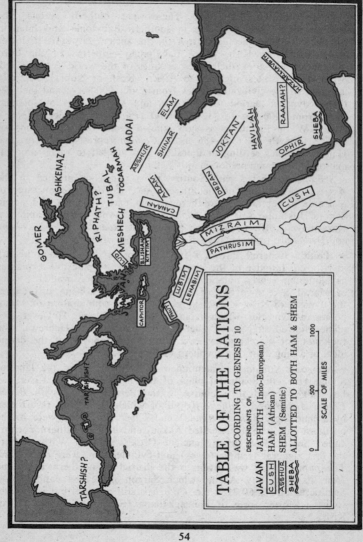

TABLE OF THE NATIONS

ACCORDING TO GENESIS 10

DESCENDANTS OF:

JAVAN   JAPHETH (Indo-European)

CUSH   HAM (African)

ASSHUR   SHEM (Semitic)

SHEBA   ALLOTTED TO BOTH HAM & SHEM

SCALE OF MILES

0   500   1000

Asshur (*Assyria*), the capital and center of Assyrian power 60 miles S of Nineveh, now called Qalat Sharqat, was excavated 1903-14 and its occupation goes back to the early third millennium B.C.

Nineveh (modern Kuyunjik), about 60 miles N of Asshur, was the later capital of the Assyrian Empire. Resurrected by modern archaeology from the grave of its oblivion, it was anciently, like New York, the center of a complex of cities including *Calah,* 18 miles S; *Resen,* between Calah and Nineveh proper; and *Rehoboth-Ir* (Rebit-Ninua), W of the capital.

Other Hamitic Nations—Descendants of Egypt, 13-14, are *Ludim* (thought by some to be for Lubim, Libyans, a tribe W of the Delta), the *Anamim, Lehabim, Naphtuhim* and *Casluhim* (all obscure). The *Pathrusim* are inhabitants of Ptores, Upper Egypt. *Caphtorim* are dwellers of *Kaptara* or Caphtor (Crete). The *Philistines* are abundantly illustrated by the monuments. They invaded SE Palestine en masse in the 12th cen. B.C.

Other Descendants of Canaan, 15-20. *Sidon* (the oldest Phoenician city, 22 miles N of Tyre) represents the Phoenicians (Sidonians). *Heth* was ancestor of the Hittites, an ancient imperial people of Asia Minor with capital at Hattushash (Boghazkeui) on the Halys River. The *Jebusites* settled in Jebus, the old name of Jerusalem (Josh 15:63; Jud 19:10-11; 1 Chr 11:4) before David's conquest (2 Sam 5:6-7).

The Amorite ("westerner") was applied by Babylonians in the sense of alien or foreigner to the inhabitants of Syria-Palestine. The *Girgashite* and *Hivite* were Canaanite tribes, which remain obscure archaeologically. The *Arkite* is represented by Tell Arka, 80 miles N of Sidon (Irkata in the Amarna Letters). The *Sinite* (Assyrian *Siannu*) is mentioned by Tiglath-pileser III as a seacoast town.

The Arvadite denotes the inhabitants of Arvad, 25 miles N of Arka (Arwada in the Amarna Letters). The *Semarite* alludes to the people of Simura (Simuros) six miles N of Arvad. The *Hamathite* represents the inhabitants of Hamath on the Orontes, excavated 1932-39.

SEMITES

Descendants of Shem, 21-31. These made up the central nations. The special importance of the progeny of Shem in redemption is attested by their double introduction to that section of the Table of the Nations that deals with their genealogy and the solemn language employed, 21-22. Their languages were Eastern Semitic or Akkadian (Babylonian and Assyrian); North Semitic, Aramaic and

55

Syriac; Northwest Semitic, Ugaritic, Phoenician, Hebrew, Moabite; South Semitic, Arabic, Sabaean, Minaean and Ethiopic.

Shem is designated "the father of all the children of Eber," 21. *Eber* includes all the Arabian tribes, 25-30, as well as Israelites (11:16-26), Ishmaelites, Midianites (25:2) and Edomites. The name Eber ("the other side, across") denotes either (1) those who came from "beyond the River" (Euphrates), i.e., Haran (Josh 24:2-3, ASV), or (2) those connected with the Habiru (*'Apiru*), well known from archaeological records.

Elam is Susiana, capital Susa (Shushan, Neh 1:1; Est 2:8), with excavated levels going back to 4000 B.C. *Asshur* is Assyria, founded by Hamites (Gen 10:11), but Semites overran the country. *Arpachshad* (ASV) is probably Arrapachitis NE of Nineveh. *Lud* (Lydians) with Semitic affinities was established by a dynasty of Akkadian princes of Asshur after 2000 B.C. *Aram* (Aramaeans) became an important people in Haran in the Habur River region of Mesopotamia and later established states in Zobah, Maacah, Geshur, Beth-Rehob and Damascus. They were conquered by David. *Uz* (desert Aramaeans S of Damascus), *Hul, Gether* and *Mash* are Aramaean desert tribes.

Descendants of Arpachshad were Shelah, Eber, Peleg and the thirteen Arabian tribes through Joktan (Arabia).

Descendants of Joktan were Arabian tribes. *Almodad* and *Sheleph* are uncertain. *Hazarmaveth* is present-day Hadramaut in southern Arabia, E of Aden. *Jerah, Hadoram, Uzal, Diklah, Obal* and *Abimael* are all archaic but unidentified. *Sheba* is a people of southwest Arabia, capital Mariaba (Saba), 200 miles N of modern Aden. *Ophir*, famous for its gold (Job 22:24; Ps 45:9; Isa 13:12) and Solomon's exotic trade (1 Kgs 9:28), is variously placed in India or coastal Africa. *Havilah* is perhaps different from that of 10:7. If the same, the Hamites held it previous to the Semitic Joktanites.

CHAPTER 11. FROM BABEL TO ABRAHAM

THE TOWER OF BABEL

The Building of the Tower, 1-4. Noah's descendants spoke *one* language, 1. They journeyed eastward (that is, southeastward) from the mountains of Ararat (Urartu, Armenia; cf. Gen 8:4) to the garden spot of the very fertile alluvial plain of Babylonia (Shinar), between the Tigris and the Euphrates about the last 200 miles of their course before they enter the sea. The rich silt of these two great rivers built up this ideal location for the cradle of post-diluvian civilization and the Babel builders, 2. After a long period of sedentary occupation in southern Babylonia, and during the life span of Eber's son Peleg (Gen 10:25), which apparently occurred well before 4000 B.C., the human race had multiplied sufficiently and developed arts and crafts to build a city and "a tower with its top in heaven." This is not mere hyperbole, but an expression of pride ("make us a name") and rebellion against God and His explicit command to "replenish *the earth*" (Gen 9:1). Self-glory, instead of God's glory, and man-made unity to replace the unity forfeited by abandoning the fear of God were evidenced. Brick (sun-dried clay) and mortar (bitumen) were ready materials in the alluvial soil of the plain, 3.

* **The Confusion of Languages, 5-9.** Babylon was undoubtedly one of the most polyglot cities in the ancient world, and the localization of the beginning of human languages there was effective. The confusion of languages was a divine judgment upon the pride and rebellion of the Babel-builders and effected their dissemination over the earth. But it was a divine act, and the precise way it was accomplished is not revealed. Gen 10 explaining the diversity of races is *much later* than the events of 11:1-9.

ARCHAEOLOGICAL LIGHT

The Tower of Babel is illuminated by the gigantic artificial mountains of sun-dried bricks in southern Babylonia called ziggurats (Assyrian-Babylonian word *ziqquratu*, meaning "pinnacle" or "mountain top"). The oldest recovered ziggurat (one of more than two dozen known today) is at ancient Uruk (Erech, Gen 10:10; modern Warka). It was a vast pile of clay buttressed on the exterior with brick and asphalt (bitumen), like similar ziggurats at Borsippa, Ur and Babylon. Built in stages, three to seven stories high, they were varicolored. On the topmost stage, the shrine and image of the city's patron deity were housed. The tower of Gen 11 was the first such tower attempted, and a symbol of man's revolt and rebellion against God. The polytheistic use of later towers, copies of the original, exemplified a more complete apostasy into idolatry so characteristic of the Sumerians and the later Semitic Babylonians of the plain of Shinar.

FROM THE FLOOD TO ABRAM

Genealogy from Shem to Abram, 10-32. Ten names are recorded. These are apparently selective and the genealogy (like the ten names from Adam to Noah in Gen 5) is symmetrically and telescopically abbreviated because: (1) The period of 427 years covered

(Hebrew), Septuagint 1307 years, is *much* too brief for known contemporary history in Egypt and Babylonia. (2) There is no evidence of a world-engirdling flood in excavated sites before at least 4500 or 5000 B.C. and to place the deluge at *c.* 2348 B.C. is archaeologically untenable. (3) Symmetry and abbreviation are characteristics of Bible genealogies. (4) The bare thread of the messianic line alone is apparently intended with representative names.

CONTEMPORARY MESOPOTAMIAN HISTORY

Period	Excavated Site	Events
Neolithic Age *c.* 5000-4500 B.C.	Earliest villages in northern Mesopotamia. Qal'at Jarma, 30 miles E of Mosul, excavated (1948) by Univ. of Chicago.	Stone implements, simple houses, no pottery.
Hassuna Period	Tell Hassuna 25 miles S of Mosul. Excavated 1943-44 by Iraq Museum. Matarrah 25 miles S of Kirkuk. Excavated by Univ. of Chicago 1948. Nineveh lowest levels. Samarra on Tigris N of Baghdad.	Crude pottery. Flint and obsidian artifacts. Development of agricultural implements, domestication of animals. Clay houses. No metal. Pottery improves. Painted pottery. Artistic height of Samarran Period.
Chalcolithic (Copper-Stone) Age. From *c.* 4500	Tell Halaf on the Habor River in northern Mesopotamia. Carchemish, 100 miles W of Tell Halaf, Tell Chagar Bazar 50 miles E of it and Tepe Gawra and Tell Arpachiya 175 miles to E of it.	Remarkable Halafian pottery. Wheeled vehicles. Copper begins to be used.
Halaf Period	Tell Abu Shahrain (Eridu) excavated 1946-47 by Iraq Dept. of Antiquities.	Settlement of southern Babylonia begun. Fine painted pottery. First prehistoric temples. Reed-clay dwellings.

Period	Excavated Site	Events
Tell Obeid Period *c.* 4000	Tell Obeid on Lower Euphrates excavated 1923-24 by C. Leonard Woolley corresponds to lowest level of Susa in Iranian highlands.	Characteristic pale-green painted pottery, lapis lazuli jewelry, stone and copper implements and weapons.
Uruk *c.* 3500	Biblical Erech (Gen 10:10), modern Warka, 35 miles up the Euphrates Valley from Tell Obeid, excavated by Germans.	Oldest stone constructions, first ziggurat (temple tower); cf. Tower of Babel (Gen 11:1-4). Introduction of the cylinder seal and writing script. Arithmetical calculations.
Jemdet Nasr *c.* 3000	Jemdet Nasr in the Mesopotamian Valley near later Babylon. Q. E. Mackay and S. Langdon *Report on Excavations at Jemdet Nasr,* Iraq, 1931. Shuruppak (Fara), Eshnunna (Tell Asmar) and Kish founded.	Greater use of metal. Bronze introduced. Writing in crude pictographs. Sculptures of men and animals. Lower Mesopotamian cities of oldest flood traditions go back to this period. Sumerian King List.
Early Dynastic Period *c.* 2800-2360	Four dynasties in Kish. Two dynasties in Ur. Three dynasties in Uruk. Dynasties in Awan, Hamazi, Adab, Mari, Akshah and Lagash.	Pictograph writings, temples, statues, arts and sciences develop and an elaborate idolatry by the Sumerians (pre-Semites in Babylonia).
Old Akkadian Period *c.* 2360-2180	Semites gain control. Sargon at Agade (Akkad) conquers Ur. Naram-Sin and his son Shargalishari rule a great empire.	Gasur (later Nuzi) important town. Efflorescence of art. Victory stele of Naram-Sin.

Period	Excavated Site	Events
Third Dynasty of Ur c. 2180-2070	C. L. Woolley excavates Ur 1922-23.	Abram born 2161 B.C. Early life in Ur. Ur-Nammu was king. Famous ziggurat at Ur.
Isin-Larsa Period c. 1960-1830	Ur destroyed.	Patriarch period in Palestine.

THE UR OF ABRAM'S DAY

Excavations at Ur. Until 1854 the site of Ur was unknown. In that year simple excavations yielded tablets stating that Nabonidus of Babylon (556-539 B.C.) had there restored the ziggurat of Ur-Nammu. Excavations by H. R. Hall (1918) and C. L. Woolley (1922-34) made Ur one of the best known sites of Babylon.

The great ziggurat at Ur was a brick stage-tower on the topmost level of which stood the Temple of Nanna. Seventy feet high, the structure was 200 feet long and 150 feet wide. (© *MPS*)

The Ur Ziggurat was a solid mass of brickwork 200 by 150 by 70 feet high, called "hill of heaven" or "mountain of God." On the top stage was the shrine of Nanna, the moon-god, patron of the city. The ziggurat stood in a *temenos* (sacred precinct) NW of the residential district, with the Euphrates skirting the city on the west and canals encircling and bisecting the town. Other temples and holy structures dominated the *temenos* of Nanna and his spouse Nin-Gal. Ur was a theocratic city-state where the moon-god deity was king as well as god, and the entire activity of the city, commercial, social as well as religious, revolved around the cult. Terah was very likely a devotee of the moon deity (cf. Josh 24:2). Abram left the city doubtless when it was at the height of its commercial prosperity.

ABRAM IN NORTHERN MESOPOTAMIA

Evidence of Patriarch's Sojourn. In spite of remarkable discoveries at Ur, especially the royal tombs (see Woolley's *Ur Excavations II: The Royal Cemetery,* 1934), no direct evidence has been found of Abram's residence there. But unmistakable evidence has come to light around Haran (see note on Gen 12:1-2). The Mari Tablets from the 18th cen. B.C., discovered in 1935, mention Nahor (Til-Nahiri, "The Mound of Nahor"), Rebekah's home (Gen 24:10). Towns near Haran include Serug (Assyrian Serugi, Gen 11:20) and Til Turakhi, "Mound of Terah." Peleg recalls later Paliga on the Euphrates. Padan-aram (Gen 25:20) is Aramaic *puddana,* "field" or "plain" of Aram. Reu (Gen 11:20) also corresponds to later names of towns in the middle Euphrates Valley.

CONTEMPORARY EGYPTIAN HISTORY

Biblical history is first laid in Babylonia, the "cradle of civilization" (Gen 1-11). Not until Egypt was hoary with age in the time of Abraham (*c.* 2050 B.C.) did its history touch the Bible narrative (Gen 12 and onward).

Egypt was founded soon after the Flood by Mizraim, son of Ham. The Amarna Tablets indicate the Canaanites called it Mizri (Misraim being dual form, preserving the ancient divisions, Upper Egypt, above Memphis, and Lower Egypt, the Delta). Early and predynastic periods extend from *c.* 5000 to 2900 B.C.

Twelve of Egypt's Thirty Dynasties. In the 3rd cen. B.C. an Egyptian priest named Manetho arranged Egyptian history into 30 dynasties from Menes, the first king of united Egypt (*c.* 2900 B.C.), to the conquest of Alexander the Great, 332 B.C.

CONSPECTUS OF EGYPTIAN HISTORY FROM THE FLOOD TO THE PATRIARCHS (DYNASTIES I-XII)

Dynasty	Date	Egyptian Events	Event in Genesis
I II	Protodynastic 2900-2700 B.C.	Menes c. 2900 B.C. Egypt united.	None
III IV V VI	Old Kingdom c 2700-c. 2200	Colossal pyramids. Pyramid Texts. Powerful central- ized government on the Nile.	None
VII VIII IX X XI	Intermediate Period c. 2200- 1989	Period of confusion and weakness.	Abram's birth 2161. Abram enters Canaan 2086. Sodom and Gomorrah destroyed c. 2065. Isaac and Jacob.
XII	Middle Kingdom c. 1989-c. 1776	Amenemes I-IV Senwosret I-III	Joseph in Egypt.

The Pyramids. Abram saw the pyramids when he went into Egypt, for they were constructed in the Old Kingdom (Third to Sixth Dynasties, about 2700-2200 B.C.). The famous Imhotep under Zoser, first king of the Third Dynasty, built the famous "step pyramid" at Saqqara, 190 feet high and the precursor of the other pyramids.

The Great Pyramid of Khufu of the Fourth Dynasty is the largest, consisting of 2,300,000 blocks of limestone with a base occupying thirteen acres, originally towering 492 feet, and each block weighing about two and a half tons. Khafre, a successor of Khufu, erected the Second Pyramid at Giza, which is almost as astonishing as the Great Pyramid. It towers 447½ feet (its present height), being only slightly less than the present height of the Great Pyramid. East of the Second Pyramid is the great Sphinx, which Abraham doubtless saw. It has a lion's body and the head of King Khafre with customary headdress and cobra (uraeus) coiled on his forehead, the royal symbol, ready to destroy the pharaoh's foes.

Pyramid Texts. The pyramids prove the high degree of civilization of the Nile Valley and the strong centralized government. Fifth and Sixth Dynasty monarchs erected a number of smaller pyramids at Saqqara containing carved inscriptions known as Pyramid Texts, which describe the prospect of a happy life after death for the deceased ruler in the presence of the sun-god. This was appropriate since the pyramids were tombs immortalizing the glory of the kings who built them.

First Intermediate Period. By Abram's time the glory of the Old Kingdom had passed, and the great pyramids were the mute mementoes of its power. Dynasties VII-XI had no strong central government, Dynasties VII and VIII ruling at Memphis and Dynasties IX and X at Herakleopolis S of Cairo.

CHAPTER 12. THE CALL OF ABRAM

The Divine Call in Haran, 1. God initially called Abram in Ur (Acts 7:2-3; Gen 11:31) and renewed the call in Haran. He confirmed it at Shechem (12:7), again at Bethel (13:14-17), and twice at Hebron (15:5, 18; 17:1-8), emphasizing how far-reaching in importance the call was. Heretofore the divine dealing had been with the whole Adamic race, now sunk into universal idolatry. God purges off a tiny rill through which he will eventually purify the great river itself.

Haran, where Abram sojourned until the death of Terah, is still in existence on the Balikh River about 600 miles NW of Ur and some 400 miles NE of Palestine. It was a flourishing city in Abram's day, as is known from the frequent references to it in cuneiform sources. Its name *Harranu* ("road") in Assyrian sources points it out as located on the great commercial arteries between Nineveh, Damascus and Carchemish. Like Ur, it was a center of the worship of the moon-god Sin.

Through Abram and the creation of the nation Israel, God established for Himself (1) a witness to the one true God in the midst of universal polytheism (Deut 6:4; Isa 43:10-12); (2) a recipient and a custodian of divine revelation (Rom 3:1-2; Deut 4:5-8); (3) a witness to the blessedness of serving the true God (Deut 33:26-29); (4) a people through whom Messiah the Redeemer would come (Gen 3:15; 12:3; 49:10; 2 Sam 7:16).

The Abrahamic Covenant Given, 2-4. The covenant, later confirmed (Gen 13:14-17; 15:1-7; 17:1-8), had seven parts: (1) *Abraham to be a great nation*—a natural progeny "as dust of the *earth*" (Gen 13:16; Jn 8:37), i.e., the Hebrew nation of the OT and the

63

restored nation of the future kingdom; and a spiritual progeny: "look now toward *heaven* . . . so shall thy descendants be," all men of faith, Jew or Gentile (Rom 4:16-17; 9:7-8; Gal 3:6-7). (2) *Abraham to be personally blessed*—"I will bless thee," materially, temporally (Gen 13:14-17; 24:34-35) and spiritually (Gen 15:6; Jn 8:56). (3) *Abraham's name to become great*—"And make thy name great." (4) *Abraham to be a personal blessing*—"Thou shalt be a blessing" (Gal 3:13-14). (5) *Those who bless Abraham will be blessed*—"I will bless them that bless thee." (6) *Those who curse Abraham will be cursed*—"I will curse him that curseth thee." Anti-Semitism has always brought God's curse and will continue to do so (Zech 14:1-3). (7) *All earth's families to be blessed in Abraham through his posterity*, Christ (Gal 3:16; Jn 8:56-58).

Abram in Canaan, 5-9. Abram's wife Sarai, his nephew Lot, and the persons (servants) he acquired in Haran migrated to the land of Canaan with him.

Shechem was Abram's first stopover in Canaan. This ancient city in the heart of Canaan is located in the pleasant valley between Mt. Ebal and Mt. Gerazim, the site of modern Nablus. Here Abram worshiped, some 30 mile N of the fortress of Jebus (later Jerusalem).

Bethel, meaning "house [dwelling place] of God," was the second place at which Abram stopped. It commanded a magnificent view of Palestine, and was an ideal spot for Jacob's later vision of the ladder. The site, less than a dozen miles N of Jebus, has been excavated and its history in Bible times traced.

Canaan (from the Hurrian "belonging to the land of the red purple"), at least as early as the 14th cen. B.C., became a geographical designation of the country in which the Canaanites or Phoenician traders trafficked in red-purple dye obtained from the murex shells on the Mediterranean coast. "Palestine" is a later Greek term (*he Palaistine*) derived from the Philistines (*Peleste*) who settled along the SW coast (Philistia, Joel 3:4, ASV).

Abram in Egypt, 10-20. Incidentally in connection with a famine in Canaan and Abram's trip to Egypt, the mighty empire on the Nile suddenly makes its debut in Bible history, but becomes common thereafter. Abram, leaving Canaan, got into difficulty over Sarah's beauty. It was common in antiquity for men of power to confiscate beautiful women. Abram's subterfuge of calling Sarah his sister was partly true. She was his half sister (20:12). Egyptian tomb monuments show bands of Semitic traders entering Egypt at early times, illustrating Abram's visit.

CHAPTER 13. ABRAM SEPARATES FROM LOT

Abram and Lot Return from Egypt, 1-4. Abram's wealth is mentioned (cf. 12:2), and his return to Bethel (see note on 12:8) near Ai (see note on Josh 8).

Abram Separates from Lot, 5-13. Abram made the choice of faith and Lot made the choice of sight, resulting in spiritual progress for Abram and spiritual declension for Lot.

Abrahamic Covenant Confirmed, 14-18. See notes on Gen 12:2-4. The possession of Canaan and a natural posterity are stressed. Abram migrated to Mamre, near Hebron, and built an altar, 18. Hebron as a city was not yet in existence in Abram's day, not being founded till "seven years before Zoan in Egypt" (Num 13:22), i.e., about 1700 B.C. Earlier the site was called Mamre and the mention of Hebron here, as in 23:19, is an explanatory note to indicate where Mamre was located.

ARCHAEOLOGICAL LIGHT

In the Middle Bronze Age (2000-1500 B.C.) the highland ridge of Palestine was heavily forested with little arable land. Cisterns were not in general use. Consequently towns were located only by springs, so there was plenty of room for seminomadic herdsmen like Abram and Lot. Archaeology has shown that Shechem, Bethel, Gerar, Dothan, Jerusalem (Salem) and Beersheba were in existence in Abraham's day, as well as the Jordan Pentapolis—Sodom, Gomorrah, Admah, Zeboiim and Zoar. Palestine was as yet thinly populated, with Canaanite towns located in the coastal plain and Esdraelon, and in the valley of the Jordan and of the Dead Sea.

CHAPTER 14. ABRAM THE HEBREW WARRIOR

Invasion of the Mesopotamian Kings, 1-12. Four Mesopotamian kings fought against five kings of the Jordan Valley, 2, and were victorious, 3-12.

Victory of Abram the Hebrew, 13-16. Abram is the first person in the Bible to be called the "Hebrew," 13. The occurrence of *Habiru* in the Mari Letters (18th cen. B.C.) and in the earlier Cappadocian Texts (19th cen. B.C.), as well as in later Nuzian, Hittite, Amarna and Ugaritic Texts (15th and 14th cen. B.C.), suggests the term is not an ethnic but a social designation describing "wanderers" or "those who pass from place to place." Placing the "Hebrews" (*Habiru*) in a much wider context is not an embarrassment to the biblical representations, since the Hebrews' ancestor Eber (Gen 11:16 f. included more than the Abrahamic line. Some of Eber's posterity remained in Babylonia when Terah left, and some in Haran when Abram migrated to Canaan.

Melchizedek and Abram, 17-24. Melchizedek, "king of Salem" ("Ursalim" in the Amarna Letters, later Jerusalem), went out to meet Abram, who was returning from his victory over the confederated kings. The king of Salem prefigured Christ as King-Priest since he offered the memorials of sacrifice (bread and wine) which point to the crucified and risen Christ. Abram glimpsed this messianic revelation of El Elyon (the most high God), possessor of heaven and earth (14:22), and paid tithes to Melchizedek in token of this recognition.

ARCHAEOLOGICAL LIGHT

Archaeology is attesting the high antiquity of Gen 14 as well as its accuracy. Examples of ancient archaic place names with scribal explanations, making them comprehensible to a later generation, are "Bela (the same is Zoar)," 2; "the vale of Siddim (the same is the Salt Sea)," 3; "En-mishphat (the same is Kadesh)," 7; "the vale of Shaveh (the same is the King's Vale)," 17, ASV.

The cities of Hauran (Bashan), Ashtaroth and Karnaim, were both occupied at this early period, as examination of their mounds has shown. The city of Ham has been found by A. Jirku and W. F. Albright to be identified with modern Ham and going back to the Bronze Age (c. 2000 B.C.).

The route of the invading kings through Hauran, eastern Gilead and Moab to SE Palestine has been shown to be historically likely by a discovery of a line of Early and Middle Bronze Age mounds running along this route where the Early Middle Bronze city of Ader was found in 1924. Later this route, called the King's Highway, was famous, but does not appear to have been used after 1200 B.C. The asphalt of the Dead Sea, and the important copper and manganese deposits of Edom and Midian, appear to have been the purpose of the invasion.

CHAPTER 15. THE ABRAHAMIC COVENANT CONFIRMED

The Divine Promise, 1. The Lord gave assurance of protection and reward for trusting Him.

The Human Predicament, 2-3. Abram was childless. His steward Eliezer was his only heir. In the natural, the situation was hopeless.

The Promise of a Son, 4-5. This also included the promise of spiritual progeny as numerous as the stars: "So [numerous] shall your [spiritual] descendants be" (RSV).

Abram's Faith, 6, grasped God's promise, which ultimately centered in the greater Isaac (Messiah) and resulted in justification (Rom 4:3; Gal 3:6).

The Covenant Confirmed, 7-21. God honored this justifying faith. The animals sacrificed pointed to Christ's atonement by which the covenant would be ratified, 7-10. The marauding fowls, 11, portrayed the nations that would harass Israel (cf. Mt 13:4, 19), while the exposed pieces represented Israel. The "deep sleep" and "horror of great darkness," 12, pictured the tribulation that would come upon Abram's posterity for 400 years, 13. (A generation at that time was reckoned as 100 years, 16.) Egypt was the "smoking furnace" (Deut 4:20; 1 Kgs 8:51), and the "burning lamp" indicated the Lord's presence with His people there. The covenant announced (12:1-4), and confirmed (13:14-17; 15:1-7) was here ratified (15:18-21).

CHAPTER 16. ISHMAEL AND ABRAM'S FALTERING FAITH

Temptation to Unbelief, 1-6. The stalwart warrior of faith in Gen 15 resorted to human means to help God out in the fulfillment of the promise. Unbelief manifested impatience in both Abram and Sarai, 2-3. Sarai pictures the covenant of grace, Hagar represents the covenant of the law "which gendereth to bondage" (Gal 4:24-25).

Results of Unbelief, 7-16. The birth of Ishmael memorialized Abram's doubt and his tampering with the covenant given him by God. Hagar was vouchsafed a promise that this son would father a prolific line, 10, and that Ishmael would be a wild, unruly, warlike man, 12. In this child of unbelief future generations were bequeathed a division, full of animosity, that is still a cause of international tension.

CHAPTER 17. THE COVENANT RECONFIRMED

Covenant Sealed by Revelation, 1-2. God revealed Himself as El Shaddai (God Almighty), the All Powerful One, able to consummate the staggering promise of a coming Redeemer to Abram, to Isaac (Gen 28:3-4), to Jacob (35:11) and Joseph (48:3; 49:22-26; cf. Ex 6:2-4).

Covenant Sealed by Change of Name, 3-8. The name Abram ("eminent father") was changed to Abraham ("father of a multitude") as a token of what El Shaddai in His redemptive power would do. Sarai's name was also changed to Sarah ("princess"), 15.

Covenant Sealed by Circumcision, 9-27. Circumcision was a sign or token of the covenant, 9-10, a seal of the righteousness wrought by faith (Rom 4:9-12). It suggested the putting away of evil (Deut 10:16; Jer 4:4), symbolizing the purification of life at its very source and thus saliently pointing to the messianic hope (through Isaac, 15-17, not Ishmael, 18-27). The greater Isaac, who Himself was to be born of woman, would· be the Redeemer and Covenant-Fulfiller. He alone would exemplify all that circumcision pointed to.

CHAPTER 18-19. SODOM AND GOMORRAH

The Lord's Appearance at Mamre, 18:1-16. Extraordinary intercourse of God with Abraham climaxed the divine promises of posterity through Isaac to culminate in messianic redemption. The Lord in human form, apparently accompanied by two angels, appeared to the patriarch, "the friend of God" (Isa 41:8; Jas 2:23) to assure

Sodom,
at the south end
of the Dead Sea.
(*Courtesy IIS*)

the promise. The Almighty (El Shaddai) would demonstrate that nothing is too difficult for Him, 14.

Abraham's Intercession for Sodom, 17-33. The Lord reveals His secrets to His own. Abraham was therefore apprised of the judgment of the wicked, that his posterity might know that what happened to them was divine judgment and not an accident. God's grace promised in the covenant to the believing is contrasted to His severity manifested toward the wicked and unrepentant. What boldness and humility combine in the patriarch's intercession for the sinners of Sodom, 23-33!

Sodom's Sin and Destruction, 19:1-38. The fearful degeneracy of the city and its overthrow serve as a warning to God's chosen people, especially in the case of the involvement of Lot and his family (cf. Lk 17:32; 2 Pet 2:6-9).

ARCHAEOLOGICAL LIGHT

The five cities of the plain (circle) of the Jordan (Sodom, Gomorrah, Admah, Zeboiim, Zoar) were located in the Vale of Siddim (Gen 14:3) at the southern end of the Dead Sea. Now covered with water, this region in c. 2065 B.C. was fertile and populous. About 2050 B.C. the salt and free sulphur in this area, which is now a burnt-out region of oil and asphalt (Gen 14:10), were miraculously mingled, apparently by an earthquake common to this region. The violent explosion hurled the salt and sulphur into the air red-hot, so that it literally rained fire and brimstone over the whole plain (Gen 19:24, 28).

The great salt mass Jebel Usdum ("Mountain of Sodom"), a five-mile-long elevation at the SW end of the Dead Sea, recalls the episode of Lot's wife being turned into a pillar of salt. The Cities of the Plain are to be found under the slowly rising water of the southern part of the Salt Sea. Their ruins were still visible until the 1st cen. A.D.

CHAPTER 20. ABRAHAM AT GERAR

Abraham's Lie, 1-18. Abraham told Abimelech Sarah was his sister, repeating the same weakness of a former year (12:10-20) and demonstrating that the near-to-be recipient of the fulfilled redemptive promise through Isaac was himself a needy subject for God's grace in view of his imperfections.

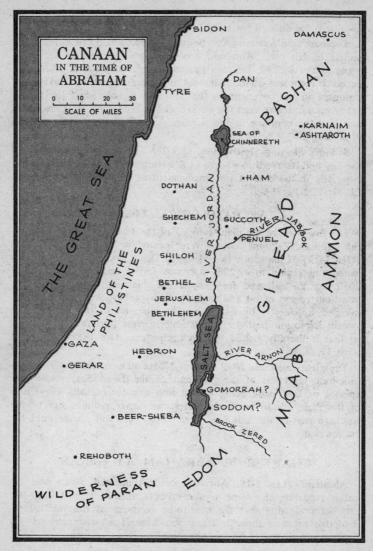

CANAAN
IN THE TIME OF
ABRAHAM

0   10   20   30
SCALE OF MILES

SIDON
DAMASCUS
DAN
BASHAN
TYRE
KARNAIM
ASHTAROTH
SEA OF
CHINNERETH
THE GREAT SEA
HAM
DOTHAN
SHECHEM
SUCCOTH
RIVER JORDAN
RIVER JABBOK
PENUEL
GILEAD
AMMON
SHILOH
LAND OF THE PHILISTINES
BETHEL
JERUSALEM
BETHLEHEM
SALT SEA
GAZA
HEBRON
RIVER ARNON
GERAR
GOMORRAH?
MOAB
SODOM?
BEER-SHEBA
BROOK ZERED
REHOBOTH
EDOM
WILDERNESS
OF PARAN

CHAPTER 21. ISAAC'S BIRTH

Birth of Isaac, 1-8. The name Isaac ("laughter") suggests the joy the child of promise was to bring not only to his aged parents but to all the redeemed through the greater Isaac, Christ.

Expulsion of Ishmael, 9-21. Ishmael mocked Isaac, made fun of the spiritual destiny of the child, and made the boy feel the importance Abraham attached to him was silly and nonsensical. Paul says Ishmael persecuted Isaac (Gal 4:29). Abraham under divine direction sent Hagar and Ishmael away (cf. a previous similar but different event, 16:5-16).

Covenant with Abimelech, 22-34. This incident shows what an influential and powerful man Abraham was under God's blessing.

CHAPTER 22. THE SACRIFICE OF ISAAC

The Supreme Test, 1-14. This event marked the highwater mark in Abraham's spiritual experience (cf. Heb 11:17-19). This, the greatest crisis of the patriarch's life, was made possible by three others which were foundational and preparatory to it: (1) His surrender of country and kindred (Gen 12:1). (2) His separation from Lot, a possible heir and fellow believer (Gen 13:5-18; 2 Pet 2:7-8). (3) His rejection of his own plan and hopes for Ishmael (Gen 17:17-18). Only with this previous spiritual commitment as a background was Abraham ready for the injunction, "Take now thy son, *thine only son* Isaac, whom thou lovest . . . and offer him . . ." (22:1). The whole incident was fraught with deep spiritual meaning. Abraham prefigures the Father who "spared not his own Son, but delivered him up for us all" (Rom 8:32). Isaac pictures Christ "obedient unto death" (Phil 2:5-8). The ram sets forth substitutionary atonement through Christ offered as a burnt offering in our place (Heb 10:5-10).

The Covenant Repeated, 15-24, dramatically and solemnly, in response to the patriarch's faith and obedience so clearly proved.

CHAPTER 23. THE DEATH OF SARAH

Sarah Dies, 1-2. Sarah's death in this richly suggestive section speaks of Israel's death nationally, consequent upon the death and resurrection of the true Isaac, the Lord Jesus Christ (Gen 22).

Sarah Is Buried, 3-18. After the death of Sarah (from whom Isaac came), her grave was secured among the Hittites (Gentiles), prefiguring Israel's burial among the nations. But the restoration of the nation is assured by resurrection, as in Ezk 37:1-14. The Lord will bring them out of their graves among the nations and bring them back to the land promised Abraham and his posterity, in fulfillment of the covenant (Gen 12:1-3; 15:7-21).

CHAPTER 24. A BRIDE FOR ISAAC

The Servant Seeks and Secures the Bride, 1-61. The deeper spiritual meaning of Gen 22 and 23 is continued and confirmed by ch. 24, which deals with the call of the bride to comfort Isaac after his mother's death. Abraham, 1-4, prefigures God the Father who would make a marriage for His Son (cf. Mt 22:2). The anonymous servant suggests the Holy Spirit, who seeks the Bride for the divine Isaac among the Gentiles (Acts 15:14-15). He does not speak of Himself but takes the things of the Bridegroom to win the Bride (Jn 16:13-14) and enriches the Bride with the Bridegroom's gifts (1 Cor 12:7-11). Rebekah beautifully illustrates the Church as the virgin Bride of Christ (2 Cor 11:2; Eph 5:25-32).

Isaac Goes Forth to Meet and Receive His Bride, 62-67. He prefigures the Bridegroom, "whom not having seen" the Bride loves through the report of the Servant (1 Pet 1:8), and who comes forth to meet and to take His Bride for Himself.

CHAPTER 25. ABRAHAM'S DEATH

Abraham Marries Keturah, 1-4. With an account of this union and its offspring the story of the great patriarch ends.

Isaac the Heir, 5-6. This reference parallels Christ as "the heir of all things" (Heb 1:2).

Abraham's Death and Burial, 7-11. The typical teaching of Gen 22—25 springs out of the fact that the blessings portrayed are connected with the Abrahamic covenant and so with the patriarch and his life.

Ishmael's Generations, 12-18. When Israel is restored, Ishmael will not be forgotten (cf. Isa 60:7).

Isaac's Generations, 25:19—35:29. It is through this line that that of the Promised One runs.

Esau and Jacob, 25:19-34. Rebekah's sterility was cured by prayer, 21-22, and she gave birth to Esau and Jacob, 23-28 (cf. Rom 9:11-13). Esau sold his birthright, 29-34, which involved (1) paternal blessing and the place as head of the family; (2) the honor of being in the promised line out of which the Messiah should come (Shem—

Abraham—Isaac); (3) the exercise of the family priesthood. Esau carnally despised all these blessings as a lover of pleasure more than a lover of God.

CHAPTER 26. ISAAC IN GERAR

Abrahamic Covenant Confirmed, 1-5.

Experience at Gerar, 6-11. There Isaac failed as his father had done (cf. 20:1-18). Gerar was SE of Gaza in Philistia (Tell Jemmeh).

Isaac the Well-Digger, 12-33. The Lord appeared to him at Beersheba ("well of the oath").

Esau's Wives, 34-35. These further showed the carnality of the despiser of the birthright.

CHAPTERS 27—33. THE STORY OF JACOB

Main Periods of Jacob's Life. (1) In Canaan, the stolen blessing, ch. 27; the flight and Bethel vision, ch. 28; (2) servitude in Padanaram, ch. 29—31; (3) return to Canaan, ch. 32—33. Jacob's life was a foreshadowing of the history of his descendants (Israelites).

Beersheba, a site prominent in the patriarchal narrative, is today a rapidly growing Israeli city. (*Courtesy IIS*)

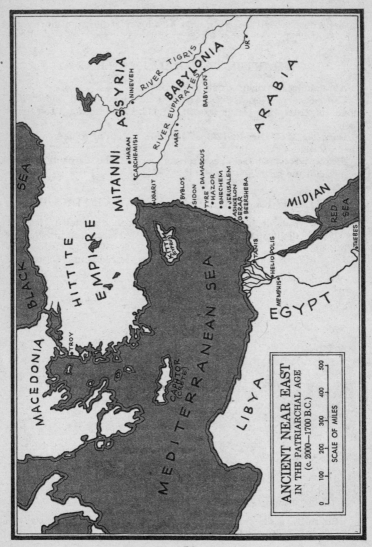

ANCIENT NEAR EAST
IN THE PATRIARCHAL AGE
(c. 2000—1700 B.C.)

SCALE OF MILES

0   100   200   300   400   500

They were once in tne land, now away from it, but will after spiritual renewal (Gen 32:30) return to it in fulfillment of the Abrahamic covenant so graphically confirmed to Jacob in the ladder vision at Bethel (ch. 28), as he was leaving the land.

ARCHAEOLOGICAL LIGHT

Haran (see Gen 11-12) was about 400 miles NE of Canaan on the Balikh River, 60 miles above the spot where it flows into the Euphrates River. It was an important junction on the rich caravan route between Nineveh, Carchemish, Mesopotamia, the Hittite Empire and Egypt via Palestine. The town played a conspicuous role in Hebrew history.

Padan-aram (Aramaic *paddana;* "field or plain" of Aram; Gen 25:20; 28:2,6), was the region in which Haran was located, and from which both Isaac and Jacob procured wives (Rebekah and Rachel) from among their relatives who had settled in Aram-Naharaim ("Aram of the two rivers").

Nahor, Rebekah's home city (Gen 24:10), occurs often as Nakhur in the Mari Tablets, discovered in 1935 and belonging to the 18th cen. B.C.

Mesopotamia is the AV translation of Aram-Naharaim ("Aram of the two rivers"; Gen 24:10, ASV marg.), which denotes the territory E of the Middle Euphrates, at least to the Habor River if not beyond. The actual term is Greek meaning "in the midst of the rivers" (i.e., the Euphrates and Tigris) and reflects a much vaster territory than the early Hebrew term Aram-Naharaim, which simply denoted the region of the Balikh and Habor Rivers which empty into the Euphrates within 200 miles of the river's course SE of Tiphsah.

PATRIARCHAL CUSTOMS

The discoveries at Nuzu SE of Nineveh near modern Kirkuk in 1925-41 have yielded several thousand cuneiform tablets illustrating such patriarchal customs as adoption (Gen 15:2,4), the relationship between Jacob and Laban (Gen 29—31), marriage (Gen 16:1-16; 30:3, 9), rights of the firstborn (Gen 25:27-34), the teraphim (Gen 31:34, ASV). The latter are now known to have been household deities, the possession of which implied family leadership. In the case of a married daughter, they assured the husband the right to the property of her father. Since Laban evidently had sons of his own when Jacob left for Canaan, they alone had the right to their father's gods. Accordingly, Rachel's stealing the teraphim was a serious offense (Gen 31:19, 30, 35) aimed at preserving for her husband the chief title to Laban's estate.

CHAPTER 34. DINAH AVENGED BY SIMEON AND LEVI

Jacob Chastened, 1-5. Although Jacob ("supplanter") had his name changed to Israel ("prince with God"), yet the patriarch's transformation in character was only gradual. He was still a man of guile and deceit. Reconciled to Esau, he told his brother he would follow him to Seir, but did no such thing. Instead he settled down at Succoth (Gen 33:18-20) among the Hivites for a sad experience.

Dinah's Defilement, 6-31. Jacob reaped what he had sown. The deceit of the father was reflected in the deceit of his sons.

PATRIARCHAL FAMILY TREE

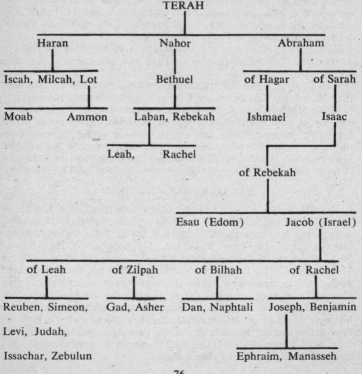

TERAH

Haran — Nahor — Abraham

Iscah, Milcah, Lot — Bethuel — of Hagar — of Sarah

Moab — Ammon — Laban, Rebekah — Ishmael — Isaac

Leah, Rachel

of Rebekah

Esau (Edom) — Jacob (Israel)

of Leah — of Zilpah — of Bilhah — of Rachel

Reuben, Simeon, Levi, Judah, Issachar, Zebulun — Gad, Asher — Dan, Naphtali — Joseph, Benjamin

Ephraim, Manasseh

CHAPTER 35. RENEWAL OF THE COVENANT AT BETHEL

Jacob Restored to Fellowship at Bethel, 1-15. The divine command, 1, was obeyed by cleansing from idolatrous contamination, 2-4. God protected on the journey, 5-6, and manifested Himself at Bethel, 7-15. Bethel ("house of God") is 12 miles N of Jerusalem and has been systematically excavated both as a Canaanite site and later prominent Hebrew town. In calling the place Bethel, Jacob (28:19; 35:15) reflected the impression the ladder vision made upon him there. Now in his deep spiritual renovation, it was the God of the place rather than the place that captivated him, so Jacob called the hallowed spot El-Bethel ("the God of the house of God").

Jacob's Sons, 16-26. Rachel died at the birth of Benjamin ("son of [my] right hand"), 16-21. Reuben, the oldest and heir to the birthright, sinned, 22, and lost the blessing (49:3-4). The other sons are named, 23-26.

Isaac's Death, 27-29.

CHAPTER 36. ESAU'S LINE

Esau's Country, 1-19. Edom was the territory S of the Dead Sea reaching to the Gulf of Aqabah. Mountains and fertile plateaus on both sides of the Arabah gave it about 100 square miles within its boundaries, which varied, however, with the fortunes of the kingdom. At the time of the Exodus the kingdom extended from the brook Zered S of Moab and the southern tip of the Salt Sea and skirted Judah in a southwesterly direction. Mt. Seir was a 5000-foot peak where Esau's descendants began their kingdom. Sela (later the Nabataean rose-colored fortress of Petra) was the early capital of the country, which developed great wealth from agriculture, metal industry, cattle raising and caravan tolls from the King's Highway which crossed its borders.

Horites, 20-43. Hori or Horim were a tribe residing in Mt. Seir in Edom, 30, thought by many to be troglodytes (cave dwellers). Other scholars identify them with the Hurrians, non-Semitic people from Mesopotamia, known from cuneiform sources discovered within the last half century. The Hurrians were conquered by the Hittites in the 14th cen. B.C. and remnants of the latter also were scattered throughout Edom (cf. Gen 26:34-35) at an early date.

The Hittites (Heb. *Hitti, Heth*) were with Egyptians, Mesopotamians and Hebrews one of the more influential peoples of early

77

OT times. Their capital was Boghazkoy-Hattushash, not far from Ankara, capital of modern Turkey. They are mentioned 47 times in the OT.

CHAPTER 37. JOSEPH INTRODUCED

The Beloved Son of Jacob, 1-11. The varicolored coat his father gave Joseph was an indication of paternal favor and apparently of Jacob's intention to make him heir of the birthright. Reuben, the oldest, had forfeited the right by incest (35:22; 49:3-4; 1 Chr 5:1-2). Simeon and Levi, next in order, were ruled out because of their violence at Shechem (34:25-30; 49:5-7). Judah, the fourth son, was the next heir. Joseph, though eleventh in order, was Jacob's firstborn by his favorite wife Rachel and his father's favorite (37:3), and so apparently was Judah's rival.

The Hatred of Joseph's Brothers, 12-27. They sold Joseph into slavery. (Cf. Judah's part, 26-27.) The old rivalry was to be perpetuated between Judah and Ephraim (Joseph's son). The division of the kingdom under Rehoboam saw Judah split from the ten tribes under Ephraim's leadership.

Joseph Sold in Egypt, 28-36.

JOSEPH THE MESSIANIC PATRIARCH

Why is so large a section of Genesis (ch. 37—48) devoted to Joseph? (1) He was the link between the *family* of Israel and the *nation* of Israel. Up to the time of Joseph the Israelites were a family. Joseph was connected with the Egyptian sojourn and the birth of the nation. (2) *He is the Bible's most complete type* of Christ—not that he was faultless, but his faults are not recorded. Numerous parallels between his life and that of Jesus may be enumerated, although it is nowhere actually stated that he was such a type. (a) Both were special objects of a father's love (Gen 37:3; Mt 3:17; Jn 3:35; 5:20). (b) Both were hated and rejected by their brothers (Gen 37:4; Jn 15:25). (c) Both made unusual claims which were rejected by their brothers (Gen 37:8; Mt 21:37-39; Jn 15:24-25). (d) In both cases brothers conspired to slay them (Gen 37:18; Mt 26:3-4). (e) Joseph was in intent and figure put to death by his brothers, as Christ actually was (Gen 37:24; Mt 27:35-37). (f) Both became a blessing among the Gentiles and acquired a Gentile bride (Gen 41:1-45; Acts 15:14; Eph 5:25-32). (g) As Joseph reconciled his brothers to himself and afterward exalted them, so at His second advent Christ will be reconciled to converted Israel (Gen 45:1-15; Deut 30:1-10; Hos 2:14-16; Rom 11:1, 15, 25, 26).

CHAPTERS 38—41. JOSEPH'S HUMILIATION AND EXALTATION IN EGYPT

Parenthetical: Judah's Shame as Progenitor of the Messiah, ch. 38. It is amazing the Spirit of God would recount this sordid story. But God's Word deals realistically with sin even in preserved family registers in the line of messianic succession.

Joseph in Prison, ch. 39. God's way up is often down, humiliation before exaltation. The Egyptian "Tale of the Two Brothers" later in the reign of Seti II bears resemblance to Joseph and Potiphar's wife.

Joseph on the Throne, ch. 40-41. He marries the daughter of the priest of On, a city of Lower Egypt, half a dozen miles from modern Cairo. The Greeks called it Heliopolis ("city of the sun") since the solar disc was the supreme deity of the Nile Valley. The worship of the sun at Heliopolis was the keynote of Egyptian ritual and the On priesthood was powerful and closely identified with the throne.

ARCHAEOLOGICAL LIGHT

Ample evidence of famines in Egypt exists. At least two Egyptian officials list among their good deeds the dispensing of food to the needy "in each year of want." One inscription (c. 100 B.C.) actually describes a seven-year famine in the days of Zoser of the Third Dynasty (c. 2700 B.C.). The titles of "chief of the butlers" and "chief of the bakers" (40:2) were those of palace officials mentioned in Egyptian documents. The entire story of Joseph swarms with correct local and antiquarian details, as well as the Egyptian narratives of Genesis and Exodus in general.

When Potiphar made Joseph "overseer of his house" (39:4) the title employed was a direct translation of a position in the houses of Egyptian nobility. Pharaoh gave Joseph an office with a similar title in the administration of the realm (41:46) corresponding precisely to the office of vizier, the chief administrator of the country, second in power to Pharaoh himself. The Egyptian office of superintendent of the granaries was pivotal and apparently filled by Joseph in addition to his duties as prime minister (vizier). Pharaoh's giving gifts to Joseph (41:42-43) on the latter's induction into office was completely in accord with Egyptian customs.

CHAPTERS 42—45. JOSEPH REVEALED TO HIS BROTHERS

This is one of the finest and most dramatic stories in all literature, filled with authentic Egyptian coloring. When Judah, who had years before engineered the selling of his brother into slavery (37:26), now climaxes the emotional throb of the story by offering himself a hostage for Benjamin (44:18-34), Joseph could no longer refrain himself (45:1-15) and made himself known.

CHAPTER 46. JACOB AND HIS FAMILY MIGRATE TO EGYPT

The Vision of God at Beersheba, 1-4. In this last appearance to the patriarch, God assured him He would bring the Israelites again out of Egypt.

Arrival in Egypt, 5-34. The descendants of Jacob are enumerated (8-26) as well as Joseph's sons who were born in Egypt, 27. Israel met Joseph, 28-30, and Joseph gave directions concerning Pharaoh (31-34).

CHAPTER 47. SETTLEMENT IN GOSHEN

Jacob Before Pharaoh, 1-10. The mighty monarch of the Nile graciously received the patriarch. In turn the aged Jacob blessed the powerful potentate, an illustration of how Israel is yet to bless the nations.

Israel's Settlement in Goshen, 11-31. Goshen was the NE section of Egypt nearest Palestine. It was called "the best of the land" and "the land of Raamses," which agrees with the character of this region, excellent for grazing and certain kinds of farming, but not particularly wanted by the pharaohs because distant from the Nile irrigation canals. This region is called Goshen only in the Bible. It was a valley some 35 miles long, centering in the Wadi Tumilat and stretching from Lake Timsah to the Nile. Joseph's wise administration is described, 13-26, and Jacob's last days, 27-31.

ARCHAEOLOGICAL LIGHT

It is noteworthy that so far no Egyptian records have been found of Israel's sojourn in Goshen. But since the pharaoh often allowed such groups to settle in Egypt, such an instance would scarcely be unusual. Besides the piece of sculpture depicting the entrance of the

Ploughing in the land of Goshen with Egyptian buffaloes. (© *MPS*)

family of Ibshe into Egypt about 1900 B.C., another Egyptian inscription indicates that it was customary for frontier officials to allow people from Palestine and Sinai to enter this section of Egypt in periods of dearth. This document (*c.* 1350 B.C.) tells of such a group "who knew not how they should live, have come begging a home in the domain of Pharaoh . . . after the manner of your [the Pharaoh's] fathers' fathers since the beginning. . . ."

CHAPTER 48. JACOB'S ADOPTION OF EPHRAIM AND MANASSEH

Joseph's Sons Presented, 1-14. As the children of the Gentile wife Asenath, Joseph's two sons were in danger of becoming gentilized and forgetting their father's house. Jacob avoided this by adopting them.

Jacob's Blessing and Last Words to Joseph, 15-22. Jacob's move was by faith (Heb 11:21), once again preferring the younger (Ephraim) before the elder (Manasseh).

CHAPTER 49. JACOB'S PROPHETIC BLESSING OF THE 12 TRIBES

Jacob's Call, 1-2. He assembled his 12 sons to prophesy their tribal future.

The Prophecy, 3-27. This covers in a remarkable manner the entire sweep of Israelite history—past, present and future. That concerning Reuben, 3-4, Simeon and Levi, 5-7, characterized the nation till Messiah's advent. Judah, 8-12, pointed to the period when our Lord was on the earth. What was said of Judah was detailed because from him was to come "Shiloh" (Heb. text), an epithet of Messiah, 10, ruling with a kingly sceptre (Num 24:17). Zebulun, 13, and Issachar, 14-15, located where sea traffic and commerce were prominent, portrayed Israel a trading people scattered among the nations. Dan, 16-18, suggests apostate Israel during the reign of Antichrist. Gad, 19, Asher, 20, and Naphtali, 21, portray the godly Jewish remnant of the Great Tribulation. Joseph, 22-26, speaks of the second advent of Messiah, and Benjamin ("son of the right hand"), of the rod-of-iron righteous rule of the King in the Kingdom Age.

CHAPTER 50. DEATH OF JACOB AND JOSEPH

Jacob's Decease and Burial, 1-13. Joseph grieved, 1-3, and had his father embalmed, 2, this being the only direct Bible reference to mummification by Hebrews. Spices were placed in certain body cavities and the body treated in an elaborate way to prevent decay. This highly developed science was practiced for 30 centuries in ancient Egypt. The Egyptains mourned for Jacob 70 days, which was the period required for mummification, while 40 days were specified for Jacob's embalming. Accompanied by a great company headed by Joseph and Egyptian officials, Jacob's body was taken to Canaan for burial, 4-13. Burial was in the cave of Machpelah.

The Return to Egypt, 14-21. Joseph's magnanimous treatment of his brothers is outlined.

Death of Joseph, 22-26. Jacob was 147 years old (47:28) and Joseph 110 when they died. Joseph's faith is shown by the oath he made his brothers take to transport his bones to Canaan (cf. Ex 13:19; Josh 24:32; cf. Gen 33:19; Acts 7:15-16; Heb 11:22).

EXODUS

THE BOOK OF REDEMPTION

The Book in General. Exodus takes its name from the Latin Vulgate through the Greek Septuagint, the word in both languages having the meaning of "departure," "a going" or "way out" (cf. Ex 19:1; Heb 11:22). The book focuses attention upon the great experience of redemption from Egypt as the type of all redemption and the constitution of the descendants of Jacob as a theocratic nation at Mt. Sinai.

The Lord, heretofore connected with the Israelites only through His covenant with Abraham, Isaac and Jacob, now brings them to Himself nationally through redemption and puts them under the Mosaic covenant with tabernacle, priesthood and the Shekinah glory of His presence. The entire book is typical of the person and work of Christ, especially the tabernacle, priesthood and sacrificial ritual as 1 Cor 10 and the book of Hebrews show.

Higher Criticism of the Book makes it (along with Genesis) a late compilation of popular traditions (Jehovistic, *c.* 850 B.C.; Elohistic, *c.* 750 B.C.; and Priestly, *c.* 500 B.C.), these being combined with the original Mosaic tradition. So the book is adjudged non-Mosaic in authorship, unreliable historically, and the miracles in it traditional rather than factual.

But the elements of the book are so intimately and closely welded together with such harmoniousness with the other Pentateuchal books and the Bible as a whole, that the critical view appears at variance with clear lines of historical and scriptural evidence supporting the unity of the entire Pentateuch. The amazingly detailed typology of the book, woven like a magnificent mosaic in God's great redemption plan from Genesis to Revelation, argues strongly against the naturalistic views of Pentateuchal partitionists.

CHAPTER 1.   ISRAEL ENSLAVED IN EGYPT

Israel's Increase, 1-14 Joseph died and several centuries elapsed. A "new king," doubtless under the powerful Eighteenth Dynasty of Egypt, came to power. His oppression of the people is prefaced by an account of the expansion of the Israelites, 1-7. This picture of expansion precedes heartless oppression, 8-14. By forced corvée, Pharaoh built Pithom (Tell er-Ratabeh) and Raamses (Avaris-Tanis) in the Delta.

Planned Extinction, 15-22. Hebrew midwives were ordered to kill all male Israelite babies, but disobeyed Pharaoh and were blessed by the Lord. Then the king ordered the populace to drown every male Hebrew baby in the Nile. Satan's attempt to destroy the promised seed and the Jewish people can be traced from Cain's murder of Abel to the time of Christ (cf. 2 Chr 21:4; 22:10; Est 3:13; Mt 2:16).

EGYPT: THE LAND AND PEOPLE

Egypt, Egypt was a country 2 to 30 miles wide, situated along the course of the mighty Nile SW of Palestine, with no significant mountains or river separating, but only the small wadi El Arish, "the river of Egypt" (Num 34:5; Josh 15:4, 47). Egypt was the Nile. And the narrow ribbon of fertile alluvial land the river deposited was watered by an annual inundation, making it the breadbasket of the ancient world. Brisk land and sea traffic with Syria-Palestine and the rest of the Fertile Crescent poured a steady stream of wealth into Egypt. The result was fabulous affluence concentrated in the splendid courts at Thebes, Memphis and Akhetaton (Tell-el-Amarna).

Store Cities. These towns were constructed to receive surplus grain in times of plenty. Hebrew forced labor was used to build a number of them, such as Pithom (Tell Retabeh) and Raamses (Tanis). These cities were also stocked with local and imported goods, and military equipment for campaigns in Syria-Palestine.

People and Language. Ancient Egyptians were Hamitic (Gen. 10:6), but later migrations, predominantly Semitic, left an imprint upon the language and culture. Earliest writing was a picture language (hieroglyphics), including representations of common objects and geometric symbols. Through the centuries this gradually gave way by the 8th cen. B.C. to a popular or "demotic" cursive script.

The Rosetta Stone, found by Napoleon's soldiers near Rosetta, Egypt, in 1799, provided J. F. Champollion with the key to decipherment of Egyptian. (*Courtesy ORINST*)

In 1799 the Rosetta Stone was discovered written in Old Egyptian (hieroglyphics), demotic and Greek. The decipherment of the stone by the Frenchman François Champollion (1822) furnished the key to the language and the foundation of modern Egyptology.

EGYPT: ITS HISTORY AND EARLY CONTACT WITH ISRAEL

Early and Predynastic Periods, c. 5000-2900 B.C.—Neolithic and later cultures previous to a United Kingdom. Manetho, a priest of the

3rd cen. B.C., wrote a history of Egypt dividing the historical period c. 2900-332 B.C. into 30 royal dynasties.

Early Dynastic Period, c. 2900-2700 B.C. Menes reigned at This below Thebes. Tombs of Thinite kings (Dynasties I and II) near Abydos have been excavated by Flinders Petrie.

Old Kingdom, c. 2700-2200 B.C., Dynasties III-VI. Dynasties III and IV were the age of the great pyramids and pyramid texts. Zoser (Third Dynasty) built the Step Pyramid at Saqqara. Khufu, founder of the Fourth Dynasty, built the greatest of the pyramids at Giza (492 feet high, 755 feet square at base, covering 13 acres, containing 2,300,000 limestone blocks each weighing two and a half tons). Khafre, Khufu's successor, constructed the second great pyramid at Giza and the Sphinx. Pyramid texts dealing with the future life of the deceased kings belong to the Fifth and Sixth Dynasties.

First Intermediate Period, c. 2200-1989 B.C., Dynasties VII-XI, ruled at Memphis and Herakleopolis, 77 miles S of Cairo. This was a period of comparative weakness. Abraham's visit to Egypt was during this time.

Middle Kingdom, c. 1989-1776 B.C., Dynasty XII, was ruled by native Thebans at Memphis and in the Fayum. It was coeval with the patriarchal period in Palestine. Probably during this period Joseph became prime minister. Jacob stood before one of the powerful rulers of this line, Amenemes I-IV or Senwosret I-III. An inscription on the tomb of Khnumhotep II, a powerful noble of Senwosret II, depicts the visit of 37 Asiatics under "sheik of the highlands, Ibshe," recalling Abraham's Egyptian visit and Jacob's going down into the country.

Second Intermediate Period, c. 1750-1570, Dynasties XIII-XVII. The strong Middle Kingdom was succeeded by a period of turmoil under Dynasties XIII and XIV, in turn followed by Hyksos, "rulers of the foreign lands." These foreign princes reigned almost 150 years, Dynasties XV and XVI, at Avaris (Tanis) in the Delta. Horse and chariot and a spirit of war were introduced. Some scholars place Joseph's rule in this period.

New Empire, c. 1570-1150 B.C., Dynasties XVIII-XX. This was the period when Egypt ruled the East, the heyday of pharaonic glory. It was the time of enslavement of the Israelites. Great pharaohs of this era include Amenhotep I (c. 1546-1525), Thutmose I (c. 1525-1508), Thutmose II (c. 1508-1504), Queen Hatshepsut (c. 1504-1482). It was the era of Moses' birth and youth. Thutmose III (c. 1490-1445) was a great builder, conqueror and enslaver of the Israelites. Amenhotep II (c. 1445-1425) was apparently the pharaoh of the Exodus. There was decline under Thutmose IV. Amenhotep

III reigned c. 1412-1375, called the Amarna period, followed by Amenhotep IV (Akhnaton), c. 1375-1359. The capital was at Akhetaton (Tell el Amarna). The Amarna Letters were discovered here in 1886. Tutankhamen's lavish tomb was unearthed in 1922. The Amarna period was perhaps coeval with Israel's wanderings and conquest of Palestine.

Many scholars place the Exodus and the Conquest under Dynasty XIX: Raamses I (c. 1319), Sethi I (c. 1319-1299), Raamses II (c. 1299-1232), Merenptah or Merneptah (c. 1232-1222). In the latter's famous stele, Israel is mentioned for the first time in Egyptian records: "the people of Israel is desolate; it has no offspring."

Dynasty XX (c. 1200-1085) had about ten rulers by the name of Raamses. Raamses III (c. 1198-1167) was the greatest. Dynasty XX was coeval with the period of the Judges in Israel. Dynasties XXI-XXX showed decline.

THE RUINS AT THEBES

Thebes (Egyptian Net, biblical No, Greek Thebai) was the capital of the powerful Eighteenth Dynasty and evidently built by Israelite slave labor. Its ruins are immensely impressive on the Nile 350 miles SE of Cairo, near the modern villages of Luxor and Karnak. The magnificent temple of Amun at Karnak is a world-wonder, and approached by an avenue of sphinxes. Its great court measures 276 by 338 feet, traversed by a double line of colossal columns. The great hall or hypostyle, 1200 feet long and 350 feet wide, was supported by 134 columns in 16 rows, the central row being 78 feet high and 33 feet in circumference. Brilliantly painted and sculptured, it is a dazzling example of Egyptian architectural skill. Another temple of Amun, located at Luxor just S of Karnak, was erected by Amenophis III and his successors.

On the west bank of the Nile near the modern village of Medinet Habu is the palace of Amenhotep III, the two Colossi of Memnon (64 feet high), the Raamaseum; a temple of Amun built by Raamses II, a temple of Thutmose III, and a number of other brilliant ruins. Amun (Amon Re) was the sun deity with a powerful priesthood centered in Thebes, against which Akhnaton rebelled when he built Amarna.

Raamses (Tanis) was called Per-Re'emasese (the House of Raamses, c. 1300-1100 B.C.). The reference to this city in Ex 1:11 is to be construed as the modernization of an archaic place name. It stands for Zoan-Avaris, where the oppressed Israelites labored centuries earlier in the Hyksos capital built c. 1720 B.C. It is difficult to imagine that such renowned conquerors and builders such as

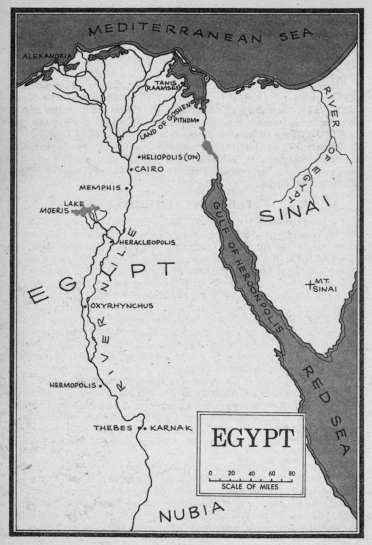

MEDITERRANEAN SEA

ALEXANDRIA

TANIS
(RAAMSES)

LAND OF GOSHEN
PITHOM

•HELIOPOLIS (ON)

•CAIRO

MEMPHIS •

LAKE
MOERIS

RIVER OF EGYPT

SINAI

GULF OF HEROONPOLIS

+MT.
SINAI

•HERACLEOPOLIS

E G Y P T

RIVER NILE

•OXYRHYNCHUS

RED SEA

HERMOPOLIS •

THEBES •• KARNAK

EGYPT

0   20   40   60   80
SCALE OF MILES

NUBIA

Thutmose III and Amenhotep II would have abandoned all interest in the Delta area, especially the rich region of Goshen so near their Asiatic domains.

CHAPTER 2. MOSES THE DELIVERER RAISED UP

Birth of the Deliverer, 1-10. Moses' parents, Amram and Jochebed (6:20), were of the tribe of Levi, later designated as the priestly line. His ark was of woven papyrus plastered with bitumen. Was the pharaoh's daughter Hatshepsut or one of the 59 daughters of Raamses II, 45 of whose names have been preserved? The Hebrew *Mosheh* (Moses) is an active participle, "the one drawing out," because Pharaoh's daughter drew the infant out of the water. But this is the interpretation given by the sacred writer. Probably the name is Egyptian *Mase* pronounced *Mose,* meaning "the child." Cf. Ahmose ("son of Ah, the god of light") and Thutmose ("son of Thot").

Flight to Midian, 11-23. At 40 (Acts 7:23), Moses cast his lot with his countrymen (Heb 11:24), in indignation killing the Egyptian taskmaster. Midian, 16-22, to which Moses fled, was a NW Arabian tribe descended from Abraham by Keturah (Gen 25:1-4; cf. 37:28 and Jud 6:2 ff.). Reuel or Jethro (he had two names as some Sabaean kings and priests) was head priest and secular head of his clan. The romantic story of how Moses won his wife Zipporah ("bird") is told. His son Gershom means "a sojourner there."

God Remembers the Covenant, 24-25. The Exodus narrative features the covenant (cf. 6:4-5; 19:5-6; 34:10).

CHAPTERS 3 AND 4. THE CALL OF MOSES

The Burning Bush, 3:1-3. Moses as a shepherd, which vocation the Egyptians despised, shared "the reproach of Christ" (Heb 11:26). The thornbush or bramble was a picture of the enslaved people. The fire was the symbol of their persecution. The indestructible character of the bush was an indication of the perpetuity of Israel because the Angel of the Lord (God the Son) was identified with them in their fiery trials (Mt 22:31-32) and graciously came to deliver them, foreshadowing the incarnation.

The Call and Commission, 4-12. "Moses, Moses" is an emphatic repetition (Gen 22:11; 46:2). The divine presence necessitated removing one's sandals, still practiced by Muslims at their mosques and the Samaritans at their sanctuary at Gerizim. It was no new god who spoke, 6, but the God of Abraham, Isaac and Jacob.

The Revelation of the Name Jehovah (Yahweh), 13-14. "I AM THAT I AM," the One who is, who was, who is to come (Rev 1:4), the Eternal, Unchanging Living One, the name of our Lord who has redeemed us. "Before Abraham was, *I am*" (Jn 8:58). W. F. Albright, however, takes the name in the causative stem: "He causes to be what comes into existence," and he cites Egyptian and Akkadian texts of pre-Mosaic times as parallels.

Directions for Deliverance, 15-22. The wilderness was et-Tih, the broad arid plateau extending from the NE border of Egypt to southern Palestine. Borrowing valuables from the Egyptians and despoiling them was not duplicity, but according to Oriental social custom. Servants, in addition to a stipend, borrowed from their masters coveted articles which they called a "gift."

Moses' Objections, 4:1-17. Moses had already pleaded *no ability,* 3:11; *no message,* 3:13; now *no authority,* 4:1; *no eloquence,* 4:10; *no inclination,* 4:13. God countered with the promise of *His presence,* 3:12; the manifestation of *His omnipotence,* 4:2-9; *enablement,* 4:11-12; and *His direction* and *instruction,* 4:14-16.

Moses' Return to Egypt, 4:18-31. Moses' wife, apparently objecting to her son's circumcision, had hindered Moses in performing a rite so closely connected with the Abrahamic covenant and the redemption of Israel back to Palestine. As deliverer, Moses was in immediate danger of being cut off for his sin. Accordingly, Zipporah circumcised her son. Moses' meeting with Aaron, 27-28, and their performance of signs signaled the progress of the redemptive plan.

CHAPTER 5. MOSES BEFORE PHARAOH

The Results of the First Encounter, 1-19. The Lord made seven demands of Pharaoh (5:1; 7:16; 8:1; 8:20; 9:1; 9:13; 10:3). The king cruelly imposed heavier burdens, requiring the same number of bricks, yet compelling the Israelites to gather their own straw. Both straw-made bricks and pure clay variety have been found at Pithom and Tanis.

Israel's Complaint and Moses' Prayer, 20-23. Darkness was experienced before the dawn.

CHAPTER 6. THE LORD'S REPLY TO MOSES' FIRST PRAYER

The Lord's Answer, 1-13. The Lord reminded Moses of His covenant with the patriarchs under the name *El Shaddai* ("God Almighty," Gen 17:1), but revealed the meaning of His personal redemptive name Jehovah *(Yahweh)*, 2-3, now that He was about to deliver them from Egyptian slavery (sin), Pharaoh (Satan) and Egypt (the world). The implication is not that the name *Yahweh* was not previously known in Genesis where it occurs many times, but simply that its meaning had not been revealed, because redemption from Egypt, typical of redemption in Christ, was not wrought out there.

The Genealogy, 14-27. Divine grace called the people by name and was intimately acquainted with their burden and concerned with their deliverance. The genealogy is obviously selective and abbreviated.

Renewed Commission, 28-30. The deliverer himself also needs constant encouragement.

CHAPTER 7. FIRST OF THE TEN PLAGUES

Moses and Aaron Assured, 1-9. "A god to Pharaoh" means Moses' declarations were to have divine authority and Aaron was his appointed spokesman (cf. 4:16).

Sign of the Rod, 10-13. Magic was inextricably bound up with Egyptian religion, which was demon-controlled idolatry of the grossest sort. The miracles performed by the magicians were manifestations of evil supernaturalism, similar to demon powers operative in spiritism and occultism today. Jannes and Jambres (2 Tim 3:8) were two of these demon-controlled miracle workers. Similar deluding signs will characterize the rise of the Antichrist and the end of this age (2 Thess 2:9-12).

First Plague: Blood, 14-25. The Nile was turned to blood, a judgment upon the river deified now as Hapi, "the giver of life," now as Osiris, the god of fertility.

CHAPTER 8. SECOND, THIRD AND FOURTH PLAGUES

The Second Plague: Frogs, 1-15. This was a miraculous intensification of a frequent natural phenomenon. After the low Nile in May–June comes the inundation in July. With the recession of the waters, leaving numerous pools of stagnant water, come the frogs in August–September. This, too, was a judgment against the innumerable gods of Egypt, the frog being worshiped as a symbol of Hekt, a form of the goddess Hathor. Plagues of frogs in Egypt are referred to by ancient classical writers.

Third and Fourth Plagues: Gnats and Flies, 16-32. Again divine miracles were performed, but based upon natural occurrences. The lice (*kinnim*) were doubtless sand flies, these stinging insects of Egypt being notorious. The flies, literally swarms, were other common pestiferous insects which plague Egypt. These judgments were a blow against the prestige of Isis, wife of Osiris, and Hathor, Egypt's foremost goddess, represented by the cow.

CHAPTER 9. FIFTH, SIXTH AND SEVENTH PLAGUES

Fifth and Sixth Plagues: Murrain and Boils, 1-12. These plagues were directed against Ptah (Apis), the god of Memphis, represented as a bull, as well as other gods represented by the goat, the ram, the cow, etc. The sixth plague, described as a boil breaking forth wi 1 blains (pustules) upon man and beast, was directed against both the idolaters and the idols they worshiped. The "Nile scab" is a popular designation of a skin disease prevalent at the rising and falling of the Nile.

The Seventh Plague: Hail, 13-35. This plague from the sky would impress the Egyptians, who saw a deity behind every natural phenomenon, that Jehovah is Lord of heaven as well as of earth. Hail is rare in Egypt. This occurred in January, as indicated by the fact that the barley was in bloom, 31-32. Each of the plagues was seasonal, but miraculous.

CHAPTER 10. EIGHTH AND NINTH PLAGUES

The Eighth Plague: Locusts, 1-20. This was a grievous visitation. Locust invasions are well-known in Syria-Palestine, but rare in Egypt. The locusts were brought by the east wind and carried away by the west wind.

The Ninth Plague: Darkness, 21-29. This miracle is thought by some to have been caused by the west wind that carried away the locusts, bringing the dreaded *Khamsin* or blinding sandstorm from the desert that creates a darkness one can feel. The darkness of this visitation was so severe it paralyzed all ordinary activities for three days.

CHAPTER 11. THE TENTH PLAGUE: DEATH
OF THE FIRSTBORN

The Climaxing Plague Announced, 1-10, and its effectiveness predicted, but its execution is not recorded until 12:26-39. The plague is called a pestilence, evidently the bubonic plague, killing the halest and best, as the firstborn was thought of in the East. Its miraculous intensity and sparing of those behind the blood-marked doors, made this wonder a fitting capstone to the other nine miracles.

CHAPTER 12. THE PASSOVER AND THE EXODUS

The Passover Instituted, 1-13. The birth of the nation and a change in the calendar were announced, 1-2. Redemption marks a new life and a new beginning. The Passover lamb slain spoke of Christ slain on Calvary. Hyssop, a common field plant, by which the blood was applied to the lintel and doorpost of believers, evidently symbolized faith in Christ's death. As the Israelites were shielded from the death angel, so the believer is shielded from the wrath of God (1 Cor 5:7). The unleavened bread (1 Cor 5:8) showed the clean-cut separation of the Israelites from Egypt and their hasty exit. The bitter herbs were apparently intended to recall their suffering in Egypt under Pharaoh's servitude.

The Feast of Unleavened Bread, 14-28. The lamb slain on the fourteenth day at sunset was followed immediately by the putting away of all leaven for seven days. Leaven in Scripture is an illustration of sin, "malice and wickedness" (1 Cor 5:8). The experience of being redeemed (the Passover) is to be followed by separation from sin and the living of a holy life.

Account of the Tenth Plague, 29-51. The death of Pharaoh's oldest son and heir to the throne was effective. The Exodus took place at once, the sojourn of 430 years to the day, 40-42, abruptly ending. The Passover was made a perpetual commemorative celebration of redemption, 43-51.

CHAPTER 13. CONSECRATION OF THE
FIRSTBORN

The Firstborn Given to the Lord, 1-16. Since the firstborn had been most miraculously delivered, the Lord enjoined that they be given to Him, 1-2. Holiness of life and redemption are inseparable. Those whom the Lord redeems, He claims for Himself (1 Cor

6:19-20). Basic to holiness, both positional and experiential, is redemption from bondage (penalty and power of sin). Salvation is unto a holy life.

Introductory to the dedication of the firstborn and as a part of the separation, Moses emphasized the importance of the Feast of Unleavened Bread (see 12:15-20) as a perpetual ordinance stressing holy separation of the redeemed, 1-10, which was to be "a sign" on their hand and a memorial "between their eyes," 9, 16 (cf. Deut 6:4-9). Upon these passages the Jews base their practice of phylacteries, using little boxes containing Scripture to fulfill by ritual what God meant to be performed by life. The requirement for the redemption of the firstborn is formally stated, 11-16.

Crossing the Red Sea, 17-22. From Succoth God manifested His power. Joseph's bones were taken along, 19. The pillar of cloud and pillar of fire were given, 21-22, symbolizing divine guidance and protection.

CHAPTER 14. THE CROSSING OF THE RED SEA

Israel's Predicament, 1-12. Shut in, perplexed and confused by the wilderness, Israel was pursued by Pharaoh's light mobile chariotry, giving the Lord a chance to be glorified in the destruction of the pursuing Egyptians.

Redemption by Power, 13-31. The Red Sea is really Reed Sea (Heb. *yam suph,* the translation "Red Sea" coming from the Septuagint). It apparently refers to the region of the Bitter Lakes N of the Gulf of Suez. These lakes were filled with sea water when the Suez Canal was built, having lain dry for centuries, but known as bodies of water in ancient Egyptian sources. The Reed or Papyrus Sea, another possibility, is referred to in an Egyptian document of the 13th cen. B.C. It was located near Tanis, which may be the site of Israel's deliverance. The great miracle at the Reed Sea was the most dramatic and far-reaching manifestation of divine power in the OT and the most memorable event in Israel's national history.

CHAPTER 15. THE SONG OF THE REDEEMED

Israel Celebrates Deliverance, 1-19. Filled with praise at their glorious rescue from the Egyptians, Israel sang ecstatically to the Lord. The great victory wrought was celebrated as the Lord's triumph, 1-10; His power, holiness and steadfast love were praised, 11-13. The terrifying effect of this great deliverance on Philistia,

Amenhotep II is often considered to be the pharaoh of the Exodus by those who hold the early date of the Exodus. *(Courtesy ORINST)*

Edom, Moab and Canaan is described, 14-16, appended with a sure promise that the Redeemer would also bring them into Canaan, 17-18.

The Women's Chorus, 20-21, under Miriam joined the praise.

Israel Tested, 22-27. The bitter trial at Marah was the brackish water. Elim, 27, gave respite in the midst of testing.

CHAPTER 16. MANNA FROM HEAVEN

The Redeemed Tested by Hunger, 1-13. The wilderness of Sin, 1, is the wide Plain of Markha beyond Elim, where the desolation presented a genuine food problem. Sin and Sinai may be derived from the name of the moon-god of Ur and Haran, or possibly from *senneh,* the thornbush where Moses had his vision (3:4). In fertile Goshen, with two crops a year, there had never been any lack of food. Now bread from heaven and quails were to be providentially supplied.

Manna from Heaven, 14-22. When the people asked in Hebrew *man-hu'* ("What is it?"), 13-15, Moses explained it was bread from heaven. The manna foreshadows Christ, the food of God's people (cf. Jn 6:33-35).

Sabbath and Manna, 23-30. The sabbath, a type of Israel's kingdom blessing (Heb 4:8-9), was enjoined upon Israel in connection with the gathering of the manna. An omer (six and a half pints) was the tenth part of an ephah, as distinguished from a homer (ten ephahs).

Manna Kept for a Memorial, 31-36, in the golden pot (Heb 9:4), speaks of the true manna which we shall eat in God's own presence in glory—"the hidden manna" (Rev 2:17), and concerning which our Lord said, "He that eats of this bread shall live forever" (Jn 6:58).

CHAPTER 17. REPHIDIM: WATER FROM THE ROCK

The Redeemed Tested by Thirst, 1-4. At Rephidim (probably the Wadi Feiran, the natural route to Sinai), the Israelites, barred by the Amalekites from marching up the valley to springs, suffered thirst and rebelled against the Lord and Moses.

Water from the Rock, 5-7. This beautifully symbolizes Christ, the Giver of the Spirit (Jn 7:37-39). The smitten rock illustrates the death of Christ resulting in an outpoured Spirit because of an accomplished redemption (Acts 2:1-4). Horeb here denotes the whole Sinaitic Peninsula. Massah ("proof") and Meribah ("strife") were the names given to the place where Israel tempted the Lord and strove with Him.

Conflict with Amalek, 8-16. This Bedouin tribe was a descendant of Esau (Gen 36:12), and Israel's implacable foe.

Jehovah-Nissi ("the Lord is my banner"), 15, assures the believer of victory.

CHAPTER 18. MOSES AND JETHRO

Jethro's Visit, 1-12. Moses rehearsed for Jethro the way the Lord had judged Egypt for Israel's sake, and the Lord's deliverance, 8. Thereupon all worshiped and fellowshiped together, 12. During the deliverance of Israel out of Egypt, Zipporah and her sons, Gershom ("a stranger") and Eliezer ("God my help"), were off the scene, 2-5. Now they appear fittingly in what may be a typical foreview of the coming kingdom (Isa 2:1-5).

Government of the Redeemed, 13-27. Here God graciously supplied governmental administration, as He had graciously supplied redemption (12:37—13:18); guidance (13:19-22); deliverance (14:1

—15:21); temporal provision (15:22—17:7); and victory in war (17:8-16).

CHAPTER 19. MT. SINAI AND THE COVENANT OF THE LAW

Israel at Sinai, 1-2. Doubtless the site of Sinai is Jebel Musa in the Sinai Peninsula, marked by the monastery of St. Catherine. However, some scholars favor Jebel Serbal near the oasis of Wadi Feiran.

Free Grace Exchanged for Law, 3-8. Pointedly the Lord reminded the people that up to this time they had been objects of His free grace, 4. The "if" of verse 5 indicates the legal method of divine dealing. Now a new economy was ushered in. The law was not set forth as a means of life, but as a medium by which Israel might become the Lord's "personal possession," "a kingdom of priests" and a "holy nation," 5-6, distinct from every other nation. Moreover, the law was not *imposed* until it had been divinely proposed and voluntarily accepted by Israel, 7-8. The Abrahamic covenant had ministered salvation and assurance because it imposed only one condition—faith. This legal covenant could not do.

Jebel Musa, traditional Mount Sinai. (© *MPS*)

The Legal Age Introduced, 9-25. This was done by the terrifying appearance of the Lord on Sinai, 9-11; by distance, 12-13; by smoke, fire, threat of death. The law was designed to school the people in God's holiness, their own sinfulness, and by its austerity and severity be a pedagogue to lead the people to Christ, to whom it pointed in detail, that they might be saved by faith (Gal 3:24).

CHAPTER 20. THE DECALOGUE

The First Table, 1-12, duties to God. These guarded His unity and spirituality against idolatry, His holiness against profanity, His worship on the seventh day against secularism, and honoring parents as His representatives against irreverence.

The Second Table, 13-17, duties to men. "You shall not kill," 13 (RSV), decrees the sanctity of life against murder. "You shall not commit adultery," 14, protects marriage and the home. "You shall not steal," 15, maintains the right of property against plunder. "You shall not bear false witness," 16, upholds the sanctity of character against slander. "You shall not covet," 17, insures the heart against wrong desires.

A Holy God Gives Instruction, 18-26. Through Moses the message was given to the people in the light of the law.

CHAPTERS 21—24. THE SOCIAL ORDINANCES

Rights of Persons, 21:1-36. Laws were given concerning the regulations of slavery, 1-11; wrongs done to a fellowman, 12-27; injuries resulting from carelessness or neglect, 28-36.

Rights of Property, 22:1-15. Laws were given dealing with theft, 1-6, and dishonesty, 7-15.

Requirements of Personal Integrity, 22:16—23:19. Proper conduct, 22:16-31, was set forth; administration of common justice, 23:1-9, and observance of the festal seasons, 10-19.

Promise and Prospect, 23:20-33. Assurance of the divine presence with Israel, 20-23, was given and a blessed future predicted, if the people remained loyal to the Lord, 24-33. These injunctions of the Book of the Covenant were for the social and religious instruction of Israel.

Acceptance of the Legal Covenant and Worship, 24:1-18. Again the voluntary acceptance of the law by Israel was stressed (cf. 19:7-8). The covenant was ratified.

CHAPTER 25. THE TABERNACLE: ARK, TABLE, CANDLESTICK

The Materials, 1-9, were supplied by the people's offering, including three metals, colored fabrics, animal skins, wood, oil and precious stones. All was by divine direction, 9.

The Ark, 10-22. This box, 3¾ feet long, 2¼ feet wide and 2¼ feet high, was made of acacia wood (commonly construed as speaking of the humanity of Christ). It was overlaid with pure gold (denoting Christ's perfect humanity). It held a pot of manna, the Ten Commandments and later Aaron's rod that budded. The ark thus envisions Christ as having God's law in His heart; Christ in resurrection, since it contained Aaron's rod that budded (Num 17:10); and Christ as Life-sustainer, since it had the pot of manna. The mercy seat was the gold lid or top of the ark, illustrating how the divine throne is transformed from a throne of judgment to a throne of grace by atoning blood sprinkled upon it. The two cherubim (winged lions with human heads known from contemporary iconography) represented guardianship of the holiness of God's throne, above which was enthroned the Shekinah glory presence of the Lord. The ark was the beginning of the tabernacle symbolism, God working outward in His outreach to man.

The Table of Shewbread, 23-30. Made of acacia wood, it was 3 feet long, 2¼ feet high and 1½ feet wide, and overlaid with pure gold. Upon it was placed the shewbread ("face-bread") made of fine wheat flour, baked in 12 loaves, renewed every sabbath to be eaten by the priests only. This bread looked forward to Christ, the Bread of life, nourisher of the believer as a priest (1 Pet 2:9; Rev 1:6; Jn 6:33-58).

The Golden Candlestick, 31-40. This was of pure gold, seven-branched; a type of Christ our Light, shining in the plenitude of the Spirit, natural light being shut out of the tabernacle. The representation on the triumphal arch of Titus may give an accurate notion of its appearance. It was worth about $35,000.

CHAPTER 26. THE TABERNACLE: ITS GENERAL CONSTRUCTION

The Linen Curtains, 1-6. Ten in all, they were white (the color of purity), blue (the color of heaven), purple (the color of royalty) and scarlet (the color of blood), speaking of various aspects of the personal work of Christ.

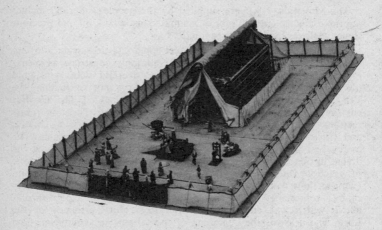

Shick's model of the Tabernacle. (© *MPS*)

The Tabernacle Coverings, 7-14; Boards, 15-30; Veil and Outer Screen, 31-37. These also doubtless portrayed aspects of the work of Christ. The veil or curtain separating the holy place from the holiest represented the "flesh" (sinless humanity) of our Lord (Heb 10:20). When Christ died "the curtain of the temple was torn in two" (Mt 27:51, RSV), opening the new and living way directly into God's presence.

CHAPTER 27. THE TABERNACLE: BRONZE ALTAR, COURT

The Brazen (Bronze) Altar, 1-8. This was the great altar for general sacrifice of animals, 7½ feet square, 4½ feet high, located at the threshold, signifying shedding of blood (atonement) is basic to man's approach to God. It is typical of the cross (death) of Christ, our whole burnt offering, who offered Himself without spot to God (Heb 9:14). The brass speaks of manifested divine judgment (Num 21:9; Jn 3:14).

The Court, 9-19. The court hangings of fine twined linen speak of righteousness required, and particularly that measure of righteousness divinely demanded by the law, of any who would come near in his own righteousness. The gate, 16 (cf. Jn 10:9), suggests Christ. He is our access to God by virtue of His redemptive work.

The Oil for Light, 20-21. The fine olive oil is symbolic of the Holy Spirit (Jn 3:34; Heb 1:9). In Christ the oil-fed light constantly burns.

CHAPTER 28. THE TABERNACLE PRIESTHOOD

Priesthood in Aaron and His Sons, 1-5. Aaron, the high priest (Heb. "great priest"), typifies Christ, who exercises His office after the Aaronic *pattern* (Heb 9), but being after the *order* of Melchizedek is an eternal deathless High Priest. The holy garments for "glory and beauty," 3, represent the glory and beauty of Christ as our High Priest. The various colors, 5, 6, 15, 33, of gold (deity), blue (heaven), purple (royalty), scarlet (blood) and white (purity) speak of various aspects of His person and redemptive work. Whereas Aaron prefigures Christ as high priest, his sons are illustrations of believers in this age (1 Pet 2:9; Rev 1:6).

The Ephod, 6-14, was an apronlike vestment worn under the high priest's breastplate, having shoulder straps, an embroidered girdle and worn over a robe. On top of each of the shoulder straps an onyx stone was encased in a filagree setting of gold and engraved with the names of six tribes of Israel. Christ bears His own on His shoulder (strength) by virtue of His present high priestly intercession.

The Breastplate, 15-29, was gorgeously embellished with precious stones engraved with the names of Israel's tribes. It illustrates Christ bearing the names of His own upon His heart in God's presence as Aaron did when he went into the holy place, 29.

Urim and Thummim, 30. The "lights and perfections" were closely attached to the breastplate. They suggest the guiding ministry of the Holy Spirit, whether they were precious stones or oracular emblems.

Robe of the Ephod, 31-35, was all of blue (color of the sky) and typifies the present heavenly priesthood of Christ. The bells and pomegranates on the skirt of the robe tell of testimony and fruitfulness in Christ's priestly intercession.

The Gold Headplate, 36-38, was inscribed with "Holy to the Lord" (RSV), a reminder of the unsullied purity of the priestly ministry of Christ.

Garments of the Regular Priests, 39-43. The ordinary vestments of the high priest and the regular priests, over which the special

101

high priestly regalia was placed, indicate that "the glory and beauty" that characterized Aaron (Christ) also characterized his sons (believer priests in this age). The linen trousers to cover their naked flesh, 42, portray the righteousness of Christ imputed to the believer, the absolute essential of access to God as a priest.

CHAPTER 29. CONSECRATION OF THE PRIESTHOOD

The Washing, 1-4. This cleansing in water symbolizes regeneration (Jn 3:5; Tit 3:5), in which Aaron had part, because he was a sinner and needed it. Our Lord as the spotless Lamb of God (Heb 7:26-28), who did not need it, nevertheless yielded to John's baptism at Jordan to identify Himself with sinners and fulfill the Aaronic pattern (Mt 3:13-17).

The Clothing and Anointing, 5-25. Clothed with his splendid garments, 5-6, and anointed, 7, symbolic of Christ's enduement with the Spirit (Mt 3:16; Acts 10:38), Aaron alone, it is to be noted, was anointed *before* the blood was shed (cf. 21). The consecration of the priests required various offerings in which the shedding of animal blood took place, 8-25. This sets Aaron off as a striking picture of Christ, who was anointed with the Spirit by virtue of what He was in Himself in His deity and sinless humanity, not by virtue of redemption, as is the case of all believers.

Special Food for Priests, 26-46. This was fitting for those, 26-37, who represented the people before God in sacrifice and worship, 38-46.

CHAPTER 30. THE ALTAR OF INCENSE AND THE WORSHIPERS

The Altar of Incense, 1-10, was of acacia wood overlaid with gold, 1½ feet square, 3 feet high. Equipped with inseparable horns and staves for transporting it, it was placed in the holy place before the veil. On it Aaron was to offer incense twice daily, 7-8. The incense fittingly symbolizes prayer, which like ascending sweet vapors, rises acceptably to heaven (Rev 5:8; 8:3). The incense altar pictures Christ as the believer's intercessor (Jn 17:1-26; Heb 7:25), through whom the believer's prayer and praise rise up to God (Heb 13:15). No "strange incense," 9, i.e., improperly compounded (cf. 30:34-38), speaking of insincere or purely formal worship, was to be used. Cf. "strange fire" of Lev 10:1-3, which refers to fire kindled in some manner other than that divinely prescribed, and typifies any religious enthusiasm gendered by merely sensuous means, or substituting something or someone for Christ as the object of devotion (1 Cor 1:11-13; Col 2:8, 16-19).

The Ransom Money, 11-16. Those who come as true worshipers must be redeemed. All are lost, all are on an equal footing, and all need redemption shown by the payment of the half-shekel of silver.

The Brazen (Bronze) Laver, 17-21. This washbasin placed between the altar and the door was used by the priests to cleanse their hands and feet, and is symbolical of washing of water by the Word (Heb 10:22; Eph 5:25-27; Jn 13:3-10; 1 Jn 1:9). True worshipers must also be continually cleansed from daily defilement.

The Anointing Oil, 22-33, a symbol of the Holy Spirit. The redeemed, those daily cleansed, and those unctionized by the Spirit alone can worship God effectively (Jn 4:23; Eph 2:18; 5:18-19) in the beauty and fragrance of holiness.

The Incense, 34-38. The ingredients are also given, as in the case of the anointing oil. Only those redeemed, 11-16; cleansed, 17-21; and anointed, 34-38, can truly worship God with genuine prayer, praise and thanksgiving, 34-38, symbolized by the incense, which in turn was to be uniquely compounded and reserved for God's adoration alone, 37. To imitate it was a crime punishable by death, showing that worship must be truly spiritual (Jn 4:23-24).

CHAPTER 31. THE WORKMEN AND THE SABBATH

The Call of the Workmen, 1-11. Bezaleel ("in the shadow of God") and Aholiab ("tent of [my] Father") were filled with the Spirit of God, with ability and intelligence, with knowledge and all craftsmanship, 2-3, to execute all the skilled labor necessary.

The Sabbath Law Restated, 12-17. Cf. 16:23-29 for the first institution of the day of rest to be kept by Israel, in connection with the giving of the manna. Shortly afterward it was re-enacted in the fourth commandment (20:8-11) linking it with the creation rest of God (Gen 2:2). The sabbath is accordingly a Jewish institution, connected with the legal or Mosaic covenant, and its infraction punishable by death. Sunday is not a sabbath, but the first day of the week, and belongs to the new age of grace which followed the death and resurrection of Christ. Sabbath keeping is to go back to the age previous to the rent veil (Mt 27:51).

Moses Receives the Tables of Stone, 18 (cf. 32:16)

CHAPTER 32. THE BROKEN COVENANT

The Golden Calf, 1-14. The legal covenant, so glibly accepted, was here shamefully infracted, showing the utter inability of the people to keep it in their own strength. This shocking return to the bull worship of Egypt, in which they copied the idol Apis, brought the wrath of the broken law upon them, 7-10, and only the intercession of Moses rescued them from wholesale destruction, 11-14.

The Broken Tablets, 15-35. A scene of terrible apostasy and debauchery met Moses, the man of God, coming down from the mountain of God with the law of God in his hands. The whole scene showed the inability of the law, itself good, to make men good. Depraved man is never saved by law-keeping, but by faith. Justification by faith is the way of salvation in every age. The law was a pedagogue to reveal man's sin and his need of God's grace and redemption. Calling on those who were on the Lord's side, the Levites leaped up and slew 3,000 of the worst offenders. Further confession and intercession by Moses, 30-35, presents a superlatively lofty scene of man's concern for the good of God's people, one of the sublimest pictures found anywhere in Holy Writ.

CHAPTERS 33—34. RESTORATION OF THE LAW

Moses' New Vision, 33:1-23. The journey to Canaan was resumed, 1-6, and the "tent of meeting" (not the tabernacle, which was later set up) was pitched outside the camp, 7-11. Moses prayed for a new vision, 12-17, and was promised it for a new task, 18-23.

Second Tables of the Law, 34:1-4. Again, the inscription was by God. The second tablets were as authoritative as the first.

The New Vision and Commission, 5-17. Moses saw the Lord pass by, 5-9, and his commission was renewed, 10-17. Here the patriarch saw the hidden nature of Jehovah.

The Feasts and the Sabbath Again Enjoined, 18-35. This is a repetition concerning the Feast of Unleavened Bread, 18; redemption of firstborn, 19-20; sabbath, 21; Feast of Weeks and Ingathering, etc., 22-27. Moses' face shone after he descended from the 40-day session with God, 28-35 (cf. 2 Cor 3:6-18).

CHAPTERS 35—39. THE TABERNACLE ASSEMBLED

The Sabbath, 35:1-3. This basic tenet of Israel's worship was once more restated and emphasized (cf. 16:23-29; 20:8-11; 31:12-17; 34:21).

Gifts and Workmen for the Tabernacle, 35:4—36:7. What was enjoined in Ex 25:1-8 concerning donations for the construction of the tabernacle was here carried out, as the people gave liberally. Bezaleel and Aholiab (cf. 31:1-11), the principal craftsmen, were again signalized and their God-given talents for the work again noted, 35:30-35. So liberally did the people give, they had to be restrained, 36:1-7.

The Tabernacle Made, 36:8—39:43. These chapters record the material and furniture of the tabernacle collected and made according to the directions given in ch. 25—31, which are here repeated. Instructions are given concerning the linen curtains, 36:8-13 (cf. 26:1-6); curtains of goat's hair, 36:14-18 (cf. 26:7); covering of rams' skins, 36:19 (cf. 26:14); boards, 36:20-23 (cf. 26:15); silver sockets, 36:24-30 (cf. 26:19); the bars, 36.31-33 (cf. 26:26); gold overlay, 36:34 (cf. 26:29); the inner veil and outer veil, 36:35-38 (cf. 26:31,36). Likewise the furniture is again detailed: the ark, 37:1-5 (cf. 25:10); the mercy seat, 37:6-9 (cf. 25:17); the table of shewbread, 37:10-16 (cf. 25:23); candlestick, 37:17-24 (cf. 25:31); altar of incense, 37:25-28 (cf. 30:1); anointing oil, 37:29 (cf. 30:23-38); altar of burnt offering, 38:1-7 (cf. 27:1); laver, 38:8 (cf. 30:18); courts, 38:9-31 (cf. 27:9,16); Aaron's high priestly garments, 39:1-43 (cf. 31:10).

CHAPTER 40. THE TABERNACLE SET UP

Built, 1-19, according to God's direction, 1-15, in perfect obedience, 16-19.

Furnished, 20-33. The ark was brought in, 20-21. The furniture was placed, 22-26. The prescribed offerings and ritual were performed, 27-33.

Divinely Accepted, 34-38. God blessed Moses and the people with His presence as the tent was filled with God's glory. So great was the splendor, Moses was not able to minister. A mob of miserable slaves in Egypt marks the beginning of Exodus. An emancipated nation in fellowship with God and on its way to Canaan ends it. This is truly "the book of redemption."

LEVITICUS

THE BOOK OF ATONEMENT

Nature of the Book. Genesis is the book of beginnings, Exodus the book of redemption, and Leviticus the book of atonement and a holy walk. In Genesis we see man ruined; in Exodus, man redeemed; in Leviticus, man cleansed, worshiping and serving. Leviticus says, *"Get right with God"* (the message of the five offerings: burnt offering, meal offering, peace offering, sin offering, trespass offering, ch. 1—7). Leviticus also says, *"Keep right with God"* (the message of the seven feasts: Passover, Unleavened Bread, First Fruits, Pentecost, Trumpets, Atonement, Tabernacles, ch. 23).

Leviticus is the book of *holiness.* (This keynote idea occurs 87 times.) God says to the redeemed, "Be ye holy as I am holy" (11:44-45; 19:2; 20:7, 26), and this book stresses the necessity of keeping the body holy as well as the soul. The redeemed must be holy, for their Redeemer is holy. A walk with God is on the basis of holiness, which is by *sacrifice* and *separation.* Leviticus as a picture book portrays Jesus our Sacrifice for sin. Every portrait prefigures the person and work of Christ.

Name of the Book. The name "Leviticus" describes the contents of the book, as the law of the priests, the sons of Levi, and is adopted from the Septuagint (*Leueitikon*) and the Latin Vulgate (*Leviticus*), characterizing it as a handbook for the ritual of the old covenant, principally associated with what in the NT is called the Levitical priesthood (Heb 7:11).

THE SACRIFICIAL SYSTEM

Origin of the Sacrifices. Although their divine origin is not explicitly declared, the fact is everywhere implicit in the Bible. The way sinful man was to approach God was revealed to Adam and Eve immediately after the Fall. They thought to approach God by self-righteous works, portrayed in their making garments of fig leaves to attempt to cover their nakedness and shame (Gen 3:7). God corrected them by showing that the guilt of sin could be covered only by shedding the blood of a victim (Gen 3:21).

Accordingly, divinely revealed and divinely ordered sacrifice is recorded in the case of Cain and Abel. Cain repudiated God's way of approach in worship. Abel accepted it and was received into God's presence on the basis of God's stipulated means of access to Himself (Gen 4:1-7; Heb 11:4). Likewise Noah (Gen 8:20), Jacob

(Gen 31:54), Job (Job 1:5; 42:8) and God's people down to the eve of the Exodus knew the way of access to God and practiced it (Ex 10:25).

When Moses led Israel out of Egypt, the sacrificial system that had at least in part existed from the beginning of the race was now expanded, given fresh meaning in the light of experienced redemption, organized, codified and written down by inspiration in the sacrificial codes of Exodus and Leviticus.

The Witness of Archaeology. Archaeology and history have demonstrated the universality of sacrifice in human religions from earliest times. Hebrew sacrifices showed both likeness and significant differences to the sacrificial ritual of the Canaanites, Babylonians, Egyptians, Greeks and Arabs. Sufficient similarity existed to demonstrate a *common origin* in a God-given revelation to the human race just after the Fall. This original source was corrupted and perverted as mankind lapsed more and more into paganism, and was reflected in the systems of sacrifice prevailing among the polytheistic neighbors of Israel. While ancient Sumerian, Babylonian, Hittite, Egyptian and Amorite records show the prevalence of sacrifices similar to those of the Hebrews in the OT, the Ras Shamra religious tablets discovered at the site of ancient Ugarit in N. Syria (1929-37 and later) have been most important in showing the similarities and differences in sacrificial terms and ritual between Israelite and Canaanite sacrifices.

The Witness of Theology. The findings of archaeology concur with the reasoning of theology and the intimations of Scripture that the sacrifices were divinely ordained at the Fall. This is true because of the character of God—infinitely holy, yet gracious in His redemptive love (Gen 3:15). It is also true because of the character of man—a fallen creature, totally unable to approach God in his own merits, or to invent a way of approach by his own ingenuity.

Meaning of the Sacrifices for the OT Worshiper

Basic Meaning. While many elements entered into the religious and spiritual value of the sacrifices, the fundamental idea to the Hebrew worshiper was that they were a *means of approach to God.* This is evident from the underlying connotation of the broadest Hebrew term for "sacrifice" (*qorban,* from the root *qrb,* "to draw near or approach"). This was the term used for a sacrificial offering either with or without blood, vegetable or animal, entirely or partially burnt (Lev 1:2-3, 10, 14; 2:1, 4; 3:1-2; 7:13; Num 5:15; 7:17; etc.; cf. Mk 7:11). Sinful, guilty man needed some way to draw near to the infinitely holy God with assurance of acceptance. This was divinely provided in a sacrificial system presided over by the Levitical priesthood.

Further Significance. Besides the basic idea of the sacrifices as a means of his approach to God, the OT believer had other important aspects of worship in mind as he presented prescribed sacrifices. These included: (1) *Self-dedication to God,* in the burnt offering (Lev 1; cf. Rom 12:1-2). In this offering the idea of a gift prevailed, because none of it was returned to the worshiper. All was consumed as the Lord's property. (2) *Generosity in giving,* in the cereal offering (Lev 2). This offering closely followed the burnt offering and featured the donation of material substance in the fruit of one's labor as the natural result of dedication of oneself to God. (3) *Thanksgiving, praise, fellowship* and *communion* of the worshiper because God had accepted his offering of gratitude, devotion or vow, in the peace offering (Lev 3), or granted some personal or national deliverance. (4) *Expiation by substitution,* in the sin offering (Lev 4), when there was sin against God with no restitution involved. (5) *Expiation and restitution,* in the guilt offering (Lev 5), where there were sin and injury involving restitution.

Classification of the Sacrifices. A twofold division is possible: (1) sacrifices used to approach God for the purpose of restoring broken fellowship—the sin offering (Lev 4) and the restitution offering (Lev 5); (2) sacrifices used to approach God for the purpose of maintaining fellowship—the burnt offering (Lev 1), the meal offering (Lev 2), and the peace offering (Lev 3).

Pagan Ideas of Sacrifice. Perverted ideas of sacrifice prevailing among Israel's heathen neighbors included the following: (1) *The food idea.* The sacrifice was thought to feed the god who needed food. (2) *The totemistic idea.* The worshiper thought he fed upon the god himself in such offerings in which the offerer partook of the sacred meal. (3) *Life-liberation notion.* Union was considered to be effected between the offerer and his god as the slain animal's life was taken. The blood was received by the god and the flesh eaten by the offerer. (4) *The magic idea.* The sacrifice was a magical rite which acted as a lever to force the god to grant what was sought.

The Typological Meaning of the Sacrifices. For the NT believer the chief import of the OT sacrifices is typological, i.e., they were symbolically *predictive,* expressing a need which they could not satisfy, but which the coming promised Redeemer they prefigured would fulfill (Eph 5:2; 1 Cor 10:11; Heb 9:14). This is the normal application of the OT sacrifices for the NT believer, although *not* their basic or practical meaning for the OT saint.

CHAPTER 1. THE BURNT OFFERING

The Bullock, 1-9. The first utterance of the Lord concerns the sweet-savor (smelling) offerings—the burnt offering, the meal offering and the peace offering. They prefigure Christ in His perfections and complete devotion to the Father's will. The non-sweet savor offerings—the sin offering and the trespass offering—set forth Christ as bearing the whole demerit of the sinner. The burnt offering pictures Christ offering Himself spotless to God (Heb 9:11-14; 10:5-7). The bullock or young ox sets forth Christ as the patient, obedient Servant, "obedient to death" (Phil 2:5-8). The offerer's putting his hand upon the head of the burnt offering illustrates the identification of the believer with his offering. The antitype is the believer's faith in identifying himself with Christ (Rom 4:5; 6:3-11) who died as his sin offering (2 Cor 5:21; 1 Pet 2:24).

The Sheep or Goat, 10-13. The sheep (lamb) portrays our Lord in willing yieldedness to the death of the cross (Isa 53:7; Jn 1:29).

The Turtle Dove or Pigeon, 14-17, speaks of sorrowing innocence (Isa 38:14; 59:11; Heb 7:26), and connected with poverty (5:7) portrays Him who became poor that we through His poverty might become wealthy (2 Cor 8:9). The fire, symbolizing the divine holiness, manifests God in that which He approves, and thus it displays the fragrance of the sweet-savor offerings; but as exhibiting the divine judgment on that which His holiness condemns, it wholly consumes the sin offering.

109

CHAPTER 2. THE MEAL OFFERING

General Meaning, 1-3. In this non-blood offering Christ is prefigured in His sinless humanity, the perfect Man. The material of the meal offering was fine flour, evenly milled, portraying the perfection which was blended in every part of Christ's humanity. The oil poured upon it speaks of Christ as anointed by the Holy Spirit (Lk 3:21-22). The frankincense, a white aromatic gum resin, symbolizes the fragrance of our Lord's divine humanity Godward. The fire may prefigure Christ's human sufferings unto death. Aaron and his sons shared this offering, 3, symbolizing our feeding upon Christ (Jn 6:51-54).

The Meal Offering Baked, 4-11. This was done in the oven, 4, in a pan, 5-6, or frying pan, 7. The oven speaks of Christ's hidden sufferings as the God-Man; the pan, of His more evident testings. No leaven, a type of insincerity and untruth (1 Cor 5:8), was to be used, setting forth our Lord's character as the Truth (Jn 14:6). Mixed with oil, 4-5, suggests Christ as *conceived* by the Holy Spirit (Mt 1:18-23; Lk 1:35).

The Offering of the First Fruits, 12-16. In connection with the first fruits, salt is mentioned with "the covenant of thy God." As such it speaks of fellowship and friendship with God. Also salt is a preservative and refers to the continuance of that fellowship in contrast to the leaven of sin (Num 18:19; Mk 9:49-50; Col 4:6). The offering of the first fruits evidently connects Christ's sinless humanity with resurrection (cf. Lev 23:9-14; 1 Cor 15:20-23).

CHAPTER 3. THE PEACE OFFERING

Offering from the Herd, 1-5. This offering presents Christ's work on the cross in the aspect of procuring peace for the sinner, God being propitiated and the sinner being reconciled. He who *made* peace (Col 1:20), *proclaimed* peace (Eph 2:17) and *is* our peace (Eph 2:14) is here typified as providing this "peace with God" (Rom 5:1) as well as "the peace of God" at the terrible cost of fire (suffering and testings) and blood (atoning death). Peace *with* God (justification) is thus the basis of the peace *of* God expressed in thanksgiving and fellowship. This makes the peace offering paramountly a thank offering (Lev 7:11-12).

Offering of the Flock, 6-17. This offering cannot be separated from the burnt offering, since it was offered on the altar *upon* the burnt sacrifice. Peace with God is inseparable from the death of Christ.

4:1—5:13. THE SIN OFFERING

The Lord's Second Utterance, 4:1-2. The first utterance (1:1-2) out of the glory that filled the completed tabernacle gave the divine direction for the sweet-savor offerings—the burnt, meal and peace offerings—setting forth the divinely appointed way of Israel's approach to God in the sanctuary (ch. 1-3). The last two offerings are the subject of the second utterance—the sin and the trespass offerings—which deal more specifically with the forgiveness of Israel's sins and restoration of fellowship with God.

The Sin Offering for the High Priest, 3-12. The sin offering pictures our Lord as the bearer of the sins of His people, "made sin for us" (2 Cor 5:21). It is expiatory and substitutionary (Lev 4:12, 29, 35) and vindicates the claims of the law through substitutionary atonement. When the high priest sinned, it was as if the whole congregation sinned.

The Sin Offering for the Congregation, 13-21. Whoever sinned, the specified sacrifice was sufficient.

The Sin Offering for a Prince (Ruler), 22-26. Sacrifices varied according to the person who sinned, but all, irrespective of position, were sinners and needed the prescribed sin offering.

The Sin Offering for a Common Person, 27-35. He too was accountable to God.

For Special Offenses, 5:1-13. Cf. Heb 13:10-13 for light on the sin offering.

5:14—6:7. THE TRESPASS OFFERING

Trespass Against the Lord, 5:14-19. This offering portrays Christ atoning for the harmful effects of sin, that is, injury done. This offering was always an unblemished ram (15, 18; 6:6).

Trespass Against Man, 6:1-7. In injury done either to God or man restitution had to be made with a fifth part of the whole being added. In the case of wrong done to the Lord, the fifth part was given to the priest; in the case of wrong done to man, to the man defrauded.

6:8—7:38. THE LAWS OF THE OFFERINGS

Law of the Burnt Offering, 6:8-13 (cf. ch. 1). This continual burnt offering with the fire that never went out portrays Christ constantly offering Himself in God's presence on our behalf as the One in whom all believers have a guarantee of their full acceptance. His

111

presence in the heavenly sanctuary is ceaseless and infinitely efficacious. Our answer to the burnt offering aspect of Christ's redemptive
work is full surrender in devotion to God.

Law of the Meal Offering, 14-23 (cf. ch. 2). The part of this
offering eaten by the Aaronic priests (type of believers) shows the
privilege of feeding upon Christ (Jn 6:53). "With unleavened bread
shall it be eaten in the holy place," 16. Such eating of the heavenly
Bread is enjoyed only in separation (unleavened) in the *holy* place.
This was a special meal offering of the high priest (19-23).

Law of the Sin Offering, 24-30 (cf. ch. 4). The sin offering had
to be killed in the place where the burnt offering was killed, showing
the inseparable connection between substitutionary atonement and
the sinless perfections of the Substitute. The priest who offered it,
ate it, typifying our Lord's identification with sinners as our Sin
Bearer, 26. The holiness of the sin offering was carefully guarded.
It was called "most holy," showing that although our Lord was
"made sin" (2 Cor 5:21) as the sin offering, He nevertheless was
Himself sinless.

Law of the Trespass Offering, 7:1-10 (cf. ch. 5). The trespass
offering was also "most holy," like the sin offering, and depended
upon shed blood.

Law of the Peace Offering, 11-38 (cf. ch. 3). Here the third of
the sweet-savor offerings is put last in the laws of the offerings,
doubtless because it represents most blessedly the result of Christ's
atoning work—peace with God for the justified believer—with communion and thanksgiving preeminent. All the details of this blessed
offering center in Christ.

CHAPTER 8. THE CONSECRATION OF THE PRIESTHOOD

The Consecration, 1-13. The basis of holiness was the five offerings of ch. 1—7. The result was the priesthood of ch. 8—10, Aaron
foreshadowing Christ, and his sons speaking of individual believers
of this age. Their priesthood was dependent on their relation to
Aaron, as the believers' priesthood is based on their relation to
Christ. Three things were done to the priests. First, they were
washed, 6, symbolizing regeneration (Jn 13:2-11; Tit 3:5; Heb
10:22). For the reason see Ex 29:1-4. Second, they were *clothed* (see
Ex 28:1-43). Third, they were *anointed* (see Ex 29:5-25).

Two important features distinguish the high priest as a prefigurement of Christ from the ordinary priests' prefiguration of believers. First, he was anointed *before* the consecration sacrifices were slain in contrast to the priests, in whose case the application of the blood preceded the anointing. As the Sinless One, Christ required no preparation for the anointing oil (Holy Spirit). Second, only upon the high priest was the anointing oil *poured,* typifying Christ's immeasurable fullness of the Spirit (Jn 3:34; Heb 1:9).

The Offerings of Consecration, 14-30. The sin offering, 14-17; the burnt offering, 18-21; the ram of consecration, 22; the blood applied, 23-26, all minutely stressed the fact that priestly function depended upon a finished redemption. The blood sanctified the body (ear, finger, toe).

The Sacrificial Feast, 31-36. The eating of the sacrifices and the bread, so frequently seen in the Levitical ritual, illustrates the necessity of believers feeding on Christ (Jn 6:50-55). The seven-day span of the feast may portray this present age when a heavenly priesthood (the Church) is feasting on Christ.

CHAPTER 9. THE PRIESTS MINISTER

Inaugurating the Ministry, 1-22. The week of priestly ordination (ch. 8), symbolic of the priestly position of believers of this age, was followed on the eighth day by a series of new offerings of the priests in which the future priesthood of converted Israel, as a high priestly nation, may be portrayed. The eighth day could represent the Millennial Age when Christ as King-Priest will appear in glory to His people Israel and they will become indeed "a kingdom of priests and a holy nation" (Ex 19:6; Zech 3:1-10; Isa 61:6). The sin offering, burnt offering and meal offering demonstrate that this future restoration of the kingdom of Israel (Acts 1:6) will be on the basis of Christ's sacrificial atoning work at His first advent.

The Manifested Glory, 23-24. Aaron had blessed the people, 22, and then he retired into the tabernacle with Moses, 23. After that he appeared to the people the *second* time, as Christ will do to Israel at His second advent. Moses, as leader (king), and Aaron, as priest, foreshadow Christ's second appearing in the dual role of King-Priest (cf. Zech 6:9-15). This will mean glory for God, for the Church, for Israel and for the earth. Then the glory of the Lord, 23, will be manifested to all the people, as when falling upon the altar it consumed the burnt offering and fat, 24. This shows that all will be prophetically consummated on the basis of Christ's atoning sacrifice.

CHAPTER 10. STRANGE FIRE OF NADAB AND ABIHU

Sacrilege Disciplined, 1-11. Nadab and Abihu offered the strange fire either ignorantly or presumptuously in kindling the fire that burned the incense. They burned it in self-will without seeking or obeying God's directive in the matter. Their sin was official, hence serious. It illustrates any unspiritual means which is used to kindle the flame of devotion and points to the believer's sin unto (physical) death (1 Cor 5:5; 11:30; 1 Jn 5:16). The seriousness of the sin is emphasized not only by the sudden death of the guilty, but by the command not to mourn for them, 6-7. The appended command against intoxicating liquor, 8-11, may give the reason for Nadab and Abihu's failure.

New Instructions, 12-15, were given the priests concerning eating the sacrifices.

Failure Forgiven, 16-20. Eleazar and Ithamar failed to eat the sin offering, but this was excusable evidently because of the judgment that fell upon Aaron's other two sons, Nadab and Abihu. This indicated that Aaron and his two living sons were not sufficiently free of sin to deserve to eat the sin offering.

CHAPTER 11. A HOLY PEOPLE—THEIR FOOD

Clean and Unclean Food, 1-23. Leviticus as a manual of holiness now sets forth the truth that *holiness is required* of God's redeemed people (ch. 11-15). The reason is, "Be ye holy; for I am holy" (1 Pet 1:16; cf. Lev 11:44-45). "Present your bodies a living sacrifice, holy, acceptable unto God" (Rom 12:1). "What? know ye not that your body is the temple of the Holy Ghost?" (1 Cor 6:19). The pre-Flood distinction between clean and unclean animals (Gen 7:2) included in the Mosaic law was based partly on reasons of physical health and religious scruples, and was designed to mark Israel's separation from other peoples. Under the Christian dispensation such distinctions have fulfilled their symbolic significance and have been abrogated, as in the case of Peter's vision when the gospel was released to Gentiles (Acts 10:9-15).

Defilement by a Dead Body, 24-47. Death, illustrative of that which is purely in the natural realm and has no place in the experience of one who serves a *living* God (cf. Heb 9:14), defiled on touch and required cleansing.

CHAPTER 12. A HOLY PEOPLE—CHILDBIRTH

Childbirth and Uncleanness, 1-8. Birth uncleanness is primarily a symbol of mankind's innate congenital depravity (Gen 5:3; Ps 51:5; Rom 5:18; Eph 2:3), indicative of the sinfulness of all human life produced. Circumcision of the male (cf. Gen 17:9-14) on the eighth day had hygienic as well as spiritual significance (Col 2:11-12). The Virgin Mary complied with the law and brought the sacrifice of the poor (Lk 2:22-24).

CHAPTERS 13—14. A HOLY PEOPLE—LEPROSY

Leprosy, 13:1-59. This dreaded disease furnishes a trenchant illustration of sin in the believer working through the old nature (Rom 6:12-14; 1 Jn 1:8), demanding confession, cleansing and self-judgment (1 Cor 11:31). It was regarded as hereditary and incurable. The leper was excluded from the camp, 45-46. The believer who permits indwelling sin to work in him is not fit for fellowship with God nor with God's people.

Its Purification, 14:1-32. This ritual assumed that the leper had been healed. The actual healing, like the forgiveness of sin, could be effected by God alone. The priest examined the leper without the camp, and if he was persuaded the sufferer was cured, he proceeded to purify him ceremonially by the two-bird ritual. The bird killed, and the live bird dipped in blood and let go, present our Lord in two aspects—"delivered for our offenses, and raised again for our justification" (Rom 4:25). It was the blood that purified from the leprosy of sin. The living bird in its upward flight bore upon its wings the blood, the badge of a finished redemptive work. So the risen and ascended Christ bore the evidences of His atonement. The other details of the ceremony, the offerings, ablutions, etc., all speak of the sinfulness of sin and the efficacy of the person and work of Christ to cleanse it away.

Leprosy in the House, 33-57. This shows how sin may contaminate a home.

CHAPTER 15. A HOLY PEOPLE—PERSONAL DEFILEMENT

Man's Uncleanness, 1-18. Human nature is hopelessly defiled and defiling. This book holds up a faithful mirror to proud humanity and leaves "the flesh" nothing to glory in before a holy God. The bodily secretions mentioned, both voluntary and involuntary, normal as well as pathological, give evidence of the deep-seated sin inherent in human nature and the curse upon it, revealing the need of continual cleansing by water (the Word) on the basis of the shed blood, 14-15 (Jn 13:3-10; Eph 5:25-27; 1 Jn 1:9).

Woman's Uncleanness, 19-33. Cf. the woman with a bloody flux (Mt 9:20-22). Fallen human nature is defiled even in its secret involuntary operations. Holiness is demanded by a holy God on the basis of redemption effected by Christ.

CHAPTER 16. IN THE HOLIEST—NATIONAL ATONEMENT

The Ritual Portraying the Lord's Objective Redemption, 1-28. *Yom Kippurim,* the Day of Atonement, the fast (Acts 27:9), on the tenth day of the seventh month (Sept.-Oct.), 'marked the climax of access to God under the old covenant. It was the most solemn day of the entire year, when the high priest (a figure of Christ) entered the holy of holies to make annual atonement for the sins of the nation, 1-5 (cf. Ex 30:10; Heb 9:7-8; 10:19). The expiation for sin was for only one year, but it looked forward to the once-for-all removal of sin by Christ's death (Heb 9:12), illustrated by the various offerings, 6-10, and the blood of the sacrificed goat being carried into the holiest, 11-19.

The offering of the high priest for himself, 6, has no parallel in the sinless Christ (Heb 7:26-27). Illustrative significance focuses on the high priest and two goats selected from the congregation for the ritual. All was done by the high priest, the Israelites supplying only the animals. ("By himself [Christ] purged our sins," Heb 1:3.) Aaron cast lots on the two goats. The goat on which the lot fell for the Lord, 8-10, 15-17, depicts that aspect of our Lord's death which vindicates the divine holiness expressed in the law (Rom 3:24-26). The live goat, which was dispatched for the scapegoat (Heb. "to Azazel") in the wilderness, 20-22, presents that aspect of Christ's atonement which expiates our sin from before God's presence (Rom 8:33-34; Heb 9:26). Azazel, for Alzalzel, may simply signify "dismissal," or complete removal of sin from the camp of God's people. The high priest's entrance into the holiest pictures Christ entering heaven itself (Heb 9:24) to present the infinite merits of His shed blood before God's throne of judgment, which is thereby transformed to a throne of grace or mercy seat.

The Ritual Picturing Man's Subjective Response for Receiving the Redemption, 29-34, "Ye shall afflict your souls," 31, later came to include fasting (Acts 27:9). The rigid rest prefigures the rest of redemption and Israel's national enjoyment of a finished atonement. As believer priests of the new covenant we enjoy a permanently "rent veil" and immediate access into the holiest place, that which Israel never knew (Heb 4:14-16; 10:19-22).

CHAPTER 17. REVERENCE FOR BLOOD

Concerning Slain Animals, 1-9. The blood was to possess sanctity because it represented life which God the Creator made. It was likewise the means of atonement, pointing to Him as Redeemer.

Concerning Eating Blood, 10-16. These injunctions were to be operative until Christ's sacrifice of Himself should fulfill the truths they pointed out.

CHAPTER 18. UNHOLY PRACTICES FORBIDDEN

A Holy Life Demanded, 1-5. About 30 times in ch. 18—22 occur the solemn words: "I am the Lord" and "You shall be holy, for I the Lord your God am holy." The holiness of the Redeemer is the all-compelling reason for the holiness of the redeemed.

Unholiness Specified, 6-23. Various unholy relationships, 6-18, render a believer unfit for worship. The vile and abominable practices of the Canaanites and other idolaters are spelled out, 19-23.

Judgment Threatened, 24-30. The panorama of history has shown God's warning consummated in judgment, both for the Canaanites and for Israel.

CHAPTERS 19—20. OTHER PRESCRIPTIONS FOR HOLINESS

Social Regulations, 19:1-37. These include honoring God and parents, 1-8; care of the poor, 9-10; commands against falsehood and theft, 11-12; oppression, 13-14; unjust judgment, 15-16; injunctions toward the love of neighbors, 17-18; and various other regulations, 19-37.

Special Sins, 20:1-27. Molech worship and demonism, 1-8; cursing parents, 9; and criminal and vile relations, 10-21, are warned against. Exhortations are given for obedience and separation, 22-27. Worship of Molech (from *melek*, "king"), a detestable deity adored by the Ammonites with sacrifice of the firstborn, offers a particularly cruel and revolting aspect of ancient Semitic paganism.

117

CHAPTERS 21—22. PRESCRIPTIONS FOR PRIESTLY HOLINESS

Holiness of the Priests, 21:1-16. The preceding laws concerned the holy nation. These special laws regulated the holiness of the priests, guaranteeing a ministry beyond reproach. Since the priesthood is illustrative of believers of this age, the various injunctions concerning ceremonial cleanliness, marriage, etc., show the importance of separation from sin on the part of Christians (2 Tim 3:16-17). The high priest's sanctity was particularly guarded.

Physical Disqualifications of a Priest, 17-24. Disabilities, such as lameness (defective walk), blindness (defective sight) and arrested growth (immaturity), barred one from priestly function but not from priestly position. These illustrated defects in a believer's life do not abrogate his position "in Christ" or his reception of grace ("He shall eat the bread of his God," 22), but they curtail his usefulness in ministry.

Personal Purity of a Priest, 22:1-16. He must regulate his own personal life discreetly, and that of his family.

Priestly Sacrifices, 17-33, must be unblemished and physically perfect. They are emblematic of the moral perfections of Christ (Heb 9:14).

CHAPTER 23. THE HOLY FEASTS

The Weekly Sabbath, 1-3. This is not one of the seven annual feasts enumerated in 4-44, but is basic to the entire festal cycle and Israel's religion, and so introduces the description of these sacred seasons or "set-times."

The Passover, 4-5 (Heb. *pesah,* "a passing over"). This memorialized redemption from Egypt, when the Lord passed over the blood-covered dwellings of Israel. This was the first feast, basic to all the rest, as all spiritual blessing rests on sinful man's redemption by Christ (1 Cor 5:7; 1 Pet 1:19) who is "our passover sacrificed for us."

Unleavened Bread, 6-8. Redemption is to be followed by a holy life and walk (1 Cor 5:7-8; 2 Cor 7:1; Gal 5:7-9). Communion with Christ, the unleavened Bread, will result in separation from evil (leaven).

Firstfruits, 9-14. These typify Christ in resurrection (the firstfruits) and those who are saved at Christ's appearing (1 Cor 15:23; 1 Thess 4:13-18).

Pentecost, 15-22. This occurred 50 days after the Feast of First-fruits, 15-16. The new meal offering, 16, looks forward to the Church. The two wave loaves (a loaf, not a sheaf of separate grains) "baked with leaven," 17, anticipate that aspect of it in which Jew (Acts 2) and Gentile (Acts 10) are united in a genuine spiritual union (1 Cor 12:13) by the advent of the Spirit at Pentecost (Acts 2:1-4). Leaven is included because in the unglorified state of the Church sin is present.

Trumpets, 23-25. The blowing of trumpets after the Church's in-gathering furnishes a picture of Israel's age-end regathering from her long worldwide dispersion (Mt 24:31; Isa 18:3, 7; 27:12; 58:1-14; Ezk 37:12-14).

Day of Atonement, 26-32. This solemn occasion prefigures the re-pentant sorrow of Israel at the time of her conversion at the second advent of Christ. This is the same day described in Lev 16 (cf. Zech 12:10—13:1). This was and is the spiritual highlight of the Jewish calendar year.

Tabernacles, 33-44. This is the last and great harvest home festival of the Jewish year. It foreshadows Israel's kingdom rest after re-gathering and spiritual conversion. It is commemorative of redemp-tion out of Egypt, 43, and prophetic of the restoration of the kingdom over Israel.

CHAPTER 24. PRIESTLY DUTIES; BLASPHEMY

Oil for the Tabernacle Light, 1-4 (cf. Ex 25:6).

The Shewbread, 5-9 (cf. Ex 25:23-30). Priests were to follow God's commands to Moses concerning these elements of the taber-nacle worship.

Blasphemy Dealt With, 10-23. This is a fleeting narrative section describing the execution of a Danite half-breed for blaspheming the name of Jehovah (*Yahweh*), a name which signifies "He *is present*" (redemptively, as in Ex 3:12-14). It shows the culprit's contempt for God's salvation itself. This adumbrates Israel's own national crime in rejecting the Lord when He became incarnate. Traditional Judaism superstitiously refuses to pronounce the holy name Jehovah (*Yahweh*), substituting *Adonai* on the strength of this passage.

CHAPTER 25. SABBATIC YEAR AND JUBILEE

The Sabbatic Year, 1-7. The sabbath of days was extended to a sabbath of years. Every seventh year was to be a year of rest for the land, 5. This was to restore the soil and provide for the poor from what grew from the untilled fields, 6, or as a humanitarian institution economically in the cancellation of debts (cf. 35-38). Primarily, however, it was a recognition of God's sovereignty over the land which He was to give them, 2 (see Lev 26:32-35). Failure to own the Lord's supremacy resulted in captivity in a foreign land. The institution pictured the coming kingdom rest and prosperity, 20-23.

The Year of Jubilee, 8-55. The cycle of seven sabbatic years was followed by the fiftieth year, 8, ushered in by the blowing of the jubilee trumpet on the Day of Atonement, 9. This portrays Israel's entrance into the blessings of the messianic reign, with the Lord in the midst of His people. But it means much more than the promised blessings to Israel. It foreshadows the blessings of Rom 8:19-23 for the entire earth. It will include a great outpouring of the Spirit, the complete fulfillment of Joel's prophecy (Joel 2:28-32).

CHAPTER 26. CONDITIONS OF BLESSING IN THE LAND

The Blessings for Obedience, 1-13. To receive blessing God's people had to be holy and maintain a holy reverence for Him according to the first table of the law given at Sinai, 1-2 (Ex 20:3-11). The vicious idolatry of the Canaanites had to be abominated. (Cf. Deut 28—30 for the conditions of the Palestinian covenant.)

The Curse of Disobedience, 14-39. This culminated in captivity and dispersion among the nations. This prediction and its fulfillment in Jewish history contain powerful evidence for the divine inspiration of the Bible.

The Restoration, 40-46. Despite disobedience to the Mosaic and Palestinian covenants, the unconditional Abrahamic covenant remains, and through grace a remnant will be restored to kingdom blessing.

CHAPTER 27. APPENDIX: VOWS

Persons and Things Dedicated, 1-25. These were voluntary obligations assumed before God, often on condition of some desired blessing, as Jacob's vow (Gen 28:20-22).

Things Intrinsically the Lord's, 26-34. These included the firstborn of animals, 26-27; and dedicated thing, 28-29; and all the tithe of the land, 30-34.

NUMBERS

WALK AND SERVICE OF GOD'S PEOPLE

Nature of the Book. Genesis is the book of beginnings, Exodus the book of redemption, and Leviticus the book of atonement and worship. Numbers, on the other hand, is the book of testing. Numbers (L. *numeri,* Gr. *arithmoi*) is so named because the Israelites were twice numbered (ch. 1 and 26), the first time at the beginning of their journey, the second time at the close of the 38 years of wandering in the desert. Numbers is a wilderness book covering the time span from the second month of the second year after the exodus from Egypt to the tenth month of the fortieth year. But the years of unbelief and wandering are mostly passed over in silence.

Authorship. Although higher criticism denies Mosaic authorship of this and other Pentateuchal books, local color and authentic wilderness background support the fact that Moses wrote the book, especially the close connection of the narrative with Exodus.

Spiritual Significance. The NT repeatedly alludes to or quotes the book of Numbers (cf. Jn 3:14 and Num 21:9). Balaam (Num 22—24) is referred to by Jude (11), Peter (2 Pet 2:15-16), and John (Rev 2:14). Jude also refers to Korah's rebellion (11; cf. Num 16; 27:3). Its rich spiritually illustrative contents are given deep meaning (1 Cor 10:1-11) and are inseparably connected with the rest of the Pentateuch, particularly with Exodus and Leviticus.

> **Outline**
> Leaving Sinai, Ch. 1—10
> Wandering in the Desert, Ch. 11—20
> Journeying to the Land, Ch. 21—36

CHAPTER 1. THE PEOPLE NUMBERED

The Numbering, 1-46. The command to number, 1-4, was given one month after the erection of the tabernacle (cf. Ex 40:17). This numbering was apparently distinct from the atonement-money census (Ex 38:25-26), although the total number is the same (603,550; see Num 1:46). The count was for military purposes, 3, according to family pedigree. In warfare for God (Eph 6:10-18), the "mixed multitude" (Ex 12:38) has no place, but only those born again and able to fight (spiritually mature) have a place (Num 11:4).

The Levites Excluded, 47-54, and separated to tabernacle service.

CHAPTER 2. THE TRIBES ARRANGED

The Command, 1-2. The camp of God's people was divinely arranged and ordered, with the tabernacle in the center (showing that God's worship and service were to be central). In the NT every believer has his appointed place in the body (1 Cor 12), with Christ as the Head.

The Ordered Camp, 3-34. On the east side were Judah, Issachar and Zebulun, 3-9. On the south side were Reuben, Simeon, Gad, 10-16. The position of the Levites was given, 17. On the west side were placed Ephraim, Manasseh, Benjamin, 18-24. On the north side were Dan, Asher, Naphtali, 25-34.

CHAPTERS 3—4. THE LEVITES ASSIGNED THEIR WORK

The Priests, 3:1-4. They are mentioned first, the worship of God (sacrifice and intercession) being centered in them as representatives of the nation.

The Levites, 3:5-39. Divine sovereign grace was exemplified in the choice of this tribe for holy tabernacle ministry (cf. Gen 34:25-31; 49:5-7). Leviticus gives a description of the work of Aaron and his sons. Here the work of the Levites in general is specified, the care of the tabernacle itself and its transportation, 5-10. Levi ("joined") was united to the Lord in holy service instead of the firstborn, 11-13. This tribe was numbered, 14-20; and the specific duties of Gershon, 21-26, Kohath, 27-32, and Merari, 33-37, are set forth. Again the sanctity of the Levites as substitutes for the firstborn is stressed, 40-51, being therefore numbered from infancy, 22, instead of 20 years of age and upward as in the case of the other tribes.

The Kohathites, 4:1-20. The priests illustrate believers in their priestly capacity. Likewise the Levites, mustered "from thirty years old and upward to fifty years," whose responsibility was to guard and transport the holy things of the Lord through the wilderness, picture believers guarding and keeping the precious things of "the faith which was once for all delivered unto the saints." (Jude 3), in their pilgrimage through the desert of this world.

The Gershonites, 4:21-28. Each Levite was divinely assigned his work according to his *birth* by tribe and maturity in *age*. Usefulness in ministry in holy things is on the basis not only of spiritual regeneration, but Christian maturity. In ch. 3 Gershon, the eldest, stands first. Here he takes a secondary place to Kohath, showing that divine grace appoints service and minutely outlines it for the believer in the will of God.

The Merarites, 4:29-49. All the Levites, in being occupied with the holy things of the tabernacle, illustrate our being occupied with Christ in fellowship with God and holy service (cf. Num 8:10).

CHAPTER 5. SEPARATION FROM DEFILEMENT

Separation from Those Unclean, 1-4. The unclean included the leper (see Lev 13—14) and the one defiled by a physical secretion (see Lev 15) or by contact with physical death. This condition incapacited one to serve the *living* God (cf. Heb 9:14), and illustrates the necessity of judging and putting away sin as a barrier to divine fellowship and service.

Restitution, 5-10. This was for wrong committed in the camp. Unconfessed sin cannot be condoned among the Lord's people. The grace of God which grants unlimited forgiveness would be tragic if it did not discipline the believer to deny "ungodliness and worldly lusts" and to "live soberly, righteously, and godly, in this present evil world" (Tit 2:12). Could anything be more calamitous than for those professedly brought near to God to have a weakening sense of the exceeding sinfulness of sin (1 Jn 1:7-9)?

Separation from Adultery, 11-31. This was scarcely a trial by ordeal, so common among ancient people and surviving in Europe till the Middle Ages, since the Mosaic law condemned popular heathen superstitions of the day. It was a simple ritual in which the Lord was to manifest His power in exposing the adulteress and punishing this serious sin in order to purge it out from among God's people.

CHAPTER 6. THE NAZIRITE

The Vow, 1-8. This was a voluntary dedication of a person of himself to the Lord, 2. It involved abstinence from wine, 3, symbolic of the natural pleasures of life (Ps 104:15), and even of grapes in any form, 4, representing earthly joys harmless in themselves but which cannot give the believer the delight in the Lord which his heart craves. This feature is therefore the outward symbol of a yieldedness which finds all its joy in the Lord. The Nazirite vow also involved long hair, 5, normally a reproach to a man (1 Cor 11:14), the outward badge that the separated one was willing to bear rejection for the Lord. The vow also entailed rigid separation from ceremonial uncleanness contracted by contact with

123

a dead body, even that of a close loved one, 6-8. Although Samson, Samuel and John the Baptist were Nazirites, yet the type finds its complete fulfillment in our incarnate Lord, who, completely devoted to the Father (Jn 1:18; 6:38), allowed no natural tie to distract Him from His heavenly mission (Mt 12:46-50) and was "holy, harmless, undefiled, separate from sinners" (Heb 7:26).

The Cleansing of the Nazirite from Defilement, 9-21. Various sacrificial rituals were prescribed, all pointing to the finished redemptive work of Christ. Defilement of a dedicated saint is cleansed only by confession and forgiveness (1 Jn 1:7-9) based on the efficacious advocacy of Christ.

Priestly Blessing of a Cleansed and Consecrated People, 22-27. This is a beautiful threefold invocation of the Lord's providence, grace and favor.

CHAPTER 7. THE GIFTS OF THE PRINCES

The Princes and Their Gifts, 1-88. The chiefs of the tribes contributed wagons and oxen for transporting the tabernacle. Although the gifts are identified for each tribe, they are recorded in detail, not primarily because repetition was characteristic of ancient oriental lists, but because the Lord takes special note of the gifts of His people, and giving in His sight is an individual matter. The Gershonites and Merarites alone received wagons and oxen according to their needs. The Kohathites were appointed to carry on their own shoulders the particularly sacred furnishings, and therefore received no oxen or wagons. Verses 84-88 give the total offering as 2400 silver shekels, 120 gold, and 240 sacrificial animals.

The Voice from the Mercy Seat, 89, manifested the Lord's pleasure in the princes' offerings at the dedication of the altar, the promise of Ex 25:22 being fulfilled.

CHAPTER 8. THE LEVITES CONSECRATED

The Lampstand Lighted, 1-4 (cf. Ex 25:31-40). The lighting of the seven-branched lampstand prefiguring Christ as the Light of the world (Jn 8:12), at the beginning of the wilderness journey focused attention upon the need of the Lord's people for the Holy Spirit (the oil in the seven branches) to shed light on the lampstand of beaten gold, 2, 4. The latter symbolizes the glorious divine Person of Christ. The Spirit reveals Christ to the believer in his pilgrimage through this world.

Purification of the Levites, 5-22. First they were sprinkled with water, symbolizing their cleansing from sin (Eph 5:26; Jn 15:3; 17:17). Next, they were to shave off the hair of their bodies, symbolizing putting off what belongs to the old nature. Then they were to wash their clothes, signifying the water of the Word cleansing their habits and ways of life. The sacrifices, 8, show that consecration is on the basis of atonement for sin, 8. The imposition of hands upon the Levites by the Israelites points to the latter's identification with the Levites, who represented them and served in their place, 9-10, as well as in place of the firstborn, 11-22.

Levitical Charge Repeated, 23-26. The period of service was 25-50 years, which is not in contradiction to Num 4:3 where 30-50 years is specified. From 25-30 they could do the heavier work, as those over 30 were exempt from these tasks. The Lord still is interested in the comfort of His servants (cf. Mk 6:31; Jn 21:13).

CHAPTER 9. GUIDANCE FOR THE REDEEMED

The Observance of the Passover, 1-14 (see Lev 23:4-5). The first Passover was held in Egypt. This second observance, held in the desert at Sinai as they journeyed toward Canaan, shows how necessary the feast of redemption with its atoning blood is to all in a walk for God. A gracious promise was made for the ceremonially unclean and the traveler, 6-14.

Supernatural Guidance Provided, 15-23. The pillar of cloud by day and the pillar of fire by night were provided to lead the people. In the trackless desert of this world of sin God's people need the guidance of the Spirit by day and by night (Ps 23:2-3).

CHAPTER 10. THE SILVER TRUMPETS; THE CAMP MOVES

The Silver Trumpets, 1-10. These were two in number and made of silver. Like the cloud and fiery pillar which were given for visible guidance, they made known the mind of the Lord in an audible way, 1-7. Aaron and the priests being in fellowship with God were to blow the trumpets and thus make known God's will to the people, 8. It was blowing the trumpets in faith in their status as a redeemed people that would assure victory, 9. In peace, the trumpets were to be blown at solemn feasts, over atoning sacrifices, at the beginning of months, to signify faith in the redemptive guidance of the Lord on behalf of His redeemed people, 10 (cf. Lev 23:24; Num 29:1; Ps 81:3; 89:15; Isa 27:13).

Departure from Sinai, 11-36. The cloud moved, 11-13, and the camp went forward, the standard of the camp of Judah in the van, 14-17, followed by that of Reuben, 18-21, of Ephraim, 22-24, and of Dan, 25-28. How beautiful and orderly the start according to the instructions of Num 1—10. But the first failure recorded is on the side of Moses, 29-32, who, acting in human wisdom and not in faith in God, leaned upon the arm of flesh. But the Lord led on and there was a shout in the camp, 33-36.

CHAPTER 11. FAILURE AT TABERAH AND KIBROTH-HATTAAVAH

Murmuring at Taberah, 1-3. This first recorded complaint of God's people so well-ordered, provided for, and led on to Canaan, is inexplicable except on the ground of the wickedness of the human heart. The chastisement was consuming fire. Therefore the place was memorialized Taberah ("a burning").

Rejection of the Manna, 4-9. "The mixed multitude" was doubtless composed of non-Israelite slaves attached to Israel, who had escaped with them from Egypt but who knew nothing of God's redemption. They illustrate those who are unable to appropriate or appreciate Christ as the Bread of God (cf. Ex 16:14-22), who lust for things pleasurable to the flesh and contrary to the Word in matters of worship and practice.

Moses' Complaint and the Appointment of the 70 Elders, 10-30. The situation was enough to tax any leader's courage. Accordingly, God directed in the appointment of 70 helpers for Moses in civil administration (cf. Ex 18:17-23), and put a portion of the Spirit that rested upon Moses upon them, so that Eldad and Medad prophesied in the camp, 26-27. Moses' humility is shown in 28-30.

Quails and the Plague, 31-35. There was abundance of quails "about two cubits [three feet] above the surface of the earth," meaning within easy reach of the people to catch. The lusting of the Israelites was punished by " a very great plague," 33, the place being called Kibroth-hattaavah ("graves of lust"), 34-35.

CHAPTER 12. MIRIAM AND AARON'S CRITICISM OF MOSES

The Mutiny of Miriam and Aaron, 1-10. The general cause for this mutiny was jealousy of Moses' preeminence, and the immediate occasion the marriage of Moses to an Ethiopian woman. Miriam the prophetess (Ex 15:20) was the leader. She was punished with leprosy, showing the seriousness of her sin of speaking against a servant of the Lord to whom the Lord revealed Himself in a uniquely intimate manner, 6-8, and yet who was at the same time so surpassingly meek, 3, a notation necessary to the narrative and not inconsistent with Mosaic authorship.

Aaron's Repentance and Moses' Intercession, 11-16. Miriam was restored to fellowship with the nation through the intercession of her brothers.

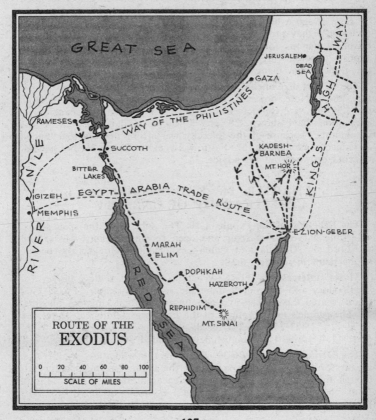

ROUTE OF THE
EXODUS

SCALE OF MILES

127

CHAPTER 13. KADESH-BARNEA:
THE EVIL REPORT OF THE SPIES

The Scouts Sent Out, 1-25. Spies were sent out to explore the Promised Land by divine command, 1-3, which was an approval of the request of the people themselves (Deut 1:19-25). Of the twelve names given, 4-15, only Joshua and Caleb appear elsewhere in the Bible. At this time Moses changed Oshea's name ("saviour") to Joshua, *Jehoshua* ("the Lord is Saviour, Deliverer"), 16. First the scouts were to go to the Negeb, the southern steppe land, and then on to the mountain or the central highland ridge, 17, in late July or early August, the time of the first-ripe grapes, 20. At Eshcol ("cluster") they procured a huge bunch of grapes, 23. The Hebron region is famous for its grapes, and clusters weighing from 12 to almost 20 pounds are found there, often carried on a pole to keep the grapes from being bruised.

The Report of Unbelief, 26-33. The land was truly all God said it was, 26-27. Note, however, the "nevertheless" of unbelief, 28. High walled cities were characteristic of ancient Palestine as archaeological excavations have shown, 28, and it was "a land that eateth up the inhabitants," because of the intercity warfare of this era that tended to reduce its population, 32. Faith was vocal in Caleb, 30, but general unbelief drowned out his advice, 31.

CHAPTER 14. KADESH-BARNEA:
THE TRAGEDY OF UNBELIEF

The Rebellion of the People, 1-10. The unbelief of the spies sowed a terrible harvest of despair and open rebellion against Moses and the Lord, 1-5. Joshua and Caleb's exhortations enraged the people to the point of murder, 6-10.

Moses' Intercession, 11-25. What an eloquent selfless prayer for God's glory and for mercy upon the rebellious people, 13-19! God heard, spared the people, and announced eventual kingdom blessing, 21. The people's ten temptings of the Lord are mentioned, 22 (cf. Ex 14:11-12; 15:23-24; 16:2; 16:20; 16:27; 17:1-3; 32:1-10; Num 11:1; 11:4; 14:2). Their punishment is hinted at in 23-25.

The Divine Sentence, 26-39. Death in the wilderness wanderings, a year for every day they spied out the land, was the penalty. Although the wilderness with its experiences of the Red Sea, Marah, Elim and Sinai was part of God's essential discipline for His people, and has its spiritual realities in a believer's experiences,

Israel's *wanderings in the wilderness were not!* The Red (Reed) Sea speaks of the cross separating us from Egypt, the world (Gal 6:14). Marah tells of God's grace to turn testings into blessings. Elim tells of God's power to grant rest and refreshment in God's way. Sinai bespeaks God's infinite holiness and our depravity (Rom 7:7-24). But from Israel's failure at Kadesh-barnea to their entrance into Canaan, all is for warning (1 Cor 10:1-11; Heb 3:1—4:16), not for imitation.

A New Sin—Presumption, 40-45. The sin of unbelieving despair in refusing to enter the conflict for the Promised Land in the strength of the promise of God was now capped with an additional sin of presumptuous confidence. They refused to believe in the severity of God's judgment by resolving to engage in conflict without God's help and purely in their own power. Their disgraceful defeat was inevitable.

SPIRITUAL SIGNIFICANCE OF KADESH-BARNEA

The people had faith to apply the redemption blood (Ex 12:28) and to leave Egypt (the world), but lacked faith to enter their Canaan rest, enjoy conquest over enemies, and victorious possession of a land flowing with milk and honey (Heb 3:1—4:16). In other words, they failed to enter into spiritual conquest and victory.

CHAPTER 15. VARIOUS LAWS

Concerning Offerings in the Land, 1-31. Two divine communications concerning offerings, 1, 17, are remarkable in that they were apparently given precisely when the people were turning in unbelief from the land of promise. What a comforting assurance of God's faithfulness in eventually bringing them into their inheritance despite their unbelief and unfaithfulness. While the great mass of people would die in the wilderness, God would bring a remnant in. They would offer these sacrifices, already described in Leviticus.

The Sabbath Breaker, 32-36. This was a case of presumptuous sin mentioned in 30-31, giving an example of the severity of the Mosaic law.

The Ribbon of Blue, 37-41, the color of heaven on the borders of the garments, was a memento that the Israelite in his pilgrimage was to live a holy, separated life, heavenly in ambition and desire, 40, as one redeemed from Egypt (the world).

CHAPTER 16. KORAH'S REBELLION

The Rebellion, 1-19. This rebellion marks another step downward in unbelief and apostasy (cf. Jude 3-11). Korah's sin was the rejection of the authority of Moses as God's mouthpiece and flagrant intrusion into the priest's office, the honor of which no one was to take to himself except "he that is called by God, as was Aaron" (Heb 5:4). Korah and the 250 insurgents who followed him attempted to create a priestly order without divine sanction (Heb 5:10). Ecclesiastical priestism is a modern analogy of this sin, in which the priesthood of every believer is denied or encroached upon.

The Punishment, 20-50. The glory of the Lord appearing, 19, dealt with this matter. Korah and the insurgents, 27-33, were swallowed by an earthquake and went down alive into Sheol. Fire from heaven devoured the 250 men who offered incense, 35, but the sons of Korah did not perish (cf. 26:11), showing God's sovereign grace (cf. 1 Chr 6:54-67; 9:19-32; 26:1-20; 2 Chr 23:3-4, 19; 31:14-18). Provision was made for a memorial of this event as a permanent warning by hammering out a covering for the altar from the bronze censers the rebels had used, 36-40. The checking of the plague against the murmuring Israelites by Aaron, 41-50, shows the necessity of the priesthood of Him who has made atonement in the presence of God to keep His people.

CHAPTER 17. AARON'S ROD THAT BUDDED

The Divine Command, 1-6. This directive for each tribal head to bring an almond rod inscribed with the name of the tribe, with the rod of Levi bearing the name of Aaron as its representative, was meant to furnish further proof of the Lord's irrevocable choice of the Levites as ministers and the Aaronites as priests.

The Sign, 7-13. Standing among the dying, "making an atonement" (16:46-48), Aaron reminds us of Christ in His redemptive work. All the tribal heads presented dead rods. The Lord caused life to spring up in Aaron's rod alone, which became a picture of Christ in resurrection, acknowledged by God as High Priest. All the great founders of ethnic faiths have died, and are dead. Only Christ was raised from the dead and exalted to be a High Priest (Heb 4:14; 5:4-10). Aaron's priesthood, so blatantly denied in Korah's uprising, was here given the permanent divine sanction, 10, silencing the rebels as Aaron's rod was laid up as a memorial in the tabernacle (Heb 9:4). The rebellion of Korah thus yielded two things for the tabernacle—the plates from the censers for the altar covering (16:38) and Aaron's fruitful rod.

CHAPTER 18. THE IMPORTANCE OF THE LEVITICAL PRIESTHOOD

It Was to Bear Iniquity, 1-7. The Levitical priests were to execute every divine regulation meticulously and make atonement for the sinfulness pertaining to the tabernacle and its priesthood. This was indispensable "that there be no wrath any more upon the Israelites," 5. Korah's rebellion was so wicked because it was directed against that which was meant to be Israel's very security. Except for the priestly service, all Israel would have been destroyed by the wrath of God. So Christ, our great High Priest, ever lives to make intercession for us, to keep us saved (Heb 7:25).

It Was to Be Properly Recompensed, 8-32. Neither the priests nor the Levites were to have any land inheritance in Israel, thus avoiding a wealthy priestly caste such as existed in Egypt and other ancient nations. The priests, however, were to receive a large part of the offerings, such as meal, sin and trespass offerings, 8-11; gifts of the firstfruits, 12-13; things devoted, 14; and money from the redemption of the firstborn, 15-19. Aaron was to have no land inheritance because the Lord was his inheritance, 20. The Levites were to get a tithe, 21-24, and to give proportionately of what they received, 25-32.

CHAPTER 19. THE RED HEIFER ORDINANCE

The Ordinance, 1-10. This ordinance is unique to Numbers and to the wilderness wandering. It was instituted because of wholesale contact with the death of so many Israelites who perished during the 40-year period in the desert (cf. 1 Cor 10:5, 8, 9). The use of the ashes of an animal in water for purification purposes is a well-known ancient religious custom outside the Bible, here invested with unique significance as it is introduced to Israel's faith.

The Meaning, 11-22. The red heifer beautifully illustrates the sacrifice of Christ as *the basis* of the cleansing of a believer from sinful defilement contracted in his pilgrim walk (1 Jn 1:7—2:2; cf. Jn 13:3-10). The choice of the red animal is due, perhaps, to an association of that color with sin (Isa 1:18). Its spotless, unblemished character, 2, speaks of the sinlessness of Christ (cf. Heb 9:13-14). It was to be an animal on which no yoke had been placed, 2, the yoke being used to restrain an animal. Christ was completely yielded to the Father's will (Ps 40:7-8; Heb 10:5-9) and needed no coercion. The heifer was killed "without the camp," 3 (Heb 13:12). The sprinkling of the blood seven times toward the tabernacle speaks of full atonement, 4. The ashes of the heifer were the memorial of an already accepted sacrifice. *Death* here typifies the polluting effects of sin in making the saint with defiled conscience unworthy "to serve the living God" (Heb 9:14).

CHAPTER 20. MOSES' SIN; DEATH OF AARON

Moses' Sin, 1-13. This chapter opens with death (Miriam's) and closes with death (Aaron's) and between recounts the failure of Moses. The long years of wandering were fraught with failure and death (cf. Amos 5:25-26; Acts 7:42-43; 1 Cor 10:1-10). Yet God's grace never forsook His sinning people (Deut 2:7; 29:5). Even Moses was contaminated with failure as he was tried by the impatient murmuring people at Meribah, 2-6, again afflicted with thirst as in Ex 17:1-7 (cf. Deut 32:51). Moses' sin was twofold: (1) *Presumptuous disobedience*. He should have spoken to the rock, not struck it once, much less twice, 10-11. (2) *Self-exaltation*, assuming authority which was not his. He should not have said, "Must *we* bring forth water?" presumptuously putting himself in God's place, 10.

Futile Negotiations with Edom, 14-22. The descendants of Esau, the brother of Israel (Jacob), denied passage to the Israelites, thus aggravating the heartless cruelty in their kinship and racial tie with Jacob's descendants.

Death of Aaron, 23-29. Aaron died on Mt. Hor. His son Eleazar succeeded him. Mt. Hor (Jebel Harun) is some 50 miles S of the Dead Sea.

CHAPTER 21. THE BRONZE SERPENT

Victory over the Canaanites, 1-3. King Arad in the Negeb, the waterless district S of Beersheba extending S and SW beyond Kadesh-barnea, was defeated and his towns placed under the ban of complete destruction.

The Bronze Serpent, 4-9. Murmuring again broke out, 4-5, and was punished by fiery serpents, 6-7. The brass serpent which Moses was instructed to make and hang on a pole, to which the people bitten were to look, prefigures Christ "made sin for us" (Jn 3:14-15; 2 Cor 5:21), in bearing on the tree the judgment of our sin (Rom 8:3). The serpent (Gen 3:14), as Satan's tool in the Fall, became God's illustration in nature of the effects of sin—from a beautiful, doubtless upright creature to a loathsome snake. The bronze speaks of judgment—in the bronze altar, of divine judgment, and in the bronze laver, of self-judgment. The bronze serpent portrays sin—judged in the cross of Christ. Looking at the serpent of brass for healing of the snake bite speaks of faith in the cross of Christ for spiritual healing from the venom of sin, 8-9. That the serpent became an object of idolatrous worship demonstrates how a means of grace can be misused (cf. 2 Kgs 18:4). King Hezekiah destroyed it about 700 B.C.

Joyful Journey to Transjordan, 10-35. After healing at the cross, joyful singing is heard, 17. There is a beautiful spiritual sequence: (1) *redemption*, 8-9 (Jn 3:14-15); (2) *water*, speaking of the Spirit given, 16 (Jn 7:37-39); (3) *joy*, 17-18 (Rom 14:17); (4) *power*, 21-35, seen in victory over Sihon, king of the Amorites, and Og, king of Bashan.

CHAPTER 22. BALAAM THE MERCENARY PROPHET

Balak Calls Balaam, 1-20. Balak, king of Moab, fearful of Israel passing by on the way to Canaan, sent for Balaam, originally a pagan diviner from Pethor, a city of Mesopotamia (Deut 23:4). Balaam was asked to curse Israel with his demonic magical powers as the Israelites were encamped in the Plain of Moab (c. 1401 B.C.). Balaam, "people's devourer," was doubtless attracted to the Lord, as Jethro (Ex 18) and Rahab (Josh 2), by the fame of Israel's deliverance from Egypt (Ex 15:14; Josh 5:1), and he determined to practice his oracular gifts in the name of Israel's God.

Balaam Goes to Balak, 21-35. The directive will of God had been known to Balaam, 12, which he did not follow. This left him to follow his own selfish inclination, as he preferred the permissive will of God, 20. The case of the speaking ass is an instance of the omnipotence of God, and is not to be explained away by unbelief (cf. the confirmation of the miracle, 2 Pet 2:15-16). That the dumb animal saw the Angel of the Lord first is in line with the frequently keener instinctive presentiments of impending danger possessed by animals over man.

Balaam with Balak, 36-41. Balaam is the type of a mercenary prophet, ambitious to exploit his gift financially. This is "the *way* of Balaam" (2 Pet 2:15). The *"error* of Balaam" (Jude 11) is the diviner-prophet's blunder in reasoning that God *of necessity* must curse the nation Israel because of its sin. He was ignorant of God's election of Israel as a nation, and the immutability of God's choice (Rom 11:29) and the nation's preservation. He failed to see how God can be "just and the justifier" of the believing sinner through the cross, to which all Israel's tabernacle ritual pointed. The *"doctrine of Balaam"* (Rev 2:14) was the teaching of the money-mad seer to abandon a separated pilgrimage for worldly conformity (Num 31:15-16; Jas 4:4).

CHAPTER 23. BALAAM'S FIRST TWO PROPHETIC PARABLES

The First Parable and Sequel, 1-12. Presented first is the sacrificial preparation, 1-6, for the prophecy itself, 7-10. It was impossible for Balaam to curse or denounce Israel whom God had blessed, 8-9. The reason is that Israel's *standing* as a redeemed people was immutable in the light of the serpent "lifted up" (21:5-9) and the water out of the struck rock (20:11). Israel's *state* was morally reprehensible, but this called for the Lord's disciplinary action against the people, not His judgment or curse upon them (Rom 11:29). Balaam saw them "from the top of the mountains," that is, from God's lofty vantage point of electing grace, 9. As such they were a *chosen nation,* different from the other nations, 9, destined for ultimate unforfeitable blessing, 10, a people set apart for a particular destiny.

The Second Parable and Sequel, 13-30. The sacrificial preparation and conversation with Balak, 13-17, are introductory to the second oracle itself, 18-24. God's immutable national election of Israel and fidelity to His Word are stressed, 18-19. God's decreed blessing could not be revoked by Balaam, 20, nor indeed by all the sinister power of heathen occultism, 23. The oracles are to be construed as literal to Israel and illustrative to Christians. Israel's *standing* because redeemed, 22, was secure and perfect, 21, though her actual *state* required the divine discipline. Likewise the believer is saved and secure through Christ lifted up on Calvary (Jn 3:14), but he may need the Father's disciplinary dealing (1 Cor 11:30-32; 2 Cor 1:4-9). All the while, however, God was *for* Israel and *against* Balak and all enemies, 23, as well as *"for"* us" (Rom 8:31). Eventually, when the kingdom is restored to Israel and she is saved, the universal testimony will be, "What has God done!" 23 (cf. Rom 11: 26-36). Because Messiah-King will one day rule over the restored nation, Balaam said, "The shout of a *king* is among them," 21.

CHAPTER 24. BALAAM'S LAST TWO PROPHETIC PARABLES

The Third Parable and Sequel, 1-14. Introductory to the third parable, 2-9, was the account of Balaam's forsaking omens and the

Spirit of God coming upon him, 1, in vision, 4, to prophesy in beautiful figures concerning Israel's future kingdom glory, 5-7. "His king," ultimately realized in the Messiah, "shall be higher than Agag," 7, the traditional name for the king of Amalek (1 Sam 15:8), Israel's inveterate enemy, and suggestive of the Antichrist and all anti-Semitic forces. King-Messiah's kingdom will be exalted and victorious as a lion over his prey, 8-9. Balaam's allusion to blessing upon those who bless Israel and cursing upon those who curse her recalls the Abrahamic covenant (Gen 12:3), the fulfillment of which is certain. Balak's angry reaction, 10, and Balaam's reply are given, 10-14.

The Last Parable and Sequel, 15-25. This is the most remarkable of the four parables, containing a magnificent messianic prophecy of "the Star out of Jacob" and a "Sceptre out of Israel," which "shall smite the corners [of the head] of Moab" and destroy "all the sons of Sheth." Although the royal symbols "star" and "sceptre" include David, whose empire encompassed the Promised Land (Gen 49:10), yet they find their fulfillment only in the greater David when at the second advent the kingdom is restored to Israel (Acts 1:6). Then Israel's foes Moab, Edom, Amalek, Asshur, Eber and Kittim, that portray the latter-day Gentile world powers, will be judged (Mt 25:31-46), before Israel's kingdom is set up.

CHAPTER 25. ISRAEL'S SIN WITH BAAL-PEOR

The Sin, 1-3. This grievous sin of fornication and idolatry was the result of Balaam teaching (Num 31:16; Rev 2:14; Jas 4:4). Although Balaam as an instrument of Satan could not turn the Lord against Israel, he could turn Israel from the Lord. Baal-peor ("lord of the opening"), worshiped near Mt. Pisgah, 3 (cf. Deut 4:3; Ps 106:28; 2 Sam 5:20), was a farm and fertility god responsible for fecundity of family, flock and field. This god was worshiped in high places or hilltops with licentious rites and ritualistic feasting.

The Punishment, 4-9. There was a great slaughter of 24,000 (the 23,000 of 1 Cor 10:8 numbering only the people who perished, with 1,000 heads of the people previously hung up before the Lord not counted).

Phinehas' Action and Reward, 10-18. Phinehas' zeal saved the people from further judgment, 11, and was rewarded by a covenant of peace and an everlasting priesthood, 12-13. He reminds us of Christ in His righteous burning zeal for God's glory. The Midianites were to be exterminated, 16-18, showing that snares to compromise and apostasy must be destroyed by God's people.

CHAPTER 26. THE SECOND NUMBERING

The Command and Its Execution, 1-51. The new census was taken after the plague and the events of the wilderness, the grand total, 51, being slightly smaller than the previous census (Num 1:46 with Ex 38:25-26).

A Fair Method of Dividing the Land, 52-65. The new revision of the military lists provided figures for a more equitable division of the land by lot-drawing. Notice the fulfillment of God's judgment, 64-65; but compare Josh 14:1 and 22:13, showing that both Eleazar and Phinehas entered Canaan. Evidently the sentence of execution applied only to the tribes which had been numbered twice previously. Levi, not having been so numbered, not having sent a scout like the others to spy out Canaan (Num 13:4-15), and apparently not having concurred in the unbelief the adverse report occasioned, was not subject to this judgment.

CHAPTER 27. ZELOPHEHAD'S DAUGHTERS; MOSES' DEATH ANNOUNCED

A Question of Inheritance, 1-11. The case of a man dying intestate and having no male heirs, only daughters, became the occasion for a further elaboration of Hebrew inheritance laws. Daughters were to receive the right of inheritance, but were to marry only within their own tribe (cf. Num 36:8).

Appointment of Moses' Successor, 12-23. Moses' death being announced, and the reason for it, 12-14, the great leader demonstrated his humility and meek selflessness in thinking only of the interest of God's people, 15-17. Joshua was divinely chosen, 18, and ordained by Moses.

CHAPTERS 28—29. THE OFFERINGS FOR FESTAL SEASONS

The Portion the Lord Was to Receive, 28:1—29:11. This was to be taken from the daily offerings, 28:1-8; the weekly offerings, 9-10; the monthly offerings, 11-15; the Passover, 16-25; the Feast of Firstfruits, 26-31; Feast of Trumpets, 29:1-6; and the Day of Atonement, 7-11. The key is 28:2: "Command the children of Israel, and say unto them, *My* offering, and *my* bread for *my* sacrifices made by fire, for a sweet savour unto *me,* shall ye observe to offer unto me in their due season." Cf. Lev 23 for the meaning of these set feasts.

Prominence Given to the Feast of Tabernacles and Its Offerings, 29:12-40. Cf. the 12 verses devoted to this feast in Lev. 23:33-44 with the 28 verses here. The seven days of this feast look forward to Israel's Kingdom Age and its worship, commemorating a finished redemption, while the eighth day of solemn rest, 35, points to the eternal state.

CHAPTER 30.   LAWS REGULATING VOWS

Vows of a Man, 1-2. The man who keeps his word, who performs all he vowed, illustrates the sanctity and importance of the vow in ancient Israel.

Vows of a Woman, 3-16. These injunctions involved vows or pledges made by women in which men were involved as the heads of households, and were exceptions to the general rule that any-one who made a vow must perform it. The vow of an unmarried daughter, 3-5, living at home might be annulled by her father, or that of a married woman by her husband, but only if the objection to it was stated at the time the vow was made, 6-8. If the woman did not fulfill it, the man had to do so. The law applied to widows and divorcees, 9-16. On vows see Lev 27.

CHAPTER 31.   WAR AGAINST MIDIAN

The Divine Command, 1-12. Vengeance upon Midian was the last official act of Moses' leadership. This was previously enjoined (Num 25:16-18), but delayed until now. The war of a holy character was to be conducted by Phinehas. It was designed to show how uncompromising God's servants must always be against idolatrous apostasy and apostate prophets like Balaam, 8. The war was to execute the vengeance of the Lord upon Midian, 3, as God will do to all apostates and especially to Israel's last-day enemies (cf. Isa 63:1-6; 2 Thess 1:7-9).

Cleansing, Spoil Gathering, and Offerings, 13-54. God gave complete victory. Israel was enriched by rooting out the danger of apostasy and thankfully offered to God the spoils of conquest over a subtle temptation to sin.

CHAPTER 32.   THE PORTION OF REUBEN, GAD AND MANASSEH

Their Request and Dispute with Moses, 1-24. The request was a selfish one, characterized by worldly convenience, 1-5. The territory they chose, moreover, was outside the Promised Land and they thereby showed unbelief and a willingness to shun war. Moses' rebuke, 6-15, warned them of the fruits of unbelief at Kadesh-barnea when the spies were sent out. Their compromise to join their brothers in fighting in Canaan before settling down, 16-19, was accepted, 20-24.

The Final Arrangement, 25-42. The tribes of Reuben and Gad and the half tribe of Manasseh, 33, obtained the rich grazing lands of Transjordan, but their choice was comparable to Lot's selfish decision (Gen 13:5-11), and manifested similar results of unbelief and worldly conformity (2 Kgs 15:29; 1 Chr 5:25-26).

CHAPTER 33. SUMMARY OF THE JOURNEY FROM EGYPT

The First and Second Stages, 1-17. This chapter shows God's concern and watchcare over His people. The first stage was from Egypt to Sinai, 1-15. The second was from Sinai to Kadesh, 16-17.

The Third and Fourth Stages, 18-49. The third stage was from Rithmah to Kadesh, 18-36, the 38 years of wilderness wandering. The fourth stage was from Kadesh to the Plain of Moab in the fortieth year, 37-49. Most of the 21 places mentioned are yet unidentified in the travelog set down by Moses.

Directions to Exterminate the Canaanites, 50-56. Idolaters and every trace of their idolatry were to be rooted out. The reason is given in verse 55 (cf. Josh 23:13).

CHAPTER 34. DIRECTIONS FOR THE CONQUEST AND ALLOTMENT OF CANAAN

Canaanites to Be Exterminated. See 33:50-56.

The Land Divided, 1-29. The boundaries of the land are given, 1-12, and the names of the men who would apportion it, 13-29.

CHAPTER 35. LEVITICAL CITIES AND CITIES OF REFUGE

The Levitical Cities, 1-8. These were 48 in all. They included six cities of refuge, which are specified (cf. Gen 49:5-7). The cities were set apart because the Levites were not entitled to a tribal inheritance (Lev 25:32-34; Josh 21; 1 Chr 6:54-81).

The Cities of Refuge, 9-34. The six cities of asylum are described

(Deut 4:41-43; 19:1-13). They restrained the tribal law of blood revenge so that a manslayer might receive a trial, 12. Murder and manslaughter are distinguished, 16-34. Murder is a terrible crime because blood pollutes the land (Gen 4:10-11) in which the Lord dwells. Therefore, the murderer's blood alone can expiate the crime (Deut 19:10-13).

The cities of refuge furnish illustration of Christ sheltering the sinner from judgment (Ex 21:13; Deut 19:2-9; Ps 46:1; 142:5; Rom 8:1; Phil 3:9). The shedder of innocent blood is reminiscent of Israel, who crucified the Messiah, and on this account has been kept out of her inheritance. Yet Israel has a city of refuge in which to flee, preserved as she will be to return to possession of the land. This will occur when Christ's priesthood in glory as now exercised ends and He comes forth to exercise the Melchizedek priesthood.

CHAPTER 36. LAWS OF FEMALE INHERITANCE

The Request of the Tribe of Manasseh, 1-4. This plea asked that tribal inheritance affected by women be kept in the tribe (cf. Num 27).

Moses' Response, 5-12. Moses approved the request. Verse 13 refers to all statutes or amendments published by Moses in the Plain of Moab (ch. 27—36).

The Dead Sea. (*Courtesy IIS*)

DEUTERONOMY

THE BOOK OF OBEDIENCE

Name of the Book. Deuteronomy is called by the Jews the "five-fifths of the law," since it completes the five books of Moses. It is logical both in its place in the canon and in the content of its message. Numbers brings the history of Israel up to the events in the Plains of Moab. Deuteronomy rehearses the law to the new generation that had come out of the wilderness and was looking to the conquest of Canaan. The name "Deuteronomy" ("second law," the inexact rendering in Greek of 17:18) should be rendered, "This is the copy [or repetition] of the law." The book, therefore, does not contain a "second law" distinct from the Sinaitic legislation, but is simply a partial restatement and explanation of previous laws of Israel to the new generation which had grown up in the wilderness. Hence in the Masorah (Heb. tradition) it is styled *Mishneh Torah,* meaning "repetition [or copy] of the law," 17:18.

Nature of the Book. This is distinctly a book of *obedience.* "Observe *to do"* was the emphasis of Moses to the people. Everything depended on this—life itself, possession of the Promised Land, victory over foes, prosperity and happiness. Blessing is the reward of obedience; the curse, the result of disobedience. It is also distinctly a book of *remembrance* and *retrospect.* It looks back to redemption out of Egypt and discipline and punishment in the wilderness, beholding both the goodness and severity of God. It is a book of *hope* and *prospect,* looking to the future in Canaan and the prophetic forecast of Israel's future. Deuteronomy was our Lord's favorite book, as the book of obedience reflecting His own perfect obedience to the Father. Significantly He quoted from this great book in repelling the disobedience suggested by the tempter (Mt 4:1-11; Lk 4:1-13; cf. Deut 8:3; 6:16; 6:13 and 10:20).

Higher Criticism of the Book. Despite the fact that the Mosaic authorship of the book is emphatically asserted (Deut 31:9, 24-26), and our Lord validated its authenticity by prominent quotations, higher critics reject its Mosaic claims and relegate it to the time of Josiah, making its publication the basis of that king's great reformation (2 Kgs 22 and 23). This claim is to be rejected, because it makes the book a pious fraud, and explains away clear evidence of the early existence of the book by arbitrary assumptions that these were later additions.

CHAPTERS 1—4. HISTORICAL REVIEW: SUMMARY OF EVENTS IN THE WILDERNESS

Introduction, 1:1-5. The synopsis of Israel's unbelief is given, 2-3. An 11 days' journey by faith was changed to 40 years' wandering by unbelief. Moses expounds (Heb. *be'er,* "explains" or "elucidates") the law to the new generation preparatory to entrance into the land (cf. 1 Cor 15:3; Heb 3:5).

Review of the Journey from Sinai to Kadesh, 1:6-46. A recapitulation of the wilderness wanderings is given. This is vital to clarify to the new generation the moral judgment of God upon Israel's unbelief and failure in these events. The command to go in to possess the land, 6-8, and the appointment of judges, 9-18, are summarized, as well as the failure of the people to possess the land, and the consequent visitation of divine judgment upon them, 34-46.

Thirty-eight Years of Wandering, 2:1-15, are merely glimpsed and stress is laid on not offending the Edomites or the Moabites.

New Period of Faith and Advance, 2:16—3:29. Israel marched on to the land of the Amorites, 2:16-23. The command to possess the land was given, 24-25, resulting in the conquest of Sihon, 26-37, and Og, 3:1-11, and the possession of Transjordan, 12-20, Joshua taking his place as Moses' successor, 21-29.

Moses' Earnest Exhortation to Obedience, 4:1-40. This speech strikes the keynote of the book (cf. 11:26-28).

Transitional Statement, 4:41-43. Cities of refuge were set apart, 41-43 (cf. Num 35, especially v. 14). There were to be six of these in all. Moses obediently set up three of them, Bezer ("defense"), Ramoth ("heights") and Golan ("their joy"), in the land already conquered. For their illustrative significance, see Num 35.

Introduction to Moses' Second Discourse, 4:44-49. The summary of the first discourse, 44-45, declares Mosaic authorship of this material and distinguishes the law into *testimonies,* declaring the Lord's will; *statutes,* expressing moral and spiritual duties; *judgments,* indicating measures designed to secure social justice. The territory conquered, 48, is now known as Transjordan, extending from the middle of the Dead Sea to Mt. Hermon and from the

Jordan to the desert. All was set for conquest of the Promised Land itself.

CHAPTER 5. REITERATION OF THE TEN COMMANDMENTS

Introduction to Moses' Second Discourse. See 4:44-49.

The Decalogue Repeated, 1-21. Moses now recapitulated the Ten Commandments (see Ex 20:1-17). These were basic to the Mosaic covenant given to Israel and expressed man's duties to God and to his fellowmen. These, together with the "judgments," governing the social life of Israel (Ex 21:1—24:11), and the "ordinances," regulating the religious life (Ex 24:12—31:18), form "the law" (Mt 5:17-18), or Mosaic covenant. Moses purposely varied the statement of the commandments; e.g., the supernatural redemption out of Egypt is presented as the basic reason for keeping the sabbath in contrast to God's creation rest in Ex 20:11.

The Meaning of the Events at Sinai Stressed, 22-33. The aged Moses, soon to depart this life, solemnly impressed his hearers with the deep significance of the giving of the law at Sinai. He recalled the fire, cloud and darkness, 22, and notably God's voice, 23. The people were deeply moved, 27-29, and Moses' role of mediator was indicated, 31.

CHAPTER 6. EXPOSITION OF THE FIRST COMMANDMENT

Summary and Exhortation to Obedience, 1-3. This section relates to the content of ch. 5.

The First Commandment, 4. This is a famous verse with orthodox Jews, who call it *Shema‘* after the first word, "Hear!" "The Lord [*YHWH*] our Elohim is *one* Lord [*Yhwh*]," the *one, 'ehadh,* expressing *compound unity* not *yahid,* meaning a *single* one, thus not supporting Jewish and Unitarian denial of the Trinity. The meaning is "the Eternally Existing One is our God and He is the unique and *only* Eternally Existing One" (see footnote of ASV).

Duties Resulting from the First Commandment, 5-25. Since He is the unique and *only* Lord God, Israel is to love Him, obey and serve Him supremely, 5-25 (cf. Mt 22:37; Mk 12:29-30). The basis for this is gratitude for redemption out of Egypt, 21-22, and into the Promised Land, 23. Likewise the NT believer is to love the Lord as his Redeemer (1 Jn 4:19; 5:3; 1 Cor 6:20). Jews have literally carried out verses 6-9, writing these words on parchment and binding them in little boxes on their forehead and hand. These were later called phylacteries (Mt 23:5; cf. Deut 11:8; Josephus *Antiquities* IV, 8, 13). But the command was not meant to be a ritual requirement, but a spiritual reality.

CHAPTER 7. POSSESSION OF THE LAND AND SEPARATION FROM SIN

Command to Destroy Idolatry, 1-11. The Canaanites were to be exterminated, 1-4, because their licentiousness was infective and their iniquity full (cf. Gen 15:16; 1 Cor 10:14). It was a question of destroying or being destroyed, being separated or polluted and ruined. Therefore both idolaters and their idolatry were to be wiped out, 5-11. The Ugaritic religious texts discovered in 1929-37 at Ras Shamra (ancient Ugarit) on the N. Syrian coast fully attest the moral depravity of Canaanite cults around 1400 b.c., and support the biblical notices and the justice of the divine severity in ordering their destruction.

Promise of Blessed Assistance, 12-26. Victory, increase and general prosperity would attend godly separation from idolatrous contamination. The same principle holds good for God's people in every age.

CHAPTERS 8-10. WARNINGS TO OBEDIENCE

Remember the Past, Anticipate the Future, 8:1-20. Recall the 40 years of God's gracious care, 1-6. Look forward to the gracious provision in the Promised Land, 7-10. Be careful not to forget the Lord, 11-20.

Warning in the Light of Former Failure, 9:1—10:11. The warning, 9:1-6, was in view of past unbelief, 7-24. Moses' intercession was presented, 25-29, and the results of former disobedience, 10:1-11, recounted to the new generation.

The Lord's Love for His People and Their Responsibility, 10:12-22. His love is set forth, 12-15, as well as His people's duty to fear and serve Him, 16-22.

CHAPTERS 11—12. THE BLESSING OF OBEDIENCE; THE CURSE OF DISOBEDIENCE

Israel's Supreme Duty, 11:1-21, was to love the Lord and to show that love by keeping the commandments.

The Blessing and the Curse, 22-32. The key word "obedience" in Deuteronomy is further elucidated. The blessings were to be put upon Mt. Gerizim and the curses upon Mt. Ebal, 29 (cf. Deut 27:12-13; Josh 8:33).

Conditions of Blessing in the Promised Land, 12:1-32. False worship had to be overthrown, 1-4; true worship of the Lord had to be maintained in a central sanctuary which the Lord would choose, 5-14. Further warning against idolatrous abominations was given, 15-32.

CHAPTER 13. FALSE PROPHETS AND THEIR DOOM

Punishment of the False Prophet, 1-5. The penalty was death, because these charlatans would lead people into idolatrous apostasy. Their signs and wonders were wrought by evil supernaturalism to delude and distort the truth.

Punishment of Blood Relatives Who Tempt to Idolatry, 6-11. So terrible is the snare of idolatry that nearest of kin found guilty were not to be spared. One is ever to exercise discernment when religious teachers claim special miraculous powers.

Punishment of an Apostate City, 12-18. If it defected to idolatry, the city should be wholly destroyed and burned with fire.

CHAPTER 14. SEPARATION OF GOD'S PEOPLE

Basis of Separation, 1-2. They are "children of the Lord" their "God . . . a holy people . . . chosen . . . to be a peculiar people above all the nations that are upon the earth" (cf. Ex 19:5-7). To them "the adoption" still belongs (Rom 9:4). God called Israel His firstborn son among the nations (Hos 11:1), and hence they have a national election in which they will be reinstated. Relationship to God is to be the basis of separation from the sinful customs of the heathen, 1-2, notably mourning customs involving self-mutilation or cutting of hair in token of a covenant or propitiatory gift for the dead (cf. Jer 16:6; 41:5 with Lev 21:5 and 1 Thess 4:13).

Separation and Distinctions in Food, 3-21. These were principally religious, no doubt in part hygienic, and some had association with pagan rites. Boiling a kid in its mother's milk was a pagan custom, the milk later being poured out as a charm to guarantee fertility of the soil.

Separation and Pure Religion, 22-29. The negative commands are followed by the positive requirements of the tithe. The tithe gave expression to the principle of the Lord's proprietorship of the people and the land they were to possess (cf. Num 18:21-32, which deals with Levites' use of the offerings). Once in three years the householder's tithe went not to the sanctuary and its established priests, but to the country Levites (Deut 18:6-8), the poor, foreigners in Israelite employ, and orphans and widows, 28-29, showing that charity toward one's fellowmen is linked with love and loyalty to God.

CHAPTERS 15—16. SABBATIC YEAR AND PRINCIPAL FEASTS

The Sabbatic Year, 15:1-11. The seventh year brought rest to the land and release from debts and obligations. An enlarged exposition of the previously given law is here noted (cf. Ex 23:10-11; Lev 25:2-7). Obedience would bring blessing to the humanitarian regulation, which breathes grace and love.

Liberation of Hebrew Slaves, 12-18 (cf. Ex 21:1-11). God's merciful love was to permeate all phases of His people's living—care of poor, treatment of slaves, etc.

Sanctification of the Firstling of the Flock, 19-23. This is supplementary to the law of the firstborn in Ex 13:1-16; Num 18:15-19. The eating of the unblemished sacrifice at the central sanctuary prefigures the believer's feeding upon the spotless Lamb of God in the presence of God the Father.

Principal Annual Feasts, 16:1-17. These feasts were Passover, 1-8; Feast of Weeks, 9-12; and Feast of Tabernacles, 13-17 (cf. Lev 23 for the full number). Moses stressed the Passover and Tabernacles as marking the beginning and consummation of God's dealing with Israel—redemption for kingdom blessing. The Feast of Weeks coming between Passover (redemption) and Tabernacles (millennial blessing) speaks of the joy and separation of God's redeemed people, anticipating greater blessing in store. Special gifts of the males were specified to be brought at the three great festivals, 16-17.

Justice Assured, 18-22, by legal provisions.

CHAPTER 17. CIVIL GOVERNMENT IN THE LAND

Appointment of Judges, 16:18—17:13. Judges were to administer civil justice, idolaters being condemned to death by stoning before witnesses, 1-7. The priests and Levites were also appealed to in default cases, 8-13.

Anticipation of a King, 14-20. The Spirit of God in Moses foresaw the eventual rejection of the theocracy and the choice of a king in the time of Samuel. Solomon disregarded the Deuteronomic law and thus invited apostasy, 16-17 (cf. 1 Kgs 9—11).

CHAPTER 18.   PROPHECY OF THE GREAT PROPHET

The Levites and the Priests' Portion, 1-8. How the people were to minister to those who were dependent upon the Lord and closely identified with them is revealed.

Interdict Against Idolatrous Divinatory Occultism, 9-14. That demonism is the source and dynamic of pagan idolatry is here revealed (cf. 1 Cor 10:19-20; 1 Tim 4:1-2; 1 Jn 4:1-6; Rev 16:13-16).

The Great Prophet to Come, 15-22. This is a wonderful prediction of our Lord as *the Prophet* (cf. Jn 1:21-45; 7:16; 8:28; 12:49-50; Acts 3:22-23; 7:37), to be immeasurably filled with the Spirit of truth as the True Prophet in contrast to the false prophets under demon inspiration (1 Jn 4:1-2). The test of false and true prophets is given, 20-22.

CHAPTERS 19—20.   LAWS FOR THE NATION IN PALESTINE

The Cities of Refuge, 19:1-13. See comments Num 35:1-34; Deut 4:41-49. Mercy was prescribed for the accidental manslayer but none for the willful killer.

Other Laws, 14-21. Removing a landmark and punishment of perjury are specified.

Future Wars of the Nation, 20:1-20. Since Israelites were the Lord's people they were to be fearless, 1-4. The fearful and fainthearted are unfit for the battle, 5-9. The law of sieges is given 10-20. Persistency and a prevailing faith are essential to take fortresses of darkness.

CHAPTER 21.   VARIOUS LAWS AND INSTRUCTIONS

The Expiation of an Unknown Murder, 1-9. Bloodguiltiness of this sort had to be atoned for by killing a heifer in a deserted valley, and by the elders and Levites washing their hands over the dead animal. An illustration of Israel's bloodguiltiness in putting the Messiah to death at His first advent seems suggested here together with the nation's expiation on the basis of Christ's death (the slain heifer), effected at the second advent when they accept Him.

Family Regulations, 10-21. These include a woman taken in war to be a wife, 10-14, and the right of the firstborn when he was the son of an unfavored wife, 15-17, polygamy being taken for granted. The case of a rebellious and intractable son and his punishment is given, 18-21.

The Burial of a Criminal, 22-23. That this case foreshadows the ignominious death on the cross suffered by our Lord in His being accounted a criminal is shown by the quotation of verse 23 in Gal 3:13 (cf. Jn 19:31). For Joshua's observance of this law in the burial of the king of Ai, see Josh 8:29.

CHAPTER 22. EXPOSITION OF LAWS FROM THE SECOND TABLE

Duty of Neighborliness and Humanity, 1-8. Love for one's neighbor is shown by guarding and preserving his property, 1-4. The law forbidding one sex to wear the clothes of the other sex was not directed principally at licentiousness or idolatrous practice, but to preserve the sanctity of the divine distinction of the sexes established at creation. Ignoring the distinctive place of male and female as intended by God is an abomination, i.e., an act characterized by shameful flaunting of God's established order.

Further laws of humanity and mercy govern a bird's nest, 6-7 (cf. Lev 22:28), and proper safety precautions to be taken on one's premises, 8.

Laws Emphasizing Separation, 9-12. Common distinctions in everyday life are presented to impress the need for separation from evil and devotion to the Lord (2 Cor 6:11—7:1).

Laws Against Adultery, Incest and Fornication, 13-30. These were given to protect the home and family.

CHAPTER 23. THE HOLINESS OF THE CONGREGATION OF THE LORD

Constitution of the Congregation of the Lord, 1-8. The congregation (*qahal*), "assembly of the Lord" (*Yhwh*), like the NT church (*ecclesia*), was to be separated from everyone and everything unclean or defiling (2 Cor 6:11—7:1), because it was the Lord's assembly. Only those truly regenerated and hence *positionally* clean (cf. Jn 13:10 with Jn 13:3-15) actually belong to it, and only those *experientially* clean by continued cleansing by the Word (Eph 5:26) enjoy the fellowship and privileges of it. The assembly of Israel in the wilderness portrays this truth by excluding the profane, the maimed or those of blemished birth, 1-2 (cf. Zech 9:6), the Ammonite and the Moabite, 3-6, prefiguring those who are at enmity

147

to the full truth of God and oppose God's spiritual children. The Edomite (the natural man) and the Egyptian (the man of the world) could enter the congregation only in the third generation (cf. Col 3:1-4).

Cleanness of the Camp in War, 9-14. Especially necessary was separation from sin and defilement in time of war, illustrating the truth that spiritual conquest and victory (Eph 6:10-18) are possible only in separation from complicity with Satan and his hosts, 14 (cf. Heb 12:1-4; 1 Cor 6:19-20).

The Law of the Escaped Slave and Harlot, 15-18. How gracious that the poor escaped slave found a refuge in the assembly of the Lord, 15, and was not to be oppressed, 16. The harlot (Heb. *qedeshah,* "female religious prostitute") and the sodomite (*qadesh,* "male religious prostitute") had a polluted role in Canaanite degraded worship. Such a one separated to sexual sin, as in the fertility cults of the heathen, and thinking to honor their god with such license, as the Canaanites did, was an abomination to the Lord. Sexual perversions under the garb of religion are abominable in the extreme, the "sodomite," 18, being termed a "dog" (Heb. *kelev*), because the practice of his vice reminds one of the sexual intercourse of animals.

Other Regulations of the Congregation of the Lord, 19-25. Usury or taking of interest was not to be practiced between brothers in the Lord's congregation, only among foreigners, 19-20. Vows, 21-23, were to be kept by God's people (cf. Lev 27:1-25; Num 30:1-16; Mt 5:33-37). The law of eating grapes and plucking corn, 24-25, demonstrated the Lord's essential ownership of the land, and He invited the hungry, as it were, to be His guests (cf. Mt 12:1; Lk 6:1). But the Lord also graciously protected the rights of the tenant.

CHAPTER 24. DIVORCE AND OTHER LAWS OF MERCY

Mosaic Concession on Divorce, 1-4. This was *not a commandment,* as the Pharisees who encountered Jesus erroneously concluded (Mt 19:7-8), but merely a concession. That is, it was something which Moses allowed because of the hardness of the Israelites' hearts. (Cf. with Mt 5:31-32; 19:3-12; Mk 10:1-12; Lk 16:18; 1 Cor 7:10-15.)

Other Regulations, 5-22. A newly wed man was free from war or business for one year to make his wife glad or happy, 5. Nothing necessary to a man's very existence, such as a millstone for grinding his daily food, was to be taken as security for a debt, 6. Manstealing, 7 (cf. Ex 21:16), was punishable by death. Laws concerning leprosy, 8-9, were to be diligently observed, as well as those concerning the taking of a pledged garment, 10-13; concerning servants, 14-15; punishment of sins, 16; justice, 17; and gleanings to be left for the poor, 18-22.

CHAPTER 25. VARIOUS LAWS CONTINUED

Corporal Punishment, 1-3. Such discipline was to be administered, but a merciful provision limiting it to 40 lashes was given. Rabbinical instructions put the maximum at 39, and Paul was punished five times in this manner (2 Cor 11:24). Paganism was cursed with cruelty. This Israelite law was merciful.

The Ox, 4. As the ox, reminding one of a slave, was to be allowed to eat when treading out the grain (cf. 1 Cor 9:9; 1 Tim 5:18), so the toiling servant of the Lord is worthy of his remuneration.

The Brother-in-Law's Marriage, 5-10. This custom was pre-Mosaic (Gen 38:8-11) and finds its outworking in the kinsman-redeemer theme in the book of Ruth. Taking off the shoe, 9 (cf. Ruth 4:7), arose from the custom of walking on the soil as a symbol of declaring one's right of acquired possession. Verses 8-9 show the law of levirate marriage was not obligatory.

Other Laws, 11-16. Prescriptions against foul play, 11-12, and dishonest weights are mentioned, 13-16.

Doom Upon Amalek, 17-19. See comments on Ex 17:8-16. Amalek, the opposer of the people of God, was to perish forever (Num 24:20). When Israel possessed the land and their enemies were defeated, then the memory of Amalek was to be blotted out. Conflict against the flesh is a holy war in the spiritual realm.

CHAPTER 26. OFFERING OF FIRSTFRUITS AND PRAYER

The Basket of Firstfruits, 1-11. Possession of the land is anticipated. This beautiful ceremony anticipated presentation of its firstfruits to the Lord at the central sanctuary (cf. Ex 23:16-19), a token of praise, worship and thanksgiving to the Lord for His faithfulness and blessing. The lovely confession, "A wandering Aramaean was my father," 5 (RSV), is a reference to Jacob's seminomadic life in contrast to Israel's anticipated settlement in the land.

Obedience and Prayer, 12-19, result in blessing.

CHAPTER 27. LAWS ON STONE: BLESSINGS AND CURSES

Dramatization of Israel's Covenant Responsibilities, 1-26. This ceremony was to be inaugurated on Mt. Ebal and Mt. Gerizim overlooking the city of Shechem, in the heart of the land. On Mt. Ebal the memorial stones were to be set up and the curses of the law pronounced. On Gerizim there were no stones engraved with the law, nor curses pronounced, but only blessings. Gerizim speaks of the grace of God. Ebal of the curse of the law (Gal 3:10). But upon Ebal, in addition to the stones plastered with the law engraved upon them, was also an altar to the Lord for burnt offerings and peace offerings for rejoicing before the Lord, 5-7. This looked forward to Christ's redeeming us from the curse of the law.

CHAPTER 28. BLESSINGS AND CURSES PROPHESIED

The Blessing Promised, 1-14. These benefits were for obedience to the Lord in the Promised Land.

The Prophesied Curses, 15-68. Prewritten history of Israel's tragic career of unbelief and sin is here outlined. The Spirit of prophecy through Moses foresaw the sufferings, tribulations and worldwide dispersion of God's ancient elect nation. Reflected in these panoramic prophecies were the siege by the Babylonians and later the siege by the Romans, 49-50. The horror of the siege of Jerusalem by the Romans was foreseen, 54-57, and Israel's present worldwide diaspora, 64-68.

CHAPTER 29. THE PALESTINIAN COVENANT AND THE CURSE

The Covenant Introduced, 1-15. This was a covenant (Palestinian) governing Israel's tenure of the Promised Land distinct from the Mosaic covenant given at Horeb, 1. Redemption was the basis of the covenant, 1-3, but the people were characterized by spiritual insensitivity, 4 (cf. Isa 6:9-10; Mt 13:14-15; Jn 12:40; Acts 7:51-52; 28:26-27), despite the Lord's wonderful care of them, 5-8. He therefore had a claim on their loyalty and love, 9-15.

The Curse Reiterated, 16-29. Warning against apostasy was again given, 16-21. All the nations would know these grievous punishments were because Israel forsook her covenant, 22-29.

CHAPTER 30. THE PALESTINIAN COVENANT DEFINED

The Terms of the Covenant, 1-10. Deut 28 and 29 introduce the Palestinian covenant (see 29:1), and are an integral part of it. This covenant, similar yet distinct from the Mosaic covenant, and governing the nation's life in Palestine, is here defined in seven prophetic declarations: (1) *Dispersion of Israel for disobedience and apostasy,* 1 (described in Deut 28:63-68). (2) *Israel's future conversion while in the dispersion,* 2. (3) *The second advent of Christ,* 3 (cf. Amos 9:9-14; Acts 15:14-17). (4) *Restoration of the land,* 5 (cf. Isa 11:11-12; 35:1-2; Jer 23:3-8; Ezek 37:21-25). (5) *Israel's future national conversion,* 6 (cf. Rom 11:26-27; Hos 2:14-16). (6) *The judgment of the nations,* Israel's oppressors, 7 (cf. Isa 14:1-2; Joel 3:1-8; Mt 25:31-46). (7) *National prosperity of the millennial nation,* 9 (cf. Amos 9:11-14). The unconditional Abrahamic covenant (Gen 15:1-18) guarantees the land on the basis of divine sovereign grace. This covenant is not to be confused with either the Mosaic or Palestinian covenants.

Final Ominous Warning Against Violation of the Covenant, 11-20. "Love . . . obey . . . cleave unto him: for he is thy life . . . that thou mayest dwell in the land which the Lord sware unto thy fathers, to Abraham, to Isaac, and to Jacob, to give them," 20.

CHAPTER 31. MOSES' FINAL CHARGE AND A SOLEMN PROPHECY

Moses' Final Charge, 1-8. He gave encouragement and tender loving exhortation to "all Israel," 1-6, and specifically to the new leader, Joshua, 7-8.

The Law Written and Delivered to the Priests for Safekeeping, 9-13. Instructions were set down for its reading every seventh year at the Feast of Tabernacles.

The Lord's Prophetic Disclosure, 14-23. Israel would apostatize, 15-21. Therefore Joshua was solemnly ordained to leadership, 14, and Moses was given a prophetic song, 19-23, as a warning and witness against the sinning people.

Moses Instructs the Levites, 24-30. The law written by Moses and delivered to the Levites was to be deposited in the ark.

CHAPTER 32. THE SONG OF MOSES

Introductory Appeal, 1-3 (cf. Isa 1:2; Mic 1:2). This magnificent prophetic ode spans the entire history of Israel—past, present and future. It is a great mountain peak of prophetic poetry like Balaam's oracles (Num 22—24; cf. with Rom 9—11).

Integrity of the Lord's Ways vs. Israel's Perversity, 4-6. The Lord is "the Rock," 4, an ancient appellation for God, 15, 18, speaking of stability and dependability. God's Word is perfect. He is a God of truth, just and right. His people, 5-6, are perverse, crooked, foolish and senseless.

The Lord's Love for Israel, 7-14. God set the bounds of the nations with Israel as the center of interest, 7-9. The divine name "Most High" is the millennial title of Deity, which He will assume when the Son receives the kingdom over Israel (cf. Gen 14:19) and this prophecy is fully realized. The Lord found Israel. He encircled, cared for, prospered and blessed her, 10-14.

Israel's Apostasy, 15-18. Like a well-fed animal, Israel rebelled against her master. "Jeshurun" ("the upright one") is an appellative applied ironically to Israel (33:5, 26). Israel took five steps downward: forsook God, 15; scoffed at the Rock of her salvation, Messiah; served strange gods, 16; sacrificed to demons, 17; was unmindful of the Rock, 18. The term "demons" refers to the gods of Canaan, since demonism is the dynamic of idolatry (1 Cor 10:19-20).

Results of Israel's Apostasy, 19-33. Again history is prewritten. The sufferings of the Babylonian captivity 587 B.C., and the world-wide woes from A.D. 70 to the second advent are reflected here.

The Lord's Final Dealing with Israel, 34-42. The sudden change, 36, when Israel is reduced to the direst extremity and the Lord arises to deliver her from complete destruction by her enemies, is a prophecy of the Great Tribulation (Jer 30:5-7; Rev 8—17). The judgment, 40-42, is that which will fall upon the nations at the second advent of the Lord.

The Final Consummation, 43. The nations will rejoice with and praise Israel, because the Lord has avenged her enemies. This envisions the full establishment of the kingdom over Israel when the nation will be the head and not the tail. Moses' song is a résumé of biblical prophecy.

The Song of Moses Taught to Israel, 44-47.

Moses' Death Announced, 48-52.

CHAPTER 33. THE BLESSING OF MOSES

The Lord's Manifestation in Glory, 1-5. This, the basis of all blessing to Israel and the earth, is a prophetic picture of the second advent.

The Tribes Blessed, 6-25. Moses' prophetic blessing envisioned

Mount Nebo and the Springs of Moses. (© *MPS*)

the benefit Israel will enjoy when the Lord will be manifested in glory. This differs from Jacob's blessing of his sons in that that prophecy embraced the panoramic history of the posterity (see Gen 49). The blessing of Moses is an inspired expansion of the concluding verse of his song (Deut 32:43, see above). The blessing of Reuben, Judah and Levi, 6-11, reveals the salvation and deliverance Israel will enjoy at the second advent. The blessing of Benjamin and Joseph, 12-17, pictures the protection and prosperity of Israel in the Kingdom Age. The blessing of Zebulun and Issachar, 18-19, tells of the joy and spiritual worship Israel will have in that day. The blessing of Gad, Dan, Naphtali and Asher, 20-25, prophesies the enlargement, victory and strength of Israel in the kingdom.

The Future Joy of Israel, 26-29. Jeshurun (see Deut 32:15-18) is happy in millennial restoration because of her incomparable, 26, eternal God. He is her dwelling place, 27; Deliverer, 28, and Saviour, 29, and He has conquered all the enemies of Israel, who now is really Jeshurun, "the upright one," restored and blessed by divine favor.

CHAPTER 34. THE DEATH OF MOSES

Moses Dies and Is Buried, 1-7. Mt. Pisgah (Num 21:20; Deut 3:27) is a headland of the rocky Abarim range in Moab (modern Jordan) jutting toward the NE end of the Dead Sea opposite Jericho. Pisgah is closely associated with its neighboring elevation Mt. Nebo, slightly NW of the latter. From Pisgah and Nebo Moses saw the Promised Land. In the valley near Beth-peor he was buried by the Lord Himself, 6. Moses' body became the subject of dispute between Satan and Michael, the archangel and protector of the people of Israel (Jude 9; Dan 12:1), probably because of Moses' appearance in a glorified body at the Transfiguration before the first resurrection (Lk 9:31).

Israel Mourns, 8, and weeps for 30 days.

Joshua Takes Over, 9 (cf. Num 27:18-23).

Moses As a Prophet, 10-12. The greatest of Israel's prophets (Num 12:6-8; Deut 18:15-22; Hos 12:13) had a touching homegoing and was honored by being the only man the Lord buried.

JOSHUA

THE BOOK OF CONFLICT AND CONQUEST

Place and Nature of the Book. Joshua is the first book in the second part of the Hebrew canon called the Prophets, the Law (Pentateuch) constituting the first part, and the Writings the third part. This book takes its name from the great religious and military leader whose exploits it recites. The name Joshua, or Jehoshua, means "the Lord [*Yhwh*] saves or delivers." Critics commonly make it a late composite work, one in literary composition with the Pentateuch, employing the term "Hexateuch." This idea of a Hexateuch, however, is lacking any traditional or historical corroboration, and is erected on the premise of unbelief in the miraculous and the prophetic. The conservative view would date the book early, probably in the time of Joshua or soon after, so that the events are historical.

Spiritual Meaning of the Book. *Anticipation* marks the book of Deuteronomy, *realization* the book of Joshua. Redemption *out of Egypt* under Moses gave the Israelites a redeemed *position*. Redemption *into the Promised Land* under Joshua gave them a redemption *experience* of victory and conquest in possessing their possessions. The two factors, *position* and *experience*, are inseparable in salvation. Salvation is basically a position or status, but it is also an experience of the blessings involved in possessing that position. In a spiritual sense the book of Joshua is the Ephesians of the OT. "The heavenlies" of Eph 1:3; 6:12 are illustrated by the land of Canaan, which is a picture of the *experience* of victory and conquest belonging to those positionally redeemed. Those who had been redeemed out of Egypt by the Passover blood now claimed the blessing of that redemption by possessing the land.

The Book of Joshua and New Testament Truth. This handbook includes illustrations of NT truth found in Joshua because it, along with the redemptive narratives in the Pentateuch, forms a connective thread in the history of redemption. The NT references to this thread present interpretive leads which cannot be limited to historical features specifically mentioned, but must logically include illustrations of spiritual truth the reality of which is found in the NT. Christians are more than students of ancient history, they are learners of the spiritual principles of life. Therefore the illustrative nature of Joshua is given a rightful place in this study.

Outline
Entrance into Canaan and the Conflicts, Ch. 1—12
Division and Settlement of the Land, Ch. 13—22
Joshua's Final Words and Death, Ch. 23—24

CHAPTER 1. JOSHUA ASSUMES COMMAND

Joshua's Commission, 1-9. Moses' successor was commanded to lead God's people into their inheritance. He was given assurance of divine presence and success, conditioned on obedience. Joshua ("Jehovah Saviour") prefigures Christ as the Captain of our salvation (Heb 2:10-11), leading His people in the power of His Spirit. Joshua succeeded Moses, who pictures Christ as the obedient Servant (Heb 3:5).

Joshua Takes Charge, 10-18. He addressed the people, 10-15, who replied, 16-18, promising obedience. The energy of faith would be necessary to possess the land. This would lead to warfare, as active advance leads to spiritual conflict in the case of every believer (Eph 6:10-20).

CHAPTER 2. THE SPIES AND RAHAB'S FAITH

The Spies and Jericho, 1. Joshua, who himself had been a spy, acted wisely in sending out the spies to learn the strategy of the enemy.

Rahab's Faith, 2-14. The harlot is an apt illustration of the power of the gospel of grace to save a sinner. "*By faith* the harlot Rahab perished not with them that believed not, when she had received the spies with peace" (Heb 11:31). She attested her saving faith by works. "Likewise also was not Rahab the harlot justified by works, when she received the messengers, and had sent them out another way?" (Jas 2:25). She gave a well-grounded reason for her faith, 10-11, and prayed for the salvation of her loved ones in Jericho, 13. Full assurance was given her, 14.

The Scarlet Line, 15-24. Bound by Rahab to the window, this line by which she let the spies escape, becomes a beautiful symbol of salvation.

CHAPTER 3. THE JORDAN CROSSED

The Ark of the Lord Leads the Way, 1-6. The ark (Ex 25:1-22), one of the most inclusive object lessons of Christ, led on and made a way through Jordan. Beautifully pictured is our Lord going through the deep waters of death to make a way for His people to advance victoriously and possess their heavenly possessions in Him. Having accomplished redemption, He takes all His people through death into resurrection life and glory by "a new and living way" (cf. v. 4; Heb 10:20).

Joshua Begins to Be Magnified, 7-8. When the Lord's people enter into the *experience* of their position in Christ, portrayed by Israel crossing Jordan, they begin to exalt and obey the divine Joshua, the Captain of their salvation.

Joshua Directs the Crossing, 9-13. Joshua's message to the people assured them that "the living God" would prove His presence among them by driving out the Canaanites, 10. The ark of the covenant is that "of the *Lord of all the earth,*" 11, 13, an appellative which Zechariah employs of the time when Israel is established in the kingdom (Zech 4:14) after all her enemies have been judged (Zech 6:5), and Messiah by right of creation, redemption and conquest is King of kings and Lord of lords. How aptly was this used when Israel was entering her possession, held by formidable and wicked enemies. The mighty miracle of the parted waters was wrought by "the living God," that is, Deity in manifested omnipotence, not a creation of naturalistic religion.

The Jordan River descends into the Dead Sea as the snake slithers, flowing over a bed of about 200 miles in the 60-mile distance between the Sea of Galilee and the Dead Sea. (© *MPS*)

The Crossing Is Made, 14-17. It was wholly the result of a miracle, whether or not an earthquake dammed up the stream above the crossing at Adam (Adamah), a town eight miles N of Succoth overlooking the Jordan. This has been identified by Nelson Glueck with Tell Damieh. Glueck also maintains that the dozen miles between Adamah and Zarethan is the only stretch in the Jordan Valley where such a damming up and going over on dry ground could have taken place

CHAPTER 4. THE MEMORIAL STONES

The Two Memorials, 1-18. Far from being the result of conflicting traditions, as critics hold, these monuments were two separate memorials, each expressive of an aspect of Christ's death. The twelve stones taken out of Jordan and erected as a monument at Gilgal, 1-8, 20, speak of redemption for Israel *into* the land and into a sphere and experience of victory and conquest. The stones left in the swirling Jordan to be overwhelmed by its waters are mementoes of Christ's death under judgment in the believer's place (Ps 22:1-18; 42:7; 88:7; Jn 12:31-33). This was the basis of victory and conquest in the land.

What Mean These Stones, 19-24? The mighty God had provided redemption and had brought His people into their inheritance. The stones in Jordan mean: We *died* in Christ (Rom 6:1-10). The stones at Gilgal mean: Let us reckon on that death and enjoy life and conquest in the land (Rom 6:11).

CHAPTER 5. ISRAEL AT GILGAL

Israel's Terror-stricken Enemies, 1. All the surrounding kings of the Canaanites, who had so terrified the unbelieving people of God a generation previously, now were terrified as Israel took territory in the land at Gilgal. A redeemed and victorious people always disheartens the enemy.

The New Generation Circumcised, 2-8. This sign of the Abrahamic covenant (see Gen 17; Ex 4:24-26), evidently in abeyance in the wilderness until the unbelieving generation should die, now again became meaningful, and the males of the new generation were circumcised at *Gibeath-hacaraloth* ("the hill of foreskins"), 5, 7. Henceforth they bore the visible token of belonging to the Lord and the Lord, in turn, being in gracious covenant relation with them. Circumcision speaks of the execution of the sentence of death upon the flesh, Christ's death being a spiritual circumcision for His people

(Col 2:11). But the fact that believers are dead to sin by the circumcision of Christ, and thus have a death-to-sin *position*, must by appropriating faith be carried out in a death-to-sin *experience*. The sharp knife must be applied to the flesh and its lusts.

Reproach of Egypt Rolled Away, 9-10. "The reproach of Egypt," which Joshua said he rolled away at Gilgal (Gilgal means "a rolling") when he circumcised the people, was their bondage to Pharaoh in Egypt. In their uncircumcised state the people were without the sign and seal of the Abrahamic covenant and were in the same condition as they were in Egypt under no covenant relationship. Having been circumcised, they were ready to keep the Passover, the feast commemorating deliverance from Egypt, 10 (see comments on Ex 12:1-28; Lev 23:4-5).

Manna and the Old Corn of the Land, 11-12. After circumcision and the keeping of the Passover, the Israelites ate "the old grain of the land." The harvest of barley was then in progress so that the people of God could begin to enjoy the fruits of redemption. They appropriated the blessings of their privileged possession.

Joshua's Vision of the Divine Captain of the Lord's Army, 13-15. The man with the drawn sword before Jericho was the Lord, the preincarnate Christ in visible form, who appeared as a man of war to undergird Joshua and to show him that He who marshals the armies of heaven was fighting for Israel. The ground was thus made holy for Joshua as it had been for Moses when the same preincarnate Christ appeared to him (see Ex 3:1-12).

CHAPTER 6. JERICHO TAKEN

Divine Instructions Followed, 1-19. The formidable walled city of Jericho, now known from archaeology to be one of the oldest occupied sites in the world, offered a real obstacle to Israel in the conquest of the land. It is analogous spiritually to the world which the believer must conquer if a life of victory is to be his. The city was to be taken in faith and obedience to God's word, and not by human wisdom or sagacious calculation. The miracle of its tumbling walls was the miracle of faith (cf. Heb 11:30). "This is the victory that overcometh the world, even our faith" (1 Jn 5:4). Joshua did not reckon with the high walls or the human impossibilities, but counted solely on the power of God. Although a military general, he was foremost a spiritual leader. Nor was he offended by the divine direction to circle the city once each day for six days and seven times on the seventh day, with seven priests blowing seven horns, and then on the seventh day the people shouting. From a purely military view this was ridiculous, if not fantastic. But walking by faith and not by sight (2 Cor 5:7) is never sensible to worldlings.

The Fall of the City, 20-21. Remains of the massive walls and the city that fell to Joshua (*c.* 1400 B.C.) have largely eroded, since Jericho was constructed of mud brick. The excavations of Kathleen Kenyon since 1952 reveal that most of the extant mound is 16th cen. B.C. or earlier. Joshua's Jericho has thus largely been washed away. It was apparently not a large city. So crowded were the living conditions that the houses, such as Rahab's, were built on the walls.

Rahab Remembered, 22-25. The scarlet line, doubtless an object of ridicule, saved Rahab and her house, while the entire city was devoted to destruction (Heb. *herem*), 17, 24. The expression *herem* refers to that which is irrevocably given over to destruction (cf. Deut 13:16) or devoted wholly to the Lord, not being used for secular purposes.

Curse Upon Jericho, 26-27. As an illustration of the world system, the fall of Jericho may well prefigure its destruction at the end of the age (Rev. 6:1—19:16). Jericho was put under the ban, *herem*. It was never to be rebuilt, except under the penalty of a curse, 26 (cf. 1 Kgs 16:34).

CHAPTER 7. ACHAN'S SIN

Defeat of Israel and the Reason, 1-15. The unity and solidarity of God's people are here stressed. The sin of one involves all. Cf. the analogous case of Ananias and Sapphira (Acts 5:1-11). The specific sin of Achan was disobedience to the command of separation from the "accursed thing," *herem* (Josh 6:17-18), that is, from Jericho (the world), ripe for and under the sentence of judgment, 1, 11 (cf. Jas 4:4; 1 Jn 2:15-17). This sin of complicity with evil was responsible for the defeat of God's people. As soon as a believer clings to worldliness, he suffers spiritual defeat and his sin affects the whole body of believers, 11-12. Instant confession and self-judgment are necessary, 13-15. Severity is necessary in a "sin unto death" (1 Cor 5:5; 11:20-32; 1 Jn 5:16) because the time, place and nature of the sin tolerated bring slander upon the Lord and peculiarly jeopardize His people, 15 (cf. 8, 9, 12). Joshua here demonstrates his typical character as the Captain of our salvation by being an advocate when his people suffered defeat, 5-9 (cf. 1 Jn 2:1).

The Sin Judged, 16-26. It was an extremely serious offense and entailed physical death (see comment on 1-15). "I saw . . . I coveted . . . and took," 21, is the story of temptation and fall. This whole episode, like the deaths of Saul, Ananias and Sapphira, and others, was not an illustration of the loss of salvation, but a warning of the discipline which befalls a sinning saint, even to the point of physical death.

CHAPTER 8. AI TAKEN

Joshua's Strategy, 1-17. The divine assurance of victory always follows self-judgment and confession of sin, 1. Divine directions can then clearly be given, understood and obeyed, 2. The ruse of the ambush was by divine direction, not Joshua's brilliance, 3-8. Implicitly obeyed, it brought the desired result, 9-18. The believer's strategy is always to be secured from the Lord and based upon the strength of his position in Him (Eph 6:10-12).

The Capture of Ai, 18-27. The Lord's command to Joshua to stretch out his spear toward the city continuously until he completely destroyed all the residents, 18, 26, betokened the presence of the Lord to effect complete victory. Joshua's faith is thus emphasized. Cf. the uplifted hands of Moses (Ex 17:11-13) in the victory over Amalek. Spiritual victory is always by faith in the Word and the Spirit of God.

The Destruction of the City, 28-29. "Joshua burnt Ai, and made it a heap," 28. Ai means "the ruin" and has been identified with et-Tell, excavated in 1933-35. It shows no traces of occupation between 2200 and 1200 B.C., but there is no indubitable proof that et-Tell is really Ai. L. H. Vincent's suggestion that Ai was merely an outpost of Bethel, and so small (cf. Josh 7:3) that it has left no traceable remains, is doubtless the case.

The Altar at Ebal, 30-35, was erected in the scenic Shechem area in the heart of the land as a commemoration of victories at Jericho and Ai, and as an act of obedience to the command of Moses (Deut 27:2-8). The law copied on stones may have been the Ten Commandments and other laws, or the blessings and cursings of Deuteronomy, or the summary of the laws of the Pentateuch. The custom of inscribing law codes on stone had hoary antiquity behind it, for such a practice prevailed in Sumerian and Babylonian times (cf. the Code of Hammurabi, c. 1700 B.C., with prologue, 282 sections, and epilogue).

CHAPTER 9. THE DECEPTION OF THE GIBEONITES

The Confederacy of the Enemy, 1-2. The kings of the hill country, the central highland ridge including Jerusalem and Hebron, of the

Shephelah or the low hills receding to the plain, and of "the shores of the Great Sea" (Mediterranean) or Maritime Plain, united to fight Israel.

The Ruse of the Gibeonites, 3-15. However, a group of Hivites, 7, a little-known ethnic group of Palestine, perhaps a subsection of the Horites or Hurrians which were a well-known people of the ancient Middle East, determined on a course of diplomacy rather than war. Their capital city was Gibeon (ej-Jib), located five miles NW of Jerusalem on the road to Joppa. They pretended to be friends. Their lie, that their wineskins had become old and worn on the long journey, their bread moldy, and their sandals worn, completely deceived the Israelites, who made a treaty with the enemy. The reason was the Israelites "partook of their provisions, and did not ask direction from the Lord," 14 (RSV), allowing them to live under peaceful treaty, 15.

The Mistake Discovered, 16-27. The Gibeonites were found to be neighbors and enemies, among those who should have been eradicated, 16-17. The result was Israel's disobedience to the Lord and enemies numbered among them. Though the Gibeonites were given menial tasks, being made woodcutters and water carriers, the fact that they were enemies remained. They are analogous to the spiritual forces that beguile us—"the wiles" or strategems of Satan, who often comes as "an angel of light" to deceive us (2 Cor 11:14), rather than attack us openly.

CHAPTER 10. SOUTHERN CANAAN TAKEN

Adoni-zedek and His Alliance, 1-6. The name of this enemy king, meaning "my lord is righteousness," occurs in connection with the first mention of Jerusalem in the Bible. He was the head of an evil coalition which was formed against Gibeon and Israel.

The War and the Miracle, 7-15. From Gilgal, Israel's first encampment, the place of self-judgment and the memorials of God's power, Israel issued forth to victory against the southern confederacy. This, the most remarkable battle in the history of Israel, is a foreshadowing of the coming day of the Lord (Hab 3:11). Following the victory, a poetic quotation from the ancient collection called the book of Jasher is preserved, 13 (cf. 2 Sam 1:18). The tremendous miracle, 12-14, the Lord performed to aid Joshua in the victory over the southern confederacy may have been the result of refraction of sunlight, producing intense cold and hailstones in a normally hot climate. Whatever the explanation, Joshua's long day involved the setting aside of the normal laws of nature's operation. The utter uniqueness of the miracle is stressed, 14, and hence may be considered scientifically inexplicable.

A Great Victory and Subsequent Conquests, 16-43. The five kings were executed, 22-27, and further conquests brought about the subjugation of all southern Palestine. Israel then returned to Gilgal (see Josh 5).

Excavations at Hazor, whose King Jabin led the northern confederation of Canaanites against Joshua. (*Courtesy IIS*)

CHAPTERS 11—12. FURTHER CONQUESTS OF CANAAN

Conquest of Northern Canaan, 11:1-15. Jabin, king of Hazor, formed a northern confederacy. Hazor (Tell el Wakkas, Qedah) was a site strategically located SW of Lake Huleh, near the headwaters of the Jordan. Joshua was divinely directed to hamstring the horses and burn the chariots, 6, 9, so that he might trust in the Lord and not in these means of warfare. Hazor was burned, but the smaller cities "that stood on mounds" (RSV, "tells") Joshua did not destroy, 13. These could be useful to the Israelites later.

Resume of the Conquest, 11:16—12:24. A general statement of the conquest is given in 11:16-23. Conquests in Transjordan are reviewed, 12:1-6, and conquests in Canaan, with a roster of the kings conquered, presented in 12:7-24.

163

CHAPTER 13. JOSHUA INSTRUCTED TO APPORTION THE LAND

The Lord's Message to Joshua, 1-7. "There remaineth yet very much land to be possessed," 1, is the sad story of Israel, and of many believers who fail to claim their full spiritual possessions. The unpossessed land is outlined, 2-7. In the foreground of undispossessed enemies were the Philistines, non-Canaanites, representing those who hinder God's people from possessing the land and thus enjoying their full inheritance.

The Inheritance of Reuben, Gad and Half Tribe of Manasseh, 8-33, is restated and confirmed.

CHAPTER 14. CALEB'S REQUEST AND INHERITANCE

Summary of the Apportionment of the Land, 1-5. Eleazar, Joshua and the tribal chieftains distributed the inheritance by lot (Num 26:55; 33:54; 34:13).

Caleb's Request, 6-15. Judah's portion was first, and Caleb stepped forward at Gilgal to present his testimony of the Lord's faithfulness, 6-12, and to receive Hebron, 13-15. (Cf. Num 13:6; 14:24, 30.)

CHAPTERS 15—16. JUDAH'S AND EPHRAIM'S PORTIONS

The Portion of Judah, 15:1-63. Judah's inheritance was specified as to the southern border, 1-4; eastern and northern borders, 5-11, and the western border, 12. In his conquest, 13-19, Caleb inherited Hebron ("communion"), but had to face giants, as everyone who wholly follows the Lord and claims his rightful possession does (cf. 14:6-12). Hebron was also called Kirjath-sepher ("city of [a] book").

The Portion of Ephraim, 16:1-10. Joseph's progeny was given a wonderful part of the land, 1-4. Ephraim ("doubly fruitful") received its territory, 5-9, but failed to possess it wholly, not expelling the Canaanites from Gezer, 10, a very ancient city on the Shephelah above the Maritime Plain, 18 miles NW of Jerusalem and 17 miles SE of Joppa. Joshua smote the king of Gezer (12:12), yet the Canaanites somehow regained control of their city with its 14-foot-thick walls. The city remained under Canaanite control until Solomon's time (1 Kgs 9:16).

CHAPTER 17. MANASSEH'S PORTION

The Names and Boundaries, 1-13. The descendants of Joseph's firstborn were given portions both in Transjordan and in Palestine, 1-6, and their boundaries specified, 7-13.

Manasseh's Complaint and Joshua's Reply, 14-18. This complaint showed selfish dissatisfaction. Joshua's courageous answer, 15, demonstrated faith and prudence and showed his faith in the promise of God (cf. Josh 1:3). Manasseh's plea of weakness, 16, revealed unbelief in looking at the iron chariots of the Canaanites in the valley of Esdraelon instead of the power of the Lord. These complainers offered a striking contrast to Caleb's faithful intrepidity, yet Joshua encouraged them, 17-18.

CHAPTERS 18—19. THE PORTION OF THE OTHER TRIBES

Tabernacle Erected at Shiloh, 18:1. Shiloh became the focal point (Deut 12) of the 12 tribes till the destruction of the city by the Philistines (1 Sam 4:11; c. 1050 B.C.) and the capture of the ark.

Failure of Seven Tribes to Claim Their Possession, 2-10. Evidently lacking faith and courage, seven tribes were urged on by Joshua to explore the land and claim their possessions by lot at Shiloh.

Portion of Benjamin, 11-28. This was a small but influential tribe located in mountainous terrain.

Portion of the Remaining Tribes, 19:1-51. The portions of Simeon, 1-9; of Zebulun, 10-16; of Issachar, 17-23; of Asher, 24-31; of Naphtali, 32-39; of Dan, 40-48; and of Joshua, 49-51, are described.

CHAPTER 20. THE CITIES OF REFUGE

Repetition of the Provision, 1-6. This provision was according to the law of Deut 19:1-13 (see also Num 35:1-34). "The avenger of blood" (or go'el), 3, 5, was the deceased man's nearest relative, upon whom the responsibility fell of avenging his death (cf. Ruth 3:9; in Prov 23:11 meaning "redeemer"). The gate of the city, 4, was the place where the council of elders convened and where town business was normally transacted. It was not merely an entrance in the city wall, but an enclosed building built into the wall with several chambers and several stories. Unintentional homicide cases were protected by the institution of the cities of asylum.

The Cities Specified, 7-9. The Pentateuch enumerates only the three cities outside the land. Here the three cities in the land are also specified as Kedesh ("sanctuary"), Shechem ("shoulder"), Hebron ("communion"), together with Bezer ("defense") Ramoth ("heights") and Golan ("their rejoicing") located outside the land. This may well illustrate our Lord's role as the sinner's place of refuge.

CHAPTER 21. THE LEVITES' PORTION

The Portion of the Levites, 1-42. Because of its religious functions, the tribe of Levi did not receive a territorial assignment like the other tribes. Although true in a sense of all the tribes, the Lord was the particular inheritance of the tribe of Levi (cf. Num 18:30; Deut 10:9; Josh 13:14, 33; 14:3-4). The Kohathites, 9-26; the Gershonites, 27-33; and the Merarites, 34-40, were distributed throughout the entire Israelite territory to exert an influence for pure worship against idolatry.

The Lord's Fidelity, 43-45, was renewed. He gave them "all the land," 43; "rest" and victory, 44. Nothing He promised did He fail to keep (Num 23:19; 1 Kgs 8:56).

CHAPTER 22. RETURN OF THE TRANSJORDAN TRIBES

Joshua Sends the Tribes Home, 1-9. Joshua commended the Reubenites, Gadites and the half tribe of Manasseh for their faithful participation in the conquest of Palestine, 1-4, and with kindly exhortation, 5-6, sent them to their own lands E of the Jordan (1:12-18). So they departed with wealth and spoil, 7-9.

The Great Altar and the Controversy, 10-29. The departing tribes built an altar in the Jordan region on the frontier of Canaan, that is, on the west side of the river, since Canaan is strictly speaking the territory W of Jordan, 10-11. The people gathered at Shiloh to make war against them, 12, assuming a blatant violation of the law of the central sanctuary (Deut 12:13-14). The altar was interpreted as an act of rebellion against Israel and the Lord. A delegation headed by Phinehas was sent to examine the matter, 13-20, expostulating with them and warning of the result of Israel's sin at Peor, 17-18 (Num 25:3-5), and the case of Achan, 20 (Josh 7:1). The explanation given was that the monument was not a real altar, but merely a memorial, a "witness," 21-29.

The Controversy Settled, 30-32. It was a testimony that the 12 tribes, though separated by Jordan, were *one* people.

CHAPTER 23. JOSHUA'S FAREWELL ADMONITIONS

Exhortations of Fidelity to the Lord, 1-13. Israel's great spiritual leader and military general, advanced in age, 1, assembled all Israel, 2, to review the goodness and faithfulness of the Lord, 3-5, and to exhort obedience to the Mosaic law, 6-11. Failure to keep clear of idolatrous unions would spell ruin, 12-13.

Concluding Appeal, 14-16. Warnings were sounded against the woes which would follow the blessings in case of disobedience and apostasy.

CHAPTER 24. COVENANT AT SHECHEM; JOSHUA'S DEATH

Historical Retrospect and Joshua's Eloquent Challenge, 1-15. All Israel at Shechem heard the review of the Lord's dealings from Abraham to the conquest, 1-13, as a basis for the challenge to serve the Lord only, 14-15. Joshua in turn indicated his own irrevocable choice.

Covenant Accepted, 16-28. Israel accepted Joshua's challenge, 16-18, and asserted her loyalty to the Lord and the covenant. The generation which conquered the land now subscribed to the covenant at Shechem, between Ebal and Gerizim in the heart of Canaan, as Joshua outlined the conditions of serving the Lord, 19-23, and set up memorials, 25-28.

Joshua's Death, 29-33. The great leader died and was buried, 29-31. Joseph's bones brought up from Egypt were buried in Shechem (cf. Gen 50:25; Ex 13:19; Heb 11:22). Record of the death of Eleazar, the priest, is also given, 33.

CANAAN
IN THE
TIME OF THE JUDGES

0   10   20   30
SCALE OF MILES

THE GREAT SEA

SIDON
TYRE
ACCHO
MT. CARMEL
BETHLEHEM
ZEBULUN
ASHER
NAPHTALI
DAN
DAMASCUS
+ MT. HERMON
DAN
KADESH
HAZOR
BASHAN
RAMAH
SEA OF
CHINNERETH
MT. TABOR
ISSACHAR
SHUNEM
JEZREEL
MEGIDDO
MANASSEH
RAMOTH-GILEAD
MANASSEH
MT. GERIZIM + + MT. EBAL
SHECHEM
RIVER JABBOK
RIVER KANAH
JOPPA
EPHRAIM
SHILOH
BETHEL
AI
BENJAMIN
JERUSALEM
JERICHO
GAD
AMMON
EKRON
ASHKELON
PHILISTINES
GAZA
GATH
LACHISH
HEBRON
EN-GEDI
BETHLEHEM
+ MT. NEBO
REUBEN
SALT SEA
CHERETHITES
JUDAH
SIMEON
CALEB
BEER-SHEBA
KENITES
RIVER ARNON
MOAB
JERAHMEEL
BROOK ZERED
WILDERNESS OF ZIN
SEIR
WILDERNESS OF PARAN
EDOM
RIVER JORDAN

JUDGES

THE MONOTONY AND MISERY OF SIN

The Name of the Book. Judges takes its name from the 12 Spirit-anointed military leaders the Lord raised up to deliver the nation. As a loose confederacy around the central shrine at Shiloh, the young nation had no stable central government, and forsaking the Lord, it became an easy prey for enemy invasion. The judges first delivered the people, then ruled over them. In their ruling role they corresponded to the *shufetim* of Phoenicia and the *sufetes* of Carthage (Heb. *shofetim*).

The Nature of the Book. Judges is a record of the dark ages of the declension and apostasy of Israel in the land. The people forsook the Lord (2:13); the Lord forsook the people (2:23). The key verse is: "In those days there was no king in Israel, but every man did that which was right in his own eyes," 17:6. The record of Israel's failure in the land covers about 350 years—from Joshua to Saul. Seven apostasies, seven servitudes and seven deliverances may be traced. The book of Judges begins in compromise and ends in anarchy and confusion.

Date. Internal evidence and tradition suggest an origin for the book of Judges during the early years of the monarchy. The era of Saul (c. 1025) is a possible time. Samuel, as a member of the prophetic school, may well have been the author-compiler.

The Book of Judges vs. the Book of Joshua

Joshua	Judges
Victory	Defeat
Freedom	Servitude
Faith	Unbelief
Progress	Declension
Spiritual vision	Earthly emphasis
Fidelity to the Lord	Apostasy from the Lord
Joy	Sorrow
Strength	Weakness
Sense of unity	Declension, anarchy
Sin judged	Sin lightly regarded

CHAPTER 1. ISRAEL'S FAILURE TO DRIVE OUT THE CANAANITES

The Question Confronting the Tribes, 1-4. The Israelites "asked" or "inquired of the Lord" by consulting the sacred lots, 1: "Who shall go up first for us against the Canaanites?" (RSV). The Lord directed Judah, 2, who apparently did not fully trust the Lord but relied on Simeon for help, 3-4.

Incomplete Victory of Judah, 5-20. Judah enjoyed some conquests, including Adonibezek at Bezek (uncertain), 5-7, and Jerusalem, which was either not actually captured, 8, or later recaptured by its inhabitants (cf. 1:21), for it was not taken until the time of David (2 Sam 5:6-7). Other victories included the Negeb and the Shephelah, 9; Hebron, 10; Debir, identified as Tell Beit Mirsim, SW of Hebron. Caleb, 20 (cf. Josh 14:13-15), was given Hebron, the most important town of southern Palestine.

Incomplete Victory of Benjamin, 21. The Jebusites were not dislodged from the fortress of Jerusalem (cf. 1:8 with 2 Sam 5:6-7).

Failures of the Other Tribes, 22-36. The house of Joseph, 22-26, took Bethel (Luz), 12 miles N of Jerusalem on the Shechem road (cf. Gen 12:8; 28:11-17). Manasseh failed to drive out the Canaanites of the valley of Esdraelon; they had iron chariots. Israel's disobedience is plainly stated, 28; Ephraim's failure at Gezer, 29; the failure of Zebulun, 30; Asher, 31-32; Naphtali, 33; Dan, 34. Joseph, 35-36, did gain control, but did not drive out the Amorites. The Ugaritic religious literature from Ras Shamra (Ugarit, 1929-37) reveals the moral depravity and degrading character of Canaanite religion. Failure to exterminate this morally debauched people was Israel's grand act of disobedience and the reason for her apostasies and defeats in the era of the judges (1400-1040 B.C.).

CHAPTERS 2:1—3:4. RESULTS OF ISRAEL'S FAILURE

The Angel of Bochim, 1-5. This was the Lord Himself who redeemed the Israelites from Egypt and brought them into the land, 1. He enjoined complete separation from the Canaanites, 2, but the nation disobeyed. Consequently Israel was told the Lord would not drive out her foes but they would be a thorn in her side and their religion a corrupting snare. Israel wept, 4, but did not repent, calling the place Bochim, i.e., "weepers," 5, and so forfeited national prosperity and blessing.

Israel's Earlier Obedience Contrasted to Present Apostasy, 6-15. The nation had been obedient to the Lord under Joshua and the elders who outlived him, 6-9. Now the apostasy of the new generation aroused the Lord's anger, 10-15. Baal and Ashtaroth were images of the male and female gods of the Canaanites, 11, 13, well known for their immoral license as seen in Ugaritic epics from Ras Shamra.

Resume of Israelite History under the Judges, 16-19. The Lord raised up "judges," i.e., military heroes, who by vitrue of their successes were entrusted with government administration during their lifetime, 16. But as soon as the Spirit-anointed (charismatic) leader died, the people apostatized and again sank into political servitude to an invader, 17-19.

Nations Left to Prove Israel, 2:20—3:4. The nations left had a twofold divine purpose: (1) to punish Israel for disobedience, 2:20-21; (2) to test and prove the faithful and instruct them in warfare, 2:22—3:4.

CHAPTER 3:5-31. JUDGESHIPS OF OTHNIEL, EHUD AND SHAMGAR

First Apostasy, Servitude and Judge (Othniel), 5-11. The story of declension is told, 5-7: compromise, intermarriage with idolaters, finally idolatry itself, serving the gods and goddesses of the Canaanites—Baal and Asherah—worshiping the various images of these deities. Punishment was meted out in Israel's being sold to Cushan-rishathaim, a kinglet of Mesopotamia, for eight years. Othniel (1:13; Josh 15:18) of Judah was raised up to deliver the Lord's people.

Second Apostasy, Servitude and Judge (Ehud), 12-30. Eglon, king of Moab, the country E of the Dead Sea, was the oppressor, 12-14. He captured "the city of palm trees," i.e., Jericho. A Benjaminite hero named Ehud slew Eglon by a ruse. The sculptured stones near the Gilgal quarries, 19, are connected in the RSV with those put there by the Israelites (Josh 4:20). Ehud's deliverance from Moab was followed by an 80-year period of peace, 30.

Shamgar, 31, slew 600 Philistines with an ox goad.

CHAPTERS 4—5. DEBORAH AND HER EXPLOITS

Third Apostasy, Servitude and Judge (Deborah), 4:1-3. The apostasy, 1, was followed by oppression under Jabin, king of Hazor, one of the most important Canaanite cities of Galilee, whose excavations have confirmed its capture in this era, 2-3. "Chariots of iron" put the Canaanites ahead of the Hebrews, who as yet did not have chariots nor were familiar with the art of iron smelting (Josh 17:16; 1 Sam 13:19-22). Jabin was the case of an old enemy revived (cf. Josh 11:1).

Deborah and Barak and Their Victory, 4-24. Deborah summoned Barak to muster an army at Mt. Tabor, 14, in Galilee N of the Plain of Esdraelon. The scene of Barak's victory was the river Kishon, a small stream flowing westward through Esdraelon N of Carmel. Zebulun and Naphtali were tribes of Galilee. Jael, 18, was another prominent woman, who slew Sisera, Jabin's commander-in-chief, 18-24. This episode shows the rough morality of the period.

The Song of Deborah, 5:1-31. This is a spirited martial poetic version of ch. 4. Graphically it ascribes praise to the Lord, 1-5; describes the condition of the people and their deliverance, 6-11; celebrates the victory and the victors, 12-22; and hails the destruction of the enemy, 23-31.

CHAPTER 6. GIDEON AND THE MIDIANITE OPPRESSION

Fourth Apostasy, Servitude and Judge (Gideon), 1-24. The Midianites, the Amalekites and the people of the East, 3, were Bedouin raiders. These desert people overran the territory of Israel for seven years. Their use of camels enabled them to take waterless journeys of several days, which earlier nomads using asses were unable to do. Israel's distress, 1-5, and repentance, 6, brought a gracious answer from the Lord through "a prophet," 7-10. Later the Angel of the Lord (Deity) appeared to Gideon, a hero of Manasseh, a member of the small clan of Abiezer, 11, 15. Gideon was called to be a deliverer as he was beating out the wheat in the wine press, instead of the usual place on the hilltop, to hide from the marauding invaders, 11-24.

Gideon's Initial Exploits, 25-40. The Lord directed Gideon to destroy the altar of Baal, the chief Canaanite deity, and the "grove," i.e., Asherah, a representation of one of the chief goddesses of Canaan, 25. An altar of the Lord was to be erected in its place, 25-26. Gideon obeyed, 27-32. The invaders pitched camp in the valley of Jezreel, 33, i.e., the eastern part of the great Plain of Esdraelon. Gideon, charismatically anointed (as were all the judges), mustered an army, 34-35, and was given the assurance of the sign of the fleece of wool, 36-40.

APPLICATION

Midian is an illustration of the world as the enemy of God and His people. It is often connected with Moab, also a picture of the world. Midian and Moab tried to persuade Balaam to curse Israel (Num 22:4), and it was Moabite and Midianite women who seduced Israel (Num 25:1-18; 31:16; Rev 2:14; Jas 4:4; 1 Jn 2:15). Amalek may well represent the flesh in the believer (Gal 4:29; cf. Ex 17:8-16; Num 24:20; Deut 25:17; 1 Sam 15:2). The world and the flesh overrun God's people and despoil them, and are routed only by the same faith as Gideon's 300.

CHAPTER 7. THE VICTORY OF GIDEON'S THREE HUNDRED

The Reduction of the Army, 1-8. Gideon ("hewer down"), now called also Jerubbaal ("contender against Baal"), with faith refined and valor strengthened by the sign of the fleece, sifted his army of 32,000 to 10,000, and finally to 300. Spiritual quality and not numbers is important if God is to work and be glorified, 2-3. The test, 4-7, of lapping water in the hand like a dog instead of drinking the natural way, separated the vigilant and watchful from the more careless, who were more concerned about natural comforts and less fired by faith to spot the enemy and press on in victory. The Lord chose the 300 who lapped water, 7, to deliver Israel.

The Midianite's Dream, 9-14. The cake of barley bread, 13, represented the Israelite farmers and homesteaders, and the tent which the barley loaf struck and flattened, the nomadic Midianite and Amalekite invaders.

The Victory of Faith, 15-25. The trumpet was the sign of the battle advance against the enemy, the harbinger of faith's victory.

CHAPTER 8. GIDEON'S FAILURE

Jealousy of the Ephraimites, 1-3. Claiming victory over the world and the flesh (routing Midian and Amalek) soon brings the test of the reality of such victory. Gideon's gracious reply (cf. Phil 2:1-5) to the jealous and selfish Ephraimites illustrates this. "The gleaning of the grapes," i.e., the taking of Midianite chieftains Oreb and Zeeb by the Ephraimites, was "better than the vintage of Abiezer," 2, i.e., the defeat of the whole invading horde in the valley of Jezreel. A soft, humble answer turns away wrath (Prov 15:1).

Complete Victory Over the Invader, 4-21. A greater test and victory followed the overcoming of internal strife. The people of Succoth and Penuel, 5-8, taunted Gideon and refused him aid, demonstrating that they were really secret allies of Midian, and treated as such by Gideon after his return.

Gideon's Failure, 22-32. Although Gideon refused the offer of hereditary kingship, 22-23, he fell into another snare in making an ephod (probably some kind of image or memorial), 24-27, and placed it in his hometown Ophrah. This became an evil to Israel and Gideon, perhaps in violation of some priestly rule.

The Fifth Apostasy, 33-35. After Gideon's death, Israel served Baal-berith.

CHAPTER 9. ABIMELECH AND HIS WICKEDNESS

The Murder of Gideon's Sons, 1-5. Abimelech ("my father was king") claimed what his father had rejected. As a product of a Canaanite union, he showed the evils of compromise and disobedience to the word of God in his foul crime of the wholesale murder of Gideon's sons, except Jotham, the youngest, who escaped. Baalberith ("the lord of the covenant") was the god of Shechem, 4.

Abimelech's Pretensions and End, 6-57. Jotham's parable, 7-21, from Mt. Gerizim, the mountain S of Shechem (Deut 11:29), incisively shows the base worthlessness of Abimelech (a worthless "bramble," 14). Abimelech's three-year reign marked a quarrel between himself and the men of Shechem, 26-49, climaxed by Gaal's rebellion, 26-41, which was put down. Abimelech died ignobly, as he had lived, besieging Thebez, about a dozen miles NE of Shechem, 50-57.

CHAPTER 10. TOLA, JAIR AND THE SIXTH APOSTASY

Tola and Jair, 1-5. No record of achievement is given for Tola and little for Jair ("enlightener"). The latter had 30 sons, heads of 30 villages, called Havoth-Jair ("the tent villages of Jair"). Riding on asses' colts, 4, indicated their high social status.

The Sixth Apostasy and Servitude, 6-18. A very serious depar-

CHAPTER 11.   JEPHTHAH DELIVERS FROM THE AMMONITES

Jephthah Rejected but Called to Be Leader, 1-11. Jephthah was a man of great valor but of blemished birth, 1. Thrust out by his family, he went to Tob, a district of Syria, N of Gilead in Transjordan. There he became a roving freebooter. When war broke out with Ammon, a central Transjordanian people whose capital was at Rabbath-Ammon (modern Amman), Jephthah was called back by the elders of Gilead and made commander. He reminds us of our Lord, rejected by His brothers, but yet to be their Deliverer.

Jephthah's Negotiations with Ammon, 12-28. This showed tact, wisdom and diplomatic skill, but was unsuccessful in averting war.

Jephthah's Vow and Its Fulfillment, 29-40. On the eve of the battle, 29, Jephthah (meaning "he opens") made a vow that whoever came forth from his house first to meet him on his victorious return, 30, would be the Lord's and he would offer "him up for a burnt offering," 31 (Heb 'olah, "an offering that ascends"; cf. Lev 1). Opinion is divided whether or not this involved an actual human sacrifice, as Jephthah's only child, a young unmarried daughter, was the first to greet the returning hero at his home in Mizpeh, 34-35. Those who believe this was an actual sacrifice argue: (1) the express terms of the narrative, 31; (2) the half pagan background of Jephthah, who in resorting to this extreme step of vowing a human sacrifice (cf. 2 Kgs 3:27) would follow a pagan custom and not be cognizant of or deterred by the Mosaic law forbidding such a practice (Lev 20:2-3), especially since his daughter concurred, 36. Moreover, Jephthah's excessive grief, 35, and the fact that there is nothing in the narrative to show that his conduct was sanctioned by the Lord argue that it was a real sacrifice. Jephthah's daughter asked for time to "lament" her virginity, 37, because no greater disgrace could befall a Hebrew woman than to die childless. Some suggest that her perpetual virginity was a fulfillment of the vow, but the text seems to indicate that she died at the hands of her father.

CHAPTER 12.   JEPHTHAH'S WAR WITH EPHRAIM

The Quarrelsome Ephraimites Punished, 1-7. This tribe, situated W of the Jordan, illustrates a spirit of divisive, sectarian strife. The people showed a similar contentious attitude toward Gideon (Jud

8:1). But in striking contrast to Gideon, Jephthah exhibited the self-ish, proud, "I-centered" attitude of sectarianism and religious cultism. "*I* and my people," 2; "*I* called you," 2; "*I* saw," 3; "*I* put my life in my hands," 3. The result was strife and war among brothers, death and long-lasting bitter feuds, so characteristic of believers who have lost the sense of the oneness of the Body of Christ (1 Cor 12:13; Eph 4:1-6). In the great strife that followed, when the Ephraimites tried to slip back to their own country across the Jordan fords controlled by the Gileadites, those who pronounced *Shibboleth* (meaning "an ear or head of grain") *Sibboleth* ("s" for "sh") were easily recognized and slain. The Ephraimites spoke a slightly different dialect of Hebrew and could instantly be detected by their inability to make the "sh" sound.

The Judges Ibzon, Elon and Abdon, 8-15. These were so-called minor judges (cf. 10:1-5), who perhaps were administrative and judicial but evidently never performed military exploits like the other judges.

CHAPTER 13. PHILISTINE DOMINATION; BIRTH OF SAMSON

The Seventh Apostasy, 1. Israel was delivered into the power of the Philistines for 40 years. There was no cry to the Lord or record of repentance. This was the last and evidently the deepest apostasy. Also the deliverance was only partial and imperfect, 5, as was the career of Samson. The Philistines were intensely religious, celebrating their victories in the house of their idols (1 Sam 31:9), often carrying their gods into battle (2 Sam 5:21). Dagon, "the fish god," was represented with the face and hands of a man and the tail of a fish (1 Sam 5:4). They also worshiped Ashtaroth (1 Sam 31:10), corresponding to the ancient Assyrian goddess of propagation, Ishtar, as well as Baal-zebub ("lord of flies"), a mocking distortion of Baal-zebul ("lord of the divine abode," 2 Kgs 1:2). Beelzebub in Jewish theology became "the prince of the demons" (Mt 12:24). Philistinism, therefore, represents religionism intermixed with paganism, mere empty ritualism without regenerating and sanctifying power, since the Philistines were uncircumcised, and hence with no covenant knowledge of God or of atoning sacrifice or forgiveness of sins. Nor did they have any assurance of salvation.

Philistinism vs. Naziritism, 2-23. Who was to be the deliverer, 7, from the Philistines? A Nazirite, or "separated one." See the comments on the Nazirite's vow and his cleansing from defilement in Num 6:1-21. Not only was the deliverer to maintain Nazirite separation from Philistinism from birth, his parents were likewise to be separated, 2-14, and as a result of the vision of God were to trust in the power of God. The Angel of the Lord, 3-23, was the pre-incarnate Christ, the same as appeared to Moses in the bush (Ex 3:1-8) and Joshua outside Jericho (Josh 5:13-15).

Samson's Birth, 24-25. Samson (Heb. *Shimshon,* "little sun") was born when his tribe Dan, 2 (cf. Mahaneh-dan, "camp of Dan," RSV), was located in the southwest near Philistia. Later the expanding Philistines forced the tribe to migrate northward (Jud 18).

CHAPTER 14. SAMSON'S EARLY EXPLOITS

Samson Kills the Lion, 1-7. Samson took the first step to compromise his Nazirite vow, 1. He went down to a Philistine city, where he fell into temptation, 1-2, in the matter of the Timnite woman. Yet the Lord overruled Samson's mistake to show His power, 4. By virtue of Samson's Nazirite status, the Spirit of God came upon him mightily, as He always operates through a holy vessel set apart for God. Samson tore the lion to death with his bare hands, 6.

The antiquities park at the ancient Philistine city of Ashkelon.
(*Courtesy IIS*)

177

But while the Nazirite did exploits and conquered Satan, as it were, on one front, he was falling a prey to the wiles of Satan on another front in becoming infatuated with the Timnite woman, 7-8.

Honey in the Lion's Skeleton, 8-9. On his trip to take the woman to wife, Samson, the Nazirite, turned in to see the lion's carcass. He found therein bees and honey, and he scraped the honey into his hands. This was a direct violation of the Nazirite oath, which forbade contact with a carcass.

Exploits Despite Compromise, 10-20. This first venture into alliance with the Philistines, although it furnished an occasion for the exhibition of Samson's strength, nevertheless was fraught with failure and frustration. His betrothed wife nagged and deceived him, and the Philistines outwitted him. The lesson is plain. Philistine alliances are the result of the wiles of the devil and result in the outwitting of the Lord's people (Eph 6:11-12).

CHAPTER 15. SAMSON IN CONFLICT WITH THE PHILISTINES

Samson's Revenge, 1-8. The marriage, which Samson believed himself to have contracted, was of the ancient type in which the husband came only periodically to visit his wife, who continued to reside at her parents' home. The kid apparently was a customary gift for sexual intimacy (Gen 38:17). The 300 foxes (jackals) with torches tied to their tails let loose in the grain and vineyards of the Philistines were apparently pure revenge, not indited by the Spirit of God. Samson's trouble was of his own making, as contamination by Philistinism *always* is.

Bound by His Own, 9-13. His own Israelite brothers, out of fear, bound Samson to deliver him to the Philistines. Lehi, 9, 14, means a "jawbone."

The Exploit with the Ass's Jawbone, 14-17. At Ramath-lehi ("the hill of the jawbone"), 17, Samson killed 1,000 Philistines. But he wisely discarded the jawbone when it had accomplished its purpose, lest like Gideon's ephod (Jud 8:27) it should become a snare. Often the instrument of God's blessing is praised instead of God who uses the instrument.

Samson's Prayer and Its Answer, 18-20. Samson's thirst and the Lord's splitting open the hollow place at Lehi so that water flowed out at En Hakkore ("the spring of him who called"), illustrates the provision of God for His servant who called on Him in his need. Thus, he was strengthened in facing the vengeance of the other Philistines.

178

CHAPTER 16.   SAMSON AND DELILAH;
HIS DEATH

Samson at Gaza, 1-3. Three Philistine women plagued the Nazirite Samson, stripped him of spiritual power and finally accomplished his ruin—the Timnite woman, 14:1-4, the harlot at Gaza, 16:1-3, and Delilah, 16:4-20. Each one silhouetted the power of the Nazirite against the dark background of the compromising sin that was destroying it. Gaza was the chief Philistine city.

Samson and Delilah, 4-19. Delilah, the instrument of Samson's downfall, is analogous to the world in its religious, gay, pleasure-loving aspects, which, like this wily woman, is bent on stripping the true Nazirite of his separation to God, the secret of power in the believer's life. Multifarious were Delilah's cunning subtleties, illustrated here, as she finally cajoled her victim into telling her the secret of his strength, 4-17. The secret *was Samson's Nazirite separation to God.* And when his locks, the badge of his Nazirite separation, were shaved off, his strength departed.

Results of Samson's Violation of His Separation, 20-25. (1) Ignorance of his spiritual powerlessness. He *did not know* that his strength had left him, 20. (2) He was taken captive by the Philistines—became a victim of Philistinism (see comments on Jud 13:1). (3) Lost his eyesight (forfeited his spiritual understanding and discernment). (4) He was enslaved by Philistinism, 21. (5) Became a scandal and a means of glorifying a pagan god instead of the Lord, 23-25. (6) Became the object of Philistine ridicule and a religious clown, 25. On Dagon, see comments on Jud 13:1.

Samson's Death, 26-31. His end was ignominious and terminated in revenge and death. His last prayer was, "Let me die with the Philistines," 30. This is the tragic result of the believer forsaking the Nazirite separation to which he is called. It *always* ends in Philistinism with its disappointment, frustration, powerlessness, enslavement, spiritual blindness, ridicule, destruction, death.

CHAPTERS 17—18.   IDOLATRY OF MICAH AND
THE DANITES

Micah and the Levite, 17:1-13. The story of the relocation of the Danites is prefaced by the story of Micah and his idolatry. On receiving money Micah had stolen from her, 2-3, his mother appropriated 200 pieces of it to make several images under pretense of devotion to the Lord, 4. Micah also had an idolatrous shrine, and had made an ephod (an image) and teraphim (images of household protective deities), and in the spirit of that lawless age installed one of his .sons as priest, 5-6. When a Levitical priest arrived from Bethlehem in Judah, some seven miles S of Jerusalem, Micah persuaded him to act as chaplain in his shrine. This lawless man-made religious arrangement, showing the spiritual apostasy of the day, was ignorantly claimed by Micah as a basis of divine blessing.

The Danite Migration, 18:1-31. The Danites in their removal to the north (cf. Josh 19:40-47; Jud 1:34; 13:2) under Philistine pressure, stole Micah's shrine, including the Levite priest, 16-20. This is another evidence of the lawless apostasy and political confusion of the period (cf. Jud 17:6; 18:1; 19:1; 21:25). Moreover, the aim of the entire appendix of the book of Judges (ch. 17—21) is to show Israel's deep internal corruption. The Levite did not object to this flagrant injustice to Micah because it meant advantage to him personally. Micah's objections against this outrage were made in the name of religion. His efforts to recover his losses came to naught, 26. Ch. 17 and 18 show Israel's religious corruption. Ch. 19-21 show the moral and political lawlessness of the period.

CHAPTERS 19—21. GIBEAH'S CRIME AND ITS PUNISHMENT

The Deed of Lust and Violence, 19:1-30. This chapter faithfully catalogs the horrible results of departure from God (cf. Rom 1:26-32; 2 Tim 3:1-5). Adopting Canaanite ways, Israel sank into the cesspool of Canaanite violence and immorality. Similar lawlessness attends present worldwide apostasy (Lk 17:28-30). The crime of the Benjaminites of Gibeah shows that the city had sunk to the level of Sodom (Gen 19:1-14).

The Harvest of War and Bloodshed, 20:1-48. Israelite chiefs gathered at Mizpah, a town on the northern boundary of Benjamin, to decide on a course of action, 1-7. They determined to punish the guilty persons by death, 12-13. Because the Benjaminites refused to surrender the criminals, a horrible civil war ensued in which thousands perished. A tragic harvest was reaped (cf. Gal 6:7). The guilty tribe was almost wiped out.

Repentance Concerning Benjamin, 21:1-25. The inhabitants of Jabesh-Gilead were smitten and the virgins left were given as wives to the remnant of Benjamin, 1-15. Benjamin was restored as a tribe and additional wives were supplied from the dancers at the annual festival at Shiloh, 16-22. Judges ends with the notation of the lawlessness of the era, 25, so fully illustrated by the book itself.

RUTH

THE RENDEZVOUS OF ROMANCE AND REDEMPTION

Place in the Canon. This beautiful love story of redemption is closely associated with the book of Judges. Its events transpired during that period, *c.* 1400-1050 B.C. (Ruth 1:1). Therefore Ruth is correctly placed after Judges. Its place in the Hebrew Bible is in the third division of the threefold canon among the five shorter books called Megilloth or Scrolls (Song, Ruth, Lamentations, Ecclesiastes, Esther). It was apparently transferred from the second to the third division for liturgical reasons, its scenery of the harvest field adapting it for the harvest festival.

Author and Date. The author is unknown, but since the genealogy is brought up to David (4:17, 22), it would appear it was written by an inspired writer during David's reign (*c.* 1010 B.C.). To place it later, particularly after the Exile, is based upon unsound critical criteria.

Typology. The rich underlying typology of this idyll makes the book of Ruth more than a pastoral story of love. It is an important link in the unfolding account of redemption, presenting in figure our Lord as the great Kinsman-Redeemer in general, but particularly as that aspect of His glorious character *will affect Israel,* His covenant people, in their future restoration. It presents an important link in the messianic family, from which our Lord came some 1,100 years later. The wonder of Scripture to the heart of faith and the discerning eye of love is the messianic pattern interwoven in the warp and woof of Holy Writ. This gorgeous mosaic of Christ's person and work is inwrought in the sacred page, making our Lord the Alpha and the Omega of God's revealed ways with men. See "Typology of the Bible" in the General Introduction to this handbook.

Outline
Ruth Deciding by Faith, Ch. 1
Ruth Gleaning Under Grace, Ch. 2
Ruth Communing in Fellowship, Ch. 3
Ruth Resting in Redemption, Ch. 4

CHAPTER 1. RUTH DECIDING BY FAITH

Naomi and Her Misfortunes, 1-5. This book is a lovely story teaching moral lessons. But it is more than that, since it deals with redemption. As the romance of redemption it prefigures in a blessed sense the dispensational ways of God with the nation Israel, and from this aspect its message will be set forth, thus connecting it as a phase of God's redemptive love for the world. Naomi ("pleasant one") reflects Israel, the chosen people. Her happiness in Bethlehem ("house of bread") married to Elimelech ("my god is king") pictures Israel's prosperity in the land, married to the Lord, faithful to Him and enjoying His favor and blessing. The sorrows that came upon Naomi as a result of the famine speak of spiritual failure and chastisement in the land. The enforced migration to Moab, a pagan nation, sets forth Israel's worldwide dispersion. The death of Naomi's husband in a foreign land illustrates Israel's national rejection during the centuries of her absence from the land, her widowhood and separation from her husband the Lord (cf. Isa 50:1-3). The death of Mahlon ("sick") and Chilion ("pining") in the foreign country shadow forth the trouble and calamities that have engulfed Israel (Naomi) among the Gentiles, where her condition is hopeless. Ruth and Orpah, Moabite wives of Mahlon and Chilion, were left widows.

Ruth and Her Decision, 6-18. Naomi's hearing that "the Lord had visited his people and given them food," 6, and her plan to return to the land suggest the time when dispersed Israel sets her face homeward, 7. Orpah, who remained in Moab, speaks of the unbelieving mass of the nation that will elect to remain among the nations in the day of Israel's return to her homeland. Ruth, however, clinging to Naomi, beautifully portrays the believing remnant of the nation, which will trust in God's provision and ultimately come into touch with the mighty Kinsman-Redeemer, through whom they will inherit the promised blessings. Both Orpah and Ruth signify the nation in dispersion and unbelief. In such a condition of national rejection they have fallen into the same situation as the Gentiles—*Lo-ammi* ("not my poeple") (Hos 1:9). The difference is that Orpah remained in that condition, while Ruth took the step of faith that eventuated in her not only being incorporated among the Lord's people, *Ammi* ("my people"), but actually becoming an ancestress of Christ.

Naomi and Ruth in the Land, 19-22. Arriving back in Bethlehem, Naomi ("pleasant one," what she should have been in faith) called herself Marah ("bitter one," what she would be in her return to the land in unbelief). The time indicated is "in the beginning of the

Reaping in the fields of Boaz. (© *MPS*)

barley harvest," 22, which signifies the end of the age (Mt 13:30, 39). When that end comes, after the Church has been glorified, Israel, like Naomi, with a believing remnant cleaving to her, represented in Ruth, will return to the land (cf. Isa 6:13; 10:21-22; Mic 4:7; Zeph 3:7, etc.).

CHAPTER 2. RUTH GLEANING UNDER GRACE

Ruth Gleaning in the Field of Boaz, 1-17. Boaz ("in him is strength"), a relative of Naomi, was introduced as "a mighty man of wealth," 1. He is typical of the Lord Jesus Christ, the wealthy one. As Him "in whom there is strength," Boaz portrays the Kinsman-Redeemer. Ruth's desire to glean in the field of Boaz to find grace in his sight, 2-3, represents the longing of the remnant at the end-time to seek after the Lord, the Kinsman-Redeemer, and to search the Scriptures to find Him in grace. Boaz' advent from Bethlehem, 4; his notice of and kindness to Ruth, 5-9; his words of grace to her, 11-12; and provision for her, 13-17, show the concern of Israel's Kinsman-Redeemer for the believing remnant of the nation.

Ruth Learns About Boaz, 18-23. Returning to Naomi with her gleanings, Ruth was told something about Boaz. She only knew him, however, as "one of our kinsmen redeemers," not as *the* kinsman-redeemer, 20. This latter revelation Ruth would learn only from Boaz himself. So Israel will not know the full story of the divine Boaz until He reveals Himself in grace and power to the remnant of His people at His second advent (cf. Zech 12:10—13:1; Isa 60:1-22; Hos 6:1-11; 14:4-9; Rom 11:26-36).

CHAPTER 3. RUTH COMMUNING IN FELLOWSHIP

Boaz Guarantees Ruth's Redemption, 1-13. Naomi instructed Ruth in the custom of kinsman redemption, 1-5, according to the regulations of Lev 25:25-28 and the marriage of a brother-in-law (Deut 25:5-12). Ruth accepted Naomi's directions, 5, and obeyed them, 6. The object was "rest," 1. Boaz' discovery of Ruth resulted in Ruth's resting at his feet, 1, 8, experiencing the truth that rest can be found only at the feet of the Redeemer, both for the individual believer (Lk 10:38-42), and the converted nation Israel (Isa 59:20; Rom 11:23-29) when that nation experiences the redemption of the Kinsman-Redeemer and enters into its kingdom rest. Boaz' occupation of winnowing barley at the threshing floor, 2, when Ruth sought him to claim her blessing, foretells the work of the divine Boaz (Mt 3:12) when at His second advent He separates among His people, and the believing remnant, like Ruth, seeks the place of rest at the feet of its Redeemer.

Ruth Reported to Naomi, 14-18, and looked for the promised redemption.

CHAPTER 4. RUTH RESTING IN REDEMPTION

The Nearer Kinsman Renounces His Right, 1-8. At the gate, 1 (Gen 23:10, 18), the normal place for transacting business, Boaz told the nearer kinsman that he could not legally redeem the property without also marrying Ruth. This the kinsman was unable to do, probably because he was already married. To raise up a son in the name of another would confuse the whole question of the inheritance of the estate. The unnamed redeemer who could redeem the land but could do nothing for the poor foreigner Ruth is illustrative of the law, ten witnesses attesting its inability. For the law required that "an Ammonite or Moabite shall not enter into the congregation of the Lord; even to their tenth generation . . . forever" (Deut 23:3). The law could only keep Ruth out, much less bring her in. The symbolic act of removing the shoe, 8, was not connected with the regulation in Deut 25:8-10 where the action served to humiliate one who refused to accept the levirate marriage. Here the shoe symbolized the right of the owner to set foot upon the land (Ps 60:8) and the removal symbolized the act of ceding the rights of possession to another.

Boaz' Redemption and the Marriage of Ruth, 9-17. Ruth the Moabitess, as a result of Boaz' action, 9-10, was officially accepted in Israel by the representatives of the city, and God sanctioned the act of redemption in the fertility of Ruth, 13-17. The marriage represents the consummation of the redemption of both the land and the people, when the redeemed remnant enters into the blessings of kingdom rest (cf Isa 4:1-6; 11:1-16; Zech 8:6-8).

Messianic Genealogy. 18-22. The abbreviated list is given from Perez (RSV), the forefather of the royal family of Judah (Gen 38:29) who was also born of a levirate marriage, to David. The latter points to the true theocratic king, Messiah (cf. 1 Chr 2:5; 9:4; Mt 1:3-6). Thus through a simple story is interwoven God's plan for the redemption of the world and the restoration of His people Israel.

1 SAMUEL

FROM THE JUDGES TO THE KINGS

Nature of the Book. Treated as one book in the Hebrew, 1 and 2 Samuel constitute some of the finest historical writing in all literature. Written largely as historical biography, these narratives differ from contemporary documents (Assyrian, Egyptian, Hittite) in not being the mere pegging out of events on the line of time. The events themselves are stressed, and the moral and spiritual repercussions of these events and of the persons involved are highlighted. Accordingly, these books have eminent ethical and didactic value. From a prophetic viewpoint they are also important in that they tell of the founding of Israel's kingdom under David. These events foreshadow the coming of Israel's true King (cf. Num 24:17-19 and 1 Sam 2:10) and the establishment of the kingdom under Messiah (Acts 1:6).

Authorship and Authenticity. While Samuel is not said to be the author, he may have been joint author with Nathan and Gad (cf. 1 Chr 29:29). The higher critical contention that 1 and 2 Samuel consist of various discordant traditions is not sustained by careful analysis and spiritually discerning exegesis of the books.

CHAPTER 1. SAMUEL'S BIRTH AND BOYHOOD

Hannah's Prayer and Vow, 1-18. The ancestry of Samuel is given, 1-2. God's sovereign working is seen in the child's birth. For similar unusual offspring of barren women cf. Sarah (Gen 17:16-19), Rebekah (Gen 25:21-26), Rachel (Gen 29:31; 30:22-24), Samson's mother (Jud 13:2-5) and Elisabeth (Lk 1:5-17). Hannah's prayer and consecration were answered.

Samuel Born and Given to God, 19-28. The name Samuel ("requested of God") was given to the child as a token of the Lord's faithfulness in answering Hannah's prayer. The child was weaned and presented to Eli, the priest, at the central shrine at Shiloh (Seilun) in Ephraim, E of the main road from Shechem to Jerusalem.

CHAPTER 2. THE FAILURE OF ELI'S HOUSE

Hannah's Ode, 1-11. This is an inspired song of praise to the Lord, 1-3, celebrating His power and grace in deliverance, 4-8, with a prophetic glimpse into the future day of the Lord preceding Israel's true King and the establishment of His kingdom, 9-10.

Failure of Eli's House, 12-36. The moral decline and lawlessness of the period of the judges were reflected in the disciplinary weakness of Eli and the flagrant wickedness of his sons, Hophni and Phinehas, 12-17. "Sons of Belial," 12, is a Hebrew idiom for "worthless fellows." While judgment was ripening for Eli's house, God's grace was manifested in the boy Samuel ministering at Shiloh, 18-26, amid the increasing laxity of Eli and the immorality of his sons, 22-25. God sent a prophet to pronounce doom upon the priestly sinners, 26-36.

CHAPTER 3. SAMUEL'S CALL

The Call, 1-18. Because of sin among God's people, the word of the Lord was "precious" (*yaqar,* "rare"); no "open [broken open] vision," that is, one broken open like an alabaster bottle of perfume and the fragrance dispersed. Samuel's call, 1-9, followed by the message from the Lord, 10-18, manifested the divine grace in supplying the need for a human instrument through whom the word of God might come.

Samuel's Prophetic Ministry, 19-21. From Dan on the northern boundary of Israel to Beersheba on the southern border, all Israel became aware of God's chosen human instrument of revelation.

CHAPTER 4. JUDGMENT OF ELI'S HOUSE

The Death of Eli and His Sons, 1-18. The Philistines (see Jud 13) were the human agents to fulfill the predicted judgment upon Eli and his sons (1 Sam 2:26-36). Israel trusted in the ark (see comments on Ex 25:10-22) rather than in Him of whom the ark spoke. Substitution of ritualism for spiritual reality always leads to domination by "the Philistines" with its dire results—(1) spiritual death, here illustrated by the physical death of Eli, Hophni and Phinehas; (2) and loss of the spiritual presence of the Lord, the

Shekinah, with Ichabod ("no glory" or "alas for the glory") the result. This is indicated by the name the widow of Phinehas gave to her newborn son.

The Tragedy of Ichabod, 19-22 (cf. Ps 78:60-61). The name "Shiloh" (Gen 49:10) is messianic. Even the critical contention that its rise in Genesis is not in the sense of a proper name cannot rule out the obvious reference in that passage to Christ.

ARCHAEOLOGICAL LIGHT

Shiloh was located nine miles N of Bethel. Such a tribal religious focal point (shrine) has numerous parallels in ancient extrabiblical cultures. Cf. the Delphic amphictyony in Greece, the Etruscan amphictyony in Italy, the temple of the moon-god Sin at Haran, and the shrine of Belit-ekalli at Qatna, as well as the temples at Nineveh, Ashur and Nippur. The destruction of Shiloh (c. 1050 B.C.) is confirmed by the Danish excavations at the site. (Cf. Jer 7:12-15; 26:6-7.)

CHAPTERS 5—6. THE ARK AMONG THE PHILISTINES AND ITS RETURN

The Ark in Dagon's Temple, 5:1-5. Dagon (apparently a diminutive of Heb. *dag*, "fish") was represented with human head and hands and the body of a fish. In Palestine he became associated with the harvest (Heb. *dagan*, "grain"), abundantly attested by the religious tablets found at Ugarit in N. Syria. Numerous places were named after him (Josh 15:41). Ashdod was one of the principal towns of the Philistine pentapolis, composed also of Gaza, Gath, Ekron and Ashkelon. The spiritual blindness of the Philistines is seen in their superstitious veneration of Dagon.

The Lord's Punishment of the Philistines, 5:6—6:21. Malignant tumors and a plague of field mice (cf. 6:4, 11, 18) were the judgments visited upon the enemies of the Lord and His people.

CHAPTER 7. SAMUEL AS JUDGE

Samuel's Message, 1-8. The judge-prophet issued a general call to genuine repentance in turning away from Canaanite idolatry. The Baalim were images of the great northwest Semitic fertility deity Baal ("lord"), and the Ashtaroth were replicas of Ashtoreth, the Hebrew name for Astarte, goddess of sexual love and fertility, 3-4. The water libation, 6, usually of wine, shows the preciousness of water to a people in a dry climate.

Victory at Ebenezer, 9-14. For the significance of the whole burnt offering which Samuel offered, 9-10, see comments on Lev 1. Repentance and faith in the Lord's redemption always bring a manifestation of the Lord as Ebenezer ("the stone of help").

Summary of the Ministry of Samuel, 15-17, the circuit-riding prophet-judge.

CHAPTER 8.   ISRAEL'S DEMAND FOR A KING

Failure of the Judgeship, 1-3. Samuel made the mistake of appointing his sons as judges. The concept of priestly or apostolic succession is wholly false and productive of much corruption among God's people.

Demand for the Kingship, 4-22. Samuel's age, the unfitness of his sons and the desire to be like other nations were the reasons given for demanding a king, 5. The evils of the kingship were pointed out by Samuel, 7-18. Unbelief and self-will were the basis of the rejection of the theocracy, 19-22.

CHAPTERS 9—11.   SAUL AND HIS ANOINTING

Saul's Anointing, 9:1—10:16. Saul's search for the lost asses of his father Kish, 1-10, furnished the occasion for his meeting with Samuel, 11-25, and his being anointed king by the prophet, 10:1-16.

Saul's Fair Beginning, 10:17-27. Samuel again warned the people at Mizpeh concerning their fault in rejecting the theocracy, 17-19. Saul was selected by lot, 20-22. His initial humility, 21-22, imposing appearance and commanding physique made him a promising choice on the human plane, 23-24. Samuel established the kingdom, 25, and Saul returned to Gibeah, 26-27.

Saul's Initial Victories, 11:1-15. The gross insult of Nahash ("serpent") the Ammonite, 1-3, to the inhabitants of Jabesh, a town of Gilead in Transjordan, was told to Saul at Gibeah (modern Tell el-Ful, excavated by W. F. Albright), 4-5. Saul was anointed by the Spirit to deliver Israel in the manner of the earlier judges, 6. He mustered Israel to arms, 7, and won both a great victory over Ammon and public acclaim in the kingship as well, 8-15. The kingdom was consequently renewed at Gilgal, symbolic of self-judgment in Israel where the reproach of Egypt was rolled away (see comments on Josh 5:2-10). Saul was making a good start.

CHAPTER 12.   SAMUEL'S FAREWELL ADDRESS

Samuel Officially Proclaims the Kingdom, 1-15. Samuel declared his integrity as prophet-judge. This took place at Gilgal before the assembly of all Israel dispersed, 1-4. He affirmed the Lord and His anointed (Saul) were witnesses to the fact that he (Samuel) had given the people no cause to be weary with government by judges, 5. He inferred that the blame for desiring the kingship rested with them. The aged prophet-judge thereupon reproved Israel for ingratitude, 6-15, as he rehearsed "the righteous acts of the Lord," 7. "Bedan," 11, should be read "Barak" with the Greek and Syriac, and "Samson" probably for "Samuel." The people's reasons for choosing a king were wrong, 12. The kingship would expose them to many dangerous temptations. Obedience to the theocratic ideal alone could save them from the consequences, 13-15.

The Lord's Sign of Israel's Sin in Asking for a King, 16-25. Thunder and rain in the wheat harvest (last of June and early July) were so rare as to be miraculous, especially without any prior indications and wholly by the word of the Lord through the prophet. The people regarded the event as such, and asked Samuel to pray for them as they confessed their wrong motives in asking for a king.

Gibeah of Saul, a few miles north of Jerusalem. (© *MPS*)

CHAPTER 13. SAUL'S FIRST GREAT FAILURE

Saul's Self-Will, 1-10. In Saul's first year, 1, the events of ch. 9, 10 and 11 took place. In his second year he was severely tested regarding his fitness to be king by a formidable invasion of the Philistines, 2-7. Would he trust God and obey His word through Samuel? Jonathan, Saul's son, 3, a striking contrast to his father, did so. But Saul showed flagrant unbelief and disobedience in intruding into the priest's office at Gilgal (of all places! See notes on Josh 5). He, a Benjamite, offered the sacrifices which only a priestly Levite might offer (Num 16:1-3, 32-40). The act was a direct violation of God's law, a proof of the unbelief of his heart and his essential unfitness to be king over the Lord's people.

The Lord's Rejection of Saul Announced, 11-23. Saul's excuse to Samuel, 11-12, revealed his unbelief and disobedience. So the prophet announced Saul's unfitness and rejection as king, 13-14. The unworthy monarch's subsequent career demonstrated the futility of trying to discharge work for God without God's electing grace and blessing.

ARCHAEOLOGICAL LIGHT

The Philistines had a monopoly on iron (1 Sam 13:19-22) which gave them military advantage. They apparently obtained the secret of smelting from the Hittites. Saul and David by their conquests broke this monopoly. Verse 21 should read with the RSV: "And the charge was a pim [two-thirds of a shekel] for the plowshares and for the mattocks, and a third of a shekel [about 11½ grams or 50 cents] for sharpening axes and setting the goads." The iron age extended from 1200 to 300 B.C.

CHAPTER 14. JONATHAN'S HEROISM

Jonathan's Great Victory, 1-23. He is one of the finest characters in sacred history, a glowing contrast to his father, a picture of genuine victorious faith, 6. King Saul was surrounded by a company, among whom were relatives of Eli, but manifested unbelief. The Lord miraculously worked through an earthquake, sending confusion and destruction among the Philistines, 15-23.

Saul's Foolish Impetuosity, 24-45. Fearful of losing this advantage over the Philistines, Saul laid an anathema on anyone tasting food till the evening. He was remiss as well as rash in failing to notify Jonathan. This episode shows how unreliable he was to be king over the Lord's people. Saul built an altar but his request was unanswered by the Lord, 35-37. Jonathan's condemnation by his own father, 38-44, and his rescue by the people, 45, again demonstrated the weak and unkingly character of Saul.

Saul's Successes and His Family, 46-52. Despite the king's unworthiness, God nevertheless graciously granted victories for the sake of His people, 46-48. Saul's pedigree and family are given in 49-52.

CHAPTER 15. SAUL'S SECOND GREAT FAILURE

Saul's Commission to Exterminate Amalek, 1-8. Samuel presented Saul with the Lord's plain command, 1, and the clear reason for the total blotting out of Amalek, 2-3. Saul's incomplete obedience was highlighted, 4-8, his stubborn self-will again cropping out. (For Amalek see notes on Ex 17.) Saul was, therefore, disqualified to lead God's people.

Saul's Disobedience and Rejection, 9-31. He spared "the best" and "all that was good," forgetting that *nothing* of the flesh is good or can please God (Rom 8:8), but must be utterly wiped out, put under the ban, destroyed in the name of religion, i.e., exterminated *with a deeper spiritual connotation* (Deut 20:16-18). Little wonder the Lord's word of rejection was once more (1 Sam 13:14) enunciated, 10-11. Samuel's tearful intercession for the king could not avail. Saul's conduct in erecting a monument to himself, 12, and the evidences of his leniency with Amalek under the pretense of piety, 13-15, proved his guilt and called for divine rejection, despite his self-defense, 16-23. Saul's superficial repentance, 24-25, only brought a dramatic episode, 26-28, emphasizing Saul's loss of the kingdom so far as God's blessing him was concerned. Saul's pride appeared uncorrected, 29-31.

Destruction of Agag, 32-33. Death alone must be pronounced upon the flesh and all that pertains to it, if the Word of God is to be obeyed (Rom 8:13; Col 3:5) and spiritual victory enjoyed.

Samuel Separates from Saul, 34-35. Samuel did not visit Saul again in any official capacity (cf. 1 Sam 19:24 and 28:11). The rejected king turned to his rustic palace at Gibeah (excavated by W. F. Albright and dating about 1015 B.C.).

CHAPTER 16. DAVID ANOINTED KING

David's Anointing, 1-13. The rejection of the king after the people's heart was followed by the choice of the king after God's own heart, 1-2, whose exile and sufferings are told in ch. 16—31. Like Jonathan, David was a man of faith, kingly in spirit, and in complete subjection to the Lord. He who was to be the type of the true King came from Bethlehem of Judah ("praise"), the royal tribe (Gen 49:10). Samuel called Jesse and his sons to a sacrificial feast, 3-5, examined each prospect, 6-10, and finally chose David and anointed him, 11-13.

Saul's Declension, 14-23. The Spirit of God departed from Saul and an evil spirit (demon) from the Lord, 14, i.e., by the Lord's permission, began to torment him. Divine sovereignty controls evil forces for God's purposes. Believers who stubbornly reject God's Word expose themselves to demon control to a greater or lesser degree (1 Tim 4:1; 1 Jn 4:1-4; cf. Mt 12:43-45). David's skill in performing on the harp, that is, the lyre, 16-23, was called upon to refresh the harassed king. After the young shepherd-king had soothed the troubled monarch and was no longer needed, he returned to his father's sheep. (Cf. 1 Sam 16:19-23 with 17:55-58, where a discrepancy has been imagined. The preoccupied Saul did not bother to ascertain the lineage of this young musician until the latter was about to become his son-in-law.)

CHAPTER 17.   DAVID AND GOLIATH

Defiance of Goliath, 1-11. The Philistines advanced, 1-3. Introduced is Goliath of Gath and his impious defiance of the Lord's people, and hence of the Lord Himself, 4-11. This Philistine giant furnishes an illustration of Satan as he defied and terrified God's people through Philistine doctrines and practices. Note the prominence of the number six, 5-7, the number of man under Satanic sway in opposition to God. Cf. also another giant (2 Sam 21:20), Nebuchadnezzar's image (Dan 3:1), and the number of the Antichrist, a triple six (Rev 13:18).

David Appears on the Scene, 12-30. In the deeper spiritual sense David, whose name probably means "leader" (as archaeological evidence from the Mari Letters discovered at Tell el Hariri on the Middle Euphrates in 1933 shows), points to the Lord Jesus. David's being sent by his father Jesse, 12-19; his obedience, 20-27; his being misunderstood and unfairly accused by his own brothers, 28-30, tell of Him whom the Father sent into the world and of His treatment by His own.

David's Victory, 31-54. The sling and the stones out of the brook illustrate the supernatural despoilment of Satan by the greater David through the cross, a means in turn just as unlikely to unbelieving man as David's humble shepherd's sling (Col 2:15; Heb 2:14).

Saul's Question, 55-58. See notes on 16:14-23 for the alleged discrepancy.

CHAPTERS 18—20. DAVID'S FLIGHT FROM SAUL

Jonathan's Love for David, 18:1-30. This noble friendship, 1-4, was beautifully silhouetted against the dark background of Saul's demonic jealousy, 5-16, and his base treachery toward David with regard to his daughter Merab, 17-19, and his other daughter, Michal, 20-30. The latter, however, became David's wife, in spite of the trap Saul set for David in arranging the marriage.

Saul's Renewed Attempt to Kill David, 19:1-24. So unprincipled had Saul become that he even tried to get Jonathan to kill David, in the face of the tender love that existed between the two, 1-6 (cf. 1 Sam 18:1). The deranged king, in spite of his oath to Jonathan, 6, was overwhelmed by his mania and tried to pin David to the wall with his javelin, 7-10. Michal by a ruse, 11-17, saved David's life, and David fled to Samuel, 18-19. The grace of God dealt with Saul, 20-24, but his disobedience was his ruin.

Jonathan Protects David, 20:1-42. What a story of selfless love! The heir to the throne, far from being jealous or envious of David, who in a sense was a throne rival, loved him as himself (1 Sam 18:1). He himself was a hero, as his valorous triumph over the Philistines proved (ch. 14). He also possessed a sterling character worthy of being a king. But he had mastered the lesson that God's will is best and that God had ordained David to be king. To this he bowed with admirable self-effacement. Jonathan's devotion to his rival is a superbly noble story and one of the finest in history.

CHAPTER 21. DAVID'S FLIGHT TO NOB AND TO GATH

David at Nob, 1-9. After leaving Jonathan, David fled to Nob not far N of Jerusalem, where Ahimelech, son of Ahitub (1 Sam 22:9), great grandson of Eli, was high priest. Hungry and unarmed David arrived on the sabbath and asked food. The Bible's fidelity in showing the seamy side of a person's character is here illustrated in David's lapse in faith and deception, 2. What a contrast to the Greater David (1 Pet 21:22). Then David and the men who were with him ate the shewbread, bread of presence (cf. Mt 12:1-8; Mk 2:23-28; Lk 6:1-5). Using this incident in David's life, our Lord justified the conduct of His disciples in plucking and eating grain on the sabbath. He was willing to set aside Jewish legal ordinances to give to His own the true Bread of life of which the bread of presence speaks. (See Ps 34.)

David at Gath, 10-15. Again a lapse in David's faith was seen. Once more his seamy side appeared, as he feigned insanity among the enemies of God's people.

CHAPTER 22. DAVID AT ADULLAM; SAUL'S VENGEANCE

David Gains Followers, 1-5. David's headquarters at Adullam SW of Bethlehem became a stronghold, 4. He committed his parents to the king of Moab for protection. Read Pss 62 and 142.

Saul's Desperate Violence, 6-23. Doeg, an unscrupulous foreigner, acted as an informer (see 21:7). Saul cruelly wiped out the entire priestly community at Nob, Abiathar alone escaping to inform David, 11-19. David therefore felt a sense of obligation to protect Abiathar, 20-23.

CHAPTER 23. DAVID DELIVERS KEILAH

David Delivers Keilah, 1-15. Abiathar had brought an ephod (a priestly garment containing the sacred lots) with him. By its use David was assured of divine help in rescuing Keilah, a few miles S of Adullam (1 Sam 22:1), from the Philistines. Also by the use of the ephod, 6-12, David was warned to flee Keilah, as Saul planned to besiege the town and kill David, 13-14.

David Is Hunted by Saul, 16-29. David was a fugitive in Ziph, a rocky, remote terrain S of Hebron, 15, where he was nobly visited by Jonathan, 16-17. The two made a covenant, 18. The traitorous Ziphites informed Saul of David's whereabouts, 19-24. Saul sought David at Maon, somewhat S of Ziph, Hachilah and Jeshimon (Josh 15:55) in the Arabah, here meaning simply "desert" or "wilderness," not the Jordan-Dead Sea depression, 24-26. Tidings of a Philistine raid distracted Saul, 26-27. David had a moment of respite in the strongholds of Engedi, 29, on the west shore of the Dead Sea, SE of Hebron. The rocky terrain here with its numerous caves offered natural fortresses.

CHAPTER 24. DAVID SPARES SAUL'S LIFE

David Spares Saul in the Wilderness of Engedi, 1-15. After relief from the Philistine raid, Saul again took up his relentless pursuit of David in "the wildgoats' rocks," 2, a graphic description of the wilderness around Engedi. In this region Saul entered the same cave where David and his men were hiding. David refused to kill "the Lord's anointed," 4-7, merely cutting off the skirt of Saul's robe, 4. He acted on faith, allowing God to deal with his enemy. David's magnanimous conduct was reflected in his words to Saul, 8-15. "A dead dog," 14, was less than nothing since a live dog was little thought of in those days.

Saul's Reply to David, 16-22. Saul was broken, but essentially unrepentant, 16-19. He knew David was God's choice to be king, 20, and begged that his descendants be spared, 21-22.

CHAPTER 25. DAVID, NABAL AND ABIGAIL

Samuel's Obituary, 1. It is brief but comprehensive and shows the great love of all Israel for this faithful man of God.

David Obtains Abigail to Wife, 2-42. David made a peaceful gesture to a wealthy Calebite whose wife was named Abigail, 2-8. Nabal ("fool") was shearing sheep in Carmel (Josh 15:55) between Ziph and Maon, SE of Hebron (not to be confused with Mt. Carmel N of the Plain of Sharon on the Mediterranean seacoast). Nabal senselessly repulsed David's men, 9-11, and played "the fool." Abigail acted wisely, 14-22, and went to meet David with provisions for him and his men, beseeching mercy in a nobly sagacious speech, 23-31. David replied just as nobly, 32-35. Nabal was struck by God and died, 36-38. Abigail became David's wife, 39-42.

David Also Takes Ahinoam to Wife, 43-44. She was from Jezreel, the Valley of Esdraelon. Explanatory note concerning Michal's relation to David is given in verse 44.

CHAPTER 26. DAVID SPARES SAUL A SECOND TIME

The Ziphites Again Inform Against David, 1-4 (cf. 24:1-8). Critics make these events conflicting accounts of the same event. But numerous details show they are genuinely reliable accounts of two separate events. The Ziphites, having betrayed David once, knew the only thing that could save them from David's wrath was his death, so they were doggedly persistent in trying to deliver him to Saul.

Second Reprieve of Saul's Life, 5-16. The whole *dramatis personae* of this incident is different from 24:1-22. Abner, Joab and Abishai appear. All of these persons were destined to play an important role in David's reign, recorded in 2 Samuel. Ahimelech the Hittite is, of course, not to be confounded with Ahimelech the priest (ch. 21). Hittites who remained in the country from earlier times (Gen 23:7, RSV; Josh 1:4) adopted Hebrew names, as Uriah the Hittite (2 Sam 11:3). The details of Saul's being spared, 7-12, are diametrically different from 24:4-5. David amusingly taunted Abner, 13-16. Even at present Bedouin shout across great distances in this way.

Colloquy Between David and Saul, 17-25. David again challenged Saul concerning the wrong of his coming out to seek his life "like one who hunts a partridge [Heb. "flea," as in 24:14] in the mountains," 17-20. Saul's confession, 21, and David's gracious reply, 22-24, are recorded. Saul's declaration to David, 25, was prophetic, "Blessed be you, my son David! You will do many things and will succeed in them" (RSV). So the enemies of the Greater David, the Lord Jesus, must confess His integrity and success (cf. Mt 27:24; Phil 2:10).

CHAPTER 27. DAVID'S LAPSE OF FAITH

Unbelief and Discouragement, 1-7. David's plaint, 1, is understandable on the human plane in the light of his long and grueling hounding by Saul. The discouragement of unbelief caused the Lord's anointed to go over to the enemies of the Lord's people, live with them, and settle down in the very city Goliath, the giant David slew by faith, came from. David was given Ziklag, located somewhere on the Judah-Philistine border, 5-7.

Deceit and Deception, 8-12. Unbelief produced other evil fruits. To court Achish's trust, David lied concerning the object of his military raids, 10.

CHAPTER 28. SAUL AND THE SPIRITISTIC MEDIUM

Saul's Desperate Straits, 1-7. The Philistines advanced, 1, into the Valley of Jezreel, eastern end of the Plain of Megiddo (Esdraelon), and encamped at Shunem opposite Mt. Gilboa near the fortress Bethshan, 4-5. Samuel had died, so there was no word from the Lord through him, 3, nor through dreams, Urim, or by prophets, 6. Heaven was closed, so to speak, to the rejected, disobedient monarch. So he resorted, as it were, to hell, 7. To make matters worse, the monarch himself in his better days had outlawed pagan occultism, 9.

Saul Resorts to Spiritism, 8-19. Saul sought out a medium, "a woman, mistress of a divining demon," 7. Disguised so as not to be recognized as the king, 8, he required the woman to call up the spirit of Samuel, that he might inquire what to do about the Philistine pressure. Samuel's spirit was brought back from the intermediate, disembodied state. But this was accomplished by God, not by the medium. The medium's fright proves this. A "god" in 13 (RSV) means a judge (Ps 82:6; Jn 10:34-35), the venerable prophet-judge Samuel, 14. This was not a case of a medium communicating with the spirit of a deceased person; it was God actually calling back Samuel in spirit form to pronounce impending doom upon Saul, 15-19. It is thus a once-for-all exposé of the fraud and wickedness of necromancy and all occultism.

Saul Takes Food, 20-25. Saul received strength to go on to his last battle on Mt. Gilboa. He serves as an illustration of the believer who sins the sin to death, i.e., physical death (cf. 1 Cor 5:5; 11:30-32; 1 Jn 5:16).

CHAPTER 29. DAVID'S DEFECTION TO THE PHILISTINES

Results of David's Lapse of Faith, 1-5. See ch. 27, which is here resumed. David not only found himself among the enemies of the Lord's people, but put in the deplorable situation of fighting against the Lord's people. Unbelief makes a sad spectacle of any believer. So much so in this case that David, as a result, became *persona non grata* as far as the Philistine lords were concerned. They still remembered the former exploits of a hero of faith, 5, and feared treachery.

Achish Dismisses David, 6-11. Achish showed his great respect for David, 6, swearing by David's God and pronouncing him blameless in his sight "as an angel of God," 9. Nevertheless he bowed to the will of his colleagues, the Philistine lords, 7. David's reply, 8, asserting his willingness to stay with the Philistines and fight against the Lord's people, showed how deeply unbelief can plunge a believer into inconsistency and spiritual treason. Only God's grace kept David from plummeting deeper into the ignominy unbelief always brings. The Philistines quickly marched on the Israelites at Jezreel (cf. 1), the Plain of Esdraelon (the Gr. form of Jezreel), from Aphek (modern Ras el-'Ain in the Plain of Sharon), from which rallying point they had captured the ark of the covenant years before (1 Sam 4:1).

CHAPTER 30. DAVID'S CHASTENING AND RESTORATION

The Plundering of Ziklag, 1-6. Achish had given David Ziklag as his residence (1 Sam 27:6). The town was about 80 miles S of Aphek, a strenuous two-day march, 1. When David with his men arrived on the third day, the plundered city was a token that the chastening hand of the Lord rested heavily upon him, 1-5. David was hard pressed and the embittered people were ready to stone him, 6. But the backslider was restored by discipline and "strengthened himself in the Lord his God," 6. He had joined himself to the enemies of God and was ready to fight against the Lord's people. Now the Lord permitted the enemy to plunder him.

The Enemy Defeated, 7-20. David consulted Abiathar's ephod (containing the sacred oracles), and received the go-sign to pursue the Amalekites, 8. With 600 men he crossed the brook Besor, S of Ziklag, 9. Four hundred were able to advance. Through the help of an Egyptian, 11-15, an abandoned servant of an Amalekite, who acted as a spy, the Amalekites (see Ex 17) were slaughtered and all David's family and possessions were retrieved, with great spoil, 16-20.

The Spoil Divided Equitably, 21-31. Thus David's fairmindedness and political sagacity were displayed especially in sending a gift to the elders of Judah, 26-31. All the places named, 27-31, were in Judah. It is no surprise David was soon to be made king of Judah (2 Sam 2:6).

CHAPTER 31. SAUL'S DEATH

Saul's Suicide, 1-7. In the battle with the Philistines on Mt. Gilboa, S of the eastern part of the Plain of Jezreel (Esdraelon), Israel was routed, 1. Saul's older sons, Jonathan, Abinadab and Melchishua, were killed, 2, and Saul was wounded, 3. He pressed his armor bearer to kill him, but committed suicide when the armor bearer refused, 4-6. This climactic tragedy followed his visit to the spiritistic medium at Endor, Saul's last step toward ruin (28:1-25). He died unrepentant, in rebellion against the Lord, as he had lived, the first suicide recorded in the Bible. Cf. also Ahithophel (2 Sam 17:23), Zimri (1 Kgs 16:18) and Judas Iscariot (Mt 27:5).

Saul's Body Dishonored, 8-10. The completely victorious Philistines beheaded Saul's corpse, put his armor in the temple of Ashtaroth (Astarte) and hung up his body and those of his sons in ignominy on the walls of Bethshan, the fortress town which guarded the eastern approach to the Valley of Jezreel.

The Men of Jabesh-Gilead Recover the Bodies, 11-13. They had now the chance to show their thanks to Saul for what he had done for them (1 Sam 11). They not only recovered the bodies of Saul and his sons, but gave them honorable burial and proper mourning.

2 SAMUEL

David King Over Judah and All Israel

Theme of the Book. Continuing the narrative (see introduction to 1 Samuel), 2 Samuel presents the biographical story of David. In 1 Samuel the failure of man is stressed as seen in Eli and Saul. In 2 Samuel the restoration of order follows the enthroning of God's king with the establishment of Jerusalem as the nation's political center (2 Sam 5:6-12) and Zion (2 Sam 5:7; 6:1-17) as the religious center. Following this arrangement the great Davidic covenant was established by the Lord (2 Sam 7:8-17), the basis of all revealed truth concerning the kingdom yet to be established over Israel (Acts 1:6). David prophetically sang of that kingdom (2 Sam 23:1-7).

Outline
David, King of Judah, Ch. 1—4
David, King of Israel, Ch. 5—10
David's Sin and Chastisement, Ch. 11—20
Historical Appendix, Ch. 21—24

CHAPTER 1. DAVID'S LAMENT FOR SAUL AND JONATHAN

The Amalekite's Report of Saul's Death, 1-16. This is not contradictory to the account in 1 Sam 31:1-6, as critics commonly claim, but supplementary. First, Saul, severely wounded by Philistine archers, begged his armor bearer to dispatch him. Refused, Saul fell upon his own sword, followed by his armor bearer who in turn fell upon his sword and died. But Saul was not completely successful. In death anguish he was transfixed and held upright by his own sword when an Amalekite in the turmoil came by. At Saul's plea the Amalekite killed him, took his crown and bracelet, and hurried from the battlefield to go to David. There is no need to assume the Amalekite lied. Saul's great sin was in sparing Amalek (cf. 1 Sam 15; cf. 28:18). An Amalekite made an end of him. David's slaying the Amalekite was dictated largely by his view of the inviolability of the person of a God-appointed leader. His allegiance to Saul showed his magnanimity of character and noble statesmanship.

David's Lament, 17-27. This superb elegy shows the deep feeling of David. It is great lyric poetry from a skilled musician (1 Sam 16:23) and talented poet (cf. the many Davidic psalms), who was a man of God and a steadfast friend even in the face of such treatment as Saul gave him.

CHAPTER 2. DAVID MADE KING OF JUDAH; ABNER'S REVOLT

David Anointed King Over Judah, 1-7. God's king at once showed faith and dependence upon the Lord, 1-3. The answer was plain. He was to go up to the cities of Judah, where he was made king. Judah was evidently living a separate existence from the other tribes. (Cf. 2 Sam 3:10; 5:5; 19:8-15, 40-43; 20:1-3 for other indications of separateness.) David's first official royal act in thanking the men of Jabesh-Gilead for their service rendered in burying Saul was an augur of David's brilliant diplomacy and political sagacity, 5-7.

Abner Sets up Ishbosheth as King, 8-11. An attempt was made by Saul's army commander to perpetuate the Saul dynasty, 8-11. Ishbosheth ("man of shame") had the original name of Eshbaal ("man of Baal") (1 Chr 8:33; 9:39). The Hebrew word for "shame" (*bosheth*) was substituted for the hated name of the Canaanite fertility god. Mahanaim was the principal town in Transjordan. The Philistines were in control W of the Jordan River. The servants of Ishbosheth under Abner and the servants of David under Joab clashed at the pool in Gibeon (Josh 9), an important city some five miles NW of Jerusalem, 12-17. Abner's killing of Asahel precipitated a blood feud between Joab and Abner, 22-23. David's forces were victorious, 29-32. This initial victory presaged further victories.

CHAPTER 3. ABNER'S DEFECTION TO DAVID AND HIS DEATH

Quarrel with Ishbosheth, 1-11. Summary statement of the war, 1, is followed by a description of David's family, 2-5, and the episode of Abner's break with Saul's house, 6-11. Ishbosheth's charge was serious, since in a harem a concubine was royal property and must be kept in the royal household. To seek to procure such a concubine was tantamount to treason (2 Sam 16:21-22; 1 Kgs 2:22).

Abner Goes Over to David, 12-30. His negotiations with David, 12, were answered affirmatively with only the condition that Michal, Saul's daughter and David's first wife, be returned, 13 (cf. 1 Sam 18:20-27). This had a political purpose in bolstering David's claim to Saul's throne as the king's son-in-law. Abner's reception by David, 20-21, fired him to campaign for David's kingship over all Israel. However, he was murdered by Joab in the blood feud occasioned by Abner's killing Asahel, 23-30.

David's Lament Over Abner, 31-39. The public mourning and wise conduct of David presaged his success in the kingship.

CHAPTER 4. ISHBOSHETH'S DEATH

Ishbosheth's Assassination, 1-7. The hopeless prospect of Saul's house by Abner's defection, 1, occasioned other disloyalty. Baanah and Rechab, two army officers, murdered Ishbosheth, 2-7. Mephibosheth, Jonathan's son, is introduced rather abruptly, 4, perhaps to show the sorry plight of Saul's house in general.

David's Punishment of the Murderers, 8-12. Bringing the head of the murdered king to David, these violent criminals tried to justify their crime by pious reference to the Lord's avenging David, 8; but David continued to honor Saul's house and to punish anyone who would harm it (cf. 2 Sam 1:14-16; 3:28-39).

CHAPTER 5. DAVID MADE KING OVER ISRAEL; CAPTURES ZION

God's King Comes into His Own, 1-5. It was a magnificent occasion when all Israel came to Hebron to turn the kingdom of Saul over to David (cf. 1 Chr 12:23-40). The united nation was gripped by a tremendous enthusiasm after Ishbosheth's death. David's stirring coronation foreshadows that day when Israel's long-rejected King, the Messiah, son of David (Mt 1:1), returns in glory to be the Shepherd-King of Israel. The great feast of rejoicing mentioned in 1 Chr 12:39-40 offers a faint foregleam of Israel's joy when her true King is enthroned (cf. Isa 25:6-9).

David's Conquest of Zion and Other Victories, 6-25. The town of Jerusalem had been taken in the time of the judges (Jud 1:8), but not the stronghold of the Jebusites. This was the southeast hill, later called the city of David or Zion. Zion is closely connected with David's being made king over all Israel. Its capture was politically important because it rooted out the last vestige of Canaanite power in the land, and provided the kingdom with a neutral capital situated between Judah and Israel, but belonging to neither. Hiram I of Tyre (c. 969-936 B.C.) showed friendship to David, 11-12. He appears in Phoenician records both as a conqueror and builder. These ties of amity continued through Solomon's reign (1 Kgs 9:10-14). David's expanding family in Jerusalem is described, 13-16, as well as his two victories over the Philistines, 17-25.

ARCHAEOLOGICAL LIGHT

The eastern hill where the Jebusite fortress was located was practically impregnable (2 Sam 5:6). It was located above the Gihon spring. Some scholars still maintain David's men gained access through the water shaft which was dug by the Jebusites to get water inside the city (cf. 5:8, RSV). Early researches of the Palestine Exploration Fund under the direction of Sir Charles Warren yielded important discoveries concerning this Jebusite water system. W. F. Albright, however, maintains the wall was scaled by a grappling hook and that this is the meaning of the word (as shown by Aramaic and Arabic) instead of water shaft.

CHAPTER 6. THE ARK BROUGHT TO ZION

The Sin of Uzzah, 1-11. Since the Philistines had captured the ark and destroyed Shiloh, the ark had had no permanent resting place (1 Sam 4—7). The Levites alone were commissioned to transport (i.e., "touch") the ark (Num 4:15; 1 Chr 13:9). Uzzah's sin was an infraction of this divine regulation. David apparently failed to inquire of the Lord, transporting the ark in a Philistine expedient and not according to the divinely prescribed manner. Obed-edom, 10-11, was a Levite (1 Chr 26:1-5), and blessing upon his house encouraged David to bring the ark to Jerusalem.

The Ark Brought to David's City, 12-19. This was done in the Mosaically prescribed manner (1 Chr 15:1-28), and blessing followed.

Michal's Mockery, 20-23. She is called not "wife of the king" but "the daughter of Saul" and displayed the pride of her father, upon which the curse of God fell. David manifested singular humility and self-abasement in contrast.

CHAPTER 7. THE DAVIDIC COVENANT

David Desires to Build the Temple, 1-3. This worthy ambition to build the Lord a house furnished the revelation through Nathan the prophet that the Lord would build David a house.

The Davidic Covenant, 4-17 (cf. 1 Chr 17:4-15). This great covenant of kingship centering in Christ provided: (1) a Davidic "house," 11, or family through which Messiah would be born (Mt 1:1, 16; Lk 3:23); (2) a perpetual kingdom, 12, and a throne, 13. This regal covenant had only one condition—chastisement for disobedience in the kingly Davidic line. The covenant, however, was not to be abrogated, 15, but was to be "established forever," 16. It was renewed to Mary by the angel Gabriel (Lk 1:31-33; Acts

Cedars of Lebanon. (© *MPS*)

2:29-32; 15:14-17). Although since the Babylonian captivity only one King of the Davidic house has been crowned at Jerusalem, and He with thorns, He will yet be given the throne of His father David and sit on His own throne, as He now sits with the Father on His Father's throne (Rev 3:21). This throne will be millennial and merge into the everlasting kingdom of the eternal state (Rev 21:1-8).

David Worshiped, 18-19, in holy humility and awe.

CHAPTER 8. DAVID'S KINGDOM ESTABLISHED

David's Conquests, 1-14. The kingly covenant in ch. 7 is followed by the account of David's great conquests. These include victories over the Philistines and Moabites, 1-2; over Hadadezer of Zobah, 3-8; over the Edomites, 12-13, as well as diplomatic victory over Toi of Hamath, 9-11.

David's Reign, 15-18. His rule of justice and equity, 15, prefigures Messiah's administration of righteousness. David's sons were not priests but rulers (cf. 2 Sam 20:26; 1 Chr 18:17). The Cherethites and Pelethites were foreign mercenaries (2 Sam 15:18; 20:7, 23; 1 Kgs 1:38, 44), probably Cretans and Philistines.

CHAPTER 9. DAVID'S KINDNESS TO MEPHIBOSHETH

Mephibosheth Brought to David, 1-6. Lame in his feet (cf. 2 Sam 4:4), a helpless cripple who was carried into the king's presence, Mephibosheth is a beautiful illustration of the sinner made helpless and worthless by the Fall, but a candidate for God's grace, 3. Hearing what kindness was to be shown him, Mephibosheth confessed his shame and nothingness, calling himself a "dead dog" (cf. 1 Sam 24:14), less even than a live dog, little enough esteemed in those days.

David's Mercy to Mephibosheth, 7-13. David, for Jonathan's sake (cf. 1 Sam 18:1-4), lifted the poor cripple to a place at the king's table as one of the king's sons. Similarly the gospel of Christ lifts us out of our shame, constituting us sons and giving us an inheritance (Rom 8:16-17).

CHAPTERS 10—11. DAVID'S GREAT SIN

Prelude to the Sin, 10:1-19. The Ammonite-Aramaean War triggered by Hanun's insult to David, 1-5, furnished the background of David's sin. Mutilation of the beard, a badge of masculine honor, and enforced shameful exposure were heinous insults. This whole incident was the result of David's not seeking God's leading, and was a harbinger of his approaching fall.

The Terrible Sin Itself, 11:1-27. While Joab and the army were besieging Rabbah (modern *Amman), David committed adultery with Bathsheba, wife of one of his army officers, Uriah the Hittite, 1-5. Thereupon David sent for Uriah, 6-13, and when subterfuge failed to hide his sin, he had Uriah murdered, 14-25, and then took Bathsheba to wife, 26-27.

CHAPTER 12. DAVID'S CONFESSION

The Confession Elicited, 1-13. The Lord's rebuke came through the message of the prophet Nathan, 1-4, showing the king's hypocrisy and guilt, 5-6, and bringing the denunciation, "Thou art the man!" 7-9. The announced chastisement upon the Lord's disobedient servant, 10-12, brought a full confession, 13.

The Chastisement Begins, 14-31, in the death of the child and David's grief, 14-23. Solomon's birth, 24-25, and the capture of Rabbah, 26-31, were mercies mingled with disciplinary dealing. Sin in the Lord's servant always brings divine discipline (1 Cor 5:1-5; 11:30-32; Heb 12:3-11). The Lord's grace spared David physical death (13; cf. 1 Jn 5:16) but not severe chastening.

CHAPTERS 13—14. AMNON MURDERED BY ABSALOM

Amnon's Sin Against Tamar, 13:1-22. As the eldest son of David (2 Sam 3:2), Amnon was in line for the throne. Tamar was his half sister, and any union was forbidden by Mosaic law (Lev 18:9). Lust and lawlessness ruled, however, and Amnon violated Tamar, full sister of Absalom.

Absalom Murders Amnon and Flees, 23-29. Incest and violence in his own family were the beginning of David's chastisements for his own twin sin of adultery and murder. Absalom not only avenged the wrong done his sister, but doubtless knew he was removing the heir apparent to the throne at the same time, 23-36. He fled to Geshur (1 Sam 27:8), the country of his maternal grandfather (2 Sam 3:3). This was an Aramaean principality under David's control (2 Sam 8:3-8; 10:6-19).

Absalom's Recall by Joab's Craftiness, 14:1-33. Joab was powerful as well as subtle, and secured Absalom's return through the ruse of the woman of Tekoa, a town just S of Bethlehem, in the home country of David and Joab, 1-20. Absalom was partially forgiven, 21-24, and finally fully reinstated to the king's favor, 25-33.

CHAPTER 15. ABSALOM'S REVOLT

Absalom's Conspiracy, 1-12. By flattery and David's failure to establish a judiciary system, Absalom won the hearts of the Israelites, 1-6. It took him four years (Gr. and Syriac versions, not the "forty years" of the Heb.) to plan his uprising, 7. He probably chose Hebron, for he had discovered disaffection there over its loss of prestige when David moved the capital to Jerusalem, 8-12.

David Flees from Jerusalem, 13-27. David apparently decided that a showdown as to the loyalty of his professed followers would be better accomplished by this move and that his spies could operate better under this arrangement. The king left part of his harem, 16. He was accompanied by his servants, the Cherethites and Pelethites (see note on 2 Sam 8:18) and 600 Gittites, i.e., Gathites, Philistines from Gath, 18. The sad trek over Kidron, 23, the eastern extremity of the city, was made. The ark of the Lord was sent back to Jerusalem, 24-30, as well as Hushai the Archite, "David's friend," 37, i.e., royal counselor, an official title (1 Kgs 4:5).

CHAPTER 16. DAVID IN FLIGHT; ABSALOM IN JERUSALEM

David Meets Ziba and Shimei, 1-14. Strangely, David believed the wily falsehood of Ziba concerning Mephibosheth, 1-4, (cf. 19:24-30), but acted with wisdom and restraint in the case of the cursing Shimei, 5-14. The latter represented an element of disaffection in Israel over the loss of the ruling house, 8. Cf. 19:16-23 for the outcome.

Absalom Follows Ahithophel's Wicked Counsel, 15-23. Absalom's shameful public violation of his father's harem (royal property) was a crossing of the Rubicon in assuming the kingship (cf. 15:16; 1 Kgs 2:17-25).

CHAPTER 17. AHITHOPHEL AND HUSHAI

Ahithophel's Counsel vs. Hushai's, 1-26. Ahithophel's advice was to aim only at the life of David, 1-4, while Hushai advocated a prepared attack taking time, 5-13. The result was that Ahithophel's good counsel, which spelled David's death, was set aside by the Lord, who, though He was chastening His servant David, would not destroy him, 14, but rather Absalom. David was apprised of the decision, 15-22. Ahithophel committed suicide, 23. Absalom pitched his camp in Gilead, 24-26, and David crossed the Jordan.

David's Friends Minister to Him, 27-29. Shobi, brother of Hanun, of Rabbah ('Amman), Machir of Lodebar (cf. 9:4) and Barzillai, an Aramaean by name and likely a non-Israelite, succored David.

CHAPTER 18. ABSALOM'S DEATH

The Battle in the Woods of Ephraim, 1-8. Absalom's hastily recruited troops were no match for David's veteran army. David wisely kept out of the battle (cf. 12:28-29; also 21:17).

Absalom's Death, 9-18. His head not his hair (cf. 14:26) is said to have been caught in the oak, 9. The huge pile of stones cast over his body, 17, has no connection with the present-day Absalom's Tomb in the Kidron Valley, dating from late Hellenistic times. "No son," 18, must mean his three sons (14:27) had died.

David's Lament, 19-33. A touching scene of paternal love for a worthless son, who deserved all he got.

CHAPTER 19. DAVID RETURNS AS KING

Judah Calls David Back as King, 1-15. Joab jolted David out of his excessive grief, 1-8. Movement in all Israel to call David back,

9-10, was followed by the king's successful overtures for Judah's initiative in the matter, 11-15.

Shimei, Mephibosheth and Barzillai, 16-40. David showed mercy to Shimei, 16-23. Mephibosheth's genuine joy, 24-30, at David's return was proof enough of Ziba's treachery. Yet David divided Mephibosheth's inheritance with Ziba, 29. Barzillai's parting with David is beautiful, 31-39. Chimham was no doubt Barzillai's son (cf. 1 Kgs 2:7).

Antagonism Between Judah and Israel, 41-43, again broke out. This deep cleavage was to come to the fore in the final disruption after Solomon's death (1 Kgs 12:16-20).

CHAPTER 20. SHEBA REVOLTS; JOAB MURDERS AMASA

Joab Regains His Position, 1-22. Sheba from the most disaffected tribe of Benjamin (16:5, 8) organized a final revolt. Israel sided with him (cf. 19:41-43). Amasa, having succeeded Joab as head commander of the army (19:13), incurred the latter's implacable jealousy. His failure to subdue the revolt was a further reason for Joab's murdering him (1 Kgs 2:31-32). Joab again proved his cruel thoroughness by hunting down the rebel and using the woman of Abel of Bethmaachah to accomplish Sheba's death. A mother city, 19, is one with dependent villages or "daughters" (Num 21:25; Josh 15:45; Jud 11:26).

A List of David's Officials, 23-26. (Cf. a similar list in 8:16-18.) On Cherethites and Pelethites, 23, see note on 8:15-18.

CHAPTER 21. FAMINE AND PHILISTINE WARS

The last four chapters of 2 Samuel are an appendix.

The Famine and the Gibeonites, 1-14. A three-year severe famine is traced to bloodguiltiness upon the land for Saul's murder of the Gibeonites, who were under a covenant of protection (Josh 9:25-27) in the Lord's name, which Saul had violated. David inquired of the Gibeonites, instead of the Lord, and in acquiescing to their demand further erred in breaking the law that children were not to be executed for their father's sins (Deut 24:16). The terrible scene of 7-9 was the result, with Rizpah's wild grief, 10-11, which was followed by the public interment of the bones of Saul and Jonathan in the ancient tomb in Zelah, 12-14.

Memoirs of the Philistine Wars, 15-22. (Cf. 1 Sam 17:4; 1 Chr 20:5.)

CHAPTER 22. DAVID'S GREAT PROPHETIC PSALM

Praise to the Lord for His Intervention, 1-28. This great ode of deliverance was placed here and also as Psalm 18 in the Psalter. It is prophetic and looks beyond the sufferings and triumphs of David to David's son and Lord, Jesus Christ. The occasion of praise, 1-4, is followed by David's sufferings as a fugitive from Saul, 5-7, presaging Christ's rejection. God's intervention, 8-20, reflects our Lord's deliverance from death "into a large place," 20. The divine approval and reward, 21-28, go far beyond the earthly David to the heavenly.

Praise to the Lord for Exaltation Over Foes, 29-51. The judgment of enemies, 29-43, and exaltation over adversaries, 44-49, will be realized only by Him into whose hands is committed all judgment (Jn 5:22). In coming kingdom glory "He will be head of the nations," 44, and in fulfillment of the Davidic covenant (ch. 7) verses 44-51 will become a reality.

CHAPTER 23. DAVID'S LAST WORDS; HIS HEROES

His Last Words, 1-7. This inspired prophecy, 1-2, celebrated again the theme of the perpetuity of the house (dynasty) of David, 5, to be realized in the righteous rule of David's Lord in the kingdom, fulfilling the royal covenant (see ch. 7). Verses 3 and 4 picture the clear morning of the Kingdom Age.

Roster of David's Heroes, 8-39. Cf. 2 Sam 21:15-22 and 1 Chr 11:11-47 for interesting points of variation in the lists.

CHAPTER 24. DAVID'S FAILURE IN THE CENSUS

The Sin and Its Punishment, 1-17. The Lord allowed Satan to move in David's heart (1 Chr 21:1) through pride (1 Tim 3:6), 1-9. David's confession, 10-14, was followed by the plague, 15-17.

The Altar and Atonement, 18-25. Araunah's threshing floor, where Abraham had offered Isaac and where the temple was to be set, was a fitting spot for mercy upon Israel.

1 KINGS

SOLOMON'S REIGN AND THE DIVIDED KINGDOM

Name and Purpose: 1 and 2 Kings are called the third and fourth books of Kingdoms in the Greek version and the third and fourth books of Kings in the Latin. Originally one book, they catalog the history of the undivided kingdom from David's death through Solomon's and Rehoboam's reigns and the divided kingdom till Israel's fall in 722 B.C. and Judah's captivity in 586 B.C.

Author: The author (or authors) was inspired to write these narratives from sources at his disposal. The result under the Holy Spirit's guidance is a historically reliable account. Although only conjecture, Jeremiah may have written all but the last chapter of Kings.

Outline
David's Decease, 1:1—2:11
Solomon's Reign, 2:12—11:43
The Kingdom Divided, 12:1—16:34
Elijah's Ministry, 17:1—22:53

CHAPTERS 1—2. DAVID'S DECEASE

Adonijah's Bid to Be King, 1:1-27. David's premature physical decline, 1-2, due to his great sin and chastenings, gave Adonijah, David's oldest living son, a chance to assert his claim of primogeniture, 5-9. Abishag, 3, was from Shunem (1 Sam 28:4) near Mt. Gilboa in the Esdraelon plain. Nathan and Bathsheba's plot, 10-14, succeeded in David's proclaiming Solomon king, 15-27.

Solomon Crowned, 28-53. Gihon, 33, now Mary's Spring (2 Chr 32:30), like En-rogel, Job's Well, 9, was a sacred place suitable for affairs of this type (2 Sam 17:17). Solomon's anointing, 28-40, resulted in Adonijah's fear and submission, 41-53.

David's Charge and Death, 2:1-11. He charged Solomon to follow the law of Moses (cf. Deut 4:40; 5:1; 11:1—12:32; 17:14-20). Elimination of Joab (2 Sam 3:27; 20:10) and Shimei (2 Sam 16:5-14; 19:18-23) was ordered.

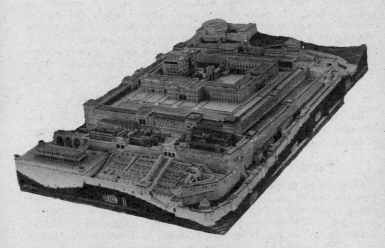

Shick's model of Solomon's Temple. (© *MPS*)

Solomon Eliminates His Enemies, 12-46. Benaiah was appointed leader of the army and Zadok priest in Abiathar's place, 35; Shimei was put to death.

CHAPTER 3. SOLOMON'S PRAYER FOR WISDOM

Solomon Marries an Egyptian Princess, 1-3. She was a daughter undoubtedly of one of the pharaohs of the Twenty-first Dynasty, since Sheshonk (Shishak), founder of the Twenty-second Dynasty, did all in his power to weaken Solomon.

Solomon Prays for Wisdom, 4-28. His reign began in wisdom and ended in folly. The "high places" were hilltop shrines. Gibeon (cf. Josh 9) was one of the most famous of these shrines (2 Chr 1:2-6). Worship at such places in itself was not evil (Gen 12:7; 22:2-4; 31:54; Jud 6:25), but was in conflict with the anticipatory provisions of Deuteronomy after the temple was established on Moriah (Deut 12:11-14).

CHAPTER 4. SOLOMON'S GOVERNMENT

His Administration, 1-34. Solomon's high officials are listed, 1-6. His new administration ignored the old tribal divisions. The system of taxation supported the king's grand style of living.

CHAPTERS 5—8. SOLOMON'S TEMPLE

Preparations to Build, 5:1-18. Hiram I of Tyre (c. 969-936 B.C.) bore the title of "King of the Sidonians." His was a common Phoenician royal name as attested by the inscriptions, such as the sarcophagus of Ahiram at Byblos, biblical Gebal, discovered in 1923-24.

Description of the Temple, 6:1—8:66. The temple was begun, 6:1, in Ziv (April-May) about 962 B.C. The specifications, pre-Greek and authentic for the 10th cen. B.C., displayed Phoenician influence, as a temple at Tell Tainat discovered in 1936 shows. Besides the temple, Solomon built his palace and administrative complexes, 7:1-51. Jachin and Boaz, 7:21, were huge incense stands with oil bowls at the top, which served to illuminate the facade of the temple.

CHAPTER 9. SOLOMON'S SECOND VISION AND SPLENDOR

Solomon's Warning Against Apostasy, 1-9. He was admonished in a second vision.

Solomon's Splendor, 10-28. His foreign diplomacy and intermarriage designed to produce peaceful neighbors are described (3:1-3;

11:1-8). His building operations at Gezer, Hazor and Megiddo are known, especially at the latter, which was the headquarters of Solomon's fifth administrative district. His stables, housing at least 450 horses and about 150 chariots, have been excavated at Megiddo. His navy, 26-28, was a refinery fleet which brought smelted copper from the colonial mines of the Phoenicians in Sardinia and Spain, Tarshish denoting a copper-refining port. Excavation of the copper refinery at Tell el-Kheleifeh (ancient Ezion-geber) disclosed Solomon's copper-smelting station on the Gulf of Aqabah.

Remains of Solomon's stables at Megiddo. Some hitching posts and mangers are still in place. (*Courtesy ORINST*)

CHAPTER 10. SOLOMON AND THE QUEEN OF SHEBA

The Queen's Visit, 1-13. Sheba is probably Saba in SW Arabia, modern Yemen, mentioned in cuneiform sources from the 8th and 7th cen. B.C. Although queens played little part in the later history of S. Arabia, they ruled large tribal confederacies in N. Arabia from the 9th to the 7th cen. B.C. Some identify this queen with a colony of Sheba in N. Arabia.

Solomon's Revenues, 14-29. His great wealth, 14-15; his famous targets and shields, 16-17; his ivory throne, 18-20, his opulence in gold and silver, 21-22; and his horse and chariot trade, 27-29, are mentioned. The horse and chariot trade was one of the sources of Solomon's vast wealth. His annual income amounted to 666 talents of gold (1 Kgs 10:14), a talent of gold equaling about $30,000. He imported horses from Kue (Cilicia) and Egypt, acting as middleman in the horse and chariot trade between Egypt and Asia Minor. At the same time he built up his army of chariotry.

CHAPTER 11. SOLOMON'S FAILURE

Solomon's Sin and Chastisement, 1-43. His sin was apostasy and idolatry because of his numerous pagan marriages for the purpose of carnal security, 1-13. Raised up by God to chastise him were Hadad the Edomite, 14-22; Rezon, founder of the Aramaean kingdom of Damascus, 23-25; and Jeroboam, who later became head of the northern kingdom, 26-40. At his death, Solomon was succeeded by his son Rehoboam, 41-43.

CHAPTER 12. REHOBOAM AND THE REVOLT

The Secession of the Northern Tribes, 1-24. The folly of Rehoboam is almost unimaginable. But sin makes fools of its victims. The harm of this division of the Lord's covenant people was never healed.

Jeroboam's Evil Plans, 25-33. He built two shrines to the Lord, one at Bethel in the S part of his country, a bare dozen miles N of Jerusalem, and the other at Dan in the north, both ancient cultic centers. His two bull calves of gold were scarcely representations of Jehovah as a bull-god, but like Israel's pagan neighbors, the deity was represented as standing on the back of an animal or on a throne borne by animals. The Lord was to be thought of as invisibly enthroned above the animal (cf. 1 Sam 4:4; 2 Kgs 19:15). The bull affiliations of Baal made this purely political plan dangerous and wicked.

CHAPTERS 13—14. JEROBOAM'S AND REHOBOAM'S REIGNS

God Sends a Prophet to Condemn Jeroboam's Plan, 13:1-34. The remarkable prophecy, 1-3, uttered by an unknown prophet, that Josiah would burn the bones of the priests on Jeroboam's false altar was fulfilled in 621 B.C. (2 Kgs 23:16-17). It served as a stinging rebuke to Jeroboam and his household, and incurred his subsequent vengeful displeasure, 4. The prophet resisted the king's attempts to get him to compromise his directive from God, 5-10. But what the king could not do in dissuading the man of God from doing God's will an old prophet from Bethel accomplished by lying and deceit, 11-22. Disobedience brought immediate judgment on the prophet,

24, and bitter remorse to the one who had been used to tempt the Lord's messenger, 29-32. Jeroboam's impenitence sealed his doom, 33-34.

Jeroboam's Punishment, 14:1-20. God's disciplining hand of judgment fell on the king's son, his most precious possession. The boy's sickness led to a deceptive scheme to ascertain the future from Ahijah the prophet, 2-6. Ahijah learned of the plot and told the wife of Jeroboam that the king's house would be utterly destroyed because of adulterous disobedience and Israel would be sent into captivity, 7-16. The child died as the prophet foretold, 17-18.

Rehoboam's Reign Over Judah, 14:21-31. This son of Solomon was a fool, driving the ten tribes to secede, and showing his folly in his 17-year reign, which catapulted Judah from the glory it had enjoyed.

ARCHAEOLOGICAL LIGHT

In Rehoboam's fifth year Shishak (cf. 2 Chr 12:2-4) invaded Judah, and Israel as well. Archaeology shows Shishak is Sheshonk I of Egypt (*c.* 945-924 B.C.), founder of the Twenty-second Dynasty, whose gold-masked body was discovered at Tanis in 1938-39. His triumphal Karnak (Thebes) inscription lists towns taken in Judah as well as in Israel and Gilead. Part of his stele was excavated at Megiddo, showing that he actually took this city, as the Karnak relief shows.

Dynasties of Israel: Nine dynasties with 19 kings. Total reign 201 years, with average reign slightly over 10 years. All these kings were bad, with Ahab and his queen the worst.

Dynasty of Judah: 20 kings, but only one dynasty, the Davidic, except Athaliah, the usurper, who invaded the Davidic line by marriage and interrupted it for five years. Total reigns 335 years, with 16 average years per reign. The good kings included Asa, Jehoshaphat, Amaziah, Uzziah, Jotham, Hezekiah, Josiah.

15:1-24. ABIJAM'S AND ASA'S REIGNS

Abijam, 1-8, or Abijah (cf. 2 Chr 13:1-12), had an unworthy reign of three years.

Asa's Rule, 9-24. He was a good king (*c.* 911-870 B.C.), who bribed Benhadad I of Syria to attack Israel to relieve him of Baasha's fortification of Ramah, a southern frontier fortress threatening Jerusalem's security. Asa cleansed the land of idolatry—pagan pillars, sun images, asherim and male cult prostitutes.

A relief of Pharaoh Shishak I, from the wall of the Temple of Karnak, depicting conquered Palestinian towns (I Kings 14:25-30). (© MPS)

ARCHAEOLOGICAL LIGHT

"Benhadad son of Tabrimmon, the son of Hezion, king of Aram [Damascus]," 18, is attested on the inscribed stele of Benhadad I discovered in N. Syria in 1940 (cf. *Bulletin of the American Schools* 87, October, 1942, pp. 23-29, 90; April, 1943, pp. 32-34).

15:25—16:28. KINGS OF ISRAEL: BAASHA TO OMRI

Nadab's Reign over Israel, 15:25-31. His was a short-lived, unworthy rule of two years.

Baasha, 15:32—16:7, warred with Asa and was cursed because of his idolatry and sin. He was buried in Tirzah, royal capital of Israel before Samaria was founded by Omri.

Elah, 8-14, was a drunkard. He reigned only two years.

Zimri, 15-20, was burned to death in his own house after a seven-day reign.

Tibni and Omri, 21-28. After the tragic death of Zimri, the people were divided, half following Tibni and half Omri. At the death of Tibni, Omri reigned over the entire nation. He was industrious, capable, energetic, founding the Omride dynasty (Ahab, Ahaziah and Joram). He built the new capital of Samaria, 24.

ARCHAEOLOGICAL LIGHT

Omri's reign (*c.* 880-874 B.C.) ushered in a new era of Israelite power. He was an astute politician, cementing ties with Phoenicia to offset Aramaean commercial monopoly. The result was the marriage of his son to Jezebel, daughter of Ethbaal, king of the Sidonians (18:18). The Moabite Stone from Dibon discloses that it was Omri who conquered N. Moab. Omri's brilliant capital, Samaria, has been excavated. Periods 1 and 2 belong to Omri and Ahab. The foundations of his palace and other evidences attest he was the founder of the city (cf. *The Harvard Excavations at Samaria 1908-10*, 2 vols., 1924, and *The Buildings at Samaria*, 1942).

Omri's fame in the world of his day is attested by the Assyrians' reference to him on the Black Obelisk of Shalmaneser III over a century later in connection with King Jehu of Israel, who is styled "son of [i.e., royal successor of] Omri," although Jehu belonged to an entirely different dynasty. After Omri, Israel moreover is styled *Bit-Humri* ("house of Omri") in Assyrian cuneiform texts.

CHRONOLOGY OF THE DUAL KINGDOM*

	Israel		Judah	
1 {	Jeroboam	931-910	Rehoboam	931-913
	Nadab	910-909	Abijam (Abijah)	913-911
2 {	Baasha	909-886	Asa	911-870
	Elah	886-885		
3	Zimri	885		
	Tibni	c. 885-880		
⌈	Omri	880-874		
4	Ahab	874-853	Jehoshaphat	873-848†
	Ahaziah	853-852	Jehoram (Joram)	853-841†
⌊	Joram (Jehoram)	852-841	Ahaziah (Azariah, Jehoahaz)	841
	Jehu	841-814	Athaliah	841-835
	Jehoahaz	814-798	Joash (Jehoash)	835-796
5 {	Joash (Jehoash)	798-782	Amaziah	796-767
	Jeroboam II	782-753	Uzziah (Azariah)	791-740†
⌊	Zachariah	753/752	Jotham	750-736†
6	Shallum	752		
7 {	Menahem	752-742		
	Pekahiah	742-740		

Israel		Judah	
8 Pekah	740-732	Ahaz	736-716
9 Hoshea	732-722		
Fall of Samaria	722		
		Hezekiah	716-687†
		Manasseh	696-642†
		Amon	642-640
		Josiah	640-608
		Jehoahaz (Shallum) ...	608
		Jehoiakim	608-597
		Jehoiachin (Coniah, Jeconiah) ..	597
		Zedekiah	597-586
		Fall of Jerusalem	586

* This chronology is that of Edwin R. Thiele in *The Mysterious Numbers of the Hebrew Kings*. W. F. Albright in the *Bulletin of the American Schools of Oriental Research #100* places the division of the kingdom at 922 B.C. and follows a slightly different system.
† Overlapping coregencies account for the seeming discrepancies.

219

16:29-34. AHAB, KING OF ISRAEL

Ahab, 29-34, was acute, sagacious, but wicked and idolatrous. Ahab reigned 22 years at Samaria, the new capital of the Omride dynasty. He outstripped his predecessors in wickedness and shrewdness, erecting an altar to Baal, the great NW Semitic fertility god, in the Baal temple which he dared to build in Samaria, 32. He also made an Asherah, 33, a wooden pole symbolic of the Canaanite fertility goddess Asherah, known from the Ugaritic tablets discovered at Ras Shamra in N. Syria, 1929-37. This Canaanite goddess, mentioned some 40 times in the OT, was a snare to the Israelites, for her cult was viciously depraved. Ahab married Jezebel, a pagan princess and daughter of Ethbaal, "king of the Sidonians," 31, i.e., of the Phoenicians. This title reflects the earlier supremacy of Sidon following Tyre's assumption of commercial and political importance after the 11th cen. B.C. (cf. 1 Kgs 5:1, 5). On 34 cf. Josh 6:26. A detailed account of Ahab's reign is given in 17:1 — 22:40 because of the tremendous religious crisis it precipitated in Israel.

ARCHAEOLOGICAL LIGHT

The Ugaritic texts from Ras Shamra (Ugarit), dating from the 14th cen. B.C., show Baal as the son of El, and the reigning king of the Canaanite pantheon, the god of the rain and the storm, whose voice thundered in the tempest. At Ugarit, Baal's consort was his sister Anath, but at Samaria in the 9th cen. B.C. Asherah appears as such (18:19, RSV). Like Anath, she was the patroness of sex and war. Snake worship, both male and female prostitution, child murder and sacrifice, and every conceivable vice were associated with Canaanite religion. Priests and prophets of Baal were official murderers of little children, and hence deserved death themselves (18:40).

The rebuilding of Jericho (16:34) is confirmed by archaeological diggings. Recent excavations trace the city's occupation from dim antiquity. Despite confusion in interpreting the evidence of Garstang's excavations of the fall of the city around 1400 B.C., the Bible stands confirmed on this point, with no occupational levels from Joshua's time to Ahab's era, when small ruins from the century point to Hiel's rebuilding the site.

CHAPTER 17. ELIJAH BEFORE AHAB

Elijah's Message to Ahab, 1-7. Baal, the Phoenician storm god, was held by Ahab, Jezebel and his other devotees to control the rain. Elijah ("my God is the Lord") abruptly announced to Ahab that Jehovah would be proved to be the one who does so. Elijah,

Samaria from the Shechem Road. (© *MPS*)

of the town of Tishbe in Gilead, disappeared, directed by the Lord to a small stream E of the Jordan.

Elijah and the Widow, 8-24. After the brook dried up, Elijah was guided to the widow of Sarepta (i.e., Zarephath, 9, on the Phoenician coast, S of Sidon, N of Tyre) out of Ahab's jurisdiction. Here the God-chosen destroyer of Baalism, whose God had power to shut the heavens for three and a half years, was miraculously fed by the ravens and then by the widow (cf. Jas 5:17). The widow's son was restored to life, 17-24. Unselfish devotion to God brings blessings of the choicest variety.

CHAPTER 18. ELIJAH ON CARMEL

The Question, 1-19. The terrible three-and-one-half-year drought was about to end. Who withheld and would send the rain? "Baal of the heavens" or the Lord? Obadiah ("servant of the Lord") showed his faith by saving the prophets of Jehovah whom Jezebel had designed for death, 3-16. Elijah met Ahab and called for the contest on Carmel, 17-19. The Baals were the local representatives of the great sky-god, 19 (RSV). Asherah, Baal's consort, had 400

The slope of Mount Carmel with the city of Haifa below.
(*Courtesy IIS*)

prophets and Baal 450, demonstrating the tremendous gain of Canaanite paganism under Ahab.

The Contest, 20-46. Elijah's faith was superb. He staked everything on Jehovah's answering by fire and rain, and both came. Jezebel, the wicked Phoenician queen, was unpersuaded and sought only to kill Elijah. Elijah uttered a masterful satire on idolatry, 27. Ritualistic gashing of the body, 28, was common (Deut 14:1; Lev 19:28; Jer 16:6; Hos 7:14, RSV). The struggle proved Jehovah's power. Elijah ran 17 miles to Jezreel, 46, Ahab's secondary capital (21:1), to herald complete victory of the worship of Jehovah over Baalism (cf. Isa 40:30-31).

CHAPTER 19. ELIJAH AT HOREB

Elijah's Flight and Despondency, 1-14. Here he demonstrated himself a man of like passions with us (Jas 5:17) by fleeing from the wrath of Jezebel to Beersheba, 130 miles S of Jezreel, well into the territory of Judah and out of Jezebel's jurisdiction, 1-3. By divine assistance he reached Horeb, 4-8, also called Sinai, some 200 miles farther S, where the law had been revealed to Moses. There God also spoke to the distraught prophet, 9-18 (cf. Ex 33:17-23), rebuking him for being where he should not have been, 9,13. What a contrast! Elijah the hero of faith on Carmel victorious over Baalism! Elijah the coward of unbelief at Horeb, self-occupied, utterly discouraged, wishing to die (cf. Rom 11:2-4), praying *against* rather than *for* God's people!

The Lord's Message, 15-21. The Lord was not in the earthquake, wind or fire but in the "still small voice" of His revealed will, which probed the prophet's failure and directed him to wind up his ministry.

CHAPTER 20. AHAB'S WARS WITH DAMASCUS

The Siege of Samaria, 1-34. The long-threatened attack from Syria came about five years before the end of Ahab's reign. Benhadad suddenly besieged Samaria with a coalition of kings. Ahab's brilliant strategy won this battle and a later more decisive battle at Aphek, 22-34, E of the Sea of Galilee on the Bethshan-Damascus road.

The Prophet's Warning, 35-43, was focused upon Ahab's foolish release of his enemy (with whom he later allied himself to fight an advancing Assyria).

ARCHAEOLOGICAL LIGHT

The Monolith Inscription of Shalmaneser III (859-824 B.C.), now in the British Museum, records Assyria's clash with a Syrian-Palestinian coalition at Qarqar, N of Hamath in the Orontes Valley, in 853 B.C. "I crossed the Euphrates; at Qarqar I destroyed 1,200 chariots, 1,200 horsemen, and 20,000 men of Benhadad, and 2,000 chariots and 10,000 men of Ahab, the Israelite. . . . "

CHAPTER 21. AHAB AND NABOTH'S VINEYARD

Ahab Murders Naboth, 1-16. Naboth was religiously and legally right in keeping his ancestral property (cf. Lev 25:10-17, 23-24, 34). Ahab realized this. However, his wicked covetousness overpowered him. Jezebel scorned Israelite religious regulations, 5-7, and devised a diabolical plan to murder Naboth and take his vineyard, 8-14. Ahab was led to ruin by a wicked wife, 15-16.

Elijah's Pronouncement of Judgment, 17-29. The dogs licked Ahab's blood at the place he had Naboth murdered, 19 (cf. 22:38), and dogs devoured Jezebel's body by the wall at Jezreel (2 Kgs 9:30-37).

CHAPTER 22. AHAB'S DEATH

Ahab and Jehoshaphat Go up to Ramoth Gilead, 1-28. They disregarded Micaiah's prophecy and listened to the demon-inspired fake prophets.

Ahab's Death, 29-40.

Jehoshaphat and Ahaziah, 41-53. Cf. 2 Chr 17—20 and 2 Kgs 1:1-18.

2 KINGS

THE KINGDOM TO THE EXILES
1 AND 2 KINGS IN CONTRAST

1 Kings	2 Kings
Begins with King David	Ends with the king of Babylon
Opens with Solomon's glory	Closes with Jehoiachin's shame
Begins with the blessings of obedience	Ends with the curse of disobedience
Opens with the building of the temple	Closes with the burning of the temple
Traces the progress of apostasy	Describes the consequences of apostasy
How kings failed to rule God's people	Consequences of that failure
Prophet Elijah introduced	Prophet Elisha presented
The long-suffering of the Lord	The Lord's sure punishment of sin

> **Outline**
> Elijah's Final Ministry, 1:1 — 2:11
> Elisha's Ministry, 2:12 — 9:10
> From Jehu to Samaria's Fall in 722 B.C., 9:11—17:41
> Judah from 722 B.C. to the Exile, 18:1—25:30

Ministries of the Prophets. During this period Hosea and Amos prophesied in Israel. Joel, Micah, Isaiah, Obadiah, Nahum, Habakkuk, Zephaniah and Jeremiah prophesied in Judah.

Period Covered. About the middle of the 9th to nearly the middle of the 6th cen. B.C.

CHAPTER 1. ELIJAH AND AHAZIAH

Ahaziah's Sickness and Death, 1-18. Coregent with his father, a Baal devotee, Ahaziah preferred Baal to the Lord. Baal-zebub ("lord of flies") was a manifestation of the great Canaanite Baal, as worshiped at Philistine Ekron. It was an intentional distortion of

Baal-zebul ("lord of the divine abode"), the epithet later being associated with Satan in Jewish theology (Mt 10:25; 12:24; Mk 3:22; Lk 11:15-19). Elijah's appearance, 3-8; the fate of Ahaziah's messengers, 9-15; and Elijah's word of doom to the Baal-worshiping king for consulting the pagan priests of the Philistines rather than the God of Israel, 16, are recorded.

Jehoram's Accession, 17-18. This last king of the Omride dynasty must not be confused with Jehoram, the son of Jehoshaphat, king of Judah (8:16-18, 25-27).

CHAPTER 2. ELISHA AND THE TRANSLATION OF ELIJAH

Translation of Elijah, 1-11. The prophet of fire (1 Kgs 18:38; 2 Kgs 1:10, 12) was translated to heaven by a "chariot of fire and horses of fire," 11-12. Enoch (Gen 5:24; Heb 11:5) and Elijah (Mt 17:3-4) were the only two men ever to be translated without dying. This Gilgal, 1, was N of Bethel. The term "the sons of the prophets," 3, 5, 7, 15, means members of the prophetic order, and has nothing to do with physical sonship. Similarly, "father" was an ancient title of a man of God, 12. A "double portion of thy spirit," 9, indicates a double share of God's Spirit that had operated through Elijah. This request was granted as Elijah's mantle fell on Elisha, 12-15.

Double Portion upon Elisha, 12-25. The waters of the Jordan were divided, 14. The spring at Jericho was healed, 22. The idolatrous lads at Bethel were killed by bears, 24, which God sent to punish the taunting of Elisha's God, not Elisha. Today the name of Elisha is attached to the finest spring in Jericho, Elisha's Fountain.

CHAPTER 3. ELISHA AND JEHORAM

Revolt of Moab, 1-20. In Jehoram's (Joram's) reign (852-841 B.C.) Moab revolted and refused to pay tribute in lambs and wool, 1-8. The famous Moabite Stone, a Louvre treasure, discovered in 1868, gives a remarkable account of the war from the viewpoint of the Moabite king Mesha. Jehoram's plan required Judah's aid and that of its vassal Edom (1 Kgs 22:47), as the plan was to attack Moab from the rear. Elisha, "who poured water on the hands of Elijah" when he washed, 11, denoting that he waited on him like a servant, prophesied a divine supply of water and victory of the coalition over Moab, 10-20.

Defeat of Moab, 21-27. The dry stream bed, 16, likely the brook of Zered (Deut 2:13), separating Edom from Moab, filled with pools and reflecting the rising sun and the red sandstone of Edom (Gen

25:30), was taken for blood. Mesha's sacrifice of his eldest son to Chemosh on the wall in plain sight of Israel, 26-27, filled the attackers with such horror that they returned to their own land without exploiting to the full their victory. This again was unbelief on their part. Human sacrifice was outlawed in Israel (Ex 22:29-30; 34:20; Deut 18:10), but was wickedly resorted to at times (2 Kgs 16:3; 21:6).

ARCHAEOLOGICAL LIGHT

The Moabite Stone, set up by King Mesha of Moab at Dibon, N of the Arnon, about 840 B.C., discloses the prominence of Chemosh, the national god of Moab. "I am Mesha, son of Chemosh . . . king of Moab, the Dibonite. . . . Omri, king of Israel . . . oppressed Moab many days because Chemosh was angry with his land. And his son succeeded him, and he said, I will oppress Moab. . . . "

CHAPTER 4. FOUR MIRACLES OF ELISHA

The Widow's Oil Increased, 1-7. The section 4:1—8:6 breaks the synchronized story of the reigns of Judahite and Israelite kings and constitutes an interlude dealing with Elisha's miracle-working ministry. In Israel a child could be sold into servitude for debt (Ex 21:7; Deut 15:12-18; Lev 25:9-34; cf. Jer 34:8-16; cf. Elijah's miracle, 1 Kgs 17:14-16).

The Shunammite Woman's Son Raised from Death, 8-37. The woman lived in Shunem, about five miles N of Jezreel. Not only did she conceive a son late in life, according to God's word through Elisha, 8-17, but the lad was raised from death, 18-37. (Cf. Elijah's parallel miracle, 1 Kgs 17:17-24. Cf. also Heb 11:35.)

The Poisonous Stew Healed, 38-41. The meal, cast into the stew to counteract the poisonous wild gourds, portrays God's power to remove evil. Through our faith He is able to remove the evil in us.

Bread Multiplied, 42-44, finds its striking parallel in our Lord's ministry (Mt 14:13-21; 15:32-38).

CHAPTER 5. ELISHA AND NAAMAN

Naaman's Healing, 1-19. Naaman ("pleasant") is a picture of the natural man, enjoying the highest and best but unregenerate. "But he was a leper," 1, leprosy vividly illustrating sin. The testimony of the captive Israelite maid was effective and Naaman went to the king of Israel for healing with "ten talents of silver and six thousand shekels of gold," probably $75,000 or more, 2-7. Naaman appears as a proud man, hurt by Elisha's curt directions to wash seven times in muddy Jordan, 8-12. His compliance is parallel to the proud sinner who accepts God's self-humbling way of salvation by grace and is cleansed of sin, 13-14, and saved, 15-19. Naaman's desire to take home "two mules' burden of earth" from Israel, 17, was due to his wrong idea that a god could not be worshiped apart from his own land. His official position required him to give lip service to Rimmon, the chief god of Syria, called also Hadad, but Naaman was really healed and saved. (Cf. Lk 4:25-27.)

Gehazi's Sin and Punishment, 20-27. Covetousness earned Gehazi the leprosy from which grace had delivered the Syrian Gentile. The greater than Elisha's salvation has been accepted by the Gentiles, while those so closely connected with the Saviour (Israel) have hardened their hearts (Rom 11:1-25).

CHAPTERS 6—7. ELISHA AND OTHER MIRACLES

The Floatng Ax Head, 6:1-7. Elisha recovered the iron ax head.

The Syrian Army Blinded and Captured, 6:8-23, by Elisha's prayers. Dothan, some ten miles N of Samaria, is being excavated by J. P. Free of Wheaton College.

Repulse of the Syrian Siege of Samaria, 6:24—7:20, by Elisha's prophecy was fulfilled by the Lord's intervention.

CHAPTER 8. ELISHA AND HAZAEL

Elisha Again Aids the Woman of Shunem, 1-6. Her story is continued from 4:8-37. Elisha predicted famine, 1-2, and sent her into Philistia (cf. Gen 26:1), where Isaac too had gone for the same reason. Elisha's influence restored her homestead in Shunem.

Elisha's Prediction of Benhadad's Death and Hazael's Usurpation, 7-15. Hazael was divinely chosen to punish Israel for her sins, so Elisha wept, 11. Hazael became king of Syria as predicted (cf. 1 Kgs 19:15-16; Hos 13:16).

ARCHAEOLOGICAL LIGHT

Benhadad I's long and energetic reign ended in 842 B.C. By 841 Hazael had usurped the throne. On a pavement slab from Nimrud (Calah) is Shalmaneser's record of his attack upon Hazael (*Haza'ilu*) of Damascus. Another text from Asshur reads: "Adadidri forsook his land, Hazael, son of nobody, seized the throne."

Jehoram's and Ahaziah's Reigns in Judah, 16-29. Athaliah was Jehoram's wife. The "lamp" (RSV) was symbolic of the permanence of the Davidic dynasty, 19 (cf. 2 Sam 21:17; 1 Kgs 11:36; 15:4).

Jehoram (Joram) was followed by his son Ahaziah, whose mother was Athaliah. Jehoram reigned 853-841, Ahaziah in 841 B.C.

CHAPTERS 9—10.   JEHU'S REIGN

Elisha Has Jehu Anointed, 9:1-37. Jehu had a long reign, c. 841-814 B.C. He was anointed (cf. 1 Kgs 19:15-16) as the rough instrument for the bloody task of exterminating the house of Ahab and Baalism. The latter was so unspeakably and viciously cruel that a person of Jehu's relentless thoroughness was necessary. Joram, Ahaziah and Jezebel were liquidated. Zimri, 31, was a brutal murderer (1 Kgs 16:8-12).

Jehu's Purge Continued, 10:1-36. By cleverness and ruthlessness Jehu wiped out the entire house of Ahab, "seventy sons," 1, no doubt including grandsons, as well as the worshipers of Baal, 1-11. Jehonadab, the Rechabite, 15-17, joined the purge. The Rechabites were a simple-living people who strictly maintained the desert way of life, avoiding the corruption of urban living (1 Chr 2:55; Jer 35). Jehu in his extermination of the priests and worshipers of Baal, 18-27, was similar to Elijah in zeal but a contrast to him in subtlety. Hazael's cruel career begins, 32-33.

ARCHAEOLOGICAL LIGHT

Like Hazael (see ch. 8), Jehu was a usurper. The Black Obelisk of Shalmaneser III, which Austen Layard found in the palace at Nimrud, shows Jehu actually kneeling before the Assyrian emperor. Following the prostrate king come Israelites bearing gifts. The inscription reads: "Tribute of *Iaua* (Jehu), son of Omri. Silver, gold, a golden bowl, a golden beaker, golden goblets, pitchers of gold, lead, staves for the bed of the king, javelins I received from him."

CHAPTER 11.   ATHALIAH'S REIGN IN JUDAH

Athaliah's Usurpation and Death, 1-16. Ironically Jehu's attempted eradication of the house of Ahab in Israel resulted in the temporary seizure of the throne of Judah by one who was not only a member of Ahab's family but a Baal devotee, 18. Jehosheba who saved Joash, the son of Ahaziah, was not Athaliah's daughter, and hence only a half sister of Ahaziah. She was wife of the high priest Jehoiada (2 Chr 22:11), and taught the young royal heir the Word of the Lord. Jehoiada led the revolt, crowning Joash king, 4-12, and ordering Athaliah killed, 13-16. The "Carites," 4,19 (RSV), perhaps a variant for Cherethites (cf. 1 Sam 30:14; 2 Sam 8:18), were foreign mercenaries.

Jehoiada's Revival, 17-21. The common people, loyal to Jehovah, destroyed the temple of Baal, 17-18.

CHAPTER 12. JEHOASH (JOASH) KING OF JUDAH

Repair of the Temple, 1-16. Joash (*c.* 835-796 B.C.) had a controversy with the priests over the repair of the temple, 4-8. The new system of collection, 9-16, secured necessary funds for repairs, but not for replacements (cf. 2 Chr 24:7).

Jehoash's Declension and Death, 17-21. Jehoash bought off Hazael by despoiling the temple, 17-18. For his further spiritual decline and his killing of Jehoiada's son, see 2 Chr 24:17-22. Jehoash's own servants conspired against him and slew him, 19-21.

CHAPTER 13. JEHOAHAZ AND JEHOASH, KINGS OF ISRAEL

Jehoahaz' Reign, 1-9. Jehoahaz (*c.* 814-798 B.C.), son of Jehu, was weak, and Israel was brought very low by Hazael of Syria. He followed the bull worship at Dan and Bethel. The Asherah, 6, was a replica of the Canaanite fertility goddess.

Jehoash's Reign, 10-25. Jehoash, also called Joash (*c.* 798-782 B.C.), warred successfully both against Syria and Judah and reestablished Israel as a real power for his son Jeroboam II (*c.* 782-753 B.C.). The death of Elisha is recounted, 20-21.

CHAPTER 14. AMAZIAH OF JUDAH AND JEROBOAM II

Reign of Amaziah of Judah, 1-22. Amaziah put to death the assassins of his father, 5-6 (cf. Ex 20:5; Deut 5:9-10; 24:16); subdued Edom, 7; and was defeated by Jehoash of Israel, 8-14. He reigned *c.* 796-767 B.C.

Jeroboam II of Israel, 23-29, reigned *c.* 782-753 B.C. and advanced the power of Israel against Damascus, lifting the northern kingdom to the apogee of its strength and prosperity. This conquest of Syria, 28, was possible because of the comparative weakness of Assyria.

ARCHAEOLOGICAL LIGHT

Excavations at Samaria have confirmed the splendor of Jeroboam II's capital. Jeroboam refortified the city with a double wall. The beautiful palace uncovered belonged to Jeroboam II rather than Ahab. The jasper seal of "Shema, servant of Jeroboam" with its magnificently executed lion, shows the effervescence of art at this era. Ahab's ivory palace was imitated by many of the wealthy of this era, as ivory finds at Megiddo and other sites attest. (Cf. Amos' prophecy, 3:15; 5:11; 1 Kgs 22:39.)

CHAPTER 15. UZZIAH AND JOTHAM; ZACHARIAH TO PEKAH

Azariah (Uzziah) of Judah, 1-7, like Jeroboam II of Israel, had a long and prosperous reign, c. 791-740 B.C. (see 2 Chr 26:6-15). When the king became a leper because of his intrusion into the priesthood, his son Jotham became regent, 5. An inscription on limestone found at Jerusalem from the 1st cen. A.D. reads: "Hither were brought the bones of Uzziah, king of Judah: not to be opened." Jotham ruled c. 750-736 B.C. Tiglath-pileser III refers in his Annals to *Azriyau of Yaudu* (Azariah of Judah) in connection with a western coalition of kings.

Zachariah, Shallum and Menahem in Israel, 8-22 (about 753-742 B.C.). Jeroboam II's son Zachariah reigned only six months in *Samaria* (753/752 B.C.) and was assassinated by Shallum, thus ending the Jehu dynasty, 8-12 (cf. 10:30). Shallum, the usurper, reigned only a month, and in turn was murdered by Menahem, 13-22, who reigned c. 752-742 B.C. The horrible practice of disembowelling pregnant women (8:12; Hos 13:16; Amos 1:13) shows the bestiality of ancient warfare and Menahem's character.

ARCHAEOLOGICAL LIGHT

Tiglath-pileser III (745-727 B.C.) to whom Menahem paid tribute, 19-20, was also known as Pul (*Pulu*), under which name he was popularly known to the Israelites. This same event is mentioned in Tiglath-pileser's Annals: "As for Menahem, terror overwhelmed him. Like a bird, alone he fled and submitted to me. To his palace I brought him back and . . . silver, colored woolen garments, linen garments . . . I received as his tribute." Menahem of Samaria (Menihummu . of Samerina) is also again mentioned in Tiglath-pileser's Annals with "Rasunnu [Rezin] of Aram."

Pekahiah's Reign, 23-26, lasted only two years (742-740 B.C.).

Pekah's Reign, 27-31 (c. 740-732). The "20 years" of 27 evidently indicate a coregency. Tiglath-pileser, who overran northern Galilee, refers to Pekah, Israel's king, in his records.

Jotham's Reign, 32-38. Rezin of Syria became a menace.

231

CHAPTER 16. AHAZ' REIGN

Ahaz' Idolatries, 1-4. Reigning *c.* 736-716, Ahaz revived Canaanite idolatry, including the horrible practice of child sacrifice (see 3:27; cf. Ex 34:20; Deut 18:10). For Ahaz' apostasy, see 2 Chr 28.

His Appeal to Assyria, 5-8. The Syro-Ephraimite war (Isa 7:1-17; 2 Chr 28:5-8) displayed Ahaz' idolatrous perfidy when he appealed to Assyria for help (2 Chr 28:16-21). The king of Assyria, happy to be magnanimously compensated by the foolish Ahaz for what he planned to do anyhow, destroyed Damascus 732 B.C., and devastated Israel (15:29). Tiglath-pileser mentions these events in his Annals.

His Trip to Damascus, 9-20, to pay homage to Tiglath-pileser III, further demonstrated his idolatrous folly.

CHAPTER 17. FALL OF THE NORTHERN KINGDOM

Hoshea's Reign, 1-23. The last king of Israel (732-722 B.C.), Hoshea was dominated and heavily taxed by Assyria. He was imprisoned for conspiracy with Egypt, his capital Samaria was besieged, and its citizens carried captive 722 B.C. The 200-year-old northern kingdom collapsed, the result of its incurable apostasies, 7-23.

Assyria Repeoples Israel, 24-41. Sargon's own records substantiate v. 24. "[The cities] I set up again and made more populous than before. People from lands which I had taken I settled there." The country became known as Samaria (not Israel), its mixed population Samaritans, 29. Its worship became a syncretism of foreign cults, 34-40. Cf. the Jewish attitude here originated which continued into NT times (Ezr 4:1-4; Lk 10:33; 17:16-18; Jn 4:9; 8:48).

CONTEMPORARY ASSYRIAN RECORDS

Pekah and Hoshea: Tiglath-pileser on an inscription says: "Pekah, their king, they had overthrown. I placed Hoshea over them. From him I received 10 talents of gold and 1,000 talents of silver." Cf. 15:30; 17:3.

Shalmaneser V (726-722 B.C.) was the Assyrian emperor who began the siege of Samaria (cf. 17:3), being the son and successor of Tiglath-pileser III. On an only inscription from this monarch's reign in the British Museum is memorialized his restoration of Nabu's temple at Borsippa in Babylonia " . . . its damage I repaired and strengthened the structure." He imprisoned Hoshea for conspiracy with So (Sibe), a petty king of the east Delta of Egypt, 3-6. It is noteworthy that neither 2 Kgs 18:9-11 nor 2 Kgs 17:3-6 states that Shalmaneser himself actually took Samaria. "And at the end of three years they [the Assyrians, i.e., under Sargon II] took it [the city]."

Sargon II (722-705 B.C.) actually took Samaria in the opening months of 722 B.C. after Shalmaneser's death. "At the beginning of my rule, in my first year of reign . . . Samerinai [the people of Samaria] . . . 27,290 . . . who lived therein, I carried away. . . ." In Sargon's "Display Inscription" at Khorsabad, where Sargon's royal palace was discovered by Paul Emil Botta in 1843, the emperor says: "I besieged and captured Samaria, carrying off 27,290 of the people who dwelt therein. . . . I caused others to take their [the deported inhabitants'] portion. I set my officers over them and imposed upon them the tribute of the former king." Before modern archaeology, Sargon's name in extant literature appeared only in the Bible and that only once (Isa 20:1). Now critics who impugned the Bible on this point are not only silenced, but must confess him one of the greatest and most powerful rulers of antiquity. Another Sargon inscription actually says: "Azuri, king of Ashdod, planned in his heart not to pay tribute. In my anger I marched against Ashdod . . . I conquered Ashdod, Gath. I settled in them people from the lands of the east. I received tribute from Philistia, Judah, Edom, and Moab."

Winged bull from palace of the Assyrian King Sargon II, probable conqueror of the Northern Kingdom. (*Courtesy ORINST*)

THE ASSYRIAN PEOPLE

Asshur and Assyria's Beginning. Located 60 miles S of Nineveh on the west bank of the Tigris River, this site (present-day Qalat Sharqat) was the original center of Assyrian power (*c*. 3000 B.C.). Named after Asshur, the national god of Assyria, the capital became the hub of the later Assyrian Empire and gave its name to the "giant among the Semites." Assyria was founded by colonists from Babylonia and periodically dominated the Tigris-Euphrates Valley. Tiglath-pileser I (*c*. 1115 B.C.) made it a great nation, but it declined during the Davidic-Solomonic era, 1010-931 B.C., making possible their empire.

The Mighty Assyrian Empire (885-612 B.C.). Its capital was Nineveh. See the book of Nahum.

Ashurnasirpal II (885-860 B.C.). His formidable fighting machine extended Assyrian might to the Mediterranean.

Shalmaneser III (859-824 B.C.) was the first Assyrian king to clash with Israel. Ahab fought against him with Benhadad at Qarqar (853 B.C.). Jehu paid tribute to him.

Shamsi-Adad V (824-815 B.C.), *Adadnirari III* (808-783 B.C.) and several weak emperors till 747 B.C., enabled Uzziah of Judah and Jeroboam II of Israel to rule long and prosperously.

Tiglath-pileser III (745-727 B.C.), "Pul," carried northern Israel into exile, 734 B.C.

Shalmaneser V (726-722 B.C.) besieged Samaria.

Sargon II (722-705 B.C.) took Samaria in 722 B.C.

Sennacherib (705-681 B.C.) was a great conqueror, but failed to take Jerusalem.

Esarhaddon (681-668 B.C.) rebuilt Babylon and conquered Egypt.

Ashurbanipal (669-626 B.C.), Asnapper (Ezr 4:10), was the last great emperor. The period 626-607 B.C. witnessed the disintegration and fall of this cruel empire.

Assyrian Annals mention contacts with some nine Hebrew kings: Omri, Ahab, Jehu, Menahem, Pekah, Uzziah, Ahaz, Hezekiah and Manasseh. Assyrian cruelty was proverbial and the Hebrews suffered severely at the hands of Assyrian kings.

CHAPTER 18. HEZEKIAH AND SENNACHERIB'S INVASION

Hezekiah's Reforms, 1-12. His actual reign, not including coregency, was *c*. 716-687 B.C. Events listed here are doubtless to be placed in the coregency with Ahaz, such as Samaria's fall, 9-12. Hezekiah destroyed the Asherim or wooden poles symbolic of the

Inscription of Sennacherib (above), which describes his military operations, including his invasion of Palestine in 701 B.C. (II Kings 18:13—19:17). (*Courtesy ORINST*)

The Black Obelisk of Shalmaneser (right) in its second register depicts King Jehu of Israel paying tribute to Shalmaneser III of Assyria. (*Courtesy ORINST*)

Canaanite fertility goddess Asherah and the bronze serpent (Num 21:6-9). Because Baal religion had the serpent symbol, the bronze serpent had pagan associations and was abused.

Sennacherib's Attack, 13-37. See Isa 36. Does this campaign belong to the first attack (701 B.C.) attested by the records of Sennacherib, or a second campaign not mentioned in the Assyrian records? "The Tartan, the Rabsaris, and the Rabshakeh" were Assyrian army officials, 17-18, military titles, such as general, colonel, captain. The language of Judah, 26, was Hebrew. Aramaic was the language of Syria which in Palestine largely superseded Hebrew after the Exile.

CHAPTERS 19—20. HEZEKIAH AND ISAIAH

Hezekiah Consults Isaiah, 19:1-37. See Isa 37. Sennacherib was finally assassinated by his sons.

ARCHAEOLOGICAL LIGHT

The Taylor Prism in the British Museum describes Sennacherib's attack on Hezekiah's realm: "As for Hezekiah, the Jew, who did not submit to my yoke, 46 of his strong walled cities . . . I besieged and took. . . . Himself, like a caged bird, I shut up in Jerusalem, his royal city. . . . As for Hezekiah, the terrifying splendor of my majesty overcame him. . . ." It is noteworthy Sennacherib did *not* claim to have captured the city, and made as good a story as possible out of the siege.

The destruction of the Assyrian army, 35, has been connected by some with a plague carried by field mice. Herodotus mentions such an onslaught in which the Assyrians suffered defeat on the borders of Egypt because the mice chewed up their bowstrings and leather equipment. Tirhakah, 9, was then a general, who later became king (690 B.C.).

Hezekiah's Sickness, 20:1-21. See Isa 38—39.

ARCHAEOLOGICAL LIGHT

Hezekiah's Pool and Conduit, 20 (cf. 2 Chr 32:2-4, 30), the rock-hewn conduit from the Gihon Spring to the Siloam Reservoir, 1,777 feet long, is one of the most amazing devices for water supply in the biblical period, comparable to tunnels at Megiddo and Gezer. In addition, Hezekiah constructed a new and larger reservoir called the Pool of Siloam (Jn 9:7-11) identical with the Pool of Shelah (Neh 3:15, RSV).

The Siloam Inscription, discovered in 1880, is a six-line inscription in classical Hebrew beautifully cut on the wall of the conduit

Entrance to Siloam Tunnel. (© *MPS*)

about 19 feet from the Siloam end of the aqueduct. It recounts the completion of the engineering feat, as workmen with wedge, hammer and pickax, digging from opposite ends, finally met.

CHAPTER 21. MANASSEH'S AND AMON'S REIGNS

Manasseh's Idolatrous Orgy, 1-18. Hezekiah's son Manasseh (696-642 B.C.), in stark contrast to his father, bent every effort to pervert the Hebrew faith by complete idolatrous contamination (cf. 2 Chr 33:1-20). The Baal cult included gay licentious dances on wooded hilltops called "high places," 3. Baal's consort Asherah was the goddess of fertility. Snake worship, male and female prostitutes, planetary worship, human sacrifices and all types of demon-inspired pagan occultism constituted features of this horrible apostasy.

ARCHAEOLOGICAL LIGHT

Piles of ashes and infant skeletons in cemeteries around heathen altars attest child murder in the name of religion. Archaeology has uncovered incantation tablets, exorcistic rituals, and abundant evidence of demon-inspired occultism in antiquity. For Manasseh and references to him in Assyrian inscriptions see 2 Chr 33.

Amon's Reign, 19-26. Wicked like his father, Amon was murdered.

CHAPTERS 22—23. JOSIAH'S REIGN

Repairing the Temple and Finding the Book of the Law, 22:1-20.
Josiah's long and godly reign lasted *c.* 640-608 B.C. Unminted metal
(money) was collected to repair the temple (cf. 2 Kgs 12:4-16). This
was 621 B.C. The outstanding event of Josiah's reign was the discovery of the book of the law, 8-10, precipitating great reformation
and revival, 22:11—23:37. It is consonant with the evidence to believe
this scroll was "the law of Moses," i.e., the Pentateuch, copies of
which during Manasseh's idolatrous reign had been destroyed. This
recovery of the Pentateuch, placed in the cornerstone when Solomon's
temple was erected (*c.* 966 B.C.), was due to the extensive repairs
of workmen.

ARCHAEOLOGICAL LIGHT

It was customary in ancient times to deposit documents in foundations of buildings. Nabonidus, a Babylonian king of the 6th cen. B.C.,
delighted to dig into foundations of buildings to recover earlier documents, doing so at the temple of Shamash in Lower Mesopotamia.
Doubtless masonry in the Solomonic temple had so cracked that
this stone had to be replaced, and the books of Moses, which had
been deposited there for three and one-half centuries, came to light.

Reforms and Death of Josiah, 23:1-30. Historians used to wonder
why Josiah advanced against Necho, 29, when the Pharaoh was
evidently on his way to attack Assyria. The Babylonian Chronicle
has put the whole matter in a new light and shows that Necho went
to the Assyrians' aid, so that v. 29 should be translated: ". . . Necho
. . . went up *to* [not *against*] the king of Assyria to the river
Euphrates."

Jehoahaz and Jehoiakim, 23:31-37. Both were evil and were dominated by Pharaoh-necho of Egypt (609 B.C.). Jehoiakim reigned
608-597 B.C.

CHAPTER 24. JEHOIACHIN AND ZEDEKIAH

Fall of Jerusalem and the First Deportation, 1-17. Egyptian control of Judah was lost at the battle of Carchemish (605 B.C.) when
the Neo-Babylonians (Chaldeans) defeated both the Assyrians and
Egyptians, 1-7. Jehoiachin thus rebelled against Nebuchadnezzar of
Neo-Babylonia. Jehoiakim, the father, had died in 597 B.C. and his
young son Jehoiachin (Jeconiah, 1 Chr 3:16; Coniah, Jer 22:24)
assumed the shaky throne. On March 16, 597 B.C., in Nebuchadnezzar's seventh year (Jer 52:28), Jehoiachin surrendered to the Babylonian monarch, as told in cuneiform sources, 10-17 (see 25:27-30).

Zedekiah Made King, 18-20, ruling 597-586 B.C. Was Jehoiachin's uncle Mattaniah; was called Zedekiah in token of his servitude.

CHAPTER 25. JERUSALEM'S DESTRUCTION AND THE BABYLONIAN EXILE

Zedekiah's Rebellion, 1-21. Despite his oath of allegiance (2 Chr 36:13), Zedekiah began to plot with Egypt and other nations. The result was that Jerusalem was laid under terrible siege and fell in 586 B.C. after frightful famine. The city was burned and the inhabitants deported or slain (cf. Jer 52:29). Temple equipment of any value was carried to Babylon, 13-17. Jeremiah gives many other details, but surprisingly the prophet is not mentioned in 2 Kings.

Gedaliah's Governorship, 22-26. His murder brought chaos and ruin (cf. Jer 40—42).

Jehoiachin's Release, 27-30. After being a political prisoner for 37 years in Babylon, Jehoiachin was set free by Nebuchadnezzar II's successor Evil-Merodach (Amel-Marduk, Akkadian, "man of Marduk"), 562-560 B.C. A vase from Susa corroborates this king and reads: "Palace of Amel-Marduk, king of Babylon, son of Nebuchadnezzar, king of Babylon." Babylonian records list "Yaukin king of the land of Yahud," i.e., Jehoiachin of Judah, as one of the recipients of royal rations. He was still considered king of Judah, even by the Babylonians themselves. Jar handles from Tell Beit Mirsim and Bethshemesh found in 1928-36 are stamped "Eliakim steward of Yaukin" (Jehoiachin), evidencing the fact that the exiled king was recognized as rightful sovereign by the people of Judah also.

THE CHALDEAN EMPIRE

Old Babylonian Period (1830-1550 B.C.). Babel dates from prehistoric times but did not itself become the capital of a great empire until this period. Hammurabi (1728-1686 B.C.), of the first dynasty of Babylon, lifted it to the height of power. Babylon and Assyria struggled till Assyrian supremacy (885-626 B.C.).

The Chaldean Empire (605-539 B.C.). This Neo-Babylonian Empire was coterminous with Judah's Captivity.

Nabopolassar (625-605 B.C.), governor of Babylon, threw off the Assyrian yoke and destroyed Nineveh, 612 B.C. He was the father of Nebuchadnezzar II.

Nebuchadnezzar II (605-562 B.C.). His first deportation of Judah (Dan 1:2) came in 605 B.C., the second in 597 B.C., and the third in 586 B.C., when he destroyed Jerusalem. He besieged Tyre (585-573 B.C.) and also invaded and desolated Moab, Ammon, Edom and

Lebanon. He invaded Egypt in 572 and 568 B.C., and died in 562 B.C., one of the most autocratic and splendid rulers of the ancient world, with his capital city Babylon (see notes on Jer 50) immortalized for its magnificence (cf. Dan 4:30).

Evil-Merodach, Amel-Marduk ("man of Marduk") (562-560 B.C.), son of Nebuchadnezzar, was slain by his brother-in-law Nergal-shar-usur.

Neriglissar, Nergal-shar-usur (560-556 B.C.), reigned only four years. His son *Labashi-Marduk* was murdered after reigning only a few months.

Nabonidus (556-539 B.C.) was one of the nobles who usurped the throne. He was called also Nabunaid ("the god Nabu [Nebo] is exalted"). His eldest son *Belshazzar, Bel-shar-usur* ("Bel protect the king"), was coregent when Babylon fell to the Persians (Dan 5) in October, 539 B.C.

THE CITY OF BABYLON

Excavations. The splendors of Nebuchadnezzar's Babylon (Dan 4:30) are now well known. From 1899 to 1914 the Germans uncovered remains of vast building projects which the king's own inscriptions describe. The Ishtar Gate led through a massive double wall of fortification decorated with bull dragon motifs done in enameled colored bricks. The Great Processional Street led from the Ishtar Gate. A dominating building was the royal ziggurat or temple tower rising to eight stages. Marduk's temple stood nearby. The famous hanging gardens were constructed in terraces and constituted one of the seven wonders of the world. Nebuchadnezzar was an avid builder and Babylon a dazzling capital (Isa 14:4).

Inscriptions. Most of the bricks found carry Nebuchadnezzar's stamp, "Nebuchadnezzar, king of Babylon. . . ." One inscription recalls his boast in Dan 4:30: "The fortifications of Esagila [Marduk's temple] and Babylon I strengthened and established the name of my reign forever."

Fall of the City. Both Isaiah (13:17-22) and Jeremiah (51:37-43) prophesied Babylon's fall. Inscriptions of Cyrus the Persian and the royal records of Babylon describe the fall of the city in 539 B.C.

Extent. Babylon's wall is said by Herodotus to have been 60 miles in length, 15 miles on each side, 300 feet high, 80 feet thick. It was protected by moats or canals, and its 250 towers were manned by soldiers. The city had 100 gates of brass, and the Euphrates flowed through the city.

Ruins. Modern excavations have largely attested the almost fabulous ancient accounts of the city. Present-day mounds are mostly found E of the river, and consist of Kasr, the central ruin, and Amran, the southern mound which contains the ruins of Esagila, the vast Temple of Marduk, the city's patron deity. The Amran mound contains the ruins of the great Tower of Babylon. Babil was the fortress guarding the northern entrance to the city and is almost a dozen miles from Kasr. These sprawling ruins attest the great size of the ancient metropolis of the world (see Jer 50—51).

1 CHRONICLES

THE REIGN OF DAVID

Name and Author. The name "Chronicles" is from the Vulgate *Liber Chronicorum* ("book of Chronicles"). The Hebrew title is *Devri Hayyammim* ("events of the times"). The Greek *Paralipomena* signifies "things leftover," i.e., from the books of Kings. The author is unknown, but may have been Ezra. The date is post-Exilic, and the books appear in the third part of the Hebrew canon, in the place where Malachi is found in the English order.

Chronicles and Kings Compared. The books of Kings were written before the Captivity, the books of Chronicles after that event (1 Chr 6:15). Kings traces the history from the *prophetic* viewpoint, Chronicles from the *priestly* approach, emphasizing the temple ritual. The blessing and grace of God toward David, as the establisher of the temple worship, and his successors on the throne of Judah are set forth in Chronicles down to the Exile. The kings of Israel are ignored and treated only as necessity dictates, in contrast to 1 and 2 Kings, which interweave the history of the dual kingdom.

Outline
The Genealogies, 1:1—9:44
Saul's End, 10:1-14
David's Kingdom, 11:1—21:30
David's Temple Ritual, 22:1—29:30

CHAPTERS 1—9. THE GENEALOGIES

From Adam to the Edomites, 1:1-54. (Cf. Gen 5,10,11,25 for these names.) The genealogies of ch. 1—9 are given to show that the Chronicles are dealing with the true Chosen People, descended through Abraham, and destined to be the line through whom the Messiah was to come.

Genealogies of Judah, 2:1—4:23. Judah is first because from this tribe Messiah was to come (Gen 49:8-12). David's line to Zedekiah is traced, 3:1-24, with additional genealogies of Judah given in 4:1-23.

Simeon, Reuben, Gad, and Half of Manasseh, 4:24—5:26. Listed are the sons of Simeon, 4:24-43; the sons of Reuben, 5:1-10; the sons of Gad and the half tribe of Manasseh, 5:11-26.

Levi, 6:1-81. Mentioned are the high priestly line, 1-15, 49-53; Levitical lists, 16-30; chief musicians of David, 31-48; and territories assigned, 54-81.

Issachar, Naphtali, Half of Manasseh, Ephraim, Asher, 7:1-40.

Benjamin, 8:1-40. Sons of Benjamin are mentioned, 1-28, and the house of Saul, 29-40.

Jerusalemites After the Return, 9:1-44. Genealogical records were carefully kept in Israel. Those in ch. 1—9 are condensed.

CHAPTER 10. SAUL'S OVERTHROW AND DEATH

Death and Burial of Saul, 1-12 (cf. 1 Sam 31). The Chronicler uses the downfall of Saul and his sons as the springboard to introduce the Lord's true king, David.

The Reason for Saul's Failure, 13-14. His disobedience and unfaithfulness to the Lord are brought into final focus by his recourse to occultism (1 Sam 28).

CHAPTER 11. DAVID'S ACCESSION AS KING

The King and His Capital, 1-9. David was anointed king at Hebron, 1-3 (cf. 2 Sam 5:1-3). He conquered Jebus (Jud 1:21; 19:10-11) and made it the capital, 4-9 (cf. 2 Sam 5:6-12).

List of David's Warriors, 10-47 (cf. 2 Sam 23:8-39). Note additional names.

CHAPTER 12. DAVID'S WARRIORS

The Benjamite Warriors at Ziklag and Others, 1-22. David's rejection and acceptance prefigure our Lord, of whom David is a prototype.

Those Who Came to Crown Him King, 23-40. How much greater the joy and the feast when our Lord is made King over all nations.

CHAPTER 13. DAVID BRINGS THE ARK FROM KIRJATH-JEARIM

A Praiseworthy Thing Performed Wrongly, 1-8. The ark, mentioned 46 times in 1 and 2 Chronicles, was to be carried on the shoulders of the Levites (Num 4:5,15), not in a Philistine expedient, a cart. Kirjath-jearim is now called Tell el-Azhar, about seven miles NW of Jerusalem. The Shihor of Egypt, 5, was the east branch of the Nile delta. The entrance of Hamath was far to the N in Syria. The cherubim, 6, were guardians of sacred areas, like the sphinx of Egypt, and were winged lions with human heads (Ezk 41:18-19; Gen

243

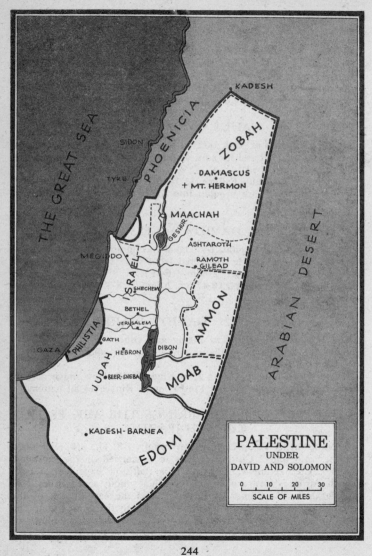

THE GREAT SEA

KADESH

SIDON

PHOENICIA

TYRE

ZOBAH

DAMASCUS

+ MT. HERMON

MAACHAH

GESHUR

ASHTAROTH

MEGIDDO

RAMOTH
GILEAD

I S R A E L

SHECHEM

BETHEL

AMMON

JERUSALEM

PHILISTIA

GATH

GAZA

HEBRON

DIBON

ARABIAN DESERT

BEER-SHEBA

JUDAH

MOAB

KADESH-BARNEA

EDOM

PALESTINE
UNDER
DAVID AND SOLOMON

0   10   20   30
SCALE OF MILES

3:24). In Phoenicia the king often appeared sitting on a cherubim-supported throne.

The Punishment, 9-14. Only Levites were to touch the ark (cf. 2 Sam 6:1-10). The breach of Uzzah was serious, punishable by death.

CHAPTER 14. DAVID'S INCREASE AND SUCCESS

His Family, 1-7. David's relation to Hiram of Tyre, 1-2, and his family are mentioned, 3-7 (cf. 2 Sam 5:11-25).

His Victories Over the Philistines, 8-17. The Chronicler's summary is given in 17.

CHAPTERS 15—16. DAVID BRINGS THE ARK TO JERUSALEM

The Right Way of Doing It, 15:1-29 (cf. 1 Chr 13 with Num 4:5, 15 and 2 Sam 6:1-10).

The Service of Dedication, 16:1-43. Described are David's sacrifices, 1-3; his choir, 4-6; his great psalm of thanksgiving, 7-36; and his appointment of the tabernacle ritual and music, 37-43. Part of the tabernacle ritual being at Gibeon indicates the confusion of the times, 39.

CHAPTER 17. THE DAVIDIC COVENANT

David's Desire to Build the Temple, 1-6 (cf. 2 Sam 7:1-3).

The Davidic Covenant, 7-15. Only in Christ, David's son and Lord (Ps. 110:1), will this great covenant be fulfilled, when our Lord returns at His second advent. Then "the Lord God shall give unto him the throne of his father David" (Lk 1:32; see 2 Sam 7:4-17).

David's Praise and Prayer, 16-27 (cf. 2 Sam 7:18-29).

CHAPTERS 18—20. DAVID'S WARS

Full Establishment of His Kingdom, 18:1-17 (cf. 2 Sam 8:1-18).

Defeat of Ammonites and Aramaean Allies, 19:1-19 (cf. 2 Sam 10:1-19).

Other Military Successes, 20:1-8. David and Joab took Rabbah, 1-3 (cf. 2 Sam 12:26-31) and defeated the Philistines, 4-8 (cf. 2 Sam 21:15-22).

CHAPTER 21. DAVID'S SIN IN THE CENSUS

Joab's Protest, 1-7 (cf. 2 Sam 24:1-9). David's pride was the cause.
The Plague and the Purchase of a Site for the Sanctuary, 21:8—

22:1. The Chronicler highlights David in his ecclesiastical and ritualistic activities in accordance with the purpose of 1 and 2 Chronicles.

CHAPTERS 22—27. DAVID'S TEMPLE RITUAL

Preparation and Charge to Solomon, 22:1-19. David chose the temple site, 1; gathered building materials, 2-5; instructed Solomon to build, 6-16; and ordered all the chiefs of Israel to help Solomon in the task, 17-19.

Preparation of the Levites and Priests, 23:1—24:31. For the 24 orders of the priests, 24:1-19, see the division of Abijah (Lk 1:5).

Preparation of Singers and Musicians, 25:1-31. The sons of Asaph, Jeduthun and Heman, 1-7, are described. They were divided in 24 divisions, like the priests.

Preparation of Other Temple Officers, 26:1—27:34. Gatekeepers, treasurers, and other functionaries were organized, 26:1-32, including officers over military and civil affairs, 27:1-34.

CHAPTERS 28—29. LAST ACTS OF DAVID AND HIS DEATH

David's Address to the Assembly and to Solomon, 28:1-21. The address, 1-10, was followed by the temple plans being given to Solomon, 11-19, with encouraging counsel, 20-21.

David's Final Words and Death, 29:1-30. He reviewed his plans and preparations for building the temple, 1-19, and invested Solomon as king, 20-25. David's death is recounted, 26-30.

2 CHRONICLES

JUDAH'S HISTORY TO THE EXILE

Scope of 2 Chronicles. Solomon is presented second only to David in importance in connection with the temple and its service, ch. 1—9. The bulk of the book, ch. 10—36, concerns the period of the dual monarchy, but centers in the Lord's gracious dealing with the Davidic house. The northern kingdom is referred to as summarily as possible. It was regarded as not representing true Israel and hence not important. Judah's apostasy from the Deuteronomic law is given as the reason for the disaster that overtook Judah.

> **Outline**
> Solomon's Reign, 1:1—9:31
> The Division of the Kingdom, 10:1-19
> History of Judah to the Exile, 11:1—36:14
> Captivity and Epilogue, 36:15-23

CHAPTER 1. BEGINNING OF SOLOMON'S REIGN

His Vison at Gibeon, 1-13 (cf. 1 Kgs 3:5-15). Gibeon *(ej-Jib),* about six miles NW of Jerusalem, was the place the tabernacle had been set up after Saul had destroyed Nob. It remained there until Solomon built the temple (1 Kgs 3:4; 1 Chr 16:39). Gibeon was excavated in 1956, walls and parts of the city water system being uncovered.

Resume of Solomon's Splendor and Wealth, 14-17 (see 1 Kgs 10:26-29; 2 Chr 9:25-28). Solomon imported horses "from Egypt and Kue [Cilicia], and the king's traders received them from Kue for a price," 16 (RSV). Cilicia, in Asia Minor, was famous for its steeds.

CHAPTERS 2—4. SOLOMON'S BUILDING OF THE TEMPLE

Solomon Prepares to Build, 2:1-18 (cf. 1 Kgs 5:1-6, 11). The king of Tyre is here called Huram instead of Hiram. "Lebanon," 8, 16, was famous in antiquity for its cedars. "Huram-abi," 13 (RSV), was the artisan Hiram of Tyre, and not to be confounded with the king of that name. The timber from Lebanon was to be floated in rafts by sea to Joppa, 16, ancient seaport of Palestine, about 30 miles NW of Jerusalem. Aliens were conscripted for forced labor, 17-18 (cf. 1 Kgs 5:13-18; 9:22).

Details of the Building Operation, 3:1-17. Mt. Moriah, 1, appears only here and in Gen 22:2. Ornan is called Araunah in 2 Sam 24:16. "Cubits of the old standard," 3 (RSV), were larger, about 20 inches in length. "Gold of Parvaim," 6, is obscure (cf. 1 Kgs 9:28). The location of Ophir is also uncertain, probably in S. Arabia. The cherubim, 10-13, were human-headed winged lions. Jachin and Boaz, 15-17, were huge fire cressets with oil containers for flares to illuminate the temple facade (see 1 Kgs 7:15-22).

The Temple Furnishings, 4:1-22 (cf. 1 Kgs 7:23-51). The altar of bronze, 1, appears in 1 Kgs 8:64 and 2 Kgs 16:14. The molten sea was a huge basin built on 12 oxen, with capacity of 2,000 baths (a bath equals six gal.) and was for ablutions, 2-6 (cf. 1 Kgs 7:23-26).

CHAPTERS 5—7. SOLOMON DEDICATES THE TEMPLE

The Ark Brought In, 5:1-14 (cf. 1 Kgs 8:1-11). The Chronicler adds the account of the priests and singers, 11-13.

Solomon's Prayer of Dedication, 6:1-42, taken from 1 Kgs 8:12-52. The address, 4-11, is followed by the prayer, 12-42.

The Lord's Presence Consecrates the Temple, 7:1-22.

CHAPTER 8. SOLOMON'S PROSPERITY

His Building Activities, 1-11. His campaign, 3, is otherwise unknown. Tadmor, 4, is Palmyra, the metropolis of the Syrian desert (cf. Tamar, 1 Kgs 9:18, RSV).

His Religious Activities, 12-18. The expression "before the vestibule," 12 (RSV; cf. 1 Kgs 9:25), is employed because only the priests could go inside. For 17-18 see notes on 1 Kgs 9:26-28. Solomon's copper smelting establishment has been excavated at Ezion-geber (Tell el Khalifa).

CHAPTER 9. THE QUEEN OF SHEBA AND SOLOMON'S DEATH

The Queen's Visit, 1-12, duplicates 1 Kgs 10:1-13 (see notes there). The Chronicler presents Solomon's good traits, as he did with David.

Solomon's Wealth and Splendor, 13-28. Taken from 1 Kgs 10:14-29.

Solomon's Death, 29-31. Cf. 1 Kgs 11:41-43, omitting unfavorable details.

CHAPTER 10.   SECESSION OF THE TEN TRIBES

Rehoboam's Folly, 1-15. This chapter closely follows 1 Kgs 12:1-19.
The Sad Result, 16-19. Rehoboam's leadership was rejected by the
northern tribes of Israel. The kingdom was divided. He reigned over
Judah c. 931-913 B.C.

CHAPTERS 11—12.   REHOBOAM'S REIGN

Beginning of Rehoboam's Reign, 11:1-23. Rehoboam was forbidden to fight against Jeroboam I, 1-4. He greatly fortified his kingdom, 5-12, and protected the priests and Levites, 13-17. His family
is given, 18-23. He was obedient to the Lord for three years.
Rehoboam's Sin and Its Punishment, 12:1-16. Declension and
apostasy resulted in Shishak's invasion (note 1 Kgs 14:21-31). Shishak
was Sheshonk I (c. 945-924 B.C.), whose invasion of Palestine-Syria
at that time is well known to archaeologists. Repentance avoided
complete destruction, 5-12. Rehoboam's acts and death are mentioned,
13-16.

CHAPTERS 13—16.   ABIJAH AND ASA

Reign of Abijah, 13:1-22 (c. 913-911 B.C.), also called Abijam
(1 Kgs 15:1, 2, 7). The Chronicler shows that the true worship of the
Lord was conducted in the Jerusalem temple, 1-12. Abijah's great
victory over Jeroboam is described, 13-22.
Asa's Reign, 14:1—16:14 (c. 911-870 B.C.). His reforms are noted,
14:2-8, as well as his great victory over Zerah, the Ethiopian. Asa's
prayer, 11, breathed the freshness of faith and resulted in triumph,
12-15. Victorious Asa was warned by the prophet Azariah, 15:1-7,
and conducted a religious reformation, 8-19. Asherah was an image
of the Canaanite fertility goddess, 16 (RSV). Asa's war with Baasha,
his apostasy and death are mentioned in 16:1-14. Verse 9 is famous
and often quoted. Asa's foot disease, 12, was severe. His funeral
was elaborate, 14.

CHAPTERS 17—20.   JEHOSHAPHAT'S
REFORMATION

Godliness and Prosperity of His Early Reign, 17:1-19. The "book
of the law of the Lord," 9, which Jehoshaphat had taught in Judah
was the law of Moses, critically alleged to have been a later fabrication of Josiah's day (2 Kgs 22:8-13; Deut 17:18-20).

Stele of Baal from Ugarit.   Stele of the Canaanite God El.

His Mistake, 18:1—19:11. Jehoshaphat's alliance with Ahab 1 Kgs 22:1-40) was a serious compromise and blunder, deserving the stinging rebuke of the prophet Jehu, son of Hanani, 19:1-3. This was effective and Jehoshaphat restored judicial justice and priestly order in Judah, 19:4-11.

His Deliverance from an Invasion, 20:1-37. The Moab-Ammon invasion, 1-2, in answer to Jehoshaphat's prayer, 3-13, was brought to nought, 14-25. Great booty was taken and Jehoshaphat returned in triumph, 26-34. His compromising trading adventure with Ahaziah (1 Kgs 22:47-49) ended in disaster. Ezion-geber is modern Tell el Khalifa where a copper smeltery has been uncovered belonging to Solomon.

CHAPTERS 21—22. JEHORAM, AHAZIAH, ATHALIAH

Jehoram's Wicked Reign, 21:1-20. Jehoshaphat's eldest son murdered his brothers and worked evil, 1-7. Edom and Libnah (Tell es Safi, some 22 miles SW of Jerusalem) rebelled, 8-10. Jehoram ordained high places, 11. His doom was pronounced by a letter which had been written by Elijah, 12-15, doubtless delivered by Elisha. His end was disastrous, 16-20.

Ahaziah's Wicked Reign, 22:1-9 (cf. 2 Kgs 8:24-29). He was slain by Jehu.

Athaliah's Usurpation, 22:10-12 (cf. 2 Kgs 11:1-3). Jehoshabeath (Jehosheba) hid Joash, Ahaziah's son.

CHAPTERS 23—24. JOASH'S REFORM AND EVENTUAL APOSTASY

Joash Becomes King, 23:1-11, c. 835-796 B.C. (cf. 2 Kgs 11:4-12).

Athaliah Executed, 23:12-15, c. 841-835 B.C. (cf. 2 Kgs 11:13-16).

Revival Through Jehoiada, 23:16-21 (cf. 2 Kgs 11:17-20).

Joash's Reign, 24:1-27. A synopsis of his rule is given, 1-2. The repair of the temple, 4-14; the death of Jehoiada, 15-16; and the apostasy of the princes and king, 17-19, are mentioned, climaxing in the stoning of Jehoiada's son Zechariah, 20-22, and the invasion of the Aramaeans of Damascus, 23-24. At Joash's death by violence, his son Amaziah succeeded him, 25-27.

CHAPTERS 25—26. AMAZIAH AND UZZIAH

Amaziah's Reign, 25:1-28, c. 796-767 B.C. (cf. 2 Kgs 14:1-2). His campaign against Edom, 5-13, and his idolatry, 14, resulted in divine wrath against him, 15-16. His mistake in hiring soldiers of Israel, 7, led to a disastrous war with Joash of the northern kingdom, 17-25, and a violent death, 26-28 (2 Kgs 14:8-20).

Uzziah's Reign, 26:1-23. The reign of Uzziah (also called Azariah) was long and prosperous (c. 791-740 B.C.). He intruded into the priest's office and was struck with leprosy (see note on 2 Kgs 15:1-7).

CHAPTERS 27—28. JOTHAM AND AHAZ

Jotham's Reign, 27:1-9. A good and prosperous king, 1-2, he built on "the wall of Ophel," 3, a fortified eminence in the eastern part of the city. He also subdued Ammon. Jotham reigned c. 750-736.

Ahaz' Great Wickedness, 28:1-27. He reigned c. 736-716 B.C. His idolatries, 1-4, brought chastisement at the hands of Rezin, king of Syria, and Pekah, king of Israel, 5-8 (2 Kgs 16:5-6). The prophet Oded reproved the Israelite invaders, 9-15. Ahaz' dealings with Tiglath-pileser, 16-21, and his further acts of wickedness are told, 22-27.

THE SILOAM INSCRIPTION,

FROM A SQUEEZE.

Inscription in the Siloam Tunnel. (© *MPS*)

CHAPTERS 29—32. HEZEKIAH'S REFORMATION

Hezekiah's Reign, 29:1—30:27 (cf. 2 Kgs 18:1—20:1; Isa 36—39) (*c.* 716-687 B.C.). He effected a great revival, 29:1-19, restoring the temple worship, 20-36, and celebrating the Passover, 30:1-27.

Other Reforms, 31:1-21. He rooted out idolatry and restored the temple ritual.

Sennacherib's Invasion, 32:1-23. (See notes on 2 Kgs 18:13—19:37, and Isa 36:1-22.)

Hezekiah's Sickness, Recovery and Embassy from Babylon, 32:24-33. (See note on Isa 38—39.)

CHAPTER 33.   MANASSEH'S AND
AMON'S IDOLATRY

Manasseh's Orgy of Wickedness, 1-10. (See notes on 2 Kgs 21:2-9.)

His Captivity and Restoration, 11-13. The Babylonian Captivity of Manasseh was historically possible since his name appears in Assyrian annals as a vassal of Esarhaddon, 681-668 B.C., and Ashurbanipal, 669-626 B.C.

His Reforms and Death, 14-20. Manasseh reigned *c.* 696-642 B.C.

Amon's Rule, 21-25 (*c.* 642-640 B.C.). He was evil like his father.

CHAPTERS 34—35. JOSIAH'S GREAT REFORMATION

Early Reforms, 34:1-7. Josiah reigned 640-608 B.C., as one of Judah's best kings. He fought against Canaanite Baal cults.

Great Revival, 34:8—35:19. This was the result of finding the Mosaic law lost in Manasseh's reign of terror. (See notes 2 Kgs 22:1—23:30.)

Josiah's Death, 35:20-27. (See notes on 2 Kgs 23:28-30.)

36:1-14. JEHOAHAZ TO ZEDEKIAH: THE END

Jehoahaz Deposed, 1-3 (cf. 2 Kgs 23:31-33; 608 B.C.).

Jehoiakim's Reign, 4-8 (cf. 2 Kgs 23:34—24:6; 608-597 B.C.).

Jehoiachin's Reign, 9-10 (cf. 2 Kgs 24:8-16; 597 B.C.).

Zedekiah, 11-14 (cf. 2 Kgs 24:17—25:7). He reigned 597-586 B.C., till the fall of Jerusalem.

36:15-23. CAPTIVITY AND CYRUS' DECREE

Fall of Jerusalem and the Exile, 15-21 (587-539 B.C.). The Chronicler reviews the Lord's grace and patience and gives the reason for the Exile. This is the only reference to Jeremiah the prophet in Kings and Chronicles (see 21). (Cf. his prophecies in Jer 25:11-12; 29:10.)

Decree of Cyrus, 22-23 (538 B.C.). See Ezr 1:1-4 in fulfillment of Jer 29:10, under divine direction (Isa 44:28—45:3).

EZRA

RETURN FROM BABYLON

Chronology of the Return

605-536 B.C.   General period of Captivity

605, 597, 586 B.C.   Leading Judean citizens deported, including Daniel and Ezekiel

538 B.C.   Edict of Cyrus permitting the return

536 B.C.   Return of 49,897 from Babylon to Jerusalem

536 B.C.   Altar rebuilt, sacrifice offered in seventh month

535 B.C.   Temple begun, but stopped

535-520 B.C.   Economic and political struggle

520 B.C.   Ministry of Haggai

520-515 B.C.   Ministry of Zechariah

515 B.C.   Temple completed

458 B.C.   Ezra returned

445 B.C.   Nehemiah rebuilt the walls

World Events During the Return

557-447 B.C.   Buddha (in India)

551-478 B.C.   Confucius (in China)

549 B.C.   Cyrus united Persia and Media

546 B.C.   Cyrus conquered Lydia

539 B.C.   Cyrus conquered Babylon

530 B.C.   Cyrus died

539-331 B.C.   Persian Empire

530-522 B.C.   Cambyses ruled

522-486 B.C.   Darius I

490 B.C.   Darius defeated at Marathon

486-465 B.C.   Xerxes I (Ahasuerus)

485-425 B.C.   Herodotus

480 B.C.   Persians defeated at Thermopylae and Salamis

470-399 B.C.   Socrates

460-429 B.C.   Golden Age of Pericles

428-322 B.C.   Plato and Aristotle

Outline

Return Under Zerubbabel
    Temple Rebuilt, Ch. 1—6
Return Under Ezra
    His Reformation, Ch. 7—10

CHAPTER 1. THE EDICT OF CYRUS

The Proclamation, 1-4. Cyrus' first year at Babylon, 1, was 539 B.C. Jeremiah's prophecy (Jer 29:10) was divinely fulfilled in Cyrus (Isa 44:28—45:3), by means of the Persian monarch's decree, 2-4. Archaeology has shown that Cyrus' concession to the Jewish exiles was not an isolated act of kindness but the general policy of a humane leader. His cylinder found by H. Rassam in the 19th cen. shows that he reversed the inhuman deportation policy practiced by Assyrian and Babylonian conquerors and restored displaced peoples and their deities to their homelands.

Gifts Provided, 5-11. These included the holy vessels appropriated by Nebuchadnezzar (2 Kgs 25:13-16). Mithredath, 8, was the temple treasurer and Sheshbazzar was the Babylonian name of a Jewish official in the Persian court.

CHAPTER 2. THE RETURNING EXILES

Register of Those Who Returned, 1-65. Enumerated are the people in general, 1-35; the priests, 36-39; the Levites, 40-54; the descendants of Solomon's servants, 55-60; other priests, 61-63. The total number was 49,897, see 64-65. Apparently others were included, and all the tribes of Israel were represented. (Cf. Lk 22:30; Acts 26:7; Jas 1:1; Ezr 2:70; 6:17; 8:35.)

The Property and Gifts of Those Who Returned, 66-70. The dram (daric) was a Persian coin equivalent to about $5.00.

CHAPTER 3. THE TEMPLE BEGUN

The Altar Erected, 1-7. In the seventh month, Tishri (Sept.-Oct.), the altar of burnt offering was set up, the first step in rebuilding the temple and reestablishing the nation. The Feast of Tabernacles was kept, 4-6, and materials to build the temple were assembled, 7. Sheshbazzar (Ezr 5:14-16) was governor.

Foundation of the Temple Laid, 8-13, in the second month (May) 535 B.C. Zerubbabel, 2, grandson of King Jehoiachin (1 Chr 3:17-19), later appointed governor by Cyrus, and Jeshua (Joshua), the high priest (Hag 1:1; Zech 3:1), were leaders in the undertaking. Great rejoicing and also weeping, 12-13 (cf. Hag 2:3) accompanied the ceremony.

CHAPTER 4. WORK ON THE TEMPLE STOPPED

Enemies Endeavor to Hinder the Building of the Temple, 1-10. These were the mongrel Samaritans, the result of foreigners from

Assyria (676 B.C.) being settled in the territory of the former northern kingdom by Esarhaddon (681-668 B.C.), 2, and by "noble Osnappar" (RSV), i.e., Ashurbanipal (669-626 B.C.), 10. The offer of help was a snare because it entailed a compromising union with semi-idolaters, 3 (cf. 2 Kgs 17:32). Ahasuerus (a royal title), 6, was evidently Cambyses (530-522 B.C.), and was the same as Artaxerxes of 7. The section 4:7-24 is not a misplacement, as critics maintain, but refers to Artaxerxes (465-424 B.C.).

Enemies Succeed and Work Is Stopped, 11-24. Accusations lodged with Ahasuerus (Artaxerxes), i.e., Cambyses, and Darius succeeded. The work was stopped till Darius' second year (520 B.C.).

ARCHAEOLOGICAL LIGHT

Esarhaddon's Annals on a cuneiform cylinder now in the British Museum recount the deportation of the Israelites and the settlement of colonists in their place.

CHAPTERS 5—6. THE TEMPLE WORK RESUMED AND COMPLETED

Haggai's and Zechariah's Ministry, 5:1-17. Darius (522-486 B.C.)

A bull capital from one of the columns of the palace at Susa (biblical Shushan). (*Courtesy, The Louvre*)

ascended the throne of Persia, and through his kindness and the prophetic ministry of Haggai and Zechariah (Hag 1:1-4; 2:1-4; Zech 4:9; 6:15) the work was resumed. Cuneiform tablets mention Tattenai, 3 (RSV), governor of the province "beyond the river."

The Temple Finished, 6:1-22. Darius found the decree of Cyrus at his summer capital in Ecbatana, 1-5 (RSV), and ordered the completion of the temple, 6-13. The house was finished, 14-15; dedicated, 16-18; and the Passover and Feast of Unleavened Bread were kept, 19-22.

Note "king of Assyria," 22. The ruler was probably so styled because Persia then ruled the former Assyria.

CHAPTERS 7—8.   THE ARRIVAL OF EZRA

Ezra Went to Jerusalem, 7:1-28, in the reign of Artaxerxes I (465-424 B.C.) to teach the law of God, 6, 10. The royal decree was made on Ezra's behalf, 11-26, who gave thanks to God, 27-28.

Ezra's Mission, 8:1-36. Ezra's companions are named, 1-14. Ahava is unidentified, but the river, 21, is certainly a tributary of the Euphrates. Casiphia is also unknown, 17. The treasure was committed to 12 priests, 24-30, and delivered to the temple storehouses ("chambers"), 29.

CHAPTERS 9—10.   EZRA'S REFORM

Loss of Separation, 9:1-15. Mixed marriages with semi-idolaters caused Ezra great pain, 1-4. His intercession and confession are recorded, 5-15.

Separation Restored, 10:1-44. The people repented and put away foreign wives, 1-17. The register is given of those who had married foreign women, 18-44. Chislev is the ninth month (Nov.-Dec.), 9, when copious rains are common. Tebet is the tenth month (Dec.-Jan.), when the work started. It was finished in Nisan (the first month, Mar.-Apr.).

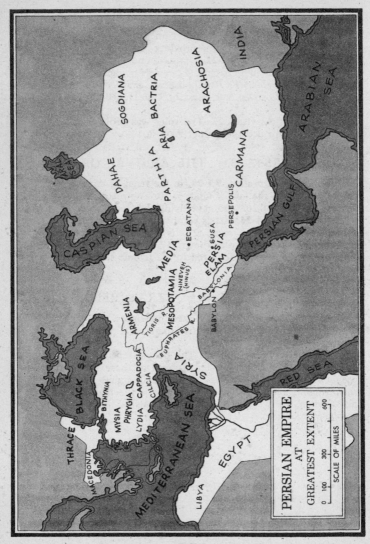

PERSIAN EMPIRE
AT
GREATEST EXTENT

SCALE OF MILES

0   100   300   600

NEHEMIAH

REBUILDING JERUSALEM'S WALLS

Name and Purpose of the Book. Nehemiah takes its name from its principal character and traditional author (1:1). The rebuilding of Jerusalem as a fortified city, the establishment of civil authority under Nehemiah, and his governorship are recounted. More civil and secular than the book of Ezra, it is nevertheless also written from the priestly viewpoint. Ezra-Nehemiah, until 1448 one book called the Book of Ezra, demonstrates God's fidelity in restoring His exiled people. The divine working is seen through great Gentile monarchs—Cyrus, Darius and Artaxerxes, and the Jews' own anointed leaders—Haggai, Zechariah, Zerubbabel, Jeshua, Ezra and Nehemiah.

The Persian Empire (539-331 B.C.). The Persian kings constituted a humane line of world rulers who permitted the Jews to return and rebuild their temple and city. Persia reversed the cruel policy of Assyria and Chaldea, and repatriated displaced peoples. Under the two-century beneficent Persian regime, Judah was a tiny province in the Fifth Persian Satrapy. Its southern frontier fortress Lachish, well-known from archaeological investigation, was controlled from the palace of the Persian administrator.

Cyrus (539-530 B.C.) united Media and Persia (549 B.C.), conquered Lydia (546 B.C.), and Babylon (539 B.C.), which was ruled by Nabonidus and the crown prince Belshazzar. His decree (Ezr 1:1-4; 2 Chr 36:22-23) permitted the return of the Jews to Palestine.

Cambyses (530-522 B.C.) conquered Egypt. His death was by suicide. (Cf. Ezr 4:7, 11.)

Smerdis (522 B.C.) was a Magian usurper who precipitated civil war (cf. Ezr 4:7, 11).

Darius I the Great (522-486 B.C.) put down the insurrection under Smerdis and saved the empire. He erected the famous Behistun Inscription on the road from Babylon to Ecbatana which furnished the key to Babylonian-Akkadian cuneiform, as the Rosetta Stone in Egypt proved to be the key to Egyptian hieroglyphics. The temple at Jerusalem was completed in 520-515 B.C. (Ezr 6:15).

Xerxes I (486-465 B.C.) was Ahasuerus, the husband of Esther. Mordecai was his prime minister. Ahasuerus warred against Greece.

Artaxerxes I Longimanus (465-424 B.C.) was favorable to Jerusalem. Ezra returned in 458 B.C.; Nehemiah became governor (Ezr 7:1, 8; Neh 2:1) in April/May, 445 B.C. The famous Elephantine Papyri from the Jewish military colony at the First Cataract of the Nile, discovered in 1903, confirm this period and mention Sanballat (Neh 2:19) and Johanan (Neh 3:1; 12:23).

Xerxes II (424 B.C.) was followed by *Darius II* (423-404 B.C.), *Artaxerxes II* (404-358 B.C.), *Artaxerxes III* (358-338 B.C.), *Arses,* (338-336 B.C.), and *Darius III* (336-331 B.C.).

Outline
Nehemiah's Restoration of the Walls, Ch. 1—7
Ezra's and Nehemiah's Reforms, Ch. 8—13

CHAPTERS 1—2.　NEHEMIAH'S CALL

Nehemiah's Concern for Jerusalem, 1:1-11. In Chislev (Nov.-Dec.) in Artaxerxes' twentieth year (445-444 B.C.; cf. 2:1), Nehemiah ("the Lord comforts") heard of the sorry state of Jerusalem, 1-3. "Men out of Judah," 2, were visitors to the Persian winter capital at Susa in Elam (Est 1:2, 5; Dan 8:2). Nehemiah's great sorrow and prayer appear in 4-11 (cf. Deut 30:1-5). "This man," 11, was Artaxerxes. The cupbearer was a royal butler who tasted the king's wine, etc., to see it was not poisoned. This office was one of high honor (Herodotus 3.34).

Nehemiah's Mission, 2:1-20. The king sent Nehemiah to build Jerusalem, 1-8. Sanballat, mentioned in the Elephantine Papyri, the governor of Samaria, and Tobiah, an Ammonite official in the hire of Persia, planned resistance, 9-10. Nehemiah inspected the walls of Jerusalem by night, 11-16, and urged immediate rebuilding, 17-18. Geshem, an Arab, 19 (6:6), king of Kedar, joined the opposition. Non-Jews had no portion, property, right, authority, or memorial, i.e., remembrance, in the Jewish community, 20.

CHAPTER 3.　JERUSALEM'S GATES AND WALLS REPAIRED

Builders of the Sheep Gate, 1-2. Eliashib (12:22; 13:4) was the grandson of Jeshua (12:10), who worked with Zerubbabel, and grandfather of the later high priest Jonathan (12:11). Through the Sheep Gate sacrificial animals were led to the altar.

Builders of the Other Gates, 3-32, are mentioned along with the builders of the walls between. *The Old Gate,* 6-12, was perhaps the Corner Gate (Jer 31:38). *The Dung Gate,* 14, was that from which refuse was removed from the city. *The East Gate,* 29-32 (cf. Ezk 43:1-2), was that from which the Shekinah glory left and by which it will return. *The Miphkad Gate,* 31 ("an appointed place; place of visitation"), may speak of the gate of judgment.

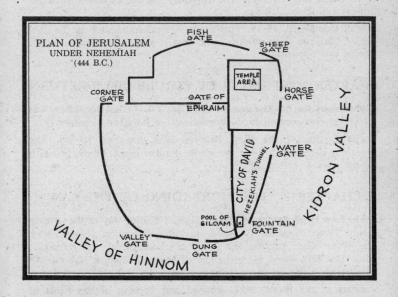

PLAN OF JERUSALEM
UNDER NEHEMIAH
(444 B.C.)

FISH GATE
SHEEP GATE
TEMPLE AREA
HORSE GATE
CORNER GATE
GATE OF EPHRAIM
CITY OF DAVID
HEZEKIAH'S TUNNEL
WATER GATE
KIDRON VALLEY
POOL OF SILOAM
FOUNTAIN GATE
VALLEY GATE
DUNG GATE
VALLEY OF HINNOM

CHAPTERS 4—5. OPPOSITION TO THE WORK

Opposition by Ridicule and Anger, 4:1-9. Ridicule, 1-3, was answered by prayer, 4-6. Anger, 7-8, was likewise met successfully by further intercession to God and vigilance, 9.

Opposition by Discouragement, 4:10-23. The spirit of defeatism, 10-13, was met by faith, 14, 20, and hard work 15-23.

Opposition by Selfishness, 5:1-19. The internal greed (Deut 23:20) and covetousness, 1-5, had a remedy in restitution, 6-13, reinforced by Nehemiah's personal example of unselfishness during his 12-year term as governor, 14-19.

261

CHAPTER 6. THE WALLS COMPLETED

Opposition by Craftiness, 1-14. For Sanballat, Tobiah and Geshem, see note in Neh 2:1-20. These wily Satanic foes tried to lure Nehemiah to Ono near Lydda, some six miles SE of Joppa, 2. Unsuccessful, they once again tried intimidation by threatening to report him to the king, mentioning "prophets," since these were often fomenters of rebellion (Jer 28:1-4). The hireling Shemaiah, 10-14, tried his strategy (cf. Zech 13:2-6).

Wall Completed, 15-19. This event was consummated on the 25th day of Elul, the sixth month (Aug.-Sept.), despite every conceivable type of evil opposition.

CHAPTER 7. REGISTER OF ZERUBBABEL'S RETURN

Provisions for the Defense of the City, 1-4. At last Jerusalem was a fortified city once again. Nehemiah set up laws for its safety.

The Census of the First Return, 5-73 (see Ezr 2:1-70). The genealogy is recorded, 5-65; the whole number given, 66-69; and gifts for the work described, 70-73.

CHAPTER 8. PUBLIC READING OF THE LAW

The Law Read Before the Water Gate, 1-8. First day of the seventh month Tishri (Sept.-Oct.) was a day of convocation (Num 29:1). The Water Gate became the place of cleansing by the refreshing power of God's Word. Here the law of Moses written in Hebrew was interpreted in the common Aramaic, 7-8.

Effect of the Word, 9-12. Revival and keeping of the Feast of Tabernacles, 13-18 (cf. Lev 23:33-44), were the results.

CHAPTER 9. SPIRITUAL REVIVAL

The Public Confession, 1-5. Reading, hearing, believing, obeying the Word always bring spiritual revival with humiliation, self-judgment, confession and true worship.

The Great Confession and Prayer, 6-38. Ezra's prayer is one of the longest recorded prayers in the Bible, 6-37. For the covenant that was made, 38, see ch. 10.

CHAPTER 10. THE COVENANT RENEWED

The Commitment to Support God's House, 9:38—10:28. Those who signed the covenant are named, 9:38—10:28. Talmudic tradition makes these signers "the Great Synagogue." "Tirshatha" means "governor," 10:1.

The Obligations of the Covenant, 29-39. These included the duty not to intermarry with Gentiles, 28-30; to observe the sabbath, 31; to support the temple ritual, 32-36; to pay tithes and priestly dues, 37-39 (see Lev 27:30; Num 18:25-32). "The chambers," 39, were the storerooms of the temple (Neh 13:12; Ezr 8:29; 10:6).

CHAPTERS 11—12. THE DEDICATION OF THE WALLS

Faithful Workers, 11:1-36. Those who lived in Jerusalem, then a place of danger and death, are specified, 1-2. Registers of Judahites, Benjaminites, priests, temple officials, Levites, Nethinim, etc., are given, 11:3-24. Registers of those who lived outside Jerusalem are also indicated, 11:25-36.

Other Faithful People, 12:1-26. Named are priests and Levites of the first return, 1-9; descendants of Jeshua the high priest, 10-11; heads of priestly houses, 12-21; and of Levitical houses, 22-26.

Dedication of the Walls, 12:27-43.

Provisions for Temple Personnel, 12:44-47.

CHAPTER 13. EVILS CORRECTED

Separation Enforced, 1-9, from a mixed crowd, 1-3, and from unholy alliances, 4-9. Eliashib was the high priest of 3:1, 20; 12:22; Ezr 10:6, who was related by marriage with Sanballat, 28.

Nehemiah Corrects Other Evils, 10-29.

His Testimony Concerning His Work, 30-31, was characterized by modesty and piety.

ESTHER

DIVINE PROVIDENCE AT WORK IN HISTORY

Nature of the Book and Author. Esther is the last of the five scrolls (megilloth) found in the third section of the Hebrew Bible called Kethubhim or "Writings." The book describes the origin of the festival of Purim ("lots"). This solemnity was celebrated on the 14th or 15th of Adar (Feb.-Mar.). Thus Esther is the Purim scroll (roll). Its author is unknown. Ezra, Mordecai, Joiakim or men of the Great Synagogue are possible authors.

Historicity. Despite the common critical contention that the story is legendary fiction, its historicity is supported (1) by its being entrenched in history and its being specifically dated (1:1, 15; 2:1, 10, 20) in the reign of Ahasuerus, i.e., Xerxes I (486-465 B.C.); (2) by the author's familiarity with Persian life—the architectural plan of the palace and court (1:5; 2:11, 21; 7:8), court etiquette (4:11; 8:11-18), palace intrigues (2:21-23; 7:9), banquet customs (1:6-8; 5:5); (3) by external evidence from excavations at Susa, etc., and evidence of a certain Marduka, an official at Susa under Xerxes.

Outline
Vashti Deposed, Ch. 1
Esther Made Queen, Ch. 2
Haman's Plot, Ch. 3
Esther's Courage, Ch. 4—7
Vengeance Executed, Ch. 8
Purim Kept, Ch. 9
Epilogue, Ch. 10

CHAPTER 1. VASHTI DEPOSED

Ahasuerus' Feast, 1-9. Ahasuerus was Xerxes I (486-465 B.C.). The third year of his reign was 483 B.C., 3. He fought the Greeks at Salamis and Thermopylae in 480 B.C. His empire, 1, extended from India (Indus Valley) to Ethiopia (modern Nubia) and included 20 satrapies (cf. Herodotus *History* III, 89) which were divided into numerous provinces. Fabulous Persian feasts are described by Greek writers, and excavations at Susa, 5, capital in Elam, have uncovered such a court. Herodotus says Amestris was Xerxes' queen (*History* VII, 61). Vashti apparently was one of the royal concubines.

Vashti's Deposition, 10-22. Her name was Elamite.

ARCHAEOLOGICAL LIGHT

Shushan (Susa), 2, was the winter capital of Persia; Ecbatana, the summer residence. Susa shows ruins dating from *c.* 4000 B.C. through A.D. 1200. Excavated ruins reveal remains from the palace begun by Darius the Great and enlarged by subsequent kings. The palace had three courts with multitudinous rooms decorated with warriors, winged bulls and griffins. The famous Code of Hammurabi was found here in the excavated area (1901). Other finds from Susa include inscriptions of Artaxerxes II (404-358 B.C.).

CHAPTER 2. ESTHER MADE QUEEN

Search for Vashti's Successor, 1-4. Between Vashti's demotion and Xerxes' marriage to Esther (478 B.C.), the monarch was absent on his ill-fated campaign against the Greek states.

Mordecai and Esther, 5-23. Mordecai was Esther's foster father (having adopted her in her childhood), as well as her cousin, 5-7. He, like Saul, was a Benjaminite, 5. His office was apparently that of a eunuch gatekeeper, since he was closely connected with the harem, 11, 19, 21 (cf. 6:10). Esther was chosen queen in the month Tebeth (Dec.-Jan.) in the seventh year (478 B.C.) of Xerxes, 16. The conspiracy of the eunuchs, 21-23, who guarded the threshold to the royal bedchamber, 21, was of the type Xerxes finally fell a victim to in 465 B.C.

CHAPTER 3. HAMAN'S PLOT

Haman's Promotion, 1-6. He was made grand vizier. All lesser officials were required to do obeisance to him. Mordecai as a Benjaminite (cf. 1 Sam 15:7-9) refused to so honor a descendant of Agag, king of Amalek, Israel's bitter enemy (cf. 10). Haman was enraged.

Haman's Plot to Exterminate the Jews, 7-15. Casting the lot (*pur,* an Akkadian word), 7, was for the purpose of determining a suitable time for the pogrom. Haman offered 10,000 talents (about 18 million dollars) to the king to bribe him to massacre the Jews. The royal signet ring, 10, 12, stamped the order of annihilation with authority (cf. 8:2, 8; Gen 41:42), although the king refused the bribe. The euict of extermination, 12, was published by couriers, 13, i.e., the renowned post service of fleet horses which Cyrus had instituted throughout the Persian Empire. The apocryphal additions to the book of Esther give the text of the edict.

CHAPTERS 4—5. ESTHER'S INTERCESSION BEFORE THE KING

Esther's Decision to Go Before the King, 4:1-17. Mordecai's mourning in sackcloth made him ritually unclean, since it was a badge of mourning for the dead among the Persians, 1-3. Esther was informed of the edict, and volunteered to go before the king, 4-17.

The King Received Esther, 5:1-14, and indicated he would grant her petition, 1-8. Haman determined to liquidate Mordecai, 9-14.

CHAPTERS 6—7. MORDECAI HONORED, HAMAN HANGED

Mordecai Honored by the King, 6:1-14. The king, sleepless, had "the book of memorable deeds," 1, read, in which Mordecai's exposé of a plot against the king's life was told, 1-3. Haman was forced to honor Mordecai, 4-11.

Haman Hanged, 7:1-10. He was charged with his wickedness by Esther before the king and incriminated by an unforeseen circumstance.

CHAPTER 8. THE EDICT OF DELIVERANCE

Mordecai's Exaltation, 1-2. It was customary for convicted criminals to have their property confiscated (Herodotus III, 29). The signet ring given to Mordecai signified his exaltation to Haman's prime ministership.

Revocation of the Edict, 3-17. Esther's ability to handle the monarch was enviable. Mordecai was authorized to make a decree that the Jews defend themselves.

CHAPTER 9. ORIGIN OF THE FEAST OF PURIM

Vindication of the Jews' Enemies, 1-16, including Haman's sons.

Institution of Purim, 17-32. It was held on the 14th or 15th day of Adar, the twelfth month (Feb.-Mar.). In later times the book of Esther was read on these festal days, while the congregation interrupted with shoutings of curses on Haman and praises on Esther and Mordecai.

CHAPTER 10. EPILOGUE: MORDECAI'S GREATNESS

The continual greatness of Xerxes and the power of Mordecai are recounted. The names of both Mordecai (Marduk) and Esther (Ishtar; Heb. Hadassah, "myrtle") are Babylonian. It was customary for native names to be given foreigners (cf. Dan 1:7).

JOB

WHY THE RIGHTEOUS SUFFER

The Book of Job and Its Order in the Canon. This great dramatic poem heads the so-called poetical books of the OT in the English order, coming before Psalms, Proverbs, Ecclesiastes and the Song of Solomon. In the Hebrew it is placed in the third section of the canon, the *Kethubhim* or Writings, third in the order—Psalms, Proverbs, *Job,* the Song and Ecclesiastes being found in the rolls. It is also part of the OT Wisdom Literature which presents the simple, pious philosophizings of the Hebrew mind on practical godly living.

The Book of Job and Hebrew Poetry. Hebrew poetry, unlike Occidental verse, does not possess meter or rhyme. Its basic structure is *parallelism* or thought arrangements rather than word arrangements. Common types of such *parallelism* are (1) *synonymous parallelism,* where the second line or stich repeats the first, giving a distich or couplet (cf. Job 3:11-12; 4:17; Ps 2:4); (2) *antithetic parallelism,* in which the second line presents a contrasting thought to emphasize the first (Job 42:5; Ps 34:10); (3) *synthetic parallelism,* in which the second and succeeding lines add a progressive flow of thought to develop the first (Job 4:19-21; Ps 1:3). Other variations of these basic forms of thought rhythm occur. In addition to parallelism Hebrew poetry possesses rhythm or pulsating beats: (1) 3+3 is *epic* or *didactic,* as in Job and Proverbs; (2) *lyric* is 2+2, as in Canticles; (3) *dirge* or *qinah* is 3+2, as in Lamentations. Hebrew poetry is also highly figurative, rich in imagery, simile, metaphor, metonymy, synechdoche, hyperbole, personification and alliteration.

The Book of Job As Literature. This poem is widely recognized, even in secular circles, as one of the world's most magnificent dramatic poems. The sublimity of its theme, the majesty of its thought patterns, the grandeur of its literary sweep are unexcelled in any piece of literature.

The Theme of the Book. It treats a perplexingly profound subject. Why do righteous people suffer? How can their sufferings be consonant with a holy, loving God? Job's three friends offered essentially the same answer, ch. 3—31. Suffering, they intimated, is the outcome of sin. In desperation Job was driven to the dilemma that God must be dealing unfairly with him. However, he struggled with the confidence that he would eventually be vindicated. At this point Elihu appeared and declared the truth that afflictions are often a means of purifying the righteous, the testings or chastenings of a loving father, in no sense the vindictive anger of an implacable God, ch. 32—37. By God's speech out of the whirlwind, ch. 38—41, Job was humbly led to detest himself before the divine majesty, 42:1-6. His self-renunciation and spiritual refining were the entrée to his restoration and blessing, 42:7-17.

Outline
Prologue: Job's Test, 1:1—2:13
False Comfort of His Three Friends, 3:1—31:40
Elihu's Speeches, 32:1—37:24
God's Discourses, 38:1—42:6
Epilogue: Job's Restoration, 42:7-17

CHAPTERS 1—2. PROLOGUE: JOB'S TESTING

Job's Testing and Integrity, 1:1-5. The land of Uz was likely Edom (cf. Lam 4:21; Gen 36:28). Job was blameless, not sinless or perfect, 1. He was a historical character (Ezk 14:14, 20; Jas 5:11). The date is unknown. The name "Job" *('iyyob)* occurs extrabiblically in the Berlin Execration Texts as the name of a prince of the land of Damascus 19th cen. B.C., and later around 1400 B.C. as a prince of Pella (modern Fahil).

Satan's Accusation, 1:6-12. "The sons of God" *(bene 'elohim)* were angels. Satan ("the Adversary") was Lucifer, "son of the morning" (Isa 14:12-14; Ezk 28:11-19). The serpent of Gen 3 was Satan. Here he appears, as often in Scripture, as the "accuser of the brethren" (Rev 12:10).

Job's Affliction, 1:13—2:13. Severe testing came. Possessions and family were wiped out, 1:13-22. Job's health was taken away, 2:1-8. His wife turned against him, 9-10. His three friends came to comfort, 11-13. The Sabeans (1:15) were Arab nomads. The Chaldeans (1:17) were Semitic Aramaeans who finally invaded Mesopotamia.

CHAPTERS 3—14. THE FIRST CYCLE OF SPEECHES

Job's First Speech, Ch. 3. He cursed the day of his birth, 1-9, and longed for death, 10-26. In the controversy that followed, Job spoke nine times, Eliphaz three, Bildad three, Elihu one, God one.

Eliphaz' First Speech, Ch. 4—5. He rebuked Job, 4:1-6, and insisted the righteous are not cut off, 7-11. His awe-inspiring vision, 12-21, fitted him for exhortation, he thought, 5:1-16. The man is fortunate whom God corrects, 17-27.

Job's Reply, Ch. 6—7. He justified his despair by the magnitude of his affliction, 6:1-7, requesting to be cut off, 8-13, at the same time reproaching his friends, 14-30. The misery of life, 7:1-7, broached two questions: Why does God deal with me in this manner? Why does He not pardon? 8-21.

Bildad's First Speech, Ch. 8. He followed the general logic of the other "Job's comforters." God was punishing Job for his sins, 1-7, appealing to the traditions of the past, 8-10, namely, the wicked cannot really prosper and God will not cast off the righteous, 11-22.

Job Answers Bildad, Ch. 9—10. God is so supremely powerful, 9:1-10, how can Job meet Him? 11-24. Job confessed his weakness and longed for a daysman (umpire) "who might lay his hand upon us both," 25-35. He bitterly complained, 10:1-17, welcoming death, 18-22.

Zophar's First Speech, Ch. 11. Job's wordiness was rebuked, 1-6, and God's greatness and omnipotence were lauded, 7-12, with exhortation that Job repent to be restored and blessed, 13-20.

Job's Reply to Zophar, Ch. 12—14. He was vexed into biting sarcasm, 12:1-6, and dwelt upon God's power, 7-25. Denouncing his "friends," 13:1-13, he appealed to God, 14-28, dwelling upon the brevity and trouble of life, 14:1-6, relieved only by a faint hope of immortality, 7-22.

CHAPTERS 15—21. SECOND CYCLE OF SPEECHES

Eliphaz' Second Speech, Ch. 15. The controversy grew more heated. Eliphaz assumed Job's culpability, charged that Job stood self-condemned, 1-6, in his conceit and pride, 7-16, and described the wicked and their end, 17-35.

Job's Reply to Eliphaz, Ch. 16—17. Job branded his "friends" as "miserable comforters," 2. "Shall windy words have an end?" 3 (RSV). Suppose you were in my place? 4-5. God had afflicted him, 6-22. Trouble upon trouble overwhelmed him, 17:1-12. Where was his hope? 13-16.

Bildad's Second Speech, Ch. 18. Harshly he reproached Job, 1-4, and attempted to frighten him by describing the doom of the wicked, 5-21.

Job's Reply to Bildad, Ch. 19. Unhumbled and acutely vexed by Bildad's words, 1-6, Job stumbled in confusion, blaming God, 7-12, and falling into a doleful lament at his pitiable condition, 13-24. But there was a flash of faith and light! The Spirit of God enlightened him and lifted him out of the doldrums of despair, 25-27, to utter one of the most superlative statements of faith in all the OT: "For I know that *my redeemer* liveth, and that he shall stand at the latter day upon the earth: and though after my skin worms destroy this body, yet in my flesh shall I see God: whom I shall see for myself . . . and not another." The *Goel*, Kinsman-Redeemer (Isa 59:20; Ruth 3:12-13; 4:4-6) is the Lord Jesus Christ, risen, coming again, Victor over death and the grave. What a witness to the blessed hope of the Lord's coming, the resurrection of the body and the glorification of the saints (1 Thess 4:13-18; 1 Cor 15:52; Ps 17:15).

Zophar's Second Speech, Ch. 20. His hasty reply, 1-3, followed proverb and tradition, and he mistakenly classified Job with the wicked and their fate, 4-29.

Job's Reply, Ch. 21. He looked to God for help and showed how the wicked often prosper in this life, 1-26, branding the conclusions of his friends as pure falsehoods, 27-34.

CHAPTERS 22—31. THIRD CYCLE OF SPEECHES

Eliphaz' Third Speech, Ch. 22. Eliphaz of Teman (apparently SW of Sela in Edom at Tawilan) concluded Job was a great sinner, 1-5, charging him with avarice and cruelty, 6-11, and hypocritically dwelling upon God's omniscience and man's wickedness, 12-20, urging Job to get right with God, 21-30.

Job's Reply, Ch. 23—24. He groped for God, proving he was not defiantly wicked, 23:1-9, wavering between faith and unbelief, 10-17. Had God failed? 24:1-12. Job gave further testimony of the frequent prosperity of the wicked, 13-25.

Bildad's Third Speech, Ch. 25. Although his arguments were exhausted, he presented a forceful description of what God is, 1-3, and what man is, 4-6.

Job's Reply, Ch. 26. He sarcastically dismissed Bildad's arguments, 1-4, and knowingly and feelingly described God's greatness, 5-14.

Job's Closing Words of Self-Vindication, Ch. 27—31. He clung to his righteousness, 27:1-6, contrasting himself with wicked people, 7-23. He described the treasures of earth, 28:1-6, and the higher wealth of wisdom, 7-22, which is known by God, 23-28. Job outlined his past blessings and honors, 29:1-10, and the good deeds he had wrought, 11-25, contrasting his present shameful humiliation, 30:1-19, with God's silence, 20-31. He ended confidently maintaining his chastity and righteousness, 31:1-12; his philanthropy, 13-23; and his integrity and hospitality, 24-34. He challenged God and man to disprove his claim, 35-40. He concluded by saying in a word: *"I am clean!"* The next time he spoke, he declared in essence, *"Behold I am vile"* (42:6). The reason for the change is recorded in the rest of the book.

CHAPTERS 32—37.   ELIHU'S SPEECHES

Elihu's First Speech, Ch. 32—33. God instructs man through affliction. Elihu ("my God is He") is introduced, 32:1-6. He was a Buzite, living near Edom, for Buz (Gen 22:21) was a brother of Uz (Job 1:1) and an Aramaean (Gen 11:26-32). Buz in Jer 25:23 was a place name in Edom. Elihu was a true daysman, in a sense the answer to Job's desire for such an umpire. Elihu's speeches thus served to prepare the way for the interposition of God Himself, ch. 38—41.

Elihu's Second Speech, Ch. 34. God's justice was vindicated against Job's insinuations, 1-30. Job had not yet learned the purpose of suffering, 31-37.

Elihu's Third Speech, Ch. 35. The advantages of piety were set forth as a refutation to Job's wrong reasoning, 1-8, showing that it does matter with God whether a man is righteous or wicked, 9-16.

Elihu's Fourth Speech, Ch. 36—37. God has a purpose in afflicting the godly, 36:1-7. He does so to wean man from pride and to show His disciplining grace and love, 8-18. Job was to take note of this, 19-21, and to acknowledge God's power and presence in nature, 22-33; in the thunderstorm, 37:1-5; and in snow and rain, 6-16. Elihu's concluding remarks stressed man's sinful frailty before God, 17-24, clearing the way for the Almighty to speak.

38:1—42:6.   GOD'S DISCOURSES TO JOB

God's First Discourse to Job, 38:1—40:5. Creation proclaims God's omnipotence. The Lord spoke "out of the whirlwind," 38:1, a frequent setting for theophanies (Nah 1:3; Zech 9:14; Ps 18:7-15; Ezk 1:4; Hab 3). Verses 4-7 antedate the entrée of sin into a sinless universe, and describe original creation, perhaps aeons before Gen 1:1-2. (See notes on Gen 1—2.) God is Creator of the sea, 8-11; of time, 12-15; He is Master of the deep, light, darkness, snow, hail, lightning, constellations, clouds and mist, 16-38; God is the Creator and Protector of animals, 38:39—39:30. Job made a confession, 40:1-5.

God's Second Discourse to Job, 40:6—42:6. God's power and man's frailty are contrasted. Job was silenced as a contender and faultfinder with God, but not as a sinner. So the divine controversy was renewed. "Will you condemn me that you may be justified?" 40:6-8 (RSV), asks the Lord in His appeal to Job, 9-14. "Behemoth," 15-24, apparently is a plural of intensity of Hebrew *behemah* ("beast") and refers probably to the hippopotamus (Egyptian *p-ehe-mou*) or water-buffalo. Figures of this huge amphibian have been found on amulets and in Palestinian temples. "Leviathan," 41:1-11, is the crocodile, but is generally interpreted elsewhere to refer to a mythical chaos-monster (Ps 74:14; 104:26; Isa 27:1). Description of leviathan, 12-24, and his remarkable strength, 25-34, is given.

Job's reply to God, *solves the problem* of suffering, 42:1-6. Affliction is God-permitted to refine man so that he may see God, 5, in all His greatness and splendor, and see himself in his despicableness and sin to the intent that man may repent of his pride "in dust and ashes."

42:7-17. GOD REBUKES JOB'S FRIENDS AND RESTORES JOB

The Lord's Vindication of Job, 7-9, against his friends. God's grace forgave Job's sin, and Job prayed for his erring friends.

Job's Fortunes Restored, 10-17. His end was peace.

PSALMS

Prayer Book and Hymnal of God's People

Nature and Number. The Hebrew title for the Psalter is "Book of Praises" (*Sepher Tehillim*). Praise, worship, confession and the outpouring of prayer characterize the Psalms. The Psalter was the hymnal of the Jewish people and is the prayer and praise manual of the Christian church. Martin Luther called the Psalter "a Bible in miniature." Our English word "Psalms," from the Septuagint *Psalmoi,* means "songs" accompanied by string instruments. In the Hebrew Bible, Psalms head the third division, called the *Kethubhim* or Writings (cf. Lk 24:44). The Hebrew Bible contains 150 psalms.

The Psalms and Hebrew Poetry. See introduction to Job on the nature of Heb. poetry.

Themes of the Psalms

1. The spiritual conflicts and triumphs of saints under the old economy constitute the basic theme, but these reflect the conflicts of God's people in every age.

2. Great prophetic themes run through the book, as NT quotations prove. These are: (a) The far-reaching predictions concerning Messiah (cf. Lk 24:44), including His first advent in humiliation; His death, resurrection and exaltation; and His second advent in glory and triumph, Ps 2, 8, 16, 22, 45, 69, 72, 89, 110, 118, 132. (b) Sorrows, trials and sufferings of a godly portion of Israel in the nation's coming time of trouble, eventuating in deliverance, restoration and glory, Ps 52, 58, 59, 69, 109, 140. (c) Future glories for redeemed Israel, the earth and all creation, Ps 72, 110.

Note: In the necessarily brief comments that follow, the focus is upon the more difficult prophetic themes, since the devotional meanings are more obvious to the reader and thus need less comment.

Authorship As Indicated by the Titles

David 73 (Book 1, 37; Book 2, 18; Book 3, 1; Book 4, 2; Book 5, 15)

Asaph 12 (Ps 50, 73-83)

Korahites 12 (Ps 42-49, 84, 85, 87 88)

Solomon 2 (Ps 72, 127)

Moses 1 (Ps 90)

Ethan 1 (Ps 89)

Classification

Five Books: Book 1, Ps 1-41; Book 2, Ps 42-72; Book 3, Ps 73-89; Book 4, Ps 90-106; Book 5, Ps 107-150.

Royal Psalms: 2, 18, 20, 21, 45, 72, 89, 101, 110, 144. They anticipate Christ as King.

Alphabetic Psalms: 9, 10, 25, 34, 37, 111, 112, 119, 145. They employ some arrangement based on the Hebrew alphabet.

Penitential Psalms: 6, 25, 32, 38, 39, 40, 51, 102, 130. These psalms breathe deep contrition for sin committed.

Messianic Psalms: 2, 8, 16, 22, 45, 69, 72, 89, 110, 118, 132. They preview the person and work of the coming Messiah.

Imprecatory Psalms: 52, 58, 59, 69, 109, 140. All of these implore God's vindication of His own against godless persecutors.

Hallelujah Psalms: 111-113, 115-117, 46-150. These psalms employ the term Hallelujah, meaning "Praise Jah [Jehovah]."

Elohistic Psalms: 42-83. They employ the name *Elohim* for God. Others use the name of Jehovah.

Ascent Psalms: 120-134. They were recited or sung as the pilgrims went up to Jerusalem to celebrate the feasts.

PSALM 1. THE GODLY MAN VS. THE UNGODLY

The godly man is happy, 1-3, because he is separated from sin, 1; Bible-centered, 2; and prosperous, 3. The ungodly, 4-6, in contrast, is unlike the godly, 4, and is doomed to judgment, 5-6. A wisdom psalm introductory to the entire Psalter.

PSALM 2. MESSIAH'S KINGSHIP AND KINGDOM

This previews Christ's present rejection, 1-3 (cf. Acts 4:25-28), which continues throughout this age and culminates in the abysmal apostasy of the Great Tribulation. Messiah's present session (cf. Ps 110:1), in disdain of His enemies, is foretold, 4-6. The future incarnate and risen Lord (cf. Acts 13:33-34) vindicates His sonship at His second advent and assumes the kingdom, 7-9. He exhorts kings and warns rebels in view of the establishment of His kingdom, 10-12.

PSALMS 3—7. TRIALS OF THE GODLY

Psalm 3. Peaceful Trust in God. In time of deep anguish when Absalom rebelled against him, 1-2, David found God his glory, as his shield (protector) and encourager, 2-3; as the One who answered his prayers, 4; and as the One who gave him peace and deliverance, 5-8.

Psalm 4. Evening Prayer Sustaining Faith results in enlargement of heart, 1; assurance of God's help, 2-3; faith, 4-5; divine approbation, 6; joy, 7; peace and security, 8.

Psalm 5. Morning Prayer Giving Courage, 1-3, bestows a sense of God's goodness and justice, 4-6; secures God's guidance, 7-8; His protection and punishment of enemies, 9-10; and His blessing upon the righteous, 11-12.

Psalm 6. Heart Cry of One Distressed. Sorely chastened, 1-3; beset by death, 4-5; and stricken with grief, 6-7, the psalmist expresses faith in God's deliverance, 8-10.

Psalm 7. Cry for Protection against cruel enemies, 1-2. Personal innocence is protested, 3-5; and punishment upon evildoers is requested, 6-16. Praise is accorded the Lord, 17.

PSALM 8. THE SOVEREIGNTY OF THE SON OF MAN (MESSIANIC)

As Son of Man, Christ appears in humiliation, a little lower than the angels (Mt 21:16; 1 Cor 15:27; Heb 2:6-9), to taste death for every man, and is now crowned with glory and honor, 1-5. Man (the first Adam being a figure of the Second Man or the Last Adam) was given dominion over creation, which was lost by sin, and which is is to be restored only by the Second Adam (Christ), 6-9. This achievement of the Creator-Redeemer will redound to God's glory, 1, 9.

PSALMS 9—15. THE GODLY AND THE WICKED ONE

Psalm 9. The Godly Praise the Most High, 1-2, for His kingdom blessings and glories, 3-12, with prayer for the Lord's intervention in the judgments preceding the establishment of the kingdom, 13-20.

Psalm 10. Supplication of the Godly for divine intervention continued, 1-2, directed against the Wicked One, 3-18.

Psalm 11. Faith's Resources are for the day of trouble ("Jacob's trouble," cf. Jer 30:5-7), when "the foundations are destroyed" in that dark hour of universal apostasy, 1-3. But the Lord will judge sinners and reward the righteous, 4-7.

Psalm 12. The Arrogance of Sinners, 1-3, is described. But God is about to judge them, 4-6, as their iniquity comes to the full, 8.

Psalm 13. The Faith of the Godly, 1-4, eventuates in victory, 5-6.

Psalm 14. Human Apostasy and Depravity are described, 1-3, especially the period preceding Christ's second advent when Israel will suffer violent persecution, 4-6. Messiah's advent, bringing salvation for Israel and joyful restoration, is prayed for, 7 (cf. Rom 11:26-27; Ps 53).

Psalm 15. The Character of the Godly. Such a saint has fellowship with God in worship, 1, and his life conforms to his profession, 2-5.

PSALMS 16—24. PROPHETIC VISTAS OF CHRIST

These nine psalms reflect the character of the godly but find their *ultimate* fulfillment in Christ, starting in Psalm 16 with our Lord in His obedience on earth, climaxing in His second advent manifestation as "the King of glory" (Ps 24).

Psalm 16. Christ Obedient Is Resurrected. He is the Obedient One, 1-3, whose path was one of complete devotion to God, 4-8, which led Him to death and resurrection, 9-11 (cf. Acts 13:35).

Psalm 17. Christ the Intercessor (cf. Jn 17). He only fits the righteous Intercessor, 1-5. His prayer for His own, 6-12, and the deliverance, 13-15, will find fruition only in the Greater David, David's Lord.

Psalm 18. God's Power Vouchsafed Christ. David as a prophet (Acts 2:30) here predicts Christ's experience of death, 1-6, and God's manifest power and glory in Christ's behalf, 7-18. He speaks not only of raising Him from the dead but giving Him glory, 19-27, subduing His enemies, 28-42, and making Him "Head of the nations," 43-50.

Psalm 19. Christ in Creation and Revelation. He appears first in creation, 1-6; then in revelation (His written Word), 7-11. Man's response follows, 12-14.

Psalm 20. Christ and His Salvation. Prayer for the earthly king's victory, 1-2, adumbrates the greater victory of Christ's salvation, the whole burnt offering, 3, typifying the death of Christ. Celebration of Christ's glorious salvation, 4-8, is climaxed by a cry of the godly in the time of trouble, 9.

Psalm 21. Christ's Kingly Glory is anticipated, 1-7, and His victory over His foes celebrated, 8-12. Then redeemed Israel will sing the anthem of 13.

Psalm 22. Christ's Sufferings and Coming Glory. The sufferings, 1-21, are a graphic portrayal of crucifixion (cf. Mt 27:27-50), and are followed by the glory, 22-31, the ode breaking from crucifixion to resurrection at 22, fulfilled in Jn 20:17, "Go to my brethren," "I will declare thy name ["Father"] unto my brethren," 22 (cf. Heb 2:12). "The kingdom," 28, is Jehovah's, and the Lord (*Adonai*), 30, rules with the purpose of restoring the kingdom to Jehovah (1 Cor 15:23-24).

"Thou anointest my head with oil." (© *MPS*)

Psalm 23. Christ the Great Shepherd. The *Good* Shepherd of Ps 22, giving His life for the sheep (Jn 10:11), appears in Ps 23 as the *Great* Shepherd "brought again from the dead . . . through the blood of the everlasting covenant" (Heb 13:20), caring for the sheep, giving them assurance, 1-3, and comfort, 4-6.

Psalm 24. Christ the Chief Shepherd. The *Good* Shepherd of Ps 22 and the *Great* Shepherd of Ps 23 now is revealed as the *Chief* Shepherd, the "King of glory," appearing to acknowledge and reward His sheep (1 Pet 5:4). Who shall dwell with Him in His kingdom advent, 1-6? What suitable welcome shall be accorded Him at His coming, 7-10?

PSALMS 25—39. SOUL EXERCISE OF THE GODLY

Psalm 25. Petition for Deliverance. This is an acrostic (cf. Ps 9, 10) in which an arrangement of the letters of the Heb. alphabet is used for a specific purpose.

Psalm 26. Prayer for Vindication against an unjust charge is presented, 1-3, with protestations of innocence, 4-7, dramatized by a liturgical ceremony, 6 (cf. Deut 21:5-8; Ps 51:7). A prayer for aid is uttered, 8-12.

Psalm 27. Prayer for Spiritual Orientation, toward God, 1-3; toward life, 4-6; toward self, 7-14.

Psalm 28. Prayer for Deliverance. The prayer, 1-5, is followed by thanksgiving for the answer, 6-9.

Psalm 29. The Storm of Judgment. Ascription of praise to the Lord, 1-2, because the day of the Lord shall come as a great tempest, 3-9, to clear the air for the calm of the Messianic Age when the Lord is King, 10-11.

Psalm 30. Praise for Healing. The recovery is noted, 1-3, and praise is offered, 4-12.

Psalm 31. Victory over Enemies. Prayer of the saint is for deliverance, 1-18, and the answer points to victory, 19-24. Jesus quoted verse 5 as He expired on the cross (Lk 23:46).

Psalm 32. The Blessing of Being Justified. This is the first of 13 Maskil psalms, i.e., psalms of spiritual instruction. The justifier, 1-5, is also a hiding place, 6-7; a Guide and a Preserver, 8-10, in whom the saint is to rejoice, 11.

Psalm 33. Praise to the Lord is rendered to Him as Creator, 1-9; as Governor, 10-17; and as Keeper and Deliverer of the righteous, 18-22.

Psalm 34. Full Praise of God's Redeemed is sung for deliverance, 1-10; for instruction, 11-14; for redemption, 15-22. Verse 20 was fulfilled in Jn 19:36.

Psalm 35. Cry for Help in Distress. This is an imprecatory psalm like 52, 58, 59, 69, 109 and 137. These must be understood as the prayers of the godly in a day of abysmal apostasy and violence. The Spirit of God prays through them for the destruction of the wicked, whose cup is full and whose judgment is executed in the day of the Lord. To see a conflict here with Jesus' teaching of love and forgiveness is to misunderstand God's holiness when His grace in Christ has been rejected.

Psalm 36. Contrast of the Wicked and the Lord. What the wicked man is and does, 1-4, is contrasted with what the Lord is and does, 5-9. The Lord is to be petitioned and trusted, 10-12.

Psalm 37. The Righteous and Wicked in Contrast (cf. Ps 1). The wicked will most surely be punished. Let the righteous who have been wronged not be discouraged.

Psalm 38. The Suffering Saint and Sin. In suffering, 1-8, looking to the Lord, 9-15, results in confession of sin and prayer, 16-22.

Psalm 39. Human Frailty. The emptiness of life, 1-6, should lead to self-judgment and prayer, 7-13.

PSALMS 40—41. DAVID'S EXPERIENCES FORESHADOW CHRIST'S

Psalm 40. The Obedient Christ (cf. Heb 10:5-7). His path of obedience, 1-12, is prefaced by the Redeemer's resurrection song, 1-3. Messiah's "pierced ears" refer to Ex 21:6. The fruit of the Redeemer's work is outlined, 13-17, as He prays as the Sin-Bearer of His people.

Psalm 41. Messiah Betrayed. David's experience, 9, foreshadows Christ's (Jn 13:18-19). Verse 13 will be redeemed Israel's shout as a result of Messiah's redemption.

PSALMS 42—49. THROUGH TRIBULATION TO KINGDOM BLESSING

These psalms open Book 2 of the Psalter, which begins with the oppression of the godly Heb. remnant of the last days and ends with Ps 72, the great Kingdom Psalm of the Psalter. The first group (42-49) presents aspects of this troubled scene and final deliverance.

Psalm 42. Longing for God in Deep Distress, 1-6, is described with the tonic of faith and the comfort of hope, 7-11. This is a Maskil (instruction) psalm for the godly remnant of that terrible time of trouble (Dan 12:1).

Psalm 43. Cry to God Against Enemies, namely, the lawless one, 2, and his wicked nation. Ps 43 is one with Ps 42 (cf. the Septuagint which makes them one psalm).

Psalm 44. Increased Cry for Help. The psalmist pleads with God to command deliverances, 1-8. The reason is the terrible trouble of the Tribulation period, 9-21 (cf. Rev 4:1—19:16). This anguish calls for help, 22-26.

Psalm 45. The Answer: King Messiah's Advent in Glory. His majesty and power, 1-5. His dominion and glory, 6-8, and those who share His kingdom, 9-17, are foreseen (cf. Heb 1:8-9 and Isa 11:1-2).

Psalm 46. Deliverance from Tribulation and the Sequel. The great time of trouble, 1-3, is followed by Messiah's advent in power and glory, 4-7, and the establishment of the kingdom, 8-11. "Selah" is a liturgical direction of some sort, the meaning of which is now uncertain.

Psalm 47. Messiah King in His Kingdom is seen among His redeemed, 1-5, the object of the praise of His ransomed people, 6-9.

Psalm 48. Nations Judged, the Kingdom Established. Jerusalem is seen as the capital of the earth in the Kingdom Age, 1-3 (cf Isa

2:1-5). The nations are judged, 4-7, and the kingdom set up, 8-14 (cf. Mic 4:1-10; Zech 14:9-21).

Psalm 49. Transiency of the Wicked and Their Wealth. The contrast is to the lot of the righteous who trust in the Lord.

PSALMS 50—51. THE RIGHTEOUS GOD AND HIS PENITENT PEOPLE

Psalm 50. God's Demands for Holiness. God comes to Israel in His revealed righteousness and demands righteousness of His people, 1-6; not mere ritualism, 7-15, but spiritual reality, 16-22, which will in turn result in the revelation of the salvation of God, 23.

Psalm 51. The Sinner in Deep Penitence. This is the greatest of penitential psalms. David's great sin of adultery and murder is confessed before God and forgiven. The sinner, 1-2, becomes the penitent, 3-11, and the forgiven, 12-17, who in turn becomes the intercessor for Zion, 18-19.

PSALMS 52—55. ISRAEL'S TIME OF TROUBLE

These four psalms are Maskil (instruction) odes reflecting afflictive experiences of the psalmist himself (David). They may also be prophetic of Israel's last-day troubles under the false Messiah (Zech 11:15-17; 2 Thess 2:7-12).

Psalm 52. The Wicked Tyrant and His Destruction. The wicked one's character (Doeg, the Edomite), 1-7, contrasting vividly with the character of the godly psalmist, 8-9, furnishes the historical occasion for a description of an arrogant tyrant who will experience the retribution of God (1 Sam 21:7; 22:9, 18, 22).

Psalm 53. An Age of Apostasy. The last day denial of God, 1; wickedness, depravity, 2-3, and persecution of God's people are forseen, 4. Judgment then falls on the apostates, 5. The godly remnant prays for the advent of Messiah and the restoration of Israel, 6. Ps 53 is almost identical with Ps 14, but uses *Elohim* instead of *Jehovah*.

Psalm 54. Petitions of the Godly. David's betrayal by the Ziphites (1 Sam 23:19-27) furnishes the historical occasion for this psalm and offers a prophetic parallel of the prayers, 1-3, of the Jewish saints previous to the advent of Messiah, 4-7.

Psalm 55. In the Vortex of Great Distress. The base defection of Ahithophel, David's trusted counselor, to the traitor Absalom (2 Sam 15:12—17:23) furnished the occasion for the psalmist's deep distress, 3, and anguish to escape the plot, 4-8. Jerusalem had become a city of violence and strife, 9-11, because of the treason of Ahithophel, 12-15. David's assurance of God's help, 16-19, was uttered while suffering from this classic treachery, 20-21. Comfort for the righteous and judgment for the wicked are indicated, 22-23 (cf. 2 Sam 17:23).

PSALMS 56—60. TRIALS OF THE SAINTS BEFORE BLESSING

Psalm 56. Praise for Anticipated Deliverance. David was hemmed in by two enemies, his own people and the Philistines while living with the latter in Gath (1 Sam 27:1—28:22). His trust and comfort, 1-9, produced assurance of deliverance, 10-13.

Psalm 57. Deliverance in Distress. David cries to God, 1-5, amid enemies and dangers when he found deliverance from Saul in a cave at Adullam (1 Sam 22:1; 24:3). When his attention shifted from present circumstances his heart became fixed on the God of mercy and truth, and triumph followed, 6-11.

Psalm 58. Judgment upon the Wicked. They must suffer punishment, 1-5. The execution of punishment is described, 6-11.

Psalm 59. The Hatred of the Wicked for the Righteous. This cruel animosity is reflected in David's lament when Saul tried to trap him in his home (1 Sam 19:10-17). It was then the psalmist experienced the hatred from sinners which all God's saints have periodically known.

Psalm 60. A National Lament. A temporary reverse of David in the war with the Syrians and Edomites (2 Sam 8:3 14) furnished a lament, 1-5, to be echoed by the Israelite remnant of the end time, 6-12.

PSALMS 61—68. THROUGH SUFFERINGS TO KINGDOM BLESSING

This series, through the experiences of the psalmist, reflects not only the heart cries of suffering saints in general, but of the godly in Israel in the period of trouble before the Kingdom Age.

Psalm 61. Prayer for the King. The personal lament of David, 1-5, perhaps penned on a distant expedition or at the time of Absalom's rebellion, expresses the heart cry of the godly in the nation who look for Messiah's advent to establish the kingdom. The petition for the king, 6-8, goes beyond King David and embraces King-Messiah, as the Targum, the ancient Jewish commentary, correctly interprets.

Psalm 62. The Saints' Waiting and Trusting for Deliverance. David's waiting in faith, 1-4, has its expectation in God alone, 5-8, not in the vanity of man, 9-12.

Psalm 63. The Saints' Thirst for God. David's burning desire for fellowship with God despite his trials in the wilderness, 1-8, prefigures the heart exercise of every true saint in trouble. The coming judgment of the godless gives encouragement in tribulation, 9-11.

Psalm 64. The Fate of the Wicked. Their bold wickedness, 1-6, will be judged, 7-9, and the godly remnant will rejoice in the Lord, 10.

Psalm 65. Millennial Restitution of the Earth. Spiritual blessings are realized, 1-5, as well as temporal and material benefits, 6-13. Psalms 65—68 describe "the restitution of all things, which God hath spoken by the mouth of all his holy prophets since the world began" (Acts 3:21).

Psalm 66. Worship and Praise in the Kingdom. God's mighty deliverances are rehearsed, 1-7, with Israel's adoration and worship resulting, 8-20.

Psalm 67. Full Kingdom Joy and Blessing. The nations know and praise God, 1-4, and worldwide prosperity ensues, 5-6.

Psalm 68. Consummation of Redemption. Israel's joy in the kingdom is the outcome of the Lord's mighty deliverances, 1-20. Verse 18 is quoted in Eph 4:7-16 of Christ's ascension ministry. Israel is regathered and her last-day enemies are destroyed, 21-23. Full and universal kingdom blessing is celebrated, 24-35.

PSALMS 69—72. CHRIST REJECTED AND EXALTED

Psalm 69. The Sufferings of the Rejected Messiah. He is hated without cause, 1-6; bears reproach, 7-12; and prays, 13-21. The retribution upon His enemies is described, 22-28. His exaltation and glory follow, 29-36. On 14-20, cf. Christ's experiences in Gethsemane (Mt 26:36-45). Verse 21 connects with the cross (Mt 27:48; Mk 15:36; Lk 23:36; Jn 19:28-29). Acts 1:20 recalls verse 25. This remarkable psalm illustrates the deep prophetic strain running through the Psalms (cf Lk 24:44).

Psalm 70. Israel's Prayer for Deliverance recalls and repeats Ps 40:13-17, David's prayer in time of great stress.

Psalm 71. Israel's Paean of Hope. The psalmist declares his faith, 1-18, resulting in spiritual reviving and victory, 19-24.

Psalm 72. The Great Kingdom Psalm. The king is invested, 1-4. The extent of the kingdom, 5-11, and its blessings are viewed, 12-20. All David's prayers, 20, will find their fulfillment in the kingdom (cf. 2 Sam 23:1-4).

PSALMS 73—83. PSALMS OF ASAPH CONCERNING THE SANCTUARY

Book 3 of the Psalter, Psalms 73-89, deals with the holiness of the Lord's sanctuary. This portion has been compared to the book of Leviticus. Eleven psalms are by Asaph, leader of David's choir (1 Chr 6:39) and composer (2 Chr 29:30).

Psalm 73. Problem of the Prosperity of the Wicked. The perplexing question is the same as in the book of Job, Why do the wicked flourish, 1-9, and the righteous suffer, 10-14? God's justice and the holiness of the sanctuary are the answer, 15-28.

Psalm 74. Desecration of the Sanctuary by the Enemy. The sight of the enemy in the sanctuary, 1-9, goes beyond the Babylonian destruction in 586 B.C., and the desecration by Antiochus Epiphanes. It will be realized in the Antichrist of the end-time (Mt 24:15). Prayer is made for divine intervention, 10-23.

Psalm 75. Divine Intervention on Behalf of the Sanctuary. Messiah, the righteous Judge, 1-7, executes His judgment at His second advent, 8-10.

Psalm 76. Divine Government Set Up. The Lord reigns in Zion, 1-3, as a result of the judgments upon the wicked, 4-12.

Psalm 77. The Troubled Saint, 1-10, finds his comfort recalling past deliverances, 11-20.

Psalm 78. God in Israel's History Is Seen, 1-55, despite continued provocation by His people, 56-64. Grace appears to David, 65-72.

Psalm 79. Prayer for Judgment upon Jerusalem's Enemies. This lament points to some great national calamity, such as Shishak's invasion, the fall of the city to the Babylonians or to Antiochus Epiphanes or the Romans. But the prophetic meaning will find fulfillment in Jerusalem under the false Messiah when the cruelties of Antiochus Epiphanes will be repeated (cf. Rev 11:3-12).

Psalm 80. Cry for Restoration of the Nation Israel. The Lord, the Shepherd of Israel (Gen 49:24), is invoked, 1-2, to restore, 3, 7, the chastened and scattered nation, 4-6. Under the figure of a vine (cf. Isa 5:1-7), the redemption of the nation out of Egypt, 8-13, is made the basis of the appeal for final pre-kingdom restoration, 14-16, through Messiah, "the man of thy right hand," 17, who will seek His scattered sheep, 18-19, to restore them, 19. (Cf. 3, 7, 19 with Ezk 34:11-31.)

Psalm 81. Israel's Regathering. The blowing of trumpets foreshadows Israel's age-end regathering, 1-5, the answer to the prayer of Ps 80:3, 7, 19. The restoration is focused against the background of deliverance out of Egypt, 6-10, and the nation's subsequent disobedience and chastisement, 11-16.

283

Psalm 82. Pre-Kingdom Judgment. God takes His place as the supreme and righteous Judge, la, to judge the nations and to administer justice in contrast to unjust judges, 1b-7. (The word "gods" is used of magistrates who represent God, Ex 21:6; Ps 58:1; Jn 10:34-36.) His right to judge is in the fact that all the nations belong to Him as He takes possession of the kingdom, 8.

Psalm 83. Israel's Enemies Overthrown. The nation's foes of the writer's day, 1-8, foreshadow the final coalition and its complete overthrow, 9-18 (cf. Isa 10:28-34; Joel 2:1-11; Dan 11:36-42; Zech 12:2).

PSALMS 84—89. PRAYER ISSUING IN KINGDOM GLORY

Psalm 84. Spiritual Vitality of the Kingdom. Revitalized worship, 1-4; faith, 5-8; and service, 9-12, are realized by the manifestation of the Lord in the person of God's Anointed, 9, Israel's sun (cf. Ps 80:3, 7, 19) and shield, 11.

Psalm 85. Promised Blessing in the Kingdom. The benefits, 1-3, realized by prayer, 4-9, include righteousness and millennial peace, 10-13.

Psalm 86. A Prayer, 1-9, and Praise, 10-17, find full realization in the Kingdom Age, as 9 shows (cf. Isa 2:1-5).

Psalm 87. Zion Attains Glory in the Kingdom. Zion (Jerusalem) is honored, 1-6, above all cities and celebrated as a fountain of blessing, 7.

Psalm 88. Soul Cry of Distress, 1-7, with no apparent answer, 8-18, pictures the dark experiences of the godly in Israel.

Psalm 89. God's Fidelity, 1-18, is manifested in the fulfillment of the Davidic covenant, 19-37 (cf. 2 Sam 7:9-14, 27), which can refer only to Immanuel (Isa 7:13-15; 9:6-7; Mic 5:2). The plea of the godly remnant (cf. Isa 1:9; Rom 11:5) goes forth for the cessation of the chastening visited upon the Davidic house, 38-52.

PSALMS 90—93. FROM SINFUL WANDERING TO REDEMPTION REST

Book 4 of the Psalter, Psalms 90-106, is compared by some to Numbers, the book of wilderness wandering (cf. Ps 90). It contains numerous psalms describing the time when the wilderness experiences of God's people end with glory for Israel and the nations.

Psalm 90. Man's Fallen Condition. Moses meditates upon man's frailty and death because of sin, 1-10. He prays for God's interposition for sinful man, 11-17.

Psalm 91. Redeemed Man in Fellowship with God. His dependence upon God, 1-2, as He walks among men "in the secret place" under "the shadow of the Almighty," results in his security, 3-8, triumph and exaltation, 9-16. Satan realized the application of this psalm to Jesus, 11-12 (cf. Mt 4:6).

Psalm 92. Song of Praise for Ultimate Rest (Song for the Sabbath Day) as a result of God's "work" of redemption, 4; His conquest of the enemies of His people, 5-9; and His favor to His own, 10-15. The application of the psalm is perennial. Its fulfillment, however, is millennial.

Psalm 93. The Lord's Millennial Reign (cf. Rev 11:15-18). The Lord begins His reign over the earth in holiness, 5.

PSALMS 94—100. JUDGMENT AND THE GLORIES OF THE COMING AGE

Psalm 94. Judgment of the Wicked. Prayer is made for divine vengeance upon the wicked, 1-13. The righteous are comforted, 14-23, as their enemies and God's enemies are destroyed.

Psalm 95. Worship and Joy in Prospect of the Advent of Israel's Saviour-King. His right to rule is by virtue of His ownership of the earth, 1-5, and man as a result of creation and redemption, 6-7a. Let those who are about to enter kingdom rest take warning against disobedience from those who forfeited the rest of Canaan, 7b-11 (cf. Heb 3:7-11).

Psalm 96. The Second Advent. The Lord is supreme, 1-6. Creation celebrates, 7-13. The "new song" is based on a finished redemption and its realized benefits for man and the earth (cf. Ps 98:1-3).

Psalm 97. The King Reigns, 1-5. The results of His reign are indicated, 6-12.

Psalm 98. The New Song of Triumph. All creation is summoned to celebrate the establishment of the Lord's kingship in the earth with a new song, 1-9.

Psalm 99. The Lord's Earthly Kingship. He is the ruler of the earth, 1-3. "Holy is he!" is the refrain, 5, 9. His rule will be just, 4-5; His dealings faithful, 6-9.

Psalm 100. Israel's Kingdom Praise. The call to worship is on the basis of the deity of the King and the redemption wrought by Him for His own, 2, and the fact of His goodness and His covenant mercy, 5.

PSALMS 101—106. THE RIGHTEOUS KING IN HUMILIATION AND GLORY

Psalm 101. The Righteous King and His Rule. David speaks as a prophet of the true King's character, 1-3, and His righteous kingdom rule, 4-8.

Psalm 102. Christ the King in His Rejection. The reference to verses 25-27 in Heb 1:10-12 demonstrates this ode predicts the soul exercise of the God-Man.

Psalm 103. Israel's Kingdom Praise is rendered for blessings of full salvation, 1-7; for the Lord's gracious character, 8-18; and for His established kingdom, 19-22.

Psalm 104. Creation's Millennial Praise to the Creator, Messiah-Christ, 1-9 (cf. 4 with Heb 1:7), for His creation works manifesting His kindness and greatness, 10-35.

Psalm 105. Historical Retrospect. The wonders of the exodus from Egypt are celebrated.

Psalm 106. Historical Retrospect. The goodness and patience of God in the desert wanderings are recalled.

PSALMS 107—108. ISRAEL'S DELIVERANCES AND PRAISE TO GOD

Book 5 of the Psalter, Psalms 107—150, is compared by some to Deuteronomy. It sets forth the divine dealing with Israel eventuating in deliverance for them, the nation, and all creation. The book ends with a Hallelujah Chorus of redemption.

Psalm 107. God's Mercies to Israel. Their final regathering and restoration, 1-9 (cf. Deut 30:1-10); their liberation from bondage, 10-16, despite their folly, 17-22, and unrest, 23-32, are reviewed. Their praise of God for His deliverances is recorded, 33-43.

Psalm 108. Israel's Praise, 1-4, for her inheritance, 5-9, through the Lord, 10-13, is offered.

PSALMS 109—113. CHRIST IN REJECTION, EXALTATION AND COMING GLORY

Psalm 109. Prediction of Christ's Rejection. David as prophet sees the despised and rejected One, 1-5, His rejecters and their doom, 6-20 (cf. 8 and Acts 1:20). The voice of the rejected One echoes in 21-25, and merges into the voice of the final remnant, 26-31, identified with Him.

Psalm 110. Christ As King-Priest. Christ, David's son and Lord (His deity), is exalted in resurrection and ascension, 1 (cf. Jn 20:17;

Acts 7:56), and waiting till His enemies are put down. His second advent, 2-3, to accomplish this and reign as King-Priest according to His eternal priesthood, is described, 4 (Heb 5:6; 6:20; 7:21). His judgments and victories prior to His kingdom glory are predicted, 5-7 (cf. Joel 3:9-17; Zech 14:1-4; Rev 19:11-21).

Psalm 111. Hallelujah! The King-Priest on His Throne (cf. Ps 110). First of the Hallelujah ("Praise the Lord") Psalms. His work of redemption is praised (Lk 1:68).

Psalm 112. Hallelujah! The Righteous Are Rewarded by the King-Priest on His Throne.

Psalm 113. Hallelujah! Praise the Lord for what He is, 1-6, and what He does, 7-9.

PSALMS 114—117. PAST DELIVERANCES AND FUTURE PRAISE

Psalm 114. The Egyptian Deliverance in Retrospect. Future deliverance is implicit in prospect (cf. Jer 16:14-15).

Psalm 115. Israel's God. Who He is, 1-3, is contrasted with what idols are, 4-8. The exalted One can be implicitly trusted, 9-18.

Psalm 116. Israel's Praise of God for Deliverance from Death, 1-9. This centers in the dark experiences of unparalleled suffering and martyrdom, 15. The godly who escape thank God, 10-19.

Psalm 117. Universal Praise in the Kingdom. The praise, 1, is followed by the reason for it, 2.

PSALMS 118—119. MESSIAH AND THE WORD OF GOD EXALTED

Psalm 118. Messiah Exalted As the Head Cornerstone. This great hallelujah psalm was sung by our Lord and His disciples in observing the Passover the night He was betrayed (Mt 26:30; Mk 14:26). He applied verses 22-23 to Himself (Mt 21:42). The psalm looks beyond the rejection of the Stone (Christ) to His ultimate exaltation in the kingdom.

Psalm 119. The Word of God Exalted. Although omnitemporally applicable, this magnificent alphabetic acrostic (each of the 22 letters of the Heb. alphabet occurs eight times in the 22 sections) will be fulfilled when Israel, under the new covenant, will have the law written "in their hearts" (Jer 31:31-33).

PSALMS 120—134. THE PSALMS OF ASCENT

Apparently these psalms were sung as pilgrims went up to Jerusalem to the sacred feasts.

Psalm 120. Suffering of the Godly. David's prayer for deliverance from enemies and persecutors breathes the same spirit as the cry of the distressed godly of all ages.

Psalm 121. Israel's Keeper and Preserver. He never fails His own, 1-8.

Psalm 122. Prayer for Jerusalem's Peace. This is a song praising Zion as the pilgrims' goal. A group of pilgrims arrives for a feast and admires the city, 1-5, and prays for its peace and prosperity, 6-9.

Psalm 123. Cry for Mercy in Distress. Humble dependence upon God, 1-2, and a plea for mercy is made, 3-4, in the face of contempt from the proud and the worldly.

Psalm 124. Answer of Prayer for Mercy. This psalm is the answer to the cry of Ps 123.

Psalm 125. Reward of the Righteous and Punishment of the Wicked. Expression of confident faith, 1-3, and prayer for help, 4-5, will be fulfilled in Israel's future blessings.

Psalm 126. Song of the Returned Captives. The joy of past favors, 1-3, inspires prayer for final restoration, 4-6.

Psalm 127. Praise God from Whom All Blessings Flow. Faith in God is basic to all real prosperity, 1-2. The gift of many male children is a blessing to an Eastern father, 3-5.

Psalm 128. Blessings Out of Zion are to be fully realized when the Lord reigns.

Psalm 129. The Lord, Israel's Preserver, has protected His people in the past, 1-4. Prayer is offered that Israel's enemies may not triumph over her, 5-8.

Psalm 130. The Lord, Israel's Faithful Redeemer. The personal experience of a believer, 1-6, is a pattern for the nation, 7-8.

Psalm 131. The Lord, Israel's Hope. The psalmist's experience of quiet submission, 1-2, is an example for the nation, 3.

Psalm 132. Messiah, David's Son, Enthroned. David's concern for God's house, 1-10, is rewarded by the Davidic covenant, 11-12. It will be realized in King-Messiah at His second advent, 13-18.

Psalm 133. The Blessings of Fraternal Harmony. Such brotherhood is good and pleasant, 1, like Aaron's anointing, 2, and refreshing dew on Mt. Hermon, 3. It is the atmosphere in which God commands spiritual blessing.

Psalm 134. Blessed Worship. The priests are called to render praise to the Lord, 1, and to bless the congregation, 2-3.

PSALMS 135—136. RESTORED ISRAEL IN PRAISEFUL WORSHIP

Psalm 135. The Nation Cleansed and Converted Worships (cf. Ex 19:4-5; Zech 3:1-7). The call is to worship, 1-4, and adore Him who controls nature, 5-7; who redeemed the nation and set it in Palestine, 8-18; who is above all gods and is therefore worthy of all worship, 19-21.

Psalm 136. The Redeemed Nation's Praise of God's Mercy. His mercy is revealed in creation, 1-9; in Israel's redemption, 10-15; in the wilderness wanderings, 16; and in the conquest of Canaan, 17-22. A summary of His mercy follows, 23-26.

PSALM 137—139. THE EXPERIENCES OF GOD'S PEOPLE IN THE LIGHT OF THEIR GOD

Psalm 137. The Experience of the Exile looks through the Babylonian Captivity to the final age-end restoration when Israel's foes are punished, 8-9 (cf. Isa 13:16; 47:6).

Psalm 138. Praise to the Lord, 1-3, culminates in full kingdom blessing, 4-6, but brings immediate blessing to the worshiper, 7-8.

Psalm 139. Israel's Creator-Redeemer is omniscient, 1-6; omnipresent, 7-12; worthy of all praise, 13-18; righteous and holy to punish sin and sinners, 19-24.

PSALMS 140—143. TRIALS AND TROUBLES OF GOD'S PEOPLE

Psalms 140—143. Prayer for Deliverance from Enemies. These reflect David's various experiences of suffering. He cries for vindication in his distress, and prays for deliverance and restoration to spiritual prosperity.

PSALMS 144—145. DAVID'S EXPERIENCES A MIRROR OF ISRAEL'S FUTURE

Psalm 144. Prayer for Manifestation of the Lord's Power. God is praised, 1-2, and His help invoked in the light of man's weakness, 3-4. Let the Lord come to deliver from enemies, 5-8. Israel's "new song" of redemption, 9-11, will be sung in kingdom blessing, 12-15 (cf. Ps 96:1; Rev 5:9; 14:3; 15:3).

Psalm 145. The Glory of King-Messiah and His Kingdom. This is an alphabetic acrostic of personal praise, 1-3; of the Lord's wonderful works, 4-7; of His love, 8-9; of His millennial kingdom, 10-13; and His providential care for His creatures, 14-21.

PSALMS 146—150. THE GRAND HALLELUJAH FINALE

Each of these five psalms opens and closes with Hallelujah, "Praise the Lord."

Psalm 146. Hallelujah! The God of Jacob, 1-2. This is the designation of Him who loves the helpless sinner in redemptive compassion, 3-4; yet who is the mighty Creator, faithful, righteous, provident, 5-7; the glorious Saviour and Protector, 8-9, and the eternal King, 10.

Psalm 147. Hallelujah! For His Power and Providential Care, 1-11, especially toward Israel, 12-20.

Psalm 148. Hallelujah! Let All Creatures Praise Him in heaven, 1-6, and on earth, 7-14.

Psalm 149. Hallelujah! Sing the New Song of Redemption. Redeemed Israel leads the Hallelujah chorus, 1-3, because the Lord has given victory, vindicating His own, 4-9.

Psalm 150. Hallelujah! Climactic Crescendo of Universal Praise. The ultimate purpose of creation is the praise of the Creator. God alone is worthy. Hallelujah!

PROVERBS

COMPENDIUM OF MORAL AND SPIRITUAL INSTRUCTION

Nature of the Book. This writing is most typical of the Wisdom Literature of the OT (cf. Job and Ecclesiastes). It is a library of moral and spiritual instruction for the young to insure a godly, happy life here and reward in the life to come. A proverb (Heb. *mashal*, from a root "to reign, rule," also "be like, represent") is a precept or sententious saying *regulating* or *governing* conduct and life, often taking the form of a resemblance or parable. Many proverbs are condensed parables.

Authorship. Many of the Proverbs stem from Solomon (1:1; 10:1; 25:1; cf. 1 Kgs 4:32; 2 Chr 1:10; Eccl 12:9); some from Agur (30:1) and Lemuel (31:1), who are unknown persons.

Recipients. The writer's son (1:8; 2:1, etc.) is presumably Rehoboam. But the precepts are for all youth (4:1), and in broadest scope for all men (8:1-5).

Proverbs and Near Eastern Literature. The section 22:17—24:34 bears special similarity to the proverbs of an Egyptian writer by the name of Amenemope (dated between 1000-600 B.C.), showing the prevalence of this type of wisdom literature outside the Bible. Proverb literature is very ancient, going back in written form to about 2700 B.C. in Egypt.

Outline

Book I.   Proverbs of Solomon, 1:1—9:18
Book II.   Various Sayings of Solomon, 10:1—22:16
Book III.   Words of the Wise, 22:17—24:34
Book IV.   Proverbs Copied by Hezekiah's Scribes, 25:1—29:27
Agur's Words, 30:1-33
Queen Mother's Counsel to Her Son, 31:1-9
The Virtuous Wife, 31:10-31

CHAPTER 1.   PURPOSE OF THE BOOK OF PROVERBS

To Promote Wisdom and Godly Living, 1-7. Verse 7 strikes the theme of the entire book. Reverence toward God is the essential prelude to all wisdom and successful living.

Home Discipline Is a Moral Safeguard, 8-19, against a life of crime.

Wisdom Personified, 20-33, as a prophetess and teacher. She shows the folly of those who reject moral instruction and discipline.

CHAPTERS 2—3. RESULTS OF THE PURSUIT OF WISDOM

The Promise of Wisdom, 2:1-22. The pursuit of wisdom brings a knowledge of God, 5; produces moral safeguards, 6-15; delivers from the loose woman, 16-19; and gives prosperity, 20-22.

The Precepts of Wisdom, 3:1-35, make for physical and spiritual well-being, 1-10. Even adversity becomes the discipline of a loving father, 11-12, and inculcates a true sense of values, 13-18, understanding of God's creation, 19-20, and practical righteousness, 21-35.

CHAPTER 4. THE PRIMACY OF WISDOM

In Both Teacher and Student, 1-19. The teacher had been taught wisdom by his parents, 1-9, and the pupil is admonished likewise to receive wisdom and profit by it, 10-19, as the principal acquirement of life.

Wisdom Practiced, 20-27, is productive of life, health and personal integrity.

CHAPTERS 5—7. MORAL RESTRAINT OF WISDOM

Restraint Against Sexual Sins, 5:1-14, is urged and marital infidelity is warned against, 15-23.

Restraint Against Various Sins, 6:1-35. Mentioned are debt, suretyship, 1-5; laziness, 6-11; irresponsible gossip, 12-15; wickedness in general, 16-19; and adultery, 20-35.

Restraint Against the Loose Woman, 7:1-27. Wisdom is personified, 4 (cf. 1:20-33).

CHAPTER 8. REMARKABLE REVELATION OF WISDOM'S IDENTITY

Personified Wisdom, 1-21. Her call, 1-5, is followed by announcement of her worth, 6-11; her authority, 12-16; her rewards, 17-21.

Revelation of Personified Wisdom's Identity, 22-31. Wisdom as a person is revealed to be the preincarnate Christ (although some scholars have denied this). Here Wisdom is revealed to be coeval and coexistent with God. "The Lord *possessed* me [not created me] in the beginning of his way, *before* his works of old," 22. This beginning, like John 1:1: "In the *beginning* was the Word . . .," is an absolute timeless beginning. This magnificent passage anticipates 1 Cor 1:30; Jn 1:1-3; Heb 1:1-3.

Renewed Appeal, 32-36. How true it is that he who finds God is "happy," 32, 34, because he finds life in Christ the true Wisdom of God.

CHAPTER 9. CONTRAST BETWEEN WISDOM AND FOLLY

Wisdom's Invitation, 1-12. Personified Wisdom (revealed to be Christ) issues an invitation (Mt 11:28-29; cf. Lk 14:15-24).

Folly's Enticement, 13-18. Folly, too, is personified, as a foolish woman, and those who choose her instead of our Lord court death and hell.

10:1—22:16. THE GODLY AND UNGODLY IN CONTRAST AND OTHER MAXIMS

Contrast in Life and Conduct Is Made, 10:1—11:31, in matters of work, diligence, ambition, speech, truth, stability, honesty, integrity, fidelity, guidance, graciousness, kindness, etc.

Contrast Is Made in Relation to Various Conditions, 12:1-28, in thought, words, in domestic relationships, etc.

Contrast in Relation to Advantage and Disadvantage, 13:1-25.

Contrast Between the Wise and Foolish, the Rich and Poor, 14:1-35.

The Better Course of Wisdom and Serving God, 15:1-33.

The Better Way of Life Through Serving the Lord, 16:1-33.

Various Maxims Regulating Good Conduct, 17:1—18:24.

Various Proverbs Regulating Personal Conduct, 19:1—22:16.

22:17—24:34. THE WORDS OF THE WISE

This section, Book 3, shows affinity to the Wisdom of Amenemope (see above). This portion is a teacher's instructions to his student ("son") who is being educated for a place of responsibility.

Introduction, 22:17-21. The Egyptian Wisdom of Amenemope also has 30 sections, of which ten have parallels here.

Various Admonitions Are Given, 23:1-35. These are concerning being a guest, 1-8; speaking, 9; removing a boundary stone, 10-11; parental discipline, 12-14, etc.

Various Admonitions Are Added, 24:1-34. These concern envy, 1-2; wisdom, etc.

CHAPTERS 25—29. PROVERBS COPIED BY HEZEKIAH'S SCRIBES

These constitute Book 4 and consist of separate proverbs guiding moral conduct. They were collected in Hezekiah's time (716-687 B.C.).

Wise Conduct Is Enjoined, 25:1-28, before a king, 1-7; in court, 8-10; in speech, 11-18; in dealing with enemies, 19-22, etc.

Other Sins, 26:1-28. Singled out are the fool, 1-12; the sluggard, 13-16; the meddler, the talebearer, 17-20, 22-23; the contentious, 21; the hater, 24-26; and the liar, 28.

Various Other Maxims, 27:1—29:27. These cover different phases of conduct.

CHAPTER 30. AGUR'S WORDS

God's Power, Truth and Centrality, 1-10, so overwhelm Agur (otherwise unknown) of Massa (cf. Gen 25:14) that he abases himself and owns his ignorance, 1-3. (Cf. Job 42:1-6 as a sequel to God's might as revealed to Job, ch. 40—41.) Such a God must have first place in Agur's life against the dangers of wealth with its pride or poverty, 7-9, with its desperation, 10.

Expose of Rogues and Extortioners, 11-17, is made by their counterparts in nature of things "never satisfied"—the leech, 15; Sheol, the barren womb, thirsty earth and fire, 16.

Expose of the Shameless Adulteress, 18-20, by four wonders in nature: the eagle in flight, a gliding snake, a sailing ship, and a man and a maid (cf. 2:16-20; 5:1-23; 23:27, etc.).

Expose of the Arrogant, Foolish, 21-23.

Expose of the Indolent, Disorderly, Cowardly, 24-33, by the industrious ant, humble badgers, orderly locusts and puny lizard; by the fearless lion, fleet greyhound, he goat and king. Warning against strife is given, 32-33.

31:1-9. A QUEEN MOTHER'S COUNSEL TO HER SON

Words of Lemuel, 1, are a twofold lesson taught him by his mother. His name is unidentifiable, and Massa could be a place name (cf. Gen 25:14), or simply "King Lemuel, an oracle."

The Maternal Warning, 2-9, is given negatively to avoid lust, 3, and strong drink, 4-7; and positively to rule righteously and impartially, 8-9.

31:10-31. THE VIRTUES OF AN IDEAL WIFE

This noble acrostic poem (each verse beginning with a letter of the Heb. alphabet) is a choice gem of Wisdom Literature. It may be a part of the queen mother's counsel to her son, 31:1-9, or a separate poem.

The Ideal Housewife's Character, 10-28. She is priceless, 10; trustworthy, 11; industrious, 12-19; charitable and unselfish, 20-22; a boon to her husband, 23; possessing business acumen, 24; strong, dignified, 25; wise, provident, 26-27; and respected and loved by her children, 28.

Writer's Appraisal of Her, 29-31. She is superlative, 29. Two appended proverbs on the godly woman are deduced, 30-31.

ECCLESIASTES

THE FUTILE THINKING AND LIVING OF THE NATURAL MAN

Place in Canon. In the Hebrew Bible the book is placed in the third division with the other rolls (Song, Ruth, Lamentations, Esther) used at special feasts. Ecclesiastes was read at the Feast of Tabernacles in the fall. In the English order, it is placed as Wisdom Literature after Proverbs. Because its meaning has been frequently misunderstood, its legitimate place in the canon has sometimes been disputed.

Difficulty of the Book. Ecclesiastes is perhaps the most perplexing and confusing book of the Bible to the average reader. Reasons: (1) Its spirit of hopeless despair, depicting the emptiness and disappointment of life. (2) Its lack of a note of praise or peace, in contrast to other Wisdom Literature of Scripture. (3) Its seeming sanction of conduct at variance with the rest of Scripture.

Nature and Purpose of the Book. The difficulties can be resolved only by a correct view of the nature and purpose of the book. (1) It must first be understood as the *book of the natural man*—his reasonings and actions apart from the Spirit of God and divine revelation (cf. 1 Cor 2:14). This is the meaning of the characteristic phrase "under the sun," occurring 29 times. This is why the covenant name "Lord" (Jehovah) is not used, only Elohim as Creator. Hence the writer is confined to natural revelation (the light which nature gives) and human reason (cf. the clause "I communed with my own heart," occurring seven times). (2) The purpose of the book must be seen to demonstrate to the natural man the complete emptiness of that which is "under the sun" apart from that which is *above* the sun, i.e., God's revelation and salvation.

Outline
The Theme: The Supreme Emptiness of Godless Living, 1:1-3
The Theme Proved, 1:4—3:22
The Theme Expanded, 4:1—12:8
The Conclusion Reached, 12:9-14

1:1-3. THE THEME OF THE BOOK

See "The Nature and Purpose of the Book" above. "Vanity of vanities" is a Heb. expression meaning the supreme or consummate "vanity" or "emptiness" ("breath"). "Preacher" (Heb. *Koheleth;* Gr. *Ecclesiastes*) suggests one who addresses or teaches an assembly (Heb. *qahal*). The feminine signifies an office or title. Koheleth (a pen name?) is intimated to be Solomon, 1, 12.

1:4—3:22. THE THEME OF THE EMPTINESS OF LIFE PROVED

By the Transitoriness of Things, 1:4-11. Generations pass on, nature continues in the same round, but nothing new results.

By the Futility of Human Endeavor, 1:12-18.

By the Emptiness of Pleasure, Wealth and Work, 2:1-26. Man's sole good is present enjoyment, argues the natural man, as later Gr. philosophers concluded by natural reason.

By the Certainty of Death, 3:1-22. Mortality robs man of the fruits of his labor (cf. 2:12-26). Man is helpless to understand or alter the predetermined pattern of his life, 1-15. Is his end not like that of the beasts, 16-22?

THEOLOGICAL NOTE

In a study of this book one must carefully distinguish between what is *revealed truth* and what is merely the *inspired record* of man's unaided reasonings. Erroneous teachings, such as annihilation, 3:16-22, and soul sleep, 9:5, 10, cannot be said to be taught by God's Word when they are recorded by inspiration as merely natural man's reasonings.

4:1—12:8. THE THEME OF THE EMPTINESS OF LIFE EXPANDED

In View of the Inequalities of Life, 4:1-16. The folly of wasting life through envy or avarice is noted, 1-6, a miser's wealth being a cheap substitute for human fellowship, 7-12. Even royal fame and power are evanescent, 13-16.

In View of Religious Insincerity, 5:1-7, and Wealth, 8-20.

In View of Man's End, 6:1-12. Both his life and his death are uncertain. The natural man without divine illumination is baffled by both.

In View of Man's Sin, 7:1-29. The "man under the sun," the natural mind unilluminated by God's Spirit, sees no advantage in being righteous, 13-21, and is hazy with regard to spiritual things and the meaning of earthly existence and its end.

In View of Life's Uncertainties, 8:1—9:18. The natural mind flounders in obscurity. It vaguely bows to wisdom 8:1, and to the king because he is absolute, 2-4. But life itself is a riddle and nothing absolute can be known about the future, 5-9, nor anything of life in general. Death is a conundrum, 9:1-16, to the spiritually unrenewed man.

In View of Life's Disorders, 10:1-20. Only divine revelation can give symmetry and meaning to life. The man "under the sun" here gives further proof of his lack of spiritual illumination.

In View of Youth, 11:1-10. Various proverbs are set forth, 1-7. The natural man needs a supernatural birth to enable him to discern spiritual meaning in life and death. Ecclesiastes proves it. The book mirrors the heart of the unregenerate man and points to his need of salvation in Christ. The meaning of youth, 9-10, is vague to Koheleth in his natural reasonings.

In View of Old Age, 12:1-8. Koheleth does rise to see the creatorship of God and urges remembrance of God as such in youth. But the natural man needs more than the knowledge of God as Creator if he is to be lifted out of his natural blindness. He needs God as *Saviour*. Symbols of the decrepitude of age are set forth, 2-6: grinders (teeth?), 4; "those that look through the windows" (eyes?), 4; "almond tree blossoms," 5, are white, suggesting the silver-white hair of the aged; "the grasshopper drags itself along," 5, the stiff-legged gait of the aged.

12:9-14. CONCLUSION REACHED—PRACTICAL PIETY IN VIEW OF JUDGMENT

"Fear [reverence] God and keep his commandments." This is the whole duty of *redeemed* man. But Koheleth does not tell how man is to be redeemed.

SONG OF SOLOMON

SANCTITY OF WEDDED LOVE

The Book and Its Author. The author was doubtless Solomon as 1:1 states, and as the local color and internal evidence sustain. However, this verse may be rendered: "The song of songs which is *about* or *concerning* Solomon" (cf. 1:4; 3:7-11; 8:11). "Song of songs" is a Heb. idiom for "chiefest" or "most superlative song" of the monarch's 1005 songs (cf. 1 Kgs 4:32). The date is about 965 B.C. It is the first of the five scrolls in the third part of the Heb. canon, and was sung at Passover in the spring. It is a magnificent literary gem, considered eminently chaste among Orientals. What a pity that such a masterpiece should sometimes be perverted.

The Purpose. Critics quibble over the question of whether it is a homogeneous poem, or just a collection of love lyrics to celebrate an Eastern wedding. We believe it is a homogeneous poem and its purposes are:

1. In a general sense to honor marriage and the joys of wedded love. The key word is "beloved" (32 times), and the theme is the love of the bridegroom for the bride.

2. Primarily, in application, to show the Lord's love for Israel, particularly His godly remnant (Hos 2:19-20).

3. Secondarily, to set forth Christ's love for the Church (2 Cor 11:2; Eph 5:25-33; Rev 19:7-9).

The Characters. There are only two. The higher critical notion of Heinrich Ewald (1826) of a third, a shepherd lover from whom Solomon despicably tries to seduce the shepherdess, is false and dishonoring.

The Background of the Story. H. A. Ironside's presentation of the setting of the poem is meaningful. King Solomon had a vineyard in the hill country of Ephraim, about 50 miles N of Jerusalem, 8:11. He let it out to keepers, 8:11, consisting of a mother, two sons, 1:6, and two daughters—the Shulamite, 6:13, and a little sister, 8:8. The Shulamite was "the Cinderella" of the family, 1:5, naturally beautiful but unnoticed. Her brothers were likely half brothers, 1:6. They made her work very hard tending the vineyards, so that she had little opportunity to care for her personal appearance, 1:6. She pruned the vines and set traps for the little foxes, 2:15. She also kept the flocks, 1:8. Being out in the open so much, she became sunburned, 1:5.

One day a handsome stranger came to the vineyard. It was Solomon disguised. He showed an interest in her, and she became embarrassed concerning her personal appearance, 1:6. She took him for a shepherd and asked about his flocks, 1:7. He answered evasively, 1:8, but also spoke loving words to her, 1:8-10, and promised rich gifts for the future, 1:11. He won her heart and left with the promise that some day he would return. She dreamed of him at night and sometimes thought he was near, 3:1. Finally he did return in all his kingly splendor to make her his bride, 3:6-7. This prefigures Christ, who came first as Shepherd and won His Bride. Later He will return as King, and then will be consummated the marriage of the Lamb.

Outline

Bride Muses in the Bridegroom's Palace, 1:1—3:5
Bride Accepts the Bridegroom's Invitation, 3:6—5:1
Bride Dreams of Separation from the Bridegroom, 5:2—6:3
Bride and Bridegroom Express Ardent Love for Each Other, 6:4—8:14

1:1—3:5. MUSINGS OF THE BRIDE IN THE BRIDEGROOM'S PALACE

She Muses on Her First Love for Solomon, 1:1-17. On the title, 1:1, see introduction. The Song begins with the bride's recollection of her first intense longings for her beloved, 2-3, and how she had first voiced her love for him, 4. She explains her dark beauty to the palace women as due to sunburn and hard work in her brothers' vineyard before Solomon's visit, 5-6, when they fell in love (see background of the story in the introduction). She reminisces on her lover (Solomon) when he first appeared at the vineyard disguised as a shepherd, 7. Verse 8 is apparently the reply of the bride's companions. She vividly recalls the king's rapturous praise of her beauty, 9-11; her praising him as her beloved, 12-14; his assuring her of his delight in her beauty, 15; and her own response to his love, 16-17.

The Bride's Musings on the Blossoming Romance, 2:1—3:5. She recalls Solomon's comparing himself and her to lovely flowers, 2:1-2, and her intense satisfaction in his companionship, 3-6. The refrain, 7 (cf. 3:5; 8:4) which the bride addresses to "the daughters of

Jerusalem," i.e., the women of the king's harem in Jerusalem, is that Solomon and the maid are not to be disturbed "till love itself shall please," i.e., run its full course. Continuing to turn leaves in her book of memory, she recalls rapturously Solomon's visit to her and his invitation to be his bride and come with him to Jerusalem, 8-17. The bride's first dream, 3:1-4 (cf. 5:2-8), is recalled in which she envisioned herself separated from her beloved at Jerusalem. After finding him, she dreamed she had led him to her humble home in the north.

3:6—5:1. THE BRIDE ACCEPTS THE BRIDEGROOM'S INVITATION

Solomon Brings His Bride to Jerusalem, 3:6-11. Her dream, 1-4, is closely connected with ch. 2 as well as 3:5 (cf. 2:7). Solomon comes for his bride and takes her from her rural home to Jerusalem, 6-11. Whether applied antitypically to Messiah's second advent in glory for Israel (Zech 12:10; 13:1, 9), or Christ's coming for His Church (1 Thess 4:13-18; 1 Jn 3:1-3), or simply the bliss of God-ordained marriage, the lessons are sublimely beautiful.

The Bridegroom Praises the Bride, 4:1-15. So will the Lord's people, whether the Church or redeemed Israel, be the object of the praise and delight of the Lord in the day of His appearance.

Anticipation of the Joys of Married Love, 4:16 — 5:1, signifying the blessings of the Lord's redeemed in manifested union and glory with Him (1 Jn 3:3; Rev 19:5-7; 20:6).

5:2—6:3. THE BRIDE DREAMS OF SEPARATION FROM THE BRIDEGROOM, BUT FINDS HIM

The Bride's Second Dream, 5:2-8 (cf. 3:1-4). The bridegroom knocks at her door, but he is not there when she opens it. She wanders about the city in search for him. This experience is evidently a dream (see 6:2).

In Praising Him to Others, She Claims Him As Her Own, 5:9— 6:3. Her dream shows how much she loves him and misses him.

6:4—8:14. THE BRIDE AND BRIDEGROOM EXPRESS THEIR ARDENT LOVE FOR ONE ANOTHER

He Praises Her Loveliness, 6:4-10. His praise of her beauty recalls his ardent praise in 4:1-15. Tirzah, 4, was a city of northern Israel, which became the capital of the northern kingdom till Omri founded Samaria.

Her Experience in the Nut Orchard, 6:11-13. This experience was an emotional elation in connection with which she is called the "Shulamite," 13, i.e., "a maid of Shunem," a small town in northern Palestine. (The "n" interchanges with "l" in place names.)

Mutual Praise and Devotion, 7:1—8:14. They both express their praise of and devotion to each other, 7:1—8:4, asserting their unquenchable love, 8:5-14.

THE PROPHETS

The Prophets' Messages. These were primarily moral and spiritual in their purpose. Israel's prophets were rugged reformers, divinely raised up to call the nation from sin and idolatry in its periods of decline. They thundered forth warnings of impending doom in the centuries preceding the fall of Israel in 722 B.C. and the fall of Judah in 586 B.C. Their weighty messages of woe, however, were frequently the vehicle for far-reaching messianic prophecies. Daniel and Ezekiel ministered hope and comfort to the exiles. Haggai and Zechariah encouraged the weak remnant that returned. Malachi sounded a somber note of warning and repentance illuminated by brilliant messianic flashes.

Excavations at Ramat Rahel on the edge of Jerusalem, where some have concluded that King Uzziah built his palace and lived during his years as a leper. (*Courtesy Howard F. Vos*)

Isaiah Through Malachi

THE PROPHETS AND THEIR AGE

Prophet	Message	Period c. 800-400 B.C.
Amos Hosea Jonah	Divine punishment follows persistent sin. God's love for Israel. Nineveh, repent! God's concern for Gentiles.	To Israel before the fall of the northern kingdom, 722 B.C.
Joel Obadiah Isaiah Micah	The day of the Lord and judgment of nations. Doom upon Edom. The coming Saviour and Israel's King. Bethlehem's King and kingdom.	To Judah during her declining years.
Jeremiah Nahum Habakkuk Zephaniah	Jerusalem's judgment and coming glory. Doom of Nineveh and Assyria. The Lord's kingdom and people will triumph. Remnant rescued for blessing.	To Judah in her last years, 634-606 B.C.
Daniel Ezekiel	The times of the Gentiles and Israel's kingdom. Future restoration of Israel and the land.	To exiles in Babylon, 606-538 B.C.
Haggai Zechariah Malachi	Restoration of temple and kingdom foretold. Messiah the Branch and King-Priest. Final judgment and warning to the nation.	To restored community, 538-400 B.C.

Contemporary Kings of Israel, Syria, and Assyria

Israel	Syria	Assyria
Jeroboam II 782-753 B.C.	Benhadad II (801 B.C.——) and a successor (?)	Ashurdan III (773-755 B.C.). Assyria weak.
Zachariah 753/752 B.C.	Rezin (c. 740-732 B.C.), Ras-unnu in the monuments, al-	Ashur-nirari V (755-745 B.C.). Assyria weak.
Shallum 752 B.C.	lied himself with Pekah against Ahaz (Isa 7:1-12) in the Syro-Ephraimite war	Tiglath-pileser III (745-727 B.C.) (Pul of 2 Kgs 15:19), to whom Ahaz appealed for
Menahem 752-742 B.C.	(735-732 B.C.). The Rezin-Pekah alliance is recorded in	aid against Rezin and Pekah, and who invaded and carried
Pekahiah 742-740 B.C.	Tiglath-pileser's inscriptions.	captive northern Israel (733 B.C.). In 732 B.C. he captured
Pekah 740-732 B.C.		Damascus and killed Rezin, and put all northern Pales-tine and Syria under tribute.
Hoshea 732-722 B.C.		

Shalmaneser V (727-722 B.C.) (2 Kgs 17:3; 18:9) conquered the Phoenician coast, received tribute from Hoshea, and laid siege to Samaria when Hoshea allied himself with So (2 Kgs 17:4), an otherwise unknown Egyptian dynast.

Sargon II (722-705 B.C.) took Samaria in 722 B.C., when 27,290 chief citizens were carried into captivity. This was the end of the northern kingdom of Israel.

Fall of Samaria 722 B.C.

Sennacherib (705-681 B.C.), great statesman, conqueror, aqueduct builder, invaded Judah in 701 B.C. He mentions Hezekiah in his annals inscribed in cuneiform on a clay prism in the British Museum (a copy is also in the Oriental Institute of the University of Chicago). (Cf. Isa 36—37; 2 Kgs 18—19).

ISAIAH

PROPHECY OF THE COMING SAVIOUR AND ISRAEL'S KING

Writer. Isaiah ("Jehovah is salvation") is the great messianic prophet and prince of OT seers. For splendor of diction, brilliance of imagery, versatility and beauty of style, profundity and breadth of prophetic vision, he is without peer. He was the son of Amoz (1:1) and traditionally said to be of royal extraction—the brother of King Amaziah, grandson of King Joash. The traditional dates for his ministry are c. 750-680 B.C.

Unity of the Book. Since the days of J. C. Doederlein (1775) the Isaianic authorship of ch. 40—66 has been commonly denied. Critics have attributed this section to an unknown "Deutero-Isaiah" of the period 550-539 B.C., and others have imagined a third author (Trito-Isaiah) for ch. 55—66, dating them around 450 B.C.

Three main arguments are advanced against the unity of the book: (a) *the literary style,* (b) *the theological ideas,* and (c) *the theme and subject matter* are supposedly different in the two (or three) main sections of the book. It is stated that these differences can be accounted for only by a difference in authorship. However, careful study reveals that *similarities in style* between the sections are more significant than the supposed differences, and even those differences are explained by the change in Isaiah's situation during the later years. As to the alleged theological differences, the germinal doctrines of ch. 40—66 can be traced in the earlier section. *No theological contradictions* between the sections can be found. The changed political conditions under the wicked Manasseh in the later years account for the new emphases which appear.

The argument that the theme and subject matter of the later chapters require another author is more serious. Ch. 1—39 are contemporary in setting, while ch. 40—66 are future to Isaiah's time. Critics argue that it is rationally untenable to hold that the prophets ever projected themselves (by divine revelation) into an ideal standpoint in the future. Since in these later chapters Isaiah sees events distinctly related to the Babylonian Captivity and the return therefrom, which have since been historically fulfilled, this material must have been added later by a "Second Isaiah" who was contemporary with the return from the Captivity. However, *futuristic prophecy has an important role* in the first section as well as in the second. In addition, the decadent age of Manasseh demanded a series of prophecies which would reveal the future glory for Israel as the light of her testimony burned low. There is nothing unnatural about the themes of ch. 40—66 when compared with ch. 1—39.

Kings of Judah Contemporary with Isaiah

Uzziah 791-740 B.C.*	Good	(2 Kgs 15:1-5; 2 Chr 26:1-23)
Jotham 750-736 B.C.	Good	(2 Kgs 15:32-38; 2 Chr 27:1-9)
Ahaz 736-716 B.C.	Wicked	(2 Kgs 16:1-20; 2 Chr 28:1-27)
Hezckiah 716-687 B.C.	Good	(2 Kgs 18:1—20:21; 2 Chr 29:1—32:33)
Manasseh 696-642 B.C.*	Wicked	(2 Kgs 21:1-18; 2 Chr 33:1-20)

* Overlapping reigns indicate coregencies.

Messianic Character of the Book. Of all the prophetic books of the OT Isaiah is the most messianic; even more so than the book of Zechariah. Only the Psalms contain a larger number of messianic predictions. Every glory of our Lord and every aspect of His life on the earth are set forth in this great evangelical prophecy: His deity, eternity, preexistence, creatorship, omnipotence, omnipresence, omniscience, incomparableness (40:12-18; 51:13); His incarnation (9:6; 7:14, cf. Mt 1:23); His lowliness and youth in Nazareth (7:15; 9:1-2; 11:1; 53:2); His appearance as the Servant of the Lord, anointed as such (11:2), and chosen and delighted in as such (42:1); His mild manner (42:2); His tender ministering kindness (42:3; Mt 12:18-20); His obedience (50:5); His message (61:1-2); His miracles (35:5-6); His sufferings (50:6); His sufferings as the gateway to His exaltation (52:13-15); His rejection by the Jewish nation (53:1-3); His shame—struck, wounded, bruised (53:4-6); His vicarious death (53:8) and burial (53:9); His resurrection (53:10); His ascension (52:13); His spiritual progeny (53:10) and present high priestly ministry (53:12); His future glory. After ch. 53 Messiah is not mentioned again as the Servant of the Lord, and His coming glory centers more into focus (59:20; 63:1-6; 66:15-19).

The Dead Sea Scrolls of Isaiah. The two Isaiah scrolls from Cave 1 at Qumran in the original discovery of 1947 constitute the most famous finds of the Dead Sea Scrolls. The first scroll contains the complete Heb. text of Isaiah. The second contains about one-third of it.

GREAT PROPHETIC THEMES OF ISAIAH STILL UNFULFILLED

Theme	References
The Day of the Lord	Some 45 times Isaiah uses the term "in that day" to describe this period of apocalyptic judgment (cf. 2:10-22; 4:1; 13:9-13; 24:1-23; 32:1-20; 63:1-6)
Blessing upon Restored Israel	2:1-5; 4:2-6; 9:7; 11:4-16; 12:1-6; 14:1-3; 25:1-12; 32:15-20; 35:1-10; 52:1-12; 59:20-21; 60:1-12; 61:3—62:12; 65:17—66:24
Restoration of Israel to Palestine	11:10-12; 14:1-2; 27:12-13; 35:10; 43:5-6; 49:10-12; 66:20
Restoration of Palestine Itself	30:23-26; 35:1-10; 49:19; 60:13; 61:4; 62:4-5; 65:21-25
Jerusalem As Capital of the Earth	1:26; 2:3; 4:2-6; 12:6; 24:23; 26:1; 40:2; 52:1-12; 60:1-22; 62:1-7
Blessing upon the Remnant	12:1-6; 25:1-12; 26:1-19; 33:24; 35:10; 43:25; 44:22; 46:13; 54:6-10; 61:6; 62:12; 66:8
Blessing upon the Nations	2:1-4; 11:3-4; 9-10; 25:6-9; 60:1-12
Blessing to Entire Creation	Isaiah had a fleeting glimpse beyond the Kingdom Age to the new heaven and earth of the eternal state (65:17; 66:22). But like John in the Revelation (Rev 21—22) he saw a blended view of millennial and eternal conditions (cf. 11:6-8 with 65:25; 66:22)

The first Isaiah scroll dates from the 2nd cen. B.C. It consists of 17 sheets, 24 feet in length and 10.2 inches high. It is amazingly similar to the standard (Masoretic) Heb. text, the earliest extant manuscripts of which date almost a millennium later. This scroll constitutes one of the great manuscript discoveries of all time and authenticates the high accuracy of Heb. textual tradition.

Outline

Prophecies from the Standpoint of Isaiah's Day, Ch. 1—35

    Prophecies Concerning Judah and Jerusalem, ch. 1—12
    Prophecies Against Enemy Nations, ch. 13—23
    Prophecies of Kingdom Establishment, 24—27
    Prophecies Concerning Judah and Assyria, ch. 28—35

Historical Interlude, Ch. 36—39

Prophecies from the Standpoint of the Exile, Ch. 40—66

    Comfort in the Message of Redemption, ch. 40
    Comfort in the Lord's Vindication, ch. 41
    Comfort in the Lord's Servant, ch. 42
    Comfort in National Restoration, ch. 43—45
    Comfort in the Downfall of Idolatry, ch. 46—48
    Comfort in the Prophecy of Messiah-Redeemer, ch. 49—57
    Comfort in the Prospect of Israel's Future Glory, ch. 58—66

Vol. I. Book of Reproof and Promise, 1:1—6:13

CHAPTER 1. THE LORD'S CASE AGAINST JUDAH (FIRST DISCOURSE)

Isaiah's Preface, 1. The prophet gives his name; the nature of the prophecy ("a vision," implying supernatural revelation); the time, c. 750-680 B.C. (see above for list of contemporary kings); and the subject, concerning Judah and Jerusalem, since Isaiah was a prophet of the southern kingdom.

The Lord's Accusation, 2-6. The charge takes the form of a courtroom scene in which the whole universe, 2, is called upon to witness the twofold accusation of base ingratitude, 2-3, and rebellious apostasy, 4, illustrated by the figure of a diseased body, 5-6.

The Lord's Chastisement, 7-9. Because of God's punishment the kingdom faced ruin, 7. Jerusalem's suburbs were overrun and forsaken, 8. A faithful remnant was the only hope against complete annihilation, 9.

The Lord's Rejection of Their Religious Externalism, 10-15. They rejected the Lord, 10. He rejected their empty worship, 11-15, as being purposeless and nauseating, iniquitous, hateful, and devoid of spiritual power, 15.

The Lord's Call to Repentance and Reformation, 16-20, is issued in a summons to cleanse themselves, 16-17, and then to reason with God, 18-20, in order to discover the equity of His way both to pardon, 18-19, and to punish, 20.

The Lord's Challenge to Contrast Jerusalem, Past and Present, 21-23. What the city had been, 21: faithful, full of justice, the dwelling place of righteousness. What the city had become, 21-23: a faithless harlot, full of unpunished murderers and dishonest judges (illustrated by the figures of debased money and diluted wine).

The Lord's Promised Restoration of Jerusalem, 24-31. This prophecy is still unfulfilled. The "afterward," 26 (when earthly Jerusalem is to be called "the city of righteousness," "the faithful city"), refers to the second advent of Christ, which will be preceded by the destruction of transgressors and sinners, 28.

CHAPTER 2. JERUSALEM AND THE DAY OF THE LORD (SECOND DISCOURSE)

Jerusalem the Center of the Earth in the Kingdom Age, 1-5. The subject of the prophecy is Judah and Jerusalem, 1; the time indicated is the futurity of the days of Israel, referring to her ultimate blessing at Messiah's second advent. This vision refers to the time when Israel is converted and restored to Palestine. It envisions Jerusalem's exaltation as the religious center, 2-3, with the site of the millennial temple established. This results in the spontaneous inflow of the nations, 2, for worship and instruction, 3, because in that day Jerusalem shall be the place where the law and the Word of God go forth, 3. Jerusalem's exaltation as the governmental center will be made possible by Messiah as the ruling King-Judge. The result will be universal peace, with armaments of war converted to implements of peace and the science of war abandoned, 4. Converted and restored, Israel encourages her people to walk in the light of the Lord, 5.

The Day of the Lord, 6-22. This is the time when the Lord visibly judges sinners in the earth (Rev 4:1—19:16), preparatory to the kingdom as outlined in 1-5. It is here described as the period when the Lord "ariseth to shake terribly the earth," 19, 21, and reveals His glorious majesty in judgment upon sinners.

CHAPTER 3. JUDAH'S SIN AND THE DAY OF THE LORD (SECOND DISCOURSE)

Isaiah's second discourse, 2:1—4:6, of which this chapter is a part, shows how chastisement for the nation's sin in the future day of the Lord can alone cleanse and equip the nation for her kingdom mission (2:1-4; 4:1-6). All classes of Judah's society are to be punished for their sin—the rulers, professional men, and others, 1-15, as well as the vain, wicked, worldly women, 3:16—4:1. The sins of the prophet's day demand the judgments of the day of the Lord before national blessing can come.

CHAPTER 4. THE GLORY AWAITING THE REDEEMED REMNANT (SECOND DISCOURSE)

The Remnant Survives the Judgment of the Day of the Lord, 1. Only one man in seven will survive so that seven women (cf. 3:16-26) will court one man.

The Remnant Accepts Messiah the Branch of the Lord (in His deity) "beautiful and glorious," and "the fruit of the earth" (in His humanity), 2.

The Remnant Is Cleansed and Converted, 3-4, and hence is called "holy." This is accomplished by the decimating judgments of the day of the Lord, 4, when the Lord cleanses Israel nationally (cf. Rom 11:16-27), and by the outpoured Spirit, if "spirit of burning" refers to the Holy Spirit.

The Remnant Is Sheltered and Protected, 5-6, by a pillar of cloud by day and a pillar of fire by night, recalling Israel's wilderness experience (Ex 13:21-22), and by a canopy over "all the glory." This will be the manifested glory of Messiah in the midst of His people. This chapter concludes Isaiah's second sermon begun at 2:1.

CHAPTER 5. GOD'S PEOPLE SHOWN THEIR SIN AND ITS RESULT (THIRD DISCOURSE)

By a Parable, 1-7. The nation Israel is represented under the figure of the vineyard of the Lord, 7. The Lord's tender care of Israel is shown by His favorable location of the vineyard "in a very fertile slope" (Palestine), 1; by intensive cultivation, choice of the finest vine, and by building a tower in it, 2. His normal expectation was of a good yield, 2; but its yield of wild grapes and the owner's complaint, 3-4, and threatened castigation of the vineyard, 5-6, necessitated the removal of its protection (hedge) and wall (overrun

311

by enemies) and temporary setting aside of the vineyard (Israel in her national election, Rom 11:1-26; cf. Mt 21:33-41).

By an Enumeration of Their Sins, 8-23. Covetousness and greed would be punished by famine, 8-10; rioting and drunken revelry, 11-12, 22, by the miseries of the Captivity, 13-17. God further revealed their presumption in sinning, 18-19; their breaking down moral distinctions, 20; their pride and conceit, 21; their self-indulgence and injustice, 23.

By a Threat of Captivity, 24-30, with general desolation, 24-25, and foreign invasion, 26-30.

CHAPTER 6. ISAIAH'S CALL AND COMMISSION (FOURTH DISCOURSE)

The Prophet Sees God, 1-4, i.e., "the glory of Christ" (Jn 12:41), about 740 B.C. in the year of Uzziah's death, 1. It may have been an initial vision to launch him on his prophetic career, or to confirm him in a career already under way. It was, in any case, of "Christ's glory"—the Lord upon His throne, with the cherubim choir.

The Prophet Sees Himself, 5. He thus abhors himself and acknowledges his sin. This is always the divine order in a call to service —a vision of God, then of self.

The Prophet Is Cleansed, 6-7, fire being the symbol of cleansing.

The Prophet Is Commissioned, 8-10. The Triune God counsels concerning the commission and the prophet accepts it, 8, whereupon God communicates the commission, 9-10. This involved a hardening and blinding judgment upon the nation (Mt 13:14-15; Jn 12:39-41; Acts 28:25-27).

The Prophet Is Given the Outcome of the Commission, 11-13. How long would this spiritual deterioration go on? To the complete blotting out of Israel's testimony to the one true God? No, came the divine answer. Only until the complete devastation of the land and the removal of its inhabitants to Babylon were accomplished. Thence a *remnant* would return to Palestine. Even this tenth part would be further reduced, yet a holy posterity would survive in whom the ultimate hope of Israel would rest and in whom the covenants and promises would be realized.

Vol. II. Book of Immanuel, 7:1—12:6

CHAPTER 7. THE GREAT MESSIANIC SIGN CONCERNING IMMANUEL (FIRST DISCOURSE)

Historical Circumstances Calling Forth the Sign, 1-2. About 735 B.C. Ahaz faced the coalition of Rezin, king of Syria (c. 740-732 B.C.), and Pekah (c. 740-732 B.C.), king of Israel. They advanced against Jerusalem to punish Ahaz for not aligning himself with them to check the growing power of Assyria, who, under Tiglath-pileser III (745-727 B.C.), was relentlessly pressing toward the Mediterranean, 1. Ahaz and his people were fearful and hard pressed, 2. The issue? Where should help be found, in Assyria itself or in God?

A Message of Encouragement, 3-9. The prophet was sent to the faithless monarch with his son Shear-jashub ("a remnant shall return") to attempt to persuade Ahaz to trust in God instead of Assyria, since the Lord had already decreed the destruction of these ungodly allies and the frustration of their plan to set their puppet over Jerusalem. For a time the status quo would prevail both in Damascus (Syria), 8, and in Israel, 9, and Judah would not be conquered. Fulfillment came within 65 years, during Esar-haddon's reign (681-668) when foreigners were introduced and took possession of both Syria and Israel, that it might be forever said Ephraim was broken so as no longer to be a people, 8.

God's Sign to Confirm the Prophet's Message, 10-13. The sign or miracle was unlimited and unrestricted, 11, but Ahaz in mock piety alluded to Deut 6:16 to cover his unbelief, already displayed in stripping the temple of treasure to bribe the king of Assyria. Thereupon the prophet reproved Ahaz as a member of the house of David, 13.

The Great Messianic Sign Itself, 14-15. This sign involved the miracle of the virgin birth of Christ: (1) It was divinely given ("the Lord Himself" shall give it). (2) It was given to the house of David ("to *you,*" plural) not to Ahaz. (3) It involved a miraculous sign, no mere human baby of that day, and embraced making the sign "deep as Sheol" or making it "high as heaven," 11 (RSV), which implied a unique and stupendous miracle. (4) It concerned the perpetuation of the house of David till the preeminent sign of the ages should be realized. (5) It concerned a "virgin" (*'almah*). The context necessitates such a one, and the inspired Word declares such to be true (Mt 1:22-23, *parthenos*). The Septuagint (c. 250 B.C.) so translates the word. Arguments alleging that *'almah* (instead of *bethulah*) cannot mean "virgin" here not only violate the context of 7:14 but the possible meaning of "virgin" for the word in Gen 24:43; Ex 2:8; Ps 68:25; Song 1:3; Prov 30:19. (6) His very name "Immanuel," meaning *"with us* [humanity] *is God* [deity]," involves the incarnation of Christ, "the miracle of the ages." (7) Although divine, He would also be truly human, eating what other children ate, growing to maturity like other children, 15 (cf. Lk 2:52).

An Appended Non-Messianic Sign, 16. This is the sign of Isaiah's small child Shear-jashub. *Before* this child Shear-jashub (7:3) is

313

three or four years older, "the land before whose two kings thou art in deadly fear, shall be rid of her two kings." This was fulfilled in Tiglath-pileser's taking Damascus in 732 B.C. and slaying Rezin (2 Kgs 16:9). Pekah, too, was slain about two years after this remarkable prophecy.

Threatened Punishment of Ahaz, 17-25. The severity of the punishment is told, 17. The instrument of punishment was to be the king of Assyria, who was trusted instead of the Lord, and he therefore would desolate the land, 17-25.

8:1—9:7. PRESENT DELIVERANCE PRECURSOR TO FUTURE DELIVERER (SECOND DISCOURSE)

The Fall of Damascus and Samaria Prefigured, 8:1-4. Three children are mentioned in connection with the Syrian-Israelite invasion of Judah: (1) Shear-jashub (7:3; "a remnant shall return"), (2) Maher-shalal-hash-baz, 8:1-4 ("hasten booty, hurry prey"), both Isaiah's sons; and (3) Immanuel, David's son and Lord (7:13-14). All three of these children portray emphases in Isaiah's daily preaching: (1) "A remnant shall return" from Babylon and from end-time worldwide Diaspora (1:9; 4:1-4; 6:13, etc.)—coming captivity and deliverance. (2) "Hasten booty, hurry prey" refers to present deliverance from Rezin and Pekah. Damascus was taken in 732 B.C. and Rezin was slain. The northern kingdom had to cede its northern provinces to Assyria (2 Kgs 15:29), and not many years later the capital city fell (722 B.C.). (3) The virgin-born Child is the future glory of the nation. Maher-shalal-hash-baz was not the type of the virgin-born Messiah of 7:14 because the prophet's wife was not a virgin at the time (7:3).

The Choice of Unbelief and Its Result, 8:5-8. The people followed Ahaz and chose Assyria rather than God's guidance and help, which were symbolized by the gentle waters of the pool of Shiloah (the Siloam of Jn 9:7, 11; Lk 13:4). In unbelief and worldly wisdom rejecting these quiet waters, the disobedient nation was to be inundated by the floodwaters of the Euphrates, symbolizing invading Assyrian armies. Yet the fact that Palestine was called "Immanuel's land," 8, brought assurance that in the light of the virgin-born Immanuel Israel would not be obliterated by this terrible flood.

The Challenge of God's Grace, 8:9-15. The Lord challenged the enemies of Judah to do their worst to destroy her, 9-10. They would be smashed against the rock of divine judgment. The reason—His grace was to be manifested in "Immanuel," 10, to His true elect people in Judah. The Lord encouraged and instructed Isaiah and His faithful adherents not to be frightened by the popular charge of conspiracy or treason, 12, hurled against them because of their opposition to an Assyrian alliance against the northern coalition. Let them "sanctify the Lord of armies" (witness to His all-sufficiency) before their tottering countrymen, 13. He promised to become a sanctuary for them, but a stumbling stone (1 Pet 2:7-8) and a snare to remove from Israel all the unfaithful and rebellious, like Ahaz, who reject Immanuel (Christ), 14-15.

The Challenge to Trust God's Grace Alone, 8:16-20. The testimony of the great tablet inscribed with the name Maher-shalal-hash-baz, 1, was to be sealed up, that its fulfillment might be objectively verified by the Lord of history, 16. The believing remnant will take its stand upon the sure Word of God and confidently await its fulfillment. The faithful prophet declared his own steadfast testimony, 18-19, and warned that those who claim inspiration or authority contrary to the Word of God in demon-controlled religion will be deprived of spiritual light, 19-20. Spiritism and general cultism were condemned to judicial error and blindness.

The Alternative to Trust in God, 8:21-22, would be the indescribable anguish and distress of Assyrian invasion and deportation.

Prophecy of Immanuel As the Great Light, 9:1-2. Prediction was made that He would providentially appear in dark, despised Galilee, 1. This was the very territory of Zebulun and Naphtali which was first brought into contempt and plunged into gloom by the ravaging armies of Tiglath-pileser (732 B.C.). Here the radiant light of the Messiah, who made His headquarters in Galilee (Mt 4:13-17), shone.

Prophecy of Immanuel As the Great Liberator, 9:3-5. He would multiply the nation and increase its joy, 3. He would liberate the nation from all its oppressors and foes, supernaturally (cf. Zech 12:1-8; 14:1-15), but in terrible final conflict, 5. This prophecy had application to the increase of the nation after the Babylonian Captivity and its victories in Maccabean times; but it will find its final fulfillment in Armageddon and the restoration of the kingdom over Israel (Acts 1:6).

Prophecy of Immanuel As the Great Lord, 9:6-7. His humanity ("a child born") and His deity ("a son given") are foretold. His government is described as prosperous, peaceful, Davidic, righteous, eternal and sure, 6-7. His messianic titles are given: (1) *Wonder of a Counselor,* giving counsel which alone can save man from sin; (2) *God-Champion,* Deity in the special character of a champion in battle; (3) *the Eternal One,* both as the possessor of eternity and the author of eternal life (Heb. "father of eternity"); (4) *Prince of Peace,* the ruler who will bring about a warless world in the coming kingdom. The Davidic covenant (2 Sam 7:8-17) will be executed in the Kingdom Age, which in turn will merge into the eternal state by authority of the Lord's zeal; for He will perform these wondrous promises of ultimate blessing for Israel and the world.

9:8—10:4. PROUD SAMARIA IS DOOMED (THIRD DISCOURSE)

Israel's pride and presumption, 9:8-10, would be punished by Syrian and Philistine invasion, 11-12; her incorrigibility under chastisement, 13, would be punished by the destructive, pitiless wrath of the Lord, 14-19, civil war, and starvation, 20-21. The Lord's hand "is stretched out still" in wrathful chastisement and not withdrawn because of refusal to reform (cf. the doleful refrain in 9:12, 17, 21; 10:4; cf. 5:25). Captivity was imminent for the ruthless ruling class in Samaria who heartlessly exploited their subjects, 10:1-4.

10:5-34. THE ASSYRIAN INVADES IMMANUEL'S LAND (FOURTH DISCOURSE)

Assyria, God's Instrument for Judging His People, Shall in Turn Be Judged, 5-19. Assyria was the divine tool for chastening God's people, 5-6. In spite of her overweening pride, 7-14, she would be irretrievably destroyed by the Lord who employed her as His scourge, 15-19.

The Return of a Faithful Remnant, 20-23. The time: "in that day," the day of the Lord (2:10-22), after Israel's *final* enemies have been destroyed. Although this had a historical fulfillment, the destruction of the Assyrian envisions a similar invasion of Palestine by "the king of the north" (Dan 11:45) in the end-time (Isa 14:24-25; 30:31-33; Mic 5:4-7; Dan 8:23-26; 11:40-45). The remnant will, like Isaiah and his followers, reject this false ruler and "lean upon the Lord, the Holy One of Israel, in truth," 20 (RSV).

Therefore Assyria Is Not to Be Feared, 24-34, by those who trust in the Lord, 24-27, even in her fearful advance on Immanuel's land, 28-32, for the Lord will make a sudden end of the Assyrian, 33-34.

CHAPTER 11. IMMANUEL-KING AND HIS KINGDOM (FOURTH DISCOURSE)

Immanuel-King's Davidic Descent, 1. He is here prefigured as "a shoot" from the truncated "stump of Jesse," showing His obscurity and lowliness, the house of David being poor and unknown at the time of Christ's nativity. He is also symbolized as a "branch" (*netzer;* cf. Mt 2:23: "And he came and dwelt in a city called Nazareth: that it might be fulfilled which was spoken by the prophets, He shall be called a Nazarene").

Immanuel-King's Enduement, 2. The Holy Spirit in His sevenfold measureless fullness (Jn 3:34) is to rest or remain upon Him (Jn 1:32-34; cf. "the seven Spirits," the one Spirit in all His plenitude, Rev 1:4; 4:5). The general enduement is "the Spirit of the Lord," which is the necessary qualification for righteous government. Its result is that Immanuel finds His delight in reverence for the Lord, 3 (RSV).

Immanuel-King's Equitable Government, 3-5. He will not arbitrate by mere external appearance, 3 (cf. 1 Sam 16:7), but judge equitably and govern forcefully, 4, ruling with a "rod of iron" (Ps 2:9; Rev 2:27; 12:5; 19:15). He will vindicate God's holy law as the second Adam against Satan-dominated mankind's pride and rebellion, which will contaminate the earth till He destroys the Satanic world system at His advent and kingdom. He will be "girded" with righteousness and faithfulness, 5.

Immanuel-King's Peaceful Kingdom, 6-9. Aggression will not be found in Immanuel's holy kingdom. So complete will be the change, even the animal creation will be affected, sharing in the glorious liberation from the vanity and evil brought in by the Fall (Rom 8:19-22). Edenic conditions will be at least partly restored, predatory beasts and noxious serpents no longer preying upon one another or upon man. The reason is that all men everywhere will know God and be completely dedicated to His will, 9.

Immanuel-King Will Bring the Gentiles into the Kingdom, 10. As a military standard or ensign, Messiah will appear "as the root of a scion of the ancient decayed family of Jesse" (Rev 5:5; 22:16), "and his rest [dwelling place] shall be *glory*"—the state of rest and security from greed and war.

Immanuel-King Will Regather the Jews, 11-16, when His kingdom is set up, 11. This will be a second (final) regathering of a remnant from a worldwide dispersion, 11-12, consummated by divine power. The old animosity between Judah and Ephraim (southern and northern kingdoms) will be abolished, and security and dominion over any adversaries assured, 13-14. Every obstacle to the final regathering of Israel will be removed—here symbolized by great geographical barriers. The tongue (bay) of the Egyptian sea is the barrier they miraculously passed through when they came out of Egypt. The river is the Euphrates (8:7).

CHAPTER 12. THE REMNANT'S SONG OF REDEMPTION (FOURTH DISCOURSE)

The Believer's Song of Redemption, 1-3. It is a paean of praise to Immanuel-Redeemer because the divine anger is turned away and comfort abounds, 1; because God is the singer's salvation, 2; and because He is his strength and song, 3. The song will be sung "in that day," 1, i.e., the day of regathering from the nations and Israel's final deliverance from the Egypt of the world, re-echoing the song of Moses and Israel after deliverance at the Red Sea (Ex 15:1-21).

The Remnant's United Song of Redemption, 4-6. This section changes from the singular to the plural "you" as each redeemed one joins the choir of all Israel's redeemed about to enter the kingdom. As a continued and amplified song of praise to God, it contains an exhortation to prayer and witnessing, 4; joyful singing, 5; and to holy exultation and joy, 6. What an ode expressing the boundless joy of Immanuel's redeemed when He comes again to rule over Zion and reign supreme over all the earth.

Vol. III. God's Oracles of Judgment upon the Nations, 13:1—23:18

CHAPTER 13. THE JUDGMENT OF BABYLON

The Confusion of the Nations Preparatory to Destruction, 1-16. Babel ("confusion") here appears symbolically to portray the political and governmental disorder which characterizes the earth during the times of the Gentiles (Lk 21:24). This is in contrast to the divine order (Isa 11) with Israel in her own land, the center of spiritual blessing and divine world government (Isa 2:1-5). Anything other than the nations blessed in association with Israel is politically Babel ("confusion"). The acme of this confusion is reached in the day of the Lord as political Babylon's iniquity becomes full, preparatory to destruction (Rev 18). Verses 12-16 focus upon the apocalyptic judgments of the day of the Lord (Rev 6—16) which eventuate in the destruction of both religious (Rev 17) and political (Rev 18) Babylon.

Prophecy of Babylon's Destruction in Isaiah's Day, 17-22. The Babylon of Nebuchadnezzar II (605-562 B.C.), which became mistress of the world and which fell to Cyrus the Persian (539 B.C.), is here in view. This Babylon with the Jew in captivity is a type of the political Babylon which will prevail until it is destroyed at the second advent of Christ.

CHAPTER 14. BABYLON'S FALL AND ISRAEL'S RESTORATION

Prophecy of Israel's Restoration Anticipates Babylon's Fall, 1-3. Israel's exaltation to her God-ordained place as witness to the nations, and her rest from her worldwide woe, cannot be realized until political Babylon is destroyed.

Israel's Song of Triumph Over Babylon's Last King, 4-11. This is not Nebuchadnezzar II nor Belshazzar, but the last-day political head of the restored Roman Empire (Rev 13:1-18), "the man of sin, the son of perdition" (2 Thess 2:3-4), "the lawless one" (2 Thess 2:8, RSV), "the little horn" (Dan 7:8, 24-27; 11:36-45). He is seen in Sheol (cf. Rev 19:20 where he is cast into Gehenna).

Satan Addressed As Energizer of Babylon's Last King, 12-17. Satan, organizer and head of this world's system governmentally, is so intimately associated with its last and most diabolical ruler ("whose coming is after the working of Satan with all power and signs and deceiving wonders," 2 Thess 2:9) that the occasion of the king of Babylon's fall furnishes the revelation of Satan's original fall and the entrance of sin into the universe. The revelation also serves to show the role of Satan in human government, especially since Israel has been outside the focus of the divine order since her captivity.

Future Destruction of the Satanic World System, 18-27. This passage goes beyond the destruction of literal Babylon, 18-24, and of the Assyrian of that day, 25, and encompasses "the whole earth," 26, in preparation for God's order in the kingdom which is guaranteed by God's immutable purpose, 27.

Oracle upon Philistia, 28-32. Philistia would be crushed by Assyrian might under Sargon and Sennacherib, but the Lord would protect His people.

CHAPTERS 15—16. JUDGMENT UPON MOAB

Moab was to be pitilessly desolated (15:1—16:9). Her arrogance and pride would be humbled by terrible devastation from Assyria, 16:10-14. Events in the day of the Lord are foreshadowed (cf. 16:5).

CHAPTER 17. JUDGMENT UPON DAMASCUS AND SAMARIA

Damascus and Ephraim (the northern kingdom) would be desolated, 1-3, but eventually Samaria would yield a remnant of true believers who would disavow idolatry, 3-8. Chastening must, however, precede blessing, 9-11, with the horrible atrocities of the approaching Assyrian invasion predicted, 12-14. Again the events of Armageddon and the day of the Lord are foreshadowed.

CHAPTER 18. THE JUDGMENT UPON ETHIOPIA

The prophet apprises Ethiopian ambassadors that the birds of prey would feed upon their corpses rotting on the battlefield, 1-6. Yet "gifts will be brought . . . to Mount Zion, the place of the name of the Lord of hosts," by Ethiopia in the millennial day, 7 (RSV).

CHAPTERS 19—20. THE JUDGMENT OF EGYPT

Civil war, drought, devastation plague Egypt as a result of Assyrian invasion, 19:1-10. Egypt's wisdom and pride turn to foolishness, 11-15. Egypt will yet be terrified by the land of Judah because of God's purpose through it against Egypt, 16-18, and Egypt will be converted and delivered to participate with Israel in God's favor, 19-25.

Yet impending conquest and captivity by Assyria (Esar-haddon) faced Egypt, 20:1-6. Isaiah walked naked and barefoot, 1-2, as a sign that the king of Assyria would lead away captive Egyptians and Ethiopians, 3-6, demonstrating to a strong party in Jerusalem who looked for help from Egypt, how foolish such expectation was.

CHAPTER 21. THE JUDGMENT OF BABYLON, EDOM, ARABIA

The Judgment of the Desert of the Sea, 1-10. The "desert of the sea" was Babylon: "utterly fallen is Babylon," 9. Media is mentioned as the instrument of judgment, 2. This event was some two centuries in the future, but the prophet envisioned the Persian conquerors advancing. Such is the accuracy of the prophetic word, history prewritten.

The Judgment of Dumah (Edom), 11-12. Dumah ("silence") is evidently an anagram (a transposition of letters) for Edom. This land S of the Dead Sea, minerally rich, is also called Seir (Gen 32:3; Num 24:18; Jud 5:4), the home of Esau's ancestors, rivals of the tribes of Jacob. The wealth of Edom was shown by the heavy tribute it paid Esar-haddon. Copper and iron made Edom wealthy, as well as the tolls over the ancient king's highway which ran to Eziongeber. The cry of the watchman and his cryptic reply were to be heard, 11-12.

The Judgment of Arabia, 13-17. The northwestern tribes along the Red Sea (Gen 25:3; Ezk 27:20; 38:13) called Dedanites, who shipped goods to Phoenician Tyre (Ezk 27:15), and the Kedarites E of Palestine and Syria, noted for their choice flocks (Isa 60:7) and their black tents, were to be driven into flight by conquering Assyrians and Chaldeans.

CHAPTER 22.   JUDGMENT UPON JERUSALEM

The joyous, world-renowned city, 1-4, invaded by armies, 5-7, was to suffer siege and calamity, 8-14. It is called the "valley of vision," 1, 5, for God revealed Himself on the hill of Zion, which was surrounded by valleys with higher hills beyond. Notice is made of the careless indulgence of its inhabitants, 13, in the face of Assyrian invasion. Shebna, the steward, 15-19, the proud materialistic usurper (type of the Antichrist), was to be thrust out of office and to be replaced by the faithful Eliakim, 20-25 (type of Christ).

This one (Christ) will be given "the key to the house of David," 22 (Rev 3:7). He possesses the right to reign, 20, as the Holy and True One. "And I will fasten him like a peg in a sure place . . . and they will hang on him the whole weight of his father's house," 23-24 (RSV) (cf. Zech 10:4). "Out of him [Judah] shall be the tent peg"—the stout peg inside the tent for hanging up items of value for display (Ezk 15:3).

CHAPTER 23.   THE JUDGMENT OF TYRE

Tyre is a type of the pomp and pride of the Satanic world system (cf. Ezk 28:12-15) in its commercial aspects. Tyre was an opulent trading emporium on the Phoenician coast which all conquerors prized. Its dazzling splendor, proud self-sufficiency and worldly wisdom had behind them the inspiration of Satan. Nebuchadnezzar, after a 12-year siege, failed to take the island city, which, however, Alexander accomplished in 332 B.C. (cf. Zech 9:2-4). Isaiah foresaw the downfall of this commercial center of the world, 1-7. God had decreed this calamity because of pride, 8-12. After 70 years of desolation she would regain her commercial ascendancy, and will be sanctified in the Kingdom Age, 18 (cf. Ezk 26—27).

Vol. IV. Book of Judgment and Promise,
24:1—27:13

These chapters form a continuous prophecy on the subject of judgment in the day of the Lord with blessing afterward. They are sometimes styled Isaiah's Apocalypse.

CHAPTER 24. THE DAY OF THE LORD AND MILLENNIAL BLESSING

The Judgments of the Day of the Lord, 1-13. The Lord will judge the earth and earth dwellers, 1. All classes of the Christ-rejecting society of the end-time will be affected, 2. The apocalyptic desolations are described, 3-13, and the reason for them specified, 5. This is the period described in 2 Thess 1:7-10; Mt 24—25; Rev 4:1—19:16; Isa 2:6-22; Zeph 1:1-18; Zech 12:1—14:15.

Interlude: The Preservation and Song of the Remnant, 14-16. Singing begins "in that day" and is heard because of the experience of God's marvelous deliverance through the Great Tribulation (Rev 7:1-8; 14:1-5).

The Judgment of the Day of the Lord Continued, 17-22. It will concentrate on the earth and wicked earth dwellers, and upon Satan and demons—"the host of the high ones on high," 21. The latter indwell and energize wicked men (Eph 6:10-12; Rev 9:1-12, 20-21; 12:7-10), and particularly "the kings of the earth" (Rev 16:13-16) for the final phase of God-defying wickedness crushed at Armageddon. The fulfillment: Satan and the demons will be remanded to the bottomless pit, 22 (cf. Rev 20:1-3), and the Beast and the False Prophet will be cast alive into Gehenna (Rev 19:20; 20:10). Wicked earth dwellers will be swept away by the seal, trumpet and bowl judgments (Rev 6:1—19:16), or destroyed at the advent of Messiah (Rev 19:11-19).

The Millennial Reign of Christ, 23. So glorious will it be that the sun and moon will be confounded when Messiah "reigns in Mount Zion and before his ancients [resurrected OT saints] gloriously."

CHAPTER 25. ISRAEL'S PRAISE FOR KINGDOM BLESSING

The Delivered Nation Praises the Lord, 1-5. Israel praises her Lord for His miraculous deliverances, 1; His punishment of her enemies, 2-3; and His help of the poor and needy, 4-5 (cf. Isa 12:1-6).

Blessings for All Nations Described, 6-8. A feast of fat things "in this mountain," i.e., Zion (cf. Isa 2:1-5), is promised; spiritual blindness will be removed, 7. Death will be swallowed up in victory (Hos 13:14; 1 Cor 15:54; Rev 20:14; 21:4). The Lord will remove the reproach of His people from all the earth, 8. The eternal state blends with this millennial scene.

Israel's Reward for Waiting, 9. Salvation and attendant joy in the Lord are promised.

Israel's Enemies Judged, 10-12, including Moab.

CHAPTER 26. JUDAH'S MILLENNIAL SONG

Praise for the Lord's Faithfulness and Mercies, 1-6. Jerusalem is celebrated as a saved city opening its gates to welcome the righteous, 1-2. The Lord's blessing upon those who trust Him, 3-4, and His humbling of the proud, 5-6, are stressed.

Experiences of Waiting During the Night, 7-11.

Assurances of Peace and Deliverance, 12-18. Israel restored and converted, enjoying the blessing of the land, expresses her worship of the Lord in glad praise and testimony.

Assurance of the Bodily Resurrection of Righteous OT Saints, 19. "Thy dead shall live, their dead bodies [the bodies of the deceased people of the Lord] shall rise" (RSV). Although the restoration of Israel as a nation is symbolized by the figure of resurrection (Ezk 37:1-11), like Dan 12:1-2, this passage evidently has in mind physical resurrection, since the first resurrection involves participation in the kingdom (Rev 20:4-6).

Glimpse of the Divine Indignation in the Day of the Lord, 20-21. A call is issued to the remnant to hide. Verse 21 graphically summarizes the judgment events of Rev 6:1—19:21.

CHAPTER 27. PUNISHMENT OF ISRAEL'S ENEMIES AND KINGDOM TRIUMPH

Destruction of Israel's Enemies, 1. These are symbolized by leviathan (Ps 74:14), the sea monster and the dragon, doubtless with implication of Satanic forces behind them as in the case of the king of Babylon (14:1-14) and Tyre (Ezk 28:12-14). (Cf. the seven-headed Lotan of the Ugaritic Literature, Rev 11:7; 12:3; 13:1.)

The Lord's Care for His Own Even in Chastening, 2-9, is indicated under the figure of a vineyard (cf. Isa 5:1-7), with Israel hereafter flourishing, 6, after the chastenings are over, 8-9.

Israel's Enemies Are Destroyed — totally and finally, 10-11.

The Return of the Remnant, 12-13. This last word of this Volume of Judgment and Promise tells of Israel's final regathering under the blowing of the trumpet (cf. Mt 24:31) and future worship in Jerusalem (cf. 2:1-5). The brook of Egypt (Gen 15:18; Ezk 47:19) is the Wadi el-Arish separating SW Palestine from Egypt.

Vol. V. Book of Woes Preceding Restoration Glories, 28:1—35:10

CHAPTER 28. WOE AGAINST EPHRAIM

Judgment upon the Ten Tribes, 1-13. Their pride and drunkenness are noted, 1, 3, 7-8. Their threatened punishment by Assyrian invasion is foretold, 2-4. The testimony of God's Word goes out to these sinners, 9-12, but they reject its warning, sealing their doom, 13. Nevertheless, a remnant shall be preserved to confess the Lord as "a crown of glory" and "a diadem of beauty" in the kingdom, 5.

Fate of Ephraim a Warning to Judah, 14-29. The scoffing rulers of Jerusalem have made "a covenant with death" and "Sheol" (probably an alliance with Egypt) to escape the Assyrian invasion, 14-15, but the messianic reference to the "stone, a tested stone" (Dan 2:34; 1 Pet 2:8) projects the prophecy to the end-time and the covenant adumbrating the time when the apostate nation enters into an agreement with the Antichrist (Dan 9:27). But all who trust in the false covenant rather than in God's deliverance through the Stone (Messiah) shall be swept away in judgment, 17-29.

CHAPTER 29. WOE AGAINST ARIEL (JERUSALEM)

Jerusalem's Last Siege, 1-4. Despite her sacred character as Ariel ("the lion of God"), associated with David, 1, a type of Jerusalem's great Deliverer ("the Lion of the tribe of Judah," Rev 5:5), the Lord Himself through His instruments of chastening (Israel's last-day enemies) will encamp against her. He will besiege her, 2-3, till the city is brought to the dust, 4-5 (cf. Zech 12:1-14; 15; Mic 4:11; 5:4-15; Dan 11:40-45).

The Lord Will Then Deal with Jerusalem's Enemies, 5-10. "In an instant, suddenly," 6 (RSV), when the tools of His chastening anger have accomplished His purpose concerning His people, the Lord will turn against them and destroy "the multitude of all the nations . . . that fight against Mount Zion," 7-8, blinding and intoxicating them for their destruction, 9-10 (cf. Zech 14:3, 12-15).

This Prophecy Is for the End-Time, 11-12. It is to be sealed because neither Sennacherib's siege nor the siege by the Romans accomplished it. Its fulfillment is still in the future.

The Condition of the People, 13-16, is one of religious blindness and empty formalism (cf. Mt 15:8-9; Mk 7:6-7). Woe is pronounced upon those who think their dark deeds are hidden from the Lord, 15-16.

Blessing for a Redeemed Remnant, 17-24. The "meek" shall obtain "fresh joy" and the "poor among men shall exult in the Holy One of Israel," 17-19. The wicked will be purged out, 20, and the house of Jacob blessed, 22-24.

CHAPTERS 30—31. WARNING AGAINST ALLIANCE WITH EGYPT

The Wickedness of the Pro-Egypt Party, 30:1-14. They fostered a foolish cause, 1-7, stultified and resisted God's word, 8-11, and calamity was to result from following their advice, 12-14.

Advice to Trust in the Lord, 30:15-33. Blessing foreshadowing kingdom deliverance and joy is promised those who believe God, woe foreshadowing the judgments of the day of the Lord for those who rebel.

The Woe of Trusting Egypt Again Outlined, 31:1-9. A repeated condemnation of the Egyptian alliance is indicated, 1-3. The Lord promises to rescue Jerusalem, 4-9. The people of Israel are exhorted to turn in faith to Him from whom they have deeply revolted, 6-7, for the Assyrian of the end time, 8, shall be supernaturally routed, 9, by Israel's messianic King.

CHAPTER 32. MESSIAH-KING AND HIS KINGDOM

Israel's Ultimate Deliverance by Messiah-King, 1-8. This chapter is part of the discourse begun in 31:1. Deliverance through God's gracious interposition, 31:1—32:20, will ultimately be by Israel's Messiah-King, 32:1-8 (not by trusting in Egypt, 31:1-9). The King (Jesus Christ) is seen as "a hiding place from the wind, and a covert from the tempest . . . a great rock in a weary land," 1-2, and His earthly rule is described, 3-8.

Israel's Interim Sins and Sufferings Outlined, 9-14. Sins of the careless women (cf. Isa 3:16—4:1, 4) are specially mentioned. The spiritual state of the women is a sensitive barometer of the moral state of any nation.

Hope for the Future — the Outpoured Spirit and the Result, 15-20. Israel's sorrow and judgment are not permanent—"until the Spirit is poured out . . . from on high," 15, fulfilling Joel 2:28-32. Results of the outpouring of the Spirit are blessing on the land, 15; prevalence of justice and righteousness, 16; peace and security, 17-20.

CHAPTER 33. PUNISHMENT OF THE ASSYRIAN, TRIUMPH OF CHRIST

The Destruction of the Assyrian Declared, 1-12. Treacherous deceivers like Sennacherib are to be divinely destroyed, 1, as a result of God's favor to His people and His answer to their prayers, 2-6. The horror of the Assyrian's cruelty and perfidy as he invades the land is described, 7-9. The Lord announces the Assyrian's destruction, 10-12.

The Plight of the Godless in the Face of the Assyrian Menace, 13-16. Their fearful trembling is the result of their sin and unbelief.

Salvation by Seeing Messiah-King in His Beauty, 17-24. This vision of the coming Deliverer will dissipate the terror of the Assyrian menace and an alien invader, 17-19. Instead, Jerusalem will be seen as a secure city, filled with the Lord's majesty and deliverance, 20-22, and the remnant will divide the spoil, 23-24.

CHAPTER 34. ARMAGEDDON AND THE DESTRUCTION OF GENTILE WORLD POWER

The Battle of Armageddon, 1-7. All nations are to be gathered to battle, 1-3. Frightful carnage results as the Lord wreaks vengeance upon the armies of the Satanic world system, centering in Edom, 4-6 (cf. Rev 19:11-21; Isa 63:1-6).

Desolation Following This Disaster, 8-15. The indignation of the Lord is then revealed upon all nations and their demon-driven armies, who are bent on destroying Israel and taking possession of the earth (cf. Rev 16:13-16).

Divine Guarantee That Israel Will Possess and Inhabit the Land, 16-17. God's promise to Israel is to be fulfilled in securing the land and causing them to inhabit it perpetually, 16-17.

CHAPTER 35. THE GLORY OF THE KINGDOM

The Restoration of the Land and the Manifestation of the Lord, 1-2. Isaiah 34 is one of the darkest chapters in the Bible. Chapter 35 is one of the brightest and most joyful. It is a grand climax to the Volume of Woes Preceding Restoration Glories, which began at 28:1. Palestine, physically and climatically changed to welcome its Redeemer and the redeemed at the second advent, is poetically personified. With lilting joy the desert, Arabah, Lebanon, Carmel and Sharon see "the glory of the Lord, the majesty of our God."

Retrospect upon the Tribulation Preceding Blessing, 3-7. The command is given to encourage the weak and fearful, 3-4, to tide them through the darkness preceding the dawn. They are to be encouraged because Messiah-King is coming to punish Israel's enemies; to reward and deliver His own, 4; to work miracles in men's bodies and souls, 5-6; and to effect wonders in nature, 6-7.

Return of the Redeemed Remnant to Zion, 8-10. This will be by an appointed way, a highway, a holy way, a plainly marked way, 8, a safe way, 9. The redeemed will return joyfully to Zion, with everlasting exultation, at last obtaining gladness, with sorrow and sighing (so long plaguing them) fleeing away, 10.

Vol. VI. Historical Parenthesis, 36:1—39:8

CHAPTERS 36—37. OVERTHROW OF THE ASSYRIAN ARMY

Chapters 36—39 form a historical parenthesis connecting the first part of the book (ch. 1—35), consisting of predictions of judgment and blessings springing out of the Assyrian period, with the second part of the book, composed of prophecies of comfort emanating from the Babylonian period. Hezekiah's name is mentioned some 35 times in this section, and it is sometimes called the Volume of Hezekiah (cf. 2 Kgs 18:13—20:19).

The Assyrian Blatantly Challenges the Lord, 36:1-22. The arrogant conqueror Sennacherib in 701 B.C. sent the Rabshakeh (his Assyrian commander-in-chief) from Lachish (the Judean fortress commanding the road to Egypt) to demand the unconditional surrender of Judah. Rabshakeh met with Hezekiah's delegation, 1-3, and in its presence taunted Judah for trust in Egypt, 4-6, and in Hezekiah's God, 7-10. He continued his blasphemous taunts before all the people of Jerusalem, 11-22.

The Lord's Reply to the Challenge, 37:1-38. Hezekiah laid the matter before the Lord in the temple, 1, and sent a delegation to Isaiah for counsel and prayer, 2-5. He received from the prophet the first assurance of deliverance, 6-7. Meanwhile, the Rabshakeh returned to find Sennacherib besieging Libnah (another fortified city of Judah N of Lachish). Hearing that prince Tirhakah (Taharka in the Egyptian king lists, who later became third king in Egyptian Dynasty XXV) was preparing to attack, 8, Sennacherib dispatched another intimidating threat to Hezekiah, 9-13. The king spread it before the Lord in the temple and prayed, 14-20. The Lord granted a second assurance through Isaiah. The God-defying monarch would

Asshur, one of the Assyrian gods. (*Courtesy ORINST*)

be crushed, 21-35. The promise was subsequently fulfilled, 36-38. This great miracle was the capstone of Isaiah's repeated prophecies (10:24-34; 17:12-14; 29:5-8, 14; 30:27-33; 31:4-9; 33:3-4, 21-23; cf. 2 Kgs 19:35; 2 Chr 32:21-22).

CHAPTERS 38—39. HEZEKIAH'S SICKNESS AND SIN

Hezekiah's Deliverance from Serious Illness, 38:1-22. Isaiah announced that Hezekiah's sickness would be fatal, 1. The monarch's prayer, 2-3, was answered and God added 15 years to the king's life and confirmed His promise by "the sign," 4-8 (explainable only as a miracle). Hezekiah's psalm of thanksgiving and praise is recorded, 9-20. The remedy used for the recovery is specified, 21.

Hezekiah's Foolish Pride, 39:1-8. Merodach-baladan, a Chaldean and the son of Baladan, pretending to congratulate Hezekiah on his recovery from illness, tried with an embassy and lavish presents to draw the Jews into a league against Assyria, 1. Hezekiah's egotistical folly in displaying all his wealth and power, 2, drew a scathing rebuke from Isaiah and a warning of the Babylonian Captivity, 3-7. The king repentantly accepted God's sentence, 8.

HISTORICAL NOTE

Merodach-baladan was twice ruler of Babylon (722-710 B.C. and 703-701 B.C.). He initiated the policy of strengthening Chaldea and set the stage for the rise of Nabopolassar and Nebuchadnezzar II, and Judah's subsequent captivity.

Vol. VII. Book of Comfort, 40:1—66:24

CHAPTER 40. COMFORT FOR DELIVERED ISRAEL

The Call and Circumstances of the Promised Comfort, 1-11. A call is given to comfort Jerusalem, 1, because her suffering is foreseen as ended with her disobedience fully chastened and her sin forgiven, 2. The precursor to the promised comfort (John the Baptist and his message), 3-8, is seen preparing the way for Messiah, Israel's only true Comforter (Mt 3:3; Lk 3:4-6; Jn 1:23). The occasion for the comfort is the revelation of God in Christ, 9-11, as the personal God, Deliverer and King, 10, a Rewarder, 10, and a Shepherd, 11.

The Character of the Comforter, 12-26. His power is limitless to comfort, 12. His wisdom is unsearchable, 13-14. His Being is incomparable, 15-17. His worship must be spiritual, 18-26. Hence idolatry is utter folly and wickedly reprehensible, 18-20, in light of the infinite greatness of Deity, 21-26, witnessed to by God's creation, 21-22, 25-26, and declared by His works among men, 23-24.

The Prescription for Present Comfort, 27-31. The prophet reproves their discomfort, 27. He then prescribes for their comfort, 28-31, by reviewing God's character, 28-29, and by recalling God's faithfulness, 29-31, especially in helping the helpless, 29, and faithfully answering their prayers, 30-31.

CHAPTER 41. THE LORD'S CASE AGAINST IDOLATRY

Idolaters Are Arraigned, 1-7. God's court is convened and His challenge presented, 1. His case against idolaters is proved by His raising up Cyrus, founder of the Persian Empire and liberator of the Jews from Babylon, 2-4. The folly of idolaters is exposed, 5-7. (For Cyrus, cf. 41:25-26; 44:24-28; 45:1-6, 13; 46:11; 48:14.)

God's People Are Encouraged, 8-20. The basis of this encouragement, 8-9, is the fact that they are God's servants, His elect people, Abraham's progeny, 8, and objects of former deliverance, 9. As such they are the objects of special encouragement, 10-20. God promises His personal presence and protection, 10; deliverance from their enemies, 11-14; conquest over their foes, 15-16; and physical blessing for the land, 17-20.

The Idols Themselves Are Arraigned, 21-24, to present proofs of their knowledge of the past or future, 21-23, and of their power to do anything—good or bad, 23. Failing to do either, they are condemned as nonentities and their worshipers as abominations, 24.

The Lord Himself Produces Proof of His Sole Deity, 25-29. He alone has irresistible power to effect Cyrus' rise, and infallible foresight to foretell it over a century and a half in advance. He therefore pronounces the verdict upon both the idols and their worshipers. They are vanity, their works nonexistent, their representations are wind and confusion, 29.

CHAPTER 42. THE MESSIAH-SERVANT OF THE LORD

God (the Father) Presents the Servant, 1-4, in relation to Himself as His Servant, His elect, and His delight, 1. He mentions the qualifications for His work (the Holy Spirit resting without measure upon Him), specifies His task and describes His Servant's character, 2-4. This is the first "Servant Song," 1-6 (see 49:1-6; 50:4-11; 52:13—53:12).

The Prophecy of the Servant's Ministry, 5-9. The description of the One who commissions the Servant to the ministry shows Him to be God (the Father), Creator of the universe, Sustainer of men upon the earth, 5. His assurances to the Servant guarantee success, 6. The description of the Servant's ministry itself sets Him forth as the Mediator of the covenant of grace, 6; as a Light to the Gentiles, 6-7; and as a Liberator of prisoners, 7. The ratification of the commission is assured, 8-9, by the deity and authority of the Commissioner, 8, and the integrity of His word, 9.

Expression of Praise and Worship to God for the Coming Servant, 10-12. This blessing requires a "new song" from humanity everywhere to the ends of the earth.

Prediction of the Servant's Vengeance, 13-17. He will triumph as a warrior over His foes, 13. He will terminate His silence at His enemies' insults, 14-15. He will treat His friends with mercy, 16; but will thoroughly discomfit idolaters, 17.

Exposure and Reproof of Israel the Unfaithful Servant, 18-25. The Lord calls His people, 18, and faithfully appraises their sad condition, 19-20. Protecting His character and His word, 20, He must of necessity chasten His people's sinfulness and unfaithfulness as a servant, 22. However, He graciously provides for their relief by counseling them to acknowledge His hand in their affliction, 23-24, and confess their provocation in His punishment of them, 25.

43:1—44:5. ASSURANCE FOR THE RESTORED NATION

Promise of Comfort for the Remnant, 43:1-7. The basis of the promise is twofold: (1) the Lord is the Creator, and (2) He is the Redeemer of the yet-to-be-restored nation, 1. The promise assures the divine presence through fire and water, 2. Past proofs of the promise, 3-4, include His purchasing them dearly, and therefore He prizes them highly. The future efficacy of the promise is vouch-safed by the fact He will be with them personally, 5, and gather them from their captivity, 5-6. He will thus vindicate His purpose in calling the nation into existence, molding it, perfecting it to glorify Himself in it, and be glorified by it, 7 (cf. Rom 11:29).

Purpose of God in the Nation, 43:8-13. It was to be a witness to the pagan nations blinded by idolatry, 8-9, of the one true God and His Servant, 10-13.

God's Sovereign Power Will Be Demonstrated by Crushing the Chaldeans and Restoring Their Captives, 43:14-21. This will bring glory to God.

The Nation's Chastisements Are the Result of Its Ingratitude, 43:22-28. This is manifested in its prayerlessness, 22; its religious indifference, 23; and its sin, 24, all in the face of God's ready grace to forgive, 25, and to plead and reason with it, 26-28.

God's Saving Grace Will Be Manifested in the Conversion of the Servant Nation, 44:1-5. As His servant and His elect nation, 1, the Lord promises to pour out His Holy Spirit upon the converted nation (Isa 32:15; Joel 2:28-32), symbolically styled Jesurun ("upright"), 2 (see Deut 32:15; 33:5-6).

44:6-28. ISRAEL A WITNESS TO THE ONE TRUE GOD

God's Declaration of His Sole Deity, 6-8. As the Lord, the King of Israel, Israel's Redeemer, the Lord of armies, 6, He declares He is the only Deity, the Incomparable One, the Omniscient One, the Rock, 7-8.

Satire on the Sheer Folly of Idolatry, 9-20. It darkens the mind and blinds the eyes to spiritual truth.

God's Nation Israel Is to Be a Witness Against Idolatry, 21-23. This is her servant role, 21, being redeemed, 22, so that God might be glorified in the nation, 23.

The Lord Decrees the Restoration of His People Through Cyrus, 24-28. He calls Cyrus "my shepherd" who shall "fulfill all my purpose," 28 (cf. 41:2-4; 44:24-28; 46:11; 48:14).

CHAPTER 45. CYRUS A TYPE OF MESSIAH

See 44:24-28 above.

The Lord Promises Irresistible Conquest to Cyrus As a Type of Messiah, 1-6. The Lord calls him "His anointed," which is the only case in which this appellative is applied to a Gentile. This, with the designation "My shepherd" (Isa 44:28), likewise a messianic title, marks Cyrus an extraordinary exception, a Gentile type of Messiah. Both are restorers of Jerusalem (Isa 44:28; Zech 14:1-11). Both are irresistible conquerors of Israel's foes (Isa 45:1; Rev 19:19-21; Ps 2:9). Both are used to glorify the name of the one true God (Isa 45:6; 1 Cor 15:28).

The Lord's Sovereignty Is Vindicated Against Human Critics, 7-25. His lordship is vindicated by what He has done, 7-12; by His raising up Cyrus as His servant, 13; by the prediction that Gentiles are to be converted as well as Israel, 14-19; and by His open invitation to the "ends of the earth" to believe and be saved, 20-25.

CHAPTERS 46—47. DELIVERANCE FROM BABYLON AND ITS LESSONS

The Helplessness of Idols in Contrast to the Lord's Omnipotence, 46:1-13. Bel (Marduk, Merodach, Jer 50:2, the patron god of Babylon) and Nebo (an influential Babylonian deity, patron of culture and learning) will be a burden to the beasts who cart them into humiliating captivity, 1-2. In contrast, God bears and carries His people from birth till old age, creating and redeeming them, 3-4. He is moreover incomparable, 5, so unlike a wrought idol which is lifeless and must be carried by the worshiper instead of the worshiper being carried by his God, 6-7. It is dumb in contrast to the omniscient God who knows the future, 8-10, and demonstrates His purpose by raising up Cyrus, 11, and calling men to accept His (the Lord's) deliverance, 12-13.

Chastisement Beyond That Which God Ordains Punishable by Enslavement in Babylon's Case, 47:1-7. Shame and enslavement shall be visited upon the proud city of the Chaldeans for excessive cruelty to God's people.

The Godless Culture, Philosophy and Religion of This World Are Doomed, 8-15. Babylon's carnal pleasure and self-security, 8-9; her pride, wisdom, and knowledge, 10-11; and her demonized occult religion, 12-13, shall be her undoing, 14-15. Her doom symbolizes the destruction of the Satanic world system at the advent of Israel's King and kingdom.

CHAPTER 48. THE LORD'S DEALING WITH DISOBEDIENT ISRAEL

The Lord Presents the Evidence of Fulfilled Prophecy, 1-8. Idolatrous, hypocritical Jews, 1-2, are confronted with the truth of fulfilled prophecy as a manifestation of the omniscient power of God against any claim they might make for their idol. Many were tempted to trust in their idol, 3-5, for the Jews "deal very treacherously" and from birth were "called a rebel," 6-8 (RSV).

God Upholds His Glory by Means of Israel's Chastening, 9-11. For His name's sake, on the one hand, He restrains His anger that His people Israel might not be utterly destroyed, 9; yet, on the other hand, He must purify them in the furnace of affliction so that His name is unprofaned and His glory guarded, 10-11.

He Will Raise up a Gentile Deliverer to Liberate His People from Babylon, 12-16. As the Eternal One, the Creator, 12-13, He assembles His erring people to foretell to them that He will raise up one beloved (Cyrus) who will do His will against Babylon, 14-16.

He Laments the Tragedy of Their Disobedience, 17-19. The purpose of His chastening is to teach them "to profit" and to lead them "in the way they should go," 17. Had they obeyed, numerous blessings should have been theirs, 18-19.

They Are to Advertise His Redemption from Babylon, 20-22. His goodness is to be witnessed both in deliverance from Babylon, 20, and in His gracious interposition in their deliverance from Egypt. They are to remember always: "There is no peace for the wicked," 22 (RSV).

CHAPTER 49. THE MESSIAH-SERVANT AND HIS MISSION

The Servant's Arresting Exclamation, 1-4. Dramatically the Lord summons the Gentiles and announces to them that His call is divine, prenatal and illustrious, 1. Then He described His qualifications for the ministry (equipped with a powerful message and protected by the divine majesty), 2, and indicates its divine attestation, 3. Nevertheless, from the purely human standpoint (and He became a man!) the Messiah-Servant laments the apparent initial failure of His task, but quickly conquers the temptation to discouragement with the conviction that He did God's will, expecting God's reward, 4.

The Lord's Assurance of the Unqualified Success of His Servant, 5-13. The Lord's character and purpose, 5, as well as the Servant's specific ministry to the Jew first, 5-6, and to the Gentile, guarantee the worldwide extent of His blessing. This follows upon His sufferings and rejection, 7. He is granted not only a blessed ministry of redemption, 8-9, but His redeemed enjoy His full-scale blessings, 10-13.

The Lord Encourages Disheartened Israel, 14-26. He has not forgotten His people; they are engraved in the palms of His hands, 14-18. He will restore and bless them in their land, 19-23, punishing their enemies, 24-26.

CHAPTER 50. DISOBEDIENT ISRAEL VERSUS THE OBEDIENT SERVANT

The Disobedient People Presented, 1-3. They are dramatically challenged by the Lord Himself to prove Him unfaithful as a husband and as a father, 1. They are charged with responsibility for their captivity and their divorce from the Lord, and decisively condemned because of their unbelief, disobedience and disregard for God's power, 2-3.

The Obedient Servant-Saviour Prophesied, 4-9. The coming of the Servant is foretold. He will come as the taught one, the docile one, the one obedient to suffering, rejection and death, 4-6 (cf. Phil 2:6-8). The Servant will conquer as a courageous champion, depending upon God, doing His will, boldly confident in its success, and defying all opposition, 7-9.

His Promise of Salvation and Threat of Doom, 10-11. The way of salvation is through faith and obedience, 10. The way of destruction is through unbelief and disobedience, 11.

CHAPTER 51. ENCOURAGEMENT FOR THE FAITHFUL

The Faithful Given Promise of Zion's Future, 1-3. They are described in their present conduct, 1; reminded of their past descent, 2; and condoled with the promise of future deliverance for Zion, 3.

The Faithful Are Assured of the Fulfillment of the Promise to Zion, 4-8. The promise will be fulfilled by Messiah's personal administration, 4-5, and perpetual salvation, 6, with the prediction of the destruction of their persecutors explicit in the promise, 7-8.

The Faithful Petition for a Demonstration of the Promise by Deliverance, 9-16. The prayer is presented, 9, and enforced by a recital of the wonders of past deliverance from Egypt, 9-11. It is answered, 12-16, with regard to the fearful, 12; the fettered, 14-15; and the faithful, 16.

Predicament of Jerusalem Portrayed, 17-20. She is in a drunken stupor, 17; destitute of helpers, 18; decimated by desolation, 19-20.

Prediction of Jerusalem's Future Redemption, 21-23. The Lord assures her that He is her God and will speedily end her affliction, 22. He will make her persecuting foes drink the same cup as she had to drink, 23.

CHAPTER 52. JERUSALEM AROUSED TO GLORY

The dark background behind this bright scene is contained in 51:17-23.

Appeal to Jerusalem to Prepare Herself for Glory, 1-2. She is to arouse herself from the humiliation of her captivities, put on her high priestly apparel (cf. Zech 3:1-8), separate herself from defilement and assume her regal position, 2.

The Case the Lord Presents for His People's Liberation, 3-6. Their oppressors paid nothing for God's property, nor acknowledged His power, and so have no claim on His people, nor are to be paid any price, 3. His people have been similarly delivered before, 4. Moreover, their captors depreciated God's glory by their excessive cruelty to His people, 5, so that God's glory will be promoted by their emancipation, 6.

Praise of Prophet and People at Zion's Liberation, 7-10. The messenger of such an emancipation is very acceptable, 7. His message is theocratic, "Your God reigns!" (cf. Zech 6:8-14, with Christ the King-Priest installed upon the throne). The recipients of the message are expectant, exultant and specially illuminated, 8. The desolated city is commanded to rejoice, 9. The Lord is glorified and His worldwide salvation published, 10.

The Importance of Their Repatriation, 11-12, demands speed and thorough separation from Babylon, 11, with their return orderly and in dependence upon God, 12.

The Preeminence of the Servant Epitomized, 13-15. He is exalted because the Lord God views the Servant as divinely commissioned and qualified, 13. The compass of His exaltation is given, from the depths of humiliation to a position "above all heavens" (Eph 1:20-23; Phil 2:6-9). The precursors of exaltation were His abysmal degradation and sufferings, 14. He startles many nations and awes kings into silence as a consequence of His exaltation, 15.

CHAPTER 53. PROPHECY OF THE MESSIAH-SERVANT AS SINBEARER

Introduction: The Preeminence of the Servant Epitomized, 52:13-15. (See above.)

The Person of the Servant Despised, 1-3. Presented first is the incredible unbelief of the Jews concerning His person, 1 (cf. Jn 1:11). They despised His person because of His quiet, unobtrusive entrance among men, His poverty and obscurity, and His lack of worldly pomp and appeal, 2; but mostly because of their own blindness and sin, 3.

The Passion of the Servant Summarized, 4-6. Although He died for mankind in general, this is the penitential confession of the future repentant nation. She will glimpse His vicarious bearing of her (and the world's) sins, as well as see His shame and misrepresentation, stripes and wounds.

The Perseverance of the Servant Particularized, 7-10. He suffered silently, 7, unjustly, for our good and in our stead, vicariously, 8, ignominiously, 9, and under the frowns of heaven, 10.

The Recompense of the Servant Is Realized, 10-12. He acquires a glorious spiritual progeny ("He shall see a seed"), enjoys a splendid victorious resurrection ("He shall prolong His days") and fully accomplishes the divine will ("the pleasure of the Lord will prosper in His hand"), 10. He is rewarded with abundant satisfaction, 11; justifies many, 11; obtains incontestable victory and universal dominion, 12; and is given an efficacious high priestly ministry, 12.

CHAPTER 54. THE RADIANT JOY OF RESTORED ISRAEL

The Blessings of the Converted Nation, 1-10. Subsequent to the cross of Christ is the singing of the redeemed. When Israel looks unto Him whom they have pierced (53:1-8), what radiant joy, spiritual fruitfulness and expansion will be theirs, 1-3. She who during her sin and faithlessness was put away as the wife of the Lord is now restored, 4-6. Her restoration will be permanent and God's covenant of peace shall not depart from her, 7-10.

The Radiant Beauty of the Restored Nation, 11-17. She is likened to a beautiful city, 11-12. Her citizens shall be spiritually taught; will become spiritually prosperous, 13-14; and be victorious and secure, 15-17.

CHAPTER 55. WORLDWIDE EVANGELICAL INVITATION

The Invitation Offered, 1. It is universal, "everyone"; qualified only by a sense of need, "everyone that is thirsty." They will find wine to revive and milk to nourish (1 Pet 2:2) their souls. Everyone is invited "to come, buy and eat." They are assured of a free, gracious communication "without money and without price"—because the salvation offered is priceless, having already been purchased by Christ's own blood (Isa 53:1-8; 1 Pet 1:19).

The Invitation Enforced, 2-4. The appeal is strengthened by a consideration of the wrong to oneself in rejecting the invitation, 2, and the benefit by accepting it, 2-4.

The Invitation Extended and Defined, 5-7. It is extended by the calling of the Gentiles, 5 (Acts 15:14-15; Rom 1:16), and unknown nations, 5. It is defined as a call "to seek the Lord," 6; to repentance and faith, 7; and to obtain pardon, 7.

The Invitation Authorized and Accepted, 8-13. It is not authorized by man, because of the utter disparity between God's thought and man's, 8-9, but by God Himself, 9-10, and this by reason of the certain fulfillment of His word, 10-11. The invitation is accepted, 12-13, resulting in Israel's heart being regenerated, 12, and her land revived, 13, with creation being delivered from the bondage of corruption (Rom 8:19-23).

56:1-8. GENTILES INCLUDED IN KINGDOM BLESSING

Latter-day Israel Admonished to Maintain a Godly Witness, 1-2. She is to observe justice, do righteousness, keep the sabbath, and refrain from doing evil. Reason: the Lord's salvation is about to be revealed, 1-2.

Blessing Is Promised to Non-Israelites, 3-8. The foreigner and the eunuch who keep the Lord's sabbath and join themselves to God's covenant people, 3-5, will share the benefits of millennial worship in the temple at Jerusalem, 2:1-5, called "a house of prayer for all peoples," 6-8.

56:9—57:21. CONDEMNATION OF THE WICKED IN ISRAEL

The Sins of Wicked Rulers in Israel Denounced, 56:9-12. The sins of Israel's prophets are denounced—their spiritual blindness, veniality, covetousness, gluttony, false self-secure optimism.

The Sins of the Wicked Populace in Israel Denounced, 57:1-13.
They pay no attention to the death of a righteous man, 1-2. They
give themselves to idolatry, 3-10, but find no benefit, 11-13.

Mercy for the Repentant, but Judgment for the Wicked, 57:14-21.
The contrite and humble are chastened and revived, 14-20, but the
wicked have no peace, 21.

CHAPTER 58. FALSE WORSHIP VERSUS THE TRUE

Hypocritical Worship and Israel's Sins, 1-5. The prophet's preaching commission, 1, is followed by a description of the sins exposed.
As the first advent of our Lord was heralded by a message of repentance from John the Baptist (Mt 3:1-11), so the second advent will
be similarly preceded by such a call (Mal 4:5-6).

True Worship Outlined, 6-7. Repentance will result in true fasting
and humiliation.

The Promises for the Repentant Remnant, 8-14. Here all the great
future blessings of the converted remnant of Israel are set forth. It
is the gist of the entire closing section of the book.

CHAPTER 59. THE COMING OF THE REDEEMER TO ZION

Israel's Unbelief and Sin of the Last Days, 1-8. The terrible
catalog of the nation's depravity (cf. Rom 3:10-18) shows what has
separated her from God.

Israel's Last-Day Confession, 9-15. They confess their spiritual
darkness, 9; their desolation and deadness, 10; their unsaved condition, 11; their sinfulness, 12; and their wickedness, 13-15.

The Lord's Gracious Intervention, 16-19. He personally interposes
in their behalf, 16, judging and punishing the wicked, 17-18. His
Spirit raises up a standard against the flood of iniquity of the
Tribulation when it reaches its full, 19.

The Second Advent of the Redeemer, 20-21. Christ appears in
person for the salvation of them who turn from sin (Rom 11:26-27).

CHAPTER 60. JERUSALEM'S GLORY IN THE KINGDOM AGE

Israel Enlightened in the Kingdom Age, 1-2. Messiah the Light
shines on Jerusalem, Jerusalem shines on the earth, 1. Observe the
close connection with ch. 58 and 59. First the call to repentance;
then the uncovering of Jacob's sin; Israel's confession; and the
answer of the Lord by His personal advent, dealing with His

enemies and appearing as Redeemer in Zion. Then the glorious light of ch. 60 breaks forth. It is the glorious day preceded by the night of universal corruption and apostasy, 2.

Israel Enlarged in the Kingdom Age, 3-14. Gentiles are drawn to the Light, 3, and Jews return to the Light, 4. They bring in their wealth, and world conversion ensues, 5-9. Rich pastoral and commercial nations shall vie with one another in building Jerusalem, 10, and enriching Zion, 11. Rebels will be cut off, 12; the temple will be rebuilt (cf. 56:7) and beautified, 13; and enemies and revilers will humbly submit, 14.

Israel Exalted in the Kingdom Age, 15-22. Her humiliation gives way to exaltation, 15; her weakness to strength, 16; her poverty to wealth, 17; her troubles to salvation and safety, 18; her darkness to perpetual light, 19-20; her sin to righteousness, 21; and her insignificance to importance, 22.

CHAPTER 61. MESSIAH'S MINISTRY FOR ISRAEL AND THE WORLD

Messiah's Ministry in His First Advent Detailed, 1-2. In its spiritual character, His ministry was anointed by the Holy Spirit of God, 1 (cf. 42:1). In its specific character, it was a ministry of gospel preaching, 1, of spiritual healing, and of gracious favor to believers at His first advent (cf. Lk 4:18-20 where Jesus stops at this point).

Messiah's Ministry in His Second Advent, 2-3. In this connection He announces "the day of vengeance of our God," 2, and comfort for all who mourn, especially in Zion, 3.

Results of Messiah's Ministry at His Second Advent, 4-9. Waste places are rebuilt, 4. Israel, lately enslaved, will be served, 5; lately abased, will be exalted as a priestly, wealthy, and honored nation, 6. Lately afflicted, she will be enriched and comforted, 7; lately scattered, will be divinely gathered and guided, 8; lately reproached, will be fully vindicated before the nations, 9.

The Joy of Messiah's Ministry Is Depicted, 10-11. He personally exults that God has clothed Him with "the garments of salvation," 10, because of what God will do before the nations.

CHAPTER 62. JERUSALEM A PRAISE IN THE EARTH

The Divine Solicitude for Zion, 1. The Lord Himself is the speaker and He resolves He will not keep silent nor rest till Jerusalem is made a praise in the earth, till her vindication goes forth as brightness, and her salvation as a burning torch. The Lord Himself is eager to see the millennial city blessed and made a blessing, 1.

The Results of the Divine Solicitude for Zion, 2-5. Zion shall be honored and admired by the nations, 2. She shall be called by a new name—a God-given, royal name. It will no longer be Forsaken or Desolate, but Hephzibah ("my delight is in her") and Beulah ("married"), 3-4. The name will be given because the Lord's delight will be in her and she shall be married, as illustrated in the simile in 5.

The Concrete Expression of the Divine Solicitude for Zion, 6-12. This is set forth in the Lord's actions ("setting watchmen upon her walls"), 6; in the prophet's exhortation to intercession for the city, 6-7; in the Lord's oath that He will protect Jerusalem from ever again being overrun by enemies, 8-9; in the call to return from Babylon, 10; in the final end-time deliverance, 11, and in the final end-time blessing. This is expressed in a fourfold name for the Lord's own—"the holy people," "the redeemed of the Lord," "sought out," "a city not forsaken," 12.

63:1-6. THE MESSIAH-AVENGER AND THE DAY OF VENGEANCE

Messiah the Avenger Interrogated, 1-2. "The acceptable year of the Lord," i.e., "the year of the Lord's favor" (61:2), is closed and fearful judgment sweeps the earth (Rev 19:11-21). Two rhetorical questions are asked: "Who is this that comes from Edom?" (Answer, 1.) "Why is thy apparel red?" (Answer, 3-6.)

Messiah the Avenger's Answer, 1-6. Conquering, the figure (Christ in His second advent glory) replies, "I that speak in righteousness, mighty to save." He moves up through Edom to the valley of Jehoshaphat (Joel 3) for the great slaughter at Armageddon. The brilliant red of His garments (Rev 14:18-19) is explained as the result of treading the winepress of wrath against His enemies, whom He vanquishes solely by His own power and zeal, in complete fulfillment of the prophetic word, 3-4. Despite the failure of His own people, 5, He accomplishes the complete overthrow of His foes, 6.

63:7—64:12. THE REMNANT'S GREAT PRAYER OF INTERCESSION

The Remnant Remembers Past Deliverances, 63:7-19. Isaiah, as the representative of the godly remnant, utters one of the greatest prayers in the Bible, to be prayed by the godly remnant in the Tribulation preceding the kingdom. The steadfast love of the Lord in general is set forth, 7-9. Specific deliverance out of Egypt is cited, 10-14. The prayer is for the Lord's help in distress, 15-19.

The Remnant Beseeches the Lord to Assert His Power Over the Nations, 64:1-4. In the dark night of the Tribulation when enemies of Israel close in, 1-2, divine interposition is pleaded for.

The Penitent Confession of the Believing Remnant, 64:5-7. They are confident that the Lord will meet them, 5, in their confession of sin, 6-7.

The Appeal for Pardon and Restoration, 64:8-12. The touching plea is from a chastened and yielded people, 8-9, reviewing their punishments, 10-11, and interceding for help, 12.

CHAPTER 65. THE LORD'S ANSWER—HIS MERCY RESERVED FOR THE REMNANT

The Sins of Latter-day Apostate Israel, 1-7. The stern rebuke of the Lord goes forth because of their rebellion in the face of open opportunity, 1, and abundant divine revelation, 2, which they scouted for idolatry, 3-4, and self-righteousness, 5. The warning of punishment concerns the day of vengeance, 6-7.

The Election and Blessing of the Righteous Remnant, 8-10. God will not destroy the remnant, because there is blessing in it, 8. He will restore it and the land for it to dwell in, 9-10.

The Judgment of Latter-day Apostate Israel, 11-12. Idolatry, covetousness, rebellion and disobedience destine the apostates for slaughter.

The Blessings of the Remnant vs. the Curses of Apostate Israel, 13-16. The state of God's servants is in sharp contrast to that of those who reject Him.

The Glories and Blessings in Store for God's Own, 17-25. The prophet glimpses the eternal sinless state, 17. In the kingdom he sees Jerusalem blessed, 18-19; longevity restored, 20; security and happiness prevailing, 21-23; prayer answered, 24; and the curse lifted, 25 (cf. 11:6-9).

CHAPTER 66. SYNOPTIC FINALE; THE ENTIRE PROPHECY IN RETROSPECT

Wicked Worship of Age-end Apostate Israel, 1-4. This final chapter restates the leading prophetic themes of the book. The apostate mass of the Jewish nation (Israel) restored in unbelief erects a temple in Jerusalem and resumes its ancient worship. This is a worship of unbelief and is an abomination to the Lord, 1-4 (cf. 2 Thess 2:4; Dan 9:27; Mt 24:15; Rev 11:1-2). "What is the house which you would build for me?" 1 (RSV). The true worshiper is in contrast, 2, to the apostate worshiper, 2-4.

The Remnant Persecuted and Encouraged, 5. The remnant trembles at God's Word and is hated and mocked by apostate brethren, who shall be put to shame, 5. In derision they taunt, "Let the Lord be glorified."

The Coming of the Lord, 6. Suddenly He comes to His temple (Mal 3:1). He appears rendering recompense to His enemies.

Israel's National Rebirth, 7-9. A people and a land are born in a day! A nation is regenerated in a moment (Rom 11:26-27).

Jerusalem's Millennial Glory and Exaltation, 10-14. The city is likened to a mother who nurses her children, 10-11. Her kingdom, prosperity and wealth are communicated to her children, 12-14 (cf. 60:1-7).

Messiah the Avenger and the Day of Vengeance, 15-17. The Lord will come with fire to render His anger in fury (cf. 61:2; 63:3-4) against His foes among the nations, 15-16, and against the apostate mass of Israel, 17.

Gentiles Brought into the Kingdom, 18-21. All nations and languages will be brought in to see God's glory, 18. Those gathered are to evangelize and bring others in, 19. Jews also will be brought in, 20-21.

The Perpetuity of Israel and the Eternal State, 22. The truth of the eternal state is used as a simile for the fact of Israel's perpetual existence.

Blessings for the Righteous, 23. All mankind will worship the Lord.

The Destiny of the Wicked, 24. Eternal perdition is their portion —"their worm shall not die, their fire shall not be quenched" (cf. the Lord's warning of Gehenna, Mk 9:44-48; Rev 20:14-15).

JEREMIAH

DEATH THROES OF A DECADENT NATION

The World of Jeremiah. Isaiah lived and prophesied under the Assyrian period. Jeremiah ministered when Assyria was tottering on the brink of ruin, and Babylon and Egypt were struggling to take over world control. He warned of Babylon's victory, but Judah failed to repent of her sin and accept his warnings. As a result Judah suffered destruction, but the prophet announced that she would one day be restored, and through Messiah would come into worldwide blessing. Babylon, however, would be destroyed, never to rise again.

KINGS OF JUDAH IN TIME OF JEREMIAH

King	Events of the King's Reign
Manasseh 696-642 B.C.	Jeremiah born under this wicked tyrant.
Amon 642-640 B.C.	Doom of Judah threatened.
Josiah 640-608 B.C.	This godly king began his reforms 627 B.C. Jeremiah's call 626 B.C. Book of the law found, followed by Josiah's great reformation 621 B.C. (2 Kgs 22—23). Scythian invasion 620 B.C. (Jer 4); growing power of Neo-Babylonia (Nabopolassar) 625-605 B.C.; fall of Nineveh 612 B.C.; Haran 609 B.C. Josiah killed at Megiddo 608 B.C. by Pharaoh-Necho.
Jehoahaz 608 B.C.	Reigned three months—carried to Egypt.
Jehoiakim 608-597 B.C.	Wicked idolater. Rise of Nebuchadnezzar II 605-562 B.C.
Jehoiachin 597 B.C.	Reigned three months—carried to Babylon.
Zedekiah 597-586 B.C.	Zedekiah visited Babylon 593 B.C. Lachish Letters 589-587 B.C. Jerusalem sacked 586 B.C. Temporary end of Davidic dynasty.

Arrangement of Book. The messages that are dated show that the book was not arranged in chronological order. For instance, messages in *Josiah's* reign are found in 1:2 and 3:6, while those in *Jehoiakim's* reign are in 22:18; 25:1; 26:1; 35:1; 36:1; 45:1. Those in *Zedekiah's* reign are in 21:1, 8; 27:2, 3, 12; 28:1; 29:3; 32:1;

34:2; 37:1-2; 38:5; 39:1; 49:34; 51:59. Two were written late in Egypt, 43:7-8; 44:1. Most of the messages were obviously given in Jehoiakim's and Zedekiah's reigns. The lack of chronological order is evidently intentional. Probably the order is to be found in the arrangement of the subject matter by contrast, not by date of composition.

Message of Jeremiah. His was principally a message of stern warning against the inevitable doom of the Babylonian Captivity (25:1-14), if the people did not repent of idolatry and sin. The menacing gloom of an iconoclastic message (1:10) was highlighted, however, by bright messianic flashes (23:5-8; 30:4-11; 31:31-34; 33:15-18). Final restoration of Israel was to be accomplished after a period of unparalleled suffering (30:3-10), through the manifestation of David's righteous Branch, the Lord (23:6; 33:15).

Outline
Prophecies Against Judah and Jerusalem, Ch. 1—45
    Under Josiah and Jehoiakim, Ch. 1—20
    At Various Periods Till Jerusalem's Fall, Ch. 21—39
    After Jerusalem's Fall, Ch. 40—45
Prophecies Against the Nations, Ch. 46—51
Historical Appendix, Ch. 52

CHAPTER 1. INTRODUCTION; JEREMIAH'S CALL

Superscription, 1-3. Jeremiah ("the Lord exalts") was a descendant of the priest Abiathar, who was banished by Solomon to Anathoth (Ras Karrubeh) about two miles NE of Jerusalem in Benjamin. Jeremiah's ministry, 2, extended from Josiah's thirteenth year (627 B.C.) to Zedekiah's eleventh year (586 B.C.).

Jeremiah's Call, 4-19. God's electing grace, 5, and the prophet's humility, 6, resulted in a definite commission three-fifths destructive and iconoclastic in a decadent age, 7-10. Jeremiah's encounter with God and his commission were buttressed by three visions, 11. The almond tree (Heb. *shakedh*) is the first harbinger of spring and was a sign that God was *watching, awaking early* (Heb. *shakedh*) to empower His word, 12. The boiling pot fanned by the north wind pictures God's judgment boiling over from the north on Judah for her sin and idolatry. God's Word is effectual (1 Pet 4:17; Heb 4:12).

Anathoth, home of Jeremiah. (© *MPS*)

2:1—3:5. SERMON 1—SIN OF THE NATION

A Faithful Lord vs. an Unfaithful People, 2:1-19. The review of
the Lord's goodness, 1-3, is followed by an exposé of the apostasy
of the nation, 4-13. Baal contamination is hinted, 11. The people
had committed two evils, forsaking the Lord, "the fountain of living
waters" (cf. Jn 4:10-15; 7:38), and by their idolatry were drinking
the polluted waters at the bottom of a cracked and contaminated
man-made cistern, 13. As a result, Israel had lost her freedom and
had become a slave of Assyria ("the lions") and of Egypt (Memphis,
capital of N. Egypt), 14-19.

The Divine Impeachment and Expostulation, 2:20-37. Israel had
become like a stubborn ox, 20; a degenerate vine, 21; a lustful prostitute, 22-25; a shameless thief, 26; a foolish idolater, 27-28; a
thoughtless, thankless people, 29-32; an impudent transgressor, 33;
a blinded nation, 34-37.

The Results of Israel's Infidelity, 3:1-5. Her callousness made her
punishment inevitable.

3:6—6:30. SERMON 2—DEVASTATION FROM THE NORTH

Judah's Apostasy Greater Than Israel's, 3:6-25. The northern kingdom's punishment in captivity and eventual destruction did not properly impress Judah, 6-11. She was a harlot, made unclean by traffic in foul Canaanite religion, divorced from the Lord. Similar chastisement as that which befell Israel (2 Kgs 17:1-18) threatened Judah; but true repentance, 10-14, would be followed by blessing, 15-25.

The Foe from the North, 4:1-31. Danger threatened in the impending Scythian invasion. Barbarian hordes from the north were threatening the hard-pressed Assyrian Empire. God's prophet saw the Lord's disobedient people chastised in these political upheavals.

Judgment and Impending Disaster, 5:1-31. The weeping prophet of Anathoth bewailed the sins of Jerusalem, his moral sensitivity pained.

Continued Warning, 6:1-30. A great destruction was coming on Jerusalem, 1-26. Let its inhabitants flee to the wilderness of Tekoa (Amos' home), some dozen miles S of Jerusalem. Jeremiah appeared as the Lord's tester or assayer to try the Lord's people, 27-30 (cf. Job 23:10).

CHAPTERS 7—10. SERMON 3—THREAT OF EXILE

This temple message, like the two preceding sermons, was a stern rebuke, warning and exhortation, but centered in the religious conditions in Judah.

Rebuke of Apostate Religionism, 7:1-34. Would these empty ritualists of Jerusalem make God's house "a den of robbers," 1-11? Let the destruction of Shiloh (18 miles N of Jerusalem, destroyed about 1050 B.C.) be a lesson, 12-14 (cf. Jer 26:6; 1 Sam 4:10; Ps 78:60). The Lord's anger burned at Jerusalem's idolatry, 15-19, and apostasy, 20-34. The "Queen of Heaven," 18, was an ancient Semitic deity, Babylonian Ishtar (Venus) (cf. 44:17-19, 25). "Tophet," 32, was a high place in the Valley of Hinnom, SW of Jerusalem, where in the Isaiah-Jeremiah era people sacrificed children to Molech, a deity of Ammon.

Further Warnings of Judgment, 8:1-22. All classes of God's people were corrupted, prophets as well as priests, 10; sinners were brazenly shameless, 12.

Jeremiah Weeps Over Sinners, 9:1-26. The prophet was torn between pity for sinners and revulsion at their sin, 1, which could not be condoned, 2-26.

The Lord and Idolatry, 10:1-25. The folly of worshiping idols is outlined, 1-16, and the judgment to be visited upon it, 17-22. A prayer is offered, 23-25.

CHAPTERS 11—13. SERMON 4—THE BROKEN COVENANT; SIGN OF THE LOINCLOTH

The Broken Covenant, 11:1 — 12:17. The rebukes, warnings and exhortations of this sermon were based upon the violation of the Palestinian covenant (Deut 28:1—30:9). Jeremiah championed the covenant, 11:1-8. The reformation under Josiah had been forgotten, 9-17, and the prophet's own countrymen at Anathoth planned to kill him, 11:18-23. This underhanded action and the prosperity of the wicked bothered the prophet, 12:1-6, and the Lord pronounced a lamentation for Judah through him, 12:7-17.

The Parable of the Loincloth, 13:1-27. This parabolic sign was acted out by the prophet, 1-11. The pure white linen garment worn next to the skin symbolized the pristine purity of the nation in fellowship with the Lord. Put off and exposed to dampness and soil at the Euphrates, 4, 6, 7, it showed the ruin of the nation away from God and in predicted captivity beyond the Euphrates in Babylon. The wine jars, 12-14, filled to the brim, symbolized the people's drunkenness and their ruin under divine judgment. The warning against pride, 15-17, was followed by the dirge for the king (Jehoiachin) and queen mother, both of whom were taken captive to Babylon (597 B.C.), 18-19. Woes were pronounced upon Jerusalem, 20-27.

CHAPTERS 14—17. SERMON 5—THE DROUGHT; SIGN OF THE UNMARRIED PROPHET

Drought and the Nation's Doom, 14:1-22. This terrible calamity, 1-6; the empty ritualistic prayers of the nation, 7-9; and their rejection by the Lord, 10-12, are described. The false prophets, 13, who had no divine credentials, were to blame, 14-16. Jeremiah lamented for the nation, 17-22.

The Lord's Answer to Jeremiah, 15:1-21. Intercession was rejected and the nation's fate was sealed, 1-9. The prophet's grief was followed by the Lord's reply, 10-21.

The Approaching Disaster, the Wages of Sin, 16:1-21. The inexorable fulfillment of God's word is shown by the Lord's denying marriage to the prophet, 1-4, and even observance of funerals and festivities, 5-9, seen as signs of impending ordeals because of Judah's apostasies, 10-13. Ultimate blessing would result after judgment, 14-21.

Judah's Terrible Sin, 17:1-27. A description of it, 1-4, with the curse and the blessing, was set before the people, 5-11. Jeremiah worshiped and prayed, 12-18. Sabbath desecration, an index of their disloyalty to the Lord, was warned against, 19-27.

CHAPTERS 18—20. SERMON 6—SIGN OF THE POTTER'S HOUSE

The Prophet's Visit to the Potter, 18:1-23. This episode furnished a lesson in God's sovereign molding of His people (Rom 9:20-24). He dealt sovereignly with them; design for evil could be substituted for design for good if His people repented, 1-11. But their brazen unrepentance was commented on by the Lord, 12-17; demonstrated by the wicked plots of the people against Jeremiah, 18; and lamented by the prophet's imprecatory prayer, 19-23. Imprecation was in order since they were ripe for divine destruction.

The Broken Earthen Flask, 19:1-15, was another sign that the Lord would smash the idolatry-ridden people. Topheth (see 7:31) was the center of the cruel Moloch cult. The Potsherd Gate (later the Dung Gate, Neh 2:13) led to Hinnom, the location of the idol Moloch, where children were offered.

Public Punishment of Jeremiah, 20:1-18. Pashur, chief temple policeman, imprisoned Jeremiah for his message on the broken flask, 1-6. Pashur's doom was announced, 6, and his name was changed to "Terror," 3 (cf. 6:25; 25:8-11; Ps 31:13). Jeremiah's severe testing produced momentary perplexity and complaint, but faith triumphed over unbelief in the prophet, 7-18.

CHAPTERS 21—24. ORACLES CONCERNING REIGNING KINGS

Jeremiah's Message to Zedekiah, 21:1-14. The inquiry of Zedekiah, 1-2 (597-586 B.C.), was made concerning Nebuchadrezzar (Akkadian *Nabu-kuddurriusur,* "Nabu protect my boundary stone," 605-562 B.C.). This Pashur was different from the Pashur of 20:1. Zephaniah, the priest, was later executed at Riblah (52:24-27). Jeremiah's reply to Zedekiah, 3-7; the people, 8-10; and the court, 12-14, was realistic and must have cut his sinful auditors to the quick.

Jeremiah's Message Concerning Other Kings of Judah, 22:1-30. This was an introductory oracle warning the Davidic court, 1-9, and comforting Shallum (Jehoahaz), who reigned only three months and was carried to Egypt (608 B.C.), 11-12. An oracle concerning Jehoiakim (608-597), 13-19, a wicked idolater and foe of Jeremiah, was presented (cf. 2 Kgs 23:24—24:7). Judgment was pronounced upon Jehoiachin, 20-30, who was deported to Babylon. (He is called Coniah here and 37:1; Jeconiah in 24:1; 27:20; cf. 2 Kgs 24:8-16; 25:27-30.)

Great Messianic Prophecy, 23:1-40. The false shepherds (unworthy rulers) of Judah, 1-2, furnished the somber background for the bright prophecy of kingdom regathering and restoration, 3-4, under Messiah, "the righteous Branch," 5, "the LORD our RIGHTEOUSNESS," 6. This will be fulfilled in the end-time and will embrace the final exodus and redemption from worldwide bondage into kingdom status, 7-8, under the Messiah (Rom 11:25-27). Jeremiah's lament, 9-14, and condemnation of the false prophets, 15-32, followed the glorious messianic flash. The recalcitrant sinners of that day were given up to shame, 33-40.

Vision of the Two Baskets of Figs, 24:1-10, directed against Zedekiah. The good figs symbolized the best of the people carried to Babylon with Jehoiachin (597 B.C.), here called Jeconiah (cf. 22:20-30). The bad figs stood for the apostates who remained in Jerusalem to support the wicked Zedekiah, and who were of a mind to resist Babylon with Egypt's help, (2 Kgs 24:10-20).

CHAPTER 25. PREDICTION OF THE 70-YEAR CAPTIVITY

The Exile Declared, 1-11. In the fourth year of Jehoiakim (604 B.C.), with the supremacy of Babylon assured by Nebuchadrezzar's defeat of Egypt at Carchemish, Jeremiah reviewed his previous 23-year ministry, 1-7. Then he announced the 70-year captivity, 8-11 (cf. Lev 26:33-35; 2 Chr 36:21; Dan 9:2).

Judgment of the Nations and the Day of the Lord, 12-38. Babylon with its king was to be punished, 12-14, as well as "all the nations," 15-29 (cf. Isa 51:17; Rev 14:10). This will usher in the "day of the Lord" and the wrath of God, 30-38. This is the future period of judgment upon apostate Israel and the nations, culminating in the glorious second advent of Christ (Mt 24:30; Rev 4—19).

CHAPTER 26. JEREMIAH FACES THREAT OF DEATH

His Prediction of the Destruction of the Temple, 1-11. It would be destroyed like Shiloh (cf. 7:12,14 with 1 Sam 4:10-11). All classes rejected the truth and persecuted the prophet.

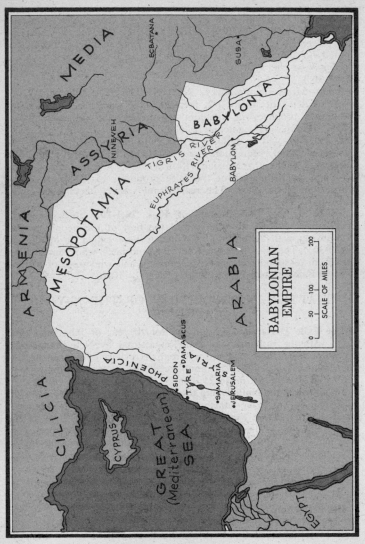

Jeremiah's Deliverance, 12-24. His brave defense and deliverance are described, 12-19, with reference made to Micah's similar ministry, 18-19 (cf. Mic 1:1), and Urijah's martyrdom under Jehoiakim, 20-24.

CHAPTERS 27—28. THE SIGN OF THE YOKES

The Divinely Imposed Yoke of Babylon, 27:1-22. Jeremiah saddled himself with an ox yoke to symbolize how Babylon would put a yoke on the neck of Jerusalem and Judah. This truth was distasteful to the people.

Opposition by False Prophets, 28:1-17. Hananiah, one of the false prophets, impudently broke Jeremiah's yoke, 10. He was punished by death, 17.

CHAPTER 29. JEREMIAH COMFORTS THE EXILES

His Letter Sent to Babylon, 1-23. He urged the people to be law-abiding, peaceful exiles and to multiply, 1-9, against the day of restoration after 70 years, 10 (cf. 25:11; 27:7). The Lord had good plans for them, 10-14. They had a future and a hope, 11, but they must refuse the false prophets among them, namely, Ahab and Zedekiah, 21, whose doom was sealed, 22-23.

Shemaiah's Attack and Jeremiah's Second Letter, 24-32. Another false prophet uttering lies and rebellion against the Lord sent a scathing letter to the new temple overseer, Zephaniah, attacking Jeremiah. Zephaniah showed the letter to Jeremiah, who then sent another letter to the exiles, condemning Shemaiah and prophesying that neither this false prophet nor his descendants would see the day of the return from exile (cf. 20:6).

CHAPTERS 30—31. RESTORATION AND MESSIANIC FOREGLEAMS

The Time of Jacob's Trouble, 30:1-17. Jeremiah's dark warnings of judgment were relieved by a prophecy of the glorious future of the nation, ch. 30—31. But this great regathering and end-time restoration, 30:1-3, is to be preceded by the Great Tribulation, 4-11, the acme of the nation's age-long sufferings, here called "the time of Jacob's trouble" because it will center in latter-day Israel, 7 (cf. Mt 24; Mk 13; Rev 7). The return of Christ, 9 (cf. Rev 19:11-16), will establish the kingdom after the sinful people have been purged, 12-17.

Israel's Restoration to Kingdom Glory, 30:18-24. They will be restored as the Lord's people, 22.

The Nation's Homegoing and Salvation, 31:1-26. The restored nation, 1-6, will sing songs of redemption, 7-14, with the preceding tribulation (as in 30:1-17, 23-24) producing genuine repentance and preparing the nation for blessing, 15-20, and assurance, 21-26.

The New Covenant and the Everlasting Nation, 31:27-40. This restoration to the Lord's blessing is based on the new covenant, 31-34. The old covenant was the law covenant grounded in legal observance. The new covenant (Heb 8:8-12) will be entirely on the basis of grace and the sacrificed blood of Christ, which will be the foundation of Israel's future inward regeneration and restoration to God's favor. Israel's entering into the blessings of the new covenant will insure her being an everlasting nation, 35-36 (cf. Rom 11:1-26).

CHAPTER 32. JEREMIAH'S FAITH IN THE RESTORATION

The Sign of the Prophet's Faith, 1-25. He purchased land in Anathoth, early in 586 B.C., before the fall of Jerusalem. Hanameel, Jeremiah's cousin, was eager to sell his land to the prophet to prevent loss of the family patrimony (Lev 25:25-28). Storage of deeds, written on papyrus, in earthen jars is known from Elephantine in Egypt, 14. Jeremiah's faith in the hour of his imprisonment, 3, became vocal in prayer, 16-25. Baruch, 12, was Jeremiah's faithful secretary.

The Lord's Answer, 26-44. The fate of the doomed city was announced, 28-35, and the future final regathering, of which the restoration from Babylon was a foreshadowing, was declared, 36-44.

CHAPTER 33. THE GREAT PROPHECY OF THE DAVIDIC KINGDOM

Jerusalem's Imminent Overthrow, 1-5. A call to prayer was issued, 1-3, as the siege of Jerusalem was begun. This picture of impending disaster furnished the dark background against which was flashed the future glory of the nation.

Future Blessing and Glory, 6-14. Cleansing is to be effected after the return, 6-8 (cf. Ezk 36:25; Zech 13:1; Heb 9:13-14; Rom 11:25-27). The joy of salvation is echoed, 9-11, and kingdom peace and prosperity are described, 12-14.

The Davidic King and His Kingdom, 15-26. "In those days" is the time of the second advent of Christ when He, "the Branch of Righteousness," will come to sit on the throne of His father David (Lk 1:31-33; cf. 2 Sam 7:8-16). Then the Lord in redemptive power will be manifested toward Israel as "the Lord our [Israel's] righteousness," 16 (cf. 33:6-8). Also temple worship (see Ezk 40—44) will be restored, 18. The inviolability of the Davidic covenant was declared, 20-22, as well as God's faithfulness to perform all the covenants and promises made to Israel, 23-26 (cf. Rom 9:4-5; 11:29).

CHAPTER 34. JEREMIAH'S WARNING TO ZEDEKIAH

The Warning, 1-7. The siege of the city (Jan., 588 B.C.) impending, Jeremiah warned Zedekiah of its fall. Lachish, the fortress city 23 miles SW of Jerusalem, and Azekah, 11 miles N of Lachish, are well known from the Lachish Letters.

ARCHAEOLOGICAL LIGHT

The Lachish Ostraca discovered at Lachish (Tel ed-Duweir) in 1935 belong to this very time. Letter No. IV says, "We are watching for the fire signals of Lachish . . . for we no longer can see the signals of Azekah." The names, places and circumstances of these 21 Heb. inscribed tablets closely resemble the times of Jeremiah just before the fall of Lachish, Azekah and Jerusalem, 589-586 B.C.

Zedekiah's Perfidy, 8-22. Freeing all Heb. slaves (cf. Ex 21:1-6; Deut 15:12-18), Zedekiah later broke the agreement, 1-11. Jeremiah strongly condemned this base conduct, 12-22, and declared punishment like that in their covenant ritual, 18 (cf. Gen 15:9-17). The infractor would suffer the same fate as the animal slaughtered to seal the covenant.

CHAPTER 35. THE LOYALTY OF THE RECHABITES

The Command Concerning Them, 1-11. A religious order inculcating the simplicity and purity of bedouin life, the Rechabites were founded by Jonadab, son of Rechab, during Jehu's reign (841-814 B.C.). They assisted in the eradication of Baalism from Israel. City life with its corrupting influences was avoided, and they lived simply in tents as shepherds, drinking no wine (cf. the similar Nazirites, Num 6:1-21).

The Lesson for the Jews, 12-19. The Rechabites refused to drink wine and were obedient to their ancestor Rechab, 6, while the Jews were utterly disobedient to the Lord's command. This vivid illustration furnished a contrast and an occasion for pronouncing doom upon the Jews and blessing upon the Rechabites.

CHAPTER 36. JEHOIAKIM'S OPPOSITION TO THE WORD OF GOD

The Reading of the Scroll, 1-20. The writing of the scroll was commanded in the fourth year of Jehoiakim (604 B.C.), 1-4. The purpose was to set before the people the evil coming upon them, so they might turn from their sin. The reading of the scroll, 5-10, was enjoined upon Baruch by Jeremiah. The occasion was the fast ordered by the king because of Nebuchadrezzar's advance against Ashkelon (Nov., 604 B.C.).

Jehoiakim Cuts and Burns the Roll, 21-26. The same Satanic spirit energizes unbelieving critics and opposers of God's Word in every age.

Indestructibility of God's Word, 27-32. The Word moves on, but its doom is pronounced upon its rejecters and would-be destroyers.

CHAPTERS 37—38. JEREMIAH'S EXPERIENCES DURING THE SIEGE

Jeremiah's Response to Zedekiah's Inquiry, 37:1-10. In the spring of 587 B.C., an army of Pharaoh-Hophra (Apries) appeared to relieve Jerusalem, and the Chaldeans withdrew, 5. Jeremiah answered Zedekiah's deputation, warning that the Chaldeans would shortly return and burn the city, 6-10.

Jeremiah's Arrest, 37:11 — 38:13. He was charged with desertion as he attempted to go to Anathoth "to receive his portion," 12 (RSV), and was imprisoned in the dungeon, 38:1-13. He was accused of treason and of "weakening the hands of . . . all the people," 4. This idiom occurs in Lachish Letter VI: "And behold the words of the princes are not good, but to weaken our hands" (see Archaeological Light, ch. 34).

Jeremiah's Final Appeal to Zedekiah, 38:14-28. The prophet's wise advice to surrender to Nebuchadrezzar, so long made, was again finally rejected.

CHAPTER 39. THE FALL OF JERUSALEM

The Burning of the City and Fate of Zedekiah, 1-10. (See also 2 Kgs 25; Jer 52; 2 Chr 36.) The Word of God through Jeremiah was vindicated. The city was destroyed, Zedekiah's sons were killed, his eyes put out, and he was carried in chains to Babylon. The Rabsaris and the Rabmag were titles of Babylonian officers (cf. 3, 13).

Kind Treatment of Jeremiah, 11-18. He was given a choice to go to Babylon or stay in Palestine. He chose the latter, 11-14, and cast his lot with Gedaliah, the governor. His oracle to Ebed-melech, 15-18, and his deliverance (continued from 38:13) are presented here to show the truth that the faithful are rewarded when judgment falls.

CHAPTERS 40—41. MURDER OF GEDALIAH

Jeremiah Chooses to Cast His Lot with Gedaliah, 40:1-8. The governor appointed by the Babylonians had his headquarters at Mizpah (apparently Tell en-Nasbeh), seven miles N of Jerusalem. In 1935 a seal inscribed, "Belonging to Gedaliah, who is over the house," was found in ashes left by Nebuchadrezzar's fires at Lachish.

Plot Against Gedaliah, 40:9-16. His wise regime prospered, 9-12, but Ishmael, a member of the royal family, was sent by Baalis of Ammon to assassinate Gedaliah, 13-16.

The Crime Perpetrated, 41:1-18. Ishmael with a company of ten men slew Gedaliah, 1-3, and a sorrowing band on the way to Jerusalem was also murdered en masse, 4-10. Ishmael fled to Ammon, 11-18.

CHAPTERS 42—43. THE REMNANT'S FLIGHT INTO EGYPT

Jeremiah the Intercessor, 42:1-22. The remnant in dire perplexity besought Jeremiah to pray for them, 1-6, but when the answer came from the Lord after ten days to the effect that they should remain in the land, they refused God's word and decided to go down to Egypt anyway, 7-22.

Rebellion Against Jeremiah and the Trip to Egypt, 43:1-7. The people took Jeremiah along to Egypt and settled in Tahpanhes, 7, the Egyptian border fortress, also called Baal-Zephon (Gr. Daphne, modern Tell Defneh).

Jeremiah's Prediction of Nebuchadrezzar's Conquest of Egypt, 43:8-13. This came true in 568 B.C. when Nebuchadrezzar, "my servant" (25:9; 27:6; cf. 43:10), invaded Egypt against Amasis (Ahmosis II) (cf. 46:13-20). Verse 13 (RSV) mentions Heliopolis (called On in Gen 41:45), "city of the sun," the center of the worship of the sun-god Re (Isa 19:18, RSV). The famous obelisks found here were characteristic Egyptian monuments, slightly tapered granite shafts, capped by a prymidion which symbolized a shaft or ray of sunlight. Jeremiah's scorn of Egyptian idolatry is seen in 12: "as a shepherd cleans [delouses] his cloak of vermin."

CHAPTER 44. JEREMIAH'S FINAL PLEA IN EGYPT

His Expostulation with the Jews in Egypt, 1-19. Jeremiah's message went to "all the Jews," 1, in Noph (Memphis, the capital of N. Egypt, 14 miles S of Cairo), Migdol (Tell el-Heir, E of Tahpanhes, see 43:7), and "in the land of Pathros," i.e., "land of the South," upper or southern Egypt, where a Jewish colony at Elephantine (now so well known from Aramaic papyri from the 5th cen. B.C.) was already doubtless in existence. The prophet's plea, 1-10, was followed by a prediction of punishment, 11-14. The diaspora at Pathros impudently defied Jeremiah, 15-16, stoutly declaring they would continue adoration of the "Queen of Heaven," 17-19 (the Assyrian Ishtar, Canaanite Astarte, Gr. Aphrodite, Rom. Venus), a polluted cult. Offerings included moon- or star-shaped cakes and replicas of the goddess of sexual love.

The Lord's Answer and Sign, 20-30. Judgment was pronounced upon these impudent idolaters, 20-28. The sign given to confirm God's word through Jeremiah was Pharaoh-Hophra (Apries, 588-569 B.C.; cf. 37:5), who was to "be given into the hands of his enemies" and slain. He was assassinated by Ahmosis II (Amasis, 569-526 B.C.), a former court official, founder of Dynasty XXVII (Libyan).

CHAPTER 45. JEREMIAH'S MESSAGE TO BARUCH RECALLED

Baruch's Initial Plaint, 1-3. This was made and Jeremiah's message given in 604 B.C., Jehoiakim's fourth year, 1. Baruch, as Jeremiah's secretary and associate, was told at the beginning of his ministry of the difficulties ahead (cf. 1:10; 36:1-4).

The Lord's Sustaining Promise, 4-5. Now as Baruch concluded his ministry with Jeremiah and his memoirs, he recalled God's promise of physical preservation through all his trials (cf. 39:15-18).

CHAPTER 46. PROPHECY AGAINST EGYPT

This section of prophecies against foreign nations, ch. 46—51, compares with Isa 13—23 and Ezk 25—32.

Prediction Concerning Pharaoh-Necho, 1-12. Necho II of Egypt, in June, 604 B.C., was routed at Carchemish at the great bend of the Euphrates 60 miles W of Haran (cf. Gen 11:31). Victorious Chaldean crown prince Nebuchadrezzar pursued his defeated foe to Egypt, 2-6. Egypt, prefigured by the Nile River, 7-8, was poised to flood the north country. She was humiliated. Put is Somaliland, and Lud is unidentified, 9 (RSV).

Nebuchadrezzar's Invasion of Egypt, 13-26. In 601 B.C. Nebuchadrezzar fought an indecisive battle on the Egyptian border, according to the Babylonian Chronicle, but in 568 B.C. this prophecy was fulfilled (see note on 43:8-13). Apis, 15 (RSV), was an idol bull-god of Egypt (Nah 3:8, RSV). Thebes, 25 (RSV), was the great metropolis of Upper Egypt, and Amon, the great sun deity adored there.

Promise of Future Blessing to Israel, 27-28. Future comfort for God's people was given.

CHAPTER 47. PROPHECY AGAINST THE PHILISTINES

The Advance of Nebuchadrezzar, 1-4. This prediction is probably to be connected with the destruction of Ashkelon, 5, 7. Apparently Tyre and Sidon, 4, were in league with the Philistines (cf. 27:3).

Results of Nebuchadrezzar's Invasion, 5-7. The Philistines (Peleste) were Indo-Europeans from Caphtor (Crete) (cf. Amos 9:7), the main wave of them settling in SW. Palestine, "the land of the Peleste," in the 12th cen. B.C.

CHAPTER 48. PROPHECY AGAINST MOAB

The Overthrow of Moab, 1-19. The advance of the enemy, probably Nebuchadrezzar, is described. Chemosh was the national deity, 7. Although protected because of her isolation from main trade or invasion routes, Moab would not escape, 11-17.

Reason for the Overthrow, 20-47. She was to reap the harvest she had sown, 20-28, and was to be punished for her pride, 29-42. After terrible devastation Moab would be restored, 43-47.

CHAPTER 49. PROPHECY AGAINST VARIOUS NATIONS

Against Ammon, 1-6. Ammon was the northern "brother" nation of Moab (Gen 19:30-38). Milcom, 1 (RSV), was the national god (1 Kgs 11:5, 33). Rabbah, present-day Amman in the kingdom of Jordan, was the capital city, 2-3.

Against Edom, 7-22. Cf. Ob 1-9 for another prophecy of Edom's punishment for cruelties inflicted and for encroachment on Judah's frontier due to Arab tribal expansion. Teman, 7, is modern Tawilan, some three miles E of Sela (Petra), the rock-cut city. Bozrah, 13, is a N. Edom fortress city.

Against Damascus, 23-27. Arpad in N. Syria, about 23 miles N of

Aleppo, is commonly mentioned in Scripture with Hamath, a well-known city-state on the Orontes River N of Damascus. The power of these city-states was broken by Assyria and further reduced by Babylon.

Against Kedar and Hazor, 28-33. Hazor (not Tell el Qedah, five miles SW of Lake Huleh, dominating the ancient trade route via Maris) is a still unknown place in the Arabian Desert E of Palestine which Nebuchadrezzar sacked in 598 B.C. Kedar (Gen 25:13) was an Arab tribe of desert bedouins descended from Ishmael. Nebuchadrezzar conducted a successful campaign against these desert dwellers (9:26; 25:23-24).

Against Elam, 34-39. Elam, E of the Tigris-Euphrates country of Babylonia, with its capital at Susa, was overrun by Nebuchadrezzar in the winter of 596 B.C. Zedekiah ascended the throne in March, 597 B.C., with the deposition of Jehoiachin. "The bow of Elam" refers to the skill of Elamite archers, 35.

CHAPTER 50. PROPHECY AGAINST BABYLON

Fall to Persia, 1-3. Two themes interlace, the fall of the historical Babylon of that day and the fall of the future Babylon (Rev 17—18). The gods of Babylon were confounded by the prophecy of Babylon's fall—Bel (Baal) and Merodach (Marduk of the monuments), the two chief deities. The disaster came out of the "north," a reference to Cyrus the Persian who took Babylon in October, 539 B.C. (cf. Dan 7:4-5).

Return of the Exiles, 4-7. This prediction included but went beyond the return from Babylon in 536 B.C. and embraced the final pre-kingdom regathering.

Fall of Babylon Resumed, 8-16. The vast ancient city of Babylon on a branch of the Euphrates near the modern town of Hilla, SW of Baghdad, was excavated by the Germans under Robert Koldewey (1899-1914) and later by Heinrich Lenzen. Its brilliant palaces, hanging gardens, temple tower, Ishtar Gate, walls and fortifications, are now well-known. Archaeology fully confirms the splendor of the city. (See notes on 2 Kgs 25.)

Israel's Restoration, 17-20. Babylon, as Assyria in an earlier epoch, would be destroyed. Israel will be regenerated and regathered in the last day.

Divine Judgment Upon Babylon, 21-32. Merathaim ("double rebellion"), 21, was a pun on *mat marrati* ("land of lagoons"), an epithet of S. Babylonia. "Pekod" ("punishment"), 21, was a play on *Puqudu,* a tribe of E. Babylonia (Ezk 23:23).

Israel's Deliverance Repeated, 33-34. Her "Redeemer" would be strong to save her.

Babylon's Downfall Repeated, 35-46. No nation can defy God with impunity .

CHAPTER 51. PROPHECY AGAINST BABYLON CONTINUED

Divine Judgment Upon Babylon, 1-5. Babylon would be mowed down and winnowed like grain, a common threshing figure indicating judgment (Isa 21:10). She was guilty of sin against "the Holy One of Israel," 5.

Address to the Remnant, 6-10. Command was issued to God's people to flee from Babylon. (Cf. the fall of ecclesiastical Babylon, Rev 17, and the destruction of commercial Babylon, Rev 18.) Babylon was the "golden cup," 7 (Rev 17:4). The whole chapter is a forecast of the destruction of the Satanic world system at the end-time previous to the kingdom-advent of Messiah.

Attack by the Medes, 11-19. Media lay NE of Babylonia. "Many waters," 13, refer to the Euphrates and the interlacing canals in S. Babylonia (cf. Rev 17:1, 15). Idolatry is satirized, 16-19, before Israel's true God, 15-16.

Babylon's Utter Ruin, 20-33. As a hammer, 20-23, Babylon was God's instrument to punish His disobedient people. But Babylon would fall like Assyria, 24-26. As Babylon conquered nations, 27-33, so nations would attack her. Ararat, 27, is Armenia, ancient Urartu, N of Lake Van. Minni embraced the Mannaeans S of Lake Urmia. Ashkenaz included the Scythians.

Israel's Deliverance, 34-40, was again reviewed.

Babylon's Fall Continued, 41-64. Sheshach, 41-43, was Babylon, which would be inundated by attackers.

CHAPTER 52. FALL AND CAPTIVITY OF JUDAH; JEHOIACHIN'S LIBERATION

The Fall of the City, 1-30. This final chapter is a historical appendix, largely a repetition of 2 Kgs 24:18—25:30 (cf. also Jer 39:1-10; 40:7—43:7). Described are Zedekiah's reign, 1-3, and rebellion, 4-11. The siege lasted more than 18 months. Riblah, 9, was in the central valley NE of Byblos. Jerusalem was burned, 12-16, August, 586 B.C. Nebuzaradan was Nebuchadrezzar's field general. The booty taken from the temple is described, 17-23, together with the death of some temple priests at Riblah, 24-27. Three deportations are enumerated, 28-30, apparently connected with Jehoiachin's exile in

597 B.C. (2 Kgs 24:12-16); the suppression of Zedekiah's revolt in 586 B.C.; and the punishment for Gedaliah's assassination (40:7—41:18).

Jehoiachin's Liberation, 31-34. See 2 Kgs 25:27-30.

One of a collection of letters found at Lachish and alluding to the final days of the Kingdom of Judah before it fell to Nebuchadnezzar. (*Courtesy Wellcome Archaeological Research Expedition*)

LAMENTATIONS

LAMENT OVER JERUSALEM'S DESOLATION

Place in the Canon. In the English Bible, following the Septuagint tradition, Lamentations comes after Jeremiah. In the Hebrew Bible it is found in the third division, the *Kethubhim* or Hagiographa, among the scrolls *(Megilloth)*—Song, Ruth, Lamentations, Ecclesiastes, and Esther. Like the others, it was read on special occasions, in this case during the fast on the ninth of Ab (Aug.) to commemorate the destruction of Jerusalem and the burning of the temple in 586 B.C.

Author. There is little doubt Jeremiah was the author. The Septuagint opens with a declaration of this fact in the words: "And it came to pass that, after Israel was taken captive and Jerusalem was made desolate, Jeremiah sat weeping and lamented with this lamentation, and said. . . ." The Vulgate follows this very ancient tradition.

Literary Form. Of the five poems, the first four are alphabetic acrostics. Poems (ch.) 1, 2 and 4 have 22 verses apiece, each beginning with one of the 22 letters of the Heb. alphabet. Poem (ch.) 3 has three verses to each letter, totaling 66. Poem (ch.) 5 has 22 verses, but is not in alphabetic order. Dirge *(qinah)* meter, $3+2$, prevails, with a lively three beat trailing away in a sad two beat.

Message. "The Lord is afflicted when His people die (Ex 3:7), He suffers when they suffer," is the theme of this book. It is because of His loving-kindness that His own are not "altogether destroyed" (3:22). "His compassions fail not. They are new every morning: great is thy faithfulness" (3:22-23). Tradition has the suffering prophet weeping in a grotto outside Jerusalem's north wall under the knoll called Golgotha where the suffering Saviour was to die. However that may be, the Spirit of Christ in the prophet made him in a real sense a prefigurement of our Lord (Jer 13:17), as the Master likewise wept over the erring city (Mt 23:36-38).

Outline
Desolated Jerusalem Cries for Pity, Ch. 1
The Lord's Chastening and Its Results, Ch. 2
Heart Cry of a Chastened People, Ch. 3
The Horrors of the Siege and Fall of the City, Ch. 4
Lament and Petition for Restoration, Ch. 5

CHAPTER 1. DESOLATED JERUSALEM CRIES FOR PITY

Her Desolation Is Described, 1-11. Only twice does the voice of the city, personified as a widow, speak in this section, 9b, 11b. The rest of the verses describe the misery of the ruined city. When she speaks, she breathes a prayer.

The Personified City Bewails Her Destruction, 12-22. This whole passage, except 17, is a lament in the first person. Jerusalem declares her woe, 11-13; professes her penitence and just punishment for her iniquity, 14-16; asserts God's equity in punishing her, 18-20; and utters a prayer for vindication against her enemies, 21-22.

CHAPTER 2. THE LORD'S CHASTENING AND ITS RESULTS

The Lord's Punishment of the City, 1-8. Jerusalem's woe was not a piece of bad luck or a mere accident. "The Lord" occurs more than seven times in this section as the author of her calamity.

The Results of the Lord's Punishment, 9-17. The city is desolated and spiritual darkness befalls its prophets and people, 9-10. The prophet Jeremiah weeps and laments because of these disasters, 11-14. Jerusalem's enemies rail, 15-16. But God's word and warning have been fulfilled, 17.

The Prophet's Exhortation to True Repentance, 18-19.

His Prayer, 20-22, as identified with the chastened people.

CHAPTER 3. HEART CRY OF A CHASTENED PEOPLE

A Psalm of Personal Faith in God, 1-24. This chapter is an acrostic in three parts with three verses allotted to each of the 22 letters of the Heb. alphabet. The prophet Jeremiah identifies himself with the chastened people, and in agony and distress pours out his heart to the Lord in faith. His plaints recall Job's exercise of soul before the Lord: verse 1 (Job 9:34); 2 (Job 19:8); 3 (Job 7:18); 4 (Job 7:5); 5 (Job 19:6,12); 6 (Job 23:16-17); 7, 9 (Job 19:8); 8 (Job 30:20); 10-11 (Job 16:9); 12-13 (Job 16:12-13); 14 (Job 30:9); 15 (Job 9:18); 16-18 (Job 19:10; 30:19).

Jeremiah Enjoins Repentance and Submission to God, 25-51. The prophet wisely counsels submission and penitential confession in view of God's righteous judgment.

Prayer for Vindication Against the Enemy, 52-66. Jeremiah recalls the Lord's faithful blessing in times past, and pleads for the punishment of Jerusalem's destroyers.

CHAPTER 4. HORRORS OF THE SIEGE AND FALL OF THE CITY

Jerusalem's Disaster Described, 1-20. The gold and stones of the temple had been desecrated, 1. Sons of Zion (Zionites), worth more than gold, were now reckoned as common clay, 2. Terrible famine stalked the city, 3-9, accompanied by horrible cannibalism, 10. Divine wrath was outpoured, 11-12, in bloody carnage and defilement, 13-15; captivity, 16; death, 17-19; and violence to the king (Zedekiah; 2 Kgs 25:4-6).

Prediction of Disaster on Edom, 21-22. Edom, too, would be punished (cf. Ob 8-14).

CHAPTER 5. LAMENT AND PETITION FOR RESTORATION

Lament Over Judah's Misery Under Babylon's Heel, 1-18. The people suffered agony and hardship, 1-14. The Davidic dynasty no longer reigned, the temple was destroyed, 15-18.

Intercession for Divine Mercy, 19-22. These verses echo Ps 74:1-2; 79:5-8; 80:1-7, and capture the plea of the faithful remnant for the establishment of the kingdom.

EZEKIEL

ROLE OF DIVINE DISCIPLINE

The Prophet. Ezekiel (*Yehezkel*, "God strengthens") was the son of a Zadokite priest. He was deported to Babylon in 597 B.C. with King Jehoiachin. The prophet's wife died the day the siege of Jerusalem began, 588 B.C. (24:1,15-18). The prophet resided at Tel-Abib, a town on the Chebar, a canal known from Babylonian sources which flowed from the Euphrates fork above Babylon through Nippur, winding back into the Euphrates near Erech.

Date. In the fifth year of Jehoiachin's exile Ezekiel began his prophetic ministry (1:1-2), i.e., 593 B.C., continuing till at least April, 571 B.C. (29:17), his last dated utterance.

Purpose. While Jeremiah in Palestine was prophesying the destruction of Jerusalem, Ezekiel, his younger contemporary in Babylon, was declaring the same fate for the apostate city (ch. 1—24). Unlike Jeremiah, however, Ezekiel, ministering principally to the exiles, had a large note of consolation in his messages. He showed his suffering colleagues that the Lord was justified in sending His people into captivity (cf. 18:25, 29; 33:17, 20). His ministry centered in showing the preventive and corrective nature of God's chastenings that His people might "know that he is God" (an expression occurring more than 30 times in the book, from 6:7 to 39:28). To this end Ezekiel showed that the Lord's people had been at fault, not the Lord (18:25). The Lord would punish the nations jubilant over Israel's fall (ch. 25—32), and eventually restore Israel to kingdom blessing.

Ezekiel and the Revelation. Ezekiel's visions bear striking resemblance to the book of the Revelation (cf. Ezk 1 with Rev 4—5; Ezk 3:3 with Rev 10:9-10; Ezk 9 with Rev 7; Ezk 10 with Rev 8:1-5). The prophet Daniel was already famous in Babylon when Ezekiel prophesied (Ezk 14:14, 20; 28:3).

Outline
Prophecies Against Jerusalem, Ch. 1—3
Prophecies Against Jerusalem, Ch. 4—24
Prophecies Against the Nations, Ch. 25—32
Prophecies of the Final Restoration of Israel, Ch. 33—48.

CHAPTER 1. EZEKIEL'S VISION OF GOD'S GLORY

Introduction, 1-3. "The thirtieth year," 1, probably means when Ezekiel was 30 years old. For Tel-Abib (Babylonian *til abubi,* "mound of the flood," a Jewish settlement near Nippur on the Chebar canal), see 3:15 and introduction. The fifth year of Jehoiachin's exile would be 593 B.C., fifth day, fourth month, July 31. "The hand of the Lord was upon him" shows Ezekiel's contact with God, 3 (3:14, 22; 8:1; 33:22; 37:1; 40:1).

The Vision of God's Glory, 4-28. This revelation of the Shekinah glory of God prepared Ezekiel for his great ministry, as in the case of Moses (Ex 3:1-10), Isaiah (Isa 6:1-10), Daniel (Dan 10:5-14), and John (Rev 1:12-19). Theophanic manifestations of God in wind (1 Kgs 19:11), cloud (Ex 19:16), and fire (1 Kgs 19:11-12) were usual. Portrayed is the preincarnate Christ. This vision is mentioned repeatedly in this book (10:1-22; 11:22-25; 43:1-7). It came "out of the north," 4, not because Ezekiel borrowed a literary figure from Canaanite (Ugaritic) mythology, according to

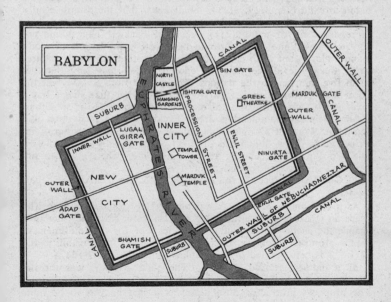

which the gods lived in the north, but because a storm cloud of divine wrath from the north (Babylon) was about to burst over Judah. The Holy One of Israel was revealed in His glory ready to deal in judgment with His apostate people. The "living creatures," 5, were cherubim (Rev 4:7) who were guardians of the holiness of God's throne (Ex 25:10-22; 1 Kgs 6:23-28, cf. Gen 3:22-24). They were winged human-headed lions or oxen, distinct from the seraphim (Isa 6:2). Both are actual beings of the celestial realm, not merely artistic creations. The four wheels symbolize mobility in all directions. The Lord enthroned above His creatures, 26-28, compares with the Lord enthroned above the cherubim on the ark (Ex 37:9; 1 Sam 4:4).

CHAPTERS 2—3. EZEKIEL'S FIVEFOLD COMMISSION

His Commission As a Prophet, 2:1-10. Whatever the reception of Ezekiel's ministry, the "rebellious house," a designation of apostate Judah in exile (Jer 2:29; 3:13), "shall know that there hath been a prophet among them," 2:5. More than 90 times the non-messianic expression "son of man" (2:1) occurs in Ezekiel. This points not only to man's finite limitation and need before the vision of God's infinite glory, but also signalizes the fact that although captive Israel was an evidence that the chosen nation had forgotten her distinctive ministry to the nations (Ezk 5:5-8; Rom 9:4-5), yet the Lord had not forgotten her. It would remind her that she is but a small part of the entire race of mankind for whom He is solicitous.

As a Fearless Denunciator, 3:1-9. Ezekiel was to feed upon and digest the Word of God, symbolized by eating a papyrus scroll inscribed with divine judgments, 1-3 (cf. Zech 5:1-4; Rev 10:8-11). The Word was "sweet" (Ps 19:10), but bitter when given to unrepentant sinners ripe for judgment, 4-9.

As God's Mouthpiece to the Exiles, 3:10-15. For Tel-Abib, Chebar, see 1:1.

As a Watchman, 3:16-21. A watchman (Heb. *sopheh*) is "one who keeps on guard or on the lookout," 17 (Isa 21:6; Mic 7:4), not only against the enemy but expectantly and in hope for the fulfillment of God's promise. Ezekiel's doctrine of personal responsibility (cf. 18:1-32) is here applied to his prophetic ministry (33:7-16).

As a Faithful Herald, 3:22-27. "The plain" (valley) was the flat alluvial southern Tigris-Euphrates country (Gen 11:2; Ezk 37:1). The prophet's protracted dumbness was a sign he was to be mute when God wanted him to be silent.

CHAPTERS 4—5. SYMBOLIC PROPHECIES OF JERUSALEM'S SIEGE

The Sign of the Brick, 4:1-3. Jerusalem was outlined on a soft mud brick with the clay dried in the sun, so common in S. Babylonia. The "iron plate" was evidently a griddle, showing how the Lord would fight against the city, not for it (cf. Jer 21:5). The captives were hoping for a speedy return to Jerusalem, but the prophet foretells Jerusalem's awful siege and fall.

Sign of the Prophet's Physical Position, 4:4-8. His discomfort for 390 days on his left side and 40 days on his right side (total 430 years, symbolically a year for a day) recalled the Egyptian servitude (Ex 12:40-41). A similar captivity would engulf both Israel and Judah. The captivity of the northern kingdom was to be longer, however.

Sign of Famine, 4:9-17. Hunger and cannibalism were to stalk besieged Jerusalem. Mixing of grains, 9, indicates scarcity. Dried cow dung is still a common fuel in the East, but human excrement was unclean (Deut 23:12-14). Dearth of water, 16, would add to the horror. En-Rogel on the south and Gihon in the Kidron Valley would fail and the cisterns would be dry.

Sign of the Shaved Head and Beard, 5:1-17. Hair of the head and face cut with a sword instead of a razor, 1 (RSV), spoke of the shameful military defeat of Jerusalem. The reason for this disgrace was Israel's abysmal failure in her favored position "in the center [navel] of the nations" as a light and witness of the one true God, 5-6 (RSV). The woes described were to come upon her for failure in her trust, 7-17.

CHAPTER 6. JUDGMENT AGAINST THE MOUNTAINS OF ISRAEL

Judgment upon the Idolatry of the High Places, 1-7. Figuratively, "the mountains of Israel," 2, stood for the high places, used as outdoor pagan sanctuaries, while the sword, 3, spoke of their destruction, with their cultic personnel and devotees. Idols, 5, were part of the cultic equipment, being images of Baal and such fertility goddesses as Anath and Asherah, corrupt deities now so well known from Ugaritic mythology. Cf. Lev 26:27-33, which is here re-echoed by Ezekiel.

The Surviving Remnant, 8-14. The remnant (Rom 11:5) would survive and learn the purpose of these terrible chastisements, 10, 14 (cf. Isa 6:10-13).

CHAPTER 7. THE END IMMINENT

The Doom of the City, 1-9. The day of judgment upon Jerusalem prefigured the coming great day of the Lord when wrath will be outpoured before Israel's restoration (Ps 2:5; Rev 6—19; cf. Joel 1:15; Mal 4:1; see Amos 5:18-20; Isa 2:11-17).

Horror in the City, 10-27. The confusion and brutality in the fallen city were portrayed.

CHAPTERS 8—9. VISION OF JERUSALEM'S SIN

Vision of Idolatry, 8:1-18. The date, 1, was September 17, 592 B.C. For "hand of the Lord," see 1:1-3. The renewed vision of God, 2-4, was a proper background for the judgment of false gods. "The gateway of the inner court that faced north," 3 (RSV), was the third gate leading N from the palace complex into the temple area. "The image of jealousy" was perhaps that of Astarte. The worship of Egyptian Osiris, who was thought of as guaranteeing a happy life after death, is apparently referred to, 7-13. Tammuz worship, 14-15, was the adoration of the Sumero-Akkadian god of vegetation, whose descent into the nether world signalized the seasonal fading of life. Tammuz (Adonis) or the worship of Re, the Egyptian sun-god, is suggested, 16-18.

Vision of Punishment for Idolatry, 9:1-11. A divine call went forth for destruction, 1-2. On the "north," see 1:4 note, from which direction the executioners came. For the mark or seal, 4-5, see Rev 7:3; 9:4; 13:16-17; 20:4; on a godly remnant, cf. Isa 1:9; Rom 11:5. the Lord's linen-clothed scribe, signifying ritual cleanness, undoubtedly represented Deity. Cf. Nabu, the god of wisdom, among the Babylonian gods.

CHAPTERS 10—11. DEPARTURE OF THE LORD FROM HIS TEMPLE

The Renewed Vision of God's Glory, 10:1-22 (cf. Ezk 1, 11, 43). The manifested glory of Israel's God was the background for the judgment of Israel's idolatry and horrible profanation of the temple. The linen-clothed personage, 9:2-4; 10:2-4, who scattered coals from the fire between the cherubim (1:13) over the idolatry-ridden city, in the light of Rev 5:1; 8:3-5 was apparently the preincarnate Christ, the Angel of the Presence, who appeared to Abraham, Isaac, Jacob, Moses, Joshua, Gideon and Daniel (Dan 10:5-6). Judgment is committed to His hands (Jn 5:22). "The glory of the Lord" (cf. Ex

16:10; Num 10:34) is the revealed holiness and power of God (Lev 9:23; Num 20:6).

Ichabod, the Glory Departs, 11:1-25. A glimpse into the wicked political leaders is given, 1-13. A message of mercy follows, 14-21, predictions yet to be fulfilled for Israel. These include a spared remnant, 14-16, and the promise of restoration to the land and spiritual conversion, 17-21. The departure of the Shekinah glory from the wicked city now follows, 22-25. The departure was gradual (cf. 9:3; 10:4) from the temple outward and from the city to the Mount of Olives, 23. (Cf. 1 Kgs 8:5-11; Ezr 3:12; and the return to the millennial temple, Ezk 43:2-5.) It was from the Mount of Olives that Christ ascended (Acts 1:10-12) and to which He will return in glory (Zech 14:4).

CHAPTER 12. THE EXILE PORTRAYED IN SYMBOL

Signs Given Through Ezekiel, 1-20. On the "rebellious house," 2, see note on 2:5 and on Isa 6:10-13. Ezekiel was to enact the exiles' fate, 1-7. Zedekiah was the prince, 10, alluded to in 17:20, who was taken to Riblah and whose eyes were put out (Jer 39:1-10; 52:10-11; 2 Kgs 25:1-7).

Message of Impending Judgment, 21-28. Unbelief in God's true prophets was the cause of judgment. God's word through His prophet could not be ignored (Hos 12:10).

CHAPTERS 13—14. CONDEMNATION OF FALSE PROPHETISM

Divine Denunciation of False Prophets, 13:1-23. They spoke falsehoods and were contaminated with paganistic divination, 1-9. Their message was as useless as whitewash on a mud brick wall to protect it against a storm, 10-16. Prophetesses (sorceresses and spiritistic mediums, 1 Sam 28:7-25) were also denounced, 17-23. They belonged to paganistic pollution.

Depravity of the Idol-Loving Elders, 14:1-23. They revealed the pitch of their depravity by daring to inquire of the Lord, 1-11, and rendered judgment imperative, 12-23.

CHAPTER 15. ALLEGORY OF THE VINE

The Allegory, 1-5. The vine branch is no good for wood. It is useful only to produce fruit. Even as fuel it is practically useless.

The Meaning, 6-8. The vine typified Israel (Jerusalem; cf. Ps 80:8-12; Isa 5:1-7; Hos 10:1). Jerusalem, an unproductive vine, was no longer good for anything but burning. This is the first of three parables in ch. 16 and 17 showing the empty hope of deliverance for the sinful city.

CHAPTER 16. THE ALLEGORY OF THE FAITHLESS WIFE

Israel's Idolatry Described, 1-52, figuratively as a waif, 1-7; as a maiden, 8-14; as a degenerate, 15-34; as a punished ingrate and harlot, 35-52. As a foundling, unrelated to God's covenant, Israel had a pagan origin, 3. The Canaanites were the Semitic-speaking residents of Palestine before Israel arrived on the scene. The Hittites, a well-known imperial armenoid people (Josh 3:10; 2 Sam 11:3), occupied Palestine with the Canaanites and Amorites ("westerners"). As a foundling Israel was to be exposed to death as female babies often were in ancient paganism. As a maid, betrothed by covenant and married to the Lord, 8-14, she attained a regal status, but lapsed into harlotries (cult prostitution and general infidelity and degeneracy), 15:34. She became a shameless harlot, 35-52, and was to be stoned (Deut 22:21, 24). She was worse than "Sodom" and her "younger sister" Samaria (Jer 3:6-11).

Promise of Gracious Restoration, 53-63. Even in this lurid setting the Lord pledged future blessing under the Palestinian covenant (Deut 30:1-10) and the new covenant (Jer 31:31-34; Heb 8:8-12).

CHAPTER 17. THE ALLEGORY OF THE EAGLES AND THE CEDAR

The Allegory of the Eagles, 1-21. The "great eagle," 3-6, was Nebuchadrezzar (Jer 48:40; 49:22). "The top of the cedar," 3 (RSV), was the house of David (Jer 22:5, 6, 23). The "young twig," 4, was Jehoiachin; the "land of traffic" (trade), Babylonia; "the seed of the land," 5, Zedekiah. "Another great eagle," 7, was Psammetichus II (594-588 B.C.), who enrolled Zedekiah and other western powers in a coalition against Babylon (Jer 27). "The east wind," 10, was Nebuchadrezzar, before whom Zedekiah, 13-21, was doomed to fall (Jer 52).

The Allegory of the Cedar, 22-24. Israel's hope for the future once again comes into view. The Lord will take a "sprig" (Messiah) from "the lofty top of the cedar" (Davidic house) and "one of its young tender twigs" (Messiah), and plant it "upon a high and lofty mountain" (Mt. Zion, Mic 4:1). (Cf. Isa 11:1; 53:2; Jer 23:5-6; Zech 3:8.) "The high tree" brought low and "the green tree" dried up, 24, symbolize Gentile world power. "The low tree" exalted and "the dry tree" revived portray the restoration of the kingdom to Israel (Acts 1:6) when the Son of David returns. Gentile world power will be broken and Israel will be restored to governmental and spiritual glory under Messiah.

CHAPTER 18. DIVINE JUDGMENT AND INDIVIDUAL RESPONSIBILITY

False Accusation Against God and the Divine Answer, 1-13. Sinners in their plight incline to blame God and their forebears for their troubles. The exiles in Babylon and the sinners in Jerusalem were doing this, 1-2. The Lord rebuked this shifting of blame, 3-4, and through Ezekiel stressed God's justice and individual responsibility for wrongdoing. The way of life, 5-9, was stressed (not conditions of eternal life, but proof of justifying righteousness to escape physical death in the impending judgment). The conditions of death were set forth, 10-13.

Ezekiel's Doctrine of Individual Responsibilty, 14-32. Eating upon the mountains, 6, 15, refers to partaking of sacred meals in pagan high places (6:1-14). The good or evil of one generation is transferable to the next, 19-20. To deny this truth is to fail to comprehend God's justice, 25-29. Israel must repent in the light of God's justice. This was the only escape from terrible judgment, 30-32.

CHAPTER 19. LAMENT FOR THE PRINCES OF ISRAEL

Lamentation for the Princes, 1-9. The princes were Jehoahaz, the first whelp, 3-4, who was taken to Egypt (Jer 22:10-12; 2 Kgs 23:30-34). The second whelp, 5-9, was Jehoiachin, who was exiled to Babylon (Jer 22:24-30; 2 Kgs 24:8-16). The "lioness," 2, was Judah. This symbol is found on Israelite seals (cf. Gen 49:9; 1 Kgs 10:18-20).

Lament for the Land, 10-14. The vine portrays Judah (Isa 5:1-7; Jer 2:21). "Its strongest stem," 11 (RSV), stands for Zedekiah (17:13), who was stripped by "the east wind," 12, Nebuchadrezzar, and "transplanted," 13, to Babylon (Jer 52:1-11).

CHAPTER 20. REHEARSAL OF DIVINE MERCY TO ISRAEL

Israel's Sins in Egypt, 1-8. Dated August 14, 591 B.C., this rehearsal was occasioned by the inquiry of the elders of the Exile, 1-4 (14:1-

11). The nation's idolatry in Egypt, 5-8, is described (cf. Ps 106). Yet God's gracious revelations are given.

Israel's Sins in the Wilderness, 9-26. A review is made of wonderful redemption wrought for God's name's sake, 9, 10, 14, with the sabbath given, 11-13, and grace shown, 14-26.

Israel's Sins in the Land, 27-49. Judgment and a future restoration are outlined.

CHAPTER 21. JUDGMENT BY THE SWORD

The Lord Unsheaths His Sword, 1-17. The sword was a common symbol of divine judgment (14:21; Isa 34:5; Jer 14:12; Rev 6:8). It is seen sharpened, indicating judgment was imminent, 8-17 (cf. Jer 50:35-37). Striking upon the thigh, 12, was an indication of mourning (Jer 31:19).

The Sword of Nebuchadrezzar, 18-32. His sword would actually be God's means of judgment, 18-19. His occultism, 21, would guide him to Jerusalem and slaughter. Divination was the pagan counterpart of prophecy. Belomancy, the tossing of arrows with names of enemies on them, and hepatoscopy, examining the liver of animals for omens, were highly developed in Babylonia. The teraphim (21, RSV) were small oracular deities. The sword would cut down Zedekiah, 25-27, and strike against Ammon, 28-32 (cf. 20).

CHAPTER 22. JERUSALEM'S INDICTMENT

Jerusalem's Violence and Abomination, 1-16. Before the retributive sword of justice fell, Jerusalem's horrible corruption was laid bare. Her iniquities included idolatry, violence, deceit, injustice, slander, sexual promiscuity (cf. 6:2-14; 14:3-5; 18:6).

The Smelting Furnace of God's Wrath, 17-31, refined all classes of corrupt Jewish society. The purpose of the smelting, 17-22, and the dross, 23-31, are indicated.

CHAPTER 23. AHOLAH AND AHOLIBAH

The Allegory, 1-4. Aholah is Samaria (the northern kingdom) and her sister Aholibah is Jerusalem (representing by metonymy the southern kingdom). The ungodly relations, politically and religiously, of these two sisters with the surrounding nations are inveighed against. There is a pun in the names: "Aholah," "she who possesses a tent" (sanctuary), i.e., Samaria, and "Aholibah," "my tent [tabernacle] is in her" (Jerusalem). This word play intimates that although Samaria had a place of worship, *the true sanctuary* was in Jerusalem.

This fact was the crucial consideration in accentuating the enormity of Jerusalem's sin.

The Meaning, 5-49. Aholah, 5-10, politically and spiritually contaminated herself with Assyria by alliances and religious syncretism. Aholibah, 11-21, likewise sinned. Their political and religious sin had to be punished, 22-35. Judgment of the lewd sisters was forecast, 36-49.

CHAPTER 24. THE BOILING CALDRON AND THE END

The Allegory of the Caldron, 1-14, was symbolic of the imminent destruction of Jerusalem. In the caldron (Jerusalem) all would be boiled, as the besiegers heaped fuel (siege apparatus) about it (cf. Jer 1:13-19). After thorough boiling, the pot would be emptied after the siege, and the bones burned (city sacked). The rust, 6, 11 (RSV), refers to the city's sin and degeneration, 12-13. The date, 1, of the beginning of the siege is given, January, 588 B.C. (cf. 2 Kgs 25:1).

Death of Ezekiel's Wife, 15-27. He was not to mourn over his wife, who died the day the siege of Jerusalem began. As death dissolved the union between the prophet and his beloved wife, so the relationship between the Lord and Jerusalem was to be dissolved so that destruction would follow. This was an object lesson to the exiles, 19-24. The day the news of Jerusalem's destruction arrived, Ezekiel's tongue would be loosed for a new message, 25-27.

CHAPTER 25. PROPHECIES AGAINST VARIOUS NATIONS

Ezekiel 25—32 corresponds to Isaiah 13—23 and Jeremiah 46—51. These nations were to be judged before Israel was restored (36:5-7).

Predictions Against Ammon, Moab and Edom, 1-14. The nations of this chapter were immediate neighbors of Judah. The Ammonites, 1-7, and the Moabites, 8-11, were racially connected with Israel (Gen 19:37-38) and inveterate enemies (cf. Isa 15:1—16:14; Jer 48:1—49:6). Edom, 12-14, also would know God's vengeance (Jer 49:7-22; cf. Deut 23:7; Amos 1:11).

Predictions Against Philistia, 15-17 (cf. Jer 47). The Cherethites, 16 (Cretans), lived in Philistia.

CHAPTER 26. PROPHECY OF TYRE'S DESTRUCTION

Judgment Announced, 1-6. Nebuchadrezzar besieged Tyre for 13 years, the eleventh year being 587 B.C. (Septuagint, twelfth year 586 B.C.), 1. Its judgment was because of its refusal to help its ally Jerusalem (Jer 27:3) and its overweening pride as the chief Phoenician sea mart (cf. 28:2-10).

Judgment Executed, 7-21. Tyre was defeated in 572 B.C. (cf 29:18), but not the insular city, which was not destroyed till taken by Alexander the Great in 332 B.C. The lament would be made by Tyre's commercial neighbors, "the princes of the sea," 15-18. The city would sink into the pit (Sheol), the realm of the dead, 19-21 (cf. Isa 14:15; Zech 9:3-4). Thus Alexander the Great fulfilled this prophecy.

CHAPTER 27. LAMENT OVER TYRE

Tyre Symbolized as a Ship, 1-24. The Tyrian commercial empire is fittingly described as a goodly merchant vessel, 3, "perfect in beauty." The ship was made of fir trees from Senir, i.e., Mt. Hermon (Deut 3:9). Lebanon ("the [snow] white") is the mountain mass composed of two parallel ranges, Lebanon and Antilebanon, famous in antiquity for its cedars, 5. The oaks of Bashan, 6, were the famous forests E of the Sea of Galilee. Elishah (Cyprus) and Gebal (Byblos) together with Arvad (an island coastal mart like Tyre) and Sidon, 20 miles N of Tyre, were the hub of Tyre's commercial center. The prose section, 10-25, describes many names elucidated by the Table of Nations (see notes on Gen 10).

Destruction of the Ship, 25-36. "The east wind," 26, is Nebuchadrezzar (cf. 19:12; Jer 18:17). But Alexander the Great (Zech 9:3-4) alone took insular Tyre.

CHAPTER 28. LAMENT OVER THE KING OF TYRE

The King of Tyre, 1-10. The "prince" or ruler of the city at that time, Ithobaal II, headed up in himself the arrogance and pride of the city, claiming to be divine, 2, and "wiser than Daniel," 3. This was not the Danel of the Ugaritic tablets, the judge of the helpless orphan and widow, as the critics hold, but the historical contemporary Daniel, then of great fame in Nebuchadnezzar's court (cf. 14:12-23). It would be unthinkable for Ezekiel to associate Noah and Job with a mythological figure.

The Spiritual Power Behind the Tyrian King, 11-19. This vast panoramic revelation, like Isa 14:12, reached beyond the human ruler to the spiritual power energizing him in the realm of human government. Satan and demons have a notable role in this sphere, as Dan 10:13 and Eph 6:12, "the world rulers of this present darkness," show. As the inspirer, energizer and the invisible dynamic behind such godless, proud rule of the world governmental systems, Satan is portrayed in his unfallen state, and this passage together with Isa 14:12-14 gives the entrance of sin into a sinless universe and Satan's fall. The vision, however, is not of Satan in his own person, but as he is connected with the governmental administration of the present evil world system. The pride, pomp and arrogation of Deity which belongs to God alone stamp the king of Tyre and the king of Babylon (Isa 14:12-14) as illustrations of the coming Antichrist, the last God-defying ruler of the Satanic world system before its destruction at the second advent of Christ (Rev 18:1—19:16). For a comment on Satan's pristine unfallen glory see note on Jude 8-10.

Judgment of Sidon, 20-26. Some 20 miles N of Tyre, Sidon (modern Saida in the Republic of Lebanon, 20 miles S of Berytus [Beirut]), was perhaps the oldest of the Sidonian (Phoenician) coast cities. After 1200 B.C. Tyre assumed ascendancy. Jeremiah also predicted Sidon's subjugation by Nebuchadrezzar (Jer 27:3, 6), which occurred when Tyre was defeated. "A pricking brier to the house of Israel," 24, refers to the Sidonian craze for Baalism which led Israel into many apostasies (cf. 1 Kgs 16:31-33; 18:17-40). Promise of restoration is made to Israel, 25-26 (cf. 11:17; 20:41; 34:13; 37:21; Isa 11:12), to be fulfilled after her enemies have been judged.

CHAPTERS 29—32. JUDGMENT AGAINST EGYPT

Egypt was to be reduced to a second-rate kingdom. This judgment was fulfilled after Nebuchadrezzar's invasions in 572 and 568 B.C.

Against Pharaoh-Hophra, 29:1-16. This prophecy is dated 586 B.C., a half year before Jerusalem fell. Hophra's advance against Nebuchadrezzar in 588 B.C. had not relieved Jerusalem. Egypt is pictured as a crocodile (sea monster), 3 (Isa 27:1). "From Migdol to Syene," 10 (RSV), is an expression indicating the northern extent (Migdol, SW of Pelusium, 30:15, RSV), and Syene (Aswan, at the first Nile cataract) the southern limits.

Nebuchadrezzar's Conquest of Egypt, 29:17-21. This is Ezekiel's last dated oracle, April, 571 B.C. Lack of booty from Tyre was compensated. The "horn," 21, is Davidic and doubtless messianic.

Egypt's Doom, 30:1-26. This prefigures the day of the Lord in an eschatological sense (Isa 2:12; Jer 30:5-7), the time of the judgment of the nations, previous to kingdom blessing. Nebuchadrezzar's Egyptian successes furnish the background.

Lament Over Pharaoh As a Cedar, 31:1-18, dated in 586 B.C., just prior to the fall of Jerusalem.

Lament Over Pharaoh As a Lion, 32:1-32, dated March, 585 B.C. The proud Egyptian ruler considered himself a kingly lion, but he was only a sea monster to be caught in a net. The lament over Egypt, dated April, 586 B.C., shows that nation in the lower world with other governments of this evil world system, 17-32.

CHAPTER 33. EZEKIEL'S RESPONSIBILITY AS WATCHMAN

Chapters 33—39 portray events preceding the restoration of the kingdom to Israel (cf. Acts 1:6), and ch. 40—48 give the description of the restoration.

A Watchman and His Responsibility, 1-20. The prophet's commission included his being a "watchman" (see note on 3:16-21). Here Ezekiel applies his teaching of God's justice and individual responsibility developed in ch. 18 to his own ministry (see notes on ch. 18). In his discussion of individual responsibility, 10-20, the prophet reinforces what he had already taught in 14:12-23; 18:1-32.

News of Jerusalem's Fall, 21-33. Ezekiel's enforced silence (3:24-27) was lifted by news of Jerusalem's fall. The message he received thereupon is given, 23-29, and the assurance of the fulfillment of the Lord's word through the prophet declared, no matter what the people's reaction to it might be, 30-33.

CHAPTER 34. FALSE SHEPHERD AND THE TRUE

Indictment of the Faithless Shepherds (Rulers), 1-19. The law of individual responsibility (3:16-21; ch. 18 and 33) is applied to the nation's leaders, metaphorically called "shepherds," who were responsible for misusing God's flock (Jer 23:13-17) and scattering them (Jer 10:21; 23:1-4). The Lord is the Good Shepherd (Isa 40:11; Jer 31:10) who will regather the flock, 11-16, and judge between the sheep (the saved Israelite remnant) and the rams and he-goats (nations who have abused Israel, 17-19 (cf Mt 25:31-46; Joel 3:11-16). This is the judgment of the nations preceding the restoration of the kingdom to Israel.

Restoration of Israel Under Messiah, the True Shepherd, 20-31. This prophecy goes beyond Zerubbabel, the civil head of Judah at the restoration from Babylon in 536 B.C., or the literal David raised from the dead at the second advent, and refers to Messiah, David's son and Lord, David's name being used typically (Jer 23:5-6;

Hos 3:5; Isa 9:6-7; 55:3-4). "The covenant of peace," 25 (cf. Jer 31:31-34; Heb 13:20), is the new covenant. The "wild beasts," 5, 25, are the nations, particularly Babylon, that have wronged Israel. The "showers of blessing," 26, are for Israel in her restoration (Acts 3:19-20), with a description of the kingdom given in verses 26-27 (cf. Isa 11:6-9; Rom 8:19-22). "The plant of renown," 29, is He who grew up as "a tender plant," as "a root out of a dry ground" (Isa 53:2), who now is manifested in His glory.

CHAPTER 35. THE JUDGMENT OF EDOM

Edom's Evil Design, 1-10. Mt. Seir, 3,7,15, is the plateau E of the Arabah in which Sela (Petra), the Edomite capital, was located (cf. 25:12-14; Isa 34; Jer 49:7-22). Edom's encroachment on southern Judah and the hatred engendered were reflected. With Israel and Judah in exile, Edom purposed to possess their land, 10 (cf. Obadiah).

Edom's Ruin, 11-15. Chapter 35 is inserted here as a background for ch. 36—37, dealing with Israel's restoration to her land.

CHAPTER 36. RESTORATION TO THE LAND

Ezekiel 36—48 is yet unfulfilled and envisions the future restoration of the land and the people of Israel.

Future Judgment of Israel's Enemies, 1-7. The "mountains of Israel" form the central highland ridge and stand for all Israel (Deut 3:25; cf. 1, 4). The judgment of enemy nations (Mt 25:31-46) must precede Israel's restoration (Joel 3:11-16; Rev 16:12-16).

Promised Return to the Land, 8-38. The sovereign "I wills" of Israel's hope and glory are spoken by the Lord 18 times in this section. The land is to be restored to its former fertility, 11. Formerly desecrated by idolatry and pagan hilltop sanctuaries with fertility cults and human sacrifice, 14, the land shall "no longer devour men" (cf. Deut 12:1-3, 29-31). Israel's past sins and chastisements are reviewed, 16-21, followed by the great promise of future restoration and gracious blessing, 22-38. The regathering, 22-24, goes far beyond the small return from Babylon. Spiritual regeneration follows, 25-29. The sprinkling with clean water, 25, refers to the water mixed with the ashes of a red heifer (Num 19; Heb 9:13-14; 10:22; cf. Zech 12:10; 13:1). The new birth, 25-29, is a prerequisite for kingdom entrance (cf. Jn 3:1-12).

CHAPTER 37. VISION OF THE DRY BONES

Scope of the Vision, 1-14. The most satisfactory view of this passage sees it as setting forth *the national and spiritual reinstatement of God's chosen people Israel in kingdom blessing.* The method of the restoration will be by divine power, 3; by the divine Word, 4-6 (cf. Mt 24:32-35; Mk 13:27-31; Jer 16:14-15); and by the divine life, 7-10. The purpose of the vision is to fulfill God's word, 14; to revive Israel's lost hope, 11, 22; to settle Israel in her own land, 12-13; and to demonstrate Israel's status as an elect nation, 12-13. The "bones" are the exiles; the valley, their dispersion; the graves, the death of their national life.

The Extent of Israel's Restoration, 15-28. It embraces the entire house of Israel (the 12 tribes), comprising the union of both Judah and Israel into one nation, 15-17. The results of the restoration will be a land forever, 25; a king forever, 24-25; a covenant of peace forever, 26; a sanctuary forever, 26-27. If there is no future for Israel, this vision is meaningless.

CHAPTERS 38—39. DESTRUCTION OF ISRAEL'S LAST FOES

The Great Last-Day Northern Confederacy, 38:1-6. Gog is the leader of the coalition, 2; Magog his land. He is said to be "chief prince" of Meshech (Assyrian "Mushku") S of Gomer (Assyrian "Gimirrai") or Cimmerians in central Asia Minor (Gen 10:2-3). Some make Gog "prince of Rosh," and identify it with Russia; but this identification is tenuous, although the general area was that now occupied by Russia ("the uttermost parts of the north," 6, RSV) and Turkey. Tubal, 3 (Assyrian "Tabali"), is W of Togarmah (Tilgarimmu) near the Halys River, SE of Gomer. Allied with this great northern power are Persia (Iran), Cush (probably connected with ancient Kish in Mesopotamia) and Put (Libya?). (Cf. notes on Gen 10:6.)

Attack on Israel, 38:7-23. The time is "in the latter years," 8, when Israel is restored (yet future) and the Lord has resumed His relationship with the nation. This invasion is evidently *subsequent* to Armageddon, when the Antichrist (Beast) of the revived Roman Empire (Dan 7:8; Rev 13:1-10; 19:19-20) has been dealt with in judgment. The Lord personally undertakes and gives triumph, 14-23.

Overthrow of Gog, 39:1-24. His complete defeat, 1-10, is followed by a massive burial of his army, 11-20, resounding to God's glory, 21-24.

Vision of Restored and Converted Israel, 39:25-29.

CHAPTER 40. DESCRIPTION OF THE TEMPLE

Chapters 40—48 constitute Ezekiel's remarkable vision of restored Israel in the land during the Kingdom Age. Envisioned are the millennial temple, ch. 40—42; the millennial worship, ch. 43—46; and the millennial land, ch. 47—49.

The Introduction, 1-4. The date, 1, was April 28, 573 B.C., on the occasion of the twenty-fifth anniversary of the prophet's exile. Ezekiel was supernaturally transported in vision to Israel, 2, and prophesied from a future idealistic standpoint "upon a very high [temple] mountain" (Mic 4:1; Isa 2:2-3).

The Vision of the Temple, 5-49. What was this temple? Various views are: (1) a somewhat idealized replica of Solomon's temple destroyed in 586 B.C. and which should have been built upon the return from Babylon; (2) a description of the kingdom of God in its final form; (3) the Christian church in its earthly glory and blessing. However, the view which seems to fit the context in Ezekiel, and the testimony of other Scripture, is that *Ezekiel's temple is a literal future sanctuary to be constructed in Palestine during the coming Kingdom Age.*

The measuring reed, 5, was about 10 feet 4 inches (the small cubit about 17.5 inches, the large cubit about 20.68 inches). The East or Processional Gate, 6, may be compared to Solomonic gateways (excavated at Gezer, Hazor and Megiddo). The outer court is described, 17-27; then the inner court, 28-37; and the tables for the offerings and chambers for the inner court, 38-47. The porch is also described, 48-49 (cf. 1 Kgs 7:15-22).

CHAPTER 41. THE ARRANGEMENT OF THE TEMPLE

The House Itself, 1-14, will be the dwelling place of the visible presence of the Lord in the kingdom. The holy place, 1-2, and the most holy place, 3-4, are described. There is no allusion to the ark, mercy seat, high priest, or tables of the law. All these will be superseded by the manifested divine glory. The chambers around the house, 5-11, are probably for the temple personnel. Specified is the separate place, 12-14.

Interior Details, 15-26. Wainscoted with wood, it is embellished with two-faced cherubim (cf. 1:6-12) and palms, symbols of victory. The face of a lion (kingly majesty) and that of a man looking on a palm tree describe the kingly role of the glorified Son of Man, the Lion of the tribe of Judah, ruling in regal splendor on David's throne.

379

The doors of the sanctuary are also decorated with the palm-cherubim motif.

CHAPTERS 42—43. THE PURPOSE OF EZEKIEL'S TEMPLE

To Demonstrate God's Holiness, 42:1-20. This is the pervading theme of the entire book (see introduction) and especially so in the purpose and details of the kingdom temple (cf. 43:10). The holiness of the Lord is further emphasized by the principle of *separation*. At the very outset the wall separating the courts and temple from all that is defiling is introduced (40:5). The cell buildings, 42:1-14, are called holy and have a similar function of separation. The established separation of the whole enclosure is set forth, 15-20.

To Provide a Dwelling Place for the Divine Glory, 43:1-17. Ezekiel sees the return of the glory to take up residence in the temple's holy of holies during the Kingdom Age, as he had seen its departure before the fall of the city in 586 B.C. (cf. 9:3; 10:4; 11:23-24). "This is the place of my throne and the place of the soles of my feet, where I will dwell in the midst of the people of Israel forever," 7.

To Provide a Center for the Divine Government, 43:7. "This is the place of my throne" (cf. Isa 2:2-3; Mic 4:2). The theocratic administration throughout the vision is stressed.

To Perpetuate the Memorial of Sacrifice, 43:18-27. This sacrifice, of course, is not rendered with a view of obtaining salvation, but it is commemorative of an accomplished redemption maintained in the presence of the revealed glory of God.

CHAPTERS 44—46. WORSHIP IN THE KINGDOM AGE

Concerning the Priests and the Prince, 44:1-31. The outward Eastern Gate for the Prince is described, 1-3, and the charge concerning aliens and rebellious tribes is set forth, 4-14. Matters concerning the priesthood (Zadokites) are given, 15-27, with a statement of the priests' inheritance, 28-31.

Portions of Other Groups, 45:1-25. The portions of the priests, Levites, the whole house of Israel, and the Prince are specified, 1-8. The Prince is discussed, 9-17, as well as the feasts (Passover and Tabernacles), 18-25.

The Worship of the Prince, 46:1-18. His personal worship, 1-8, and other instructions for worship are given, 9-15. The Prince's sons and servants are noted, 16-18.

A Final Description of Places in the Temple, 46:19-24.

CHAPTERS 47—48. THE MILLENNIAL LAND

The River of the Sanctuary, 47:1-12 (cf. Zech 14:8-9; Rev 22:1). The reality of this river is of one piece with the vision of the temple, the land and the people of Israel. It must be a literal river, as well as the blessed healing it accomplishes. It constitutes part of the topographical changes in Palestine when the covenants and promises made to Israel are fulfilled and the curse is lifted.

The Boundaries of the Land, 47:13-23. The north boundary is traced from "the great sea" (Mediterranean), the way of Hethlon (Heitala) E of Tripolis in Lebanon, 15, and Hamath (present day Nahr el-'Asi) on the Orontes in Syria N of Damascus. The general borders are to be compared to the promise to Abraham in Gen 15:18-21 and instructions to Joshua in Josh 13:1—19:51.

The Apportionment of the Land, 48:1-29. The term "entrance to Hamath" (cf. Num 34:8) describes the ideal limits of the Promised Land. Solomon's kingdom extended from the brook of Egypt (Wadi el-'Arish) to the "entrance of Hamath" (1 Kgs 8:65; cf. 2 Kgs 14:25; Amos 6:14). The term "Labo-hamath" is likely the name of a town (modern Lebweh) on the Orontes below Riblah. The general assignment by tribes, 1-9, is followed by the allotment for the priests and Levites, 10-20, and for the Prince, 21-29.

Jerusalem in the Kingdom Age, 48:30-35 (cf. Rev 21:10-27). Ezekiel sees the city as it will exist in the coming age, while the apostle John in Revelation has in view the eternal state, which will follow the coming last ordered age in time. Since the kingdom will be eternal, the temporal kingdom merges into the eternal. Jerusalem's kingdom name is *Yhwh-shammah*, "The Lord is there," 35.

DANIEL

PROPHECIES OF THE TIMES OF THE GENTILES

Daniel the Prophet. Daniel is called a prophet by our Lord (Mt 24:15), and His predictions are of immense importance, constituting the indispensable introduction to NT prophecy. Daniel was of princely extraction (1:3), a circumstance itself remarkably foretold by Isaiah (Isa 39:7; cf. 2 Kgs 20:18). He was contemporaneous with Jeremiah, Ezekiel, a fellow exile (Ezk 14:20), and Joshua and Zerubbabel of the restoration. His long career extended from Nebuchadnezzar (605 B.C.) to Cyrus (530 B.C.).

Authenticity of the Book. From the days of Porphyry, a neo-Platonic philosopher of the 3rd cen. A.D., to the present, the authenticity of the book of Daniel has been denied. Many have made it a pious forgery of the Maccabean era (167 B.C.). Two principal reasons exist why Danielic authorship is denied: (1) the minutely accurate picture of the Seleucid-Ptolemaic wars and the career of Antiochus Epiphanes (ch. 11), which is unthinkable as genuine prophecies to the rationalistic critic; and (2) alleged historical inaccuracies in the book. The first objection rests on pure unbelief, and the second rests on arguments from silence, plausible but erroneous presuppositions, insufficient data or untenable interpretations. Many alleged difficulties have been cleared up by archaeological and historical advance, but the book seems designed as a battleground between faith and unbelief.

The Message of the Book. The book is the key to all biblical prophecy. Apart from the great eschatological disclosures of this book, the entire prophetic portions of the Word of God must remain sealed. Jesus' great Olivet Discourse (Mt 24—25; Mk 13; Lk 21), as well as 2 Thess 2 and the entire book of the Revelation, can be unlocked only through an understanding of the prophecies of Daniel. The great themes of NT prophecy, the manifestation of the Antichrist (the man of sin), the Great Tribulation, the second advent of Messiah, the times of the Gentiles, and the resurrections and judgments are all treated in Daniel.

CHAPTER 1. DANIEL THE MAN AND HIS CHARACTER

Beginning of Judah's Exile, 1-2. The third year of Jehoiakim was 605 B.C., but Jeremiah makes the fourth year of Jehoiakim Nebuchadnezzar's *first* year (Jer 25:1). He was evidently using the Palestinian system, not reckoning the year of accession as the first year as in the Babylonian scheme, which Daniel apparently used. This early capture of Jerusalem by "King" Nebuchadnezzar (Daniel uses the term "king" proleptically since Nebuchadnezzar did not ascend the throne until later), although not authenticated by positive extra-biblical evidence, nevertheless stands absolutely unimpugned by any negative evidence.

This date, 605 B.C., marks the beginning of the times of the Gentiles (Lk 21:24), the prophetic period when Jerusalem is under Gentile control. It is plain from 2 Kgs 24:1-4 and 2 Chr 36:6 that Judah from this moment on was subservient to Gentile rule. The Jew has remained so, even to a degree in the heyday of Maccabaean power, and will remain so to the second advent. Nebuchadnezzar's god, 2, was Marduk (Bel, the head of the Babylonian pantheon). Shinar is Babylonia (Gen 10:10; Zech 5:11).

Daniel's Great Moral Decision, 3-21. In this deportation Nebuchadnezzar (the Jewish form of the Babylonian Nebuchadrezzar; Akkadian *Nabû-kudurri-usur,* "Nabu protect my boundary") took only the most noble and promising. Daniel was of royal birth, highly gifted and showed great promise. His moral faith and spiritual courage were proved in his decision for godly separation from the defilement of Babylon. The name Daniel ("God judges") occurs with Noah and Job (cf. Ezk 14:14, 20; 28:3). Higher critics connect Ezekiel's references to Daniel with the legendary judge of the widow and orphan in the religious texts from Ras Shamra (Ugarit) named Danel. But Daniel had ample time to establish his truly great reputation in Babylon by the time of Ezekiel, who did not begin his ministry until some 13 or 14 years after Daniel's deportation. It is, more-

Reconstruction of Babylon as Daniel would have known it. (*Courtesy ORINST*)

over, unthinkable that Ezekiel would link Noah and Job with a pagan legendary figure (see note on 2:46-49). For Daniel's companions, also see note on 2:46-49. On Daniel's Babylonian name "Belteshazzar," see 10:1.

CHAPTER 2. NEBUCHADNEZZAR'S COLOSSUS VISION

The Forgotten Dream, 1-28. The dream came to the king in his "second year," commonly considered to conflict with 1:5, 6, 17, 20. The solution is probably that the three years of training were not three full years, but parts of three years, and that the first year of training was the accession year of the king, the second year his first year, and the third year of training "the second year" in which the dream occurred. The Chaldeans were a caste of wise men, associated with others in a category of diviners and occultists, 2-5. The crux was that the king forgot the dream. If the dream could be recalled, dream and omen lists could be consulted, as extant cuneiform divinatory tablets attest, 6-9. But to recall a forgotten dream was a matter beyond human or demonic ability, 10-16. Daniel and his friends prayed and received help from "the God of heaven," 17-23, and Daniel stood before the king, 24-28.

The Revelation and Interpretation of the Dream, 29-45. By divine help in answer to prayer, Nebuchadnezzar's forgotten dream was revealed by Daniel, 31-35, and interpreted to the king, 36-45. The great image or colossus, as interpreted by Daniel, symbolizes the entire period known in prophecy as the times of the Gentiles (Lk 21:24, see note on 1:1). This is the long era when Jerusalem is politically subservient to the nations, among whom the chosen people are not to be reckoned (Num 23:9). It began with Judah's initial captivity to Babylon in 605 B.C., and will extend to the second advent of Messiah, the Smiting Stone, 34-35, who will destroy the Gentile world system catastrophically.

Then, and not till then, will the Stone (Christ) become a mountain (the millennial kingdom, Isa 2:2, since a mountain symbolizes a kingdom, Rev 13:1; 17:9-11) and fills "the whole earth," 35. This is the "kingdom which shall never be destroyed . . . and shall stand forever," 44; for after it has run its temporal course (Rev 20:4-5) it will merge into the eternal kingdom of the eternal state (1 Cor 15:24-28).

The four metals symbolize four empires—Babylon, Media-Persia, Macedonian Greece and Rome, 37-40. The fourth kingdom (Rome), 40-44 (cf. 7:7), is envisioned panoramically, as it would exist in its ancient imperial glory, as divided into Eastern and Western empires in A.D. 364 (the two legs). These two divisions will enjoy a last-day political revival in a ten-kingdom European United States of dictatorships (iron) 'and democracies (tile), 43. Then the supernatural Stone will strike and destroy Gentile world power and restore the kingdom to Israel (Acts 1:6).

Daniel's Promotion, 46-49 (cf. Ezk 14:14,20; 28:3). The scope of this passage is sufficient to prove that Ezekiel's Daniel is not to be equated with the mythological Babylonian hero Danel of the Aqhat Epic of Ras Shamra (Ugarit), and that the historical Daniel has no connection with such a legend. Shadrach is perhaps *Shudur-Aku* ("command of Aku," Sumerian moon-god) or just a corruption of Marduk. Meshach is perhaps Akkadian *Mishaaku* ("Who is what Aku is?"). Abednego is for *Abednebo, Abdi-Nabu* ("servant of Nabu," god of wisdom).

CHAPTER 3. THE FIERY FURNACE

The Image of Gold, 1-7. Nebuchadnezzar's pride manifested in this act of idolatry and deification of man marks the spirit that prevails in the times of the Gentiles (see notes on 1:1-2; 2:36-45). The image was 60 cubits (90 feet) high and six cubits (nine feet) wide, evidently in the form of an obelisk, grotesque indeed, as man's idolatry and self-deification are in the sight of the God in heaven.

"The plain of Dura" (Akkadian *dûru,* "wall," "circuit") is perhaps Tulul Dura, a few miles S of Babylon. The music, 5-6, was to stir up the religious emotions to aid in the idolatrous worship.

The Faithful Three and Their Deliverance, 8-25. Shadrach, Meshach and Abednego were saved through the furnace of tribulation. "The form of the fourth" person walking unscathed in the fiery furnace "like the Son of God" or "a Son of God," 25, was evidently the preincarnate Christ, not a mere angel as the king thought, 28. In the presence of tribulation the Lord's own are assured of His presence and deliverance.

The King's Confession and Decree, 26-30. Here is another step in the king's progressive apprehension of the one true God (cf. 2:47; 3:28; 4:34-35).

CHAPTER 4. NEBUCHADNEZZAR'S INSANITY

The King's Salutation, 1-3. He fully comprehended the universality of his rule, 1 (cf. 3:29).

The Tree Vision and Its Interpretation, 4-27. Nebuchadnezzar sees a great tree, 4-18, a symbol of his pride and imperial self-exaltation (cf. 3:1-25; Ezk 17:22-24; 31:3-9; Mt 13:31-32). Daniel, whose Babylonian name was Belteshazzar (Akkadian *balusu-usur*, "may he [Bel] protect his life"), interprets the true vision, 19-27.

ARCHAEOLOGICAL LIGHT

Nebuchadnezzar was a great builder. For comment on his boast recorded in 30, see notes on 2 Kgs 25, where the excavations of his capital city, Babylon, are mentioned; also notes on Jer 50—51. The king's inscriptions closely parallel Dan 4:30.

The Vision Fulfilled, 28-37. The king was punished for his pride by temporary mental derangement (lycanthropy), in which the victim imagined himself to be a wild beast, a type of pathological aberration known in all eras of history. Berossus, a Babylonian priest of the 3rd cen. B.C., notes that Nebuchadnezzar after he had reigned 43 years "was suddenly invaded by sickness" (*Contra Apionem* 1:20), obviously referring to some unusual malady. Eusebius in his *Praeparatio Evangelica* (9:41) quotes from Abydenus concerning Nebuchadnezzar in his last days "being possessed by some god [demon] or other" and who having uttered a prophecy concerning the coming of the Persian conqueror "immediately disappeared." Critics disregard these allusions and maintain that Nebuchadnezzar's madness is a fictitious element of Daniel. But if history *were* silent, that in itself would not be sufficient evidence to reject the historicity of this chapter. The "seven times," 16, are "seven years." A Dead Sea Scroll text identifies such a mental malady with Nabonidus. Why then would it be impossible for Nebuchadnezzar? The king was restored, 34, and abased himself and praised "the Most High," 34, confessing Him King of heaven, 37.

CHAPTER 5. BELSHAZZAR'S FEAST

Belshazzar's Licentious and Blasphemous Celebration, 1-9. The moral decline of the nation is evident. The holy vessels from the Jerusalem temple were desecrated by drunkenness, debauchery and idolatry. Babylon's iniquity, like the Amorites' (Gen 15:16), was full and judgment struck. Belshazzar (Akkadian *Bel-shar-usur*, "Bel protect the king"), as is now well-known from modern archaeology, was the son of, and coregent with, the king, Nabonidus. What is unique in cuneiform literature is that Belshazzar is so recognized as coregent. Two legal documents dated to the twelfth and thirteenth years of Nabonidus record oaths sworn by the life of the king and of *Bel-shar-usur*, the crown prince. Nabonidus (Nabunaid, Akkadian

Nabû-na'id, "Nabu is inspiring") was the last king of Babylon, 556-539 B.C. In the Persian Verse Account it is stated that in his third year Nabonidus entrusted the kingship to his son Belshazzar, and he himself took up residence at Tema (in Arabia). The mysterious writing on the wall, 5-9, turned the feast into a nightmare of terror.

The Forgotten Daniel and His Message of Doom, 10-28. At this juncture the queen (probably the aged widow of Nebuchadnezzar) recalled Daniel, who had played so great a role in her husband's regime, 10-16. Daniel, the aged saint, was called in. Belshazzar confessed that in Daniel dwelt "the Spirit of the holy God" or "holy deity," 14 (not as the RSV renders, "the spirit of the holy gods"). Daniel, knowing the impending doom, refused the empty honor of "third ruler," 16, 29, in the realm. Why *third* ruler? Because Belshazzar as coregent was himself the second.

Daniel became more than an interpreter of the handwriting. He was God's messenger of judgment and disaster upon Belshazzar and the Chaldean Empire. The writing, "Mene, Mene, Tekel, Upharsin," 25, means literally: *mene,* "numbered, numbered," i.e., "thoroughly numbered," where the repetition emphasizes the thought; *tekel,* "weighed"; *upharsin,* "and divided." *Peres,* past participle of "divided," is a word play on *Parus* ("Persia") or *perasin* ("Persians"). The Heb. text thus takes all these forms as past participles, i.e., as verbs. It does not, as some critics hold, permit the explanation that these are substantives denoting weights: *mene,* a mina; *tekel,* a shekel; *parsin,* two half-minas, meaning that Nebuchadnezzar weighed a mina, Neriglissar his successor a mina, his successor Labashi-Marduk only a shekel, Nabonidus and Belshazzar but half a mina each. The import of the riddle is that the Chaldean Empire was completely numbered, weighed, and divided among the Medes and Persians. For the figure of weighing in a balance, see Job 31:6; Ps 62:9; Prov 16:2.

The Reward of Daniel and Belshazzar's Death, 29-31. Critics attack the historicity of the narrative on the basis that Belshazzar was so unconcerned as to reward Daniel at once. But the king was merely keeping his word and showing that he believed Daniel's prophecy. Moreover, there was no reason why Daniel at this juncture should refuse the honors, since he had proved his disinterestedness. Critics also object that the fall of Babylon and Belshazzar's death are unauthentic. But there is nothing in the Gr. sources—Herodotus, Xenophon, Berossus, or the cuneiform records—the Nabonidus Chronicle or the Cyrus Cylinder that indicates this would not be in keeping with the statement of the murder of Belshazzar. For the problem of Darius the Mede, see 6:1, 9, 25; 9:1.

CHAPTER 6. DANIEL IN THE DEN OF LIONS

Darius the Mede and Daniel, 1-28. Daniel was now an old man, certainly well over 80 years of age. Darius himself was in his sixties. It is maintained that Darius is to be identified with Gobryas (Gubaru), who took charge of Babylon immediately after the death of Belshazzar, and who appointed satraps and presidents, including Daniel, to assist him in governing the extensive territory. He probably ruled about two years, until Cyrus was free to take over (6:28; 9:1; 11:1). That the Bible should record another name for the interim ruler Gubaru (or Cyaxares, the Median father-in-law of Cyrus, if Josephus' contention is correct) is not surprising. It was customary to have a Babylonian name in addition to one's native name (cf. Daniel and his three Jewish colleagues, 1:6-7).

Daniel's long diplomatic career and his prediction of a Medo-Persian victory were doubtless reasons why Darius placed him over the government. Daniel's faith and courage, 10-15, were the prelude to a mighty miracle, accentuated by the climactic struggle with pagan idolatry. This signal demonstration that the Lord of the captive Hebrews was really God had a great effect upon Darius, as is seen in his decree, 25-28, and doubtless also affected Cyrus favorably to issue his decree a few years later to permit the Jews to return to Jerusalem.

CHAPTER 7. DANIEL'S FOUR-BEAST VISION

The Vision of the Beasts, 1-8. The date was evidently 553 B.C. when Belshazzar began to act as coregent for his father, 1. The "sum" is the main substance of what the prophet saw. The four winds stirring up the "sea" (the nations, Rev 17:15) speak of evil celestial (demonic) powers (Dan 10:13; Eph 6:12), who have a conspicious role in the government of fallen man. The four beasts trace the same four world empires as in the image of 2:37-45, with this difference, that the colossus presents the outward dazzling brilliance of world governments in their political, economic, social aspects, while ch. 7 gives their intrinsic selfish and beastlike character.

These four empires, as in ch. 2, are Babylon, Medo-Persia (not a separate Median kingdom as higher critics posit), Greece and Rome. The lion prefigures Babylon, the bear Medo-Persia, the leopard Greece, and the nondescript iron beast admirably portrays Rome. The ten horns of ironlike Rome are ten kings, 7-8 (cf. 24), and correspond to the ten toes of 2:40-44. The "little horn," 8, prefigured by Antiochus Epiphanes (8:23-25), is the latter-day Antichrist, "the man of sin" in 2 Thess 2:3-8, "the king" of Dan 11:36-45, "the Beast" of Rev 13:4-10, the last terrible ruler of the times of the Gentiles, who will be destroyed by Messiah at His second advent (Rev 19:20).

The Vision of Messiah's Second Advent, 9-14. This is the OT counterpart of Rev 19:11-16. "The Ancient of days," 9, 13, is God. "One like the Son of man," 13, is Christ invested with the kingdom and returning to earth as King of kings and Lord of lords (Rev 19:16). He will bring to an end the times of the Gentiles and Gentile world dominion, setting up His righteous rule over Israel and the nations. The Messiah's investiture with the kingdom in heaven, 13-14, is presented. This will take place *before* His coming portrayed in 9-12, and is identical with Rev 5:6-10. Daniel describes the judgment of the nations and the setting up of the kingdom, 10, 26-27 (cf. Mt. 25:31-46; Rev 20:1-6). The vision of the destruction of the "little horn," 11 (cf. 8) is fulfilled at the second advent (Rev 19:20; 20:10).

The Interpretation of the Vision, 15-28. "The saints of the Most High" who "possess the kingdom," 18, 22, 25, 27, are the saved Jewish remnant who pass through the Great Tribulation and inherit the kingdom and the covenants and promises made to Israel in connection with it. Note that the kingdom will be *eternal,* 18. The *mediatorial* and *temporal* aspects of it, i.e., the thousand year reign of Christ (Rev 20:4, 7), merge into the eternal state when Christ, after His reign on the earth, "delivers up the kingdom to God the Father . . . that God may be all in all" (1 Cor 15:24-28). It is important that the designation of God as the Most High, possessor of heaven and earth (Gen 14:18-22), is used when the Messiah comes to make good that title in His kingdom rule, 27. It is essential to see that the "fourth beast," 23, and the ten-kingdom confederation growing out of it, 24, are *not* Macedonian Greece and Antiochus Epiphanes, 25-26, as critics commonly assert, but last-day revived Rome, since the whole context involves the *second* advent of Messiah and His subsequent rule.

CHAPTER 8. THE RAM, THE HE-GOAT AND THE LITTLE HORN

The Vision, 1-14. Dated two years later than the beast vision (7:1), the time would be 551 B.C., and the place Shushan (Susa), which became the winter capital of the Persian kings. The Ulai River is the Eulaeus of classical writers, 2, 16, an artificial canal (Akkadian *U-la-a*) that flowed close by Susa on the N and NE, and connected the Kerkha and Abdizful Rivers. The Assyrian emperor Ashurbanipal claims to have reddened it with his enemies' blood when he invaded the province of Elam, E of Babylonia.

The ram, 3-4, with two horns (Media and Persia) is the Medo-Persian Empire, 539-331 B.C. The he-goat is Macedonian Greece in its lightninglike conquests under Alexander the Great, "the conspicuous horn" of the goat, 5 (RSV). Alexander's conquest of the Persian Empire is prophetically symbolized, 6-7, in the decisive battles of Granicus (334 B.C.), Issus (333 B.C.) and Gaugamela (331 B.C.). His untimely death in Babylon (323 B.C.) and the division of his world empire among his four generals are prefigured, 8. This resulted in three great Hellenistic empires by 275 B.C.: Macedonia, Egypt (Ptolemies) and Syria (Seleucids).

The career of Antiochus Epiphanes (175-163 B.C.) is prophetically outlined, 9-14. In 167 B.C. he conquered Palestine, defiled the sanctuary and dedicated it to Zeus Olympus. In 164 B.C. the temple was purified. This is the period of the "2300 evenings and mornings," 14 (RSV). As the "little horn," 9, he must not be confused with the "little horn" of Dan 7:8, 24-26, who is the Antichrist of the end time, although Antiochus Epiphanes foreshadowed him, 24-25. Both are similar in their idolatry and desecration of the temple (cf. 2 Thess 2:3-4; Rev 13:1-18), but are distinct as the context proves and as the book of the Revelation attests.

The Interpretation of the Vision, 15-27. The angel Gabriel's interpretation shows clearly that the vision of Antiochus Epiphanes is a foreshadowing of the future tribulation, called "the time of the end," 17, "the last end of the indignation," 19, "when the transgressors are come to the full," 23.

CHAPTER 9. THE PROPHECY OF THE SEVENTY WEEKS

Daniel's Prayer, 1-19. The date of the prophecy, given as a result of Daniel's deep penitential prayer, is "the first year of Darius" (538 B.C.), "son of Ahasuerus" (Xerxes). Daniel was stirred to intercession for the restoration of his people by reading Jeremiah's prophecies of the 70 years (Jer 25:11-12; 29:10).

The Answer—the Prophecy of the Seventy Weeks, 20-27. Jeremiah's prophecy of the 70-year Babylonian captivity is made the basis of a newly revealed panoramic prediction of the entire history of Daniel's people, the Jews, from the rebuilding of Jerusalem's walls until the ultimate establishment of Messiah's earthly kingdom.

The figure of 70 weeks is employed. The weeks (Heb. *heptads,* "sevens") are *heptads* of years. The total given is 70 *heptads,* or 490 years. It is a *historically complete* answer to Daniel's prayer, (1-19), when Israel's national chastisement will be ended, prophetic vision sealed (closed) because it will be fulfilled (cf. Acts 3:21), and everlasting righteousness brought to Israel when she accepts her Messiah at His second advent, 24.

The total of 70 weeks ("sevens") is first divided into *seven weeks* or 49 years, 25. At the beginning of this time "the commandment to restore and to build Jerusalem" was issued in the decree of Artaxerxes I to rebuild Jerusalem's walls (Nisan, Mar.-Apr., 445 B.C., Neh 2). During this period (445-396 B.C.) "the street shall be built again, and the wall, even in troublous times."

The next division is *62 weeks* or 434 years, 26. After this period (plus the first seven weeks, cf. v. 25) "Messiah shall be cut off" (396 B.C. to Mar.-Apr., A.D. 30). The 62-week period ended and Christ the "Messiah-Prince" was cut off in death and had nothing, i.e., nothing which was rightly His, no kingdom.

Following the 62 weeks an *unreckoned period* is prophesied, a time of Israel's national rejection, during which "the people of the prince that shall come [the Beast, world ruler of the Gentile endtime, cf. 7:8; Rev 19:20] shall destroy the city and sanctuary," 26b. The Romans under Titus destroyed Jerusalem in A.D., 70, the city has since been trodden down by the Gentiles (Lk 21:24), the Jews have been scattered, and "wars and desolations" have characterized the age.

The *final week* of seven years constitutes the climax of Jewish history prior to the establishment of the messianic kingdom, 27. It is divided into two half periods (three and a half years each). During the *first half* the "prince" (world ruler, "little horn" of 7:8, 24-25) will make a covenant with the Jews, who are restored in Palestine with a resumption of temple worship. In the *middle of the week* the covenant is broken, worship for the Jews ceases (2 Thess 2:3-4), and the time of Great Tribulation ensues. The *advent of Christ* the Messiah consummates this period of desolation, bringing everlasting righteousness to Israel, 24, and judgment upon the "desolator," the prince, and his hosts (Rev 19:20).

CHAPTER 10. THE ROLE OF DEMONIC POWERS IN GOVERNMENTS

The Vision, 1-14. This chapter is the prologue for the vision of ch. 11, while ch. 12 is the epilogue. "The third year of Cyrus" was 535 B.C. "Belteshazzar," Daniel's Babylonian name, was apparently an abbreviated form of the Akkadian *Bel-balasu-usur* ("may Bel [i.e., Baal] protect his life").

Verse 1 should be translated: ". . . and the thing [revealed] was true [truth], and it was a conflict [involved a spiritual struggle or warfare]." The battle involved a spiritual tussle with demon powers operating in the government of the world system, 13. Daniel's three-week prayer and fasting, 2-3, challenged these "wicked spirits [demons] in the heavenlies" (cf. Eph 6:12), i.e., evil spirits connected with governmental administration operating through Cyrus, 13. "The prince of the kingdom of Persia" was the evil spirit of government working in and through Cyrus (not Cyrus himself), to hinder him in his good intention to repatriate the Jews. Michael, 12-13, the arch-angel and patron of Daniel's people the Jews, 12:1, came to Daniel's assistance in the conflict precipitated by believing prayer. Hiddekel, 4, is the Tigris (cf. Gen 2:14). Uphaz, 5, is unknown.

The Meaning of the Vision, 15-21. The world governments of the times of the Gentiles (Lk 21:24) are operated by unseen evil spirits or demons in the Satanic world system. These tried to hinder Daniel's prayer for His people, whose ultimate restoration in the kingdom will be preceded by the end of the times of the Gentiles and the imprisonment of Satan and his demons (Rev 20:1-3) to make possible the perfect government of Messiah in the Kingdom Age.

CHAPTER 11. KINGS OF THE NORTH AND SOUTH

The Wars of the Ptolemies and Seleucids, 1-35. This marvelous prewriting of history by the Spirit of prophecy through Daniel of the 6th cen. B.C. seems impossible to rationalistic critics and is a chief reason for the rejection of the genuineness of the book of Daniel. History has minutely verified these prophecies fulfilled by Persian kings, 2; Alexander the Great, 3-4; the Ptolemies of Egypt, 5; "the kings of the south" and the Seleucids of Syria, "the kings of the north," 6-35. Even the Romans, 30, in "ships of Kittim" (Cyprus), mentioned in the description of Antiochus IV (Epiphanes), 21-45, and the "abomination that makes desolate," 31, which he set up when he profaned the Jerusalem temple, exactly fulfilled these prophecies (cf. notes on 8:1-14). But our Lord in Mt 24:15 referred not to this passage but to 12:11. The 11:31 passage was fulfilled then, but 12:11 is still future.

The End-Time and the Man of Sin, 36-45. Between 35 and 36 spans an unreckoned period of time, from the historical fulfillment of these prophecies in Antiochus Epiphanes and the victorious

Maccabees to the still future fulfillment of 36-45, fulfilling 10:14. The willful king of these verses is the Antichrist of the last days, the man of sin of 2 Thess 2:3-4, the lawless one of Rev 13:1-10, adumbrated by Antiochus Epiphanes. "He shall prosper till the indignation is accomplished," 36 (12:1), i.e., God's wrath outpoured (Mt 24:21; Rev. 6—19). His lawless, God-defying character, 36-39, is unfolded. His latter-day activity preceding his doom is outlined, 40-45 (cf. Rev 19:20; 20:10), and described in 2 Thess 2:3-10. The last day attack by the kings of the north and of the south shall not destroy him. Only the direct judgment of God upon him by the returning victorious Christ shall seal his doom. While he reigns, he is invincible.

CHAPTER 12. THE GREAT TRIBULATION AND ISRAEL'S DELIVERANCE

The Great End-Time Period of Trouble, 1. "At that time" (twice in v. 1) is the time of the end, the last half of Daniel's seventieth week (see notes on 9:27), the terrible period of "Jacob's trouble" (Jer 30:5-7) preceding the return of Christ. This time is outlined in Rev 12:7-17, culminating in the terrible bowl judgments of Rev 15—16, and the destruction of the Satanic religions and political world system (Rev 17—18). It climaxes in the appearing Messiah (Rev 19:11-16). This "end" time is referred to in Dan 8:17-19; 9:26; 11:35, 40; 12:4, 6, 9. "Thy people," 1, are Daniel's people the Jews. Those "found written in the book" are those delivered from physical death (Isa 4:2-3) and regenerated to enjoy kingdom blessing. For Michael's ministry on behalf of Israel in the end-time, cf. Rev 12:7-12 and Dan 10:21 (delivering the remnant of Israel from the wrath of Satan, who has been cast down to the earth).

Israel's Resurrection, 2-3. That this resurrection is predicated of *Israel,* and the idea of a general resurrection of all the dead is excluded, is shown by the following: (1) The context, which concerns "Daniel's people, the Jews, 1. (2) The term "many," not all. (3) The partitive preposition "out from," "from among" a category "who, sleep" (the sleep of physical death) in the "ground of dust" or "land of dust," a figurative term for the grave (cf. Job 20:11; Gen 3:19). (4) The verb "awake" to denote physical resurrection (Isa 26:19) from the sleep of death (2 Kgs 4:31; Jer 51:39, 57; Job 14:12). (5) The phrase "to life everlasting," showing that it is physical resurrection to eternal life. (6) The fact that Daniel himself (with all the OT saved) will participate in it, 12:13. (7) Not necessary that resurrected Israelites will be a part of the earthly population in the millennium any more than resurrected believers will be, but they will arise at this time and realize their ancient hopes as saved Israelites. (8) Fulfillment of such statements of our Lord as Mt 8:11; 19:28. (9) The "some [these] . . . and some [those]" does not mean that unsaved Israelites will be resurrected at this time (cf. similar thought in Jn 5:28-29). The first category refers to all saved Israelites raised at that time, while the second embraces those left for the second resurrection (Rev 20:11-15). (10) Verse 3 refers to rewards of the resurrected OT saints.

The Final Consummation, 4-13. The character of the intervening period, especially its latter part, 4, 9, was revealed to Daniel by the Lord, 5-8. But the prophecy was to be sealed up (not understood) to the end-time, 4. Verses 11 and 12 give the time of the setting up of Antichrist's image (9:27) in the Jerusalem temple (2 Thess 2:3-4), and the duration of the great time of wrath. The added period is specified as 1260, 1290 and 1335 days, for those who reach its end will be spared death. Resurrection, 3, occurs after the 1335 days.

THE MINOR PROPHETS

The 12 so-called Minor Prophets are distinguished from the Major Prophets—Isaiah, Jeremiah, Ezekiel and Daniel. In the Heb. canon they are grouped together as *one* book called the Twelve, and with the first three major prophets make *four* books, known as the Latter Prophets. The Former Prophets are also reckoned four in number—Joshua, Judges, Samuel, Kings. The Heb. Bible then has eight prophets in its second section, called the Prophets *(Nebhi'im)*. Daniel was placed in the third section among the Writings *(Kethubhim)*. From Augustine's time (late 4th cen.), the Latin church has employed the term Minor Prophets because of their brevity (not their unimportance) as compared with the Major Prophets.

The Habakkuk Commentary from the Dead Sea Scrolls. (© *Shrine of the Book, Jerusalem, Israel, MPS*)

THE MINOR PROPHETS AND THEIR MESSAGE

Prophet	General Message	Approximate Time
Hosea	The Lord loves Israel despite her sin.	c. 755-715 B.C.
Joel	Judgment precedes Israel's future spiritual revival.	c. 835-796 B.C.
Amos	God is just and must judge sin.	c. 765-750 B.C.
Obadiah	Sure retribution must overtake merciless pride.	c. 848-841 B.C.
Jonah	Divine grace is universal in its sweep.	c. 780-750 B.C.
Micah	Bethlehem-born Messiah will be mankind's Deliverer.	c. 740-690 B.C.
Nahum	Doom is to descend on wicked Nineveh.	c. 630-612 B.C.
Habakkuk	Justification by faith is God's way of salvation	c. 625 B.C. or earlier
Zephaniah	The day of the Lord must precede kingdom blessing.	c. 625-610 B.C.
Haggai	The Lord's temple and interests deserve top priority.	520 B.C.
Zechariah	The Lord will remember His people Israel.	520-515 B.C. Ch. 9—14 after 500 B.C.
Malachi	Let the wicked be warned by the certainty of judgment.	c. 433-400 B.C.

HOSEA

The Love of God for His Erring People

The Prophet and His Times. Hosea began his ministry toward the latter part of the prosperous and morally declining era of Jeroboam II of Israel (782-753 B.C.,) and continued on after the fall of Samaria (722 B.C.) into the troubled reigns of Jotham, Ahaz and Hezekiah (1:1). His ministry followed closely upon that of Amos. The latter thundered forth his scathing prophecies as a southerner to a prosperous dissolute Israel, while Hosea spoke with the heart passion of a native son. Jonah was the northern kingdom's foreign missionary, while Hosea was its home missionary. With the brokenness and passion of Jeremiah, Hosea had a sensitiveness of heart that made him the apostle of love in the OT. Although the theme of judgment for apostasy runs through the book, it is interwoven by the golden strand of mercy and love. And Hosea's exposure of sin and impending judgment are not the fiery denunciations of Amos, but a mournful, solemn elegy that breathes the deep love of the Lord for His sinning people.

CONTEMPORARY KINGS

Israel				Judah	
Jeroboam II	782-753	B.C.	Hosea	Uzziah*	791-740 B.C.
Zachariah	753-752	B.C.	begins	Jotham*	750-736 B.C.
Shallum	752 B.C.		Anarchy		
Menahem	752-742	B.C.	and		
Pekahiah	742-740	B.C.	civil war		
Pekah	740-732	B.C.	(Hos 1:4)	Ahaz*	743-716 B.C.
Hoshea	732-722	B.C.			
Fall of Samaria	722 B.C.			Hezekiah	716-687 B.C.

*Coregencies included

> **Outline**
> Israel's Rejection as an Unfaithful Wife;
>   Her Future Reception and Restoration, Ch. 1—3
> Messages of Judgment Mingled with
>   Pleadings of Love and Mercy, Ch. 4—14

CHAPTER 1. THE PROPHET'S MARRIAGE ILLUSTRATES ISRAEL'S SIN

Introduction, 1. Hosea means "salvation" or "deliverance." The fundamental conviction of Heb. prophecy is here expressed in the divine inspiration of the human agent and the consequent authority of the message.

Hosea Divinely Commanded to Marry a Harlot, 2-9. Hosea took the prostitute Gomer, and she bore him children. He gave them names, 2-9, which were historically and prophetically meaningful. Jezreel, the son, means "the Lord sows," 3-5, and pointed back to the blood of Jezreel shed by Jehu (1 Kgs 19:15-17; 2 Kgs 10:1-14) and the approaching punishment of the Jehu dynasty of which the then reigning prosperous Jeroboam II was a member. Jezreel also pointed forward to Israel's future restoration, 2:21-23. The birth of a daughter, Lo-ruhamah ("unpitied") is announced, 6-7. The little girl would be a living reminder that because of her harlotry Israel would no longer be pitied. The name of the third child (another boy), Lo-ammi ("not my people"), made him a living reminder why the Lord would no longer pity. The Lord broke the covenant relation between Himself and Israel. "My people" refers to Israel as God's elect nation in the OT, while "not my people" has reference to the temporary setting aside of this national election (cf. Rom 11:1-5). The "Lo-ammi" period of Israel (the northern ten tribes) would end with the nation's conversion and her reunion with Judah.

Future Restoration of Israel, 10-11. Cf. Rom 9:23-26 for the divine commentary on God's sovereignty and Israel's reinstatement. Verse 11 is still unfulfilled. "The [great] day of Jezreel" will be Armageddon's slaughter, a prelude to the destruction of Israel's last-day enemies, and restoration, 11.

MORAL PROBLEM

(1) Did the Lord command Hosea to marry a harlot, or (2) did she become a harlot after his marriage, or (3) is the incident only an allegory? Since Israel, the Lord's adulterous wife, was not always unchaste, number two is possible. But the text apparently supports number one and does not impinge upon the holiness of a sovereign God. Number three is a makeshift.

CHAPTER 2. ISRAEL'S SUFFERING FOR HER HARLOTRY

Appeal and Warning, 1-13. The godly remnant is addressed, 1, and urged to plead with faithless Israel (their mother), 2, who is dis-

owned by the Lord as His wife because of her infidelity. The Lord Himself dramatically threatens His unfaithful spouse with grievous punishments, 3-13.

Israel to Be Restored, 14-23. The valley of Achor ("trouble"; Josh 7:26; Isa 65:10) is SW of Jericho (modern el-Buqe'ah). Israel, the disowned, will be restored. She who has immorally taken Baal as her husband and engaged in the foul fertility rites of the Canaanites, 6-7, shall return to the Lord (*Ishi*, "my husband"), and no longer call Baal that detestable designation *Baali* ("my Baal," Lord), 16. These verses present a glorious future for Israel. (For v. 23, cf. Rom 9:25-26.)

CHAPTER 3. ISRAEL'S FUTURE RESTORATION

Israel's Past Symbolized, 1-3. Hosea bought back his unfaithful wife, disciplined her, as the Lord has done for Israel, and affirmed his undying love for her. "Even as the Lord loves Israel, though they turn to other gods," 1 (RSV), expresses the central theme of Hosea's prophecy—God's undying love for His covenant people. "Cakes of raisins" (RSV) were used in pagan festal worship (Isa 16:7; Jer 7:18). Although Hosea bought his wife back (implying Christ's ransom price paid at Calvary), she was not to live with him as his wife, but must sit as a widow in sorrow and discipline until he would one day take her to himself, after her cleansing.

Israel's Present Described, 4. During this period of disciplinary dealing in a virtual state of widowhood, Israel would be deprived of her ceremonial and civil institutions, as has been the case. The ephod speaks of the priesthood; the teraphim (household gods), of insight into the future; the king, of millennial blessing.

Israel's Future Indicated, 5. This is unfulfilled and will take place in the latter days of Israel, before kingdom restoration (Acts 1:6), when the adulterous wife is cleansed (Zech 12:10; 13:1) and restored.

CHAPTER 4. EPHRAIM'S ATTACHMENT TO IDOLATRY

Fruitage of Idolatry, 1-11. A general category of sins, 1-5, is augmented by the willful ignorance of the Lord's people, 6-11.

Description of Ephraim's Idolatry, 12-19. What an indictment of the foolishness and foulness of Canaanite cults! Beth-aven ("house of wickedness or vanity"), 15, is apparently a condemnatory name for Bethel (5:8; cf. 10:8), a center of Canaanite idolatrous pollution (cf. 10:5, "calf of Beth-aven"). "Ephraim" became the designation of

Israel after the Syro-Ephraimite war (734-732 B.C.) when the northern kingdom lost its peripheral territories to Assyria and was reduced to its central rump state. Ephraim's pathetic occupation with idols, 17, resulted in inevitable judgment, 19, the wind having caught the people in its power to scatter them in exile.

CHAPTERS 5—6. MESSAGE OF REBUKE AND FUTURE MERCY

The Favor of the Lord Withdrawn, 5:1-14. Israel's leaders (priests and civil rulers), 1, had been a trap to the people and judgment was due. Tabor seems to have harbored a pagan shrine on its heights as well as Mizpah, N of Jerusalem (1 Sam 7:5). Ephraim (see note on 4:12-19) was so addicted to idolatry (4:17) she was unable to return to the Lord. "Stranger [alien] children," 7, were offspring unfaithful to the Lord.

Future Return and Blessing, 5:15—6:3. The Lord withdrew from Israel. Her interim affliction resulted and will continue till He returns at His second advent, 5:15. The heart cry of the believing remnant of the last days is expressed, 6:1-3 (cf. Isa 1:9; Rom 11:5), their cry just before the return of the Lord declared in 5:15. The "two days," 2, prefigure the long period of Israel's affliction (5:15). "The third day," 2, is her day of spiritual resurrection (regeneration) and consequent spiritual blessings (Joel 2:28-29).

The Lord's Reply, 6:4-11. He mourned over Ephraim and Judah, 4-6, exposing their sin, 7-11, which had caused their calamities.

CHAPTERS 7—13. THE LORD'S INDICTMENT OF ISRAEL

Her Moral Depravity, 7:1-16. The horrible harvest of her idolatry, 1-7, in mixing with the polluted paganism of the surrounding nations, 8-16, is excoriated.

Judgment Upon Her Apostasy, 8:1—9:9. The judgment announced, 8:1-7, upon her apostasy, 8-14, is followed by warnings against a spirit of self-security, 9:1-9.

Retrospect of the Nation's Sin and Woe, 9:10—11:11. How Israel requited the Lord's love, 9:10-17, incurring awful guilt, 10:1-11, is told. Exhortations and rebuke were administered, 10:12-15. God's mercy is set forth, 11:1-11.

Ephraim's Indictment, 11:12—13:13. She is brought face to face with her polluting idolatrous contamination, 11:12—12:2. Past mercies are recalled, 12:3-6, in view of Israel's present plight, 7-14. Her former greatness is contrasted with her shame and spiritual death, contaminated by impure Baal worship, 13:1-6. The Lord has had to turn against her as a leopard, 7, as a lion 7, and as a bear robbed of her whelps, 8. Israel's ruin is in the fact that she is against the Lord, who is her help, 9-11. Could her kings save her from the destruction she had incurred by turning against the Lord? Ephraim's sin is held on to, bound up and hidden like a treasure, 12.

Israel's Future Resurrection, 13:14-16. This is a glorious promise of physical resurrection (1 Cor 15:55) for saved Israelites preceding the kingdom .(Dan 12:2). Physical resurrection for the faithful is an unchangeable fact of divine certainty. "Repentance [change of mind] concerning it is hid from my [God's] eyes," 14.

CHAPTER 14. KINGDOM RESTORATION OF ISRAEL

Call to Return, 1-3. God's Spirit through the prophet calls apostate Ephraim to come back to the Lord in repentance and faith. "Calves" (bulls) means "fruit" in the sense of young oxen as thank offerings.

The Lord's Gracious Response, 4-8. Sovereign love expresses itself in three "I wills," 4-5. In kingdom glory Israel, "the lily" and "the olive tree" (cf. Rom 11:16-24), will flourish. The olive is a symbol of Israel in her spiritual blessing.

Concluding Statement, 9. The spiritually wise will understand these things, but not sinners.

JOEL

THE GREAT DAY OF THE LORD

Author and Date. Joel means "the Lord *(Yahweh)* is God." The name of his father is given, but merely to distinguish him from others of the same name. He leaves even the time he prophesied to be guessed at. Although modern critics date him late (post-Exilic), conservative scholars place him as perhaps the earliest of the minor prophets, during the reign of Joash (*c.* 800 B.C.).

Outline
The Locust Plague—The Day of the Lord, 1:1-20
Events of the Day of the Lord, 2:1-32
The Judgment of the Nations, 3:1-16
Kingdom Blessing, 3:17-21

CHAPTER 1. THE LOCUST PLAGUE—THE DAY OF THE LORD

The Desolation of the Land, 1-7. The prophet is presented, 1. Description is given of an unprecedented locust plague, which was to be unforgettable in the future, 3. The plague was utterly destructive in its results. Four names are given to the locusts portraying their decimating destruction. "The leavings of the *gnawer* the *multiplier* ate, and the leavings of the *licker* the *devourer* ate" (Keil and Delitzsch), 4. The nation's drunkards are called to bewail the calamity, 5. The locusts point to something still more terrible and form a prophetic picture of a greater disaster. They prefigure an invading army, 6-7 (cf. 2:25) and its desolation of the land. Both the vine (Ps 80:8, 14; Hos 10:1; Isa 5:1-7) and the fig tree symbolize Israel in her spiritual privilege and national election (Hos 9:10; Mt 24:32-33; Lk 13:6-7; Rom 11:17-24).

Appeal to Lament the Plague, 8-13. All people, 8-10, especially the farmer and vinedresser, 11-12, the priests and spiritual leaders of the nation, 13, are called to mourn.

Call to Self-Humiliation and Repentance, 14. Fasting and prayer must give evidence of genuine repentance.

The Plague a Prophetic Symbol of the Day of the Lord, 15-20. Just as the Spirit of prophecy frequently uses some local circumstance as the occasion of a far-reaching prophecy (cf. Isa 7:1-14 in the case of the virgin-birth prediction), so the locust plague is made a symbol of the yet future day of the Lord (Isa 2:12-22; 4:1-6; Ezk 30:3; Rev 19:11-21). In this apocalyptic period (Rev 6—19), the Lord will manifest His power in putting down His enemies actively and publicly in order to set up His mediatorial kingdom over Israel. It is the period described graphically in Ps 2.

CHAPTER 2. EVENTS OF THE DAY OF THE LORD

The Invading Army from the North, 1-10. Joel 2 conducts us at once to the closing times of the Gentiles and the historical enactment of the day of the Lord, 1. It is still future, as is ch. 3. The invading army is preparatory to Armageddon (Rev 16:13-16). Blowing the trumpet (*shophar,* a carved horn) signaled the danger of invading forces (Hos 8:1; Jer 4:5; 6:1). "My holy mountain" (Ps 2:6) is Moriah, the temple hill. The day of the Lord and the terrible destructiveness of the army are described, 2-10, the locust (army) plague being in the background of the imagery.

The Lord's Army Appears, 11. This involves the second advent of Christ and is a phase of the titanic struggle at Armageddon (3:9-13; Rev 16:14). The saints and angels will constitute the Lord's "camp." For the expression "utter his voice," cf. Rev 19:15.

The Repentant Remnant, 12-17. The Lord calls upon the remnant in the land genuinely to repent, 12-13, and to receive the Lord's blessing, 14. All classes, 15-17, are included. None is excused, not even the newlywed bridegroom (cf. Deut 24:5).

The Lord's Response to the Repentant Jews in the Land, 18-27. Instead of His fiery wrath burning against them, the Lord's fiery jealousy will flame for them and His mercy go out toward them, 18. He promises temporal prosperity, 19; military deliverance, 20; joy and gladness, 21-23; restored rainfall and abundant harvests, 24-26; restored fellowship, 27. Scholars have translated 23 as "the former rain moderately" (AV). Others render it, "the teacher of righteousness," giving it a messianic connotation.

The Promise of the Outpoured Spirit, 28-32. Keil takes the outpouring of the Spirit as a second and later result of the gift of "the teacher of righteousness" (cf. 23). The "afterward" and "in the last days," 28 (Acts 2:16), refer to the days of Israel's exaltation and blessing in the opening era of the kingdom (Isa 2:2-4; Mic 4:1-7). The term "pour out" signifies communication in rich abundance (cf. Isa 32:15; Ezk 39:29). Peter's use of this prophecy at Pentecost (Acts 2:15-21) was illustrative of what the Spirit of God can do. Its fulfillment awaits the introduction of the Kingdom Age. The reason Peter quoted Joel was to show that the evidences of the outpoured Spirit at Pentecost were just a sample of what the Jew could expect when the OT promised kingdom is introduced. The kingdom outpouring is to be universal, 28-29, and is to be connected with the climactic phase of "the day of the Lord," 30-31, with preceding signs announcing the dispossession of wicked men at the setting up of Christ's kingdom on the earth, 32.

CHAPTER 3. THE JUDGMENT OF THE NATIONS

Israel's End-Time Restoration, 1. "In those days and in that time" denote that phase of "the day of the Lord" which will witness Israel's restoration (Isa 11:10-12; Jer 23:5-8; Ezk 37:21-28; Acts 15:15-17). This passage is introductory to the primary theme of the judgment of the nations, 2-8, inasmuch as that event is a necessary prerequisite to Israel's reinstatement. The nations that have persecuted Israel must be judged before Israel can be brought into safety and blessing (cf. Mt 25:31-46; Rom 11:25-27; Zech 6:1-8; Rev 16:14).

The Nations Judged, 2-16. The Lord Himself is the speaker, 2-8. He announces what He will do to Israel's enemies when He restores His people (note "My people," 3). The place of the judgment is said to be "the valley of Jehosaphat," 2, 12. This is usually taken as a symbolical rather than a geographical name, as inferred from the etymology, "*Yahweh* shall judge" and from 14, where the same valley is called the "valley of decision," in the sense of a judicial sentence or verdict (rendered against the wicked nations judged there). However, both Joel and Zechariah (cf. Zech 14:4) evidently regarded this theater of judgment as the Kidron Valley and the widening mountain basin to the S of the city beyond Hinnom. Kidron is now also known as the valley of Jehoshaphat, called so as early as Eusebius, but evidently on the basis of the Joel and Zechariah passages.

The basis of the judgment will be "on account of *my* people . . . my heritage Israel," 2. The sin of the nations has been their mistreatment of the Jew (cf. Ps 79:1-13; 83:1-18; Isa 29:1-8; 34:1-3; Jer 25:13-17; Zech 1:14-15; 12:2-3; Mt 25:31-46). Joel 3:2-3 indicates the crime of the nations, with special condemnation resting upon the Phoenicians and Philistines, 4-8. The Sabaeans, 8, were traders of SW Arabia. The judgment of the nations connects with Armageddon, 9-14 (Rev 16:13-16; 19:11-21), and 15-16 parallels 2:30-32. Verses 9-16 summarize 2:9-32.

Full Kingdom Blessing, 17-21. At last unbelieving Israel receives the Messiah, the true basis of their holiness, 17 (cf. Zech 14:20-21).

"My holy mountain" is Moriah, the temple hill (cf. Ps 2:6; Dan 11:45; Ob 16; Zech 8:3). The kingdom prosperity of Palestine, 18, is a common prophetic theme toward which all the prophets gravitate (cf. Isa 35:1-3). The related themes of the destruction of Israel's enemies, Egypt and Edom, 19 (cf. Zech 14:18-19), and the restoration of Judah, 20-21, are also prominent.

AMOS

Impending Judgment

The Times of Amos. Amos' ministry occurred in the latter part of the reign of Jeroboam II (*c.* 782-753 B.C.), when this prosperous and idolatrous sovereign ruled contemporaneously with Uzziah (Azariah) of Judah (*c.* 791-740 B.C.). Therefore 765-750 B.C. would be approximately the time of Amos. It was an age of economic boom with luxurious living, moral corruption and rampant idolatry. Amos directed his fiery oratory against these sins.

The Prophet. Amos ("burden") was a simple shepherd and dresser of sycamore fruit (7:14) from Tekoa, a hill country town about 10 miles S of Jerusalem. He was called to be prophet to the whole house of Jacob (3:1, 13), but chiefly to the northern kingdom (7:14-15) at the main sanctuary at Bethel (7:10). He met the opposition of the high priest Amaziah, who reported the fearless preacher to Jeroboam II. Amos doubtless reduced his prophecies to writing shortly after his return to Tekoa.

Outline
Judgment on Israel, Judah and Surrounding Nations, 1:1—2:16
The Lord's Indictment of the Whole House of Jacob, 3:1—9:10
    Four Condemnatory Sermons, 3:1—6:14
    Five Symbolic Predictions of Punishment, 7:1—9:10
Kingdom Blessing for Restored Israel, 9:11-15

1:1—2:3. JUDGMENT UPON SURROUNDING NATIONS

Superscription, 1:1-2. The earthquake is mentioned again in Zech 14:5. The Lord "roars" as a lion in mounting wrath against increasing sin. Carmel ("the garden or orchard"), a prominent headland jutting into the Mediterranean, was famous for its luxuriant growth of plants in antiquity.

Judgment Upon Six Nations, 1:3—2:3.

Judgment upon Damascus, 3-5. Damascus was the capital of a powerful Aramaean city-state that harassed Israel (*c.* 900-780 B.C.), especially under Benhadad I (*c.* 880-842) and Hazael (*c.* 842-806). "For three transgressions . . . and for four," 3, 6, 9, 11, 13; 2:1; 2:4, 6, means sin multiplied on sin, more than enough (cf. Prov 30:18; Job 33:14). It was Hazael, the usurper, 3-4, who threshed Gilead in Transjordan "with threshing sledges of iron" (2 Kgs 10:32-33; 13:7). The bar of Damascus, 5, was the bar of its gates (Jer 51:30). The strongholds of Benhadad, 4, were the fortresses of Benhadad II, son of Hazael (2 Kgs 13:3). The valley of Aven, 5, is the valley of On, not far from Damascus. Beth-eden (AV, "house of Eden"; Bit-idini of the Assyrian tablets) was situated by the Euphrates River, called Eden (Ezk 27:23).

ARCHAEOLOGICAL LIGHT

On Hazael, see comments on 2 Kgs 8. Kir is in Mesopotamia and is the place from which the Aramaeans migrated (9:7), and to which they were exiled (2 Kgs 16:9).

Judgment upon Philistia, 6-8. Gaza, Ashdod, Ashkelon and Ekron were judged because they sold the Israelites into slavery to Edom (2 Chr 21:16-17; Joel 3:4-8).

Judgment upon Tyre, 9-10. Cf. Joel 3:4-8 for its inhuman cruelty against Israel. "Covenant of brotherhood" refers to the covenant David and Solomon made with Tyre (cf. 1 Kgs 9:13).

Judgment upon Edom, 11-12. Though closely related to Israel ("his brother"), 11, yet he was pitiless in his hatred and cruelty (cf. Mal 1:2; Ob 1-21). Teman is doubtless Tawilan SE of Sela (Petra), and Bozrah is in north central Edom.

Judgment upon Ammon, 13-15 (cf. Zeph 2:8-11). The Ammonites, N of Moab, with capital at Rabbah (modern Amman), ravaged neighboring Gilead.

Judgment upon Moab, 2:1-3. So fierce was their hatred they desecrated the body of the Edomite king by cremation (cf. 2 Kgs 3:26-27).

2:4-16. JUDGMENT UPON JUDAH AND ISRAEL

Judgment upon Judah, 4-5. Judah and Israel were as guilty as the nations around them and would be punished.

Judgment upon Israel, 6-16. Israel's judgment was put in the same literary form and was more detailed because she enjoyed greater light and was more privileged.

CHAPTER 3. ISRAEL'S GREATER PRIVILEGE AND GUILT

Israel's Culpability Because of Her Greater Privilege, 1-11. She was a nationally elect nation, redeemed out of Egypt and under covenant responsibility (Ex 19:4-6; Deut 6:7; Lk 12:48). Her failure would therefore be severely judged, 1-2. Let Israel make an appointment to walk with the Lord, 3, to hear His warnings of judgment through His prophets and approaching calamity, 4-8, because as the Lord's elect nation she had been such a poor example to her pagan neighbors, 9-11.

The Thoroughness of the Divine Judgment, 12-15. This is vividly set forth, 12. The calamity would center upon the paganized altars at Bethel, 14, and the polluted wealth of the prosperous sinners of Jeroboam II's reign. "Houses of ivory," 15 (cf. 1 Kgs 22:39), were so called because they were lavishly decorated with ivory inlays. Numerous fragments of such inlay have come to light in the archaeological diggings at ancient Samaria in the "Samaritan ivories."

CHAPTER 4. PREPARE TO MEET THY GOD, O ISRAEL

Indictment of the Wealthy Women of Samaria, 1-3. These greedy, vain women (cf. Isa 3:16-26) were called "cows of Bashan," 1 (cf. Ps 22:12). This was a rebuke for their responsibility in making unnecessary demands upon the men for the luxuries of life. Bashan was a fertile area E of the Sea of Galilee known for its sleek, fat cattle.

Israel's Abominable Ritualism, 4-5. They loved empty idolatrous ceremonialism in the name of religion. Bethel was the idol-ridden royal sanctuary and Gilgal was another polluted shrine.

Israel Must Face God's Judgment, 6-13. Failing to respond to God's chastening love, 6-11, Israel must now get ready to face God's justice and wrath, 12, and realize how great He is in His power, wisdom and justice, 13.

CHAPTER 5. SEEK THE LORD AND LIVE

A Lament for the Fallen and Forsaken Nation, 1-3. She who had once been a virgin, separated to the Lord, was now fallen into harlotries and abominations, unable to help herself, and was due for impoverishment by enemy invasion and death.

Seek the Lord, 4-17. If they would be spared national death, let them seek the Lord, not the idolatrous ritualism at Bethel, Gilgal and Beersheba. Idolatry was a criminal abomination in the light of who the Lord was, 8-9, and its practice productive of every type of immorality, 10-13. Therefore, they were to forsake it and seek the Lord, 14-17.

Be Warned of the Day of the Lord, 18-20. How wrong they were to think of it piously as a day of vindication against their foes. It would engulf them in its gloom.

The Lord's Hatred of Their Empty Religionism, 21-27. To avert disaster, justice must "roll down like waters, and righteousness like an overflowing stream," 24 (RSV)—the essence of Amos' message. Sakkuth and Kaiwan, 26 (RSV), were Assyrian gods (Acts 7:42-43), designations of Saturn. "Tabernacle of your Moloch" (AV) should read "Sakkuth your king."

CHAPTER 6. CALAMITY UPON THE SELF-SECURE

Warning to Self-Indulgent Sinners, 1-7. Let the secure in Zion (Jerusalem's temple hill, i.e., Judah) and in the mountain of Samaria (the hill of Shemer, upon which Samaria was built, i.e., by metonymy, the northern kingdom) take warning, 1, from the fate of Calneh in N. Syria and Hamath on the Orontes in Syria (the latter now well known from the Danish excavations there conducted by H. Ingholt). The dissipating indulgence, 4-5, and spiritual unconcern, 6, of the carnal rich in Samaria would result in early captivity to Assyria, as happened to Calneh and Hamath. "Beds of ivory" (cf. 3:12-15 note) speak of the prosperity of Israel.

Punishment Is Inevitable, 8-14. The solemn certainty was emphasized by the Lord's oath sworn by Himself, 8 (cf. Gen 22:16-17). Pride and injustice could not go unpunished. Entrance of Hamath, 14 (cf. 1 Kgs 8:65; 2 Kgs 14:28), marked Israel's ideal N boundary, while the "Brook of the Arabah" (RSV), probably the brook Zered (Wadi el-Hesa, which flows into the SE end of the Dead Sea), marked its extreme S border.

CHAPTER 7. THE LOCUST PLAGUE, THE DROUGHT AND THE PLUMB LINE

Amos presents five symbolic predictions of punishment, 7:1—9:10.

The Locust Plague, 1-3. Impending judgment was prophesied by the Lord's "forming locusts in the beginning of the shooting up of the latter growth . . . after the king's mowings," 1 (RSV). So terrible was it, the Lord repented (cf. Joel 1—2).

The Drought, 4-6. This is evidently the meaning of this judgment by "fire" (cf. Joel 1:19). Amos' plea for mercy stayed this plague also.

The Plumb Line, 7-9. The Lord, however, declared the irrevocable sentence of destruction, after having measured His people with a plumb line (2 Kgs 21:13-15), and finding them so irremediably warped by sin as to be past correction.

Amos and Amaziah, 10-17. Amos' bold prediction against the house of Jeroboam of the Jehu dynasty, 9, aroused the weak crown-loyal official priest of the royal sanctuary at Bethel to report Amos to the king. This weak religious conformist urged Amos to flee to Judah. Amos' reply showed his magnificent spiritual stature in that decadent syncretistic age, 16-17. There was one brave soul at least who would buck the tide of iniquity and easy conformity. He was God-called and not a mere man-pleasing ecclesiastic.

CHAPTER 8. THE FRUIT BASKET

The Basket of Summer Produce, 1-3. The basket of perishable produce of the land symbolized the immediacy of Israel's end.

The Reason for the End, 4-14. Israel's terrible sin called forth scathing indictment. Crooked businessmen chafed at the sacred festal seasons and at the sabbath, because they caused a lull in their dishonest money-making activities, 4-5, and their oppression of the poor, 6 (cf. Isa 1:13-17; Lev 19:35-36; Deut 25:13-16). The judgment detailed for "Jacob's pride," 7, embraced mourning, 8-10, and famine of the word of the Lord, 11-14. Idolatry and pride put out the light God gave through His word.

Dan and Beersheba were pagan shrines in the farthest northern and southern limits of the land, 14. The patron deities of these idolatrous centers would be powerless to help in the coming calamity. "The sin [*ashimah*] of Samaria," 14, is rendered "Ashimah of Samaria" in RSV, representing a deliberate Heb. distortion of the name of Asherah, the Canaanite mother goddess, to conform to the Heb. word for "guilt" (*'asham*).

9:1-10. THE LORD AT THE ALTAR

The Lord at the Altar, 1-6. The Lord standing "beside" (rather than "upon") the altar pronounced judgment. Properly symbolizing mercy because of judgment executed upon an interposed sacrifice, the altar, desecrated by idolatry and despised, became a place of poured-out judgment (Jn 12:31). This was the reason for the relentless pursuit of these sinners by the justice of God, 2-4. Because the Lord is the mighty God He is, 5-6, He must punish those who reject His mercy.

The Lord and Sinful Israel, 7-10. The Lord would destroy every sinful kingdom, Israel not excepted. His chosen nation had no special privilege in the moral sphere. The prophet tempered his teaching on election (3:2) with his doctrine of universalism (ch. 1—2). Caphtor, 7, was Crete. Kir was somewhere in Mesopotamia (Isa 22:6).

9:11-15. FUTURE KINGDOM BLESSING

Messiah's Return and Reign, 11-15. "The tabernacle [booth] of David" is the Davidic dynasty the Lord will raise up in the Person of the Christ returning in glory at His second advent to establish the kingdom over Israel (Acts 1:6). James quoted this great prophecy at the first church council (Acts 15:15-17). The Holy Spirit on that momentous occasion employed it to unfold the divine program for the future; that is, in this present age God is calling out a people for His name. After that the Lord will return and reestablish the Davidic dynasty in Christ, 11-12, and millennial prosperity, 13, will result in a restored Israel, 14-15.

OBADIAH

GOD'S RETRIBUTIVE JUSTICE

Nature of the Book. This is the shortest prophecy and the smallest book of the OT. Its author was Obadiah, whose name means "the servant of the Lord." The prophecy is wholly taken up with the condemnation of Edom for its treachery toward Judah, with a prophecy of its utter destruction and Judah's salvation in the day of the Lord.

Date. Although numerous critics deny the unity of the prophecy, placing it in the Chaldean period after Jerusalem's fall in 586 B.C. or later, it is best to hold to the authenticity of the book and date it during the reign of Jehoram (c. 848-841 B.C.). At that time the Philistines and Arabians invaded Judah and plundered Jerusalem (2 Chr 21:16-17; Joel 3:3-6; Amos 1:6). The Edomites were also bitter enemies of Judah in that period (2 Kgs 8:20-22; 2 Chr 21:8-10). Thus, the requirements of Obadiah's having written this prophecy are satisfied in the historical context.

Obadiah and Amos. Amos (c. 760 B.C.) shows acquaintance with Obadiah (cf. 4 with Amos 9:2; vv. 9, 10, 18 with Amos 1:11-12; v. 14 with Amos 1:6, 9; v. 19 with Amos 9:12; v. 20 with Amos 9:14). Jeremiah apparently used this prophecy also (cf. Jer 49:7-22 with Ob 1-6). This gives additional support for an early date for the prophecy.

Outline
Edom's Destruction Foretold, 1-9
Cause of Edom's Fall, 10-14
The Day of the Lord, 15-21

1-9. EDOM'S DESTRUCTION FORETOLD

Dislodged from Her Mountain Fortresses, 1-4. Obadiah ("servant of the Lord") is unknown, identifiable with none of the dozen or so men in the OT who bore the same name. Edom ("the red region") was Israel's neighbor on the SE, S of Moab and the Dead Sea. Its copper- and iron-rich territory extended S to the Gulf of Aqaba. Its entire boundary was dotted with a series of fortresses. North Edom ranges from 5,000 to 5,300 feet above sea level with one of its chief forts at Bozrah (modern Buseireh). Southern Edom with its mountains and plateaus rises from 5,300 to 5.700 feet above sea level, its chief fortress being Teman (Tawilan). Edom's pride, 3, was to be humbled. The expressions, "the clefts of the rock" (Sela, Gr. *Petra*), 3, and "nest set among the stars," 4, admirably fit the country and the people.

Plundered and Deserted Completely, 5-9. Esau, 6 (Gen 25:30; 36:1), was the progenitor of the Edomites. Since he was Jacob's twin brother, there was close kinship between the Edomites and the Israelites (cf. "brother Jacob," 10). Esau's treasure was enormous wealth from iron and copper mines, and caravan·trade, 6. Edom was famous for her wise men (Jer 49:7).

10-14. CAUSE OF EDOM'S FALL

"For the violence done to your brother Jacob," 10 (RSV), describes Edom's failure to help his brother in distress. Edom became as culpable as those who attacked Jerusalem, 12; in fact, it did share in the attack, 13-14 (cf. Num 20:14-21; Ps 137:7; Ezk 35:5).

15-21. THE DAY OF THE LORD

In verse 15 the prophet links the future with the past in a prediction still unfulfilled, "For the day of the Lord is near upon *all the nations*" (RSV). All nations will be judged as to their treatment of Israel, as Edom was (cf. Mt 25:31-46; Rev 16:13-16; with Joel 3:1-14). Jacob's deliverance and salvation, 17-20, are described (cf. Joel 2:32). "The south," 19, is the Negeb, the semi-desert region S of Judah. The inhabitants of the Judean foothills (Heb. "falling off [region]" or "Shephelah") shall inherit the Philistine plain, 19. Gilead was in Transjordan. "Halah," 20 (RSV), referring to "the captivity of this host," is in Mesopotamia (cf. 2 Kgs 17:6). Sepharad, 20, is uncertain; it may be Sardis in Asia Minor. Zarephath was a Phoenician town between Sidon and Tyre. Israelite "saviours" in the Kingdom Age shall administrate Edom. The Lord Himself in kingdom power shall rule over all (Ps 22:28; 103:19).

JONAH

ISRAEL'S MISSION TO THE NATIONS

Jonah the Man. Jonah ("dove") was the son of Amittai who came from Gath-hepher (Khirbet ez-Zurra⁰) some three miles NE of Nazareth. A short distance to the N of this site is located the traditional tomb of Jonah at a village called Meshhed. Jonah's ministry shortly preceded that of Amos under Jeroboam II (782-753 B.C.), and predicted victory over the Syrians and the largest extenson of Israelite border control (2 Kgs 14:25).

The Book. The book is more than biographical history. It is *predictive typical history,* written by a prophet and possessing a prophetic motif. As such it prefigures Christ as the Sent One, suffering death, being buried, and after being raised, ministering salvation to the Gentiles (Mt 12:39-41; Lk 11:29-32).

Joppa, ancient town from which Jonah set sail. (© *MPS*)

CHAPTER 1. JONAH'S CALL AND DISOBEDIENCE

The Divine Call and Attempted Escape, 1-3. "Nineveh, that great city" is aptly designated. At this period it was the capital of the Assyrian Empire at its height, and until its fall in 612 B.C. was the greatest city of the time. Its excavated ruins are marked primarily by two large mounds, Quyunjiq and Nebi Yunus (Prophet Jonah), enclosed by walls almost eight miles in circumference sprawling on the east bank of the Tigris across the river from modern Mosul. Nineveh's wickedness is amplified by Nahum (Nah 3).

Jonah's proposed flight to Tarshish, 3, in open rebellion against the Lord, 3-4, represents the most distant point the disobedient prophet could go. It was probably Tartessus in S. Spain near Gibraltar, a trading station visited by Tarshish or smelting fleets that traded in smelted copper. Joppa (modern Jaffa) was Palestine's ancient seaport 34 miles NW of Jerusalem, then the only harbor between Mt. Carmel and Egypt.

The Storm at Sea, 4-7. The Lord violently "hurls a great wind upon the sea," 4 (RSV), to retrieve the recalcitrant prophet. The heathen sailors (Heb. "salts"), 5, were well-seasoned mariners and rebuked the snoring Jonah, insensible of his peril, 6. Disobedience to God's word always brings spiritual torpor and frequently results in rebuke from the unsaved.

Jonah's Witness and Fate, 8-17. In identifying himself he confessed his own sin, but even this furnished a witness to the pagan seamen. They realized the gulf between his creed and his conduct. The calmed sea evidently was a means of their conversion. Five "greats" occur in the book: the *great* refusal, 3; the *great* fish, 17; a *great* city, 2; a *great* jealousy, 4:1; and a *great* God, 4:2b. Jonah, however, was not "a *great* prophet."

CHAPTER 2. JONAH'S PRAYER AND DELIVERANCE

His Prayer of Thanksgiving, 1-9. Remarkably this prayer is not petition of desperate entreaty but thankful praise for escape from physical death. His severe chastening to the point of physical death (cf. 1 Cor 5:5; 11:31-32; 1 Jn 5:16-17; Heb 12:4-11) resulted in renewed spiritual life. Jonah's praise is reminiscent of the Psalms. (Cf. 2:2 with Ps 120:1; 2:3 with Ps 42:7; 2:4 with Ps 31:22; 2:7 with Ps 143:4; 2:8 with Ps 31:6; 2:9 with Ps 3:8.)

His Deliverance, 10. When he had learned his lesson, he was delivered to do God's will. The course of disobedience Jonah took proved to be the roughest distance between two points involved in God's will.

CHAPTER 3. JONAH'S RENEWED COMMISSION

Jonah's Obedience, 1-4. Verse 3 should read, "Now Nineveh was an extremely large city requiring three days' travel." That is, to go around the complex of suburbs that made up the great metropolis required three days (cf. notes on 1:2 and Gen 10:11-12). The long buried and forgotten city has amazed the archaeologist in its resurrection from dust since 1843. It was a complex of cities like modern New York, including Calah to the south, Resen between Calah and Nineveh proper, and Rehoboth-Ir (Rebit-Ninua) W of the capital. Other suburbs included Tarbisu and Dur-sharrukin (Sargonsburg). The latter swelled the size but was not yet built when Jonah preached to the Ninevites.

Nineveh Repents, 5-10. Under Adad-nirari III (810-782 B.C.), there was an approach to monotheism in the worship of the god Nabu (Nebo). Either in the closing years of this reign or early in that of Ashur-dan III (772-755 B.C.), Jonah appeared in Nineveh. Whether the total eclipse in 763 B.C., regarded as a divine portent, or the plagues of 765 and 759 B.C., recorded in Assyrian history, prepared the Ninevites for monotheism cannot be known. Sackcloth, 5, rough goat's hair worn over the naked body, was a garb of mourning. Nineveh was spared, 10 (cf. Amos 1—2).

CHAPTER 4. JONAH'S REACTION TO THE REVIVAL

Jonah is Angered, 1-5. The pagan emperor of Assyria (3:7-9) sets a better example than the selfish, narrow-minded prophet.

The Prophet Rebuked, 6-11. He must be shown that God loves all His creatures, not only sinful Ninevites but even dumb cattle.

MICAH

PERSONAL AND SOCIAL RIGHTEOUSNESS

Micah the Poet and Isaiah. Micah's prophecy is a beautiful and moving example of classical Heb. poetry. Like his contemporary, Isaiah, Micah possessed great literary power. While Isaiah was a court poet, Micah was a rustic from an obscure village. Isaiah was a statesman; Micah, an evangelist and social reformer. Isaiah was a voice to kings; Micah, a herald for God to the common people. Isaiah addressed himself to political questions; Micah dealt almost entirely with personal religion and social morality.

Great Emphases of Micah. (1) Back to Bethlehem (5:2), back to David, back to Messiah, David's son and Lord. (2) Back to ethical righteousness (6:8), the practice of justice, kindness, compassion, mercy and humility. (3) Back to the coming Prince of Peace (4:3), "this man" who shall be "our peace" (5:5), the world's only hope of permanent peace.

Outline

General Prediction of Judgment, Ch. 1—3
The Coming Messianic Kingdom, Ch. 4—5
The Lord's Controversy with His People and Final Mercy,
Ch. 6—7

CHAPTER 1. JUDGMENT UPON SAMARIA AND JUDAH

Introduction, 1. The name Micah is apparently a shortened form of *Mikayahu,* "who is like the Lord" (cf. 7:18; Jer 26:18). He was a native of Moresheth, a small village, identified with Tell ed-Judeideh, about 20 miles SW of Jerusalem near Gath in N. Philistia (cf. 14 where it is called Moresheth-gath). Micah was contemporary with Isaiah (see Isa 1:1), prophesying in the days of Jotham (750-736 B.C.), Ahaz (743-716 B.C.), and Hezekiah (716-687 B.C.).

Judgment upon Samaria, 2-7. The city of Samaria was founded by Omri (1 Kgs 16:24), about 857 B.C. So prosperous did this new city become it soon gave its name to the entire northern kingdom, of which it was the capital. This splended city, whose brilliance has been revealed by archaeology, became a heap of rubble and her stones rolled down the hill of Shemer upon which it was built. This happened in 722 B.C., when Sargon of Assyria took the city. In his Khorsabad annals Sargon (722-705 B.C.) says: "At the beginning of my rule, in my first year of reign . . . Samerinai [the people of Samaria] . . . 27,290 . . . who lived therein, I carried away. . . ."

Lamentation over Samaria and Judah, 8-16. As a sign of the impending Assyrian invasion, Micah went naked, predicting the judgment of enemy invasion up to the very gates of Jerusalem, 8-9. In 701 B.C. Sennacherib's army took all the walled cities of Palestine and laid siege to Jerusalem itself. Micah, the poet, graphically predicted the terrors of the coming invasion by a series of lively puns, 10-14. Moffat freely translates this: "Weep *tears* at *Tear*town [Bochim], grovel in the *dust* at *Dust*town [Beth-ophrah]," 10. "*Fare* forth stripped, O *Fair*town" (*Shaphir,* "fair"). "*Stir*town [Zaanan] dare not stir," 11. "Harness your steed and away, O *Horse*town [Lachish] . . ." 13. "Israel's kings are ever *balked* at *Balk*town [Achzib]."

CHAPTERS 2—3. JUDGMENT UPON VARIOUS CLASSES

The Leaders of Samaria and Jerusalem Mislead, 2:1-11. They devised wickedness at night and performed it by day, 1-5. Seer and prophet preached lies, 6-11. Social and moral sins of the nation cried for judgment.

Mercy upon a Remnant, 2:12-13. The Lord would gather out His own.

Denunciation of Various Classes, 3:1-12. The oppressors of the poor are indicated, 1-4. Their terrible greed is forcefully pictured by the figures of wild beasts tearing their victims, and a butcher cutting up meat for boiling. The mercenary prophets and seers, who huckstered their solemn office to please sinners, were to be cut off from God, the true source of revelation, 5-7. Micah, by contrast, was filled with the Spirit and faithful in the deliverance of his message, 8. Mercenary priests were also upbraided and judgment was focused on Jerusalem, 9-12, fulfilled in the fall of the city in 586 B.C.

CHAPTER 4. THE ESTABLISHMENT OF MESSIAH'S KINGDOM

Character of the Kingdom, 1-5. Ch. 4 and 5 present Israel's glorious future and the restoration of the Davidic kingdom. Verses 1-3 are

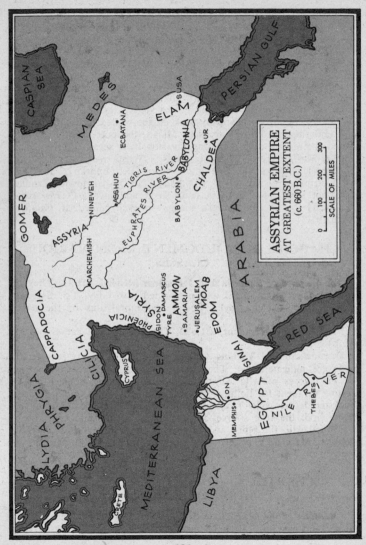

ASSYRIAN EMPIRE
AT GREATEST EXTENT
(c. 660 B.C.)

SCALE OF MILES
0   100   200   300

duplicated by Isaiah (2:2-4). Both prophets received this message by divine inspiration, as they were contemporary. The mountain is Zion, 1, and the house is the millennial temple (Ezk 40—42). The prediction is that Jerusalem will be exalted in the kingdom to be the religious and governmental center of the earth, 2. The people are the nations which will "flow" into Jerusalem spontaneously like a river, 1. The character of the restored Davidic kingdom, 3-4, its justice and peace, 3, and its security, 4, are presented. Verse 5 should read: "For all the peoples walk [i.e., now are walking] each in the name of his god, but *we* will walk in the name of the Lord our God [i.e., free from idolatry] perpetually." The verse predicates that Israel will be free from idolatry in the kingdom, but does not say or even imply that the nations will not be free also.

Establishment of the Kingdom, 6-13. Israel is to be regathered into the kingdom, 6-8 (Isa 11:11-16), the Babylonian Captivity, 9-10, intervening and typifying the final regathering. The manner of the setting up of the kingdom after the end-time assault of the nations upon Jerusalem is set forth, 11-13, eventuating in the battle of Armageddon. Jerusalem's victory, 11-13, is outlined as she threshes the sheaves (the hostile nations) gathered against her. "The Lord of the whole earth" is a kingdom appellative of Christ when He returns as King of kings and Lord of lords (Rev. 19:16) to take possession of the earth, *His* by virtue of creation and redemption (cf. Gen 14:19, 22; Josh 3:11, 13; Zech 4:14; 6:5; Rev 11:4).

CHAPTER 5. THE FIRST AND SECOND ADVENTS OF MESSIAH

Prospect and Retrospect, 1. The future siege of Jerusalem by the end-time northern invader is in prospect in 1a (cf. Joel 1), connecting with the preceding context. The smitten Judge is in retrospect in 1b (cf. Mt 26:67; 27:30), presenting in the rejected Messiah the reason for Israel's long history of woe, culminating in the event prophesied in 1a. Smiting upon the cheek was the acme of insult (1 Kgs 22:24; Job 16:10).

His First Advent and Rejection, 2. Verse 2 tells who the "smitten Judge" of 1 is. He is the Bethlehem-born preexistent, eternal One (cf. Isa 9:6-7). The Davidic family is significantly denoted as Ephrathites (Ruth 1:2; 1 Sam 17:12), that is, residents of Ephrath, a suburb of Bethlehem, which later became incorporated into the town. The double designation here not only connects Messiah with the Davidic line, but both Bethlehem ("house [place] of food") and

Ephratah ("productivity") are reminiscent of the fertility of the region.

Interval Between the Advents, 3. Verse 2 is parenthetical, "therefore" of 3 connecting with the rejection of Israel's Judge, 1b. "Therefore will he [the Lord] give them up" refers to Israel's woes because of her rejection of Messiah. "She who travaileth" does not have reference to Israel as bringing forth the Messiah but to her last-day tribulation travail in bringing forth a believing remnant, here called "the remnant of his [Christ's] brethren," as in Mt 25:31-46.

The Second Advent, 4-6. The rejected One now becomes the Shepherd of Israel, standing and feeding in "the strength of the Lord," 4, for He is the Lord. Therefore "they" (the saved remnant) shall dwell securely as He extends His kingdom sway over the redeemed earth. "This man shall be the peace," 5 (cf. Isa 9:6-7; Zech 9:10), who made peace by the blood of His cross, and is our peace (Eph 2:14-15), as well as Israel's (Isa 9:7). The reference here is to the peace He has purchased and dispenses to His restored people Israel, the peace attained by striking down the northern invader of the end-time, 6, the last-day Assyrian from "the land of Nimrod" (Assyria, Gen 10:9-11).

The Blessed Remnant and the Kingdom, 7-15. The twofold character of the remnant is given as: (1) a spiritual witness and blessing, 7, and (2) an avenger of wrongs and destroyer of enemies, 8-9. Instruments of war shall be done away with, 10-11; and all demonic cults and idolatry, such as "Asherim" (pagan cult objects of Asherah, fertility goddess), shall be rooted out, 12-15.

CHAPTERS 6—7. FINAL CONTROVERSY AND MERCY

The People's Ingratitude and Sin, 6:1—7:6. The Lord's controversy was with His people, 6:1-8, because they had forgotten His mercies of old and the practice of common piety. The Lord must judge them, 6:9-16. Micah exposed their sin, 7:1-6.

Confession, Petition and Thanksgiving, 7:7-20. This echoes the voice of the remnant in the end-time through the prophet who identified himself with Israel (cf. Dan 9:3-19). Those in Israel who kept faith, like himself, had an unquenchable trust in the Lord's faithfulness to restore the nation eventually in fulfillment of all His promises.

NAHUM

GOD'S HOLINESS VINDICATED IN JUDGMENT

Nahum's Theme. The prophet has one theme, judgment upon Nineveh, the capital of the mighty Assyrian Empire (see notes on Jon 3:1-4), and hence on Assyria, the "giant among the Semites." Its tyrannical cruelty scourged the ancient world periodically from 850 B.C. till its fall in 612 B.C. Nahum's ministry was exercised between the conquest of No-Amon (Thebes) in Egypt (3:8) in 661 B.C. and Nineveh's fall in 612 B.C. The book is a classic of Heb. poetry, exceedingly fine and vivid in its descriptions. Critical attempts to deny part of the poem to Nahum have not been very successful.

> **Outline**
> A Psalm of God's Majesty, Ch. 1
> Prophecy of Ninevah's Fall, Ch. 2—3

CHAPTER 1. GOD'S MAJESTIC HOLINESS

Superscription, 1. Nahum ("consoler" or "comforter") was a native of Elkosh (unknown). His prophecy of judgment upon wicked Nineveh and his indication of God's mercy to His own constitute him a "consoler" to those who do good. A "burden" is a prophecy full of weighty judgment.

Character of God in Judgment, 2-11. On one hand God is jealous, the source of His passion being in His love for His people, 2. Yet on the other hand He is also infinitely holy and must manifest His vengeance against those who wrong His people. He must punish the wicked, 3. His manifestation of His character in judgment is revealed, 4-6. The Lord is also good to those who trust in Him, 7, but severe in His dealings with His enemies, 8. Let none of His people vainly imagine He will not punish His enemies in a thorough-going fashion, 9. The judgment of the Assyrian was assured, 10, from whom "a wicked counsellor" (Rabshakeh, 2 Kgs 18:13-37) came, 11.

The Fall of Nineveh Announced, 12-15. The Lord (through the prophet) announced Nineveh's coming doom, 12, 14, and deliverance for Israel, 12b, 13. Israel's glad proclamation of the good news of Nineveh's fall is a prefigurement of the fall of Israel's enemies in the last days and the joyous announcement of the final deliverance of Israel for kingdom blessing and worship, 15 (cf. Isa 52:7; Rom 10:15).

CHAPTER 2. SIEGE AND DESTRUCTION OF NINEVEH

The Overthrow of Nineveh Predicted and Described, 1-12. In superb poetry Nahum dramatically portrays the city's siege. Under the combined attacks of the Medes of the north and the Chaldeans from southern Babylonia, Asshur, the ancient capital of the empire, fell in 614 B.C. In 612 B.C., Nineveh collapsed, ending Assyrian sway. Some scholars believe Nineveh's patron goddess Ishtar is referred to in 7.

The Reason for Nineveh's Destruction, 13. The Lord was *against* her.

CHAPTER 3. NINEVEH AN EXAMPLE OF GOD'S JUDGMENT

Her Sins Reap Their Harvest, 1-17. Her violence, 1-3, her deceptions and false dealings with other nations are outlined, 4-7. The case of No-Amon (Thebes), the great Egyptian city, was a warning when it fell in 661 B.C., 8-10. Nineveh's fortifications and armaments would be useless, 11-13, her efforts to ward off disaster would come to nought, 14-17. She was doomed.

Lament over the King of Assyria, 18-19. Dramatically he was addressed in the first person. His destruction was declared, 18; and the joy it would cause is outlined, 19. (See note on Jon 3:1-3.)

HABAKKUK

THE JUST SHALL LIVE BY FAITH

The Prophet and His Message. Practically nothing is known of the prophet Habakkuk. It can be inferred, however, that he lived in the period of the rise of the neo-Babylonian Empire (*c.* 625 B.C.), for the Chaldean invasion of Judah was threatening (1:5-6) and the iniquity of Judah was mounting. Habakkuk's theme centers in the theological question of how God's patience with evil can square with His holiness. The answer the prophet received is valid for all time. A sovereign God has the incontestable prerogative of dealing with the wicked in His own time and way. "But the righteous shall live by his faith" (2:4, RSV).

Literary Beauty. Habakkuk, like Nahum and Isaiah, is couched in sublime poetry, reflecting the classical era of Heb. prophecy. The magnificent lyric ode of ch. 3 contains one of the greatest descriptions of the theophany in relation to the coming of the Lord which has been given by the Holy Spirit, awaiting fulfillment in the day of the Lord (cf. 2 Thess 1:7-10).

Outline

Judah's Judgment Through the Chaldeans Announced, Ch. 1
Ultimate Judgment upon the Chaldeans Predicted, Ch. 2
The Prophet's Vision of the Coming King, Ch. 3

CHAPTER 1. JUDAH'S JUDGMENT BY THE CHALDEANS

Problem: Why the Lord Had Not Judged Judah's Sin, 1-4. Habakkuk ("embrace") takes hold of the Lord and raises the question of the Lord's just government of the world. How can a holy God tolerate the sin of His own people Judah, 1-4?

The Divine Solution, 5-11. The Chaldeans would judge Judah. According to Acts 13:37-41, verse 5 anticipates the redemptive work of Christ. The Chaldeans, or neo-Babylonians, ruled the ancient Near East 612-539 B.C., tyrannically administering a justice all its own and worshiping its own might (cf. 11, RSV, "whose might is their god"). The Chaldeans were aggressive Semitic-Aramaean nomads who gradually settled in southern Babylonia (Chaldea from Akkadian *Kaldu*). Nabopolassar (625-605 B.C.) was the founder of the Chaldean Empire, inherited by his son Nebuchadnezzar II (605-562 B.C.). Verse 10 accurately portrays the military practice of the Chaldeans in throwing up earthen ramparts to take fortresses.

Problem: Why the Wicked Chaldeans Were Used to Punish Judah, 12-17. How could the Lord employ people more wicked than His own sinning people as a rod of punishment? The question of God's holy character is discussed in the light of His silence in this matter, 12-13. The ruthless savagery of the Chaldean is pictured. Like a fisherman with rod and net, the Babylonian sat beside a pond which God had abundantly stocked with human fish, 14-15. Pulling up fish after fish, and eating to heart's content, he dumped out the surplus on the bank to die, 17. How long would this outrage of waste of human life go on and this brutality go unchecked by God's righteous intervention, 17?

CHAPTER 2. THE LORD'S SOLUTION—JUDGMENT OF THE CHALDEANS

A Righteous Remnant to Be Preserved, 1-5. The prophet takes his stand to watch and stations himself on "the tower" (place of quiet solitude where God could break in upon his listening soul and answer his perplexities), 1. The Lord's answer: "Write the vision; make it plain upon tablets, *so he may run* who reads it," 2 (RSV), i.e., as a messenger of the vision (cf. Zech 2:4-5). Those not upright in soul, 4, shall fall, "but the righteous shall live by his faith" (the godly remnant).

The Chaldeans Themselves Shall Be Punished, 6-19. The five woes of this indictment fall upon the nation that plunders "peoples," 6-8; obtains gain by violence, 9-11; erects "a town with blood," 12-14; debauches its neighbors, 15-17; and trusts in idols, 18-19. Noteworthy is the fact that in the midst of these woes the prophet catches a glimpse of the future Kingdom Age, 14, when all these evils will be extirpated (cf. Isa 11:9, which fixes the fulfillment of this prophecy when David's righteous Branch [Christ] has set up the kingdom): The transfiguration in Lk 9:26-29 was a preview of this happy event. "The glory of the Lord," 14, will be Christ revealed in kingly splendor (Mt 24:30; 25:31).

The Sovereign Lord Is Ruling, 20. This is part of the Lord's answer to the prophet. The Lord has not absconded His holy temple (cf. Zeph 1:7; Zech 2:13.), nor does His habitation cease to be holy. This is sufficient for the entire globe to be silent before Him, because His sovereign power and righteousness are operative in *all* the earth.

CHAPTER 3. VISION OF THE LORD'S COMING AND KINGDOM

The Prophet's Prayer, 1-2. The prophet is thankful for the revelation of God's work and stands in awe of it. In anticipating the final consummation in the day of the Lord, he pleads for mercy in the midst of wrath. "Shigionoth," 1, is unknown.

The Coming of the Lord as Judge and Warrior, 3-15 (cf. Deut 33:2; Ps 18:8-19; 68:8; 77:17-20; Isa 63:1-6; Rev 6:1—19:16). Paran lay SE of Edom, and Mt. Paran is a prominent peak of the Sinai wilderness highlands, 3. Teman is in south central Edom near Sela (Petra), 3. Cushan, 7, is in Midian, S of Edom and E of the Gulf of Aqabah. "Selah" is a pause for a musical interlude.

The Effect of the Theophany upon the Prophet, 16-19. His reaction and quiet trust reflect the attitude of the future godly remnant during the Great Tribulation, 16. He professes his deep faith in God, despite outward sufferings to be endured, 17-19.

ZEPHANIAH

A WARNING OF JUDGMENT

Date. Zephaniah, a contemporary of Jeremiah, exercised his ministry during the reign of Josiah (640-608 B.C.). He was doubtless instrumental in Josiah's revival (2 Kgs 22—23; 2 Chr 34—35), but the spiritual movement proved superficial with the captivity impending (cf. Jer 2:11-13). Zephaniah had access to the royal court and had an influence on King Josiah's policies.

> **Outline**
> Judah's Coming Doom, 1:1-18
> Judgment upon Surrounding Nations, 2:1—3:8
> Israel in Kingdom Blessing, 3:9-20

CHAPTER 1. JUDAH'S DOOM AND THE DAY OF THE LORD

Judgment of the Whole Earth, 1-3. Zephaniah ("the Lord hides or protects") was perhaps a great grandson of Hezekiah. The scope of these verses embraces a worldwide judgment of the day of the Lord (cf. 1:17; 2:11, 14, 15).

Judgment of Judah and Jerusalem, 4-13. The Lord will destroy Judah's ungodly religious syncretism. Chemarim, 4, were apostate idolatrous priests contaminated with the worship of Baal, the great god of the Canaanite pantheon. Milcom, 5 (RSV), was the chief Ammonite deity. The Assyrians adored "the host of heaven."

The Day of the Lord, 14-18. The imminent invasion of the Chaldeans under Nebuchadnezzar is treated as a prefigurement of the apocalyptic day of the Lord in which all earth judgments culminate (cf. Isa 2:10-22; Joel 1—2; Rev 19:11-21).

2:1—3:8. THE JUDGMENT OF THE NATIONS

The Call to Repentance, 2:1-3. The "shameless nation," i.e., apostate Israel, 1 (RSV), is called upon to repent (cf. Jer 3:13). This section is a call to the Jewish remnant of the end-time just preceding the judgment of the nations. "Be hid," 3, is a play upon

Zephaniah's name (see 1:1) and constitutes a promise to the faithful remnant.

Judgment upon the Philistines, 4-7. The chief cities of Philistia in southwest Palestine are named (cf. Joel 3:4-8). Cherethites, 5, were evidently Cretans living in Philistia (1 Sam 30:14; 2 Sam 8:18; Ezk 25:16). "Canaan" (meaning traffic in blue purple dye obtained from the shells of a murex mollusk of coastal Palestine) is the older name for Palestine. The later term Palestine is a Gr. corruption of the land of the Philistines (Gr. *Palaistinē*).

Judgment upon Moab and Ammon, 8-10. They shall be destroyed because they jeered at the Lord's people and boasted against the Lord (Isa 15—16; 25:10-12; Jer 48:1—49:6; Ezk 25:8-11; Amos 1:13—2:3).

Judgment upon Other Nations, 11-15. Ethiopians will be slain, and the proud Assyrians brought low. Nineveh's fall is predicted (cf. Nah 3; see note on Nineveh, Jon 3:1-3).

Judgment upon Jerusalem, 3:1-8. Four charges are made against the city: disobedience, opposition to correction, unbelief and godlessness. Threatened punishment is indicated by the Lord, 6-8.

3:9-20. ISRAEL IN KINGDOM BLESSING

Salvation and Deliverance in the Kingdom, 9-13. The gift of a pure speech removes the curse of Babel (Gen 11:1-9) and anticipates the great outpouring of the Spirit (Joel 2:28-32), of which Pentecost (Acts 2:1-11) was an illustration. The redeemed remnant is graphically described, 12-13 (cf. Ezk 34:13-16; Zech 8:3, 16).

Praise in the Kingdom, 14-20. Israel's renown and praise of God fulfills the promise of the Abrahamic covenant (Gen 12:1-3).

THE POST-EXILIC PERIOD

HAGGAI, ZECHARIAH AND MALACHI

Date (B.C.)	Palestine	Persian Empire	Greece
549		Cyrus the Great united Persia and Media	
546		Lydia conquered	
539		Crown Prince Belshazzar ruled Babylon	
538	Edict of Cyrus		
536	Jews return		
536-34	Altar laid		
	Economic and spiritual poverty		
530-22		Cambyses	
525		Egypt conquered	
522-486		Darius I	
520	Haggai		
	Zechariah		
	Temple rebuilt		
535-15			Greek ascendancy
490		Defeated by Greeks at Marathon	Defeated Persians under Darius I

Date	Biblical / Jewish events	Persian kings	Greek figures
486-65		Xerxes I (Ahasuerus) Esther's husband	Herodotus, Father of History; Defeated Persians under Xerxes I
485-25	Zechariah's later ministry (Zech 9—14)		
480		Defeated by Greeks at Thermopylae and Salamis	
470-399			Socrates
465-24		Artaxerxes I	
460-29			Golden Age of Pericles
458	Ezra's return		
445	Nehemiah rebuilt walls		
435	Malachi		
428-348			Plato
424-23		Xerxes II Darius II	
423-04			
404-358		Artaxerxes II	
384-22			Aristotle
358-38		Artaxerxes III	
338-36		Arses	
336-31		Darius III	
336-23		Kingdom fell to Alexander	Rise of Alexander

HAGGAI

CALL TO COMPLETE THE UNFINISHED TEMPLE

Historical Background. Cyrus' decree (538 B.C.) permitted the Jews to return home and rebuild their temple at Jerusalem (Ezr 1:1-4). The monuments give clear evidence of this noble spirit of Cyrus. The remnant laid the foundation (Ezr 3:1-3, 8-10), but from c. 535 B.C. to 520 B.C. failed to go on to complete the edifice. Through Haggai and Zechariah's combined ministry (520 B.C.), the temple was completed (520-515 B.C.). The circumstances of the construction of the temple gave rise to panoramic messianic predictions by the two prophets, especially Zechariah (q.v.).

Outline
Call to Rebuild the Temple, 1:1-15
Prophecy of the Millennial Temple, 2:1-19
Prophecy of the Destruction of Gentile World Power, 2:20-23

CHAPTER 1. CALL TO REBUILD THE TEMPLE

Call to Face Sinful Neglect, 1-6. The date was August-September, 520 B.C., the second year of Darius I the Great (522-486 B.C.), the archaeologically famous monarch of the Behistun Inscription. Haggai means "festal." Zerubbabel had succeeded Sheshbazzar as the governor under Persian overlordship (Ezr 1:8-11). Joshua ("the Lord is salvation") was the high priest (Ezr 2:2; 3:1-13). The rulers and the people at large were faced with their failure, 1-6.

Declaration of the Lord's Judgment, 7-11. Economic stress, drought and unemployment (cf. Zech 8:9-13) were directly traceable to neglect in building the temple, 9.

The People's Response, 12-15. Rulers fell in line first, and then the people gladly responded, 12. Haggai forthwith gave a word of encouragement from the Lord, 13, and the people resumed construction on the twenty-fourth day of the same month Haggai began his ministry, 15 (cf. 1).

2:1-19. PROPHECY OF THE MILLENNIAL TEMPLE

The Prediction of the Temple, 1-9. This, the second prophetic oracle, was delivered September-October, 520 B.C. Human disparagement of the modest plans for the second temple engendered pessimism and discouragment, 1-3. Haggai gave assurance of the divine presence and success of the venture, 4-5 (cf. Ex 29:45-46; Isa 43:1-7). The restoration temple, in process of building at that time, furnished the background for the far-reaching prophecy of the kingdom temple, 7-9. The "shaking of all nations" refers to the end-time Tribulation, 7 (cf. Heb 12:26; Dan 12:1; Rev 16:18-20). The translation of the phrase, "the Desire of all nations," 7, usually follows the Septuagint: "The desirable things [*hamudoth*] of all nations shall come," i.e., their costly treasures brought to beautify the millennial temple. But the Masoretic Heb. text has "desire [*hemdath*]" feminine singular with a plural verb. Thus it is more properly translated as "the Desire of all nations" shall come, construing the passage as messianic. Messiah is objectively the Desire of all nations because through Him, and Him alone, can the nations be blessed with the righteousness and peace they yearn for.

Promise of Present Blessing, 10-19. This, Haggai's third discourse, is dated November-December, 520 B.C. By a ritual comparison, 10-14, the prophet demonstrated that the ruined and neglected temple, as an insult to God, had rendered all their worship and giving unclean. While one holy thing does not sanctify others, that which is unclean contagiously corrupts everything it touches. So it was with the people. Becoming clean, as it were, would bring the Lord's favor and constitute a solution to pressing economic problems among them, 15-19.

2:20-23. DESTRUCTION OF GENTILE WORLD POWER

The Shaking of the Nations, 20-22. This, the fourth and final sermon excerpt, is dated November-December, 520 B.C., and is still entirely unfulfilled and prophetic. The shaking of the heavens and the earth, 21, and the destruction of the kingdoms of the nations, refer to the future Tribulation, as does 2:7-9. This shaking will destroy the throne of kingdoms, so that the kingdom of Messiah may be set up. He is the "stone" (Dan 2:44-45) that smites the image and destroys it.

The Promised Ruler, 23. Zerubbabel, a son of David (Shealtiel was of the posterity of David, Mt 1:12; Lk 3:27), typifies Christ, the son of David. In that day Christ will receive His Davidic throne and be made a signet ring—a mark of honor, a badge of royal authority possessed by kings and conferred on their administrative agents. Here Christ is pictured as being invested with all rule and authority. Zerubbabel himself may share as one of Messiah's prime ministers in the kingdom (cf. Dan 12:2; Mt 19:28).

ZECHARIAH

ISRAEL, THE NATION GOD REMEMBERS

Nature of the Prophecy. This book is unique in its messianic emphasis among the minor prophets and in its unfolding of events connected with the first and second advents of Christ. It has been called the most messianic, the most truly apocalyptic and eschatological of all the writings of the OT.

Important Messianic Predictions. These predictions include: the Lord's Servant, the Branch (3:8); the Man, the Branch (6:12); the King-Priest (6:13); the True Shepherd (11:4-11); the True Shepherd vs. the false shepherd—the Antichrist (11:15-17; 13:7); the betrayal of the Good Shepherd (11:12-13); His crucifixion (12:10); His sufferings (13:7); His second advent in glory (14:4).

1:1-17. VISION OF THE MAN AMONG THE MYRTLES

Preface, 1. The time was October-November, 520 B.C., the second year of Darius I the Great (522-486 B.C.) of the Behistun Inscription (cf. Hag 1:1). Dating a Heb. prophecy by a Gentile king indicates that the times of the Gentiles (Lk 21:24) were in progress. Zechariah means "whom the Lord remembers," and appropriately this book is a testimony of that fact to the prophet and his (and the

Grand entrance to the palace at Persepolis, capital of the Persian Empire. (*Courtesy ORINST*)

Lord's) people. He was the son of the priest Iddo (Ezr 5:1; 6:14; Neh 12:16).

The Call to Repentance, 2-6. This is the spiritual keynote sounded so that the remnant of less than 50,000 might be spiritually prepared for the great visions given to them through the prophet. Zechariah enunciates divine wrath, 2, and also divine grace, 3, citing a warning from Heb. history, 4-6. "The former prophets" had continually stressed repentance (Isa 1:16-20; 30:15; 55:6-9; Jer 3:12; Joel 2:12-13; Hos 7:10). Zechariah was imbued with knowledge of these prophets and their messages.

The Man Among the Myrtle Trees, 7-17. This vision signifies hope for scattered and downtrodden Israel. The date of this and the other seven visions, all given the same night, was Shebat (Feb.) 24, 519 B.C. The red horse rider is the Lord in theophanic form, 8 (cf. 13), the color red speaking of Him who wrought redemption at His first advent and will come to "judge and make war" at His second advent (Rev 19:11). The patrol scouts are angelic agents who ascertain the condition of the earth as this affects Israel's restoration to kingdom blessing, 11-12 (cf. Hag 2:21-22). The myrtle trees symbolize Israel as the covenant people and the object of God's covenants and promises of restoration. The bottom (deep glen), 8, expresses her condition of deep humiliation during the times of the Gentiles (605 B.C. to Christ's second advent). The meaning of the vision, 9-12, is that the worldwide trouble which is to be a precursor to Israel's restoration is not in prospect (cf. Hag 2:21-22); but "good and comforting words," 13, are given through the prophet, assuring the people of God's great love for them, 14; His great indignation at the persecuting nations, 15; and the future final restoration in the kingdom, 16-17.

1:18-21. VISION OF THE FOUR HORNS AND FOUR SMITHS

Israel Triumphant Over Her Foes, 1:18-21. The prophet first sees four horns, 18-19. These represent hostile nations, i.e., the four great world powers of the times of the Gentiles (cf. Dan 2:37-45; 7:2-8, 17-28), namely, Babylon, Medo-Persia, Greece and Rome (the latter to be revived at the end time, Dan 2:42-44; 7:7, 8, 20; Rev 13:1).

The Lord then shows the prophet four smiths, 20-21. These artisans (technicians) symbolize kingdoms which the Lord used to cast down the persecutors of His people Israel. Three of these "smiths" (Medo-Persia, Greece, and Rome) were horns, which *in turn* became smiths. The fourth smith is the kingdom set up by the returning King of Kings and Lord of lords (Rev 19:16) who destroys the ten-kingdom confederation of the end time (Dan 2:44). Both the Babylonian (Jer 25:9; 27:6; 43:10) and Persian (Isa 44:28—45:1) as well as the Macedonian Greek power (Zech 9:3-4) were controlled by the Most High ruling in the kingdom of men. He used them first as a horn to chasten His people, and later as a smith to destroy the horn when its divine purpose had been accomplished.

CHAPTER 2.   VISION OF THE SURVEYOR

The Measuring Line, 1-3. This vision presents Jerusalem in millennial glory. The surveyor is probably the same divine Person as the red-horse rider of the first vision. His surveying activities intimate the growth and prosperity of Jerusalem, not only at that time, but ultimately to be fulfilled in the Kingdom Age, as 4-13 demonstrates.

Promises Proceeding from the Vision, 4-13. Jerusalem is promised prosperous expansion, 4; divine protection and glory, 5; restoration, 6-7; vindication against her enemies, 8-9, in an earth prepared for full blessing, 10-13, when Palestine will be called "the Holy Land." Verse 13 is a grand synopsis of Rev 6—19.

CHAPTER 3. VISION OF JOSHUA'S CLEANSING

This vision sets forth the restoration of Israel as a high-priestly nation.

Israel As Defiled and Condemned, 1-3, is pictured under the representative figure of Joshua, the high priest. As such she is accused as a criminal, 1-2, because she attempted to minister before the angel of the Lord (the Lord Himself), and because her sinful condition gave place to the devil (cf. Eph 4:27) who resisted her. Her "filthy" (excrement-covered) garments represent her self-righteousness in not submitting to the righteousness of God (cf. Rom 10:1-4). Satan, however, is effectually reprimanded by the angel (the Lord) on the basis of God's sovereign electing grace, 2, despite Israel's sin, 3.

Israel As Pardoned and Repositioned, 4-5. This portrays the conversion of the nation at Messiah's second advent. First comes the negative aspect of salvation, 4, the forgiveness of sin (cf. Rom 3:25; Eph 1:7). Then the positive bestowal of divine righteousness and reinstatement into full priestly function are given, 4-5 (cf. Ex 19:5-7; Rom 1:16-17; 3:22, 26; Zech 12:10—13:1). Ex. 28 shows how the high priest was clothed when he ministered.

Covenant of Priesthood Renewed with Joshua, 6-7.

Prediction of Restored Israel Under the Figure of Messiah, the Branch, 8-10. Joshua and his colleagues were "men of predictive omen," i.e., men who in their person signified future events for Israel, 8. "Messiah the Branch" portrays Christ in the redemptive aspects of His first advent, 8 (cf. Isa 53:1-10; Phil 2:6-8), the basis of Israel's cleansing and restoration at His second advent. The omniscient "stone," a precious carved gem, portrays the Messiah in His glorious second advent when Israel will be converted, 12:10. The carvings signify the scars and wounds His precious body received when He purchased redemption on the cross. The vision ends in full kingdom blessing, 10 (cf. Mic 4:4 with 1 Kgs 4:24-25).

CHAPTER 4. VISION OF THE GOLDEN LAMPSTAND

This vision portrays Israel as the light of the world under Messiah King-Priest.

The Symbolism of the Vision, 1-5. The prophet prepared, 1, is presented with the vision, 2-3. The lampstand of pure gold (Ex 25:31-40) typifies Christ our Light (Jn 8:12; Mt 5:14). He is manifested in His deity (pure gold) in the plentitude of the power of the sevenfold Spirit (Heb 1:9; Rev 1:4), prefigured by the seven lights (fullness of testimony). Israel was the *one* nation so chosen by God to be a witness to the one true God. The seven-branched lampstand *in the midst* of her (and it was never a symbol in the midst of any other nation) therefore symbolizes the realization of Israel's divine vocation to be a witness and a testimony of God's salvation in Christ to the unbelieving pagan nations around her. Thus Israel is prefigured in full fellowship with God as she was meant to be, and as she will actually be in her millennial restoration.

The Purpose of the Vision, 6-10. The prophet's inquiry, 4-5, elicits the angel's reply concerning the purpose, 6-10. The temple was to be completed by divine power, 6, with every obstacle removed, 7. Zerubbabel was to accomplish this, 7, 9. The word of God would be fulfilled, 9; critics would be silenced, 10; well-wishers would rejoice, 10; and God would be magnified, 10.

The Prophet Favored with a Full Explanation, 11-14. The prophet's double question, 11-12, brings the angel's definite answer, 13-14. The two olive trees portray the civil (kingly) and priestly office. The two olive branches represent the present incumbents, Zerubbabel and Joshua. The two golden pipes symbolize these two offices united in Christ as King-Priest. The gold (oil) is the exquisite operation of the Holy Spirit through the medium of the King-Priest to the restored nation as lightbearer. "The Lord of the whole earth" (Gen 14:19; Josh 3:11, 13; Mic 4:13; Zech 6:5; Rev 11:3-4) is Messiah's kingdom appellative when He returns as King of kings and Lord of lords (Rev. 19:16). He will destroy His enemies and assume absolute ownership and control of the earth, now potentially His by virtue of creation and redemption (Eph 1:13-14). Regeneration, ch. 3, is followed by witness, ch. 4.

CHAPTER 5. VISIONS OF THE FLYING SCROLL AND THE EPHAH

The flying scroll, 1-4. The sixth vision, 1-2, is a flying roll or scroll 30 feet long and 15 feet wide, illustrating the rod-of-iron rule of the kingdom. The meaning of the vision, 3-4, is that the scroll symbolizes the curse of God against sinners. The scroll involves both tables of the law and can only curse (Deut 27—28; Gal 3:10-14). The flying motion denotes the worldwide extent of the curse, 3, and the subjects mentioned are representative of all sinners, 3. Enforcement of the curse portrays Messiah's iron rule at His second advent and in His subsequent reign (Ps 2:9; Rev 2:27; 12:5; 19:15).

The Ephah, 5-11. This seventh vision portrays the removal of commercial and ecclesiastical wickedness from the earth. The ephah,

6, is a Heb. dry measure (1.05 bushels) and speaks of commerce, godless business and inordinate gain. It is symbolic of commercial Babylon (Rev 18). The ephah (commerce; cf. Jas 5:1-3) is associated with a talent (also a commercial figure) of lead (heavy metal), 7. The woman introduced as sitting contentedly in the ephah, 7, is personified wickedness (cf. Mt 13:33; Rev 2:20; 17:3-7). The woman symbolizes ecclesiastical Babylon (the religious aspects of the Satanic world system), i.e., religionism settled down in and nurtured by ungodly commercialism (cf. the harlot of Rev 17, which represents her in a more developed stage of iniquity). The reason the woman suddenly desires to get out of the ephah is because she wishes to escape its fate, 10-11, but her complicity in evil commercialism (the talent of lead) imprisons her and her sin becomes her undoing (cf. Prov 5:22). Shinar, 11, is Babylonia (Gen 10:10; 11:1-9; Dan 1:2).

6:1-8. VISION OF THE FOUR CHARIOTS

This vision presents the judgment of the nations preparatory to Messiah's reign. The findings of the scouts in vision one are now executed.

The Vision Presented, 1-3. "*The* two mountains" (Olivet and Zion) are "mountains of bronze" (i.e., mountains from which divine judgment issues), since bronze (copper and tin) is typical of manifested divine judgment. (Cf. the bronze altar, Ex 27:2; Jn 12:31-33; Jn 3:14 with Num 21:9.) The four chariots are pictured with their horses, 2-3. The *red* horses portray war and bloodshed (Rev 6:4); the *black* horses, famine and starvation (Rev 6:5-6); the *white* horses, victory and conquest (Rev 6:2); the *grisled* and *bay* horses ("hail-spotted" and "strong" horses) portray death (Rev 6:8).

The Vision Explained, 4-8. Attention focuses on the horsed *chariots,* not the horses. The interpretive key is given in 5. These horsed *chariots* represent "the four spirits" (angelic ministers, not "winds"; cf. Dan 7:10; 1 Kgs 22:19; Ps 103:20-21; 104:4; Heb 1:7; Lk 1:19) who are the celestial agents executing judgment against the nations. The *horses* portray the judgments; the chariots, the *angelic* executors administering these judgments (as in Rev 8:2, 7, 8, 10, 12; 9:1, 13; 11:15; 15:1; 16:1-3) to dispossess wicked earth squatters for possession by "the Lord of the whole earth," 5 (see comments on Zech 4:14). The message concludes with a note of hope for the prophet's own day, 8. The word "spirit" in 8 has the specialized meaning of anger (Jud 8:3; Isa 33:11; Eccl 10:4).

6:9-15. CROWNING THE HIGH PRIEST

The eight visions have ended. Now follows an actual historical event—Joshua's coronation—for which the eight visions were preparatory. This symbolic occurrence constituted the summation and climax of these visions.

The Historical Event and the Prophetic Symbolism, 9-11. The arrival of the deputies from Babylon with gifts for the temple constituted an event with symbolic and prophetic significance. Zechariah, prepared by the visions, was instructed to receive as a gift for the temple the gold and silver brought by the returned exiles, namely, Heldai ("[the Lord's] world"), Tobijah ("the Lord is good"), Jedaiah ("the Lord knows"), at Josiah's ("the Lord supports") house. In 14 Josiah is nicknamed "Hen" ("graciousness"), perhaps because of his hospitality. Zechariah was enjoined to make "*a* crown" (singular, the preferred reading rather than "crowns" plural). The singular significance of the whole episode was that the crown was to be placed upon the head of the high priest Joshua, *not* Zerubbabel, despite the rigid separation of the priestly and kingly offices in Israel (cf. 2 Chr 26:16-21). The reason was that *all* eight night visions pointed to the kingdom restored to Israel under Messiah King-Priest (Heb 7:1-3; Ps 110:4).

Messianic Import of the Prophetic Symbolism, 12,13,15. Messiah the Branch (see notes on 3:8) will appear as Joshua's antitype, 12a (cf. Jn 19:5; cf. Isa 53:2; Jer 33:15; Ps 2:6). This is Messiah in His humanity. Messiah the Branch shall build the millennial temple, 12-13 (Ezk 40—42; cf. Isa 2:2-4; Mic 4:1-2). He Himself (and no other) shall bear the glory (*hodh*, which is used almost exclusively of the divine splendor, Ps 8:1; Isa 45:3; Ps 148:13; Hab 3:3; Rev 19:16). He will be a King-Priest, the Son of Man, the "last Adam," the second Man (1 Cor 15:45-47), with regained dominion over the earth lost by the first Adam. Messiah will combine in one Person the two offices in perfect harmony, 13, binding together in unity both Jew and Gentile, 15, vindicating the word of God and demanding unflinching obedience, 15.

Provision for a Permanent Memorial, 14. The crown, as a prophetic symbolism, is to be kept as a memorial.

CHAPTER 7. THE QUESTION OF THE FASTS

The Question Raised, 1-3. The date is Chislev (Dec.), 518 B.C. (cf. 1:1). The city of Bethel, 12 miles N of Jerusalem, sent a delegation to Jerusalem "to entreat the favor of the Lord," 2 (RSV), and to inquire concerning observing certain fasts (cf. Lev 23:27; Joel 1:13-14). The question betrayed an attitude of ritualism rather than of spiritual reality. The fast of the fifth month mourned the destruction of Jerusalem (2 Kgs 25:8-9; Jer 25:13; cf. Zech 8:19); that of the seventh month marked the murder of Gedaliah (Jer 41:1-2); the fourth month (Tammuz) recalled the breaching of Jerusalem's walls (2 Kgs 25:3; Jer 39:2-4); the tenth month (Tebeth) marked the beginning of the siege (2 Kgs 25:1).

The Motive of Selfishness Exposed, 4-7. The prophet rebuked meaningless ritualism, 4-6 (cf. Isa 1:10-15), and urged obedience to the word of God, 7, spoken by "the former prophets," Isaiah and Jeremiah in particular, but also including Joel, Amos, Hosea, Micah.

Call to Repentance Proclaimed, 8-14. The divine command was to put the word of the Lord into practice, 8-10, and to take warning of the refusal of the pre-Exilic nation to obey that word, 11-12, with the dire results that followed, 13-14.

CHAPTER 8. WHEN THE FASTS BECOME JOYFUL FEASTS

Present Partial Restoration Harbinger of an Eventual Full Restoration of Israel, 1-8. This full restoration is guaranteed by God's word and God's electing love, 1-2, the latter truth vehemently declared. The results of this future restoration will be: (1) *the Lord's return*, 3 (cf. 1:16; Hos 5:15; 6:3; Mt 23:39); (2) *the permanent divine presence*, 3 (cf. Ezk 11:22-25; 43:2-5); (3) *the exaltation of Jerusalem*, 3 (cf. Isa 1:26; 60:14; 62:12); (4) *her increase in size and security*, 4-5; (5) *the manifestation of God's power*, 6. In 7-8 the promise of future regathering and restoration, 1-6, is repeated.

Encouragement Amid the Hardships of the Present Partial Restoration, 9-17. Added to the subjects of encouragement, 9, are listed the reasons for their discouragement, 10, with details given for their hope, 11-15, and the practical use they were to make of it, 16-17.

Prediction of Full Millennial Restoration, 18-23. Fasts will one day give way to feasts, 18-19. The nations of the kingdom will eagerly seek the Lord, 20-22. The Jew will enjoy special divine favor, 23. Such an emphatic assertion of the reinstatement of the Lord's covenant nation summarizes and climaxes worthily the scope of the eight night visions (1:7—6:8) and that of the symbolic crowning of the high priest (6:9-15), as well as giving a satisfactory answer to the question of the fasts in ch. 7—8.

9:1—10:1. HUMAN WORLD RULER VS. DIVINE
PRINCE OF PEACE

Sudden Rise of Alexander the Great, 9:1-8. A "burden" is an oracle admonitory or threatening in character. The land of Hadrach, 1, is the region of Hatarika mentioned in the Assyrian annals. It is an Aramaean country against which Assyria campaigned in the 8th cen. B.C. The well-attested city and region were in the hinterland of Phoenicia beyond the Antilebanon Mountains in the vicinity of Hamath on the Orontes and Damascus about 100 miles to the S. Tyre (the leader) and Sidon, 20 miles N on the coast about the same latitude as Damascus, were the prominent Phoenician cities taken in the whirlwind conquests of Alexander (333 B.C.), 2-3. Tyre's siege and fall to the conqueror are graphically predicted, 3-4, and dramatically fulfilled in Alexander's conquest of the insular city after an eight-month siege. Prophecy against the Philistine strongholds, 5-7 in SW Palestine indicates the conqueror's victorious sweep in Egypt. Of the Pentapolis, only Gath is omitted. The fate of Gaza is fully recorded in Alexander's annals after its five-month siege. Like Tyre, it dared to resist because of its strength, but suffered a violent destruction. Verse 8 is a prophecy, wonderfully fulfilled, of Jerusalem's escape from Alexander's destruction, 8a (cf. Josephus *Antiq* XI. 8.3). At the same time it is a harbinger of a complete future deliverance under Messiah at His second advent, 8b.

First Advent of Israel's Humble King and Saviour, 9:9. The joyful announcement of His coming, 9a, is followed by a featured account of His character and condition, 9b. He is to be "just" (righteous), showing Himself a Saviour; and "lowly," shown by His riding a humble beast, which no king at that period would ever ride.

Second Advent of Israel's Glorious King, 9:10—10:1. He establishes peace, 9:10. Suffering Israel is encouraged in the light of the nation's future hope, 11-12. The Maccabean conflict with godless paganism (175-130 B.C.) was an illustration of Israel's final conflict, 13-15, with the nation's end-time deliverance and blessing predicted, 9:16—10:1.

10:2-12. DIVINE PRINCE OF PEACE
AND DELIVERER

The Second Advent and the Cure of the Nation's Deception, 2-4. The types of Israel's deception are outlined, 2, 5. The dire result of that deception is that the people have strayed like sheep, being severely afflicted, 2. However, the nation's oppressors will be punished and eventual national restoration and victory over enemies are assured, 3. The cure of the nation's deception, 4, is in Messiah's coming as (1) Cornerstone (Isa 28:15-16); (2) Tent Peg (Isa 22:15-25); (3) Battle Bow (cf. Ps 45:5; Rev 19:11).

The Second Advent and the Nation's Triumph Over Its Foes, 5-12. The Lord promises His presence with His people, the remnant, 5, and guarantees their empowering and repatriation, 6-7. He will gather Israel out of her present worldwide dispersion, 8-9, unto her own land, 10; remove every impediment, 11, and effect Israel's complete renovation, 12.

CHAPTER 11. ISRAEL'S REJECTION OF THE GOOD SHEPHERD

Impending Devastation of the Land, 1-3. This destruction due to the predicted rejection of Messiah at His first advent begins in the Lebanon region in the north, 1-2, and sweeps on into Bashan in Transjordan, noted for its splendid forests of oak (Isa 2:13). The devastation proceeds from the plateau of Bashan to the plain and on into the lower Jordan Valley, 3, whose pride is a luxuriant growth of tamarisks, willows, grasses and cane; a favorite haunt of lions in antiquity (2 Kgs 17:25; Jer 49:19; 50:44).

Prediction of the Rejection of the Good Shepherd, 4-14. This is accomplished by the prophet's commission to perform an actual prophetic symbolic act before his contemporaries, 4. It would portray the ruin of "the flock destined for butchery," because of their scurrilous treatment of him as representing their future treatment of Messiah Himself, 4-6. The two rods "Graciousness" and "Unity" symbolize the Lord's final efforts to reclaim apostate Christ-rejecting Israel, 7-8. The breaking of these rods symbolizes the cessation of the Lord's gracious and patient dealing with the nation, and the loss of internal brotherhood and unity after the betrayal and rejection of the Lord, 9-10. This prediction marvelously envisioned the pitiable state of internal dissension and hatred which characterized the Jews from the crucifixion to the fall of Jerusalem in A.D. 70. For "thirty pieces of silver," 12, see Ex 21:32, and Mt 27:3-10. "Casting it to the potter," 13, is a meaningful construction for "throw it down to the potter," i.e., that it may wind up in the possession of a potter.

Prediction of the Acceptance of the Bad Shepherd, 15-17. Zechariah's commission to enact a second symbolic act, 15, looks forward to Israel's acceptance of the Antichrist, whose wicked character is outlined, 16, and whose doom is indicated, 17. The rejection of the

Good Shepherd is connected with the first advent, as the acceptance of the evil shepherd is with the second advent (Jn 5:43; Rev 19:20; 20:10).

CHAPTER 12. ISRAEL'S DELIVERANCE AND NATIONAL CONVERSION

Future Siege of Jerusalem, 1-9. The authentication of the second prophetic oracle (ch. 12—14) is given, 1. The nations attack Jerusalem, 2-3, and are confounded, 4. This is "in that day," i.e., the day of the Lord, denoting that future period when the Lord will openly and publicly manifest His power in delivering Israel from her enemies and establishing her in peace and prosperity. Judah's signal faith in the Lord, 5, and His response to that faith, 6-7, result in her triumph, 8, and the doom of her enemies, 9.

Vision of the Crucified Messiah and the Result, 10-14. The revelation of the Pierced One (cf. Rev 19:13) produces a great effusion of the Spirit, 10 (cf. Joel 2:28-32; Ezk 39:29), and a sweeping national conversion, 11-14, that thoroughly purges out idolatry and sin, 13:1-5. Peter's quotation in Acts 2:16-21 was an illustration of the Spirit's effusion which is here fulfilled.

CHAPTER 13. ISRAEL'S NATIONAL CLEANSING

Prophecy of Israel's National Cleansing, 1-6. The prophecy was realized in the fountain of cleansing, 1, opened at Calvary for sin and uncleanness (cf. Rom 10:3). The prophecy of Israel's national cleansing is illustrated in the extermination of idolatry and its concomitant false prophecy, 2-5 (cf. Deut 18:20-22; Jer 14:14-15). In 6 the Cleanser from idolatry (Christ) is revealed, resuming the subject broached in 12:10 after the parenthesis of 12:11—13:5.

Provision for Israel's National Conversion, 7. This is Messiah, who was introduced with such dramatic abruptness in 6. He is now described by the Lord (the Father) in His *death,* 7a, and in His *deity,* 7b, "the man that is my fellow," i.e., "the man *My equal,* a human being closely conjoined or united to Me." Here appears the divine-human person of our Lord in the OT—deity united to humanity in one unique Person.

Prelude to Israel's National Conversion, 7-9. The sheep are to be scattered, and the faithful warned of persecution and death, 7, with the predicted Great Tribulation eventuating in the deliverance of a remnant, 8-9.

The Appropriation of the Provisions for Cleansing, 9. The remnant calls on the Lord, is delivered, and testifies to salvation, 9.

CHAPTER 14. MESSIAH'S SECOND ADVENT IN GLORY

Last Enemy Siege Against Jerusalem, 1-3. The time is the day of the Lord, 1 (see note on 12:1-9). The enemy apparently is triumphant, 2, and the imminent destruction of the city and the remnant threatened. But the Lord intervenes in deliverance, 3.

Personal Advent of Messiah, 4-7. The *place* is the Mount of Olives; the *result,* a gigantic earthquake, effecting topographical changes, 4. The *purpose* is to deliver His people and destroy their foes, 5. The *manner* is with His saints, 5 (Acts 3:21; 1 Thess 3:13; Jude 14; 1 Jn 3:2), including both angels and glorified men. The *time* is the second advent, 6-7.

Messianic Kingdom Established over Israel, 8-21. The temporal and spiritual blessing of the kingdom, 8, and the absolute lordship of the King, 9, center in Jerusalem as the capital of the millennial earth, 10-11. Retrospectively the destruction of Israel's enemies is described, 12-15 (cf. Ezk 38—39). Millennial worship and government, with Jerusalem as the religious and political capital of the earth, 16-19, are predicted. The prophecy closes with Israel's holiness as a high-priestly nation (cf. ch. 3—4) set forth, 20-21.

MALACHI

THE LORD'S LOVE FOR HIS SINNING PEOPLE

Name of the Prophet and Date. It is best to take the term Malachi ("My messenger") as a personal name rather than an appellation based on 3:1. Malachi is later than Haggai and Zechariah. The temple had long ago been completed and the priesthood and worship had been in operation for a number of years. The question is, how long? Evidently some time after Ezra's and Nehemiah's correction of current abuses, for decline had set in again. A date about 433-425 B.C. is perhaps not far afield.

Message of Malachi. The last prophetic voice of the OT rings out over the years intervening till the coming of the forerunner, John the Baptist, and the King at His first advent. But Malachi's prophetic emphasis is on the day of the Lord with its judgment of the wicked and the deliverance of a righteous remnant from the sinful mass. These vast themes connect Malachi with the great stream of Heb. prophecy. His immediate message deals with the sins of the priests and the people of his day. These sins form the background for his prophecies of judgment certain to fall in the future.

Outline

Preamble: The Lord's Love for Israel, 1:1-5
Oracle Against the Priests, 1:6—2:9
Oracles Against Jewish Laymen, 2:10—4:3
Concluding Warning, 4:4-6

1:1-5. THE LORD'S LOVE FOR ISRAEL

Declaration of That Love, 1-2. For "burden" (oracle), see Zech 9:1; 12:1. For the name "Malachi," see above. The message to Israel, God's ancient chosen nation, is "I have loved you," 2 (cf. Deut 10:15; 33:3; Amos 3:2). The record of this love is inscribed on every page of the OT. Their brazen questioning of this love, 2, shows their apostasy and ingratitude in the face of their deliverance from Egypt, restoration from Babylon, and many other tokens of divine care.

Contrast to Esau (Edomites), 3-5. The descendants of Esau, Jacob's twin brother, had fully merited the divine "hatred," while Jacob's posterity, on the other hand, had *not* fully merited the divine love. It was a gracious electing love in one case, but not an ungracious electing hate in the other, since it is not said in the book of Genesis, where Esau's career is described, "Esau have I hated." Only in the book of Malachi is the declaration made and then only after Edom's wicked character had been fully manifested (cf. Rom 9:13).

1:6—2:16. ORACLE AGAINST THE PRIESTS AND PEOPLE

The Impenitence of the Priests, 1:6-14. The Lord as a father and a master rightly expected becoming conduct, 6. Yet the priests despised Him and denied their sin, 6, brazenly offering polluted food, and blind or lame animals, 7-8, which were unacceptable for sacrifice (Lev 22:17-25; Deut 15:21); an insult to man, much more to God, 9. They were lazy and mercenary, 10-13. Verse 11 will yet be fulfilled, as it would have been if Israel had been true to her God in OT times. The conduct of the priests was utterly reprehensible in the light of who the Lord is and His reputation among the nations, 14.

Their Impenitence to Be Punished, 2:1-9. If they would not repent, 1, their blessings would be cursed, 2 (Deut 27:26; 28:15). The curse is spelled out, 3. The command to repent, 1, was to protect the covenant with Levi, 4-5 (cf. Num 25:12-13) and to restore the historical Levitical character of the priesthood with faithfulness of speech, uprightness of walk and usefulness of service, 6-7. Repentance would preserve the true Levitical ideal of knowledge and authority, and expose their present shameful conduct, 8-9.

First Oracle Against the People, 2:10-16, involved their treachery against men, 10, and God, 11. They would be chastened, 12. The results of this treachery were seen in divorce, infidelity, and violence, 13-16.

2:17—4:6. PROPHECY OF MESSIAH'S ADVENT

The Occasion of the Prophecy, 2:17. This is the second oracle against the people, 2:17—3:6. The occasion of the prophecy was the prophet's rebuke of the people's insincere religious profession and unbelief, particularly their unbelief in divine judgment, 2:17.

The Prophecy Itself, 3:1-6. "My messenger" is a prediction of the forerunner of the Messiah, John the Baptist (cf. Mt 11:10). "The

Lord whom you seek," "the messenger of the covenant," is Messiah envisioned particularly in His second advent in judgment, 2-5, in answer to the question of 2:17. (Cf. Mt 3:10-12; Isa 4:4; Mal 4:1; Rev 6:17.)

The People's Sin of Robbing God, 3:7-12. This is the third oracle against the people, upbraiding them for withholding the Lord's tithe (cf. Neh 13:10, 12; Lev 27:30-32; Num 18:21, 24).

The People's Sin of Criticizing the Lord, 3:13—4:3. This is the fourth oracle against the people. The charge is that they had said it doesn't pay to serve God; wickedness is the way to prosperity, 3:14-15. The answer to this calumny draws from the prophet the prediction of the godly remnant and its reward, 16-18, and the judgment to come in the day of the Lord, 4:1. This will culminate in the second advent of Christ, 4:2-3, when the wicked will be punished.

Concluding Warning, 4:4-6. The wicked priests and people are to remember the law of Moses, 4, and to expect the coming judgments of the great and dreadful day of the Lord as a punishment of sinners, 5. Elijah (cf. Rev 11:3-6) is promised to appear before that time and call out a righteous remnant from the apostate mass. Our Lord confirmed the still unfulfilled character of Malachi's prediction when He declared, "Elias [Elijah] truly shall first come, and restore all things" (Mt 17:11). Thus Malachi, in remonstrating with priest and people of his day concerning their sins, has a message for us in our day when similar sins prevail. His messianic flashes (3:1-6; 4:2) prepare us for the NT revelation and focus our attention on Him who alone is the world's hope.

BETWEEN THE TESTAMENTS

The Four Hundred Silent Years

From Malachi (*c.* 400 B.C.), the last prophetic voice of the OT, to the advent of Jesus, divine revelation as it developed in the production of canonical Scripture was in abeyance. The result was the completion and delimitation of the Hebrew canon. According to Josephus, a Jewish historian of the second half of the 1st cen. A.D., this took place in the reign of Artaxerxes I Longimanus, 465-424 B.C.

Importance of Intertestamental Period. Among many other important events of this 400-year period was the translation of the OT into the Greek language. The version was produced *c.* 280-150 B.C. and was called the Septuagint. It released the great truths of OT Scripture from the narrow isolation of the Hebrew language and people, and gave them to the Graeco-Roman world in the common speech of the day.

Qumran caves where many of the Dead Sea Scrolls were found. (© *MPS*)

EVENTS OF THE INTERTESTAMENTAL PERIOD

Date	Jewish History	Contemporary Scene
424-331 B.C.	Malachi, last OT prophet. Palestine a tiny province (satrapy) under rule of Persian governor (satrap). Palestine fell within the bounds of the Fifth Persian satrapy with the capital at Damascus or Samaria.	**Persian Empire** Xerxes II (424-423 B.C.) Darius II (423-404 B.C.) Artaxerxes II (404-358 B.C.) Artaxerxes III (358-338 B.C.) Arses (338-336 B.C.) Darius III (336-331 B.C.) **Macedonian Empire** Philip (359-336 B.C.) gained control of Greek states. Victory at Chaeronea (338 B.C.). Power of Greek city-states broken.
359-323 B.C.	Jews enjoyed comparative peace and prosperity under their Persian overlords.	
338-323 B.C.	Jews were torn between allegiance to Persian overlords and threat of Alexander's conquests. *Alexander* swept into Syria taking Palestine, Tyre (332 B.C.), Gaza. Jews submitted to Alexander and were treated well. Alexander conquered Egypt (332 B.C.). Alexandria was founded.	Alexander the Great (336-323 B.C.) conquered Persian Empire in three decisive battles: Granicus (334 B.C.), Issus (333 B.C.), Gaugamela (331 B.C.), reached India (327 B.C.); died in Babylon (323 B.C.). Alexander's generals struggled for power.
323-277 B.C.	Dissemination of Greek language culture and philosophy by Alexander's conquests.	

451

Date	Jewish History	Contemporary Scene
		Ptolemaic and Seleucid Empires
	Palestine Under the Ptolemies (323-198 B.C.)	Ptolemy I (323-285 B.C.)	Seleucus I (312-280 B.C.)
	Ptolemy I favored Jews and settled many in Alexandria, which he raised to economic and cultural heights.		Antiochus I (280-262 B.C.)
	Ptolemy II favored Jews. Began translation of OT into Greek (Septuagint). Letter of Aristeas.	Ptolemy II (285-246 B.C.)	Antiochus II (261-246 B.C.)
	Hellenization of Alexandrian Jews continued. Palestinian Jews rigidly traditional.	Ptolemy III (246-221 B.C.)	Seleucus II (246-226 B.C.) Seleucus III (226-223 B.C.)
	Painted tombs of Marisa	Ptolemy IV (221-203 B.C.)	Antiochus III (223-187 B.C.)
	Palestine Under Seleucids (198-165 B.C.)	Ptolemy V (203-181 B.C.)	Seleucus IV (187-175 B.C.)
198 B.C.	*Antiochus III* the Great expelled Egyptians from Palestine and annexed it to the Seleucid Empire.		
	Book of Ecclesiasticus written (c. 180 B.C.). Septuagint completed (c. 150 B.C.).	Ptolemaic line continued under Roman domination until	Antiochus IV Epiphanes (175-163 B.C.)

452

Date	Jewish History	Contemporary Scene
167-165 B.C.	Enforced Hellenization of Jews. *Antiochus IV* sacked Jerusalem, profaned the temple, offered sacrifices to Olympian Zeus on altar of burnt offering. Maccabean revolt led by aged priest Mattathias and his five sons.	Antiochus V (163-162 B.C.) Egypt was incorporated into Roman Empire as a province (30 B.C.) Demetrius I (162-150 B.C.)
166-134 B.C.	**Palestine Under the Hasmonaeans** (166-63 B.C.) *Judas* (166-160 B.C.) defeated Syrian armies, cleansed and rededicated the temple (166-165 B.C.).	
	Jonathan (160-142 B.C.) diplomatically, and militarily made great strides toward Jewish independence.	Struggle between Demetrius II and Alexander Balas for throne. Alexander Balas (150-145 B.C.)
	Simon (142-134 B.C.) inaugurated period of Jewish independence (143-63 B.C.). Expelled Syrian garrison from Jerusalem, conquered Gezer and Joppa. Books of 1 Maccabees, Tobit, Judith.	Demetrius II (145-139) recognized Simon as high priest and granted Jews practically full independence (143 B.C.).
134-104 B.C.	*John Hyrcanus* (134-104 B.C.), son of Simon, embarked on a career of conquest in Transjordan, in Samaria (destroyed rival temple on Gerizim) and in Edom, ruling over a small empire from Lower Galilee to Negeb and from the Mediteranean to Nabatea.	Antiochus VII (139-134 B.C.) invaded Judea, took Jerusalem, imposed heavy tribute, but his death (134 B.C.) marked the virtual end of the Seleucid power over Palestine.

Date	Jewish History	Contemporary Scene
	Rise of the two great parties in Judaism— Pharisees and Sadducees—as well as the Essenes known from Philo, Josephus, Pliny and the Dead Sea Scrolls.	The weak uninfluential kingdom of Syria continued until Pompey took over area and made it a Roman province (64 B.C.).
104-69 B.C.	*Aristobulus I* (104-103 B.C.), a son of John Hyrcanus, seized control, but died shortly after.	Khirbet Qumran, headquarters of the Essenes on the NW shores of the Dead Sea, founded c. 110 B.C. and flourished until about 37 B.C.
	Alexander Jannaeus (103-76 B.C.), ruthless conqueror, sealed fate of Hasmonaean dynasty by alienating the Pharisees.	Many of Dead Sea Scrolls date from this period and later (*c.* 1 B.C. to A.D. 70).
	Alexandra (76-67 B.C.), Alexander Jannaeus' wife. Golden Age of Pharisaism. Probable date of Book of the Wisdom of Solomon, Sibylline Oracles, Book of Enoch, Book of Jubilees, 2 Maccabees.	Hyrcanus, elder son of Alexandra, was high priest. At her death Antipater, governor of Idumaea, persuaded Hyrcanus to flee to Petra and engage the aid of the Nabatean prince Aretas to win the throne of Judea for him against the rival claims of his brother Aristobulus. In the ensuing struggle Rome was appealed to and took over, ending the
	Aristobulus II (66-63 B.C.) deposed and carried to Rome to grace Pompey's triumph.	

Date	Jewish History	Contemporary Scene
		Hasmonaean monarchy. Catiline's conspiracy, Cicero's career, Catiline slain (62 B.C.).
63 B.C.	*Pompey* brought Palestine under Roman control and organized the Decapolis league in Transjordan to balance the power of Judea which was reduced to its former smallness.	
62-41 B.C.		Pompey, Caesar and Crassus formed First Triumvirate (60 B.C.). Caesar's Gallic Wars (58-51 B.C.). Civil war (Caesar vs. Pompey) ended in Caesar's assassination (44 B.C.).
	Palestine Under the Romans (63 B.C.—A.D. 135)	Second Triumvirate: Antony, Octavian, Lepidus (43 B.C.). Battles at Philippi (42 B.C.) and Actium (31 B.C.) left Octavian (Augustus) sole ruler.
	Antipater the Idumaean ruled Palestine under Roman grant (55-43 B.C.).	
	Herod and Phasael, Antipater's sons, were tetrarchs (41 B.C.).	
40-4 B.C.	*Antigonus,* Aristobulus' son, was high priest and king by aid of the Parthians (40-37 B.C.).	Augustus emperor (27 B.C.—A.D. 14).
	Herod the Great was king of Judea by Roman senatorial grant (37-4 B.C.).	Revival of Khirbet Qumran, Essenic headquarters near the Dead Sea, which flourished during the ministry of John the Baptist, Jesus and Paul.
	Birth of John the Baptist and Jesus (c. 6 or 5 B.C.).	

455

The Apocrypha

The Apocrypha is the name given to 14 books which originated in the period between the OT and the NT *after* the OT canon had closed (see "How the Bible Came to Us" in the Appendix to this handbook). These apocryphal books were *never* in the OT Hebrew canon. They were included in the Septuagint and the Latin Vulgate, being placed between the OT and NT. The Roman Catholic church receives 11 of the 14 as so-called "deutero-canonical" books, declaring them a part of Scripture by the Council of Trent in A.D. 1546. Protestants deny the canonical status of these books on the basis both of internal and external evidence. They were never recognized as Scripture by the Jews, nor by Jesus, nor by the NT, nor by any of the Church Fathers who objectively examined the evidence. The books in the Apocrypha are listed below and described.

1 Esdras. This book essentially covers the same historical material found in canonical Ezra, Nehemiah and 2 Chronicles. However, it contains an extended portion (3:1—5:6) that has no parallel in the Hebrew Bible. This portion consists mainly of a legendary story of a competition between three Jewish pages at Darius' court to ascertain the meaning of true wisdom. Zerubbabel was the winner and claimed as his prize the royal permission for the Jews to return and rebuild Jerusalem. The book is dated *c.* 100 B.C.

2 Esdras. This is a composite prophetic apocalyptic work completed *c.* A.D. 100. Ch. 1—2 are an anti-Jewish addition to the original Jewish Ezra Apocalypse, ch. 3—14. This latter consists of (1) the Salathiel Apocalypse, ch. 3—10, dealing with the problem of evil and its solution in the life to come; (2) the eagle vision, ch. 11—12, dealing with the Roman Empire and Messiah's coming; (3) the vision of the man (Messiah) rising from the sea, ch. 13; and a legend relating how Ezra rewrote the sacred literature, ch. 14. The last two chapters, 15—16, contain verbal echoes of the NT and were written later, probably as late as A.D. 270.

Tobit. This story, dated *c.* 150 B.C., is religious fiction. It is a didactic romance concerning a pious Jew of the Assyrian dispersion named Tobit, who is blinded accidentally in the course of giving decent burial to his fellow countrymen killed under Assyrian kings. In his distress Tobit prays for divine help and sends his son Tobias to recover a sum of money (about $20,000) he had deposited with a relative named Gabael. The angel Raphael, disguised as a dependable kinsman, accompanies Tobias, not only in answer to blind Tobit's prayer but also to help Sarah, the daughter of Raguel and Edna, in Ecbatana. Her seven husbands had been successively slain on the bridal night by the jealous demon Asmodaeus. Encamped on the Tigris, Tobias catches a fish. At Raphael's instruction he burns its heart and liver, exorcises the demon and marries Sarah. Raphael, meanwhile, goes on to Raguel, gets the money, and returns to conduct Tobias and his newly wed wife back to Tobit and his spouse Hannah at Nineveh. Their great distress at Tobias' long absence gives way to joy as they greet their beloved son and his bride. Their poverty is relieved by the money, and Tobit's blindness is cured as Tobias, at Raphael's direction, places the fish's gall on his aged father's eyes and his sight is restored. The angel Raphael reveals his identity and vanishes.

Judith. This is another fictional narrative with didactic value dating from the 2nd cen. B.C. Judith is a beautiful and devout Jewish widow of Bethulia (a pseudonym for Shechem), who by her valor saves her city from Nebuchadnezzar's invading army under Holophernes. When the city's elders decide to surrender if no help is forthcoming within five days, the noble Judith leaves the city and goes into the camp of Holophernes, beguiling him by her beauty and promises, until she returns to Bethulia with the general's head in her handbag. The result is that the defenders of the city sally forth and the vast army of Holophernes is routed and destroyed in the ensuing confusion. The high priest, Joakim, and the elders of Jerusalem come to Bethulia to do honor to the heroine, Judith.

The Remainder of Esther. These are passages composed in Greek that were inserted in the canonical book of Esther in the Septuagint version to show the hand of God in the narrative by putting the word "God" into the text. These additions consist of: (1) A dream by Mordecai and an account of his foiling a conspiracy against the king—a chapter of 17 verses preceding ch. 1 of the Hebrew canonical book. (2) A royal letter ordering the destruction of all Jews in the kingdom. This follows 3:13 of the Hebrew text. (3) Prayers of Mordecai and Esther, following ch. 4 of the Hebrew. (4) Esther's dramatic audience before Ahasuerus, adding 14 verses to ch. 5. (5) A royal letter telling of Haman's death, praising the Jews, and permitting them to defend themselves, following 8:12 of the Hebrew. (6) Interpretation of Mordecai's dream and a final word on the meaning of the feast of Purim. These follow the last chapter of the Hebrew Esther.

The Wisdom of Solomon. This is one of the most attractive and interesting of the apocryphal books, dating from about 50 B.C. The first section, 1:1—6:8, has been called "the book of eschatology" and sets forth the truth of immortality by contrasting the destiny of the righteous and the unrighteous. The second section, 6:9—11:1, is a panegyric of Wisdom, eloquent and beautiful, put upon the lips of Solomon. The third section, 11:2—19:22, is inferior to the first two sections. It presents a historical retrospect of Israel in Egypt and in the wilderness, interrupted by a discussion of the origin and evils of idolatry, ch. 13—15. The book is considered composite and anonymous.

Ecclesiasticus. This book of 51 chapters belongs to the *Hokmah* or Wisdom Literature of the Hebrews. This is the only book of the apocryphal literature whose author is known. He was Jesus the son of Sirach of Jerusalem (50:27), and he wrote about 175 B.C. His grandson translated the Hebrew original into Greek in 132 B.C., as is known from the Prologue. The traditional Latin name, Ecclesiasticus, designates it as *the* "church book" *par excellence* among the apocryphal books, attesting the high moral and spiritual character of its aphorisms or "wise sayings" and its general popularity among Christians from early times.

1 Maccabees. A historical and literary work of high quality, 1 Maccabees is an account of the Maccabean struggles from the revolt at Modin (167 B.C.) to the murder of Simon Maccabeus (134 B.C.). It catalogs the thrilling patriotic uprising of the sons of Mattathias of Modin, Judas, Jonathan, John, Eleazar and Simon, against Antiochus Epiphanes and his immediate successors.

2 Maccabees. This work covers in part the same period as 1 Maccabees (175-160 B.C.) but is inferior to it in historical worth, being to some extent a mythical panegyric of the Jewish revolt against Greek paganism. It claims to be a condensed account of a work by a certain Jason of Cyrene, of whom nothing is known.

Baruch. A work professing to have been written in Babylon by Jeremiah's secretary, Baruch. The first half (1:1—3:8) is written in prose, the second half (3:9—5:9) in poetry, echoing Isaiah, Jeremiah, Daniel and other prophets. The book contains prayers and confessions of the Jews in Exile, with promises of restoration.

The Song of the Three Children. This apocryphal addition to canonical Daniel was inserted after the story of the fiery furnace (Dan 3:23). It contains an eloquent prayer of Azariah, an account of miraculous deliverance, and a psalm of praise in which all three join.

Story of Susanna. This is another apocryphal addition to the canonical Daniel, telling how Susanna, a chaste Babylonian matron, was cleared of the trumped-up charges of adultery by the wisdom of the young man Daniel. It appears before ch. 1 in the Greek version and as ch. 13 in the Latin Vulgate.

Bel and the Dragon. These legends were designed to ridicule idolatry. They constitute the third apocryphal addition to Daniel. It was claimed that the statue of the idol Bel was a living deity because it supposedly devoured large amounts of food placed beside it each night. By scattering ashes on the temple floor, Daniel proves to the king that the priests of the god are the real consumers of the offerings. Thereupon the king destroys both Bel and his priests.

The other legend concerns a dragon worshiped in Babylon. Daniel, summoned to do it homage, feeds it a mixture of pitch, hair and fat, which causes it to explode. The enraged populace compels the king to throw Daniel in the den of lions, where he is fed on the sixth day by the prophet Habakkuk, who is angelically transported to Babylon by the hair of his head while carrying food and drink to the reapers in Judea. On the seventh day the king rescues Daniel and throws his would-be destroyers to the hungry lions.

The Prayer of Manasses. This is a purported penitential prayer of Manasseh, the wicked king of Judah, when he was carried away prisoner to Babylon by the Assyrians. It was inserted after 2 Chr 33:19, and dates probably from the 1st cen. B.C.

The Pseudepigrapha

In addition to the Apocrypha there are writings called the Pseudepigrapha ("false writings"). These are religious compositions penned under a false claim of authorship during the period 200 B.C.–A.D. 200, being attributed to such OT worthies as Adam, Enoch, Noah, Moses, Zephaniah, Baruch, etc. Unlike the Apocrypha (11 of the 14 of which are accepted as canonical by the Roman church), the Pseudepigraphal literature never vied for canonicity. These books are mainly apocalyptic, didactic and legendary. A word of description of some of the most important books follows.

Assumption of Moses. This consists of alleged predictions of the great lawgiver spoken and entrusted to Joshua shortly before Moses' death. The book was written by a Pharisee about A.D. 15 as a protest against the growing secularization of the Pharisaic party of his day.

Ascension of Isaiah. This work consists of three parts—the Martyrdom of Isaiah, the Vision of Isaiah, and the Testament of Hezekiah. The long-lost Testament of Hezekiah (2:13—4:18) gives a useful insight into the spiritual condition of the Christian church at the close of the apostolic period. The Vision of Isaiah (6:1—9:40) gives valuable insight into 1st cen. beliefs on the Trinity, the incarnation, the resurrection, and heaven. The Martyrdom of Isaiah is fragmentary (1:1, 2, 6-13; 2:1-8, 10; 3:12; 5:1-14). It recounts the death of Isaiah at the hands of wicked Manasseh by being sawed to pieces.

Book of Enoch. This is a fragmentary work consisting of revelations reputedly given to Noah and Enoch concerning Christ's coming and future judgment. It is by unknown authors and was written in the first two centuries B.C.

Book of Jubilees. Dividing the history of the world into Jubilee periods of 50-year cycles (Lev 25:8-12), the Pharisee author of this work (153-105 B.C.) wrote to save Judaism from the demoralizing effects of Hellenism by extolling the law and presenting the Hebrew patriarchs in an irreproachable light.

Sibylline Oracles. These oracles originated in the Maccabean era. Dealing with the downfall of empires and the advent of the messianic age, they are modeled after the prophetic sayings of the Greek Sibyls. The original Sibyl of Cumae is first alluded to by Heraclitus of Ephesus (500 B.C.).

Psalms of Solomon. These consist of 18 psalms stemming from the middle of the 1st cen. B.C. Apparently penned by an anonymous Pharisee, they tell of the coming Messiah.

Testaments of the Twelve Patriarchs. These 12 testaments allege to record the dying speeches of Jacob's twelve sons, being inspired by Gen 49. In its final form the book dates perhaps as late as A.D. 250, though it includes material composed as early as the 2nd cen. B.C.

The Targums

The Targums are free renderings of the Hebrew Scriptures into Aramaic after the latter had become the common language of Palestine in the post-Exilic period. They were first oral, the Hebrew Scriptures being read and the Aramaic rendering given. The earliest written Targums, such as Onkelos on the Pentateuch and Jonathan on the Prophets, date from Christian times.

The Talmud

This is a body of Hebrew civil and canonical laws based on the Torah of Moses. It is the condensation of the thinking of rabbis from c. 300 B.C. to A.D. 500. The Talmud ("teaching") consists of the *Mishnah,* or traditional oral law deduced from the written law of Moses itself, and the *Gemara,* a commentary on these legal traditions. The Aramaic language is used in the Gemara. Closely connected with the Talmud is the Midrash, the earliest synagogue sermons in Hebrew and Aramaic, expounding the Hebrew OT Scriptures. The Midrash flourished 100 B.C.–A.D. 300.

The Synagogue

The synagogue (from the Gr. *synagōgē,* "a gathering" or "assembly") had its origin evidently first in homes in Babylon (cf. Ezk 8:1; 20:1-3). The "house synagogue," like the first Christian churches which met in homes, after the Exile gradually developed into formal assemblies for instruction, public worship and prayer. They replaced the temple worship, which was now no longer possible for the Jews who were scattered far beyond Palestine. Every town harboring any considerable number of Jews in the Graeco-Roman world of 300 B.C.–A.D. 300 had its synagogue for worship and instruction in the law and the prophets (cf. Lk 4:16-30). These were the repositories of the Hebrew Scriptures and were among the first places the Christian gospel was proclaimed (Acts 13:5, 14; 14:1). Since the dispersion was widespread, the synagogue was a common institution in the Roman world.

The Sanhedrin

The Sanhedrin was an aristocratic body possessing powers of jurisdiction, doubtless going back in principle to King Jehoshaphat's time (cf. 2 Chr 19:5-11). It developed into the supreme native court of the Jews by Jesus' day and functioned in both civil and religious realms till the fall of Jerusalem (A.D. 70). A council in the Ezra-Nehemiah era (450-400 B.C.) known as the Great Synagogue is echoed in popular tradition and is thought to have given way about 250 B.C. to the 70-membered Sanhedrin (Aramaized form of Gr. *synedrion,* "a sitting together" or "assembly") presided over by the high priests.

The Pharisees

During the Maccabean period in the reign of John Hyrcanus (134-104 B.C.), the conflicting parties in Judaism, the Pharisees, Sadducees and Essenes, came into existence. The Pharisees were apparently successors to the Hasidim ("the pious"), who stood true to the law under Antiochus Epiphanes' proscription of Judaism in 168 B.C. They were rigid legalistic separatists, with watchwords of prayer, repentance and charitable giving. From an admirable beginning in the fires of Maccabean suffering, they gradually degenerated into empty, unprincipled religionists in Jesus' day.

The Sadducees

Probably Zadokites, partisans of Solomon's priest Zadok (1 Kgs 2:35), the Sadducees were chiefly aristocratic, worldly-minded priests, who obeyed the letter of the law but denied resurrection and future retribution. They welcomed Hellenic culture and were willing to gain earthly advantage through military strategy or adroit diplomacy. Their deep cleavage with the Pharisees continued until Jesus' day, after their differences had wrecked the Hasmonaean kingdom years before.

The Scribes and Essenes

The scribes were copyists of Holy Scripture, intimately conversant with the Mosaic law, hence also called lawyers. During the inter-biblical period they became influential and appear prominently in Jesus' day.

The Essenes were a monastic sect rather than a party such as the Pharisees and Sadducees. Until the discovery in 1947 of the Dead Sea Scrolls, Philo, Josephus and Pliny were the only sources of information on this communal monastic order. A similar if not identical group is now well known as a result of the excavation of its headquarters at Qumran on the NW shore of the Dead Sea. The recovery of their book of rules and order has corroborated ancient sources and added to our knowledge of sectarian Judaism from about 200 B.C. to A.D. 70.

Preparation for the Greek New Testament

The interbiblical period witnessed the development of the various Greek dialects into a *lingua franca* of the Hellenistic world through the conquests of Alexander the Great. This universal language affected vitally the Jews of the diaspora and eventuated in the translation of the OT into Greek (the Septuagint). This translation became an important factor in the formation of the NT, and with it, constituted the Bible of early Christianity.

Moreover, Greek learning and culture, Roman law and Roman roads, Jewish monotheism and Jewish synagogues (the latter wide-spread as a result of the Jewish diaspora), and Jewish apocalyptic and messianic hopes prepared the world for the coming of Christ and Christianity. Divine providence can be traced everywhere in the long interval between the Testaments. The goal was the incarnation and birth of the long-awaited Messiah and Saviour of the world, prophesied so often in the OT. To this great event all preceding centuries of world history, especially Jewish history, pointed.

Introducing the New Testament

The OT constitutes the *preparation* for Christ and contains prophecies of His divine person and redemptive work. The NT is the account of the realization of these predictions in the *appearance* of the Redeemer and the provisions of His glorious gospel.

In the Gospels Christ is *manifested* to the world and His gospel *provided* in the death, resurrection and ascension of the Redeemer. In the Acts Christ is *proclaimed* and His gospel *propagated* in the world. In the epistles His gospel is *expounded* in its doctrinal and practical meaning. In the Apocalypse all the redemptive purposes of God in and through the Redeemer are *consummated* for time and eternity. The NT is thus the capstone and fulfillment of the prophetic and redemptive truths contained in the OT, the OT forming the foundation for the completed edifice of revealed truth found in the NT.

THE NEW TESTAMENT AT A GLANCE (27 BOOKS)

Historical	Doctrinal	Prophetic
THE FOUR GOSPELS	**PAUL'S EPISTLES**	**THE REVELATION**
Portraits of the Person and Work of Christ	Romans 1 Corinthians 2 Corinthians Galatians Ephesians Philippians Colossians	1 Thessalonians 2 Thessalonians 1 Timothy 2 Timothy Titus Philemon	Apocalypse of Jesus Christ
Matthew—Christ as King Mark——Christ as Servant Luke——Christ as Man John——Christ as God		Foreview of: (1) Church, 2:1—3:22 (2) Tribulation, 4:1—19:10 (3) Second Advent, 19:11-21 (4) Millennium, 20:1-10 (5) Eternal State, 20:11—22:21
ACTS OF THE APOSTLES	**GENERAL EPISTLES**	
History of the Birth and Early Life of the Church	Hebrews James 1 Peter 2 Peter	1 John 2 John 3 John Jude	

THE FOUR GOSPELS

WHAT THE GOSPELS ARE

The four Gospels are neither histories of the life of Christ nor biographies. They are rather portraits of the person and work of the long-promised Messiah, Israel's King and the world's Saviour. As portraits they present four different poses of *one* unique personality. Matthew by the Holy Spirit presents Christ as King, Mark as Servant, Luke as Man, and John as God.

Although featuring Christ as King, Matthew sketches His role as a King in closest connection with His character as Servant, as Man, and as God. Likewise, although featuring Him as Servant, Mark depicts Christ's servant role in closest connection with His character as King, Man and God. Similarly Luke focuses the spotlight on Christ as Man and John as God, but like the other evangelists they do not separate Him from His full-orbed character. Thus all four writers present the one and same unique Person, the God-Man, Servant of the Lord, King of Israel, humanity's Redeemer.

THE PURPOSE OF THE GOSPELS

In their fourfold portraiture of Christ's person as King, Servant, Man and God, the Gospels center in Messiah's threefold ministry of Prophet, Priest and King. As Prophet, fulfilling Moses' great prediction (Deut 18:15-19), He was *the* Prophet *par excellence* by virtue of the uniqueness of His person. He not merely spoke *for* God as other prophets who preceded Him, but God spoke *through* Him as Son (Heb 1:1-2). In contrast to the OT prophet who was a voice for God, the Son, being God, was the voice of God Himself. As a Priest Christ became both the Sacrifice and the Sacrificer as He died on the cross to save sinners (Heb 9:14), and through His resurrection lives eternally to make intercession for them (Heb 7:25). As Israel's King He was rejected at His first advent, but will reign in that office at His second advent, fulfilling the Davidic covenant (2 Sam 7:8-16; Lk 1:30-33; Acts 2:29-36; 15:14-17).

THE MEANING OF THE WORD "GOSPEL"

As applied to the four portraitures of Christ, the term "gospel" (cf. Mk 1:1) is used in the sense of the good news of salvation provided by the death, burial and resurrection of Christ (cf. 1 Cor 15:1-3). The Gospels, strictly speaking, are not an exposition of the gospel, although occasional expository notations occur, as in John.

They are *an account of the provision of the gospel* for needy sinners in the person and work of Christ. For the historical outworking of the divinely provided gospel we must go to Acts. For a doctrinal exposition of the gospel we must go to the epistles, notably the 13 Pauline letters.

WHAT THE GOSPELS ACCOMPLISH

Describing the eternal preexistence, human birth, death, resurrection and ascension of Jesus the Christ, as well as His life and teachings, the four Gospels present a living, dynamic, unique personality, God become man, to work out man's redemption from sin. These four portraits present Him as Lord and Saviour, rather than describing all He did and in the precise order in which He did it. They introduce us to Him, rather than to His life as a whole.

The Gospels are designedly incomplete as a story, but marvelously complete and purposeful as a divine *revelation of the Son of God our Saviour!* And this is faith's need. It is also unbelief's stumbling block.

THE KEY TO THE CORRECT INTERPRETATION OF THE GOSPELS

It is necessary to realize that the period described is culminative of the OT age, preparatory to and predictive of the new age, but *not* the new age itself. Not until the ascension of Christ and the consequent advent of the Spirit at Pentecost (Acts 2) did the new age of the church begin.

THE JEWISH BACKGROUND OF THE GOSPELS

The fabric of the Gospels is woven out of OT type, allusion and quotation (cf. Mt 1:1; Lk 24:27, 44, 45). Our Lord was "made under the law" (Gal 4:4), ministered primarily to the Jews in the legal age (Mt 10:5-6; 15:23-25), and was "a minister of the circumcision for the truth of God, to confirm the promises made unto the fathers" (Rom 15:8).

As King and Messiah He was announced by John the Baptist, offered the kingdom to Israel and was rejected by them (Mt 1—12). As Prophet He predicted the new age (Mt 13), and His second advent (Mt 24—25). As Priest He died and rose again, fulfilling the law and bringing in grace (Jn 1:17).

Up to the cross the Gospels are an extension of the OT economy, seen in their strong Jewish coloring, which did not end till the veil of the temple was torn supernaturally at Christ's death (Mt 27:51).

THE GOSPELS AND HUMANITY

The four Gospels are slanted toward the various classes of society which existed in the 1st cen. A.D.: Matthew toward the Jews, Mark toward the Romans, Luke toward the Greeks, and John toward those neither Jews nor Gentiles (cf. 1 Cor 10:32) but believers on the Lord Jesus Christ.

COMPARISON OF THE FOUR GOSPELS

Matthew	Mark	Luke	John
The Prophesied King	The Obedient Servant	The Perfect Man	The Divine Son
Lionlike	Oxlike	Manlike	Eaglelike
Prophetic	Practical	Historical	Spiritual
To the Jew	To the Roman	To the Greek	To the Church
The Davidic King	The Servant of the Lord	The Son of Man	The Word of God
David's Righteous Branch (Jer 23:5-6)	My Servant the Branch (Zech 3:8)	The Man the Branch (Zech 6:12)	The Branch of the Lord (Isa 4:2)

OFFICIAL			PERSONAL
King	Servant	Son of Man	Son of God
	Synoptic		Supplementary
Outward, public, Galilean, earthly			Inward, private, Judean, heavenly

CHRIST'S WORDS IN THE FOUR GOSPELS

	Matthew	Mark	Luke	John
Verses, AV	1071	678	1151	879
Verses, RSV	1068	661	1149	866
Verses of Christ's words	644	285	586	419
Approx. percentage	60%	42%	50%	50%

Of the 3779 verses (AV), 1934, or more than 50%, were spoken by our Lord.

THE FOUR GOSPELS AND THE OT

	Matthew	Mark	Luke	John
Quotations from OT	53	36	25	20
Allusions to OT	76	27	42	105

POLITICAL BACKGROUND OF NT TIMES

Roman Emperors

Date	Emperor	Biblical Event
27 B.C.–A.D. 14	Caesar Augustus	Birth of Jesus, boyhood at Nazareth.
A.D. 14-37	Tiberius Caesar	Public ministry, death, resurrection of Jesus.
A.D. 37-41	Caligula	Growth of church, conversion of Paul.
A.D. 41-54	Claudius	Early missionary labors of Paul.
A.D. 54-68	Nero	Paul's later labors; martyrdom at Rome.
A.D. 68-69	Galba, Otho, Vitellius	Jewish Roman war in Palestine.
A.D. 69-79	Vespasian	Fall and destruction of Jerusalem and the Jewish state. Jews scattered.
A.D. 79-81	Titus	
A.D. 81-96	Domitian	John's probable exile to Patmos. The Revelation.

Herodian Rulers

37-4 B.C.	Herod the Great	King of Jews, great builder, Hellenizer.
4 B.C.–A.D. 6	Archelaus	Son of Herod, ethnarch of Judea, cruel.
4 B.C.–A.D. 39	Herod Antipas	Tetrarch of Galilee and Perea. Killed John the Baptist.
4 B.C.–A.D. 34	Philip	Tetrarch of Iturea and Trachonitis.
A.D. 37-44	Herod Agrippa I	Ruled tetrarchy of Philip, Judea, Perea and Galilee (41-44).
A.D. 50-93	Herod Agrippa II	Ruled former tetrarchy of Philip and Lysanias and parts of Galilee and Perea.

Procurators of Judea and Palestine

Judea, A.D. 6-41		Palestine, A.D. 44-66	
A.D. 6-9	Coponius	A.D. 44-c.46	Cuspius Fadus
A.D. 9-12	M. Ambivius	A.D. c.46-48	Tiberius Alexander
A.D. 12-15	Annius Rufus	A.D. 48-52	Ventidius Cumanus
A.D. 15-26	Valerius Gratus	A.D. 52-60	Antonius Felix
A.D. 26-36	Pontius Pilate	A.D. 60-62	Porcius Festus
A.D. 37	Marullus	A.D. 62-64	Clodius Albinus
A.D. 37-41	Herennius Capito	A.D. 64-66	Gessius Florus

MATTHEW

THE GOSPEL OF THE SON OF DAVID

The Author. The writer of this Gospel is anonymous, but from a very early period he has been identified as Matthew or Levi, the publican, a Galilean Jew who became one of Jesus' disciples. Modern criticism disfavors authorship by Matthew and a traditional early date, generally positing an unknown Christian as the writer sometime after A.D. 66. It is held that the anonymous author used a collection of sayings compiled by Matthew, to which Papias refers (*c.* A.D. 140), and so the name of Matthew came to identify this Gospel. This position, however, lacks proof. It seems best to hold to the traditional authorship by Matthew and date the book around the middle of the 1st cen.

The Scope and Theme. Matthew is a Jewish Gospel, rooted in OT prophecy relating to the coming of Messiah-King and His kingdom. It sets forth the King in His lineage from David, His birth and His royal infancy. Introduced by His herald, the King is presented in His public ministry. His rejection as King is followed by His death as the son of Abraham and His resurrection as the Son of God.

Since this Gospel is Jewish, the key to the interpretation of Matthew is an understanding of God's program for Israel and her Messiah. This involves the great focal prophecy of Israel's future earthly kingdom under Messiah. It was rejected at the first advent but is to be established (Acts 1:6) at the second advent. The theme of Matthew is the Saviour-King and His kingdom.

> **Outline**
> The King Manifested and His Kingdom Rejected, Ch. 1—12
> The Rejected King, His Teaching and Ministry, Ch. 13—25
> The King's Passion and Death, Ch. 26—27
> The King's Resurrection and Commission, Ch. 28

CHAPTER 1. THE GENEALOGY AND BIRTH OF THE KING

His Royal Descent, 1-17. The King is *first* named "son of David" in the kingly line, true heir to David's throne, 1; then "son of Abraham," the seed through whom the whole earth will be blessed. The order is significant because to the Jew (and this Gospel is slanted to the Jew) the Lord was first to present Himself as *King,* after that as Saviour (cf. Jn 1:11-12). The genealogy, 2-17, has three divisions of 14 generations each, David alone being designated explicitly as king, 6 (cf. 2 Sam 7:8-16). Matthew's genealogy shows Jesus' *legal* right to the Davidic throne through the line of Solomon and Joseph, the latter being the supposed father of Jesus (Lk 3:23; 4:22). If Jesus had been the son of Mary without her being legally the wife of Joseph, a son of Solomon, His royal claim would have been rejected from the outset. Luke's genealogy presents Jesus as the Son of Man, and a descendant of David by Mary, but through the house of Nathan (not Solomon). As the virgin-born son of Mary, however, He had no legal right to the throne. This had to come through Joseph.

His Virgin Birth, 18-25. The genealogy, 1-17, proves that Jesus was born legal King of the Jews, the son of David, the son of Abraham. The account of His conception by the Holy Spirit in the womb of a virgin, 18-25, shows Him also to be the Son of God, the Eternal Word, who was with God and was God (Jn 1:1-2) yet became man (Lk 1:26-35; 2:1-7; Jn 1:14), fulfilling Isa 7:14 (cf. Mt 1:22-23). The God-Man alone could be "Jesus" (Gr. form of Heb. "Jehoshua," Joshua, the Lord-Saviour). Verses 18-25 indicate Jesus was conceived by the Holy Spirit, and hence had a sinless human nature joined to Deity. Thus Jesus is able to "save his people from their sins," 21.

CHAPTER 2. THE INFANCY OF THE KING

The Visit of the Magi, 1-12. This visit of believing Gentiles to worship the newborn King particularly fits this Gospel of the King and hence is recorded only here. It occurred perhaps months after the nativity, while the holy family, however, was still residing in Bethlehem. The magi were a learned class in Persia. Herod the Great, an able and cruel Idumaean, ruled Judea as king by grant of the Roman senate from 37 to 4 B.C. At this time he was an aged, failing tyrant, notoriously jealous and unprincipled, a stark contrast to the true "King of the Jews," 2. The glimpse given here of the wicked wretch, insanely insecure, accords perfectly with what is known of him from history and archaeology. He who even murdered some of his own family appears as the murderer of the innocent children of Bethlehem and as the would-be murderer of Messiah. The star, 2, 7, 9, was probably not the conjunction of Jupiter and Saturn in 6 B.C., nor an exploding star (nova). It was rather a totally supernatural astronomical phenomenon, as supernatural and humanly inexplicable as the birth of Him whom it signalized (cf.

"*his* star," 2). The Gentiles (cf. Lk 2:32) brought gold, bespeaking the King's deity; frankincense, indicating the fragrance of His life; and myrrh, used in embalming the dead, hinting of His mission to die.

Flight into Egypt, 13-23. Demon powers through Herod, and later through the leaders of His own nation, resisted the King. Satan centered His attack against God's plans in Christ for the earth. Egypt, which saw the great enslavement of Israel, now became the refuge of Israel's Deliverer and the world's Redeemer in the form of a helpless baby.

CHAPTER 3. THE KING'S HERALD AND BAPTISM

The King's Herald, 1-12. John the Baptist, predicted in the OT, 3 (cf. Isa 40:3-5; Mal 3:1), now appears as the King's forerunner. John's birth and mission are described by Luke (Lk 1:5-80). His message, "Repent ye: for the kingdom of heaven is at hand," 2, was an announcement of the messianic kingdom as foretold by OT prophets to be set up on the earth over which David's son and Lord is to reign. It was "at hand" from the commencement of John's announcement here to the rejection of the King (Mt 12:1-45; cf. notes on Mt 4:17), and the announcement of a new brotherhood (Mt 12:46-50). It is the "kingdom of heaven" (the heavens) because it is the administration of the heavens upon the earth (Mt 6:10), being a term derived from Daniel (cf. Dan 2:34-35, 44; 7:23-27).

John's baptism was not Christian baptism (cf. Acts 19:1-7), but an outward act signifying the repentance of the candidate and identification with John's message, 11. In 11 and 12 the two advents blend. As a result of the first advent and Christ's finished redemption, He baptized with the Holy Spirit, in the sense that Pentecost (the initial occurrence of the baptism, Acts 2:1-4) was a result of Christ's atoning work. The baptism with fire (judgment) awaits the second advent.

The King's Baptism, 13-17. Why should the Sinless One insist on a ceremony that signified confession of sin and repentance, 13-14? The answer was, "to fulfill all righteousness," 15, i.e., the righteous requirements of the Mosaic law. Since Jesus was here being consecrated to His public ministry of King, Prophet and Priest, the essence of which was to center in His priestly work of redemption, it is His setting apart to His work as Priest that here comes into clearest focus. The Levitical law required that all priests be consecrated when they "began to be about thirty years of age" (Lk 3:23;

cf. Num 4:3) by washing, then anointing (Ex 29:4-7; Lev 8:6-36). Aaron shared in the washing, being a sinner and needing it, and thus furnishes the type of the baptism of Christ, who not being a sinner Himself and not needing it nevertheless identified Himself with sinners and fulfilled the Aaronic type. Jesus' baptism (washing), 14-15, was followed by His anointing, when the heavens were opened and the Holy Spirit came upon Him, 16, the Father's voice sealing His threefold ministry, 17. This was the priestly anointing (cf. Ex 29:5-7, where the anointing followed the washing) of Him who was thus divinely consecrated for the work of redemption (Acts 4:27; 10:38), as well as that of King and Prophet.

CHAPTER 4. THE TESTING OF THE KING

The Testing by the Devil, 1-11. This testing of the "last Adam" (1 Cor 15:45) in the wilderness was in striking contrast to that of the first Adam in paradise. The first Adam, as lord of the first creation, acting from himself in disobedience to God, fell and lost all. But the second Adam, as Servant in submission to the Father, acted wholly in dependence upon the Father, and thus resisting the

While the superstructure of this Capernaum synagogue certainly dates after Jesus' day, the foundations are thought by many to have existed when He taught there. (*Courtesy IIS*)

473

threefold temptation of the devil, regained all. He thus proved His worthiness and ability as the Sinless One to redeem sinners as Priest; as the True One, rejecting Satan's lies, to declare truth as the Prophet; and rejecting Satan's false kingship, to be the true King of kings and Ruler of the redeemed earth. The Man of obedience conquered Satan by the Word of God in Deuteronomy, the book of obedience (cf. Deut 8:3; 6:16; 10:20).

The King Begins His Public Ministry, 12-25. Jesus resided in Capernaum, 12-13 (Tell Hum), a populous, bustling fishing port on the NW shore of the Lake of Galilee. His incipient ministry fulfilled Isa 9:1-2. The King's message (also that of His forerunner) was, "Repent: for the kingdom of heaven is at hand," 17 (cf. notes on Mt 3:2). This expression "at hand" or "has drawn near" meant that the King was then present and that a bona fide offer of the kingdom was being made to Israel on the *one condition* of her repentance. The nation's failure to repent, even with its true King in its midst, and the consequent rejection of both the King and the kingdom were part of the divine plan to demonstrate the nation's inveterate sinfulness and the necessity of the King's atoning death as a prerequisite for the future establishment of the kingdom. The good news of the kingdom is called "the gospel of the kingdom," 23. The call of the disciples Peter and Andrew, 18-20 (cf. Mk 1:16-20; Lk 5: 2-11), and James and John, 21-22, is given. On Decapolis, 25, see note on Mk 7.

CHAPTERS 5—7. KINGDOM PROCLAMATIONS OF THE KING

Character of the Citizens of the Kingdom, 5:1-16. Ch. 5—7 present the Sermon on the Mount, uttered by the King when "the kingdom of the heavens" was being announced "at hand." The beatitudes, 1-12, give the character of those who inherit the kingdom. Such who really "repent" become also "the salt of the earth," 13, as well as "the light of the world," 14-16.

The King and the Mosaic Law, 5:17-48. The King fulfilled the law, confirming and emphasizing its deeper spiritual meaning. By so doing, He condemned every natural, spiritually unrenewed man, and showed that the kingdom of the heavens will be established only through a King who must also become the Saviour of those who will be His citizens. Only then will they enjoy such righteousness, love and perfection as the King here describes. That day will be fully realized at His second advent when the kingdom will come and His will will be done on earth as it is in heaven (Mt 6:10).

Heirs of the Kingdom and Prayer, 6:1-18. Heirs of the kingdom are to be motivated by true inner righteousness, which they are to possess and practice. This righteousness brings them into fellowship with God as their Father (used 12 times in this chapter). Such fellowship and consequent righteousness anticipate the cross where their possession was made possible. The model prayer, 9-13, related to the kingdom of the heavens as at hand, and was, strictly speaking, for the Jewish disciples of that era who anticipated the establishment of the kingdom (cf. 10). Its petitions, however, are applicable in every age and as such have relevancy to the church today.

Heirs of the Kingdom and the World, 6:19-34. How those who have the true motive of righteousness, who move in the sphere of the Father's presence, are to act toward worldly wealth and cares is here outlined.

Heirs of the Kingdom and Censorious Judging, 7:1-14. Judgment of motives is here forbidden (cf. 1 Cor 4:5; 5:12-13). On verse 6 cf. 2 Pet 2:22, where "dogs" and "swine" symbolize unregenerated externalists. Prayer is the cure for censorious judging, 7-11, and the "golden rule," 12, summarizes proper human motives. The two ways, 13-14, recall Ps 1.

Heirs of the Kingdom Warned Against False Teachers, 7:15-29. The fruits of false teachers attest them, 15-20, not their empty profession, 21-23, which is illustrated by those who build upon a rock and upon sand, 24-29.

CHAPTERS 8—9. THE MANIFESTATION OF THE KING

The King's Power Over Sickness, 8:1-17. Miraculous signs demonstrated to Israel that the kingdom was at hand. A leper was healed, 1-4; the centurion's slave, 5-13; Peter's mother-in-law, 14-15, and many others, 16-17. Matthew arranges these miracles unchronologically (cf. Mark and Luke) to emphasize the Jewish character of his Gospel. The first miracle recorded here, that of the cleansed leper (Mk 1:40; Lk 5:12-14), portrays the sinful nation (Num 12:13; 2 Kgs 5:1-15; Isa 1:5-6) which should have manifested the faith of this leper, but, like the priest to whom the cleansed leper was sent, failed to declare that the Lord, the King, had come to His people. The centurion, a Gentile, manifested greater faith than Israel and speaks of the Gentiles of this age who will believe. The King's healing of Peter's mother-in-law illustrates Israel's restoration after this present age, while the healing of all the sick, 16-17, may preview kingdom blessings at the second advent.

The King's Power Over Nature and Demons, 8:18-34, showed Him Lord of creation and controller of the demon world. (Cf. note on Sea of Galilee in Mk 6.)

The King's Power to Forgive Sin and Other Signs, 9:1-38. The palsied man's healing showed the King's power to forgive sin, 1-8. Matthew's call, 9, and the King's eating with publicans, 10-13, demonstrated His mission to call sinners to repentance. The new cloth and new wine skins, 16-17, prefigure the better righteousness of grace contrasted with the old cloth and wineskins of legal ordinances (cf. Mk 2:21-22; Lk 5:36-39). The ruler's daughter, 18-26, pictures Israel who will be raised after the period of the Gentiles. His kingdom proclamation was being rejected, 27-34, despite the miracles accompanying it, 35-38, and the shepherd heart of the King.

CHAPTER 10. THE KING'S AMBASSADORS

The Twelve and Their Commission, 1-15. The King sent forth His 12 disciples, endued with miraculous powers, to proclaim the kingdom to Israelites only, 1-6. Their message was identical with that of John, the King's forerunner, 7 (cf. Mt 3:2 and comment) and of the King Himself (Mt 4:17 and comment). Their commission was to confirm the gospel of the kingdom with miraculous powers. Both the commission and the message were temporary and ended with the official rejection of the kingdom by Israel (ch. 11-12).

Resumption of the Commission, 16-42. The scope of 16-23 goes beyond the kingdom ministry of the 12 and is prophetic of the preaching of the Jewish remnant in the dark persecution-ridden days of the Great Tribulation preceding the second advent, when the gospel of the kingdom will again be proclaimed. Verse 23 will be fulfilled then. Verses 24-42 give encouragement to true disciples of the King.

CHAPTER 11. REJECTION OF THE KINGDOM MESSAGE

John the Baptist Rejected, 1-19. Jesus' kingdom ministry incited an inquiry from the forerunner, 1-6. John's imprisonment may have given rise to his doubts, but the miraculous evidences of Jesus' person were intended to calm his fears. The King's praise of John was gracious and eloquent, 7-19. He that is least in the kingdom of heaven, 11, when it is established on earth, will be greater in position (not in moral grandeur) than John, who did not enter the kingdom but merely announced that which was then rejected. Verse

12 emphasizes the violence the kingdom suffered from opposers and sinners. Had Israel repented, John would have fulfilled the prophecy of Elijah's coming (Mal 4:5). But that generation in its unbelief could not be pleased, and rejected both the forerunner of the King and the King Himself, 16-19.

The King Rejected, 20-24. The kingdom of heaven, announced by John, preached and authenticated by the King and His ambassadors by miraculous signs, was morally rejected, so the King announced judgment. Chorazin (Kerazeh) was located scarcely two miles N of Capernaum (Tell Hum) in the area on the NW shore of the Lake of Galilee, where extensive ruins remain, including a synagogue known for two centuries. Bethsaida was the fishing quarter ("Fisherton") of Capernaum, the name meaning "houses," i.e., place of (fish) catching. It evidently spread on both sides of the Jordan as the river entered the lake. Capernaum was the thriving populous metropolis of the region on the NW shores of Galilee.

The New Message of the King, 25-30. This was a crisis in the King's ministry. He turned from the rejecting, unrepentant nation, and offered rest and service to individuals in the nation who were repentant and conscious of need.

CHAPTER 12. REJECTION OF THE KING CONSUMMATED

The King in Rejection, 1-21. The events of this chapter focus upon the full rejection of the kingdom and mark the great turning point in Matthew's Gospel. No longer was the kingdom preached to Israel. Rejection of the kingdom messengers was seen in the accusation of the Pharisees concerning breaking the sabbath, 1-8. As the rejected *King,* our Lord aptly referred to what David did in rejection (1 Sam 21:6). He declared Himself Lord of the sabbath, and healed the man with the atrophied hand on the sabbath, 9-14. In demonic hate the leaders planned to murder Him, 14. The rejected King of Israel intimated a future turning to the Gentiles, 15-21 (cf. Mt 10:5-6; Isa 42:1-4). This would await His official rejection manifested in His crucifixion (Mt 26—27) and the final rejection of the resurrected Christ (Lk 24:46-47; Acts 9:15; 13:46; 28:25-28).

The King and the Unpardonable Sin, 22-45. The healing of the demoniac, 22-23, precipitated the blasphemy of the Pharisees, 24, who committed the unpardonable sin of attributing the mighty works of the incarnate King to Satanic (demonic) power, rather than to the Holy Spirit, 25-32. Announcing judgment once more, 33-42 (cf. 11:20-24), the King uttered a panoramic prophecy of the nation Israel under the figure of a demoniac, 43-45. That generation in its

Pharisaic externalism was like a demoniac in the undemonized state — empty, swept, furbished. The entrance of seven worse demons predicted the demon control of the nation in the last days, when it will fall under Antichrist's sway (Dan 9:27; Rev 9:1-12; cf. 2 Thess 2:8-10; Jn 5:43).

The King's New Relationship, 46-50. King and kingdom message rejected, the King refused to see even His own, symbolizing the fact that His relationship to His own nation, to which He had come as promised King, was now abrogated. A new message and relationship obtained (ch. 13).

CHAPTER 13. THE REJECTED KING TELLS OF THE INTERIM KINGDOM

The King at the Seaside, 1-2. The King began to teach in parables. These parables, reported in full only in Matthew, portray the mysteries of the kingdom of the heavens. This was now no longer the kingdom so clearly promised to Israel by OT prophets, preached as at hand by the forerunner, the King Himself and His heralds (ch. 3—12), and rejected (ch. 11—12). It was the kingdom of the heavens in its mystery form, setting forth spiritual conditions that will prevail on the earth between Israel's rejection of the King and His kingdom and her future acceptance of it. These mysteries were not revealed in the OT (cf. Mt 13:11, 34-35), in contrast to that kingdom which had just been rejected by the nation and was well known from full OT revelation (e.g., Isa 9, 11, 35; Mic 4, etc.).

The Seven Parables (Mysteries) of the Kingdom, 3-52. They are called "mysteries" because they contain truth previously not revealed. The seven parables deal with the present age when Israel, the vineyard, is untended (Isa 5:1-7). *Parable 1* reveals that our Lord sows the seed of the Word in the field (the world), 3-23. *Parable 2*, the good seed and the tares, 24-30, interpreted in 36-43, shows Satan's activity and deception during this age in counterfeiting the wheat, the true children of the kingdom, with false professors (Mt 7:21-23). *Parable 3*, the mustard seed, 31-32, symbolizes the rapid growth of the mystery form of the kingdom. *Parable 4*, the leaven hidden in three measures of meal, 35, warns of the permeation of the truth of the Word with the error of leaven by false teaching (the woman) during this age (cf. Mt 16:11-12; Mk 8:15; 1 Cor 5:6; Gal 5:9). *Parable 5* portrays our Lord who gave all He had to possess the treasure (Israel) hid in the field, 44 (cf. Isa 53:4-10; Ps 22:1; 2 Cor 8:9). He will reinstate this treasure on the basis of His atoning death. *Parable 6* shows our Lord as a merchant, who found "one pearl of great price" (the Church, Eph 5:25-27) and sold all at Calvary to purchase it, 45-46. *Parable* 7 presents the net gathering both good and bad, 47-52, which will remain together during this age until separated at its consummation.

Further Evidences of the King's Rejection, 53-58, as He returned to Nazareth.

CHAPTER 14. THE MARTYRDOM OF THE KING'S HERALD

John's Martyrdom, 1-14. Herod Antipas, a son of Herod the Great by a Samaritan woman, Malthace, therefore non-Jewish by birth, was tetrarch of Galilee (Lk 3:1) and Perea (4 B.C.—A.D. 39). He made himself odious to his Jewish subjects by his incestuous marriage to his niece Herodias, former wife of his half-brother Herod Philip. This wickedness was denounced by John the Baptist and resulted in his beheading.

Jesus' Ministry of Mercy, 15-36. He fed the 5,000, 15-21 (Mk 6:30-44; Lk 9:10-17; Jn 6:1-14), and stilled the raging sea, 22-36 (Mk 6:45-56).

CHAPTER 15. FURTHER MINISTRY OF THE REJECTED KING

His Denunciation of the Scribes and Pharisees, 1-20. They accused Jesus of violating man-made traditions, 1-2. He scored their setting aside the Word of God by their traditions, 3-6, exposing their hypocrisy and corruption by quoting Isa 29:13, and denouncing their wicked externalism, 7-20.

He Ministers to a Gentile, 21-28. After having been rejected by His own, Christ had hinted of His wider ministry to Gentiles (Mt 12:18; cf. Isa 42:1-4). Now began a precursive fulfillment. As the rejected son of David, He ministered to a non-Israelite of Phoenicia, here called "the coasts of Tyre and Sidon" after its two principal seaports. The "dogs" were Gentiles, outside the pale of Jewish spiritual privilege denoted by "the children's bread." When the Canaanite woman addressed Him as "Lord," and took the place of humble faith, as it were, among "the *little* dogs," she obtained her request. This episode prefigured Gentile salvation in this age.

He Ministers to the Multitudes, 29-39. The healing of the multitudes, 29-31, represented the blessings of "Israel's God" on all who come to Him by faith. Feeding the 4,000 further showed the compassion of the King for the multitudes, 32-39 (cf. Mk 8:1-9).

CHAPTER 16. THE REJECTED KING PREDICTS HIS DEATH

The Leaven of the Scribes and Pharisees, 1-12. Another exposé of the wickedness of the Jewish leaders was given, 1-4, as they tempted Jesus, asking for a sign after they had disbelieved and rejected all His previous miraculous works. The sign of the prophet Jonah concerning His resurrection, 4, was the only one He gave them (cf. Mt 12:39-41; Lk 11:29-32). This served to aggravate their guilt. Jesus proceeded to interpret the symbol of leaven as evil doctrine, 6-12 (cf. Mt 13:33; 1 Cor 5:6). The leaven of the Pharisees was hypocritical externalism, that of the Sadducees rationalistic unbelief. Both rejected the King and His kingdom.

Peter's Confession, 13-19. On Caesarea Philippi, 13, see note on Mk 8:27. The confession of Peter involved the full deity of Jesus, "Christ, the Son of the living God," 16. This revelation to Peter, or anyone else, is not by human wisdom or ability but through God the Father, 17. Moreover, this truth of the deity of Christ ("the Son of the living God," not "the son of David") was to be the foundation of the Church, 18, and not Peter himself. "Thou art Peter [*petros*, a stone] and upon this rock [*petra*, great ledge of rock] I will build my church" (cf. 1 Pet 2:4-6, where the apostle made it clear he was never to be thought of as "the rock"). "The keys of the kingdom of heaven," 19, are to be thought of in the sense of Mt 13 (see note on Mt 13:1-2). Peter used these keys in opening gospel opportunity to Israel at Pentecost (Acts 2:38-42), to the racially mongrel Samaritans (Acts 8:14-17), and to Gentiles at Caesarea (Acts 10:34-44). This was the limit of their use by Peter.

Christ Foretells His Death, Resurrection and Return, 20-28. The King enjoined His disciples not to tell anyone "that he was Jesus the Christ," 20, because they had been preaching Christ as the King of a covenanted kingdom promised to Israel and "at hand." The Church, on the other hand, must be built upon the proclamation of Him as the crucified, risen and ascended Lord (Eph 1:20-23). Although the former testimony had ended, the new message was not yet ready, inasmuch as the blood of the new covenant had not yet been shed. Therefore, our Lord at this turning point of vast importance predicted His death, resurrection, 21, and second advent, 28. Little wonder Peter and the other disciples, hitherto preaching about and looking for the King to come into His kingdom, could not understand Christ's sudden prediction of His sufferings and death, 22-23. They thus had to be instructed in the rigors of true discipleship, 24-26, and rewards at the second advent when the

King and His kingdom would be accepted by Israel, 27-28. Some of them saw this future kingdom presented in an audio-visual demonstration in ch. 17.

CHAPTER 17. THE REJECTED KING AND HIS COMING GLORY

The Transfiguration, 1-21. See also comments on Lk 9:18-62. In 16:28, which belongs to this chapter, Christ had announced His second advent in glory (cf. 16:27) to establish the kingdom so lately rejected (Mt 3—12). He predicted that some who were with Him then (Peter, James and John, 1) would not die till they saw "the Son of man coming in his kingdom" (16:28). This prediction was fulfilled a week later in Christ's transfiguration, which was a portrayal of this glorious future event in miniature (2 Pet 1:16-21). All the essential details of the picture are present: (1) Christ as Son of Man, not in the humiliation of His sinless humanity but in glory; (2) Moses glorified, representing the redeemed who have entered the kingdom via death; (3) Elijah, likewise glorified, but representing the redeemed who have entered the kingdom by translation (1 Thess 4:14-17; 1 Cor 15:50-53); (4) Peter, James and John, unglorified, representing in the vision the Jewish remnant at the end who will enter the kingdom in unglorified bodies; (5) the crowd in its need at the foot of the mountain, 14-21, portraying the nations to be brought into the blessings of the kingdom after its restoration to Israel (Acts 1:6; Isa 11:10-12), with manifestation in deliverance from Satan and demon powers (Rev 20:1-3).

Jesus' Repetition of His Approaching Death, 22-23 (cf. Mt 16:21; Mk 9:30-32; Lk 9:43-45). This was necessary because it was a prerequisite to His second advent and the kingdom. See also notes on Mk 9:1-13.

The Tribute Money, 24-27. This miracle of the tax money retrieved from the fish's mouth at the busy lakeside metropolis of Capernaum demonstrates the humility and subjection of the omnipotent and omniscient Lord of the universe who had so recently revealed His glory in His coming kingdom. The tax in question was an ecclesiastical one, for the support of the temple (Ex 30:13; 2 Chr 24:6, 9). Our Lord was actually saying, "This is a tax for supporting My Father's house. As His Son, then, this tax is not incumbent upon Me. I am free."

CHAPTER 18. INSTRUCTIONS OF THE REJECTED KING—FORGIVENESS

Character of Citizens of the Kingdom, 1-14. The disciples were interested in holding office in the kingdom, 1. Jesus stressed the importance rather of being a citizen of the kingdom by being converted, 2-3, and by showing the humility of a child, 4-5. Jesus then discussed offenses (things and attitudes that harm others or cause others to sin), 6-10. These offenses must be dealt with severely, as denoted by Jesus' hyperbolic use of the figure of self-mutilation, which of course is not meant to be taken with bold literalness. Citizens of the kingdom have guardian angels, 10, and are the recipients of the saving shepherd ministry of the Son of Man, 11-14.

Discipline and Prayer in the Kingdom, 15-20. It is the mystery aspect of the kingdom which is in view in this passage (see note on Mt 13:1-2). Since this form of the kingdom is largely, though not entirely, coterminous with the Church, the Church is here anticipated as in Mt 16:18. The complete concept of the Church is not given until it is revealed through Paul (cf. Eph 3:1-10).

Discipline in the church is to take a certain pattern so that the injured member will know how to respond. This is the procedure of love and patience, bathed in prayer.

Forgiveness in the Kingdom, 21-35. Seventy times seven is 490, implying that genuine forgiveness is beyond calculation. The parable of the kingdom (cf. the seven of Mt 13) teaches the importance of forgiveness (cf. Eph 4:32).

CHAPTER 19. INSTRUCTIONS OF THE REJECTED KING—DIVORCE

Concerning Divorce, 1-15. Jesus left Galilee to begin His Perean ministry, 1-2 (ch. 19 — 20). A question by the Pharisees gave occasion for His teaching about divorce, 3-12 (cf. Mt 5:31-32; Mk 10:2-12; Lk 16:18, and Paul's discussion in 1 Cor 7). Monogamy is God's standard, 4-6, but certain accommodations to human frailty were permitted by the Mosaic law, 7-8 (Deut 24:1-4). Christ seems to allow only fornication as a ground for divorce, 9, but also takes into consideration men's weakness, 10-12. He had in mind the interest of little children, the sufferers from divorce, 13-15. Children before the age of accountability are reckoned in the kingdom, 14.

The Rich Young Man, 16-26. Religious and moral but unsaved, lacking spiritual reality, this young man pictures the case of many in Christendom. They think it is necessary to *do* something (works) in order to be saved, rather than to *believe* the gospel that Christ has done something for them. The Lord did not promise the young man eternal life by doing, but told him to perform an act which would prove to him his lack of saving faith and the spuriousness of his claim of keeping the law (Mk 10:17-30; Lk 18:18-30).

Rewards in the Regeneration, 27-30. This regeneration (re-creation) refers to the renewal of the earth in the mediatorial Davidic kingdom offered and rejected (Mt 3 — 12), but restored at the second advent (Mt 25:31). This kingdom will evidently be administered over Israel by the 12 apostles, 28 (cf. Isa 1:26).

CHAPTER 20. INSTRUCTIONS OF THE REJECTED KING—THE LABORERS

Parable of the Laborers, 1-16. This parable illustrates the truth Jesus declared in 19:30 and repeated in 20:16, to correct Peter's self-occupation and bargaining spirit (19:27). God does not evaluate man's service as man evaluates it. Some who are prominent and apparently successful in Christian work, whom we look upon as greatly used by God, will appear near the bottom of the Lord's list of faithful servants, while humble, self-effacing servants, little recognized by men, will appear at the top. Moreover, we are to be interested in the Lord's service primarily, not in the reward; in the quality, not the length of our service.

Jesus Again Predicts His Death and Resurrection, 17-28. This is the fourth prediction of these events (Mt 12:38-42; 16:21-28; 17:22-23). In the light of the foretelling of Jesus' suffering and death, 17-19, the selfishness of the request of the mother of James and John appears. She desired eminence for her sons in the promised kingdom, misunderstanding its essential character.

Two Blind Men Healed, 29-34. These called upon Jesus as "son of David," 30-31, and were healed outside Jericho (Tulul el- 'Alayiq on the Wadi Qelt, 17 miles from Jerusalem). They recognized His messianic authority and may foreshadow the future conversion of the Jewish remnant who will accept the Messiah at His second advent. (Cf. Mk 10:46-52; see note there on Jericho.)

CHAPTER 21. THE REJECTED KING ENTERS JERUSALEM

The Royal Entry into Jerusalem, 1-11. He came to Jerusalem as King to fulfill the prophecy uttered by Zechariah (Zech 9:9). Although acclaimed superficially by excited mobs, He was still the rejected King, for the official representatives of the nation gave Him no welcome in this His final and official offer of Himself to them. Moreover, even the Hosanna-shouting (Ps 118:26), garland-waving throngs answered in terms of rejection to the question of who He really was, 11. Instead of the promised King-Messiah, Jehovah-Jesus, God-Saviour, they replied, "Jesus the prophet of Nazareth of Galilee." But since the King and the kingdom (Mt 3—12) were rejected in the Galilee region, it was necessary that Jerusalem, the royal city, be given an opportunity to accept Him. And this was it!

Second Cleansing of the Temple and the Fig Tree Cursed, 12-32. The first cleansing of the temple was at the beginning of His ministry (Jn 2:13-17); this was at the end, 12-13. There it was His zeal for God's house, here He acted with kingly prerogative and miraculously ministered to the needy in its cleansed precincts, 14 (cf. Isa 56:7; Jer 7:11; Lk 14:21). The cursing of the barren fig tree, 18-22, is a type of Israel (Joel 1:7), here symbolized in national rejection. Lk 13:6-9 is contrasted with Mt 24:32-33, where symbolic prophecy indicates that Israel shall again bud (be brought back to her national election, Rom 11:1-26). The questioning of Jesus' authority by the nation's leaders, 23-27 (cf. Mk 11:27-33; Lk 20:1-8), as well as the parable of the two sons, 28-32, demonstrates further their hatred and rejection of the King.

Parable of the Householder, 33-46. The householder (God) planted a vineyard (Israel, Isa 5:1-7). The servants were the prophets, who were ill-treated. Finally God sent His Son (Messiah) and they put Him to death, 37-39. The events of the Roman-Jewish war A.D. 67-70 were prophesied, 40-41. Jesus aptly quoted prophecies referring to Himself as the Stone rejected (Ps 118:22-23), and showed that the kingdom of God in the larger sense of spiritual light and salvation would be taken away from Israel nationally and given to the Gentiles (Rom 9:30-33; 11:1-24). In verse 44 our Lord referred to Himself in judgment as the Smiting Stone of destruction (Dan 2:34).

CHAPTERS 22—23. THE REJECTED KING CLASHES WITH THE LEADERS

Parable of the Marriage Feast, 22:1-14. This parable portrays how the King and the kingdom were offered to the nation, 1-2, but were refused, 3. Verses 4-6 represent the repeated offer and its further rejection, the statement "all things are ready" hinting at the death of Christ and its salvation benefits. After Christ's atoning death the nation had a chance to repent (Acts 1—8), but refused. The world-wide offer to Gentiles was predicted, 8-10, after the events of A.D. 67-70 were described, 6-7. The wedding garment, 11-14, is the righteousness of Christ. Many have the invitation to salvation extended to them, comparatively few accept, 14 (cf. Rom 8:30).

The Nation Further Shows Its Rejection, 22:15-46. The Herodians were Jews in external religious forms, but a bitter offense to the nation as a whole in their devotion to easygoing, world-conforming Hellenism, so avidly espoused by the Herods, 15-22. In hatred to Jesus they made common cause against Him with the Sadducees, 23-33, the religious rationalists, and the Pharisees, 34-40, empty externalists. Jesus confounded the blind Pharisees by asking them about Ps 110:1, which has reference to His own divine-human person, 41-46. All three parties, representative of all Israel, being silenced, were unrepentant. No further message was left them but one of impending doom.

The Doom Pronounced and Lament Made Over Jerusalem, 23:1-39. The thunderous "woes" of the righteous wrath of the rejected son of David melted in tears as He announced blessing and hope for the repentant remnant who will greet Him at His second advent with the messianic welcome of Ps 118:26: "Blessed be he that cometh in the name of the Lord."

CHAPTERS 24—25. THE REJECTED KING'S OLIVET DISCOURSE

Prophecy of the Destruction of the Temple, 24:1-3. The rejected King as Prophet predicted, in this discourse, the events of that still future time when He will resume dealing with Israel (cf. 23:39) just before His return to earth in glory. The gorgeous edifice, 1-2, which provoked this great prophetic discourse was the Herodian temple. It was so superlatively beautiful that even the Romans, out of regard for its magnificence, were anxious to spare it when the city fell in A.D. 70. It was in clear view from the superior height of the Mount of Olives as the Prophet par excellence foretold its doom and the doom of the Jewish state that would occur in A.D. 70. The disciples asked three questions, 3. "When shall these things [destruction of the city and temple] be?" The answer is found in Lk 21:20-24. "What shall be the sign of thy coming, and of the end of the age?" The answer is in Mt 24:4-34.

Events of the Tribulation, 24:4-26. These prophecies deal with Israel in the period of Tribulation just prior to the return of Messiah-King to establish His earthly kingdom, although the end of the present age will be characterized by the general conditions mentioned in 24:4-8. A comparison of 4-8 with Rev 6 gives evidence that these verses have particular reference to the first half of the Tribulation period when Israel herself will dwell in relative safety because of the covenant made with "the prince that shall come," Antichrist (Dan 9:27a).

Verses 9-26 describe the events of the last half of the Tribulation after the world leader (Antichrist) has broken his covenant with Israel and forces idolatrous worship of himself (Dan 9:27b; 2 Thess 2:4; Rev 13:15-18). This period will be characterized by great persecution, 9-10, 17ff. (Rev 12:12-17), desolation of the temple and its worship, 15 (Dan 9:27), unbelieving Israel being deceived by false prophets, 11-12 (Rev 13:11-18), and believing Israel witnessing to the good news of Messiah's kingdom, 14. The advent of Messiah will terminate these events, 27.

Second Coming of Messiah, 24:27-30. The chronology of events is furthered by a description of the second advent. It follows immediately after the Tribulation, 29, preceded by a particular sign, 30. The coming will be sudden, 27, and evident to all, 30.

Regathering of Israel, 24:31. The event following the second advent will be the national regathering of Israel's elect through special angelic ministries.

The Certainty of Messiah's Coming, 24:32-36. The parable of the fig tree illustrates the certainty of the second advent, for the fulfillment of the signs that are to be given in the Tribulation will announce Messiah's coming as certainly as new shoots on the fig tree announce the approach of summer.

Exhortations to Watchfulness, 24:37-51. All three illustrations emphasize the unexpectedness of the Lord's coming by showing that the individuals concerned were occupied with the usual cares of life without giving thought to Messiah's return. Believing Israel is exhorted thereby to be prepared for that day.

The Judgment of Israel, 25:1-30. "Then," 1, prepares for the next event following Israel's regathering, her judgment just prior to the establishment of Messiah's kingdom. This judgment is illustrated in the parables of the ten virgins, 1-13, and of the talents, 14-30. The ten virgins represent Israel at the end of the Tribulation. The five wise symbolize the believing remnant, the five foolish the unbelieving segment who only profess to look for Messiah's advent, 1-5. They will be without oil (a symbol of the Holy Spirit) and will be shut out of the messianic kingdom which is about to be set up, 6-10.

In the parable of the talents, 14-30, the man traveling in a far country represents Christ during His absence from the earth. He entrusted gifts to His servants (Israel during the Tribulation). The five and two talent servants are believers who enter into "the joy of the Lord" (kingdom blessing), 21, 23. The one talent servant, a mere professor, is excluded from the kingdom ("outer darkness") and swept away in judgment with the ungodly, 24-30.

The Judgment of the Nations, 25:31-46. The rejected King in concluding His great prophetic discourse presented a picture of that for which Israel had been looking in His first advent, Messiah sitting upon the Davidic throne of glory, 31. The time of this event is certain from the context, viz., at His coming in *glory*. The occasion is the judgment of the nations, 32-33, consisting of sheep and goats. The sheep are individuals who receive the gospel of the kingdom (Mt 24:14) and treat kindly "these my brethren," the believing remnant of Jews, 34-36. The goats are the wicked who reject the gospel of the kingdom and persecute the Jewish remnant, 41-46, thus showing their league with Satan, 41, the Beast, and the False Prophet (Rev 13:1-18). Those who thus align themselves against the 144,000 preachers of the coming kingdom (Rev 7:1-8; 14:1-5) will share Satan's fate, 41 (Rev 20:10).

CHAPTER 26. BETRAYAL AND ARREST OF THE REJECTED KING

His Anointing for Death, 1-16. The King for the last time predicted His death, 1-2 (cf. Mt 12:38-42; 16:21-28; 17:22-23; 20:18-19). This prediction formed a prelude to the wicked counsel of the chief priests and scribes to kill Him, 3-5, and to His anointing by Mary of Bethany, 6-13 (cf. Mk 14:3-9; Jn 12:1-8). She alone seemed to have understood the meaning of His death. Matthew, recording the Gospel of the King, relates that Mary anointed His head, as Samuel anointed the head of David (1 Sam 16:13), while John, recording the Gospel of the Son of God, mentions only the anointing of Jesus' feet, the only suitable approach of the finite to the Infinite. This worshipful scene reveals Judas' base character (Jn 12:4-5) and is an introduction to his selling the Lord, 14-19 (cf. Mk 14:10-11; Lk 22:3-6). The price he received was 30 pieces of silver, the price of a common slave, about 17 dollars (cf. Zech 11:12-13; Ex 21:32).

The Passover and the Lord's Supper, 17-35. The Passover, commemorative of Israel's deliverance out of Egypt by the blood of the slain lamb (Ex 12), was to be fulfilled in Christ's death, as the true Paschal Lamb. At the last Passover, 17-25, the King therefore introduced the new memorial, the Lord's Supper, with the new meaning, 26-30, "This do in remembrance *of me*" (1 Cor 11:24-25). The dividing line between the OT and NT is not the blank page between Malachi and Matthew, but Jesus' "blood of the new testament, which is shed for many [those who receive Him] for the

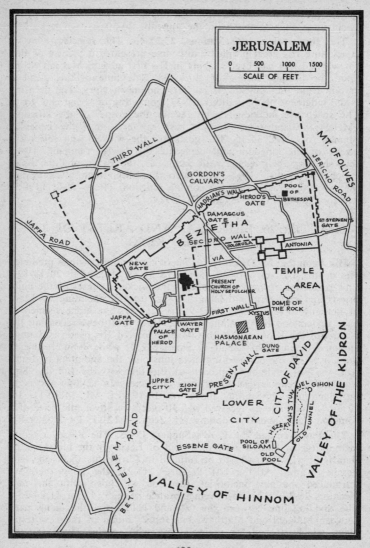

JERUSALEM

0   500   1000   1500
SCALE OF FEET

THIRD WALL

GORDON'S CALVARY

HADRIAN'S WALL

HEROD'S GATE

DAMASCUS GATE

POOL OF BETHESDA

MT. OF OLIVES

JERICHO ROAD

ST. STEPHEN'S GATE

B E Z E T H A

SECOND WALL

JAFFA ROAD

NEW GATE

VIA DOLOROSA

ANTONIA

TEMPLE AREA

DOME OF THE ROCK

PRESENT CHURCH OF HOLY SEPULCHER

FIRST WALL

XYSTUS

JAFFA GATE

WATER GATE

PALACE OF HEROD

HASMONAEAN PALACE

PRESENT WALL

DUNG GATE

UPPER CITY

ZION GATE

PRESENT WALL

CITY OF DAVID

GIHON

LOWER CITY

HEZEKIAH'S TUNNEL

OLD TUNNEL

VALLEY OF THE KIDRON

BETHLEHEM ROAD

ESSENE GATE

POOL OF SILOAM

OLD POOL

VALLEY OF HINNOM

488

remission of sins," 28. The King promised He would not drink the wine of this supper again with His disciples till the kingdom is established at His second advent. Thereupon Jesus foretold Peter's denial and His own resurrection, 31-35.

Gethsemane's Agony, 36-56. This involved no fear of death, but the contact of His sinless soul with the sin of the whole world as its vicarious Bearer and Expiator through the death on the cross (Isa 53:10; 2 Cor 5:21). This was the cup He prayed might pass from Him, 39, but *only* in the Father's will. His was an infinite anguish, as His infinitely holy soul faced the ordeal of "being made sin" and knowing the prospect of the hiding of the Father's face (Ps 22:1; Mt 27:46). The betrayal and arrest of Jesus followed the great spiritual struggle in the garden, but the victory was won there and Calvary was a spontaneous outcome.

The King Before Caiaphas and the Sanhedrin, 57-68. In the trial the rejected King claimed to be the Son of God, 64 (cf. Dan 7:13-14). He was accused, accordingly, of blasphemy (Jn 10:31-36). The conduct of the leaders in the nation's supreme court bore every evidence of the working of demonic powers.

Peter's Denial, 69-75, displayed the infirmity even of one who knew the Lord yet failed to see his own weakness.

CHAPTER 27. THE TRIAL AND DEATH OF THE REJECTED KING

Jesus Before Pilate, 1-32. The Sanhedrin handed over Jesus to Pontius Pilate, the Roman procurator of Judea (A.D. 26-36), since Rome was the final authority. Pilate's headquarters were at coastal Caesarea, but he came to Jerusalem on Jewish feasts because of the danger of uprisings. His praetorium or palace was apparently part of the Tower of Antonia near the present Via Dolorosa. Meanwhile, Judas had repented of his foul deed, and taking the 30 pieces of silver (cf. Zech 11:12-13; Jer 18:1-14; 19:1-3) cast them in the temple, and then committed suicide, 3-10. Pilate's weakness and his unavailing attempt to get out of crucifying Jesus were pathetic. The choice of Barabbas, a notorious criminal, 15-23, further accentuates Pilate's cowardice, as well as his washing his hands as a token of his innocence, 24. The insensate yell of verse 25 has been terribly fulfilled on the Jewish people. Scourging, 26, was pitiless lashing with a whip of leather thongs imbedded with pieces of metal. It usually preceded capital punishment. Evidently Pilate hoped that this severe punishment would satisfy the crowd and they would not further insist on crucifixion. Mocking the King, 27-31, shows the height of impious wickedness and the moral insensitivity of that brutal age. On "the common hall," 27, see "Praetorium" in Mk 15:16. Simon, pressed into carrying Jesus' cross, 32, was probably a Jew since many Jews lived in Cyrene, the capital city of the N. African district of Cyrenaica.

The Crucifixion of the King, 33-44. "Golgotha" is the Aramaic for "skull" (L. *Calvaria*, "Calvary"; Gr. *kranion*, Lk 23:33). Since 1842, when Otto Thenius of Dresden located Calvary on a rocky hill 250 yards NE of the Damascus Gate, this spot has been popularly identified as the location of the crucifixion. Gall was a bitter and poisonous herb, offered to Jesus as an anodyne, but it was refused. Crucifixion had been practiced by Phoenicians and Persians and was taken over from them by Rome, where it could be inflicted only on slaves and non-Romans. In Palestine this shameful and slow tortuous form of death served as a public reminder of the Jews' servitude to Rome, and was inflicted for robbery, tumult and sedition. The gambling soldiers fulfilled Ps 22:18. The complete accusation or charge from the combined Gospel narratives was: "This is [Matthew and Luke] Jesus [Matthew and John] of Nazareth [John] the King of the Jews [all]." Over the head of every victim of crucifixion was inscribed his crime. In the King's case it was meant to be mockery. How little did His blind crucifiers realize He *really was* Jesus the King of the Jews. Even their taunts were truer than they knew. "He saved others; himself he cannot save," 42. If He was to be the world's Saviour He could *not* save Himself. (See notes on "Passion Week" and "Trials of Jesus," Lk 23.)

The Death of the King, 45-50. The three-hour darkness was a supernatural phenomenon when the Father hid His face from the Son as He became sin for us and cried out, 46, the pitiable words of Ps 22:1. The slow agony of physical torture was the least of our Lord's suffering as He became the Sin-bearer, for the Father turned His face from Him as His sinless soul felt the crushing load of the world's sin. The King willingly "dismissed his spirit," 50 (cf. Jn 10:18). His death, as an act of His own will, made it different from the physical death of any other man.

The End of the Legal Age, 51-56. The supernatural tearing of the huge curtain that separated the holy place, into which the priests might enter, from the most holy place, which only the high priest could enter once a year on the day of atonement (Ex 26:31; Lev 16:1-34), signified that a "new and living way" had been opened for all believers into the very presence of God by Christ's death (cf. Heb 9:1-8; 10:19-22). A new age was dawning in which bloody sacrifices, a temple, and a special Aaronic priesthood were no longer needed.

The resurrection mentioned in 52-53 was *after* Christ's resurrection (cf. Lev 23:10-12), since He is the firstfruits (1 Cor 15:20). The Roman centurion recognized the crucified King as "the Son of God," 54 (cf. Mk 15:39-41; Lk 23:47-49).

The Burial of the King, 57-66. Tenderly and lovingly was He buried in a new tomb provided by a rich man (Isa 53:9). Joseph was from Arimathea, about ten miles SE of Antipatris in the Shephelah. The precautions His enemies took to "make the sepulchre sure, sealing it and stationing a guard," 62-64, only resulted in God's overruling the plans of the wicked and offering indisputable proof of the King's resurrection.

CHAPTER 28. THE RESURRECTION OF THE REJECTED KING

The Resurrection, 1-10. The sabbath (Saturday) ended at 6:00 P.M., and just before daybreak on Sunday, the first Easter (cf. Jn 20:1), the women came to the tomb to anoint Jesus' body. They thus showed much love but little faith in His resurrection (Mk 16:1, 11), being last at the cross and first at the tomb. Mary of Bethany evidently didn't come because she believed He would die as He said (Mt 26:6-13), also that He would arise as He said. The power and majesty of God were manifested in the earthquake, the angel who rolled back the stone and the stunned guards, 2-4. The stone, it is to be noted, was rolled away *after* the King was raised that the disciples might *look in, not* that the Lord of glory might come *out.* He had already risen in a body of glory (cf. Phil 3:20-21), which was no longer subject to natural laws. The sturdy Roman guards were not seeing a hallucination when they "trembled" before this manifestation of God's power "and became as dead men." The angel announced the Easter message of joy: "He is not here: for he is risen, as he said," and then the further proof of the reality of the event, "Come, see the place where the Lord lay," 6. Slain because He claimed to be King of the Jews, He was now raised because He was King of kings and Lord of lords (Acts 2:20-36). Rejected by Israel at His first advent, He will be accepted as King at His second advent (Zech 12:10—13:1; Isa 9:1-7; 11:1-16; 52:13—53:12). After the angelic message, the risen King Himself appeared to the disciples, 8-10. For order of events see Mk 16. See note on Jn 20 for "The Resurrection Authenticated."

The False Report of the Jews, 11-15. The last crowning act of treachery by Israel's Christ-rejecting leaders displayed their terrible wickedness. They had first-hand proof of the resurrection, 11, but

491

rejected it, 12, bribing the soldiers to lie about the whole matter. But God overruled and used the instance to give further proof of the resurrection. If the Roman soldiers fell asleep, 13, they were liable to death. And if they did so, of what value was their testimony?

The Great Commission, 16-20. The risen King gave the 11 disciples the great commission, couched in terms applicable to the present form of the kingdom (cf. note on Mt 13:1-2). His authority, which extends to every realm, supported His commission, which involved enlisting men under His lordship ("make disciples," ASV), identifying them with Himself and His followers in the rite of baptism, and teaching them the truths of His Word, 18-20. The Gospel ends with the promise of the Lord's continued presence with His own, 20b.

MATTHEW AND MARK COMPARED

Matthew	Mark
Jesus as King	Jesus as Servant
Jews in mind	Gentiles in mind
Jesus predicted miracle-working King	Jesus the miracle-working Servant
Rooted in OT prophecy	Much fewer OT prophetic references
Key is God's purposes for Israel	Key is God's purposes for the world
Deity of the King by birth, fulfilled prophecy, works	Deity of the Servant by mighty works
Events recorded concerning the King —His genealogy, birth in Bethlehem, visit of wise men, childhood in Nazareth	All these omitted as not appropriate to the Servant portrait
Sermon on Mount, spoken as King, giving the principles of the kingdom	Omitted
Many parables included which belong to this Gospel of the King but not appropriate to the Gospel of the Servant	Omits many of the parables—five of those in Mt 13; numerous others, and notably those of Mt 25
Presents the King of the Jews rejected, the mystery form of the kingdom from His rejection to His second advent to restore the kingdom to Israel	Presents the Servant of the Lord in life, death, resurrection bringing salvation to mankind

MARK

THE GOSPEL OF THE SERVANT OF THE LORD

Author. The early church ascribed the second Gospel to John Mark, the son of a certain Mary of Jerusalem (Acts 12:12). He accompanied Paul and Barnabas on the first missionary tour (Acts 13:5), but for some reason left them at Perga (Acts 13:13). Later Paul and Barnabas separated because Paul refused to have Mark on the second tour. Mark accordingly went with Barnabas. Later Paul and Mark were reconciled (Col 4:10-11). That Mark is the author of this Gospel is mentioned by Papias about A.D. 135, Justin Martyr about A.D. 150, as well as by Clement of Alexandria and Irenaeus somewhat later. Like Luke, Mark was not an apostle, as were Matthew and John.

Nature and Purpose of Mark's Gospel. This is the briefest of the four Gospels. It is a narrative of dynamic movement and action, "straightway" and "immediately" being used more than 40 times. It presents Jesus acting rather than speaking. It is slanted not to the Jew as is Matthew, but to the Roman world, giving a portrait of Jesus as the powerful Son of God whose word was law in the natural as well as the supernatural realm. The paradox is that this strong Son of God is Servant of man, Saviour, Ransomer (Mk 10:45).

Place and Date. Early church writers declare that Mark wrote his Gospel while in Rome, as a disciple of Peter. It is to be dated, therefore, between A.D. 64 and 68. It is critically regarded as the earliest of the Gospels. It has been calculated that it contains about 93 percent of the material the three Synoptic Gospels (Matthew, Mark and Luke) have in common. But dependence of the other Synoptic Gospels upon Mark is *not* a necessary conclusion. The Spirit of God inspired each writer independently, so that Matthew's Gospel is actually earlier (*c.* A.D. 50) than Mark's, as well as Luke's (*c.* A.D. 58). See "Synoptic Gospels," introduction to Luke.

Outline

The Servant's Coming, 1:1-13
The Servant's Work, 1:14—13:37
The Servant's Death, 14:1—15:47
The Servant's Resurrection, 16:1-20

1:1-13. THE SERVANT'S COMING

The Servant's Identity, 1. He is "Jesus [see note on Mt 1:18-25] the Christ [Messiah the Anointed One], the Son of God," i.e., Deity incarnate. The deity of the Servant is first stressed. This is "the gospel," the good news. Apart from the fact of His being the Son of God He could not have been the perfectly obedient Servant, nor the triumphant miracle worker and the world's Saviour. His sonship and service are closely related.

The Servant's Coming Promised and Announced, 2-8. Malachi foretold His advent, 2 (Mal 3:1), as well as Isaiah, 3 (Isa 40:3); and John the Baptist, His forerunner, announced His coming (see notes on Mt 3:1-12). John's ministry, it must be remembered, was to Israel. His baptism, as a prophet of Israel, was not Christian baptism (cf. Acts 19:1-6). It was to prepare Israel for the offered kingdom and the reception of the divine King. Mark briefly refers to John's ministry merely to introduce the Servant. In contrast to Mt 3:11 and Lk 3:16-17, Mark mentions only the baptism of the Holy Spirit, 8, effected at the first advent (cf. Acts 1:5 with 2:4 and 11:16), but omits the baptism "with fire," connected with judgment at the second advent. The reason is that Christ, as the humble Servant, did not execute judgment, as He will when coming as King (Matthew) and Son of Man (Luke) (see notes on Mt 3:11; cf. Lk 3:16-17).

The Servant's Baptism, 9-11 (see notes on Mt 3:13-17 and Lk 3:21-22). The Sinless One as Servant-Saviour submitted to the baptism of sinners to identify Himself with them and with their need. The essence of His ministry was to seek and to save the lost (Mk 10:45). His baptism was His induction to this priestly redemptive work.

The Servant's Testing, 12-13. This was a divine necessity, because His humanity had to be tried as a Servant, 12 (cf. Mt 4:1-11; Lk 4:1-13). Here, in combat with Satan (from Heb. *satan,* "adversary"), He proved victorious in conflict to be fit to "give his life a ransom for many." "The wilderness," 12, and the "wild beasts," 13, witness of a creation marred by sin, showed the self-humbling of the Creator, who came to triumph over the fallen creature, Satan, and overcome amid conditions effected by the Fall.

1:14-45. MINISTRY IN GALILEE

The Servant's Message, 14-15. Matthew reports that both John (Mt 3:2 see note) and Jesus (Mt 4:17 note) preached the same message, involving repentance and the kingdom of heaven at hand.

Mark, slanted toward Gentiles, uses the larger, more embracive term "kingdom of God," 14, as being more appropriate. The simplest distinction may be that the kingdom of God is universal, including God's own of all ages (Lk 13:28-29; Heb 12:22-23), in contrast to the kingdom of heaven which is Davidic, mediatorial and messianic, having its goal in the establishment of the kingdom of God on the earth. "The gospel," 15, is the good news of the kingdom, not the Christian gospel based on the death and resurrection of Christ.

The Servant Calls Helpers, 16-20. As a humble Servant Himself, He called lowly fishermen, 16-20, "to become fishers of men," 17. Of the 12, four at least—Simon, Andrew, James and John—were fishermen (cf. Mt 4:18-22; Lk 5:1-11). These had believed earlier (Jn 1:35-42) and now were called to commitment of life to service. (Cf. note on "Lake of Galilee" in Mk 6.)

The Servant Casts Out Demons in Capernaum, 21-28. The Servant's ministry was dynamic, not ritualistic, 21-22. Immeasurably filled with the Holy Spirit (cf. Jn 3:34), He challenged unclean spirits, 23, i.e., demons (cf. Lk 4:33; Mk 5:1-20 and note on Demonism).

CAPERNAUM

This busy fishing port on the NW shore of the Lake of Galilee, two and one half miles SW of the spot where the Jordan enters the lake, is identified with modern Tell Hum, where extensive ruins exist (cf. Mt 11:23). It was also a toll-collecting station (Mt 9:9; 17:24-27), gathering tax revenue from caravans en route from Damascus to the Mediterranean coast and Egypt. Jesus' headquarters were located here. Excavations at Tell Hum have yielded one of the finest white limestone synagogues in Palestine, restored by the Franciscans. Ornamented with motifs of centaurs, lions, eagles, palm trees and vines, it is dated 2nd or 3rd cen. A.D. It was probably built on the site of the synagogue in which Jesus ministered.

Other Ministries of the Servant, 29-45. These ministries included the healing of Peter's mother-in-law, 29-31 (cf. Mt 8:14-15; Lk 4:38-39); the healing of many, casting out demons, 32-34 (cf. note on Mk 5:1-20); the Servant's prayer life, 35; His tour of Galilee, 36-39; and the healing of a leper, 40-45.

CHAPTER 2. FURTHER MINISTRY IN CAPERNAUM

Healing the Paralytic, 1-12. The Servant returned to His head-quarters in Capernaum (see note above). His healing of the paralytic was proof of the deity of the Servant, for He alone could forgive sins, 5. The scribes, copyists and theorists of the Scriptures, realized this but refused to believe in His deity which had been manifested by His mighty miracles, 6-7. His miracles were slanted to prove this, 8-11. The humble Servant was the world's Saviour, 10, who healed physical and mental sickness because He could deal with the great underlying problem of the forgiveness of sin, 12 (cf. Mt 9:1-8; Lk 5:18-26).

Calling Matthew, 13-22. As a publican (tax collector for Rome), Levi was despised and counted as a common sinner, 14. Jesus' love for sinners, His holy desire to save them, 15, and His wonderful humility in associating with them advertised His character as a true Servant, 16-17, and aroused the ire of the scribes and Pharisees. The legalistic question of fasting revealed that Christ was "the bridegroom," 18-20 (Jn 3:29), the bringer of God's grace. While the grace-bringing Bridegroom was with them, there was no occasion for mourning and fasting. Grace would supersede law. The occasion called for joy. The parable, 21-22, further elucidates the approaching change from the OT legal economy. The old cloth and old wineskins (legalistic Judaism) must not be mixed with the new cloth and new wine (the gospel of grace, Jn 1:17, to be brought in by Christ). (See note on Mt 9:16-17; cf. Lk 5:36-39.)

The Servant and the Sabbath, 23-28. Closely connected with the coming change of dispensations is the episode showing the Servant as "Lord also of the sabbath," 28. As Creator He rested on the seventh day. As a sign of His covenant with His people Israel, the sabbath had become meaningless to them in its spiritual import. As the redeeming Servant, by His death and resurrection He was to supplant it by the Lord's Day. (See note on Mt 12:1-8.)

CHAPTER 3. THE SERVANT FURTHER DISPLAYS HIS DEITY

Man with the Withered Hand Healed, 1-12. By this miracle in the synagogue the Servant proved what He had said about the sabbath in 2:27-28. The empty legalism and utter hypocrisy of the Jews, 1-4, evoked His righteous anger, 5. They refused to believe, and the hardness of their hearts was what grieved the Lord. Pharisees (legalists) made common cause with Herodians (Hellenizers and world conformers) in common rejection and hatred of the Servant, 6, who went to minister to those who would receive His gracious ministry, 8-12.

The Choosing of the Twelve, 13-19 (cf. Mt 10:1-4; Lk 6:12-16; Acts 1:13).

Peter. His name Peter means "stone" (Gr.). Cephas is Aramaic. He was married (Mt 8:14; Mk 1:30; Lk 4:38). Although he came from Bethsaida (Jn 1:44), he lived in Capernaum, and was a fisherman in partnership with James and John. He was a strange combination of cowardice and courage, impulsiveness and fearlessness. His association with the Servant, however, refined his character, making him an outstanding Christian.

James. Brother of John, both nicknamed Boanerges ("sons of thunder"). They and their father Zebedee conducted a fishing business partnership with the brothers Simon Peter and Andrew. James suffered martyrdom under Herod (Acts 12:2).

John. See introduction to John's Gospel.

Andrew. One of the earliest of the Servant's converts, who led his brother Peter to Christ (Jn 1:40-42).

Philip, with Peter and Andrew, hailed from Bethsaida, a lake town NE of Capernaum. Philip brought Nathanael to Christ.

Bartholomew. Little is known of him. Some identify him with Nathanael.

Matthew. See introduction to Matthew's Gospel.

Thomas ("twin") displayed zeal (Jn 11:16), but also a spirit of skepticism regarding Christ's resurrection (Jn 20:24-25). This, however, was completely dissipated by proof furnished by his contact with the living Christ.

James the Son of Alphaeus. Some connect James (Heb. Jacob) with the James of the first church council (Acts 15) and writer of the book of James (cf. Acts 21:18). He was called "James the little" (Mk 15:40), evidently because he was shorter in stature than James, the son of Zebedee.

Thaddeus. This is a Gr. form of Theudas, his surname being Lebbaeus (Mt 10:3). He is called Judas by Luke in Luke and Acts.

Simon the Zealot had been a member of an extremely nationalistic sect of Judaism. Matthew the publican represented the opposite extreme. It is interesting that Jesus chose men of such diverse background.

Judas Iscariot. Judas is the Gr. form of Judah. He was the black sheep of the 12. Avaricious, greedy, ambitious, he chose to deny the Lord when hope of kingly position and reward failed (Mt 26:14, 47; 27:5; Acts 1:18).

The Unpardonable Sin, 20-30. See note on Mt 12:24-37.

The Servant's New Relationship, 31-35. See note on Mt 12:46-50.

CHAPTER 4. THE SERVANT'S SEASIDE TEACHING

The Parable of the Sower, 1-29. Mark develops only two of the seven parables elucidated in Mt 13, and connects them with the present kingdom of God, 11, 30, rather than, as in Matthew, with the kingdom of the heavens. This is because Mark is presenting the Gospel of the Servant, not the King, and the servanthood of Christ is related to the broader context of the inclusive kingdom of God rather than to the more national kingdom of the heavens, which involves the ultimate divine purpose for Israel.

This parable has to do with the reception given the Word of God (seed) in the world. Such truth was presented in a parable so that believers might be instructed without revealing the content of instruction to those who are spiritually blind and lack spiritual understanding, 11-12. The vivid contrast between mere profession and genuine possession of the Word may be clearly noted throughout the parable. Not only is the gospel to be appropriated, but it must shine forth in testimony, 21-25, and grow to fruitfulness, 26-29.

The Parable of the Mustard Seed, 30-34. Here the Servant describes the rapid growth of the present kingdom of God, for the common mustard seed is extremely small but when planted grows into an herb twelve feet high. The reference to the birds may suggest that as the kingdom grows things unsuitable for God's kingdom may attempt to lodge there (cf. Dan 4:20-22).

The Servant and the Storm, 35-41. The storm is a fitting close to this chapter which anticipates this present age. The Servant was with His servants in the boat. His fate was theirs, and His presence their security. His rebuke of the winds showed His power and deliverance, which are available for His own. (Cf. Mt 8:23-27; Lk 8:22-25.) See note on "Sea of Galilee" in Mk 6.

5:1-20. THE SERVANT'S POWER OVER SATAN

The Servant's sinless humanity challenged the demons. The place where the demoniac was healed, 1, is called Gadara in Matthew (8:28, RSV). Luke (8:26, RSV) mentions "the country of the Gerasenes," and ancient textual authorities vary, calling the inhabitants of the region "Gerasenes," "Gadarenes" or "Gergesenes." Some locate Gergesa (present-day Kersa, a tiny place) on the eastern shore of the Lake of Galilee just below the Wadi es-Semak, where steep hills jut into the lake. However, Gadara (Umm Qeis), five miles SE of the southern end of the lake, may be indicated. This Decapolis town may well have extended to the lake shore in that period. See note on Decapolis in Mk 7.

DEMONISM

Demons are evil or unclean spirits (cf. Mk 1:23 with Mk 1:32-34; Rev 16:13-16), and are fallen angels, servants of Satan (Mt 12:26-27; 25:41). There is only one devil, but myriads of demons who serve the devil and make his power practically universal. A demoniac (Mk 5:1-20) is a person whose personality has been invaded by one or more demons, who at will can speak and act through their human victim, deranging both his mind and body. A number of such victims of Satan were delivered by the Servant (see "Expulsion of Demons" below). The unhindered power of God working through the sinless humanity of the Servant challenged the supernatural world of evil and explains the outburst of demonism during His earthly ministry.

The reality and personality of demons are attested in all eras of history since the Fall, as in the case of Saul and the spiritistic medium of Endor (1 Sam 28:7-20), in the case of ancient idolatry of which demonism was the dynamic (Ps 106:36-37; 1 Cor 10:20), in ancient divination and magic, and in ancient necromancy and modern spiritism.

Demons can derange mind and body (Mt 12:22; 17:15-18; Lk 13:16). They know the deity and lordship of Christ in the spirit world (Mt 8:31-32; Mk 1:24; Acts 19:15; Jas 2:19), and realize their predestined fate (Mt 8:31-32; Lk 8:31). They have a conspicuous role in the government of the Satanic world system (Dan 10:13; Eph 6:12), in promoting cultism and false doctrine (1 Tim 4:1-3), and in opposing God's program and God's people (Eph 6:12; 1 Jn 4:1-6). Demons are of two classes: (1) the free demons and (2) those imprisoned. The latter will be let loose as part of the judgments upon wicked men in the Great Tribulation (Rev 9:1-21; 16:13-16). Prayer is the believer's resource against Satan and demons (Eph. 6:10-20). See also comments on "Demonism" in Lk 11:14-28.

EXPULSION OF DEMONS

(SPECIFIC INSTANCES)

Demoniac in the synagogue at Capernaum, Mk 1:21-28; Lk 4:31-37

Dumb demoniac, Mt 9:32-34

Daughter of the Syrophoenician woman, Mt 15:21-28; Mk 7:24-30

Gadarene demoniacs, Mt 8:28-34; Mk 5:1-20; Lk 8:26-39

Blind and mute demoniac, Mt 12:22; Lk 11:14

Epileptic child, Mt 17:14-21; Mk 9:14-29; Lk 9:37-43

5:21-43. THE SERVANT'S POWER OVER DISEASE AND DEATH

He the sinless Son of God, Lord of the spirit world, 1-20, having displayed His authority over Satan and demons, now displayed it over that which sin has introduced into the human race—disease and death.

MIRACLES OF PHYSICAL HEALING

A leper, Mt 8:2-4; Mk 1:40-45; Lk 5:12-15
A paralytic, Mt 9:2-8; Mk 2:3-12; Lk 5:18-26
Fever (Peter's mother-in-law), Mt 8:14-17; Mk 1:29-31
Nobleman's son healed, Jn 4:46-53
Physical infirmity, Jn 5:1-9
A withered hand, Mt 12:9-13; Mk 3:1-6; Lk 6:6-11
Deafness and dumbness, Mk 7:31-37
Blindness at Bethsaida, Mk 8:22-25; in Jerusalem, Jn 9; Bartimaeus, Mk 10:46-52
Ten lepers, Lk 17:11-19
Malchus' severed ear, Lk 22:47-51
Hemorrhage, Mt 9:20-22; Mk 5:25-34; Lk 8:43-48
Dropsy, Lk 14:2-4

MIRACLES OF RESURRECTION

Jairus' daughter, Mt 9:18-26; Mk 5:35-43; Lk 8:41-56
Widow's son, Lk 7:11-15
Lazarus of Bethany, Jn 11:1-44

MIRACLES IN THE NATURAL REALM

Water converted to wine at Cana, Jn 2:1-11
Stilling of a storm, Mt 8:23-27; Mk 4:35-41; Lk 8:22-25
Supernatural catch of fish, Lk 5:1-11; Jn 21:6
Multiplying food: 5,000 fed, Mt 14:15-21; Mk 6:34-44; Lk 9:11-17; Jn 6:1-14; 4,000 fed, Mt 15:32-39; Mk 8:1-9
Walking on water, Mt 14:22-33; Mk 6:45-52; Jn 6:19
Money from a fish, Mt 17:24-27
Fig tree dried up, Mt 21:18-22; Mk 11:12-14

METHOD AND PURPOSE OF THE SERVANT'S MIRACLES

Jesus did not work miracles solely by virtue of His deity, but in the person of His sinless humanity united to Deity. It was the Holy Spirit working in unhindered power through the medium of Jesus' undefiled human nature who wrought these mighty signs by spoken word, asserted will or occasionally by means of clay or saliva.

The purpose of the Servant's miracles was to authenticate the King (Matthew), the Servant (Mark), the Man (Luke) and God (John) as the Creator-Redeemer, God become man, the eternal Word become flesh, Israel's King and the world's Saviour. Jesus' miracles were outward proofs of His deity and messiahship (cf. Jn 15:24). They also were the expression of His love for and identification with the human race, performed for its redemption from suffering, sin and death.

Most of Jesus miracles are unrecorded (cf. Mt 4:24; Lk 4:40; Mk 6:53-56; Lk 6:17-19; Mt 15:30-31; Jn 21:25). Those that are recorded, as in John's Gospel (cf. Jn 20:30-31), are highly selected for a specific purpose—to arouse faith in Jesus as "the Christ, the Son of God; and that believing ye might have life through his name."

CHAPTERS 6—7. THE SERVANT'S REJECTION

In His Hometown, 6:1-6. Unbelief in His person and work here expressed itself. The people saw Him as Joseph's actual son, as a carpenter, 3, as a mere sinful man with brothers and sisters (cf. Lk 4:16-30).

He Sends Forth the Twelve, 6:7-13 (cf. Mt 10:5-42; Lk 9:1-6).

John the Baptist's Martyrdom Described, 6:14-29 (see note on Mt 14:1-14; Lk 9:7-9). Herod Antipas, son of Herod the Great, ruled Galilee and Perea as tetrarch 4 B.C.—A.D. 39. His incestuous marriage with his niece Herodias, former wife of his half-brother Philip, resulted in his murder of John the Baptist.

Miracle of the Five Thousand Fed, 6:30-44. See note on "Miracles" in Mk 5.

Miracle of Walking on the Water, 6:45-52 (cf. Mt 14:22-32; Jn 6:15-21). The Servant is the mighty Son of God.

Healings at Gennesaret, 6:53-56. Gennesaret is the fertile plain on the NW corner of the Lake of Galilee, where the rim of mountain wall flattens out. Though rejected by those of His own hometown and others, the Servant graciously continued to discharge His service to seek and to save the lost (cf. Mt 14:34-36).

THE SEA OF GALILEE

In Jesus' day this beautiful body of fresh water, 13 miles long and seven and one half miles wide, was dotted with populous towns, such as Capernaum (see note on Mk 1:21-28), Bethsaida, Chorazin, Magdala and Tiberias. The lake lies in a depressed cup 700 feet below sea level and enjoys a healthful semitropical climate. It was subject to sudden and violent tempests as the cold air from snowy Lebanon collided with the warmer air above the lake.

The lake abounds in fish, with fishing an important industry (cf. Mt 4:18-22; Mk 1:16-20). The sunny climate, with health-giving sulphur springs near Tiberias, made it a mecca for the sick, and a fruitful scene for Jesus' healing ministry (Mk 1:32-34).

The Empty Religionism of the Pharisees, 7:1-23. Concerned with mere outward forms of traditionalism, but devoid of faith or spiritual reality (2 Tim 3:5), the Pharisees were blinded in their rejection of and opposition to the Servant Son of God. They fulfilled Isa 29:13 (see 6-7; cf. notes on Mt 15:1-20).

The Servant and the Syrophoenician Woman, 7:24-30. See note on Mt 15:21-28. The Servant could not be hid, 24, because He was here manifesting His serving ministry (cf. Mk 10:45). This foreshadows the gospel going out to Gentiles after Israel's rejection of the King and the kingdom. Notice Mark does not allude to the woman's calling Jesus son of David, properly recorded in the Gospel of the King (Mt 15:22). See note on "Demonism," Mk 5:1-20, and on "Miracles," Mk 5. Tyre was on the coast, 25 miles N of Ptolemais, 20 miles S of Sidon.

The Healing of the Deaf and Dumb Man, 7:31-37 (cf. Mt 15:29-31). See note on "Miracles" in Mk 5, and on "Sea of Galilee" in Mk 6.

THE DECAPOLIS

The Decapolis (Ten Cities) was situated in the region SE of the Lake of Galilee. It was a confederation of Hellenistic towns (originally ten in number). All of them except Scythopolis (Beisan), just W of the Jordan at the entrance to Esdraelon, were located in Transjordan, S of tetrarch Philip's Gaulonitis, E of the N half of Herod Antipas' Perea and W and N of Aretas' sprawling kingdom of Nabatea. Pliny, a contemporary Roman historian, lists these Decapolis cities as Damascus, Philadelphia (Amman), Raphana, Scythopolis, Gadara, Hippos, Pella, Gerasa, Dion, and Canatha. (Cf. Mt 4:25; Mk 5:20; 7:31.)

CHAPTER 8. THE SERVANT PREDICTS HIS DEATH

Miracle of Feeding the Four Thousand, 1-9 (cf. Mt 15:32-39). See note on "Miracles" in Mk 5.

The Wicked Unbelief of the Pharisees, 10-21. Cf. comments on Mt 16:1-12, noting "leaven" there. "Dalmanutha," 10, is uncertain.

After feeding the 4,000 somewhere in the NE regions of the lake, Jesus took a boat to Magdala (Mt 15:39, AV; Magadan, RSV), the "district of Dalmanutha" (Mk 8:10), probably to be identified with Mejdel, three miles NE of Tiberias and located between it and Capernaum.

The Blind Man Healed at Bethsaida, 22-26. This was not the city just E of the place where the Jordan River enters the Lake of Galilee, enlarged by Philip the tetrarch, calling it Bethsaida Julius, but the town in close proximity to Capernaum, just W of where the Jordan enters the lake. These two Bethsaidas can be illustrated by Kansas City, Kansas, and Kansas City, Missouri. (See Mk 1:16-17; Jn 1:44; 12:21.)

Peter's Confession of Faith, 27-38. See notes on Mt 16:21-28.

CAESAREA PHILIPPI

Caesarea Philippi, i.e., Caesarea of Philip, was rebuilt and enlarged by this son of Herod the Great. Its name had been Panias, in honor of the nature god Pan worshiped there, but was changed to Caesarea in honor of the then-reigning Caesar Tiberius. It was thus distinguished from the city of Caesarea built by Herod the Great on coastal Palestine. At this center sacred to paganism in proximity to the Paneion grotto in the foothills of Mt. Hermon, at the main source of the Jordan, it is significant Jesus broached the subject of His deity (see notes on Mt 16:13-16; Lk 9:18-20). Nearby was an exquisite temple of marble built by Herod the Great in honor of Caesar Augustus.

CHAPTER 9. THE SERVANT'S COMING GLORY

The Transfiguration, 1-13. In one sense this was a confirmation of Peter's confession of Christ as the Son of the living God. It was a demonstration of the full deity of the Servant to three of the most discerning disciples, to prepare them against the shock of the Servant's approaching death. In another sense the transfiguration was a celestial testimony and climactic proof that this Jesus was the Christ—the Messiah, Servant, and Saviour to whom all OT prophecies pointed and in whom they were fulfilled. Again it was a visual illustration of the coming of the kingdom of God in power to the Gentiles (cf. notes on Mt 17:1-21).

The Demon-Possessed Boy, 14-29. See notes on "Demonism" in Mk 5:1-20 and "Miracles" in Mk 5:21-43. See also notes on Mt 17:14-19; Lk 9:37-43.

The Servant Again Predicts His Death, 30-41. Cf. notes on Mt 16:21-28. This subject was one of gradual unfolding to the disciples after the King and His kingdom were rejected, although it had been hinted at to Nicodemus at the beginning of Christ's ministry (Jn 3:14; cf. Mt 16:21; 17:9; 17:22-23; 20:17-19). The disciples quarreled among themselves who should be the greatest, 33-37, and their party spirit shows how little they understood the Lord's approaching death or its meaning, 38-41. On Capernaum, 33, see note on Mk 1:21-28.

The Servant Warns of Hell, 42-50. This is Gehenna, eternal hell, the "lake of fire" (Rev 19:20; 20:10, 14-15), "the second death" (Jn 8:24; Rev 21:8), signifying eternal separation from God. Gehenna was the place in the valley of Hinnom, SW of Jerusalem, where human sacrifices were offered in OT times (2 Chr 33:6; Jer 7:31). Later it became a dumping ground where the worm never died and the fire never was quenched, a graphic picture of the eternal destiny of the Christ-rejecting. Gehenna is in contrast to Hades (Lk 16:23), the intermediate state of the wicked dead before judgment.

CHAPTER 10. THE SERVANT'S PEREAN MINISTRY

Question of Divorce, 1-16. Perea, 1, was the territory across Jordan from Samaria, extending from the Decapolis E of the Sea of Galilee and S to the Dead Sea. It was ruled by Herod Antipas (see note on Mk 6:14-29). Jesus taught a monogamous standard on the subject of divorce, 6-8 (cf. Gen 1:27), teaching that God joins man and woman in marriage, 9, and that easy divorce is adultery, 10-12. Jesus' blessing of little children, 13-16, is closely connected in the context. They are the real victims of the hurt of divorce and adultery (Mt 19:13-15; Lk 18:15-17).

The Rich Young Ruler, 17-31. See note on Mt 19:16-26 (cf. Lk 18:18-30).

The Servant Again Foretells His Death, 32-34 (cf. Mt 20:17-19; Mk 9:30-37).

James' and John's Selfish Ambition, 35-45. Their desire to be served is contrasted with the Servant's aim to serve, 45. This verse is the key to Mark's presentation of the Son of God as Servant.

Bartimaeus Receives His Sight, 46-52 (cf. Mt 20:29-34; Lk 18:35-43). This miracle occurred near Jericho. See note on "Miracles," Mk 5:21-34.

JERICHO

Jericho of Jesus' day was Herod's winter palace. He and his son Archelaus elegantly beautified it with magnificent Hellenistic buildings—palace, theater, fortress and hippodrome. Ancient ruins excavated from 1950 on the site of present Tulul Abu el-'Alayiq lie one mile W of the modern city. The architecture and plan of the city resemble other cities of the Graeco-Roman world of the time. Herodian Jericho was a splendid city 17 miles from Jerusalem, 1,000 feet below sea level in the Jordan Valley, with a delightful winter climate.

CHAPTER 11. THE SERVANT'S ENTRY INTO JERUSALEM

His Presentation As King, 1-11. This is in fulfillment of Zech 9:9 (cf. comments on Mt 21:1-11). It was a popular but super- ficial demonstration. The King and His kingdom had in reality already been rejected (cf. notes on Mt 3:2; 4:17; 13:1-2). The fickleness of the sinful human heart is here displayed. A few days later many of the same mob would jeer Him, proving they were not ready to receive the King nor the principles of His kingdom.

The Barren Fig Tree, 12-14. See notes on Mt 21:18-22. The fig tree of Palestine, if it has kept its leaves through the winter, usually contains figs also. The figure portrays the spiritual barrenness of the nation that would soon crucify the King it now so glibly hails.

The Cleansing of the Temple, 15-21, is another proof of the apostasy of the nation (see note on Mt 21:12-16). The withered fig tree symbolizes this spiritual bankruptcy.

Faith Contrasted with Wicked Unbelief, 22-33. The prayer of faith, 22-26 (cf. Jas 5:15), starkly focused upon the unbelief of the scribes and elders who questioned Jesus' authority, 27-33, as further proof of their rejection of the King-Servant.

CHAPTER 12. THE SERVANT'S TEACHING IN JERUSALEM

Parable Giving a Resume of Israel's Spiritual History, 1-12. Israel, the vineyard (Isa 5:1-7), brought forth only wild grapes. The OT prophets and John the Baptist are alluded to, 2-5, as are Jesus Himself, 6-8, and the destruction of Jerusalem (A.D. 70), 9-10 (cf. Ps 118:22; 1 Pet 2:8). Verse 10 quotes Ps 118:22-23. (Cf. notes on Mt 21:33-46; Lk 20:9-18.)

Question of the Tribute, 13-17. The Pharisees and Herodians joined to trap the Servant. Jesus with omniscient sagacity declared the principle of the separation of church and state, and so silenced both (see note on Mt 22:15-22; cf. Lk 20:19-26).

The Servant Silences the Sadducees, 18-27. The wealthy, rationalistic materialists disbelieved in bodily resurrection. Their trap question seemed to favor polygamy in heaven. Jesus settled the question with one stroke—no marrying in heaven, but there is a resurrection, because Scripture so declares, and He quoted from the Pentateuch which the Sadducees claimed to believe (cf. Ex 3:6).

The Great Commandments, 28-34 (cf. Deut 6:4-5; Lev 19:18). God is to be first in our affection, our neighbor second (see Mt 22:34-40; Lk 10:25-37).

The Servant Questions the Pharisees, 35-40. From Psalm 110:1 He showed this psalm was penned by David, was inspired, was messianic and that He was David's son (man) as well as David's Lord (God). He silenced them and at the same time revealed their unbelief.

The Widow's Mite, 41-44. A mite was one-fourth of a farthing, about one-eighth of a cent. This widow first gave herself (2 Cor 8:5; Lk 21:1-4).

CHAPTER 13. THE SERVANT'S OLIVET DISCOURSE

Prediction Concerning the Temple, 1-4. On Olivet in full view of Herod's resplendent edifice, Jesus predicted its destruction. It is significant that from Olivet's strategic summit Titus poised his invincible legions for the seige of the city that was to eventuate in the complete ruin of the temple in fulfillment of Jesus' ominous words (cf. Mt 24—25; Lk 21).

Events of the Tribulation, 5-23 (see note on Mt 24:4-26).

Second Coming of the Son of Man, 24-26 (see note on Mt 24:27-30).

Regathering of Israel, 27 (see note on Mt 24:31).

The Certainty of Christ's Coming, 28-33 (see note on Mt 24:32-36 and note below on "Time of the Second Coming").

Exhortations to Watchfulness, 34-37 (see note on Mt 24:37-51).

TIME OF THE SECOND COMING

Did the Son not know the time of His second coming? "But of that day and hour knoweth no man, no, not the angels of heaven, *but my Father only*" (Mt 24:36). Mk 13:32 adds, "neither the Son." In Mark the Lord takes the place of complete humiliation as a Servant and the servant is properly presented as he who "knoweth not what his lord doeth" (Jn 15:15). After His servantship was discharged in death and He was raised in glory, the glorified Son omnisciently knew all, having this particular disclosure given to Him (Rev 1:1).

CHAPTER 14. EVENTS LEADING TO THE SERVANT'S DEATH

The Plot, 1-2. On the Passover (cf. Ex 12:1-28). This feast of redemption and that of unleavened bread which followed it speak typically of Him who was now being betrayed to die (Mt 26:2-5; Lk 22:1-2).

The Servant Anointed for Death, 3-9. See comments on Mt 26:6-13; Jn 12:1-8. Mary of Bethany was the "woman," 3. She alone understood the full import of His approaching vicarious death, and only those who sit at His feet as she did (Lk 10:39), likewise understand.

Judas' Plans to Betray Jesus, 10-11 (Mt 26:14-16; Lk 22:3-6).

The Last Passover and the Lord's Supper, 12-25. The Paschal feast of redemption was prepared, 12-16 (cf. Ex 12:8), and celebrated, 17-21. Then the Servant instituted the Lord's Supper, a

The Mount of Olives with the Garden of Gethsemane in center foreground. (© *MPS*)

memorial speaking of His death and second coming (1 Cor 11:23-26), superseding and fulfilling the slain lamb typology of the Passover.

Peter's Denial Predicted, 26-31 (cf. Mt 26:31-35; Lk 22:31-34: Jn 13:36-38).

Gethsemane's Agony, 32-42. See notations on Mt 26:36-56.

GETHSEMANE

Above the present road from Jerusalem to Bethany four traditional sites vie for the site of Jesus' agony, all of them containing ancient olive trees. None of the sites is certain. Somewhere on the Mount of Olives Jesus agonized in prayer. Gethsemane is assumed to mean "press of oils," but Jerome connected it with Heb. *ge'e shemanim*, "valley of oils" or "fertile valley," and may be correct in hinting that it was in a valley in which there were many olive trees.

Judas' Betrayal and Arrest of Jesus, 43-52. Judas' base betrayal, 43-46 (cf. Mt 26:47-56) was followed by Peter's flashing ire and show of courage, 47-52. Who the young man was who followed Jesus, 51-52, is not known.

Jesus Before the Sanhedrin, 53-65 (cf. Mt 26:57-68; Jn 18:12-24).

Peter's Denial, 66-72 (cf. Mt 26:69-75; Lk 22:56-62; Jn 18:16-27).

CHAPTER 15. THE SERVANT'S DEATH AND BURIAL

Jesus Before Pilate, 1-15. Pontius Pilate was Roman procurator of Judea (A.D. 26-36). Procurators were governors of the equestrian order subject to the emperor. They could summon help from the legate of Syria, if needed. They resided in Caesarea, but found it prudent to take up residence in Jerusalem on important feasts of the Jews. Procuratorial government proved unhappy. Roman business-men were unable to understand a volatile and ceremonially bound religious Oriental people and often resorted to cruelty, as Pilate did, when their patience was exhausted. Jesus' silence before Pilate, 5, fulfilled Isa 53:7. On Barabbas, 7-15, see Mt 27:15-23. See note on "Trials of Jesus," Lk 23.

The King of the Jews Mocked, 16-23. Pilate's praetorium, 16, is probably to be identified with Herod's palace on the western side of the city wall, graced by the gorgeous towers Hippicus, Phasael and Mariamne. However, later tradition links the praetorium with the fortress of Antonia at the NW corner of the temple area. This structure was rebuilt by Herod the Great from an earlier Maccabean structure and named in honor of Mark Anthony. On Golgotha, 22, see comments on Mt 27:33-44.

The Crucifixion, 24-41. See comments on Mt 27:33-56.

ORDER OF THE EVENTS OF THE CRUCIFIXION

1. Arrival at Golgotha (Calvary), Mt 27:33; Mk 15:22; Lk 23:33; Jn 19:17
2. Offer of a benumbing drink, Mt 27:34
3. The crucifixion, Mt 27:35
4. Cry, "Father, forgive . . .," Lk 23:34
5. The parting of Christ's garments, Mt 27:35
6. Jesus mocked, Mt 27:39-44; Mk 15:29
7. The thieves rail on Him, but one believes, Mt 27:44
8. Second cry, "Today shalt thou be with me . . .," Lk 23:43
9. Third cry, "Woman, Behold thy son," Jn 19:26-27
10. The darkness, Mt 27:45; Mk 15:33
11. The fourth cry, "My God, my God . . .," Mt 27:46-47; Mk 15:34-36
12. Fifth cry, "I thrist," Jn 19:28
13. Sixth cry, "It is finished," Jn 19:30
14. Seventh cry, "Father, into thy hands . . .," Lk 23:46
15. Jesus dismisses His spirit, Mt 27:50; Mk 15:37

The Burial, 42-47. See Mt 27:57-61.

CHAPTER 16. THE SERVANT'S RESURRECTION

His Resurrection, 1-8. See notes on Mt 28:1-10. How gracious is the report of the angel of Jesus' resurrection, 6-7, with the appended note to Peter, the denier, who must have thought surely he was disowned—"But go your way, tell his disciples *and* Peter . . .," 7. See note on "The Resurrection Authenticated," Jn 20.

ORDER OF THE EVENTS OF THE RESURRECTION

1. Mary Magdalene, Mary the mother of James, and Salome start for the tomb, Lk 23:55—24:1
2. They find the stone rolled away, Lk 24:2-9
3. Mary Magdalene goes to tell the disciples, Jn 20:1-2
4. Mary, the mother of James, draws near and sees the angel, Mt 28:1-2
5. She goes back to meet the other women following with spices
6. Meanwhile Peter and John arrive, look in and depart, Jn 20:3-10
7. Mary Magdalene returns weeping, sees two angels, then Jesus, Jn 20:11-18
8. The risen Christ bids her tell the disciples, Jn 20:17-18
9. Mary (mother of James) meanwhile returns with the women, Lk 24:1-4
10. They return and see the two angels, Lk 24:5; Mk 16:5

11. They also hear the angel's message, Mt 28:6-8
12. On their way to find the disciples, they are met by the risen Christ, Mt 28:9-10

His Post-Resurrection Appearances, 9-20. This portion is not found in the Sinaitic and Vatican manuscripts. Others have it only in part. Probably Mark's original copy was transcribed and became a textual tradition before he finished it. Later he finished it, giving rise to another text (the fuller one, consisting of verses 9-20). This latter text is referred to by Irenaeus (c. A.D. 170) and is found in the Alexandrian and Cambridge manuscripts.

POST-RESURRECTION APPEARANCES

1. To Mary Magdalene, Jn 20:14-18; Mk 16:9
2. To the women returning from the tomb, Mt 28:8-10
3. To Peter later in the day, Lk 24:34; 1 Cor 15:5
4. To the disciples going to Emmaus in the evening, Lk 24:13-31
5. To the apostles (except Thomas), Lk 24:36-45; Jn 20:19-24
6. To the apostles a week later (Thomas present), Jn 20:24-29
7. In Galilee to the seven by the Lake of Tiberias, Jn 21:1-23
8. In Galilee on a mountain to the apostles and 500 believers, 1 Cor 15:6
9. At Jerusalem and Bethany again to James, 1 Cor 15:7
10. At Olivet and the ascension, Acts 1:3-12
11. To Paul near Damascus, Acts 9:3-6; 1 Cor 15:8
12. To Stephen outside Jerusalem, Acts 7:55
13. To Paul in the temple, Acts 22:17-21; 23:11
14. To John on Patmos, Rev 1:10-19

L U K E

THE GOSPEL OF THE SON OF MAN

The Author. The writer is Luke, "the beloved physician" (Col 4:14; cf. Phm 24; 2 Tim 4:11). He with Mark was a companion worker of Paul, shown by the "we" sections of Acts 16:10-11; 20:5f.; 21:1ff. That he wrote the Gospel of Luke is shown by comparing Lk 1:1-4 with Acts 1:1-3 and by tradition. Luke wrote his Gospel very likely while he was in Caesarea during Paul's imprisonment there (Acts 27:1), about A.D. 58, and before Acts was penned, about A.D. 63.

The Synoptic Gospels. Matthew, Mark and Luke constitute the Synoptic Gospels. Synoptic means "seeing the whole together at a glance." These three Gospels, in contrast to John, present a common story and relate substantially the same incidents in the life of our Lord, with of course some omissions, additions and differences. How to explain the Synoptic problem still occupies the energy of critical scholars. Many hypotheses have been devised, which deny the authentic historical nature of the narratives, the miracles, etc.

The position which best fits the facts and honors the Christ of the Synoptics is that the Holy Spirit presents, without contradiction, through three different human writers, the *one* Messiah-King, Servant-Saviour, God-Man. Each presents Him under a different aspect for a particular purpose, but the threefold presentation is of the one and same divine-human Person.

So multi-faceted is the glory of Christ's person and so far-reaching are the ramifications of His finished redemption that one Gospel account could not portray His full-born splendor. To view these accounts as mere human productions, mechanically pieced together from existing traditions, is to forfeit any real sense of their spiritual purpose and meaning. The so-called Synoptic problem that results from such a view is both unresolved and unresolvable.

Outline
Birth, Childhood, Early Ministry, 1:1—4:13
Galilean Ministry, 4:14—9:50
Journey to and Ministry in Jerusalem, 9:51—21:38
Rejection and Death, 22:1—23:56
Resurrection and Ascension, 24:1-53

CHARACTERISTIC FEATURES OF LUKE'S GOSPEL
LUKE COMPARED WITH MATTHEW AND MARK

Luke	Matthew	Mark
The Human Gospel	The Kingly Gospel	The Servant Gospel
Perfect manhood of Christ	Divine kingship of Christ	Divine servantship of Christ
Basis of the saviourhood and present intercession (Heb 5:1-2)	Basis of His offer of Himself to Israel and His coming kingdom (Acts 1:6)	Basis of His giving His life a ransom for many (Mk 10:45)
Moral perfections and tender sympathies of the perfect Man	Kingly power and humble grace of Israel's Saviour-King	Miraculous power in service to man of the God-sent Servant
Our Lord in prayer (cf. Lk 3:21; 5:16; 6:12-13; 9:18), stressing His dependency as a man	Our Lord in kingly manifestation	Our Lord in Spirit-empowered service
Appeal to Greek	Appeal to Jew	Appeal to Roman

INCIDENTS AND EVENTS EXCLUSIVE TO LUKE

1. Zacharias' vision and Elisabeth's conception, 1:5-25
2. Mary's salutation, 1:26-38
3. Mary's visit to Elisabeth, 1:39-56
4. John the Baptist's birth and Zacharias' hymn of praise, 1:57-80
5. The enrollment decree of Caesar Augustus, 2:1-3
6. Christ's nativity in Bethlehem, 2:4-7
7. Details of the Christmas story, 2:8-20
8. The circumcision of the Child Jesus, 2:21
9. The presentation of Christ in the temple, 2:22-24
10. The story of Simeon and Anna, 2:25-38
11. The silent years at Nazareth, 2:39-40
12. Jesus at the Passover and among the rabbis, 2:41-52
13. Dating of the beginning of John's public ministry, 3:1-2
14. John's success, 3:10-15
15. Human genealogy of Christ from Mary, 3:23-38
16. Christ's rejection at Nazareth, 4:15-30
17. Details of the call of Peter, James and John, 5:1-10
18. Discourse of Christ on the plain, 6:17-49

513

CHAPTER 1. BIRTHS OF JOHN AND OF JESUS FORETOLD

Introduction, 1-4. In polished Greek this prologue shows how spontaneous and adaptable to the human instrument divine inspiration is. "Theophilus" ("God-lover") connects this Gospel as well as the book of Acts (1:1) with Luke as the author. He was Luke's literary patron, doubtless a Roman or Greek of high rank, as his title, "most excellent," indicates.

Birth of John the Baptist Foretold, 5-25. The silence of the four centuries from Malachi to Matthew was broken. The ministering priest Zacharias (Zechariah, "whom the Lord remembers") heard from God through Gabriel, the archangel. This same angel had communicated to Daniel the vision of the seventy weeks (Dan 9:21). John was to be born of a barren couple and was to minister in the spirit and power of Elijah (1 Kgs 21:20; 2 Kgs 1:8; cf. Mal 4:5-6).

Birth of Jesus Also Foretold, 26-45. Gabriel visited Mary at Nazareth, 26-27, announcing the most glorious event of human history, 28-33. Verses 32 and 33 are yet unfulfilled, and will be realized at the second advent (cf. Dan 7:27; Gen 12:2-3; Isa 9:6-7). Here was "the virgin" of prophecy (Isa 7:14). Here was the divine-human Person whom Isaiah said was to be "a child born" (human) and "a son given" (divine) (Jn 3:16; 2 Cor 9:15). How could this be? 34-38. "The Holy Spirit shall come upon thee," 35, means that the human nature of Christ (absolutely holy) was produced in the womb of the virgin by a creative act of God the Spirit (cf. Mt 1:18-20). "The power of the Highest shall overshadow thee," 35, means that the eternal Son of God (the Most High) united Himself with the miraculously generated human nature in the womb of the virgin. The result was "that holy thing" uniquely unclassifiable—deity and humanity united for the redemption of the fallen race. Therefore His name was to be "Jesus," Lord-Saviour (cf. note on Mt 1:18-25).

Mary's Ode of Praise, 46-56. Filled with OT Scripture and the Spirit of God, the virgin burst forth in praise, echoing Hannah's song (1 Sam 2:1-10; cf. Ps 34:2-3; 103:17; 111:9).

Birth of John and Zacharias' Prophetic Joy, 57-80. Zacharias' tongue was loosed, as Israel's will be when they see and believe, 57-64. His prophecy, 67-79, like Mary's magnificat, was immersed in OT promises, which he saw would be fulfilled in the person and work of the coming King.

The traditional site of the birth of Christ is marked by the Church of the Nativity. (© *MPS*)

2:1-20. BIRTH OF JESUS

Enrollment of Quirinius, 1-3. That Luke's census was part of an empire-wide enrollment is suggested by Egyptian papyri which tell of a periodic fourteen-year census. Moreover, evidence suggests also that Quirinius (RSV) was twice governor of Syria, the first time about 8 B.C., when the first census was made. Household enrollment is also attested by the papyri, so there is every indication from increased archaeological knowledge that Luke is accurate in this passage frequently questioned by various NT critics.

Birth in Bethlehem, 4-20. God's providence working through Caesar Augustus and the imperial enrollment decree made it possible for Mary and Joseph, living in Nazareth of Galilee, to fulfill the prophecy of Micah relating to Messiah's birth in Bethlehem (Mic 5:2).

Luke, presenting the perfect Man, omits the visit of the wise men and the flight into Egypt, which Matthew, describing the King, includes (Mt 2:1-21).

BETHLEHEM

This ancient picturesque town, seven miles S of Jerusalem, called Bethlehem-Ephrath in Mic 5:2, was the original home of the

Davidic family, called Ephrathites (Ruth 1:2; 1 Sam 17:12), since they were residents of Ephrath, an early suburb of the city. Memories went back to Boaz and Ruth, ancestors of Christ. Ruth gleaned in the fertile fields of Bethlehem ("house of bread"). Under the ancient Church of the Nativity, originally built in the 4th cen. by Helena, mother of Constantine, tradition points out the manger room, which it also connects with the ancestral home of David, Boaz and Ruth. Just E of the town is the Shepherds' Field where the angels sang the joyous advent of *"the* Saviour who is Christ the Lord," 11.

DATE OF CHRISTMAS

Our traditional date of December 25 as the day of Christ's birth was set in the 4th cen. It was the day settled upon by the Western Church. The Eastern Church celebrates January 6. Actually the day is unknown. Apparently the nativity did not occur in the winter, since shepherds in Palestine customarily do not remain in the open with their flocks, except from spring to autumn.

2:21-38. THE INFANCY OF JESUS

The Circumcision and Presentation, 21-24. These rites were prescribed in the Mosaic law (Lev 12:3; Ex 13:12, 16; Num 8:17).

Augustus Caesar ruled Rome when the edict was issued for the empire-wide census that brought Joseph and Mary to Bethlehem. (*Courtesy Howard F. Vos*)

They demonstrated that the perfect Man "made of a woman" was "made under the law" to redeem them "that were under the law" (Gal 4:4-5). The circumcision made Him who was "a minister of the circumcision for the truth of God, to confirm the promises made unto the fathers" (Rom 15:8) "debtor to do the whole law," which He alone could fulfill. Fulfilling it He redeemed us from its curse, "being made a curse for us" (Gal 3:13). For His name "Jesus," see Mt 1:21; Lk 1:31. The type of presentation offering indicates the poverty of Mary and Joseph (cf. Lev. 12:8).

Simeon's and Anna's Prophecies, 25-38. These two aged saints belonged to the faithful remnant who believed the Word and waited for Christ at His first advent. Simeon recognized the Babe as the prophesied One, as God's "salvation" and "a light to lighten the Gentiles" (first advent) and "the glory of thy people Israel" (second advent), 32 (Isa 42:6-7). Simeon's remarkable prophecy, 34-35, found fulfillment in Jn 19:25 (cf. 1 Jn 2:9; 1 Cor 11:19). Anna, 36-38, is a beautiful picture of devotion. She came in at the glorious moment, 38, to see the Babe, her faith in Him who could bring redemption being rewarded.

CHRONOLOGY OF THIS PERIOD

6-5 B.C.	John's birth announced to Zacharias	Lk 1:5-25
6 months later	Jesus' birth announced to Mary Mary goes to see Elisabeth	Lk 1:26-38 Lk 1:39-56
3 months later	Mary returns to Nazareth Joseph receives a message John born	Lk 1:56 Mt 1:18-24 Lk 1:57-80
5 B.C.	Jesus born	Mt 1:25; Lk 2:1-7
8 days later	Jesus is circumcised	Lk 2:21
33 days later	Jesus presented in the temple	Lk 2:22-38
4 B.C.	Magi visit the King Flight to Egypt Murder of Bethlehem's children	Mt 2:1-12 Mt 2:13-15 Mt 2:16-18
3 or 2 B.C.	Return to Nazareth	Lk 2:39; Mt 2:19-23

CORRECTED CALENDAR

In the 6th cen. A.D., when the Christian calendar which reckoned time before and after the birth of Christ was replacing the old Roman calendar, dating from the founding of Rome (753 B.C.), the monk Dionysius Exiguus made an error of at least four years in his reckoning. This mistake was not detected till long after the Christian calendar had been established in popular use Dionysius reckoned 748 or 749 B.C. instead of 753 as the date of Rome's founding. Hence 5 or 4 B.C. must be reckoned as the birth of Christ.

2:39-52. THE BOYHOOD OF JESUS

Synopsis of His Boyhood Years, 39-40. Little is told about Jesus' childhood, in contrast to the ridiculous legends of the Apocryphal Gospels. Certainly the large family knew poverty and sacrifice, and Jesus knew the weariness of common toil, no doubt at the carpenter's bench.

His Visit to Jerusalem at Twelve, 41-52. This is unique to Luke's account. Jesus must have regularly attended the three great feasts of Passover, Pentecost and Tabernacles, from 12 years of age and on. This incident is pivotal as our Lord's first self-witness to His deity. His mother had declared, *"Thy father and I* have sought thee sorrowing," 48. He corrected His fallible mother by declaring that God was His Father: "Do you not know that I must be about My Father's business?" 49, and that His divine mission took all precedent. He accompanied them to Nazareth, and as the obedient One submitted to His parents.

NAZARETH

Nazareth was a small little-known place (cf. Jn 1:46) until immortalized in the NT as the boyhood home of Jesus. Archaeology has shown that the town was not very old. There is no evidence of potsherds beyond Iron II (600 B.C.). It was just a small village of farmers and artisans, such as the carpenter Joseph. While not situated on the great trade routes from Damascus to Egypt, it did lie on a spur of road from Sepphoris on the N. While it was not a bustling emporium, it was far from being isolated from the busy Galilean towns and the stirring events of the day. Its scenic beauty and its opportunities for solitude made it an ideal spot for Jesus to grow up. Situated at an altitude of 1150 feet the view above the village commanded a majestic panorama of snow-capped Hermon on the N, nearby Tabor on the E, the extensive Plain of Esdraelon on the S and Mt. Carmel and the blue Mediterranean on the W. At Nazareth Jesus received the regular training of a Jewish lad in home and synagogue (Lk 4:16).

Present-day Nazareth is a fair-sized town of about 22,000, the site of the synagogue traditionally marked by the Church of the United Greeks, but the Orthodox Greeks locate the site where the Church of the Forty Martyrs stood.

3:1-20. JOHN'S MINISTRY

John's Ministry, 1-14. In a passage remarkable for its accuracy and comprehensiveness, 1-2, Luke pinpoints the beginning of John's ministry. Tiberius (A.D. 14-37) succeeded Caesar Augustus (27 B.C.– A.D. 14). The fifteenth year of Tiberius was *c.* A.D. 29. Pontius Pilate was procurator of Judea (A.D. 26-36). Herod Antipas (4 B.C.–A.D. 39), who killed the Baptist, was tetrarch of Galilee and Perea. Herod Philip (4 B.C.–A.D. 34) was tetrarch of Iturea and Trachonitis. Lysanias ruled Abilene, capital Abila, on the Barada River NW of Damascus. Joseph Caiaphas was appointed to the high priesthood by the procurator Valerius Gratus (A.D. 15-26) and was the acting official, while Annas was *ex officio* high priest, but very influential. Luke gives the fullest account of John's ministry, but cf. Mt 3:1-12; Mk 1:1-8; Jn 1:6-8, 15-36. John's rugged preaching of repentance (see note on Mt 3:2; 4:14) prepared the way for the ministry of Jesus. However, John's message was not the Christian gospel (cf. 14 with Acts 16:30-31) nor John's baptism Christian baptism (cf. Acts 19:4-5). But John did prepare the way for these by announcing the Messiah-Saviour and His salvation.

John's Testimony to Christ, 15-20. The baptism of the Holy Spirit (Acts 1:5; 2:4; 11:14-16; 1 Cor 12:13; Rom 6:3-4; Gal 3:26-27; Eph 4:5) is connected with Christ's death, resurrection and ascension at His first advent, 16-17. The baptism "with fire," 16, is connected with judgment at His second advent (see note Mt 3:11; Mk 1:8). On Herod Antipas and John's imprisonment see note on Mt 14:1-11.

3:21-38. BAPTISM AND GENEALOGY OF JESUS

The Baptism of Jesus, 21-22. See comments on Mt 3:13-17 and Mk 1:9-11. Luke adds the detail that Jesus was praying when He was baptized and the heavens were opened, 21. Luke's Gospel of the perfect Man often pictures Jesus praying, as the expression of human dependence upon God.

JESUS' PRAYERS IN LUKE

At His baptism, Lk 3:21
In the wilderness, Lk 5:16
Before calling the 12, Lk 6:12-13
At Caesarea Philippi, Lk 9:18
Before the transfiguration, Lk 9:28-29
When He instructed in prayer, Lk 11:1-4
For Peter, Lk 22:31-32
In Gethsemane, Lk 22:41
On the cross, Lk 23:34
At Emmaus, Lk 24:30

The Human Genealogy of Jesus, 23-38. In Luke we have Mary's genealogy in contrast to the one in Matthew where Joseph's genealogy is presented (see note on Mt 1:1-17). Matthew's genealogy goes back to David and Abraham (presenting Christ's legal right to the throne of David and relating Him to the Abrahamic covenant). In giving Mary's line Luke presents Jesus' blood descent, "the son of David, according to the flesh" (Rom 1:3). In Mt 1:16 Joseph is called "the son of Jacob," in Luke "the son of Heli" (Lk 3:23), by which Luke means son-in-law of Heli, who like Joseph was a Davidic descendant. Cf. for this usage 1 Sam 24:16.

4:1-13. JESUS' TEMPTATION

The Temptation, 1-12. Luke presents the *order* of the temptation as it affected Christ's human nature, body, soul and spirit, in the perfect Man. The first temptation, 2-4, concerned the body; the second the soul, 5-8; the third the spirit, 9-12. The whole man was tested. Cf. notes on Mt 4:1-11; Mk 1:12-13. Matthew's order is different.

The Devil Routed, 13. The accuser, however, left only temporarily. Satanic temptation in this life is not continuous but constant.

SATAN

He was disguised under the Edenic serpent, Gen 3:1-14
He is the serpent's seed, Gen 3:15
He was Lucifer, son of the morning, before his fall, Isa 14:12
He was the anointed cherub that covers, Ezk 28:14
He energized David to evil, 1 Chr 21:1
He accused and afflicted Job, Job 1:7—2:10
He opposes unbelieving Israel prefigured by Joshua the priest, Zech 3:1-9
He is the tempter, Mt 4:3

He is the prince of the demons, Mt 12:24; Acts 10:38

He instigates false doctrine, 1 Tim 4:1-6

He perverts the Word of God, Mt 4:4; Lk 4:10-11

He works in demon possession, Mt 12:22-29

He is Satan, the adversary, Zech 3:1

He is the devil, the slanderer, Lk 4:13

He caused Judas to betray Christ, Jn 13:2, 27, and Ananias to lie, Acts 5:3

He blinds people spiritually, 2 Cor 4:4

He seeks to harm believers, 1 Pet 5:8

He heads a celestial hierarchy of evil, Eph 6:11-12

He indwells the unsaved, Eph 2:2, who are his "sons," Jn 8:44

He works diabolic miracles, 2 Thess 2:9

He was branded "a liar" and "the father of it" by Jesus, Jn 8:44

He is a murderer, Jn 8:44

He is the prince of this world, Jn 12:31; 14:30

He binds people physically and spiritually, Lk 13:16

He is a fallen angel, Mt 25:41

He sows tares, Mt 13:38-39, and snatches away the Word, Mt 13:19

He will be bound during the millennium, Rev 20:1-3

He is "the enemy," Mt 13:39, "the evil one," Mt 13:38

He is routed by Spirit-directed prayer, Eph 6:10-20

He is overcome by faith, 1 Pet 5:8-9

He hinders God's will in believers, 1 Thess 2:18

He is the deceiver, Rev 12:9

He is the dragon, that old serpent, Rev 12:9; 20:2

He fell from a sinless high estate, Lk 10:18

He viewed Simon Peter as a target, Lk 22:31

He has a synagogue of legalists who deny God's grace in Christ, Rev 2:9

His children are unsaved people, 1 Jn 3:8, 10

His ultimate fate is Gehenna, Mt 25:41; Rev 20:10

4:14-44. JESUS BEGINS HIS GALILEAN MINISTRY

He Begins the Galilean Ministry, 14-15. This ministry, 4:14—9:50, curtailed by Luke is given more attention in Matthew and Mark (cf. Jn 1:43—2:25; 4:1-54).

Rejection at Nazareth, 16-30. Jesus' reading from Isa 61:1-2 is broken off at the point following the prediction of His first advent and the outgoing of the gospel of grace to Gentiles, 17-20. "Is not this Joseph's son?" 22, is a precursor of His rejection. His preaching

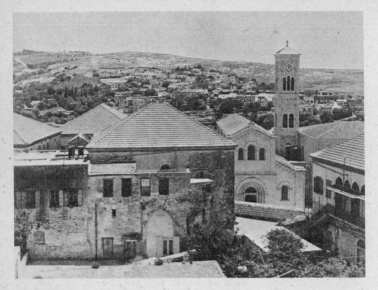

Nazareth with the Church of St. Joseph in right foreground.
(*Courtesy IIS*)

that divine grace is not confined to Israel, but will reach to Gentiles as in the case of Naaman and the widow of Zarephath, filled the people with wrath, 25-27 (cf. 1 Kgs 17:9; 18:1; 2 Kgs 5:1, 14). But His perfect manhood overawed them. They were unable to kill Him.

The Demoniac Healed, 31-37 (cf. Mk 1:21-28). See note on "Demonism" in Mk 5:1-20, on "Miracles" in Mk 5:21-43, on "Capernaum" in Mk 1:21-28, on "Satan" in Lk 4:1-13.

Peter's Mother-in-Law Healed, 38-44 (cf. Mt 8:14-17; Mk 1:29-38). See note on "Demonism" in Mk 5:1-20. On the kingdom of God, 43, see note on Mk 4:1-29. Jesus preached in "the synagogues of Galilee," 44.

THE SYNAGOGUES OF GALILEE

Excavations in Capernaum (see note on Mk 1:21-28) have yielded the ruins of one of the finest white limestone synagogues in Palestine. The Franciscans have restored this structure. According to custom, the synagogue building was oriented toward Jerusalem. Rectangular in shape the interior was 70 x 50 feet. It had a balcony for women, and colonnades on three sides. Other synagogues have been unearthed at Chorazin, Bethsaida Julias, Kefr, Birim, Meiron and Beth Alpha in the Plain of Esdraelon. All date from the 2nd cen. That at Beth Alpha is famous for its mosaics. See also note on "The Synagogue" in the section "Between the Testaments."

CHAPTER 5. MIRACLES AND TEACHING IN GALILEE

The Call of Peter, James and John, 1-11 (cf. Mk 1:16-20). On the Lake of Gennesaret, 1, see note on Lk 8:1-3. The miraculous catch of fish demonstrates the perfect Man's, the last Adam's, lordship over the animal creation lost by the first Adam. Peter's sinfulness was revealed. Cf. the other miracle of a large catch of fish in Jn 21, occurring after the resurrection.

The Leper and the Paralytic Healed, 12-26. See Mk 1:40-45; Mt 9:2-8; Mk 2:1-12. See note on "Miracles" in Mk 5:21-43.

Call of Levi (Matthew), 27-29. See comments on Mt 9:9; Mk 2:13-14.

Scribes and Pharisees Answered, 30-39. See notes on Mt 9:10-17; Mk 2:16-22. For the parables of the garments and the wineskins, 36-39, see comments on Mt 9:16-17; Mk 2:21-22.

CHAPTER 6. THE TWELVE CHOSEN; THE BEATITUDES

The Sabbath Question, 1-11. See comments on Mt 12:1-8; Mk 2:23-28. The healing of the atrophied hand (cf. Mt 12:9-14; Mk 3:1-6) showed our Lord transcended mere religious externalism. Religionism gloats in the letter, but ignores the spirit, 6-11. On the synagogue, 6, see note on Lk 4:44.

Choosing the Twelve, 12-19. The perfect Man spent the whole night in prayer to God, 12, before this momentously important task. See notes on Mt 10:2-4, and especially Mk 3:13-19. On His miraculous healing ministry and expulsion of demons, 17-19, see notes on "Demonism" in Mk 5:1-20 and "Miracles" in Mk 5:21-43.

The Beatitudes, 20-49. Many of the sayings echoed here are in the Sermon on the Mount (Mt 5—7), which are presented by Matthew as the proclamation of the King concerning the moral and spiritual principles which were to rule in the kingdom He proclaimed (see notes of Mt 5—7). See note on kingdom of God in Mk 4:1-29.

7:1-35. MIRACLES OF MERCY

The Centurion's Servant Healed, 1-10. See notes on Mt 8:5-13. On "Capernaum" see note in Mk 1:21-28.

ROMAN CENTURION

The Roman centurion, corresponding roughly to a captain, commanded about 100 men ("century") which was one-sixtieth of a Roman legion of 6,000 men. Although a centurion often drilled and inspected men under him, his duties frequently corresponded to a non-commissioned officer. The centurion was the backbone of the Roman army and was required to be a good, brave, level-headed leader.

The Widow of Nain's Son Raised, 11-18. This episode is unique to Luke. Nain (Nein), still called by this name, is a Galilean town situated five miles S SE of Nazareth in the corner of Jebel Duhy (Little Hermon) two miles W SW of Endor. Its elevation (1690 feet) gives the hamlet a superb view of the Esdraelon plain on the S and SW and of Mt. Tabor on the NW. It is a cluster of ruins containing ancient sepulchers.

Jesus' Testimony to John, 19-35. John's languishing in prison tested his faith, 19-20, but the perfect Man strengthened it with a marvelous demonstration of miracles of healing and demon expulsion (see notes on Mk 5), followed by warm praise for John, 24-29, and an exposé of the irrationality of unbelief, 30-35.

7:36-50. JESUS ANOINTED

The Anointing by a Sinful Woman, 36-50. This woman was neither Mary of Bethany (Jn 12:1-8) nor Mary Magdalene. She was an unchaste woman, 37, a prostitute likely converted under John's or Jesus' ministry, who gave public evidence of her conversion and gratitude for salvation. The Oriental banquet was in a Pharisee's house. Guests reclined, so it was easy for the woman to wash Jesus' feet with her tears and anoint them. The parable, 41-50, was a rebuke to criticism of the woman's demonstration of penitence.

CHAPTER 8. DELIVERANCES AND INSTRUCTIONS

Women Who Ministered to Christ, 1-3. This is unique to Luke's Gospel. The women were particularly demonstrative of their affection and devotion to the one who had delivered them. Mary Magdalene was "Mary of Magdala" (Mejdel), three miles NW of

Tiberias and situated between it and Capernaum at the S end of the Plain of Ginnesar (Gennesaret). The Lake of Galilee was sometimes called the Lake of Gennesaret (Lk 5:1).

Parable of the Sower, 4-15. See comments on Mt 13:1-23; Mk 4:1-20.

Parable of the Lighted Candle, 16-18 (cf. Mt 5:15-16; Mk 4:21-23; Lk 11:33).

The New Relationship, 19-21 (cf. Mt 12:46-50; Mk 3:31-35).

Jesus Stills the Storm, 22-25 (cf. Mt 8:23-27; Mk 4:36-41).

Demoniac of Gadara, 26-39. See comments on Mt 8:28-34, and note on "Demonism" in Mk 5:1-20 and "Miracles" in Mk 5:21-43.

A Woman Healed and Jairus' Daughter Raised, 40-56. See comments on Mt 9:18-26; Mk 5:21-43.

9:1-17. THE TWELVE SENT OUT

The Ministry of the Twelve, 1-9 (cf. Mt 10:1-42; Mk 6:7-13). They were given power "over all demons" and "to cure diseases," 1. There is one devil but many demons (see note on "Demonism" in Mk 5:1-20 and "Miracles" in Mk 5:21-43). On Herod the tetrarch, 7-9, murderer of John the Baptist, see note on Mt 14:1-11 and on Mk 6:14-29 (cf. also Lk 3:1-2).

Feeding of the Five Thousand, 10-17. This miracle is told by all the Gospel writers (see Mt 14:13-21; Mk 6:30-44; Jn 6:1-14). Bethsaida, 10 ("house or place of fishing"), was the hometown of Philip, Peter and Andrew (Mk 6:45; Jn 1:44; 12:21). The NT presents the Sea of Galilee dotted with thriving towns in Jesus' day, including Capernaum, Chorazin, Magdala, Bethsaida and Tiberias. On Bethsaida see Mt 11:20-24.

9:18-62. PREDICTION OF DEATH AND COMING GLORY

Peter's Confession, 18-26. See comments on Mt 16:13-20; Mk 8:27-30. Peter's confession of the perfect Man's deity, 20, did not settle his spiritual problem. So Jesus instructed in discipleship, 23, and its law of self-sacrifice and self-giving, 24-25, in the light of His approaching rejection and death, 22, 31, 44.

The Transfiguration, 27-36. In the transfiguration, the three most spiritually apperceptive disciples, Peter, John and James, 28, were given an audio-visual lesson in the law of self-losing to self-gaining, 24. The glory of Christ's outshining deity, 29, and the appearance of Moses and Elijah in glory, 30, talking about His "exodus" or death at Jerusalem, 31, were meant to show the disciples that the only way to glory for our Lord, as well as His disciples, was through self-giving to God's will and to others. Peter and the other disciples wanted the glory without the suffering and were living on the plane of self-saving, not self-losing. Hence the selfish suggestion of the three tabernacles, 33, and the cloud and fear, 34, relieved only by, "This is my beloved Son: hear him," 35, which is in striking contrast to Peter's misguided prattle, 33.

Demonstration of the Futility of the Self-Saving Attitude, 37-50. The self-centered powerless disciples, 37-43, are contrasted with the selfless powerful Christ, who again announced His death, 44-45. Results of the disciples' selfishness were the clash of believer with believer, 46-48; group with group, 49-50; race with race, 51-56. The only cure was self-losing, 24, manifested in genuine dedication to the kingdom of God, 57-62.

Journey Toward Jerusalem, 51-62. When Jesus finally left Galilee, 51, His ministry until the time of His death was performed in Perea, the territory ruled by Herod the tetrarch, E of the Jordan, and in Judea, under the Roman procurator Pontius Pilate, 9:51—19:27. Luke extensively details this Perean-Judean ministry, while Matthew relates only a few incidents (Mt 19—20), Mark one chapter (Mk 10), and John five chapters (Jn 7—11).

CHAPTER 10. THE SEVENTY SENT;
THE GOOD SAMARITAN

The Seventy Sent Out, 1-24. This sending of the 70 was in addition to Christ's sending out the 12 some nine months before. His purpose was to complete the proclamations of the King and the kingdom, so that those who disbelieved, 13-24, might have no plea they had not heard. (Cf. Mt 10:1-42; 11:20-24.) Our Lord's beholding "Satan as lightning fall from heaven," 18, was a prediction (cf. Rev 12:8-9). Satan will not be cast out of the heavenlies till the second advent and the establishment of the kingdom (Rev 20:1-3), of which great event the 70 were announcers and precursors.

The Lawyer's Question, 25-29. "Who is my neighbor?" furnished the introduction to the parable following (cf. Mt 22:34-40; Mk 12:28-34).

The Good Samaritan, 30-37. This superb parable, exclusive to the Gospel of Luke and reflective of the manhood of our Lord, although it illustrates who our neighbor is, in its deepest sense points toward Him. He is the Good Samaritan. The poor traveler, fallen among thieves, represents sin-despoiled humanity. The failure of the priest and the Levite to assist illustrates the inability of the law and the ordinances to save man out of his sad plight. With superlative love and superb grace and kindness the perfect Man came to the place where the unfortunate man was and "had compassion on him," bound up His wounds pouring in oil (typifying the Holy Spirit) and wine (speaking of the cleansing blood). The inn, 34, symbolizes the church, and the two pence speak of the rewards for those who minister in behalf of men's salvation. The promised coming again with a greater reward, 35, looks to the second advent.

Mary vs. Martha, 38-42. This is another Lukan exclusive, which shows the primacy of spiritual worship over service. Service, if it is not to degenerate into mere fleshly busyness spoiled by vexations and tensions, illustrated by Martha, must be grounded in true spiritual worship of Christ, illustrated by Mary, 39. Note that "Mary *also* sat at Jesus' feet," 39, in addition to her service. Bethany is nestled on the eastern slope of Olivet about one and five-eighths miles from Jerusalem.

11:1-13. JESUS' DOCTRINE OF PRAYER

Jesus Praying, 1. This Gospel often presents the perfect Man in prayerful dependence upon God. See note on Lk 3:21-22, "Jesus' Prayers in Luke."

Jesus Instructing in Prayer, 2-4. This is more correctly the disciples' prayer rather than the Lord's prayer, since He was sinless and could never Himself pray, "Forgive us our sins." See comments in Mt 6:9-13. The prayer is based on the Father relationship and may serve as a pattern for all those in His family.

The Parable of the Importunate Friend, 5-13, another Lukan exclusive, teaches persistence in petition. Prayer grounded in the Fatherhood of God by His children, 11-13, exhibits faith in this relationship. Verse 13 was fulfilled at Pentecost. To ask for the Holy Spirit now that the gift has been given, is like asking a friend for something he has already given you.

11:14-54. DEMON EXPULSION AND WARNINGS

Jesus Instructs in Demonism, 14-28. His expulsion of a demon, 14, brings the blasphemous accusation that "He casts out demons by Beelzebub, the prince of the demons," 15 (RSV), another name of Satan. See note on "Demonism" in Mk 5:1-20, "Miracles" in Mk 5:21-43, "Satan" in Lk 4:1-13. Satan is a king, 17-18, ruling over a kingdom of evil fallen spirits, 17-19. The kingdom of God, i.e., the rule of God upon mankind, comes upon a person when Satan and demons are cast out by the stronger than he (Jesus the Christ), 20. This is in response to believing prayer, 11:1-13 (cf. "deliver us from evil," 4, and the spiritual conflict which necessitates Spirit-directed intercession in the believer, Eph 6:10-20). The illustration of the demoniac, 24-28, is applied to the nation Israel by Matthew (see comments on Mt 12:43-45). Luke, however, applied the teaching to humanity in general, demonstrating the uselessness of self-reformation to save. External cleaning up without true regeneration invites Satan to return with seven viler spirits.

The Sign of Jonah, 29-32 (cf. Mt 12:39-42; Mk 8:11). "The queen of the south," 31, was the Queen of Sheba (1 Kgs 10:1-13).

Parable of the Candle, 33-38 (cf. Mt 5:15-16; Mk 4:21-22; Lk 8:16).

The Pharisees Denounced, 39-44 (cf. Mt 23:13-35).

The Lawyers Denounced, 45-54. "Lawyer" (*nomikos,* "of the law") denotes one who was expert in the law of Moses and traditional Jewish law (Mt 22:35; Lk 7:30; 10:25; 11:45-46, 52; 14:3). "From the blood of Abel," 51 (cf. Gen 4:8), "unto the blood of Zacharias" (2 Chr 24:20-21), follows the Hebrew order of books where Genesis opens the Scriptures and 2 Chronicles is the last book.

CHAPTER 12. PARABLES AND WARNINGS

Warning Against False Doctrine, 1-12. Leaven (Ex 12:8, 15-20; Mt 13:33; 1 Cor 5:7-8) represents corrupt teaching. The teachings of the empty ritualists, the Pharisees, were nothing but sham and hypocrisy, 1-3 (see Mt 16:1-12). The Lord encourages His own, 4-14. He who has power to cast into hell, Gehenna, is Satan, who tempts to sin and Christ-rejection, 5. Five sparrows for two farthings, one-half cent, with no "forgotten sparrow" before God, 6, shows His care of even the least of His creatures. For blasphemy against the Holy Spirit, 10, see note on Mt 12:31-32.

Warning Against Covetousness, 13-34. A request from a man in the crowd, 13-15, occasioned the parable of the rich fool, 16-21, and a general warning against this cardinal sin of covetousness, 22-34 (cf. Mt 6:25-33; Col 3:5). On "seek the kingdom of God," 31-32, see note on Mt 3:2; 4:17; 13:1-2.

Watching for the Second Advent, 35-48. See notes on the Olivet Discourse, Mt 24:37—25:30.

Christ a Divider of Men, 49-59. Christ's "baptism," 50, was His vicarious death for sinners (Mt 20:18, 22; Mk 10:38-39). He causes people to choose between good and evil, light and darkness. Therefore He is a divider.

13:1-21. TEACHINGS AND DELIVERANCES

Teaching on Repentance and Censorious Judging, 1-5. This again is exclusive to Luke. Pontius Pilate (A.D. 26-36) frequently lost his Roman temper and severely dealt with the difficult Jews. Here is an example, which Jesus used to enforce the necessity of repentance (Mt 3:2). He also referred to the collapse of the tower in Siloam in which 18 people perished.

The Barren Fig Tree, 6-9. Cf. Isa 5:1-7 and notes on Mt 21:18-20. The nation Israel was the fig tree. Because the nation displayed no repentance, the tree was to be chopped down. Cf. the budding fig tree, Jewish nationalism, before the "summer" of the Kingdom Age (Mt 24:32-34, see notes).

The Woman Delivered from Infirmity, 10-17. On the synagogues, 10, 14, see "The Synagogues of Galilee" in Lk 4:44. This episode is unique to Luke's Gospel. Satan is represented as having bound this Jewish woman, called "a daughter of Abraham" (see note on "Satan" in Lk 4:1-13). The epithet indicates this woman had Abraham's faith.

Parables of the Mustard Seed and the Leaven, 18-21. See notes on Mt 13:31-33; Mk 4:30-32.

13:22-35. TEACHINGS ON THE WAY TO JERUSALEM

How Many Will Be Saved? 22-30. This is also unique to Luke. The question was given a practical turn by the Saviour, 24, to avoid presumption, 25-30. He would teach us to "make our calling and election sure" (cf. 2 Pet 1:10).

Jesus Warns of Herod Antipas, 31-33. He was in Perea, which was Antipas' realm. Jesus called the wiley and wicked murderer of John the Baptist "that fox." The expression "today and tomorrow" describes Christ's healing and delivering ministry. The "third day" refers to His resurrection when He would be "perfected" (Jn 17:4-5; 19:30; Heb 2:10; 5:8-9). On Herod Antipas, see notes on Mt 14:1-14; Mk 6:14-29; Lk 9:7-9.

Jesus' Lament Over Jerusalem, 34-35. The tender love of the perfect Man, the last Adam, shines through. (Cf. Mt 23:37-39; Lk 19:41-44.)

CHAPTER 14. THE COST OF DISCIPLESHIP

Healing on the Sabbath, 1-6. The Lord Jesus answered Pharisaic hypocritical ritualism and empty sabbath observance with a miracle of healing (see note on miracles in Mk 5:21-43).

Parable of the Ambitious Guest, 7-15. This teaches the wisdom of humility, 11, and is peculiar to Luke's Gospel. The phrase "recompensed at the resurrection of the just," 12-14, hints at two resurrections, one to life (Rev 20:6) and the other to death (Rev 20:11-15).

Parable of the Great Supper, 16-24 (cf. Mt 22:1-14). The self-righteous (unbelieving Jews), especially the Pharisees, made excuses to get out of attending the great supper of salvation provided by God, 18-20. All things were "ready," 17, looking forward to the finished work of the cross. The harlots and sinners, 21-23, speak of the Gentiles to be brought in and the shutting out of self-righteous Israel, 24.

Condition of Discipleship, 25-35. So primary was to be the disciple's love for Christ that his affection for his closest kin, and even himself, was to be as hatred in comparison, 26. This devoted love would weed out the superficial multitude, 25, and prepare for inevitable persecution, hardship and cross-bearing, 27. Let the cost be counted! This is illustrated by the parable of the man building a tower, 28-29, and a king waging war, 31-33, and the savorless salt, 34-35.

CHAPTER 15. PARABLES: LOST SHEEP, LOST COIN, LOST SON

Occasion of the Parables, 1-2. The Lord answered the hypocritical complaint of the Pharisees, 2, illustrating the golden text of Luke's Gospel: "For the Son of man is come to seek and to save that which is lost" (19:10). The resort of publicans and sinners to hear Him, 1, proved His mission and elicited the complaint.

The Lost Sheep, 3-7. The ninety-nine sheep represented the carping Pharisees; the one lost sheep, the publicans and sinners the Son of man came to save. The parable severely rebuked the Pharisees' empty religiosity and proud self-righteousness.

The Lost Coin, 8-10. Again the one lost piece of silver represented the publicans and sinners. The woman's rejoicing was like the rejoicing of the angels of God in heaven over one sinner who repents, 10, a severe rebuke again to the carping Pharisees.

The Lost Son, 11-32. The prodigal represented the publicans, 11-22; the elder son, 25-32, the Pharisees. His self-righteousness and self-sufficiency were evident. He had never done anything wrong and considered himself above the poor sinful wastrel who had returned home. The rebuke of the Pharisees' criticism of Jesus as the Saviour and Friend of sinners was obvious.

CHAPTER 16. THE DISHONEST STEWARD;
THE RICH MAN AND LAZARUS

The Parable of the Dishonest Steward, 1-18. In this illustration Jesus commended the steward's provident foresight, not his dishonesty. The parable not only furnished an occasion to teach the right use of money, but afforded a means of rebuking the wrong, selfish use of it by the covetous Pharisees, who yet maintained they believed in the future life. If so, let them demonstrate their faith in the hereafter and use their money to befriend others, who would be at heaven's door to welcome them home, 9. Right use of money in this life demonstrates the genuineness of our salvation and will be rewarded in the life to come. The Pharisees' scoffing ridicule of Jesus' teaching about money, 14-17, proved their faith was empty and their belief in heaven an empty sham. Their covetousness proved it. Their boasted veneration for the law was also a farce, since they set aside the clear teaching of the law on divorce, 18, and granted it on trivialities.

The Rich Man and Lazarus, 19-31. This is not a parable but an actual historical illustration, also aimed at the sneering, unbelieving, self-righteous Pharisees. They boasted in their alleged law-keeping (cf. 15-17), and considered their wealth, which they covetously garnered, as evidence of this. Jesus proved the fallacy of this reasoning. The rich man's great wealth was, on the contrary, not the evidence of divine favor, for he went to hell (Hades, Sheol, intermediate abode of departed human spirits between death and the resurrection). Lazarus, a penniless beggar, nevertheless went to "Abraham's bosom," 22, i.e., paradise, where the souls of all OT saved went. He had no chance to make friends for himself by using the "mammon of unrighteousness" (Jesus' epithet for money), so as to welcome him to the "everlasting habitations" (heaven) (cf. 9). Yet he was there! And between him and the rich man was an impassable gulf, separating the lost from the saved. Let the covetous Pharisees take warning!

HEAVEN AND HELL

Jesus lifted the curtain to the life hereafter, revealing the place of departed souls, both saved and unsaved, between death and the resurrecton.

Hell (Gr. "Hades," Heb. "Sheol") is the place all dead went in OT times of "Moses and the prophets," 29. The righteous, however, went to "Abraham's bosom," 22, but were separated from the wicked OT dead by a "great gulf," 26.

531

The believing thief (Lk 23:43) was to be that day with Christ in paradise, which circumstance, in the light of Eph 4:8-10, seems to indicate that since the ascension of Christ, paradise, or "Abraham's bosom," has been transferred to the "third heaven" (2 Cor 12:1-4), the immediate presence of God (1 Cor 15:53; 1 Thess 4:13-18; 2 Cor 5:2, 8; Phil. 1:23).

The unsaved both of the OT and NT period, however, still go to Hades, or intermediate hell, in conscious torment (Lk 16:24).

At the sinners' judgment (Rev 20:11-15) the wicked dead are raised and cast into eternal hell, together with death and Hades (Rev 20:14). This is the "second death" or eternal separation from God (Rev 20:14), the final state of the wicked.

CHAPTER 17. FORGIVENESS; SECOND ADVENT FORETOLD

Instruction in Forgiveness and Service, 1-10. Those who cause others to stumble, especially the young, are doomed to severe punishment, 1-2. Forgiveness and kindness are to be practiced if we are controlled by faith (cf. Eph 4:32). Service ought to be spontaneous and natural to one who owns the lordship of Christ, 7-10.

The Cleansing of the Ten Lepers, 11-19. This episode is found only in Luke. All ten lepers were miraculously cured. Nine obeyed Christ's word and went to the priests (Lev 13—14). The tenth, a Samaritan, who did not go, but returned to worship at Jesus' feet, became an illustration and an earnest of the new age Jesus was to inaugurate. He turned away from the ceremonial law to own the grace of the Lord and prefigures the new people of God who will worship God not in the mountain of Samaria or the temple in Jerusalem but everywhere in grace and truth (Jn 4:22-24). His faith secured not only his physical healing but his spiritual salvation as well, 19.

When the Kingdom of God Should Come, 20-37. The question of the Pharisees, 20, was answered by our Lord's declaration that the kingdom of God came not with outward show but was among or in the midst of them, 21, i.e., in the Person of the King, whom the Pharisees rejected. Christ then turned to the disciples and gave further instruction concerning the external manifestation of the kingdom's coming, at the time the King is accepted, 22-37. Then His coming will be evident to all, 24. However, His mission included suffering and rejection first, 25. Judgment would immediately precede the King's visible return, 26-37. Verses 34 and 35 refer to the instantaneous gathering out of offenders to end-time judgment. Verse 37 describes the terrible carnage of Armageddon (Rev 16:14; 19:17).

CHAPTER 18. PARABLES AND INSTRUCTIONS

Parable of the Unscrupulous Judge, 1-8. This parable occurs in the context of Christ's second advent (17:20-37). Verse 8 asks this question, "Nevertheless when the Son of man cometh, shall he find faith on the earth?" In the dark apostate days of the Tribulation, faith will be found only in the faithful remnant of God's people. These, His elect, will suffer great persecution and cry continuously to Him for deliverance. He will avenge the remnant against their persecutors by His second advent.

The Parable of the Pharisee and Publican, 9-14. Like the preceding, this parable is exclusive to Luke's Gospel. It was directed against the pride and empty ritualistic self-righteousness of the Pharisees, 9. The Pharisee was filled with egotism. Five "I's" in this short prayer were directed to himself and not to God, 11-12. The publican was filled with humble contrition. "God be merciful to me a sinner," 13, had the mercy seat in mind (Ex 25:17-22; Heb 9:5), and means "God be propitiated" or "be toward me as You are when You look upon the blood-sprinkled mercy seat." In Christ God is propitiated and merciful.

Jesus Blesses Little Children, 15-17 (see Mt 19:13-15; Mk 10:13-16).

The Rich Young Ruler, 18-30 (cf. Mt 19:16-30; Mk 10:17-31).

Jesus Again Predicts His Death, 31-34 (cf. Mt 20:17-19; Mk 10:32-34).

The Blind Man Healed Near Jericho, 35-43 (cf. Mt 20:29-34. See note on Jericho in Mk 10:46-52).

19:1-27. ZACCHAEUS; PARABLE OF THE POUNDS

Conversion of Zacchaeus, 1-10. As a rich publican, Zacchaeus was despised by his fellow Jews, 1-2. He sought to see Jesus, 3-4, but much more Jesus sought to see him, 5-6. Jericho streets in NT times were lined with sycamore trees, and wood has been preserved which archaeologists have analyzed as such. Zacchaeus' restitution, 8-9, proved the reality of his spiritual experience and admirably illustrates the fact that "the Son of man is come to seek and to save that which was lost," 10, the golden text of the Gospel of Luke.

The Parable of the Pounds, 11-27. This parable was given to correct the false notion that the kingdom of God would immediately appear, 11. On the term "kingdom of God" in Mark and Luke, see note on Mk 4:1-29. In this particular context Luke uses the term "kingdom of God"; however, in the restricted sense in which Matthew employs the designation "the kingdom of the heavens," see notes on Mt 3:2; 4:17; 13:1-2. The kingdom, then rejected, is delayed (Lk 17:21;

Acts 1:6-8), but will come in due time with visible manifestation (see notes on Lk 17:20-37). Therefore, in the parable the Lord Jesus is the "certain nobleman," 12, who goes into a far country (heaven) to receive for Himself a kingdom, to be established at His second advent. The ten servants represent the same groups as the ten virgins of Mt 25:1-13. Verse 27 describes the wrath of the Lamb and the slaughter of His foes in "the day of the Lord" (Rev 6—19). The second advent will result in the reward of the righteous and the punishment of the wicked.

19:28-48. TRIUMPHAL ENTRY; SECOND CLEANSING OF THE TEMPLE

The Triumphal Entry, 28-40. See comments on Mt 21:1-9; Mk 11:1-10; Jn 12:12-19. Luke gives the interesting detail, "The whole multitude of disciples began to rejoice and praise God . . . for all the mighty works that they had seen," 37. Luke also reports their shout, "Blessed be the King that cometh in the name of the Lord: peace in heaven, and glory in the highest," 38. Peace in heaven will come when Satan is cast out of the heavenlies (Rev 12:7-12) and bound in the bottomless pit (Rev 20:1-3). Peace on earth, the angelic announcement at Christ's birth (Lk 2:14), will be realized only at the second advent.

The Perfect Man Weeps over Jerusalem, 41-44. See notes on Mt 23:37-39. What tenderness and kindness our Lord manifested! His heart of compassion overflowed (Lk 13:34-35) as He prophesied the destruction of the city, 43-44 (cf. Lk 21:20-24). This was fulfilled in A.D. 70.

Second Purification of the Temple, 45-48. See notes on Mt 21:12-16; Mk 11:15-18. Contrast the first cleansing at the beginning of Christ's ministry (Jn 2:13-17). The "house of prayer," 46 (cf. Isa 56:7), was made "a den of thieves" (Jer 7:11).

CHAPTER 20. CLASH WITH THE JEWISH LEADERS

Jesus' Authority Questioned, 1-8. See notes on Mt 21:23-27; Mk 11:27-33. Jesus exposed the empty hypocrisy and unbelief of the Jewish leaders by the test question concerning John's baptism, 1-4. Their inability to reply showed the quandary into which their sin forced them, admission that they had refused to follow God's messenger or exposure to public disfavor.

Parable of the Vineyard, 9-18. See exposition of it in Mt 21:33-46. Christ was the Stone rejected, 17 (Ps 118:22-23). At His second advent He will be the "headstone of the corner" (Zech 4:7). Whoever "falls upon that stone" in faith shall be broken in contrition and forgiveness, but "upon whomsoever it shall fall" (in judgment), "it will grind him to powder," 18, a clear reference to the Smiting Stone destroying Gentile world powers previous to the establishment of the kingdom (Dan. 2:34-35).

Question of the Tribute, 19-26. See Mt 22:15-22; Mk 12:13-17.

Sadducees Silenced, 27-38. See Mt 22:23-33; Mk 12:18-27.

The Scribes Interrogated, 39-47. See Mt 22:41-46; Mk 12:35-37.

CHAPTER 21. THE OLIVET DISCOURSE

The Widow's Mite, 1-4 (cf. Mk 12:41-44).

The Olivet Discourse, 5-38. Contrast Luke's record with Matthew's (ch. 24 and 25). The latter gives the fullest account (cf. also Mk 13). While Matthew gives full details of the end of the age immediately prior to Christ's second advent, Luke surveys this period, 5-19 and 25-36, but punctuates it with the prediction of the fall of Jerusalem (A.D. 70), 20-23, and the worldwide dispersion of the Jews during the intervening period, called "the times of the Gentiles," 24. During this period Jerusalem will be under Gentile dominion, and will not be fully delivered till the return of the Lord, 25-28, when this era, begun with the captivity of Judah under Nebuchadnezzar (606 B.C.), will end. "The fig tree," 29, is Israel. "All the trees" are other nations that will also see a revival before the Lord comes—nations under the revived Roman Empire. "Summer," 30, is the mediatorial form of the kingdom of God under Messiah, 30, at His advent. "This generation," 32, is the indestructible, unassimilable Jew, who will be preserved to fulfill God's prophetic word, 33. See notes on Mt 24 and 25; Lk 13.

22:1—23:26. EVENTS PRIOR TO THE CRUCIFIXION

Plot to Kill Jesus, 22:1-2 (cf. Mk 14:1-2).

Judas' Treachery, 3-6 (cf. Mt 26:2, 14-15; Mk 14:10-11).

Preparation for the Passover, 7-13 (cf. Mt 26:17-19; Mk 14:12-16).

The Last Passover, 14-18 (cf. Mt 26:20; Mk 14:17; Jn 13).

The Lord's Supper, 19-20 (cf. Mt 26:26-29; Mk 14:22-25).

Announcement of the Betrayal, 21-23 (cf. Mt 26:21-25; Mk 14:18-21; Jn 13:18-30).

The Apostles' Place in the Future Kingdom, 24-30 (cf. Mt 19:28; Rev 3:21). Cf. notes on Mt 3:2; 4:17; 13:1-2.

The Via Dolorosa, the traditional route to Calvary. (© *MPS*)

Jesus' Prediction of Peter's Denial, 31-34 (cf. Mt 26:33-35; Mk 14:29-31).

Warning of Coming Conflicts, 35-38.

Jesus in Gethsemane, 39-46. See notes on Mt 26:36-46; Mk 14:32-42.

The Betrayal, 47-53 (cf. Mt 26:47-56; Mk 14:43-50; Jn 18:3-11).

The Arrest, 54-65 (cf. Mt 26:69-75; Mk 14:53-72).

Before the Sanhedrin, 66-71 (cf. Mt 26:59-68).

Before Pilate and Herod, 23:1-26 (cf. Mt 27:1-15; Mk 15:1-5; Jn 18:28-40).

23:27-56. THE CRUCIFIXION AND BURIAL

The Crucifixion, 27-38. See notes on Mt 27:33-38; Mk 15:22-28; Jn 19:17-19. The cross of Christ not only judged the world (Jn 12:31) but uncovered what the world is. The people in general just stared in stolid indifference, 35; the professional religionists scoffed, 35; the brutal mocked, 36; the convicted sinner prayed, 42; materialistic unbelievers gambled (Mk 15:24); the believing centurion glorified God, 47; the disciples stood afar off, 49.

The Repentant Robber, 39-45. Here is the case of a deathbed repentance that was genuine. On "paradise," 43, see Lk 16:19-31 with notes. The story of the penitent thief is unique to Luke (cf. Mt 27:44; Mk 15:32).

Jesus Dismisses His Spirit, 46-49, voluntarily an act of sovereign will, differentiating the death of the God-Man from all other cases of physical death, 46 (Mk 15:37; Jn 19:30). "No man taketh it from me, but I lay it down of myself" (Jn 10:18).

Jesus' Burial, 50-56. See notes on Mt 27:57-61; Mk 15:42-47; Jn 19:38-42. Joseph was a member of the council, 50, i.e., the Sanhedrin, the official Jewish court, composed of 70 priests, scribes and elders, presided over by the high priest. "Looking for the kingdom of God," 51 (RSV), indicates his messianic expectation, according to the great promises of the OT (see notes on Mt 3:2; 4:17; 13:1-2). The sabbath, 54, began at sunset. Luke, slanted toward non-Jewish readers, desires to explain the urgency of the burial according to Jewish custom.

PASSION WEEK
(April, A.D. 30)

Saturday: Supper at Bethany

Sunday: Disciples bring a colt
Triumphal entry into Jerusalem
Jesus in the city and temple
Retirement to Bethany

Monday: The fig tree cursed
Second cleansing of the temple

Tuesday: The last day in the temple
Christ's authority challenged
Parable of the two sons
Parable of the wicked husbandman
Parable of the rejected stone
Parable of the marriage feast
The question of tribute to Caesar
The question of the resurrection
The greatest commandment
David's son and Lord
Denunciation of the scribes and Pharisees
Lament over Jerusalem
The poor widow's gift
Greeks desire to see Jesus
The Olivet Discourse
    Parables: The fig tree
              The porter
              The master of the house
              The faithful and evil servants
              The ten virgins
              The talents
              The sheep and the goats
Judas bargains to betray Jesus

Wednesday: Day of quiet at Bethany

Thursday: Preparation for the Passover
The Paschal meal and the Lord's Supper
Jesus washed the disciples' feet
Judas signaled as the traitor
Apostles warned against desertion
The great upper room discourse (Jn 13—17)

The great intercessory prayer (Jn 17)
The agony in Gethsemane (see note on Mt 26:36-56)
The betrayal and arrest
Peter and the healing of Malchus' ear

Friday: First Jewish trial: before Annas
Second Jewish trial: before Caiaphas
Third Jewish trial: before the Sanhedrin
Jesus declared His messiahship
Jesus mocked; Peter's denial and remorse
First Roman trial: before Pilate
Second Roman trial: before Herod
Third Roman trial: before Pilate again
Pilate handed over Jesus to the Jews
Pilate again attempted to rescue Jesus
Judas' suicide
The road to the cross
On the cross

First three hours:	9:00-12:00 A.M.
Three sayings:	"Father, forgive them . . ."
	"Today shalt thou be with me in paradise"
	"Woman, behold thy son"
Second three hours:	12:00-3:00 P.M.
Four sayings:	"My God, my God . . ."
	"I thirst . . ."
	"It is finished"
	"Into thy hands I commend my spirit"

Supernatural phenomena accompanying Jesus' death:
darkness, earthquake,
rending of the temple veil
Burial of the Body in Joseph's tomb

Saturday: Body in the tomb, spirit in Sheol

Sunday: The resurrection (see "Order of Events" in Mk 16)

TRIALS OF JESUS

Trial	Scripture	Judge	Decision
RELIGIOUS TRIALS (JEWISH)			
1st	Jn 18:12-14	Annas	Go signal given to liquidate Jesus
2nd	Mt 26:57-68	Caiaphas	Death sentence, charge of blasphemy
3rd	Mt 27:1-2	Sanhedrin	Death sentence made legal
CIVIL TRIALS (ROMAN)			
4th	Jn 18:28-38	Pilate	Not guilty
5th	Lk 23:6-12	Herod	Not guilty
6th	Jn 18:39—19:6	Pilate	Not guilty, but turned Jesus over to the Jews

CHAPTER 24. RESURRECTION AND ASCENSION

The Resurrection, 1-12 (cf. Mt 28:1-6). For "Order of the Events of the Resurrection" see note in Mk 16:1-8; cf. Jn 20:1-17. See note in Jn 20 for "The Resurrection Authenticated."

Post-Resurrection Ministry to the Emmaus Disciples, 13-35. Emmaus was 60 furlongs (one furlong equals 582 feet), hence about seven and one-half miles from Jerusalem. The village is probably to be identified with El-Qubeibeh which is about the distance specified by Luke W of Jerusalem. Its connection with NT Emmaus is very ancient and pre-Crusade. Luke alone reports in full this tender and sympathizing ministry of the risen Christ. "Moses," 27, refers to the Pentateuch, so full of messianic prophecy and typology; and "all the prophets," 27, was the second part of the Hebrew Scriptures: Law, Prophets, Writings. The third division was also called "Psalms," 44, since this section was headed by Israel's devotional treasury.

Post-Resurrection Appearance to the Eleven, 36-43. The resurrected Christ proved He was not a spirit but possessed a glorified *body* of flesh and bones (no corruptible blood), 39. Proof resides in the fact they touched Him, talked to Him, and He ate before them, 43. All this befits the Gospel of the manhood of Christ. The NT teaches clearly the physical resurrection of Christ. See note in Jn 20, "The Resurrection Authenticated." For "The Post-Resurrection Appearances" of Christ see note in Mk 16:9-20.

The Worldwide Commission, 44-49. The glorified Son of Man explained that Scripture promises and predictions concerning Him had to be fulfilled, 44. He illuminated their minds to comprehend this, 45, and the meaning of His death and resurrection, 46. The end in view was "that repentance and forgiveness of sins should be preached in his name *to all nations,*" 47. Thus Luke's narrative ends on its note of universal proclamation—salvation offered to *the whole world.*

The Ascension, 50-53. "The promise of the Father" (the Holy Spirit) was to be given (Acts 2:1-4). Until they were thus clothed with power from on high they were to stay in the city (Jerusalem) and not attempt to fulfill their superhuman task by merely human means. The ascension was the final climax, 50-53 (see Mk 16:19-20; Acts 1:9-11). Bethany, 50, was a small village about one and five-eighths miles E of Jerusalem on the E slope of the Mount of Olives.

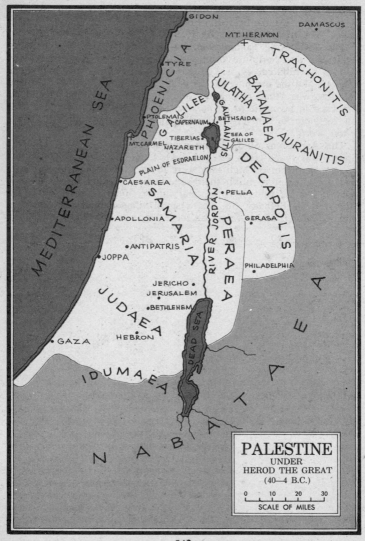

PALESTINE
UNDER
HEROD THE GREAT
(40—4 B.C.)

0   10   20   30
SCALE OF MILES

J O H N

THE GOSPEL OF THE SON OF GOD

The Author. From the time of the Church Fathers the fourth Gospel has been ascribed to John, the beloved disciple. Theophilus of Antioch (*c.* 180), Irenaeus (*c.* 200), Clement of Alexandria (*c.* 220), Tertullian (*c.* 220) and Origen (*c.* 250) were in agreement on Johannine authorship. Even Porphyry and Julian the Apostate, two early inveterate enemies of Christianity, apparently did not question the Johannine authorship. This they would have certainly done had there been grounds to deny the authenticity of the Gospel which so signally emphasizes the absolute deity of Christ.

John the Beloved. Both John and his brother James were Galilean fishermen, and members of a prosperous family, for their father Zebedee employed servants (Mk 1:20). John and his brother were fiery and impetuous. They earned the epithet "sons of thunder" (Mk 3:17). John was in the inner circle close to Jesus (Mk 5:37; Lk 8:51; Mt 17:1).

The Author in the Gospel. (1) At the Last Supper John leaned on Jesus' bosom (Jn 13:23). (2) At the cross he stood faithful and was entrusted with the care of Jesus' mother (Jn 19:26-27). (3) At the tomb he was first to believe in Jesus' resurrection (Jn 20:1-10). (4) On Galilee's shore he was the first to recognize the Lord (Jn 21:1-7).

Date of the Gospel. The date of John's Gospel is *after* the Synoptic Gospels but not later than A.D. 85 or 90, shown by the following reasons. (1) It supplements the Synoptics. It omits much that they record and records much that they omit; full where they are concise and vice versa. (2) It shows a maturity of Christian consciousness, unlikely in the earlier period of the church. (3) It shows no reference to the fall of Jerusalem in A.D. 70, either in prospect or retrospect, so was certainly written a number of years after that event. (4) Archaeology supports this sound dating, as shown by the following paragraphs.

THE DEAD SEA SCROLLS

Discovered since 1947, these documents have shown the NT to be Jewish in background, with less Greek influence than Hebrew. They also furnish evidence to date the Synoptic Gospels, dating Mark between A.D. 60-65 and John not later than A.D. 90. The recovery of the Essenic literature from Qumran, the site on the NW shore of the Dead Sea where the first and most phenomenal manuscripts were discovered in 1947, demonstrates that John's Gospel reflects the genuine Jewish background of John the Baptist and Jesus, and not the Gnostic background of the late 2nd cen. A.D. This is attested by the remarkable parallels to the conceptual imagery of the fourth Gospel found in the Essenic literature from Qumran. These archaeological findings have discredited the rationalistic criticism which had removed John's Gospel from the traditional date of the apostolic age (between A.D. 90-130), and thus treating it as essentially apocryphal.

GNOSTIC LITERATURE FROM NAG HAMMADI

In 1945 thirteen codices containing 49 Gnostic documents were found in Upper Egypt at ancient Sheneset-Chenoboskion in the vicinity of Nag Hammadi, 32 miles N of Luxor. Dating from the 3rd cen. A.D. and written in Coptic, this material, rivaling the Dead Sea Scrolls in importance, proves that Gnosticism was much later than the Gospel of John, and that the Gnostics based much of their material on this Gospel, rather than the fourth Gospel being a late Gnostic treatise.

Purpose of the Fourth Gospel. The purpose is revealed in Jn 20:30-31: to set forth the messiahship and deity of Jesus by adducing irrefutable proof from His miraculous signs, in order to engender faith in men's hearts that they might receive eternal life. To achieve this goal careful selection and meticulous omission were followed. This was done that the Jew might be convinced that the historical Jesus is "the Christ," and that the Gentile might accept this same Jesus as "the Son of God," Saviour of mankind. It is "the Gospel of Belief."

Material Peculiar to John

About 92% of the content of the fourth Gospel is unique to John and is not found in the three Synoptic Gospels. By comparison Matthew has 42%, Luke 59%, and Mark only 7% which is unique to their Gospels.

Miracles in John's Gospel. Only eight of the 35 miracles of Christ recorded in the Gospels are mentioned by John. Six of these are peculiar to the fourth Gospel.

Miracles of the Fourth Gospel	Meaning
(1) Turning water to wine, 2:1-11	Nature of eternal life
(2) Healing the nobleman's son, 4:46-54	Condition (faith) of eternal life
(3) Healing the infirm man at Bethesda, 5:1-9	Power to live the life
(4) The feeding of the 5,000, 6:1-14 (also in Mt 14:13-21; Mk 6:32-44; Lk 9:10-17)	Food for the life
(5) Walking on the sea, 6:15-21 (also in Mt 14:22-36; Mk 6:45-56)	Guidance for the life
(6) Sight restored, 9:1-41	Light for the life
(7) Raising of Lazarus, 11:1-44	Victory of the life over death
(8) The catch of fish, 21:1-14	Full fellowship of the life

Discourses in John's Gospel. Twelve discourses are unique to this Gospel.

1. On spiritual regeneration, 3:1-21
2. On eternal life, 4:4-26
3. On the Source of eternal life and its witness, 5:19-47
4. On the true Bread of life, 6:26-59
5. On the Source of truth, 7:14-29
6. On the Light of the world, 8:12-20
7. On the true Object of faith, 8:21-30
8. On spiritual freedom, 8:31-59
9. On the Good Shepherd, 10:1-21
10. On the unity of the Godhead, 10:22-38
11. On the world's Redeemer, 12:20-36
12. Upper room teaching:
   On the approaching separation, 13-31—14:31
   On union with Christ, 15:1-27
   On the Holy Spirit and the future, 16:1-33

These discourses fall into two categories: (1) Christ's *public instruction,* ch. 1—12, presenting Himself to the world as *the ultimate reality;* and (2) Christ's *private teaching,* ch. 13—16, disclosing Himself to His own as *the eternal sufficiency.*

Outline

Introduction, 1:1-51
Public Ministry of the Son of God, 2:1—12:50
Private Ministry of the Son of God, 13:1—17:26
Death and Resurrection of the Son of God, 18:1—20:31
Epilogue, 21:1-25

1:1-18. THE PROLOGUE: THE WORD—WHO HE WAS AND WHAT HE BECAME

The Word—Who He was, 1-13. These verses declare eight great truths concerning our Lord Jesus Christ. (1) He was and is the Eternal One, who always existed before time and matter: "In the beginning *was* the Word." (2) He was and is a Person distinct from God the Father: "The Word [the preincarnate Christ] was *with* God" (the Father). (3) He was and *is* God: "The Word *was* God," 1. (4) He was coexistent with God (the Father) from eternity, 2. (5) He was the Creator of the universe, 3. (6) He is the Source of all life and light (both physical and spiritual), 4, 5, 9 (not to be confused with John the Baptist, 6-8, who was merely a witness to Him as the "true Light," 9). (7) He is the self-revealing God to a fallen universe and His self-disclosure is invincibly victorious, 5. (8) He entered the world of men and they ignored Him, 10. His people Israel rejected Him, 11. But those who receive Him are granted spiritual regeneration, 12-13.

The Word—Who He Became, 14-18. "The Word [the Eternal Creator God] became flesh [man]," 14. The mystery of the ages! God became Man, the God-Man. Deity united Himself to humanity in one glorious theanthropic Person forever and "tented" in a tabernacle of flesh among us, 14. Those who saw the God-Man saw the glory of "the only Son from the Father," as John the Baptist bore witness, 15 (cf. 6-8). They actually saw God, who is invisible, in "the only Son," who made God known, 18, and introduced a new era of grace and truth, 17.

1:19-51. THE TESTIMONY OF JOHN AND OF JESUS' FIRST DISCIPLES

Testimony of John the Baptist, 19-34. The Jewish religious authorities of Jerusalem inquired, "Who are you?" 19, 22. John denied he was the Christ, or Elijah (2 Kgs 2:11), who was expected to return before Christ, or "the Prophet," i.e., Messiah foretold in Deut 18:15 (cf. Jn 6:14; 7:40). John declared he was merely "a voice" (Isa 40:3) prophetically announcing Messiah's advent, 23. The Jewish authorities then demanded why John was baptizing or performing an official rite without official status, 24. His answer was that the water ceremony he was performing was not an end in itself, but introductory and preparatory to a spiritual operation of far greater importance to be performed by Him whose way he was preparir?, and whose sandal thong he was unfit to untie (a slave's job).

Jesus was the sacrificial Lamb of God, 29 (Ex 12; Isa 53:7; 1 Pet 1:19), outranking John because He existed before John, 30 (cf. 1-18). John's knowledge of Jesus' messiahship was divinely authenticated at Jesus' baptism by the dovelike Spirit coming and remaining upon Him, 31-33, confirming Him as "he who baptizes with the Holy Spirit," 33, the Son of God, the Messiah, 34 (cf. 49; 11:27). John evidently recognized Jesus as the sacrificial Lamb who would die, 29, be resurrected and ascend to heaven, to give the gift of the Holy Spirit at Pentecost (Acts 2:1-5). This gift would contain the baptizing ministry of the Spirit (Acts 1:5; 2:4; 11:14-16). Since this ministry was made possible by Christ's redemptive death, He, the Redeemer, is styled "he who baptizes with the Holy Spirit." *After* the advent of the Spirit at Pentecost the Spirit Himself is the Agent of the spiritual baptism (1 Cor 12:13).

Testimony of Jesus' First Disciples, 35-51. John's testimony to Jesus' messiahship, 35-37, resulted in Andrew's conversion, 38-40. Andrew's testimony in turn won Simon, whose name Jesus changed to Cephas (Aramaic "stone"; Gr. *petros,* "Peter"), 42. Philip was called, 43. He was of Bethsaida, on the Lake of Galilee near Capernaum, 44. He testified of the Messiah and won Nathanael, 45-51, of Cana near Nazareth (21:2). Nathanael was an Israelite in whom was "no guile," that is, he did not possess the wily traits Jacob had before he became Israel (Gen 27:35; 32:28).

CHAPTER 2. WATER TURNED TO WINE; THE TEMPLE CLEANSED

The First Miracle, 1-12. "This, the first of his signs," 11 (RSV), illustrates the basic *nature* of the *newness of life* which Christ came to give (cf. 20:30-31). This blessing of eternal life received by faith is seen in the water turned to wine at Cana, near Nazareth in Galilee. "Signs" are mighty works or miracles *which symbolize spiritual truths.* The first sign shows that the Bestower of life is the

PALESTINE
DURING JESUS'
MINISTRY

SCALE OF MILES

omnipotent Creator of ch. 1, able to change water to wine. The wine is typical of the joy and ministration of the grace which He came to bring (1:17) and which issues in life. The Creator alone can be our spiritual Re-creator. He alone can bestow the joyous exhilarations of eternal life prefigured by the wine (cf. Isa 55:1; Eph 5:18-20). It served as an exhibition of the glory of His person, 11.

The Temple Cleansed, 13-25. This was the first cleansing of the temple at the commencement of Christ's ministry, not the second at the close mentioned by the Synoptists (see notes on Mt 21:12-17; Mk 11:15-18; Lk 19:45-48). This act of Jesus manifested His authority as the Son of God and fulfilled Ps 69:9 ("my Father's house," 16). The Jews surmised this and asked for a "sign," 18, and Jesus gave that of His death and resurrection, 19, which was completely misunderstood by His foes (cf. Mt 26:61), and not understood by His friends till after His resurrection (Mt 26:61; 27:40; cf. Jn 10:18).

CHAPTER 3. NICODEMUS AND THE NEW BIRTH

Discourse on Regeneration, 1-21. From Jn 2:23 through 17:26 the Son of God imparts eternal life and describes what it is and what it does. "Many believed in his name" (2:23-25). In His interview with Nicodemus, a rigid moralist and a Sanhedrin member, 1, Jesus showed the necessity of regeneration, "You *must* be born again," 7, and the necessity of His death to accomplish a basis for this spiritual transaction, "so *must* the Son of man be lifted up," 14. In a most solemn fashion, "Verily, verily" (truly, truly), 3, 5, Jesus declared that no one can "see," 3, or enter, the kingdom of God except he is "born of water" (figure of the cleansing Word, Eph 5:26; 1 Pet 1.23; Jas 1:18) and of the Spirit (the Holy Spirit, the Agent in regeneration), 5. This is a supernatural imparting of eternal life on the basis of Christ's death, typified by the Mosaic serpent in the wilderness, 14 (see notes on Num 21:5-20; 2 Cor 5:21). The theme of John's Gospel is clearly displayed in verse 16.

John the Baptist's Testimony, 22-36. "Aenon near Salim," 23, is probably SE of Sychar. Here Jesus' disciples baptized under His direction (cf. 22; 4:2). John owned himself merely the "friend of the bridegroom" (Christ), 29. Verses 31-36 constitute John's keen insight into the person and work of the Messiah, who had the Spirit in immeasurable fullness upon His sinless humanity, 34.

CHAPTER 4. THE SAMARITAN WOMAN AND ETERNAL LIFE

Jesus and the Samaritans, 1-45. The hostile Pharisees, 1-3, evidently necessitated Jesus' leaving for Galilee and going through Samaria, which lay between. Samaria was populated by a mixed people, remnants of the northern tribes who had been taken captive when Israel fell in 722 B.C. They used the Pentateuch and worshiped the Lord. Racially and religiously mongrel, they were abhorred by the Jews, 9. Jesus' witness to the woman at the well of Sychar, in the heart of the Plain of Shechem under the shadow of Mt. Ebal, showed His compassionate concern for the lost which transcended all social and religious prejudices. The incident elicited His second great discourse, on the water of life, 4-26, following His first on regeneration (3:1-21). The woman's testimony had a remarkable effect upon the Samaritans, 27-39, and opened the way for Jesus' two-day ministry among them, 40-45.

The Second Sign, 46-54. The healing of the nobleman's son sick at Capernaum illustrates faith as the *condition* for receiving eternal life. On Capernaum see note on Mk 1:21-28.

CHAPTER 5. INFIRM MAN HEALED

The Third Sign in John's Gospel—the Infirm Man Healed at Bethesda, 1-9. This illustrates the divine power granted to live the new life (see introduction to John's Gospel). This infirm cripple presents a vivid picture of man's complete helplessness as a sinner, and Christ's power to save and enable him to live the new life. Bethesda ("house of grace") was a rectangular spring-fed pool with five porticoes. It is likely the pool discovered in 1888 near St. Anne's Church in the Bezetha quarter of Jerusalem near the Tower of Antonia and the Sheep's Gate. It has a five-arched portico with faded frescoes of Christ's healing.

Opposition of the Jews, 10-18. The Jews' empty ritualism carped at the healing and the healed man carrying his bed on the sabbath, 10-11, and vented its rage on Jesus, 16. Christ claimed a unique relation to Deity, "my Father," 17, the Jews comprehending clearly that Jesus was claiming to be God, 18 (cf. Jn 10:30, 33; Phil 2:6).

Discourse on the Source of Eternal Life, 19-47. In answer to Jewish opposition Christ set forth His unity in person and work with the Father, 19-23. This passage alone is sufficient to dispel foolish notions that Jesus never claimed to be God, or cult contentions that the Son is not very God of very God. He who is then one with the Father, God Incarnate, is the Source of eternal life. Verse 24 tells how eternal life is received; verses 25-26 show the effect of eternal life on physical death and resurrection. Verse 28 teaches literal physical resurrection. There will be a resurrection of the righteous (1 Cor 15:52; 1 Thess 4:13-18) and a separate resurrection of the unrighteous (Rev 20:4-6, 11-14).

Christ presented four witnesses to Himself as the Source of eternal life, 33-47: (1) John the Baptist, 33-35; (2) His mighty signs or works, 36; (3) the Father, 37-38 (cf. Mt 3:17); (4) the Holy Scriptures, 39-47 (cf. Lk 24:27, 44-46). For other discourses see introduction to John's Gospel.

CHAPTER 6. FIVE THOUSAND FED; DISCOURSE ON THE BREAD OF LIFE

Feeding the Five Thousand, 1-21. See note on "Miracles" in introduction to John's Gospel (cf. Mt 14:13-21; Mk 6:32-44; Lk 9:10-17). This furnishes the setting, after the episode of Jesus' walking on the sea, 15-21 (cf. Mt 14:23-36; Mk 6:45-56), for the next great discourse.

Discourse on the Bread of Life, 22-59. See note on "Discourses" in introduction to John's Gospel. He who could walk on the sea was indeed the Bread of God who came down from heaven, and gave life to the world, 33. Clearly and unequivocally Christ an-

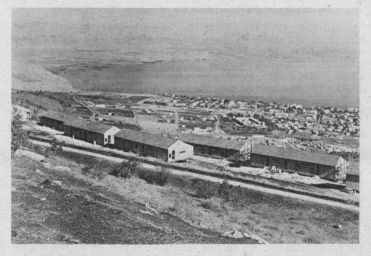

On the shore of the Sea of Galilee stood Tiberias, capital of Herod Antipas, whom Jesus described as "that fox." (*Courtesy IIS*)

Meditating on the shore of the Sea of Galilee. (*Courtesy IIS*)

nounced Himself as the Divine One, the nourisher and sustainer of the eternal life which He gives. The unbelieving Jews could neither understand His deity, 42, nor how believers could feed upon Him spiritually, 52-58. On "manna," 31, 58, see Ex 16:14-22 comments. Christ fulfilled the type as giver and sustainer of life (cf. also Ex 16:35). On the Capernaum synagogue, 59, see note on Mk 1:21-28.

Discipleship Tested: Peter's Confession, 60-71. Judas was never saved, 70-71.

TIBERIAS AND THE SEA OF TIBERIAS

John refers to the Sea of Galilee (6:1; cf. 21:1) as the Sea of Tiberias, and the city is mentioned in Jn 6:23. The city founded by Herod Antipas was named in honor of the then reigning Emperor Tiberius (A.D. 14-37). It was built before A.D. 25, and was located on Galilee's western shore about six miles from the lower end of the lake where the Jordan River exits. Herod moved his court there from Sepphoris, N of Galilee. The lax Hellenistic Roman atmosphere of the hot bath resort did not attract the Jewish-slanted ministry of our Lord. Soon the city became so important that for a time it gave its name to the lake. After the fall of Jerusalem (A.D. 70) Tiberias became a Jewish metropolis and the center of rabbinical learning.

CHAPTER 7. THE PROPHECY OF THE SPIRIT'S ADVENT

Jesus Delays to Go to Jerusalem, 1-13. He remained in Galilee because the Jews in Jewry (Judea) sought to kill Him, 1. His brothers taunted Him in their unbelief, 2-5, urging Him in a selfish, worldly spirit to advertise and exploit His works for personal aggrandizement. He rebuked their spirit of selfish independence of action and showed the difference between them and Him in the matter of God's will, 6-9. But when the time was ready in the Father's will, He went up to the Feast of Tabernacles, 10-13. This section of the Gospel, 7:1—11:53, introduces the period of conflict about His person—the unbelief of His brothers, 3-9, the bewilderment of the people, 10-13.

Jesus at the Feast, 14-36. The Feast of Tabernacles or Booths (Lev 23:33-44, see comments) was the harvest festival memorial of redemption for Israel, prophetic of kingdom rest and blessings through Israel to the nations. The conflict over Jesus' person continued, as He taught in the temple. He propounded a paradox, asserting both His authority, 14, and subordination, 16, issuing in a controversy, 21-24. The confused reaction of the people appears in 20, 25-32, 35-36, Jesus' fifth discourse, on the Source of truth, 14-29, is given (see "Discourses" in introduction to John's Gospel).

The Prophecy Concerning the Holy Spirit, 37-39. The last day of Tabernacles (Lev 23:36) was the most solemn and climactic of the entire festal cycle. It was the eighth day of rest and holy assembly. During the seven days prefiguring their wilderness wandering, water was drawn from the pool of Siloam and then poured out, commemorating the water supplied Israel in the desert. The eighth day signified the enjoyment of the springs of the land itself and no water was poured out. That was the memorial aspect. The prophetic aspect looked forward to the regathering of Israel after her present worldwide dispersion and the fulfillment of the kingdom ode of Isa 12:1-6, when the nation "with joy" shall "draw water out of the wells of salvation" (Isa 12:3; cf. Zech 14:8; Joel 2:28-32). Jesus stood and offered the spiritual reality of the kingdom to individual believers, 39, but national fulfillment to Israel of all that the festal ritual signified awaits His second advent. Verse 39 shows that the prophecy was realized in the advent of the Spirit at Pentecost (Acts 2:1-4). The idiom in 39 is, "the Spirit was not yet." After Pentecost, when Jesus was glorified by resurrection and ascension, it could be said, "The Spirit now is" (cf. Acts 19:2 where the same idiom occurs and is explained as referring to the advent of the Spirit at the introduction of a new era).

The People's Confusion, 40-53. The conflict over Christ was focused here in its intensity.

CHAPTER 8. THE ADULTEROUS WOMAN; DISCOURSE ON THE LIGHT OF THE WORLD

The Woman Taken in Adultery, 7:53—8:11. Many textual critics omit this incident on evidence from the oldest manuscripts. The RSV includes it, but sets it in small type to distinguish it from the main text. Others place it after Lk 21:38. Still others think it was omitted in certain manuscripts on purpose because the grace in dealing with the woman was unpalatable to legalists. Certainly it highlights our Lord's tender compassion for the sinner.

Discourses on the Light of the World, 12-20, and on Faith, 21-30. These were Christ's sixth and seventh discourses in the Gospel. Unbelief which rejects Him involves eternal separation from God, 21-25. Who He is, is the acid test, 25-29. Many believed on Him, the true Object of faith, 30.

Discourse on Spiritual Freedom, 31-59. This is the eighth discourse in John's Gospel. Faith in Christ manifested by continuance in His word, 31-32, is the gateway to spiritual freedom, not ritualism or human descent, 33. Whoever is enslaved by sin, 34, is not free. Only the Son can set the sinner free, 36. The Jews boasting in Abrahamic descent were children of the devil, 44. Jesus declared His eternity, 58. He was the "I AM" (Ex 3:14; Isa 43:13) who existed before Abraham. The Jews proved their slavery to sin by their reaction to the Liberator from sin.

CHAPTER 9. THE BLIND MAN HEALED

The Blind Man Restored to Sight, 1-34. This is the sixth miraculous sign in the Gospel, illustrating light and illumination for the new life to be found in Christ, 5. The clay and the spittle did not effect the healing, but symbolized what the creative power of Christ, the Creator-Redeemer, did, 6. The washing in the Pool of Siloam, 7, suggests the sign had the purpose of spiritual regeneration, 36-38 (cf. Eph 5:26). When Judaism cast the healed man out, 27-34, it cast him into the arms of a loving Lord.

Jesus Reveals Himself to the Man, 35-41. This sign, like the other signs and discourses in John, anticipated the position of true Christianity outside the pale of Judaism and that which has rejected Christ (Heb. 13:13).

CHAPTER 10. DISCOURSE ON THE
GOOD SHEPHERD

The Discourse Itself, 1-21. This ninth discourse sprang out of the miracle of Christ's healing the blind man, who was cast out of Judaism. The true sheep of Christ, it is evident, would be cast out of the Jewish fold. The blind man restored to sight was so cast out, and became one of His sheep. Our Lord, therefore, gave parabolic instruction of the new order of God's sheep. Israel, as the Lord's true elect OT people in covenant with Him, were His sheep and He their Shepherd (Ps 23:1; 95:7; 100:3; Ezk 34:1-31; Zech 11:7-9; 13:7). In the parable, 1-6, Judaism was the sheepfold, 1. Christ the true Shepherd had come through the appointed door (the prophesied messianic line) into the sheepfold, 2. The porter (Holy Spirit) opened the fold to Him and His sheep responded (as the blind man of ch. 9) and He led them out, 3, of the apostasy and unbelief Judaism had degenerated into by rejecting Him, its true Shepherd, 4-5.

The lessons drawn from the parable, 7-21, are: (1) Christ (not Judaism) now becomes the door of the sheep—a new order, 7. (2) All other presumed saviours (the leaders of apostate Judaism) are thieves, 8. (3) He alone is Saviour, Sustainer, Life-giver, 9-10. (4) He is the Good Shepherd who will die for the sheep (Israel), 11-15. (5) The Good Shepherd has other sheep (Gentiles), who with the Jews will be brought into one fold (the Church) with one Shepherd (Christ), 16 (cf. 1 Cor 12:13; Eph 4:4-6). (6) This will be effected by the Good Shepherd's unique and voluntary death for the sheep, 17-18. Unbelief, 19-21, was incapable of anything except confusion and wicked blasphemy.

Discourse on the Unity of the Godhead, 22-39. The tenth discourse of John's Gospel was delivered at the Feast of Dedication, 22, celebrated the 25th day of Chislev (Nov.-Dec.). It commemorated the reconsecration of the Jerusalem temple by Judas Maccabeus in 165 B.C. During the eight-day festival, the Jews demanded a statement of our Lord, if He were the Christ. His reply, 25-38, asserted: (1) Christ's sheep, whom the unbelieving Jews were not, know His deity and messiahship, 25-27. (2) His sheep are saved, safe and secure, 28-29. (3) Jesus asserted His unity of essence with the Father, hence His unequivocal deity, 30 (cf. 14:9; 20:28-29), and the Jews so understood Him, 31. (4) He defended His deity by His works and by the Scriptures, 32-39. If Israel called its judges "elohim" ("gods"), 34-35, because they represented God (Ps. 82:6), why should they stumble at the true Son of God whom the Father sent, 36?

Jesus at the Place Where John Had Baptized, 40-41. Many believed on Jesus because of the testimony John the Baptist had borne concerning Him.

CHAPTER 11. THE RAISING OF LAZARUS

The Son's Power Over Death, 1-44. This is the seventh sign-miracle of John's Gospel, authenticating the Son of God as Life-giver (cf. 20:30-31). It was the last and greatest of Jesus' public miracles recorded by John proving His claim to be the resurrection and the life. The episode is supported by the most convincing evidence of details. Bethany was just beyond the brow of the Mount of Olives less than two miles from Jerusalem. Jesus declared Lazarus' illness was "not unto death," i.e., to result in death alone, but "for the glory of God, so that the Son of God may be glorified by means of it," 4 (RSV), through resurrection from the dead. Jesus waited till Lazarus died and had lain in the grave four days, so that He might perform a great and incontrovertible miracle. The great declarations of verses 25 and 26 will find their fulfillment in 1 Thess 4:13-18; 1 Cor 15:22-23.

The Effect of This Climactic Sign, 45-57. Many Jewish friends of Mary believed, 45. Others went to report the sign to the Pharisees, 46, who forthwith called the Sanhedrin, 47, and plotted to put Jesus to death, 48-57. Caiaphas' prophecy that one man should die for the nation rather than that the whole nation should perish, 49-52, was amazing, especially 52, that the one who died "should gather together in one the children of God that were scattered abroad," i.e., the Gentiles (Ps 22:27; Jn 10:16; Rom 1:16; Eph 2:14-17). The city of Ephraim, 54, was a remote, isolated village N of Jerusalem.

CHAPTER 12. SUPPER AT BETHANY; ACCLAIM AT JERUSALEM

The Anointing by Mary, 1-11. See notes on Mt 26:6-13; Mk 14:3-9; cf. Lk 7:37-38. Martha as usual was serving. Mary as usual was worshiping. Others had come to His feet to have their needs met. Mary came to render Him His due. She anointed Him for His approaching death, 7, which she possibly glimpsed as a result of her worshipful communion. Judas' perfidy stood out in stark contrast, 4-6, as well as the wickedness of the chief priests, 10, in plotting to put Lazarus to death because of their venomous hatred of Jesus, 11.

The Triumphal Entry, 12-19. See comments on Mt 21:4-9; Mk 11:7-10; Lk 19:35-38. Ps 118:25-26 was shouted, 13, by the populace who had been stunned by Lazarus' being raised from the dead, 17-19. Zech 9:9 was fulfilled, 15. John adds the details of the reason for the public display of Palm Sunday—excitement over the climactic sign wrought at Bethany.

Discourse on the World's Redeemer, 20-36. This is the eleventh discourse in John's Gospel. The occasion was the inquiry of "certain Greeks," 20, to see Jesus, 21-22, suggesting the outgoing of the gospel to the whole world as a result of Jesus' death, 23-24, authenticated by a voice from heaven, 28 (cf. Mt 3:17). In verse 31 the judgment of Jesus Christ as bearing the believer's sins is alluded to, resulting in the casting out of Satan, "the prince of this world" (Satanic world system). The sins of believers would be judged in the person of Christ lifted up on Calvary, 32. The result would be the justification of the believer, here embracing the extension of the gospel to the Gentile world.

Jesus' Final Words, 37-50. Notice the prominence of Isaiah's prophecy in the quotations in 38 (Isa 53:1) and 40-41 (Isa 6:10).

JOHN AND ISAIAH

Subject	Isaiah	John
The Shepherd and the sheep ..	40:11	10:1-21
Water for the thirsty	41:18; 44:3; 48:21; 49:10; 55:1	4:13-14; 6:35; 7:37
Food for the hungry	49:10	6:35
Guidance	42:16; 48:17	14:6
The divine Comforter	51:12	14:16
The gift of the Spirit	59:21	14:26; 15:26; 16:13
Worldwide salvation	43:19; 45:22; 49:12; 56:7-8; 60:3	4:21-24; 10:16
Freedom from fear	41:10; 51:7	14:1
Sight for the blind	35:5; 42:7	9:39
Liberty for the bound	61:1	8:36
Divine teaching	50:4-5	14:10; 17:6-8

CHAPTER 13. WASHING THE DISCIPLES' FEET

The Meaning of the Lord's Action, 1-20. The Lord's washing of the disciples' feet illustrates the believer's continual need of cleansing after the once-for-all bath of regeneration. "He who has bathed [the washing of regeneration, complete ablution] does not need to wash, except for his feet, but he is clean all over [because of regeneration]; and you are clean, but not all of you," 10 (RSV) (Judas being unregenerate). The figure is of a person returning from the public bath to his home. His feet would become defiled. So the believer is once-for-all cleansed in the bath of regeneration (Heb 10:1-12), but must confess the sins involved in his daily walk in a sinful world (Eph 5:25-27; 1 Jn 1:9). A defiled saint, 8, cannot have communion with Christ; that is why Peter had to have his feet washed. The command, 14, involves the exercise of a spirit of forgiveness of one saint toward another (Eph 4:32).

Prophecy of the Betrayal by Judas, 21-35 (see Mt 26:20-25; Mk 14:17-21; Lk 22:21-22). Judas was never regenerated, 10 (cf. Jn 6:70-71; 13:27). He so surrendered himself to Satanic ambition and was so taken over by evil power that he is called a devil (Jn 6:70). Jesus' choice of him was an instance of divine overruling of evil for good. The name Judas (Gr. form of Judah) became popular after the time of Judas Maccabeus (166 B.C.).

Prophecy of Peter's Denial, 36-38 (cf. Mt 26:33-35; Mk 14:29-31; Lk 22:33-34). Impetuous and well-meaning, Peter had to learn the hard way to gauge his weakness. His example is very human and therefore very helpful.

CHAPTER 14. THE SECOND ADVENT AND THE SPIRIT'S COMING

Christ's Return for His Own, 1-6. This is part of the upper room discourse (ch. 14—16), involving the private instruction of Christ directed to His own whom He was soon to leave. His return here declared is His coming *for* His own (1 Thess 4:13-17; 1 Jn 3:1-3), not His return in glory *with* His own (Mt 24:29-30). It was Jesus' first instructions concerning the believer's heavenly hope (cf. Phil 3:20-21).

Christ Expounds His Deity, 7-15. He declared His union with the Father, 7-11. Cf. the tenth discourse of John's Gospel on the unity of the Godhead, 10:22-38. There our Lord had enunciated the same truth, "I and my Father are one" (essence or substance, *not* one Person), 10:30. He who saw the visible Son saw the invisible

Father (cf. 1:18). The "greater works," 12, are possible because our Lord in the flesh was confined to one place at a time. Now with the outpoured Spirit (Acts 2) "all that Jesus began both to do and teach" (Acts 1:1) can be continued worldwide by His faithful followers. Also the new promise and privilege in prayer, 13-15, makes the promise of verse 12 possible.

The Promise of the Spirit, 16-26. The Paraclete ("one called alongside to assist") was the Holy Spirit, called "another Comforter," 16, because He would continue the ministry of Christ through His disciples after the Lord's death, resurrection and ascension. Called "the Spirit of truth," 17, because of His revelatory ministry in truth, the Holy Spirit was said "to indwell *with*" the disciples, but at some future time (Pentecost, Acts 2) was promised to be *"in"* them (cf. Rom 8:9; 1 Cor 6:19). The advent of the Spirit would make up for Christ's departure, 18. "At that day" (Pentecost), the disciples would be enabled to understand Christ's union with the Father because they would be baptized by the Spirit in vital union with Christ, 20. "I in you" was the Spirit's predicted indwelling, 20. "Ye in me" was the Spirit's predicted baptism. Verse 26 hints at the teaching ministry of the promised Spirit.

The Bequest of Peace, 27-31. Cf. Phil 4:7.

CHAPTER 15. UNION WITH CHRIST AND FRUIT-BEARING

Abiding and Fruit-Bearing, 1-17. The believer's relation to Christ is here prefigured as that of *union* (position) and *abiding* (experience). The *union* would be effected by the death, resurrection and ascension of Christ, and advent of the Spirit (Acts 2) to baptize the believer into Christ (Rom 6:3-4), and into His Body, the Church (1 Cor 12:13). The Spirit came at Pentecost to accomplish this (Acts 1:5 with Acts 11:14-16). The *experience* of *abiding*, 4, 5, 7 (Rom 6:11), is the result of knowing and reckoning in reality on that position of union (Rom 6:1-10). The result is "fruit," 2, 4; "more fruit," 2; "much fruit," 5, 8. As "the true vine," 1, Jesus was the true Israel, fulfilling the vocation in which the nation Israel had failed (Isa 5:1-7; Jer 2:21; Ezk 19:10-14). The branches are the new people of God, the Church, issuing from union with Christ by the baptism of the Spirit. Fruit springs from abiding, or reckoning on that union, in faith, 5, and is manifested in prayer, 7, and loving obedience, 9-10; resulting in joy, 11, *love* toward fellow believers, 12-14, and a new intimacy as friends, not merely servants, 15-17.

The Believer and the World, 18-27. The world will hate and persecute the true abiding and fruit-bearing disciple. This refers to the evil Satanic world system organized under Satan's principles of greed, ambition, self-will and pleasure (Mt 4:8-9; Jn 12:31; 14:30; Eph 2:2; 6:12; 1 Jn 2:15-17). Satan is its organizational head; Satanic principles underlie it. It is in deadly opposition to Christ and all joined to Him in *position* and in *practice*.

CHAPTER 16. THE WORK OF THE PROMISED SPIRIT

Disciples Warned of Suffering, 1-6. These verses connect with 15:18-25. Leaving His disciples shortly, the Lord was faithful to warn of dangers.

Threefold Work of the Coming Spirit, 7-11. Jesus plainly announced that His death and ascension were necessary prerequisites for the Spirit's advent at Pentecost, 7. He outlined the promised Spirit's work with the unsaved, 8-11: convicting sinners (1) "of sin," 8, "because they believe not on me," 9, the one damning sin of rejecting Christ as Saviour; (2) "of righteousness," 10, because the Son's return to the Father was the evidence of the provision of a perfect righteousness for sinners through faith in Christ, without which there is no acceptance before a holy God; (3) "of judgment," 11, because rejection of Christ and His purchased righteousness results in the sinner sharing Satan's doom (Mt 25:41, 46).

Teaching Ministry of the Spirit, 12-15. This embraces Christ's pre-authentication of the NT Scriptures to be written, 12-13, including "things to come," additional prophecies such as 2 Thess 2 and the Revelation. The Spirit to come at Pentecost was promised to guide into all truth, i.e., lead in the way to all the truth, the full NT revelation. He is the divine Teacher in this age.

Jesus Predicts His Death, Resurrection and Second Advent, 16-33. A new order in prayer, "in Jesus' name," was indicated, 26. This involves a new access to the Father on the basis of the finished work of Christ and the believer's position of dignity and power in union with Christ, the beloved Son.

CHAPTER 17. CHRIST'S GREAT HIGH PRIESTLY PRAYER

The Seven Petitions, 1-26. (1) That the Son might be glorified, 1. *This involved our salvation.* He glorified the Father in His life and His finished work, anticipated in verse 4. In this our salvation resides. He had power to give eternal life to as many as the Father had given Him, 2. Our Lord defined salvation, 3. (2) Restoration to His preincarnate glory in union with the Father, 5. *This involved His glorious person.* He alone could be an efficacious Saviour. (3) Safety of His own from the world, 11, and the "evil one," 15. *This involved the security of the saved sinner.* (4) Sanctification of believers, 17. *This insured their fellowship with God and usefulness in this life.* (5) The spiritual oneness of believers, 11, 20-21. *This involved the advent of the Spirit* at Pentecost (Acts 1:5; 2:4; 11:14-16) to baptize all believers into vital union with Christ (Rom 6:3-4) and with one another in Him (1 Cor 12:13). (6) That the world might believe, 21. *This involved recognition of the oneness of the Church in its union with Christ* and with all born-again believers, 20. (7) That believers might be with Him in heaven to behold and share His glory, 24. *This involved the security and assured eternal felicity of all who are His.*

CHAPTER 18. THE SON OF GOD BEFORE HIS ENEMIES

The Arrest in Gethsemane, 1-11. See comments on Mt 26:36-56; Mk 14:32-50; cf. Lk 22:39-53. In John's account there is nothing about the agony and the bloody sweat. These belong to a description of His humanity. The Gospel of Christ's deity, however, describes what the Synoptics omit—the momentary outflashing of deity of Him who was the great "I AM," 5-6 (cf. Ex 3:13-14), prostrating the men who came to arrest Him. No power could touch Him till *His hour* had come!

Trial Before Annas and Caiaphas, 12-27 (see Mt 26:57-68; Mk 14:53-65; Lk 22:66-71). Annas had been deposed as high priest by the Romans (A.D. 15) and had been succeeded by Caiaphas, his son-in-law, but Annas still wielded great influence, 12-13. During the trial Jesus was brought from the residence of Annas to the palace of Caiaphas, 24. The latter had predicted that Jesus should die for the nation (11:49-52). On Peter's denial, see 15-18, 25-27; cf. Mt 26:69-75; Mk 14:66-72; Lk 22:54-62.

Trial Before Pilate, 28-40 (cf. Mt 27:1-14; Mk 15:1-5; Lk 23:1-7, 13, 16). See note on "Passion Week" and "Trials of Jesus" in Lk 23. Jesus told Pilate that His kingdom (Ps 45:3, 6; Isa 9:6-7; Zech 9:9) was not from this world, i.e., of this Satanic world system, based on its principles of pride, lust and war, 36. If His kingdom were such, then would His servants fight. Jesus was emphasizing the true nature of His kingdom in stark contrast to Rome and other world governments.

CHAPTER 19. THE SON OF GOD CONDEMNED, CRUCIFIED, BURIED

Pilate Brings Jesus Before the Populace, 1-15. The scourging was a pitiless Roman atrocity, often itself fatal, 1. Pilate's words, "Behold the man!" 5, recall Zechariah's prophecy: "Behold the man . . . The BRANCH" (Zech 6:12), and John the Baptist's words: "Behold the Lamb of God, which taketh away the sin of the world" (Jn 1:29). What shame and mockery were heaped upon Him who was the God-Man, especially the crown of thorns, the emblem of the curse being borne by Him who would someday come into His kingdom by bearing the curse of sin (Rev 19:12). Verse 7 reveals the full blind unbelief of the Jews: "He *made himself* the Son of God" (cf. Lev 24:16). Verse 15, "We have no king but Caesar," uncovers the full terrible apostasy of the nation. The "Pavement" (Aramaic *Gabbatha*), 13, was an exquisite inlaid floor, 2,500 meters square, designed as a parade ground for Roman military pomp and as the approach to the procurator's judgment hall. It was near the ancient Tower of Antonia, apparently part of the NW part of the temple area, now located under the present-day Church of the Dames de Sion.

The Crucifixion, 16-30. See notes on "Passion Week" in Lk 23 and "Order of Events on the Crucifixion" in Mk 15. Above the cross, as was customary when executing criminals, the accusation was written in Hebrew (Aramaic), Latin and Greek, the three common languages of Palestine. Pilate apparently worded the charge differently in the three languages. Evidently Matthew and John report the Hebrew title, Mark gives the Latin and Luke the Greek, 19-20. The seamless robe (tunic), 23, a picture of Christ's perfect righteousness, was not torn, but gambled for, 24, fulfilling Ps 22:18. Jesus' loving committal of His mother to the beloved apostle John, 25-27, is unique to this Gospel and exquisitely tender. The "vinegar" was sour wine, 29.

Fulfillment of Scripture, 31-37. The "high day" was especially holy since it fell on the Passover (Ex 12:16). "The preparation," 31, 42, was the day before the sabbath. Empty Jewish ritualism, 31 (cf. Deut 21:23), was overruled to fulfill prophecy: "A bone of him shall not be broken," 36 (Ps 34:20; cf. Ex 12:46; Num 9:12). "They shall look on him whom they pierced," 37 (Zech 12:10) was *not* fulfilled then, but will be at the second advent (Rev 1:7). Breaking a criminal's legs was to hasten a horrible death that sometimes lingered for days.

THE BLOOD AND THE WATER

Jesus' death was certainly unique and thought by many to be due to heart rupture, i.e., a "broken" heart. The suffering and pressure of His sinless humanity in becoming a sin offering was too much for His physical body to stand, and so His heart ruptured, the blood collecting in the pericardium and separating in a sort of bloody clot and watery mass, 34.

Jesus' Burial in a Garden, 38-42. Nicodemus, 39, must have become a real believer and here appears so (cf. Jn 3:1-2; 7:50-52). The burial of Jesus by these wealthy friends shows the reality of Christ's death.

JEWISH BURIAL CUSTOM

There is no reference to a Jewish practice of embalming. Instead, the body was washed (Acts 9:37) and swathed in bandagelike wrappings of linen (*othonia,* "linen cloths," 40; 20:5-7; Lk 24:12). Hippocrates and Aristophanes employ the word for "bandages." Thick layers of aromatic preservatives were enclosed in the folds of the wrappings (Mt 27:59; Lk 23:53; cf. Jn 11:44).

Because evening was imminent with the high festal sabbath commencing at 6:00 P.M., Joseph and Nicodemus chose a nearby garden tomb belonging to the former. Tomb burials were common. Ancient tradition from the early 4th cen. locates Jesus' tomb beneath the dome of the Church of the Holy Sepulchre. Archaeological excavations, except for showing that this spot was located outside the city walls in that era, however, have not confirmed this site otherwise. Ossuaries (stone boxes) holding the bones of the deceased when tombs were emptied for new burials have been found in large numbers in Jerusalem excavations dating from this era, and common names such as Jesus, Judas, Ananias, Lazarus, even a Jeshua (Jesus) son of Joseph were found. These names are carved in the ossuaries in Hebrew, Aramaic or Greek.

GORDON'S CALVARY AND THE GARDEN TOMB

Another site known as the Garden Tomb near Gordon's Calvary rivals the Church of the Holy Sepulchre as the place of Jesus' entombment. Located outside the present north wall, this rock-cut chamber, originally sealed with a large rolling stone, has been authenticated as a Jewish tomb of the Roman period. However, epigraphic or archaeological evidence is lacking to prove it was Jesus' tomb. The exact location of these holy spots has been lost, probably by divine providence, God knowing the inveterate superstition of the human heart which tends to attach glory to places, while glory belongs to Him alone.

CHAPTER 20. THE RESURRECTION

Evidence of the Resurrection, 1-29. This stupendous event, the consummating fact of Christian faith, the capstone of the Gospel of the deity of Christ, is here authenticated: (1) *By the open tomb,* 1-2. Its discovery was made by Mary, 1, who hastily returned to Jerusalem to report to Simon Peter and the other disciple, 2. Conclusion: "They have taken away the Lord," 2. Reason: The huge stone which sealed the rock-hewn tomb was found moved. (2) *By the grave clothes,* 3-8. The two disciples Peter and John raced to the tomb and saw the linen clothes, 6-7. John *saw* and *believed,* 8. The disciples, convinced, left the tomb, 9-10. (3) *By the self-revelation of the Lord* to Mary Magdalene, 11-18. Her attitude of gloom and desperation was changed by the revelation of the risen Saviour to her. Jesus appeared also to the discouraged disciples, 19-20, Thomas being absent, 24-25; then a week later to the believing and rejoicing disciples when Thomas was present, 26-29. The latter's doubt answers the uncertainty of every honest skeptic ever since.

THE RESURRECTION AUTHENTICATED

1. The open tomb, Jn 20:1-2
2. The recovered grave clothes, Jn 20:3-8
3. The revelation of the risen Lord
   (a) To Mary Magdalene, Jn 20:11-18; Mk 16:9
   (b) To women returning from the tomb, Mt 28:8-10
   (c) To Peter later in the day, Lk 24:34; 1 Cor 15:5
   (d) To the Emmaus disciples, Lk 24:13-33
   (e) To the apostles—Thomas absent, Lk 24:36-43; Jn 20:19-24
   (f) To the apostles—Thomas present, Jn 20:26-29
   (g) To the seven by the Lake of Tiberias, Jn 21:1-23
   (h) To a multitude of believers on a Galilean mountain, 1 Cor 15:6
   (i) To James, 1 Cor 15:7
   (j) To the eleven, Mt 28:16-20; Mk 16:14-20; Lk 24:33-53; Acts 1:3-12
   (k) At the ascension, Acts 1:3-12
   (l) To Paul, Acts 9:3-6; 1 Cor 15:8
   (m) To Stephen, Acts 7:55
   (n) To Paul in the temple, Acts 22:17-21; 23:11
   (o) To John on Patmos, Rev 1:10-19

4. Pilate's sealing and guarding the tomb, Mt 27:62-66
5. Removal of the stone by an angel, Mt 28:1-3
6. The terror of the Roman guards, Mt 28:4
7. The message of the angel to the women, Mt 28:5-6
8. The report of the guards to the chief priests, Mt 28:11
9. The chief priests' bribe to the Roman guards, Mt 28:12-13
10. The Roman guards spread the lie that Christ's body was stolen, Mt 28:15
11. The certainty of Christ's death, Jn 19:34-42
12. The certainty of His burial, Mk 15:42-47
13. The certainty His body was not stolen:
    (a) If His enemies had done so (Mt 28:4-15) they would have produced it
    (b) If His friends had done so they would not have preached a lie nor been willing to die for it
14. A hallucination? How could doubting Thomas have a hallucination, or 500 people imagine something at the same time?
15. A hoax? How does one then account for the wonderful change in all the disciples from deepest gloom to radiant joy, cowardice to valor, timid disciples to powerful witnesses?
16. The miracle of the Christian faith, personal regeneration
17. The conversion of Saul of Tarsus

Purpose of John's Gospel, 30-31. See "Purpose of the Fourth Gospel" in the introduction to the book. The miracles reported are highly selected with practical intent: (1) to prove Christ as the Messiah, the God-Man; (2) to show Him as the Saviour and Lifegiver; (3) to cause men to believe on Him; (4) that they might receive eternal life.

This purpose explains the fragmentariness and unity of the book, its imagery, its symbolism and its characters, as well as its distinctive presentation of the Messiah, the Son of God.

CHAPTER 21. EPILOGUE: INSTRUCTION IN SPIRITUAL SERVICE

Post-Resurrection Appearance, 1-2. The resurrected Christ directs our service for Him, 1-2. This can result only when the risen Lord reveals Himself to His own. For Sea of Tiberias, 1, see note on Jn 6:1.

Peter Instructed in Spiritual Service, 3-25. Peter's "I am going fishing" smacked of the old life of self-directed service before He yielded to Christ's call to leave his nets. The disciples, following human self-directed leadership, that night caught nothing, 3. Jesus'

565

appearance, 4-5, tested their labors as fruitless (cf. Jn 15:1-17 comments). Service directed by Christ is fruitful, 6-11; revelatory of the inadequacy and shame of self, 7, and of the all-sufficiency of the risen Lord, 12-14 (cf. Lk 22:35; Phil. 4:19). Love for the person of the risen Lord manifested in the primacy of His will in the life, 15-17, is the only acceptable motive for spiritual service (2 Cor 5:14; Rev 2:4-5). Peter was probed on the matter of the quality of His love for Christ. "Feed my sheep" is pastoral work and demands love for the Good Shepherd of the sheep as the primary qualification.

Spiritual service also demands death to self, 18-19. Death in verse 19 was primarily not the martyr's death (although this would eventually follow in Peter's case), but death to sin and self, anticipatory of the position Peter and the other disciples would receive after Christ's ascension and gift of the Holy Spirit (Acts 2:1-4). The Spirit would baptize them "into Christ" (Rom 6:1-10) and their knowledge of and faith in this new position would make possible the transition from the spiritual immaturity of verse 18a to the spiritual maturity of 18b.

Our Lord also instructed Peter about physical death, 20-25. If the Lord returned, His servant would be translated not to see death (1 Cor 15:51-52; 1 Thess 4:13-18). But this was in the Lord's hands.

ACTS

THE GOSPEL TO THE ENDS OF THE EARTH

Author. The author of Acts is the same as the author of the Gospel according to Luke. This is indicated by Lk 1:3-4 and Acts 1:1. "The former treatise" addressed to Theophilus (Acts 1:1; Lk 1:3) is the third Gospel. Internal evidences, particularly the "we" passages of Acts (16:10-17; 20:5—21:18; 27:1—28:16), confirm Lukan authorship. Luke was a physician (Col 4:14), and presumably a Gentile, since his name in Colossians occurs after mention of those of the circumcision (cf. Col 4:11). As a Gentile, he wrote to Gentiles through a Gentile patron, Theophilus, narrating the extension of gospel privilege to Gentiles.

Date. This book was apparently written about A.D. 63, since it terminates with Paul's two-year imprisonment in Rome (28:30). Since Luke devotes so much space to the account of Paul's trial and appeal to Caesar, it would have been very unlikely had the book been written later for the author not to have alluded to the outcome of the apostle's trial.

Scope and Contents. The book of Acts, called the Acts of the Apostles since about the middle of the 2nd cen. A.D., bridges the period between the four Gospels and the later epistles. In dealing with the history of Christian origins, it is the natural sequel to the Gospels, and at the same time it is an indispensable introduction to the Pauline labors and epistles.

1. *The book shows the progress of Christianity* from Jerusalem, to all Judea, and Samaria, and to the end of the earth (1:8). This commission of the risen Lord had already been reported incipiently by Luke (Lk 24:46-49). Here it is again described and traced in its outworking as a result of the advent of the Spirit.

2. *The book continues the acts of the risen Lord through the Holy Spirit.* "In the former treatise" (the Gospel of Luke) Luke says he dealt with "all that Jesus began both to do and teach" (Acts 1:1). In the Acts he describes what Jesus *continued* to do and teach through His Body (the Church), brought into existence at Pentecost (Acts 2), and indwelt by the Holy Spirit. This activity of the risen Christ in heaven working through the Holy Spirit on earth suggests the name "The Acts of the Risen Christ" or "The Acts of the Holy Spirit," rather than merely "The Acts of the Apostles," who were only human agents. This truth of Christ in glory working on the earth through the believer indwelt by the Holy Spirit, seen in historical

outworking in Acts, is the subject of doctrinal revelation in the Pauline epistles. In addition to the human instruments in Acts, two supernatural Beings are found working: Christ in heaven, and the Holy Spirit on earth. Besides these, there is Satan, everywhere operating to hinder and thwart the work of God.

CHRONOLOGICAL CHART OF ACTS

Events	Dates
Ascension (1:9-11)	A.D. 30
Pentecost (2:1-41)	A.D. 30
Early church (2:42—6:7)	A.D. 30
First persecution (4:1-31)	A.D. 31
Second persecution (5:17-42)	A.D. 32
Third persecution— Stephen's martyrdom (6:8—8:4)	A.D. 35-36
Philip's ministry in Samaria and to the Ethiopian (8:5-40)	A.D. 36
Paul's conversion (9:1-21)	A.D. 37
Paul in Damascus, Jerusalem, Tarsus (9:22-30)	A.D. 39
Peter at Caesarea (10:1—11:18)	A.D. 41
Founding of Gentile church at Antioch (11:19-24)	A.D. 41
Paul in Antioch (11:25-26)	A.D. 43
Martyrdom of James; Peter imprisoned (12:1-19)	A.D. 44
First missionary journey (13:1—14:28)	A.D. 45-47
Jerusalem council (15:1-29)	A.D. 50
Second missionary journey (15:36—18:22)	A.D. 51-54
Third missionary journey (18:23—21:19)	A.D. 54-58
Paul arrested in Jerusalem (21:20—23:22)	A.D. 58
Paul a prisoner at Caesarea (23:23—26:32)	A.D. 58-60
Paul's journey and arrival in Rome (27:1—28:31)	A.D. 60-61

Outline
From Jerusalem to All Judea, Ch. 1—7
To Samaria, Ch. 8
To the Gentiles, Ch. 9—12
To the End of the Earth, Ch. 13—28

CHAPTER 1.   THE FORTY DAYS

Post-Resurrection Teaching, 1-8. On Luke's introduction, 1-2, see notes on author and date of the Acts, above. In verses 3-8 Luke presents a résumé of our Lord's 40-day post-resurrection ministry in which He instructed His own concerning the kingdom of God, 3. This teaching centered in "the promise of the Father," i.e., the gift and advent of the Spirit, 4, to be realized at Pentecost (Acts 2). Thereupon our Lord mentioned the one unique ministry of the promised Spirit that would characterize the new age, 5, the Spirit's baptizing work, by which the Church, Christ's Body on earth, shortly would be brought into existence (1 Cor 12:13; Rom 6:3-4; see notes on Acts 2). John the Baptist foretold this baptism of the Spirit (Mt 3:11). The reason Jesus omitted reference to the baptism with fire, which John also had foretold, was because this would be in connection with judgment at the second advent (Mt 3:12). The question of the restoration of the kingdom to Israel, 6 (cf. v. 3), was a natural query for a Jew, since instruction concerning the new age evidently had left this truth untreated (cf. notes on Mt 3:11; 4:17; 13:1-2). So far from denying such a restoration of the kingdom to Israel, our Lord reiterated His repeated teaching that the time was still future and was God's secret (Mt 24:36, 42-44; 1 Thess 5:1; cf. Mt 25:13; Mk 13:32).

The Ascension and Promised Return, 9-11. Christ's ascension, 9, was the capstone of His death and resurrection, as was His predicted second advent, 10-11. Each forms an unbreakable link in an inseparable chain of events. The "cloud" which received Him, 9, was evidently the cloud of the Shekinah glory, so often seen in the OT, and to be seen when He returns again (Mt 26:64; Rev 1:7).

The Ten-Day Wait for the Spirit, 12-14. The disciples waited and prayed, and the Holy Spirit came on prophetic schedule to fulfill the divine type and timetable.

Choice of Matthias, 15-26. This is not to be considered a mistake with Paul being regarded as the rightful twelfth apostle. The twelve had a ministry of witness to the entire Jewish nation. Not until Israel's final rejection of the testimony, as witnessed by Stephen's death (Acts 7), was Paul chosen as the Apostle to the Gentiles and that by direct divine revelation (1 Cor 15:5-8).

CHAPTER 2.   THE SPIRIT'S ADVENT—
BIRTH OF THE CHURCH

The Advent of the Spirit, 1-13. This is a pivotal chapter opening a new era, witnessed by the wind, 2, fire, 3, and supernatural tongues,

4 (see notes on Acts 11). Pentecost marked: (1) The advent of the Spirit (Jn 16:7-8, 13). (2) The giving and reception of the gift of the Holy Spirit (Jn 14:16; Acts 2:38-39). (3) The copious pouring out of the gift (Acts 10:45). The advent and giving of the gift involved the performing of all His ministries for' this age, including (a) regenerating the believer; (b) baptizing him into the Church as Christ's Body (cf. Acts 1:5; 11:16; 1 Cor 12:13) and into Christ the Head (Rom 6:3-4); (c) indwelling the believer (Jn 14:17); (d) sealing him (Eph 4:30); (e) giving him the privilege of infilling (Acts 2:4; Eph 5:18). (4) Thus Pentecost signaled the beginning of the Church since it marked the first historical occurrence of the baptism of the Spirit by which operation the Church alone could be formed (Acts 5:13-14; 1 Cor 12:13). (5) It opened gospel opportunity to the Jew or Jewish proselyte (Acts 2:5). (6) It indicated Peter's first use of the keys of the kingdom of the heavens (Acts 2:14; cf. note on Mt 16:19). (7) It furnished an illustration of spiritual outpouring (Acts 2:16) prophesied upon Israel when restored to kingdom blessing in the coming age (Joel 2:28-32). (8) It signaled the worldwide proclamation of the gospel of grace to every race, prefigured by the supernatural languages (Acts 2:4-11), in fulfillment of the program of evangelization for the new age commanded by the risen Lord (1:8). See notes on Acts 8; 10; 11:1-18; 19:1-7.

The Results of the Advent of the Spirit, 14-47. The reception of the gift of the Spirit as a deposit in the newly formed Church was far-reaching. It furnished the dynamic for Peter's great sermon declaring the messiahship and lordship of Christ, 14-36. Three thousand were converted and became recipients of the blessings of the gift of the Spirit, 37-41. It brought power and unity to the newly formed community of believers, 42-46, and a sustained growth and increase, 47.

CHAPTERS 3—4. THE FIRST MIRACLE AND ITS RESULTS

The Healing of the Lame Man, 3:1-11. The miracle was a further testimony to the unbelieving Jewish nation of the lordship and messiahship of Him whom they had crucified, as Peter's sermon had been (2:14-36). It witnessed to the fact that the Crucified One was risen and ascended to glory, and that His omnipotence had been revealed through His name, 12-16, in the instant healing of the lame man.

Peter's Second Sermon, 3:12-26. His words were addressed to the nation Israel. The nation was called to repent, 19, of its crime of killing the Prince (Author) of life, 15. Repentance would have resulted in national deliverance, described as "times of refreshing," 19 (cf. Joel 2:28-32) and "the restoration of all things, whereof God spake by the mouth of his holy prophets that have been from of old," 21 (ASV), i.e., the restoration of the kingdom to Israel alluded to in Acts 1:6 and the great theme of OT prophecy. The nation's official answer was complete impenitence (ch. 4), so that "the heavens must receive" Israel's coming Saviour till this present age is past, 21. The outcome of not hearing the Prophet Jesus Christ (Deut 18:15-18) was to be utter destruction, 22-23, consummated in national decimation by the Romans in A.D. 70.

The Result, 4:1-37. The nation rejected the message of the miracle and of Peter's appeal, arrested the apostles, 1-4, and forbade preaching in Jesus' name, 13-22. Peter's address to the Sanhedrin, 5-12, was fearless, climaxed by a quotation, 11, from Ps 118:22, and a call to salvation, which was rejected. The high tide of spiritual life in the Jerusalem church appears in verses 23-37.

CHAPTER 5. DISCIPLINE AND PERSECUTION

Ananias and Sapphira's Sin, 1-11. Like Samson and Saul, Ananias and Sapphira sinned the "sin unto [physical] death" (1 Cor 5:1-5; 1 Jn 5:16; cf. 1 Cor 11:30). It was a direct yielding to Satan in the sense of lying to the Holy Spirit, 3, and tempting Him who was operating in such fullness of power in giving witness of the power of a crucified and risen Christ to the Jewish nation, 9. Peter was prominent in the discipline meted out (cf. Mt 16:19; 18:18).

Powerful Witness to the Jewish Nation, 12-42. The place was prominent—Solomon's portico in the temple, 12. The results were public to the nation and miraculous, so much so that even Peter's shadow effected cures, 12-16. Jesus' works were continued by the Spirit through the apostles (1:1) as a further witness to the Jewish nation. These mighty miracles were directed toward Israel to give the nation a last chance to repent. They were only for the beginning of the age to authenticate the gospel of a crucified and risen Christ to Israel, and later to the first Gentile converts before the NT Scriptures were given. When these purposes were met, the miracles and sign gifts were superseded by a written revelation, which was to be the object of faith. Jewish rejection is seen in the second persecution, 17-42. Gamaliel was a well-known rabbi, 34-39. Theudas is mentioned by Josephus (*Ant.* XX. 5. 1). Judas revolted A.D. 6.

CHAPTER 6. THE FIRST DEACONS

Choosing the Seven, 1-7. The Hellenists (Grecians), 1, were Jews who adopted the Greek language and customs. The Hebrews clung to Aramaic and Jewish practices. "To serve tables," 2, included financial and temporal duties. "Prayer and the ministry of the word," 4, are always primary in a presbyter or bishop. The deacon's office was to guard this calling from encroachment by other necessary functions of a minister of Christ. A proselyte, 5, was a Gentile convert to Judaism prior to becoming a Christian. The growth of the Jerusalem church, 7, is indicated. These converts were "added to the Lord" (5:14; cf. Rom 6:3-4). The laying on of hands, 6, speaks of simple identification of the apostles and the assembly with the chosen deacons in their work (cf. Lev 3:2).

Stephen's Ministry and Arrest, 8-15. Stephen's Spirit-filled and miracle-attested witness to the nation's leaders was rebuffed, bringing final Jewish rejection of the testimony of the Triune God—God the Father in the OT, God the Son in the Gospels, now God the Spirit in powerful appeal through Stephen. The Libertines, correctly "freedmen," 9, were Jews who had been Roman slaves but were subsequently freed. The reference is apparently to a Jerusalem synagogue frequented by Jews from a number of the lands of the dispersion—Cyrene in N. Africa W of Egypt, Alexandria in Egypt, Cilicia NW of Syria and proconsular Asia.

CHAPTER 7. STEPHEN'S MARTYRDOM

Stephen's Sermon, 1-53. He was the chosen instrument to deliver the Lord's final testimony to the nation. He, the accused, became the accuser. He, the one judged by the nation, became the nation's judge. His defense cited Abraham's history through Isaac and Jacob, 2-8; Joseph's history, 9-16; Moses' rejection and deliverance, 17-38; Israel's apostasy, 39-50. His arraignment of his judges and sentence upon the nation follow, 51-53.

Stephen's Martydrom, 54-60. The first martyr was remarkably like his Lord. He was filled with the Spirit and did "great wonders and signs among the people," 6:8. Like Christ he was accused of speaking against Moses, the law, and the temple, 6:13-14, and was put to death as a blasphemer, 7:56-58. Like Christ he was arraigned before the Sanhedrin and faced false accusers, 6:11-13. He gave witness to the truth of our Lord's confession that He was to sit at God's right hand, 7:55-56, seeing Him there. Like Jesus he prayed for his enemies' forgiveness and that the Lord might receive his spirit, 7:59-60. The first martyr was transformed wonderfully by the Spirit into Christlikeness (2 Cor 3:18). Three manifestations of the glorified Christ are recorded: to Stephen (Acts 7:55-56); to Paul (Acts 9:3-6; cf. 7:58 with 8:1); and to John (Rev 1:10, 12-16).

CHAPTER 8.   THE SAMARITANS ADMITTED TO GOSPEL PRIVILEGE

Philip's Ministry in Samaria, 1-25. The occasion was persecution, 1-3, resulting in the outgoing of the gospel to non-Jewish regions (Acts 1:8). Philip's ministry in Samaria, 4-13, prepared the Samaritans for admission into gospel privilege and the gift of the Holy Spirit, 14-25. Real significance must be attached to Peter's coming to Samaria to pray for and lay hands upon the believing disciples that they might receive the Holy Spirit, 15. The case involves the introduction of the gospel to another people (as to the Jew at Pentecost) and the initial bestowment of the Spirit upon them. Hence Peter's presence was necessary. To him alone was given the "keys of the kingdom of heaven" (Mt 16:19). As he opened the gospel to the Jew (Acts 2:14) and to the Gentile (10:34), so in a similar sense he opened the gospel privilege to the racially and religiously mongrel Samaritans, who were a bridge to the Gentiles. The episode was *not* a second experience after salvation, but marked the initial giving of the Holy Spirit to the Samaritans as an ethnic group. Until the Spirit was given to Jews at Pentecost, to Samaritans (Acts 8), and to Gentiles at Caesarea (Acts 10), no regenerated soul enjoyed the "so great salvation" in the sense now experienced by every Christian, including (besides regeneration) baptism by the Spirit into Christ (Rom 6:3-4), sealing (Eph 4:30), and permanent indwelling (1 Cor 6:19-20) with the privilege of continuous infilling (Eph 5:18).

The Ethiopian Eunuch, 26-40. "Candace," 27-28, was a title of the queens of Nubia, the country on the Nile from the first cataract to the vicinity of Khartoum. A eunuch, or castrated male, was placed under serious religious disabilities by the Mosaic law (Deut 23:1; cf. Lev 22:23-25). The eunuch's conversion illustrates the outgoing of gospel privilege beyond those racially and religiously related to the Jews and their religion (like the Samaritans), to those simply religiously related (like the eunuch). He was apparently a non-Jew, a proselyte of the gate, who had embraced Judaism. The grace offered in Christ now overleaped all racial barriers and legal disabilities, and granted full salvation to men who, although of noble position, had been excluded from the congregation of the Lord's people by the law of Moses.

Roman theater at Caesarea, capital of Palestine in Paul's day and place where he was imprisoned for two years. (*Courtesy IIS*)

CHAPTER 9. CONVERSION OF THE APOSTLE TO THE GENTILES

Saul's Conversion, 1-19. Acts 1—8 presents the spread of the gospel from Jerusalem to "all Judea and Samaria" (1:8). The rest of Acts is concerned with the preparation of the great evangelist to the Gentiles, ch. 9; the official introduction of the gospel to the Gentiles, ch. 10—11; and the extension of gospel witness "to the end of the earth," ch. 12—28. The conversion of Saul of Tarsus is significantly recounted *immediately after* the completed official opening of the gospel to Jews and Samaritans and *just before* the account of the introduction of gospel grace to Gentiles. Saul saw the risen, ascended Christ, 1-8, basic to his later apostleship; was filled with the Spirit, 17; and was baptized to show his identification with Christ and His people, 18-19.

Damascus and the Beginning of Saul's Ministry, 20-25. Saul's fearless preaching stirred Jewish persecution, 20-24. He was let down over the wall in a basket, 25. Damascus was a free city, a member of the Decapolis of free cities, but at this time may have been under Nabatean rule, for "the governor under King Aretas guarded the city" (2 Cor 11:32, RSV) at the time. Aretas IV's (9 B.C.—A.D. 40)

574

ethnarch probably waited outside the city, hoping to catch Saul as he emerged.

Saul's Return to Tarsus, 26-31. This was preceded by a visit to Jerusalem, 26-29. Intense hatred and persecution, 29, necessitated Saul's return to his hometown Tarsus via Caesarea, provincial capital and Judea's seaport. Tarsus was in Cilicia in SE. Asia Minor across the Gulf of Issus from Antioch's seaport Seleucia. It was an important free city and a center of commerce.

Peter Prepared for Gentile Evangelism, 32-43. Peter healed the paralytic Aeneas at Lydda (present-day Ludd, 11 miles SE of Joppa), 32-35. At Joppa he restored Dorcas to life and resided "with one Simon a tanner," 36-43. Jewish law regarded a tanner as an outcast and his work defiling. Joppa was stoutly Jewish, a pharisaical center highly suitable for Peter's revelation of those clean and unclean, as an indispensable prerequisite for his ministry to Gentiles, 9:43—10:33.

CHAPTER 10. THE GENTILES ADMITTED TO GOSPEL PRIVILEGES

Cornelius and Peter, 1-33. The case of Cornelius, as a representative Gentile, 1-8, marked the giving of the Holy Spirit to the Gentiles. Cornelius, although devout and pious, did not enjoy the common salvation of the new age opened up at Pentecost (Acts 11:14). Peter's soul-transforming vision, 9-16, set forth the truth that Gentiles, unclean and long shut out from religious opportunity as "dogs" (Mt 15:24-27), symbolized by the various ceremonially unclean animals, were to receive the "like [identical] gift" God had given to the Jews at Pentecost (Acts 11:17; see notes on Acts 2 and 8).

Peter's Last Use of the Keys, 34-48. For the last recorded time Peter used the keys of the kingdom of heaven (Mt 16:19). It was he who preached the sermon, 34-44 (cf. Acts 2:14; 8:14), which opened the gospel and the gift of the Holy Spirit to Gentiles, establishing *the norm for the age.* With the events of verses 44-48, Jew, Samaritan and Gentile had been introduced to the gift of the Holy Spirit. Resident in the Body of Christ, the Church, the Spirit becomes the blessing of *every one* who exercises faith in Christ as Saviour.

CAESAREA

This brilliant capital of the Roman government in Judea was built (25-13 B.C.) by Herod the Great. He dedicated the city to

Caesar Augustus in 12 B.C., changing the name Straton's Tower to Caesarea in honor of the emperor. Made a fine seaport, Caesarea had ready access to all parts of the Roman world. A huge sea mole 200 feet wide in 120 feet of water was constructed, remains of which are still visible. In 1960 the harbor was explored by the Link Expedition to Israel, opening up a chapter in underwater archaeology or aqueology. A coin depicting the harbor as two ships enter contains the letters KA, an apparent abbreviation for Caesarea.

Fine Graeco-Roman buildings included a forum, stadium and amphitheater. The latter was located by Israeli archaeologists by aerial photography. It was 300 feet by 200 feet, larger than the Colosseum at Rome. It was the scene of bloody gladiatorial contests when Herod inaugurated the town in 10 B.C. Here Graeco-Roman culture and customs prevailed in Palestine. Luke does well to highlight Caesarea in his account of the gospel outreach.

11:1-18.   PETER DEFENDS HIS MINISTRY TO GENTILES

Peter Called to Explain His Ministry to Gentiles, 1-3. The fact that Gentiles received the Holy Spirit and were admitted to gospel privilege required explanation. The circumcision party, 2, composed of conservative Jewish believers, came into existence as soon as Gentiles were saved (15:1-5; 21:20).

Peter's Explanation, 4-18. He recounted his experiences at Joppa and Caesarea, 4-14 (cf. 10:1-33). His interpretation to his Jerusalem colleagues, 15-18, included the following facts: (1) Salvation thereby was granted to Cornelius and his household as the first representative Gentiles, 14. (2) The Holy Spirit fell on the Gentiles as on the Jews at Pentecost, 15, referring to the mighty *infilling* (2:4) that characterized the initial giving of the Spirit at Pentecost and the introduction of the gift to Samarians (8:16) and Gentiles (10:44). (Cf. the term "poured out" gift, 2:17; 10:45.) (3) The baptism of the Spirit, 16, was connected initially with Pentecost by Peter, as a comparison with Acts 1:5 shows, and also with the events of Acts 10. This demonstrated that the Church began at Pentecost, since it was formed by this "one [spiritual] baptism," as 1 Cor 12:13; Rom 6:3-4; Gal. 3:26-27 show. (4) Peter declared the gift of the Spirit granted to the Gentiles was "the same," i.e., identical with the gift initially given to Israel in Acts 2. This included supernatural languages (2:4; 10:46; 19:6).

SPEAKING IN TONGUES

There are two aspects in the manifestation of tongues: first, the tongues (languages) in Acts 2, 10, 19 (and probably in ch. 8); second, the gift of tongues (known languages) in the early apostolic church. The gift under the second aspect evidently was not permanent (1 Cor 13:9-13), nor given to every believer. It required the concomitant gift of interpretation (1 Cor 12:10; 14:1-40). This sign gift with interpretation was meant to instruct the church before the completed NT Scriptures were given.

Under the first aspect tongues were a means by which the Holy Spirit witnessed to Israel on the day of Pentecost (2:4-13). They were a sign of the truth that Jesus was the Messiah and an indication of the new age of the Spirit.

The Jews were again challenged by the Samaritans' receiving the Holy Spirit (Acts 8:14-17), and, although this is not specifically mentioned, they may have been given the evidence that the despised Samaritans had actually received the same gift as the Jews, by the sign of their supernatural utterances (cf. 11:17).

This is the use of tongues in the introduction of the gift of the Holy Spirit to Gentiles (Acts 10:44-47). Nothing could have been more convincing to skeptical, unbelieving Peter and his Jewish colleagues than the fact that Cornelius and the other Gentiles spoke in supernatural languages just as the Jews at Pentecost.

The disciples of John the Baptist who received the Holy Spirit and spoke in languages they had never learned (Acts 19:6-10) were a similar witness to the strong Jewish community at Ephesus. For the disciples of John the Baptist, whom the Jews generally accepted as a God-sent prophet, to be blessed by the Holy Spirit after being baptized in the name of the rejected Messiah, was of the deepest significance. Yet "they [the Jews] would not hear" as Isaiah (Isa 28:11-12) had predicted (1 Cor 14:22. Cf. notes on 1 Cor 14).

11:19-30.   THE CHURCH AT ANTIOCH

The Disciples Called Christians, 19-26. The gospel began to be preached to non-Jews at Antioch, on the Orontes in Syria, 19-20. Great numbers of Gentiles were converted, 21, after the introduction of gospel privilege to them (see notes on Acts 10, 11). Barnabas (4:36) was from Cyprus and many Cypriots resided in Antioch, 20. He brought Saul from Tarsus, 25-26 (see note on 9:26-31). Believers were called Christians first in Antioch, 26. The term *Christiani* ("partisans of Christ") was probably an official name of Jesus' disciples given by Roman officials at Antioch. (Cf. *Pompeiani*,

Sullani, Herodiani, Mt 22:16, and other party names.) See note on Antioch in ch. 13.

Relief Sent to Jerusalem, 27-30. The famine in the days of Claudius (A.D. 41-54) occurred probably in A.D. 46. Prophets like Agabus, possessing a supernatural gift of prediction, were common in the early church before a completed canon, as well as persons gifted with speaking in tongues and possessing other sign gifts.

CHAPTER 12.   HEROD'S PERSECUTION AND DEATH

Arrest of Peter and His Deliverance, 1-19. James the son of Zebedee was martyred. Peter was arrested. His persecutor was Herod Agrippa I, grandson of Herod the Great and the Maccabean Mariamne. Agrippa was made king over Judea and Samaria by Emperor Caligula, and from A.D. 41-44 ruled over practically the same territory as his grandfather, Herod the Great. For "angel," 7, cf. Gen 48:16; Mt 18:10.

Death of Herod at Caesarea, 20-25. On Caesarea see note on Acts 10:34-48. Herod evidently was in Caesarea to participate in the quadrennial festival in honor of the Roman emperor, which took place in the spring of A.D. 44. Josephus (*Ant.* XIX. 8.2) relates how the king was struck with a deadly malady after being hailed as divine.

13:1-12.   FIRST TOUR—CYPRUS

Antioch the Birthplace of Foreign Missions, 1-3. Antioch-on-the-Orontes in Syria was the third largest city in the Roman Empire in Paul's day. The large Gentile church there was not only blessed with gifted teachers, 1, but with the free operation of the Holy Spirit, 2-3, who launched the pivotal gospel witness in the West. Seleucia, 4, was Antioch's seaport, situated five miles up the Orontes River from the Mediterranean. Two giant moles jutting out into the sea are mute witnesses of the important harbor which connected with the port town and inland city by walls.

The Tour of Cyprus, 4-12. Time: spring of A.D. 45. Destination: Salamis, 130 miles SW of Antioch on the E coast of Cyprus, third largest island in the Mediterranean. It was 148 miles long and 15 to 20 miles broad. It had a long pagan cultural history including the licentious worship of Aphrodite. Salamis, 4, was the largest city on the island, with a large Jewish population, 5. Paphos, 6, present-day Baffo near modern Ktima, was on the western part of the island. It was a cult center, capital of the senatorial province of

Cyprus, residence of the proconsul (practor) and mecca for the polluted worship of Aphrodite. Elymas (from the Arabic *alimun,* "wise," "learned," or Aramaic "powerful") was a demon-energized occultist, not pagan but Jewish, 8. At Soli, a city on the NW coast of Cyprus, a Greek inscription dated A.D. 52-53 was found reading, "Under Paulus the proconsul." It doubtlessly refers to Sergius Paulus, Paul's famous convert.

ANTIOCH-ON-THE-ORONTES AND ARCHAEOLOGY

Founded in 300 B.C. by Seleucus I Nicator, three centuries of cultural history prepared the great city for its famous role in Christian missions. Its suburb of Daphne was known for license and pleasure, the playground of the dissolute city. The seed of the gospel of grace found needy soil here, for Daphnic morals were notorious even in blasé Rome.

The present-day site of Antakiyeh, in numerous excavations since 1932, has yielded gorgeous floor mosaics, as well as buildings, walls and other remains, enabling the history of the city to be outlined. The claim was formerly made that the famous Chalice of Antioch, found in 1910, contained the earliest figures of Christ and the twelve apostles and belonged to the latter part of the 1st cen. The inner chalice was supposedly the original communion cup of Christ. Scholars now generally place it anywhere from the 2nd to the 6th cen., as a product of early Christian art.

Famous churches excavated at Antioch include the octagonal edifice of Constantine and a cross-shaped edifice, both from the late 4th cen., showing that Christianity left its impress on Antioch's architecture. The city's patron deity was Tyche, whose memory is preserved in the exquisite marble replica in the Vatican.

GOSPEL OUTREACH

Acts 1—12	Center: Jerusalem	Chief Person: Peter	Gospel to: Judea and Samaria	Evangelism: Jewish
Acts 13—28	Center: Antioch	Chief Person: Paul	Gospel to: the end of the earth	Evangelism: Gentile

13:13-52. FIRST TOUR—PERGA AND PISIDIAN ANTIOCH

From Paphos to Perga, 13. Crossing the 180 miles of water from Paphos, Paul and Barnabas landed at Perga, chief city of Pamphylia in Asia Minor. This site, now called Murtana, is notable for the completeness and intactness of its ancient ruins. Artemis, the nature goddess, was worshiped here, as Pergan coins show. At Perga John Mark decided to quit the tour, 13 (cf. 15:38; 2 Tim 4:11).

From Perga to Pisidian Antioch and Iconium, 14-52. The 100-mile trip to Pisidian Antioch was through rugged robber-infested terrain. Sir William Ramsay has adduced numbers of inscriptions from this area proving its banditry (cf. 2 Cor 11:26). But in bringing the gospel to Pisidian Antioch, Paul and Barnabas were planting the witness in a communication nerve center in the heart of Asia Minor through which an E-W traffic artery ran. Westward it connected with Apamaea, Colossae, Laodicea, Magnesia, Ephesus and the Greek world of the Aegean. Eastward it gave access to Lystra, Derbe and via the Cilician Gates led on to Tarsus, Issus and Antioch-on-the-Orontes. In verses 16-41 Paul's great message on justification by faith is reported in detail. Jewish rejection came into prominence.

ANTIOCH OF PISIDIA

This city was one of 16 founded by Seleucus Nicator (312-280 B.C.), together with Antioch-on-the-Orontes in Syria. It is now commonly referred to as Pisidian Antioch because in the late 3rd cen. A.D. it was made the capital of a newly created province called Pisidia. In Paul's day it was a part of the Roman province of Galatia, district of Phrygia. Inscriptions point to Phrygian occupation. Rome took over the city when Galatia became a Roman province in 25 B.C. Augustus realized its strategic military location and made it one of his chief military colonies, officially calling it Colonia Caesarea Antiochia. The military highway, the Royal Road, linked it with a sister military colony of Lystra, 120 miles SE. Antioch had a large Roman military personnel, numerous Greeks, and many Jews (13:14, 50) and Jewish proselytes (13:16, 26, 43). Members of the ruling military class ("coloni") included the devout women of honorable position and the chief men (13:50).

PISIDIAN ANTIOCH AND ARCHAEOLOGY

The site was discovered in 1833 on the right bank of the Anthios River, on the slopes of a mountain called Sultan Dagh, near the Turkish town of Yalovach. Ruins of an ancient Roman aqueduct are still visible. Coins display the river-god Anthios. Sir William Ramsay in 1910-13 excavated the sanctuary of Men, the city's chief deity. The huge altar, 66 by 41 feet, was bounded by a sacred area 241 by 136 feet, enclosed by a 5-foot wall. Men was emblemized by a horned bull's head and was paired with Artemis (Diana), a Hellenized form of Cybele. Here the Phrygian mystery rites were celebrated (cf. Col 2:18). A significant inscription found at Antioch is engraved, "To Lucius Sergius Paullus, the younger," an important official at Antioch, who may have been a son of the Cyprus proconsul (13:7).

Later excavations have uncovered an Augustan city and other buildings from the era of Tiberius. A magnificent frieze recovered depicts Augustus' victories by land and sea, adorned with Tritons, Poseidon, dolphins and other marine symbols. Representations of Men, symbolized by bulls' heads garlanded with leaves and fruit, graced the Square of Augustus and furnish very fine examples of Graeco-Roman art. Terra-cotta pipes of the water system of Antioch have been uncovered. These conducted the water from the aqueduct.

CHAPTER 14. FIRST TOUR—ICONIUM, DERBE, LYSTRA

Iconium, 1-5. Forced out of Antioch by malicious unbelieving Jews, Paul and Barnabas took the Royal Road toward Lystra, but turned aside to visit Iconium (present-day Konia) in Phrygia, 6. Archaeology has shown from inscriptions that the city was predominantly Phrygian racially and Galatian administratively. When Paul came to the town, it was one of the important cities in the southern part of the Roman province of Galatia. It attracted many Jews, being the center of a thriving weaving industry, for which the highland flax and Taurus sheep and goats furnished raw material. The city was also on a commercial artery, connecting it with Ephesus on the W and the Mesopotamian world on the E.

The Work at Lystra, 6-19. Driven out of Iconium by unbelieving Jews, the missionaries came to Lystra and Derbe, two other towns in the Roman province of Galatia. The site of Lystra was ascertained in 1885 by an inscribed Roman altar, still standing, which bore the name of the city in Latin—*Lustra*, with the notice that it had been a Roman colony under Augustus. Few if any Jews were there in Paul's time, as it was unimportant commercially. The uneducated

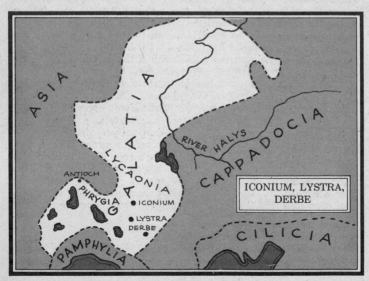

ICONIUM, LYSTRA, DERBE

and superstitious nature of the Lycaonians, not Greeks or Romans, is illustrated by their native cult, here appearing under a thin guise. Barnabas was viewed as Zeus and Paul as Hermes, 12. One inscription from Lystra found in 1909 lists several priests of Zeus. Another refers to Hermes and Zeus. The brutal stoning of Paul by the natives distinguishes them from the educated Greek and Roman society of the colony. (Cf. 2 Cor 11:25; 2 Tim 3:11.)

Work at Derbe and the Return to Antioch of Syria, 20-28. Derbe was the last town in distinctively Roman territory on the road running through southern Galatia to the E. It was therefore a custom station, as Strabo declares. Paul visited it because of its strategic position on the great E-W military and commercial artery. Roman milestones dotted the road. Beyond Derbe on the E lay Commagene, under a Roman vassal but independent. The cult of Mithras prevailed there, and Paul avoided areas where kings were protectors of certain cults and could act drastically. The return trip to Antioch-on-the-Orontes, 23-28, covered the same ground the missionaries had crossed, as they visited and confirmed the churches established. At Perga, 25 (see notes on Acts 13:13), they preached and set sail for Syria at the port of Attalia, founded by Attalus II Philadelphus (159-138 B.C.).

15:1-35. THE COUNCIL AT JERUSALEM

The Council and the Issue, 1-12. The question was whether Gentiles could be saved apart from circumcision and the legalism of the Mosaic system, 1, 5. That they could, and had been so saved, had been fully demonstrated on the first missionary tour, as Paul had reported to the Antioch church. The door of faith opened to the Gentiles (14:27) was an announcement that the gospel, apart from circumcision and Mosaic legalism, had been divinely authenticated as the medium of salvation to the nations. It was a summary declaration that Christianity was an international religion, completely separated from the legalism and narrow isolationism of the Hebrew faith, reaching out to the uttermost part of the earth (1:8). The church at Antioch was to send a delegation to the mother church at Jerusalem, 2-4, and thus also witness the struggle of Christianity with Judaism (cf. Gal 2:1-10). Peter saw the futility of insisting that Gentiles had to become Jews to be saved, 7-11. He comprehended the irrationality of the Judaizers who desired to open the door to the Gentiles only halfway, admitting only those who in addition to faith in the Messiah submitted to Jewish rites, notably circumcision. Paul and Barnabas added their testimony, 12.

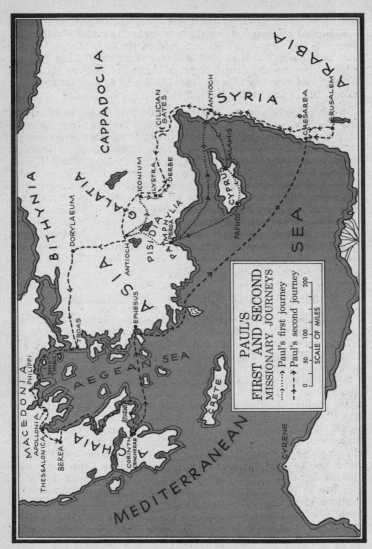

PAUL'S
FIRST AND SECOND
MISSIONARY JOURNEYS
······· Paul's first journey
–·–·–➤ Paul's second journey

SCALE OF MILES
0   50   100   200

The Council and the Decision, 13-35. The question of the first church council was happily settled in the form of the gospel of free grace Paul had seen so signally authenticated. James summarized the decision: "Therefore my judgment is that we should not trouble those of the Gentiles who turn to God," 19 (RSV). They were merely enjoined to abstain from idolatry, from fornication, and from things strangled and from blood, 20-21. This decision was communicated by a delegation of the Jerusalem council to Antioch and to the Gentile world, 22-35.

IMPORTANCE OF THE FIRST CHURCH COUNCIL

The immense significance of the first church council consists, first, in saving the gospel from Judaistic mixture, thereby setting Christianity on its own course as a universal spiritual movement transcending all social, racial and religious barriers, offering spiritual regeneration to everyone who believes; and second, in the revelation of God's gracious purposes for the present age and the age to come, 14-18. The purpose of the present age is to take out of the Gentiles a people for God's name, 14, the "called-out" ones, the Church, the Body of Christ. "After this I will return," 16, that is, Christ's second advent. When the called-out number is completed, Christ will return. Then Israel will be restored: "I will build again the tabernacle of David . . . I will set it up," 16 (cf. 1:6; 3:21 with notes). The kingdom will be established—the world converted, 17, and God's plan for the ages will be fulfilled, 18.

15:36—16:11. SECOND TOUR—ASIA MINOR AND THE CALL TO EUROPE

Paul and Barnabas Separate, 15:36-41. This epoch-making tour, which was to bring the gospel to Europe, began in sharp dissension. Paul and Barnabas separated over John Mark (Acts 12:12, 25; 13:13; 2 Tim 4:11). Barnabas, with Mark, sailed to his homeland of Cyprus. Paul and Silas set out for Asia Minor, this time by land via Mt. Amanus, the Syrian Gates, into Cilicia and on into Galatia, via the Cilician Gates (modern Gulek Bogaz), 3,575 feet above sea level across the Taurus Mountains.

Paul Finds Timothy, 16:1-5, as he revisits Derbe and Lystra (see notes on ch. 14). This name is a shortened form of Timotheus ("God-honorer"). Timothy became Paul's "beloved son" (1 Tim 1:2-18; 2 Tim 1:2) and "fellow laborer in the gospel" (1 Thess 3:2). Apparently converted on Paul's first tour, Timothy was chosen as Paul's secretary and helper on the second tour. Paul's circumcision of Timothy, 3, was a matter of wisdom and loving concern for the salvation of his Jewish brothers, not compromise.

The Call to Europe, 6-11. Careful leading by the Holy Spirit, 6-7, indicates the tremendous spiritual import of the gospel going W into Europe. Asia, 6, was the province of proconsular Asia. Mysia and Bithynia were N of Asia. The Holy Spirit led to Troas, gateway by sea to Europe, 8, where the Macedonian (European) vision was given, 9. Following the Spirit's direction always leads to effective witnessing. Luke, the beloved physician and author of Acts, joined Paul's party, 10-17 (cf. 20:5—21:18; 27:1—28:16). Paul set sail from Troas, an old seaport town on the Aegean, a Roman *colonia* and a free city from the Augustan age, present-day Eskistanbul, where extensive ruins of the Roman period have been uncovered. Paul's ship touched at Samothrace, an Aegean island, roughly midway on the 175-mile trip between Troas and Neapolis, 11 (modern Kavalla), on the European mainland, the port of Philippi and terminus of the great Egnatian Road which ran through Philippi, and thence across Macedonia to Dyrrachium (Durazzo) opposite Brundisium in Italy. Across the Adriatic the Appian Way led to Rome.

16:12-40. SECOND TOUR—PHILIPPI

First European Convert, 12-15. This convert was not a man, as in the vision, but a business woman of ability and means, 14. She was a dealer in purple dye, a native of Thyatira in the extreme S of Mysia, a colony of Macedonians and a thriving market for purple. Lydia's home became the first private home to be used as a meeting place for Christians in Europe. For two centuries the homes of wealthier Christians were to serve as places of Christian assembly. No synagogue apparently existed at Philippi because the Jewish element was small. Sabbath meetings were held by the Gangites River where Jews or proselytes gathered in an "oratory," mainly women, 13. The first effect of the gospel in Europe was a happy harbinger of its emancipation of womanhood by Christianity in striking contrast to paganism and even Judaism.

Clash with Demonism at Philippi, 16-24. The progress of the gospel in strategic Europe was bound sooner or later to evoke Satanic opposition, 16-19. How could the gospel advance against the strongholds of paganism and not be challenged by demonism, the dynamic of heathenism (Deut 32:17; Ps 96:5; 1 Cor 10:20-21)? The young woman, 16, was a spiritistic medium, with powers of oracular utterance, 16, not a fake. The real enemy was not the girl but the evil spirit controlling her and giving her divinatory powers. Therefore Paul addressed "the spirit" (demon), 18, not the girl, expelling the "Pythian spirit" or divining demon controlling her. In Greek mythology Python was the legendary dragon which was thought to guard Delphi, the most famous pagan oracular shrine of antiquity. "The Pythian spirit" became a generic term for the alleged source of inspiration of diviners in general. The Delphic seeress was originally a young woman from the surrounding countryside, and the god was claimed to enter the body and speak through the maid. Scripture recognizes the reality of this in its doctrine of demonism (1 Tim 4:1-6; 1 Jn 4:1-4).

Persecution at Philippi, 25-40. Lethargic paganism was aroused when the promoters of the spiritistic medium saw their profit gone. The Roman element was prominent in Philippi, as would be expected in a Roman colony, 12. The term "praetor" (Gr.), 20, is correctly employed by Luke as a courtesy title for the chief magistrate of a Roman colony. It was an office of great dignity (below a consul) and out of respect used instead of the more usual term *duumvir*. The "lictors" (Gr.), 35, 38, were Roman, carrying the fasces or bundle of rods with an ax. With these rods the lictors soundly beat Paul and Silas. Two lictors attended each praetor, protecting him and executing his orders. The violation of the rights of Paul's Roman citizenship, 37, was a real cause for the praetors' fear, 38. The *lex Porcia* (248 B.C.) protected a Roman citizen from scourging for any reason whatsoever. Condemning a Roman citizen without regular trial and defense was also contrary to Roman law. But Paul used his citizenship not for selfish gain but to proclaim the gospel.

PHILIPPI AND ARCHAEOLOGY

The present-day site called Felibedjik was excavated by the Ecole Française d'Athènes between 1914 and 1938. Ruins mostly dating later than Paul have been recovered, including baths, a theater, the forum, and notably the colonial archway to the W of the city. This was probably the archway mentioned in Acts 16:13, "outside the *gate* to the riverside" (RSV), under which the Via Egnatia ran as it left the city.

17:1-14. SECOND TOUR—THESSALONICA, BEREA

Paul at Thessalonica, 1-9. Thessalonica lay 70 miles SW of Philippi on the Egnatian Way, running through Amphipolis and Apollonia. Under the Romans Thessalonica (modern Salonika with a population of more than 200,000) was a great emporium on the Thermaic Gulf, a center of trade both by land and sea. It attracted Jews, and

THE ACTS

Paul gained an entrée for the gospel through the synagogue, 1-4. The rulers of the city were "politarchs," a Macedonian term shown by inscriptions to be accurate. The Vardar Gate inscription particularly vindicates Luke's accuracy. Thessalonica was a free city with a *demos* or "people's assembly" led by five or six politarchs, 5-9. Jason, 6, Paul's friend, was apparently a Jew whose Semitic name Jesus was complemented by a Greek name roughly comparable. Use of double names among Jews of the diaspora was common in this period (cf. Saul and Paul, Eliakim and Alkimos, Jesus and Justus, Col 4:11). Paul and Silas' labors resulted in a strong church in the city. The rabble-rousers, 5, employed by the Jews were common in the agora or forum of Graeco-Roman cities. They gravitated around a rostrum, applauding or heckling according to those who paid them. Cicero aptly styled them *subrostrani* ("those-under-rostrum").

Paul at Berea, 10-14. About three days of travel on the Egnatian Way brought Paul to Berea, an "out-of-the-way city," according to Cicero. It was E of the Thermaic Gulf, about 35 miles inland. Paul's experience here was a refreshing contrast to the treatment from the Jews elsewhere. "Well-born" or "noble," they searched the Scriptures with an open mind to see "whether these things were so," 11. Many believed, including some prominent Gentiles, 12.

17:15-34. SECOND TOUR—ATHENS

Paul and Athenian Idolatry, 15-18. While Paul waited in Athens for Silas and Timothy, "he was exasperated to see how the city was wholly given to idolatry," 16. To the apostle the artistic magnificence and cultural refinements of the city were seriously tarnished by superstition and spiritual ignorance. Since the Jewish community here was evidently small, Paul had discussions in the agora (marketplace), 17. Luke accurately depicts the marketplace crowd in words which agree with pagan writers from Demosthenes and Thucydides to Pausanias: "Now all the Athenians and foreigners who lived there spent their time in nothing except telling or hearing something new," 21 (RSV). The Epicureans, 18, followed Epicurus (342-271 B.C.) in abandoning the search for pure truth by reason as hopeless and giving themselves to present pleasure. The Stoics, 18, followed Zeno and Chrysippus (3rd cen. B.C.) and embraced a philosophy of stern self-repression on the basis of human self-sufficiency. Paul had the answer for both in Christ's redemptive work. They called him a babbler (*spermologos*), meaning a loquacious person with nothing important to say.

Paul's Sermon to the Areopagus, 19-34. This court met on the 377-

foot hill, the Areopagus, Hill of Ares, god of war, a little NW of the Acropolis. In Paul's day this body functioned in matters pertaining to religion, culture and education. They evaluated the competence of visiting lecturers to speak, and so heard Paul as a promoter of a new religion. Paul's sermon to the court itself, whether assembled on Mars Hill or in the Stoa of Zeus Eleutherios or in the Temple of Apollo Patroos, was a masterpiece of sagacious adaptability to the Greek mentality. He quoted one of the Greek poets, Aratus, a Stoic of the 3rd cen. B.C., 28, arguing first from human reason, 22-29. When he went to revelation, preaching repentance and faith in a risen Christ, 30-32, these intellectual sophisticates viewed the matter as an amusing joke, 32 (cf. 1 Cor 1:18). Little spiritual result was visible, 33-34.

ARCHAEOLOGY AND ATHENS

The marketplace or agora, 17, was the hub of Athens' culture. Its excavation since 1930 by the American School of Classical Studies constitutes an illustration of some of the finest examples of archaeological study in the world. Among the famous buildings (some later than Paul's day) are the Odeion or Music Hall, the Stoa of Attalos, Stoa of Zeus, Temple of Apollos Patroos, the Bouleterion or Assem-

Mars Hill, foreground, overlooking modern Athens. (© *MPS*)

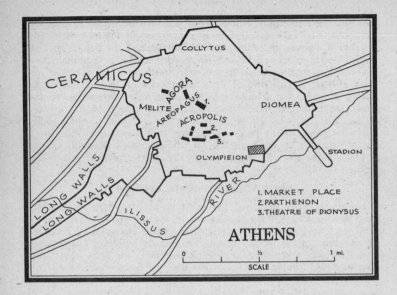

COLLYTUS

CERAMICUS

AGORA
MELITE
AREOPAGUS 1.
ACROPOLIS
2.
3.

DIOMEA

STADION

OLYMPIEION

RIVER

LONG WALLS

LONG WALLS

ILISSUS

1. MARKET PLACE
2. PARTHENON
3. THEATRE OF DIONYSUS

ATHENS

0 — ½ — 1 mi.
SCALE

bly of the Athenian Council of Five Hundred, the Tholos, the Temple of Ares (Mars), the Roman Forum and the Horologium or public clock.

On the 512-foot acropolis are the ruins of the splendid temple of Athena, Athens' patron goddess, called the Parthenon. There also are the Propylaea and the celebrated temples, the Erechtheum and the shrine of Athena Nike. The bronze statue of Athena, forged from the spoils of Marathon, towered above the Acropolis.

Below the Acropolis was the concert hall, the Odeion of Pericles, the Theater of Dionysus and SE toward the Ilissus River the huge Temple of Olympian Zeus 354 by 135 feet and 90 feet tall, one of the largest temples in antiquity.

18:1-22. SECOND TOUR—CORINTH

Founding the Church, 1-11. See 1 Cor 1—4 for Paul's own account. His ministry in this dissolute thriving metropolis was begun in spiritual and financial testing. There was no word from Silas or Timothy concerning the permanence of the work in Macedonia and little encouragement at Athens. What about Corinth? Paul's finding

Aquila and Priscilla, with whom he lodged and found employment as a tent weaver, was providential, 2-3. Claudius' decree about A.D. 49 resulted in Aquila becoming Paul's employee. Prosperous Corinth attracted numerous Jews. A stone inscribed "Synagogue of the Hebrews" was uncovered at the foot of the Propylaea. Paul's ministry to the Jews was rejected, so he turned to the Gentiles. The conversion of Justus and Crispus, 7-8, was a signal victory. Paul's encouraging vision from the Lord assured the success of the work in the city, 9-11.

Paul Before Gallio, 12-17. Gallio was proconsul, 12, in the summer of A.D. 51. This is now known from an important inscription found at Delphi in the form of a letter sent from Emperor Claudius containing a reference to Gallio "as Lucius Junius Gallio, my friend, and the proconsul of Achaia. . . ." The date of the letter is A.D. 52, and Gallio must have arrived earlier to take up his office in A.D. 51, since he had been in office long enough to have given the emperor information important to the people of Delphi. Paul's arrival in Corinth was still earlier, in A.D. 50. The Jewish charge against Paul, 13, was treated lightly by Gallio, 12-17. He was unconcerned in a Roman court about altercations over minutiae of Jewish practice. His decision was a judicious one that saved Paul from the rage of Jewish bigotry.

End of Second Tour, 18-22. Paul left Corinth by its seaport Cenchraea on the Aegean (c. autumn A.D. 51) for Syria. He landed at Ephesus and went on to Caesarea and to Jerusalem, and then back to Antioch.

CORINTH OF PAUL'S DAY

Corinth lay only one and a half miles from the narrow isthmus joining central Greece with the Peloponnesus. It was a great emporium with two seaports—Cenchraea on the E, and Lechaeum on the W. Sea cargoes were hauled overland across the strategic four-mile strip. This spared mariners the hazardous 200-mile jaunt around Cape Malea to the S.

The Corinth canal was not built till 1881-93, although Nero attempted such a venture in A.D. 66. Lust and material gain were two vices that plagued the city. Its brisk commercialism fostered one; the entrenched cult of Aphrodite fostered the other. The goddess of love (lust) had her temple above the Acrocorinth, served by more than a thousand religious prostitutes. Voluptuous and vicious forms of the goddess' worship made Corinth a notorious center of immorality (cf. the Corinthian letters, especially 1 Cor 5:1-5). Such terms as "to corinthianize," "Corinthian sickness," etc., were reminiscent of the moral debauchery of the city.

18:23—19:7. THIRD TOUR BEGUN— JOHN'S DISCIPLES

Beginning the Third Tour, 18:23. Paul visited and reported to his home church at Antioch the results of the second tour as he had done on the first trip (14:26-28), giving a permanent lesson for missionary method, 23.

Apollos at Ephesus, 18:24-28. Apollos was born in Alexandria, Egypt, 24, and although well-taught in the OT messianic Scriptures, 24, he knew only John's preparatory and introductory baptism, 25 (Mt 3:11; Mk 1:8; Lk 3:16) and nothing about the baptism of the Holy Spirit which occurred at Pentecost (Acts 1:5; 2:1 ff.). Aquila and Priscilla, carefully taught in the gospel by close association with Paul (18:2-3), expounded to him the way of God more accurately, 26, i.e., gave him precise teaching in the gift of the Holy Spirit, particularly how the believer is now baptized into Christ and His Body, the Church, the moment he believes in Christ.

Apollos' Disciples Become Christians, 19:1-7. When Paul came to Ephesus, he found certain disciples of Apollos, 1. These disciples, because of Apollos' limited knowledge, knew nothing of the giving of the Holy Spirit (see note on Jn 7:39), nor of the ministries He undertakes for every believer. Paul's question is correctly rendered, "Did you receive the Holy Spirit *when ye believed*?"2. The trouble was not that the Ephesian disciples did not believe. It was *what* they believed, i.e., John's introductory and now superseded message of the coming Spirit. As a result of John's limited message, the disciples did not even know "that the Holy Spirit was," 2 (cf. the same idiom in Jn 7:39). Now that the Spirit *had* come, Paul proclaimed Jesus Christ and a finished redemption, 4-5. The result of faith in the gospel was that "the Holy Spirit came on them," which means they were introduced to NT salvation. The speaking in tongues, 6, was a sign to the large Jewish element at Ephesus that these Jewish men were admitted to gospel privilege. (Cf. notes on 11:1-18.)

19:8-41. THIRD TOUR—EPHESUS

Paul's Powerful Ephesian Ministry, 8-22. Paul first ministered in the synagogue, 8, then in the school of Tyrannus, 9, who apparently was a Greek rhetorician. Probably busy at his loom from dawn till about 11 A.M., Paul rented the lecture hall for the rest of the day. The Greek *scholē* ("school"), 9, was a place for intellectual pursuits and instruction, and attained its finest use when Paul used it to teach Christ, the wisdom of God, 10. Paul's Spirit-empowered ministry of miraculous signs advertised the truth among "all who resided in Asia," 10, i.e., the Roman province of proconsular Asia. It also clashed with the demonism energizing the city's idolatry and its paganistically contaminated Judaism. The result was the exposé of Jewish exorcism, 13-17, and the demon control in apostate Judaism (Mt 12:43-45) that had rejected the Messiah as well as the witness of Stephen. The clash also with demon-energized paganism resulted in the wholesale destruction of occult literature for which Ephesus was famous, 19. These scrolls were the *Ephesia grammata*, a term familiar in the Graeco-Roman world for magical writings in general. These magical formulas were associated with mutterings of temple soothsayers, and constituted an industry in the city. Fifty thousand drachmas of silver (about 9,200 gold dollars) was a large sum for those times, 19.

Clash with the Cult of Diana, 23-41. The religious life of Ephesus centered around the worship of the fertility goddess Artemis or Diana, Magna Mater (the Great Mother), worshiped in a temple that was one of the seven wonders of the ancient world. Paul's success at Ephesus was so great that the cult of Artemis and its mighty temple were seriously affected, 25-27. Demetrius, apparently head of the silversmith guild or union, manufactured miniatures of the temple and the goddess. The rioters rushed to the theater, well-known from archaeology and inscriptional reference. The crowd's yell, "Great is Diana of the Ephesians," 28, is archaeologically corroborated. The title "great" for a deity was common in antiquity. Many images and other objects of Artemis have been found and references to them occur in inscriptions.

The town clerk (*grammateus*) is known from nonbiblical sources to have been an important administrative official in the city, 35-41. He drafted decrees submitted to the popular assembly and acted as chairman of popular meetings, often held in the theater. Such an authoritative voice was successful in quelling the riot.

When the town clerk called the city of Ephesus "the temple keeper" (*neokoros*) of Diana, 35, he was using a commonly attested term both for individuals and cities as temple keepers to a god. The crowd in the theater was called "an assembly" (*ecclesia*), 32, 39. This term also was used popularly, and frequently occurs on inscriptions from Ephesus. The designation "Asiarchs," 31 (RSV), was an honorific title given civic benefactors in the Roman province of Asia.

THE CITY OF EPHESUS

Ephesus in Paul's day was the metropolis of proconsular Asia and vied with Alexandria of Egypt and Antioch of Syria among the top three cities of the East. Its ruins located at the mouth of the Cayster

River three miles from the Aegean have been carefully explored and excavated. Its dredged harbor gave the city access by sea, and its easy connection with interior Asia by interlacing highways brought it commercial prosperity by land as well. The population has been estimated at 250,000.

EPHESUS AND THE WORSHIP OF ARTEMIS

The worship of Artemis was the most distinctive source of Ephesus' prestige. The temple of Artemis was called the Artemesion. This vast edifice was 340 feet long, 160 feet wide and was decorated with 100 columns more than 55 feet high. Richly adorned with treasures of art, the temple was also a bank, an asylum for fugitives and the center of an elaborate cult. It was located between two hills, Ayasoluk (Seljuk) and Mt. Pion.

The discovery of the long-buried temple is an epic in archaeological research. Excavations and search began May 2, 1863, but not till December 31, 1869, at a depth of 20 feet, was the white marble pavement of the temple itself uncovered. During the next five years the fabulous finds that now adorn the Ephesian Gallery of the British Museum were dug up, including such exquisite works of art as Hercules struggling with the Queen of the Amazons, as well as hundreds of ritual inscriptions dealing with the cult. Later excavations (1904-5) uncovered a treasure trove of rich deposits of the goddess found under the pedestal which held the image of the deity.

EPHESUS AND OTHER ARCHAEOLOGICAL DISCOVERIES

Continuous archaeological exploration has revealed the long checkered history of the city from its founding about 1044 B.C. The great theater of Paul's day, where the populace rioted, was situated in the hollow slope of Mt. Pion, and could accommodate about 24,500 spectators. Present-day ruins represent a reconstruction after Paul's time.

The chief street of Ephesus called the "Arkadiane," marble-paved and monumented, was gorgeously colonnaded, shop-lined, and connected with the harbor by the beautiful Harbor Gate. The Greek agora (marketplace) lay S and SW of the theater. The larger Roman forum was situated N of the Arkadiane. The Magnesian Gate lay in the SE part of the city, NW of which was the odeum or lyric theater. Southeast of the Artemesion was the so-called Cave of the Seven Sleepers. Numbers of Christian churches of a later period attest the effectiveness with which Christianity took hold of the city. These include Justinian's Church of St. John and the double Church of the Virgin Mary.

CHAPTER 20. THIRD TOUR—
MACEDONIA TO MILETUS

Last Visit to Greece, 1-6. After leaving Ephesus Paul returned first to Macedonia, revisiting the churches planted there, 1-2. He then went on to Greece, where he stayed three months. From Corinth he apparently wrote the Epistle to the Romans. He planned to observe the Passover at Jerusalem. Discovery of a plot to kill him, probably as the ship was about to sail from Corinth's eastern port Cenchraea, 3, made him change his plan and return to Macedonia, celebrating the Passover and Unleavened Bread at Philippi. He then set sail from Neapolis to Troas (16:11-12), returning over the route by which he had entered Europe on the second tour.

From Troas to Miletus, 7-16. At Troas Paul had received his great vision to evangelize Europe (16:8-10). Here the incident of the sleeping Eutychus falling out of a window occurred, and the Christians are seen celebrating the Lord's Supper on the first day of the week, 7 (cf. 2:42). For physical exercise, relaxation and spiritual communion Paul chose to go by foot from Troas to Assos, normally a six- to eight-hour walk, likely by the road through a valley from the N. Assos was a beautiful town on a high hill, with an admirable harbor sheltered by the island of Lesbos, occupying one of the most scenic sights in proconsular Asia. It has yielded rich archaeological treasures and numerous architectural remains, notably the Doric Temple of Athena. Mitylene, 14, the next stop, was the most important town of Lesbos, located on the eastern coast of the island. Chios and Samos, 15, picturesque islands in the Aegean Sea, were passed as the ship headed for Miletus, modern Palatia. Miletus was an important port at the mouth of the Maeander River, 17, vying in importance with Ephesus at the mouth of the Cayster. In the great pagan theater there an inscription reads, "Place of the Jews, who are also God-fearing," which shows the secularization of the Jews of the city.

Farewell to the Ephesian Elders at Miletus, 17-38. Paul's touching speech to them and through them to the Ephesian church was his third discourse thus far reported by Luke. The first was addressed to *Jews* in the synagogue at Pisidian Antioch (13:16-41). The second was addressed to *Gentiles* in Athens (17:22-31). The third was addressed to the *church* (20:18-35). It was a masterful testimony of a true servant of Christ utterly yielded to his Master, and a touching warning against false doctrine and false teachers. Verse 35 is a quote from Jesus not found in the Gospels.

CHAPTER 21. END OF THIRD TOUR— ON TO JERUSALEM

From Miletus to Caesarea, 1-14. Coos and Rhodes, 21, are islands in the southernmost Aegean Sea NE of the island of Crete. Rhodes was both the name of the island and its capital city in the NE extremity of the island where Paul gazed upon one of the seven wonders of the world—the colossus of Helios, the sun-god, towering 105 feet above the fine harbor of the city. Strabo, the Greek geographer, lauded Rhodes' harbor, streets and walls. Patara was the seaport of Lycia, near the mouth of the Xanthos River, 1-2, a mecca for trading ships, a center of Apollo worship, and now a rich site for archaeological ruins. A triumphal arch reads: "Patara the metropolis of the Lycian nation." For Cyprus, 3, see notes on 13:4-12. At Tyre, 4-6, believers warned Paul of approaching trouble. This ancient city-state was a free city till 65 B.C. when it was annexed to Rome. Ptolemais is modern Acre, near Haifa, OT Accho (Jud 1:31). At Caesarea, capital of the province of Judea and contiguous regions, Paul was entertained at the home of Philip the evangelist, one of the seven deacons (6:1-7; 8:5-12). Agabus (11:28) imitated OT prophets in performing a symbolic act, 10-12 (cf. Isa. 20:2-6). Caesarea was a magnificent Hellenistic town (see ch. 10). The fine harbor was called Port of Herod in honor of the city's builder, Herod the Great.

Paul in Jerusalem, 15-40. The apostle's success among the Gentiles was narrated to James and the elders, 17-20. But a crisis came. Paul conformed to Judaism, 23-26, to allay suspicions of Jewish believers zealous for the law. The result was a strange sight: the apostle who had taught deliverance from the law in union with Christ (cf. Gal 1—2; Rom 6—7) was back in the temple going through dead ritual which was ended by the death of Christ. The result was disastrous. He was arrested and taken prisoner. Agabus' prophecy was fulfilled. But in it all the apostle showed his tremendous love and concern for his Jewish kinsmen and proved that what he declared in Rom 9:1-5 were not idle words, spoken for mere rhetorical effect.

ARCHAEOLOGY AND PAUL'S ARREST

Had the charge been true that Paul had brought Gentiles into the temple, i.e., into the court of Israel in the inner precincts, to which only Jewish men who were not priests or Levites were admitted, it would have constituted a capital offense. On this point even Roman authorities were so conciliatory of Jewish scruples that they permitted the death penalty for this offense, even when infracted by a Roman citizen.

The warning notices in Greek at the gates to the inner courts read: "No alien may enter within the barrier and wall around the temple. Whoever is caught [violating this] is alone responsible for the death [penalty] which follows." One of these stones from Herod's temple was recovered in a cemetery in 1871. Another turned up near St. Stephen's Gate in 1935.

CHAPTER 22. PAUL'S DEFENSE BEFORE THE POPULACE

Paul Gives His Testimony, 1-21. He addressed the throng in Hebrew (Aramaic), 21:40, to show the Jews that their tongue was not alien to him, and to capture their attention. Gamaliel (5:34-37) was a famous rabbi, the grandson of Hillel, a Pharisee, 3. On Tarsus, 3, see note on 9:26-31. For Damascus, 5, see 9:20-25.

Paul Appeals to His Roman Citizenship, 22-30. The examination by scourging, 24, was not for punishment but to get evidence. A Roman citizen uncondemned was protected from this cruel practice (cf. notes on 16:37-38). In the reign of Claudius (A.D. 41-54) Roman citizenship was frequently purchased for a large sum of money, 28.

CHAPTER 23. PAUL'S DEFENSE BEFORE THE SANHEDRIN

Before the Sanhedrin, 1-10. The tribune set Paul before the supreme Jewish court, not to try him but to get evidence, 22:30. Ananias, 2, was high priest in the reigns of Claudius (A.D. 41-54) and Nero (A.D. 54-68). He was assassinated in A.D. 66. "Whitewashed wall" was an apt metaphor to apply to the hypocritical high priest, who broke Jewish law by commanding Paul to be struck even before he was proved guilty. It suggested a tottering partition whose rotten condition had been disguised by a generous coat of whitewash. Such undignified conduct obscured Paul's recognizing the high priest, 4-5 (cf. his quote of Ex 22:28). Paul used wit and humor, 6-10, even though hard pressed. Sadducees were rational critics who denied resurrection.

Plot to Kill Paul, 11-22. Paul was sustained in his trials by a vision of the Lord, 11; even in the face of the plot to kill him, 12-22.

Paul Sent to Caesarea, 23-35. On Caesarea see notes on ch. 10; 21:8. The third hour was 9:00 to 10:00 P.M. The large bodyguard for Paul, 23, shows the seriousness of the tumult against him and the plot to kill him. Felix the governor, 24, was appointed procurator of Judea by Claudius (A.D. 52). He was cruel and had little moral principle. The letter of Claudius Lysias, 26-30, has the epistolary flavor of the period. Herod's praetorium, 35, was the sumptuous palace built by Herod the Great to grace his Hellenistic city of Caesarea. It was taken over by the Romans and used as the headquarters of the Roman procurators of Palestine.

CHAPTER 24. PAUL BEFORE FELIX

Before Felix the First Time, 1-23. Ananias the high priest here appears again in a bad light in hiring the orator Tertullus, who made the charge against Paul before Felix, 2-9. "Sect of the Nazarenes," 5, refers to Christians as followers of Jesus of Nazareth, but the term does not occur elsewhere in early Christian literature. Paul's defense before Felix is given in 10-21. "The way," 14, 22, i.e., the true way of the Lord (Jn 14:6), was one of the first designations of Christianity (cf. 9:2). Verse 22 should read: "But Felix, having a rather accurate knowledge of the Way" (RSV).

Before Felix the Second Time, 24-27. Felix's wife Drusilla was sister of Herod Agrippa II and Bernice (25:13). Felix's behavior was similar to that of Herod Antipas (Mk 6:20). Concerning him Tacitus declared, "He exercised the power of a king with the mind of a slave" (*Annals* XII. 54). Felix's treatment of Paul's case well bears out this character analysis. He deliberately sacrificed duty and justice for his own selfish ambition. Paul had to languish in prison for two years or his account, 27.

CHAPTERS 25—26. PAUL BEFORE FESTUS AND AGRIPPA

Before Festus, 25:1-12. Porcius Festus was procurator A.D. 60-62. He showed the same compromising weakness, 9, as Felix. Paul, knowing the calamity of being turned over to a Jewish court, chose Caesar's tribunal, 9-10. He appealed to Roman justice in the person of the procurator. Festus decided the emperor himself should hear the matter. The apparent weakness of procuratorial government is seen in the conduct of Paul's case.

Paul Before Agrippa, 25:13—26:32. Agrippa, 13, was Herod Agrippa II (A.D. 50-93). He and his sister Bernice were children of Herod Agrippa I (cf. ch. 12). In an attempt to clarify the case, Festus enlisted Agrippa's aid. The audience in the beautiful hall of the praetorium was a glittering affair, 23-27. After hearing Paul's testimony again, 26:4-23, Festus' conclusion was that Paul was unbalanced but harmless, 24. Both Festus and Agrippa agreed Paul was guilty of no crime worthy of death or even imprisonment, 30-31. Agrippa's famous words, "Almost thou persuadest me to be a Christian," 28 (AV), are rended in RSV: "In a short time you think to make me a Christian!"

CHAPTER 27. PAUL'S JOURNEY TO ROME— CAESAREA TO MALTA

From Caesarea to Myra, 1-6. Paul's case was now out of the hands of the procurator of Judea. As a prisoner of Rome he had chosen to appeal to the emperor at Rome. Italy at this era had come to denote the entire Italian peninsula from the Alps on the N to the heel of the boot on the S, with the imperial city on the Tiber the governmental metropolis. The centurion commanded about 100 men, the basic unit of the Roman army. The Augustan band was the imperial cohort, one of the five cohorts stationed at or near the provincial capital. The term is attested in secular history. Caesarea was doubtless the port of embarkation. Sidon, 3, was on the Phoenician coast less than 70 miles N. This ancient Phoenician emporium had a Christian church and friends, whom Julius permitted Paul to visit. Cyprus, 4, brought a flood of memories of the first tour (13:4-13). The lee of Cyprus, 4 (RSV), was N and E of the island, since the westerly winds prevailed. Myra, 5, in Cilicia (modern Dembre) boasts imposing ruins today and was the maritime gateway to the eastern Mediterranean in early Christian times. There the centurion found an Alexandrian grain freighter bound for Italy and put Luke (indicated by the "we" passage) and Paul's party aboard.

From Myra to Crete, 7-12. Adverse winds made the 130-mile trip to Cnidus (a fine harbor) difficult and lengthy. The time of the fast (Oct. 5), 9, signalized that dangerous weather had set in, which could be expected after September 14. Phoenix, 12 (RSV), is probably Lutro, a harbor 34 miles W of Cape Matala in Crete; but Phineka, just W of Lutro on the other side of the peninsula of Muros, is likely the place.

The Storm, 13-44. This account is a classic of graphic precision and accuracy. The tempestuous NE gale which struck the ship, 14, was called by a hybrid Greek-Latin term *Euraquilo,* from *euros* ("east wind") and Latin *aquilo* ("north wind"), i.e., an east by northeast wind. Clauda, 16 (modern Ghaudo, Gozzo), is an island some 23 miles SE to the leeward. The Syrtis, 17 (RSV), were the shallow quicksands off the African coast W of Cyrene. Paul displayed faith and moral strength in the terrible ordeal, 21-26, and was strengthened by God through an angel. The distance from Clauda to Malta is

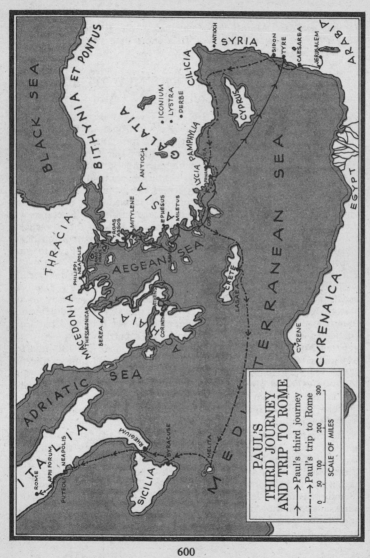

PAUL'S
THIRD JOURNEY
AND TRIP TO ROME

→ Paul's third journey
-·-·-· Paul's trip to Rome

SCALE OF MILES

0   50 100   200   300

476 miles, and the ship's forward progress averaged about one and a half miles per hour. By midnight of the fourteenth day the ship would be less than three miles from St. Paul's Bay on Malta. The sea of Adria, 27, was the central portion of the Mediterranean bounded by Italy on the N, Sicily on the W, the Cyrene coast of Africa on the S and Crete on the E. The Gulf of Adria was the smaller sea between Italy and Greece.

28:1-16. MALTA TO ROME

Paul in Malta, 1-10. Melita, 1, is the Greek name of Malta, S of Sicily in the mid-Mediterranean. Melita, a Phoenician word meaning "escape," was adopted by later Greeks from early Phoenician sailors to whom this island had often proved a haven of escape. The natives ("barbarians" in the sense of speaking a Punic dialect from Phoenician ancestors, not uncivilized), 2, welcomed the bedraggled victims of shipwreck. Publius ("first man"), 7-8, was the propractor's immediate subordinate in Malta, since Malta was under the province of its propraetor Sicily, only 60 miles away. Paul's experience with the viper was providential. His healing of Publius' father and others gave the apostle opportunity to show his gratitude for Publius' kindness, 7-9. Maltese fever, due to an organism in goats' milk, is a notorious sickness on the island.

Malta to Puteoli, 11-13. Another ship of Alexandria, doubtless also a grain freighter, had been forced to winter in Malta, probably in the harbor of Valetta. Around March 5, with the opening of the navigation season, Paul sailed for Sicily, 11. "The Twin Brothers," Castor and Pollux, were worshiped by sailors. As legendary sons of Zeus, they were patrons of distressed mariners. Connected with the constellation Gemini, the Twins, the two chief stars being Castor and Pollux, if glimpsed in a storm, were considered harbingers of good fortune. Syracuse, 12, was described by Cicero as "the greatest of the Greek cities and the most beautiful of all cities" (*In Verrein* IV, 52). Rhegium, 13, was on the toe of Italy (modern Reggio di Calabria), across the strait of Messina, some six miles from Messina on the Sicilian side. Puteoli, 13, is modern Pozzuoli near Neapolis (Naples). In Paul's time, Puteoli was the gateway to Rome for large grain ships before Ostia was dredged sufficiently a little later to become Rome's port, supplanting Puteoli.

Puteoli to Rome, 14-16. The first Augusteum (temple of the imperial cult) was located at Puteoli. Little remains of the old port city, except ruins of the mole where Paul first stepped on Italian soil and the amphitheater where Nero performed as an actor. The

601

Forum of Appius, 15, was 43 miles from Rome. Here an official welcoming party of Roman Christians greeted Paul. Three Taverns, 15, was 33 miles from Rome. Both were on the famous Appian Way which Paul had taken to Capua, from which point it was 132 miles to Rome. Some of the delegation were so eager to meet the apostle they came the extra ten miles to the Forum of Appius.

28:17-31. PAUL IN ROME

Paul Contacts the Jews, 17-22. He doubtless entered by the Porta Capena. At last he was in the world's capital. Although a prisoner, he trusted for an open door to all parts of the empire (cf. Rom 15:23-28). His great love for his kinsmen the Jews was demonstrated. Despite their terrible treatment of him in many parts of the East and especially in Jerusalem, his concern went out to them in Rome (Rom. 9:1-5). These Jews desired to hear his views.

Final Jewish Rejection of the Gospel, 23-31. This is the last demonstration in Acts of the principle "to the Jew first." Paul's "chain," 20, was a proof of his love for Israel; but here in Rome the final crisis was reached. Rejection of the message of him who was such a trophy of grace and who manifested such love toward Israel could result only in judgment. What insight and wisdom were revealed as Paul opened up "the kingdom of God," 23, the new order for the age as it affected the Gentiles particularly. He expounded from Moses and the prophets, 23. Unbelief caused Paul to quote Isa 6:9-10 and to announce the outgoing of the gospel to Gentiles (cf. 13:46; 18:6). This final appeal to Jews in the world's capital constituted a scene of immense significance. It was a signal that the new age was fully established and God's purpose for it, to visit the Gentiles, fully launched (cf. 15:14-15).

ROME OF PAUL'S DAY

Size of the City. In Paul's day Rome was the greatest city in the world. An inscription discovered at Rome's seaport Ostia in 1941 gives the population of the capital as 4,100,000 in A.D. 14. Although this figure is more than three times the usual estimate, it at least gives an idea of the vast size of the metropolis on the Tiber. Most of these teeming millions lived in large tenement houses, multistoried, called *insulae*. The wealthy lived in *domi*, with rooms opening on an inner court.

Palaces and Temples. The forum was a maze of exquisite temples and altars. The Palatine Hill was graced with the palaces of the emperors, notably the house of Augustus' wife Livia, with its superb murals, and the fabulous palace of Nero, which sprawled to the foot of the Esquiline and was one of the wonders of the empire. The Temple of Apollo and the Temple of Cybele also adorned the Palatine. Innumerable temples graced the city, such as those of Jupiter, Augustus, Saturn, and the Divine Julius.

Avenues and Hills. Built on seven hills, the city was famous for its roads and scenic avenues which interwove among the hills and along the Tiber. The more famous hills were the Palatine, the Esquiline, the Coelian, Aventine, and Capitoline. Famous roads and avenues, often 15 to 20 feet or more in width, opened up into the heart of the city. These included the Via Appia, Via Flaminia, Via Nomentana, Via Salaria and Via Pinciana, Via Ostensis, Via Latina, Via Labicana and Via Tiburtina.

Theaters and Places of Pleasure. The Rome of Paul's day was given to pleasure. "Bread and circuses" were the concern of the populace, according to Juvenal. Holidays amounted to 159 a year, with 93 supplied with public spectacles at government expense. Famous circuses included the mammoth Circus Maximus, enlarged to seat some 200,000 in Nero's time. Others were the famous Circus of Caligula, Circus Flaminius and the Circus of Nero, so-called.

Theaters of Paul's day included Pompey's Theater (55 B.C.) seating 10,000, Theater of Balbus (13 B.C.) seating 8,000, Theater of Marcellus (11 B.C.) seating 14,000. Amphitheaters such as the Colosseum, except that on the Campus Martius (29 B.C.), date after Paul's time. Rome rapidly degenerated and bloody orgies became common from Nero's day on.

Gardens and Public Parks. Numerous recreation areas dotted the city. In the Vatican district the estates of Domitia, Nero's aunt, were fabulous and became known as Nero's Gardens. Sumptuous public baths (*thermae*) were also common. Many of these with impressive ruins date after Paul's time, such as the Thermae of Titus, the Thermae of Trajan and the Thermae of Diocletian.

Paul's Life

Early Life

Born in Tarsus (Acts 22:3), *c.* A.D. 10
Educated in Judaism (Acts 22:3), A.D. 20-30
Saw Stephen's death (Acts 7:58), *c.* A.D. 35
Persecuted Christians (Acts 9:1-2), A.D. 35-36
Conversion near Damascus (Acts 9:3-18), A.D. 37
Sojourn in Arabia (Gal 1:17), A.D. 37-39
Visit to Jerusalem (Acts 9:26-29), A.D. 39

Return to Tarsus (Acts 9:30), A.D. 39
Brought to Antioch (Acts 11:25-26), A.D. 43

First Tour

Cyprus crusade (Acts 13:4-12), A.D. 45
Perga (Acts 13:13)
Pisidian Antioch (Acts 13:14-50), A.D. 46
Iconium (Acts 13:51—14:5)
Lystra (Acts 14:6-19)
Derbe (Acts 14:20)
Return to Lystra, Iconium, Pisidian Antioch
    (Acts 14:21-24), A.D. 47
Perga, Attalia (Acts 14:25), A.D. 47
Syrian Antioch (Acts 14:26-28), A.D. 47-50
Jerusalem Council (Acts 15), A.D. 50

Second Tour

Antioch by land through Syria and Cilicia
    (Acts 15:41), A.D. 50
Derbe and Lystra (Acts 16:1-5)
Phrygia and Galatia (Acts 16:6)
Troas, Samothrace, Neapolis, Philippi
    (Acts 16:8-40)
Thessalonica (Acts 17:1-9)
Berea (Acts 17:10-14)
Athens (Acts 17:15-34)
Corinth (Acts 18:1-17)
    1 and 2 Thessalonians
Ephesus, Caesarea, Jerusalem (Acts 18:18-22)
Return to Antioch (Acts 18:22), A.D. 53 or 54

Third Tour

Galatia and Phrygia (Acts 18:23), A.D. 54
Ephesus (Acts 19:1-41), A.D. 54-57
    1 and 2 Corinthians, Romans, Galatians
Macedonia and Achaia (Acts 20:1-5), A.D. 57
Troas (Acts 20:6-12), A.D. 58
Miletus (Acts 20:13-38)
Journey to Jerusalem (Acts 21:1-17), A.D. 58
Arrested in Jerusalem (Acts 21:27-36), A.D. 58

Prisoner and Death

Prisoner at Caesarea (Acts 23:23—26:32), A.D. 58-60
Journey to Rome (Acts 27), A.D. 60
Arrival in Rome (Acts 28:16), A.D. 61
First imprisonment, A.D. 61-63
    Prison epistles: *Philemon, Colossians, Ephesians,
    Philippians*

Release, A.D. 64-67 (?)
  1 Timothy, Titus
Spain (?), Crete (Tit 1:5)
Asia (2 Tim 4:13)
Macedonia (1 Tim 1:3)
Greece (2 Tim 4:20)
Second arrest (?), A.D. 67
  2 Timothy
Martyrdom, A.D. 68

THE EPISTLES OF PAUL

Probable Order	Approximate Date
1 Thessalonians	A.D. 52
2 Thessalonians	A.D. 53
1 Corinthians	A.D. 55
2 Corinthians	A.D. 56
Romans	A.D. 57
Galatians	A.D. 58
Philemon	A.D. 61-62
Colossians	A.D. 61-62
Ephesians	A.D. 61-62
Philippians	A.D. 62
1 Timothy	A.D. 64-66
Titus	A.D. 64-66
2 Timothy	A.D. 64 or 67

DISTINCTIVE CHARACTER OF PAUL'S EPISTLES

The Pauline epistles present the calling, hope and destiny of the Church of Jesus Christ. In the four Gospels the person and work of Christ are presented historically, eventuating in our Lord's death, resurrection and ascension. In the Acts the result of these historical events is traced in the founding and growth of the church. In the Pauline epistles the *doctrinal* revelation and *theological* significance of all these events are expounded.

To Paul was given the disclosure of God's heretofore hidden purpose (Eph 3:9) for this present era between the ascension of Christ and His return. This involves the calling out principally from the Gentiles a people for God's name to be the Body and the Bride of Christ (cf. Acts 15:14-15). In Mt 16:18 our Lord had preannounced this divine purpose concerning the church. However, the how, why and when of this new spiritual entity, as well as its position, relationships, duties and destiny were wholly unexplained. To Paul was given the distinctive revelation of these matters.

To Paul also was given the revelation of the doctrinal meaning of the cross and salvation by faith *alone* through grace (Eph 2:8-10). By him the gospel of God's grace was fully expounded in the great doctrines of justification, sanctification and glorification (Rom 1—8) as these affect every believer, including the Jew (Rom 9—11), and also as they relate to the law of Moses (Gal 1—6).

ROMANS

The Revelation of the Gospel of God

Importance. Romans is the greatest and most influential of all Paul's epistles, the first great work of Christian theology. This doctrinal exposition of the meaning of the cross of Christ has had an immense effect on the thought of the West from Augustine's time on. It was the bulwark of the Reformation, the great corrective against the errors of Romanism, the protective against modern cultism. The divinely revealed gospel of God in Romans is the antidote for the babel of false gospels of our day or any day. Called the profoundest and yet the simplest document, the epistle is for sinful mankind *as it is*. It points out how lost, helpless humanity can find deliverance in Christ and what this deliverance includes. All focuses in Christ's cross. Christ's redemption is shown to be humanity's *only* hope. But what a glorious, exhilarating hope!

Place and Occasion of Writing. The epistle was apparently written from Corinth after the contribution Paul had been collecting from the Gentile churches of Greece and Asia Minor had been completed (Rom 15:25-27; cf. 1 Cor 16:3-5). He was waiting to go to Jerusalem with it, intending afterward to visit Spain (Rom 15:28), and on the way to visit the church at Rome. He wrote his doctrinal masterpiece to the members of the church in the Imperial City to announce his intention to visit them and to enlist their prayer and interest in evangelizing the West. The epistle is dated about A.D. 57, toward the end of the third missionary tour.

Outline

Doctrinal, Ch. 1—8

  Introduction, 1:1-17
  The Sin of Man, 1:18—3:20
  Justification of the Sinner, 3:21—5:21
  Sanctification of the Believer, 6:1—8:39

Dispensational (the Case of Israel), Ch. 9—11

  God's Past Purpose for Israel, 9:1-33
  God's Present Purpose for Israel, 10:1-21
  God's Future Purpose for Israel, 11:1-36

607

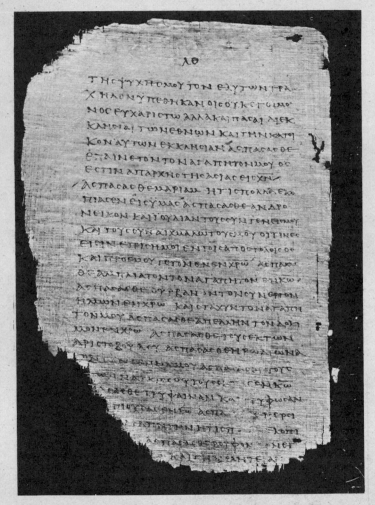

A page of Romans from a Beatty-Michigan manuscript dating about A.D. 200. (*Courtesy UML*)

1:1-17.   THE THEME—THE GOSPEL OF SALVATION

Paul and His Gospel, 1-6. The author of the epistle presents him-self as "servant" in his personal relation to Jesus Christ, "apostle" in his official relation to Him, "separated unto the gospel of God," 1, and in relation to the message committed to him. The "gospel" or good news he expounds, 1-6, is *divine* in origin, "the gospel of God," 1; *promised* in the OT prophetic Scriptures, 2; *centered* in the incarna-tion, death and resurrection of the Son, 3-4; *accredited* and *authen-ticated* by the Son for worldwide proclamation, 5-6.

Paul and His Readers, 7-17. The salutation of grace and peace is made to his readers at Rome, 7, with thanksgiving for them, 8; petition concerning his proposed trip to them, 10; desire to minister to them, 11-15; and conviction that "the gospel of Christ" presented to them is worthy of pride even at imperial Rome, 16, because it is effective to save and is a revelation of the divine righteousness on the basis of faith (cf. Hab 2:4). On Rome of Paul's day see note on Acts 28:17-31. In Paul's statement of his theme, 16-17, the great words of the epistle emerge—"the gospel," "power of God," "salvation," "faith" (believe), "revealed," "righteousness," "live." Paul's comprehension of the glory of the gospel was the basis for his enthusiasm for it. "From faith to faith," 17, means faith is the sole condition of salvation.

1:18—2:16.   THE REVELATION OF MAN'S SIN—
THE GENTILE

God's Wrath Against Man's Sin Revealed, 1:18-32. This divine wrath is a revelation God has made. It is not based on fallen man's faulty reasonings as to his own supposed goodness. The divine arraignment of the fallen race is on two counts: man's guilty aban-donment of God's glory, 18-23; and his progressive moral declen-sion, 24-32. Hence man is under God's wrath, 18, i.e., under the necessary expression of divine displeasure against human sin because of God's infinite holiness. The reason: (1) man changed the divine glory into idolatry, 19-23; result, God gave him up to uncleanness,

609

24; (2) man changed the truth of God into a lie, 25; result, God abandoned him to gross immoralities, 26-27; (3) man forsook the knowledge of God, 28; result, God abandoned him to a base mind and perverted conduct, 29-32. What a horrible picture of human depravity!

The Sin of the Gentile Revealed, 2:1-16. Immediately the Gentile begins to plead "not guilty" to God's indictment of his sin, seeking to gloss over it with the claim of morality. This claim is refuted because unsaved man really has no consistent morality. He does the things he condemns, 1. The divine sentence, 16, in contrast to man's judgment, is on the basis of truth, 2-5; according to deeds, 6-10; without personal bias, 11-15; and in accord with the gospel, 16.

2:17—3:20. THE REVELATION OF MAN'S SIN— THE JEW

The Sin of the Jew Revealed, 2:17—3:8. Immediately the Jew under the Mosaic law also begins to plead "not guilty," attempting to gloss over his sin with the claim of religion, boasting in his spiritual privileges, 17-20. Yet his unchanged life nullifies any such claim, 21-29, netting him only increased condemnation, 21-22, as he causes God's name to be evilly spoken of by the Gentiles, 23-24. Being victimized by mere ritualism, 25-26, he thereby abrogates any claim of superior religious standing, 27-29.

Several Jewish objections are offered, 3:1-8. Has the Jew then no profit or advantage, 1? The answer is, "Much in every way," chiefly in the fact "that unto them were committed the oracles of God," 2. They were not made a mere Bible depository, but as Jews God gave them promises *peculiarly their own, and yet to be fulfilled* (cf. ch. 9—11). But does not Jewish unbelief nullify God's faithfulness, 3? By no means, these promises will yet be fulfilled (cf. 11:29). There *is* a future for Israel based upon OT covenants and promises made to the nation (ch. 11). The unbelief of some will not make God untrue to His promises to the nation, 4 (cf. Ps 51:4). Then another Jewish objection is raised, 5. "But if our wickedness serves to show the justice of God . . . [is not] God unjust to inflict wrath on us?" (RSV). Paul's answer, "Then how could God judge the world?" 6. For the world is unrighteous, too, and sin reveals God's love toward it. Such false reasoning would rule out God's righteous judgment toward Jew or Gentile.

The Universality of Sin, 3:9-20. Man's condemnation under sin is summarized. God's case is proved, 9. "All," both Jew and Gentile, are "under sin." Sin is demonstrated to be universal, 10-12, and total,

13-18, involving man's speech, 13-14; his actions and deeds, 15-17; and his vision, 18. The final verdict, 19-20, is that all opposition is removed, 19, no flesh is justified, and the whole world is found guilty before God, 20.

3:21-31. JUSTIFICATION DEFINED

Justification Involves the Revelation of God's Righteousness, 21-23. This righteousness which God's infinite holiness requires is apart from the law, 21; it is by grace, yet is witnessed to by the law and the prophets, i.e., the OT Scriptures. From Genesis to Malachi the grace of Christ is prefigured by symbol, sacrifice, promise and prophecy. This righteousness is not only apart from the law of Moses, 21; it is made available to all, 22, and needed by all, 23.

Justification Involves the Imputation of God's Righteousness, 24-28. Justification is God's act of declaring the sinner righteous, so that the divine righteousness is judicially reckoned to his account. This divine transaction is on the basis of *grace,* or the unmerited favor of God the Father revealed in Christ, which provides it, 24; *blood,* or the death of Christ, which procures it, 25-27; *faith,* produced in man by the Spirit, which appropriates it, 28. This all-sufficient basis for the sinner's being justified, 26, strips away all ground for human boasting, 27.

Objections to Justification Answered, 29-31. Justification is a universal remedy for sin. By this means God justifies *all,* both Jew and Gentile, 29-30. Justification honors the law, 31. How it establishes the OT Scriptures is seen in ch. 4.

CHAPTER 4. JUSTIFICATION ILLUSTRATED

By God's Dealings with Abraham, 1-5. In defending justification from the OT Scriptures, the apostle shows it was a well-established principle in God's dealings with men as far back as Abraham, so that it was not some novel idea the apostle had invented. Moreover, it was in operation prior to the Mosaic law, so it is not dependent upon legal observance. Abraham was so justified, 3 (cf. Gen 15:6), and righteousness was "reckoned" or "imputed" to him, 4 (cf. Phm 18), on the basis of grace, 4-5.

By the Case of David, 6-8. David was not only devoid of the works of righteousness but loaded down with sins of adultery and murder. Out of this awful plight he could claim forgiveness because he was justified by faith (Ps 32:1-2).

By the Case of Abraham Resumed, 9-25. He was justified by faith, not by religious rites, 9-12, before he was circumcised, 9-10. His subsequent circumcision was indicative of the acceptance with God he already enjoyed, 11-12, so that he might be "the father of all them that believe," 11. Abraham was justified by faith, not by legal observances, 13-25. The promise given to him was long before the giving of the law, 13. This was a necessity because of the intent and effect of the law, 14-15. Moreover, the law was confined to one nation, but the promise of faith through Abraham extends to all, 16-21 (cf. Gen 17:5). Through Isaac, the child of faith, came Christ, the Justifier. He was "delivered for our offenses" and "raised again for our justification," 25. His resurrection, ascension and intercessory session at God's right hand (cf. Heb 9:24) are the proof that our sins are remitted. Because His work is completely accepted by the Father, we stand fully acquitted in Him.

5:1-11. THE RESULTS OF JUSTIFICATION

Our Present Possessions, 1-5. "Therefore being justified by faith, we have *peace*," i.e., reconciliation or a state of harmony with God, 1. We have *"access* in this grace," 2. We also have joyful *"hope* of the glory of God," 2, since that hope is based on what *God* has done for us, not what we may or may not do for Him. This certainty of our destiny in Christ gives spiritual backbone in suffering, 3; for we realize that tribulation for Christ cannot be futile in the life to come, or unrewarding in its beneficial effects in this life, 3-5.

Our Future Security, 6-11. Justification gives conviction of security. It gives assurance of salvation by contrasting what we were *before* being justified, 6, 8, 10, with what we are *after* being justified, 9-11. The climax is a twice-repeated "much more . . . we shall be saved," 9-10. "Saved from wrath," 9, expresses what we have been saved *from.* "Saved by his life," 10, expresses what we have been saved *to*—a life of holiness and power through the manifestation of His resurrection life in us (8:11). The word "atonement," 11, is reconciliation, which is manward, and removes our enmity toward God. It is that which we need and receive in justification.

5:12-21. JUSTIFICATION SUMMARIZED
CONDEMNATION AND JUSTIFICATION CONTRASTED

	Condemnation	Justification
Source	From one: first Adam	From one: Second Adam

	Condemnation	*Justification*
Extent	To all: the many	To all (by faith): the many
Cause	Disobedience Trespass	Obedience Grace
Nature	Judgment deserved	Free gift undeserved
Measure	Abounded	Abounds much more
Result	Sin Death	Righteousness Life

The gracious results of justification are brought to a climax in this incisive contrast to what the sinner was in condemnation and what he becomes in justification. This prepares the way for the higher subject of sanctification.

The New Headship. The concept of "in Adam" relates one to the fallen race in sin. "In Christ" is the new position in the "Second Adam," the Head of the new creation. This new position is the ground for a holy life as unfolded in ch. 6. It is an effective answer to the objection that justifying grace leads to looseness of life.

6:1-11. SANCTIFICATION—THE METHOD

Positional Sanctification by Union with Christ, 1-10. The problem raised against God's method of saving men by justifying grace, 1, is answered, 2-11. Similar objections are dealt with in 6:15; 7:7; 7:13. The first objection is: A wholly-by-grace salvation will encourage men to go on living in sin, taking advantage of free, exhaustless grace as a wastrel son presumes upon a father's generosity. The answer given in verse 2 involves the principle of being cut off from sin by "death." In His birth Christ became identified with us, that we might become identified with Him in His death. This is effected by our union with Christ by the baptism of the Spirit, 3-4 (cf. 1 Cor 12:13), which places us in the Body (1 Cor 12:27) with Christ Himself the Head. This is the position of the justified believer, i.e., his status as God sees him and as he is in God's purpose.

This divinely administered baptism of the Spirit, of which water baptism is an outward symbol, constitutes us one with Christ in a Body that has passed through death, burial and resurrection into new life, 4. Thus we are no longer "in Adam" but "in Christ."

"Planted together," 5, means caused to grow together as a graft, so that life and nature merge into one. The "old man," 6, is what we were in Adam. The "body of sin" which was "destroyed," i.e., made inoperative, is the human body as it was enslaved by sin in its unjustified state in Adam. Verse 7 declares that "he that died is delivered from sin." Since this is the justified believer's position, 2-10, he is delivered from sin's domination and enabled to live a holy life in resurrection power, 8. He is united to the risen Christ, who won a judicial victory for him over sin in the flesh, 10 (cf. 8:3).

Experiential Sanctification by Knowledge and Faith, 11. Converting our position, i.e., what we are in God's sight, into possession, i.e., what we enjoy in our experience, is on a twofold basis: we must know what we are in our position in Christ, 2-10; and we must act in faith on what we know. "Reckon," 11, means keep on counting as true (present tense), a word of *faith* based on knowledge. As we count on the twin truth that we are "dead indeed to sin" and "alive unto God in union with Jesus Christ our Lord," our position becomes an experiential reality. Justified believers *are* "dead to sin" and "alive to God" unchangeably in their position. They become so in their experience only as they momentarily count upon their position in faith. This requires yielding, 13, to God's will.

THE BIBLE TEACHING ON SANCTIFICATION

Largely misunderstood and abused, sanctification (a setting apart for God's worship and service), as taught by the Scripture, is in three aspects: past, present, future. The following chart will illustrate.

6:12—7:6. SANCTIFICATION BY GRACE AND LEGALISM

Sanctification by Grace Dispenses with the Problem of Legalism, 6:12-23. The gospel of grace which Paul expounds *does not give license to sin,* 12-14. "Sin," personified as a master, "shall not exercise lordship over you, because you are not under law [the legal principle] but under grace [grace principle]," 14. Law says, "Do and live." Grace says, "Live and do," conferring blessed enablement so that deeds and fruit may follow.

The abuse of God's declaration that the believer is not under a principle of legalism, 15, is answered by the truth that not only does sanctification by grace not give license to sin, 14-15, but *actually provides freedom from sin,* 16-23. The servitude it delivers from and the freedom it gives are contrasted: *with regard to masters,* 16-20, and *with regard to results,* 21-23. The two masters, "Sin" personified,

Past Aspect of Sanctification	Present Aspect of Sanctification	Future Aspect of Sanctification
Positional (1 Cor 1:2, 30). *All* believers were so sanctified as saints, the youngest as well as the oldest, the most carnal as well as the most spiritual.	Experiential. Depends upon our knowledge of and faith in our position in Christ (Rom 6:1-11), converting our position into experience.	Final. When we see the Lord and are made like Him— sinless, sickless, deathless (1 Cor 4; 15:54; 1 Jn 3:2).
Static, unalterable, inseparable from justification, and the result solely of our union with Christ.	Progressive, changeable, depends upon yieldedness to God's will (Rom 6:13) and conformity to God's Word (Rom 12:2).	Eternal. Will result in our final state in eternity (Phil 3:21).
As God sees us in Christ (1 Cor 1:2, 30, with Phil 1:1, etc.).	As we are in our conduct (2 Thess 2:13).	As we shall be in glory (Rom 8:29; 1 Cor 15:49).

16, and God in Christ, are contrasted. The servitude is unto death, but the freedom is unto life. Men are either "slaves of sin" or "servants of righteousness." The *results* are either death, 21, with no fruit, or "fruit unto holiness" and "everlasting life," 22. The "wages of sin," death, 23, is contrasted with the "gift of God," eternal life, 23.

Sanctification by Grace Delivers from the Principle of Legalism, 7:1-6. In ch. 6 sin is viewed as a master to whom the sinner belongs as a slave. This bond is dissolved by death of the slave. In 7:1-6 the figure of the marriage bond is introduced to show the believer's relation to the legal principle. Sanctification by grace delivers from the legal principle *by the death of the believer,* 4a, and *by the marriage of the believer,* 4b. The illustration of the law of marriage simply points out that death dissolves legal obligation. The marriage bond is for life. Only the death of husband or wife annuls it. But in this case who dies? The law? Christ? The believer? Although Christ died, His death is not in view except as it effected the believer's death in union with Him. Therefore, the believer "died" and so becomes released from the legal principle by incorporation into the body of Christ, 4.

But the release of the believer from legalism by death is only half of Paul's illustration. The believer is now free to be "married to another," 4, that is, to Christ, the New Man, risen from the dead. But if we died, how can we be married? The point is that our union (in resurrection) is with the risen Lord, who has obtained through death and resurrection a bride akin to Himself (Eph 5:25-32). What a climax of Christian revelation! Married to the risen Christ! Sharing His past triumphs, His present life, His future glory! The Father has taken the hand of His Son and that of His child and joined them for time and eternity.

7:7-25. FALSE SANCTIFICATION—ITS DEFEAT

Sanctification by Grace and the Law, 7-14a. Another objection (cf. 6:1, 15; 7:13) arises. If the law arouses sin, 5, is it not sinful, 7? Paul dismisses this error with abhorrence and shows the good purpose of the law in revealing man's sin, 8-9. The law is blameless, 12. It is sin that is to blame. Just because the law cannot sanctify, but only reveals false sanctity, does not make it sinful, 9-11. So the law reveals sin to be sinful, 7-13, and condemns the carnal nature, 14.

False Sanctification by the Self-Effort of Legalism, 14b-24. Whether legalism is the law of Moses for the Jew or the general moral law of the non-Jew, sanctification cannot be realized by legalistic self-effort. A new standard of conduct is obtained. Not an external standard (law) to live up to, but an indwelling Person to please. Not self-occupation, but occupation with Christ. Not what I am in myself, but what I am in Him. Not I, but Christ. This is the struggle of self to live the Christian life. In this section the pronoun "I" occurs 38 times. "I" trying to sanctify itself is the reason for the dismal defeat here outlined. The story is "I" the new man attempting to live the Christian life, but defeated by "I" the old man. Portrayed is the struggle of the new nature over the old. The defeat is that of legalistic self-effort or false sanctification.

True Sanctification, 25. Victory alone is "through Jesus Christ our Lord." Not through suppression of the old nature (futile legalism); nor eradication (pure imagination), since if this were true one could not sin if he wanted to, for the new nature never sins (1 Jn 3:9). The answer is the deliverance which Christ has wrought, expounded in Rom 6 (see comments). Defeat is due to failure to realize and act upon our gracious position in Christ, converting it by faith into experiential reality.

8:1-25. TRUE SANCTIFICATION—ITS VICTORY

The New Law, 1-4. The victory is by knowing and acting on our position of grace in Christ and thus experiencing its power. This involves triumphant life in the Spirit. No objections are offered, no defeat appears in Rom 8. Basic to all victory is the assurance of "no condemnation" in our new position in Christ, 1. "Therefore" is cumulative of the truth presented in ch. 1—7. The words "who walk not after the flesh, but after the Spirit" obscure the radiant truth of verse 1, and are interpolated from verse 4, where they belong. The new "law of life," 2, is the Holy Spirit operating in the sphere of the believer's new position in Christ as a higher principle, counteracting and overcoming the lower "law of sin and death," producing righteousness and life. What the law of Moses, or any legal principle, was unable to do because of human sin, God accomplished through the incarnation of His Son, 3. He, through His sinless humanity, condemned sin as a master criminal and secured a judicial sentence against it. Accordingly, God can righteously undertake to fulfill the just requirements of the law in us through the gracious operation of the Holy Spirit, 4.

The New Victory, 5-25. The Holy Spirit takes over the conflict with sin, 5-13. The combatants are *the flesh,* mentioned 13 times in this general context, and *the Spirit,* mentioned 21 times. The Spirit supplants the "I" of ch. 7, and victory instead of defeat is the result. Proof is abundant that true sanctification is by grace through faith (6:1-11) which brings the power of the Spirit in victorious operation against the "flesh," i.e., sin working through the human body. The new victory brings also a new realization of sonship, 14-17. Not only does the believer become a child by birth, but a son by adoption (cf. Gal 4:5), with mature status and full legal rights; with guidance, 14; full filial fellowship, 15; assurance, 16; heirship and stamina to suffer, 17, in view of coming glory, 18-25. Creation itself will be delivered, 20-22. "The sons of God," 19, will be revealed with God's Son Jesus Christ. Our adoption, 23, is our future physical resurrection of which our present spiritual adoption is a pledge and prospect, 15. "Saved by hope," 24-25, is the future aspect of our salvation as we who are in Christ look toward the glory ahead, 14-23. Faith produces this hope. Without faith there is no such hope.

8:26-39. TRUE SANCTIFICATION—ITS POWER AND ASSURANCE

True Sanctification—Its Power in Prayer, 26-27. Acting on our position in Christ brings the power of the Spirit in the realm of our prayer life, enabling us to overcome our notable weaknesses in this area, making possible the Spirit's intercession *in* us on behalf of the saints according to God's will, 26-27. (Here the Holy Spirit prays *in* us. Cf. 33-34 where the Son intercedes *above* us, His "sons.")

True Sanctification—Its Assurance, 28-34. In these verses the Father provides *for* us. His providence includes "all things," 28, 32. "And *we know*. . . ." True sanctification gives assurance amid life's providences of God's unfailing purposes for good toward us. But the magic lens which enables us to see all things working together for our good is love. "To them that love God," 28. His love for us in Christ, 32, which gives us "all things," evokes our love for Him, enabling us to trust Him through trials. The basis for this assurance is His sublime purpose toward us spanning eternity. He foreknew us, 29*a*; predestined (foreordained) us to Christlikeness, 29*b*; called us, 30*a*; justified us, 30*b*; glorified us, 30*c*, the latter even put in the past tense to show the certainty and immutability of His age-spanning plans for us. The conclusion is, "God is for us!" Who then can be against us, 31? The grand proof of this is the sacrificial gift of His Son "for us all," 32. This supreme demonstration of His love in the greater realm is a guarantee that such love may be trusted to "freely give us all things," 32, for our good in this earthly sphere—to defend us, keep us safely, and bring us to Himself in glory, 33-34.

True Sanctification—Its Climactic Triumph, 35-39. So wonderful are the notes of triumph just sounded, 33-34, that the apostle breaks forth into ecstatic exultation. Man's awful condemnation (1:18—3:20), triumphed over by God's glorious justifying grace (3:21—5:21), logically leads up to the exultant triumph of sanctification (6:1—8:39). Marked is the note of the safety and security of the believer. The new life in Christ is inseparable from Christ, 35-39. Every possible type of experience that might be conceived of as separating from Christ is called up. The conclusion is ". . . *more than* conquerors through him who loved us," 37. Nothing in time or eternity can separate one from God's love manifested in Christ, 38-39. This is the dramatic and soul-thrilling climax to the grand exposition of "the gospel of God," 1:1. This is the summit where *true* sanctification leads.

9:1-13. GOD'S PAST PURPOSE IN ISRAEL—HER POSITION

Romans 9—11 is parenthetical. In the unfolding of the gospel of grace, what about the Jew? The gospel as "the power of God unto salvation to every one that believeth" had been announced in the apostle's theme (1:16) to be "to the Jew *first*." What about the Jews' rejection of Messiah at the cross as well as their rejection of the program "to the Jew first" (Acts 13:46)? Are the covenants and promises God made with His ancient people empty words? Has God failed them because they failed Him? How do they fit in to God's glorious plan of salvation (ch. 1—8)?

Israel's National Position, 1-5. Paul's deep love and intense anguish of heart for Israel are expressed, 1-3. His words are strikingly reminiscent of Moses' intercession (Ex 32:1-34) and recall our Lord's weeping over rebellious Jerusalem (Mt 23:37-39). The same Spirit that gripped the heart of Moses and that of our Lord for Israel gripped Paul's heart.

Now follows a statement of Israel's position as distinct from any other nation, 4-5. Eight distinguishing privileges are mentioned: (1) the adoption or sonship (Ex 4:22; Deut 14:1); (2) the glory—on Mt. Sinai and among the people in the holiest place (Ex 40:34-35; Ps 147:20); (3) the covenants—the *Abrahamic* (Gen 12:1-3; 13:14-17, etc.), the *Mosaic* (Ex 20—31), the *Palestinian* (Deut 29—30), the *Davidic* (2 Sam 7), the *new* (Jer. 31:31-33); (4) the law at Sinai; (5) service of the tabernacle; (6) the promises, the messianic kingdom, etc.; (7) fathers—the patriarchs to whom God revealed Himself; (8) Christ—born of Israel as her anointed Saviour-King and given as the world's Redeemer.

Israel's Spiritual Election, 6-13. God has not failed in Israel's unbelief, 6. This people is distinctively *His*. This truth is expounded as the basis of the absolute sovereignty of God over those who are so peculiarly His chosen ones. The spiritual remnant of the nation, 6-7, are the recipients of the promise, 8, descended from a supernaturally generated posterity through Isaac, 9. In addition, from among this line God makes a sovereign choice, selecting Jacob the younger, and setting aside Esau the elder, 10-13. The conclusion? Israel is His. He is sovereign over His people.

9:14-33. GOD'S PAST PURPOSE IN ISRAEL— HIS SOVEREIGNTY

An Objection Offered, 14. God's righteousness (justice) is challenged. Has Jewish unbelief placed God in the position of not being able to keep His word and agreements?

The Objection Answered—God's Righteous Sovereignty, 15-29. Since Israel is distinctively His, 6-13, cannot God do as He wishes with His *own*? Is He not free to show His mercy, 15-16, or power and wrath, 17-18, as the case may warrant in the divine wisdom? *His* is the clay. The divine Potter can make of it that which He sees fit, 21-24. Moreover, the Potter had proclaimed His purpose through the prophets, 25-29, to show that the Gentiles were to become "vessels of mercy," 25-26 (Hos 2:23; 1:10; cf. 1 Pet 2:10). At the same time the Jews were forewarned against becoming "vessels of wrath," 27-29 (cf. Isa 10:22-23 with Isa 1:9).

Israel's Rejection of God's Righteousness, 30-33. In His infinite wisdom and love the Potter selected the cross as the mold for His redemptive purposes. The Gentiles in faith accepted that mold and obtained the "righteousness of faith," 30. In contrast, Israel stumbled through unbelief, seeking legalistic righteousness by works, 31-33. Rejecting the principle of faith, even declared in their own Scriptures (Hab 2:4), they stumbled at the stumbling stone (cf. 1 Pet 2:8), plunging headlong out of their land to be weary wanderers over the earth ever since.

CHAPTER 10. GOD'S PRESENT PURPOSE FOR ISRAEL

Israel's Present Condition, 1-5. As individuals they need salvation, 1, which is the burden of Paul's heart (cf. 9:1-3). They are zealous, but ignorant of God's righteousness, 2-3 (cf. 3:21—5:11). They are busy seeking their own righteousness by law, and have bypassed God's righteousness, 3. "For Christ is the end [termination] of the law for [with a view to] righteousness to every one that believeth," 4.

Present Salvation for Both Jew and Gentile, 6-21. This requires no effort, 6-7, such as bringing Christ from above or from beneath. The righteousness of faith, which is judicially reckoned to all who trust Christ, has as its key words, 8, "believe," "confess," "call upon the Lord," 9-13. It results in salvation and is available to both Jew and Gentile without any distinction, 12. This divine plan for bringing God's righteousness to everyone, 14-15, involves the sending of men to preach, 15. People are to hear and believe, 14. Believing they are to call, and calling they are to be saved, 13. This method of gospel propagation renders man's unbelief inexcusable, 16-21. Faith is produced by hearing God's Word, 17, in the case of "all the earth" (the Gentiles), 18 (cf. Ps 19:4). Israel, from her Scriptures, should have known of the outgoing of this message to the Gentiles (Deut 32:21; Isa 65:1; cf. 42:6-7). While Gentiles have found God, 20, the Jews have rejected God's righteousness through disobedience and contrariness, 21 (cf. Isa 65:2).

CHAPTER 11. GOD'S FUTURE PURPOSE FOR ISRAEL

Israel's National Setting Aside Not Final, 1-10. God's faithfulness is guaranteed in a future restoration of the nation. The present setting aside of Israel in her national election is only temporary, 1, because: (1) Paul himself as a Jew was saved in this age, 1; (2) the Lord foreknew Israel's unbelief, 2; (3) God has always had a remnant of faithful believers as in Elijah's day, 2-4; (4) in this present age God has a saved remnant "according to the election of grace," 5. This remnant is composed of believing Jews who become one with Gentiles in the Body, the Church, and obtain the blessing, 6-10, while the rest of Israel is blinded and hardened in unbelief (cf. Isa. 29:10; Ps 69:22). Hence Israel's present blindness is only partial.

Israel's Present National Rejection Has a Divine Purpose, 11-24. (1) It has brought salvation to the Gentiles, 11, hence has been beneficial to the world. (2) The future restoration of the Jews will also bring untold world blessing even as their present rejection has, 11-15. (3) Gentile salvation will provoke Israel to jealousy, 11. (4) Their rejection serves as a warning to the Gentiles, 16-26. The "dough" and the "root" (Num 15:19-20; Jer 11:16-17) symbolize the patriarchs through whom Israel has been consecrated. The good olive tree prefigures Israel in covenant relation with God through Abraham (Gen 12:1-3), the root. The tree is ever green as the covenant is unchangeable. The broken-off branches represent the nation's unbelief. The wild olive graft represents Gentiles brought into spiritual privilege. Unless Gentiles cherish their privilege, like unbelieving Israel they will be broken off. God will graft back the real olive tree, Israel, when unbelief gives way to faith. Christendom will be judged in apostasy prior to Israel's restoration.

Restoration of the Nation Certain, 25-36. It is assured *by special revelation*, 25. A "mystery" is a truth once hidden but now revealed. This truth is that of Israel's partial blindness during this age, which is to last till "the fullness of the Gentiles" is effected, 25. This means the completion of God's purpose in calling out a people from the Gentiles in this age (Acts 15:14). The restoration of the nation is the *subject of prophecy*. The kingdom is to be restored to Israel, 26 (Acts 1:6; 15:15-17). All Jews living at the second advent will be saved when Christ the Deliverer shall come out of Zion, 26, as Isaiah predicted (Isa 59:20-21). The new covenant with converted Israel, 27, was foretold by Isaiah (27:9) and Jeremiah (31:31-37; cf. Heb 8:8; 10:16). The restoration of the nation is *according to the divine plan*, 28, and *the divine principle*, 29. Although she is temporarily hostile to the gospel, the election of Israel as a nation is irrevocable. God has not changed His mind about the covenants and promises made to the nation. The restoration of the people will constitute a *fulfillment of God's purpose*, 30-32, and *redound to God's glory*, 33-36.

CHAPTER 12. PRACTICAL CHRISTIAN SERVICE

The last five chapters constitute the practical part of the epistle. Now the doctrine of salvation is to be worked out in experience. Service is to be expressed in the outliving of the inliving Christ.

Christian Service and Self, 1-2. Self is to be sacrificed. The body is to be presented to God the Father. This is a privilege. "I beseech" expresses exhortation and responsibility. "Therefore" is logical because of God's salvation, ch. 1—11, and "the mercies of God" in redemption. The sacrifice is "living," involving our life. It is "holy, acceptable" because cleansed by Christ's blood. It is "reasonable" because of all that Christ has done for us. The results will not be a conforming to or fitting into the mold of the world, 2, but a change of mind so that we may know and prove the will of God, the only valid sphere of spiritual, God-glorifying service.

Christian Service and Gifts, 3-8. Exercise of spiritual endowments in service calls for humility and proper evaluation of oneself, 3. In relation to the Church, the Body of Christ, we are to remember we are many members, with different duties and functions, 4-5. Our varied service is to be discharged as a gift from our Lord, 6-8.

Christian Service and Fellow Believers, 9-16. Love is to be genuine. Evil is to be hated. That which is good is to be held fast, 9. Love is again enjoined, 10. "Never flag in zeal, be aglow with the Spirit" in serving the Lord, 11. "Distribute to the necessity of the saints," 13, means contribute to the needs of poor Christians. Verse 16 should be rendered, "Live in harmony with one another. Do not be haughty, but associate with the lowly; never be conceited."

Christian Service and Unbelievers, 17-21. General exhortations to kind conduct toward Christians are followed by special pleas to loving forbearance under provocation from unbelievers. It is God's part to administer wrath, 19. Man's responsibility is to serve in love, 20.

CHAPTER 13. CHRISTIAN SERVICE AND GOVERNMENT

The Christian and the State, 1-7. This important relationship requires submission to governing authorities, 1. The reason? Human government represents God's authority, 1-7. To resist it is to resist

God, 1-2, and to incur judgment. Governmental authorities are agents of God for good, 3-4. Good citizenship is required of a Christian, 5-7, to avoid God's displeasure and to have a good conscience.

The Christian and Good Citizenship, 8-14. God's law of love is a potent force for a law-abiding life, 8-10. It crystallizes our duty to fellow citizens, 9-10, and fulfills the law of God, 10 (Lev 19:18; cf. Ex 20:13-17). The urgency of the times is a call to good citizenship, 11-13. It is time to awake, 11-12, time to live soberly, 13. "For now is our salvation *nearer* than when we believed," 11, means we are closer to the full result of salvation in glorification. The essence of good citizenship is outlined, 14, involving putting on Christ as a garment, putting off lusts as a soiled garment.

14:1—15:3. CHRISTIAN SERVICE AND QUESTIONABLE THINGS

The Principle of Personal Liberty, 14:1-13. This problem involves the Christian and doubtful practices, 1-2. The strong believer has a duty to welcome a weak believer, but not "for disputes over opinions," 1, such as eating or not eating certain foods, 2. In matters of conduct over which Christians differ, 2-6, the principle of personal liberty is to operate, 3-13a. This prohibits our despising or judging a weaker brother, because (1) God has received him as a believer, 3; (2) he is the servant of Another (Christ, the Master) not us, 4; (3) there are allowable conscientious differences, 5-6; (4) we answer to the lordship of Christ under whom we live, 7-9; (5) we shall be judged at the judgment seat of Christ, 10-12; (6) human judgment, therefore, is not to limit our brother's liberty in Christ, 13a.

The Principle of Our Neighbor's Welfare, 14:13b-21. This consideration rules out putting a stumbling block in his path, 13b-15, even though something may seem good in itself, 16-20. The weaker believer's welfare must be valued above one's own desires, 21.

The Principle of God's Glory, 14:22-23. God the Father is to be glorified in a life of faith, 22. We are to live in God's sight by faith, 22a, free from a spirit of condemnation, 22b-23 (cf. 1 Cor 10:31).

Plea to Observe These Principles, 15:1-3. The strong believer ought to put up with the failings of the weaker brother, sacrificing personal pleasure, 1b (the principle of personal liberty). Furthermore, the strong believer is to please his neighbor for his good and upbuilding, 2 (principle of our neighbor's welfare). He also is to imitate Christ's example for God's glory, 3b (principle of God's glory).

15:4-13. CHRISTIAN SERVICE AND GOD'S WORLDWIDE GLORY

The Hope of God's Worldwide Glory, 4-7. All Scripture inspires hope, 4, by instructing us in the divine redemptive purposes for man and the earth. Human relationships of God's redeemed ones are to glorify the Father, 5-7, promoting His praise and honor. Harmony among God's people is for the purpose of a united voice of praise to God.

The World Is the Ultimate Outreach of the Gospel, 8-13. God's plan embraces gospel extension to the entire globe in which both Jew and Gentile are glorifying God. For this purpose Jesus ministered to one nation, 8, so that eventually in the future kingdom all nations might join in glorifying God the Father, 9-12. As "a minister to the circumcision [Israel] for the truth of God," 8, Christ had as His ultimate purpose not only the outcalling of a people for His name in this age but the confirming (not abrogating) of His promises to the patriarchs. These promises guarantee worldwide Gentile conversion when the kingdom is restored to Israel. Their fulfillment awaits the second advent. The promises are taken from the Psalms (18:49; 117:1), from Moses (Deut 32:43), and the Prophets (Isa 11:10). They show that God's goal all the while is the nations of earth glorifying Him in worldwide adoration. The apostle appends his quotation of these promises with a benediction of hope, 13.

15:14—16:27. CHRISTIAN SERVICE AND CHRISTIAN FELLOWSHIP

Paul Greets the Saints in Rome, 15:14-33. (On city of Rome, see note on Acts 28:17-31.) The apostle expresses assurance of their spiritual growth, 14. In order not to be misunderstood he outlines his devotion to his ministry for Christ, 15-21. Its source is in God, 15-17. Its accreditation is by miraculous signs, 18-19a. Its extent is broad, 19b. Its aim is to be a pioneer for Christ, 20-21. What a confession of a faithful ministry! Paul also expresses his longing to visit the church in Rome, 22-29, and the circumstances delaying his visit. He makes request for their prayer support, 30-32, ending with a benediction of peace, 33.

Closing Greetings and Warnings, 16:1-27. He mentions many saints by name—trophies of the gospel of God, 1-16 (cf. 1:1). His salutations are full of the grace and the love of Christian fellowship. He warns against schismatics and false teachers, 17-20. He asserts they will be defeated, 20a, and breathes a triumphant benediction, 20b.

The apostle includes his colleagues in his salutation, 21-23. His closing benediction ends in an outburst of praise to God, 25-27.

GOD'S GLORY LOST AND REGAINED

	In the Bible As a Whole	In the Book of Romans
Paradise lost	*Ruin* Gen. 1—3	God's glory forfeited, 1:18—3:8; whole world under sin, 3:9-20
God's plan of salvation	*Redemption,* Gen 4—Rev 20	Gospel of God, 1:1—justification, 3:21—5:21; sanctification, 6:1—8:28; glorification, 8:29-39
Paradise regained	*Restoration,* Rev 21—22	Glory of God regained, 15:9-12; 16:27

1 CORINTHIANS

CARNAL VS. SPIRITUAL CHRISTIAN LIVING

Date and Purpose. This epistle was written from Ephesus, probably in A.D. 55. It was penned to instruct recent converts from the lowest and grossest paganism with its vice and sin, so notably practiced at Corinth. See note on the city in Acts 18:1-17. It was not easy for these converts to break with their degraded past. Their carnality and spiritual immaturity needed patient instruction on the part of the apostle. As a center of commerce and wealth, covetousness and unbridled lust. Corinth, with its vain worldly wisdom, offered a challenge to Christianity. If a church could be planted here where East and West met on the crossroads of the Graeco-Roman world, its influence could be expected to be far-reaching. Moreover, a large Jewish element in the city challenged the apostle's policy " to the Jew first" (Rom 1:16).

Outline

The Unity of the Church vs. Divisions, Ch. 1—3
The Order of the Church vs. Disorders, Ch. 4—11
The Gifts and Doctrines of the Church vs. Their Abuse, Ch. 12—16

CHAPTER 1. CHRIST THE BASIS OF UNITY

The Preeminence of Christ, 1-9. The spotlight is focused upon Christ in these opening verses. He is the basis of the church's unity and of the individual believer's position, i.e., the sphere in which God sees the believer and deals with him. This is set forth as "in Christ," 2. Christ must be central and preeminent in any church to correct its abuses. This is the lesson of the epistle. Correction of faults in the assembly must begin, as Paul begins, with the fact of Christ—(1) His authority—"an apostle of Jesus Christ," 1; (2) His power to give us a new position—"sanctified in Christ," "called saints" (those set apart as holy), 2a; and (3) to effect spiritual unity of believers everywhere, 2b; (4) His granting of grace and peace, 3; (5) His giving the believer full sufficiency, 4-5; (6) His being the object of the believer's witness, 6, and (7) the believer's expectation, 7; (8) His being the confirmer of the believer's destiny, 8, and (9) the fact of the believer's fellowship, 9. Therefore, the believer's position in Christ, 1-9, is the basis of appeal to correct these faulty practices.

The Presence of Factions, 10-17. The faults and abuses in the Corinthian church were due to Christians behaving as unregenerate men, as carnal believers instead of spiritual. The result was disunity, occasioning a plea for unity, 10, against the evil of factionalism, 11, brought about by a perversion of Christian liberty, 12-13. The legitimate likes and dislikes of teachers and leaders were perverted into parties and cliques. The corrective is Christ. Is He "divided," 13? See comments on 1:1-9. Let Christ be central! Party spirit will flee! To this end Paul stresses the priority of preaching Christ, 14-17. Paul's primary duty was to gospelize, to evangelize, not ceremonialize. He was not belittling baptism, but He was exalting Christ. Only in Christ does the church's true unity appear. Occupation with Him and not with ceremonies is the only sure cure for divisions in the Body of Christ, the Church.

The Corrective of the Cross, 18-31. Only at the cross can the sin of dividing over men instead of uniting around a message be avoided. Only the cross can save us from man's philosophies and bring us the true wisdom of God. The preaching of the cross is "foolishness" to the lost, 18, but "the power of God" to the saved. The futility of worldly philosophy, 19-20 (cf. Isa 29:14), is contrasted to the triumph of preaching the cross, 21-25. Faith in the message of the cross releases both the wisdom and the power of God that humanity might not boast before God, 26-29. God is the source of our life in Christ Jesus. God has made Him our wisdom, our sanctification and redemption, 30. He who boasts must therefore boast in the Lord Jesus, 31 (cf. Jer 9:23-24), i.e., in his position in Christ, not in what he is in himself.

CHAPTER 2. THE HOLY SPIRIT THE AGENT OF UNITY

The Spirit Reveals True Wisdom, 1-13. This wisdom, the touchstone of Christian unity, is not to be obscured by fine rhetoric and molded by human philosophy to make it palatable to the unregenerate, 1. It centers in the person and death of Jesus Christ, 2; is nurtured in human weakness, 3; marked by the effective witness of the Holy Spirit, 4; and concentrates faith in God's power, 5. This wisdom is distinctly God's wisdom, 6-7, "a mystery . . . hidden" and revealed only by the Holy Spirit, 7. It is in striking contrast to the wisdom of this world and that of the intellectual leaders of this age, 6. It is comprehended only by the mature or adult believer, 6.

The proof that the leaders of this world were ignorant of this true wisdom is the fact they crucified the Lord of glory, who is the true wisdom of God, 8. This wisdom is absolutely dependent upon the Spirit's revelation and illumination. "But, as it is written, 'What no eye has seen, nor ear heard, nor the heart of man conceived, what God has prepared for those who love him,'" 9 (RSV; cf. Isa 64:4), this He "has revealed to us through the Spirit," 10. Therefore, apart from the teaching ministry of the Spirit (cf. Jn 16:13-15) true wisdom is unknown and unknowable, 11-13. These truths are imparted "in words not taught by human wisdom but taught by the Spirit," by whom spiritual truths are inculcated in "those who possess the Spirit," 13 (RSV).

The Unregenerate Man Is Totally Ignorant of True Wisdom, 14-16. The "natural man," i.e., the unbeliever, who does not possess the Spirit (Jude 19), does not receive true wisdom, because it is mere folly to him, nor does he comprehend it, because it is discerned or understood only on the basis of the teaching ministry of the Holy Spirit, 14. By contrast, the *pneumatikos* ("the mature believer controlled by the Holy Spirit") discerns or comprehends "all things," i.e., true wisdom, yet he himself is judged or discerned by no one except God. No one can instruct God, but the believer can be taught by God because he possesses "the mind of Christ." Unity resides in Him, 16.

3:1-8a. THE SPIRITUAL CHRISTIAN

The Spiritual vs. the Carnal Christian, 1-3a. The carnal and spiritual believers are in contrast, 1-2. (1) The "carnal" or fleshly believer lives under the power of the Adamic or old nature working through the human body. The spiritual believer lives under the power of the new or Christlike nature with his body controlled by the Holy Spirit. (2) The carnal believer is a "baby in Christ," 1, i.e., born again but immature and undeveloped in the Christian life when he should be mature. The spiritual Christian *is* mature. (3) One can feed only on milk, simple teaching. The other can take the solid food of full doctrinal instruction with personal application.

The Results of Carnality, 3b-8a. Jealousy, bickering and divisive cliques were formed, the result of walking after the manner of men, 3, i.e., as unregenerate men instead of mature Christians. Following human leaders, 4, was a direct violation of the principle of the unity of the Lord's people, 5-8. Christian servants, although possessing different tasks to perform, are one—have one Lord, one aim, one goal, 8. Spiritual maturity alone realizes Christian unity.

3:8b-23. THE JUDGMENT OF THE BELIEVER'S WORKS

Christian Service to Be Judged, 8b-9. This judgment will determine the believer's reward, 8b, or loss of reward, 15. In *no sense* does this judgment involve the issue of sin, condemnation or eternal life (Rom 8:1; Jn 5:24). It concerns works solely, *not* salvation. It involves the issues of the carnal and the spiritual believer, but *only the believer* and the quality of his life and service after salvation (cf. 2 Cor 5:10; Rom 14:8-10). It judges the faithfulness or unfaithfulness of the believer as a *servant*, hence God's fellow *workers*, God's farm or plantation, God's building 9. We work *for* God, but also *with* Him in dignity. More than that, He works in us, through us and upon us for His glory, 9.

The Believer's Judgment for Service, 10-15. The basis is the gospel of salvation from sin through Christ. Christ is the foundation, 10. Building upon Him as a foundation is a metaphor for Christian service which is only for born-again believers, 11. There exist two kinds of service. One is illustrated by gold, silver and precious stones, built by the spiritual believer, and is indestructible by the fire of judgment, 12. The other is set forth by wood, hay, stubble, built by the carnal Christian. This is destructible and will not stand up before Him whose eyes are like a flame of fire (Rev 1:14). The issue for the truly born-again servant will be either reward for the spiritual believer, 14, or loss of reward for the carnal believer, 15. However, the fleshly worker will still be saved, since the issue is not sin, condemnation or eternal life. Yet he will be saved so as through fire with all his works burned up, as a man escapes with his bare life.

Solemn Warning to Carnal Believers, 16-23. The body of *every* believer is a sacred temple in which the Holy Spirit dwells, 16. If a carnal believer scandalously (cf. 5:1-5) desecrates this holy precinct, God will destroy him by *physical* death, 17 (cf. 1 Cor 5:5; 11:30-31; 1 Jn 5:16). Not only are fleshly sins of the body warned against, but intellectual sins, 19-23. (Cf. v. 19 with Job 5:13; v. 20 with Ps 94:11.) Christians are not to be ensnared by worldly wisdom, nor are they to glory in men, but in the Man Christ Jesus, in whom the believer possesses everything, 21-23 (cf. Rom 8:16-17).

CHAPTER 4. THE CHURCH AND ITS LEADERS

The Sin of Judging God's Servants, 1-8. The church's leaders are to be highly esteemed as ministers of Christ and stewards of the truths revealed by God, 1. Their supreme duty is to be faithful to

God in this trust, 2. They are to be judged in this matter by Him alone, and not by any human being, 3-4. Therefore judgment must be suspended till the coming of the Lord and the divine assessment of the believer's works, 5 (cf. 3:11-15). The Corinthians must cease their carnal judging of their church leaders, 6-7, prompted by carnal pride, which the apostle rebukes with keen sarcasm, 8.

The Holy Dedication of the Apostles, 9-21. Apostolic sacrifice and suffering are used to shame the carnal self-secure critics in the Corinthian church, 9-13. Paul writes incisively but lovingly, 14, appealing to his begetting them in the gospel, 15, his sacrificial example of life, 16, and his concern for them in sending Timothy, 17. Nevertheless he sternly warns the unrepentant, 18-21.

CHAPTER 5.   THE PROBLEM OF THE IMMORAL BELIEVER

Carnality Blinds to the Presence of Gross Immorality, 1-5. A case of vile incest, even alien to voluptuous Corinth, was reported in this church, 1. The apostle directed the disordered saints, completely unconcerned about disciplinary action, 2, on their responsibility, 3-5.

The Temple of Apollo overlooking the agora of ancient Corinth, with the acropolis of Corinth in the background. (© *MPS*)

The incestuous brother was to be abandoned to Satan "for the destruction of the flesh" (physical death, cf. 1 Cor 11:30; 1 Jn 5:16) that "the spirit may be saved," i.e., he might be disciplined as a believer possessing eternal life, 5.

The Principle of the Leaven of Sin, 6-13. Leaven, as a type of sin in Scripture, spreads through the whole batch of dough, 6. Sin condoned or unjudged likewise spreads, 6. It must, therefore, be purged out, 7. The reason? Christ, the Passover Lamb, who takes away the sin of the world (Ex 12:1-13; Jn 1:29), has been offered, by which the believer is saved. The result is the Feast of Unleavened Bread, which the Paschal sacrifice inaugurated (Ex 12:12-22). This is typical of the Christian life to be lived in separation from sin, 8. Therefore, the incestuous brother must be excommunicated, 9, 11. Yet personal separation must be on the principle of "in the world but not of it," 10-11. Discipline is to be exercised within the church, but judgment of those outside the church rests with God, 12-13.

6:1-8. THE DISORDER OF LEGAL SUITS

Christian Suing Christian, 1-8. Christian going to law against fellow Christian in pagan courts before pagan judges, 1, is a violation of Christian truth. The "saints" are to judge the world (unsaved humanity), 2, and even the fallen angels, 3 (cf. 2 Pet 2:4; Jude 6). Since this judicial dignity is a result of the believer's union with Christ, the Judge, are there not wise saints to act as judges in cases involving Christian with Christian, 4-5? The carnal Corinthians clearly manifested their carnality in going to law against each other and wronging each other, 7-8.

6:9-20. THE SNARE OF FORNICATION

The Christian Tempted by Fornication, 9-20. This problem was acute in this church because it had been recently saved out of the polluted moral atmosphere of Corinth. As a commercial emporium this city united East and West in a veritable cesspool of uncleanness. The apostle warns that believers failing to separate from this polluted paganism, 9-10, "shall not inherit the kingdom of God," i.e., shall suffer loss of reward (cf. 3:11-15), even inviting premature physical death as the penalty of scandalous sin. Fornication is utterly at variance with the Christian because: (1) He has been sanctified and justified from this and other sins in *his position* (as God sees him in Christ), and is to realize his position in *his experience* (as he acts toward men), 11, under grace, 12. (2) The believer's body is for the Lord's use, 13, and when so used the believer can claim the Lord's care of his body. (3) The body is holy and is to be resurrected, 14. (4) The body is joined to Christ, 15-17, not to a harlot. (5) Fornication is a sin against the sanctity of the believer's body, 18. (6) The believer's body is "a temple" (*naos, "a dwelling place of God"*), specifically the most holy place or inner sanctum where the Shekinah glory was manifested in the tabernacle and temple, 19. (7) The believer's body is God's property, 19. (8) It is for God's glory, 20. (9) God-ordained marriage is the antidote against fornication, 7:1-3.

7:1-24. REGULATIONS OF CHRISTIAN MARRIAGE

The Purpose of Christian Marriage, 1-9. The unmarried state is good; but Christian marriage is for the purpose of avoiding fornication and establishing a mutually satisfactory monogamous relationship, 2-3, in which both partners express full bodily powers in normal satisfactory physical union. Depriving either partner of sexual intercourse is to be only by mutual consent for the purpose of special spiritual exercise, 5a, after which normal sexual union is to be enjoyed in order to avoid Satanic temptation to some illegitimate sexual outlet, through reduced self-control, 5b. This is a concession to human weakness, rather than a divine commandment, 6. Celibacy is best for some, 7-8, but marriage is God-ordained, and designed to meet physical and psychological needs as constituted by the Creator, 7, 9.

Regulations Governing Christian Marriage, 10-24. Marriage of believers is for life, 10-11. The Christian wife is not to leave her husband. If she does, she is to forfeit marrying again. Likewise the Christian husband is not to leave his wife. Loose pagan views of marriage must be abandoned. These regulations, so far from not being inspired, are associated with our Lord's instructions, 12 (cf. Mt 5:31-32; 19:5-9), and designed to meet new situations arising with the outflow of the gospel to the Gentiles. The general principle is that insofar as possible every effort is to be made to maintain the *status quo* at the time of becoming a believer, 12-24. Applied to the marriage union, it means the saved partner is to do everything possible to maintain the union, and win the unsaved partner to the Lord. The children are privileged to be in a circle of Christian instruction when even one parent is saved, 14.

7:25-40. MARRIED VS. THE UNMARRIED STATE

The General Principle, 25-31. The general rule is that the unmarried are well-off as they are, particularly at times when believers are subject to economic and social stress, 25-26. At such times they are to remain in the general state in which they were when saved, 27-28. There are, however, certain advantages of the unmarried state for a believer. He is free from economic cares, 26. He is spared trials and troubles "of the flesh," i.e., the inevitable responsibility of the health and welfare of his family, 28. He is in a better position to realize the brevity of life in the light of eternity, 29-31.

Contrast Between the Married and Unmarried State, 32-40. The unmarried believer of either sex is more at liberty to please the Lord, 32-34, and to serve Him without distraction, 35. Physical and psychological makeup may require one to marry, 36. On the other hand, those who can, are to remain single, 37-38. Marriage is till death parts, 39-40. Remarriage is limited to those whose former mates have died, and then only between believers. Even in such cases, remaining single is the better course.

CHAPTER 8. CHRISTIAN LIBERTY

The Law of Love the Solution, 1-3. Paul faces the problem of a Christian's eating food offered to idols, which involves the principle of a believer's liberty in non-moral questions. In such matters knowledge about an issue is common, but love is often lacking when viewing the actions of others, 1. Knowledge may be incomplete and superficial, leading to pride. It cannot solve such problems as those involved in the limitations of Christian liberty. Love, however, does solve these problems, 3, and God is fully cognizant of the principle operative in His own.

The Law of Knowledge Inadequate, 4-13. To most believers, the knowledge of the nothingness of an idol and the sole existence of the one true God was such an obvious fact of revelation, 4-6, that they were not offended by eating meat first dedicated to a heathen deity, as was often the case in a pagan city like Corinth. Other weaker believers did not have this conviction of the nothingness of an idol, and were offended, 7. Love must control over knowledge if a weaker brother is not to be offended, 8-13. Christ in love died for him, 11, and Christ's love is to rule our hearts, 12, as it did the apostle's heart, 13.

CHAPTER 9. THE CHURCH AND ITS WORKERS

Church Leaders Are to Be Honored and Supported, 1-15. Paul had to defend his office as an apostle before a carnal, critical element at Corinth. This ought not to have been the case. Rather, God-ordained church leaders ought not only to be honored as such, but financially supported as well, 7-18. As illustrations of the latter the apostle uses the cases of the soldier, the farmer, and the dairyman, 7, and the law of Moses, 8-9 (cf. Deut 25:4). Even the ox is not muzzled when he stamps out the grain, so that he can eat his fill as a reward for his labor. Plowing and threshing are in hope of a return for labor, 10; and so it ought to be in the spiritual realm, 11. Paul forbears this privilege for a definite purpose, 12, 15, but uses another illustration, the temple and its Levitical priesthood, 13, to prove the thesis "that they which preach the gospel should live of the gospel," 14.

True Church Leaders Are to Be Rewarded, 16-27. They are under a divine commission and constraint, 16; and if they serve willingly, they will be rewarded in this life, 18, and in the life to come, 19-27. This calls for work performed as a genuine "servant to all," to win more for Christ, 19. This is dedicated adaptability, 20-23, for the high purpose to "save some," i.e., be the human medium through which the divine Spirit moves in regeneration, 22-23. Reward at the judgment seat (*bema*) of Christ will crown such dedicated service, 24-27 (cf. 1 Cor 3:11-15; 2 Cor 5:10). Paul uses the athletic figure of the famed Isthmian games, 25, held near Corinth. The footrace, 24, 26, and the boxing match, 26, are selected. Self-control and rigid discipline, 25, are necessary to win a perishable victor's crown. Verse 27, "I keep under [buffet] my body, and bring it into subjection: lest that by any means, when I have preached to others, I myself should be a castaway [disapproved]" (*adokimos*, "disqualified for reward"), concerns rewards, *not* salvation.

10:1-15. THE CHURCH'S HERITAGE

OT Typology and Its Lessons, 1-5. The Egyptian redemption, the wilderness wandering and entrance into the land were types or shadows of spiritual truths applicable to NT saints. 6, 11. Moses prefigures Christ, 2, while Israel's passing through the cloud and sea were typical of the baptism of the Spirit into Christ (Rom 6:3-4). The "fathers" prefigure NT saints, and the bread they ate and the water they drank in the desert point to Christ, 3-4 (Ex 13:21; 14:22; Ps 105:39; Ex 17:6).

The Warning, 6-15. But Israel fell into idolatry, 5, 7, 8 (cf. Ex 32:6; Num 25:1, 9); tempted the Lord, 9 (cf. Ex 17:2, 7; Num 21:6); murmured, 10 (Num 14:2); and were destroyed, 9-10 (cf. Num 25:1-9). Verse 8 says 23,000 fell "in one day" (cf. Num 25:9 which gives 24,000, the *complete* number that fell). The warning against proud self-sufficiency follows, 12, together with encouragement to trust God, and an injunction to flee from idolatry, 13-14. Appeal is made in verse 15 to a wise course.

10:16-33. THE LORD'S SUPPER

Fellowship at the Lord's Table Requires Separation, 16-22. The communion, symbolizing the death of Christ and the fellowship of the Body of Christ, 16, portrays our oneness as believers in union with Christ, 17. The apostle uses the example of the Israelite priesthood fellowshiping at the altar by eating of the sacrifice as a case in point of separation and communion, 18. Hence, believers must be separate from idolatry, not because the idol is anything, 19, but because idolatry is demon-energized, 20, and represents fellowship with demonic powers, 21. Behind the lifeless idol is the demon, 21, from which the Lord's Supper in all that it portrays demands rigid separation. Complicity is folly, since the Lord is righteously jealous of sole worship and is omnipotent to deal with offenders, 22.

The Law of Love and Christian Liberty, 23-33. The believer is not under a legalistic principle, but the law of unselfish love, 23-24. "The shambles" (*makellon*, "public market") was the place where meat and all kinds of food were displayed for sale (L. *macellum*). A Christian is not to quibble over eating what might have been offered to idols, since he recognizes the earth is the Lord's by creation and redemption, 25-26 (cf. Ps 24:1). If, however, the circumstance involves offense to a weaker believer, he is to abstain (cf. Rom 14:1-23). A believer must always act to God's glory, 31, giving no cause for stumbling, 32, in a spirit of selfless love, 33.

11:1-16. THE CHURCH AND ITS WOMEN

The Headship of the Man, 1-10. Verse 1, urging the Corinthian believers to be followers (*mimētai*, "imitators") of the apostle, belongs to the preceding chapter. In urging the headship of the man, 3 (cf. Gen 3:16), Paul presents the woman's headdress as a symbol of her subordination to the man, as the man in turn is subordinated to Christ, 4-6. The apostle uses the OT to show that man is made in the image and for the glory of God (Gen 1:27), and when praying or preaching he should not have his head covered, in token of God's order among the sexes, 7. Man was created first. The woman was made from man, 8. Hence, man's headship. Therefore, the Christian woman ought to have the badge of her husband's authority on her head "because of the angels," 10, i.e., because of the divine order that prevails among the elect unfallen angels (cf. Ps 103:20), who are looking on the human scene.

Order Under Grace, 11-16. "In the Lord" man and woman are one, and mutually dependent, 11-12. Order and propriety are to be observed, 13-15, but not in any legalistic sense, 16. The freedom of grace is never to be compromised, but believers ought to be willing to submit to that which is proper, even if it is not mandatory.

11:17-34. DISORDERS AT THE LORD'S SUPPER REBUKED

The Disorder Exposed, 17-22. The holy ordinance of the Lord's Supper was marred by irregularity, 17; schisms, 18; divisive sects, 19; and gluttony, 20-22.

The Disorder Corrected, 23-34. The sacred institution of the supper is indicated, 23-25 (see notes on Mt 26:26-29; Lk 22:17-20). Its doctrinal import is specified. It declares the Lord's death (retrospect) until He comes (prospect). It looks backward to salvation provided in redemption and forward to salvation realized in glorification, 26. Its violation is described, 27, as partaking of it not "unworthily" (no one is "worthy") but "in an unworthy manner." This means in an attitude of unconfessed sin, and thus being "guilty of the body and blood of the Lord," transgressing against the very essence of the meaning of Christ's death, which liberates the believer from sin, 27. Self-examination is necessary, 28, to avoid condemnation and consequent chastening, entailing physical weakness, sickness and even death, 30. This judging of self, with consequent confession not only avoids the Lord's disciplinary action against the sinning saint, but is for the distinct purpose of sparing him as a son from condemnation (eternal hell), the portion of every unbeliever, 32. Hence let the believer avoid abuse of the Lord's table, 33-34.

12:1-11. THE BELIEVER AND THE SIGN GIFTS

The Giver of the Gifts, 1-3. The apostle now sets forth much needed instruction on the operations and manifestations of the Spirit through the individual believer. The Corinthian Christians were appallingly ignorant of this subject. Abuses abounded among them since they were saved so lately out of paganism and gross demon-inspired idolatry, 2 (cf. 10:20-21). They who had been controlled by demon spirits must now be taught the operations of the Holy Spirit, called also the Spirit of God, to emphasize the importance of His working in the believer in the manifestation of gifts, 3. Let them also beware of demonic counterfeit.

The Enumeration of the Gifts, 4-11. There are *numerous* and various gifts, but only *one* and the same Spirit who gives the gifts and operates them through *each* believer, 4. There are numerous and different administrations or operations of these gifts through gifted men, but the same Lord, 5 (cf. Eph 4:4-6). *The Spirit* gives the gifts to men for service. *Christ* gives the gifted men to the church (cf. Eph 4:8-12). *God the Father* controls the numerous and various operations or workings, 6. Thus the Triune God works in each believer, to whom the Spirit's manifestation is given for profit and edification, 7.

Some of the various gifts are enumerated, 8-11. Although under the sovereign control of the Spirit, 11, these are mainly and more particularly the *sign* or *miraculous* gifts with which the early church was endowed before the full NT written revelation was given to guide believers. They included: (1) *intellectual gifts*—wisdom, knowledge, 8, and faith, 9, chiefly to instruct the church before it had the authoritative, complete, once-for-all written revelation; (2) *volitional gifts*— healings, 9; miracles, as a sign to the Jews and authentication to Gentiles, and prophecy, chiefly a supernatural receiving and declaring of truths not yet given in full and final written form; (3) *emotional gifts*—"differentiating spirits," 10 (cf. 1 Jn 4:1-4), given to ascertain whether supposed truth was from God the Holy Spirit or from Satan (1 Tim 4:1-4); speaking in supernatural tongues (languages), as a sign to the Jews (cf. Acts 2:4; 10:46; 19:6 and notes); and "interpretation of tongues," giving the content of the supernatural message in the common parlance of the people.

12:12-31. THE CHURCH AND THE SIGN GIFTS

The Church As the Body of Christ, 12-27. The *unity* of the Church is presented under the illustration of a human body, 12a. One body but *many* members of that one body is the figure used to portray Christ, 12b. This is not Christ merely as a person, but also in His people united to Him (Rom 6:3-4) by the baptism of the Holy Spirit, 13. Just as the human body is a unit with many members, 14, such as the foot, the hand, the ear, 15-16, so also is the Church,

Judgments Mentioned in Scripture

Judgment	Nature	Occasion	Result
Of Jesus Christ, Jn 12:31	Bearing the believer's sins, 2 Cor 5:21; Heb 9:26-28; 1 Pet 2:24; 3:18	Christ lifted up on the cross, world judged, Satan defeated, Jn 12:31	Death of Christ; justification and security of the believer, Jn 5:24; Rom 5:9; 8:1; 2 Cor 5:21; Gal 3:13
Of the believer's works, 2 Cor 5:10	Quality of the believer's life as a servant, 1 Cor 3:11-15; Mt 12:36 (in *no* sense for sins, Heb 10:17)	At the coming of the Lord, 1 Cor 4:1-5; 9:24-27; Rom 14:10; Gal 6:7; Col 3:24-25; 2 Tim 4:8	Reward for faithful service; loss of reward for unfaithfulness, 1 Cor 3:8, 14-15; Rev 22:12
Of the believer by himself, 1 Cor 11:31-32; 2 Sam 7:14-15	The believer's condemnation of himself for permitting his own sinful ways and habits, 2 Sam 12:13-14	Self-judgment of the believer as a son to avoid chastisement by his heavenly Father, Heb 12:7	If neglected, the Father's chastening follows, but never condemnation, 1 Cor 11:32; 5:5
Of the nations, Mt 25:31-46; Joel 3:11-16	Point of testing is the treatment of Christ's "brothers," i.e., the Jewish remnant of the end time	At Christ's return in glory to set up the kingdom over Israel, Acts 1:6	Entrance or exclusion from the kingdom as individuals in the nations

Of Israel, Ezk 20:33-44	Subjects will be living Israelites at the end time regathered from worldwide diaspora	Similar on the Israelite plane to the judgment of the nations with regard to the Gentiles	Entrance or non-entrance into the land for kingdom blessing, Ps 50:1-7; Mal 3:2-5; 4:1-2
Of the fallen angels, Jude 6; 2 Pet 2:4; 1 Cor 6:3	Subjects will be the angels who rebelled with Satan, Rev 12:3-4. May include angels who cohabited with human women at time of the Flood, Gen 6:1-6	Evidently after the millennium, at the end of history	Satan and evil angels relegated to the lake of fire, Gehenna, eternal hell, Rev 20:10
Of the unsaved, Rev 20:11-15	Only the wicked dead. Perhaps Satan and fallen angels are finally judged also at this time	Basis of judgment is according to works to determine degree of punishment of the lost	Second death or lake of fire—*not* annihilation, Rev 19:20; 20:10, 14-15

the Body of Christ, 27. *One* Church, *one* body, *many* members, *many* functions, but all a vital part of the *one* Body.

The Church and the Sign Gifts, 28-31. As the apostle had related the individual Christian to the sign gifts, 1-11, he now relates the Church, the Body, the aggregate of individual believers, to these gifts. Although some of the permanent gifts are again included, the list stresses once more the temporary sign gifts, such as apostles, prophets, miracles, gifts of healings, diversities of tongues, 28. Note particularly that all do not have the same gift, 29-30, nor are they expected to have.

CHAPTER 13. THE CHURCH AND THE PERMANENT GIFTS

Love Must Control the Exercise of All Spiritual Gifts, 1-8a. This is true of the sign gifts as well as the non-sign or permanent gifts of the church. The "best gifts," 12:31, are the permanent, necessary, edifying gifts. These are to be earnestly sought. The "more excellent way" is the "love" way, which the carnal, emotional Corinthians had completely missed in their childish desire for the showy gifts to be used for selfish ends. In this classic passage, 1-8a, love is shown to be the *sine qua non* of the exercise of all gifts, such as tongues, 1, prophecy, 2, knowledge and faith (cf. 12:8-11)). Even charitable almsgiving and martyrdom are useless without love, 3. Love is personified and its excellencies detailed in 4-8a.

Permanence of Love, 8b-13. Love is contrasted with the gifts which would be superseded and would cease, 8. They would cease because a time of complete or perfect knowledge and prophecy would come, 9, when the NT Scriptures would be completed. The partial revelation through *direct inspirational* knowledge, prophecy, and tongues would then give way to that which is perfect (Gr. "the complete and final thing"), 10, meaning the completed written Scriptures, as the context shows. Paul illustrates the period of the church's infancy, when it had to depend on piecemeal revelation through special gifts, by the figure of a child growing into adulthood, 11, and a person seeing himself indistinctly in a metal mirror which reflected only a blurred image, 12. However, faith, hope, and especially love would remain and always be necessary, 13, in contrast to the impermanent gifts.

CHAPTER 14. ABUSE OF THE SIGN GIFTS

The Superiority of Prophecy Over Tongues, 1-11. "Keep on pursuing love," 1, and "earnestly desire spiritual gifts"—particularly prophecy, i.e., inspired verbal utterances of truth not yet written down. This is superior to speaking in tongues by contrast, because it is more *comprehensible* to men, 2, 6 (cf. the illustration of the trumpet, 7-9), than are difficult sounds or voices, 10-11; and it is *edifying* to the church, 3 (cf. 12; Rom 14:19; Eph 4:29).

Correction of the Abuse of Tongues, 12-40. The corrective for the situation in the primitive church where there were liberty and a need for the ministry of all the gifts outlined in 1 Cor 12:8-11 includes the following important regulations. (1) The believer was to desire the superior edifying gifts, such as prophecy, and was to seek to abound, i.e., be richly furnished or abundantly gifted, in these gifts to the upbuilding of the church, 12, 23-26. (2) The believer was to pray for the gift of interpretation if he had the gift of tongues, 13-18. (3) The church was to use tongues only with great restraint, 19, and in any case, only if an interpreter was present, 27-28. (4) Childish immaturity manifested in the abuse of this gift was to be outgrown, 20. (5) The purpose of the gift, 21-22 (cf. Isa 28:11-12) as a *sign* to unbelieving Jews was to be held in mind (Acts 2:6-13; 10:45-46; 11:15-18). (6) Prophecy, especially in its character as a vehicle of revelation before the objective written Word was completed, was to be given the prominent place, but also regulated orderly, 29-33. (7) In public meetings women were to keep silent, 34-35, not only in the matter of tongues, but in declaring divine revelation (i.e., prophesying). (8) Tongues and the sign gifts were seemingly to cease after the initial need for them in the apostolic church was met, 19, 21-22. (9) These injunctions were to be recognized as divinely corrective, 36-37. (10) Decency and order were to prevail, 40.

CHAPTER 15. THE DOCTRINE OF RESURRECTION

15:1-19. THE FACT AND IMPORT OF CHRIST'S RESURRECTION

The Fact of Christ's Resurrection, 1-11. The doctrine of the resurrection of the body was specially denied by the pagan intellectualism of Corinth. By contrast Paul presents Christ's resurrection as central in the gospel of salvation which he proclaimed and which the Corinthians received, 1-4a. It was a fulfillment of Scripture, 4b (cf. e.g., Ps 16:10), and authenticated by Cephas (the Aramaic name of Peter); the Twelve, 5; more than 500 brethren; James; all the apostles, 7, and by Paul himself. He considered himself a Hebrew prematurely born to be a type of the nation's spiritual rebirth at the second advent, 8b, a trophy of the grace of God which was manifested through the death and resurrection of Christ, 9-11.

Christ's Resurrection the Basis of Ours, 12-19. Some Corinthian believers were contaminated with the prevailing pagan denial of bodily resurrection, 12. The apostle argues for the importance of the doctrine by facing the alternatives of denying it. These are: (1) Christ would not be risen, 13; (2) Paul's preaching would be useless, 12, 14; (3) the Corinthians' faith would be empty, 14, 17; (4) the apostle would be a false witness, 15-16; (5) the Corinthians would still be unsaved, 17; (6) the dead in Christ would have perished, 18; (7) hope would be limited to this life, 19; (8) the Christian's lot would be most pitiable, 19. So ridiculous are the alternatives, Paul uses these arguments as the basis for his declaration of the doctrine in the verses following.

15:20-23. CHRIST'S RESURRECTION AND OURS

Christ's Resurrection a Guarantee of Ours, 20-23. It is declared a fact, 20*a*, which guarantees our resurrection, 20*b*. Christ is the "firstfruits of them that slept." On the Feast of Firstfruits (Lev 23:10-14), the first sheaf of ripened grain was presented to the Lord on the day after the sabbath (the day of Christ's resurrection), a pledge of the ingathering of the whole harvest ("they that are Christ's at his coming"), 23 (1 Thess 4:13-18).

Christ's Resurrection the Divine Remedy for the Fall, 21-23. "By man [Adam] came [physical] death, by man [God incarnate] came also the resurrection of the [physically] dead," 21. All in Adam, i.e., all members of the human race, die (physically). All in Christ, *all* saved or redeemed humanity, will enjoy victorious resurrection. OT saints, NT saints and Tribulation martyrs will enjoy the benefits of Christ's resurrection (cf. Dan 12:2; Rev 7:9, 13), but will be raised in the various steps of the first resurrection, "each in his own order." But Paul here is thinking in particular of Christian believers, and so limits the complex picture of resurrection to that which affects them, namely, the coming of Christ for the Church (1 Thess 4:13-18; 1 Cor 15:53-54).

15:24-28. RESURRECTION AND THE FINAL CONSUMMATION

The Final Abrogation of Death, 24-26. "The end," 24, is not the commencement of Christ's earthly reign at His second advent, but the end of that reign. It is the termination of time and its ordered ages, and the dawn of the eternal state, and has as its goal the restoration of the divine authority in all creation, 24-25, with the abolition of death, 26. The destruction of death is the last result of Christ's mediatorial reign, and the climax to His initial victory over death in His own resurrection.

The Eternal State, 27-28. This will entail paradise regained (Rev 22) as it was lost in Gen 1—3. Satan, demon powers, and unregenerate men, as well as sin and death, will be done away. "God all in all" (absolutely supreme) will be realized in a sinless, deathless universe *glorifying the one Triune God,* with all evil confined and quarantined in *one* place (Rev 20:14-15), never to disturb a sinless universe again.

15:29-34. CHRIST'S RESURRECTION AND NEW INCENTIVES

The Incentive to Be Baptized for the Dead, 29. If Christ's resurrection is not a fact, and ours consequently not a living hope, 12-19, then what purpose is there for the rite of Christian baptism? What course of action shall believers take who through this introductory water ceremony have publicly taken their places in the ranks left vacant by believers who have died, 29? If there is no resurrection, and really no divinely authenticated Saviour and gospel of salvation, might they not better give up a rite that portrays their identification with such a Saviour and such a salvation?

The Incentive to Live Dangerously, 30-34. "Why stand in jeopardy every hour?" If Christianity is a mere resurrectionless, hopeless religion, why risk one's life, as the apostle did, in fighting against violent beastlike opposition such as that at Ephesus (Acts 19:23-41)? Why not renounce Christian sacrifice and get all the selfish enjoyment possible out of a life in which death ends all? But the apostle knows the reality of the gospel of the resurrection and "dies daily," 31, i.e., exposes himself constantly to physical death for Christ (Rom 8:36-37). Moreover, he separates himself from evil, 33 (cf. Prov 13:20; Eph 4:29) and bestirs himself to righteousness, 34.

15:35-58. RESURRECTION AND CONQUEST OVER DEATH

The Character of the Resurrection Body, 35-49. The question of the "how" of the resurrection is broached, 35. The process is described as death, 36. Death is the prelude to life. In nature nothing lives except it dies (cf. Jesus' illustration in Jn 12:24). The product of this resurrection process is a new kind of body fitted for a new type of life. Three illustrations from nature are used to demonstrate the reasonableness of the new resurrection body: plants, 37-38; flesh, 39; heavenly bodies, 40-41. The resurrection body will likewise be similar to and different from the natural body, 42, but will be a spiritual body, 42-44, freed from the characteristics of corruption, dishonor and weakness of the natural body. It will spring from Christ, the Head of the new creation, the Lord from heaven, 45-49, and will bear His heavenly image.

The Change That Produces the Resurrection Body, 50-58. The need for the change is indicated by the creation of our bodies for the natural realm and their fallen corrupt nature, 50. The mystery of the resurrection is set forth, 51, a divine secret that becomes known to the one who enjoys eternal life. All believers will be changed, but all will not "sleep" (die, since death is really no more than a nap for one redeemed), 51. The change will take place in a split second, at the "last trumpet" (cf. 1 Thess 4:1? 18), which has no connection with the last of the seven judgment trumpets sounded by angels (Rev 11:15-19). This blowing is a trumpet of blessing sounded by God. The imperative necessity of the resurrection, 53, preludes the triumph of the event, 54-57, producing the great incentive to holy steadfastness and achievement in the Christian life.

16:1-4. THE DOCTRINE OF STEWARDSHIP

The Principles Involved, 1-2a. The occasion of the instruction here given is an offering for the poor believers in persecution-ridden Judea, 1. Giving to God involves: (1) The principle of *regularity*. It is to be done periodically. "Upon *the first day* of the week," 2. (2) The principle of *personality*. "Let *everyone of you* lay by him in store." Specifically, every believer is to be a steward. The *giver* is as important as the gift. (3) The principle of *proportion*. "*As* God hath prospered him." The basis is to be according to personal prosperity. Periodic, personal, proportionate giving is not to be mere legalistic tithing, but certainly presupposes giving a tenth as a minimal standard. It is rather a gracious giving of all, on the basis of love for the Saviour.

The Reason and Application, 2b-4. "That there be no collections when I come," 2b. Christian giving is not to be upon the basis of emotional appeals or under pressure of financial crises. It is to be a spiritual ministry based on scriptural principles. The application, 3-4, involves the very highest motive for giving and wise handling of the gift. Paul calls the anticipated offering "a liberality," anticipating that being scriptural—periodic, personal and proportional to prosperity— it would be liberal.

16:5-24. THE ILLUSTRATION OF BROTHERLY SERVICE

Brotherly Concern, 5-14. This is illustrated by the mention of three contemplated visits, 5-9: Paul's own visit, 5-9; that of Timothy, 10-11; that of Apollos, 12. It is emphasized by an appeal to manliness and maturity on the part of the Corinthians as they serve, 13-14. True growth will manifest itself in such service (cf. 13-18).

Service and Final Salutation, 15-24. Verses 15-18 offer a beautiful illustration of brotherly service, as do the closing salutations, 19-24—one from the churches, 19-20, and the other from the apostle, 21-24. "Maran-atha," 22, is Aramaic, meaning "Our Lord, come!" (cf. Rev 22:20).

2 CORINTHIANS

THE GLORY OF THE CHRISTIAN MINISTRY

Author and Genuineness. Evidence that Paul is the writer and that the letter is genuine is strong. Polycarp, Irenaeus, Theophilus of Antioch, Clement of Alexandria, Tertullian, Cyprian, Marcion and the Muratorian Canon all testify to Pauline authorship. The intimate details of Paul's life and ministry contained in the epistle are beyond the reach of the forger. Links with 1 Corinthians, Galatians, Romans and Acts abound in the biographical touches. It is saturated with characteristic Pauline concepts. The epistle was likely written shortly after 1 Corinthians, in A.D. 56, from Macedonia (cf. 2:13; 7:5-7; 8:1; 9:2-4).

Character of the Epistle. It is the most personal and the least doctrinal of all the Pauline epistles, Philemon excepted. It lays bare the life and ministry of the great apostle. In intensity of emotion, expression of the writer's idiosyncrasies, and individuality of style it stands in the forefront of Paul's letters.

Contents. Attacked by critics, Paul presents a grand defense of his life and ministry in ch. 1—7. Chapters 8 and 9 concern the collection for the impoverished believers in Jerusalem, with instructions in proper giving. Chapters 10—13 further defend Paul's apostleship and authority against false legalistic teachers. While the apostle is forced by enemy attack to lay bare his life and ministry, the occasion furnishes the highest instruction and inspiration to every minister of Christ.

Outline
Introductory, Personal Testimony, 1:1—2:13
The Glory of the Christian Ministry, 2:14—7:16
The Glory of the Ministry of Giving, 8:1—9:15
The Glory of the Christian Ministry Defended, 10:1—13:14

1:1-11. DIVINE COMFORT AND ITS PURPOSE

God's Comfort Abounding in Trouble, 1-7. After a usual salutation, 1-2 (cf. Rom 1:1-7; 1 Cor 1:1-3), the apostle presents a benediction to God as (1) "Father of our Lord Jesus Christ," (2) hence "Father of mercies," since all divine grace flows through the Son, and (3) "the God of all comfort," since comfort follows grace.

Comfort (Gr. *paraklesis*, "a calling alongside") is divine aid which comes to our side to help us in extremity or sorrow (cf. Jn 14:16, 26; 15:26; 16:7; 1 Jn 2:1). The purpose of God's comfort is that we in turn may go to the side of a needy one and help him in the strength of the divine consolation and solace which we have received, 4. When extremities and sufferings abound, experience of God's comfort multiplies, and so does our usefulness in comforting others, 5-7.

Thanksgiving for Recent Deliverance, 8-11. Paul's harrowing experience in proconsular Asia at Ephesus (cf. Acts 19:23—20:1) is selected as an example of the tribulation through which God's servant passed, 8. Its severity was almost to the point of death, 9, but comfort abounded through concerted prayer, 11.

1:12—2:13. TESTIMONY OF SINCERITY

Paul's Reason for Joy 1:12-24. This was "the testimony of his conscience" concerning the simple, sincere manner of his life and specially of his conduct toward the Corinthian believers, 12-14. "The day of the Lord Jesus," 14, is the time of blessing and reward for the saints at Christ's coming for His own (cf. 1 Cor 1:8; 5:5; Phil 1:6, 10; 2:16). "The day of the Lord" by contrast refers to the era of earth judgments in the Great Tribulation (Rev 4—19).

The "second benefit" (*charin*, "blessing"), 15, the only use of this expression in Scripture, has reference to an additional spiritual benefit that would accrue to the Corinthians as the result of another visit from Paul, 16-24. The sealing of the Spirit, 22, is the guarantee of the believer's security (Eph 1:13; 4:30); the Holy Spirit is the "seal." A seal signifies ownership (Jer 32:11-12; 2 Tim 2:19), security (Est 8:8; Dan 6:17; Eph 4:30), and a completed transaction (Jer 32:9-10; Jn 17:4; 19:30).

Paul's Desire to Visit Them in Joy, 2:1-13. To avoid a sad visit, 1-2, he wrote to them correctively, 3-13. The case of the incestuous brother, 6-8 (cf. 1 Cor 5:1-5), needed further direction from the apostle, and he gives such instruction. The apostle's mention of Satan's devices or stratagems, 11 (cf. 2 Cor 11:3; Eph 6:10-12), shows the crucial importance of the believer's knowledge of biblical demonology.

2:14-17. THE GLORY OF THE MINISTRY— ITS TRIUMPH

The Christian's March of Triumph, 14. The figure is that of a triumphal march through the city of Rome to honor a Roman conqueror. The public honor was voted by the senate. The procession included victors and victims. The conquerors, with the commander at the lead, were followed by the conquered led in chains to death or captivity. Perfume of incense ascended from multitudinous censers borne by captives and from aromatic herbs strewn along the way. The scent of victory's perfume filled the air. Such is an illustration of the Christian minister-warrior's constant victory march.

The Christian's Powerful Influence, 15-17. Every true minister of Christ is a censer of sweet incense wafting Christ's fragrance abroad upon a corrupt and ill-smelling world—not only as a future anticipation but as a present experience. This influence of gospel presentation has a twofold effect. To them "who are being saved," i.e., who *have* accepted Christ and *are* walking in Him, it is "a perfume of life unto life," giving life and fullness of life (Jn 10:10). To them "who are being lost," who have rejected Christ and continue to reject Him, it becomes "a perfume of death unto death," bringing eternal death and confirming the rejecter in death. So vital is a true minister's vocation, involving such tremendous issues for eternity, that the question is, who is sufficient (Gr. *hikanos,* "qualified" or "adequate") for such a task, 16? The answer, only those whom God calls and equips. Only those who do not "huckster" or "traffic in the Word of God" for personal profit, 17, but declare it with utmost sincerity as in God's omniscient presence.

3:1-6a. THE GLORY OF THE MINISTRY— ITS ACCREDITATION

It Is Not Accredited by Self-Commendation, 1. The apostle found it both unwise and unnecessary to justify himself or commend himself by letters of commendation to them or from them. Personal performance for Christ is to be a self-evident credential and our best recommendation.

It Is Accredited by Paul's Witness and Work, 2-3. His Corinthian converts were Paul's credentials, 2, as well as Christ's credentials, 3. They were his "letter," written in his heart, which everyone could see, 2. They were also Christ's "letter," written not with pen and ink but by the supernatural working of the Spirit upon human hearts, 3.

It Is Accredited by God, 4-6. Paul's qualification was divine. His ministry was attested by Christ, 4, dating back to the Damascus road experience. It was made possible by divine enablement, 5. His sufficiency (cf. 2:16) was *from* (*ek*) God. It had its source in God. God "made" him sufficient as a minister, 6a.

3:6b-11. THE GLORY OF THE MINISTRY—
ITS MESSAGE OF GRACE

Its Message Was Spiritual and Life-Giving, 6b-11. As the gospel of grace is energized by the Holy Spirit, it is contrasted with the law of Moses as a code written on stone. The power of the minister of the new covenant does not lie in the letter of the law, the old covenant, which convicts of sin and serves only to manifest our death, but in the Spirit of God who grants us eternal life. The old legal covenant that kills is thus "a ministration of death," 7, "of condemnation," 9, since it merely points out our sin. The new covenant of grace "gives life," 6, as a "ministration of the Spirit," 8, and as a "ministration of righteousness," since it also provides for the removal of our sin, 9. One is graven on stones, 7; the other on the human heart. One is glorious, 7; the other is much more glorious, 8-11.

3:12-18. THE GLORY OF THE MINISTRY—
ITS TRANSFORMING POWER

It Is to Exercise Great Boldness, Illumination and Liberty, 12-17. The glory of the Christian ministry engenders such hope that plainness without fear is demanded when proclaiming its message, 12. Ministers of the new covenant are not to be like Moses, who put a covering over his face after he received the law on Sinai (Ex 34:28-35). The glory that suffused his face was a fading, temporary glory that represented the law, which was to pass away, 13. In its place the gospel of grace would come to reflect the face of Christ with a permanent glory. Judaism has a veil over it (Ps 69:22; Isa 6:9-10; Rom 11:7-12), which veil has been done away in Christ, 14-15. "Nevertheless when it [the heart of Israel] shall turn to the Lord, the veil shall be removed," 16 (Zech 12:10—13:1; Rom 11:26-27). Meanwhile, the believer who gives Jesus Christ His rightful place finds himself moving in the realm of liberty. Instead of the regulation of outer law, he finds the dynamic of inner law, 17, "the law of the Spirit of life in Christ Jesus" (Rom 8:2).

It Is to Enjoy Wonderful Transformation, 18. Three steps are involved: (1) *the seeing*—"beholding," having a clear image presented of the glory of the Lord with an unveiled or uncovered face (unlike Moses); (2) *the changing*—"are being changed into his likeness from one degree of glory to another" (RSV); (3) *the transforming*—"by the Spirit of the Lord," the change being God's work in us, not our own work or effort.

4:1-7. THE GLORY OF THE MINISTRY— ITS SINCERITY

It Renounces All Sin and Sham, 1-2. Such a ministry is grounded in a personal experience of God's mercy in Christ. This becomes the powerful incentive for unselfish service in carrying the message to others,1. Negatively, it rejects every semblance of a false life; and positively, commends itself by a true testimony lived before God as well as men, 2.

It Advertises Jesus Christ, 3-7. He must be proclaimed and set forth, for unless He becomes visible, our gospel is veiled to those that are lost, 3. Satan, the god of this present age (cf. Jn 12:31), has blinded the minds of unbelievers to the light of the gospel. It is, therefore, essential that if this blindness is to be penetrated, Christ, not we ourselves, must be proclaimed. He is the divine source of light, 5 (cf. Jn 8:12). We are the human source, 6 (cf. Mt 5:14). The light must shine from God through us. "The treasure" of the indwelling Spirit is "in clay pots," fragile earthen containers (the believer's body), that the excellency of the power might be from God, and not from us, 7.

4:8-18. THE GLORY OF THE MINISTRY— ITS SUFFERINGS

It Suffers but Is Spiritually Benefited, 8-11. "Troubled . . . yet not distressed [straitened or crowded into a narrow place]; perplexed, but not in despair [hopeless]; persecuted, but not forsaken," 8-9. The believer experiences suffering and death, as did his Lord, so that Christ's life may be revealed and seen in him, 10-11.

It Has an Inner Secret of Spiritual Stature, 12-18. This secret comprehends self-crucifixion, 12; intense faith, 13; radiant hope, 14; self-forgetfulness, 15; spiritual strength, 16; proper perspective, 17; and a wise life goal, 18.

5:1-13. THE GLORY OF THE MINISTRY— ITS FEARLESSNESS IN THE FACE OF DEATH

Its Conviction of the Resurrection of the Body, 1-8. The Christian has the strong assurance, 1, 6, of a future life. His redeemed body is called "an earthly tent house." Death is the taking down of the tent,1. The resurrection body is called "a house not made with hands." Immortal, it is described as "eternal in the heavens," 1. The believer's earnest desire for the resurrection body, 2-4, is answered in God's redemptive work for him in Christ, particularly the Spirit of God indwelling the believer's body as a forepayment and guarantee of the glorification of the body, 5. This fact of the gospel of redemption gives great confidence, 6-8. Whether still in this body (life) or absent from the body (death), we are of good courage, boldly cheerful in the face of our glorious hope. Faith, not sight, becomes the manner of our living, 7. We know that what we do not see is often more important and lasting than what we do see (cf. 4:17-18). Absent from the body (death) for the believer means to be present with the Lord (in heaven). Could there be a greater incentive to valor?

Results of the Conviction of Bodily Resurrection, 9-13. (1) It makes us labor, i.e., constantly bend every effort to be well-pleasing to the Lord, 9. (2) It makes us reckon on the fact that all believers must face a judgment of their life and works since they have been saved. This is to be the *bema* (judgment seat) of Christ. Reward or loss of reward (cf. 1 Cor 3:12-15; 4:5; 9:27) will be the issue, 10. (3) In the light of the judgment of our works before Christ, we plead with believers to be faithful to the Lord in their life and testimony, 11. "The terror of the Lord" is reverential awe and deference due Him. (4) It leads to selfless, dedicated service to God and men, 12-13.

5:14-21. THE GLORY OF THE MINISTRY— ITS MOTIVES AND DIGNITY

Its Glorious Motive, 14-17. This is "love" (cf. 1 Cor. 13:1-8), both Christ's love for us and our love for Christ. This mighty dynamic constrains or impels us. Love is the constant drive of the true minister of Christ. He concludes that because one (i.e., Christ) died, all (believers) died *in Him,* by virtue of spiritual union with Him (1 Cor 12:12-13; Rom 6:3-4), and are thus "dead" in their position, i.e., as God sees them. Therefore, love should be the impelling motive, since we know one another as fellow members of Christ in spiritual union and not after the flesh, 16. Being in Christ involves a new creation with a *completely* new order, 17.

Its Wonderful Dignity, 18-21. We have been reconciled to God, 18. We have been given the ministry of reconciliation, 18-19. Reconciliation describes the effect of Christ's death upon man as a sinner alienated and estranged from God by the Fall. In response to the believing sinner's faith in Christ, divine power works in him a complete transformation toward God from enmity and aversion to loving trust. We are Christ's ambassadors, 20-21. To be an ambassador means to represent one's country (heaven) and government (the Lord) with prestige, wisdom, maturity and dignity.

6:1-10.   THE GLORY OF THE MINISTRY—
ITS CHARACTER

It Is to Be Blameless, 1-3. (1) Because it involves cooperation, both with God and with fellow Christian workers, 1a. (2) Because it entails the proclamation of the free grace of God, 1b-2 (cf. Isa 49:8), which can be so easily abused by license—the grace of God received "in vain"—to *no purpose* in practical holiness. (3) Because there is an urgency in Christian evangelism that must not be nullified by inconsistency in the evangelist, 2. (4) Because the ministry is peculiarly liable to criticism and blame from sinful men, as well as from carnal believers, 3. Stumbling blocks are easily erected by wrong conduct.

It Is to Be Approved, 4-10. Negatively, the ministry is to be blameless, 1-3. Positively, it is to be highly approved, 4-10, by the loftiest type of devoted and selfless service to God and man. The apostle names *nine testings of a minister* in which he is to honor God: in afflictions, necessities, distresses, stripes, imprisonments, tumults (mob violence), labors (rigorous toil), watchings (vigils) and fastings (hunger and thirst willingly endured), 4-5. Then he proceeds to indicate *nine ways by which the minister of Christ is to be characterized*: by purity, by knowledge, by long-suffering, by kindness, by the Holy Spirit, by sincere love, by the word of truth, by the power of God, by the armor of righteousness, 6-7. He lastly names *nine paradoxes,* 8-10, which occur in the life of the true minister who honors God in the nine testings and nine characteristics just outlined. These paradoxes are: by honor and dishonor, by evil report and good report, as deceivers and yet true, as unknown yet well known, as dying yet living, as chastened yet not killed, as sorrowful yet constantly rejoicing, as poor yet enriching many, as having nothing yet possessing everything. The blameless and approved ministry is one of miracle and paradox. It gives the God of miracle and paradox a chance to work.

6:11—7:1.   THE GLORY OF THE MINISTRY—
ITS PURITY

Purity Is the Basis of Affection Among Believers, 6:11-13. Paul pleads for the complete affection of the Corinthians. He poured his sincere love upon them. He pleads for a return in kind. But this manifestation of love among believers is dependent upon their separation from sin and from alliances with unbelievers. To achieve Christian unity and to love one another, God's people must be separate from that which is contaminating.

A Plea for Purity, 6:14—7:1. The unequal yoke is anything that unites a believer with an unbeliever in a common purpose, 14 (cf. Deut 7:2-3; 22:10). It undermines fellowship and communion, 14, concord and agreement among Christians, 15-16. Separation is not from *contact* with evil in the world, but from complicity with it and conformity to it (Jn 17:15; Gal 6:1). The result of separation from evil is the full manifestation of God's fatherhood, with unhindered worship and communion, 17-18; therefore the exhortation to cleansing from all uncleanness, 7:1, in the light of the promise of blessing in the preceding verses.

7:2-16. THE GLORY OF THE MINISTRY— ITS REFLECTION IN PAUL'S LIFE

Paul's Loving Concern for the Corinthian Believers, 2-11. He urges them to open their hearts toward him, 2, protesting his interest in their welfare, 3-7. He mentions his severe dealing with them in a former letter, 8, but rejoices that it produced godly sorrow, 9, which works repentance to salvation in contrast to the sorrow of the world which produces only death, 10. The apostle is glad because the Corinthian believers really were sorrowful to repentance, 11.

He Desires Them to Be Assured of His Love, 12-16. He was solicitous concerning their recognition of the fact that he cared for them, 12. Their welcome of Titus assured the apostle that his confidence in them was not misplaced, 13-16.

8:1-15. EXAMPLE AND EXHORTATION IN GIVING

Christian Giving and the Example of the Macedonian Christians, 1-8. Paul uses the example of the generous Macedonian churches in inculcating the grace of giving, 1. Their giving was miraculous for its rich liberality out of deep poverty, 2-4. The reason was basic, they *first* gave *themselves* to the Lord, 5. All charity and Christian giving should begin where the Macedonian believers began. It was there that the Corinthian believers were exhorted to begin, 6-8. Giving ourselves to the Lord should always be done *first*. If God *has us*, He has our *all*, including our pocketbooks.

Christian Giving and the Example of Christ, 9-15. The apostle sets forth: (1) The *grace of giving*, i.e., a disposition wrought in the heart by the Holy Spirit, 9 (cf. v. 7). (2) *The example of Christ in giving*: "Though he was rich, yet for your sakes he became poor, that ye through his proverty might be rich," 9b. (3) *Pledging in giving*, 10-11. A pledge to aid in the offering for the impoverished saints in

Jerusalem had been made by the Corinthians a year previously. Something had hindered. Let them now keep their pledge. (4) *Willingness in giving,* 12. This is a prime requisite. Spiritual giving is willing giving based on what we have, not on what we do not have. (5) *Equality in giving,* 13-15 (cf. Ex 16:18). One is not to be burdened while another is eased. There is to be willingness to share abundance with the needy.

8:16—9:5. INSTRUCTION IN WISE HANDLING OF FUNDS

The Lord's Money Is to Be Handled in a Manner Above Reproach, 8:16-24. Funds are to be administered by approved men of integrity, 16-18. These men are to keep such records as can be mutually checked, 19. The management of funds is to be in such a business-like manner as to avoid any blame or suspicion, 20, in accordance with principles of strict honesty before the Lord as well as before men, 21. The character of the men chosen to administer the offering, 22-24, should be sufficient evidence of integrity of management.

The Corinthians Are Urged to Meet Their Share, 9:1-5. Paul tactfully commends them, 1-2, yet sends delegates to them to make sure they will be ready, 3-4, and their gift in hand, 5.

9:6-15. PRINCIPLES OF SPIRITUAL GIVING

The Principle of Harvest, 6. The apostle has already hinted at the principle of readiness, 1-5. Now he adds the principle of sowing and reaping. A bountiful sowing will mean a bountiful reaping. More is reaped than is sown.

The Principle of Free-Will Donation, 7. There is to be no constraint, no pressure, no high-powered clever methods. Giving is to be a matter of personal decision. Joyful, spontaneous gratitude to God for what He has done for us in Christ alone can make a "cheerful" (hilarious) giver. This is the kind of giving that delights God, because its motive is love.

The Principle of Grace, 8-10. Spiritual giving taps God's boundless resources. The grace He is able to make abound toward us is His blessing in our lives, that will enable us in His sufficiency to minister to needy people in their deficiency, 8-9 (cf. Ps 112:9). He gives to us that we may give to others. This is a tremendous promise opening up new vistas of challenge to *every* believer, 10.

The Principle of Thanksgiving, 11-15. Observing the law of spiritual giving and spiritual receiving engenders an attitude of gratitude to God, 11. Not only is the receiver blessed, but the giver also, 12 (cf. Acts 20:35). The receiver is particularly positioned to glorify God, 13, and to be stirred up to prayer, 14. Thanksgiving ultimately goes back to God's supreme gift of salvation through Christ, 15, the ground of all spiritual grace. This gift is so wonderful it is said to be "inexpressible," "unutterable," "incapable of being described," 14.

CHAPTER 10. THE GLORY OF THE MINISTRY DEFENDED—COMMENDED BY THE LORD

The Minister Commended by His Attitude, 1-6. He is to be characterized by "the meekness and gentleness of Christ," 1, yet by godly boldness, 2, and a martial prayer life, 3-4 (cf. Eph 6:10-20), that is highly effective in spiritual results, 5. This prayer power overthrows human reasonings and leads every thought into submission to Christ. It also imparts spiritual stamina to punish disobedience, 6.

The Minister Commended by His Authority, 7-11. The authority is not idly presumptuous or dependent upon outward appearance, 7-10, but is from the Lord and genuinely real, 11. It is for the purpose of "edification" (upbuilding) and not for "destruction" (downpulling), 8.

The Minister Commended by the Lord, 12-18. Self-commendation as well as comparison with others is unwise and not to be engaged in, 12. Like Paul, our ministry is to be reviewed not in the light of our own self-elected standards but according to Christ's norm, 13-14, not claiming credit for others' labors, 15-16, but glorying in the Lord, 17. The fact must be recognized that he is approved whom the Lord approves, not the one who commends himself, 18.

11:1-15. THE GLORY OF THE MINISTRY DEFENDED BY SINCERITY ATTESTED IN SERVICE

The Sincere Motives of Service, 1-6. Like Paul, the true servant of Christ is often criticized falsely and wrongly accused. Sincerity, which is one of the greatest assets in life, is here referred to by the apostle as a quality to answer his critics and to show that his life was right. He was sincere in his jealous love for the spiritual welfare of the Corinthians, and it was his desire that they might be chaste and pure in Christ, 2, unspoiled in the "simplicity that is in Christ," 3, by false teachers, 4. Against these Paul pits his eminence and knowledge as an apostle, 5, and also the proof of his faith in Christ exhibited by his works for Christ and for the Corinthians, 6.

The Rewards of Sincere Service, 7-11. Sincere service abases self and serves unselfishly, 7-9. It enables the servant of the Lord to boast in the Lord and to be offenseless in his service for others, 10. It proves the reality of the servant's love for those to whom he ministers, 11.

The Counterfeits of Sincere Service, 12-15. The apostle determines to persist in a blameless ministry, thereby cutting off occasion for criticism from counterfeit servants who eagerly look for some cause to attack him, 12. He describes these insincere ministers, branding them in their true colors as "false apostles, deceitful workers," 13, under Satan's delusive, transforming power, 14, whose end will be according to their evil works, 15.

11:16-33. THE GLORY OF THE MINISTRY DEFENDED BY SINCERITY ATTESTED BY SUFFERING

Paul Answers His Critics, 16-23a. The apostle resorts to a legitimate type of ridicule and satire to answer his critics forcefully and to prove to them his utter sincerity. They boasted. He also would boast for argument's sake, 16, even though foolishly, 17. They gloried in the flesh. He also would glory for argument's sake, 18, and adds a note of penetrating sarcasm to shame the Corinthians out of being imposed upon by false, insincere ministers, 19-21. They boasted what they once were, 22. They prided themselves in being Hebrews racially, nationally and religiously. He could claim the same and more! They prided themselves in what they were now, 23. They boasted of being "ministers of Christ." He could claim the same and more! How? By citing his sufferings and testings for Christ.

Paul Cites His Sufferings to Prove His Sincerity, 23b-33. In these verses he summarizes his entire ministry and glories in his sufferings for Christ in contrast to the false apostles who gloried in themselves and their personal accomplishments. Adversity is the real test of sincerity in spiritual matters. The multitudes follow the easy road; only the sincere glory in their sufferings for Christ. Acts 13—28 is a commentary on Paul's sufferings here cited to answer his carnal critics.

12:1-10. THE GLORY OF THE MINISTRY DEFENDED BY EXPERIENCE OF GOD'S DEALING

The Experience of God's Glory, 1-6. Experience is important in any work or job. So it is in commending the Lord's servant. Paul uses his sublime experience of God's revealed glory to him, 1, to defend his ministry against false workers. Paul recounts one of his many visions and revelations. "A man in Christ" was the apostle himself, 2-3. He was caught up to "the third heaven," the place of God's abode, 2, or paradise, 4 (see notes on Lk 16:19-31). Paul could not tell whether he was "in the body," i.e., still alive in the flesh, or momentarily dead, with his soul and spirit released temporarily from the physical body. This may have occurred when he was mercilessly stoned at Lystra and dragged out of the city for dead (Acts 14:19-20). Besides the experiences of God's glory are experiences of his testing and chastening.

The Experience of God's Testing, 7-10. Paul's "thorn" (Gr. *skolops,* "anything pointed," like a stake for impalement or a sharp brier to prick) was a real pain or experience of suffering with a definite purpose to keep him humble, 7. In the case of God's servants, suffering is never pointless. It tests to strengthen or chastens to correct, after acting as a deterrent to sin. In this case it was an angel or messenger (*aggelos*) of Satan—perhaps some physical weakness or disability caused by Satanic or demonic power, but permitted by God. What it actually was is pure conjecture, for it is not specified. It was in God's will and not removable by prayer or faith, 8. Its purpose was to teach that: (1) God's grace is fully sufficient for His tested servant; (2) divine strength is fully realized only in human weakness; (3) God's servants are to glory in human weakness so that God's power may rest upon them; (4) when they are weak in themselves, they are strong in Christ, 9-10.

12:11-21. THE GLORY OF THE MINISTRY DEFENDED BY EXPERIENCE OF EFFECTIVE SERVICE

Ministry for Christ Is to Be Effective for Christ, 11-12. We either help or hinder the cause of Christ. Simply because we claim to be a minister, 11, is no proof that we produce the true works of a minister. Paul authenticated his apostleship by the genuine works of a true apostle, including miracles and the sign gifts, 12 (cf. 1 Cor 12:8-11).

Effective Service Excels in Helping Others, 13-19. It does not seek its own advantage and good, 13, but the good of others, as a father seeks the welfare and security of his children, 14. It willingly spends and is spent for others, irrespective of the requital of love, 15-16. It acts in sincerity before God in Christ for the edifying of God's people, 17-19.

Effective Service Warns Against Sin, 20-21. It does not gloss over sin in the saints, but demands a clean break with iniquity.

13:1-10. THE GLORY OF THE MINISTRY DEFENDED —COMMENDED BY HONESTY

Honesty to Correct Faults, 1-6. The true minister is no coward. He is willing to face a battle. He will not back down to sin, 1-2. Witnesses must support a testimony against a sinning saint (cf. Deut 19:15). The apostle gave proof of Christ's speaking through him and the power of God operating in him, 3-4. He pleaded for self-examination (1 Cor 11:28; 1 Jn 3:20). This was not a morbid introspection, but a healthy scrutiny and taking stock of one's spiritual condition. There is such a thing as a believer being "reprobate" (*adokimos,* "disapproved" or "disqualified") in the race, 5-6 (1 Cor 9:27), facing loss of reward or possible physical death (1 Cor 3:14-15; 5:5; 1 Jn 5:16).

Honesty to Demand Honesty, 7-10. He was honest himself and demanded honesty in those to whom he ministered, 7. He warned that truth cannot be fought against successfully, 8. His delight was the strength and maturity of God's people, 9, and he would not compromise to achieve this goal, 10.

13:11-14. BENEDICTION AND FAREWELL

The Exhortation, 11-13. The apostolic call is to be "perfect" (i.e., mended in one's ways), of good comfort, of one mind, to live in harmony and to enjoy God's love and peace.

The Benediction, 14. The blessing of the Triune God is evoked upon the Corinthians.

GALATIANS

MAINTAINING OUR FREEDOM IN CHRIST

Date and Occasion. Written by the apostle Paul about A.D. 58, the epistle was necessitated by serious defection among Paul's converts in the Roman province of Galatia made on his first (Acts 13:4—14:28), second (Acts 16:6) and third (Acts 18:23) missionary journeys. The apostle is called upon to defend the gospel of free grace which he had proclaimed to the Gentiles (Acts 14:27). Judaistic teachers had come in to adulterate Paul's gospel with a mixture of human works and some form of legalism.

The Purpose. The situation made it incumbent upon Paul to defend his apostleship as genuine, the gospel he preached as divinely authoritative, the doctrine of justification by faith alone apart from any admixture of works or law-keeping as valid, and the principle of Christians living on the basis of freedom in Christ, and by faith appropriating their resources in Him as effective in practice.

Contrasts Presented in the Epistle. The apostle presents the gospel in a series of contrasts or opposites, things that ought not to be mixed because they are incongruous. The cross of Christ produces the contrasts.

CONTRASTS IN GALATIANS

Ch. 1—2	Lost in Adam	Saved in Christ
Personal	All die physically in Adam	All live spiritually in Christ
	Another (false) gospel	The genuine gospel
	Man's reasoning	God's revelation
Ch. 3—4	Law	Grace
Doctrinal	Works	Faith
	The curse of death	The blessing of life
	Condemnation by works	Justification by faith
	Servants in bondage (defeat)	Sons in freedom (victory)
	The old covenant (symbolized by Hagar)	The new covenant (symbolized by Sarah)
Ch. 5—6	Living in the flesh	Walking in the Spirit
Practical	Works of the flesh	Fruit of the Spirit
	Falling from grace	Standing firm in grace
	World or self the object of glorying	The cross the sole object of glorying

> **Outline**
> PERSONAL—Gospel Revelation, 1:1—2:14
> DOCTRINAL—Justification, 2:15—4:31
> PRACTICAL—Sanctification, 5:1—6:18

1:1-9. SALUTATION AND THEME

The Greeting, 1-5. The apostle combines his personal greeting with that of his colleagues in gospel ministry, 1-2. He stresses the divine origin of his apostleship, because his enemies in Galatia attacked both him and the gospel he preached. His salutation, 3-5, stresses the redemptive self-giving of Jesus Christ (Gal 2:20; 1 Cor 15:3; 1 Pet 2:24) issuing in deliverance from this "present evil world." In this phrase Paul refers to this age or era in which evil is allowed to work and Satan, demons and evil men are permitted a large sphere of activity. From all this Christ has rescued and set us free.

The Theme—the Gospel the True and the False, 6-9. The apostle is astounded or amazed that his converts in Galatia have been so quickly changed over to or transferred from the gospel of free grace

(salvation by grace alone) to "another [*heteros*] gospel, which is not another" (*allos*, of the same kind; but heterodox, not of the same class or category), nor just as good. It is a false gospel and hence not the gospel at all, only a perversion of it, 7. Here for all time Paul finalizes and fixes the true gospel of redeeming grace from any admixture of legalism or human works, 8-9. His solemn "anathema" does not express narrowness or personal pique, but emphasizes the tremendous importance of safeguarding the gospel, which involves issues of eternal destiny.

1:10—2:14. PAUL'S TRUE GOSPEL— A DIVINE REVELATION

Proved by Paul's Early Experiences and Ministry, 1:10-24. The Galatians had the fact fully demonstrated to them that the apostle was not a man-pleaser, 10. He backs up his declaration of the divine origin of his gospel of grace with his character, which had been fully manifested to the Galatians, 11-12. Paul declares that he himself had once been a foremost protagonist of the "Jews' religion" (*Ioudaismos*, "Judaism"), which his legalistic foes were trying to mix with the gospel of grace, 13-14, but he had left it for something better. He had divinely received the revelation of grace and proclaimed it long before he saw any of the other apostles, 15-24.

Proved by Paul's Later Experiences and Ministry, 2:1-14. Nothing was added to the divine revelation of Paul's gospel of grace by subsequent contacts with the apostles, 1-6. His apostolic authority and message were fully owned by them, 7-10. If appeal was made to Peter's authority, his course of action among Gentile believers, and his failure to claim any such authority when rebuked, were sufficient answers that Paul's message was completely independent of men, 11-14.

2:15-21. JUSTIFICATION AND THE JEWISH LAW

Jews (Not Just Gentiles) Must Be Justified by Faith, 15-18. Paul here proves to the Galatians that whatever false claims were made by the legalistic perverters, he and Peter were both in complete concord doctrinally. Paul cites his words to Peter, 15-16, when he rebuked that apostle's inconsistent practice at Antioch, 11-14, to emphasize the fact of their mutual agreement that justification by grace through faith is entirely apart from observance of the Mosaic law, 16. In verses 17-20 Paul's declaration may be thus paraphrased, "But

661

if we *Jews* [cf. Rom 3:19-23], in trusting in Christ fully to be justified, are thus placed in the position of being lost sinners like the Gentiles, is it therefore Christ who makes us sinners? Of course not! It is rather by placing ourselves again under law after being justified freely by Christ, that we build again that which we destroyed and constitute ourselves transgressors against the gospel of grace."

Justification by Faith Cuts Us Off from Legalism, 19-21. "Dead to the law," 19, means to be completely out of the sphere of and cut off from communication with the law of Moses or any principle of legalism. This is accomplished through the law which has already executed its sentence of condemnation upon the one who trusts in Christ, 19. Thus, the law has no more claim on the Christian. The result of being "dead to the law" is enablement to "live unto God" (Rom 7:4), because of a new position in Christ of co-crucifixion and co-resurrection, whereby the inliving Christ lives out His life in the believer, 20. The principle is faith (Rom 6:11) in the believer's new position in the Son of God. As I believe *I am what I am* in union with Him, I enjoy the experiential reality of that new position, 20. This is the Christ life. To mix law works with this grace frustrates it, i.e., sets aside or abrogates it. In a fallen sinner, God's imputed righteousness can come only by Christ's death. Otherwise His death was useless, 21.

3:1-5. JUSTIFICATION AND THE HOLY SPIRIT

The Gift of the Spirit Is by Faith, 1-3. The Galatians in lapsing from grace into legalism were senseless or irrational and bewitched or deluded by its spell. Especially so since Christ's all-sufficient death had been so fully and distinctly expounded before them, 1. Paul in contrasting several completely antithetical principles—law vs. grace, works vs. faith, flesh vs. Spirit—asks several pivotal questions. Upon what principle had they "received the Spirit"? (Cf. Acts 2:38-39; 8:14-15; 10:45, and see notes on these passages.) The answer is, the Spirit from the time of Pentecost has been given purely on the basis of faith in a crucified and risen Redeemer.

Christian Living Is by Faith, 4-5. They began the Christian life in faith, relying on the Spirit. Were they to be made mature or complete in it by the flesh, 3? Was all their suffering for Christ to no purpose, 4? Was the apostle's dynamic ministry among them by faith to be ignored and counted as mere fleshly activity and law keeping? Or did the Spirit of God minister to him and through him to them?

3:6-9. JUSTIFICATION AND THE ABRAHAMIC COVENANT

The Abrahamic Covenant Is on the Basis of Faith, 6-9. Abraham believed God, 6 (cf. Gen 15:6), and so was justified, as are all those who like him believe God, 7. The Scripture foresaw the justification of the Gentiles by faith and proclaimed the gospel in the Abrahamic covenant promises, 8 (cf. Gen 12:3). This has been realized in the justification of Gentile believers, 9.

3:10-18. JUSTIFICATION AND BLESSING

Redemption from the Curse, 10-13. What is "the curse," 10 (cf. Deut 27:26)? It is the result of the law's requirement of obedience from men who are sinners by nature, 10 (cf. Jas 2:10). Breaking one of its commands is being guilty of breaking the whole law. The purpose of the law was not to justify, 11 (cf. Hab 2:4), or to be a way of salvation. The law was intended to demonstrate man's helpless sinfulness, 12 (cf. Rom 3:20; 7:13), that he might be saved by Christ, 13. The curse of the law fell upon our Lord, 13. By His death on the tree (the cross) the Sinless One became the Sin Bearer, the Sin Offering (2 Cor 5:21; 1 Pet 2:24; cf. Isa 53:4, 11; Ps 22:1). He took the curse that was ours because of a broken law and bore it in His sinless person, thereby buying and setting us free from the curse and condemnation of the law.

Reception of the Blessing, 14-18. The blessing of justification includes:

(1) *"The blessing of Abraham,"* 14-16, the benefit accruing from faith, 8 (cf. Rom 4:2-5). Abraham is the great example of faith, "the father" of all those who believe (Rom 4:13-25). He honored God by faith that credits God and God's word. He believed in the promise concerning Isaac and a physically impossible posterity which was the link to faith in the promised Seed, Christ. The blessing of salvation Abraham enjoyed has come to the Gentiles through Christ. This salvation described with regard to the Holy Spirit (cf. Lk 24:49; Acts 2:38-39, see comments) is called "the promise of the Spirit," 14. The reason is that the salvation brought by Christ entails a wider and fuller bestowment of the Spirit (cf. Jn 7:37-39; Lk 24:49; Acts 1:5-8; 2:1-4) than was ever possible in pre-Pentecost experience.

(2) *The promise through faith,* 14. The "promise" is important (cf. its recurrence, 14, 16, 17, 18, 21, 22, 29). Neither law nor law-keeping offered any real promise, since fallen man could not keep

its injunctions. But grace and faith bring promise upon promise. Abraham and his Seed (Christ) is the one channel through which the promises pass, 16.

(3) *The covenanted blessing of an inheritance*, 17-18. An inheritance is not worked for or earned. It is entirely by one's birthright or adoption. The promise to Abraham, confirmed to Jacob when he went down to Egypt, was given 430 years before the law at Sinai (cf. Ex 12:40-41). The law therefore does not disannul the promise. Grace and faith precede law and works and supersede them in Christ to fulfill Abrahamic promises. The covenant blessing, therefore, is *wholly by faith*. Salvation is by faith *plus nothing*.

3:19-29. JUSTIFICATION AND THE PURPOSE OF THE LAW

The Question, 19a. If justification is by faith plus nothing, 14-18, and not at all by works of the law, what then is the purpose of the law?

The Answer, 19b-29. (1) It was "added" (i.e., put or placed by the side of grace) "for the sake of transgressions," i.e., for the divine purpose that it might *clearly reveal sin* as transgression or personal guilt (Rom 5:13). Also it was to show the inveterate sinfulness of man's old nature, since the law could not keep man from sinning, but actually provoked him to sin more. Its introduction after covenant grace was to be *strictly* temporary, "until the Seed [Christ] should come." The promise channeled through Him would then be realized. (2) It was added to conclude all, both Jew and Gentile, "under sin," 22 (cf. Rom 3:19-23). (3) It shut up sinful men to faith as the only medium of salvation, 23.

(4) Dispensationally it marked a period of child-training for the Jew. It was a pedagogue to train him as a minor with childish "do's" and "don'ts," till he came to the period of spiritual adulthood in Christ, 24-25, when the responsibility of love responds spontaneously to the benefits conferred by grace. (5) It was thus introductory to the present age of spiritual adulthood, 25-29, in which (a) "faith [the faith principle of salvation, faith plus nothing] has come," i.e., has been proved by the law of Moses to be the *only* way of salvation for guilty sinners, 23, 25; (b) all believers have the adult status of "sons [*huioi*] of God" under faith and not mere "children" as under law, 26; (c) all believers have been baptized by the Holy Spirit into spiritual union with Christ, 27 (cf. Rom 6:3-4); (d) and thus "have put on Christ," 27. The figure is that of laying aside the garment of a boy (Mosaic law observance) for the adult toga (faith in Christ). Spiritual union with Christ means all human distinctions

are laid aside, 28, and the believer inherits through Christ the promises of faith given to Abraham, 29.

4:1-7. JUSTIFICATION AND SONSHIP

Sons Under Faith vs. Servants Under the Law, 1-3. The apostle illustrates the difference between the Mosaic (legal) age and the gospel (grace) age inaugurated by the death and resurrection of Christ with the figure of a child heir in a family. Although the child is heir, as long as he is a minor he does not differ from a slave, despite the fact that he is destined to inherit all. He is under child-training discipline ("the pedagogue," 3:24) until the father constitutes him heir. The comparison is to the Jews ("we") who when under the law were children and servants—not sons—and in servitude to the legalistic elements of the world, not free in the grace of Christ, 3.

Sonship by Redemption from the Law, 4-7. Christ's incarnation was in "the fullness of time," i.e., when the law had fully discharged its task as a pedagogue to bring us to Christ, 4. Then God sent His Son to redeem us from the law, that we might have the placement of full grown sons in the new age of grace. Placement as full adult sons (*huiothesia,* Rom 8:15; Eph 1:5) means full deliverance from the child-servant status of the legal age with the Spirit sealing the filial relationship, 6-7.

4:8-18. JUSTIFICATION AND FREEDOM

Losing Our Liberty in Christ, 8-14. Before they became acquainted with God, the Galatians were in bondage to the enslaving deities of paganism, 8. Being set free by a knowledge of the one true God revealed in Christ (cf. Jn 8:32, 36), will they again be victimized by a religion of *doing something* to gain favor with the Deity? Will they revert to the status of religious slaves, victims of a system of works and merit (weak and beggarly elements) to acquire salvation, 9? These elementary religious regulations are stated, 10, badges of religious bondage, insignia of pagan religions and false cults (cf. Col 2:14-17). Their lapse back into their rudimentary ceremonies has caused the apostle concern, 11. The result in conduct contrasts sharply with the Galatians' original joyous reception given Paul and his message of grace, 12-14.

Losing the Blessing of Liberty, 15-18. What a boon is liberty, especially spiritual emancipation! How easily lost! How jealously to be guarded! The Galatians once enjoyed this blessing and were willing to prove it by any sacrifice, 15. Would their loss of that liberty result in rejection of the apostle and the liberating truth he proclaimed, 16? The legalists made a show of affection; however, not for the good purpose of liberating but enslaving. Indeed, they were determined to shut out or separate their victims from the liberating truth of the grace of Christ that their dupes might show them obedient affection, 17. But obedient affection must be shown in a good thing (the liberating grace of Christ), not in a bad thing (the enslaving legalism of the false teachers), 18.

4:19-31. THE NEW COVENANT VS. THE OLD

The Illustrating Allegory, 19-26. The allegory, 22-27, is directed as an illustration to deluded but justified *believers,* 19-21, who were attempting to mix two mutually exclusive systems, law and grace. For the fifth time in this letter the question of whether the believer is under the law is broached (cf. 2:19-21; 3:1-3; 3:25-26; 4:4-6; 4:9-31). The allegory presents Sarah and her son versus Hagar and her son, 22-24 (cf. Gen 21:9-21). The two mothers represent two covenants, Sarah the new covenant, Hagar the old covenant; one gracious, the other Mosaic and legal (Jn 1:17). Their sons, Isaac and Ishmael, are the children of these covenants, with their spiritual status fixed before God.

ALLEGORY: LAW VS. GRACE

Hagar	*Sarah*
Old covenant (law)	New covenant (grace)
Mt. Sinai	Mt. Calvary
Bondage, her children were slaves performing the rites of the Sinaitic law	Freedom
Jerusalem that now is	Heavenly Jerusalem (cf. Heb 12:18-24)
Bondwoman	Freewoman
After the flesh	Divine promise
Her children born into slavery	Her children born into freedom
Powerless to change their status	Dignity of sons with a preferred status
Works	Faith

The Meaning of the Allegory, 27-31. (1) The believer loosed from the law is free in Christ under grace. (2) Sarah (the new covenant of grace) is productive of a great spiritual progeny, occasioning intense joy, 27, in contrast to Hagar (the old covenant), now unproductive and spiritually barren (cf. Isa 54:1). (3) As Sarah's posterity, believers are "children of promise," 28. The new covenant is a covenant of promise—promise of divine favor, of life eternal, of the Holy Spirit, of sonship, of freedom, etc. (4) Sarah's descendants are persecuted by Hagar's descendants. There is bitter antipathy between the children of the Spirit and the children of the flesh, between the spiritual believers free in Christ and the carnal believers enslaved by legalism, 29. One suffers persecution, the other avoids it (cf. 2 Tim 3:12). (5) The believer is to realize his freedom from the law, 30-31. Therefore as the epistle proceeds from *doctrine* to *duty,* his privilege and obligation is not to the Mosaic law, nor indeed to any principle of legalism, but to live out his freedom in Christ by the power of the Spirit.

5:1-9. THE PERIL OF FALLING FROM GRACE

Falling from Grace, 1-3. The apostle now leaves the *doctrinal* discussion, 2:15—4:31; to deal with the *practical* issues of experiential sanctificaton, ch. 5—6. Having proved the truth that the believer is not under law but under grace (cf. notes on 4:19-26), the apostle warns of the peril of being entangled once more or held fast in "the yoke of bondage." By this latter expression Paul means legal rites or ceremonies of Judaism, particularly circumcision, 2-6. Given as a sign of the Abrahamic covenant (Gen 17:9-14; Rom 4:11) and a part of the Mosaic covenant (Lev 12:3), the reality of all that this sign of separation in the flesh stood for was fulfilled in Christ (Col 2:8-10). The legalists were declaring that circumcision was necessary to salvation in addition to faith in Christ (Acts 15:1).

The Sad Results of Falling from Grace, 4-9. (1) This meant leaving the principle of faith plus nothing to be saved. They had "fallen away from grace," 4 (cf. 4:9). (2) It meant being entangled again in the yoke of bondage, and (3) nullifying the full efficacy of Christ's atonement, 4. (4) It meant losing sight of the position of spiritual oneness in union with Christ, 6, and (5) the importance of one thing—"faith working through love," 6. (6) It meant losing the race, 7; (7) disobeying the truth, 7; (8) listening to false teachers rather than the Spirit; and (8) accepting the dangerous "leaven" of false doctrine (legalism) that could corrupt the whole gospel of truth, 9 (cf. 1 Cor 5:6-8; Mt 16:6, 12).

667

5:10-15. THE CALL TO FREEDOM UNDER GRACE

The Call, 10-13a. The apostle expresses assurance that the Galatians will heed his warning and the false teachers will be dealt with as they should, 10-12. He shows how the legalists avoid persecution and "the offense of the cross," 11 (1 Cor 1:23; 2 Tim 3:11-12), by insisting on circumcision and law-keeping.

The Warning Against License, 13b-15. The call is to "liberty." But Christ-bought liberty is not to be used as an opportunity for fleshly indulgence or as a cloak for sin, but for love manifested in service, 13. The law is thus fulfilled in love (Lev 19:18). But a lack of love will result in biting and devouring one another (Jas 3:13-16) and mutual destruction, 15 (Isa 9:18-21).

5:16-18. SANCTIFICATION AND THE HOLY SPIRIT

The Human Condition, 16a. "Walk in [by] the Spirit." This involves not fleshly striving, legalistic ordinances, or works of the law, but simple adjustment to the Spirit. The imperative (command) is in the present tense and involves a *continuous* reliance upon the Spirit, i.e., faith in the Spirit's operation. *"Keep on* walking" (a figure of living), in which each *step* is a potential fall as the body is momentarily thrown off balance. "Walk by the Spirit" (RSV), i.e., by means of (agency) the Spirit, indicates the divine agent and dynamic of victory under grace. Sanctification is thus by faith not by works; by the Spirit of God, not by morality or self-effort.

The Divine Undertaking, 16b-18. "Ye [by the aid of the Holy Spirit] shall not fulfill the lust [keen desire] of the flesh," i.e., the body as controlled by the old, unrenewed nature, which always exists side by side with the new nature in the believer, 17b. When we believe, God undertakes. But it is God, not we ourselves, who does the sanctifying work. The unceasing struggle between the old nature and the new, 17, and the futile self-effort of the flesh versus the effective inworking of the Spirit, demonstrate that those who are *"by the Spirit* continually conducted,"* alone have complete victory, 18. They alone are delivered from the bondage of self-effort which seeks to please God by law-works.

5:19-26. WORKS OF THE FLESH VS. FRUIT OF THE SPIRIT

The Works of the Flesh Listed, 19-21. These are the outcome of unbelief—failing to walk by means of the Spirit, which involves faith.

They are works or fleshly operations because they are the results of the activity of the old, unrenewed nature being made manifest (i.e., being openly revealed), laying its defiled nature bare through the vehicle of the human body. *All* these sins may be manifest in a believer unless he walks continually by the Spirit. The old nature in him is just as vile as the old nature in the unregenerate. If he commits or practices such fleshly sins in not walking by the Spirit, he may expect the heavy chastening of God in this life (1 Cor 5:5; 11:30-32; Heb 12:5-11), and the forfeiture of rewards and honors in the life to come (1 Cor 3:11-15; see notes on 1 Cor 6:9-12). "Inherit" the kingdom of God is not the same as "seeing" or "entering" the kingdom of God (see notes on Jn 3:3, 5).

The Fruit of the Spirit Specified, 22-26. "Fruit" is in contrast to "works." One is by faith, the other by human effort; one by the Spirit, the other by the flesh. One is holy, the other polluted. One springs out of the renewed nature, the other is produced by the old nature. One is singular "fruit," a blended whole; the other is plural "works," discordant confusion. One is contrary to law because it is criminal; against the other there is no law because it is virtuous, 23. The basis for the production of the fruit is the believer's once-for-all recognition of the fact of his death-to-the-flesh *position* in Christ and his *reckoning* on that position, 24 (cf. Rom 6:11), permitting the Spirit to produce the fruit. "If we live by means of the Spirit [instrumental], let us walk [frame our conduct in accordance with this truth] by the Spirit," 25. This will liberate us for the Spirit's production of "the fruit," not the flesh's production of its "works," 26.

6:1-18. SANCTIFICATION IN ACTION

Dealing with Fellow Christians, 1-6. The spiritual believer, i.e., one in whom the fruit of the Spirit is produced (5:22-23), and who is being sanctified experientially by the Spirit, is instructed in his conduct toward the *erring* fellow believer, whom he is to restore with humility, considering his own exposure to temptation and sin apart from the Spirit's ministry. The *burdened* fellow believer, 2-5, is to be helped, 2, in all humility, 3, and faithfulness, 4, realizing everyone has a burden to bear, 5. "The law of Christ," 2, is the law of love for one's neighbor (Lk 6:27-38). A *teaching* brother is to be supported financially by one who is benefited by his ministry, 6.

Sowing to the Spirit, 7-9. The new life in Christ is presented under the figure of farming or husbandry. Deception is easy for a believer. He is not to forget that the inexorable law of sowing and reaping applies to him as spiritual or carnal, as well as to the unsaved, 7-8 (cf. Jas 1:16; 1 Cor 3:10-13). The spiritual believer is, therefore, not to become weary in the work of faith, 9 (1 Cor 15:58; 2 Thess 3:13). He will reap at the time of harvest (Jas 5:7-8) if he does not faint or despair, i.e., be unloosed or exhausted spiritually, 9 (Heb 12:3, 5).

Manifesting Spirituality, 10-13. Spirituality is shown by doing good to all, particularly to fellow believers, 10 (cf. 6:1-6; cf. Rom 12:13; 1 Jn 3:17), and by exemplifying a spirit of sacrificial love, 11-13. This the apostle did in the matter of fidelity to the gospel of grace against legalistic contamination (insistence on circumcision as necessary to salvation). Verse 11 refers to the apostle's writing this epistle in very "large letters," possibly because of poor eyesight (cf. Gal 4:13-15). He wrote it himself, rather than dictating it, as a token of his sacrificial love for the Galatians.

The Basis of True Spirituality, 14-18. This is the cross, 14 (cf. 1 Cor 1:18). The reason is that it separates the world from the believer by his death-to-sin position in Christ (Gal 1:4; 2:20), and the believer from the world, i.e., the Satanic world system which is the chief foe of true spirituality, 14-15. In this "new creation," Christ is all. Human merit and legalistic self-effort are nothing, i.e., are of no use or relevance. The "Israel of God," 16, are saved Jews who believe that salvation is by grace through faith, totally apart from the works of the law (Rom 4:12; 9:6-8; Eph 2:8-10). For this truth the apostle has suffered, proving his utter sincerity in proclaiming the message of grace. The brands or scars in his body, the tokens of his suffering for the gospel of grace, are the evidence. He closes with a benediction, 18.

EPHESIANS

BLESSED IN THE HEAVENLIES IN CHRIST

Date and Author. This magnificent epistle was evidently addressed to the church in Ephesus (cf. Acts 19), but intended also as a circular letter to neighboring churches. The omission of the phrase "at Ephesus" (1:1) in two of the oldest manuscripts suggests that early copyists shied away from localizing the letter when it was intended for reading in other churches in the vicinity. Paul had spent three years in the Ephesian metropolis (see notes on Acts 19:8-41). He wrote this letter about A.D. 61 or 62 from prison in Rome, the first of his so-called Prison Epistles, and sent it to Asia together with Colossians and Philemon.

Significant Words in Ephesians

In occurs about 90 times. It stresses the truth of the believer's union with Christ in death, resurrection, ascension and present session. The fact of the believer's position *"in* Christ" permeates the entire thought of the epistle.

Grace occurs 13 times, showing that this epistle is an exposition of "the gospel of the grace of God" (cf. Acts 20:24).

Spiritual (or *Spirit*) occurs 13 times, defining both the sphere of truth dealt with in the epistle and the realm of life in which believers are living.

Body occurs eight times. It is a metaphor describing our positional union with Christ (ch. 1—3).

Walk is found eight times. Our walk is our behavior within the Body of Christ, how we act in union with Him, the Head. This term is the heart of the practical appeal of the epistle.

Heavenlies is found five times, setting forth the exalted *sphere* of the believer's *position* in Christ and the *realm* of his walk and warfare.

Mystery is found five times. The term does not denote something inscrutable, but a hidden truth held in secret till the proper time for its revelation in the divine program.

Outline
Our Position in Christ, Ch. 1—3 (What we are before God)
   The Believer as God's Child, 1:1-23
   The Believer as a Member of Christ's Body, 2:1-18
   The Believer as God's Building, 2:19—3:21

Our Practice of Christ, Ch. 4—6 (How we are to act before men)
A Worthy Walk, 4:1—6:9
A Continual Conflict, 6:10-24

1:1-6. CHOSEN IN CHRIST BY THE FATHER

Blessed, Chosen and Adopted in Christ by the Father, 1-6. After
the salutation, 1-2, the apostle presents God the Father's role in
our salvation, 3-6. This includes: (1) Blessing us with all spiritual
blessings in "the heavenlies," 3, i.e., in the realm of the believer's
position and experience as a result of his being united to Christ by
the baptism of the Spirit (1 Cor 12:13; Rom 6:3-4). (2) Choosing
us for Himself (election) *before* the foundation of the world (earth)
"in Him" (the Son), 4*a*, as "the Lamb slain *from* the foundation of
the world" (Rev 13:8). (3) Choosing us for glory hereafter "that
we should be holy and without blame before him," 4*b*. (4) Fore-
ordaining us in love to sonship by adoption, 5*a*, or "placement as
adult sons" (cf. 1 Jn 3:2), according to His sovereign will and
pleasure, 5*b*. (5) Assuring us of His present and future delight, the
goal of His electing love being centered in Himself, the Chooser, 6.

DIVINE ELECTION

This is the sovereign act of God in grace by which from eternity
certain are chosen from the human race for Himself (Jn 15:19;
Eph 1:4). Election pertains only to God's people, not to the lost.
Men are not elected to perdition. Christ is the Chosen of God par
excellence (Isa 42:1-7). God the Father chose us in eternity past in
Him. All elect are selected to a holy life of separation to the Chooser
(Jn 17:16; Eph 1:5). Election may be *corporate,* as in the case of
the nation Israel (Isa 45:4) or the Church (Eph 1:4), or *individual*
(1 Pet 1:2), being based on divine decree and foreknowledge.

FOREORDINATION

Foreordination is that exercise of the divine will by which that
which has been determined by God from eternity past is brought
to pass by Him in time. It is our guarantee that what He has predetermined for us shall not be nullified.

FOREORDINATION AND FREE WILL

Foreordination concerns only God's people. So far as the human
race is concerned, every man may not only accept Christ as Saviour

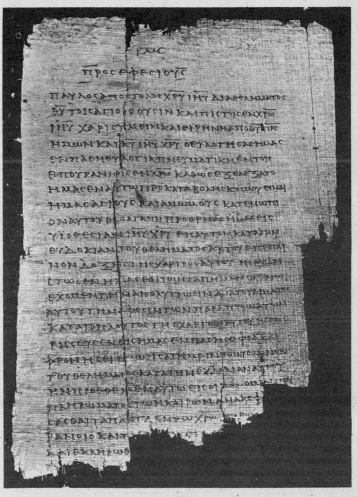

The first page of Ephesians from a Beatty-Michigan manuscript dating about A.D. 200. (*Courtesy UML*)

but is urged and invited to do so. The ground of this invitation is the work of the incarnate Son which made the human race savable (Heb 2:9; Jn 3:16). Free will concerns the man outside of Christ. Once he accepts the gospel and is "in Christ" his viewpoint changes, as God from His side shows him why the believer is accepted. Divine foreordination and human free will are humanly irreconcilable, but like two parallel lines that meet in infinity, they have their solution in God. Only when the sinner exercises personal faith in Christ and enters the portals of salvation does he discover emblazoned on the inside of the doorway "Chosen in him before the foundation of the world" (Eph 1:4).

1:7-12.   REDEEMED BY THE SON

Purchased by Christ's Blood, 7. Our redemption was *planned* by the Father, 3-6, and *provided* by the Son. Christ's role in our salvation is now outlined, 7-12. "Redemption" is deliverance by means of a price paid, in this case Christ's blood (Lev 17:11; Mt 20:28). The result is "forgiveness of sins," 7 (cf. Heb 9:22), because His blood, being that of the God-Man, was infinitely efficacious (Jn 1:29) and accomplished a completed redemption (Jn 19:30).

Enlightened by His Grace, 8-10. The wisdom and knowledge of God center in Christ, 7b-8 (Mt 11:27; Jn 1:18; 14:8-9; 1 Cor 1:30). His redemption purchased us out of the ignorance of the slave-to-sin category into the intimacy of son relationship and revelation (Jn 15:15). The purpose is that during the last of the ordered ages of time, He might "gather into one all things in Christ," thus making way for the eternal state (1 Cor 15:24-28, see notes).

Given an Inheritance in His Purpose, 11-12. The Authorized Version renders verse 11, "We have obtained an inheritance." How wonderfully true! (Cf. Rom 8:17; 1 Cor 3:21, 23.) The expression, however, may mean that we were made a heritage, His inheritance in us being meant rather than our inheritance in Him. The purpose is "that we should be to the praise of his glory," 12. *He* shall be glorified in us, as well as we in Him.

1:13-14.   SEALED BY THE SPIRIT

The Spirit Energizes Faith to Salvation, 13a. The Father planned, 3-6; the Son provided, 7-12; and the Holy Spirit *applies* our salvation in persuading us to appropriate it (cf. Jn 16:13-15). "The word of truth" is called "the gospel of your salvation" since it results in deliverance on the basis of faith.

The Spirit Seals the Believer, 13b-14. The Spirit Himself indwelling the believer is the seal. This marks: (1) *Ownership*—that we belong to God (1 Cor 6:19-20). In this connection the Sealer is called "the Spirit of promise," since He is the pledge or earnest (part payment guaranteeing a complete transaction) of full possession of that which has been purchased (cf. 2 Tim 2:19). (2) *Security*, guaranteeing safe delivery to heaven (Eph 4:30) and assurance of full redemption in glorification. (3) *A completed transaction* (Jer 32:9-10; Jn 17:4; 19:30).

SALVATION IN PANORAMA—
WORK OF THE TRIUNE GOD

	Father	Son	Holy Spirit
Past	Chose us in the Son	Purchased us with His blood	Persuaded us to believe the gospel
Present	Places us as sons	Reveals the Father's purpose and will	Seals us as God's own
Future	Will fully accept us in Christ	Will inherit us as His own	Will claim us in final possession

1:15-23.   PRAYER FOR REALIZATION OF THE BELIEVER'S POSITION IN CHRIST

The Apostle's Prayer Interest, 15-16. The faith and love of God's people aroused prayer and thanksgiving on the part of the apostle.

The Apostle's Prayer, 17-23. He petitions (1) for *knowledge* on the part of God's people concerning their position and possessions in Christ and concerning Christ's position toward them and inheritance in them, 17-18; and (2) for *power* of that position to be manifested in their lives by faith, 19-23 (cf. Rom 6:11). The basis of that power is the resurrection, ascension and exaltation of Christ "far above" every power, angelic or demonic, 20-22, and Christ's leadership of the Church, 23, His Body, composed of all those baptized into vital union with Him (1 Cor 12:13) the Head (Rom 6:3-4).

2:1-7.   THE BELIEVER AS A MEMBER OF CHRIST'S BODY

The Body Defined, 1:22-23. See above.

The Body Brought into Being, 2:1-7. All in the body are regenerated, 1-5. They were dead in sins, 1; disobedient to God, 2-3a; and deserving of wrath, 3b. This is *what they were*, 1-3, utterly lost, cut off, helpless, fallen under demon control and divine displeasure. *What God has done* in Christ, 4-7 (cf. Rom 3:21—5:21), is summed up in His marvelous *remedy* in Christ. This comprehends God's mercy, 4 (cf. Ps 103:8-18), His love, 4, and grace, 5. Mercy is God's love in action, resulting in grace, which is His undeserved favor toward lost, helpless sinners, the objects of His love. The results of the operation of grace are threefold—past, present and future, 5-7. (1) *Past*— we *were* raised from the dead *with* Christ, 5-6a. In the plan of God this occurred when Christ was raised. By virtue of our union with Him by the baptism of the Spirit (Rom 6:3-4), we were raised with Him. So all in the Body are not only *regenerated*, 1-5, but also *baptized by the Spirit* into union with Christ, 6. This is what is meant to be saved, 5 (cf. 8). (2) *Present*— we *are now* seated in the heavenly realms *in union with* Christ, 6b. This is true because we have been baptized by the Spirit into Christ's Body (into union with all other believers in Him, 1 Cor 12:12-13), and into union with Him the Head of the Body (Rom 6:3-4). Hence we share the death, burial and resurrection position of the Body. (3) *Future*— God will display to the universe the unfathomable wealth of His gracious kindness to us *through* Christ, 7. The divine triumph over sin through grace will be put on exhibition to every created being—fallen and unfallen alike. The divine glory will thus be demonstrated.

2:8-10. THE WAY OF SALVATION IN THE BODY

Saved by Grace, 8-9. This is the indubitable conclusion resulting from verses 1-7. The emphasis is (1) on the *divine method* of salvation—"by grace"; (2) on its *assured certainty*—you have been saved (a past fact and present certainty) and are being saved (a continuous unfailing present operation), no uncertainty or lack of assurance here; (3) on its *human medium*—"through faith"; (4) on its *non-meritorious basis*—"not of yourselves," not "of works"; (5) on its *free, undeserved character*—"the *gift* of God"; (6) on its *God-glorifying end*—"lest anyone should boast."

Saved to Serve, 10. Saved *apart* from works, but unto good works. These truths emerge: (1) To be saved, "created in Christ," is for the purpose of entering God's plan for the redeemed life, "unto good works." (2) This plan has been divinely foredetermined for us, and is not a hit-or-miss proposition, "which *God has foreordained* that we should walk in them."

2:11-18. THE BODY MADE ONE BY CHRIST'S BLOOD

What We Were in Ourselves, 11-12. Salvation, as it pertains to the individual, 1-10, now is seen as it affects the collective. The race in its twofold division, Jew and Gentile, comes into view. The sacrifice of Christ goes beyond meeting the individual's need and meets that of society, removing all obstacles to the unity of the new Body in doing away with all distinctions of race, class, or even sex (cf. Gal 3:28). The moral and spiritual plight of the individual seen in 2:1-3 is now applied to the corporate, and we are seen to have been dispensationally and collectively undone as well, being (1) "Gentiles in the flesh," 11a, and belonging to the vast unsaved mass of humanity (cf. Rom 1:18-32); (2) outside of Jewish spiritual privilege through the Abrahamic covenant sealed by circumcision, 11b; (3) without Christ, without hope, without God; (4) aliens to the covenants and promises made to Israel, 12.

What We Are in Christ, 13-18. In strong contrast to what we were: (1) We are now united to Him instead of being separated from Him. (2) We have been brought near by Christ's finished work instead of remaining far off as unsaved Gentiles. He has broken down "the middle wall of partition," referring to the outer court of the temple for the Gentiles separated from the inner court into which Jews alone might enter. (3) We are given full acceptance with God through Christ apart from legal ordinances, 15a. (4) We have been made a new community of His people, the Church, Christ's Body, here called "the new man," 15b (cf. Eph 1:22-23; 1 Cor 12:12-13; Col 3:10-11; Heb 12:23). (5) He has abolished the old enmity between Jew and Gentile by being "our peace," 14-15a, and preaching "peace," 17, reconciling both to God. (6) Both have been given access to God by one Spirit, 18 (cf. 4:4-6).

2:19-22. THE BELIEVER AS GOD'S BUILDING

The Building Described, 2:19-22. Believers also are constituted "one building." This involves the Triune God. It is God the Father's "household" into which the believer is born, 19. The holy "temple" into which the believer is corporately built is the Lord's, the Son's 21. The "habitation" or abode which He has chosen to indwell is the Spirit's, 22. The Lord's "temple," 20-21, has its foundation in both the Old Testament and the New Testament "apostles and prophets," in the truth entrusted to these men concerning the one foundation (cf. 1 Cor 3:10-11). Jesus Christ Himself is the chief cornerstone (Ps 118:22). All prophecy and the apostolic message center in Him, who binds the building together. The building is composed of "living stones"—born-again Jews and Gentiles made *one* "in Christ." Completion of the building will be at the Lord's coming. It (not any earthly cathedral or shrine) is the real building of God in this age.

3:1-12. THE FORMATION OF THE BUILDING REVEALED

The Mystery and Its Meaning, 1-6. It was revealed to the apostle Paul, now a prisoner, 1, 3. It involves the dispensation (economy) of the grace of God, 2, and is called "the mystery of Christ," 4, "hidden in God," 9. It is the divine purpose to make both Jew and Gentile a new entity called the Church, the Body of Christ, formed by the baptism of the Holy Spirit (cf. 1 Cor 12:12-13). This mystery was latent in OT typology and prophecy but not revealed, and was foretold by Christ (Mt 16:18). The revelation of its meaning was divinely made known to Paul, who expounds the mystery of the Church in his epistles.

The Mystery and Paul's Ministry, 7-12. Paul was especially equipped and constituted a minister of the mystery, 7-8. The mystery involves the unsearchable (unexplorable, incomprehensible) riches of Christ, 8, including His person, His work, His intercession, His coming again, His eternal kingdom, His inheritance in us. The purpose of this ministry, 9-12, is to make known now "the fellowship of the mystery" (that Gentile with Jew had become one by faith in Christ) to all the earth and to all the heavenlies.

3:13-21. PRAYER FOR KNOWLEDGE AND POWER

The Petition, 13-19. The prayer is addressed to the Father, 14-15, seeking the threefold fullness of the Triune God, 16-19. Paul asks that God's *Spirit* would make the Ephesians strong in the inner man, 16; that by *Christ's* indwelling their hearts by faith, 17a, and rooting and grounding them in love, 17b, they would know His full love consonant with their position in grace, 18-19a; and that they would be "filled to all fullness" by *God the Father,* 19b. This threefold fullness of God is the believer's *state* in Christ. The apostle prays for an experiential comprehension of this position with its resultant *power* realized in everyday living.

The Benediction, 20-21. The practical realization of the believer's position in Christ is made possible by our omnipotent God. He is willing and able to bring this about in response to our knowledge of and faith in this truth, 20. Such a God and Saviour is worthy of all glory, 21.

4:1-6. A WALK WORTHY OF CHRIST

The Walk Described, 1-3. "Walking" is a common figure for everyday living. Living in accordance with one's *position* in Christ is "walking worthily." This is the believer's gracious privilege, the response of his love to God's love displayed in saving him with the wonderful salvation outlined in ch. 1—3. Hence the language of the book is that of beseeching or imploring, not legalistic commanding. The virtues of humility, meekness, long-suffering, and forbearing love, 2, are basic in maintaining the practical unity of the Body of Christ. The Spirit alone can effect this experiential oneness—hence it is "the unity *of the Spirit*," 3.

The Basis of the Worthy Walk, 4-6. Sound doctrine, 4-6, always underlies right conduct, 1-3. Doctrinal defection forfeits a worthy walk. The doctrinal *sine qua non* of such a walk is the recognition of: (1) "one body" composed of *all* who are born again; (2) "one Spirit"—the Holy Spirit of God; (3) "one hope of your calling," the divine call to sainthood ("called saints," 1 Cor 1:1); (4) "one Lord," Jesus Christ, the Head of the Body and the center of our unity; (5) "one faith," that body of truth "once for all delivered to the saints" (Jude 3), and focusing in the death and resurrection of Christ (1 Cor 15:3-4); (6) "one baptism," that of the Spirit (1 Cor 12:13), which forms the "one body" in union with Christ the Head (Rom 6:3-4), the entity of the unity; (7) "one God and Father of all [believers], who is above all [created intelligences], and through all [His plans], and in you all [believers]." This is scriptural ecumenicity.

4:7-16. THE MINISTRY AND A WORTHY WALK

Christ's Gifts for a Worthy Walk, 7-11. Every individual in the Body is given grace or spiritual enablement and blessing to walk worthily of his high calling and position in Christ. This is made possible according "to the measure of the gift of Christ," 7, i.e., His great ascension gift of the Holy Spirit (Jn 14:16-17; Acts 2:38-39). This gift of the Spirit was the direct result of Christ's glorious victory, 8-10, over all His foes and ours, none excepted, 9-10. His ascension, a proof of His resurrection, marked His *complete triumph* in that He "led captivity captive" (Ps 68:18). By His redemptive conquest He made captive the powers of evil that once held us captive. It also resulted in His *dispensing "gifts to men*," 8. *The* gift par excellence, 7, is the Spirit (Lk 24:49), but other gifts which make possible a worthy walk are also included, notably gifted men,

11. They all remain except "the apostles," which were meant to be temporary. Cf. 1 Cor 12:8-28 where the gifts or spiritual enablements (not the men) are in view.

Purpose of the Gifts, 12-16. In general the gifts (including gifted men) are given for "perfecting" (mending or equipping) the saints for the work of ministering on the Lord's behalf and building up the Body of Christ, 12, and producing maturity, 13, especially in doctrinal matters, 14, manifested by love, 15-16. As a result Christ becomes the center of unity and the object of occupation.

4:17-29. THE NEW MAN AND A WORTHY WALK

The Old Man Put Off, 17-22. "The old man," 22, is the unregenerate man ruled by his corrupt, fallen nature (Rom 6:6). Verses 17-22 describe his conduct characterized by (1) a heathen or pagan way of life, 17a; (2) "vanity" or futility of thinking, 17b; (3) a darkened mind alienated from God, 18a; (4) spiritual ignorance and blindness, 18b; (5) moral insensitivity and ethical debasement, 19. In God's reckoning, the old man *in the believer* has been crucified and is dead. As an old, worn-out soiled garment the old man has been put off through learning Christ, having been taught by Him, 20-21. It is "truth" in Jesus, i.e., positional truth concerning our union with Him as Saviour from sin, which constitutes the basis of deliverance from the corruption of the old nature, 22.

The New Man Put On, 23-29. "The new man," 24, is the regenerate man with a new nature in whom Christ is formed (Col 1:27). In the reckoning of God, the believer has put on the new man as a clean garment. This new man is characterized by a renewed mind, 23, in contrast to the blind ignorance of the old man, 18; and he is divinely created in the likeness of God, in true righteousness and holiness. This new position is the basis for deliverance from falsehood, 25; sinful anger and grudges, 26-27; theft and laziness, 28; and impure speech, 29. Deliverance comes by claiming our in-Christ position by faith, making it an experiential reality.

4:30-32. THE HOLY SPIRIT AND A WORTHY WALK

The Holy Spirit Is Grieved by an Unholy Walk, 30. He is the dynamic of a worthy walk. Stop grieving Him or causing Him pain or distress! Why? (1) Because He is the *holy* Spirit. Unholiness distresses Him. (2) He is the "Holy Spirit *of God*," a divine person. (3) He has sealed or stamped us as God's own, and God's honor is brought into disrepute by our sinning. (4) He has sealed us "to the day of redemption" (full glorification). Our safety and security are not to be abused by license.

The Holy Spirit Effects a Holy Walk, 31-32. He enables us to put away sin—bitterness, wrath, anger, clamor, evil speaking and all ill will, 31. He enables us to be kind, compassionately tenderhearted, forgiving, because He makes us acutely conscious we have been forgiven by grace, 32 (Col 2:13).

5:1-17.   IMITATORS OF GOD AND A HOLY WALK

Imitating God As Children of Love, 1-7. Since "God is love" (1 Jn 4:8), family likeness requires that we imitate our Father in a worthy walk as children of love, 1-2. God's love is most clearly revealed in the sweet savor offering of Christ, 2 (Lev 1:9, 13). Sexual impurity, covetousness, 3; filthiness, idle prattle and silly levity, 4, are unsuitable to children of love because they are harmful to others. Thus they deny the very essence of love to God and to one's neighbor (Lev 19:18). These sins characterize the unsaved, 5-7, upon whom the wrath of God rests, 6 (cf. Rom 1:18). Should they characterize the professing believer, if truly regenerate, he forfeits any reward or inheritance in the kingdom of God, 5 (see notes on 1 Cor 3:12-16; 6:9-12); if one is still unsaved, he merely deceives himself with an empty profession.

Imitating God As Children of Light, 8-17. Since God is light (1 Jn 1:5), family resemblance necessitates that we imitate our Father in a worthy walk as "children of light," 8 (cf. 1 Thess 5:5). This means (1) walking "in the light" (1 Jn 1:7); (2) exhibiting the fruit of the Spirit, 9 (cf. Gal 5:22-23); (3) ascertaining what is well-pleasing to the Lord, 10; (4) separating from fruitless works of darkness; (5) reproving such works, 11-13; (6) enjoying spiritual alertness, 14 (cf. Isa 60:1-2); (7) living wisely and exemplarily, 15; (8) taking every opportunity to do good, 16 (Col 4:5); and (9) clearly perceiving the will of God, 17 (Rom 12:2).

5:18-20.   THE SPIRIT-FILLED LIFE AND A WORTHY WALK

The True Elixir of Life and the False, 18. Paul warns against intoxicants that give momentary natural exhilaration and often lead to excess, 18a. He contrasts the true stimulant of God, the Holy Spirit. The injunction is to be continually filled with Him (completely submitted to His presence and control), instead of wine.

The Results of Being Spirit-filled, 19-20. These are productive of the greatest good, and involve a life overflowing with joyful song and praise to the Lord, and a thankful spirit, the result of clear appreciation for all God's blessings given to us in Christ's redemption, 20 (cf. Ps 34:1; Phil 4:6).

5:21-33. HUSBANDS, WIVES AND A WORTHY WALK

The General Principle, 21. We are to submit to one another "in the fear of God." This is a broad guiding directive involving all earthly relationships of believers as husbands-wives, 22-23; children-parents, 6:1-4; and servants-masters, 6:5-9.

The Duty of Wives, 22-24. Christian wives are to be in subjection to their husbands as "to the Lord," 22*b*, because the husband is the head of the wife, 23*a* (cf. Col 1:18). The illustration used is the relation between Christ and the Church. Christ is the Head of the Church, 23*a*. He is its Saviour, 23*b*, since He purchased it with His own blood, 25. A Christian wife is to be in subjection to her Christian husband "in everything." The dominating note is love—a loving subjection to "your own," not a mechanical "obey," a word reserved for children, 6:1, and servants, 6:5.

The Duty of Husbands, 25-33. They are to love their wives, 25, as Christ loved the Church and died to sanctify and glorify it, 25-27, because a husband is joined to a wife as one and is one flesh with her, even as the Church is united to Christ in one body joined to the Head, 28-31 (cf. Gen 2:24). Taken from Adam's side, Eve was actually his flesh and bones. But also being his wife, in a relationship that made the "two . . . one flesh" (Mt 19:5-6), she typifies the Church as Christ's Bride. This is a mystery, 32, a glorious, God-revealed secret unfolded in the NT. The union of Christian husband and wife is to be permanent, intimate, and indissoluble, 31, not marred by divorce.

6:1-4. CHILDREN, PARENTS AND A WORTHY WALK

The Injunction to Children, 1-3. Family relations are to be such as to reflect our position in Christ. Children are to obey parents, the only qualification being "in the Lord." This injunction contextually applies to saved parents and children. Children are to obey, providing such obedience does not violate prior duty to God. The Decalogue is cited to enforce the command, 2-3 (cf. Ex 20:12; Deut 5:16).

The Injunction to Fathers, 4. This is twofold: negatively, do not provoke your children to wrath by unreasonable demands (Col 3:21); positively, rear them in the discipline and admonition (warning) which the Lord gives in His Word against sin and wrongdoing.

6:5-9. SERVANTS, MASTERS AND A WORTHY WALK

Servants Are to Obey, 5-8. Slavery was rife in the ancient biblical world. Many slaves were converted to Christ. They are enjoined to obey their masters, living for Christ in the social status in which they were saved, 5a. This obedience is to be genuine, "in sincerity [singleness] of heart," not with "eyeservice, as menpleasers," working only when watched to impress people, but as obedient to Christ Himself, as "servants of Christ, doing the will of God from the heart," 5-7. The servant is to be fully conscious of the reward for good service which belongs to *every* believer, whether slave or freedman, 8 (Col 3:24-25; cf. 1 Cor 3:11-16).

Masters and Employers, 9. The same sincere, Christ-honoring conduct is enjoined upon masters as upon slaves. They are to omit or "leave off" threatening, perhaps suitable for pagan but not Christian conduct. They are to act in the light of Christ's mastery over their lives, bearing in mind there is no respect of men's persons or earthly positions with Him (cf. Acts 10:34).

6:10-20. SPIRITUAL CONFLICT AND A WORTHY WALK

The Warrior's Resources, 10-12. The Christian, in his walk, inevitably engages the opposition and spiritual resistance of Satan and his hosts. Thus, as a Spirit-filled warrior he must continually "be strong" or strengthen himself with the armor provided for him. The ground of the warrior's strength is his position "in the Lord." His strength is "the power of His might." When the Christian takes into account his position in Christ and appropriates the provided armor, the Holy Spirit empowers him to make good the new life in resisting Satanic attack.

The Warrior's Use of His Resources, 13-20. The believer's resources are described under the figure of a Roman soldier's equipment in full battle dress. His secret of victory in spiritual battle is reckoning or counting by faith on those resources which are actually his in Christ, the Victor (Col 1:13; 2:15). "Take unto you the whole armor" emphasizes the responsibility of so reckoning, 13. This the Christian must do if he is to wage effective warfare.

Christ is the believer's defense and therefore all pieces of the armor may speak of Him, but they also speak of the resources which are given to the believer by Him. The girdle of truth gives confidence against the onslaught of error, while the breastplate of righteousness (the practical outgrowth of imputed righteousness) gives protection against the subtle temptations of unrighteousness, 14. The good news of peace with God produces firm-footed stability when facing the enemy, 15, and the shield which consists of faith offers a defense against the devious attacks of Satan, 16. Salvation constitutes the helmet or headgear, protecting the vital organs which have to do with the believer's thought life and spiritual senses, 17a. The only offensive weapon is the sword which the Spirit provides, the Word of God, 17b. Personal knowledge thereof is used by the Holy Spirit both offensively and defensively (e.g., Mt 4:1-11; Heb 4:12).

Prayer is the capstone of the believer's armor in that it is to be his uninterrupted activity. It is in this realm that the armor Christ has provided is appropriated to the immediate conflict being waged, 18. Paul makes personal application in verses 19 and 20.

6:21-24. PERSONAL NOTE; CLOSING SALUTATION

Personal Note, 21-22. Tychicus, a beloved brother and faithful helper of Paul, is mentioned and his ministry make known.

Closing Salutation, 23-24. Peace, love, faith and grace are mentioned in benediction and blessing.

PHILIPPIANS

THE JOY OF KNOWING CHRIST

Author and Theme. This epistle is one written while Paul was a prisoner at Rome, perhaps A.D. 62. Its theme is the adequacy of Christ for all the experiences of life—privation, persecution, hardship, suffering, as well as prosperity and popularity. Christ gives joy and triumph whatever may come, if He is allowed to be the center of life. This is mottoed in Paul's testimony: "For to me to live is Christ" (1:21).

Historical Background. The account of the Philippian mission (Acts 16:6-40) shows the church there was founded under divine leading (Acts 16:6-7) as a result of a directing vision (8-11). It was born in a prison (Acts 16:25-34), and this letter written to it a decade or so later was penned from a prison. A note of triumphant joy in Christ permeates it, despite the apostle's severe testings in the interim (cf. 2 Cor 11:23-33). The note of joy is sounded more than 18 times in the course of the short letter. "Rejoice in the Lord alway: and again I say, Rejoice" (4:4) may be taken as the golden text.

> **Outline**
> The Joy of Christ Our Life, Ch. 1
> The Joy of Christ Our Example, Ch. 2
> The Joy of Christ Our Goal, Ch. 3
> The Joy of Christ Our Sufficiency, Ch. 4

1:1-11. PAUL THE PASTOR'S JOY IN CHRIST

His Pastoral Salutation, 1-2. Paul addresses the local church in Philippi, Macedonia (cf. Acts 16:6-40). It was organized with "bishops" (overseers) and "deacons" (cf. Acts 6:1-7). He greets it as composed of "saints . . . in Christ," but it doubtless, as other local churches, contained some professing members who were not born again.

His Pastoral Joy, 3-11. Paul's remembrance and prayer ministry for the Philippians were characterized by joy, 3-4 (1) because of their continued fellowship in the gospel, 5; (2) because of the apostle's assurance of God's effectual working in them until "the day of Jesus Christ," i.e., the time of judgment of the believers' works at the

Lord's coming when the rewards for faithful service are dispensed, 6; (3) because they shared with Paul his experience of the joy of Christ as the believer's life, which the apostle calls "my grace," 7; (4) because of his great interest in their spiritual welfare, 8-11.

1:12-30. PAUL THE PRISONER'S JOY IN CHRIST

His Confident Joy in Tribulations, 12-20. He is assured his sufferings will result in promoting the gospel, 12, even in the emperor's court itself, 13 (cf. 4:22). His imprisonment in Rome has inspired a fearless confidence in many to speak the Word, 14. He even rejoices that the Word is proclaimed by those who preach Christ contentiously, opposing him, 15-19. Paul's confidence is confirmed by his realization that Christ will be magnified in his body, whether he lives or dies, 20.

The Secret of Paul's Confident Joy, 21-30, is his Christ-centered life. For him "to live is Christ," 21. Outwardly his one goal was Christ, inwardly Christ was living out His life through him. Living, he was blessed with radiant joy. Dying was "gain" because it meant "to be with Christ," which was "far better," 22-23. To remain in this life was, however, more needful for the spiritual progress of the Philippians, 25-26. In the light of his own conflicts, the apostle admonishes them to endure sufferings joyfully, 27-30.

2:1-11. EXHORTATION TO UNITY AND HUMILITY

The Exhortation, 1-4. The basis for the exhortation is the Philippian believers' position in Christ, 1. If they act upon this position they will fulfill the apostle's joy, 2, by realizing their unity which will be effected by genuine selflessness and meekness, 3-4.

The Example of Christ, 5-11. His self-humbling, 5-8, led to His exaltation by the Father, 9-11. This great "kenotic" or self-emptying passage is the basis for the apostle's exhortation, 5. "Let this mind," i.e., settled state of mind or attitude, be in you which was in Christ. The passage teaches (1) the deity of Christ. He was in the "form of God," the second Person of the Godhead, absolute Deity, "equal," i.e., on an equality with God, 6b. (2) This equality was His by right of His glorious person, not something to be grasped after because it was not His by virtue of who He was. (3) As God "he emptied himself," not of His deity but of His heavenly glory and privilege, 7a, (4) becoming incarnate in order to be a "servant," 7b, (5) as a man among men, 7d. (6) He then humbled Himself further, 8a (Ps 40:6-8), by dying, (7) even to the point of dying for sinners on the cross, 8b. (8) As a result, He was gloriously exalted in resurrection, ascension and His heavenly session. This exaltation will be furthered still more in His return and subsequent mediatorial reign, defeating His enemies and bringing great glory to the Father, 9-11 (cf. Heb 2:9; Rev 3:21; Ps 2:8-12).

2:12-16. WORKING OUT INWROUGHT SALVATION

The Exhortation, 12-13. Working *out* salvation is vastly different from working *for* salvation. Salvation can be worked out only by those to whom God has first given it (Eph 2:8-10). Personal salvation is God-inwrought—by faith apart from works. Working it out in daily experience is on the basis of obedience to God's Word, 12a, and by "fear and trembling." Fear is necessary because of the ever-present threat to fail to work out that which is inwrought *by* God. God works in us by the Spirit to enable us to work it out.

The Result, 14-16. This will be: (1) spiritual accomplishment without complaining and friction, 14 (cf. 1 Cor 10:10); (2) blamelessness of life, character in keeping with the position of God's *sons,* 15; (3) proper testimony by light-bearing—"shining as lights" (lumi-

The theater at Philippi, dating back to the New Testament period.
(*Courtesy Howard F. Vos*)

naries) in a sin-darkened world made perverse by sin; (4) effective soul-winning in holding forth, as exhibited wares, "the word able to give life" to those dead in sin; (5) furnishing the apostle joy "in the day of Christ" (cf. notes on 1:3-11).

2:17-30. PAUL'S EXAMPLE OF HUMBLE SERVICE

The Joy of Such Service, 17-18. To realize fully such joy, the apostle is willing to be poured out as a drink offering sacrificially in service, 17, and desires the joy of the Philippian believers to be realized in such a manner also, 18.

The Service Exemplified, 19-30. In Timothy, 19-23, in himself, 24, and in Epaphroditus, 25-30 (cf. Phil 4:18), joyful self-humbling service is seen.

3:1-6. CHRIST THE TRUE GOAL VS. FALSE GOALS

The True Goal in Life Presented, 1. Christ is the true end in life. He alone brings genuine joy. All real rejoicing concentrates in Him and what He has done, 1a (cf. 1 Thess 5:16). To point this out and warn against spiritual counterfeits which steal away this joy is not tedious for the apostle, and is safe for the Philippian believers.

False Goals Warned Against, 2-6. Those who proclaim these false goals, particularly legalistic teachers, violate grace and detract from the all-sufficiency of Christ. They are termed "dogs," 2, "evil workers," since they cause much harm to believers in God's grace. "The concision" refers to the false circumcision and means "the cutting up" or mutilation (*katatomē,* a pun on *peritomē,* "a cutting around" or "circumcision"). The legalists said one had to be circumcised and keep the law to be saved, in addition to faith in Christ (Acts 15:1; Gal 5:1, 3). Paul shows that true circumcision involves faith in Christ without any adulteration of legalism, 3. He uses his own example as a warning against the false goal of trusting in legal righteousness instead of the righteousness of Christ alone, 4-6.

3:7-9. CHRIST THE ONE GOAL IN LIFE

Counting All Lost, 7-8. All the things Paul formerly valued "in the flesh" as a natural religionist, 4-6, which were gains in the old unregenerate life, he now reckons total loss, pure liability, "for Christ," 7. He counts all loss, as excrement, 8b.

Reckoning the Gain, 8b-9. On the credit ledger appears (1) "the excellency" or "surpassingness" of knowing Jesus Christ as his Lord;

(2) winning Christ as the ultimate prize or treasure; (3) "found in him," a position of perfect acceptance in the righteousness of God gained by faith, 9.

3:10-14. CONCENTRATION OF SPIRITUAL PURPOSE

The Object of Concentration, 10-11. The apostle's object is Christ. His purpose is to know Him in broad life experience in a threefold way: the power of His resurrection (victory over sin and death); and what is inseparable, the fellowship of His sufferings (the cross); and what follows, to be "made conformable," i.e., being continually molded into the form of Christ's death. Thus he will possess the experience *of* Christ.

The *"out-resurrection* from among the dead," 11, has reference to the resurrection of believers when separation from sin will be final and conformity to Christ complete. This was Paul's prospect while his life hung in the balance, a prospect deepened by his life purpose, 10. "If by any means" voiced no uncertainty as to his participation in the resurrection, but simply echoed his desire to submit to any means (imprisonment, suffering, death) which would hasten the day of complete conformity to Christ.

The Reason for Concentration, 12-14. Paul did not presume to have gained absolute or final knowledge of Christ as outlined above. Rather, such requires diligent and constant pursuit, having as the ultimate goal the possession of Christ as He had taken possession of Paul, 12. Although the apostle's wonderful career for the Lord was drawing to a close and he had not yet seized in experience the fullness of what he was in Christ, still he exerted the utmost concentration in pursuing the goal of God's upward call in Christ Jesus, 13-14. This probably has reference to the *bema,* or judgment seat of Christ, when the believer's works shall be judged. Paul's aim was evidently to possess such intimate knowledge of his Lord, and his position in Him, that the day of judgment would be one of approval and victory instead of shame and defeat. Every effort was bent with this focus in view.

3:15-19. ANOTHER APPEAL FOR UNITY

The Appeal, 15-16. Those who are "perfect" (*teleioi*), i.e., mature or grown-up both doctrinally and experientially, are to be in the attitude of mind expressed by the apostle in the preceding context, 15 (see comments on 10-14; cf. Gal 5:10). Unity is essential and patience necessary with dear saints who are yet ill-taught on the subject of perfection, 16.

The Example, 17-19. The apostle is able to offer his own walk (manner of life) as an example. "Become co-imitators of me," 17a (cf. Eph 5:1). He urges continual marking or noting of those who walk by God's grace, 17b, because many do not walk thus. They are "enemies of the cross of Christ," i.e., they are hostile in some degree to the complete sufficiency of the death of Christ as the basis of justification before God, adding some other requirement to grace through faith as the way of salvation (Eph 2:8-9). Paul strongly denounces them, 18-19.

3:20-21. CHRIST THE BELIEVER'S EXPECTATION

Our Heavenly Citizenship, 20a. Our commonwealth or native land is in heaven. We are a heavenly people (Col 3:1-4), citizens of a country in keeping with our "high calling."

The Privileges of Our Citizenship, 20b-21. We are expecting or awaiting our Saviour from heaven (Acts 1:9-11; 1 Thess 1:9-10; 4:13-18). He will then complete our salvation in its future sense of glorification, 21. This involves changing "our body of humiliation," i.e., our present physical body still subject to sin, disease and death, 21. This remodeling or transforming will result in "a body of glory," like the resurrection body of our Lord (cf. 1 Thess 4:13-18; 1 Cor 15:52; Lk 24:39). It will be deathless, diseaseless, sinless, indestructible, designed for heaven and the spiritual world. Such a change will be effected by Christ's omnipotence.

4:1-5. STANDING FAST IN CHRIST'S SUFFICIENCY

The Reason for the Injunction, 1. "Keep on standing firmly [present imperative], constantly persevere in Christ." Why? Because we are a heavenly people enjoying a sure salvation (3:20-21) and are to be rewarded for such firm adherence to our position in Christ. "My *joy* and crown" refers to Paul's fruitage in lives, which will be recompensed at the Lord's coming, 1b.

The Result of the Injunction, 2-5. Their constant perseverence will heal personal rifts and grant the "mind of Christ," 2 (cf. 2:5). It will produce a spirit of helpfulness among believers, i.e., those whose names are "in the book of life," 3 (Col 1:27), and will produce double joy, 4. Rejoicing in anything or anyone other than in Christ and in the matter of His atoning work of salvation, always decreases joy. A firm stand also generates "moderation" (gentleness of Christ) and the expectation of the imminent return of the Lord, 5 (cf. 3:20-21).

4:6-9.   THE SECRET OF GOD'S PEACE

The Prescription for Receiving God's Peace, 6-7. The direction is twofold: don't worry about anything, and pray about everything in a spirit of thanksgiving and gratitude, 6. The result will be "the peace of God." This is the peace with which God fills the believer as he stands firmly in his position in Christ, 1. It is to be distinguished from "peace with God" which is the result of justification (Rom 5:1) and the portion of *every* believer. This deeper peace of walking with God is said to be incomprehensible to the merely natural mind. It overtops or surpasses anything the unspiritual mind can grasp; it "keeps on guarding," protecting the mental, emotional, and spiritual life from enemy intrusion of that which would spoil God's peace.

The Prescription for Maintaining God's Peace, 8-9. The secret is (1) to guard our mental life, i.e., what we allow ourselves to think upon or ponder, 8. We are to meditate continually on the things that are true, honest (honorable, reputable), just (righteous), pure, lovely (acceptable), of good report (commendable, laudable). (2) To practice the things which were taught by the apostle and were exemplified in his personal contact with them. The result will mean not only possessing "the peace of God," 7, but "the God of peace" Himself, 9.

4:10-23.   PAUL'S TESTIMONY OF GOD'S PEACE

His Contentment in the Lord, 10-14. He rejoices greatly that the Philippians' care for him has flourished once again, like vegetation revived by a shower, 10. He stresses the fact that he has learned to be satisfied in whatever state he found himself while in the pathway of service for the Lord, 11-12. In Christ he has unlimited potential, 13 (cf. Jn 15:5; 2 Cor 12:9). He is grateful for help in time of necessity, 14.

His Gratitude for Benefit Received, 15-23. He commends the early liberality of the Philippian church, 15-17, and is grateful for their recent gift via Epaphroditus, 18. They are assured that God will honor them as they honor Him in their giving, 19 (cf. Ps 23:1). Paul closes with a benediction, 20, 23, and personal salutation, 21-22. The saints of Caesar's household were converts from the imperial Roman court itself.

COLOSSIANS

THE SUPREME GLORY OF CHRIST'S PERSON

Date and Author. One of the Roman Prison Epistles written by the Apostle Paul (1:1), this letter was dispatched to proconsular Asia by Epaphras, who also delivered Ephesians and Philemon. This letter therefore dates about the same time, probably A.D. 61 or 62.

Purpose and Theme. This epistle was penned to the church at Colossae, a town near Laodicea and Hierapolis. The apostle had learned of two specious doctrinal errors that were threatening the church. One was a form of ascetic legalism (2:14-17). The other was a type of unsound mysticism (2:18-23). To combat both, the epistle exalts Christ in His person and work and the believer's union with Him as the answer for all time to errors of this sort.

Outline
Paul's Interest in the Colossians, 1:1-14
The Glory of Christ's Person and Work, 1:15-29
Christ the Answer to Doctrinal Errors, 2:1-23
Union with Christ the Basis of Christian Living, 3:1—4:18

1:1-8. THE APOSTOLIC GREETING

Paul's Pastoral Solicitude, 1-3. Paul associates Timothy with himself, 1, in this introductory greeting to the believers at Colossae, a small town in Asia Minor. He did not establish the church there but greets it as his own, 2, and declares his earnest prayer interest in it, 3.

Reasons for Paul's Interest, 4-8. He was impressed with their faith in Christ, their love for Christ's own, 4, and the fruitfulness of the gospel in their lives, 6. He also had a personal connection with them through Epaphras, 7, who had made known their "love in the Spirit," 8.

1:9-14. THE APOSTOLIC PRAYER

The Petitions Made, 9-11. Paul's prayer for the Colossians was continuous, 9 (cf. 3). The apostle intercedes (1) for full knowledge of God's will and spiritual perception, 9; (2) that this knowledge might be translated into a "worthy" walk of life (cf. Eph 4:1), productive of good works (cf. Eph 2:10); (3) that further knowledge might be granted, 10; (4) that spiritual power might be given, 11a; (5) that Christian virtues such as patience and long-suffering might be exercised with joyfulness, 11b.

The Name in Which the Petition Is Made, 12-14. The prayer is directed to God the Father, who is said to have qualified us to share the portion which is the inheritance of the saints who dwell in the realm of light, 12 (cf. 1 Jn 1:5). He has rescued us from the dominion of Satanic and demonic power, 13a (cf. Eph 6:10-20) and "has translated us into the kingdom of the Son of his love," 13b. In this One we possess redemption through His death, namely, "the forgiveness of sins," 14.

1:15-17. CHRIST'S DEITY AND CREATORSHIP

Christ's Deity, 15a. He is the image (*eikōn*), the exact likeness or representation, of the invisible God. He is very God of very God, one with the Father, so that he who sees the Image sees the identical likeness of God reflected (Jn 14:9). Apart from the Image, God the Infinite Spirit cannot be seen by a human being (Jn 4:24; Rom 1:20). In Christ preincarnate and then incarnate, God became visible to man (Jn 1:1, 14, 18).

Christ's Creatorship, 15b-17. As Creator, (1) Christ is *prior to all creation,* being the Creator Himself—"the firstborn of," antecedent to, every creature or all creation, 15b. He is "before all things," 17a (cf. Jn 17:5), having existed eternally before all creatures and creation. (2) He is the *Agent of creation*—"for *by* him were all things created," 16a. This statement is repeated, 16b. (3) He is the *Goal of creation.* "All things were created for him," 16c. All creation centers in Him and has its consummation in Him. (4) He is *the Sustainer of creation.* "*Through him* all things hold together." Apart from Him atomic fission would explode the universe. He keeps it together in the form in which He created it (cf. Heb 1:3).

1:18-19. CHRIST'S HEADSHIP OVER THE CHURCH

He Is Head of the Church, 18a. The Church is *His Body.* As the head of the human body is one with the body, so Christ is corporately one in life and destiny with His redeemed of this age. The Holy Spirit baptizes the believer into the Body (1 Cor 12:13) and at the same time into Christ the Head (Rom 6:3-4). As the head directs and controls all the activities of the human body, so Christ directs and controls all the activities of the Church, His spiritual Body (1 Cor 12:12; Eph 1:22).

He Is the Beginning of the New Creation, 18b-19. As the crucified and risen Redeemer He is "the firstborn from among the dead" and as such "the beginning" of the new creation (2 Cor 5:17; Rev 1:5). As "the firstborn of every creature," 15, He is the Creator and imparts natural life. As "the firstborn from among the dead" He is the Redeemer and imparts new resurrection life. Through His redemptive work the "new creation" is brought into being, by virtue of which He is its Head. He is "to have the preeminence" in everything "because in him all the fullness of the Godhead was pleased to dwell," 19. He was very God become man, to create a new people through redemption.

1:20-23.   CHRIST'S WORK OF RECONCILIATION

The Meaning of Reconciliation, 20-21. Reconciliation is Christ's making peace between God and man, who was alienated from and at enmity with God as a result of the Fall. This was accomplished by the blood (Christ's death) on the cross, 20a. Alienation and enmity were centered in man's mind (his thoughts) and were expressed in wicked works, 21. The sinner is reconciled (thoroughly changed) by divine power from a state of hostility and aversion toward God to loving trust (cf. Rom 5:10; 11:15; 2 Cor 5:18-20).

The Purpose of Reconciliation, 22-23. The end in view in Christ's reconciling work, realized in His finished sacrifice, is to present the believer holy, faultless and unreprovable before God, 22 (cf. Eph 5:27).

1:24-29.   CHRIST'S GLORY PROCLAIMED IN PAUL'S MINISTRY

By Paul's Sufferings, 24-25. The apostle rejoices in these sufferings, which are for God's people, 24a. By so doing he "fills up" or completes that which is lacking in his afflictions for Christ endured in his physical body for the sake of Christ's mystical Body, the Church, 24b. Of this Church Paul has become a "minister" (*diakonos*) in accordance with the stewardship or apostolic commission divinely vouchsafed to him for the Colossians' benefit, that he might thereby fully execute the preaching of God's Word, 25c.

By His Fulfilling the Word of God, 25d-29. The complete preaching of the Word of God, 25d, involves the revelation and exposition of the "mystery," 26. This mystery, or divine truth now made known, was unrevealed in ages previous to the Church period, 26a (cf. Eph 3:2-6). It is now revealed through the apostle, 26b, and contains "the riches" of God's glory among the Gentiles, involving their salvation, 27a (cf. Acts 15:14). The quintessence of this mystery is "Christ in you," which is the truth that the crucified, resurrected and ascended Christ dwells in the believer, 27b. It comprehends the fact that Christ is formed in the regenerate or "new man" (cf. Gal 2:20; 4:19; 1 Jn 4:12; cf. Eph 4:24). The indwelling Christ is the believer's "hope of glory," 27c (Col 3:3-4), since the believer is identified with Him and made one with Him in life and glorious destiny. Christ's glorified humanity in heaven is the guarantee that the believer will be glorified for eternity (1 Jn 3:2). The goal involved in proclaiming this mystery is adulthood or maturity in Christ, 28. It requires labor and conflict, but is wrought by the power of God, 29.

2:1-7. CHRIST THE ANSWER TO DOCTRINAL ERROR

The Conflict with Error, 1-2. This involves intense conflict (Gr. *agōnia*, "agony"), 1a, because of demonic opposition directed against God's truth (cf. 1 Tim 4:1-5; 1 Jn 4:1-4), especially against that so sublimely glorious as "the mystery of God," 2. This spiritual struggle was to the end that God's people at Colossae and Laodicea (see introduction) might be comforted or consoled by the truth, 2a; that they might be united in love, 2b; that they might have full assurance of salvation brought by understanding the mystery of God, which centers in the grace of God in Christ, 2c. Error never gives full recognition to grace or produces solid assurance in Christ.

The Answer to Error, 2c-7. This is "the mystery of God," 2, which is *Christ,* in whom the fullness of the Godhead became incarnate for the redemption and reconciliation of man. In the incarnate One are "concealed *all* the treasures of wisdom and knowledge," 3 (cf. Eph 1:9; 3:9). God incarnate is thus the answer to all error (cf. 1 Jn 4:2-3), including persuasive speech and plausible discourse that shove Christ from the center of spiritual thought and activity, 4. Paul's desire is that the Colossians will not make this mistake, 5, but will continue to walk (live) with Christ focal in their doctrine and conduct, as they had received Him, 6-7.

2:8-13. THE PERIL OF FALSE PHILOSOPHY

The Warning, 8. "Beware" means to possess and use the faculty of sight in the sense of being cautious. "Philosophy," literally, love of knowledge, is here any system of religious thought that does not place the person and work of Christ central. Unless the believer is extremely wary, he will be "despoiled," i.e., victimized by imposture, carried off as the prey of such empty delusion. Such vain systems of thought are built on that which has been handed down by learned but unbelieving men, framed according to the elementary principles of the Satanic world system "and are not after Christ." In Him alone are hid *all* the treasures of wisdom and knowledge, 3.

The Remedy, 9-13. The remedy to false religion centers in Christ and involves: adherence to the truth of His *full* deity in humanity, 9 (Jn 1:14; Col 1:19); recognition of the believer's complete spiritual life in union with Him, 10*a*; recognition of Christ's authority as Head of the Body, the Church, as well as of all created intelligences, 10*b*; recognition that union with Christ gives the believer a *new* position. This new position is that of true spiritual circumcision, i.e., the putting off of "the body of sin." The believer is now able to live a life of victory over sin because he has been made alive by the resurrection life Christ has imparted to him, 11-13.

2:14-17. THE PERIL OF LEGALISM

Legal Observances Were Done Away in Christ, 14-15. When the veil of the temple was ripped from top to bottom at Christ's death (Mt 27:51; Jn 1:17; Heb 9:3-8; 10:19-20), the termination of the legal age was indicated. Christ fulfilled the law (Mt 5:17), and by His death liberated us from its condemnation, 14. He erased or blotted out the legal ordinances that condemned us, nailing as it were the document that was against us as sinners to the cross (cf. Eph 2:15-16). Moreover, He despoiled Satanic and demonic powers which bound us (Eph 6:12; Heb 2:14), making a public spectacle of them in His triumph, 15. In Him we have full emancipation.

The Conclusion, 16-17. Therefore, no believer is to pass judgment upon another believer in matters of food, observance of a festal day, monthly new moon, or sabbath, 16 (cf. Rom 14:3). The believer is complete in Christ and has been accepted by Him, 10. No brother is, therefore, to reject such a believer because of non-observance of legal minutiae. These legal ceremonies were only types or shadows of the real things that were to come in Christ. Therefore they can neither add to nor subtract from the completeness which the believer enjoys in Him, 17.

2:18-19. THE PERIL OF FALSE MYSTICISM

The Form of the Error, 18. This pseudo mysticism took the form of Gnosticism, a spurious knowledge (Gr. *gnosis*) which inculcated an assumed humility and a worship or veneration of angels, 18*a*. In doing so it looked upon Christ as merely the highest in rank in the order of spirits, impinging upon the full dignity of His person and work by venerating angels. Paul's warning against it had called forth magnificent statements of Christ's sublime person (1:15-19) and complete work (1:20-23; 2:9-10). Now he brands its false teachers as audacious intruders, prying into a realm of which they were ignorant and impelled by inflated pride, 18*b*.

The Reason for the Error, 19. This false mysticism resulted from "not holding fast" or adhering to the supreme Headship of Christ, 19*a*. Only when the absolute supremacy of Christ is adhered to can the Body, the Church, function normally and grow. As in the case of the human body, the Head must direct all the other functions of the Body, 19*b*.

2:20-23. THE PERIL OF ASCETICISM

The Believer's Emancipation from Legalistic Ordinances, 20*a*. The medium of emancipation is death, a complete separator. This is the *position* the believer enjoys in Christ by virtue of identification with Him (Rom 6:3-4). This position of death to legalism of any sort is to be reckoned on (Rom 6:11) and converted into the *experience* of deliverance from legalistic "do's" and "don'ts." These the apostle calls "the rudiments," simple elements of the *kosmos*, the world system. It inculcates a works-merit basis of acceptance with God in opposition to a grace-faith basis founded on the all-sufficiency of Christ's person and work. The tendency is for these rudimentary elements to produce a legalistic asceticism, dishonoring to the freedom Christ has purchased for those in Him.

Result of This Emancipation, 21-23. If freed, why then be subject, i.e., suffer laws to be imposed on oneself or permit oneself to be bound by ordinances, 20*b*? On the contrary, let there be a thorough separation from such regulations as "Do not touch, do not taste, do not handle," 21. Such legalistic ordinances (as those under the Mosaic law) were divinely intended "for mortality," in the sense of cessation after Christ came, being used up or consumed in their using when they had discharged their intended functon, 22*a*. The imposition of such ordinances now, under grace, is the result of men's commandments and teachings, not God's, 22*b*. It has a wordy show (*logon*), a mere talkative demonstration, but no real manifestation of wisdom, i.e., true wisdom which makes Christ all in all, 23*a* (cf. 1 Cor 1:30). It is mere "will worship," not Spirit-directed communion with God; false humility, not true submission to the grace of God in Christ, 23*b*. Grace humbles man and exalts God. Such asceticism neither honors God, nor does it gratify the flesh, 23*c*. It is futile in every direction.

3:1-4. UNION WITH CHRIST AND A HEAVENLY WALK

Basis of a Heavenly Walk, 1. The basis is the *fact* of union with Christ in resurrection, 1*a*, and in His present heavenly session, 1*b* (Rom 6:5; Eph 2:6; Col 2:12; Ps 110:1). The "if" is not conditional but inferential. "*Since* you are therefore risen with Christ." Our union is heavenly (*position*). Therefore, our walk or manner of life (*experience*) is also to be heavenly.

Exhortations to a Heavenly Walk, 2. These involve: (1) a continuous seeking or striving for spiritual attainments, "*the things above* [emphatic] keep on pursuing," 1*a*; (2) a continuous "setting one's thought life upon" *the things above*, "*the things above* [doubly emphatic by word position and by repetition] set your mind upon," 2*a*; (3) a clear-cut break with earthly or material things, "*not* on things on the earth."

Reasons for These Exhortations, 3-4. These are: (1) because of the believer's death-to-sin position in Christ, sin has no more claim on him, 3*a*; (2) because his life is now Christ's and thus "hid [laid up in store] with Christ in God," 3*b*; (3) because Christ is the believer's life, 4*a*; (4) because Christ's manifestation in glory will mean our manifestation with Him, 4*b*. A heavenly walk is possible *now* if we *know* and act on our position in Christ. It is assured *in the future* by our glorification.

3:5-7. PRONOUNCING DEATH ON A SINFUL LIFE

Death Sentence Declared, 5a. "Mortify your members upon the earth," or once for all pronounce the death sentence upon any organ or part of the body which may be yielded to sin before the redeemed body has been glorified (cf. Rom 8:13; Gal 5:24).

Results of Failure to Pronounce the Death Sentence, 5b-7. The organs or members of the redeemed body will fall into the sins enumerated in 5*b*. "Fornication" is any illicit sexual intercourse, "uncleanness" any sexual or bodily perversion. "Inordinate affection" is any perverted or unnatural lust indulged in (Rom 1:26). "Evil concupiscence" is the insatiable craving or burning desire generated by such indulgence. "Covetousness," the desire to have more and more, is idolatry because it relegates God to a secondary place or ostracizes Him altogether (Eph 5:5). These sins bring "the wrath of God" upon the unsaved, 6. Pollution by them will result in severe chastening of believers, 7 (cf. 1 Cor 3:12-17; 5:1-5).

3:8-17. PUTTING ON THE NEW MAN

Putting Off the Old, 8-9. "The old man" is the unregenerate man with his corrupt human nature (Rom 6:6; Eph 4:22). In position, as *God sees* the believer in Christ, the old man was crucified and *is* dead. The believer is here exhorted to make this good in his *experience* by reckoning or counting it so as a once-for-all act of faith, 8a. The figure of an old soiled garment laid aside is used to describe the old life of anger, wrath, malice, evil speaking, filthy talk, and falsehood which has been abandoned, 8-9.

Putting on the New, 10-17. For the new man see note on Eph 4:23-30. He is put on as a fresh clean garment, 10. The new man involves (1) a new divine nature (regeneration), 10b; (2) a new unity transcending race, social position, etc., 11a; (3) a new sphere where Christ is absolutely central, 11b (Eph 1:23). His behavior is to be based on the fact that God has chosen, loved and sanctified him, 12a; therefore every Christian virtue and grace should be manifested, 12b-17.

3:18—4:6. A HEAVENLY WALK AND DOMESTIC RELATIONSHIPS

Wives, Husbands, Children, 3:18-21. Wives are to act under two principles: (1) submission to their husbands (cf. Gen 3:16) and (2) what is suitable or proper "in the Lord," 18 (cf. Eph 5:22; 1 Pet 3:1). No Christian wife is to give blind submission to an unsaved husband if such obedience violates her conscience before God. The supreme duty of a husband is to love his wife, 19 (Eph 5:25), and everything else will follow in due order. Children are to be obedient in all things, because this particularly pleases God, 20 (cf. Eph 6:1). Fathers are to be reasonable with their children to avoid exasperating them and thus discouraging them, 21.

Servants, Masters, 3:22—4:1. This lengthy instruction must have been partially dictated by the experience of Philemon, a Christian at Colossae, with his runaway slave Onesimus (cf. 4:9; also book of Philemon). Servants (slaves) are to act under a Christian spirit of service, obedience, fidelity and sincerity, 3:22-25. Masters are to act in light of the example set by their supreme Master in heaven, 4:1 (cf. Eph 6:5-9).

General Principles, 4:2-6. Prayer is to be practiced, 2-4. Wise conduct toward the unsaved, 5a; discreet use of time, 5b, coupled with sound gracious speech, are to be cultivated, 6.

4:7-18. A HEAVENLY WALK AND CHRISTIAN FELLOWSHIP

The Commendation of Fellow Workers, 7-15. A heavenly walk generates warm Christian fraternity.

Instructions and Salutation, 16-18. Directions are given concerning the public reading of the letter to the Colossians at Laodicea, a nearby town. Paul also requests that the epistle from Laodicea (contents unknown to us) be read at Colossae. Archippus is admonished, 17 (cf. Phm 2). A closing word of greeting is given by Paul, 18.

1 THESSALONIANS

PICTURE OF AN EXEMPLARY CHURCH

Writer and Date. The first letter to the Thessalonians is the earliest of the Pauline epistles. It was penned from Corinth not long after Paul left Thessalonica on his second missionary tour (Acts 16—17), perhaps A.D. 52.

Purpose of the Epistle. This letter was written to encourage and establish a young church in the basic truths of the gospel, to inspire it to progress in the power of holy living, and to instruct it in the matter of the coming of the Lord for His own and the relation of this event to the events of the day of the Lord.

Outline
An Exemplary Church, 1:1-10
A Model Minister, 2:1-20
A Holy Life, 3:1—4:12
The Coming of Christ and the Day of the Lord, 4:13—5:28

1:1-4. AN ELECT CHURCH

A Model Assembly, 1-3. Thessalonica was a very important city on the Thermaic Gulf, SW of Philippi. The apostle, however, seems to take pride in the Christians there rather than in the great city. The model church recently established, 2, was cause for thanksgiving because of its "work of faith" (faith manifested in works), its "labor of love" (love proved by toil) and "patience of hope" (in waiting for God's Son from heaven, 1:10), 3.

An Elect Assembly, 4. Election is both individual and corporate. The latter is in view here. The divine order is foreknowledge (1 Pet 1:2), election (choice) and predestination. The foreknown are elected, and the elect are predestinated. This election is certain to every believer. It is wholly by grace (Rom 9:11; 11:5-6) apart from human merit, and proceeds from the divine will (Jn 15:16; cf. Eph 1:5).

1:5-8. A MISSIONARY CHURCH

Objects of Effective Evangelism, 5. The gospel which Paul and his fellow workers preached, called "our gospel," did not come to the Thessalonians in word only, i.e., merely theoretically, but effectively—"in power," "in the Holy Spirit," and in "great assurance," 5a. Paul himself was an example of this manifestation of God's power, 5b.

Subjects of Effective Missionary Work, 6-8. Their effective conversion led to: (1) their following Paul and his fellow workers, and the Lord, 6a; (2) their receiving the Word of God in the midst of tribulation with the joy the Holy Spirit gives, 6b (cf. Acts 13:52); (3) their becoming an example of what Christians should be like to the believers in Macedonia and Greece, 7; (4) their missionary zeal in spreading the gospel to the regions beyond, 8 (cf. Rom 10:18).

1:9-10. A SERVING AND WAITING CHURCH

They Served God, 9. To do this they manifested their "work of faith," 3, in that "they turned to God from idols," and their "labor of love" in that they served "the *living* and *true* God" in contrast to the false, dead idols.

They Waited for Christ, 10. They manifested their "patience of hope" in that they waited "for God's Son from heaven." He will deliver us from the wrath which is to come upon the unsaved.

The Egnatian Way, highway across Greece which Paul traveled, passed through Thessalonica. Today "Egnatian Way" is one of the main streets of the city and follows the ancient route. (*Courtesy Howard F. Vos*)

2:1-4. MODEL MINISTERIAL CONDUCT
UNDER PERSECUTION

Boldness Engendered by Suffering, 1-2. It was well known among the Thessalonians that the entrée of the gospel to them was not fruitless or ineffectual, 1. It was characterized by "boldness." The suffering which Paul and his associates endured at Philippi (Acts 16:12-40), which involved cruel beating and imprisonment, had emboldened them to declare the gospel of God with great confidence. The result was twofold: effective spiritual fruitage, 1*b*; and "much contention" (Gr. *agonia*), spiritual struggle and warfare, 2. Far from being cowed or silenced, persecution spurred Paul on to greater liberty and power in preaching.

Faithfulness Called Forth by Responsibility, 3-4. Paul's hortatory instruction, i.e., his earnest entreaty, was not "of deceit." It did not have its origin in the desire to deceive or defraud, nor in "uncleanness," i.e., in impurity of motive; nor "in guile," i.e., it had nothing in it to bait or entrap its hearers by insidious artifice, 3. Far from such a show of infidelity, it was a model of fidelity. It viewed the gospel as a sacred trust and its heralds solemnly entrusted with it as something exceedingly valuable and easily despoiled, 4. Its heralds viewed themselves as "permitted by God" to be entrusted with the gospel only after rigid testing and approval. Therefore they spoke boldly, not pleasing men but God, who tests men's hearts (Jer 11:20) and who had approved them for this gospel trust.

2:5-8. UNSELFISH MINISTRY IN LOVE

The Proof of Selfless Love, 5-7. *Negatively,* Paul and his colaborers never employed flattery, i.e., insincere praise for unworthy ends, such as a cloak or front (that which appears in front or is put forward to hide the true state of things) for covetousness. They never flattered people for material gain, as so many ministers are tempted to do. They could call God to witness this fact, 5. They never sought men's glory, 6*a*; never were financially or otherwise burdensome, which they might have been under the circumstances, 6*b*. Positively, they were gentle, i.e., mild or kind as a nursing mother who nourishes *her own* (not someone else's) little born ones and hence showers real love upon them, 7.

The Expressioin of Selfless Love, 8. Having a strong love for the Thessalonians, Paul, Silvanus and Timothy (1:1) were heartily willing (took delight or pleasure) to communicate not only the gospel but their very own lives. Why? Because the Thessalonians became "dearly loved" to them. Love gives the magic touch to ministry for God and others.

2:9-20. DEVOTED MINISTRY FOR OTHERS

Devoted Ministry Described, 9-12. It is marked (1) by sacrifice, labor and self-denial for others' good and the success of gospel witness, 9; (2) by blamelessness in one's personal life, 10; (3) by fatherly love and patience in instructing and comforting, 11; (4) by the high goal of establishing believers in a walk (life) "worthy of God" and His high calling to His "kingdom and glory,"12.

Results of a Devoted Ministry Indicated, 13-20. Such service is always God-blessed and fruitful, as with the Thessalonians. (1) They received the Word preached as the Word of God, not the word of men, 13a, it operating effectually in them in response to faith, 13b (1 Pet 1:23). (2) They became followers (imitators) of the churches of God in Judea, which likewise suffered persecution from apostate Jews, whose unbelief and sins are mentioned, 14-16 (cf. Acts 7:52; 17:5, 13; 18:12). (3) They endeared themselves to the apostle who so earnestly desired to see them again, 17, but was hindered by Satan in his proposed visit, 18. (4) They were Paul's "hope, joy, and crown of rejoicing," his reward at the judgment seat of Christ, when the Lord rewards His saints at His coming, 19-20 (1 Cor 3:12-15; 4:5; 2 Cor 5:10).

3:1-8. STANDING FAST IN THE LORD

The Apostle's Concern, 1-5. When Paul had been conducted to Athens (cf. Acts 17:15; 18:5), he so desired the Thessalonians' spiritual welfare that he preferred to remain alone, 1, in order that Timothy might be sent to look after their spiritual interests, 2, and to steel them against the afflictions they were called to endure, 3 (2 Tim 3:12). On Paul's visit to Thessalonica he had warned them concerning suffering tribulation, 4. Now he is anxious to find out how they had fared. He knew the subtlety of Satanic temptation (2 Cor 11:2-3) and how the results of spiritual labor could be brought to nought, 5b (cf. Gal 4:11).

The Apostle's Reward, 6-8. His godly concern for them was rewarded by a good report from Timothy. He "brought good tidings" of their faith and love, indicating that the Thessalonians held the apostle in happy memory and that they were as earnestly desirous of seeing him as he was of seeing them, 6. This greatly consoled the apostle, 7. He declared, "For now we *live,*" i.e., live fully and joyfully, "if *you* [emphatic] go on standing firmly in your position of union with the Lord," 8 (Eph 6:13-14; Phil 4:1). Such standing is the key to spiritual health. It is the antidote against all error.

3:9-13. APOSTOLIC PRAYER FOR HOLINESS

The Question, 9-10. The petition, 11-13, is prefaced by a question, 9-10. How can God be thanked enough for all the joy the Thessalonians have given Paul by their spiritual perseverance, 9? This thanksgiving accompanies his request to see them again that he might "perfect" or mend (repair) anything that might be deficient in their faith, 10.

The Petition, 11-13. He prays that God might direct or make straight his way to them, 11. Further, he asks that the Lord might make them "increase" (have abundance) and "superabound" in love, 12, to the end that God might establish their hearts blameless in holiness (separation to God). The time of reckoning before God will come at the second advent when those who have died in Christ (as in 4:14) are brought with the descending Lord when He catches His living saints up to meet Him in the air (4:13-17).

4:1-8. DIVINE CALL TO HOLINESS

The Authority Behind the Call, 1-3. The authority is God's. "We request . . . we implore *by the Lord Jesus,*" 1. Cf. *God* has called us . . . *to* holiness," 7. He therefore that rejects this call rejects *God,* 8.

The Call Itself, 4-8. We are called to a life ("walk") pleasing to God, 1. This involves a life set apart unto God (experiential sanctification), 3*a*, which is characterized by abstention from sexual immorality, 3*b*; by sexual temperance, 5; and by rigidly avoiding adultery, 4-5. This call to holiness in the realm of sex is to be obeyed because: (1) the Lord is the avenger (punisher) of all who practice sexual promiscuity, 6; (2) He has called us to holiness, 7, emphatically *not* to uncleanness; (3) His authority is behind the prohibition, 8*a*; (4) God has provided the Holy Spirit to give each believer victory and sanctity in this area of life, 8*b*.

4:9-12. THE ELEMENTS OF A HOLY LIFE

The Basic Element of Love, 9-10. "Brotherly love" is so indispensable and obvious to a holy life that the apostle declares the Thessalonians have no need for written instruction. They have been taught by God to love one another, 9 (cf. Jn 15:12, 17; Jas 2:8;

1 Jn 3:11-18), and are commended for the exhibition of their love, but urged to increase more and more, 10.

Other Elements Enjoined, 11-12. (1) *Quietness.* "Bend every effort to be quiet," i.e., to live peaceably or have a tranquil spirit. (2) *Industry.* "Do one's *own* business" (1 Pet 4:15), not be a meddler or a busybody in others' affairs. (3) *Responsibility.* "Work with one's hands," i.e., not be lazy, shiftless, nor a parasite on others, 11-12*b* (cf. 2 Thess 3:10-12). (4) *Honesty* in one's walk (life and testimony) toward the unsaved, 12.

4:13-18. THE BELIEVER'S HOPE

The Blessed Hope, 13-15. Hope is faith-produced confidence and expectation of the future. The great obstacle to hope for the unbeliever is death. This obstacle is removed in Christ. Believers do not really die, they merely "fall asleep," 13. This is true because Jesus died and rose again (1 Cor 15:20, 52). Therefore, since believers are united to the risen Lord (Rom 6:4; Col 3:1-4), when they die physically they fall asleep "in Jesus." When Christ returns He will bring their souls and spirits with Him to be united with their risen bodies, 14. But the saints still alive physically when the Lord returns for His own shall not "go before" them who have fallen asleep in Jesus, 15.

The Lord's Coming, 16-18. The answer to the Christian's hope is the return of the resurrected, ascended Christ to raise the bodies of those who died in the Lord and to glorify the living saints. "The Lord himself," personally, bodily, "shall come down from heaven with a shout, with the voice of the archangel and with the trumpet of God." The "shout" is the shout of triumph over death (1 Cor 15:54-57), manifested in the raising of the dead saints and in the instantaneous glorification of the living saints, who will never taste physical death. "The voice of the archangel" is evidently that of Michael (cf. Dan 12:1-2). The dead in Christ rise *first,* then immediately the saints who are living when the Lord comes and remain to that hour "shall be caught up," suddenly conveyed away in the "clouds" to meet the Lord in the air. In this manner the saints will forever be with the Lord. This is the comfort and hope of the Christian, 18.

5:1-11. THE DAY OF THE LORD

The Day of the Lord—What It Is, 1-3. The apostle has just described the coming of the Lord for His own. This ' ᵔugurates "the day of Christ" with glorification and reward for the translated Church saints (1 Cor 1:8; 5:5; 2 Cor 1:14; Phil 1:6, 10; 2:16). Now Paul turns to the subject of "the day of the Lord." By contrast, it concerns the restoration of the kingdom to Israel, 1a (Acts 1:6-7; 3:19-21), and the earth judgments which take place prior to the setting up of that kingdom (cf. Isa 2:6-22; Jer 30:5-9). It was no new revelation, hence Paul had no need to write about it, 1b. It will come unexpectedly, like a thief, upon the ungodly, i.e., those in darkness (cf. Mt 24:36-51; 25:5), when mankind will have hoped to attain world peace, 3.

The Day of the Lord and the Believer, 4-11. These earth judgments and the outpoured divine wrath do not fall upon believers, 4, because they are sons of light, 5-8 (cf. Eph 5:8), and because God has not appointed them to wrath but to "salvation through our Lord Jesus Christ," 9. The wrath of God will not fall upon those "in Christ," 10, because they will be glorified and removed (1 Thess 4:13-17) before these end-time manifestations of God's wrath (Rev 3:10). This is their comfort and edification, 11.

5:12-15. EXHORTATIONS TOWARD MUTUAL HARMONY

Showing Honor to Those in Places of Responsibility in the Lord, 12-13. Believers are to regard or recognize these brethren with the favor and respect due them: (1) because of their consecrated labors in the cause of Christ, 12a; (2) because of their God-ordained position as those set or appointed with authority over believers, 12b; (3) because of their wisdom and counsel (they "admonish," i.e., put in mind or warn, God's people), 12c; (4) because of their good "works," 13a.

General Admonitions for Harmony, 13b-15. (1) The basic principle of living in peace is to rule in all relationships, 13b. (2) Believers are to admonish or warn the unruly, that is, those neglectful of duties, derelict in responsibility, 14. The word "unruly" (*ataktos*) is used of soldiers who desert their ranks. Other responsibilities include: (3) comforting the fainthearted or discouraged (*oligopsuchoi*), literally "little souled"; (4) supporting or exercising a zealous care for, the weak, the infirm, those deficient in mental, moral or spiritual strength; (5) being patient (long tempered) toward all (cf. Eph 4:2); (6) seeing (take care, see to it) that none render evil for evil, 15a (cf. Prov 20:22; 24:29; Mt 5:39, 44), "but follow by pursuing that which is good," 15b.

5:16-22. VARIOUS EXHORTATIONS

Rejoice, Pray, Be Thankful, 16-18. "*Always* [the emphasis] keep on rejoicing," 16 (cf. Phil 3:1; 4:4). "*Unceasingly* [emphatic] go on praying," 17. "*In everything* be grateful." The reason is that thankfulness is God's will for His people, 18.

Do Not Quench the Spirit, 19. We *grieve* (pain) the Spirit by unconfessed sin (Eph 4:30). We *quench* (stifle, dampen) the Spirit by disobedience to God's will.

Other Injunctions, 20-22. "Do not despise [treat with contempt or scorn] prophesyings," the truth of God as declared by a prophet, 20. "Test or approve by rigid trial all things." Adhere to the good, 21. "*From every semblance of evil* [emphatic] keep yourself," 22.

5:23-24. SANCTIFICATION FOR THE WHOLE MAN

The Whole Man Set Apart for God, 23. To be set apart for God is the idea of the Gr. adjective *hagios* ("holy") which in its verbal form means sanctify or make holy. This work of sanctification is the operation of "the very God," i.e., God Himself. It is not a human accomplishment.

Sanctification results in "the peace of God" (Phil 4:7); therefore the divine Sanctifier is called "the God of peace." It involves the whole tripartite nature of man: *body,* the material tent (2 Cor 5:1-8) in which man pilgrims in this world and with its five senses has communication with the natural world; *soul,* the seat of affections, desires, will and emotions (Mt 11:29; 26:38; Jn 12:27); *spirit,* the higher part of man which knows (1 Cor 2:11) and has communion with God (Job 32:8; Ps 18:28; Prov 20:27).

Sanctification itself is in three tenses: *past,* the believer *was* sanctified positionally in Christ at regeneration (1 Cor 1:2), so that every believer is a called saint; *present,* the believer experientially should be continually being set apart unto God (2 Thess 2:13); *future*—full conformity to Christ in glorification (1 Jn 3:1-3).

The Certainty of Complete Sanctification, 24. God effects sanctification. He guarantees our past unchangeable position as complete in Christ and thereby makes certain our future glorification. The Holy Spirit makes it possible for the believer to realize the present experiential or practical sense of sanctification in his daily walk (1 Cor 10:13; 2 Thess 3:3; Gal 5:16).

5:25-28.   CLOSING CHARGE

Request for Prayer, 25-26. "Brothers, keep on praying for us," 25. The Lord's servants need the constant prayers of God's people. "Greet all the brothers with a holy kiss," 26. This was customary among early Christians, especially in the high tide of spiritual love which often prevailed.

Charge Concerning Reading, 27-28. "I charge [adjure] you that this epistle be read to all the holy brothers," 27. The closing salutation, 28, is characteristic of the Pauline epistles.

2 THESSALONIANS

COMFORT IN PERSECUTION

Writer and Occasion. Paul was the writer (1:1). The occasion was a misunderstanding among the Thessalonians regarding the coming of Christ for His own (1 Thess 4:13-17) and the day of the Lord (1 Thess 5:1-10). Because these believers were being persecuted severely, they erroneously concluded that the day of the Lord had arrived (2:2). Paul writes to correct this misconception.

Date. This epistle was written after 1 Thessalonians in the early 50's.

Outline

The Coming of the Lord and Comfort in Present Persecution, Ch. 1

The Coming of the Lord and the Day of the Lord, Ch. 2

The Coming of the Lord and Practical Christian Living, Ch. 3

1:1-4. THE CHURCH COMMENDED

The Greeting, 1-2. As in the first epistle, the apostle associates Silvanus and Timothy with himself in saluting "the church of the Thessalonians" (see 1 Thess 1:1).

The Commendation, 3-4. Paul was bound to express thanks to God for the Thessalonians because their faith was growing and their love was abounding toward one another, 3. The result was that the apostle was able "to glory" (2 Cor 9:2), i.e., to boast rejoicingly, in them, and thus give a laudatory testimony concerning them in the church of God (local assemblies) for their patient and faithful conduct under persecution, 4 (cf. Jas 5:11).

1:5-10. THE CHURCH COMFORTED

The Reason for Their Sufferings, 5-6. Their tribulations were not an accident or piece of ill luck but clearly the will of God, "an evident token" (a proof or evidence) of the righteous decision of God, 5a, to test or prove them worthy of the kingdom of God, 5b.

It was really for the kingdom of God that they suffered, 5c (1 Thess 2:14; Heb 10:32-33).

The Basis of Comfort, 7-10. The second advent of Christ in glory, 7-8, will witness the vengeance of God on those who do not know Him and have not obeyed the gospel of salvation by believing, 8. Those who persecuted the Thessalonians belonged to this category. This will involve eternal dismissal (not annihilation) from God's presence in a separate eternal isolation ward reserved for sinners (cf. Rev 20:10-15) called Gehenna or eternal hell, which is eternal separation from God, 9-10.

1:11-12. INTERCESSION FOR THE CHURCH

The Prayer, 11. Paul constantly interceded for the Thessalonians, asking that God would count their conduct and Christian achievement worthy of their high calling (cf. Eph 4:1-3; Col 3:1-4), each believer fulfilling God's will in His power through faith manifested by good works.

The Purpose, 12. That the Lord might be magnified in them and they in the Lord according to the grace given them.

2:1-5. THE CHURCH'S OUTTAKING AND THE DAY OF THE LORD

A Misunderstanding Exposed, 1-2. The Thessalonians thought their sufferings (1:5-12) meant that the day of the Lord had arrived, 2, that the end-time period of worldwide judgment (Rev 6—19) had dawned, making way for the setting up of Christ's kingdom (Rev 19:16—20:10). The apostle pleads against this mistake by citing again the truth that Christ's coming would be *before* the day of the Lord, 1, a teaching he had outlined in the first epistle (4:13-18). He warns clearly against the speciousness of the error, 2-3a, and describes the first phase of Christ's coming *for* His saints as the personal presence (*parousia*) of our Lord Jesus Christ, coupled with our gathering together to Him (*episunagogē*), as outlined in 1 Thess 4:13-17.

The Error Refuted, 3-5. *Before* the day of the Lord bursts upon a Christ-rejecting world, there must *first* come the apostasy or falling away. This is not departure from the faith often characterizing the Church Age (1 Tim 4:1-5; 2 Tim 3:1-8; Rev 3:14-22), but the wholesale rebellion and thoroughgoing lapse into error and demonism of the period just preceding Christ's advent in glory (Lk 18:8; Rev

711

9:20-21). There must also come the revelation of the Antichrist, here called "the son of perdition," the lawless one, the last great demon-inspired world ruler (Dan 11:36; Rev 13:1-10; 19:20; 20:10). He will arrogate to himself divine honors and deceive end-time Jewry regathered to Israel, 4. The apostle had plainly taught these truths when he founded the Thessalonian church, 5.

2:6-9. THE CHURCH'S OUTTAKING AND THE MAN OF SIN

The Church's Outtaking and the Holy Spirit, 6-7. "That which re-strains," or the One who holds back the full development and manifestation of the demonic forces of evil in this era (cf. 8-10), is the Holy Spirit, a Person—"He who holds in check." He has been forming and indwelling the Church ever since Pentecost (Jn 14:16; Acts 2:1-4; 1 Cor 6:19), and will do so until "He is taken out of the way," literally comes out of the midst, when He leaves in the distinctive sense in which He came at Pentecost. This takes place at the time the Church, indwelt by the Spirit, is taken to meet Christ in the air (1 Thess 4:13-17). Only when the divine Restrainer is taken away with the glorified Church can and will *the* Antichrist be made manifest, 6, and "the mystery of iniquity" come to the full.

The Church's Outtaking and the Man of Sin, 8-9. "Then," *after* the Holy Spirit is taken out of the way, the lawless one will be revealed. This sinister personage sums up "the mystery of iniquity," or the full development of last-day miracle-working demonism (Rev 9:1-21; 12:7-17; 16:13-16). He will be destroyed by Christ's advent in glory (Rev 19:20; 20:10) and Satan will be bound in the abyss (Rev 20:1-3).

2:10-12. THE CHURCH'S OUTTAKING AND LATTER-DAY TRUTH REJECTERS

The Doom of Truth Rejecters, 10. Demonic deception, operative during the Church Age in a restricted sense because of the Holy Spirit's restraining operation, 6-9 (cf. 1 Tim 4:1-4; 1 Jn 4:1-5), will burst forth with irresistible power. Those "who are perishing," 10a, are the unsaved multitudes still living on the earth after the Church is translated. Rejecting truth when it was available results now in demonic delusion "because they did not receive *the love* of the truth, that they might be saved," 10, i.e., before the Church was glorified.

The Reason for Their Doom, 11-12. Because they did not love and accept the truth when it was available, 10b, God sends them "strong delusion," an inworking or energy of deception, to believe "the lie," i.e., the supreme deception of accepting the Antichrist, 11 (Jn 5:43; Rev 13:8, 16-18). The delusion is sent so that they all might be judged and found guilty for not having believed the truth, but having had pleasure in unrighteousness instead, 12.

2:13-17. THE CHURCH'S OUTTAKING AND THE THESSALONIANS

The Thessalonians Were a Cause for Thanks, 13-14, because they were God's beloved and elect (see notes on "Divine Election" and "Foreordination" in Eph 1:1-6). They were chosen to salvation and sanctification. In contrast to the deceived of the last days, they loved and hence believed "the truth." They were saved under the preaching of Paul's "gospel," 14a, to obtain the glory of our Lord Jesus Christ, i.e., to be sharers of Christ's glory, 14b (Rom 8:17; 2 Tim 2:12).

They Were Objects of Exhortation and Prayer, 15-17. The exhortation is to steadfastness and fidelity to the "traditions" taught them, i.e., what had been transmitted to them in teaching, 15. The prayer is for comfort and establishment or grounding "in every good word" (doctrine) "and work" (practice).

3:1-5. APOSTOLIC REQUEST FOR PRAYER

The Request, 1-2. The petition is twofold: (1) That the Word of God may run without obstruction and victoriously, as an athlete in a race (1 Cor 9:24, 26), that it may progress freely and advance rapidly and be glorified. The Word is always glorified when it has free course because the God of the Word is thereby exalted. (2) That the apostle might be delivered (rescued) from "unreasonable" men, men out of place or order, i.e., not being where God would have them. Being unoriented toward God they are troublesome and wicked. Being without faith (cf. Heb 11:6), they lacked the starting point for deliverance from sin and orientation toward God.

The Basis for the Request, 3-5. The Lord's faithfulness and Paul's confidence in the Thessalonians constituted the ground for the apostle's prayer, 3-4. He asks that the Lord would direct, i.e., guide them aright in a straight path into "the love of God" and into "the patience of Christ." Since this last phrase is an objective genitive, it is better translated "patience for Christ," meaning patient expectation for His return, 5 (cf. 1 Thess 4:13-17; 2 Thess 2:1-3).

3:6-15. INSTRUCTION CONCERNING DISCIPLINARY SEPARATION

The General Principle of Separation, 6. The injunction is to withdraw oneself from every believer who goes on walking (living) disorderly, neglectful of the common duties of life like a soldier who deserts his regiment, and who disregards "the tradition," i.e., the transmitted teaching (cf. 2 Thess 2:15) he has received from the apostle, 6.

The Apostolic Example, 7-9. Paul gave not only doctrine to guide, but his life as an example, 7-8. He toiled with his own hands as a tentmaker that he might not be an expense or burden upon any of those to whom he ministered, 8. He did this not because he had no right to expect support, but in order to furnish an example that the Thessalonians might follow, 9.

The Disorder Specified, 10-12. A disturbing attitude was evidently present among the Thessalonian believers. It was apparently a presumptuous piety that attempted to be heavenly-minded but shirked the common duties of earthly existence, such as working and supporting oneself and one's dependents. Paul gives a straightforward cure. No work—no food, 10. He puns on the word "work," 11—not just workers (*ergazomenoi*) but workers-around (*periergazamoi*), i.e., intensive workers in the wrong way or "busybodies," 11*b* (cf. 1 Tim 5:13; 1 Pet 4:15).

The Cure Indicated, 13-15. The cure was plain. (1) First, they were to "work *with quietness*" (emphatic), not complaining, gossiping, or prying into others' business. (2) Secondly, they were to eat *their own* food and not be a parasite on others, 12. (3) The orderly believers were to be unwearied in continuance of their well-doing, furnishing an example to the disorderly, 13. (4) The obstinately disobedient were to be marked or noted, 14*a*. (5) The faithful were not to mix or associate intimately with the disorderly, in order to shame them, 14*b*. (6) Yet such a disorderly brother was not to be reckoned as an enemy, but warned as a brother, 15 (cf. 2 Cor 6:14-17; Lev 19:17).

3:16-18. CONCLUDING BENEDICTION

The Benediction, 16, 18. "The Lord of peace" (Jn 14:27; Heb 13:20) was to grant them peace by His personal presence, 16. "The grace of our Lord Jesus Christ" is pronounced upon "all" (God's people), 18.

The Salutation, 17, was Paul's own signature, which was the token or pledge and assurance of the genuineness of his letters.

1 TIMOTHY

DIRECTIONS FOR CHURCH ORDER

The Writer and Date. Paul is the writer (1:1). The epistle is one of the pastoral letters and dated later in Paul's life, how late depends upon the question of whether the apostle had one or two imprisonments. If there were two, it was apparently written during the interval between the two, not later than A.D. 66. If there was but one, the letter was penned not long before the apostle's last trip to Jerusalem, probably A.D. 64.

The Theme. The central thought of 1 Timothy is on church order, soundness of faith, and ecclesiastical discipline (ch. 1—3). This was natural after numerous churches were established and the government of local assemblies came to the fore. It was also inevitable that instruction to settled pastors should be given after churches were founded (ch. 4—6).

Outline
The Discipline of Sound Doctrine, Ch. 1
The Discipline of Prayer and Public Worship, Ch. 2
The Discipline of Church Government, Ch. 3
The Discipline of the Local Pastor, Ch. 4—6

1:1-7. THE PASTOR AND SOUND DOCTRINE

The Pastor and Unsound Teachers, 1-4. Paul greets Timothy as a pastor and as his "own [genuine, true] son in the faith," 1-2. In such a capacity he urges the younger man to assume responsibility against unsound teachers, 3-4. A pastor must first be sound himself before he can assume such responsibility. Timothy was urged to remain at Ephesus (cf. Acts 20:1-3) that he might "charge" (entreat solemnly) the leaders that "they teach no other doctrine," i.e., "other" in the sense of different from and at variance with sound Christian truth, 3; and that they "neither give heed to [take up with] fables," i.e., religious fictions, such as the myths that honeycomb paganism nor "endless [interminable] genealogies," in which Judaism prided itself. Why? These unprofitable exercises offer only fruitless questionings rather than the acceptance of God's stewardship, i.e., the discharge of His plan and purpose as seen in the gospel. This stewardship is known by faith, 4.

The Pastor and Legalists, 5-7. In contrast to the unsound teachers' empty legalism, the goal of Christ's commandment (cf. Jn 13:34; 15:12; Gal 6:2) is love, born out of a pure (clean) heart, out of a good conscience, and out of unfeigned (unhypocritical) faith, 5. Those who have missed the mark through legalism have turned aside to vain or empty jangling—mere clang of meaningless words, 6. Desiring to be law-teachers, they are characterized by ignorance of true knowledge or genuine experience, 7.

1:8-11. THE LAW AND THE GOSPEL OF CHRIST

The Purpose of the Law, 8-10. The law itself is good, 8*a* (cf. Rom 7:12), but it must be employed (made use of) lawfully, i.e., properly or legitimately, in line with the glorious gospel committed to Paul's trust, 11. Its purpose is to convict the sinner (the unrighteous) and to lead him to the Saviour that he might be declared righteous by faith (Rom 3:21-28; Eph 2:8-10). In no sense is the law to be used

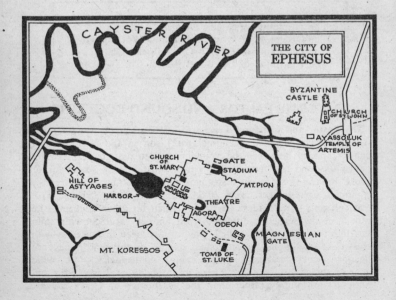

THE CITY OF **EPHESUS**

CAYSTER RIVER

BYZANTINE CASTLE

CHURCH OF ST. JOHN

AYASSOLUK TEMPLE OF ARTEMIS

CHURCH OF ST. MARY

GATE

STADIUM

MT. PION

HILL OF ASTYAGES

HARBOR

THEATRE

AGORA

ODEON

MAGNESIAN GATE

MT. KORESSOS

TOMB OF ST. LUKE

for the righteous (justified) man, either to justify him or to sanctify him. It is intended to reveal to the sinner his sin and its penalty apart from Christ, 9-10.

The Purpose of the Gospel, 11. It is "the gospel of the glory of the blessed God," 11*a*. It is the good news which heralds God's excellence in manifesting His gracious love for sinners by providing for their salvation (Jn 3:16). What the law could never do, grace does (Jn 1:17; Tit 3:4-5).

1:12-17. THE GOSPEL OF CHRIST AND THE SINNER

Salvation and Commission of Paul the Sinner, 12-15. The apostle's ministry of salvation was the result of God's saving grace, 12, manifested toward a great sinner, a blasphemer, a persecutor of God's people and "injurious" (an overbearing, wantonly violent person), 13*a* (Acts 8:3; 1 Cor 15:9). He received God's mercy because he committed his sin in ignorance and unbelief, 13*b*, the abundance of God's grace being shown toward him, 14. Paul was an illustration of the great truth that the incarnation of God in Christ was for the purpose of saving sinners, in which category he placed himself first, 15. This grand fact is a "faithful word," i.e., fully trustworthy, true and indubitably sure, worthy of hearty reception and universal cordial assent.

Paul's Salvation an Example for all Believing Sinners, 16-17. The apostle was to be a pattern of God's gracious patience and love toward sinners in Christ, 16. God is "the King, eternal, incorruptible, invisible [Jn 1:18], the only wise God" to whom all honor and glory are to be given forever, 17, because of the salvation He has provided in Christ.

1:18-20. THE CHARGE TO TIMOTHY THE PASTOR

The Charge, 18-19a. The solemn exhortation and injunction to Paul's "child" Timothy, since he was evidently Paul's convert, is that he might wage a successful spiritual conflict, 18*b* (cf. 2 Tim 4:2; Heb 9:14). Predictions of such a ministry were made earlier in the younger man's life and would not fail to be realized in him.

The Warning, 19-20. The case of Hymenaeus and Alexander (2 Tim 2:17-18) offers an example to the contrary. Teaching error concerning the resurrection, Hymenaeus had destroyed the faith of some. By apostolic authority Paul had delivered these false teachers to Satan, 20 (cf. 1 Cor 5:5; 11:30-32; 1 Jn 5:16). This involved serious chastening (Heb 12:6), even to the point in some cases of physical death.

2:1-8. THE CHURCH AND PUBLIC PRAYER

The General Injunction, 1-2a. Prayer both public and private has a primacy. Paul exhorted, therefore, that *"first of all,* supplications [earnest requests and petitions], prayers [wishes or earnest desires], intercessions [prayer as a meeting or rendezvous with God], and giving of thanks, be made for all men," 1, especially for civil rulers and authorities, *2a* (Rom 13:1).

Reasons for Prayer, 2b-8. (1) That Christians may lead a tranquil and quiet life in godliness and gravity, *2b,* in accord with God's will, 3. (2) Because God's desire is the salvation of men in which prayer has an important place, 4. (3) Because the incarnation and redemptive work of Christ gave new power and outreach in prayer, 5-6 (cf. Jn 16:23-28). Paul was divinely commissioned as a preacher (herald or proclaimer) and an apostle (delegated one) of these truths concerning prayer, 7. He was to instruct believers in the proper prayer attitude and exercise, 7-8.

2:9-15. THE ORDER OF WOMEN IN
CHRISTIAN SOCIETY

A Christian Woman's Demeanor and Dress, 9-10. As the Christian man's life is to be adorned by prayer, so the Christian woman is to beautify herself with the proper "cosmetic." Positively, this is well-ordered (i.e., proper) dress. Without, there is to be befitting dress; within, proper adornment of heart manifested by modesty and reflected in a reverent countenance and in a serious attitude toward her place in Christian society, *9a.* Negatively, to spell out the positive injunction, Christian women are not to adorn themselves with "braided" hair (from root *pleko,* to interweave or plait), or with costly jewelry, *9b.* This does not suggest drab dress, but modest adornment, becoming a woman's position as a Christian and her station in life. That which is worldly or unbefitting these criteria is to be avoided, whether a woman is queen or commoner. Positively again, the real adornment or cosmetic of the godly woman is to be her good works.

A Christian Woman's Relation to Men, 11-15. A Christian women is to be characterized by a spirit of teachableness and of quiet submission to her husband, 11 (1 Cor 14:34-35; cf. Gen 3:16). The opposite attitude is most unbecoming to a woman professing godliness. Paul himself did not permit women to teach men or usurp authority over them, in the sense of acting in independent power or domineering over them, 12. Women have a wide sphere of teaching, but not where men are involved. New cults have frequently been started or abetted by women who refused to be in subjection to God's Word on this point.

The reason for subjection is outlined, 13-15. (1) Adam was created as federal head of the race before Eve was formed, 13. (2) Eve was formed from Adam, not Adam from Eve. (3) The woman, not the man, was deceived, 14, and is still peculiarly subject to doctrinal deception. (4) She will be "saved," i.e., be rescued and preserved from the dangers of insubordination, deception, and teaching doctrinal error which the apostle hints at, by cultivating her highest call of homemaking and childbearing. Her real salvation is in producing and training godly offspring, 15.

3:1-7. THE QUALIFICATIONS OF ELDERS

The Honor of the Office, 1. It is a fact that if anyone earnestly desires, in the sense of setting his heart upon, the office of an elder (*episkopēs,* "overseer"), he desires "a good work" (office, position of watching over the flock of God).

The Qualifications of the Office, 2-7. The overseer must be: (1) blameless, not to be laid hold of by some blot on his character, irreprehensible; (2) a one-wife man, not an adulterer, divorced or polygamous, although he may be an unmarried man; (3) vigilant, watchful, circumspect; (4) sober, serious-minded; (5) of good behavior, well-ordered with a symmetry-adorned life focused on Christ; (6) given to hospitality, literally a stranger-lover; (7) gifted and qualified to teach, 2; (8) not addicted to wine and hence not intemperate and quarrelsome; (9) not a "striker," that is, not a violent, quick-tempered person apt to give a blow in a fit of anger; (10) not covetous or greedy, i.e., no money-lover, not mercenary; (11) patient, mild or gentle; (12) not a brawler, literally a non-fighter; (13) one who controls his own family well, having his children well-disciplined, 4. If a man is defective in the control of his own family how can he be qualified to take care of the house of God (the local church), 5? (14) An elder must not be a novice, one newly planted in the Christian church, a new convert. Such an inexperienced, untested believer is peculiarly exposed to the sin of pride that caused Satan's original fall and still characterizes him, 6 (Isa 14:12-14; Ezek 28:12-19; 1 Tim 6:9; 2 Tim 2:26). (15) He must also be one having a good report (testimony) among the unsaved, 7.

719

3:8-13. THE QUALIFICATIONS OF DEACONS

Their Qualifications, 8-12. The deacons were charged with the financial and temporal administrations of the local church, as the overseers were charged with the more directly spiritual aspects. The deacons' qualifications are largely the same as the overseers, 8-10, 12 (cf. 2-7). The qualifications of their wives, 11, doubtless also apply to overseers' wives.

Their Reward, 13. They who discharge the office well acquire (gain or earn) for themselves a "good degree," literally a step, stair, in the sense of dignity of rank and standing. They also attain boldness and freedom of speech which the Spirit gives to those who gain confidence and assurance by virtue of fidelity to a Christ-centered faith.

3:14-16. THE CHURCH AND REVEALED TRUTH

The Church and Its Relation to Revealed Truth, 14-15. Paul intends Timothy to be instructed in church management and discipline. If the apostle cannot do this orally, he will write, 14-15a. It is important to know how one, particularly a pastor, ought to conduct himself in the house of God (the local church). "The church of the living God" (the Body of Christ) is the pillar or column in the sense of the support holding up the roof of truth. It is also the ground or foundation of truth in that the Holy Spirit teaches the revealed truth of God (the Bible) only to believers, members of the true Church.

The Gist of Revealed Truth, 16. This verse refers to the basic body of divine revelation made known in Scripture and may well have constituted an early Christian hymn. It is avowedly "great" because it embraces God's eternal plans and purposes in Christ centering in redeemed man. It involves a "mystery," i.e., revealed truth previously hidden but now made known, which still transcends man's full comprehension. This mystery has its goal in godliness, that is, restoring lost mankind to a state of godlikeness where man is united to Christ and enabled to fellowship with and worship his Creator. It centers in Christ: (1) His *incarnation*—God "manifest in the flesh" (Jn 1:1, 18); (2) His *resurrection* by the power of the Holy Spirit vindicating and proving true all His claims (Rom 1:4); (3) His *post-resurrection appearances* witnessing to the spirit world of His person (Mt 28:2-7); (4) His *gospel*—"preached to the nations" (Gal 1:16); (5) His *Church and Body*—constituted by those who "believe on [Him] in the world"; (6) His *ascension*—"received back in glory" (Acts 1:9-11).

4:1-6. THE PASTOR AND DOCTRINAL ERROR

Demonism the Source of Doctrinal Error, 1-2. The well-instructed pastor must know the *real* origin of false teaching to deal with it adequately. Therefore the Holy Spirit speaks plainly on this point. He declares unequivocally that error is instigated *not* primarily by the false teacher but by the evil spirits or demons energizing the false teacher. This truth is enunciated by the fact that when some depart from the faith (Jude 3), they are said to give heed to (take up with) seducing spirits (wandering demons) rather than the false teachers. The result is doctrines of demons—not teachings about demons (demonology) but errors originated by demons. These teachers, teaching falsehoods in hypocrisy, are mere insincere actors or pretenders, whose conscience is cauterized into insensitivity to differentiate good from evil, error from truth.

An Illustration, 3-6. The apostle selects a current error, a type of legalistic asceticism, to illustrate the fact that false doctrine is demon-originated. It forbids marriage (as if this God-ordained institution were evil, and thus incriminates God), and the eating of certain foods, which the apostle shows were created by God to be received with thanksgiving and prayer, 3-5. The demonic impress in this doctrine is apparent, displaying Satanic pride (Isa 14:12-14), slander of God's goodness (Gen 3:5), and clear falsehood (Gen 3:4). As a good pastor Timothy is to show the source of error and teach truth, 6.

4:7-16. THE PASTOR AND SELF-DISCIPLINE

Self-Discipline in Public Ministry, 7-11. This involves faithfully teaching truth (cf. 6); refusing or rejecting "old wives' fables" (silly, superstitious stories such as garrulous old women tell, mere myths or figments of the imagination) which are "profane," not being connected with holiness or godliness; and exercising toward a goal of godliness rather than toward mere physical conditioning, the benefits of which are temporary in contrast to both the temporal and eternal benefits of godliness, 8. This is a completely reliable directive, 9, for the reason given in 10. Our hope is in the "living God," who through Christ's sacrifice has made humanity "savable," and who actually *saves* those who believe. Self-discipline also involves the diligent teaching of these things, 11.

Self-Discipline in Private Ministry, 12-16. Timothy, the young man, is to give no occasion for anyone to look down upon his youth. He is rather to be an example or model to God's people, 12. In his ministry he is to emphasize reading (scholarly study of the Scripture), exhortation (preaching) and doctrine (teaching). He is not to neglect the spiritual gift he possesses. There is evidently reference here to the charge given him at his ordination, 14. He is to meditate or continually bestow careful thought upon these matters, so that his progress or advancement in spiritual maturity may be apparent to everyone. This means he must pay particular attention to his living as well as to his teaching. In persevering in these matters he will "save himself" in the sense of deliverance from pastoral pitfalls, and rescue the people to whom he ministers from common snares in the Christian life.

5:1-16. THE CARE OF WIDOWS

Conduct Toward Various Christians, 1-2. *Elders* are not to be the objects of verbal violence. The *young men* are to be treated as "brothers," the *older women* with parental respect and love. Sisterly purity is to mark Timothy's relations with the *younger women*.

Treatment of Christian Widows, 3-16. Widows who are really destitute are to be "honored" and provided for, 3. Those who have children or other relatives ought to be supported by them, 4. Real widows trust God, 5, something which is not true of those who live in voluptuous pleasure and luxury, 6-7. Such are not to be supported by the church. Relatives are under obligation to support widows within their families, 8. No widow under 60 is to be church-supported. Those who are, must fulfill certain conditions, 10. Younger widows are not to be supported for various reasons, 11-13, but are encouraged to marry and bear children, 14-15. Insofar as possible the church is to be responsible only for "real" widows, 16.

5:17-22. CONCERNING ELDERS

Honor Due Them, 17-20 (cf. 5:1). Teaching elders (pastors) are to be considered worthy of "double honor" — honor of position and honor of financial support, 17-18 (cf. Deut 25:4; 1 Cor 9:7, 11; Lk 10:7). They are not to be irresponsibly accused, 19 (cf. Deut 19:15). However, those who sin are to be publicly rebuked for the sake of others who may be tempted, 20.

Timothy's Responsibility, 21-22. Like all pastors, Timothy is solemnly warned against partiality and prejudice in dealing with God's people, 21 (cf. Jas 2:1-12). He is also warned against ill-advisedly ordaining young men to the ministry, 22 (cf. Acts 13:3).

5:23-25. PAUL'S PERSONAL ADVICE TO TIMOTHY

Regarding Timothy's Health, 23. Paul suggests that Timothy no longer be a water drinker, i.e., no longer confine himself to drinking water only, but use a little wine (perhaps to be mixed with water) for its medicinal value, 23.

Regarding the Question of Men's Sins and Good Works, 24-25. Some men's sins are so plainly manifest and evident that they precede the sinner to judgment. In the case of others, their sins follow after or catch up with them and appear as the sequel to their evildoing, 24. In like manner the good works of some believers are obvious and manifest. However, those good works and deeds of love which are not open to everyone's sight cannot be hid, certainly not from God, and not even altogether from men, 25.

6:1-5. DIRECTIONS FOR SERVANTS AND MASTERS

The General Directive, 1-2 (cf. Eph 6:5-9 with comments). The apostle takes the social custom that prevailed and inculcates the Christian ethic as applicable to the prevailing institution, as wrong as the institution itself may have been, 1-2. (Cf. also Col 3:22—4:1 with comments.)

Denunciation of False Teachers, 3-5. Those who reject wholesome (sound) words and doctrines which result in godliness, 3, are described in their true light. They suppose that gain is godliness, 4-5.

6:6-10. WARNING DIRECTED TO THE RICH

The Blessing of Godly Contentment, 6-8. Gain is not godliness, 5, but godliness with contentedness is *great gain* (emphatic), 6. Contentment is satisfaction with one's lot in the will of God (Heb 13:5). Since we brought nothing material into this world nor do we take anything material out, 7, having food and clothing we should be satisfied, 8 (cf. Gen 28:20-21).

The Curse of Ungodly Wealth, 9-10. The curse is not in wealth itself, but in the wrong attitude toward it. They that "will," or make a deliberate choice to be rich, select a course of life motivated by the desire for worldly wealth. As a result they pay the penalty of falling into temptations others never have to face. Such ungodly wealth also proves to be a snare. Like a trap that deprives an animal of freedom and life, it traps men in "numerous foolish [senseless, brutish] lusts" so keen they become irresistible and result in personal and moral ruin. Instead of bringing contentment it is *"a root"* (emphatic) of all sorts of evils, such as covetousness, apostasy from the faith, and piercing sorrows.

6:11-16. WARNING DIRECTED TO THE MAN OF GOD

His Ambition, 11-12. The man of God is to run away from the snares of worldly wealth, to shun them in rigid separation (2 Cor 6:14-17; 2 Tim 2:19-21). He is to diligently pursue Christian virtue, 11. He is also to fight, 12a, and this means spiritual conflict (Eph 6:10-20; 2 Tim 2:3-4). The battle rages around the good fight of faith. Lastly, he is to lay hold of eternal life, 12b. This suggests the athletic figure of running for a prize (Phil 3:12-14), the reward being the full realization of the meaning of eternal life in the believer's earthly race, 12c.

The Apostle's Charge to Him, 13-16. Paul charges the man of God, i.e., the person who permits God to control his life, to keep this commandment, 14, concerning worldliness and worldly wealth (6-13) without stain or cause for rebuke till Christ's appearing (1 Thess 4:13-17). His life ambition is to be above reproach.

6:17-19. INSTRUCTIONS FOR WEALTHY BELIEVERS

The Charge, 17-18. They are solemnly enjoined not to be conceited (proud), nor put their faith in (fix their hope on) material wealth, which is always characterized by a degree of uncertainty and insecurity. Faith is to be reposed rather in the bounty of the *living* God, 17. They should rather be rich in good works, ready to use their wealth to advance God's work and to share with poor believers, 18.

The Purpose, 19. The goal in view is: (1) *Future reward* for faithfulness (cf. 1 Cor 3:9-15; 9:23-27; 2 Cor 5:10-11). They are to lay up in store (hoard) the treasure of a good foundation (imperishable eternal wealth) for "the time to come." (2) *Present enjoyment of the spiritual life.* "That they may lay hold on life indeed" (cf. Phil 3:14), that is, life more abundant here and now (Jn 10:10).

6:20-21. APPEAL TO TIMOTHY

The Positive Injunction, 20a. "Keep [guard as something very valuable] that which is committed to your trust." The young pastor was entrusted with a life and ministry which he was commanded to watch over jealously.

The Negative Warning, 20b-21. He was to avoid or shun worldly and empty discussion and pointless argumentation. He was likewise to avoid points of controversy with pseudoscience, the realm of false knowledge. Man's unproved theorizing has many so-called conflicts with revealed truths. The wise minister will shun these and give himself wholly to proclaiming God's revealed truth, 20. Some, however, in Paul's day as in ours, became involved with man's theorizing and subsequently "missed the mark" in the sense of going astray from the faith, 21a (Jude 3). The closing benediction follows, 21b.

2 TIMOTHY

A GOOD SOLDIER OF JESUS CHRIST

The Writer and Date. Second Timothy was written, as was 1 Timothy, by Paul the apostle to his "dearly beloved son" Timothy (1:1-2). If there was only one imprisonment of Paul, this touching epistle containing the last recorded words of the apostle was penned about A.D. 64. If there was another and later imprisonment it was penned about A.D. 67.

The Purpose. The letter was written to outline the course of a true servant of Jesus Christ in a time of doctrinal declension. The churches in Asia (1:15) had defected from the gospel of grace which the apostle had proclaimed and had lapsed into legalism. Paul encourages Timothy to use the divine resources available to the faithful pastor in such a time of apostasy.

Outline
Apostasy and Pastoral Fidelity, Ch. 1
Apostasy and Spiritual Conflict, Ch. 2
Apostasy and the Word of God, Ch. 3
Apostasy and a Faithful Lord, Ch. 4

1:1-5. THE INTEGRITY OF A FAITHFUL PASTOR

Paul's Love and Prayers for Timothy, 1-4. In his greeting, 1-2, Paul calls Timothy his "dearly beloved son [child]," showing his deep affection for this true child in the faith. His interest in Timothy is revealed by his constant prayer on his behalf, 3, and his love is displayed by his earnest desire to see him, 4 (cf. 4:9, 21), which in turn would fill him with joy. This is one of the great friendships of Scripture.

Paul's Confidence in Timothy, 5. He calls to mind Timothy's "unfeigned faith," and how genuinely real it was, with no hypocrisy or make-believe sham. He was persuaded with full confidence that the same genuine faith which resided in his mother and grandmother was present in Timothy also.

1:6-8. THE AFFLICTIONS OF A FAITHFUL PASTOR

Afflictions Demand a Spirit of Courage, 6-7. In the light of Timothy's background and faith, he was to "stir up the gift of God" in him. This divinely conferred endowment (*charisma,* 1 Cor 12:4, 9, 28) was bestowed upon him through the laying on of the apostle's hands (1 Tim 4:14) at his ordination as a pastor. "Stir up" means to "kindle up a dormant fire," to fan into a flame in the sense of stirring up or cultivating one's powers, 6. A spirit of ardent courage is needed to combat declension in a day of apostasy. Timothy's God-given endowment was not a spirit (attitude) of fear (Rom 8:15; 1 Jn 4:18), but of power (the dynamic inworking of an omnipotent God), love and a sound mind. This last phrase refers to a tranquil mental health that displays fearless courage to stand for truth and righteousness, 7.

Afflictions Are Part of Faithful Gospel Testimony, 8. Timothy was accordingly to expect afflictions and not try to avoid them by being ashamed of "the testimony of our Lord," which involves the full declaration of Christ's person and saving work. Nor was he to be ashamed of Paul, "His prisoner" ("His" because Paul was imprisoned for his faithfulness to Christ). The "afflictions of the gospel" are inseparable from the declaration of the good news itself. When they are endured for the sake of the truth, the power of God can be expected to be manifested in the ministry of the one afflicted.

1:9-11. THE APPOINTMENT OF A FAITHFUL PASTOR

The Gospel Described, 9-10. Several phrases describe the gospel or good news which the faithful pastor must proclaim, and to which he is appointed. Essentially it is a message which declares the parallel work of God in saving and calling the sinner. The call is emphasized here as being: (1) *divine,* God "called us"; (2) *sanctifying,* "an holy calling" setting the called ones apart for God's own possession and use; (3) *gracious,* "not according to our works, but . . . grace"; (4) *purposeful,* "according to his own purpose"; (5) *preplanned,* "given us . . . before the world began"; (6) *revealed,* or made known, by Christ's incarnation. God's call was effected through the work of the divine-human Son, who rendered death powerless and provided life eternal and incorruptibility. These great gifts are brought into clear light through the gospel.

The Appointment Illustrated, 11. Paul himself furnishes an illustration of one who has been divinely appointed as a herald, an apostle —delegated one—and an instructor of the gospel.

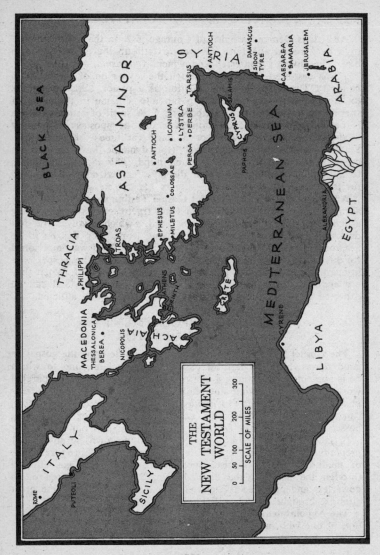

THE
NEW TESTAMENT
WORLD

SCALE OF MILES

0   50 100   200   300

1:12-14. THE HOLY CONFIDENCE OF A
FAITHFUL PASTOR

The Testimony of Assurance, 12. "I suffer . . . nevertheless I am not ashamed," 12*a*. Why? The apostolic confidence is the answer. "I know . . . I have believed . . . I am persuaded." Assurance is basic to an effective witness. It is the believer's unswerving conviction not only that he possesses salvation, in which he will be eternally kept through the merits of the work of Christ alone, but that the committal of his life to the Saviour will be safely guarded and his investment blessed and increased.

The Results of Assurance, 13-14. One sound in the faith himself is able (1) to enjoin soundness of doctrinal teaching and terminology on others — "Hold to the form [type, outline, impress] of words that are sound," 13*a*; (2) to put sound (healthful) doctrine into practice, 13*b*; (3) to guard or keep his ministry for Christ intact, 14*a*. This is accomplished by means of the Holy Spirit (not self-effort) "who dwells at home" in the believer, 14*b* (cf. 1 Cor 6:19).

1:15-18. THE TRIALS AND JOYS OF A
FAITHFUL PASTOR

The Trials, 15. The churches of proconsular Asia had declined doctrinally. They had "turned away" from the apostle, i.e., from his message of grace, going back to some degree of legalism. To that degree the apostasy had already set in 15*a*. Two who had defected are especially named, 15*b*.

The Joys, 16-18. The household of Onesiphorus is mentioned on the other side of the pastoral ledger. This brother had refreshed the apostle by not being ashamed of Paul's imprisonment in Rome, and by previous help at Ephesus, 17-18.

2:1-3. THE MESSAGE OF GRACE AND
SPIRITUAL WARFARE

Strength Is Required to Proclaim the Gospel of Grace, 1-2. "*You* [emphatic] then, be strong [or strengthen yourself] in the grace that is in Christ Jesus" (RSV), because the Asian churches have defected from it, 1 (see 1:15). This injunction was especially necessary because the truth that salvation is wholly the result of the finished work of Christ without any admixture of works, human merit, or legalistic observance is subject to Satanic attack (cf. 1 Tim 4:1-5).

The truth of grace was divinely revealed to the apostle (Eph 3:1-10) and committed to Timothy in the presence of many witnesses. Timothy, in turn, was to transmit this truth to other faithful men who would, in like manner, instruct others, 2. This is the biblical pattern for Christian education, the method of promulgating the gospel to the ends of the earth.

Preaching Grace Arouses Conflict, 3. An adherent to this message may expect opposition. Paul enjoins Timothy to suffer opposition along with him, as a good soldier of Christ Jesus.

2:4-7. SEPARATION AND SUCCESS IN GOD'S WORK

The Necessity of Separation, 4. The military figure of a soldier, 3, continues. No one who serves as a soldier in performing military duty entangles or implicates himself with the business and affairs of this life. The purpose is that he might be pleasing to the one who enlists troops. In the conflict which the message of grace arouses there must be disentanglement from worldly pleasures and pursuits on the part of the Christian soldier, for his singular aim must be that of pleasing his Lord (2 Cor 5:9).

The Necessity of Obedience and Effort, 5-7. Reward for achievement in the Christian race demands (1) separation from sin (Heb 12:1); (2) discipline and obedience to God's Word (the figure of an athlete running according to the rules of the contest), 5 (cf. 1 Cor 9:25-27); and (3) labor and effort (the figure of a hard-working farmer who must labor first before sharing the fruits of his toil), 6. (See the distinction between salvation and rewards in 1 Cor 3:10-15.) The apostle implores spiritual comprehension of these examples as a result of the Lord's tuition, 7.

2:8-10. SUFFERING AND SOUL-WINNING

The Cause for the Suffering, 8-9a. Paul's gospel of grace, at the very center of which were the doctrines of the resurrection of the incarnate Christ and His messiahship (of the posterity of David, 8; Rom 1:3-4), led him to suffer hardship even to the extent of imprisonment (Eph 6:20).

The Results of the Suffering, 9b-10. He was in chains, but the Word of God was not, 9b. As a result, the unbound Word which he had preached would effect salvation in the lives of many. "The elect" are believers or believers to be (Eph 1:4-6). He endured suffering that these elect might be saved and be eventually glorified (Rom 8:29-30).

2:11-14. UNION WITH CHRIST AND COMING GLORY

The Believer's Position of Union, 11. This is a faithful saying, i.e., a reliable fact, that the believer has been baptized (placed) by the Holy Spirit into a *position* of union and identification with Christ in death, burial and resurrection (Rom 6:3-4; 1 Cor 12:13; Col 2:8-10; Gal 3:27). Here the apostle dwells on the death and life aspects of that position. "If [since] we have *died* with him . . . we shall also *live* with him" (Gr.). The death aspect is inseparable from the life aspect. As the believer died in Christ to sin, so he also possesses life in and with Him.

The Believer's Experience of Union, 12a. If we suffer in our experience of living in Christ, we shall also reign with Him, both presently as an experience of power and authority (Phil 3:10-15), and hereafter as a reward (Rev 2:26-27; 20:6).

The Problem of the Believer's Unfaithfulness, 12b-14. "If we deny him, he also will deny us" — reject us, count us as disqualified for a prize, disapproving us for reward in the Christian race (1 Cor 9:27, see notes). If we continue to be unfaithful, so that our experience is inconsistent with our position, yet "he remains faithful: he cannot deny himself," 13 (cf. Num 23:19). He cannot go back on His word, His promise of our safety and security in Christ (Jn 10:28-29; Rom 8:1). Timothy was to remind his flock of these truths of grace, meanwhile warning them against petty debates which result in the subversion and ruination of the hearers from "the grace that is in Christ Jesus," 14 (2:1).

2:15-19. BIBLE STUDY AND GODLY LIVING

A Discerning Use of Scripture—the Antidote to Error, 15-18. Study, be diligent or zealous, to present yourselves "approved" (qualified) before God. The workman is not to be ashamed or embarrassed by faulty workmanship, for he is to "rightly divide," literally "cut straight," the revealed Word of God, here called "the word of truth." This setting forth of divine revelation without distortion, perversion or contradiction is possible only as God's workman diligently labors to discern the various subjects in Scripture and to make application accordingly. Only in this way can error and cultism, 16-18, be answered, illustrated here by the false teaching mentioned concerning the resurrection.

Bible Study—the Key to Godly Living, 19. Revealed truth discloses that "the foundation of God," the essence of His character, stands firm, steadfastly immoveable. This divine foundation has a twin seal (mark or token) guaranteeing it: (1) the Lord knows His own (Num 16:5; Jn 10:14); and (2) the Lord's own are to be separated from iniquity. Holy living is to be the external evidence of one's personal relationship to God. These two principles run through the warp and woof of all Scripture.

2:20-23. SEPARATION AND SPIRITUAL USEFULNESS

The Principle Illustrated, 20-21. The illustration is that of a large household with many utensils, some valuable, others less so. Some are for honorable uses, others for dishonorable purposes. The "servant of the Lord" is a vessel. If he is to be used by God, he must separate from evil—"purge himself" from the dishonorable utensils. He will then become a vessel for honor, experientially as well as positionally sanctified (made holy), "prepared for every good work."

The Principle Enunciated, 22-23. "Flee youthful lusts" (the intense burning desires or passions of youth), but "follow" (pursue diligently) Christian virtues practiced by those "who call on the Lord." Only by such means can a pure (clean) heart be maintained. Foolish and unprofitable questions are to be avoided, for they produce only quarrels and dissensions, 23.

2:24-26. SPIRITUAL VICTORY

The Servant of Jesus Christ, 24-25a. Here the pastor is called "the servant of the Lord." Although called to spiritual battle, he must not strive—quarrel or dispute in a natural sense. Rather he must display traits of victory over himself, being gentle, gifted and trained to teach, enduring, and patient under evils and injuries, 24. With gentleness he is to instruct and correct those that are of an opposite opinion to his, 25a.

The Servant's Conquests over Satan, 25b-26. The servant's personal victory, 24-25a, has a twofold strategy: (1) that the Lord might grant his opponents repentance, leading them to a full comprehension of the truth, 25b; (2) that they might "recover themselves," recover their senses. Those caught in the devil's snare of false doctrine become infatuated and intoxicated. When in such a state they are captured by the devil at his pleasure, 26.

3:1-5. THE APOSTASY

The Time of the Apostasy, 1. The importance of this revelation is seen in the phrase "This *know* also." It was something to which

Timothy was to give special attention. The time described as "the last days" often refers in Scripture to the messianic period. NT writers viewed Christians as living in the last days, which were to be days of departure from the truth. Within the period of these "days" were to be "dangerous seasons" which would be particularly spiritually and morally trying. Conditions will become progressively worse as the Church Age draws to a close (v. 5).

The Nature of the Apostates, 2-5. The difficult seasons, 1, are made so by the character of the people involved. They will be: (1) self-lovers; (2) money-lovers; (3) boasters who are ostentatiously arrogant; (4) proud, haughty; (5) blasphemers, impiously irreverent toward God and holy things; (6) disobedient to parents, self-willed and undisciplined; (7) unthankful, ungrateful for blessings received from God and man; (8) unholy, repudiating the distinction between good and evil; (9) without natural affection, devoid of love for their own kindred; (10) trucebreakers, unwilling to be placated, irreconcilable; (11) false accusers, slanderers who are literally devils; (12) incontinent, intemperate and uncontrolled, lacking mastery of self; (13) fierce, savage or ferocious in attitude and action; (14) despisers of those that are good, literally nonlovers of the good; (15) traitors, betrayers; (16) heady, headstrong ones who rush forward pursuing their own will; (17) high-minded, besmoked, imbued with the fumes of conceit, puffed up; (18) pleasure-lovers rather than God-lovers; (19) "having a form of godliness, but having renounced the power of it," possessors of mere formal religion which resembles the real, but continuing to reject the genuine dynamic which energizes the Christian life.

The Attitude Toward Apostates, 5b. Rigid separation (cf. 2:4-5, 20-23) is enjoined: *"From such turn away."* This injunction needs to be pondered in our day.

3:6-9. RESULTS OF APOSTASY

Immorality and False Intellectualism, 6-7. Apostates gravitate into immorality (2 Pet 2:10-14; Jude 4, 8, 10). Here they are represented as entering homes and seducing weak, silly women. Literally, these are "little women," small in respect to true womanhood, laden with sins and led away from virtue by various lusts, 6 (cf. Tit 1:11). Apostates also are victimized by false intellectualism. They are ever learning (philosophical and kindred disciplines) but are never able to come to any accurate or real knowledge of the truth.

Opposition to the Truth, 8-9. Not only are apostates unable to arrive at the precise knowledge of the truth, they "resist" or stand against the truth in stout opposition, as Jannes and Jambres (cf.

733

Ex 7:11-12). These names are preserved in Hebrew extrabiblical tradition as opposers of Moses. (Cf. those who suppress the truth, Rom 1:18.) They are men in a state of corruption, perverted in their thinking, reprobate concerning the faith, 8 (Jude 3). Their judgment and doom are indicated, 9. Apostasy is irremediable and awaits divine judgment.

3:10-13. PERSECUTION AND APOSTASY

Apostasy Leads to Persecution, 10-11. The apostle's life and ministry are an example, 10. Persecutions and troubles befell him at Antioch in Pisidia, 11 (Acts 13:45-50), Iconium (Acts 14:5-6), and Lystra (Acts 14:19). In his patient endurance he saw the Lord's delivering hand.

Godliness and Persecution, 12-13. All those who determine to live in a godly manner in union with Christ Jesus, i.e., determine to realize their *position* in Christ by an *experience* of Christ, shall suffer (endure) persecution, 12. This will be particularly true in the difficult seasons preceding Christ's return, because evil men and impostors (literally diviners) shall grow worse and worse, deceiving, and being deceived, 13.

3:14-17. SCRIPTURE AND APOSTASY

The Role of Scripture in Timothy's Life, 14-15. He had learned Scripture and been assured of its truths by his grandmother, mother (1:5-6) and the apostle himself (1 Tim 1:1-2; 2 Tim 1:1-2). From childhood he had been taught the holy writings (the OT). These have the power of making one wise to salvation through faith centered in Jesus Christ (Rom 10:17).

The Inspiration and Use of Scripture, 16-17. The sound rendering of this pivotal passage is: "All scripture is God-breathed and profitable. . . ." This declares: (1) The full inspiration of the entire OT and by implication all canonical Scripture. (2) All Scripture is a product of God—God-breathed. God actually produced it, "breathed it *out*." It remains so whether man believes it or not. It has this unchanging quality *objectively* inherent in it. (3) As God-breathed it is inerrant and fully authoritative, since God produced it and actual error is inconsistent with God. (4) The whole of Scripture is useful: (a) for doctrine (teaching); (b) for reproof or censure of wrong and sin; (c) for correction, setting aright or reformation; (d) for instruction (disciplinary education) in righteousness, both God's inherent righteousness and the righteous conduct He requires of His own; (e) that "the man of God may be perfect" in the sense of complete with nothing lacking, completely equipped and furnished "for all good works." This view of the full inspiration of the Bible is the citadel against error and apostasy, both in life and in doctrine.

4:1-4. THE PREACHED WORD AND APOSTASY

A Solemn Charge, 1-2. Paul enforces the command, "Preach the word," 2a, with a most serious and weighty appeal to the divine witnesses, God the Father and Christ Jesus the Judge of all, 1 (cf. Jn 5:22). So pivotal is the matter of heralding the Scripture, 2, that the apostle stresses the accounting which Christ's ministers will render as to how they have handled the Word of God. The preacher is to have *one* ambition—to herald and proclaim *the Word*. This means the systematic and orderly exposition of the plans and purposes of God for lost humanity centering in Christ. Such a task is to be executed "in season" (opportunely, conveniently) as well as "out of season" (inopportunely, inconveniently); in other words, *always.*

The Reason for the Charge, 3-4. The Word of God alone is the antidote against apostasy. In these verses apostasy is described as it relates to Scripture. (1) Apostates will not endure healthy teaching ("sound doctrine"). (2) They will "heap up" teachers who will pander to their lusts. (3) They will have "itching ears," burning to be titillated by some novel error, 3. (4) They will turn their ears from the truth (the Word) to fables or myths.

4:5-8. THE REWARD OF THE FAITHFUL PREACHER

Advice for a Faithful Preacher, 5. The advice is: (1) "watch," be watchful and alert; (2) "endure afflictions," suffer hardship patiently (2:3); (3) "do the work of an evangelist" (an announcer of the good news that Jesus died to save sinners); (4) "make full proof" of your ministry. Serve God in full measure, completely discharging your service through maximum effectiveness.

Testimony of a Faithful Preacher, 6-7. This is the triumph of one who preached the Word. Paul states that he is "now ready to be offered," i.e., to pour out his life as a libation or drink offering, having spent it in sacrifice to make known the gospel (cf. Phil 2:17). The time of his departure by death was at hand. He had fought a good fight (*agonia*, a spiritual struggle, cf. Eph 6:10-20), and now had finished his course. "Course" (*dromos*) refers to a race in the public games and is used figuratively of one's career or ministry. The apostle had "kept the faith" (Jude 3), guarded it against error and apostasy.

The Reward of the Faithful Preacher, 8. Here faith becomes vocal in radiant hope. "The crown of righteousness" is a reward for faithfulness and is reserved for those who particularly love Christ's appearing. "The crown" is the *stephanos* or victor's crown, the chaplet of wild olive or pine, given to the winner in the Greek games.

4:9-15. PERSONAL WARNINGS OF A FAITHFUL PREACHER

Advice Concerning Fellow Workers, 9-13. Timothy is urged to bend every effort to come to the apostle immediately, 9. The reason was that Paul was almost alone. Demas had abandoned him because of love for the present age (or world system). Crescens had gone to Galatia in Asia Minor, Titus to Dalmatia across the Adriatic Sea from Italy, 10. Only Luke remained. Paul requests Mark to be brought, 11 (cf. Acts 15:37-39). Paul had sent Tychicus (Tit 3:12) to Ephesus, 12. He asks for "the cloak," a warm coat with hood used in travel, and "the books," the scrolls (*biblia*), but especially the "parchments," vellums, made of polished fine leather, 13.

Warnings Concerning Evil Workers, 14-15. Timothy is warned to beware of Alexander the coppersmith because he had stoutly resisted (rejected) Paul's message, 15.

4:16-18. TESTIMONY OF THE LORD'S FAITHFULNESS

Man's Unfaithfulness, 16. At his first defense (preliminary hearing) before Caesar all had abandoned Paul and no one vouched for him and his statements. Although disappointed, he was not vengeful, and prayed that their neglect would not be held against them.

God's Faithfulness, 17-18. By contrast, the Lord stood with Paul and strengthened him, apparently securing his acquittal and further ministry. Deliverance out "of the mouth of the lion" refers evidently to the Roman power. Paul's confidence in the Lord's continued faithfulness is asserted, 18.

4:19-22. GREETINGS AND CLOSING SALUTATION

Greetings, 19-21. Among others, Priscilla and Aquila, Paul's colaborers in the gospel and in the trade of tentmaking in Corinth and Ephesus (Acts 18:2-3), are named, together with "the household of Onesiphorus" (1:16-18), Erastus (Acts 19:22) and Trophimus (Acts 21:29).

Closing Salutation, 22.

TITUS

THE ORDER OF GOD'S HOUSE

Writer and Date. The author is Paul (1:1). His letter to Titus was written about the same time as 1 Timothy (see discussion there), approximately either in A.D. 64 or in 66, depending on whether Paul had one or more imprisonments.

Theme. Titus had been left on the island of Crete to organize the churches there (1:5). The letter therefore has much in common with 1 Timothy, but with greater emphasis on church organization and administration.

> **Outline**
> Scriptural Church Organization, Ch. 1
> Pastoral Ministry Toward Various Groups, Ch. 2
> Pastoral Ministry and General Teaching, Ch. 3

1:1-4. GREETING TO TITUS

Paul's Ministry Defined, 1-3. The apostle defines his offices as being those of God's bond-servant and Christ's apostle. His performance of these offices was to be evaluated in accord with "the faith of God's elect" (the personal faith which the believers possessed) and "the knowledge of the truth" which had produced godliness and assurance of eternal life in the lives of the Cretan believers. Paul views his commission as being the proclamation of God's promise of eternal life as embodied in the redemption and life which Christ the divine Word provides, 2-3.

Paul's Greeting to Titus, 4. He is called a "true [genuine] child after the common faith," called common because it was meant for all sinners to embrace and enjoy (cf. 1 Tim 1:1-2).

1:5-9. QUALIFICATIONS OF ELDERS AND BISHOPS

Titus' Task Outlined, 5. Paul left Titus in Crete to organize the assemblies there according to divine order and appoint church officers (elders and bishops). These officers are called bishops (*episcopoi*, "overseers") and deacons (*diakonoi*, "servers") in 1 Tim 3:1-13. Bishops and elders (*presbuteroi*) are terms apparently used to designate the same office of one who both preached and taught, in addition to being an administrator. Deacons, on the other hand, were

737

concerned with finances and benevolences (Acts 6:1-7). However, evidently not all elders were teaching elders or more specifically pastoring elders, with the chief oversight of a church.

Qualification of Elders, 6-9 (see 1 Tim 3:1-13). "Steward of God," literally God's steward, is one who holds a commission from God to serve in the gospel, a trustee of spiritual truth, 7. Among other essential qualifications, he must adhere firmly to the faithful Word of God, 9. This is possible only as the teaching elder is a careful Bible student. He will then be able by healthful teaching to exhort and convince opposers, 9.

1:10-16. WARNING AGAINST FALSE TEACHERS

The Legalists Especially Cited, 10-13a. The churches in Crete were endangered by many who were "unruly," rebellious to the authority of the Word and hence lawless and disorderly; "vain talkers," given to empty arguing and trivial disputation; "deceivers," leading people astray in their thinking. Especially guilty were those of the circumcision, i.e., Jewish legalists. Paul asserts that a curb or muzzle *must* be applied to their mouths to silence them. They "subvert" (corrupt or overturn) whole families, teaching "things which they ought not" for vile or dishonorable financial gain, 11. Paul quotes one of their own prophets (Epimenides, *"de oraculis"*) as saying: "Cretans are always liars [delinquents], evil beasts [wicked brutes], slow bellies [lazy, idle gluttons]." Paul agrees, 13.

The Remedy, 13b-16. A severe reprimand is called for. "Rebuke them sharply, that they may be sound in the faith" and unlegalistic, 13b-14 (cf. 1 Tim 1:4). Then a positive note is sounded: Inculcate purity. "To the pure [clean] all things are clean. But to the defiled and unbelieving nothing is pure [clean]." The reason for impurity is that they are not regenerated, 15-16a. "Easy believism," 16a, not supported by works, is no credential of being saved (2 Tim 3:5, 7; cf. Jas 2:14-20).

2:1-4a. THE AGED ADORNING THE GOSPEL

Aged Men, 1-2. The general responsibility of a true pastor is to teach that which is proper for sound doctrine, 1. Older men are to be "sober" (temperate); "grave" (serious-minded, dignified); "temperate" (sensible, discreet); "sound [hale and hearty] in faith, in love, in patience" (perseverance, the quality of remaining under a trial gracefully).

Aged Women, 3-4a. Older women are to be reverent in their behavior; "not false accusers" or malicious gossips (literally, not devils, controlled by the devil the accuser [from *diaballo*, "to accuse"]); not enslaved to excessive wine; teachers of what is good to the young.

2:4-6. THE YOUNG ADORNING THE GOSPEL

Young Women, 4-5. The older Christian women are to train the young women to be "sober" (serious-minded); lovingly devoted to their husbands and to their children; "discreet"; holy or chaste; home-workers; "good"; subjecting themselves to their own husbands. The purpose or motive for such action is that God's Word may not be blasphemed because of unruly, insubordinate wives.

Young Men, 6, are also exhorted and urged to be serious-minded (sensible). This quality is expected of all ages (cf. 1:8; 2:2, 5) and is a mark of spiritual maturity.

2:7-8. TITUS, THE PASTOR, ADORNING THE GOSPEL

The Pastoral Example, 7-8a. Titus was to be an example for the young men, 6, to imitate (1 Cor 11:1). "In all things" he was to be a model of good works, 7; displaying the quality of not being corrupted or vitiated by error in doctrine. His attitude or manner was to exhibit "gravity" (serious-minded dignity) and "sincerity" (genuineness). "Sound speech" included all his conversation and meant that nothing capable of being condemned should be found in it, being irreproachable.

The Purpose of the Pastoral Example, 8b. Titus was to be so exemplary that "he that is of the contrary part" (an enemy or opponent) would be put to shame, having nothing bad to say concerning the young pastor.

2:9-10. SERVANTS ADORNING THE GOSPEL

Their Conduct Enjoined, 9-10a. Servants were to be voluntarily submissive to their own masters, pleasing them in everything without being impudent or insubordinate, 9. Pilfering or stealing was forbidden, but displaying all good faith was enjoined, 10*a*.

The Purpose Stated, 10b. "That they [common slaves] may adorn the gospel of God." How significant it is that lowly domestics should be selected for this high purpose of being an ornament to the gospel, i.e., to honor or dignify it, decorating or embellishing it, so that men can see its glory displayed in humble human lives. The word "adorn" (*kosmeo*) gives us our English word "cosmetic."

When Titus went to Crete its ancient glory was gone. Here is a section of the palace at Knossos, dating before 1400 B.C. (Courtesy *Mimosa*)

2:11-15. THE GOSPEL AND ADORNED LIVING

The Basis of Adorned Living, 11-14. "The grace of God"—the unmerited divine favor and mercy bestowed upon helplessly lost sinners who trust in Christ's vicarious atonement (Rom 3:24)—constitutes the foundation of godly conduct. This grace, which brought salvation and was displayed in Christ's person and work, teaches by disciplining and instructing us as a child is instructed, 11-12a. Its lesson is that we are saved by His grace from sin to righteous holy living, and are thus to deny or reject ungodliness and worldly lusts. This life is to be a positive one, characterized by a mind set in proper balance ("soberly"), by conduct which meets with God's approval ("righteously"), and by reverence toward God ("godly"). The sphere of this activity is "this present world" or age, the testing ground of our faith, 12.

Motivation for godly conduct is to be found in the believer's anticipating Christ's return for the saints ("blessed hope and glorious appearing"), 13. This hope is even more blessed when the work of the Coming One is realized. His was a vicarious sacrifice. By His atoning death He paid the ransom to rescue sinners from the slavery of sin ("redeem") so that they might be uniquely His own possession ("peculiar people"), zealous of good works, 14. Such grace demands a life of adorned living in response.

The Injunction to Enforce These Truths, 15. Paul emphasizes the need to continually urge the foregoing directives upon Christians, using whatever authority necessary. They are incumbent on every believer ("let no one disregard you").

3:1-7. ADORNING THE GOSPEL BEFORE THE WORLD

The Nature of Exemplary Behavior, 1-2. (1) Believers are to remember that they are subject to established government (Rom 13:1) and are to obey civil authorities, being ready to assist in worthy civic or educational projects, 1. (2) They are to speak evil of no one. (3) Instead of being contentious, a Christian must be "gentle," displaying all meekness to all men (both believers and unbelievers), 2.

The Reason for Exemplary Behavior, 3-7. First of all, the gospel of grace is to be adorned before the world because *we ourselves* (emphatic) were once in the same unsaved state, 3. Thus we are to be examples of God's grace, not judges of the world. We ourselves were once "foolish" (unwise, without spiritual understanding); "disobedient" (refusing to believe and submit to God's will); "deceived" (led astray, caused to wander in spiritual darkness); "serving" (enslaved by) various lusts and pleasures; "living in malice and envy" (in ill will and jealousy); "hateful" (detestable to others); "hating one another" in distrust. People in this state need the gospel advertised to them *by life,* if they are to see the glory of God's grace.

The second reason for proper behavior is seen in the realization that our present condition is entirely due to the grace of God alone, 4-7. This involves: (1) our understanding God's love for men ("kindness and love of God," *philanthrōpia,* i.e., God's special love for mankind), 4; (2) our understanding that salvation is a free gift given, entirely apart from human merit, on the basis of God's mercy and grace, 5a; (3) our realizing that Christ is the exclusive channel of salvation and secures for us "the washing of regeneration" (the cleansing of the believer from the guilt of sin) and "renewing of the Holy Spirit" (the impartation of new life in the person of the indwelling Holy Spirit), 5b-6; (4) our realizing the possessions which are ours in Christ, 7. These include "being justified" (having been pronounced guiltless from sin), "made heirs" (in line for the full inheritance of salvation), "according to the hope of eternal life" (the hope which eternal life gives).

741

3:8-11. ADORNING THE GOSPEL
WITH GOOD WORKS

The Continual Affirmation of Profitable Things, 8. Paul sets forth
a basic principle based on the summary of truth given in 4-7: good
works are to follow personal faith. Those who "have believed in
God" must be careful to take the lead in the diligent practice of good
works. Such a fact is to be "affirmed constantly" (strongly asserted).

The Avoidance of Unprofitable Things, 9-11. Legalistic snares such
as "foolish questions," with which Judaism was honeycombed, and
"genealogies," to which the Jews attached great importance (1 Tim
1:4, 2 Tim 2:23) are to be shunned because they have no value and
are useless. "Strivings" (contentions and arguments) about the law
are also to be avoided, for they too are without value and gain no
end, 9.

A heretic, one who creates factions and fosters divisions as a result
of false doctrine, is to be shunned after he fails to respond to a first
and second admonition or warning (cf. Mt 18:17). Such a one is a
serious sinner because he destroys the unity of God's people (cf. Eph
4:3-6). He is a divisive person who is "subverted" (turned aside or
away from the truth) and goes on sinning, being self-condemned, 11.

3:12-15. CLOSING GREETINGS

Instructions Concerning Fellow Workers, 12-13. Paul desires Titus
to come to Nicopolis, where the apostle plans to spend the winter.
This may have taken place between the first imprisonment and the
possible second (see introduction to 1 Timothy). Zenas and Apollos
are to accompany Titus, 13.

Instruction Concerning Christian Industry, 14-15. "And let ours
[i.e., our Christians] learn to maintain [to practice diligently] good
works for essential needs." There is to be no abuse of grace; no
thinking that because one is saved by grace apart from works and
human merit therefore there are to be no good works produced.
One is saved without works (Eph 2:8-9) but "to good works" (Eph
2:10). A practical result also appears. Believers must have funds for
essential needs. Their lives are not to be unfruitful and barren of
the rewards of common labor. A closing benediction is given, 15.

PHILEMON

CHRISTIAN FELLOWSHIP IN ACTION

Writer and Date. The Apostle Paul is the author of this personal epistle, 1, written probably in A.D. 61 or 62. The letter is one of the so-called Prison Epistles (see introduction to Ephesians and Colossians). It was dispatched by Paul from his prison in Rome by Tychicus, as were Ephesians and Colossians.

Theme. Philemon was a Christian of Colossae, a small city in Asia Minor SE of Laodicea and S of Hierapolis. His slave, Onesimus, had robbed him and consequently fled to Rome. There the renegade slave came in contact with Paul and was saved. The apostle sent him back to his master with this priceless letter preserved for us.

Outline
Paul's Greeting and Commendation of Philemon, 1-7
Paul's Intercession for Onesimus, 8-21
Concluding Word and Greeting, 22-25

VERSES 1-3. PAUL'S GREETING TO PHILEMON

The Greeting, 1-2. Paul describes himself as a "prisoner of Jesus Christ," 1a, not of the Roman emperor (cf. Eph 3:1; 4:1), for he viewed his imprisonment as being the direct will of God. He calls Philemon "our dearly beloved" and "fellow laborer," identifying him as one with himself in the fellowship of the gospel. Mentioned is the church which met in his house. The homes of believers were the customary meeting places of all the early assemblies.

The Benediction, 3, is characteristic of the Pauline letters (cf. Eph 1:2).

VERSES 4-7. PAUL'S COMMENDATION
OF PHILEMON

Philemon's Love and Faith, 4-5. Paul thanks God and commends Philemon for his love and faith directed toward the Lord and toward all believers.

Paul's Prayer for Philemon, 6-7. The apostle prays that "the communication" or "sharing" (RSV) of Philemon's faith may become "effectual" in the sense of being efficiently adapted to work toward others in blessing (cf. Jas 2:14, 17). As a result others may acknowledge every good thing in him in Christ Jesus (cf. Phil 4:8; 2 Pet 1:5, 8). Paul further commends Philemon for his love because the "bowels" (Gr. for tender affections) of the saints had been refreshed by his testimony.

VERSES 8-13. PAUL'S PLEA FOR ONESIMUS

The Plea, 8-10. Philemon's runaway slave is the object of Paul's intercession. Although by virtue of his apostolic authority, Paul was free to "charge" Philemon concerning the proper action to take with regard to Onesimus, 8, yet out of Christian love he rather pleads with him, as the "aged" friend and "the prisoner of Jesus Christ." Paul calls Onesimus "my son," literally, "my very own child whom I have brought to spiritual birth while imprisoned," 10 (1 Cor 4:15).

Paul's Defense of Onesimus, 11-13. The apostle freely acknowledges that Onesimus had been unprofitable (unuseful) in the sense that he caused his master loss. But he also stresses the change conversion

ROME

0   ½ mi.   1 mi.
SCALE OF MILES

makes in a life and asserts, "But now [he is] highly profitable both for you and me as well." Paul would have desired to keep Onesimus because of his usefulness in assisting and encouraging him while in prison, and also because of the deep affection Paul had for him, but gives him back to his master, 13. It is a powerful plea for Philemon to forgive and reinstate his runaway slave.

VERSES 14-16. NOT AS A SERVANT BUT AS A BROTHER

Paul's Courteous Tact, 14. "But without your consent [agreement] I would do nothing, that your displayed kindness [toward Onesimus in taking him back] might not be the result of coercion or pressure, but purely voluntary." Forced service for Christ is not genuine. Paul's aim was to motivate the best in a man.

Paul's Skillful Analysis, 15-16. The apostle suggests a deeper purpose in the matter (cf. Rom 8:28). Maybe Onesimus was separated from Philemon for a while that his master might have his complete loyalty and permanent service, 15. This was now possible because Onesimus was no longer just a servant (a common slave or bondman), but above a slave a "brother beloved" in Christ and united with Philemon in a bond stronger than any other, the Body of Christ— the Church. Onesimus was especially beloved to Paul because Paul was his spiritual father. How much more beloved was he to Philemon, his master, because "in the flesh" (on the natural plane) he was now a dependable Christian servant and "in the Lord" (on the spiritual plane) he was a fellow believer, 16.

VERSES 17-19. RECKON TO MY ACCOUNT

Receive Him as Me, 17. Paul gives a further appeal, "If you therefore count [esteem] me a fellow partner [sharer of salvation, a partaker of eternal life with you], receive Onesimus as myself," 17. The "if" does not express a doubtful contingency. "Therefore, since you do esteem me as a fellow partner in salvation, esteem your repentant slave as a fellow believer also, for such he is now."

Put Any Demerit to My Account, 18-19. This is a beautiful illustration of the principle of imputation by which the sinner's sins are reckoned or imputed to Christ's account, and His righteousness is credited or imputed to the sinner's account, all by faith. The apostle states, "Receive him as myself"—reckon *to him my merit*. "If he has wronged you or owes you anything"—put that on my account—reckon or impute *to me his demerit*. (Cf. Jas 2:23.) Paul will pay any debt owing, 19*a*; but he tactfully suggests that Philemon owes himself to him for the benefit not only of returning a runaway slave, but even more, now a brother in the Lord. It may be that Philemon also was a convert of Paul's, in which case an even greater debt was owed the apostle.

VERSES 20-21.   PAUL'S CONFIDENCE IN PHILEMON

The Request, 20. Philemon's reception of Onesimus would bring joy to Paul in that his action would gladden him and refresh his inmost self.

The Confidence, 21. Paul has confidence that Philemon will do even more than has been suggested to him.

VERSES 22-25.   A REQUEST AND CLOSING GREETINGS

The Request, 22. The imprisoned apostle asks Philemon to find him lodging, for he, in faith, looks forward to release.

The Greetings, 23-25.

THE JEWISH-CHRISTIAN EPISTLES

Hebrews	1 Peter	Jude
James	2 Peter	

These inspired epistles are addressed principally to Jewish believers. In the case of Hebrews the purpose is to set forth the finality of Christ's salvation and warn against the peril of Jewish believers going back to the fulfilled types and superseded ritualism of Judaism. James instructs them in the practical virtues familiar to OT saints. First Peter is also addressed to Jewish Christians of the dispersion (1:1-2). Second Peter and Jude are more general, like the catholic (universal) epistles of 1, 2 and 3 John.

All these Jewish-Christian writings differ from the Pauline epistles in their omission of those distinctive elements which were revealed particularly to the Apostle to the Gentiles, such as the nature, position, and destiny of the Church, the Body of Christ. For instance, the Epistle to the Hebrews presupposes these truths but it does not expound them. Instead, it approaches our "so great salvation" from the point of its superiority to Judaism, since the letter is directed primarily to Jews, not Gentile believers as were the Pauline letters.

It may be said that these Jewish-Christian epistles deal more with the inculcation of the practical expression of salvation in consistent living grounded in the basic doctrines of biblical Christianity. By contrast, the Pauline letters base the same conduct on the more complex disclosures of the Christian's *position* and *possessions* in union with Christ (Eph 4:1-3), in His death, resurrection, ascension, and return in glory (Rom 6:1-11; Eph 1:1-14; Col 3:1-4). The difference then is not that of disagreement or conflict in any sense. Both present the same Christ, the same salvation and the same hope. But the distinction is that of development and extension.

HEBREWS

CHRIST SUPERIOR TO ALL

Authorship. This great epistle is anonymous. Paul has been claimed as author (cf. 2 Pet 3:15; Heb 13:23), and there is internal evidence pointing to this possibility. But in the absence of direct statement or indubitable proof, the question must remain unsettled. This, however, does not affect the genuineness of the epistle. No book contains grander truth, nor attests itself as being more divinely inspired.

Theme and Date. Hebrews meets a pivotal need in showing the relationship of Christianity to Judaism, a question which has been a burning issue in the Christian church since the apostolic period. The book was written before the destruction of Jerusalem and the temple by the Romans in A.D. 70 (cf. 10:11).

Outline
Superiority of the Son to Prophets and Angels, 1:1—2:18
Superiority of the Son to Moses and Joshua, 3:1—4:16
Superiority of Christ's Priesthood, 5:1—8:5
Superiority of the New Covenant to the Old Covenant,
   8:6—10:39
Superiority of Faith, 11:1—13:25

1:1-3. THE SON SUPERIOR TO THE PROPHETS

The Ministry of the Prophets, 1. The word through the OT prophets came in many ways and in various modes (dreams, visions, audible voice, theophany, angels, men, etc.). Although it was the inspired, infallible Word ("God spoke"), it was ministered by weak, fallible men ("the prophets") to those who proved disobedient ("the fathers").

The Superior Ministry of the Son, 2-3. The Son's ministry is superior to that of the OT prophets because of His glorious person and His creative and redemptive work. That superiority is seen in the following declarations. *Christ's eternal deity* is seen in the reference to "Son," 2a, the Word who was God and who became flesh (man), the only begotten of the Father (Jn 1:1, 14). He was *God's full and final revelation* of Himself to man, for "God has spoken through a Son," 2a; not through mere man but through Himself become man.

"Whom he [God] hath appointed heir of all things," 2b, has reference to *the Son's eternal heirship*. God's heir is Christ (Rom 8:17). His inheritance is over all things and is eternal as well as universal. The Son is also superior because of *His creatorship*, 2c, for He not only created the material universe but fashioned the ages of time. *His full divine glory* is that which is referred to when it is said that He was "the effulgence [the full outshining] of God's glory," 3a. Christ is the absolute expression of the collective attributes of Deity (Jn 1:18; Rom 9:5). All that God is and does is revealed in full splendor in the divine Son.

"The express image of his person," 3b, has reference to the Son's being the *exact representation of God's nature*. God is seen, or is made visible, in the person of Jesus Christ. The Son is also *the sustainer* (Col 1:17b) *and the maintainer of the universe*, "upholding all things by the word of his power," 3c. In His redemptive act He did what no other priest had ever done, He completely removed sin from the sinner, not merely covering it temporarily (Jn 1:29; 19:30; Heb 5—7). "He . . . by himself purged our sins," 3d. His was *a finished redemption*. Finally, it is said that He "sat down on the right hand of the Majesty on high," 3e, becoming, in *His present session*, an interceding priest on the basis of an accomplished redemption (Heb 8:1-2; 10:12; 12:2).

1:4-14. THE SON SUPERIOR TO THE ANGELS IN HIS PERSON AND WORK

Superior in His Person, 4-9. He is *uncreated* Deity; the angels are mere creatures, though lofty celestial spirits. He has "by inheritance obtained a *more excellent name*" than the angels, 4 (cf. 1-3). He received this name as the result of His incarnate redemptive work (Rom 1:4; Phil 2:5-8). It is an inheritance of the Father who has highly exalted Him and given Him this "*name* which is *above every name*" (Phil 2:9).

God addresses Him "my Son" (Deity), 5, in Father-Son relationship (2 Sam 7:14), which is in contrast to the angels (mere creatures) who are never so addressed. Furthermore, Christ is styled "firstborn," 6, a title of uncreated Deity (Col 1:15), and "all the angels of God" are commanded as creatures to *worship Him*, their Creator. They are designated His (created) "spirits" and His "ministers" or "servants," 7 (Ps 104:4). The Son is addressed "as God" in verses 8-9; attributes of Deity are ascribed to Him; His

749

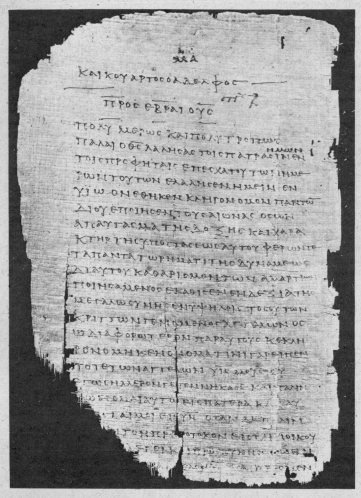

The first page of Hebrews from a Beatty-Michigan manuscript dating about A.D. 200. (*Courtesy UML*)

righteous kingdom rule is intimated; and His immeasurable anointing with the Holy Spirit is noted (Ps 45:6-7).

Superior in His Work, 10-14. Christ is superior to angels in His work as *Creator,* 10-12, and *Redeemer,* 13-14. As the crucified and risen Lord He sits at the Father's right hand, until His enemies are made the footstool of His feet (Ps 110:1). No angel was ever addressed in this fashion, 13. Angels have a blessed but much lower status, 14. As creatures they are all engaged in sublime but subordinate service, "ministering [serving] spirits," delegated and sent forth to assist "those who will [in the sense of a sure and settled futurity] inherit salvation."

2:1-4. WARNING AGAINST DRIFTING

The Warning, 1. "Therefore," since the infinitely superior Son of God has spoken, we ought of necessity to give the more earnest attention to the things which we have heard from Him and concerning Him (the Gospels and the Acts). If Hebrew believers thought the OT prophets should be heard, how much more the Lord of glory Himself! The danger was that they might imperceptibly *drift away* from these truths in the strong currents of legalistic ritualism.

The Reason for Warning, 2-4. The writer now argues from the lesser to the greater. If judgment fell on those who transgressed the law given through the mediation of angels, how much more serious will be the state of the one who rejects the word of God's Son! Then an unanswerable question: "How shall we escape if we neglect so great salvation?" 3. Those who perished under the judgment of the Mosaic economy serve as a warning to us. This word of "great salvation" was first proclaimed by Christ Himself; then by His commissioned disciples, attested by miraculous signs and gifts of the Holy Spirit (1 Cor 12).

2:5-9. THE SON SUPERIOR TO THE ANGELS IN HIS AUTHORITY

The Son's Kingdom Authority, 5. "The world to come" refers to the inhabited earth in the coming age when Christ the Son returns in His glorified humanity to rule as King of kings and Lord of lords (Rev 19:16). This future world will not be subject to angels, but to Christ in its totality. Such authority is His alone.

The Basis of the Son's Authority, 6-9. This quotation from Psalm 8:4-6, referring to the original estate of the first Adam (man), is applied to Christ the "second man" (1 Cor 15:47). Adam, the representative man, forfeited his earth-dominion through sin, but the last Adam (Christ, the perfect man) regained it by virtue of His humiliation and death for every man. He was made "a little lower than the angels," 9, God becoming man, submitting to human limitations to which angels are not subject, and foregoing the glories which were His as the Prince of heaven. Undergoing the suffering of death, He, the Sinless One, tasted death for every man. His was a vicarious and a substitutionary death for sinners. From such humiliation He arose to the heights of exaltation and is crowned with glory and honor, far above that of angels.

2:10-13. THE SON SUPERIOR TO THE ANGELS IN HIS PERFECT HUMANITY

Bringing Sons to Glory, 10. It was the purpose of God the Father "in bringing many sons unto glory," i.e., consummating their salvation in resurrection and glorification, to make complete the work of the Captain (Leader) of their salvation through suffering. He was thus advanced to completeness in His role of suffering Redeemer. Because He suffered He is qualified to serve as the File Leader of those who are heirs of salvation, those being brought to glorification.

Union of the Redeemer and the Redeemed, 11-13. Both "he that sanctifieth" (the Son through whom the Father is bringing many sons to glory) and "they who are sanctified" (the sons who are being brought to glory) are "all of one," 11. They have a common origin in God; therefore, because of this unity, the Son is not ashamed to call them His brothers. As sons of glory, 10, they are destined for glorification even as Christ their Captain is already glorified.

The reference to Psalm 22:22 in verse 12 prophetically sets forth the eternal priestly work of Christ in which He continually reveals God's name to us and sings the praises of God among us "His brothers" (cf. Jn 20:19). "I will put my trust in him," 13a (cf. Isa 8:17), expresses the personal faith of the Son in the Father. "Behold, I and the children whom the Lord hath given me" (Isa 8:18) actually refers to Isaiah's two sons, but is here, 13b, applied by the Holy Spirit to represent the unity of the Son with His brethren. The angels do not sustain such unity with the redeemed; such uniquely belongs to the perfect Man, the Redeemer.

2:14-18. THE SON SUPERIOR TO THE ANGELS IN HIS CONQUEST OF SIN AND DEATH

The Purpose of the Incarnation, 14-16. This purpose is threefold: (1) that the Incarnate One might "render null, void and completely powerless" the devil's power over death (Gen 3); (2) that such might be accomplished through the death of the Incarnate One, 14; (3) that those who were held in slavish bondage to the fear of death all their lives might be delivered, 15. Help was not given to angels, but to the seed (posterity) of Abraham, and for such a task the incarnate God-Man was necessary, 16. Only He could fulfill the great divine purposes of the Abrahamic covenant (Gen 12:1-3).

The Purpose of His Priesthood, 17-18. The Son's incarnation was a necessary prelude to His priesthood. He must, in order to be a qualified high priest in behalf of men before God, "be made like His brothers," whom he was bringing to glory. This involved His becoming a human being, laying aside His heavenly splendor and glory, and sharing man's sufferings and temptations, 17a, 18. Only thus could He be a "merciful and faithful high priest." As such, Christ made "propitiation [satisfaction] for the sins of the people" at the cross (Jn 19:30), giving man access to God, 17 (ASV).

3:1-6. THE SON SUPERIOR TO MOSES

Holy Brethren, 1. For the first time the readers are addressed as "holy brethren, partakers of the heavenly calling," 1. They were no longer simply Jews with an earthly inheritance but members of the Church, the Body of Christ, with a "heavenly calling." This is emphasized throughout the book.

Consider the Son, 1-2. The exhortation here is to consider Christ, to contemplate our faithful High Priest so as to perceive and fully understand Him as the delegated One sent by the Father. He is the High Priest of our "confession" (not "profession"), the One to whom confession is made by believers, 1.

In comparing Christ with Moses, emphasis is given in verse 2 to the faithfulness each exercised in his calling. Christ "was faithful to him [God the Father] that appointed him, as also Moses was faithful in all his house" (Num 12:7; Mt 26:42).

The Son Contrasted with Moses, 3-6. Christ is esteemed, deserving of more honor than Moses, for although both were faithful in administrating the divine economy (the spiritual household) committed to them, Christ built the house (the divine economy) while Moses only served therein, 3-5a. Moses was faithful as a free and dignified servant; Christ was faithful as Son. Moses' ministry was typical and prophetic of Christ, and of the truths and blessings to be realized in Him, 5 (Deut 18:15, 18-19). He was the fulfillment of all that Moses and the law looked forward to in redemption. The saved now constitute God's "house" (1 Cor 3:9; Eph 2:19-22). Their faith is expressed by their confidence in Christ, which constitutes their hope until the day of complete redemption, 6.

3:7-19. WARNING AGAINST DEPARTING FROM THE LIVING GOD

The Sin of Heart-Hardening, 7-10. This warning is addressed to the brethren of verse 1. It is *urgent* ("today") and *authoritative* ("even as the Holy Spirit saith," ASV). Faith and obedience to God's Word ("if ye shall hear his voice," Ps 95:7-11) are involved, 7 (ASV). The danger is that of an omnitemporal peril—hardening the heart—becoming stubbornly insensitive and rebellious against God, 8a. Illustrated by God's people in the wilderness, 8b, the warning concerns "tempting God," refusing to believe Him in the face of gracious signs and miraculous provisions, and at the same time evidencing unbelief by demanding new signs and miracles, 9. Such sin leads to error, wandering, and ignorance of God's ways, 10.

The Penalty—Forfeiture of God's Rest, 11. Unbelief, 7-10, stirs up God's anger, 11, and provokes His oath, i.e., the suitable response of His gracious and infinitely holy nature. God's "rest" is the quiet inner assurance and triumphant sense of peace He gives those who trust Him. It is the reward of believing God and is typified by Israel's entrance into Canaan.

The Deceitfulness of Sin, 12-16. So treacherous is sin in rendering the heart insensitive and unresponsive to God and His Word, that constant exhorting and urging are necessary while opportunity affords, 13. That those addressed were genuine believers is indicated by the fact that they had been made "partakers of Christ," 14. They must continue to hold to the full efficacy and finality of Christ's priesthood, not lapsing back into Jewish ritualism. To do so would have been to harden their hearts as in "the provocation"—Israel's rebellion in the desert for 40 years, 15-16 (Ps 95:8; Ex 17:1-7; Num 14:1-45).

The Tragedy of Unbelief, 17-19. "They sinned . . . they believed not." The result was they "provoked," 16, and "grieved" God, 17. Their "skeletons" fell in the desert. They forfeited God's rest, 18, because of unbelief, 19. Redemption, typified by sprinkling the Passover blood (Ex 12:12-13) and crossing the Red Sea (Ex 14:13-31), was meant to have its consummation in "rest," illustrated by the conquest and settlement of Canaan. This aspect of salvation was forfeited because of unbelief. The chastening which resulted was physical death—their corpses fell in the desert (cf. 1 Cor 11:30-31; 1 Jn 5:16).

4:1-8. THE SON SUPERIOR TO JOSHUA IN THE REST HE GIVES

The Gospel, the Source of Rest, 1-3b. "Fear," 1, is a believer's godly concern lest he die in unbelief in the "wilderness" like Israel, and never enter Canaan, the place of rest (cf. Num 14). Canaan rest (Mt 11:28-30) is that *full trust* in the finished work of Christ, both for salvation of the soul and sanctification of life, which brings not only "peace with God" (Rom 5:1) but the "peace of God" (Phil 4:7). The gospel is the source of this peace, because it centers in the atoning work of the Son. It (the good news) was preached to "us," as well as "to them," referring to Israel in the OT. The difficulty was that it was not believed ("united with faith") by those who heard it. The gospel then pointed forward to the atonement of Christ as it now points back to it (1 Cor 15:1-4). Faith in the gospel is the key to this rest, 3*a* (Ps 95:11).

God's Creation Rest Is a Type, 3c-8. On the seventh day of creation God rested and was refreshed (Ex 31:17; cf. Gen 1:31—2:3). This serves as a type of the rest that the believer may enter spiritually now, in the midst of persecution and conflict, as he fully relies on the finished work of Christ. This rest was not entered into by the generation that came out of Egypt (except Caleb and Joshua) because of unbelief, 6. Neither did Joshua (here called Jesus, the Gr. form of Joshua) give Israel this rest from the harassment of their enemies. Only Jesus Christ, the greater Joshua, can provide true rest, 8.

4:9-13. THE SON SUPERIOR TO JOSHUA IN THE REDEMPTION HE PROVIDES

Redemptive Rest Is Available for God's People, 9-10. These verses refer to the rest called sabbath-keeping (*sabbatismos,* "a state of rest from labor"), 9. It involves the believer's resting completely in a perfect work of redemption (3-4) as God rested from a perfect work of creation, 10. This rest of redemption reposes *wholly* in the work of the cross, and ceases from all self-effort, human merit or legalistic claim as a means either to salvation or sanctification, 10 (cf. Eph 2:8-10). It projects the victory of faith in conquest over spiritual enemies (the world, the flesh and the devil).

This Rest to Be Diligently Realized, 11-13. The believer is exhorted to be eager to enter into this rest through quiet believing with the reminder that some in Israel failed to enter the rest of the Promised Land because of their unbelief, 11. Faith is necessary in order to possess the rest which Christ provides, while unbelief will rob us of such blessing.

The instrument which God uses to bring men into the rest of faith is the living and dynamic Word of God, 12-13. This Word, keener than a sharp two-edged sword, severs to the point where attitudes and motives are laid bare, where one's innermost thoughts are judged, 12. It strips away all pretense and sham, revealing us as we truly are, 13. Faith that leads to rest in Christ is distinguished thereby from mere assent and formalism.

4:14—5:10. CHRIST'S PRIESTHOOD SUPERIOR TO AARON'S

Our Great High Priest, 4:14-16. Christ, our "great high priest," is great because of *His finished work of redemption,* attested by His having "passed through the heavens," 14 (ASV). This means that worship and intercession are now carried on in the heavenly sanctuary alone, the believer being brought directly into God's presence (Heb 10:19; Phil 3:3).

Christ is also great because *He is Jesus, the Son of God,* qualified to represent man before the throne of God the Father. He is "touched with the feeling of our infirmities," or sympathizes with our weaknesses, because He was tested in all particulars as we are, sin excepted; that is, He had no connection with sin (cf. 7:26). He was tempted in every way as the absolutely Sinless One, perfect man.

Further, Christ is great because *He transforms God's throne* of holy judgment against sinners *to a throne of grace* for believers, His blood being sprinkled thereupon. There the believer finds a continual supply of mercy and grace for help in all times of need, 16. The greatness of our High Priest calls for adhering to (holding fast) our confession to Him, 14. He is the One to whom confession is made, and to whom we may draw near with confident assurance that grace may be expected from His throne, 16.

Qualifications of Aaronic Priests, 5:1-4. Israel's high priest (1) was *chosen from among men,* 1*a*; (2) was ordained or *appointed to* *minister on behalf of his fellowmen* before God, 1*b*; (3) *offered gifts and sacrifices* for sins, representing the sinner, 1*c*; (4) was *compassionate with sinners* because he himself was "clothed with" sinful weakness, 2; (5) also *offered sacrifice for his own sins* as well as those of the people (Lev 16:11) because he, too, needed atonement, 3; (6) was *God-called,* not self-chosen (Ex 28:1; Num 16:40).

Superiority of Christ's Qualifications, 5:5-10. Christ was fully qualified to be a high priest because He was: (1) *divinely chosen* by God the Father, 5; (2) *divinely appointed* to be *an eternal High Priest* of the Melchizedek order, 6; (3) a *true man* with a genuinely human nature "in the days of his flesh," therefore able to represent men, 7*a*; (4) the *actual sacrifice* or offering for sin, facing death for sinners, 7*b*; (5) the *final victor* over sin and death in His resurrection, 7*c*; (6) the *perfect substitute* for man and his sin in that Christ's sufferings taught Him the full obedience necessary for His redemptive work, 8. As a result of His perfect qualifications, He became the "author" or "provider" of eternal salvation, not a mere covering for sin (as did the Aaronic high priest's sacrifice). His salvation is eternal because His status as a priest is eternal—after the order of Melchizedek (see Heb 7), 9-10.

5:11-14. APPEAL TO MATURITY

Characteristics of the Immature, 11-13. Before developing the truth of the Melchizedek priesthood of Christ the writer introduces another warning or rebuke in the epistle, this time concerning spiritual immaturity. Many of the Hebrew believers addressed were characterized as being sluggish (dull) of hearing in their acceptance and understanding of the truths of the faith, 11. They were still untaught at a time when they should have been qualified to be teachers of the deeper truths, such as the Melchizedek aspect of Christ's priesthood, 12*a*. As babes, they could receive only milk, or elementary truths, and were unqualified because of a lack of knowledge of and experience in the truth of the Word, 12*b*-13.

Contrast of the Mature, 14. Those "of full age" have an adult diet, able to take the solid nourishment of the Word as applied to life and doctrine. They are those who are trained athletes in the spiritual life because of the discipline under which they have gone. In addition, they are doctrinally discerning, able to distinguish between truth and error because their mature experience has made them spiritually discriminating.

6:1-3. PRESSING ON TO FULL GROWTH

Exhortation to Spiritual Progress, 1a. "Therefore [because of the danger of immaturity, 5:11-14], leaving the elementary teaching about the Christ, let us press on to maturity" (Gr.). "Leaving," in this passage, means advancement—advance beyond the elementary truths concerning Christ toward completeness or full growth (*teleiotes*). Perhaps the writer had in mind advancing to the experiential knowledge of Christ's life, death and resurrection, etc., beyond the simple historical facts, to the realization of one's position and possessions in Christ as revealed in the NT epistles.

Danger of Spiritual Retrenchment, 1b-2. The peril endangering maturity is that of relaying the foundation instead of proceeding to build the superstructure thereupon. Those basic truths constituting the foundation, while absolutely necessary but not ends in themselves, are: (1) "repentance from dead works," 1c, i.e., those works which were involved in obedience to the Mosaic law, "dead" because they were valueless in obtaining eternal salvation (Acts 15:10; cf. Deut 6:24-25 with Gal 3:11-12); (2) "faith toward God," 1d, not faith in their privileges as Jews (1 Pet 1:18-21); (3) "the doctrine of baptisms," 2a, which for the addressees included OT washings and purification rites as well as Christian water baptism; (4) "laying on of hands," 2b, a ceremony symbolizing identification and transfer in the OT (Lev 16:21) with similar meanings in the NT (Acts 5:12; 8:17-19; 9:41; 13:3; 19:6; 1 Tim 4:14; 2 Tim 1:6); (5) "resurrection of the dead," 2c, a doctrine believed in the OT (Job 19:25; Ps 16:10; Dan 12:2) and a cardinal element of NT preaching which proclaimed the believer's hope (Lk 24:39, 43; 1 Cor 15:20-22); (6) "eternal judgment," 2d, the teaching that lost mankind and rebellious angels will experience eternal punishment (Mt 25:41; Rev 20:10).

The Dynamic of Spiritual Progress, 3. With God's permission, these Jewish believers must press on toward maturity, advancing from the elementary doctrines just mentioned. God can only allow such blessing as believers trust Him in faith and allow Him to work in them. "Pressing on" is the Christian's working out God's inwrought salvation (Phil 2:12).

6:4-8. THE SIN OF LAPSING BACK INTO JUDAISM

The Subjects—Hebrew Believers, 4-5. These verses give evidence that those being discussed were believers, but they had drifted away from the experiential knowledge relating to Christ's person and work, thereby neglecting to claim God's rest and remaining immature.

The Nature of the Sin—Defection from the All-Sufficient Nature of Christ's Death, 6. This sin involved their falling away from grace (salvation in Christ by faith alone) to Judaistic ordinances in the maintaining of their relationship to God. It was a denial of the Hebrew believer's initial repentance from the dead works of the law, which in reality was a denial of the complete efficacy of Christ's death for all sin (Jn 19:30). Evidently the Christians in view were those who fell back on Judaistic ritual and sacrifices to atone for their sins. This was tantamount to crucifying the Son of God again, considering Him an impostor and subjecting Him to great indignity and public shame because it slighted both His person and His work. For such there was no repentance, no about face, only divine judgment.

The Result of the Sin—Divine Rejection, 7-8. Defection calls forth God's disciplinary action because there is lack of fruitfulness in the life, 7, and instead, the presence of unbelief and sin ("thorns and briers" being tokens of unbelief and the curse of sin), 8. The result is rejection (*adokimos*), disapproval or disqualification (1 Cor 9:27) for a prize, and the believer's works being burned, as wood, hay or stubble, at the judgment seat of Christ (1 Cor 3:13-15).

6:9-12. THE CONTRAST OF MATURITY IN CHRIST

The Better Things of Salvation, 9-10. Although very much aware of the dangers which were present to thwart these Hebrew Christians in their growth toward maturity, the writer expresses his confidence in them. Their past lives gave him a basis for this confidence, 10. Not only he but God Himself would not forget their many acts of kindness which they had shown toward their Christian brethren even in the face of tribulation and temptation. "Things that accompany salvation" evidently has reference to the fruitful works which resulted from their inwrought faith.

The Author's Desire, 11-12. It was the writer's longing that their good start (9-10) might continue toward full maturity, 11. This would be accomplished by each manifesting through outward conduct the same earnestness which had been displayed to this point. Such diligence would result in the full assurance that they would possess or inherit the promises in the end, at the consummation of the age. There would be the temptation to slothfulness or sluggishness, but they were to be imitators of those saints who inherit the promises, 12.

6:13-20. ENCOURAGEMENT TO MATURITY IN CHRIST

God's Faithfulness to Abraham, 13-18a. Those who anticipated inheriting the promise, 12, had God's covenant with Abraham as their assurance. This patriarch is introduced here to serve as an example of perseverance in waiting for the promise of God. Abraham persevered because God guaranteed by His own name the covenant He made with Abraham, 13. The divine oath, 14, involved a Hebraism, "Surely blessing I will bless [superabundantly bless], and multiplying I will multiply [superabundantly multiply] thee." Given to encourage Abraham in patience, it accomplished its purpose and he obtained the promise, 15, that is, he received the full guarantee of its complete fulfillment.

Using the human custom of an oath as a settlement of a controversy, 16, God being more abundantly willing to demonstrate the unchangeableness of His purpose, confirmed His promise by an oath. Having sworn by His own name, it was impossible for God to lie. His authority and integrity were at stake. His oath, thereby, gave Abraham absolute guarantee of fulfillment, 17-18. Since God is unchangeable, we have as strong encouragement as did Abraham.

God's Faithfulness in Christ, 18b-20. Christ, who is the fulfillment of the Abrahamic covenant, is our assurance, the object of our hope, 18b. This hope we continually have as an anchor (emphatic) of the soul which keeps us from drifting. It (Christ) is within the veil in the heavenly sanctuary, 19, and He, as our Forerunner and High Priest, enables us to follow after Him and through Him to enter within the veil—heaven itself, 20.

7:1-3. MELCHIZEDEK, THE TYPE OF CHRIST AS KING-PRIEST

The Identity of Melchizedek, 1-3a (cf. Gen 14:17-24). This man, 4, was "king of Salem," an ancient name for Jerusalem, in the patriarchal era. But more important, he was "priest of the most high God" (*El Elyon*, "possessor of heaven and earth," Gen 14:19, 22), 1a. His eminence or superiority to Abraham is revealed in his blessing, 1b, and in his receiving tithes from Abraham, 2a. Perhaps a clue to his character is given in the translation of his name, which means "king of righteousness," and in the meaning of his title as "king of Salem, that is, king of peace," 2b. Neither Melchizedek's parentage nor his genealogy is recorded; nor are his birth and death specified, because such is extraneous to his priestly office in being "like unto the Son of God," 3.

Melchizedek, a Type of Christ, 3b. Melchizedek was made like, or made to resemble, Christ in description and typical significance. The focus is thus placed on Christ's royal authority and the unending duration of His priesthood, which, in turn, are based on His person (the eternal Son of God) and His work in redemption (as King of righteousness, Rom 3:25-26; then as King of peace, Rom 5:1). Our King-Priest now sits "on the right hand of the Majesty in the heavens" (8:1) "ever living to make intercession" (7:25b).

7:4-22. THE SUPERIORITY OF MELCHIZEDEK'S PRIESTHOOD TO AARON'S

Aaron Paid Tithes to Melchizedek, 4-7, 9-10. The reader is urged to "consider" (*theōreite*, "keep on contemplating with attentive discernment") the eminence of Melchizedek, who was so great that even Abraham gave him tithes of the best of the firstfruits and produce of the land, 4. The theme emphasized is that Melchizedek's priesthood was greater than Aaron's because the Aaronic priests (who received the tithes of the people) as descendants of Abraham offered tithes through Abraham to Melchizedek, the greater. In this manner Melchizedek, "the better," blessed the Levites, "the less."

Aaron's Priesthood Was Transitory, Melchizedek's Permanent, 8. The Levitical, or Aaronic, ministry was temporary because it was served by mortal men who died. By contrast, the Melchizedek priestly ministry was enduring and contained no hint of death. Christ, the antitype, is emphasized in the last phrase. His ministry is eternal because it is served by the immortal, death-conquering King-Priest.

The Aaronic Priesthood Was Limited, 11-14. The Levitical priesthood lacked "perfection" in the sense of finality of function and completeness of operation and effect. It could neither remove sin, nor grant righteousness or favor and position with God, 11a. This lack of perfection is recognized: (1) in the need which existed for "another priest," i.e., one of a *different* order, the order of Melchizedek, 11b; (2) in the necessity of a change in the law with which the Aaronic priesthood was unseparably bound, 12; and (3) in the need for a change in the exclusive regulations of the law which limited the priesthood to the tribe of Levi, and thereby excluded Christ on the human plane from serving since He was from the tribe of Judah, 13-14a. Moses gave no priestly authority to Judah, 14b.

The Melchizedek Priesthood Is Final, 15-22. Christ's priesthood, after the order of Melchizedek, is final and complete because of: (1) its superior nature, 15 (cf. 4-11); (2) its qualification by the power of an indissoluble life and not by physical regulations, 16; (3) its institution by the authority of the Word of God, 17; (4) its bringing in a better hope with immediate access to God, 19; (5) its finalization by a divine oath establishing and ordaining Christ's eternal

761

priesthood, 20-21; (6) Christ, the guarantee of a new and better covenant by virtue of the oath's better validity, 22 (Jer 31:31-33; Mt 26:28; 1 Cor 11:25).

7:23-28. THE SUPERIOR EFFICACY AND PERPETUITY OF CHRIST'S PRIESTHOOD

Its Perpetuity, 23-24. The Aaronic priests were many in number, death necessitating that they frequently be replaced by their descendants. They contrasted to Christ's one permanent priesthood (*aparabaton*, "not to be superseded" in the sense of not passing from one to another), because He continues forever (never dies), 24.

Its Superior Efficacy, 25-28. The superior nature of the efficacy of Christ's priesthood, based on its perpetuity ("wherefore," 25*a*), consists, first, in its *complete ability to save forever* ("to the uttermost," *eis to panteles,* "through all time,"), 25*b*. This is possible because those coming to God through Him enjoy His uninterrupted intercession which guarantees their salvation forever. "He ever lives to make intercession," never interrupted by death.

Second, it is superior because *its Priest is perfectly suited to our need,* 26. He is: (1) "holy," perfectly aligned with God's will in reverent piety (Ps 16:10); (2) "harmless," in the sense of blamelessly free from evil; (3) "undefiled," in the sense of being unstained by blemish from sinful men; (4) "separate from sinners," or better translated, "having been separated from sinners," being in a different class from sinners when He was on earth and now separate from them as their High Priest in heaven above (cf. Lev 21:12); (5) "made higher than the heavens," for He literally "passed through" the heavens (4:14, ASV).

Third, the *sacrifice* of this priesthood *is final,* 27. In contrast to the day-by-day sacrifices of the Aaronic priests (9:6; 10:11; cf. Ex 29:38-42), Christ's sacrifice was a *once-for-all* offering of Himself. He did not need to offer daily, nor to offer for His own sins. He offered Himself as a final and complete efficacious sacrifice, the Sinless One alone offering for the sinful (cf. Lev 16:11).

Fourth, the efficacy of Christ's priesthood is superior because *it is sealed by divine oath,* 28. In contrast to the Mosaic law, which constituted men priests who themselves were sinners, God's oath in Ps 110:4 (which was made after the law was given) makes the sinless Son Priest perfected forevermore.

8:1-5. CHRIST, HIGH PRIEST IN THE HEAVENLY SANCTUARY

The Reality of His Ministry, 1-2. The "main point in what has been said is" that Christ "has taken His seat at the right hand of the throne of the Majesty in the heavens" (Gr.), completely superseding the Levitical priesthood, 1. He is infinitely above all other priests, exercising His priesthood in heaven, not on earth (10:12). The high priest, even when he entered the holiest annually, only *stood* for a moment before the *symbol* of God's throne. By contrast, our Lord *ever sits* on the throne of the Majesty on high till His enemies are made His footstool (Ps 110:1). Further, Christ sits as a "minister of the sanctuary"—the administrator of the holy things in the real tabernacle in heaven. The earthly tabernacle was a mere foreshadow of the heavenly, being pitched not by man but by the Lord, 2.

The Typical Foreshadowing of His Ministry, 3-5. "Every high priest . . . appointed to offer both gifts and sacrifices" (Gr.) was a type of "this One," who must also have something to offer, 3, viz., He offered Himself once for all as a completed, final sacrifice to remove sin. As the high priest did not enter the most holy place apart from blood, so Christ did not enter the holiest (heaven) apart from His own blood (1 Pet 1:2). He ministers thus in heaven. If He were here on earth He would not even be a priest, not being from the tribe of Levi, 4. But He ministers the real, while the Levitical priests ministered only "a copy and shadow of the heavenly," 5 (Ex 25:40).

8:6-13. THE SATISFACTORY NATURE OF THE NEW COVENANT

The Limitations of the Old Covenant, 6-9. The "old covenant" refers to the legal or Mosaic covenant. It was *enacted on promises inferior* to those upon which the new covenant was established, 6. These promises entailed conditions ("if ye . . .," Ex 19:5-7), with promises of blessing following obedience, but furnishing no dynamic for such obedience. By contrast, the new covenant is unconditional, final, and irreversible, since God does everything, 8-10. It rests upon the finished work of Christ and secures eternal blessedness, under the Abrahamic covenant, to all who believe (Gal 3:13-29).

The old covenant *lacked finality*, 7. It was not "faultless," i.e., not without defect. The law as a method of divine dealing "made nothing perfect" or final (Rom 8:3; Heb 7:18-19) because of man's sinfulness.

Had the old covenant been satisfactory, a second covenant would not have been needed.

The old covenant also *lacked efficacy,* 8-9. It provided no power to the sinner to keep its conditions. Although a standard for conduct was provided, enablement to maintain it was lacking, and Israel disobeyed and fell under the judgment of God, 8*a,* 9*b.*

The Satisfactory Nature of the New Covenant, 10-13. In contrast to the old, the new covenant is *gracious and unconditional,* 10*a.* This is the result of what God does sovereignly and unconditionally for Israel at the second advent, not what they helplessly attempt to do for God (cf. the "I wills," 10-12). The new covenant is also *spiritually efficacious,* 10*b*-11, resulting in spiritual regeneration, 10*b,* and universal knowledge of the Lord, 11. Then, too, this covenant is *faultless and final,* 12, based as it is upon the complete redemption of Christ, settling forever Israel's sin question and superseding the old covenant, 13 (see notes on 10:15-17).

9:1-10. THE TYPICAL NATURE OF THE OLD COVENANT

The Ordinances of the Sanctuary Under the Old Covenant, 1-5. The ministry of the priests under the Mosaic covenant is described in relation to the pieces of furniture in the tabernacle. This sanctuary (the tent or tabernacle) is called "worldly" because it involved worship on this earth, i.e., an earthly sanctuary, 1. It is selected for special description here because the priestly ordinances were observed therein. The outer room (the holy place) is described in 2, the inner room (the holy of holies or the holiest of all) in 3-5. Each piece of furniture spoke typically of Christ, His person and work (see notes on Ex 25—30).

The Sacrifices of the Old Covenant, 6-10. The daily repeated activities relating to sacrifice and worship which were performed by the priests in the holy place, 6, and the sacrifices on the Day of Atonement which were offered by the high priest once a year in the holy of holies, 7, intimated that the way of access directly to God for every believer was not yet open, 8. These were "carnal ordinances," 10, earthly and external observances related to an imperfect tabernacle. Such ordinances served as symbols, or typical illustrations, for that pre-cross era of the future glorious ministry of Christ and the spiritual realities which He would effect, 9. They were external and temporal symbols imposed by the old covenant (Mosaic law) until the time of rectification (of setting things right) by the new covenant in the death of Christ, 10.

The Covenants of Scripture

Covenant	*Significance*
Eternal Covenant (Heb 13:20)	The redemptive covenant before time began, between the Father and the Son. By this covenant we have eternal redemption, an eternal peace from the "God of peace," through the death and resurrection of the Son.
Edenic Covenant (Gen 1:26-28)	The creative covenant between the Triune God, as the first party (Gen 1:26), and newly created man, as the second party, governing man's creation and life in Edenic innocence. It regulated man's dominion and subjugation of the earth, and presented a simple test of obedience. The penalty was death.
Adamic Covenant (Gen 3:14-19)	The covenant conditioning fallen man's life on the earth. Satan's tool (the serpent) was cursed (Gen 3:14); the first promise of the Redeemer was given (3:15); women's status was altered (3:16); the earth was cursed (3:17-19); physical and spiritual death resulted (3:19).
Noahic Covenant (Gen 8:20—9:6)	The covenant of human government. Man is to govern his fellowmen for God, indicated by the institution of capital punishment as the supreme judicial power of the state (Gen 9:5-6). Other features included the promise of redemption through the line of Shem (9:26).
Abrahamic Covenant (Gen 12:1-3; confirmed, 13:14-17; 15:1-7; 17:1-8)	The covenant of promise. Abraham's posterity was to be made a great nation. In him (through Christ) all the families of the earth were to be blessed (Gal 3:16; Jn 8:56-58).

765

Covenant	Significance
Mosaic Covenant (Ex 20:1—31:18)	The legal covenant, given solely to Israel. It consisted of the commandments (Ex 20:1-26); the judgments (social) (Ex 21:1—24:11) and the ordinances (religious) (Ex 24:12—31:18); also called the law. It was a conditional covenant of works, a ministry of "condemnation" and "death" (2 Cor 3:7-9), designed to lead the transgressor (convicted thereby as a sinner) to Christ.
Palestinian Covenant (Deut 30:1-10)	The covenant regulating Israel's tenure of the land of Canaan. Its prophetic features include dispersion for disobedience (Deut 30:1), future repentance while in dispersion (30:2), the Lord's return (30:3), the restoration (30:4-5), national conversion (3:6), judgment of Israel's foes (30:7), national prosperity (30:9). Its blessings are conditioned upon obedience (30:8, 10), but fulfillment is guaranteed by the new covenant.
Davidic Covenant (2 Sam 7:4-17; 1 Chr 17:4-15)	The kingdom covenant regulating the temporal and eternal rule of David's posterity. It secures in perpetuity a Davidic "house" or line, a throne, and a kingdom. It was confirmed by divine oath in Ps 89:30-37 and renewed to Mary in Lk 1:31-33. It is fulfilled in Christ as the world's Saviour and Israel's coming King (Acts 1:6; Rev 19:16; 20:4-6).
New Covenant (Jer 31:31-33; Mt 26:28; Mk 14:24; Lk 22:20; Heb 8:8-12)	The covenant of unconditional blessing based upon the finished redemption of Christ. It secures blessing for the church, flowing from the Abrahamic covenant (Gal 3:13-20), and secures all covenant blessings to converted Israel, including those of the Abrahamic, Palestinian, and Davidic covenants. This covenant is unconditional, final and irreversible.

9:11-14. REALITY UNDER THE NEW COVENANT

The Essence of the Reality, 11-12. Christ's appearance as High Priest fulfilled the types of both the Melchizedek and the Aaronic priesthoods in bringing "the good things to come," 11*a*. He fulfilled the type of the high priest's entering the holiest once a year (Lev 16) by having entered *once for all* into the *real* holy place in the tabernacle in heaven, 11*b*. There He presented His own infinitely efficacious blood on the heavenly mercy seat, showing His *one* sacrifice to be incomparably superior to the *many continued* sacrifices of the blood of goats and calves, 12*a* (cf. 9:13-14). This once-for-all sacrifice secured eternal redemption, not merely a temporary covering and passing over of sin for the time being, as under the old covenant, 12*b*. "Eternal redemption" has reference to the safety and security which the believer possesses in Christ, and his future eternal glorification.

The Meaning of the Reality, 13-14. This eternal redemption, purchased by Christ's own blood, purifies not only externally and ceremonially (as did the Levitical sacrifices on the Day of Atonement), but inwardly and vitally for service rendered to a "living God." "If," or "since" (the Gr. indicative indicating the reality of the case), the sprinkling of ceremonially defiled persons with animal blood and the ashes of a red heifer (Num 19:16-18) could purify outwardly to any degree, to how much greater degree shall the blood of Christ effect inward cleansing and obtain an eternally complete salvation, 14?

9:15-22. THE NEW COVENANT SEALED BY CHRIST'S BLOOD

Christ's Death a Necessity, 15-17. The sacrificial offering of Christ in death constituted the beginning of a new covenant based thereon. Without His death there could have been no covenant, 16, nor could He have become the Mediator, acting between a holy God and guilty sinners to the end that they might be reconciled, 15*a* (cf. 8:6; 1 Tim 2:5). As a result of His redemptive death, those whose sins were simply covered under the old covenant (Rom 3:24-25) have now received "the promise of eternal inheritance," 15*b*.

In the OT the only way a covenant could be sealed was by the blood of sacrifice, 16. Similarly, Christ's death sealed the new covenant and set it in force (made it valid), 17. Even among men, a covenant (*diathēkē,* testament or will) is invalid until the testator dies, and then it becomes operative.

The Necessity of Christ's Death Foreshadowed by the Law, 18-22. The first or legal covenant was inaugurated by blood, 18, beginning only when Moses had sprinkled with blood both the book of the law and the people, 19, and had pronounced the words, "This is the blood of the testament which God hath enjoined [commanded] you," 20 (Ex 24:1-8). The tabernacle and all the vessels of worship were similarly blood-sprinkled, 21 (Ex 29:12, 36), as were practically all things under the old dispensation, 22a, thus typically showing the necessity of Christ's death. (For exceptions see Ex 19:10; Lev 15:5, etc.) This emphasized the great truth, "Without shedding of blood [death] there is no remission [forgiveness] of sins" (no "dismission," *aphesis*, "no sending off or away," i.e., no separation of sin from the sinner, cf. Mt 26:28), 22b.

9:23-24. THE BETTER SANCTUARY OF
THE NEW COVENANT

The Mosaic Tabernacle Purged with Animal Sacrifices, 23a. This tent and its personnel and ritual were only "patterns" (in the sense of copies and suggestive tokens) of the heavenly things in the heavenly tabernacle. Animal sacrifices might typically purify this inferior earthly sanctuary, but not its antitypical and superior sanctuary in heaven, 23.

The Heavenly Tabernacle Purged with Better Sacrifices, 23b-24. "The better sacrifices" (plural) comprehend and sum up the *one* final sacrifice of Christ. This *one* sacrifice is more than equivalent to all the numerous Levitical sacrifices. Our Lord, as both Priest and Sacrifice, has entered into "heaven itself," to present Himself in the immediate presence of God on our behalf, 24, thus securing eternal redemption.

9:25—10:4. THE BETTER SACRIFICE OF
THE NEW COVENANT

Christ's Sacrifice Is Final, 9:25-28. This finality is indicated by Christ's complete and unrepeatable offer of Himself in contrast to the earthly high priest who entered the holiest every year "with blood not his own," 25 (Lev 16). If Christ's sacrifice had not been final He would then often have had to suffer, since the continued sins of men would entail repeated suffering on earth "from the foundation of the world," 26a. But His sacrifice once for all at the "consummation of the ages" (ASV marg.) has put away and abolished sin—thus there is no need for further sacrifice, 26b.

The sacrifice of Christ is final because: (1) it involved the blood of His own glorious person, 26c, satisfying all the claims of an infinitely holy God against sinful men; (2) it perfectly meets the needs of the sinner who faces death and judgment, 27; (3) it perfectly meets the needs of the believer. Christ was once offered to bear the believer's sins, 28a (1 Pet 2:24; 1 Cor 15:3), and the believer will never have to face the sin question again (Jn 5:24). Christ's coming for His own will not involve the sin question, but rather "salvation," consummating in glorification (1 Cor 15:51-57; 1 Jn 3:1-2), 28b.

Levitical Sacrifices Imperfect and Repeatable, 10:1-4. These sacrifices were directly related to the law of Moses and were only "a shadow" (*skia,* "a dim shadowing forth") of "the good things to come" (cf. 9:11), i.e., the blessings of Christ's salvation, 1a. They lacked the perfection and finality of Christ's once-for-all sacrifice, 10b, in that these typical sacrifices continued to be offered and never really cleansed away the consciousness of guilt and sin in the worshipers, 2. On the contrary, they only brought a fresh remembrance of sins to be atoned for, 3, because of the utter inability of animal blood to remove sin and guilt, 4.

10:5-10. THE NEW COVENANT BASED ON CHRIST'S PERFECT SACRIFICE

Christ's Perfect Sacrifice Foretold, 5-7. His sacrifice was prophesied in Ps 40:6-8 by David, who expressed the truth that animal sacrifices were powerless to remove sins (see v. 4). This prophecy envisioned the coming of One who would enter the world (by incarnation) to effect the removal of man's sins. 5a, and enunciated God's dissatisfaction with the sacrifices and offerings of the Levitical system, 5b-6. It predicted the incarnation, "but a *body* hast thou prepared for me," 5c (RSV). The Heb. has, "my ears hast thou opened" ("pierced," Ps 40:6), alluding also to the incarnation and willing servitude of Christ (Ex 21:5-6).

Verse 7 predictively sums up our Lord's redemption work: God the Son entering the world to become incarnate, "Lo, I have come" (cf. Lk 1:35); and His utter obedience to the Father's will, even to death, "to do thy will, O God" (cf. Lk 22:42; Phil 2:8).

Christ's Perfect Sacrifice Annuls the Old Order, 8-10. The Father's dissatisfaction with the Levitical ritual, 8, is contrasted with His will for the Son, 9. This will involved the Son's sacrifice of Himself in order to establish the new covenant of perfect redemption. It also has resulted in the formation of a new company of redeemed, those who are positionally sanctified (set apart unto God as holy) through the once-for-all offering of Christ's own body, 10.

10:11-14. THE NEW COVENANT SUPERIOR BECAUSE OF CHRIST'S PRESENT SESSION

The Inferior Position and Ministry of the Levitical Priests, 11. The incompleteness and inefficacy of the Levitical priest's ministry were seen in the repetition of his ritual and in his position as standing before the altar. The repeated offering of the same sacrifices could never *take away* sins (could never remove sins in the sense of stripping them away expiatorily, as one would strip off an old soiled garment closely wrapped around a body).

The Superior Position and Work of Christ, 12-14. In striking contrast to the inadequacy of the Levitical priesthood, Christ offered *"one* sacrifice," a single efficacious sacrifice for sins which availed for all time, 12a. The completeness of His work was signified by His having "sat down," thus assuming an exalted position of authority and priestly service "at the right hand of God," 12b. He now awaits the wider results of His redemptive work, when His enemies will be vanquished and His rule established throughout the whole earth, 13. The superior efficacy of Christ's sacrifice is noted in that "by one offering He has perfected *for all time* those who are sanctified" (Gr.), 14. See note on verse 10.

10:15-18. THE NEW COVENANT IS SUPERIOR BECAUSE OF THE FINALITY OF CHRIST'S SACRIFICE

The Witness of the Spirit, 15-17. The Holy Spirit's testimony to the finality of Christ's sacrifice is quoted from Jer 31:33-34. This prophecy of the new covenant envisions Israel's conversion at the second advent, but inasmuch as the new covenant is based on the finality of Christ's sacrifice its blessings are enjoyed by both the church (Mt 26:28; 1 Cor 11:25) and Israel. Christ in His sacrificial atoning death accomplished remission of sins and transformation of life for all who place their faith in Him, 16-17. It was to this that the Spirit gave witness.

A Summary Statement, 18. Christ's sacrifice is final and complete because it secured "remission" (*aphesis,* complete "dismission") of sin from the sinner in the sense of unqualified forgiveness. The guilt and penalty of these ("sins and iniquities," 17) were cancelled. Where these sins are completely remitted a need no longer exists for further "offering for sin."

10:19-25. APPEAL TO A LIFE OF FAITH

The Basis for the Appeal, 19-22. Underlying this exhortation, 22, is the description of all that Christ is and has done as found in the preceding argument of this epistle. Boldness (assurance, perfect confidence) is enjoined for these fellow Hebrew believers as they enter the very presence of God because: (1) the blood of Christ—eternally acceptable to God and totally sufficient—has made such access possible, 19; (2) Jesus has inaugurated ("consecrated") a new and living way through the veil into the immediate presence of God, 20; and (3) we have a High Priest, superior to all other priests, who serves "over the house of God," the real sanctuary in heaven, 21 (see notes on 9:11-12, 23-24). Such privileges enable the believer to "draw near [come to God intimately and frequently] with a sincere heart in full assurance of faith," freed from the doubts of an evil conscience and cleansed from defilement, 22.

The Further Appeal, 23-25. In appealing to a life of faith, the writer not only emphasizes the necessity of possessing assurance to enter God's immediate presence (19-22), but urges: (1) steadfastness in the hope Christ has given us, 23, i.e., complete reliance on God's faithfulness in giving the future inheritance He has promised (1 Pet 1:3-5); (2) consideration for one another, 24, which will result in stimulating each other to love and good works; and (3) constancy in public worship, 25, which will encourage ("exhort") one another in view of the Lord's coming ("the day") and His judgment of the believers' works.

10:26-31. WARNING AGAINST LAPSE INTO JUDAISM

The Problem of Presumptuous Sinning, 26-29. This sin, which faced the Hebrew believers to whom the epistle is addressed, consisted of a willful and deliberate course of action against the full knowledge (*epignōsis*) which they had received of the truth—Jesus Christ and His salvation as the way to God (cf. 2:1-4; 3:7-19; 5:11—6:20; 12:3-17, 25-29), 26a. It evidently involved a return to worn-out forms and ceremonies to atone for sins, things that had been fulfilled in Christ's sacrifice. Rejecting His *one* and *only* sacrifice, "there remains no more sacrifice for sins"—no other sacrifice is left on which to depend, 26b. Such sin incurs the judgment of God, a fearful and terrifying thing which all adversaries (those opposed to God's method of salvation by grace through faith in the atoning death of Christ) may expect, 27. The charge placed against these rejectors included: (1) trampling under foot (spurning and treating shamefully) the Son of God, who purchased so great salvation; (2) rejecting as common and unholy the covenant blood of Christ by which the believer is consecrated; and (3) insulting the Holy Spirit who imparts the gracious blessing of God, 29.

The Punishment, 30-31. If one who despised the old covenant faced severe judgment, 28 (Deut 17:2-6), how much worse will be the punishment of those who despise the new covenant, 29? Deut 32:35-36 is quoted to give additional evidence of the judgment which rejectors may expect, 30. This punishment is in reference to "his people," and may be executed by present disciplinary action or at the future judgment seat of Christ (see notes on 1 Cor 3:11-17). In either case it involves falling into the hands "of the living God," the Judge of all the earth, 31, a terrifying and fearful thing.

10:32-39. A CALL TO PATIENT FAITH

The Call to Remember Their Early Faith, 32-34. These vacillating Hebrew believers, endangered by a return to Mosaic ordinances and ritual, are called upon to remember the days past, in which, after they had been spiritually enlightened concerning Christ's eternal redemption, they *proved* their faith by enduring a "great conflict of sufferings" (Gr.), 32. This involved being publicly exposed to abusive insult from unbelieving Jews, or sincerely sharing in sympathy with those fellow believers who were so treated, 33. They had further *demonstrated* the genuineness of their faith in Christ by expressing sympathetic compassion for those imprisoned (including the writer of the epistle) and by accepting with joy the seizure of their property—looking with the eye of faith at a better and abiding possession, 34.

The Call to Continue in Patient Faith, 35-39. These believers, in the light of their expression of past faith, are urged not to "fling away" their intrepid confidence in Christ, which carries with it a great reward, 35. Their present need is "patience" (*hupomonē*, that quality of remaining under trial and difficulty with persevering endurance), so that having accomplished the will of God they may "receive the promise," the promised reward related to the imminent return of the Lord, 36-37.

Faith is to be the theme of the believer's life, not legalistic forms and works (Hab 2:3-4; Rom 1:17; Gal 3:11). But if any, to escape persecution or ostracism, draw back from professed faith to legalism, God shall voice His displeasure, and judgment may be expected (cf. 26-31), 38. The writer realizes his readers have genuine faith that will not permit them to draw back to eternal ruin ("perdition"); rather, they are "of those who believe to the preserving of the soul," 39.

11:1-3. THE SUPERIORITY OF PERSEVERING FAITH

The Definition of Persevering Faith, 1. The faith here defined is not faith in its widest sense or entire nature but specifically persevering faith. It is urged upon tried and tested believers so that they might go on to perfection (6:1-20), avoiding defection (10:19-39). Such faith is said to be: (1) the "substance" (*hupostasis*, that which stands under as a foundation or basis, giving assurance of realization) of things hoped for—hope being faith in action with regard to the future reality of present promises; and (2) a settled conviction or persuasion of things not yet actual but certain to become so (cf. 2 Cor 5:7).

The Accomplishments of Persevering Faith, 2-3. Faith enables men *to receive divine approval,* 2, and *to understand spiritual truth,* 3. We believe, therefore we know, through a Spirit-enlightened intellect. Such knowledge brings understanding concerning God's creative acts and His ordering of the ages for His own purpose and glory.

11:4-40. FAITH THAT ENVISIONED THE PROMISE— CHRIST
ABEL AND ENOCH

Abel's Sacrifice of Faith, 4. His sacrifice was "more excellent" in the sense of being greater and of higher value. It involved the shedding of atoning blood, bespeaking Abel's faith and obedience to God's revelation that fallen man was a sinner and needed the interposition of a substitute (Gen 3:15, 21; Heb 9:22). Cain's bloodless offering was a presentation of his own works and secured no acceptance with God (see notes on Gen 4). In contrast, Abel's sacrifice secured God's declaration that he was righteous, and testified to all men for all time that salvation is by faith in the atoning death of an acceptable substitute (Jn 1:29).

Enoch's Walk of Faith, 5-6 (cf. Gen 5:23-24). His walk in unbroken fellowship with God resulted in his being translated to heaven without so much as a glimpse of death. The character of his life had been such that God could testify that Enoch had pleased Him, 5. Thus, his life was an illustration of the truth that the way of faith is the *only way* of pleasing and approaching God, 6.

NOAH

Noah's Action of Faith, 7. Noah built the ark because of his faith in God's predictive word concerning events of which there was as yet no visible sign. As a result of this act: (1) his household was saved from judgment; (2) his 120-year witness condemned the world because of its unbelief; and (3) he became an heir (possessor) of righteousness because of his faith (later exhibited in his offering, Gen 6:13-22).

ABRAHAM AND SARAH

Abraham's Obedience of Faith, 8-10. In leaving his home in Ur, and later Haran (Gen 11:31—12:4), for Canaan, Abraham displayed an obedient faith which was *unwavering* in that the land he set out for was still not promised to him, and when it was, the Canaanites still possessed it. His was also an *unquestioning* faith, for he did not know where he was going, 8b, and a *pilgrim* faith in that he lived in a foreign land without a permanent dwelling, 9. *Expectantly* in faith "he waited for" the city which has foundations, whose Architect and Maker is God, 10 (Rev 21:19-20; cf. Jn 8:56; Heb 11:16; 12:22; 13:14).

Sarah's Strength of Faith, 11-12. By faith Sarah received physical strength to conceive Isaac, the child of promise in the line of Christ, even when she was long past the age of childbearing, because she considered God, who had given her the promise, faithful and trust-worthy in keeping His word, 11 (cf. Gen 17:19; 18:11-14; 21:1-2). Because of their trust in God, Abraham and Sarah, even though physically they were "as good as dead," became the parents of multitudes as numerous as the stars of the sky and the sand of the seashore, 12. All Jews trace their physical lineage to them, and all believers trace their spiritual lineage to this blessed couple.

THE REALITY AND HOPE OF FAITH

Its Reality, 13-15. The genuineness of the faith of OT saints is shown: (1) by *their death,* "all died in [according to] faith," for they were controlled and energized to the end by their confidence in God, 13a; (2) by *their unwavering trust,* despite the fact that they did not receive the visible fulfillment of the promises, 13b (Gen 3:15; 12:1-4, 7); (3) by *their separated and pilgrim walk,* as a result of their having been given the promises, 13c (cf. Gen 23:4; Ps 39:12); and (4) *by their words and actions,* proving they sought a heavenly fatherland, 14-15, for they had ample opportunity to return to Meso-potamia and Ur had they desired.

Its Hope, 16. The genuine faith of the OT saints expressed itself in their hope for a better fatherland (heaven). God responded by being identified as the God of Abraham, Isaac, and Jacob (Ex 3:6, 15; 4:5). In fulfilling their hope "he has prepared for them *a city*," the New Jerusalem (Isa 2:2; Ezk 40—48; Heb 12:22; 13:14; Rev 21—22).

ABRAHAM AND ISAAC

Abraham's Severely Tested Faith, 17-18. The supreme test of Abraham's faith was his presenting of Isaac as a sacrificial offering (Gen 22:1-10). In intention he actually did sacrifice his "only begotten" son, typifying the Father "who spared not his own Son, but delivered him up for us all" (Rom 8:32). The test was intensified because God had said to Abraham face to face, "*In Isaac* shall thy posterity be called" (Gen 21:12).

Abraham's Uniquely Triumphant Faith, 19. His faith met the supreme test because: (1) it conquered the fear of death, "he *considered* that God is able to raise men even from the dead" (Gr.); and (2) it retrieved Isaac from death by what was a parable of the resurrection, in the sense that Isaac was figuratively dead by being potentially sacrificed.

ISAAC, JACOB AND JOSEPH

Isaac and Jacob's Blessing of Faith, 20-21. Isaac by faith, when blessing Jacob and Esau, assigned things still in the future as if they were present (Gen 27:27-29, 39-40). Jacob had the precedence because his blessings were spiritual. "By faith Jacob, when he was dying, blessed each of the sons of Joseph" (Gen 47:29; 48:8-20). Unable to distinguish them by sight, he did distinguish them by faith and intentionally placed his right hand on Ephraim, the younger, faith showing him that Ephraim would be greater than Manasseh. The aged dying Jacob did this, not "leaning upon" but "worshipfully bowing in prayer over the top of his staff," the emblem of his God-sustained pilgrimage to the heavenly city.

Joseph's Instructions of Faith, 22. "By faith Joseph, when he was dying, made mention of [by reminiscing upon the promise of God] the exodus of the children of Israel, and gave orders concerning his bones" (Gr., Gen 50:24-25). His exalted position did not blind him to the fact that Egypt was not his home (cf. Josh 24:32). He believed God would keep His word in bringing about the exodus and Israel's restoration to Canaan (Gen 15:13-21), and ultimately would resurrect his physical body for the heavenly Canaan.

MOSES IN EGYPT

His Parents' Act of Faith, 23 (cf. Ex 1:22—2:2). Moses' beauty as a babe was likely the divinely appointed sign by which God aroused the faith of Moses' parents to the conviction that this boy was destined to be the deliverer—because "they saw [by faith] that he was a proper [beautiful] child" (Acts 7:20, "fair to God").

Moses' Choice of Faith, 24-26. After he was grown, Moses willingly refused to be identified as "the son of Pharaoh's daughter" together with the eminence and royal position which would have been his (Ex 2:10), 24. He preferred to share the hardships and endure ill treatment with God's people rather than enjoy the passing pleasures of a sinful life, 25. This choice was made because faith gave him a glimpse of the Messiah to come, and Moses considered suffering for Him to be "greater wealth than all the treasure of Egypt," 26.

MOSES' QUITTING EGYPT

Moses' Flight of Faith, 27 (cf. Ex 2:14-15). Had Moses stayed in Egypt and renounced his allegiance to his fellow Israelites, his high status would have doubtless secured his pardon. But his flight represented the irrevocable choice of faith that forever severed him from Egypt and joined him to God's people as their deliverer. He fled without fear of Pharaoh, enduring because he saw "him who is invisible." He acted as though he were dealing not with men but with God alone, who was ever in faith's eye.

Moses' Passover of Faith, 28-29. Simple faith in God prompted Moses to institute the Passover and the sprinkling of the blood on the doorposts, so that the destroyer of the firstborn might not touch the Israelites (Ex 12:21-30). By the same trust in God Israel crossed the Red Sea with walls of water on each side. What was faith to God's people was presumption to their enemies, who were engulfed in the sands as well as the waves of the sea (Ex 14:21-31; 15:12).

JOSHUA AND RAHAB

Joshua's March of Faith, 30. By faith the walls of Jericho fell down after the Israelites had marched around them seven days, in contrast to sieges which often lasted for years. Faith, not the marching or the trumpet blaring, released the power of God to level the walls (Josh 6:12-21).

Rahab's Hospitality of Faith, 31. Rahab, the Jericho prostitute, did not perish with her unbelieving fellow inhabitants of the city, because she received the Israelite spies into her home and thus exhibited personal faith in her confession (Josh 2:9-11).

FROM GIDEON TO SAMUEL AND THE PROPHETS

Other Heroes of Faith, 32. In summary, the writer mentions Gideon (Jud 6—8), Barak (Jud 4—5), Samson (Jud 13—16), Jephthah (Jud 11—12), David (1 Sam 16—30; 2 Sam 1—24, 1 Kgs 1—2), and Samuel (1 Sam 1—16).

Their Exploits, 33-34. These who were robust in faith: (1) conquered kingdoms—e.g., David (2 Sam 8); (2) performed acts of righteousness—e.g., Samuel (1 Sam 12:3-23; 15:33) and David (2 Sam 8:15); (3) obtained promises—e.g., the prophets (Josh 21:45; 1 Kgs 8:56); (4) shut the mouths of lions—e.g., Samson (Jud 14:5-6), David (1 Sam 17:34-37), Benaiah (2 Sam 23:20), Daniel (Dan 6:22); (5) quenched the power of fire—e.g., the three Israelites (Dan 3:25); (6) escaped the edge of the sword—e.g., Jephthah (Jud 12:3), David (1 Sam 18:11; 19:10), Elijah (1 Kgs 19:1-2), Elisha (2 Kgs 6:14-17); (7) from weakness were made strong—e.g., Samson (Jud 16:28-30); (8) mighty in war . . . routing armies—e.g., Barak (Jud 4:14-15), Maccabees (1 Macc 1—5); (9) women received back their dead by resurrection—e.g., the widow of Zarephath (1 Kgs 17:17-24), the Shunammite (2 Kgs 4:17-35).

Their Sufferings, 35-37. Many of the faithful suffered by: (1) being tortured—e.g., Eleazar (2 Macc 6:18; 19:20, 30), who was "broken on the wheel" by being stretched out and beaten to death—and not accepting release in order that they might attain a better resurrection, i.e., the first resurrection to life, their martyrdom being the supreme proof of their saving faith; (2) being scourged and imprisoned—e.g., Hanani (2 Chr 16:10); (3) being stoned—e.g., Zechariah, son of Jehoiada (2 Chr 24:20-22; Mt 23:35); (4) being sawed in two—e.g., Isaiah by Manasseh, according to tradition; (5) various other inflictions such as being tempted to sin, put to death by the edge of the sword, ill-treated, destitute.

Their Evaluation, 38. The world was not worthy of them. In treating them as it did the world condemned itself.

THE FAITH OF OLD TESTAMENT SAINTS AND OURS, 39-40

Old Testament saints "obtained a good report," i.e., they won divine approval as a result of their faith; but they did not receive the realization of Christ's complete salvation nor the fulfillment of the new covenant with its personal and national blessings. This perfection will come for both OT and NT saints when Christ returns to complete salvation and reign as King of kings and Lord of lords.

12:1-4. THE RACE AND GOAL OF FAITH

The Race of Faith, 1. The figure of an amphitheater filled with OT saints (11:4-38) witnessing NT believers run the race of faith constitutes an incentive for the Christian as he runs. "Wherefore," since we have surrounding us such a great company of OT witnesses who themselves performed so well in their lives, "let us keep on running with patience [endurance] the race [*agōna,* a contest demanding full expenditure of energy] set before us." To run with full energy demands that we first lay aside every encumbrance, as a runner would strip off clothing, "and the sin which so easily entangles us."

The Goal of Faith, 2-4. The goal is "Jesus," the all-sufficient Saviour; therefore sight is to be *fastened on Him* during the entire course of the race. The believer is to run "looking to [*aphorontes,* off-looking, or looking away to] Jesus," away from every other would-be saviour, because: (1) He is the only Saviour, 2*a*; (2) He is the originator and the perfecter of our faith, 2*b*; (3) He is the supreme example of steadfast faith—"who for the joy that was set before Him endured the cross, lightly esteeming the shame," 2*c*; (4) He won the race and as a result He is "set down at the right hand of the throne of God," 2*d*; (5) His example is the antidote against discouragement, 3; (6) His struggles were infinitely greater than ours, yet He was victorious, 4.

12:5-11. CHASTENING AS AN INCENTIVE TO FAITH

The Discipline of Faith, 5-9. Divine chastening is an encouragement to press on toward the goal because it is a token of the Lord's love for His own, 5-6 (cf. Prov 3:11-12). Therefore, it is not to be regarded lightly, or wrongly interpreted as being ground for discouragement. The Lord's chastening is a necessary discipline in the Father's treatment of His sons, 7, the absence of which would prove that we were illegitimate children and not genuine sons, 8. If a human father's discipline of his son is beneficial, of how much greater value is it for us to be submissive to our heavenly Father's discipline and thus receive fullness of life, 9?

The Results of Disciplined Faith, 10-11. The first result is our permanent eternal good, not merely temporal welfare, which may have seemed fit to our human father, 10*a*. The second result is the sharing of God's holiness, 10*b*. Chastisement is inflicted so that we may share God's holiness experientially (2 Pet 1:4), here and now, in preparation for future glorification in His presence, 10*b*, 14 (cf. 1 Jn 3:2-3). To those so trained, discipline seems painful rather than pleasant; later it yields the peaceful fruit of righteousness, 11.

12:12-17. A WARNING FROM ESAU

The Exhortation, 12-14. In light of the great incentives to run the Christian race with patience, 1-11, the Hebrew believers are urged to lift up their drooping hands and strengthen their weak knees, 12 (cf. Isa 35:3). They are to make straight paths for their feet so that "what is lame" (the weak believer tempted to forget grace) may not be "put out of joint" by yielding to such temptation, but rather be "healed" by being encouraged to persist in the gracious race of faith, 13 (Gal 6:1; Rom 14:19).

The call is to "follow peace" in the sense of constantly and diligently pursuing it, 14a (cf. Ps 34:14), so as to live harmoniously with everybody. Urged also is the diligent pursuit of holiness, 14b. Believers are to be daily set apart as holy unto God (present sanctification) by earnestly pursuing a course of separation from sin, claiming by faith their position in Christ and converting it into the experience of Christ (Rom 6:11-12) through yieldedness to the Holy Spirit. Only as the Holy Spirit sanctifies us are we fit to see the Lord, in the final sense, and be ever with Him. A right relation with God must be coupled with a proper relation with fellow believers.

The Warning, 15-17. Verse 15 is a warning against defaulting from the grace of God, resulting in a bitter spirit which poisons many in the Christian community. An illustration is given in the example of Esau, 16-17, whose "profanity" (godless or secular interest) through the forfeiture of his birthright led to a hopeless condition (Gen 27:30-40). He exchanged spiritual well-being for momentary fleshly gratification. Default from God's grace back to Mosaic ceremonialism leads to similar despair. Believers may, through carnal sin and unbelief, miss the privileges of their access into the holiest through their great High Priest and the promises of blessing in Him.

12:18-24. THE RESULT OF FAITH THAT HAS OBTAINED THE PROMISE

It Delivers from a Law of Terror, 18-21. The realities of the old covenant are contrasted with the glories of the new, pointing out once more the advantages of "going on in Christ" over a return to Judaism because of persecution. God's presence, under the law, brought fear and trembling, even to Moses, 21.

It Brings the Blessings and Relationships of Grace, 22-24. Grace, under the new covenant, brings Hebrew believers to *Mount Zion,* the city of the living God, the New Jerusalem, in contrast to the earthly Jerusalem and the fearful Mount Sinai, 22a (cf. 11:10; Rev 21:2ff.). They are also brought into the company of *"myriads of angels* in festal assembly, and to the *church of the firstborn* who are enrolled in heaven" (Gr.), 22b-23a. The firstborn is a reference to Christ (Rom 8:29; Col 1:15-16; Heb 1:6), and the Church is His Body, His possession, the members of which are heavenly citizens (Eph 2:19; Phil 3:20). These relationships also include one of access to *God, the Judge* of all men, 23b; association with *just men made perfect,* 23c, a reference to OT saints now made perfect by the cross of Christ (11:39-40); and identity with *Jesus, the Mediator* of the new covenant, 24a, and His *sprinkled blood* which has obtained eternal forgiveness from sin, 24b.

12:25-29. WARNING AGAINST REFUSING TO HEED GOD'S VOICE

The Danger of the Sin, 25-27. Warning is given lest some refuse to hear the voice of Christ through the gospel of grace and therefore shun Him, 25a. For such there is no escape, 25b-27, judgment will come. If the Israelites who refused to listen and obey Moses' warning on earth suffered the judgment of God, how much greater peril do those face who refuse to heed the voice of God's own Son from heaven, 25b? Then reference is made to the day of judgment when the impermanent will be shaken and only the permanent and eternal will remain, 26-27, including the kingdom which will be the inheritance of believers, 28a.

The Preventive Against the Sin, 28-29. Realizing that they are heirs of the unshakable kingdom, believers are to show their gratitude for the grace they have received through the gospel by serving God with reverence and awe. "God is a consuming fire," 29, but Christ is our haven from judgment. Recognition of the blessings one has in Christ will prevent the sin of refusal (25).

13:1-6. THE EXPRESSION OF FAITH IN DAILY LIVING

In Social Relationships, 1-4. Faith must have its outward manifestations in the believer's relations with others. *Love for the brethren* is to be a normal course of action, 1, which may express itself in such ways as the offer of hospitality to strangers—who might indeed be angels (Gen 18:1-8; 19:1-3), 2, and in caring for those in prison and others who have been persecuted or ill-treated, 3. The thought is that of genuine sympathy, true identity, with these brethren, suffering as if you were in their place. The *marriage bond,* and the *sexual life* within that bond, are to be held in high honor, 4. Those who break such, face the judgment of God.

In Financial Matters, 5-6. The life of faith makes no provision for covetousness. Freedom from the love of money ("not money-loving") and contentment with present possessions are to characterize the believer's way of life. He is to take comfort in the Lord's presence and provision, both of which are constant.

13:7-9. FAITH'S EXPRESSION IN A STABLE TESTIMONY

The Example, 7-8. Both the spiritual leaders who had spoken the Word of God to these Hebrew believers and the Lord Jesus Himself constitute examples of stability. The outcome of the lives of such leaders as Stephen, James the brother of the Lord, James the brother of John (Acts 12:2), and others who faced suffering and martyrdom, testifies to their faithfulness to the end. Their faith is to be imitated, 7. The immutable Christ, always the Changeless One, serves as the perfect example for all believers.

The Exhortation, 9. "Do not be carried past the truth into error and deception by varied and alien teachings" is an obvious reference to Judaism. Such legal observances as the dietary laws brought no lasting spiritual benefit, while, in contrast, the heart *is* strengthened by God's grace. Legalism was barren of spiritual reality, grace is full of it. Feeding on grace will lead to stability of life and testimony.

13:10-14. FAITH EXPRESSED IN SEPARATION FROM JUDAISM

The Basis of Separation, 10-12. The life of faith was no longer related to the practices of Judaism. Instead, the distinctiveness of Christianity from Judaism, shown by a new and different altar, 10, and a greater and antitypical sacrifice (Christ's), 12, makes faith and legalism mutually exclusive under the new covenant.

The Exhortation to Separation, 13-14. "Let us go out to Him outside the camp" (Gr.) meant separation, for these Hebrew believers, from Judaism to Christ. It would entail persecution and rejection by the Jews, and this was the reproach they would have to bear, 13 (Acts 5:41; Heb 11:25-26). Separation would also require pilgrim faith, fixing their hope not on the temporal but on the eternal, "the city which is to come," 14.

13:15-17. FAITH EXPRESSED IN SPIRITUAL
WORSHIP AND OBEDIENCE

Sacrificial Worship, 15-16. The believer-priest (10:19) is to offer continually spiritual sacrifices to God. These include: the *sacrifice of praise* in joyful ascription of glory to God, called "the fruit of the lips" because the lips are a sensitive spiritual barometer of the condition of the heart, 15; and the *sacrifices of substance and of good works,* 16, sharing oneself with others in need. With such sacrifices God is pleased because they are proof of spiritual reality in worship (Phil 4:18).

Humble Obedience, 17. Believers are urged to be submissive to their leaders because "they keep watch over your souls, as those who will give an account" (Gr.). Obedience to them will result in spiritual maturity, bringing joy in the day of reckoning to those in authority.

13:18-25. CONCLUDING BENEDICTION

Personal Request, 18-19. The writer requests specific prayer from the addressees of this epistle, particularly for honorable conduct and for restoration to their immediate company.

Benediction, 20-21. This prayer of the writer contains essential elements for the spiritual well-being of the Hebrew believers to whom he has been writing: (1) "the God of peace," who has established or made peace between man and Himself through the sacrifice of Christ, and who gives peace of mind and soul to those who trust in Him; (2) the hope of resurrection founded on God's raising Christ from the dead; (3) the shepherd care of Christ for His own; (4) the assurance of covenant relationship based on Christ's shed blood; (5) a request for each believer's fitness for his task in the will of God—"make you perfect" or "make up in you what you lack"; (6) a request to allow the indwelling Christ to work in the believer that which is pleasing to God. Such matters would have particular relevance for Hebrew believers, who would contrast them with the inferior blessings of Judaism.

Concluding Salutation, 22-25.

JAMES

THE NECESSITY OF A LIVING FAITH

The Author. There is strong evidence for the traditional view that James the half brother of our Lord (Mk 6:3) was the author of this epistle. He was an unbeliever during our Lord's earthly ministry (Jn 7:3-10), and after the crucifixion he apparently remained in Jerusalem with his mother. Following the resurrection, Christ appeared to him also (1 Cor 15:7), doubtless in connection with his conversion, for he was among those in the upper room (Acts 1:14). Paul, after his stay in Arabia, visited him in Jerusalem, about A.D. 35 or 36 (Gal 1:18-19).

By A.D. 44 James was a leader in Jerusalem (Acts 12:17), heading up the first church council (Acts 15:13, 19; Gal 2:1, 9-10) and overseeing the Jewish church there (cf. Gal 2:12). Paul talked with him on his last fateful visit to Jerusalem (Acts 21:18-25). According to Josephus and Eusebius, James was martyred at Jerusalem in A.D. 62 or 63.

The Date and Character of the Epistle. Several considerations place this book as one of the earliest, if not the earliest, epistle addressed to (Jewish) Christians, dated possibly as early as A.D. 45.

The internal evidence. The church order and discipline it displays are very simple. The leaders are called "teachers" and "elders," with no mention of "bishops" or "deacons." Believers still met in the synagogue, Christian-controlled of course, with little organization since various members set themselves up as teachers.

The doctrinal character of the letter. The epistle is silent with regard to the relation of the Church to the non-Jewish world and doctrinally is elementary in character. It shows no evidence of the Church as the Body of Christ. Indeed, in the Judaic tone displayed throughout the epistle the question of the admission of Gentile believers does not even seem to have come up, indicating a date of authorship before the Jerusalem council A.D. 48 or 49.

There is no more Jewish book in the NT. If the several passages referring to Christ were eliminated, the whole epistle would be as proper in the canon of the OT as it is in the NT. In fact, the epistle could be described as an interpretation of the OT law and the Sermon on the Mount in the light of the gospel of Christ.

The external evidence for the acceptance of the book. It tallies with what appears concerning James in Josephus (*Ant.* XX, ix), in the Acts (15:13-21; 21:17-25), in Galatians (1:19; 2:9-10), and from the known circumstances of Jewish Christians in the dispersion.

In the East the epistle early appeared in lists of accepted books from Asia Minor and Egypt. Not being written by an apostle, or addressed to Gentile churches, and seeming to contradict Paul, the question of the epistle's reception at Rome and Carthage until the 4th cen. can be better understood.

> **Outline**
> Living Faith Tested by Trial, Ch. 1
> Living Faith Proved by Works, Ch. 2
> Living Faith Evidenced by Conduct, Ch. 3—4
> Living Faith Exercised by Persecution, Ch. 5

1:1-4. THE PURPOSE OF TRIALS

The Author, 1. Although the brother of our Lord (see introduction) and one of the most prominent and influential leaders in the early church of Jerusalem and Judea, James humbly styles himself simply "a servant [*doulos,* "slave"] of God and of the Lord Jesus Christ." He addresses Jewish believers as Peter (1 Pet 1:1) and the author of Hebrews do. As leader of the Jerusalem church James was overseer of Jewish believers everywhere, since these came annually to the great feasts held in the capital city (cf. Acts 2:5-11) from every part of the Roman Empire.

His Message, 2-4. James' chief ministry was to comfort Jews who had turned to Christ. These were targets of intense persecution and ostracism from their unbelieving countrymen. Addressing these sufferers for Christ as "brothers," James urges them to "count [as] *all joy*" (emphatic), unmingled by any regret, the occasion of becoming involved for Christ's sake in diversely manifold temptations. These are actually experiences that test or prove by trial, calamity or affliction the reality of their faith in Christ and are designed to strengthen it, 2. Therefore they are to rejoice because: (1) testing gives knowledge and experience, 3a ("*knowing* this"); (2) testing brings conviction that the trial (*dokimion,* "testing to prove") of faith continually produces and results in patience, the quality of "gracefully remaining under" trial until such testing has worked out its divinely designed blessing; and (3) testing leads to full maturity of Christian character, 4. "But let patience have her *perfect* [complete] work" in order that you may be perfect (mature) and whole (all parts fully developed), being deficient in nothing, 4.

1:5-12. WISDOM FOR TRIALS

The Need and Supply of Wisdom for Trials, 5-8. In no sphere is wisdom so essential and folly so disastrous as in the matter of life's reverses. If anyone is deficient in the matter of this God-given faculty let him: (1) ask or petition it *from God,* its source and bounteous Bestower, 5*a* (Prov 2:3-5), who does not "upbraid" the ignorance of the petitioner as a teacher might scoldingly censure a dull student, 5*b;* (2) ask "liberally," for God bestows bounteously, 5*c*; (3) ask believingly, for God gives in response to faith, 5*d*-6. He who doubts and hesitates because of mental reservations is as unstable as a wave of the sea, at the mercy of the wind and utterly changeable. Such a person is not to imagine "he shall receive anything from the Lord," 7, being "double-minded," hence inconstant and fickle because one mind continually counteracts the other. Thus he is characterized by an unsettled state of disorder in all his ways, i.e., all the roads of life he journeys.

The Rewards of Exercising Wisdom in Trials, 9-12. (1) Wisdom enables the brother "of low degree" (he who is in a poor or depressed condition in this life) to see and rejoice in his high and exalted position as Christ's own, having a place of eminence and dignity with his Saviour, 9. (2) Wisdom enables the rich brother, on the other hand, to see and rejoice in his lowliness apart from his salvation, the low estate of all his wealth apart from God (Isa 57:15), in the light of the transiency of mortal life and material possessions, 10-11. (3) Wisdom reveals the blessedness of the believer who endures testing, because it shows him that when he is approved as the result of his wise reaction to testing, he shall be rewarded, 12*a*. The "crown of life" is the reward of those who love the Lord and prove it by trial even to death, 12*b*. See notes on 1 Cor 3:12-17; 9:25-27; 2 Cor 5:10 for rewards.

1:13-18. GOD AND TRIALS

God Tempts No One to Sin, 13-15. Wisdom (cf. 5-12) alone can show us God's relation to temptation, which is employed in this context in two senses: (1) testing under trial, 2-12 (cf. Gen 22:1; Lk 22:28; 1 Pet 1:6); (2) solicitation to evil, 13-15 (cf. Gen 3:1-6; Mt 4:1; 1 Cor 10:13; 2 Cor 11:3-4). Wisdom shows us that *solicitation to evil is not of (from) God* as the source and initiating agent. He is "untemptable with evil," being infinitely holy, nor does He tempt (solicit anyone to evil), 13. *The cause of sin is in ourselves,* 14. Each one is tempted (solicited to evil) by his own peculiar lust, that intense impure desire proceeding from sin working through the old fallen nature and expressing itself in the flesh (the body). This occurs "when one is being drawn away [allured] and enticed" (entrapped as with a snare, or caught as a fish with bait). *The progress of sin is inexorable,* 15. "Then when the lust [personified as a harlot] has conceived, it gives birth to sin [expressed in word and deed], and sin when it reaches maturity produces death, both spiritual and eternal."

God Is Good to Men, 16-18. Under trial and temptation it is easy to be misled or deceived on this point, 1*b*. But do not be led astray about the source of temptation; it is in ourselves, not in God. His goodness is shown *by His gifts,* 17. So far from bringing temptation and sin into our lives, He is the Bestower of every benefit we enjoy. "Every beneficent gift and every perfect present [perfected boon] is from above, and comes down from the Father of lights" (Creator of the lights of heaven as well as the spiritual lights in the kingdom of grace). Because He "is light, and in him is no darkness at all" (1 Jn 1:5), He cannot be the author of sin, 13, nor be characterized by variation, not even the shadow of a turning as when the sun is eclipsed by the body of the moon and the moon by the shadow of the earth.

God's goodness is further shown *by His greatest* gift of eternal life in Christ (Jn 1:12-13; 3:16), which becomes ours as He gives us birth by the word of truth (the gospel), 18*a* (1 Pet 1:23). Thus born again, we become "a kind of firstfruits of his creatures," 18*b*, the pledge and earnest of a redeemed race (Rom 8:19, 23). The figure goes back to the OT consecration of the firstfruits of man, cattle and fruits to God (Ex 23:16-19; Deut 26:1-19).

1:19-25. GOD'S WORD AND TRIALS

God's Goodness and the Believer's Responsibility, 19-21. "Wherefore," 19*a*, because God graciously grants wisdom to face the testings of life, 5-12; does not tempt us to sin, but rather tests us to strengthen us against sin, 13-16; and has made us His children through the new birth, 17-18, let us heed the injunctions of verses 19-21. These are: (1) be quick to listen; (2) be slow to talk; (3) be slow to get angry, for man's anger does not promote the righteousness God requires; (4) get rid of everything vile and the remains of evil, as a dirty garment is discarded; (5) receive the Word of God which cleanses (Jn 15:3) and which, engrafted and living in the heart, is able to save the soul by separating from sin so that the believer may enjoy fullness of life in Christ (Jn 10:10).

God's Word and the Believer's Obedience, 22-25. So important is

God's Word in living and facing life's trials that we must be "doers," practiced exponents, of it rather than mere "hearers" who know the Word only theoretically (cf. Heb 4:2) and are deluded by the logical fallacy that mere hearing is enough. Such a deceived reader is like a man looking at his face in a mirror (the Word, which shows us ourselves), but goes away and immediately forgets what he looks like, 23-24. In contrast, whoever looks carefully into the flawless law of liberty, i.e., the law of Christ which is applied to those freed from the law of sin (cf. Gal 6:2; 1 Jn 2:7, 8, 15; 2 Jn 5), and habitually does so, will become an active doer who obeys and will find happiness (blessedness) in his obedience, 25.

1:26-27. TRUE RELIGION AND TRIALS

False Religion, 26. *Outward* religious service (religion) may be genuine and thus the expression of true faith, or it may be false and the expression of dead works. Since man is created religious, he is so even in his fallen state. Therefore the world is full of vain religion. James gives a sample. If anyone seems or appears to be religious, meticulously observant of the externalities of his faith, and does not curb or bridle his own tongue, as a bit controls a horse, this person's religion is vain (deceptively useless, fruitlessly barren and ineffective). Religion (external) must be accompanied by godliness (internal) to be genuine.

True Religion, 27. The practice of genuine religious service, in contrast to mere external ritual, 26, is exhibited in compassionate love (looking after orphans and widows in their trouble) and in separation from sin (keeping personally free from the world's smut).

2:1-9. DEAD FAITH MANIFESTED IN PARTIALITY

How the Sin Nullifies Genuine Faith, 1-5. Partiality is the sin of displaying undue respect or disrespect for certain persons. It nullifies genuine faith by violating equality within the Christian brotherhood ("my brethren," 1*a*), and by detracting from God's glory revealed in Christ, 1*b*. "Do not have [possess] faith in our Lord Jesus Christ, the Glory, with respect of persons." Christ is "the Glory" (Heb 1:3), taking the place of the Shekinah of the OT, and in His presence earthly distinctions disappear. Regarding mere external appearances, such as social status and wealth, ignores internal and more basic considerations, 2-4 (cf. Acts 10:34; Rom 2:11).

Why the Sin Is Serious, 6-7. Partiality belies God's choice, 5*a*. "Hath not God *chosen* the poor of this world to be rich in faith and to be heirs of the kingdom?" This choice is spurned by those showing

787

partiality. It also ignores inner spiritual worth, 5b, that these who are poor outwardly are rich in faith inwardly; though refused on earth they are heirs of heaven; though unloved by believers, they belong to those who love Christ. Furthermore, it dishonors the poor, 6, and honors the rich, who so frequently are oppressive and godless, 7.

Partiality Breaks the Royal Law, 8. This is the law of love, "royal" or "kingly" because it is the monarch of all laws, the quintessence of the Ten Commandments. It is the law of God, the great King, who is love and whose royal law of love reigns supreme as He Himself. The sign of partiality infringes upon this royal law, "You shall love your neighbor as [you love] yourself" (Lev 19:18, RSV).

The Royal Law Convicts of Guilt, 9. "But if you display respect of persons by paying regard to mere external appearances, you are committing sin, all the while being convicted by the law as transgressors," 9.

2:10-13. DEAD FAITH RESULTS IN JUDGMENT

The Reason for Judgment, 10-11. Under the Mosaic system infraction of any part of the law makes one a lawbreaker and a guilty sinner before God. The law is like a chain. The chain is broken when *one* link of the chain is broken, 11. A man is a guilty sinner before an infinitely holy God under the legal principle whether he breaks the royal law of love, 8-9, or some minor offense. Unless man has saving faith in Christ, he stands condemned by the law, 12. Dead faith cannot save him.

The Reason for Mercy, 12-13. The man who has faith that saves is not under the Mosaic law of condemnation, but under "the law of liberty," 12, i.e., the principle of free grace and mercy in Christ. Therefore he is to so speak and so act as those who are to be judged under the grace principle, 12. This means, although he will never be judged (condemned) as a sinner (Jn 5:24; Rom 8:1), he will be judged for his works as a believer (cf. note on 1 Cor 3:11-15; 9:27; 2 Cor 5:10). Because God has shown him mercy, he is to be merciful in his dealings with others, 13.

2:14-20. DEAD FAITH IS USELESS

The Principle Stated and Illustrated, 14-16. What is the advantage, James asks, if someone claims to possess faith but does not possess works? Can *such a faith* save him, 14? Combatted is the Jewish tendency (transferred to Christianity) to substitute a lifeless knowledge of the law for a practical holiness of life, as if justification before God could be secured in this manner (Rom 2:3, 13-23). The uselessness of dead faith is illustrated by the case of a fellow believer who is destitute, 15-16. The believer is particularly obligated to lend assistance to this brother, yet he not only does not help him but uselessly tells him to be fed and clothed.

The Inseparability of Faith and Works, 17-20. Faith is declared to be "dead being alone," literally dead in itself when separated from works, 17. James concerns himself here with proving that faith and works are inseparable. He does not question that faith is *the* way of salvation, and *the only way*. But he does question that such saving faith can ever be divorced from works, which prove its existence. To offer God a faith separated from works is little better than the faith of demons who believe and shudder, but such faith produces no good works of repentance or virtue, 19-20.

2:21-26. LIVING FAITH PROVES A MAN RIGHTEOUS

The Case of Abraham, 21-24. James adduces two examples of living (saving) faith—faith with works: Abraham, one of the greatest men of faith in the Word of God, 21-24; and Rahab, the harlot, 25. He asserts that Abraham was justified by works when he offered up Isaac, 21 (Gen 22:9-12). That James is not contradicting Paul, who declares that Abraham was justified by faith apart from works (Rom 4:2-4), appears from the following considerations.

(1) James uses the term "justified" in the sense of actually proved or demonstrated to be righteous *before men;* Paul uses the term in the sense of being judicially declared righteous *before God.* James is speaking manward, Paul Godward. (2) James offers the corrective of an abused truth, Paul sets forth the truth itself. (3) James' epistle is aimed toward Jewish believers tempted with a tendency to substitute a head knowledge of the law for a heart experience manifested in holiness of life. Paul's epistles are aimed toward Gentiles lost in sin with no legal righteousness to offer God. (4) James' justification by works does not contradict Paul's justification by faith, because Abraham enjoyed the latter blessing (Gen 15:6) long before he enjoyed justification by works as a result of his offering of Isaac (cf. Gen 22:1-12).

The Case of Rahab, 25-26. Her saving faith was proved before men when she hid the spies, sent them back another way, and hung out the red cord (Josh 2:1-21; Heb 11:31). The analogy is given in verse 26. As the body is lifeless when the spirit departs in death, so faith separated from works is dead (cf. 17-20), being a lifeless, useless thing which cannot secure our righteous standing before God or demonstrate that position before men.

3:1-5. LIVING FAITH AND THE INFLUENCE OF THE TONGUE

Our Weighty Responsibility for What We Say, 1-2. The tongue has great influence for good or bad. For this reason James warns against haste in becoming a teacher, 1a, since a teacher instructs and influences lives to a large extent by what he says. He therefore should be conscious of his tremendous responsibility, "knowing that we [teachers] shall receive the greater judgment" if we discharge our heavy obligation wrongly or influence people against God and His Word.

The sins of the tongue are commonest and hardest to control, 2. "We all stumble" (*ptaiomen*), in the sense of making a slip of the tongue, and so transgress, 2a. "If any one [believer] does not stumble in what he says, he is a *perfect* man" (*teleios*), spiritually developed, 2b and "able to bridle [control, as a horse is controlled by a bit] the whole body as well."

The Power of the Tongue Illustrated, 3-5. Three analogies are employed to illustrate that in the natural world a great effect can be produced by a relatively insignificant cause: the horse's bit, 3; the ship's rudder, 4; and the spark of igniting fire, 5.

3:6-12. LIVING FAITH AND THE TREACHERY OF THE TONGUE

Its Unruly Nature, 6-8. Not only is the tongue powerful and influential but treacherous as well. Its treachery is shown by: *its distinctive character* as a fire, a blaze uncontrolled and devastating; *its defiling character,* defiling or staining the whole body as smoke tarnishes and soils; *its corrupting quality,* being "a world of iniquity" in the sense that it sets on fire the whole machinery of existence, reacting harmfully on both the speaker and on the hearer; and *its evil source,* it is kindled by Gehenna, eternal hell (Mt 5:22). Unlike any beast, 7, the human tongue is untamable, 8a, being "an unruly evil, full of deadly [death-causing] poison," 8b.

Its Unpredictable Inconsistencies, 9-12. The tongue is used both to bless God, our Lord and Father, and to curse men, who are made in God's likeness, 9 (cf. Gen 1:26; 1 Jn 4:20). From the same mouth proceed blessing and cursing. This is a glaring inconsistency which ought not to be, 10. James shows how inconsistent this is by illustrations from nature. The sweet-water spring does not send forth the brackish water of the mineral spring, nor does the fig tree bear olives or the grapevine produce figs. Neither can salt water yield fresh. Yet the tongue is guilty of that which is absolutely contrary to nature, 12.

3:13-18. LIVING FAITH AND WISDOM

Earthly Wisdom, 13-16. The wise man (*sophia*), the technical term for teacher (cf. 1), as well as every believer, must choose which wisdom will control his life, earthly, 13-16, or heavenly, 17-18. Earthly wisdom cannot produce a truly wise teacher, endued with discreet knowledge (*epistēmōn*), who demonstrates by good behavior his works with genuine humility, 13. It rather produces bitter jealousy and selfish ambition, boasting, and disloyalty to the truth, i.e., to the Word of God as centered in Jesus Christ, 14 (Jn 14:6; Eph 4:21). Moreover, such wisdom is not "from above," not taught by the Holy Spirit (Jn 16:13). Rather, it is earthly, belonging purely to this natural terrestrial sphere. It is sensual or animal-like (*psuchichē*), the learning of the natural, unregenerate, purely *soulish* man (Jude 19), and is devilish (demoniacal), having its origin in Satanic and demonic activity, 15 (cf. 1 Tim 4:1-5; 1 Jn 4:1-4). As a result such wisdom produces confusion and every evil work, 16 (cf. Gal 5:17-21).

Heavenly Wisdom, 17-18. The teacher, and every believer, is to be controlled by heavenly wisdom (1 Cor 2:6-7), which is divine in its origin and tuition, literally, "the *from above* [emphatic] wisdom." It is *pure* in the sense of being chastely modest, blameless from the sin of intellectual pride, so characteristic of teachers; *peaceable,* tending to tranquility and concord, not divisive and heretic; *gentle,* patiently mild so as always to be modestly fair and reasonable; *easily entreated,* being pliant so as always to be bendable to further truth and increased light; *full of mercy and good fruits* of the Spirit (Gal 5:22-23); *without partiality,* or better translated, "without uncertainty," manifesting conviction on matters of truth; *without hypocrisy,* stripped of the actor's role and utterly sincere, 17. True or heavenly wisdom, which has righteousness as its fruit, sows in peace because possessors of this wisdom are those who make peace, 18.

4:1-5. LIVING FAITH AND WORLDLINESS

The Manifestation of Worldliness, 1-4. This sin rooted in unbelief is evidenced by: (1) *tensions,* which are generated by the lustful pleasures that are at war, as an army of soldiers, in the members or organs of the physical body, 1; (2) *dissatisfaction,* 2a, the result of yielding to the lusts of the flesh with their insatiable cravings even to the point of committing potential murder by hating (cf.

1 Jn 3:15); (3) *prayerlessness,* 2*b;* (4) *prayer with the wrong motive,* 3, asking only for selfish and lustful gratification; (5) *spiritual adultery,* 4*a,* disloyalty to the Lord; (6) *hostility against God*—love (*philia*) for the Satanic world system is hostility against God. He who chooses to be the world's friend constitutes himself the Lord's enemy.

The Cure for Worldliness, 5. This is adjustment to the Holy Spirit who resides in the redeemed body of every believer (1 Cor 6:19), allowing Him to control the whole life. "The Spirit who dwells at home in us has keen desire [for our spiritual welfare] to the point of jealousy." The Spirit's dynamic in the life is the sure cure of worldliness in the believer.

4:6-10. LIVING FAITH AND HUMILITY

The Source of Humility, 6. God is the source of this grace which is greater than anything the world can bestow.

The Way to Humility, 7-10, is to submit to god, 7*a*; resist the devil, 7*b*; draw near to God, 8*a*; separate from evil, 8*b*; repent in abject contrition, 9; submit or abase yourself, 10, and God will grant His grace of humility, and will then "exalt" you.

4:11-12. LIVING FAITH AND EVIL SPEAKING

The Injunction, 11a, is to stop speaking loosely against fellow believers in a spirit of criticism and calumniation (cf. ch. 3). Such a practice is not the result of living faith.

The Reason for the Injunction, 11b-12. Such evil speaking is sinful because it not only is against Christian brothers, 11*a,* but against the law. It makes the speaker a self-appointed judge of the law. God alone is the one Lawgiver and Judge whose prerogative it is to judge another. He has the authority to save and to destroy, 12. The man who judges his neighbor does not have such authority, thus he has broken the law when he usurps this authority.

4:13-17. LIVING FAITH AND SECULARISM

The Spirit of Secularism, 13. Supreme and well-nigh exclusive attention to the affairs of this life with little or no thought of God is denounced. Such secularism is the result of a lack of living faith.

The Folly of Secularism, 14-17. Secularism is foolish because: (1) it is presumptuous and based on ignorance of the future—"Whereas you do not know about tomorrow," 14*a,* (2) it is a violation of the meaning of life, which is to serve God, not self, 14b; (3) it forgets the brevity and uncertainty of life, 14c; (4) it forgets God and His will, 15; (5) it is guilty of arrogance and pride, 16; (6) it is sinful. "Whoever knows what is right to do [to put God first in the life] and fails to do it, for him it is sin," 17.

5:1-6. LIVING FAITH EXERCISED BY PERSECUTION

Oppressors' Doom Predicted, 1-3. These oppressive rich people represent the unsaved. They persecute genuine believers ("brethren," 7), victimizing them by the sin of secularism, which was denounced in 4:13-17. Both they and believers are confronted by the coming of the Lord, 7-9, which will right all wrongs and judge all unrighteousness (cf. Rev 19:11-16). Oppressors will face judgment in the last days, 3, i.e., the end of this present age (1 Jn 2:18).

Oppressors' Crimes Exposed, 4-6. Their oppression of the godly poor has reached the ears of "the Lord of hosts." This expression, common in the prophets, is a prophetic appellative of Christ in His role of coming Conqueror and Restorer of righteousness upon the earth. The same spirit that led these wicked men to crucify the Righteous One leads them to persecute the righteous ones who belong to Him, 6. Therefore, their judgment is sure (cf. v. 3).

5:7-11. LIVING FAITH EXERCISED BY PATIENCE UNDER PERSECUTION

Ground for Patience, 7-9. Note the double, and therefore emphatic, exhortation: "Be patient . . . be patient," 7-8. Why? Because such patient endurance and longsuffering will surely receive its reward at the *parousia,* the personal presence or coming of the Lord. The certainty of this reward is illustrated by the farmer who waits for the precious fruit of the earth, being patient until the ground receives the early (Oct.-Jan.) and latter (Feb.-Mar.) rains. James refers to the coming of the Lord as being "at hand," the Gr. expressing present time and a settled state, so that the event is always imminent ("near"), 8, with the Judge (the returning Christ) standing at the doors (cf. Mt 24:33). He will judge all wrongs, right all inequalities; thus believers are not to try to do what is the Lord's prerogative alone to do, 9.

Encouraging Examples of Patience, 10-11. James cites the case of the OT prophets, who were especially persecuted and therefore signally blessed, 10-11a. The case of Job is the classic illustration of

God's purpose in the trials and afflictions of His people and man's steadfast endurance, 11*b*.

5:12. LIVING FAITH EXERCISED BY AVOIDING OATH-MAKING

The Warning, 12a. "But above all" do not swear (Mt 5:34, 37), because swearing or cursing manifests impatience and pride which are foreign to the meek endurance just enjoined. Let your "yes" be "yes" and your "no" be "no," avoiding oaths. In everyday speech simple affirmation or denial is to be considered sufficient to establish one's word, and it will result in a reputation for honesty.

The Reason for the Warning, 12b.

5:13-18. LIVING FAITH EXERCISED IN PRAYER

Exhortation to the Suffering, 13. Affliction or calamity of any sort is to lead the suffering saint to prayer, while those cheerful or joyous in mind are to sing psalms (of praise), as Paul and Silas did in the Philippian jail (Acts 16:25).

Instructions for the Physically Ill, 14-15. This passage concerns what is commonly called divine healing. The sick believer was to call the elders of the assembly, never one elder. The use of oil for anointing the sick was a general Jewish practice, as shown by the Talmud, and a Jewish custom the Lord's disciples adopted (Mk 6:13). It was also a common medicinal remedy in the ancient East (Isa 1:6; Lk 10:34), and its use here may symbolize the employment of means used in healing. However, the emphasis is not on the oil, but on "the prayer of faith" which saves the sick. Such a prayer is divinely given and operates *when it is God's will to heal*. Chastening, testing and other factors condition the Lord's healing of a Christian's sicknesses (cf. 1 Cor 11:30-32; 2 Cor 12:7-9; 1 Tim 5:23; 2 Tim 4:20).

DIVINE HEALING

1. Does the Lord heal today? Of course He can, and does heal today, but *not always*.

2. God is completely free to heal or not to heal according to His will (cf. 1 Jn 5:13-15).

3. His will may include physical infirmity and sickness in His plan for the testing, strengthening or chastening of His own (1 Cor 11:30-32; 2 Cor 12:7-10). A Spirit-filled believer may be thus tested.

4. The principle of optimum benefit for the believer is the divine method.

Exhortation to Persevering Prayer, 16. "Confess your sins to one another [if you have offended someone], and pray for one another, that ye may be healed" (of bodily sicknesses). Power in prayer is evidently conditioned upon one's being in fellowship with both the Lord and fellow believers. This being met, the persevering prayer offered by a "righteous man," one accepted by God on the basis of his faith in Christ, "avails much in its working."

The Example, 17-18. Elijah so prayed, being a man of like passions with us, 17a. He prayed earnestly ("prayed with prayer," a Hebraism for "prayed intensely," cf. 1 Kgs 17:1); he prayed effectively, with God's glory in mind for a national drought in recompense for a national sin (1 Kgs 19:10). His prayer was also answered for the removal of the drought, 18 (1 Kgs 18:42-45).

5:19-20. LIVING FAITH EXERCISED BY A DILIGENT WITNESS

The Need for Witnessing, 19. The blessing of reclaiming a brother who errs in being led astray from the truth of the gospel and its precepts is set forth. One who brings such a one back to the truth has performed a useful service, to God and to the church.

The Results of Witnessing, 20, are twofold: (1) the salvation of the sinning brother from physical death (1 Cor 11:30), and (2) the hiding of his multitudinous sins, such sins being covered before God (or forgiven) by Christ's finished work on the cross.

1 PETER
LIVING IN THE LIGHT OF FUTURE GLORY

Authorship. That the epistle was written by the apostle Peter is indicated by the intimate acquaintance the author shows with the life of Christ and His teachings (cf. 5:5 with Jn 13:3-5; 5:2 with Jn 21:15-17). He enlarges on the sufferings of Christ as an eyewitness (5:1; cf. 3:18; 4:1), and features the person of Christ in relation to these sufferings (2:19-24; cf. 4:13). There is also a noteworthy similarity between Peter's speeches in Acts and his words in the epistle (Acts 2:32-36; 10:34, 41 with 1 Pet 1:21; Acts 4:10-11 with 1 Pet 2:7-8; Acts 10:34 with 1 Pet 1:17). Petrine authorship of the epistle was universally recognized by the early church. Polycarp quotes 1:8; 2:11; 3:9 in his Epistle to the Philippians. Irenaeus quotes it by name in *Against Heresies* (IV:9, 2; IV:16, 5; V:7, 2). Other evidence is abundant.

Occasion and Date. The epistle is predominantly, if not entirely, addresssed to Jewish believers (but cf. 4:3-5). It was written perhaps as late as A.D. 65, for the letter shows knowledge not only of very early epistles such as James, 1 Thessalonians and Romans, but seems also to be acquainted with Paul's later Prison Epistles (Colossians, Ephesians and Philippians). The date, of course, depends on the time of Peter's martyrdom, which Eusebius places in Nero's thirteenth year, A.D. 67-68.

Theme. The subject of the epistle is "suffering," with seven different words used for it in the one letter. Hope in the midst of suffering is engendered by the prospect of a future inheritance (1:4-5) and the coming of the Chief Shepherd (5:4). Suffering is purposeful (1:6-7; 2:19-20; 3:14; 4:14). It is to be expected (4:12), not to be dreaded (3:14); borne patiently (2:23; 3:9) and rejoiced in (4:13). The sufferings of Christ are featured (1:11; 2:21; 5:1) as the believer's example (2:21; 4:1-2). Suffering is in God's will (4:19).

Peter's Later Life and Ministry. At Pentecost Peter's preaching opened gospel opportunity to the Jews (Acts 2:14-41). Later, at the temple he and John healed the lame man (Acts 3:1-10), following which he preached a sermon on the theme of the future fulfillment of Israel's covenants (3:11-26). News of his distinctive ministry and message spread and he, along with John, was arrested and tried before the Sanhedrin (Acts 4:1-22). As the leader of the church at Jerusalem the responsibility of dealing with Ananias and Sapphira fell on his shoulders (Acts 5:1-11). Peter, along with other apostles, was subject to further persecution and imprisonment by the Jewish leaders following a period of spectacular power in the early church (5:12-41).

Peter was the chosen instrument (Mt 16:16-18) to open gospel opportunity to the Samaritans (Acts 8:14-25), and later to the Gentiles (Acts 10—11). The desire to placate the Jews led Herod Agrippa I to kill James, the brother of John, and to imprison Peter, between A.D. 41 and 44 during his reign over Judea (Acts 12:1-17). After his miraculous release, and following Paul's first missionary journey, Peter took a leading role in the first church council in Jerusalem (Acts 15:7-11; Gal 2:6-10). At Antioch he was rebuked by Paul for hypocritically withdrawing from fellowship with Gentile believers (Gal 2:11-14). He traveled extensively, often with his wife (1 Cor 9:5), apparently visiting Asia Minor, especially Pontus, Cappadocia and Bithynia, areas Paul did not visit. Peter's martyrdom is hinted in John 21:18-19.

The tradition that Peter was the founder of the church at Rome and its first bishop lacks historical evidence. The Bible gives no indication of such. In fact, there is no historical proof that Peter was ever in Rome, although historians grant the possibility of his going there toward the very end of his life. If so, he probably suffered martyrdom there.

The *Quo Vadis* tradition represents Peter as fleeing from Rome to avoid martyrdom. On the Appian Way he met Jesus, and asked, *"Quo Vadis?"* ("Where are you going?") Jesus replied that He was returning to the city to be crucified. Thoroughly rebuked at his own cowardice, Peter returned to be crucified head downward, considering himself unworthy to be crucified as his Lord was.

Outline

Present Suffering and Future Inheritance, 1:1-25
The Christian's Suffering in View of Christ's Passion, 2:1—4:6
The Christian's Suffering in View of Christ's Advent, 4:7—5:14

1:1-5. ENCOURAGED FOR SUFFERING

A Basis for Courage, 1-4. The strangers (sojourners) of the dispersion were believing Jews (spiritual pilgrims) scattered throughout Roman provinces in Asia Minor. These believers were often subject to severe persecution from fellow Jews. Their spiritual wealth provided a basis for courage in the midst of their trials. It included: (1) their *election,* 2, for God had sovereignly chosen them for His very own possession; (2) their *sanctification* by the Holy Spirit, 2, giving the believer the holy position of being set apart unto God, the result of "the sprinkling of the blood of Jesus Christ," which is to issue in "obedience"; (3) their *new birth*, 3, a result of God's abundant mercy; and (4) their future *glorification* and *inheritance*, 3-4. This "living hope" is "incorruptible" (immortal); "unfadable" (not subject to decay); "undefiled" (inviolately intact); "reserved in heaven," or, better translated, "which has been and is reserved [laid up in trust] for you."

Present Status of the Sufferers, 5. Further encouragement was given by the reminder that these believers were "kept by the *power of God*" in the sense that they were continually guarded as though garrisoned with a military contingent and thus maintained in a state of security. Their response was to be "through faith" in the provision God had made. The full revelation of this salvation awaits "the last time," i.e., the coming of the Lord.

1:6-9. TESTED FOR SUFFERING

The Proper Attitude Toward Suffering, 6. Suffering should be *endured with joy*, 6a. The word "rejoice" is strong, i.e., "in this be exuberantly glad." Salvation is a thing so vitally present as to cause exhilarating joy, despite present trials. Furthermore, suffering should be *seen as transient*, 6b, "though now for a season" (Gr. "for a little while"), viewed in the larger perspective of coming glory. Suffering should also be *in the will of God*, 6c, "if need be," i.e., "if it is necessary" that we suffer, for it is not always God's will that we do so. Self-inflicted pain outside God's will is never virtuous (cf. 2 Tim 3:12). One may expect suffering in God's will to be *severe and variegated*, 6d.

The Purpose of Suffering, 7-9. God's aim in suffering is that the believer's faith may be *proved genuine*, 7a; that this genuine faith may *result in "praise, honor,* and *glory"* to Christ at His unveiling (second coming), 7c; that the believer may see the great *external value of his faith*, "more precious than gold," 7b; that the believer may *grow in his love for the Lord*, thus knowing Him as the *source of full joy*, 8. As the outcome of his genuine faith in Christ, the believer receives the salvation of his soul, a present reality, 9.

1:10-12. SALVATION AND SUFFERING

The Search of the Prophets, 10-11. The OT prophets were intrigued by the plan of salvation which was hinted in their prophetic utterances concerning God's grace, 10. This grace was to be displayed in the vicarious sufferings of Messiah-King, 11, something which was a mystery to the Jews. The readers of this epistle, with their Jewish background, were brought back to the subject of suffering by this reference to the sufferings of Christ. The grace of God involved Christ's sufferings to secure salvation. So also may His grace involve suffering for those who possess His salvation.

The Benefactors of the Prophetic Message, 12. It was revealed to the prophets that their message and ministry were intended for a future age (ours). The marvelous gospel of God's grace to sinful men was prophesied by OT prophets who failed to comprehend its truths; it was preached by NT Spirit-filled apostles, and is of great wonder to angels.

1:13-21. HOLY LIVING AND SUFFERING

The Exhortation to Holy Living, 13-17. This so great salvation 10-12, demands a once-for-all attitude of separation from sin. Such holiness of life involves mental alertness ("gird up your minds"), 13a; sobriety or seriousness, 13b; mature patience in light of future blessing, 13c; obedience, 14a; nonconformity to former passions, 14b; a likeness in behavior to the holiness of God Himself, 15-16 (cf. Lev 11:44-45); recognition of God's justice amid persecution, 17a; and conduct prompted by godly fear, 17b.

The Reason for Holy Living, 18-21. Our great redemption is the essential basis for a holy life. The apostle again reminds his readers of its greatness by reference to: (1) *its infinite cost and worth,* 18-19; (2) *its effectiveness* in redeeming the believer from empty legalistic religion and mere human piety, 18b; (3) *its Redeemer, Christ,* whose blood is "precious" (infinitely valuable and inestimably costly) in that He was "without blemish" in His own character and "without spot" from contact with men, thus He was able to redeem, 19, and whose redemptive work was in the eternal plan and purpose of God, 20, its efficacy being sealed by His resurrection and subsequent glory, 21b; (4) *its impartation to man* through faith in Christ, 21a, totally apart from human merit.

1:22-25. REGENERATION AND BEHAVIOR

The Responsibility of Regeneration, 22. The new birth, 23a, is to be manifested in transformation of character. The addressees of this epistle had realized the cleansing of their souls, effected by obedient response to the truth of the gospel. This had issued in a genuinely sincere or unhypocritical love for fellow believers. Now they were enjoined to continue the practice of this same principle as evidence of their new birth. Such love is to be "from the heart"—a genuine and permanent attitude—and "fervent" (*ektenōs*, "with internal earnestness").

The Means of Regeneration, 23-25. Being "born again" (Jn 3:1-5), that is, being given spiritual life and birth by God, rests on the authority and the testimony of the Word of God. This Word is characterized as imperishable, living and eternal, outlasting all natural phenomena (Isa 40:6-8). Realizing its character gives assurance to the believer, 25b.

2:1-3. THE BELIEVER'S GROWTH AND SUFFERING

Separation from Evil, 1. Successfully meeting the trials of the believer's life, so prominently featured in this epistle, is possible only in the case of the spiritually mature. Accordingly, Christian growth calls for a negative and a positive response from the believer. Negatively, he is to exhibit a distinct separation from evil, 1, being permanently done with "all malice" (ill will), "all guile" (deceit), "hypocrisies" (insincere acts for outward effect), "envies" (jealous thoughts), and "all evil speakings." These violate the principle of love which is to characterize the behavior of the regenerate (1:22).

Desire for the Word of God, 2-3. Positively, the believer is to exhibit an intense appetite for the Word of God, 2. It is the nourishment which makes growth and development possible. Growth is the anticipated response of those who have tasted God's grace, 3.

2:4-10. SPIRITUAL IDENTITY,
AN ENCOURAGEMENT IN SUFFERING

Identity with Christ, 4-8. The apostle now brings to his Jewish readers assurance that, though they may be ostracized by the world and by unbelieving Jews, they are gloriously identified with their Lord and His Church in a personal and intimate way. The figure of a building is used to describe this relationship. Christ is the chosen, precious living stone, 4. Believers, possessing His life, are living stones which constitute a spiritual house (in contrast to the earthly temple) of priests who offer acceptable sacrifices to God, 5. Their superiority to the order of the old covenant is obvious. Jesus Christ is the cornerstone, the keystone, of this building made up of living stones (the Church), 6-7. He is the superlatively precious one to believers, 7a, but "a stone of stumbling" and "a rock of offense" to those Jews who rejected Him, 7b-8. (Cf. Isa 28:16; Acts 4:11.)

This doubtless explains why many Jewish believers were subject to suffering for His sake.

Identity with God's Own, 9-10. Identification with Christ also brings one into living relationship with the whole company of believers. Peter refers to this body as *"a chosen* [elect] *race"* (a select kind of people), *"a royal priesthood"* (priests of royalty directly related to the King with immediate access through Him to God), *"a holy nation"* (a sanctified nation, set apart in Christ unto God, as Israel was meant to be but never was), *"a peculiar people"* (a greatly prized people for God's own possession), *"the people of God"* who are recipients of His mercy. "Not a people . . . who had not received mercy" refers to their former condition as alienated from God in the dead religiosity of Judaism.

The responsibility of those who possess such a relationship is to declare the gracious goodness of God in calling lost men out of spiritual darkness into His "wonderfully admirable" light, 9b. The light of redemption is to shine from those who are so lighted.

2:11-20. THE BELIEVER'S PILGRIMAGE AND SUFFERING

Pilgrim Character Described, 11a. In a threefold designation Peter describes his Jewish fellow believers as: (1) "beloved," showing his love for them; (2) "strangers" (*paroikous*, "temporary residents") on earth with heaven as their real home; and (3) "pilgrims" (*parepidēmous*, "residents in a country not one's own").

Pilgrim Conduct Enjoined, 11b-18. This includes abstaining from "fleshly passions" 11b (cf. Gal 5:19-21), because these "fight against" the regenerated soul by opposing its high endeavors (Rom 8:13). Pilgrims are to maintain good "conduct among the Gentiles," among whom these Jewish believers were scattered, that the unsaved might glorify God by the good works of His own in the "day of visitation," the day of Christ's coming in judgment, 12. Also expected from these sojourners are: submission to constituted civil government, 13-14 (cf. Rom 13:1, 7); a good defense against those who wrongly accuse them, 15; the exercising of the freedom God's own have in submitting to His mastery, not using such freedom as pretext for evil, 16; giving honor to all men, 17; love for fellow believers; reverence for God; giving honor to the king; obedience to masters, 18 (Eph 6:5).

Pilgrim Conduct and Suffering, 19-20. Maintaining a good conscience toward God as a pilgrim, often calls for "enduring pain," suffering unjustly, 19. This sort of suffering "finds favor with God" (Gr.), 20.

2:21-25. THE BELIEVER'S SUFFERING AND CHRIST'S EXAMPLE

The Believer's Call to Suffering, 21a. Suffering righteously is an intrinsic part of the Christian vocation.

The Example of Christ's Suffering, 21b-25. Believers are called to suffer in the same spirit of placid faith and patient endurance Christ displayed. He left us an example for imitation, a pattern for guidance, desiring His redeemed ones to "follow [closely] in his steps," 21b. Christ was absolutely sinless and guileless, 22 (Isa 53:9), yet suffered, and that with calm trust and patient endurance, 23 (Isa 53:7; Mt 26:59-68; Jn 18:19-23). So far from suffering for wrongdoing Himself, His suffering unto death vicariously redeemed us sinners, making Him much more than a mere example. He, alone being able and willing, sacrificially carried and offered up *our very own sins* in His own body on the cross, 24a, providing us not only redemption from the penalty of sin but also deliverance from the power of sin, so that we might live righteously, 24b (Rom 6:1-11; 8:3-5). Thus His sufferings unto death provided us spiritual healing, 24c, and spiritual restoration, 25.

3:1-7. GOD'S PATTERN FOR WIVES AND HUSBANDS

Pattern for Wives, 1-6. Wives are to be in subjection to their own husbands so that an unbelieving husband might be won to Christ by the godly behavior of his wife, 1-2. She is to be outwardly *pure* in life, *reverential* in her attitude toward her husband, *modest* in dress, 2-3, and inwardly *spiritually adorned* "with the incorruptible, fadeless charm of a gentle and tranquil spirit which is priceless in God's estimation," 4. Following OT examples, particularly Sarah (Gen 18:12), she is to be a woman of faith, inner adornment, submission, obedience, and courage, 5-6.

Pattern for Husbands, 7. The husbands are to live with their wives in understanding recognition of what marriage means ("according to knowledge"). They are to purposefully bestow honor on the woman as the physically weaker sex, recognizing that both are equal heirs of God's gracious bestowment of life, physical and spiritual. Domestic tranquility is to prevail, so that their prayers may be unhindered; thus they may enjoy the blessing of united faith.

3:8-12. THE BELIEVER'S SUFFERING
AND HARMONIOUS LIVING

Requirements for Harmonious Living, 8-11. In order for believers to live harmoniously, especially under trial, they must be likeminded in the faith, sympathetic in their attitude toward one another, brotherly, compassionately tenderhearted (Eph 4:32), courteous (Gr. "humbleminded," since humility and love are basic ingredients of spontaneous civility), 8; not vengeful toward others, but beneficent, and thus in line for personal blessing, 9 (Ps 34:12-15).

Reason for Harmonious Living, 12. Using the words of the psalmist in Ps 34:15-16 the apostle assures believers that *they* are the objects of the gracious care of the Lord, not enemy pawns. Living harmoniously under suffering may invite the cruelty of their enemies, but it also invites the Lord's personal attention.

3:13-17. MAINTAINING A GOOD CONSCIENCE
UNDER SUFFERING

The Way to a Good Conscience, 13-15. One's conscience may be considered good when void of offense toward God and man (Acts 24:16; 1 Tim 1:5), or it may be considered evil when it is defiled (1 Tim 4:2; Tit 1:15; Heb 10:22). Keeping a good conscience entails: (1) personal integrity, 13; (2) a proper attitude toward suffering righteously, 14a; (3) facing persecution fearlessly, 14b; (4) giving God the proper place in your life, 15a, for Christ must be reverenced as *Lord* before the conscience can be void of offense toward God; (5) maintaining a proper witness before men, 15b.

The Result of a Good Conscience, 16-17. A good conscience will put persecutors to shame, 16a; it will prompt good behavior, 16b; and it will give the persecuted believer conviction of the value of suffering righteously, 17.

3:18-22. CHRIST'S EXAMPLE OF TRIUMPH
AND ENCOURAGEMENT

Christ's Triumph Over Suffering, 18. Christ's example argues for patience under suffering because He Himself chose not to be exempt from suffering. If He was not exempt from suffering, even to death, why should believers expect to be? He was sinless; we are sinners. He was to expiate sin and reconcile us to God; we are merely to be tested and corrected. He was to enter into glory; we are soon to follow Him.

Christ's Encouragement in Suffering, 19-20. The Jewish believers to whom Peter wrote were almost engulfed in the pagan world around them. He encourages them by a reference to Christ's ministry to the antediluvian generation through Noah. This ministry was by the same Spirit, 18 (Rom 8:11), that effected Jesus' resurrection, 19*a*. It was a preaching ministry in which Christ went by special operation (Gen 11:5; Mic 1:3) and preached "to the spirits now in prison" (Gr.), those who were sinners in the flesh in Noah's day. Christ, through His Spirit (Gen 6:3), preached to them through Noah. Their sin was that they "were disobedient" (rebellious and unpersuadably unbelieving), their crime being aggravated by God's patient long-suffering during the 120 years that the ark was being built, 20. This rebellion resulted in their bodies being drowned and their spirits cast into "prison" (called *Tartarus,* 2 Pet 2:4-5; Job 1:6; see notes on Gen 6:1-6), 19.

Christ's Triumph in Providing Salvation, 21-22. Christ's sufferings resulted in our salvation. This makes our suffering not only bearable but glorious. The outward figure of this salvation is water baptism. The ark on the flood waters is the type; our salvation in Christ (the true Ark) the antitype. The water simply cut off the righteous from the sin and sinners of that day. The ark alone saved. So baptism is for the saved, but cannot itself save, except as a picture ("figure") of the *saved* candidates having been cut off from sinners and their doom. Christ alone can save, and that by virtue of His resurrection (Rom 4:25), 21*c*. No mere external rite can save— "not the putting away of the filth of the flesh," 21*b*: "but the answer of a good conscience toward God"—by the consciousness of sin *removed* by Christ's blood (cf. Heb 9:14).

4:1-6. SUFFERING AND CHRIST'S EXAMPLE FOR VICTORIOUS LIVING

The Basis for Victorious Living, 1-2. As Peter has previously used Christ's example to enforce patience in suffering, he now employs it to urge mortification of sin. The believer is to arm himself, as a soldier putting on his armor, "with the same mind" (attitude and purpose) Christ had—purposing to suffer rather than to sin (cf. Phil 2:5-8), 1. As physical death frees a man from sin ("suffered in the flesh," 1*b*), so he who identifies himself with Christ's redemptive suffering should reckon thereon, no longer responding to the strong sinful passions of men while he lives on earth, but responding to the will of God for his life, 2.

The Case Against Sinful Living, 3-6. The apostle goes on to contrast the lustful living of the Gentiles with the life lived in the will of God (cf. v. 2). Such sinful living took its toll before conversion and should be given no further opportunity, 3a. Six sins are cataloged, 3b, characteristic of the unregenerate. Believers, because of their changed lives, bring condemnation to the ungodly, resulting in Christians being maligned for their purity of life, 4. However, unbelievers are sure to face the judgment of God, both in this life (the "living") and in the final Great White Throne judgment to come (the "dead," Rev 20:11-15), 5. Because unregenerate man must face God's judgment, the good news (the gospel) has been preached, even to those who are now dead. If a man believes the gospel, even though he is judged in this life according to the judgment of men, he lives spiritually according to the will of God, 6.

4:7-11. JUDGMENT AND SERVICE AMIDST SUFFERING

Living in the Light of Coming Judgment, 7. Peter's statement, "But the end [consummation] of all things is at hand" (cf. Jas 5:8-9), still has the subject of judgment in mind (cf. 5:6). In light of its nearness the believer is enjoined to "be of sound judgment and sober spirit for the purpose of prayer" (Gr.).

Serving in the Spirit of Love, 8-11. Foremost is the injunction to "exercise fervent love toward one another, because love covers a multitude of sins," 8. Lack of love broadcasts and uncovers these sins to the detriment of God's work. Peter is speaking merely of a loving spirit of forgiveness versus an unloving spirit of criticism, not of the expiation of sins. He also enjoins the practice of ungrudging hospitality, 9, and the use of one's spiritual gifts (cf. 1 Cor 12:8-12) for the welfare of one another, 10 (cf. Rom 12:6, 8; 1 Tim 6:17-18). Such service is to bear the marks of God's authority and of humility, 11. The goal of all service is to be God's glory, 11c.

4:12-19. THE LORD'S RETURN AND TRIALS

The Source of Courage for Trials, 12-14. A proper attitude toward trials, and understanding of their purpose and benefits for the Christian, will engender courage. They are to be expected, not viewed as unusual in the believer's life, and are allowed in order to test the genuineness of his faith, 12. Continual rejoicing under trial is enjoined, because one thereby now has fellowship with Christ in His suffering, 13a, and at His revelation (coming) will have cause for

805

even greater joy, 13b. Present trials bring special happiness or blessedness because the Spirit of God therein effects spiritual unction and testimony to God's glory, 14.

Courage for Trials and Christian Duty, 15-19. The believer's responsibility is to avoid suffering which is the outcome of sin, 15. Also, he is not to be ashamed of suffering as a "Christian," a contemptuous nickname invented by the Gentiles at Antioch (Acts 11:26; 26:28). By suffering righteously he honors the name "Christian" (a believer in and a follower of Jesus Christ the Messiah), and glorifies God thereby, 16.

The Christian is to realize that the judgment of his works at the Lord's return is imminent, 17 (cf. 1 Cor 3:11-15; 4:1-6; 2 Cor 5:10), and if he, a member of God's household, is subject to judgment, the ungodly have an even more severe judgment to anticipate. Perdition alone can be their portion since they do not know Christ and are lost sinners, 18. The apostle summarizes this section by stating that suffering is to be welcomed when it is "according to God's will," and the sufferers are to commit their souls to a faithful Creator, who made them and can certainly take care of them in suffering, bringing them through it to His glory, 19.

5:1-5. THE LORD'S RETURN AND DAILY DUTY

Duty of Elders, 1-4. The elders (or bishops, evidently the same office) are exhorted to tend the flock of God, assuming the responsibility of overseeing "the flock" (the body of believers) voluntarily, not under compulsion, and eagerly without being motivated by thoughts of personal (base) gain, 1-2. They are to prove themselves examples for the flock to follow, not exerting autocratic domination over those placed under their supervision, 3. The reward for faithful shepherding will be "an unfading crown of glory" (a reward) when Christ the Chief Shepherd appears for His own (cf. 1 Cor 3:11-15; 2 Cor 5:10), 4.

Duty of the Young, 5. The young are to be subject to their elders (1-4), and all members of the flock are to clothe themselves with humility toward one another (Prov 3:34; 18:12; Jas 4:6).

5:6-11. THE LORD'S RETURN AND CHRISTIAN MATURITY

Developing Maturity, 6-9. This entails a spirit of continued submission to God, 6-7, and an attitude of continued resistance to Satan, 8-9. With respect toward God, believers are to *humble them-*

selves in full submission "under the mighty hand of God," 6*a*, no matter what of weal or woe it may at the moment seem to mean in suffering (cf. Isa 57:15); *trust God* to exalt them at the proper time, 6*b*; *cast all their anxieties on Him,* 7*a*, assured that He cares about them, 7*b* (Ps 55:22).

With respect to Satan, believers are to be sober (serious-minded) and *vigilant* (alertly watchful) because their opponent the devil prowls around "like a roaring lion" in search of some one tc devour, 8. The believer must be firm in the faith to "resist him" who resists them (cf Zech 3:1; Rev 12:10). For the believer's encouragement he is to realize that it is a sign of God's favor, rather than disfavor, that Satan is permitted to hound him as he did Job. All fellow believers have the same conflict in the world (where Satan operates), 9.

Enjoying Maturity, 10-11. This is possible because: "the God of all grace" deals graciously with us, 10*a*; He has called the believer to His eternal glory in Christ, 10*b*, assuring him of ultimate perfection; His purpose in allowing suffering is to "perfect" (mature) the Christian, to "establish, strengthen and settle" him as a foundation is securely laid, 10*c*. The response of the believer in all of this is to be perpetual recognition of God's glory and lordship ("dominion"), 11.

5:12-14. CONCLUDING SALUTATION

Personal Testimony, 12. Exhortation and sincere explanation have been given throughout the epistle; now Peter adds personal testimony: "I have written . . . exhorting and *testifying that this is the true grace of God,* wherein ye stand," 12. Peter wrote with ringing authority because he himself was a brilliant trophy of God's grace. Silvanus is Silas, one of Paul's companions (Acts 15:22, 40).

Final Greetings, 13-14. "The church [or she, see ASV] that is in Babylon" probably refers not cryptically to the city of Rome but to the church (2 Jn 1) of Jewish converts at Babylon on the Euphrates (Acts 2:9), the center from which the Asiatic Jewish dispersion was derived. It was the location of a large Jewish community in the apostolic era, according to both Philo and Josephus. Marcus is John Mark (cf. 2 Tim 4:11; Col 4:10). "The kiss of love," 14, has singularly been discontinued by most Christians (Rom 16:16; cf. Acts 20:37).

2 PETER

GROWING IN GRACE

Authorship. Because of a difference in style between 1 and 2 Peter, some of the early fathers, reformers, and modern critics have questioned the Petrine authorship of 2 Peter. It was not generally recognized as an authentic writing of the apostle Peter until Origen's time (*c.* A.D. 250) or later. However, the evidence seems to favor its having been written by the apostle (1:1).

The lack of recognition by the early church and the consequent neglect by the Christian public are explained by the brevity of the epistle, its general nature (not being addressed to any specific person or church), and the fact that it contains little new material. Some have charged that Simon Peter's name (1:1) is a forgery or interpolation, but this charge lacks support and is rather improbable. It is quite unlikely that a forger writing in the interest of truth to warn against false teachers should himself be a deceiver. On the other hand, there is no real motive for pseudonymous authorship. The epistle is orthodox, advancing no new teaching. It tells nothing new of Peter, in contrast to the spurious Gospel of Peter and the Apocalypse of Peter. The autobiographical allusions are true to fact (cf. the reference to the transfiguration, 1:16-18, and Peter's martyrdom, 1:12-14, the latter written before Jn 21:18-19 which predicts it). The Christian earnestness, the apostolic zeal and the general worth of the epistle, in contrast to the valueless products of those who forged the name of an apostle, argue for the genuineness of 2 Peter. Jude apparently alludes to 2 Peter (cf. 2:6—3:3; Jude 4-16).

Occasion and Date. Second Peter was evidently penned to the same people as 1 Peter, namely, Jewish Christians (see note on 1 Pet 1:1). It was apparently written after 1 Peter and before Jude, as the doctrinal defection it describes is not as fully developed as in Jude. The date is probably A.D. 66 or 67.

Outline
Secret to Christian Growth, Ch. 1
Antidote to Error, Ch. 2
Key to Certainty of the Future, Ch. 3

---

1 PETER AND 2 PETER IN CONTRAST

1 Peter	2 Peter
Emphasis—suffering	False teaching and false teachers
The sufferings of Christ	The glory to follow
Redemptive title—Christ	Title of dominion—Lord
Consolation	Warning
Hope to face trial	Full knowledge to face error
Seven different words for "suffering" occur, and theme occurs over and over again	The word "know" and its cognates occur 16 times: 1:2, 3, 5, 6, 8, 12, 14, 16, 20; 2:9, 20, 21 (twice); 3:3, 17, 18

1:1-4. THE BASIS OF CHRISTIAN GROWTH

The Common Faith of Believers, 1-2. Simon is the Gr. form of the Heb. *Symeon* ("hearing") (Acts 15:14; cf. Mt 16:16-18), and identifies Peter as a Jewish Christian, 1. The use of his earlier name is in keeping with the purpose of this second letter, which is to warn against the rise of false teachers through the testimony of original apostolic eyewitnesses, counteracting the error of the false teachers with the "full knowledge" of Christ, 2.

The apostle addresses those who have received "like precious faith," that is, a faith equally precious to all believers. This faith, the basis of Christian development and growth, is obtained or received from God, and is not a human attainment. It rests on the basis of the righteousness of God through the redemptive work of Christ (cf. 1 Cor 3:11). "Grace" and "peace" are multiplied (increased) to believers through "the full knowledge of God, and of Jesus our Lord," 2.

The Spiritual Endowment of Believers, 3-4. Facilitating Christian growth, this endowment consists of: (1) "his divine power" (the dynamic of the Holy Spirit), bestowing on us "all things" necessary for the realization of life and godliness, 3a; (2) "knowledge of him," 3b, full, personal, accurate knowledge (*epignosis*) of Christ, made possible by the Spirit's teaching ministry (Jn 16:13-15); (3) His Word, 4a, infinitely valuable and exceedingly great promises having been given to us; (4) a new (regenerate) nature, 4b, "partakers [*koinōnoi*, "fellow partners"] of the divine nature" (Jn 3:1-5); (5) ability and means to live in a holy manner, 4b, "having escaped [by the preceding resources] the corruption that is in the world through lust."

1:5-9. THE WAY TO CHRISTIAN GROWTH

Employment of One's Spiritual Endowment, 5-7. "For this very reason," because of the spiritual endowment God has vouchsafed to us, 3-4, let us "bend every effort" to cooperate with Him. This involves supplying in your faith (the starting point of all spiritual knowledge and growth) "moral excellence, and in your moral excellence, knowledge [of God's truth and will]; and in your knowledge, self-control, and in your self-control, perseverance, and in your perseverance, godliness [devotion to God in fellowship and service, so your perseverance is not mere stoicism, but the outflow of the indwelling life of God]; and in your godliness, brotherly kindness, and in your brotherly kindness, Christian love" (Gr.). Love fittingly completes the choir of graces as in Col 3:14, and comprehends them all, being the badge of spiritual adulthood (cf. 1 Cor 13).

The Resultant Manifestation of Spiritual Maturity, 8-9. This adulthood will reveal itself in fruitfulness, 8, and will shield the believer from spiritual shortsightedness (*muōpadzon,* a state of being dimvisioned, seeing only what is near at hand), 9. A shortsighted person has forgotten that he was purged from his sins (cleansed once for all, at the time of regeneration, Jn 13:10; Heb 10:2).

1:10-15. THE CONSUMMATION OF CHRISTIAN GROWTH

Assuring Our Calling and Election, 10. "Therefore [because of the danger of lapsing into spiritual shortsightedness, 9], brethren, be all the more diligent to make certain about His calling and choosing you" (Gr.). Although their election was certain from the divine point of view, being the result of God's sovereign choice and based on the efficacy of Christ's finished redemption, believers are to employ their spiritual resources, 5-7, in manifesting maturity, 8-9, in order to make their calling and election certain to men. The result will be that "you will *in no wise* [*ou me*] fall," stumble so as to fail in the Christian life, 10b. (See notes on Eph 1:1-6.)

Entering the Eternal Kingdom, 11-15. Believers spiritually enter the kingdom of God when they are born again (Jn 3:5). The entrance spoken of here is the actual entrance into the eternal kingdom of our Lord and Saviour Jesus Christ at the resurrection of the body and its consequent glorification (1 Thess 4:13-17; 1 Jn 3:1-3; Phil 3:20-21). The work of grace in this life shall be crowned with the reward of grace in the life to come.

This glorious future demands constant reminding in order to arouse God's people, 12-13. Peter's reference to "the truth" means the gospel truth now present, formerly promised to OT saints and now in NT times actually present with and in believers as an arrived reality. Furthermore, the apostle considers his reminding ministry urgent in view of his impending death, 14. As a result of such responsibility he assures his readers that after his death his writings will serve to call to mind the truths of the gospel which he had taught them, 15.

1:16-21. CHRISTIAN GROWTH AND BIBLICAL AUTHORITY

The Authority of Apostolic Testimony, 16-18. Peter himself points believers to the real authority of the Word of God, declaring that the inspired testimony of the apostles rules out deception or imposture ("For we have not followed cunningly devised fables," i.e., myths devised by human wisdom in contrast to Holy Spirit inspiration, cf. 1 Cor 3:13), 16a. Furthermore, apostolic testimony comprehends the revelation of the power and coming of Christ, embracing the evidence of eyewitnesses, 16b (Mt 17:1, 5). To have seen the risen Christ was a requirement for being an apostle (Acts 1:21-22). On the Mount of Transfiguration Peter was such an eyewitness "of that great One's majesty" (this is the emphasis in Gr.). The transfiguration was the second advent in miniature (see notes on Mt 17:1-8; Mk 9:2-10; Lk 9:27-36). Peter also heard the voice of "the Majestic Glory" (God) when he, with James and John, was in the "holy mountain," 17-18.

The Authority of the Written Word, 19-21. This is now the sole and all-sufficient authority for faith and practice. The written Word not only contains and preserves the authority of apostolic testimony (16-18), but it has been proved inspired by fulfillment, 19a ("And we have the prophetic word [the OT Scriptures] made more sure," attested or confirmed by fulfilled NT events concerning the first advent and by the transfiguration concerning the second advent). The prophetic Scriptures are to be diligently heeded in our hearts, 19b. The Daystar (Gr. the Morning Star) is Christ in His coming for His own (Jn 14:1-3; 1 Cor 15:51; 1 Thess 4:13-18). The Scriptures also are of divine origin, for they are divinely inspired, 20-21. An expanded translation of the Gr. text would read: "For *not by the will of man* [emphatic] was any prophecy ever borne to us, but, on the contrary, men being borne along by the agency of the Holy Spirit spoke *from God* [emphatic]," 21.

2:1-3a.   FALSE TEACHERS—THEIR RISE

Their Activity, 1. In contrast to the true prophets who spoke for God, Peter refers to the opposition of false prophets (Mt 24:5; 1 Tim 4:1; Jude 4). They would stealthily introduce destructive heresies, even denying the very Lord who bought them, i.e., made them savable.

Their Influence, 2-3. The influence of these false prophets is shown by their popularity ("many will follow their lascivious ways"), 2*a*; their apparently *successful opposition* to the truth ("by reason of whom the way of the truth shall be blasphemed"), 2*b*; and their *financial exploitation* of their victims ("and motivated by greed, with feigned words [*plastois,* "formed" or "fashioned" to deceive, "fabricated" to be counterfeit] they will exploit you"), 3*a*.

2:3b-9.   FALSE TEACHERS—THEIR DOOM

Their Certain Judgment Declared, 3b. The sure ruin of these false teachers is emphasized by the following graphic personification: "Their judgment from long ago [in God's purpose and plan, Jude 4] is not idle, and their destruction is not asleep" (Gr.).

Their Certain Ruin Illustrated, 4-8. The first illustration is that of the *fallen angels,* 4. These were evidently those who at the time of the Flood intermarried with mortal women, corrupting the race, and breaking down God's orders of being (Gen 6:1-6; Jude 6). Their doom was imprisonment in "Tartarus." The second example is that of the *ancient world,* 5. Only Noah and his family were saved (Gen 6:1—8:22). The third illustration is that of *Sodom and Gomorrah,* 6-8, in which righteous Lot was spared (Gen 19:1-29; Jude 7).

The Divine Principle Enunciated, 9. The Lord is at no loss for means to rescue the godly from temptation (trial) nor to keep the unrighteous "under punishment" (Gr. "being punished," as the fallen angels are, 4), and actually under judgment, awaiting its final execution at the final day of judgment (Rev 20:11-15).

2:10-16.   FALSE TEACHERS—THEIR PRESUMPTION AND GREED

Their Sin of Presumption Specified, 10-12. These ungodly teachers, kept under judgment, 9, are given particularly to *sensuality,* indulging the flesh (the corrupt sinful nature) in the lust of moral defilement, 10*a*. They are given to *lawlessness,* despising authority—especially that of God and His Word, 10*b*. Both of these sins, however, seemingly stem from the more basic sin of *presumption,* 10c-12. Because they are presumptuous (Gr. "darers") and self-willed, seeking to please themselves in willful obstinance, they are not afraid to speak evil of angelic dignities (the order of angels). On the other hand, "angels, though being greater in strength and power [than these lawless human beings], do not bring a railing accusation against them [the false teachers] before the Lord," 11. Such presumption leads these false teachers to malign those things of which they have no knowledge, 12a.

The Punishment of Their Sin, 12b-13a. They shall be destroyed in their own corruption, the same Gr. word expressing the seed "corruption" and the fruitage "destruction," 12b. Their recompense will be the reward of unrighteousness, 13a.

Their Moral Obliquity, 13b-14. The false teachers' love of luxurious pleasure leads to lives addicted to dissipation, 13b-14a. They are moral blots and blemishes, disgraces to society, living in riot and revelry, and deceptively feasting together with believers at their love feasts. Their mercenary character is revealed by their "having a heart trained in covetousness [greed]."

Their Mercenary Character Illustrated, 15-16. Having abandoned the right path of obedience to the Lord, they have gone astray, following the way of Balaam—the course of easy world conformity taken by this hireling prophet who was eager only to commercialize his spiritual gift. They are like him "who loved the wages of unrighteousness" and was willing for gain from Balak to curse Israel whom God had blessed. Failing this, he was willing to lure Israel into idolatry and fleshly lust in order to realize material gain. The dumb ass spoke with a man's voice to rebuke "the prophet's madness" (Num 22:21-31). What a contrast — a dumb brute reproving an inspired prophet!

2:17-18. FALSE TEACHERS—THEIR EMPTY INTELLECTUALISM

They Are Devoid of God's Spirit, 17. Several metaphors show this emptiness: (1) wells (springs or fountains) without water, water being a symbol of eternal life by the Spirit (Jn 4:14; 7:37-39); (2) tempest-driven mists, unalterably unstable in spiritual issues; (3) "to whom the gloom of darkness is reserved," thus doomed to spiritual ignorance.

They Are Snared by Empty Intellectualism, 18. These teachers of error employ pompous, swelling language with a view to deceive. Their appeal is to the base desires of the flesh whereby they entrap young converts, those who have scarcely escaped from those who live in the ungodly world.

2:19-22. FALSE TEACHERS—THEIR BONDAGE
TO SIN

Their Empty Promise of Liberty, 19-20a. This promise is worthless because they themselves are enslaved by sin, 19a. They are common slaves (*douloi*) of moral depravity, and thus helpless to free others. Having rejected the truth of the gospel, they have spurned the only source of true liberty (Jn 8:32; Gal 5:1, 13; Rom 6:12-22). The liberty they offer is spurious. It is not a deliverance from sin, but a promise of liberty from every yoke, as if the service of God were not perfect freedom. Such a promise appeals to mere professors of the faith, 20, those who have in their outward conduct escaped the pollutions of the world because of fear, but as unregenerate still hanker after the old lusts.

The Plight of Their Victims, 20b-22. As enlightened but unsaved moralists, the followers of these false teachers at least avoid the more obvious sins, but by rejecting the light of Christ they are exposed to greater darkness and deeper sins (Phil 3:18-19). Having turned from "the holy commandment delivered to them" (failing to repent toward God and exercise faith toward Christ), they are like the dog turned again to his own vomit (Prov 26:11) and like the sow, after a washing, turning again to her wallowing in the mire, 22. The washing of the swine speaks of mere outward reformation.

3:1-7. LAST-DAY SCOFFERS AND
THE SECOND ADVENT

The Warning Concerning Scoffers, 1-3. Peter refers to "this second epistle," which we call 2 Peter, in which he again seeks to arouse his readers spiritually by reminding them of "the words spoken beforehand by the holy prophets [of the OT] and the commandment of the Lord and Saviour spoken by your apostles" (Gr.). (Cf. Mt 24:11; 2 Tim 3:1-9; 1 Jn 4:1-6.) His specific purpose in writing was to alert them to the peril of last-day scoffers, scorners and mockers who laugh at or make jest of anything (Jude 18).

The Nature of Their Scoffing, 4-7. These mockers will scorn the truth of the second advent, 4a, saying, "Where is the promise of his coming?" After all these centuries Christ's coming has not occurred and their sneer is, "It never will!" They boldly question the veracity of God's Word, which has this truth emblazoned in the pages of OT prophecy as well as NT. Furthermore, they espouse a natural order of events versus supernatural catastrophism, 4b, assuming that all things in the natural world "continue *as they were* from the creation of the world." The inference is, "All things will always continue thus." Such an assumption is *refuted by Bible history,* 5-6, *and Bible prophecy,* 7. The restoration of the earth (Gen 1:1-31), the Noahic flood, 6, and the coming earth-renovating catastrophe by fire, 7, exhibit the truthfulness of God's Word versus the scoffer's claim, 4.

3:8-10. GOD'S PATIENCE AND THE DAY OF THE LORD

God's Time Schedule, 8-9. The apostle proceeds to answer the scoffers, pointing out that our time concepts are not the limited context in which God operates to bring His purposes to pass. He quotes from Ps 90:4 to show that God works in eternity and is not bound by time limitations as is man, 8. Yet God is always on time, 9. He is not "slack," i.e., He does not delay in the sense of being indecisive or slow in keeping His promises, as some men by natural reasoning reckon the matter. By contrast, "He is long-suffering, not wishing that any should perish, but that all should come to repentance" (Mt 20:28; 1 Tim 2:4; cf. Gen 6:3; 1 Pet 3:20).

The Certainty of the Day of the Lord, 10. Peter gives a new revelation concerning the day of the Lord as it relates to the cataclysm of fire (cf. v. 7). OT prophecy clearly related that day to judgment, the second advent, and the subsequent reign of Messiah (Isa 2:6-22; 4:1-6; cf. Rev 4—19, etc.). This new revelation focuses on the *consummation* of the day, its climactic final catastrophe in the atomic fission of the earth for a fire bath, as it had a flood bath in Noah's day. The tremendous heat generated will effect the change indicated by Peter, an event which can be rather clearly visualized in this atomic age.

3:11-13. PRESENT CONDUCT AND THE ETERNAL STATE

The Impetus to Holy Living, 11-12a. The coming judgments of the day of the Lord furnish ample reasons for godly living. Such piety will be exhibited by a constant anticipation of and desire for the arrival of "the day of God," 12a. This "day" is the final event of time when death, sin and hell are fully conquered and Christ surrenders the mediatorial kingdom to the Father (1 Cor 15:24-28; Rev 20:7—22:21).

The Glorious Expectation, 12b-13. This anticipated event will put an end to the mockery of all scoffers (v. 4). Promised by God's own Word, 13*a*, and expected by faith, 13*b*, it entails a sin-cleansed universe, 13*c* (Isa 65:17; 66:22; Rom 8:21; Rev 21:1, 27). As the Noahic flood resulted in a renovated earth purged of sinners, so the baptism of fire will cleanse the earth for the habitation of man wholly delivered from the curse; thus righteousness will dwell therein, 13*d*. The heavens will be cleansed of Satan and demonic forces (Eph 6:10-12; Rev 20:1-3, 10) and the earth of wicked men (Rev 20:11-15). The lake of fire will be the place of eternal confinement of all evil, so that righteousness alone may fill the universe in eternity (Rev 20:10; 21:1-4, 8).

3:14-18. THE BELIEVER'S HOPE AND GROWTH IN GRACE

The Incentive to Growth, 14-17. The realization of this hope (of new heavens and a new earth in which righteousness dwells) is a further stimulus for a holy life, 14. In the meantime, the believer is to understand that our Lord's long-suffering is designed for sinners' salvation, 15*a*. Peter refers to the enunciation of these foregoing truths in Paul's epistles, 15*b*-16, a statement which authenticates the Pauline letters as inspired of God. Peter concludes by warning that error must be avoided, 17.

The Plea for Growth, 18. Believers are urged to "keep on growing in grace"—God's method not only of saving men but maturing them—and "in knowledge of our Lord and Saviour Jesus Christ," the twofold sphere of true spiritual growth.

1 JOHN

FELLOWSHIP OF FATHER AND CHILDREN

Author. The writer was the apostle John, also the author of the fourth Gospel. This fact is demonstrated by such internal evidence as a similar vocabulary in both the Gospel and the epistle. They contain such expressions as *light, new commandment, works of the devil, take away sins, eternal life, love, abide, lay down one's life, Paraclete, Saviour of the world, begotten by God*. Both also have the same simple, direct Hebraic style, employing similar types of parallelism and sentence construction.

Johannine authorship is also attested by external evidence which is both early and substantial. Polycarp, Papias, Irenaeus, Clement of Alexandria, Tertullian, Cyprian, the Muratorian fragment, the Peshitta Syriac, Origen, Dionysius of Alexandria and Eusebius all lend their testimony to the authenticity of the epistle and Johannine authorship.

Occasion and Date. The epistle was written about A.D. 85-90, apparently from Ephesus, where Irenaeus says John lived during the latter part of his life, and where he seems to have overseen surrounding churches (cf. Rev 2—3). We gather from Irenaeus that it was occasioned by the invasion of several errors. One was associated with moral laxity and the Nicolaitans, whom Irenaeus tenuously connects with Nicolaus (Acts 6:5, RSV; cf. Rev 2:14-15). The other was an error concerning the person and work of Christ, attributed to Cerinthus who taught a form of Gnosticism.

EMPHASIS OF JOHN AND PAUL COMPARED

John	*Paul*
Regeneration	Justification
Sonship in the family	Membership in the Body
Sin as a child's offense against the Father	Sin as unworthy of position in Christ
Our private relation as born-ones ("bairns") of the Father	Our public position as sons

> **Outline**
> Family Fellowship and the Father, Ch. 1—3
> Family Fellowship and the World, Ch. 4—5

1:1-4. THE BASIS OF FELLOWSHIP

The Incarnation and Eternal Life, 1-2. The apostle John presents his authority as an eyewitness to the central fact of the gospel, viz., the incarnation of the Eternal Living Word (Jn 1:1, 14; Prov 8:23). He particularly refers to the evidences which the senses provide in proving the *real* humanity of Christ, the Living Word, thus refuting the Gnostic claim that Christ was not truly human. "The Word of life," 1, is a reference to Christ as the One who came to bring eternal life to sinners dead in sin (Jn 3:16). He was eternally coexistent with the Father, 2, and manifested to men in the incarnation (Jn 1:1-2).

The Incarnation and Fellowship, 3-4. The purpose of the incarnation was to give "life," which constitutes the basis, or necessary prerequisite, of fellowship between regenerated sinners and God the Father and God the Son. The aim of John, as well as the other apostles, in writing was that their Christian readers might have fellowship (*koinōnia,* partnership in common participation of an experience) with them in sharing intimate contact and communion with God, 3, which in turn would bring "filled full" joy, 4. Fellowship with the Father and the Son brings such joy!

1:5-10. THE CONDITIONS OF FELLOWSHIP

Walking in the Light, 5-8. This walk of fellowship "in the light" (a metaphor for life) depends upon the believer's having a *right concept of God,* i.e., that "God is light" (Jn 3:20-21; 1 Tim 6:16), 5. He is absolute holiness without taint of evil, "no not even one iota of darkness" (Gr). What light is to the world of nature, so God is to the world of the spirit. Other requirements for a walk in fellowship are: having *a life separated from sin,* 6; *claiming the cleansing power of Christ's sacrifice* from daily sins of defilement, 7; and *recognizing the presence of the old nature,* 8, lest believers lead themselves astray, shutting out the light because of self-deception. The apostle states, "If we say that we have no sin [nature, principle or root], we deceive ourselves, and the truth is not in us."

Each requirement cited above is revealed by the apostolic message, 5a. This Word must be believed if one is to act thereon and thus "walk in the light."

Confessing Our Sins, 9-10. Confession of our sins to God brings forgiveness and cleansing. Such involves our frankly admitting and openly avowing our known sins, 10, realizing they spring from the old sin nature which is still with us (v. 8), and also realizing that they have broken our fellowship with an infinitely holy God. In true confession admission must be accompanied by repentance, a turning from our sins to the sacrifice of Christ as the means of cleansing from their defilement. God promises, in response to such confession, to remove these sins as a barrier to our fellowship through the blood of Christ (v. 7), for He bore our sins in His redemptive work—sins past, present and future (Rom 3:4, 25-26; 2 Cor 5:21; 1 Jn 5:10), 9.

Personal confession involves an acknowledgment that we have sinned in act. Failure to admit this makes God a liar, for His Word clearly states that man has sinned. The life of victory and fellowship is possible only when sin is admitted, confessed, and forsaken.

2:1-2. THE ADVOCACY OF CHRIST AND FELLOWSHIP

Fellowship Maintained Godward by Christ's Advocacy, 1. The apostle gives his readers to understand that what has been said in the foregoing chapter about sin and its forgiveness was stated "in order that you may not sin" at all! He now proceeds to explain the nature of the remedy for sin when a believer does commit an act of sin through infirmity, because the old nature can still be active unless continually reckoned dead (Rom 6:6). This remedy is based upon the work of *a continually present advocate* who is none other than Jesus Christ the righteous. An advocate is one who is summoned alongside to serve as a helper. Advocacy, then, is that work of our Lord in heaven carried on before the Father's throne by which He represents sinning saints on earth and restores them to fellowship with the Father on the basis of His eternally efficacious sacrifice (Ps 23:3; Jn 13:10). He pleads the cause of the believer against Satan, the "accuser of the brethren" (Rev 12:10). It is because our Lord is *righteous* that He can plead with the righteous Father.

The Efficacy of Christ's Advocacy, 2. Christ Himself is the all-sufficient Advocate because *He Himself* (Gr. intensive) is the personal "Propitiator." Propitiation means satisfaction, and Christ is the satisfaction for our sins. His redemptive sacrifice constituted the satisfaction which God demanded for sin, and it was sufficient for the sins of the whole world, the entire human race (making them savable). God the Father does not break fellowship with the sinning believer, because Christ the Advocate pleads the satisfaction of His sacrifice as sufficient for all the believer's sin.

2:3-6. OBEDIENCE AND FELLOWSHIP

Assurance of Being in Fellowship, 3-5. The believer may be assured, or may know, that he is in fellowship by the proof of obedience, 3-5.

Knowledge of Christ is inseparably linked to obeying Him and loving Him, 5b.

The Duty of the Believer Claiming to Be in Fellowship, 6. The Christian is *bound* ("ought") to imitate Christ in His walk (humility and self-sacrifice) if he claims to "abide in Him." *Abiding* may be defined by using John's definition in 3:24: habitual fellowship maintained by continual obedience to His commandments. "Even as" or "in the same manner" indicates that the imitation of Christ is to be exact and true to pattern.

2:7-11. BROTHERLY LOVE AND FELLOWSHIP

Love, the Expression of Fellowship, 7-8. This indispensable ingredient of fellowship in one sense does not involve a new commandment, 7. It is "the one we had from the beginning" (Lev 19:18; Deut 6:5; Mt 22:37-40; Mk 12:28-31; 2 Jn 5). Yet in another sense it does involve a new commandment, 8. Jesus also called it "new" and gave it a new motive, "Love one another *as I have loved you*" (Jn 13:34-35; 15:12). It was new with a fresh dynamic, because it was realized in Christ, and is realized in the believer when he walks as Christ walked, 8b.

Hatred, the Denial of Fellowship, 9-11. Hatred destroys fellowship because it belongs to the spiritual realm of darkness where fellowship with the God of light is impossible, 9. Love, on the other hand, belongs to the realm of light where fellowship with God and with the brethren flourishes, 10. The loving Christian gives no occasion for a fellow believer to stumble because of him. Hatred not only kills fellowship but breeds spiritual ignorance and blindness, 11.

2:12-14. SPIRITUAL MATURITY AND FELLOWSHIP

The Father's Family, 12. The addressees of this letter of John's were all God's children. He describes them as "little children" (*teknia*, "born-again ones," "God's bairns") whose sins have been remitted. Thus, they all have the privilege of fellowship in the family, irrespective of growth or maturity.

Fellowship and Christian Growth, 13-14. Those who develop spiritually and enjoy the full privilege of fellowship are described in these verses from the most mature to the babies. The mature, "fathers," are characterized by a seasoned knowledge of Christ—"him that is from the beginning" (Jn 1:1, 14). This knowledge is experiential and the result of intimate fellowship with the Father and the Son. The "young men," those growing in maturity, are commended because they emphatically overcome the wicked one (Satan), the outcome of being strong spiritually and of having "the word of God abiding in them." The immature, "little children" (*paidia,* "infants"), are spiritually undeveloped and are to be distinguished from the "dear sons" (*teknia*) of verse 12. Although some are immature, all believers are in the family of God and know Him as Father and Christ as the Forgiver of their sins, 12. The need is for all to grow up and enter the full privileges of fellowship.

2:15-17. THE PERIL OF WORLDLINESS AND FELLOWSHIP

The Peril Warned Against, 15a. This warning is couched in a twofold command: (1) "Do not love the world" (*kosmos*), the world system under which Satan has organized fallen mankind upon his God-opposing principles of pride, selfishness and ambition (Mt 4:8-9; Eph 2:2; 6:12); (2) "nor the things in the world," such as its wealth, pleasure or honors. It is useless to claim we do not love the world yet love what it offers.

The Reason for the Warning, 15b-17. (1) Love for the world excludes love for God, 15*b*-16. "If any one goes on loving the world, love for the Father is not in him!" So contrary is the evil world to all that God is, both cannot be loved at the same time. "The world" embraces "the lust of the flesh," the keen desire of the unregenerate man centered upon self and opposed to God (Rom 7:18); "the lust of the eyes," those keen appetites which master our body, soul and spirit through the eye gate (2 Sam 11:2; Josh 7:21; Ps 119:37); "the pride of life," i.e., the vainglorious display of godless living. Thus the evil world is completely at variance with our infinitely holy God, 16*b*. (2) The world is fleeting and impermanent, 17*a*. It it even now passing by, in a state of transition like a parade and it will soon be gone, as well as "its lusts." By contrast, the doer of God's will is destined for permanence, 17*b*. "But he who continually does God's will remains forever," even as God abides forever (Ps 90:2), for he is linked eternally with God in Christ and in present unbroken fellowship.

2:18-23. LOYALTY TO THE FAITH AND FELLOWSHIP

Doctrinal Defection, the Foe of Fellowship, 18-21. John again addresses "little children," perhaps emphasizing their immaturity in contrast to the writer's authority and spiritual experience. He reminds them that "it is the last time," 18*a,* or literally "the last hour," furthering the idea of the passing away of the present world (v. 17). This entire present age may be characterized as "the last hour" with an acceleration of defection as the second advent draws nearer (1 Tim 4:1-5; 2 Tim 3:1-5; Jude 17-18). The apostle then identifies the source of much opposition to the truth by affirming both the presence of many *antichrists* in his day and the coming of *the* Antichrist at a future time (2 Thess 2:3-10; Rev 13:1-10). "Antichrist" means one who is opposed to Christ but under the guise of Christ, 18.

These Christ-opposers belonged to the church outwardly, but "were not of us"—not organically identified with the body of believers, 19. For them defection or apostasy was natural and "they went out." Their *defection proved their false profession.* Fellowship with Christ and His church is never possible for those who deny Him.

On the other hand, God's children are protected from the peril of defection and the influence of false teachers by the unction (anointing) of the Holy Spirit given by "the Holy One"—Christ Himself. This anointing enables believers to discern between truth and error, and to discover those who are antichrists, 20, by the Spirit's help. This epistle was written because of the existence of the antichrists who stood opposed to the truth and because John's readers knew the truth, 21.

The Essence of Doctrinal Defection, 22-23. Writing against the background of the Gnostic heresy, John identifies the defectors as those who deny the deity of Jesus, 22. The Gnostics (liars) denied that Jesus was the God-Man, stating that the Christ-spirit came upon Jesus at His baptism and departed before His death. By denying the Son they also denied the Father, since the Son is the revelation of the Father and the only way to the Father (Jn 14:6, 9), 22*b.* This last thought is given emphasis in 23. Fellowship with God the Father and the Son is never possible to those who deny the Son. To deny Him by refusing to accept His deity is to forfeit the privilege of a living relationship with Him. Doctrinal defection gives evidence of personal rejection.

2:24-29. ABIDING IN CHRIST AND FELLOWSHIP

Adherence to the Truth, 24-26. In contrast to those who promote error (18-23), believers are to allow the foundational truths of the gospel ("that which ye have heard from the beginning") to abide in them. Such adherence results in fellowship (abiding) with the Son and the Father, 24. The promise and present possession of those who abide, is eternal life, 25. In addition, adherence to the truth will deliver believers from "them that seduce you"—those actively attempting to lead you astray, 26.

Reliance Upon the Holy Spirit, 27-29. The Holy Spirit is the anointing ("unction, v. 20) which believers receive at the time of conversion. He abides in the believer and teaches him "all things," guiding him into "all truth" (Jn 16:13), 27. Abiding results in one's having confidence and in not being ashamed at the coming of Christ, 28. The fruit of abiding is the practice of righteousness, which gives evidence of one's relationship to and fellowship with the Righteous One, Christ, 29.

3:1-10. RIGHTEOUS LIVING AND FELLOWSHIP

God's Bestowed Love, an Incentive to a Holy Life, 1. The germane thought of 2:29 concerning righteous living is expanded in 3:1-10. John states that there are two reasons why the Christian's life should be a holy one. The first is related to God's past work for us (v. 1), the second is related to His future work (vv. 2-3).

The apostle calls attention to the marvel of God's bestowed love by the use of "Behold!" It should call forth continual admiration and praise. God's bestowal of His superlatively excellent love in making us His children (*teknia*, "bairns") should lead to behavior which befits the family likeness. Such a relationship is unknown by the world because it does not know the Saviour, and such knowledge comes only through personal experience.

Christ's Coming, an Incentive to a Holy Life, 2-3. God's future work of transforming the believer by glorification at the coming of Christ should also motivate him to a righteous life. Because we are "children of God" (v. 1) we shall be glorified when Christ is visibly manifested. This glorification includes a new resurrection body, sinlessness, complete righteousness, and full purity, 2. Whoever has this hope "resting on him" continually purifies himself in his daily walk, 3.

A Holy Life, the Intent of Salvation, 4-5. Sin is lawlessness, and it follows that everyone who continually practices sin transgresses the law (law in its broadest scope), 4. Christ appeared as the answer to the sin problem—to remove sins, making a holy life possible for those who possess His salvation, 5. He, the sinless Saviour, is our example, 5b.

A Holy Life and Fellowship, 6-10. The person who is abiding in Christ does not sin habitually (present tense, "does not go on sinning continually"), 6a. On the other hand, the one who sins continually (also present tense) has never seen Christ with the eye of faith nor known Him experientially as his own Saviour, 6b. Righteous deeds are the fruit of a righteous character and proof of regeneration, 7. Such *holiness is the family likeness*, 7b.

As righteousness is the family image for God's family, so the continual practice of *sin is the image of the devil's family*, 8a. Sin has been the constant mark of Satan's character, 8b, "from the beginning" (Isa 14:12-14; Ezek 28:11-15). Since Christ's redeeming work was purposed to destroy Satan's works, Christians cannot practice what their Lord and Saviour came to destroy, 8c. Furthermore, no member of God's family (God's "bairn ones," 9a) habitually practices sin, because the new nature (God's "seed") abides in him and he cannot sin as a pattern of life, 9. The new nature (bestowed at the time of regeneration or new birth), by its very presence in the believer, will never permit continual sinning. The apostle then climaxes this section by furnishing the criterion for distinguishing the redeemed from the unconverted—the family of God from the family of the devil, 10. That standard is *the practice of righteousness*. which is expressed through brotherly love.

3:11-18. BROTHERLY LOVE AND FELLOWSHIP

The Fellowship of Love, 11-15. A constant exhortation of God's Word is, "Love one another," 11. The fellowship of God's family is to be permeated by the atmosphere of love. The example of Cain is given as an illustration and warning of one who was unregenerate, of the Evil One (the devil, cf. 8, 10), and thus without God's love, 12. His hatred found its logical outcome in murder, proving his deeds evil and his brother's righteous (cf. Gen 4:1-16; Heb 11:4). The attitude of the world toward God's own is one of hate because love is alien to it—the prince of this world (Satan) being the father of hate (v. 10), 13. Love gives evidence of regeneration and new life, 14, while hate furnishes evidence of spiritual death, 15.

The Manifestation of Love, 16-18. The supreme manifestation of love was Christ's incarnation and death (Jn 3:16; Rom 5:8), which furnishes an example of love in action, 16. Such evidence of love should be practical, not merely theoretical, 17-18. "To lay down our lives" may take the practical turn of sacrifice for others in need, 17. Loving "in word or speech" with intention but without deed is hypocrisy, not genuine love, 18 (Jas 1:22).

3:19-24. CHRISTIAN ASSURANCE AND FELLOWSHIP

The Nature of Assurance, 19-21. Assurance, or certainty of salvation and acceptance with God, depends on the practice of genuine love, 19. By our loving "in deed and in truth" (v. 18) we know that we are really Jesus' disciples and belong to the truth as it is in Jesus, and shall reassure our hearts that all doubts as to our acceptance before God have been removed. *But* if our "heart" (the seat of our emotions and will, our inner judge) accuses us because our brotherly-love life is too lenient or too strict, "God is greater than our heart," since He is omniscient, 20. We then appeal to Him for correct judgment about ourselves. If, on the other hand, our hearts do not condemn us, then we have double assurance of approach and freedom of speech ("confidence") before God, 21.

The Realization of Fellowship, 22-24. Experiential communion with the Father is enjoyed through a *dynamic prayer life* and *constant obedience,* 22-23. This latter involves believing in Christ's finished redemptive work and the subsequent practicing of brotherly love. Obedience results in abiding in Him, 24. The Christian knows he is abiding when he is obeying. The Holy Spirit witnesses to Christ's abiding in the believer (cf. Jn 14:16-21; 15:1-10).

4:1-6. DISCERNMENT OF ERROR AND FELLOWSHIP

The Presence of Error, 1. Error threatens the fellowship of God's own. Believers are here enjoined to "try the spirits"—those spiritual powers which energize all teachers—"because many false prophets have gone into the world" and the consequent threat to the fellowship is a grave one. The origin of all teachers must be tested, "whether they are from God." Teachers who are not from God are false prophets, energized by demon spirits which give them their zeal.

The Acid Test of Error, 2-6. The essence of this test is the confession of *Christ's deity* and *incarnation,* and it is this confession which distinguishes between those energized by the Spirit of God and those false teachers empowered by the spirit of error (Antichrist), 2-3a. Every Christian heresy can be traced to a faulty view of Christ's person and consequent work. The immediate danger of error is again stressed by the reminder that the spirit of Antichrist is already in the world, 3b. However, God's own have living in them a greater power (the Holy Spirit) than that at work in the world (Satan's power), and the Spirit enables them to overcome false teachers, 4, whose source of speech is "from the world" and whose audience is "the world," 5. A teacher's hearers are a further test of his source of power—only those who are increasing in the knowledge of God continue to listen to the apostles ("us"), 6.

4:7-18. LOVE AND THE MANIFESTATION OF FELLOWSHIP

Love, a Family Characteristic, 7-8. This is the third time the apostle has dealt with the subject of love (2:7-11; 3:10-18). It is introduced at this point perhaps because love is the great bond of fellowship which binds believers to one another, and to their Lord, in the face of Satan's threats. True love (*agapē*) has its source in God and is a characteristic of every one who has been begotten of God, those who personally know Him, 7. Their behavior is to reveal their character in their loving one another, 7a. On the other hand, those who do not habitually love as a pattern of life reveal the fact that they are unrelated to God, not having experiential knowledge of Him, 8a. God, by His very nature, is love, 8b. His children bear this likeness.

The Supreme Manifestation of Love, 9-10. The greatest manifestation of God's love for men was His giving of His only begotten Son (Jn 3:16), 9a. Christ was His only born Son in a totally unique sense, sent so that we who were dead in sin might live through Him, 9b. The nature of God's love is seen in His loving us apart from any reciprocal love on our part—it is impossible for fallen men to love God, 10a. Because He is such love, God sent Christ to be the satisfaction ("propitiation") for our sins, 10b.

The Obligation to Love, 11-12. Believers have a moral obligation ("ought") to love one another since God loved us to the extent of giving His only born Son, 11. Since no one has ever beheld God, the only way He who is love can be seen is by His children's loving one another and thus revealing the family likeness, 12a. By our so doing, His love (the love which is His nature) accomplishes its full purpose ("is perfected"), 12b.

Love and the Indwelling Presence of God, 13-16. The Holy Spirit, who indwells each believer, imparts knowledge of God's presence and of our union with Him (cf. Jn 15:1-10), 13. As a result the Spirit enables us to testify of Christ's saviorhood, 14. Confession of Christ's deity (implying also surrender to Him) establishes union with God, 15. Those who respond to God's love find that love becomes a working force in their lives, bringing the attendant blessings of fellowship ("abiding") with Him and His abiding presence in them, 16.

The Perfection of Love in Us, 17-18. The Holy Spirit brings the love which God produces in us to maturity and full development so that we may have confidence, or boldness, in the day of the judgment seat of Christ, 17. *Mature love results in the assurance* that we will be unashamed in that day because of our likeness to Christ—particularly with reference to love ("as he is, so are we"), 17*b*. Also, mature love *gives fearlessness,* for fear and love cannot be mixed, 18. Love involves the self-giving of one for the highest good of another; fear involves shrinking from another because of guilt. God's love has removed our guilt, thus fear of punishment is also gone.

4:19-21. THE INCENTIVE TO LOVE AND FELLOWSHIP

The Incentive to Love, 19. God's love for us, demonstrated by His giving His Son, is the great incentive for our loving continually (present tense). If His love was so great "first," then it is expected that His children will love as a result.

The Fellowship of Love, 20-21. Our love for our brother proves our love for God. It is humanly easier to love one whom we can see than God whom we cannot see. Then how inconsistent to say that we love God but hate our brother. We cannot love God if we hate our brother. The circle of fellowship is complete when we show our love for God by loving our brother. This is the express command of God, 21. (Cf. Lev 19:18; Mt 22:39; Jn 13:34; 15:12.)

5:1-5. FAITH AND FELLOWSHIP

Faith Introduces Us to Fellowship, 1-3. Faith in Christ, bringing the experience of the new birth, is the basis of fellowship, 1. This is *a fellowship of love,* 1*b*-2*a*. "Everyone who loves the parent [God the Father] loves the child [the believer]." It is also *a fellowship of obedience,* 2*b*-3. The proof that we love God and His children is that we also keep His commandments (2:3; 3:22-24; 2 Jn 6). Observing God's commandments is not "grievous" (Gr. *bareiai,* "severely oppressive" or "hard to be borne"), because we love God and show our love for Him by obedience.

Faith Gives Victory, 4-5. Faith operates through believers to overcome the world, the foe of God's family, 4*a*. "Overcomes" is in the present tense and conveys the thought of habitually conquering in a continuous victory, wrought by faith. This victorious faith is centered in the person of Christ, 5. He conquered the world Himself (Jn 16:33); therefore we overcome the world through Him.

827

5:6-12.   TESTIMONY AND FELLOWSHIP

The Testimony Concerning the Son, 6-10. The *first witness* is external and is to Christ's righteousness and to His redemption, 6. "This is He who came through water and blood." "Through water" refers to the inauguration of our Lord's public ministry by His baptism in the Jordan (Mt 3:13-17), by which He identified Himself with a ministry of *righteousness.* "Through blood" refers to His vicarious death on the cross (Heb 9:12) by which *redemption* from sin was accomplished.

The *second witness* is internal and is that of the Holy Spirit, 6b. He continues to bear witness to Jesus' righteousness and redemption, and because He is truth His testimony is absolutely true. Verse 7 is not in the oldest and best manuscripts and should be omitted.

The witness to Christ's person and work is threefold and consistent, 8. Accordingly, there are three witnesses, "the Spirit, the water, and the blood, and these agree" (Gr. "attest the same truth"). This witness is wholly reliable, 9, for if we receive the testimony of men on the strength of two or three witnesses (Deut 19:15; Mt 18:16; Jn 8:16-18), how much more should we receive the greater and better attested witness of God concerning His Son? Furthermore, when received by faith this testimony becomes one's own personal witness, 10a. But refused, it means the unbeliever, in rejecting God's plan of redemption, makes God a liar, 10b. In effect the rejecter is saying, "I don't believe it!"

God's Testimony Believed, 11-12. The testimony is: "God has given us eternal life, and this life is in His Son" (Gr.), 11. The result deduced is that he who has the Son possesses eternal life. The converse is also true, he who rejects the testimony does not have the Son of God and hence does not possess eternal life, 12. God's entire program of salvation is centered in His Son. Man must make a choice regarding Him!

5:13-15.   PRAYER AND FELLOWSHIP

The Importance of Assurance, 13. The apostle's purpose in writing to believers was that they might have assurance of eternal life. Such confidence provides the basis for joyful prayer and fellowship.

Power in Prayer, 14-15. Assurance of salvation gives: (1) confidence of access to God's presence (*pros,* "face to face with Him"), 14a; (2) breadth of petition, 14b, "if we ask *anything*"; (3) consciousness of God's will, 14c, "according to His will"; (4) faith to believe, 14d, "confidence . . . He hears us"; (5) confidence we will receive an answer to the requests made, 15.

5:16-21. PRAYER FELLOWSHIP AND THE SINNING CHRISTIAN

Prayer and the Problem of Serious Sin, 16-17. It is possible for a true believer to fall into sin, 16a. If and when this happens, a fellow believer is to pray for him, 16b. As a result God will give the sinning Christian preservation of physical life (not eternal life, for this life is eternal and unforfeitable). However, this intercession is effective only in the case of sin not unto physical death, 16c.

"There is a *sin unto death*," 16d. This is persistent, willful sinning in a believer in which "the flesh is destroyed" (physical death) so "that the spirit might be saved" (1 Cor 5:1-5; Acts 5:1-11; 1 Cor 11:30). Both Saul and Samson are types of this very severe chastening in the OT. This sin is *not to be prayed for* because it involves the execution of an immutable law of God unaltered by prayer, 16e. Sin has different degrees of seriousness, 17. "All unrighteousness is sin, but there is a sin which is not unto [physical] death" (involving lesser chastisements, cf. 1 Cor 11:30).

Sin and Its Remedy, 18-20. The primary remedy for habitual sin is *the new birth*, 18. "We know that everyone who has been born of God does not go on practicing sin as a habit. He having been begotten of God, this divine life keeps him from continually practicing sin, and Satan does not touch him." The believer's *new position* is also a remedy for sin, 19. He is born of God and into His family. In contrast, the world (all unsaved) is in the power of Satan, 19b. Finally, *our understanding of the truth* is a deterrent to habitual sin, 20. Truth and life mark the realm of the child of God.

Concluding Charge, 21. The aged apostle adds a final note for his "little children": "Guard yourselves from idols." An idol is anything that usurps God's place in one's life. Ephesus was full of idolatry and its practices, making these words very appropriate.

2 JOHN

WALKING IN TRUTH AND LOVE

Writer and Destination. Second John is a personal note, sent by the apostle John to "an elect lady and her children." The identity of this woman (or church?) is not known, though some scholars maintain the name is "*Lady Electa*" (the Gr. for "chosen," or *kyria,* the Gr. word for "lady"). This Christian matron lived somewhere in the circuit of churches over which the aged apostle John had the oversight. That John was the writer is apparent from the style and content of the note, which strikingly resembles 1 and 3 John and the Gospel of John.

Date and Purpose. There is no suggestion of any great interval between the writing of 1 John and 2 John. John's purpose in penning the letter was to warn this influential and esteemed lady (1-2) against false teachers. She apparently sponsored meetings with visiting preachers in her home (10), like Nympha (RSV) in Laodicea (Col 4:15). The apostle encourages her and warns against unsound doctrine by suggesting she sponsor no one who teaches less than the full deity and humanity of Christ.

VERSES 1-6. WALKING IN TRUTH AND LOVE

The Salutation, 1-3. John, in this more intimate epistle, styles himself simply "elder" (Acts 11:30; Tit 1:5-9), using a less authoritative designation than "apostle." He professes to "love the elect lady and her children in the truth," 1a. True Christian love rests on "the truth," i.e., the revealed Word of God focused in the person and work of Christ (Jn 14:6), and contrasts with false teaching, which errs at this point (see 7-11). Fellowship in the truth produces a breadth of love as wide as the communion of faith, 1b. Such truth is the only sure basis of genuine love, both in the present and in the future, 2. Grace, mercy and peace have their source in God the Father and Jesus Christ the Son, 3. Thus, they are founded in truth and love.

The Exhortation, 4-6. The apostle greatly rejoiced that he found some of her children walking (living their entire daily lives) in truth—the truth of the gospel. Their conduct conformed to the truth as it was manifested in Christ. John urges the practice of Christian love as the natural outcome of the truth, as he did in the first epistle (see notes on 1 Jn 2:7-8).

VERSES 7-13. REFUSING THE FALSE FELLOWSHIP
OF ERROR

The Presence of Error Indicated, 7-9. "For," 7a, emphasizes the contrast between the preceding verses and those which follow, showing that error violates the revealed truth of God and the commandment of love. Such false teaching is promulgated by "many deceivers" who "have gone forth into the world," 7b. Essentially, their error is a refusal to "confess Jesus Christ is come in the flesh," thereby denying the *possibility* of the incarnation and by implication also denying both advents of Christ.

The presence of error also calls for self-examination on the part of the believers, lest the false teachers undo in the fellowship what the apostles had accomplished, thus resulting in loss of reward for the Christian, 8. Those who go on ahead (perhaps, "lead on ahead" in the sense of spiritual leadership) in professing identity with the Christian fellowship must also be examined, especially when they "fail to remain in the doctrine of Christ." To so fail indicates lack of relationship to God and spiritual bankruptcy, 9.

Refusal to Admit False Teachers, 10-11. Evidently the above teachers of error were being entertained in Christian homes under the cloak of hospitality. The apostle sternly forbids the continuance of this practice and commands believers not to grant such fellowship and Christian hospitality, 10. Even the giving of a customary greeting is forbidden, for this would show identification and participation with the person's evil deeds, 11. Separation from error is necessary (2 Cor 6:14-17).

Conclusion, 12-13. The apostle anticipates a personal visit, 12, and sends greetings from "the elect lady's" sister, 13.

3 JOHN

Help and Hospitality Toward Itinerant Ministers

Author. Similarity of tone, ideas and style, as well as evidence from Irenaeus, Clement of Alexandria, Dionysius of Alexandria, Cyprian and others, indicates that this epistle was written by the same author as 1 John, namely, John the beloved disciple.

Date and Place of Writing. According to Eusebius (*Ecclesiastical History* 3:25) John returned from the Patmos exile to Ephesus after the death of Domitian (A.D. 96), spending his closing years visiting the Asiatic churches (cf. 2 Jn 12; 3 Jn 10, 14), ordaining elders and ministering. Therefore, 2 John and 3 John were written after the Apocalypse, if Eusebius is correct.

VERSES 1-8. GAIUS' EXAMPLE OF WALKING IN TRUTH AND LOVE

The Apostle's Salutation to Gaius, 1-4. The epistle is addressed from "the elder" (see 2 Jn 1) to "the well-beloved Gaius," who was possibly Gaius of Derbe (Acts 20:4), Gaius of Corinth (Rom 16:23; 1 Cor 1:14), Gaius of Macedonia (Acts 19:29), or Gaius the bishop of Pergamos (mentioned in the *Apostolic Constitutions* 7:40). Whoever is meant, the apostle professes his genuine love for him, 1; wishes him physical health, 2a; and expresses confidence in his spiritual vitality, 2b. John's greeting includes a prayer for Gaius' spiritual and physical well-being, and expresses joy for his walk in the truth, 3-4 (cf. 1 Thess 2:19-20).

Gaius' Walk in the Truth, 5-8. This walk, or manner of daily living, is demonstrated by *the good works such a faith produces,* 5, for the brethren, especially traveling Christian workers ("strangers") who were dependent on the church for support rather than on pagans; *the hospitality and love such a life shows,* 6; *the consideration such a life displays,* 7.

VERSES 9-11. EXAMPLE OF A CONTRARY WALK

The Example, 9-10. Diotrephes, in contrast to Gaius and Demetrius, 1-8, 12, did not walk in love and the truth because he was carnally ambitious, 9. John had written to the church of which Diotrephes was a member. The latter had rejected some suggestions the apostle had made, "loving to have the place of preeminence." He also manifested the works of the flesh, 10*a*, and was uncharitable and domineering, 10*b*.

The Warning, 11. Diotrephes' life was evil and not to be imitated. He was not "of God" nor had he "seen God," his evil life proving this.

VERSES 12-14. DEMETRIUS' GOOD EXAMPLE

Demetrius' Good Report, 12. The good testimony to the walk of Demetrius (unknown) was universal, including the witness of the truth itself and that of John. This was in stark contrast to the report given of Diotrephes.

Closing Observations, 13-14 (cf. 2 Jn 12).

JUDE

CONTENDING FOR THE FAITH

The Author and Attestation. The author was evidently the brother
of James, who was the bishop of Jerusalem and the writer of the
Epistle of James (Jas 1:1; cf. Mt 13:55; Mk 6:3), and the (half)
brother of our Lord, 1. At first an unbeliever (Jn 7:3-8), he became convinced of Jesus' deity (Acts 1:14). Some scholars, however,
identify him as the apostle Judas (Jude, Mt 10:2-3), called Lebbaeus
or Thaddaeus (Lk 6:16; Acts 1:13). Echoes and allusions to the
epistle occur in the writings of Hermas, Polycarp, Athenagoras,
Theophilus of Antioch and Tertullian, so that Jude has stronger
external attestation than 2 Peter.

Occasion and Date. Little is known of the circumstances or date
of writing, except that the declension it inveighs against is more
developed than in 2 Peter and hence appears to be written later,
after A.D. 66 or 67. The deep apostasy it describes furnishes background for the Apocalypse, before which it is placed in English
Bibles. The Spirit of God gave both Jude and Peter a similar note
of warning, so sorely needed by the church.

VERSES 1-4. CONTENDING FOR THE FAITH

Salutation, 1-2. Jude addresses believers in general, citing their
election, their preservation, and their status as "beloved in God the
Father."

The Occasion of the Epistle, 3-4. The author's original purpose
was to write a doctrinal epistle, 3a, "concerning our common salvation." This "common" (*koinēs*, "belong equally to more than
one") salvation was for *all* believers. False teachers threatened the
teaching of this general truth involving Christ's person and finished
work. Jude, therefore, found it necessary to switch to *an exhortation
to militantly defend the faith,* 3b. "The faith" is that which was once
for all delivered to the saints. No other revelation or faith is needed,
for it is complete and final. It is the answer to those who claim
revelation and truths in addition to the canonical Scriptures. The
intrusion of false teachers brought error concerning the doctrine
of the person and work of Christ, especially with respect to His
sovereignty and lordship, 4. This is the primary error of all false
teaching (cf. 2 Pet 2:1).

VERSES 5-7. HISTORICAL WARNINGS OF GOD'S JUDGMENT

The Israelites in the Wilderness, 5. Since those addressed in this epistle already knew all the facts once for all, Jude needed only to remind them of these things, 5a. These facts are: that "the Lord, having saved [delivered] the people out of Egypt, afterward destroyed them that did not believe," i.e., at Kadesh-barnea (Num 14:1-45; 1 Cor 10:1-5; Heb 3:17-19). This divine judgment for disobedience was upon God's own people and involved the sin unto physical death (cf. 1 Cor 5:1-5; 11:30-32; 1 Jn 5:16).

The Fallen Angels, 6. Evidently, the sin of these specially designated angels was that they "did not keep their first estate," their own initial distinctive order as purely spirit beings, but "abandoned their proper sphere of dwelling" by cohabiting with mortal women and thus producing the condition which necessitated the Flood (Gen 6:1-6; 2 Pet 2:4-5). Their punishment for disobedience is imprisonment in Tartarus (see 2 Pet 2:4). Their judgment will be at "the great day," probably in association with Satan's judgment (Rev 20:10).

The Sinners of Sodom and Gomorrah, 7 (cf. Gen 19; 2 Pet 2:6-8). Their sin, "in similar manner" to the angels of verse 6, was sexual immorality and perversion, "giving themselves over to fornication [promiscuity], and going after strange [Gr. different] flesh," i.e., unnatural vice. Their judgment served as an example to warn others of the judicial punishment of eternal fire. The literal fire by which they were consumed is a symbol of the eternal fire to which the wicked have been consigned (Rev 19:20; 20:10, 14; cf. Mt 25:41).

VERSES 8-16. FALSE TEACHERS

Their Presumption Indicated, 8. This sin of false teachers (v. 4) is revealed by their *failure to heed the historical warnings* of divine judgment illustrated in 5-7 (Gr. "in like manner notwithstanding" the warnings given), 8a; their *dreaming state*—dreaming, as natural men who are spiritually asleep; their *sexual immorality*—"defile the flesh" (cf. v. 7); their *insubordination*—they "despise authority," particularly that of God's Word; their *slander*—they "speak evil of dignities" (earthly and heavenly dignitaries).

Their Presumption Illustrated, 9-10. When Michael the archangel contended with the devil about the literal body of Moses, because it was raised for the transfiguration (Mt 17:3-4) previous to its allotted time, he did not presume to bring an abusive judgment upon Satan, out of reverence for his former dignity (v. 8c), but simply said, "The Lord rebuke you" (Zech 3:2). In contrast, these men revile (scoff at) anything which they do not understand, showing no reverence for any authority. By those things that they do know, by animal instinct, they corrupt themselves and are destroyed.

Reasons for Their Woe, 11. These teachers of error are *self-willed religious naturalists,* "running riotously in the way of Cain" (Gen 4:3-8). Cain was a type of the religious natural man who rejects blood redemption and molds his own religion of human merit and works to suit himself, 11a. They are *mercenary religious moralists,* having "abandoned themselves for the sake of gain to Balaam's error," 11b (RSV; Num 22—24). This error was the mistake of supposing that a righteous God must curse sinning Israel and displayed ignorance of the higher morality of the cross whereby God can be righteous and at the same time eternally justify the believing sinner (cf. 2 Pet 2:15; Rev 2:14). They are also *lawless religionists,* having "perished in the rebellion [like that] of Korah" (Num 16:1-50; 26:9-11). Korah's sins were a denial of God's authority through Moses as His chosen mouthpiece, and Korah's consequent intrusion into the priests' office. Rejection of the authority of God's Word is characteristic of all false teachers.

Their Spiritual Sterility, 12-13. The spiritual emptiness of these teachers is indicated by their *peril,* 12a. "They are hidden rocks" (ASV) on which the Christians' love feasts were in danger of being wrecked by their selfish and carnal carousing (cf. 1 Cor 11:30-32). Their sterility is also seen in their *barrenness,* 12b. They are "waterless windswept clouds, trees without fruit, twice [doubly] dead, uprooted," being spiritually lifeless to begin with, and when plucked up by the roots, visibly proved dead. Their *shame,* 13a (Isa 57:20), and their *deception,* 13b, further reveal the lack of spiritual reality.

Their Judgment Predicted, 14-15. This prophecy, preserved as tradition in the noncanonical book of Enoch (1:9), is here given by the Holy Spirit as divine truth. Jude declares that Enoch prophesied of these false teachers in dim antiquity, and that judgment will take place at Christ's second advent when latter-day apostates will be judged, 15.

Their Character Reviewed, 16. False teachers are declared to be inveterate "murmurers" (grumblers); "complainers" (malcontents); "walking after their own lusts" (loose-livers); boastful (arrogant talkers); and empty flatterers (flattering people to gain advantage).

VERSES 17-25. EXHORTATIONS AND
CLOSING BENEDICTION

Exhortations to God's Own, 17-23. The children of God are to remember the apostolic prophetic warnings, 17-18 (such as 1 Tim 4:1-6; 2 Tim 3:1-10; 2 Thess 2:1-12; 2 Pet 2:1-22). They are to evaluate false teachers correctly, as those who "cause divisions," who are "natural," sensual, without the new nature, and "having not the Spirit" (Rom 8:8-9), hence unsaved.

Believers are to cultivate spiritual growth, 20a, and a Spirit-energized prayer life, 20b; to keep themselves in the sphere of God's love, 21a; to be keenly expectant of God's mercy in the consummation of eternal life, 21b; to show compassion toward those who have honest doubts regarding the faith, those probably influenced by false teachers, 22; to be evangelistic, 23a; and to separate from carnal sins, 23b.

Closing Benediction, 24-25. Praise is ascribed to God for His ability to keep us from stumbling into sin and to present us in a glorified state in His glorious presence. Our safety and security in Him are indeed causes for praise!

REVELATION

CHRIST'S UNVEILING AND KINGDOM

The Title. This great prophetic unfolding is called "the Revelation [Gr. *Apocalypse*] of Jesus Christ." It is *His* revelation given to Him by the Father to be made known to His servants, 1:1. The title "Apocalypse of John" is a traditional designation early used to differentiate it from other apocalypses, the epithet St. John "the Divine" being added in the 4th cen.

Attestation and Authorship. Clear attestation comes from Justin Martyr, Irenaeus, Tertullian and Hippolytus, both as to genuineness and authorship by "John, the apostle and disciple of the Lord." The same is true of Clement of Alexandria, Origen, Victorinus (who wrote a commentary on Revelation), the Muratorian Fragment, Ephraim Syrus, etc. Rejection of the book as non-apostolic by the reformers Luther, Zwingli and Erasmus, in the face of early evidence, seems arbitrary and weightless. Johannine authorship is established by the writer, who calls himself John (1:1, 4, 9; 22:8). The early Church Fathers Clement of Alexandria, Irenaeus and Eusebius declared it was John the apostle who was banished to Patmos (1:9).

Background and Date. Evidence both internal and external (e.g., Irenaeus) places the book toward the end of Emperor Domitian's reign (A.D. 81-96). It was Domitian who had the apostle banished to the rocky island of Patmos in the Aegean Sea (1:9).

Nature of the Book. Revelation is the central terminal where all the great trunk lines of the prophetic Word converge, and is thus the consummation of all revealed truth. It was meant to be understood for the following reasons: (1) It is revelation (an apocalypse), "a making known" or "unveiling." (2) It promises blessing to those who read, hear, and keep its words of prophecy (1:3). (3) The book is not sealed (1:3*b*; 22:10; cf. Dan 12:9). (4) A simple key is furnished to understand the book (1:19). (5) The apocalyptic symbols of the prophecy, which are the vehicles of its interpretation, are found explained elsewhere in Scripture, which in turn furnishes the commentary on this crowning book of consummation.

GREAT PROPHETIC THEMES CONSUMMATED HERE

1. The Lord Jesus Christ, the central subject of all Scripture (Gen 3:15; Rev 1:1).
2. The Church (Mt 16:18; Rev 2—3).

3. The resurrection and glorification of the saints (20:4-6).
4. The Great Tribulation (Deut 4:29-30; Jer 30:5-7; Rev 4—19).
5. Satan and the world system (Isa 14:12-14; Ezk 28:11-18; Rev 12:3-17; 20:1-3, 10).
6. The judgment of the nations (Joel 3:1-10; Mt 25:31-46; Rev 16:13-16).
7. The Antichrist (Ezk 28:1-10; 2 Thess 2:7-10; Rev 13:1-10; 19:20).
8. The kingdom of Messiah over Israel (Isa 11:1-16; Acts 1:6; Rev 20:4-7).
9. The times of the Gentiles (Dan 2:37-44; Lk 21:24; Rev 6:1—19:16).
10. Paradise lost (Gen 3), and paradise regained (Rev 21—22).
11. Israel's covenants (Abrahamic, Gen 12:1-3; Palestinian, Deut 30:1-10; Davidic, 2 Sam 7:4-17; new, Jer 31:31-33).
12. The second advent of Christ (Zech 14:1-14; Rev 19:11-16).
13. The judgment of the wicked (Ps 9:17; Rev 20:11-15).
14. The eternal state with the new heaven and earth (Isa 65:17; 66:22; Rev 21—22).

METHODS OF INTERPRETATION

The Spiritualizing Method. This interpretation takes a mystical or allegorical approach to most of the book. Clement of Alexandria, Origen, and later Augustine and Jerome, followed this method. Recent interpreters who accept this method find the book dealing primarily with the general struggle between the church and evil throughout the entire age, thereby giving encouragement to tested saints. Such an interpretation, however, fails to expound the book meaningfully, and practically ignores the claims to its prophetic nature (1:3; 10:11; 22:7, 10, 18-19). It fails to recognize the interpretive key to the book (1:19) and the focus of Revelation on the second advent, including the climactic events which follow (1:7; 3:11; 16:15; 22:7, 12).

The Praeterist Method. This interpretive school holds that the book has already been practically fulfilled. The older praeterist view maintained it was fulfilled in the defeat of the Jewish enemies of the early church and in the reign of Nero (ch. 6—11), the remaining chapters being vaguely future. From the 17th cen. on, praeterists have held that the church's conflict with Judaism (ch. 4—11) and with paganism (ch. 12—19) is depicted, ch. 20—22 describing her present triumph. This position ignores the interpretive key of 1:19, gives arbitrary meanings to the symbols found in the book, and fails to account for the indications of a *short* span of time covering the events of ch. 4—19 preceding the second advent.

The Continuous-Historical Method. Those who hold to this method maintain that Revelation covers the entire span of church history from John's time to the end of the world. The view has been popular since the time of Berengaud (9th cen.) and Joachim (12th cen.). Wycliffe, Luther, Joseph Mede, Isaac Newton, Bengel, Barnes, and others held it. The inadequacies of the preceding two methods apply to this interpretation as well. It fails to correlate the book with Bible prophecy as a whole, and leaves the details of Revelation without adequate explanation.

The Futurist Method of Interpretation. This school uses the key of 1:19 as a guide in placing most of the book (ch. 4—22) still in the future, grounding interpretation in OT prophecies, such as those relating to "the day of the Lord" (Isa 2:10-22; 4:1-6; 34:1-17), the kingdom (Isa 35:1-10), and Christ's second advent (Zech 14). NT prophecies which refer to Christ's return are correlated with the events recorded in Revelation (e.g., Mt 24—25; Mk 13; Lk 21).

View of the Early Church. The early Church Fathers evidently favored the futurist view because of their belief in the imminent return of the Lord, His subsequent earthly kingdom (cf. Acts 1:6), and in a period of great trouble preceding and inaugurating that kingdom. Justin Martyr, Irenaeus, Hippolytus, Tertullian, and Victorinus held literal views of the future kingdom.

Outline

The Patmos Vision, Ch. 1 (*The Things Seen,* 1:19*a*)

Letters to the Seven Churches, Ch. 2—3 (*The Things Which Are,* 1:19*b*)

Climactic Events of History, Ch. 4—22 (*The Things Which Shall Be Hereafter,* 1:19*c*)

    The Divine Throne in Heaven, Ch. 4—5

    The Great Tribulation on Earth, Ch. 6—18

        Seal judgments, 6:1—8:1

        Trumpet judgments, 8:2—11:19

        Seven personages, 12:1—13:18

        Preview of the end of the Great Tribulation, 14:1-20

        Bowl judgments, 15:1—16:21

        Judgment of Babylon, 17:1—18:24

    The Second Advent and Armageddon, Ch. 19

    The Millennium, the Last Judgment, the Eternal State, Ch. 20—22

1:1-3. INTRODUCTION

The Nature of the Book, 1-2. It is *the* Revelation, the great unveiling *par excellence* of the future, which is *"from* Christ" (subjective genitive), "which God gave unto him." In no sense is Revelation a sealed book, nor a book which is not to be studied and understood. It deals with things which "must" come to pass "shortly" or "soon," and so are of vital import to God's people *now*. It is an unveiling from Christ, given through an angel to John in signs or symbols.

The Purpose of the Book, 3. Its purpose is to bless or make happy the one who reads its words and also "those who hear the words of this prophecy and keep what is written in it." The reason given for so doing is because the time of the fulfillment of its predictions is near. Hearing and keeping will result in faith and stabilizing hope while facing the trials and persecutions of this sinful age, in view of the triumph of Christ and the ultimate triumph of His own.

1:4-8. SALUTATION FROM THE AUTHOR

The Author and Recipients of the Book, 4a. John the apostle is evidently the human author. The recipients are *seven* representative churches in the Roman province of Asia in western Asia Minor. These are representative of conditions in the universal church in every locality during the *entire* Church Age.

Benediction From the Triune God, 4b-8. "Grace and peace" are the two great possessions of the church in Christ (2 Thess 1:2). They come from (1) *God the Father, 4b*, "Him who is and who was and who is to come," a periphrasis for the ineffable name Jehovah (Yahweh), the unchangeable, eternally self-existing One (Ex 3:13-14); (2) *God the Spirit, 4c*, symbolized in the completeness and totality of His activities as "the seven Spirits which are before his [God's] throne" (cf. Isa 11:2; 1 Cor 12:4, 13); (3) *God the Son—Jesus Christ, 5-8*. Jesus, as the center of the book, is described in full detail, including (a) *His obedient earthly life, 5a*, "the faithful witness" (Isa 55:4); (b) *His glorious resurrection, 5b*, "the first begotten [firstborn] from among the dead" (Col 1:18); (c) *His future title and kingdom glory, 5c*, "prince [ruler] of the kings of the earth" (Ps 2:2, 9); (d) *His redemptive work, 5d*, "to him who loved [Gr. 'loves'] us and washed us [the oldest MSS. have 'freed' or 'loosed us,' as from a bond] from our sins in his own blood" (Rom 3:25-26; 1 Pet 1:18-20); (e) *His redemptive accomplishment, 6a*; "and [He] constituted us a kingdom, even priests to His God and

Father" (Gr.); (f) *His worthiness of all praise*, 6b; (g) *His second advent*, 7; (h) *His personal testimony*, 8, "I am the Alpha and the Omega" (the first and last letters of the Gr. alphabet, like our "A to Z"). Hence He is the beginning and end of all things which are consummated in this book (Isa 44:6). He is the real Author of the Revelation (1:1).

PART I. THE THINGS SEEN— THE PATMOS VISION, 1:9-20

1:9-20. THE CIRCUMSTANCES AND THE VISION

The Circumstances, 9-11. The apostle was in banishment on Patmos, an Aegean island ten by six miles, about 37 miles SW of Miletus, off the coast of Asia Minor. He was exiled there by Emperor Domitian in A.D. 95, according to Eusebius, because of his loyalty to the Word of God, 9. The trumpetlike voice is that of Christ, 10, the Alpha and Omega. The seven churches are listed by name, 11 (see notes on ch. 2—3).

The Vision Itself, 12-16. Christ, the glorified One, appears intimately associated with His church on earth, 13. He is "in the midst" of the church, denoted by the seven lampstands or light-holders, Christ Himself being the Light (Jn 8:12). He appears as "Son of Man," here primarily as Judge, evaluating the service of His church on earth.

His snow-white hair, 14a, portrays His eternity, His infinite wisdom, experience and venerableness of character. *His flaming eyes*, 14b (cf. 19:12), bespeak His omniscient insight as Judge, while *His feet like burnished bronze*, 15a, speak of Him who not only walks in the midst of His church to evaluate her service, but who will "tread the winepress of the wrath of Almighty God" (19:15) at His advent to judge sinners and to make war against Satan and the Antichrist (19:11). *His voice like the sound of many waters*, 15b, symbolizes the awe-inspiring pronouncement of the Judge's verdict, whether of commendation of His own (Mt 25:34) or condemnation of the wicked (Mt 25:41). *His right hand*, 16a, once nail-pierced and still bearing the scars as credentials of His divine-human person and finished work (Jn 20:27), qualifies Him for judgment. *His mouth*, 16b, out of which proceeds His sharp two-edged sword of judgment and justice (19:11-15), sets forth the truth that He will pronounce judgment and execute justice on the basis of the Word of God (Eph 6:17; Heb 4:12). *His countenance like the sun,* 16c (cf. Mt 17:2), sets Him forth in the glory of His second advent as Judge (Mal 4:2) and as He will appear in His eternal glory (Rev 21:23).

John's Response to the Vision, 17-18. Prostrated at the sight of the glorified Son of Man appearing as Judge, 17 (cf. Isa 6:1-10), John is given assurance by the resurrected and glorified Christ, who accordingly has "the keys of death and hell" (Hades, the unseen realm where the dead go at death), 18. "The keys" (Mt 16:19) are emblems of authority and access, showing that He alone can open and shut the unseen world, having conquered death Himself.

The Key to All the Visions of the Book, 19. This verse, indispensable to the correct interpretation of Revelation, suggests a threefold division of the book: (1) "The things which you *saw*," i.e., the vision of the Son of Man as Judge (1:10-20); (2) "The things which *are*," i.e., the seven churches then existing in the Roman province of Asia, representative of the church during the entire Church Age (ch. 2—3); (3) "The things which *shall be* afterward"

THE SEVEN CHURCHES OF ASIA

PERGAMOS (REV. 2:12-17)
THYATIRA (REV. 2:18-29)
SARDIS (REV. 3:1-6)
PHILADELPHIA (REV. 3:7-13)
SMYRNA (REV. 2:8-11)
EPHESUS (REV. 2:1-7)
LAODICEA (REV. 3:14-22)

MACEDONIA
ACHAIA
AEGEAN SEA
PATMOS
CRETE
MEDITERRANEAN SEA

843

(Gr. "after these things"), i.e., after the church period ends (ch. 4—22).

The Meaning of the First Vision, 20. The "mystery," a truth previously hidden but now revealed, which nevertheless still has an inscrutable element in it (cf. Mt 13:11), is twofold. (1) *The seven stars* are the messengers, probably not actual angels but more likely men, sent by the seven churches to Patmos to ascertain the aged apostle's condition, and who subsequently became bearers of his message. (2) *The seven lampstands* are the churches (see 1:4, 11). "Stars" and "lampstands" are the luminaries of this dark age, symbols of God's people who are to reflect the One who is the Light of the world (Mt 5:14; Jn 8:12; Eph 5:8; Phil 2:15).

THE SEVEN SEVENS OF THE APOCALYPSE

1. The Seven Churches, 2:1—3:22
2. The Seven Seals, 6:1—8:1
3. The Seven Trumpets, 8:2—11:19
4. The Seven Personages, 12:1—13:18
   The woman, 12:1-2
   The dragon, 12:3-4
   The Man Child, 12:5
   The archangel Michael, 12:7
   The remnant, 12:17
   The beast out of the sea, 13:1-8
   The beast out of the earth, 13:11-18
5. The Seven Bowls 15:1—16:21
6. The Seven Dooms, 17:1—20:15
   Ecclesiastical Babylon, 17:1-18
   Political Babylon, 18:1-24
   Antichrist and the false prophet, 19:20
   Antichristian nations, 19:21
   Gog and Magog, 20:8-9
   Satan, 20:10
   The wicked dead, 20:11-15
7. The Seven New Things, 21:1—22:21
   New heavens, 21:1
   New earth, 21:1
   New city, 21:9-23
   New nations, 21:24-27
   New river, 22:1
   New tree, 22:2
   New throne, 22:3-5

PART II. THE THINGS WHICH ARE—
THE CHURCH AGE, CH. 2—3

2:1-7. EPHESUS—THE LOVELESS CHURCH

Salutation and Commendation, 1-3. The letter is addressed to the "angel" (messenger, see note on 1:20) of the church in Ephesus, the great metropolis of proconsular Asia and the Vanity Fair of the ancient world (see note on Acts 19:8-41 and "Ephesus and Archaeological Discoveries"). The message is from the glorified Judge (Christ), "who holds the seven stars in his right hand" and "walks in the midst of the seven golden lampstands" (His church on earth). The church is commended for its good works, patient endurance and intolerance of evil, especially evildoers and impostors, 2-3 (cf. Acts 20:29-30).

Complaint and Warning, 4-5. The Ephesian church's sin was departure from its initial heartfelt affection for the Lord. "Nevertheless, despite your other excellencies [v. 2], I have this against you that you have abandoned, by imperceptibly quitting, your first love" (the spontaneous affection you had for Me at the first), 4. The warning is sounded in verse 5. They were to *remember* whence they were fallen, 5a. Spontaneous love for the Lord is the height of true spirituality. To leave it is the first step toward a very serious fall. The Lord further enjoins them to *repent,* 5b (change their attitude), and *"do the first works,"* 5c, as a proof of the genuineness of their love. The alternative is forfeiture of testimony, 5d.

Praise and Promise, 6-7. The church is again commended for detesting "the deeds of the Nicolaitanes," a symbolic name apparently of a party attempting to introduce a false freedom into the church. They abused grace, which led to licentiousness, 6 (cf. v. 2; 2 Pet 2:15-16, 19; Jude 4, 11). Some take this symbolism, however, as indicating the origin of clericalism (*nikaō,* "conquer," and *laos,* "people"), making them a group that early favored a clerical system which later developed into the papal hierarchy. To the individual overcomer is promised reward in the eternal state (cf. Gen 2:9; Rev 22:2, 14).

2:8-11. SMYRNA—THE PERSECUTED CHURCH

The Persecution, 8-9. The risen Christ as the Conqueror of death, 1, is the speaker. Smyrna (modern Izmir) is 40 miles N of Ephesus. The city was called the "glory of Asia" because of its planned development, its beautiful temples and ideal harbor. It was a center of Caesar worship and included a large Jewish community among its populace. The Jews of "the synagogue of Satan," 9 (3:9), were Jews nationally but not spiritually. They bitterly blasphemed Christ as "the hanged one" and opposed Christianity, so that in rejecting the truth their synagogue became that of Satan (cf. 1 Tim 4:1-4; 1 Jn 4:1-4). Contrast "the congregation of the Lord" (Num 16:3; 20:4).

The Encouragement, 10-11. The exhortation given is not to fear, 10a (Gr. "Do not fear these things which you are about to suffer"). Why? (1) *God will overrule the devil's temptations.* "Behold, the devil [accuser] will throw some of you into prison that you may be tempted" to renounce your faith, 10b. On God's side, however, you will be "tested" to be approved and rewarded. (2) *The time of the persecution will be short,* 10c. The "ten days" (cf. Dan 1:12) symbolize a short period (cf. Gen 24:55). (3) *Faithfulness even to physical death will be rewarded by "the crown of life,"* the martyr's reward, 10d (cf. Jas 1:12). (4) *The overcomer will not be hurt by the second death,* 11. This is the lake of fire, Gehenna, the place of eternal separation from God (Rev 20:6-15; 21:8).

2:12-17. PERGAMOS—THE WORLDLY CHURCH

Where Satan's Throne Was, 12-13. Pergamos (Pergamum) was a notable center of idolatry and demon-controlled religion, with splendid temples to Zeus, Athena, Apollo and Esculapius (the god of healing). It was located on the Aegean Sea about 60 miles N of Smyrna. As a brilliant center of pagan religion, including Caesar worship, it was linked with "Satan's throne" and "where Satan resides" (cf. 1 Cor 10:19-20; Rev 9:20-21; 16:13-16 for the connection of idolatry with demonism). Antipas was one of the faithful martyrs.

The Doctrine of Balaam, 14. This was Balaam's teaching Balak to corrupt God's people who could not be cursed (Num 31:15-16; 22:5; 23:8). The strategy was to entice them to intermarry among the Moabites, violate their separation from the world and give up their pilgrim walk.

The Doctrine of Nicolaitans, 15. What were hated "deeds" of the Nicolaitans in Ephesus (2:6) was a strongly held doctrine in Pergamos (see note on 2:6).

Warning and Promise, 16-17. The *warning* is to "repent," 16 (cf. 2:5). The alternative of repentance for the Nicolaitans was the Lord's fighting against them with the sword of His mouth (cf. 1:16).

Reconstructed theater at the health center of New Testament Pergamos. (*Courtesy Howard F. Vos*)

The sword alludes to the drawn sword with which the angel confronted Balaam (Num 22:23) on his way to curse Israel, and was an earnest of the sword by which he and the deceived Israelites eventually fell. The *promise* entails Christ as "the hidden manna," 17 (Jn 6:31-35), His glorified humanity preserved in the heavenly tabernacle until manifested at His second advent. The promise also embraces the "white stone." It may refer to the precious diamond on the high priest's breastplate, the "new name" engraved upon it being Christ's (3:12), containing some new revelation then to be made known.

2:18-29. THYATIRA—THE PAGANIZED CHURCH

Commendation and Complaint, 18-23. Thyatira was a commercial center honeycombed with pagan religion. Its many trade guilds periodically sponsored idolatrous feasts. Christ, depicted again as Judge (1:14-15; Dan 10:6), 18, charges the church with tolerating the false prophetess Jezebel, 20, even though it was a church of works, 19. This woman is so designated because she resembled

847

Ahab's wicked consort who introduced depraved Phoenician cults into Israel (1 Kgs 16:31-32; 2 Kgs 9:22, 30-33).

Promise to the Overcomer, 24-29. "The deep things of Satan," 24, is an arresting reference to the shocking depth of demonism (1 Tim 4:1-6; 1 Jn 4:1-6; Rev 9:20-21; 16:13-16) and false doctrine (2 Tim 3:1-8; Jas 3:15; 2 Pet 2:1-3) to which this system sank. Overcomers will participate in Christ's messianic rule, 27 (Ps 2:8-9).

3:1-6. SARDIS—THE LIFELESS CHURCH

Dead Orthodoxy, 1-3. Located 50 miles NE of Smyrna, Sardis was noted for its wealth because of its textile and jewelry industries. The church there "had a name" (reputation) for spiritual life, just as the city had a "name" historically and politically; but Christ the Judge who has "the seven Spirits" (i.e., the Holy Spirit in sevenfold fullness) and holds "the seven stars" (the messengers of the seven churches) adjudges it spiritually dead, 1. It is called upon to "awake," to "strengthen what remains," 2, to "remember" what it "has received and heard" (recovery of God's Word), keep it, and repent (change its present course toward total spiritual death), 3. Failure to do so will mean unsuspecting judgment instead of blessing, at the Lord's coming, 3*b*.

Blotting Names out of the Book of Life, 4-6. The church is characterized by nominal Christianity (v. 1), with perhaps many admitted to the fellowship mechanically without regeneration, hence the bold figure of "erasing" or "blotting out" names from "the book of life," 5. This symbolism refers to the ancient practice of a city enrolling its citizens with the names of the dead erased. So, by analogy, those who have "a name that they live" (as belonging to the visible church) but are "dead" (unregenerate) are "erased from" God's roll of heavenly citizens. They are in the book in the sense of being *called* to salvation, their erasure being in the sense of *not* being *chosen* for salvation. "The book of life" in 20:15 and 21:27 appears, however, strictly as the book of the elect alone, those whose names remain after the erasure of mere professors (Mt 22:14). The few true believers in Sardis, the "overcomers," are those "who have not soiled their garments" by dead works, but "are worthy" because they trust in Christ and are in Him, 4, clothed in the white garments of His righteousness, 5. The importance of the garment industry in Sardis doubtless led to this double use of the term "garments."

3:7-13. PHILADELPHIA—
THE MISSIONARY CHURCH

An Open Door of Witness, 7-9. This letter, together with the one addressed to the church at Smyrna, contains no word of rebuke. The name of this city, located 25 miles SE of Sardis, means "brotherly love." Although threatened by severe earthquakes, almost to the point of complete destruction, the city still remains and a Christian group meets regularly there. Christ, the "holy" (Lk 1:35; Jn 10:36), the "true" (Jn 14:6; Rev 19:11), the One who has "the key of David" (Isa 22:22), set before this church an open door, 7, and it was impossible for anyone to shut it, 8a. Because it had "a little strength" (*dunamin*, "spiritual power") to take advantage of the opportunity for witness, it had kept Christ's Word and had not denied His name, 8b. The Philadelphian church's vigorous missionary activity won many Jews of the city, resulting in the violent opposition of the local Jewish populace, whose members, though claiming to be the people of God, were proved by their actions to be of Satan's synagogue (see note on 2:9).

Kept from the Hour of Testing, 10-13. This promise, 10b, seems to indicate that the Church, of which the Philadelphian church was representative, will be glorified and taken to heaven before the Great Tribulation begins, 10. The promise applies to all who are Christ's, "because you have kept [observed, obeyed] the word of My patience," i.e., the gospel of Christ's death by which one becomes a Christian. The expression, "I also will *keep you from*," means to "protect someone from something" (Prov 7:5; Jn 17:15). Since that "hour" from which they are to be kept is worldwide and inescapable for all earth dwellers, 10c, "kept from" suggests removal from the scene upon which the "hour" transpires. The "trouble" or "testing," 10d, has reference to the day of the Lord, Daniel's 70th week, the final seven years of terrible trouble which will engulf the earth, the time described in Rev 6—19. The promise relates to Christ's advent for His own, 11a (Jn 14:1-3; 1 Thess 4:13-17; 1 Cor 15:51-52) and the rewards of Christians, here called overcomers, 11b-13. Believers will be clearly identified as God's own possession and the inhabitants of the New Jerusalem, 12 (cf. 21:2-3, 10). Christ's "new name" will then be revealed.

3:14-22. LAODICEA—THE LUKEWARM CHURCH

Insufferable Lukewarmness, 14-19. Christ as Judge is here styled "the Amen," 14 (cf. 2 Cor 1:20), "the faithful and true witness" (in contrast to this church's compromising infidelity). "The beginning of the creation of God" denotes Christ's sovereignty over all creation (cf Col 1:15-18). He gives no commendation to this inclusivist church in the proud and wealthy city of Laodicea, located near Colossae (Col 4:13-16) and about 40 miles from Ephesus. This city's wealth was so great that in A.D. 60, when it was almost completely destroyed by an earthquake, its citizens refused Rome's aid and rebuilt the city at its own expense. As an industrial center, it was known for the production of fine black wool, and its Phrygian powder, used to treat eye diseases, and hot mineral springs made it a medical center as well. These features are used in the letter to illustrate the Laodicean church's true spiritual condition; for Christ calls its lukewarm profession nauseating, 15-16, and utterly deceptive of its true spiritual condition, 17. He advises the church "to buy gold tried in the fire," 18, the real wealth of a divine-human Saviour cleansing the heart and thus giving the "white raiment" of a truly regenerated and sanctified life, and the "eye salve" of faith granting true spiritual insight and knowledge. Chastening is promised for those in Laodicea who are Christ's, 19. They are to repent of the compromising disloyalty of their unbelief.

Christ Shut Out, 20-22. The church had ousted their Saviour and Lord. He was not even missed by this worldly-wise group. He therefore appears on the outside knocking on the doors of individual hearts, waiting for them to receive Him and to enter into fellowship with Him, 20. To the overcomer is promised the right to sit with Christ on His own throne in the coming kingdom, 21.

PART III. THE THINGS WHICH SHALL BE HEREAFTER, CH. 4—22

The Divine Throne in Heaven, Ch. 4—5

Chapters 4 and 5 introduce the source of the visions and judgments which are to follow. The setting is in heaven and the chief personage is Christ. The actual chronology of the book commences with ch. 6.

4:1-5. THE THRONE INTRODUCED

The Heavenly Door, 1. "After this" (Gr. "after these things"), 1*a*, refers to the Church Age represented by the seven churches in ch. 2 and 3. The scene is changed from earth to heaven, 1*b*, as the trumpet call of Christ summons John to heaven (cf. 1:10-13).

The Heavenly Throne, 2-5. Christ now occupies the throne of God the Father, 2, until His second advent (3:21). God's glory is symbolized in terms of precious gems, 3 (Ezk 1:26-28; cf. 1 Jn 1:5). The rainbow, 3*b* (Ezk 1:28), is a token of God's mercy based on the accepted sacrifice of His Son, as the Noahic bow was the sign of a covenant based on the sacrifice offered by Noah (Gen 8:20-22) which looked forward to Christ. John's bow was emerald colored (green) guaranteeing God's fidelity to His covenant with Noah not to destroy the earth again, as in the Flood, despite the terrible judgment to come (ch. 5—19) and despite the fact that the throne is a throne not of grace but of judgment, 5.

4:4, 10-11. THE TWENTY-FOUR ELDERS

These "elders" evidently represent redeemed OT and NT saints, for the term "elder" is never applied to angels or other heavenly and unfallen order of beings, nor do angels have crowns or occupy thrones; only redeemed men are promised such (Mt 19:28; 2 Tim 4:8; 1 Pet 5:2-4; Rev 2:10; 20:4). The crowns they wear are *stephanoi* (victor's crowns), 4, and the thrones they occupy show that these saints are viewed as having already been judged for their works (see notes on the believer's judgment, 1 Cor 3:11-15; 2 Cor 5:10) and have received their rewards (cf. Dan 7:9-10). Their "being clothed in white garments," 4, displays them as a *redeemed* royal priesthood (1 Pet 2:9), engaged in priestly services (Rev 5:8). They await *judicial* and *royal* functions to be given them at Christ's second advent (20:4-6).

The term "elder" is commonly employed in Scripture of the representative head of a nation, tribe, city or family. The number 24 represents the OT saints under the 12 tribes of Israel and the NT saints by the 12 apostles of the Lamb (cf. the 12 foundation stones of the 12 apostles of the Lamb and the 12 gates of the 12 tribes of Israel, Rev 21:10-14). The number 24, moreover, is thus representative in a redeemed priestly capacity. When David formed the priests into courses, he founded 24 heads of priestly families, and made these representative of the entire priesthood (1 Chr 24:1-19).

THE REVELATION

4:6-11. THE FOUR LIVING CREATURES

Their Identity, 6-8. They are a *special order* of created beings associated with the throne of God, apparently combining characteristics both of the cherubim, concerned with the public *governmental glory of God* (Gen 3:24; Ex 25:17-20; Ezk 10:1-22), and the seraphim, concerned with the *holiness of God* (Isa 6:1-7). Their intelligence and insight into God's plan for the earth are seen in their being "full of eyes," 6, 8. Their likeness to animals and man indicates the character of God's judicial government toward the earth, since the whole earthly scene is about to be visited with judgment (ch. 5—19).

Their Worship, 8-11. They adore the Lord God Almighty, 8-9, and are joined in worship by the 24 elders, 10-11.

5:1-4. THE SEVEN-SEALED BOOK

What the Book Is, 1. The seven-sealed book is the *title deed* to the forfeited inheritance of the earth lost by Adam when he fell. This legal document, guaranteeing the dispossession of Satan and wicked men from the earth (cf. Eph 1:13-14; Rom 8:22-23), and provided by Christ's atoning death, is seen lying "upon" (Gr.) the opened right hand of the One sitting on the throne (God the Father), 1a. "The scroll [ancient book] written within and on the back" implies completeness of legal provision for dispossession, 1b. "Sealed with seven seals" symbolizes the completeness of the sealing till one legally qualified to open the tightly closed legal document should appear.

Who Is Worthy to Open It? 2-4. This question looms large, 2. "No one" was able to open it. Not angelic beings, because the inheritance was lost by a human being and a man must therefore open it. Not any of Adam's descendants, because they are all sinners. John's keen desire to know the revelation promised herein seems frustrated, 4.

5:5-10. THE ONE WORTHY TO OPEN THE BOOK

The Lion of the Tribe of Judah, 5-6. He alone is worthy because (1) He is "the Lion of the tribe of Judah" (the royal tribe), a second advent appellative of Messiah as "King of kings" (19:16; Gen 49:8-10), who in majestic might would secure the blessing of Israel and the whole earth and in His lionlike character crush His foes; (2) He is "the Root of David" (*divine*, David's Lord and Creator, Ps 110:1; Mt 22:42-45; and "the offspring of David," 22:16, i.e., *human*);

852

(3) as the God-man He "has prevailed" (overcome) to open the scroll, 5; (4) He is the Lamb "slain," 6. The death of Christ is the basis of the redemption not only of sinners but of the earth (Rom 8:18-22). "The seven horns" denote the fullness of efficacy and "the seven eyes" completeness of intelligence in the Spirit's judicial administration over the earth, based on Christ's redemption, 6.

His Sublime Action, 7-10. "And he [Christ] came and took the book [scroll] out of the right hand of him [God] that was sitting [Gr] upon the throne" (cf. Dan 7:13-14, where the same grand scene is envisioned). It was the case of a kinsman (the God-man) being able to do what no one else could do (3-4; cf. Lev 25:23-34), the redemptive price being Christ's own blood (1 Pet 1:18-20; cf. Ruth 4:1-12). This act calls forth the worship of the living creatures, 8-10.

5:11-14. UNIVERSAL WORSHIP OF THE LAMB

Worship of the Heavenly Beings, 11-12. This great scene depicting the kingdom rights and glories of Christ (ch. 4—5), climaxed by His taking the seven-sealed book to claim possession of the earth, evokes the praise and worship of myriads of angels, the living creatures and redeemed humanity in heaven, 11. Their great theme is "Worthy is the Lamb" (cf. 5:2-3, 9; cf. Phil 2:9-11).

Participation of All Creation, 13-14. All creation worships and praises the Lamb. This adoration is repeated by the four living creatures, 14a, and the elders, 14b (see 4:4).

The Seven-Sealed Book Opened, 6:1—8:5

6:1-17. SEALS ONE TO SIX

Seals One and Two, 1-4. The opening of the seals precipitates the day of the Lord and the period of tribulation on the earth to dispossess Satan and wicked men. With each of the first four seals, one of the living creatures associated with God's judicial government toward the earth cries, "Come!" (ASV). Thus they call forth the first judgments, symbolized by four horsemen. The rider on the white horse, 2, is the Antichrist who imitates Christ (19:11), the "bow" and "crown" symbolizing his great *conquests*. The rider on the red horse, 3-4, symbolizes *war* and carnage (cf. Zech 1:7-11; 6:1-8).

Seals Three and Four, 5-8. The rider on the black horse symbolizes *famine,* which follows war. Bread is rationed: "A measure [one quart] of wheat for a denarius [a day's wage], and three measures [three quarts] of barley for a day's wage," 5-6. The rider on the pale horse represents *pestilence* and is called "Death," 7-8 (cf. 20:14).

Seal Five, 9-11. The souls under the altar (the altar of sacrifice where the sacrificial blood was poured out) represent *martyrs* of the first half of the Tribulation period. "The word of God" is that for which they suffered death, and their "blood" cries for vengeance, 10 (cf. Gen 4:10). They are the Jewish remnant whose cry is that of the prophetic imprecatory Psalms 35, 55, 59, 94, etc. The "white robes" indicate the redemption of their souls. They are to rest for a little season (the short period of the Great Tribulation on earth, Dan 9:27) until "their brothers" (fellow believing Jews) should share their martyrdom (cf. Rev 20:4-6).

Seal Six, 12-17. This seal apparently symbolizes *governmental anarchy* under the figures of earthquake, darkening of sun and moon, and the falling of stars. The collapse of all human government occasions awful terror as "the great day of God's wrath" arrives (cf. 14:10; 15:1; 16:1; 19:14).

(First Parenthesis, Ch. 7)

7:1-8. THE SEALING OF ISRAELITES

A Remnant of Israel Preserved, 1-3. These elect on the earth are preserved from the end-time Tribulation judgments which befall the earth, 1. The preservation is symbolized by a "seal," 2*a* (cf. Eph 1:13-14). It is a public preservation, for "the servants of our God" are to be sealed "upon their foreheads," 3, involving no secret discipleship. The sealing angel ascends from the east, 2, the direction of Palestine from someone in the Aegean area (cf. 1:9-11).

The Number of Sealed Israelites Specified, 4-8. These are earthly Israelites living in the time of "Jacob's trouble" (Jer 30:5-7). Though the tribal genealogies have ceased, God knows who the tribes are and where they are (Isa 11:11-16), and will preserve an elect remnant, returning them to the restored kingdom (Acts 1:6). The event will occur when "the times of the Gentiles" have run their course (Lk 21:24) with the full number of Gentiles gathered in (Acts 15:14; Rom 11:25). In the enumeration the tribes of Dan and Ephraim are omitted, probably because of their complicity in idolatry (Deut 29:18-21; 1 Kgs 12:25-30, but cf. Ezk 48:1-7, 23-29).

7:9-17. THE SALVATION OF GENTILES

Elect Gentiles Preserved, 9-14. This company of saved people is an elect body of Gentiles, like the elect body of Jews, 1-8, which will be preserved through the end-time tribulation, 14, to enter the kingdom. Like the sealed remnant of Israel, they show that in the midst of His wrath God remembers mercy (Hab 3:2). They are apparently *unglorified people on the earth,* envisioned as "saved" and therefore seen "before the heavenly throne and the Lamb, clothed with white robes, and palms," a symbol of millennial joy and triumph, 9 (Lev 23:40; Jn 12:13). They have experienced unparalleled suffering in the Great Tribulation, 14 (Dan 9:27; Mt 24:15-51; 2 Thess 2:1-12), having been brought to salvation by the preaching of the gospel of the kingdom (Mt 24:13-14; also called the "everlasting gospel," Rev 14:6).

Their Kingdom Bliss Assured, 15-17. They are "before the throne of God," denoting not their local place but their moral position, and they serve God ceaselessly "in His temple" (The millennial temple, Ezk 40—44), 15a. God will dwell among them (Gr. *scēnosei ep autous,* "shall be a tabernacle over them"), 15b (cf. 21:3; Lev 26:11; Isa 4:5-6). The sufferings of their tribulation experiences will be past, 16, and Christ the kingdom Shepherd (Ezk 34:23) will provide for them, 17 (Ps 23:1-6; Isa 12:1-6).

8:1-5. SEAL SEVEN

Seal Seven Opened, 1. This concludes the complete opening of the seven-sealed book (5:1) so that its full contents (the trumpets and bowls) might be released upon the earth and its wicked inhabitants. The half hour of silence is the lull after a preceding tempest and the prelude to a more terrible one.

The Prayer of the Saints Answered, 2-5. "Another angel," 3, is taken by some to be Christ, but probably the incense offerer is an angelic being acting in priestly capacity. The saints' prayers are answered by earth judgments upon the wicked.

The Seven Trumpets Blown, 8:6—11:19

8:6-13. TRUMPETS ONE TO FOUR

Trumpet One, 7. The first six trumpets introduce more severe judgments, perhaps beginning the second half of the Tribulation period.

Trumpet one is blown resulting in hail and fire mixed with blood being thrown to the *earth*, which affects vegetation and suggests *severe drought*.

Trumpet Two, 8-9. The second trumpet results in judgment upon the *sea*, affecting the sea *food supply* and the ocean *transportation* lines.

Trumpet Three, 10-11. The blowing of the third trumpet affects the *fresh water* supply, a third of which is *made* deadly *bitter* by the drug "wormwood."

Trumpet Four, 12-13. The *heavens* themselves are affected by the judgment resulting from the blowing of the fourth trumpet. Creation is reversed as a third of the *lights of heaven* are touched and *darkened*, 12. Three calamities ("woes") are announced, 13, which are terrible judgments falling directly on men. These three woes constitute the final three trumpet judgments.

9:1-12. THE FIFTH TRUMPET—THE FIRST WOE

The Abyss Opened, 1. The seer sees "a star *fallen* from heaven." This "star" is the angel custodian of the pit of the abyss, the prison house of the demons (Lk 8:30-31). That he cannot be Satan, or even an evil angel, is shown by the fact that he is the same angelic personage who once again opens "the pit of the abyss" to bind and imprison Satan prior to the millennium (20:1-3). He is an angel *fallen* from heaven, not a fallen angel, the past participle "fallen" describing the swiftness of the angel's descent and the suddenness with which this first woe bursts upon wicked earth dwellers.

The Loosing of Myriads of Demons, 2-12. The symbolism, 2-11, is descriptive of the invisible spirit world in terms visible and comprehensible to men. The locusts represent demons and the way they will possess, drive and torment men in the end time. (See note on "Demonism," Mk 5:1-20.) While multitudes of demons have been free to torment the human race during previous ages (Lev 19:31; 20:6; 1 Sam 28:3-25; Mk 1:23-27; 5:1-17; 1 Tim 4:1-6; 1 Jn 4:1-4), many of them are so viciously depraved and harmful that God has imprisoned them in the abyss. These are the terrible demons let loose under the first woe. The name of the king of the demons is *Abaddon*, meaning "destruction," 11 (Job 26:6; Prov 15:11), or in Gr. *Apollyon*, meaning "destroyer" (cf. 2 Thess 2:7-12).

9:13-21.   THE SIXTH TRUMPET—THE SECOND WOE

Gathered Armies Loosed, 13-19. From the altar of intercession, the golden altar of incense, God answers the prayers of His suffering and martyred saints. Toward the altar their prayers ascend (8:3). From it the answer goes forth, 13, specifically from the "four [expressing universality] horns" (denoting power and efficacy of the saints' prayers and the answer). This loosing of the armies is effected by the release of the four angels (ministers of judgment under divine control). The place of their loosing, the Euphrates, was the location of ancient Babylon. The very hour of their release is determined as well as the extent of their destruction, 15. The number of the cavalrymen is 200,000,000, as John heard it, 16. Some think the description of the army, 17-19, like the locusts, indicates denizens of the spirit world. Such armies of the spirit realm appear in Scripture (cf. 2 Kgs 2:11; 6:13-17; Rev 12:7; 19:11-16). Belonging to the sphere of the spirit world, which is ordinarily invisible to men, the torment and destruction of this infernal host will be so much more terrible. Others feel that the event of Daniel 11:44 is referred to here.

The Purpose of the Woe, 20-21. The divine design is twofold, punishment and reformation. But those who survive this dreadful calamity do not repent of their evil works and idolatry. The rampant demonism of that day (1-12) turns them away from worship of God to worship of demons. The awful results of demon-energized idolatry are enumerated: murders (violence), sorceries (traffic in demonism), fornication (sexual uncleanness), and thefts (robbery), 21.

(Second Parenthesis, 10:1—11:13)

10:1-7.   THE ANGEL AND THE LITTLE BOOK

The Identity of the Mighty Angel, 1-6. This angel is an *actual* angel who symbolizes Christ (cf. 5:2; 8:3). As representative of Christ, the angel reflects His glory and bears the insignia attributed in 1:15-16 and 4:3 to Christ Himself, 1. His stupendous act of setting his foot on land and sea shows Christ's right to claim the earth as His own, 2 (Ps 95:5; Eph 1:13-14). The angel's loud cry and the seven thunders give full testimony to Christ's authority over the earth, 3-4a. His oath that "there should be no more delay" shows Christ's divine sovereignty and control in these matters of judgment, 6.

The Mystery of God Fulfilled, 7. "The mystery of God" is the theme of the "little book," and concerns Christ as incarnate Redeemer of the earth. It is a previously hidden truth, now fully revealed, which focuses upon Christ, in whom God's plan for this earth is centered and unfolded. This truth is the grand theme of the rest of Revelation where "the mystery of God" is "finished," i.e., completed. It will be "as He [God] has declared [Gr. 'evangelized; announced the good news'] to and by His servants the prophets," who declared the grand themes of Christ's redemption, kingdom and eternal glory.

10:8-11. JOHN AND THE LITTLE BOOK

What the Little Book Is, 8-10. The little scroll (book) is not only the record of the fulfillment of the mystery of God, 7, and distinguished from the seven-sealed book of 5:1, but it seems to be, in part at least, the book Daniel was told to seal up till the time of the end (Dan 12:4, 9). This passage in Daniel appears to be the foundation for these verses. This is the reason the scroll was "sweet as honey" when first eaten (Ezk 2:8-9; 3:1-3; Ps 19:10; 119:103), but when digested, "bitter" (Jer 15:10; 20:14-18). The bright promises of deliverance for Daniel's people were preluded by terrible suffering and judgment.

Its Effect on John's Ministry, 11. As a result the seer must prophesy again, as he had done in the previous section, "concerning many peoples."

11:1-2. THE END OF THE TIMES OF THE GENTILES

Restoration of Temple Worship, 1-2a. This point marks the Lord's dealing again with Israel and its worship in a restored temple in "the Holy City," Jerusalem (cf. 2 Thess 2:3-4). This is symbolized by the seer's measuring "the temple of God" and "the altar, and them that worship therein," 1. A reed (about 10 feet) was used as the measuring instrument. "The staff" (rod) is a figure for firmness (Isa 14:5). Whereas the Lord accepts the godly remnant, the true worshipers, the apostate Jews who have linked themselves with the Gentiles (symbolized by the outer court) God rejects.

End of the Times of the Gentiles, 2b. This period, which began with Judah's captivity under Nebuchadnezzar (605 B.C.), will not end until the second advent (Dan 2:34-35, 44; Rev 19:11, 21). During this time Jerusalem has been subject to Gentile rule (Lk

21:24). Divine recognition of temple worship signalizes the swift close of "the times of the Gentiles," specified as 42 months. This is the middle of Daniel's seventieth week (a week of seven years, Dan 9:27) with the last three and a half years yet to run (cf. Dan 7:25; Rev 12:14; 13:5).

11:3-13. THE TWO WITNESSES

Their Identity, 3-7. Although the two witnesses are commonly identified as Moses and Enoch or Moses and Elijah, such identifications are scarcely tenable since both of the witnesses are killed and resurrected, something which could not be true of these OT prophets as glorified men (Mt 17:3). These witnesses are evidently two members of the latter-day remnant. They are Christ's witnesses, 3, "my witnesses" referring to the mighty Angel (Christ) of ch. 10. They preach "clothed in sackcloth," a symbol of mourning, because they identify themselves with Israel's grievous sin and Jerusalem's wickedness, 3b, 8 (cf. Joel 1:13; Jer 4:8). Their *message* is Christ's lordship over the earth, 4, proclaiming the soon coming of the King of kings to take possession of the earth. "The two olive trees and the two lampstands" (Zech 4:2-3) connect them with testimony that Messiah as King-Priest (the two olive trees in Zech 4 denote these two offices) will shortly reign over restored Israel as the light of the world. They have *miraculous powers* like Elijah and Moses, 5-6. Fire comes out of their mouth (cf. 2 Kgs 1:10, 12; Jer 5:14; cf. Lk 9:54-55). They command drought like Elijah, 6a (1 Kgs 17:1; Jas 5:17); turn water to blood (Ex 7:19) and work other signs like Moses, 6b (Ex 7—10). They are *killed by the beast* (head of the revived Roman Empire, Rev 13:1-10; 17:8), who ascends out of the abyss (cf. 9:1-12), but not until they have completed their testimony, 7.

Their Destiny, 8-13. Their corpses are dishonored in Jerusalem, 8, but God resurrects, 11, and translates the two witnesses in "*the* cloud," 12, i.e., the Shekinah glory (cf. Ezk 10:19; Mt 17:5). Meanwhile their enemies are punished with an earthquake that kills 7,000 and destroys one-tenth of Jerusalem, 13, which causes those who remain to give glory to the "God of heaven" because of His power, not because of their repentance.

11:14-19. THE SEVENTH TRUMPET— THE THIRD WOE

Anticipation of Christ's Worldwide Kingdom, 14-18. The second woe (9:13-21) is here repeated after the parenthesis, 10:1—11:13, to bridge the gap of the parenthesis and to connect the first two woes with the third and final woe, 14. This woe is said to come "quickly," and includes all the remaining judgments prior to the establishment of the kingdom (11:14—20:3). Verses 15-19 give a panorama of the rest of the book, future events being seen as already present. They envision the establishment of Christ's worldwide kingdom and reign, 15-17; the judgment of the raging nations at Armageddon, 18a; the judgment of the dead (20:11-15) when the destroyers of the earth will be destroyed, 18c; and the rewarding of prophets and saints in millennial positions of rule and dominion, 18b (20:4-6).

God's Temple in Heaven Opened, 19. "The ark of His covenant" seen within the temple speaks of God's faithfulness to His covenants and promises to Israel (Rom 9:4-5). The last apocalyptic judgments and the second advent will realize the consummation of all these commitments made to God's covenant people Israel. (See "The Covenants of Scripture," Heb 9.)

Seven Personages Performing During the Last Days of the Tribulation, Ch. 12—13

12:1-2. PERSON ONE—THE WOMAN, ISRAEL

The Woman, 1. The characters who will be on the stage during the final days before Christ's return are introduced. Not only are the outward events of the final conflict recorded, but the hidden spiritual aspects as well. The great "wonder" (a sign or symbol) is the "woman," 1. She evidently symbolizes Israel, for she is dressed in regal and governmental splendor, the 12 stars illustrating her 12 tribes, as Joseph's dream shows (Gen 37:9). Israel was often portrayed as a married woman in the OT (Isa 54:1), and as an adulterous divorced wife in her sin and rejection (Isa 47:7-9; 50:1; Jer 3:1-25; Hos 2:1-23).

The Woman's Travail, 2. This travail refers to Israel's agony during the Great Tribulation, as the context clearly illustrates. The symbol of birth was a common OT figure used to portray acute suffering, especially "the time of Jacob's trouble" (Jer 30:5-7; Isa 26:15-18; 66:7). During this supreme travail the nation will give birth to the godly Jewish remnant, 17 (cf. Mic 5:2-3), which will be closely associated with the Male Child, Christ, 5.

12:3-4. PERSON TWO—THE DRAGON, SATAN

The Dragon in Prophetic View, 3. The dragon is identified as that "old serpent [cf. Gen 3:1-10], called the Devil [accuser] and Satan" (opposer) in verse 9. He is "the great red dragon," which symbolizes him as the proud, cruel energizer of "the beast." "Red" portrays his murderous character (Jn 8:44), which is now featured. His seven diademed heads and ten horns identify him with the final form of Gentile world power centered in the beast (13:1-10; cf. Dan 7:8).

The Dragon in Historical Perspective, 4. This includes a panoramic sketch of his original fall, 4a (Isa 14:12-14; Ezk 28:12-15), suggested by verses 7-9, and of Satan's hostility to the woman's posterity, 4b (Gen 3:15; Mt 2:16).

12:5-6. PERSON THREE—THE MALE CHILD, CHRIST

The Male Child, 5. Four things are declared: (1) *His birth, 5a*; (2) *His destiny, 5b,* which is to break His foes to pieces (Ps 2:9) and then to rule in righteousness; (3) *His ascension, 5c*; (4) *His position* on God's throne, *5d* (3:21). He is destined to rule yet. Satan knows this, and pursues the woman (godly Israel).

The Woman's Flight, 6. The hiatus of the Christian centuries is between verses 5 and 6. Verse 6 describes Israel's flight into the wilderness (possibly Petra in Edom; cf. Mt. 24:16; Dan 11:41), to be sustained for three and a half years during Satan's terrible persecution, which he effects through the beast (2 Thess 2:3-7).

12:7-12. PERSON FOUR—MICHAEL, THE ARCHANGEL

Michael, 7-9. Michael is the special protector of Daniel's people the Jews, 7a (Dan 12:1; cf. Dan 10:13-21). He is involved in the war when Satan's expulsion from the heavenlies is at hand, 7b. Since his original rebellion, Satan and his hosts have been loose in the heavenlies (Job 1:6; 2:1; Gen 3:1-10; Eph 2:2; 6:10-12). In the middle of the Great Tribulation he and his angels will be expelled and cast on the earth, 7-9 (cf. Dan 10:10-14).

Rejoicing Over Satan's Expulsion, 10-12. This joyous shout is a prelude to the establishment of Christ's kingdom, 10a, which begins with the return of Christ. Victory over last-day malignity will be on the basis of the accomplished sacrifice of Christ, 11a, by a faithful testimony, 11*b*, and by martyrdom, 11*c*. Satan's expulsion means terrible woe to the earth, 12. His wrath is spurred on by the shortness of the time (cf. 10:6; 11:14).

12:13-16. SATAN PERSECUTES THE WOMAN

Reason for Satan's Persecution, 13-14. Knowing that his defeat has been occasioned by the exaltation of the Man Child, Christ, the dragon vents his fury upon the sun-clothed woman (Israel) who gave the Man Child birth, 13. The eagle wings given to the woman to escape to the wilderness recall how the Lord delivered Israel from Egypt and bore her "on eagles' wings" (Ex 19:4; Deut 32:11-12; Isa 26:20; 27:1). This is the period of the "abomination of desolation" (Dan 9:27) and the Great Tribulation spoken of by our Lord (Mt 24:15-22; Lk 21:20-24).

Israel's Preservation, 15-16. The serpent (Satan) cast out of his mouth "water like a river," 15, symbolizing Gentile nations (17:15) energized by Satan with anti-Semitic hatred to destroy the Jew. "The earth opened her mouth, and swallowed the flood" (river), 16. This points to friendly nations, who having heeded the preaching of the gospel of the kingdom, protect these persecuted Jews.

12:17. PERSON FIVE—THE ISRAELITE REMNANT

The Godly Remnant, 17. Satan now turns against the godly remnant of Jews still in the land (cf. Isa 1:9; 6:13; Rom 11:5). These are individual godly Jews who had not escaped to safety when the Tribulation broke out (Mt 24:15-20). These "keep the commandments of God," the mark of godliness common to true believers of all ages, and "have the testimony of Jesus," i.e., bear faithful witness to Him.

13:1-10. PERSON SIX—THE BEAST OUT OF THE SEA

The Beast—the Roman Prince, 1-5. This last great ruler of Gentile world power arises out of an unsettled political condition ("the sea," Isa 57:20), 1*a*. He heads a confederated ten-kingdom empire covering the sphere of the ancient Roman Empire, Daniel's fourth beast (Dan 7:24-28). The "ten horns" are ten kingdoms (kings, 17:12) and the "diadems" on the horns speak of despotic power. The dragon having "seven heads and ten horns, and diadems upon his heads" (12:3) is the dynamic behind the beast, 1*b*, 2*b*. The beast is in complete defiance of God indicated by the "names of blasphemy" upon his seven heads, 1c. His empire partakes of all the beastly qualities of the preceding world empires of "the times of the Gentiles," 2 (cf. Dan 7:4-6)—leopardlike agility of conquest (Macedonian), bearlike voracity (Persian), lionlike strength (Babylonian). His kingdom represents the restoration of the imperial power of the Roman Empire, 3b. "The head" wounded to death symbolizes the seventh (and last) form of government of the Roman Empire, the imperial, destroyed in war; but "the deadly wound" yet to be healed indicates the imperial form of government will be restored under the beast (Dan 7:8). The beast is worshiped together with the dragon who energizes him, 4. He becomes utterly God-defiant and destructive during the final three and a half years of the Great Tribulation, 5.

The Beast's Wicked Career, 6-10. He blasphemes God and those who are His, 6. To this end he wars against the saints, 7a (Dan 7:21-22; Rev 11:7, 12). He is permitted unrestrained power over all earth dwellers except over the elect, 8-10 (cf. Mt 24:13, 22). He is the Antichrist, the man of sin (2 Thess 2:3-12; 1 Jn 2:22; 4:3).

13:11-18. PERSON SEVEN— THE BEAST OUT OF THE EARTH, THE FALSE PROPHET

This third member of the unholy trinity arises out of the earth, 11a. He is the first beast's (Antichrist's) prophet, 11b, though disguised as a lamb. As such he directs worship to "the first beast" by miraculous powers, 12-14, giving life to the image of the beast and killing those who do not worship the image, 15 (cf. Dan 3:1-30). He compels men to be branded with "the number of man" and incompleteness, 16-17. The number 666 is a triad (the number "three" indicates completeness from God's viewpoint) symbolizing the climax of man's failure and wickedness, 18.

Foreview of the End of the Tribulation, Ch. 14

14:1-5. THE LAMB AND THE 144,000

The Identity of the 144,000, 1-3. These are evidently the living Jewish remnant spared from death and moral contamination during the Great Tribulation. They are associated with "the Lamb" (Christ) upon Mount Zion, 1a, the earthly Zion in Jerusalem, the seat of royal power in the kingdom. It seems evident that the 144,000 here are identical to the Israelites of 7:1-8, who have been sealed for preservation from death during the Tribulation (7:3). They belong to the Lamb and have His mark on their foreheads, 1c. Having gone through great tribulation, their song of God's grace is a "new song," a song of redemption at the cost of the Lamb's blood, 3 (cf. Rom 3:24).

Their Character and Destiny, 4-5. Their practical godliness is shown in: (1) *their separation* in virgin purity from the wickedness and idolatry around them, 4a (cf. 9:20-21); (2) *their obedience and discipleship,* 4b; (3) *their redemption,* 4c; (4) *their destiny,* 4d, to be "the firstfruits to God and the Lamb," an earnest of earth's coming kingdom when all will bow to God and the Lamb; (5) *their truthfulness,* 5a, clinging to the truth of God's Word by profession and life when the whole world believes "*the* [devil's] lie" (2 Thess 2:11).

14:6-8. THE FALL OF BABYLON FORESEEN

Proclamation of the Everlasting Gospel, 6-7. This gospel proclaims *mercy in the midst of judgment,* calling men in this terrible period to abandon the worship of the beast and reverence God (Prov 1:7), giving glory to Him, not the beast, "for the hour of His judgment has come."

Fall of Babylon Anticipated, 8. Babylon is a symbol of the Satanic world system, the center of all that is false and evil, of idolatry and oppression. It consists of the order of unregenerate humanity organized under evil principles with Satan as its head (cf. 1 Jn 2:15-17), with emphasis given to the ecclesiastical (ch. 17), political and commercial (ch. 18) aspects of this system. "Fallen, fallen" is a Hebraism for "completely fallen."

14:9-13. THE PUNISHMENT OF THE WICKED

Worshipers of the Beast and Their Fate, 9-11. The doom of these rebels is announced by an angel "with a loud voice" so all may hear and be without excuse, 9. It entails the full fury of God, 10a (Gr. "He also shall drink of the fury of God prepared unmixed in the cup of His wrath"). "Unmixed" means without any alleviating circumstances (Isa 51:17; Jer 25:15; Ps 75:8; Job 21:20). Unutterable anguish is symbolized by the "fire and brimstone" (sulphur), 10b (cf. Isa 30:33; Rev 20:10). Eternal punishment is portrayed by "the smoke of their torment" rising up "forever and ever" ("the ages of the ages"), 11. Ceaseless torment is prefigured by the expression "day and night."

The Bliss of the Martyrs, 12-13. In this dread day "the endurance of the saints" will be supremely tested. Perseverance is by the remnant's "keeping the commandments of God" and maintaining "faith in Jesus," 12. The blessedness of those who die rather than worship the beast is indicated, 13.

14:14-20. PREVIEW OF ARMAGEDDON

The Harvest, 14-16. This is heaven's view of the climax of God's judgment. The figure of the harvest portrays judgment which separates the righteous from the wicked. The judge is the one who sits upon "a white cloud," white signifying the purity and absolute righteousness of the judgment to take place, the cloud indicating the divine presence (10:1; Ezk 10:4; Mt 17:5; 24:30). The judge is the Son of Man, the title under which Christ deals with the earth and earth dwellers (Mt 25:31; Jn 5:27) and claims universal dominion (Dan 7:13-14; Rev 1:13-14). His divine kingship is shown by the golden crown on His head (Rev 19:12), the "sharp sickle" being a symbol of a thorough harvest (Joel 3:13). The judgment proceeds from the temple, 15a, the immediate presence of God, and the call is for immediate reaping because the harvest is "over-ripe" and the appointed time has arrived, 15b-16. The angels are the actual reapers (cf. 19; Mt 13:39); the Son of Man reaps through the instrumentality of the angels, 16 (Joel 3:9-14).

The Vintage, 17-20. This is God's wrath outpoured on sinners. It issues from God's presence, the temple, 17, and from the altar, 18, i.e., the brazen altar of sacrifice. The angel who comes out has power over fire, for this altar of sacrifice has now become the altar of judgment, 18 (cf. 16:5, 8). The judgment of the wicked is fully ripe, 18b (cf. 2 Thess 2:7-12). It is unsparing, signified by the figure of "treading the winepress" in which unmitigated divine wrath falls upon sinners (19:15; cf. Isa 63:3-6), and is executed "without the city" (Jerusalem), 20, in the valley of Jehoshaphat (Joel 3:12-13). The terrifying carnage of Armageddon is symbolized by the blood flowing as high as a horse's bridle for 1600 stadia (about 200 miles), 20b. Vast destruction over a circumscribed area centering in Palestine-Syria is indicated.

The Seven Bowls, Ch. 15—16

15:1-8. PREPARATION FOR THE FINAL PLAGUES

The Sign of the Seven Angels, 1. This sign (symbol) is called "great and marvelous" because these angels have the seven last plagues and in them the fury of God is completed. Attention is directed in this sign to the Antichrist, who attempts to take over the earth for himself and destroy the woman (Israel).

The Victorious Martyrs, 2-4. The fire mingled with the glass recalls the tribulation martyrs' fiery persecution under the beast, 2. The harps of God symbolize their victorious joy as a result of their triumph over the beast (5:8). The song of Moses (concerning redemption out of the Red Sea, Ex 15) combines with the song of the Lamb (redemption from sin and the exaltation of the Lamb of God). The subject of the song, 3-4, is the equity of God's works and ways as "King of nations." The reverence and glory due the name of Him whom all nations will soon worship, are celebrated as His final judgments are revealed, 4.

Ministers of God's Wrath, 5-8. These final judgments (11:19—18:24) originate from God's temple because they are severer than those earlier judgments which originated from His throne, 5-6. The angels' clothing of pure white linen (cf. 19:8, 14) shows the righteous character of their mission, 6a. They come to sacrifice to the offended holiness and justice of God. The golden vials (bowls) were temple vessels for pouring drink offerings, and here describe the fullness (seven) of God's wrath poured out. The four living creatures (see notes on 4:6-11), as executors of the judicial government of God, perform accordingly, 7. The smoke is the result of the fire of God's wrath, now hiding His grace because sin is fully ripe and must be judged without mercy, 8.

16:1-12. BOWLS ONE TO SIX

Bowls One and Two, 1-3. The bowl judgments are the consummation of the wrath of God poured out on the wickedness of men and are characterized by severity, finality and brevity. Evidently they continue to the very end of the Tribulation period, for the angels do not return to the temple in heaven. Chronologically, the next event following the outpouring of the bowls is the coming of Christ in victory, ch. 19.

The command from heaven, 1, indicates that God's long-suffering is ended and His judgment can no longer be delayed. His glory demands that His name be vindicated. The *first bowl*, 2, is poured out upon the earth—organized government under the leadership of the beast. A grievous ulcer is inflicted on those bearing the mark of the beast. This constitutes God's judgment on those who have rejected His grace and rebelled against His worship. The affliction may well be moral and spiritual as well as physical. The *second bowl*, 3, is poured out upon the sea, which becomes blood and is symbolic of the complete moral and spiritual death of godless society.

Bowls Three and Four, 4-9. Fresh waters become blood in the pouring out of the *third bowl*, 4. But in the midst of such judgment there is a proclamation of the righteousness of the Eternal God who has judged, 5. The sympathy of the heavens is with the Judge! Justice has been done, for earth dwellers on whom such retribution falls have shed the innocent blood of prophets and saints, 6; thus they deserve to drink blood. The altar adds its testimony, 7, perhaps because the prayers of the saints (6:9-10) under the altar are now answered. God's absolute authority over creation is exhibited in the *fourth bowl*, 8, increasing solar heat so that men in their frightful anguish cry out in blasphemy, 9. Their hearts are hardened thereby, and their true character revealed.

Bowl Five, 10-11. Darkness falls over the empire of the beast, 10, as his center of power (throne) is affected and God's answer to the taunt of the beast's followers is given (13:4). Morally, politically and spiritually his kingdom is plunged into solitary darkness, and men gnaw their tongues in fearful agony. Their blasphemy, 11, reveals the completeness of their spiritual blackout.

Bowl Six, 12. The drying up of the Euphrates River, 1,780 miles in length, the largest stream in western Asia, symbolizes the removal of every barrier for the advance of "the kings from the east" to Armageddon. This great river formed the eastern boundary of the Roman Empire and is stipulated as the eastern limit of enlarged Palestine (Gen 15:18). It was a natural barrier in antiquity to invading armies from the east. No longer shall it be a barrier when the Lord gathers the hosts to Armageddon or when He gathers Israel back into the kingdom (Isa 11:15-16). The kings from the east are the rulers of powers east of the Euphrates.

(Third Parenthesis, 16:13-16)

16:13-16. THE THREE FROGS

Satanic Trinity and Armageddon, 13-14, 16. "Frogs" symbolize the demons who will be the *spiritual dynamic* behind Armageddon (cf. 1 Kgs 22:20-28). The dragon (Satan), the beast (the Antichrist) and the false prophet symbolize the Satanic trinity of evil, the source of "the spirits of demons," 14, i.e., demon spirits. (See note on "Demonism," Mk 5:20.) These demons form the delusive means of persuading the nations to gather for the supreme folly of Armageddon—man's insensate fight against God and Christ's sovereignty over the earth. Armageddon, "Hill of Megiddo," is the ancient battlefield and site of several decisive battles in Israel's history (cf. Jud 5:19; 2 Kgs 9:27; 2 Chr 35:22), It symbolizes the place of the *gathering* of the nations, as the valley of Jehoshaphat (Joel 3:2, 12) symbolizes the place of *slaughter* in the final age-end battle. This battle decides the governmental question of the sovereignty of the earth.

The highly cultivated Valley of Jezreel (Megiddo, or Armageddon).
(*Courtesy IIS*)

Warning to the Remnant, 15. This is a parenthesis between verses 14 and 16. So dense will be the darkness and deception of that hour, that earth's hordes gathered at Armageddon will be suddenly surprised by Christ's glorious advent (1 Thess 5:2-3). The saints of Israel (7:1-8; 14:1-5) and the saints from among the Gentiles (7:9-17) will need warning and encouragement in these days of gross darkness (Isa 60:2) to watch their conduct and be prepared for Christ's advent.

16:17-21. THE SEVENTH BOWL

The Consummation of Judicial Wrath, 17-18. The seventh angel pours out his bowl "upon the air," the realm of Satan (Eph 2:2), who now has been driven out of the heavenlies onto the earth (12:9) and operates through the beast, the false prophet and their followers. The judgment (hailstones, 21) falls on the organized systems of evil on the earth. "It is done!" announces the completion of the wrath of God upon those who have refused the cry from the cross, "It is finished!" (Jn 19:30). God's voice from both temple (*naos*, place of His presence) and throne (seat of His administration) is heard. His judicial action symbolized by voices, thunders and lightnings, precedes the great earthquake, 18. This earthquake is a physical reality, for in no other way could there result the complete overthrow of which all previous judgments have been precursors. Other prophecies foretell such an earthquake (cf. Zech 14:4-5), and indicate results which only a literal cataclysm could effect.

The Results of God's Wrath, 19-21. Jerusalem, "the great city," is divided into three parts. "The cities of the nations" also fall. "Great Babylon," the counterfeit political and religious center of ch. 17 and 18, experiences God's full wrath, 19*b*. The earthquake is worldwide, 20, and only *one* kingdom escapes, for it cannot be shaken (Dan 2:44). The great hail (about 100 pounds in weight), 21, recalls the defeat of Israel's enemies at Bethhoron (Josh 10:1-11). Doubtless this too has a literal meaning.

Judgment of Babylon, Ch. 17—18

17:1-6. THE VISION OF THE HARLOT, ECCLESIASTICAL BABYLON

The Harlot and Her Identity, 1-5. Chapters 17 and 18 fully supplement the previous passing prophetic notices (14:8; 16:19). The harlot represents ecclesiastical Babylon (personified religious revolt against God) in its final form, ripened for judgment. (1) *She stands for corrupt religionism*, 1, a "great harlot" (Nah 3:4), denoting a religious system that compromises truth for worldly power. Scripture often uses a woman to symbolize that which is religiously out of place (Mt 13:33; Rev. 2:20). (2) *She exploits the peoples* ("waters") *of the earth*, 1. (3) *She is guilty of prostituting truth and purity*, 2c, intoxicating men by her doctrines and practices which violate the Word of God. (4) *She is spiritually destitute*, 3a. The wilderness (desert) symbolizes the place of drought, where those who are thirsty (cf. Jn 7:37-39) can never be satisfied. (5) *She dominates and uses the state whenever possible*, 3b. She rides into power on political Babylon, the beast's kingdom, the final form of Gentile world government (13:1-10, see notes). (6) *She heads up the corrupt religious system of the end time*, 4. Scarlet denotes her sin and adultery (Isa 1:18). She is rich and influential. The "golden cup" being filled with "abominations" (idolatries) and "filthiness of her fornication" tells of her gross infidelity to God and His Word. (7) *She represents in fullest scope all apostate religious movements,* from their inception in the ancient Babylon of Nimrod (Gen 10:8-10) to their terrible consummation in apostate Christianity, and other evil religious forces of the last days, 5.

The Woman and Her Crimes, 6. Her most horrible sin is her murder of the true saints of God. Both OT "saints" and NT "martyrs of Jesus" suffered under this harlot. In the end-time persecution, this evil system will participate with the beast in the wholesale murder of the true followers of Jesus.

17:7-18. THE HARLOT AND HER DOOM

The Instrument of Her Doom, 7-14. The *revived* Roman Empire with its end-time emperor (the beast) appears as the agent of the harlot's destruction. (16-18). Its last-day revival is predicted, 8a. It "was" (it existed) in John's day, "and is not" (was prophesied to cease, and did as a united empire in A.D. 476). It returns in the end-time worse than ever with Satanic powers from the abyss (cf. 2 Thess 2:8-9; Rev 9:1-12; 11:7; 13:2), but its continuance is brief, 8b. It shall go into perdition at Christ's advent (19:20). This revival of the Roman power under the beast will occasion great wonder and deception, 8b-9 (13:3-4; 2 Thess 2:8-12). The woman (ecclesiastical Babylon) has her headquarters in the beast's capital, 9b, which is the seven-hilled city of Rome (cf. 18).

The type of government of the revived Roman Empire is indicated,

10. The seven heads are not only seven hills (on which Rome is built and the harlot sits, 9), but they are also seven kings. These "seven kings" evidently refer to seven distinct forms of government which characterized the empire (32 B.C.-A.D. 476). The "five of which have fallen" are kings, consuls, dictators, decemvirs, tribunes. "One is," the imperial form of John's day. "The other," the seventh as following the sixth *imperial* form of government, has yet to come, and when it comes it must remain "only a little while" (its full power is only three and a half years, 13:5).

The last ruler of the revived empire is specified, 11: "And as for the beast which was and is not [the revived empire, 8a], even *he* [*autos*, 'he himself,' the personal beast-emperor now coming into view] is the eighth, and is of the seventh [the imperial government, 10], and he goes into perdition" (Gr.; cf. 8). This diabolical head is unique, 12-14. He rules over a ten-kingdom federation, 12-13, unknown to imperial Roman government, and makes war against the Lamb (16:14; 19:19) in the gigantic conflict for sovereignty over the earth (19:16; cf. 1 Tim 6:15).

The Account of Her Doom, 15-18. The harlot who has dominated and exploited the peoples of the earth, 15, and who has ridden into last-day power on the beast, shall find the beast turning against her at the end to utterly destroy her, 16. This will occur by God's providential overruling to fulfill His Word, 17. Destruction is her judgment (18:6) because of her evil desire to dominate earthly rulers for her own selfish and deceptive interests, 18.

18:1-24. JUDGMENT OF COMMERCIAL BABYLON

Her Destruction Announced, 1-8. A great angel announces her utter ruin, 1. She "is fallen, is fallen" (completely fallen) because of her corrupting sin of commercialism, 2-3. God's people are commanded to separate from her (2 Cor 6:14-17), 4, for her iniquity is full, 5, and her pride calls for full and immediate punishment, 6-8.

Her Destruction Is Lamented, 9-19. Those who grew wealthy on her traffic bewail her, 9-11. Her rich commerce is outlined, 12-19 (cf. Isa 13:21-22), and echoes from the taunt songs in Isa 23—24, 47; Jer 50—51; Ezk 26—27.

Her Destruction Is Effected, 20-24. All heaven is summoned to rejoice over her destruction together with "saints and apostles and prophets." The reason for such joy is that "God has avenged you on her." This shows that God alone is the real destroyer of the Satanic world system, both ecclesiastical and commercial. The "millstone" thrown into the sea symbolizes Babylon's utter destruction, 21-23, for she is guilty of the blood of God's people, 24.

BABYLON

The Babylon of ch. 18 is the Satanic world system in its godless commercial and economic aspects. This system honeycombs all phases of the life of unregenerate mankind organized as a system under Satan. Chapter 17 highlights the religious aspects of Babylon, but its ramifications are cultural, scientific, educational and governmental as well. The Satanic world system of Babylon is mentioned in more than 30 NT passages. Satan is its directing head (Jn 12:31; 14:30; 16:11; 1 Jn 5:19; Rev 2:13). The system is pronounced by God as wholly evil (Gal 1:4; Col 1:13; 2 Pet 2:20; Jas 4:4; 1 Jn 4:3). It is shown to be limited and temporary (1 Jn 4:4), as Rev 17—18 proves. It is doomed to destruction at Christ's second advent (1 Jn 2:17; Rev 17—18; 19:11-16; 20:1-3). It is characterized by greed, pride and war (Jas 4:1-4), and is a perpetual snare to God's people (1 Jn 2:16; Rev 18:4-5).

The Return of Christ, Ch. 19

19:1-5. REJOICING AT BABYLON'S FALL

Heaven Rejoices, 1-4. Ecclesiastical Babylon (ch. 17), together with commercial Babylon (ch. 18), must be judged before the true Bride (19:6-10; 21:9-21) is revealed, 1a. Wicked earth dwellers lament (18:9-19) but heaven rejoices (18:20—19:6) over Babylon's fall. Heaven's rejoicing is celebrated by the great multitude (representing all the glorified saints in heaven), angels, and the 24 elders. They ascribe deliverance, glory and power to God, 1c, employing the Heb. word "hallelujah" (Gr. "alleluia"), "praise Yah" (i.e., Yahweh, the Lord), 1, 3, 4, 6, in celebration of Babylon's eternal ruin, 2-4.

The Throne Speaks, 5. This symbolizes God Himself speaking from the center and source of His government. A new cause for rejoicing, too, comes into view. The marriage of the Lamb is about to be announced.

19:6-10. THE MARRIAGE OF THE LAMB

The Wedding, 6-8. This grand event is preluded by the announcement that God Almighty assumes kingly power in Christ, 6a, and occasions the fourth and last "hallelujah," 6b, and supreme exultation, 6c-7a. It calls for honoring the Lamb, for this event is not said to be the marriage of the Bride, but "of the Lamb." The Bride, spoken of as "wife" to be, represents the NT Church (Jn 14:3; 1 Thess 4:13-17; Eph 5:32). The figure of "wife" symbolizes the glorified Church joined to Christ her Head in royal administration and dignity in the kingdom. The figure of marriage symbolizes the outward, public consummation of the inner spiritual union between Christ and His Church (1 Cor 12:13; Rom 6:3-4; Gal 3:27; Eph 5:25-27, 30; Rev 21:9). The Bride making herself ready presupposes her being made fit by God through Christ (Col 1:12) and having her works reviewed at the *bema* (judgment seat) of Christ (see notes on 1 Cor 3:11-14; 2 Cor 5:10). The Bride's robes prefigure the righteousness of Christ (Rom 3:21-22), graciously given to her both by imputation and sovereignly on the basis of Christ's works ("righteous acts") performed in and through her (Phil 2:13), 8 (ASV).

The Guests, 9-10. This feature of the wedding is important, hence the command to "write," 9a. The bliss of the invited guests is stressed in 9b, "Blessed [happy] are they who are called." They are clearly distinguished from the Bride, evidently OT saints (Jn 3:29). It is called a "marriage supper," 9b, as it is a blessed reward for God's own in contrast to the supper of judgment (19:17). John the seer is overwhelmed by both the message and the messenger, and is reminded that the focus of prophecy is in Jesus, 10.

19:11-16. CHRIST'S SECOND ADVENT

The Conqueror and His Victorious Army, 11-14. Christ's coming is described in a symbolic vision. John sees "heaven opened," 11a (cf. 4:1 where only "a door was opened in heaven"). The vision is the departure of Christ from heaven with His saints and angels to claim His kingship over the earth. His victory is denoted by His sitting "on a white horse," 11b, symbolic of victorious conquest (cf. 6:2; Ps 45:4). His triumph is on the basis of His being faithful and true to the will of God in an unqualified sense, 11c (Phil 2:5-11). He comes to judge and wage war, 11d; but contrary to many other warriors, when Jesus comes He comes absolutely "in righteousness." He exercises omniscient judgment, 12a, symbolized by His "eyes as a flame of fire" (cf. 1:14; 2:18), and has absolute authority, 12b, shown by His many diadems. These saints wear a victor's crown (*stephanos*), not a monarch's crown (diadem) (4:4-10). Christ has a humanly inscrutable name, 12c (cf. Mt 11:27). He comes in vengeance upon His enemies, denoted by His garment "dipped in [His enemies'] blood," 13a (cf. Isa 63:1-4). His name is "the Word of

873

God," 13b, proclaiming Him as God and Creator (Jn 1:1, 3) as well as Redeemer (Jn 1:14), and hence with double right to rule the earth as Creator-Redeemer (Eph 1:13-14; Rev 5:1-7). The armies of heaven (saints and angels) are associated with Him in His victory, 14. He comes on a white horse in victorious conquest. His redeemed share His triumph, and are also seen coming on white horses.

The Conqueror and His Conquest, 15-16. *He conquers supernaturally, 15a.* The "sharp sword" is the omnipotent, irresistible Word of God that spoke the universe into being. It slays His enemies (Isa 11:4; cf. Jn 18:5-6; Heb 11:3). *He rules with stern inflexibility, 15b.* He shall rule peacefully, as a shepherd, but those who are rebellious will find His shepherd's staff a rod of iron (12:5; Ps 2:9), a symbol of unflinching severity against sin. *He will deal with unsparing vengeance on evil, 15c* (cf. 14:17-20). The figure of the vintage signifies the unrelieved judgment of evil (cf Isa 63:3, 6; cf. Mt 21:44). *He comes with absolute royal sovereignty,* 16. Universal dominion is His (Ps 45:3; Rev 1:5; 17:14; cf. 1 Tim 6:15). His name, denoting His full kingship and lordship over all the earth and men, is His right as Creator and Redeemer. The appellative "King *par excellence* and Lord *par excellence*" is on His "garment," and on His "thigh," where one would expect His sword (instead of issuing from His mouth, 15). This fact intimates that His sovereign dominion is that which is His by the word and will of God, not that which He must win through a literal sword.

19:17-21. ARMAGEDDON

The Great Supper of God, 17-18. This "great supper" contrasts with "the marriage supper of the Lamb" (19:9). One denotes the blissful fellowship and glorious destiny of the righteous in heaven. The other symbolizes the destruction of Christ's enemies on earth (cf. Dan 7:5; Ezk 32:21-32). The catastrophe of Armageddon (see 16:13-16) is effected by the word from the mouth of the returning Christ. Five times in this context the word "flesh" is used for the food of birds of prey. Armageddon will be a vivid demonstration of the sinfulness of "the flesh" (Rom 7:18), its transiency (Isa 40:6) and shameful end (cf. Ezk 39:4, 17-20).

The Total Destruction of Christ's Foes, 19-21. The beast (see 13:1-10) and his confederate kings and armies are seen gathered to make war against the Lamb. The beast and the false prophet (13:11-

18, see notes) are both cast alive into Gehenna (eternal hell, the eternal abode of *all* evildoers, 20:15), 20. "Brimstone" signifies terrible torment (14:10). The portrait of the fearful slaughter is repeated, 21.

The Millennium and Final Judgment, Ch. 20

20:1-3. SATAN BOUND

The Vision of the Angel, 1. This vision symbolizes an event which is the natural outcome of the events of ch. 19. Satan, the prime instigator of earth's evils and opposition to God, must be dealt with before Christ's kingdom can be established on earth (4-6). "The angel" represents the agent of God's authority over the underworld. The "key" and the "chain" portray in figurative language the divine authority itself.

The Binding of Satan, 2-3. This is signified by an angel's laying hold of the dragon in the sense of subduing and vanquishing him. The angel is seen "coming down" from heaven to take Satan, because Satan has been expelled from the heavenlies to the earth (cf. Eph 6:10-12; Rev 12:9). Satan's character is represented by: (1) "the dragon," to denote his cruelty; (2) "the serpent," to represent his cunning deception; (3) "old," because he operated thus in Eden (Gen 3:1); (4) "the devil," to indicate his malicious slander (12:10); (5) Satan ("opposer"), because of his rebellion against God's will, 2. The duration of Satan's binding is the length of the millennium. This binding is necessary because the kingdom has for its object the restoration of the divine authority over the earth (Acts 15:14-17), against which Satan is the chief opponent and the principal rebel. The place of imprisonment is the abyss, the prison of the demons (Lk 8:31; Rev 9:2; 17:8). Satan is loosed for a final revolt after the millennium (7-9); then cast into eternal hell, Gehenna (10) to share the fate of the beast, the false prophet (19:20) and unsaved men (20:15; Mt 25:41).

20:4-6. THE SAINTS REIGN

Classes of Saints Reigning With Christ, 4. *The first company, 4a,* consists of all the redeemed from Abel to the translation of the Church (1 Cor 6:2-3; cf. Dan 7:9-10, ASV). *The second company, 4b,* consists of the souls of the martyrs of the early part of the Tribulation period in their disembodied state (cf. 6:9-11). The reason for their death is their "witness of Jesus" and their faithful adherence, as a remnant, to the Word of God. *The third company,* 4c, consists of the individuals (souls) who had not worshiped the beast (13:15-17) and belong to the martyrs of the last part of the Tribulation period.

The First Resurrection, 4d-6. "And they," the martyred of the Tribulation period, 4b, c, "lived," i.e., were resurrected. Their resurrection thus occurs *after* the marriage of the Lamb (19:7-9) and at the beginning of the kingdom. Hence they are distinct both from the Bride (the Church) and the guests (OT saints), but all three companies (4a-c) comprise those in the *first resurrection,* 6a, who are "blessed and holy." They are to be distinguished from the unsaved ("the rest of the dead") who are not resurrected till the second resurrection to perdition (11-15) after the millennium, 5 (cf. Jn 5:29). "The second death," Gehenna (the lake of fire), has no power over these, 6b, but they shall be king-priests of God associated with Christ the King-Priest (Zech 6:9-15), and shall reign during the thousand-year Kingdom Age, 6c (cf. 11:15).

20:7-10. SATAN LOOSED

Satan's Last Rebellion, 7-9. Verse 7 resumes the history of Satan begun in verse 3, interrupted by the account of the saints' reign during the millennium. After His thousand-year imprisonment, Satan is liberated from the abyss to test man's loyalty to God under the ideal conditions of the last of God's ordered ages, before the eternal state, 7. The result is his successful deception of "the nations" in the final human confederacy. This postmillennial rebellion will be similar to the premillennial one (Ezk 38—39) and therefore metaphorically called "Gog and Magog" (see notes on Ezk 38—39). However, this rebellion will be worldwide and comprise the final coalition against God, His people and the Holy City, Jerusalem, 8-9. The rebels will evidently be individuals among the nations who, to a large extent, yielded only feigned allegiance to Messiah's iron rule (Ps 2:9; 18:44; 66:3; 81:15). Israel will be loyal to her Messiah (Jer 31:31-34; Rom 11:26). The result of the revolt will be the complete supernatural destruction of the rebels and the end of divine toleration of evil upon the earth, 9.

Satan's Final Doom, 10. Satan's predestined judgment (Gen 3:15) is now executed. First cast out of the heavenlies (12:9); then imprisoned in the abyss (20:1-3), he is now consigned to his eternal fate, the lake of fire. "Fire and brimstone" speak of inexpressible torment (14:10; Isa 30:33). The lake of fire will contain (1) the beast and the false prophet, who are already there, 10, preserved "with fire" (Mk 9:49) and punished in proportion to their sin; (2) "the devil and his angels," and (3) the unsaved (Mt 25:41).

20:11-15. THE FINAL JUDGMENT

The Throne and the Judge, 11. This scene of judgment closes the millennium and marks the beginning of eternity. The judgment concerns the wicked dead. "A great white throne" describes the *greatest* judgment ever held, "white" depicting divine purity and righteousness, which characterize God's decisions, 11a. "Him that sat on it" is Christ (Jn 5:22), to whom all judgment is committed, 11b. The living He has already judged (Mt 25:31); now He is about to judge the dead (cf. 2 Tim 4:1).

The Dead and Their Judgment, 12-15. The subjects of this judgment are those who are both physically and spiritually dead, 12a. *All the unsaved are included*—"small and great," no matter what their position on the earth may have been, 12b. They stand, in the agony and shame of their sins, before a throne which is "great" and "white." They have neither altar nor blood for forgiveness. Each sinner is face to face with God alone, 12c. They are faced with their works, 12d, but are lost because they did not accept God's salvation. As lost souls, they are judged on the basis of what they did (Eph 5:6). The book of life is opened, 12e, which is the register of the saved (13:8; 17:8). It contains the name of not one unsaved person, demonstrating that this is purely the sinner's judgment, 15. The wicked dead are raised, 13, as death holding the body and Hades the soul surrender their prisoners (cf. Jn 5:28-29). Death and hell (Hades) are finally done away with, 14, at the completion of the first resurrection (1 Cor 15:26). The doom of the unsaved is the "lake of fire . . . the second death," the place of the isolation of evil and all sinners from God in eternity.

The City of God and the Eternal State, 21:1—22:5

21:1-8. THE ETERNAL STATE

Eternity and the Righteous, 1-7. Revelation 21:1-8 belongs with 19:1—20:15, to which it forms the natural conclusion in a sequence of events issuing in the eternal state (cf. Isa 65:17; 66:22; 1 Cor 15:24-28; Eph 3:21; 2 Pet 3:13). Eternity is characterized by a new heaven and a new earth, 1. The old heaven and earth are completely renovated by fire, not annihilated (2 Pet 3:10; Rev 20:11).

The renovation includes the elimination of the oceans, necessary now and in the kingdom, but not in the eternal state. The New Jerusalem, 2, represents the glorified Church (3:12) *after* the millennial reign. She is called "holy" because she is glorified and sinlessly joined to Christ in administrative and ruling dignity (1 Jn 3:2; Rom 8:29; Phil 3:21). She comes "out of" heaven, her home (Col 3:1-4), 2. God's dwelling with men, 3, is now possible (1 Cor 15:24-28) because Adam's curse has been removed, Satan judged, the wicked punished, and the universe sinless, except for "the lake of fire" (20:15). In the millennium God spread His tabernacle *over* His people (7:15, ASV); now He tabernacles *with* them. All traces of sin are removed, 4. The authentication of this grand finale of divine redemption is by God Himself, 5. Meanwhile, an offer of salvation is made to the sinner, 6 (cf. Jn 7:37-39), and of rewards to the saint who overcomes, 7, all in the light of eternity.

Eternity and the Unrighteous, 8. God's sinless, blissful eternity will have only one isolation ward for sin and sinners. It is "the second death" or "lake of fire" (20:14). This is the eternal abode of the wicked. It is called "second" in reference to the sinner's preceding physical death while in a state of spiritual death and because it represents eternal death in separation from God. It is as eternal as the throne of God (Heb 1:8) is eternal (cf. 19:20; 20:10). The unsaved, who are described at length, 8, are its tenants.

21:9-10. THE VISION OF THE CITY INTRODUCED

The Angelic Invitation, 9. "One of the seven angels," the same angel who had invited John to view the judgment of ecclesiastical and political Babylon (17:1), here invites the seer to view the Lamb's wife, the Bride. This is a reference to the city of the Lamb, an orientalism which saw the city of a ruler as wed to him.

The View of the Great City, 10. John is carried away in "the spirit," i.e., in the vision, to a suitable vantage point from which he views the descent of the holy Jerusalem. The greatness of the city is seen in the following dimensions and splendor, 11-23. This city takes the place of and supersedes the historical Jerusalem which passed away with the first earth, 1b, and becomes part of the new earth, 2a.

21:11-21. A DESCRIPTION OF THE CITY

Her Identity, 11-14. The city is the magnificent symbol of the eternal abode and destiny of the redeemed of all ages. God's saints have always envisioned such a city (Heb 11:10, 16; 13:14; Jn 14:1-3). Its inhabitants will be God the Father in full revelation of divine light and glory, 11, glorified OT saints (Heb 11:40), NT Church saints (the Bride, the Lamb's wife), myriads of unfallen angels, and our blessed Lord Himself (Heb 12:22-23). Both Israel and the Church appear prominently in the city, 12c, 14, the great high wall, 12a, denoting the safety and security of all its inhabitants, who are bathed in God's radiant and unveiled majesty.

Her Size, 15-17. The dazzling city's measurements reveal a solid cube of golden construction 12,000 furlongs (1500 miles) broad, wide and high. This could mean 2,250,000 square miles on each tier of the cube extending 1500 miles upward, like a huge skyscraper with innumerable floors.

Her Splendor, 18-21. The glorious destiny of the redeemed in eternity is symbolized by the city's adornment with every divine beauty, her wall being of jasper, and the city itself of pure gold, both crystal-clear, 18. Each of the 12 foundations is a spectacular gem of unusual brilliance and color, 19-20. These foundations are not sections divided into three on each side of the city, but 12 layers, each of which encircles the city. Looking at them would give a rainbow or prism effect of symmetrical beauty. Each gate is a pearl, 21, and the street is transparent gold.

21:22—22:5. LIFE WITHIN THE CITY

Her Temple, 22. No visible temple will adorn the city of God, for there is no need for a place of worship. God the Almighty and Christ the Lamb dwell in the midst of the redeemed and there is direct access. Indirect approach through a temple with its altar is entirely unnecessary.

Her Light, 23-24. There is no need for the heavenly luminaries to give light, for the radiant glory of God will illuminate the city. All will be bright with His light.

Her Honor, 24b, 26. The nations and kings of the earth will bring their glory to her, and her authority will be universally acknowledged.

Her Gates, 25. Her gates need never be closed, for her enemies have all been destroyed, and there is no darkness to hide them, if there were enemies.

Her Citizenry, 27. Nothing unclean will find lodging in the city, for moral and spiritual uncleanness will be unknown within her walls.

The redeemed righteous, totally free from sin's defilement and presence, will constitute her inhabitants. Their names are on God's roll, "the Lamb's book of life."

Paradise Restored, 1-5. The complete removal of the curse brings even more than paradise ever enjoyed before the Fall. The environment will be perfect. Fullness of life ("river of the water of life") flows from the source of eternal life, God the Father through the Son (the Lamb), 1. It is readily available to all ("in the middle of its street"), 2a. Every desire is met in the kinds of fruit available, 2b, and spiritual blessing becomes a reality for all, 2c. The curse is removed and with it all the laborious toil, futility, and rebellion which marked and marred man's history, 3. The redeemed will readily submit to the Lord's sovereignty, and as His bond servants they will serve Him, seeing His face in intimate fellowship and being identified by His name on their foreheads, 4. What perfect occupation! Light will mark life in the eternal state, resulting in complete happiness and fellowship, with the redeemed reigning for endless ages, 5. In all this the Lamb is focal!

Closing Testimonies, 22:6-21

22:6-11.   THE TESTIMONY OF THE ANGEL AND OF CHRIST

The Angel Authenticates the Prophecy, 6. The truth of these great predictions is attested, 6a, and the OT foundation and NT fulfillment are declared, 6b. The same God who inspired the ancient seers has sent His angel to reveal these prophecies to His NT servants, because the prophecies are soon to be fulfilled, 6c.

Christ Himself Announces His Soon Coming, 7 (cf. vv. 12, 20). The blessing of him who treasures the words of the Apocalypse is promised and repeated (cf. 1:3; 22:7).

The Angel Pronounces the Book Unsealed, 8-11. John made a similar mistake previously of worshiping an angel, 8-9 (19:10). Worshiping any creature is an affront to the Creator. The angel declares the book of the Revelation is to be unsealed, 10, in contrast to the command to seal Daniel's prophecy (Dan 12:4, 9). The reason for not sealing this prophecy is that "the time is at hand" (Gr. "is near"). Verse 11 describes the permanency of human destiny. There is no second chance after death or the Lord's return.

22:12-21. THE CONCLUDING TESTIMONY
OF CHRIST

His Coming and Rewards, 12-15. Christ announces once again the certainty and nearness of His coming, 12a. He declares the rewards He will render for works, 12b. These rewards are dispensed at the judgment seat of Christ (see notes on 2 Cor 5:10; 1 Cor 3:11-15; 9:24-27). He, the Rewarder, is the eternal Christ, 13. Living faith in Christ alone gives access to the tree of life (Jn 3:16; Eph 2:8-9) and entrance into the eternal city, 14. Unsaved people are debarred, 15.

His Person and Relationships to Mankind, 16-19. He who has sent His angel to testify "these things" (the whole content of the book) to the churches, 16a, describes Himself *in His relation to Israel,* 16b: "*I* [emphatic] am the root and offspring of David." As the "root" He is divine, David's Lord. As the "offspring" He is human, David's son (Ps 110:1). By virtue of who He is, the crown of Israel is His, both by promise and prophecy. Born as King of the Jews (Mt 2:2), He died as King of the Jews (Mt 27:37). He will yet reign as King of the Jews (Zech 9:9). *In His relation to the Church,* 16c, He is "the bright and morning star" (cf. 2:28). This presents Him in His second advent when He returns for His Bride before the dawn of the millennial day. *In His relation to every soul that thirsts,* 17, He invites them to come and take of "the water of life freely" (cf. Jn 7:37-39). He warns against taking away or adding to the book of the Revelation, 18-19. "The book of life," 19, is not in some ancient texts.

Christ Declares His Soon Coming, 20a. "Behold, I come quickly" (soon, shortly). These words are His final message to the Church. They assert His soon coming, repeated (for emphasis) for the last time.

The Church Replies to Her Lord, 20b. John, representing the Church, as well as his own keen desire, cries, "Amen. Come, Lord Jesus," or, "Yes, indeed, come, Lord Jesus."

The Closing Benediction, 21. John, the beloved apostle and seer, also adds a benediction. "The grace of our Lord Jesus be with you all" (the saints). So ends this magnificent prophetic panorama of God's ways with man, as well as the completed sacred revelation itself.

HOW THE BIBLE CAME TO US

THE EARLIEST HEBREW SCRIPTURES

The OT Scriptures were penned over a period extending more than a millennium, from c. 1450 to c. 400 B.C. According to conservative scholars, Moses was the first inspired writer, producing the Pentateuch around 1450-1400 B.C. (see pp. 34-35, "Authorship of the Pentateuch"). Malachi, the last of the OT writers, wrote not later than 400 B.C. For a discussion of more technical matters relating to authorship, date, etc., of the various OT books, see Gleason L. Archer, *A Survey of Old Testament Introduction* (1964), and Merrill F. Unger, *An Introductory Guide to the Old Testament* (1952).

THE TEXT OF THE OLD TESTAMENT

The earliest parts of the OT were originally inscribed on leather or papyrus in old Hebrew with the archaic prong-shaped letters similar to the script of the earliest recovered Phoenician inscriptions, e.g., b=𐤁; h=𐤄; m=𐤌. This archaic writing gradually developed, after 400 B.C., into the round-bellied letters found in the Dead Sea Scrolls, later Hebrew MSS., and in printed Hebrew Bibles since 1477, e.g., b=ב; h=ה; m=ם.

CANONIZATION OF THE OLD TESTAMENT

The canon of Scripture is a phrase by which the catalog of the authoritative sacred writings is designated. The word for the expression, of Greek derivation, *kanōn*, originally signified a reed or measuring rod. Actually it indicated "that which measures," that is, a standard, norm or rule; specifically, "that which is measured" by that standard or norm. Those books which were measured by the standard or test of divine inspiration and authority, and were adjudged to be "God-breathed," were included in "the canon."

Conservatives hold that inspired Scripture had the impress of canonical authority from the moment of inspiration by the Spirit of God, independent of formal collection or mere human recognition. The higher critical view, however, is that canonization took extensive time. According to this theory, the Law was first canonized by 444 B.C., the Prophets not until 300-200 B.C., and the Writings about 165-100 B.C. (see "Order of Books in the Hebrew Old Testament," pp. 3-4). Higher criticism thus assumes that the threefold division of the Hebrew canon is due principally to chronology. It is held that the

Prophets did not become popular until after 300 B.C., and as a result their writings were collected and canonized within the next century. Alleged "Second" and "Third" Isaiah (ch. 40—66 mainly) were attached to Isaiah because their authors were completely forgotten. Daniel was supposedly not written until 167 B.C. and assumed to be too late to be included in the second or prophetic section. Other books, such as Esther, 1 and 2 Chronicles, and Ezra-Nehemiah, are said to have been composed too late to be included in the historical section.

Conservative criticism, however, maintains that the threefold division of the Hebrew canon can be explained by either the status of the writer, or the arrangement of the books for liturgical convenience. Early dates for the OT books which maintain their integrity are accordingly held. Strict adherence to the Jewish canon has always been the Protestant position.

THE WORK OF THE MASORETES

Before A.D. 500 Hebrew manuscripts had no system of vowel indication, except certain consonants to indicate long vowels. Between A.D. 600 and 950 Jewish scholars, called Masoretes (Traditionalists), invented a full system of vowels and accents to punctuate the text. They also standardized the text, including marginal readings (called *keri*) and textual variants (called *kethiv*). The work of the Masoretes on the Hebrew Bible providentially prepared it for the advent of the printing press five centuries later.

PRINTED HEBREW BIBLES

The Psalter was the first part of the Hebrew Bible put into print. It appeared in 1477. In 1488 the first edition of the entire Hebrew OT appeared printed with vowels and accents.

THE EARLIEST CHRISTIAN SCRIPTURES

For almost two decades after our Lord's ascension, the OT Scriptures, mainly in Greek, constituted the only Bible in existence (see pp. 1-5). The first NT book was apparently James, written perhaps as early as A.D. 45. The Apocalypse is commonly viewed as the latest, dating about A.D. 95. During this early period the church employed the OT as its Bible. Peter preached from the OT (Acts 2:14-36), as did Stephen (Acts 7:2-53), Philip (Acts 8:32-35) and Paul. *All* the NT writers were imbued with the OT and their inspired writings were grounded in its inspired revelation.

ORIGIN OF THE NEW TESTAMENT BOOKS

The gospel (1 Cor 15:3-4) was first preached by word of mouth and interpreted in the light of OT history and prophecy. Oral accounts of the life and work of Christ were written down and finally gave way to the inspired Synoptic Gospels sometime before A.D. 70. The need for doctrinal interpretation of Christ's person and work soon became a necessity, accentuated by the need to define Christianity against such errors as legalism and antinomianism. The Pauline and other epistles were written to meet this need. The demand for a historical sketch of the development of the church was met by the book of Acts. The Apocalypse was penned to consummate the revelation of God's plan and purposes for time and eternity.

CANONIZATION OF THE NEW TESTAMENT
Some Early Noncanonical New Testament Books

1 Clement, an epistle penned by Clement of Rome (*c.* A.D. 96) to the Corinthian church, was highly esteemed. It was considered of canonical authority by some and was publicly read in the church at Corinth around 170. Various writers in Egypt used it, such as Clement of Alexandria and Origen. It was attached to Codex Alexandrinus.

2 Clement was an epistle also attached to Codex Alexandrinus. It was falsely ascribed to Clement of Rome and never was widely read. Neither it nor 1 Clement ever enjoyed canonical recognition in the West.

The Didache (The Teaching of the Twelve Apostles) (*c.* 120) was regarded as Holy Scripture by some in Egypt, notably Clement of Alexandria and Origen. It had a wide circulation.

The Epistle of Barnabas (*c.* 130) was included in the Codex Sinaiticus and was accounted authoritative in Egypt. Jerome (*c.* 400) regarded it as apocryphal, and it gradually lost any claim to the status of Holy Scripture.

The Shepherd of Hermas (*c* 140) was written by Hermas, the brother of Pius, bishop of Rome. It was also included in Codex Sinaiticus and was looked upon highly by the Muratorian Canon, but never established itself as Holy Scripture.

Apocalypse of Peter (*c.* 145), of less importance than the preceding books, was nevertheless highly regarded in the East and known in the West. It was not approved by the Muratorian Canon and regarded as spurious by Eusebius.

Acts of Paul (*c.* 170) was circulated widely and viewed by some as canonical, but enlightened scholarship saw its apocryphal nature and gradually it was rejected.

Numerous other later gospels, acts, epistles and apocalypses appeared under apostolic names. These were obviously forgeries and never received serious consideration of the church.

Factors Fostering New Testament Canonicity

The recognition of 1 Clement, the Didache, the Epistle of Barnabas and the Shepherd of Hermas as canonical or semi-canonical, especially in the East, by the end of the 3rd cen. focused attention on the need of a clearly defined canon. Also, the incomplete canon of the heretic Marcion (c. 140) was being widely subscribed to. Marcion was a Gnostic and on doctrinal grounds accepted only Luke's Gospel and ten of the Pauline epistles, after seriously mutilating them. The appearance in time of other apocryphal and pseudepigraphal books clamoring for recognition demanded a clearly delimited canon. Somewhat later the edict of Emperor Diocletian (303), ordering the burning of all sacred books, necessitated carefully defining the canon.

Criteria for New Testament Canonicity

The first criterion was *apostolicity*. Was the writer a bona fide apostle? If not, did he have close associations with an apostle, as was true of the writers of the Gospel of Mark, the Gospel of Luke, the book of Acts and the Epistle to the Hebrews?

The second criterion was *content*. Were the subject matter and the treatment of it of the high order and spiritual stamp demanded by the test of Holy Scripture? By this criterion the spurious books were eliminated.

The third criterion was *universality*. Did the church as a whole receive the book? Did it have a universal appeal?

The fourth criterion was *divine inspiration*. Did the book give unmistakable evidence of being "God-breathed" (2 Tim 3:16)? And did the Holy Spirit give this conviction to men of God that this was true? This was the final test. Without providential interposition the NT canon would never have been correctly delimited.

Books Early Received As Canonical

These recognized books were called by Origen (245) *homologoumena* ("confessed" or "acknowledged" books). They were the NT writings universally owned as inspired Holy Scripture. Origen included the four Gospels, Paul's epistles, 1 Peter, 1 John, Acts and the Apocalypse. Although he did not include Hebrews among the *homologoumena,* he cited the epistle as Pauline, and canonical. In fact, the only books he did not cite as Scripture were Jude and 2 and 3 John.

Eusebius of Caesarea (*c.* 300-325), the church historian, included among the *homologoumena* the four Gospels, Acts, the Pauline epistles, 1 John, 1 Peter and the Revelation. He seems to have inadvertently omitted Hebrews.

New Testament Books at First Questioned

Origen called these questioned books the *antilegomena* ("spoken against" or "disputed"). Among these he placed Hebrews (see above), 2 Peter, 2 and 3 John, James, Jude, and the apocryphal Epistle of Barnabas, the Shepherd of Hermas, the Didache, and the Gospel of the Hebrews.

Eusebius of Caesarea divided the *antilegomena* into (1) those merely disputed or questioned—James, Jude, 2 Peter, 2 and 3 John; (2) those actually spurious or uninspired—Acts of Paul, the Shepherd of Hermas, the Apocalypse of Peter, the Epistle of Barnabas, and the Didache.

Reasons for Doubting Certain New Testament Books

The seven books that at first were challenged are James, 2 Peter, Hebrews, 2 John, 3 John, Jude and the Revelation. The hesitancy of some early church leaders to accept these books is explainable on the basis of their peculiar internal evidence. (1) James and Jude style themselves mere "servants" of Christ, not apostles, while the author of 2 and 3 John refers to himself as a "presbyter" or "elder," not an apostle. John in the Apocalypse calls himself "servant" and "brother." (2) Hebrews is anonymous and differs in vocabulary and style from the recognized Pauline epistles. Peter's second epistle, while not anonymous, differs from 1 Peter in the same way. (3) James, too, was written to early Jewish converts and not addressed to the great universal Gentile church. (4) Jude was questioned also because it allegedly quoted from the apocryphal book of Enoch (1:9; 5:4; cf. Jude 14-15). Gradually, however, all these controverted though genuine books came to be universally accepted by the church. In the West this was accomplished by A.D. 400 and in the East by 500.

Early Growth of the Canon in the West

The Witness of Clement of Rome (*c.* A.D. 96). In his highly revered letter (known as 1 Clement) to the church at Corinth while bishop of Rome, he shows knowledge of Matthew, Romans, 1 Corinthians, and refers over and over again to Hebrews.

The Witness of Marcion (*c.* 140). As a Gnostic heretic he accepted only Luke's Gospel and ten of Paul's epistles. But his testimony, though erroneous, is illuminating and constitutes an important milestone in the church's collection and approval of the present NT canon.

The Witness of Hermas (*c.* 150). As the reputed author of the highly revered Shepherd of Hermas he authenticates Matthew's Gospel, Ephesians, and apparently Hebrews and James, and notably the Apocalypse.

The Witness of Irenaeus (*c.* 140-203). As one who in his youth came in contact with Polycarp at Smyrna and as later bishop of Lyons in Gaul, he bears witness to the four Gospels, Acts, 1 Peter, 1 John, all Paul's letters except Philemon, and the Revelation.

The Witness of the Muratorian Canon (*c.* 172). The fragment was discovered by Muratori, an Italian, in the Ambrosian Library at Milan in 1740. The mutilated beginning contained apparently Matthew and Mark. It attests all the NT books except 1 Peter, 2 Peter, James and Hebrews.

The Witness of the Old Latin Version before 170. It attests all the books except James and 2 Peter, Hebrews being added before Tertullian's time.

The Witness of Tertullian (*c.* 150-222). This voluminous Latin writer of Carthage attests the four Gospels, 13 Pauline epistles, Acts, 1 Peter, 1 John, Jude and the Apocalypse. He rejected Hebrews, however, holding that Barnabas was the author.

The Witness of Cyprian (*c.* 200-258). As bishop of Carthage he closely followed Tertullian regarding Hebrews, and did not quote from Philemon, James, 2 or 3 John, or Jude.

Later Growth of the Canon in the West

The Witness of Jerome (*c.* 340-420). The great translator of the Latin Vulgate and renowned scholar attested *all* our canonical NT books. He accepted Hebrews as written by Paul, and explained how James and 2 Peter came to be recognized. His opinion is of superlative value.

The Witness of Augustine (354-430). His opinion, unlike Jerome's, was clouded. Although he accepted all the seven books which had been questioned, he posited different degrees of scriptural authority and was largely responsible for the wider OT canon of the Roman Catholic Church, including the Apocrypha.

Action of Church Councils. The delimitation of the NT canon was not the work of any council or councils. The inspired worth and intrinsic authority of each individual book were the deciding factors. This fact is strong proof of the genuineness and authenticity of the books that have come down to us in the canon. Not until the close of the 4th cen. did any council make any pronouncement on the subject.

The Third Council of Carthage (397) rendered the first decision on the canon. One of the canons of this body stipulated that only "canonical" books be read in the churches. Then it listed exactly our present-day 27 books. Hebrews was recognized on the ground of being Pauline. The Council of Hippo (419) repeated the list of the Third Council of Carthage. The selection of the canon was thus a spontaneous process that went on in the church till each book proved its own worth.

Growth of the Canon in the East

Ignatius, bishop of Antioch (*c*. 116); Polycarp, bishop of Smyrna (*c*. 69-155), and Papias, bishop of Hierapolis (*c*. 80-*c*. 155), testified to Matthew, John, Paul's epistles, 1 Peter, 1 John and likely Acts.

The Didache (*c*. 120) features Matthew and knows of Luke, as well as the majority of our NT books.

Melito, bishop of Sardis (*c*. 170), quoted from all the NT books except James, Jude, 2 and 3 John.

Theophilus of Antioch (*c*. 115-*c*. 188) adhered to most of the NT books and held them in the same esteem as the OT canon. However, his successor Lucian (martyred 312) in his "Antioch Canon" excluded Revelation, 2 Peter, 2 and 3 John and Jude in his revised OT and NT text.

Basil the Great of Cappadocia (*c*. 329-379) and Gregory of Nazianzus (*c*. 330-390) recognized all the books of our present canon, except the Revelation, although he quoted it by John.

John Chrysostom (347-407) accepted all but 2 Peter, 2 and 3 John and Revelation.

Theodore of Mopsuestia (*c*. 350-428) rejected the Catholic Epistles and the Revelation. The opinion of this part of the church was thus strongly influenced by the canon of Constantinople, which rejected 2 and 3 John, 2 Peter, Jude and Revelation, and which developed from the "Antioch Canon" of Lucian.

The Peshitta (411-435) likewise followed the canon of Constantinople. Not until Philoxenus (c. 508) had the Syriac Peshitta revised to add these rejected books was the unsound influence of the canon of Constantinople broken.

Early Growth of the Canon in Egypt and Palestine

Justin Martyr (c. 100-165) gave important testimony concerning the Revelation, which he considered the work of the apostle John. He also knew Hebrews and probably referred to Mark's Gospel under the title "Memoirs of Peter."

Clement of Alexandria (c. 155-c. 215) was very well read and accepted all the books in our NT, including Jude, Hebrews, the Catholic Epistles and the Revelation.

Origen of Alexandria (c. 185-c. 253) shows evidence of having accepted the books commonly disputed (Hebrews, 2 Peter, 2 and 3 John, James, Jude). He held the Apocalypse to be among the accepted books (homologoumena).

Later Growth of the Canon in Egypt and Palestine

The Chester Beatty Papyri from the 3rd cen., edited in 1933-37 by Sir Frederic Kenyon, authenticate the four Gospels, the Acts, the Pauline epistles and Hebrews (which comes after Romans), and the Revelation (only the portion 9:10—17:2 is preserved, however).

Dionysius of Alexandria (c. 200-265) authenticated Hebrews as Paul's epistle, as well as owning James and 2 and 3 John and the Revelation as inspired Scripture.

Athanasius of Alexandria (298-373) applied the term "canonical" to the exact 27 books of our canonical NT.

Summary of the Formation of the New Testament Canon

The NT canon was formed spontaneously, not by the action of church councils. The inspiration and intrinsic authority of each individual book were the determining factors in their eventual recognition and canonization. By A.D. 200 the NT contained essentially the same books as we have today. These were regarded with the same authority and finality by Christians then as they are now.

In the 3rd cen. the antilegomena were debated. The book of Revelation was opposed in the East. Hebrews was controverted in the West. By the end of the 3rd cen. practically all the extra-canonical books had been dropped from authoritative lists.

During the 4th cen., debate on questions of the canonical status of certain books practically ceased in the West, due to Jerome's and Augustine's influence and the clear distinctions made regarding the canon by Athanasius in Egypt. The Third Council of Carthage (397) sealed the decision reached, and from that time on no appreciable opposition to any of the NT books continued.

Debate in the East persisted, however, for some time longer. But the example of the West, of Athanasius in Alexandria, and the influence of the Cappadocian fathers swept away all opposition. With the addition of 2 and 3 John, 2 Peter, Jude and the Revelation to the Peshitta (Syriac Bible), the question of the canon was settled for the East also. Thus the canonicity of the NT was settled, for all practical purposes, in the West around A.D. 400 and in the East by A.D. 500.

History of the Canon Till the Present

Apart from a few very minor differences, the verdict of the first four centuries on the NT canon has remained the verdict of the church down to the present. During the Reformation the reformers insisted on the authority of an infallible Bible over against the alleged authority of an infallible church.

However, concerning the OT canon, the Roman Church at the Council of Trent in 1546, by the *Decree Sacrosancta,* declared 11 of the 14 apocryphal books canonical. These are Tobit, Judith, Wisdom of Solomon, Ecclesiasticus, Baruch, 1 and 2 Maccabees, the Song of the Three, Susanna, and Bel and the Dragon. They also accepted additions to the book of Esther.

TEXT OF THE NEW TESTAMENT

No other document from antiquity has influenced the Western world as much as the NT. Nor is the text of any ancient document so well attested. It exists in almost 5,000 Greek manuscripts (hand-written copies) and in more than 10,000 manuscripts which are copies of the early versions, besides in thousands of quotations from the Church Fathers. The problem of textual criticism is to use these copies in order to determine by study and comparison the pure original text.

SOURCES FOR NEW TESTAMENT TEXTUAL CRITICISM

The papyri. As a result of a century of archaeological research, more than 75 papyrus fragments of the NT text now exist, designated by the letter P, with index numbers, as P[1], P[2]. These date from the 2nd to the 8th cen., covering parts of 25 books, about 40 percent of the NT text. P[52] contains parts of John 18:31-34, 37-38 and dates around A.D. 135, being the oldest. P[45], P[46], P[47] belong to the Chester Beatty Papyri I, II, III (*c.* A.D. 200). P[66] is the famous Bodmer Papyrus II of John's Gospel, dating *c.* A.D. 200. P[75] is the newly acquired Bodmer Papyrus XIV-XV of John and Luke, dating *c.* A.D. 200.

Uncials. These are written on parchment in a semi-capital style letter, and were used in NT MSS. until *c.* 800. About 300 uncials exist.

Minuscules. Manuscripts of this class were executed in a cursive or running script and date from the 9th to the 18th cen. A total of 2,647 minuscules have been cataloged.

Versions. The most valuable are those executed from the original Greek prior to 1000. Of these, the most important are the Old Latin (2nd cen.), the Vulgate (Latin) of Jerome (382-84), the Syriac (4th, 5th cen.), Coptic (2nd-4th cen.), Armenian (early 5th cen.), Old Georgian (5th cen.), Ethiopic and Gothic (mid 4th cen.).

Lectionaries. These are church service books containing Scripture lessons to be read throughout the year. About 2,000 lectionaries exist, both uncials and cursives. They date from *c.* 280 to *c.* 1600.

Ostraca and Talismans. Twenty-five ostraca and nine talismans (amulets) are now known engraved with portions of the NT text. They date from about the 4th to the 13th cen.

Quotations from the Church Fathers. More than 86,000 of these are known.

OLDEST OLD TESTAMENT MANUSCRIPTS

The Oldest Masoretic Hebrew MSS. date not earlier than the later 9th cen. These are the Cairo Codex of the Prophets (A.D. 895), the Aleppo Codex of the whole OT (*c.* 925) and the Leningrad Codex (completed A.D. 1108). This latter is used as the text of Kittel's *Biblia Hebraica.* The Dead Sea Scrolls, notably the two Isaiah MSS., discovered since 1947, however, give us a Hebrew text a millennium earlier, together with fragments of all but one of the OT books dating from the 2nd to the 1st cen. B.C.

OLDEST NEW TESTAMENT MANUSCRIPTS

Codex Sinaiticus (אּ), 4th cen. The NT is complete on 148 leaves. It was discovered by Tischendorf in the monastery of St. Catherine at Mount Sinai in 1844 and 1859. Also it contains fragments of the OT in Greek.

Codex Alexandrinus (A), 5th cen. It contains most of the OT and NT. It was presented by the Patriarch of Constantinople to Charles I of England in 1627, and transferred to the British Museum in 1757.

Codex Vaticanus (B), 4th cen. This has been in the Vatican Library at Rome since 1481. It contains almost the complete OT and NT, except for Heb 9:14—13:25, the Pastoral Epistles, Philemon and the Revelation.

Codex Ephraemi (C), 5th cen. It contains 145 leaves of NT out of 238.

Codex Bezae (D), 5th cen. Not all the NT remains.

Chester Beatty Papyrus I (P[45]), early 3rd cen. It contains 30 leaves of the original papyrus codex of the Gospels and Acts.

Chester Beatty Papyrus II (P[46]), early 3rd cen. Eighty-six of original 104 leaves of papyrus codex of Paul's epistles are in existence.

Chester Beatty Papyrus III (P[47]), late 3rd cen. Ten leaves of original 32 of papyrus codex of Revelation are extant.

Bodmer Papyrus II (P[66]), early 3rd cen. One hundred fifty pages of a papyrus codex of the Gospel of John are in existence.

Bodmer Papyrus XIV-XV (P[75]), early 3rd cen. All 144 pages out of an original 144 pages of the Gospels of Luke and John were found.

ENGLISH VERSIONS OF THE BIBLE

Early Anglo-Saxon Versions. Caedmon, by 680, had rendered Bible stories in common speech in poetic paraphrase, according to Bede. Bede (died 735) is credited with a translation of John's Gosple. King Alfred (848-901) had portions of the Bible translated into the vernacular. But until the time of Wycliffe (14 cen.) and Tyndale (16th cen.), the Bible was translated into English only sporadically and piecemeal.

Wycliffe's Version (1382). This was the first complete translation into English, revised *c.* 1400, condemned and burned in 1415. At least 170 MS. copies have survived. Its weakness was that it was based on the Latin Vulgate instead of the original Greek.

Tyndale's Translation (1525-35). Translated from the original Hebrew and Greek, the significance of Tyndale's version lies in its being first in a line of translations, so creative and impressive in its style that it formed the backbone of the Authorized King James Version of 1611.

The Coverdale Version (1535). Miles Coverdale leaned on Tyndale's scholarly work. He supplemented it, where it had not been finished, by his own translation from German and Latin. He presented the first completed English Bible in print.

The Thomas Matthew Bible (1537). Largely a revision of Tyndale by Tyndale's friend John Rogers, it was nevertheless published under the name of Thomas Matthew.

The Taverner's Bible (1539), a revision by Richard Taverner of the Matthew Bible minus most of the notes and polemic data.

The Great Bible (1539) was the first authorized Bible, called "great" from its size. It was also styled the "Cranmer Bible" because of Archbishop Cranmer's preface to the second edition (1540).

The Geneva Bible (1560) was a revision of the Great Bible.

The Bishops' Bible (1568) was the second authorized English Bible and was intended to supersede the Geneva Bible, the Bible of the people, and the Great Bible, the pulpit Bible of the churches. The translation work was done mainly by scholarly bishops.

The Douay Version (1609-10) was the first Roman Catholic Bible in English.

The King James Version (1611) was the culmination of these preceding early translations and revisions, and became the third "authorized" English Bible, sponsored by James I of England. It employed the chapter divisions of Stephen Langton, archbishop of Canterbury in the 13th cen., and the verse divisions of Robert Estienne (1551). This version reigned supreme from 1611 to 1881.

The Revised Version (1881-85). A revision of the King James Version based on a literal translation of the Greek and Hebrew texts by sixty-five English scholars.

The American Standard Version (1901). An American edition of the Revised Version of 1885, including preferred readings and format changes, by a group of American scholars under the direction of William H. Green of Princeton Seminary.

The Revised Standard Version of the Bible (1952); *New Testament* (1946). Authorized by the National Council of Churches of Christ in the U.S.A., widely used by denominations in that group and many not in its membership. Although this version has many excellencies, it is weak and obscure in its translation of certain key OT messianic passages.

The New English Bible: New Testament (1961). A completely new translation by English scholars under the direction of C. H.

893

Dodd of Cambridge. It is aimed at rendering the original Greek into idiomatic English, free from archaisms and from transient modernisms. It has enjoyed an enthusiastic reception in the U.S., but not without question by many evangelicals.

MODERN SPEECH TRANSLATIONS

The Twentieth Century New Testament (1898-1901, revised 1904), by an anonymous group of scholars.

The New Testament in Modern Speech (1903), by Richard F. Weymouth, which has been revised twice by others.

The New Testament: A New Translation (1913), by James Moffatt. His Old Testament appeared in 1924 and a final revision in 1935.

The New Testament: An American Translation (1923), by Edgar J. Goodspeed, in American colloquial language.

The Riverside New Testament (1923, revised 1934), by William G. Ballantine.

The New Testament: A Translation in the Language of the People (1937), by Charles B. Williams.

The New Testament: The Berkeley Version in Modern English (1945), by Gerrit Verkuyl. The Old Testament was completed in 1959 by a group of conservative scholars.

The New Testament in Plain English (1952), by Charles Kingsley Williams.

An Expanded Translation of the New Testament (1956-59), by Kenneth S. Wuest.

The New Testament in Modern English (1958), by J. B. Phillips. Four previously published translations, beginning with *Letters to Young Churches* (1947), were published as a single volume New Testament in 1958.

The Amplified Bible: New Testament (1958), *Old Testament* (1962-64). The complete Bible was published in one volume in 1965. An attempt to add clarifying shades of meaning to the single-word English equivalents of key Hebrew and Greek words.

The New American Standard Bible: New Testament (1960-63). A revision of the American Standard Version (1901) by a group of conservative scholars.

Living Letters: The Paraphrased Epistles (1962), *Living Prophecies: The Minor Prophets Paraphrased with Daniel and Revelation* (1965), by Kenneth N. Taylor.

The New Testament in the Language of Today (1963), by William F. Beck.

Appendix

BIBLE STATISTICS

Old Testament. Thirty-nine books, 929 chapters, 23,214 verses, 593,493 words. Middle book, Proverbs; middle chapter, Job 29; middle verses, 2 Chr 20:17-18; shortest book, Obadiah; about 30 extrabiblical books mentioned.

New Testament. Twenty-seven books, 260 chapters, 7,959 verses, 181,253 words. Middle book, 2 Thessalonians; middle chapter, Romans 13; middle verse, Acts 17:17; shortest book, 2 John; shortest verse, John 11:35. The name "Jesus" occurs 700 times in the Gospels and Acts, less than 70 times in the epistles. The name "Christ" occurs 60 times in the Gospels and Acts, some 240 times in the epistles and the Revelation.

The Bible. Middle book, Micah; largest book, Psalms; shortest book, 2 John. The name Jehovah (Yahweh, Lord) occurs 6,855 times. The human authors number about 50. Chapter and verse divisions are of comparatively later origin. Johann Gutenberg completed the first Bible printed from movable type in 1456. First American edition of the Bible was printed in Boston about 1752.

BIBLE WEIGHTS AND MEASURES

Measures of Length (OT)

finger	0.72 in.
handbreadth (4 fingers)	2.91 in.
span (3 handbreadths)	8.74 in.
cubit (2 spans)	17.49 in.
Ezekiel's cubit (7 handbreadths)	20.37 in.

Measures of Length (NT)

cubit (*pēchus*)	about 1.5 ft.
fathom (*orguia*)	about 72.4 in.
furlong (*stadion*)	about 606 ft.
mile (*milion*)	about 4,879 ft.
Sabbath day's journey	about 3/5 mile

Measures of Capacity (OT)
(Dry Measures)

kab	
omer (1 4/5 *kabs*)	1.159 qts.
seah (3 1/3 *omers*)	2.087 qts.
ephah (3 *seahs*)	6.959 qts.
lethech (5 *ephahs*)	20.878 qts.
kor ⎱ (2 *lethechs*)	3.262 bu.
homer ⎰	6.524 bu.

Measures of Capacity (NT)
(Dry Measures)

choinix	0.98 qts.
modios (Lat. *modius*)	7.68 qts.
saton (Heb. *seah*)	6.95 qts.
koros (Heb. *kor*)	6.52 bu.

Measures of Capacity (OT)
(Liquid Measures)

log	0.674 pts.
kab (4 *logs*)	1.349 qts.
hin (3 *kabs*)	1.012 gals.
bath (6 *hins*)	6.073 gals.
kor (10 *baths*)	60.738 gals.

Measures of Capacity (NT)
(Liquid Measures)

xestes (Lat. *sextarius*)	1.12 pts.
batos (Heb. *bath*)	6.07 gals.
metrētes (Jn 2:6)	10.3 gals.
koros (Heb. *kor*)	60.73 gals.

Weights (OT)

gerah	8.81 grains
bekah	{ 10 *gerahs* 88.10 grains
shekel	{ 2 *bekahs* 176.20 grains
maneh	{ 50 *shekels* 20.148 oz.
talent	{ 60 *manehs* 75.558 lbs.

Weights (NT)

shekel (silver)—4 Rom. *denarii* 4 Gr. *drachma* about	$ .64
shekel (gold)—15 silver *shekels* about	$9.60
mina (silver)—50 (silver) *shekels* about	$32.00
mina (gold)—50 (gold) *shekels* about	$480.00
talent (gold)—3,000 *shekels* about	$28,800.00
litra (Jn 12:3; 19:39)—a Rom. pound (12 oz.)	

OUTLINE OF
CHURCH HISTORY

The Basis of Church History

Definition. Church history is the chronological account and interpretation of the impact of Christ and His gospel upon mankind.

Preparation. (1) The Greek language, as a common tongue of the Graeco-Roman world, provided a suitable vehicle for the writing and preaching of the NT. (2) Roman law, and Roman political unity and granting of citizenship bound men together. The Roman peace (*Pax Romana*) and road system facilitated 1st cen. evangelism. (3) Jewish monotheism provided the OT messianic hope and the basis for the NT revelation.

Periods of Church History

I. Early Church Period (A.D. 30-590)
  1. Apostolic Period (30-100)
  2. Sub-Apostolic Period (100-150)
  3. Conflict with Roman Empire and with Error (150-313)
  4. Growth of the Old Catholic Imperial Church (313-590)

II. Medieval Church Period (590-1517)
  1. Christianity in the West (590-1054)
  2. Golden Age of Papal Power (1054-1305)
  3. Early Movement Toward Reformation (1305-1517)

III. Modern Period (1517 to the Present)
  1. Protestant Reformation (1517-1648)
  2. Catholic Counter Reformation (1546-1648)
  3. Colonial Christianity and Revival (1648-1789)
  4. Christian Expansion in Britain and America (1789-1914)
  5. The Church in the Twentieth Century (1914 to the present)

PART I. EARLY CHURCH PERIOD (30-590)
APOSTOLIC PERIOD (30-100)

Political	Religious
Tiberius (14-37)	Founding of the church by the Holy Spirit.
	The gospel to Jerusalem, Judea and Samaria (Acts 1—12).
	Preaching of a crucified, risen Saviour in Jerusalem.
	Evangelization, persecution, Stephen's martyrdom.
	Samaria evangelized.
Caligula (37-41)	Paul's conversion.
Claudius (41-54)	Cornelius converted.
	The gospel to the ends of the earth (Acts 13—28).
	Missionary outreach from Antioch in Syria.
	Paul saved Christianity from legalism, evangelized cities of
Nero (54-68), first emperor to persecute Christians	Roman Empire and wrote his great epistles.
Galba (68-69)	Peter's epistles, Synoptics, Epistle to Hebrews.
Otho and Vitellius (69)	
Vespasian (69-79)	Jerusalem destroyed (70).
Titus (79-81)	
Domitian (81-96), persecutor	John banished to Patmos.
	Christians persecuted.
Nerva (96-98)	
Trajan (98-117), persecutor	NT books completed.

SUB-APOSTOLIC PERIOD (100-150)

Political	Religious
Hadrian (117-38) persecuted Christians.	**Apostolic Fathers.** Among these were: Clement, bishop of Rome Ignatius, bishop of Antioch, martyred Papias, bishop of Hierapolis Polycarp, bishop of Smyrna, martyred
Antoninus Pius (138-61) also persecuted Christians.	**Early Writings.** Some of the more reliable: *Epistle to the Corinthians* by Clement *Epistle of Barnabas,* which presented Christ's death as alone sufficient for salvation apart from the Mosaic law. *Shepherd of Hermas* (apocalyptic literature) stressed responsibility and repentance.
Before 250, persecution was local and scattered, fomented by Jews, pagan intellectuals, and some of the emperors.	*The Didache* (catechetical) was written to instruct new converts.

CONFLICT WITH ROMAN EMPIRE AND WITH ERROR (150-313)

Roman Emperors.

Marcus Aurelius (161-80) persecuted Christians; Justin Martyr and Polycarp among those martyred.

Commodus (180-92)

Septimius Severus (193-211)

Severe localized persecution, many being martyred in Alexandria, Egypt, N. Africa and Gaul. Christians were tortured, beheaded, burned and thrown to wild beasts.

Caracalla (211-17); Elagabalus (218-22); and Alexander Severus (222-35); all tolerated Christians.

Maximin (235-38) put to death many prominent Christian leaders; Origen barely escaped.

Gordian (238-44) and Philip (244-49) favored Christians.

Decius (249-51) inaugurated the period of violent and general persecution after 250; multitudes of Christians perished by cruel measures throughout the empire.

Valerian (253-60) fostered intense persecution; Cyprian was slain. Diocletian (284-305), in an attempt to exterminate Christianity, inaugurated the most severe imperial persecution the church had yet faced.

Doctrinal Errors. *Gnosticism* positing dualism taught that matter was inherently evil and thus Christ could not have a real body. *Neoplatonism* was a religious philosophy claiming that a divine substance pervaded and animated all objects worshiped in various religions, but denied this quality to Christianity. *Montanism* was an attempt by Montanus to counteract overdependence upon human organization and formalism in the church. He claimed direct revelation of the Holy Spirit and stressed the immediacy of Christ's advent. *Monarchianism* stressed the unity of God, denying a trinity of Persons.

Apologists. Wrote to government officials seeking legal recognition of Christianity. Justin Martyr, the foremost apologist, defended the moral and spiritual value of Christianity and championed its being legalized in his *First Apology*. He also defended it against Judaism in his *Dialogue with Trypho*.

Polemicists. Wrote against heresies. Irenaeus in *Against Heresies* upheld the deity and resurrection of Christ against Gnosticism. Origen, an allegorist, authored *De Principiis,* the first systematic theology, and the *Hexapla,* a monument of textual criticism. Tertullian formulated the doctrine of God's triunity in *Against Praxeas.* Cyprian formulated the doctrines of apostolic succession and Peter's primacy.

Church Development. (1) Idea of the primacy of the bishop of Rome was born out of the need for leadership in time of persecution and in combating heresy. (2) The NT canon began to crystallize by A.D. 200. (3) Church calendar developed, with Christmas and Easter the principal festivals. (4) The early form of the Apostles' Creed became a symbol of orthodoxy.

Persecution. The basic reason for attack from the Roman state was the fear that separatist Christianity would jeopardize a pagan, religiously syncretistic state.

Archaeological Light. The catacombs of Rome were caves of refuge for Christians. These great caverns contain thousands of inscriptions from this period.

GROWTH OF THE OLD CATHOLIC IMPERIAL CHURCH
(313-590)

Political Religious Developments.

Constantine (306-37) was converted to Christianity (312) and published the Edict of Milan (313).

Sylvester I became bishop of Rome.

Constantine's three sons ruled the empire (337-61).

Julian "the Apostate" (361-63) led a short-lived pagan reaction.

Jovian (363-64) restored the Christian faith.

Theodosius the Great (379-95) suppressed heathenism and made Christianity the legal state religion (380).

The imperial church of the 4th and 5th cen. became a different institution from the pilgrim church of the first three centuries.

Christianization of the Empire. The severe persecutions (250-311) not only failed to stamp out the faith but witnessed its phenomenal growth. Constantine established Sunday as a day of rest and worship (321); imperially favored Christianity; encouraged church building; moved his capital to Byzantium (Constantinople); ordered 50 Bibles on finest vellum to be prepared by Eusebius; reformed slavery and many pagan customs. This was a period when the church, no longer purified by persecution, was imperiled by the inrush of the world. The church's prosperity became her greatest peril. This era paved the way for the ecclesiastical corruption of the Dark Ages to follow. Instead of separation from paganism, the imperial church adapted itself to it.

Conversion of the Barbarians. The Goths, Vandals, and Huns overthrew the empire. Some were Christianized but their conversion was nominal and helped introduce pagan practices into the church. Celtic Britons were evangelized by Roman Christians, the Irish by Patrick, the Goths by Ulfilas, the Scots by Columba, who established a monastery on the offshore island of Iona (563).

Creedal Controversies (325-451).

Concerning Christ's Person. Arius taught that Christ was a creature distinct in essence from God. Athanasius maintained He was coexistent and coeternal, of the same essence with the Father. The Council of Nicaea (325) condemned Arianism, deciding in favor of Athanasius' position.

Concerning Christ's Two Natures. Council of Constantinople (381) dealt with Apollinaris' heresy that Christ's human spirit was replaced by the Logos. Nestorius separated the two natures and over-emphasized the human, which was dealt with at the Council of Ephesus (431). The Council of Chalcedon (451) answered the Eutychian view that Christ's two natures were fused into one—the divine. The *Definition of Chalcedon* states the orthodox view of two natures united in one Person.

Concerning Divine Grace and Human Free Will. Augustine of Hippo held to total depravity and the utter necessity for divine grace for salvation. Pelagius denied that view and insisted man was able to cooperate with divine grace.

Still other ecumenical councils dealt with doctrinal problems. Constantinople (553) dealt with the Monophysite controversy and Constantinople (680) with the two wills of Christ (Monothelitism). Nicaea (787) dealt with image worship.

Post-Nicene Fathers.

Eastern Fathers. Chrysostom, the Golden Mouthed (345-407), was a great preacher and bishop of Constantinople. Theodore, bishop of Mopsuestia, championed sound grammatical-historical interpretation of the Bible. Eusebius of Caesarea (264-340), the Father of Church History, wrote an account of the fortunes of the church to his day (323).

Western Fathers. Jerome (340-420) translated the Latin Vulgate, which became the Bible of Christendom for more than a thousand years. Augustine of Hippo (354-430) was an outstanding theologian. His *City of God* envisioned a universal Christian empire and his *Confessions* continue a classic in devotional literature.

Division of the Empire (after 364)

West (Rome)	East (Constantinople)
Valentinian I (364-75)	Valens (364-78)
Valentinian II (375-83)	Theodosius (378-95)
Theodosius the Great (383-95)	
Honarius (395-423)	Arcadius (395-408)
Valentinian III (423-55)	Theodosius II (408-50), etc.

West (Rome)	East (Constantinople)
Western Empire fell under inflow of barbarians (476).	Anastasius (491-518), etc. Justinian (527-65), etc.
Dark Ages Papal Empire emerges from the ruins of the Western Empire.	Eastern Empire lasted till the fall of Constantinople to the Turks (1453).

Rise of the Papacy. The title "Pope" is Italian for "Father." Earlier it had been applied to all Western bishops, but by 500 it began to be restricted to the bishop of Rome, then gradually to "universal bishop," based on the Roman doctrine of apostolic succession and the primacy of Peter. Leo I (440-61) obtained recognition as primate of all bishops from Emperor Valentinian III (445). With his successor Hilarus (461-68), he advocated an exclusive universal papacy. The fall of the Western Empire (476) left the popes free to make advantageous alliances with the various new barbarian kingdoms that emerged. During the period from Simplicius (468-83) to Pelagius II (578-90), the authority of the popes increased greatly, preparing the way for the medieval and modern papacy.

Rise of Monasticism. It began in Egypt with Paul of Thebes and Anthony about 250 and spread throughout the empire. Their aim was holiness by isolation from the world. In Europe monks lived in monasteries and in the Middle Ages developed education, learning, literature and farming.

PART II.   MEDIEVAL CHURCH PERIOD (590-1517)

CHRISTIANITY IN THE WEST (590-1054)

Growth of the Papacy. Gregory I (590-604) was one of the most enlightened and finest of the popes. He laid the foundation of the medieval church about to be built on the ruins of the Roman Empire. As a theologian he synthesized Roman theology, emphasizing the concept of purgatory and the sacrificial character of the mass. He initiated the evangelization which won Britain to Roman Christianity through the efforts of Augustine of Canterbury.

Rise of Islam. Muhammad was born in 570. In 610 he declared himself a prophet. Forced to flee Mecca in 622 (Hegira), he later conquered the city, making it his capital. He died in 632. In a short time western Asia and N. Africa came under Islam, a religion of the sword and hate—Syria in 634, Jerusalem in 638, N. Africa and Spain in 711. Charles Martel at the Battle of Tours (732) turned Islam back and saved Europe for Christianity.

Empire Revived in the West. Pope Zacharias (741-52) helped Pepin the Short, Charlemagne's father, to become the king of the Germanic Franks. At the request of Stephen II (752-57), Pepin led his army into Italy, conquered the Lombards, and donated their lands to the Pope (754). This papal kingdom developed into the Papal States, which lasted till 1870. Charlemagne (742-814) built up a European empire and was crowned "Emperor of the Romans" by Pope Leo III in 800. This event caused questions and problems regarding delegated authority in the church-state issue. In 962 Otto, a German ruler, was crowned Holy Roman Emperor over a kingdom that lasted till 1806.

Missionary Expansion. Growing monasticism provided the bulk of the missionary force during this period, especially from Ireland and the island of Iona. Aidan carried the gospel to the Northumbrians in northeastern England (c. 634). At the Synod of Whitby (663) King Oswy decided in favor of Roman Christianity, prominent in the S as a result of Augustine of Canterbury's mission (596). Columbanus went to the Bergundians on the continent (589), Boniface (Winfrid) exerted the influence of the gospel on the Teutonic tribes (modern Germany) after 700. Willibrord, an Englishman, won Friesland for the papacy (692). Ansgar (801-65), the "Apostle to the North," reached Denmark and Sweden. Mid 9th cen. saw Cyril and Methodius, "Apostles to the Slavs," invent a Slavic alphabet, translate the Scriptures, convert the Bulgarians and Moravians to Christianity.

There was little missionary activity in the Eastern Church, which was engaged in defending itself against Islam.

Papal Degeneration (858-1054). Nicolas I (858-67), first pope to wear a crown, claimed papal supremacy by citing the Pseudo-Isidorian Decretals. Appearing in the mid 9th cen. the Decretals claimed to be letters and decrees of bishops, Constantine and church councils of the early centuries. They were later proved to be forged attempts to demonstrate the historicity and antiquity of the claims of the papacy. The corrupting influence of the concept of a papal kingdom and temporal power, in addition to weak, immoral successors, called for reform.

The Eastern Schism of Christendom. Tension between the popes and the patriarch of Constantinople led to a split between the Eastern and Western churches. Disputes over the date of Easter, images in the churches, *filioque* (double procession of the Holy Spirit) and use of unleavened bread in the mass caused the Schism of 1054 and the formation of the Greek Orthodox Church of the East.

GOLDEN AGE OF PAPAL POWER (1054-1305)

Summit of Papal Power. The popes of the 11th to the 14th cen. instituted reforms and humbled kings. Hildebrand (Gregory VII), whose concept of the papacy is outlined in the *Dictatus Papae*, reigned 1073-85. He put down clerical immorality, simony (sale of church offices), and humbled Henry IV of Germany (1077).

Innocent III (1198-1216) brought the medieval papacy to its greatest power by forcing the submission of the kings of France, England and the Holy Roman Empire. He assumed many titles, such as "Vicar of God," "Vicar of Christ," etc., and subordinated the state to the church. Through the Fourth Lateran Council (1215) he decreed the necessity of auricular confession and the doctrine of transubstantiation. He initiated papal inquisition, exterminated heretics (Albigenses), and sponsored the Fourth Crusade. The church countered the Albigenses and Waldenses with crusades, the Inquisition and a ban on the Scriptures.

Decline of the Papacy. Weak popes succeeded Innocent. Boniface VIII (1294-1303) engaged in a power struggle with Philip the Fair of France during which he issued the papal bull *Unam Sanctum*. It stated that temporal authority was to be subject to the spiritual (the church, i.e., the pope); that there is "one Holy Catholic and Apostolic Church and outside this church there is neither salvation nor remission of sins . . ."; that "it is altogether necessary to salvation for every human creature to be subject to the Roman Pontiff." Before he could be excommunicated, Philip had Boniface taken captive for a brief time, and he died shortly after his release. In 1309 Pope

Clement V (1305-14), a Frenchman, moved the papacy to Avignon, beginning the "Babylonian Captivity" of the papacy (1309-77).

The Crusades. Purpose: to recover Palestine from the Muslims, drive out the Moors in Spain, wipe out the Albigenses of France. The First Crusade, preached by Urban II, succeeded in setting up the Latin Kingdom of Jerusalem (1099-1187). The seven crusades in all did not accomplish the permanent freedom of the Holy Land but contributed to the weakening of feudalism, enhanced the power and prestige of the papacy, gave rise to the monastic military orders, stimulated East-West trade, and facilitated cultural exchange. The Fourth Crusade, diverted to Constantinople, set up the Latin Kingdom of Constantinople (1204-61), weakening the Eastern Empire and deepening the East-West church cleavage.

Attempted Reform Movements. (1) The Albigenses, called Cathari, around the city of Albi in southern France, resembled the Gnostics. (2) The Waldenses followed Peter Waldo (c. 1150) in a simple back-to-the-Bible movement within the church. (3) Monastic reforms were led by Bernard of Clairvaux, of the Cistercian order, and by the Knights Templars and Knights Hospitallers. The Mendicant orders, i.e., the Franciscans founded by Francis of Assisi (1182-1226) and the Dominicans founded by Dominic (1170-1221), also stressed reform.

Medieval Theology. Scholasticism employed Aristotelian logic and philosophy to systematize Christian truth. (1) Anselm of Canterbury (1033-1109), "The Father of Systematic Theology," was a realist, believing faith preceded reason. He wrote on the existence of God and the satisfaction theory of the atonement. (2) Thomas Aquinas (1225-74) became the foremost Catholic theologian, especially in his *Summa Theologica*. He was a moderate realist, stressing the use of reason and Aristotelian logic to gain a degree of truth supplemented at a certain point by faith and revelation. (3) John Duns Scotus (c. 1264-1308) opposed Aquinas and elaborated the theory of the immaculate conception of Mary. (4) Others contributing to this era and development were Abelard (1079-1142), Bernard of Clairvaux (1091-1153), Peter Lombard (c. 1100-1160), Albert Magnus (c. 1206-80), William of Occam (c. 1300-49).

EARLY MOVEMENT TOWARD REFORMATION (1305-1517)

Need for Church Reform (1305-1517). Immorality of the clergy, sale of indulgences and church offices; heavy papal taxes; papal interference in state affairs; the "Babylonian Captivity" of the papacy at Avignon, France (1309-77); the Great Schism of 1378-1417, with rival popes at Rome and Avignon, all indicated the need for reform.

Pressures Toward Reform. (1) Groups more biblically oriented, like the mystics, the Friends of God, and the Brethren of the Common Life, exerted a wide influence. (2) John Wycliffe (*c.* 1329-84), "Morning Star of the Reformation," translated the Bible into English and vigorously attacked papal authority and the mass (1378). (3) John Huss (*c.* 1369-1415), Bohemian reformer, influenced by Wycliffe's *Dideas,* condemned the sale of indulgences and proposed reform in the church. (4) Savonarola (1452-98), a Florentine monk, preached against papal vice. (5) Series of councils between 1409 and 1439 aimed at reform. (6) The Renaissance of learning and the new interest in the Hebrew and Greek Scriptures exposed the unscriptural accretions of the medieval church. (7) The rise of strong national states (especially England and France), and disenchantment with papal corruption, interference, taxation, and land ownership by the church, all favored reform.

PART III.   MODERN PERIOD
(1517 TO THE PRESENT)

PROTESTANT REFORMATION (1517-1648)

Popes of the Reformation Era. Pope Leo X (1513-21) dispatched John Tetzel to Germany to sell indulgences to raise funds to complete St. Peter's basilica in Rome. It was Leo's bull of excommunication which Luther burned on December 10, 1520. Pope Leo was followed by Pope Adrian V (1522-23) and Clement VII (1523-34). Pope Paul III (1534-49) authorized the formation of the Jesuits and instigated a war against German Protestants (1546-49), which was continued through the reign of Julius III (1550-55).

Luther and the Break with Rome. Martin Luther (1483-1546), an Augustinian monk, became the greatest human emancipator since the apostle Paul.

Influences shaping his life. (1) Strict, superstitious peasant background. (2) Scholastic education in preparation for a career in law. (3) The sudden death of a friend, a narrow escape during a severe thunderstorm, and a deep consciousness of sin caused him to enter a monastery of the Augustinian order in 1505. He was ordained two years later. (4) While training for a professorship he received spiritual counsel and encouragement from Johann von Staupitz, the vicar-general of his order. (5) November, 1510 to April, 1511, he was shocked at corruption and practices in Rome, while there on business for his order. (6) Studied Scripture, St. Augustine, J. Tauler (mystic) and the *Theologia Germanica.* (7) Became convinced of the authority of the Bible and justification by faith *alone* as he lectured at the University of Wittenberg as doctor of theology and professor of Scripture. By close of 1516 Luther was assured of his own salvation, and the watchword became "The just shall live by faith" (Rom 1:17).

The Growing Break. (1) October 31, 1517, Luther posted his Ninety-five Theses against the abuse of the indulgence system. This was prompted by extravagant preaching of Johann Tetzel (1470-1519), an agent of Albrecht of Brandenburg, archbishop of Mainz and archbishop of Magdeburg, who had been authorized by Pope Leo X to sell indulgences for construction of St. Peter's in Rome. (2) Engaged in several debates, he was forced to the logical conclusions of his basic premises (regarding faith and Scripture). (3) June 15, 1520, Pope Leo X gave Luther 60 days to submit in the papal bull, *Exurge Domine.* (4) He wrote three treatises, *Address to the German Nobility, Babylonian Captivity* and *On the Freedom of Christian Men* (1520). (5) Famous "Here I Stand" speech at Diet of Worms was made in April, 1521. Put under imperial ban, he was kidnapped by friends.

Rise of Lutheranism. (1) In 1522 Luther translated the NT into German while in hiding at Wartburg Castle. (2) On June 13, 1525, Luther married Katherine von Bora (1499-1552). (3) At Diet of Speier in 1529, Lutheran princes read their *Protestation,* hence the word protestant. (4) In 1529 at the Marburg Colloquy, Luther and Zwingli disagreed over the words "this is my body" in the communion. The *Small Catechism* was published. (5) In 1530 the Augsburg Confession, the first Protestant confession, was drawn up stating the Lutheran position. Philip Melanchthon (1497-1560) was the chief author. He also wrote *Loci Communes,* the first Protestant theology, in 1521. (6) Lutherans began to ordain their own clergy (1535). (7) Schmalkaldic wars in Germany began the year Luther died (1546). They were concluded at the Peace of Augsburg (1555), which extended legal rights to Lutherans as well as Roman Catholics. The principle of two religions in Germany, *cuius regio, ejus religio* ("In a prince's country, the prince's religion") was established. (8) After Luther's death controversies marred the unity of the Lutherans until they agreed on the Formula of Concord, completed in 1577 and published in 1580 as the *Book of Concord,* the definitive statement of Lutheran theology. (9) By the sixth decade of the 16th cen. Lutheranism had spread to all the Scandinavian countries and its reformational ideas to other countries.

The Rise of the Reformed Faith. *In Switzerland.* Reformation came to Berne and Zurich through Ulrich Zwingli (1484-1531), who successfully opposed the Roman practices of indulgences, mass, celibacy, images and other unscriptural practices of his day in his *Commentary on True and False Religions* (1525). Geneva joined the Reformation under the preaching of Guillaume Farel (1489-1565), a French Protestant, and the teaching and organizing ability of John Calvin (1509-64), who after 1536 became the leader of the Reformed faith. Calvin's *Institutes of the Christian Religion* (1536) and his *Ecclesiastical Ordinances* (1541) remain classics today.

In France. French Protestants created a Reformed Church in 1559 at a synod which adopted the Gallican Confession of Faith. After 1560 they were called Huguenots and became the target of persecution and religious wars until the Edict of Nantes (1598) granted religious freedom. The terrible massacre of St. Bartholomew was begun in 1572 and in all, between 10,000 and 20,000 were killed. Admiral Coligny, leader of the Huguenots, was one of those murdered, apparently at the instigation of Catherine de Medici, a niece of Pope Clement VII.

In Scotland. Patrick Hamilton (1504-28) preached reform and was consequently burned in 1528, and George Wishart (1513-46) was burned for his faith in 1546. John Knox (1513-72) between 1560 and 1567 secured the aid of Scotch nobility and merchants, defeating the attempt of Mary Stuart (Queen of Scots) to keep Scotland in Rome's fold. Knox established the Presbyterian Church in Scotland in 1567.

In Holland. Religious freedom from Rome was linked with the struggle for political freedom from Catholic Spain. The Reformed Church was established in 1571 and political emancipation in 1581. William of Orange was the political liberator. James Arminius (1560-1609) rejected Calvinism, making divine grace resistable and the atonement unlimited. Although the Calvinistic Synod of Dort (1618) pronounced against Arminianism, it survives in some branches of Protestantism today.

In Northern Ireland. James I of England (1566-1625), who sponsored the Authorized or King James Version of the Bible (1611), colonized Scotch Presbyterians in Northern Ireland after 1603 to reduce potential revolt. This resulted in the religious division of Ireland into Protestant North and Catholic South.

In the rest of Europe. Calvinism and the Reformed faith also spread into Bohemia, Hungary and the German Palatinate.

The Anabaptist Movement. This group rejected a state church and infant baptism. Emerging from the Zwinglian movement in Zurich in 1525 under the leadership of Conrad Grebel (*c.* 1490-1526), they required the rebaptism of all adult believers. They were called Anabaptists (baptize over again) as a term of derision. The movement spread to Germany and Moravia. Menno Simons (*c.* 1496-*c.* 1561) was converted to Anabaptist teachings from the Roman priesthood in 1536 to become the leader of the movement in Holland which bears his name (Mennonites). Basic beliefs of the Anabaptists include the authority of the Scriptures, believers' church, baptism of believers (no uniformity in mode among early movement), and separation of church and state.

England's Break with Rome. Henry VIII (reigned 1509-47) declared the church in England independent of the pope in the Act of Supremacy (1534), which made the king and his successors the only supreme head on earth of the church in England. He confiscated monastic properties, and gave the people the Scriptures in common English (the Great Bible). During the reign of Edward VI (1547-53) the ecclesiastical reform begun by Henry became essentially Protestant. Thomas Cranmer drew up the Forty-two Articles and the *Book of Common Prayer.* Mary Tudor (Bloody Mary, 1553-58) vainly sought to reinstate Catholicism. Large numbers of Protestants were martyred for their faith, Cranmer, Ridley and Latimer among them.

The Elizabethan Settlement under Elizabeth I (1558-1603) reestablished Protestantism as Anglicanism, the "Middle Way." The *Book of Common Prayer* was revised, and the Forty-two Articles were revised and reduced to Thirty-nine Articles, being then made the creed of the Church of England by Parliament in 1563. The papacy retaliated by excommunicating Elizabeth (1570), establishing a Jesuit training school at Douai in Flanders to train missionaries to recapture England, and enlisting the aid of Philip of Spain, who sent the great Spanish Armada against England. This effort was defeated in 1588, reducing the threat of the papacy.

The Puritan Movement. Puritanism arose out of dissatisfaction with the Elizabethan Settlement. Advocating a more thorough break with Romanism, some wanted to purify the state Anglican Church further, change its polity to Congregationalism or Presbyterianism or separate entirely from it in the interest of doctrinal or ecclesiastical purity. Various Baptist groups also emerged, such as General Baptists (affusionists and Arminians) and the Particular Baptists (immersionists and Calvinistic). In 1604 James I called the Hampton Court Conference to satisfy Puritan requests for further reform. The only result was authorization of the translation of the Scriptures, the celebrated King James Version (1611).

Many Puritans migrated to America between 1629 and 1640. Others engaged in civil wars (1642-49) which left Puritans dominant. The Westminster Assembly met 1643-53 and formulated the Calvinistic Westminster Confession. Charles I was executed in 1649, and after the establishment of the Commonwealth Oliver Cromwell emerged as Lord Protector.

CATHOLIC COUNTER REFORMATION (1546-1648)

Within less than half a century the Protestant movement made tremendous gains in Europe. Most of the Continent, except Italy and Spain, appeared lost to the papacy. France was being threatened. To counteract the Protestant gains the Roman Church sought to regain lost adherents, keep others from leaving the fold, and reform the church, thus removing some of the causes for the Reformation. Important to the movement are the following: (1) The impetus given to the reform movement by the Oratory of Divine Love. (2) The Jesuit order was founded by the Spaniard Ignatius of Loyola (1491-1556) and sanctioned by Pope Paul III in 1540. It required absolute, unquestioning obedience to the pope, thus providing the Roman Catholic Church with one of its most effective weapons with which to stop defections, reclaim lost followers and deal with heresy. (3) The Council of Trent (1545-63), dominated by Italians, among other things dogmatized the medieval theology of the Scholastics. It made the Latin Vulgate, including 11 OT apocryphal books, the authorized Bible, and declared Scripture *and* tradition as ultimate authority. (4) The Inquisition, although of earlier origin, was employed as a means of dealing with heresy and defectors by papal bull in 1542. Ruthless tactics were employed to secure confessions and convictions of the accused. (5) The Index, a list of books not to be read by the faithful, was drawn up as early as 1543.

The Thirty Years' War (1618-1648). This was a struggle of Protestantism against Catholic intolerance in the Holy Roman Empire. The Bohemian and Danish phase (1618-29) was a victory for Rome. The Swedish phase (1630-34) saved Protestantism as the army of Gustavus Adolphus of Sweden defeated the Catholic armies. The final phase (1635-48) was a struggle of the House of Hapsburg against France, with the latter emerging as the strongest state in Europe. The Treaty of Westphalia (1648) gave legal status to Lutheranism and Calvinism, allowing lands which were Protestant prior to 1624 to legally remain so.

COLONIAL CHRISTIANITY AND REVIVAL (1648-1789)

Colonization of the Western Hemisphere. (1) Columbus' discovery of the New World (1492) had as one goal wider fields where the church might be planted. (2) English explorers took possession of the Atlantic seaboard. (3) Pilgrims settled at Plymouth in 1620. (4) John Endicott and the Puritans settled at Salem, New England (1628). (5) Connecticut was settled (1636-62). (6) Maryland was founded by Cecil Calvert in 1634, a Roman Catholic. (7) The Quakers under William Penn settled in Pennsylvania in 1681. (8) Georgia was settled by James Oglethorpe. (9) Protestantism was destined to predominate in North America, Catholicism in South America.

Higher Education in the Colonies. A number of colleges were founded, such as Harvard (1636), William and Mary (1693), Yale (1701), Princeton (1746), Brown (1764), Rutgers (1766) and Haverford (1833).

Roman Catholic Missions. Spanish conquest of Mexico (1520) was followed by "conversion" of the natives to Roman ceremonies. French Jesuits (Joliet, Father Marquette and La Salle) planted mission stations in the Mississippi Valley taking possession for France, calling the territory Louisiana.

Religious Revival in America. In New Jersey in 1726 under Theodore Frelinghuysen revival came among the Dutch Reformed people and spread to the Scotch-Irish Presbyterians under Gilbert Tennent and then through the Middle Colonies. George Whitefield furthered the revival in 1739. In New England Jonathan Edwards (1703-58) preached with power. The revival in the Southern Colonies was predominantly spread by the Baptists and Methodists. As a result, new life was infused into the churches and many were converted. This provided impetus to missions and education, created schisms, and demonstrated the possibility of intercolonial cooperation, thus aiding the War of Independence which was to follow.

Forms of Revival in Europe. Pietism developed as a reaction to the cold orthodoxy of Lutheranism in Germany. Founded by Philip Spener (1635-1705), the University of Halle became the center of the movement, which turned out a number of missionaries. In addition to infusing new life into Lutheranism, it contributed also to the Moravian awakening under Count von Zinzendorf (1700-1760).

Spiritual Awakening in England. The Wesleyan Revival under John Wesley (1703-91) and his hymn writer brother Charles influenced England after 1738. George Fox (1624-91) had founded Quakerism in 1648 and Robert Barclay, Quaker theologian, declared the inner light provided continuing direction and inspiration.

Rationalism and Deism. Descartes (1596-1650) founded modern philosophy. Spinoza (1632-77) advocated pantheism. Deism taught a transcendent God and stressed man's goodness and perfectibility. This was a result of advance in science and the rationalistic philosophy of Locke, Leibnitz, Kant, Voltaire, Rousseau and Lessing. Deism developed in England and then spread to France and Germany. Deism and Unitarianism spread to America.

PROTESTANTISM AND ROMANISM (1789-1914)

American Christianity in the National Era. The War of Independence weakened the churches. Deism and infidelity became rampant (1775-1800). Thomas Paine's *Age of Reason* (1794) and the anti-religious aspects of the French Revolution had their bad effect. The expanding frontier had a great demoralizing influence, thus creating an extensive spiritual need.

The Second Great Awakening. This began in several eastern colleges after 1786 and went up and down the seaboard. It spread to the western frontier beginning in Logan County, Kentucky, about 1800. Results were seen in new believers and churches, schism and new denominations, new sense of church freedom, moral reform, frontier camp meetings, new colleges, new seminaries such as Princeton and Andover, a spread of domestic and foreign missionary work (Adoniram Judson and others), and the formation of numerous Bible and tract societies.

Concerns for Social Reform. As a result of the spiritual awakening and a growing concern about existing conditions, the church became more actively involved in social activities. (1) Churches sponsored temperance and antislavery campaigns (the slavery question split Methodists, Presbyterians and Baptists). (2) YMCA and gospel mission work was projected. (3) Growth of the Sunday school was helped. This was a great boon to American Christianity. (4) Mormonism, Seventh-Day Adventism, Christian Science and Spiritualism came on the scene capitalizing on human and social concerns. (5) The "social gospel" of Walter Rauschenbusch (1861-1918) advocated education and legislation rather than evangelism as the means of spiritual advance.

The Papacy and the French Revolution. Rousseau, Montesquieu, and Voltaire attacked the Roman Church in France. Church lands were declared public property in France (1789). The church was ignominiously humiliated during the Revolution.

The Papacy and Napoleon. The Concordat of 1801 recognized the Catholic religion as the religion of the majority but not as the established faith, nor did it return church property taken in 1790.

British Christianity. This became a vital force in the 19th cen. (1) Missionary work was projected in many lands, beginning in India with William Carey (1793) and in Africa with David Livingstone (1813-73). (2) Charles Haddon Spurgeon (1834-92) and others preached to multitudes in England. (3) Booth's Salvation Army (1865), John Darby's (1800-1882) Plymouth Brethren and other smaller nonconformist groups arose. (4) The Church of England had an influential segment represented by William Wilberforce (1759-1833) and John Newton (1725-1807), who were concerned with evangelism and social reform, especially the abolition of the slave trade (1807) and slavery itself (1833), as well as social and economic reforms among laborers.

Foes of Christianity. (1) Rationalistic biblical criticism developed, based on the philosophy of Immanuel Kant (1724-1804), Georg Hegel (1770-1831), Albrecht Ritschl (1822-89). Denial of Mosaic authorship and the authenticity of the Pentateuch were advanced by Johann Eichhorn (1752-1827), Hermann Hupfeld, Karl Graf and Julius Wellhausen. The Wellhausen theory makes the Pentateuch a compilation of late unreliable documents from about 800-500 B.C.

Unity of Isaiah was attacked, as well as the historicity of Daniel. (2) Evolution was fostered by Darwin's *Origin of the Species* (1859) and *The Descent of Man* (1871). (3) Communism was rooted in the materialistic philosophy of Karl Marx (1818-83) and of Friedrich Engels in the *Communist Manifesto* (1848).

Papal Gains (1815-70). (1) The Jesuits (disbanded by papal action in 1773) were restored by Pius VII (1814). (2) This period of Romanticism was favorable to the colorful ritualism of the Roman Church. (3) Metternich, the powerful Austrian chancellor, favored Rome, and the Congress of Vienna, over which he presided, restored the papal states to the pope. (4) The Oxford Movement in the Anglican Church saw more than 600 prominent Anglicans and 250 Anglican clergymen return to the Roman faith between 1845 and 1862. (5) The reign of Pius IX (1846-78) resulted in two outstanding declarations: the doctrine of the Immaculate Conception of Mary (1854); and the decree of Papal Infallibility (1870) by the First Vatican Council. This doctrine claims that whenever the pope speaks *ex cathedra* (i.e., as the head of the church on earth), he is infallible in matters of faith and morals.

Papal Losses (1870-1914). (1) Almost immediately after the declaration of papal infallibility, anticlerical hostility developed. (2) When Italy was unified the pope lost his temporal power, retaining only the Vatican properties. (3) To build a strong unified Germany, Iron Chancellor Bismarck stripped the church of much of her power in 1871. (4) In France a severe blow was administered in the Separation Law of 1905, which separated church and state. Even church property was confiscated by the state. The Roman Catholic Church has not to this present time been able effectively to regain France for the papacy although her population is nominally Catholic.

PROTESTANTISM AND ROMANISM (1914 TO THE PRESENT)

Liberal-Fundamentalist Controversy (1920-34). Liberalism was opposed by conservatism in theology. Evolution was attacked (Scopes Trial, 1925). J. Gresham Machen in 1929 withdrew from Princeton Seminary to champion orthodoxy. The Bible conference and Bible institute era was launched: Nyack Missionary College (1882) and Moody Bible Institute, Chicago (1886). Nearly 40 Bible institutes were founded between 1930 and 1940. Christian colleges come to the fore (Wheaton, Calvin, etc.).

Neoorthodoxy. Karl Barth and Emil Brunner adopted liberal biblical criticism, rejecting biblical inerrancy and full authority of the Scriptures. The movement, while unsound, did not produce the theological sterility of old-line liberalism. The Roman Church met liberalism by an attempt to adapt Aquinas' theology to the modern scientific era (neo-Thomism).

Advance of Cults. Christian Science, Mormonism and Jehovah's Witnesses are growing at a rapid rate throughout the world to further complicate the complex 20th cen. religious scene.

Present-Day Popes. Pope Leo XIII (1878-1903) was an ardent claimer of papal infallibility. He denounced Protestants as "enemies of the Christian name." Leo XIII was followed by Pius X (1903-14), Benedict XV (1914-22), and Pius XI (1922-39). During the reign of Pius XII (1939-58) the dogma of Mary's Bodily Assumption was promulgated (1950). He with his immediate predecessor lacked the ecumenical emphasis exhibited by John XXIII (1958-63) and John's more conservative successor, Paul VI (1963).

Ecumenicity. This is a movement toward Christian unity. Within Catholicism, it seeks to attract "non-Catholic Christians" back to the fold. Among Protestants, ecumenism is largely American inspired and led. Various groups have engaged in organic union or confederation in the quest of Christian unity. In some cases elements of the same denomination have united to form a united body (United Presbyterian Church in the U.S.A., etc.). Other groups have crossed denominational lines to create an entirely new denomination (United Church of Canada). Liberal and neoorthodox leaders reason that all church members are believers, therefore all church members are one in Christ. The latter support the liberally orientated National Council of Churches of Christ in America and the World Council of Churches. Conservatives, realizing that true Christian unity is not predicated on organic unity, doctrinal relativity and uniformity, sponsor such organizations as the National Association of Evangelicals (1950) and its international organization, the World Evangelical Fellowship (1951), or the American Council of Churches (1941) and its International Council of Christian Churches (1948).

PRINCIPAL RELIGIONS OF THE WORLD

Source: Britannica Book of the Year, 1965

TOTAL WORLD POPULATION	3,178,155,000
TOTAL CHRISTIANS	950,550,000
ROMAN CATHOLIC	584,493,000
EASTERN ORTHODOX	142,055,000
PROTESTANT	224,065,000
JEWISH	13,121,000
MUSLIM	455,785,000
CONFUCIAN	350,835,000
BUDDHIST	161,856,000
HINDU	395,191,000
SHINTO	67,155,000
TAOIST	51,305,000
ZOROASTRIAN	147,000
OTHERS, INCLUDING PRIMITIVE OR NONE	732,210,000
COMMUNISM CONTROLS MORE THAN	800,000,000

Jewish Faith (Judaism) is the doctrines and rites of the descendants of Jacob as prescribed in the laws of Moses.

Islam (Muhammadanism) is the religion, doctrines and precepts of Muhammad (died 632) found in the Koran.

Confucianism is the ethical and philosophic system involving ancestor worship taught by Confucius of China (551-478 B.C.).

Buddhism is a system of ascetic self-abnegation that worships the deity Buddha, who is claimed to have become incarnate about 600 B.C.

Hinduism, the religion of India, is a syncretism of Brahmanism and Buddhism with a multitude of deities thought of as residing in animate and inanimate objects.

Shintoism, one of the two great religions of Japan, is a mixture of the worship of nature, particularly the sun as supreme god, and ancestor worship.

Taoism is based on the ethical teachings of Lao-tse, a Chinese philosopher (*c.* 604 B.C.).

918

Zoroastrianism, the religion founded by Zoroaster, was the national faith of ancient Persia, and is embodied in the Zend-Avesta. It teaches a dualism of good (Ahura-Mazda) and evil (Ahriman).

Animism is the belief that material objects possess life and are indwelt by spirits.

Communism is an atheistic philosophical system of godless materialism which opposes religion.

North America*

Population	280,876,000
Protestant	79,110,000
Roman Catholic	117,055,000

South America

Population	158,528,000
Protestant	2,708,000
Roman Catholic	140,549,000

Europe

Population	605,684,000
Protestant	115,855,000
Roman Catholic	253,387,000
Eastern Orthodox	130,673,000

Asia

Population	1,840,357,000
Protestant	9,984,000
Roman Catholic	42,428,000
Buddhist	161,538,000
Confucian	350,529,000
Hindu	394,030,000
Muslim	346,490,000
Shinto	67,018,000
Taoist	51,261,000
Zoroastrian	147,000

Africa

Population	276,067,000
Protestant	7,697,000
Roman Catholic	27,703,000

*Includes Central America and West Indies.

Muslim	95,545,000
Hindu	680,000
Others, including primitive and no religion	144,442,000

WORLD JEWRY AND THE ISRAELI STATE

Estimated Jewish world population	13,121,000
North America	5,896,000
South America	685,000
Europe	3,917,000
Asia	2,266,000
Africa	285,000
Population (1964 est.) of Israeli state (created in 1948)	2,523,400
Jewish	85.4%
Muslim	7.0%
Christian	2.2%
Arab and others	5.4%

RELIGIONS IN THE UNITED STATES

Source: Yearbook of American Churches, 1965

Population (est. 1965)	195,000,000
Protestant (224 bodies)	66,854,200
Sunday school enrollment (223 bodies and 281,593 schools)	45,805,074
Roman Catholic	44,874,371
Jewish	5,585,000
Baptists (29 bodies)	22,692,017
American Baptist Convention	1,559,103
Southern Baptist Convention	10,393,039
Lutherans (10 bodies)	8,697,119
American Lutheran Church	2,468,407
Lutheran Church in America	3,227,157
Lutheran Church—Missouri Synod	2,591,762
Methodists (21 bodies)	12,823,399
Methodist Church	10,234,986
African Methodist Episcopal Church	1,166,301

Presbyterians (10 bodies)	4,381,278
Presbyterian Church in the U.S.	937,558
Cumberland Presbyterian Church	80,455
United Presbyterian Church in the U.S.A.	3,279,240
Other Large Groups	
Assemblies of God	543,003
Christian Churches (Disciples of Christ), International Convention	1,834,206
Churches of Christ	2,250,000
Church of the Nazarene	342,032
Latter-Day Saints (5 groups)	1,955,350
Protestant Episcopal Church	3,336,728

SELECT SUBJECT INDEX

923

925

927